FLORIDA BEACHES

FOGHORN OUTDOORS

FLORIDA BEACHES

Second Edition

The Best Places to Swim, Play, Eat, and Stay

Parke Puterbaugh and Alan Bisbort

FOGHORN OUTDOORS: FLORIDA BEACHES

The Best Places to Swim, Play, Eat, and Stay
2nd Edition

Parke Puterbaugh and Alan Bisbort

Published by
Avalon Travel Publishing
5855 Beaudry Street
Emeryville, CA 94608, USA

ISBN: 1-56691-347-0
ISSN: 1534-7834

Editor: Lynne Lipkind, Marisa Solís
Series Manager: Marisa Solís
Proofreader: Asha Johnson
Graphics: Melissa Sherowski
Design: Darren Alessi
Production: Darren Alessi, Karen McKinley
Map Editor: Mike Balsbaugh
Cartography: Mike Morgenfeld, Mike Balsbaugh
Indexer: Valerie Sellers Blanton

Front cover photo: Clearwater Beach © Richard Cummings/Photophile

Distributed by Publishers Group West

Printed in the USA by R.R. Donnelly

Please send all comments, corrections, additions, amendments, and critiques to:

**Foghorn Outdoors:
FLORIDA BEACHES
AVALON TRAVEL PUBLISHING
5855 BEAUDRY ST.
EMERYVILLE, CA, USA
email: atpfeedback@avalonpub.com
website: www.travelmatters.com**

Printing History
1st edition—1998
2nd edition—November, 2001
5 4 3 2 1

Contents

Florida's East Coast

South Florida

The Keys

Florida's West Coast

Big Bend

The Panhandle

Beach Bits: Lists, Tips, and Trivia

MAPS

Florida's Coastal Counties

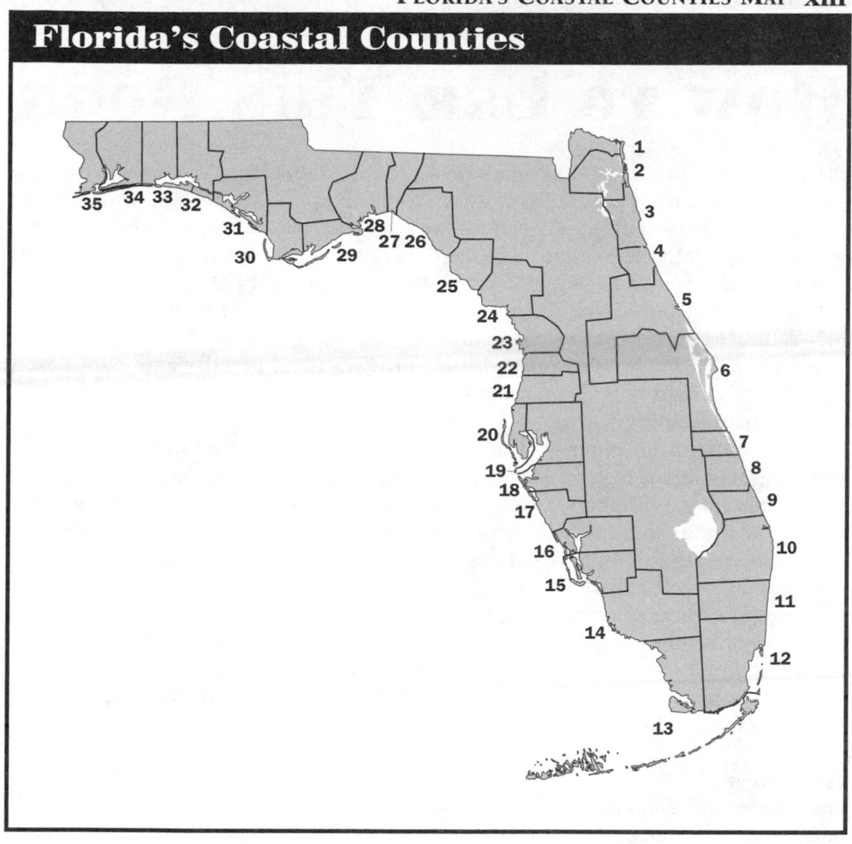

HOW TO USE THIS BOOK

Florida Beaches proceeds in a clockwise direction around Florida's coastline, from north to south down the East Coast, south to north up the West Coast, and then negotiating the interior elbow (known as the Big Bend) before making a final east-to-west run across the Panhandle. The book is divided into six regions (East Coast, South Florida, the Keys, West Coast, Big Bend, and the Panhandle) and further subdivided by county. The county functions as the basic organizational unit of *Florida Beaches,* serving as its chapters. There are 35 counties in Florida that touch the coast. Some are long and have lots of beaches (e.g., Pinellas and Palm Beach Counties), while others claim only a sliver of coastal access (e.g., Hillsborough and Jefferson Counties).

Each chapter includes a map of the county's coastline. Numbers that point to individual beaches on the map correspond to a table of contents on the facing page. Write-ups of each coastal community, park, or area follow. Each entry begins with a general essay about a given locale. We delve into any and all subjects—physical description, history, sociology, attractions, high and low culture, chance encounters—to help orient the reader and to paint a picture of what a locale looks and feels like, who goes there, what we consider its principal pros and cons, and so forth. Additional information follows under these headings: Beaches (public beaches), Shore Things (goods and services), Bunking Down (where to stay), Coastal Cuisine (where to eat), Night Moves (where to hang out after dark), and Contact Information. Here are more detailed descriptions of these headings:

Beaches

Beaches are the raison d'être of this book. We describe their natural features and what can be done there, and ante up any facts or observations that distinguish one beach from another. We've also put together "beach boxes": boxed listings of practical information, including how to get there, where to park, fees, hours, activities, facilities, an overall rating, and a contact number. Below the beach name in each box is a space with activity symbols on the left side and a rating between one and five on the right. The ratings should be interpreted as follows:

- ⑤ — extraordinary; beach heaven
- ④ — excellent; an above-average beach
- ③ — good; a decent beach that's well worth a visit
- ② — fair; a below-average beach
- ① — abysmal; keep driving

The activity icons indicate that certain activities—beyond the beach basics of swimming, sunbathing, and surfcasting—can be done here. These special activity icons look beyond the beach basics. There are eight of them:

Beach driving (🚙) — This symbol indicates that driving on the beach is permitted. It's not a good idea from an environmental standpoint, and if ghost crabs could unionize, beach driving would probably be prohibited. In Florida, beach driving is pretty much limited to the Daytona Beach area (and has been increasingly restricted there of late).

Camping ( ) — This symbol denotes a developed campground or that primitive camping is permitted.

Diving/snorkeling ( ) —A good diving and/or snorkeling spot.

Hiking ( ) — The hiking symbol denotes the presence of a marked trail (or trails) for nature observation and/or exercise.

Jetty ( ) — A jetty is often found at the mouths of harbors and marinas, creating good fishing, snorkeling, and surfing.

Pier ( ) — A pier is a wooden or concrete structure extending into the water, upon whose length people fish or stroll. But you knew that.

Surfing ( ) — A beach where waves are sufficiently sizable and well formed to draw more than the occasional surfer.

Volleyball ( ) — Volleyball nets and standards are staked into the sand.

Near the bottom of each beach box is a line marked "Facilities." We list the following facilities, if present, for each beach: concessions (food and drink), lifeguards (year-round, unless otherwise noted), restrooms (anything from portable toilets on up), showers (mostly outdoor showerheads), and a visitor center (any indoor facility with exhibits, maps, brochures, and staff personnel).

Shore Things

This handpicked listing of up to 12 goods and services is a kind of selected Yellow Pages for some of the larger communities on the Florida coast. The template for "Shore Things" is as follows:

- **Bike/skate rentals** (where to rent bicycles, in-line skates, and other fun stuff)
- **Boat cruise** (sightseeing trips out on the water)
- **Dive shop** (where to rent/buy scuba equipment or book a dive trip)
- **Ecotourism** (canoe/kayak outfitter or guide, or a park where ecotourist outings can be taken)
- **Fishing charters** (guided fishing trips)
- **Lighthouse**
- **Marina** (boat dockage)
- **Pier**
- **Rainy-day attraction** (something to do when the weather is inclement)
- **Shopping/browsing** (an interesting shopping district, area, or mall)
- **Surf shop** (surfboards, surf gear, swimwear)
- **Vacation rentals** (realtors that rent vacation cottages, condos, and beach houses)

Bunking Down

This section offers a general overview of lodgings you can expect to find in a given locale, plus specific commentary on hotels, motels, inns, and resorts we deem worthy. It is by no means an exhaustive accounting, though it grows with each edition, and we welcome your feedback and input.

Room rates fluctuate according to day of week, time of year, holidays and special events, and what the market will bear. We use between one and four dollar signs to give a general indication of the price range for a standard room (two persons, two beds) in the high season. Since everything is relative and changeable, these are offered merely as a gauge to be interpreted as follows:

$ = inexpensive (under $80 per night)
$$ = reasonable ($80–120 per night)
$$$ = moderately expensive ($120–170 per night)
$$$$ = very expensive ($170 or more per night)

This leads us to the question: What is the high season in Florida? The answer depends on where you're talking about. The farther south you travel down the peninsula, the more the term "in season" is likely to mean the winter months—usually from Christmas to Easter. Somewhat ironically, the low season, when rooms are cheapest, is summer. This may seem backward, but most folks come to Florida to escape winter's cold, not to experience summer's heat (which has been intensifying yearly as global warming kicks in). This makes for incredible summer bargains. We've seen Daytona Beach awash in rooms for $15. Up on the temperate Panhandle, the seasons conform more closely to convention, with spring and summer being the busiest times of year and fall and winter tapering off.

Finally, if you'd prefer to rent a cottage, condo, or beach house rather than stay at a hotel, motel, inn, or resort, we've picked a realtor for many locales in the "Vacation Rentals" heading under "Shore Things."

Coastal Cuisine

Our restaurant writeups highlight favorites of ours. As with accommodations, we've tried to provide an overview but make no claims of being exhaustive. We look for restaurants that emphasize seafood and/or regional cuisine. In Florida, regional often signifies Caribbean and Cuban influences, as well as "cracker" cooking: gator, catfish, fried food, and the like. We cast a favorable eye on restaurants that have been around for a while and enjoy a solid reputation for consistency and quality. In Florida, competition is keen, people value the dining experience, and restaurants that can't make the grade come and go quickly. With few exceptions, we don't have much to say—or much good to say—about franchised restaurants except that they take consistency to predictably uniform and often mediocre extremes. Instead, we cast our net for restaurants that evince honest regionalism and/or innovation. This can mean anything from a down-home hole-in-the-wall to an upscale dining room with a trained chef.

Again, we've provided dollar signs to indicate the cost of an average entrée:

$ = inexpensive (under $8)
$$ = reasonable ($8–14)
$$$ = moderately expensive ($14–20)
$$$$ = expensive (over $20)

A final note: When dining in Florida, try to order local catches. It makes little sense to choose salmon from the North Atlantic or halibut from the distant Pacific when snapper, grouper, mahi-mahi, and more are plucked fresh from nearby waters. Likewise, Florida spiny lobster (when available; the season is brief and numbers declining) is preferable to Maine lobster, and stone crab claws should be snapped up when available. Finally, be sure to order key lime pie for dessert. That's an order.

Night Moves

Night moves means nightlife, and to us that signifies people gathering during or after sunset. Some folks like to sit and talk over drinks, while others shake their booty to live or deejayed music in a club setting. We've staked out and described the after-hours landscape around the whole of Florida's party-mad perimeter. While we're dismayed about the current state of nightlife—too many troubadours still singing "Margaritaville," too many one-man bands singing to programmed accompaniment, too many deejayed nightclubs blaring mindless dance music—we dutifully hit the bars in hopes of finding convivial places to hang out. Which we did, from time to time, happily reporting our experiences. All the same, whereas we used to party like it's 1999, now that 1999 is behind us we're more likely to retire before midnight in anticipation of an early-morning jog on the beach or kayaking trip around an estuary. Still, if you love the nightlife and want to boogie, we'll point you in the right direction.

OUR COMMITMENT

We are committed to making *Florida Beaches* the most accurate, comprehensive, and fun-to-read guide to the Sunshine State, its beaches, and beach communities. Every beach, attraction, restaurant, hotel, nightclub, crab shack, and tiki bar mentioned herein has been personally visited for review, and our information is as up-to-date as we could make it at the time of publication. Our opinions—and they are plentiful—are entirely our own. We do not rely on interns, publicists, hirelings, or other published materials. In researching *Florida Beaches,* we have placed our own four feet on every Florida beach that's accessible by car, foot, or ferry.

Despite our best efforts at being timely, we cannot control price fluctuations or the fact that seemingly solid establishments may go out of business or change owners or names from time to time. So if you're planning a beach vacation based on recommendations we've made herein, it is always a good idea to call ahead to verify prices and policies.

If you want to provide feedback or share a travel tip, please feel free to write us in care of the publisher. Finally, we represent to you, our readers, that we had a fantastic time researching and writing this book, and we expect you'll find plenty in here that's useful and entertaining.

Correspondence may be addressed:
***Florida Beaches,* 2nd Edition**
Avalon Travel Publishing
5855 Beaudry Street
Emeryville, CA 94608
U.S.A
email: atpfeedback@avalonpub.com
(please put "Florida Beaches" in the subject line)

ACKNOWLEDGMENTS

We have been visiting Florida since we were old enough to make sand castles, and we've spent the last 17 years traveling and writing about the state for books and magazines. During our research for *Florida Beaches* we have come in contact with many helpful natives. There are far too many to mention by name, but some are worth singling out for going that extra mile for and with us. We'd like to thank Michelle Holder (Amelia Island); Robin Lake Miller (Ponte Vedra Beach); Susan McLain, Bill Bussinger, Dan Ryan, and Pamela Hasterock (Daytona Beach); Don Simmons (New Smyrna Beach); Melissa Tomasso (Kennedy Space Center); Eric Jacoby and Peter Wynkoop (Cocoa Beach); Bill Pullen (Jensen Beach); Jane Grant (Fort Lauderdale); Gerry Quinn (Miami Beach); Michael David Cushing (Everglades); Julie Perrin (Islamorada); Vin and Phil Depasquale (Naples); Jeanne Biggs (Fort Myers Beach); Jay Halcrow (Sanibel Island); Dick Dunham (Palm Island); Gail Rubenfeld (Siesta Key); Laurie Pike-Adkins (Sarasota); Amy Bressler Drake (Longboat Key); George Billiris (Tarpon Springs); Jayna Leach (Panama City Beach); Bruce and Judy Albert and Dave Rush (Seaside); Sherry Rushing (Destin); Gina Sholtis (Sandestin); and Sheilah Bowman (Pensacola).

We'd also like to thank several past and present employees of Visit Florida, the official state tourism organization, who have been extremely helpful: Doug Luciani, Kelly Grass, Brandy Henley, and Lisa Sloan. Special thanks to John and Leigh Forrester, old friends in Ponte Vedra Beach who routinely put us up and fed us spreads worthy of Paul Prudhomme. We're also much obliged to Mark Kohler, a rockin' journalist friend from Florida who helped stir the cauldron in St. Lucie County. Hugs to our agent and longtime friend, Anne Zeman. Thanks and love, too, to Helen Puterbaugh and Penny Bisbort, and to all our in-laws, siblings, nephews, and nieces.

Between the first and second editions of *Florida Beaches*, our publisher, Foghorn Press, was acquired by Avalon Travel Publishing. We're pleased to be part of this sharp new organization. From the "old" Foghorn, we'd like to remember and thank Vicki Morgan, David Morgan, Kyle Morgan, Holly Haddorff, Jean-Vi Lenthe, Donna Leverenz and Dawn Lish. From the new crew, we feel privileged to be working with a super-competent and friendly group of people, starting at the top with publisher Bill Newlin and associate publisher Donna Galassi. Our in-house editor, Marisa Solís, has been a pleasure to work with and has come up with some great ideas for this edition. Lynne Lipkind edited the book with a sharp yet sympathetic eye. We're also indebted to Amanda Bleakley in marketing, Mary Beth Pugh and Keith Arsenault in publicity, and Darren Alessi in design.

As always, our wives—Carol Hill Puterbaugh and Tracey O'Shaughnessy—have been understanding and supportive. One of these years, we might even take them to some of these nice places we've written about! Finally, we'd like to dedicate this book to our kids, Hayley Anne Puterbaugh and Paul James Bisbort, in the hope that they may themselves grow up to become beach bums. This assumes, of course, that we as a people will become better stewards of our wonderful beaches so that they'll be there for future generations to enjoy.

INTRODUCTION

Our votes are in and no recount is needed. Florida beaches have won the election, fair and square. Indeed, Florida's beaches have absolutely nothing in common with Florida's electoral process or political landscape. They are inviting, uplifting, reliable and, for the most part, civil. We have criss-crossed the coastline of the Sunshine State so many times that we feel like we know them better than our own hometowns. We've made friends all over and have always been made to feel welcome.

Perhaps this is why we still shake our heads in disbelief over the events of 2000. In fact, while researching this book we unwittingly found ourselves caught up in the madness of the election campaigns, as we crossed paths with numerous limo-and-cop-chopper processions as candidates of both major political parties dashed from one fundraiser, photo op, and sound-bite op to another. Seldom was heard an encouraging (or honest) word. All the more reason to ignore Florida politics and embrace her beaches.

The book you are holding is the completely reworked, rewritten and re-researched second edition of *Florida Beaches*. We were shocked by how extensively things—from individual businesses to the state itself—changed in the few years that have passed since the publication of the first edition in 1998. But this is, after all, one of the fastest-growing and changing states in the country, so maybe we shouldn't have been surprised. The state's population, for instance, grew by 23% in one decade!

Florida Beaches is our fourth book on the subject of beaches and the second devoted exclusively to the coast of a single state. In that regard, *Florida Beaches* was preceded by *California Beaches* (Foghorn Press, 1999). With these two books we've written more than half a million words on the states that are synonymous with the word *beach*. We're quite certain no one has covered or traveled these coastlines as exhaustively as we have. The first edition of *Florida Beaches* occupied us for the better part of three years. This improved, expanded second edition took another two years. Now that it's finished, we need a vacation. We mean a real vacation: one without notepads, laptops, and 16-hour days spent sight-seeing and writing about what we saw, heard, and did.

We're only half-joking when we refer to ourselves as America's beach bums. Given the economic consequences of quitting solid jobs as writers/editors at *Rolling Stone* and the Library of Congress for a life of itinerant beachcombing 17 years ago, we can vouch for the fact that the "bums" part of the handle, at least, is accurate. Still, we can't deny that there are worse things we could be doing with our working lives than traveling around Florida, which has become a second home to us. Just for the record, we've been vacationing and/or visiting friends and relatives in Florida well before we were old enough to write our own names. And now we're writing massive books about it.

Because this peninsular state is surrounded by water on all sides but one, it has not one but several coastlines: the East Coast, facing the Atlantic Ocean; the West Coast, facing the Gulf of Mexico; the Panhandle, running alongside the Gulf of Mexico on an east-west axis; and the Florida Keys, extending for a hundred miles into the Straits of Florida. We almost forgot the Dry Tortugas, seven island specks to the west of Key West. Florida never seems to end, and its seeming endlessness has been a running joke to us for a long, long, deadline-breaking time. (On the other hand, we're not so sure our editors are amused.)

How much beach is there? Incredibly, Florida has more miles of sandy beaches than almighty California. Florida is a 447-mile peninsula. It has the longest tidal coastline in the lower 48 states. When the undulations around its bays and inlets are figured in, Florida's shoreline totals 8,462 miles. As the crow flies, Florida claims 1,800 miles of coastline, and 1,100 miles of that are sand beaches.

Much of Florida is low-lying and peninsular, fringed by long, narrow barrier islands. It is a coastline more influenced by waves than tides, making it conducive to the formation of sandy-beached barrier islands and barrier spits. The exception is the "Big Bend" along Florida's Gulf Coast, whose low-energy coastline is muddy and mucky. On the Panhandle and the northern peninsula, fine-grained quartz sand is supplied by rivers and reworked by waves and currents. Farther south, the sand is shellier in composition. Some Florida beaches are pure quartz, others are made of shelly material, and many are a combination of the two. Still others are not natural beaches at all, since they have been "renourished" with sand dredged from offshore—a procedure necessitated by beach erosion due to human interference with sand-deposition processes.

By and large, we're enthusiastic champions of Florida's sandy beaches. How can you not love Florida, with its subtropical climate and generally relaxed lifestyle? Florida is sunshine and beaches, palm trees and coral reefs, Panama hats and flip-flops, citrus fruit and limestone springs, alligators and manatees. The very word Florida seems to warm up a room. The balmy winter weather triggers an annual migration of snowbirds—both of the winged and two-legged variety—from the frigid north. To college kids around the United States, Florida means a Spring Break migration to whatever beach towns will have them. Many own second residences (often condos) in Florida. Senior citizens come in droves to retire. One of our grandmothers referred to Florida as "God's waiting room." She died in Fort Lauderdale at the ripe old age of 94.

In this book, we've written about every publicly accessible beach in the state, which we've broken down into six regions: East Coast, South Florida, the Keys, West Coast, Big Bend, and the Panhandle. "Public beach access" is a key concept in this book. According to state law, descended from a principle of common law dating back to Roman times, the beach is public property seaward of the mean high-tide line. That is to say, the wet-sand portion of the beach—much of which is not inundated most of the time—is "held in public trust" for all, and therefore everyone has a right to be on it. But there's a catch. Getting onto the public part of the beach means crossing private property, and without access in the form of easements or public ownership of a beach parcel by a municipality, county, the state of Florida, or the federal government, the beach is inaccessible.

We have therefore focused on public beaches and beach access points. If you are staying at an oceanfront hotel, motel, cottage, or condo, beach access may be of little concern. For everyone else, however, the issue of access is critical. The first edition of *Florida Beaches* represented the first comprehensive inventory of Florida's public beaches and beach accesses in 15 years, and this second edition has helped us fine-tune our inventory and add some new entries. But this is more than an access guide. We also offer a window into the soul of the communities along the coast. We talk about history and sociology, flora and fauna, roads and bridges, food and drink, sun and sand, rock and roll, and all the other nuts and bolts that make beach life what it is.

Florida Beaches is a book for tourists, natives, and people who like to read about other places. We've packed it with facts, stats, and hard information, including the lowdown on where to play, stay, eat, and go out at night. At the same time, we've provided subjective commentary, humorous asides, and plainspoken opinions—plenty of opinions. We've also stocked *Florida Beaches* with sidebars—a hundred stand-alone essays on various Florida-related subjects that caught our fancy, amused us, or rubbed us the wrong way. In the candid spirit that has been our hallmark, we hereby declare this book a Disney-free zone. No mouse ears will ever divert us from our chosen turf: the beaches of Florida.

We want *Florida Beaches* to be the kind of book people can pull off the shelf as an informational travel guide or read from cover to cover as an entertaining travelogue. Pull up an armchair and hitch a ride as we trek around the bountiful coast of Florida in a clockwise direction. We begin our odyssey at Fort Clinch, butting up against the Georgia border on Amelia Island, which has flown under eight flags in its stormy history. We inch our way south along the East Coast, passing through Cocoa Beach (NASA headquarters) and Daytona Beach (NASCAR country) while lingering at wonderful wilderness beaches like Canaveral National Seashore and John D. MacArthur Beach State Park.

Then it's on to South Florida, a tri-county area that spans wealthy, glamorous, and populous Palm Beach, Fort Lauderdale, and Miami Beach. We sail out to the Keys, a grouping of narrow coral-spined islands that barely poke above sea level. Next, it's up the West Coast, home to appealing cities like Naples and Sarasota, not to mention gorgeous sunsets over the Gulf of Mexico. One of the most interesting and least visited areas is the Big Bend, along Florida's inside elbow. Sand beaches are scarce but natural beauty is abundant. Finally, we traipse the snow-white beaches of the Panhandle, from St. George Island west to Perdido Key, finishing up on the Alabama state line.

Despite the crush of humanity in a state whose 16 million residents make it the nation's fourth most populous, Florida teems with wildlife and abounds in natural areas. No other state can match Florida's bounty of parklands and preserves, which includes two national seashores, three national parks (all of which border the coast), 16 national wildlife refuges (10 of which are on the coast), and 153 state parks. Many of Florida's coastal counties and municipalities have done a commendable job of seeding the shoreline with beach parks and accesses. It is easy to understand why Florida rates so highly with beachcombers—not to mention anglers, golfers, boaters, divers, surfers, and others who play by the sea—and why tourism is the state's leading industry.

We've visited and written about nearly 400 beaches in Florida's 35 coastal counties. We apologize if any shell has been left unturned, but it's not because we weren't diligent in our research. For each beach, we've provided information on location, parking, fees, facilities, and activities. We've also supplied contact information (including website addresses) and rated each beach for overall merit. We do everything but spread out beach towels and mix margaritas.

So what are you waiting for? Turn the page and storm the beaches!

—Parke Puterbaugh and Alan Bisbort, November 2001

Florida's East Coast

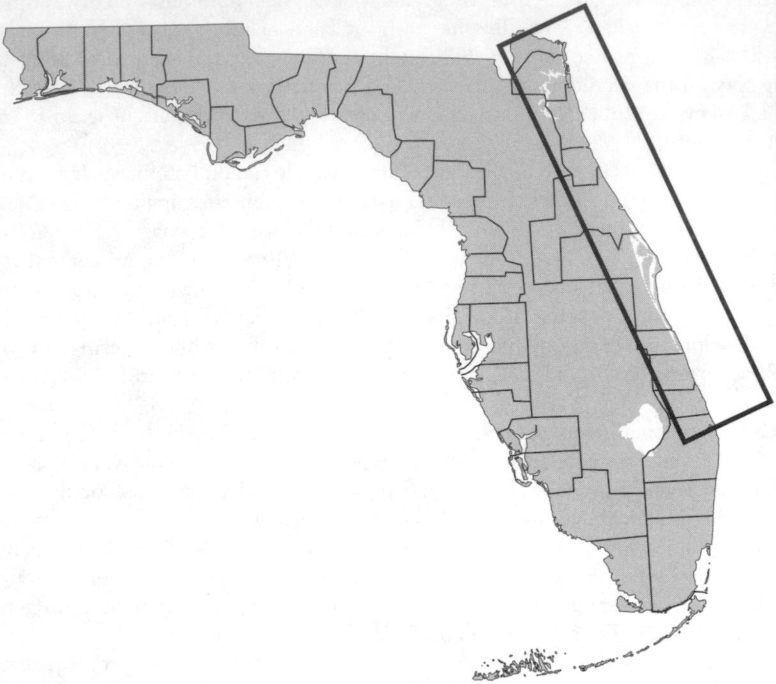

Key to the Symbols

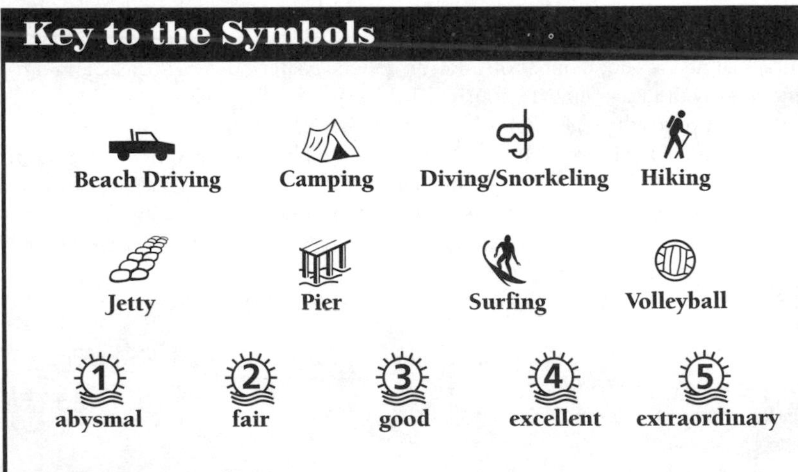

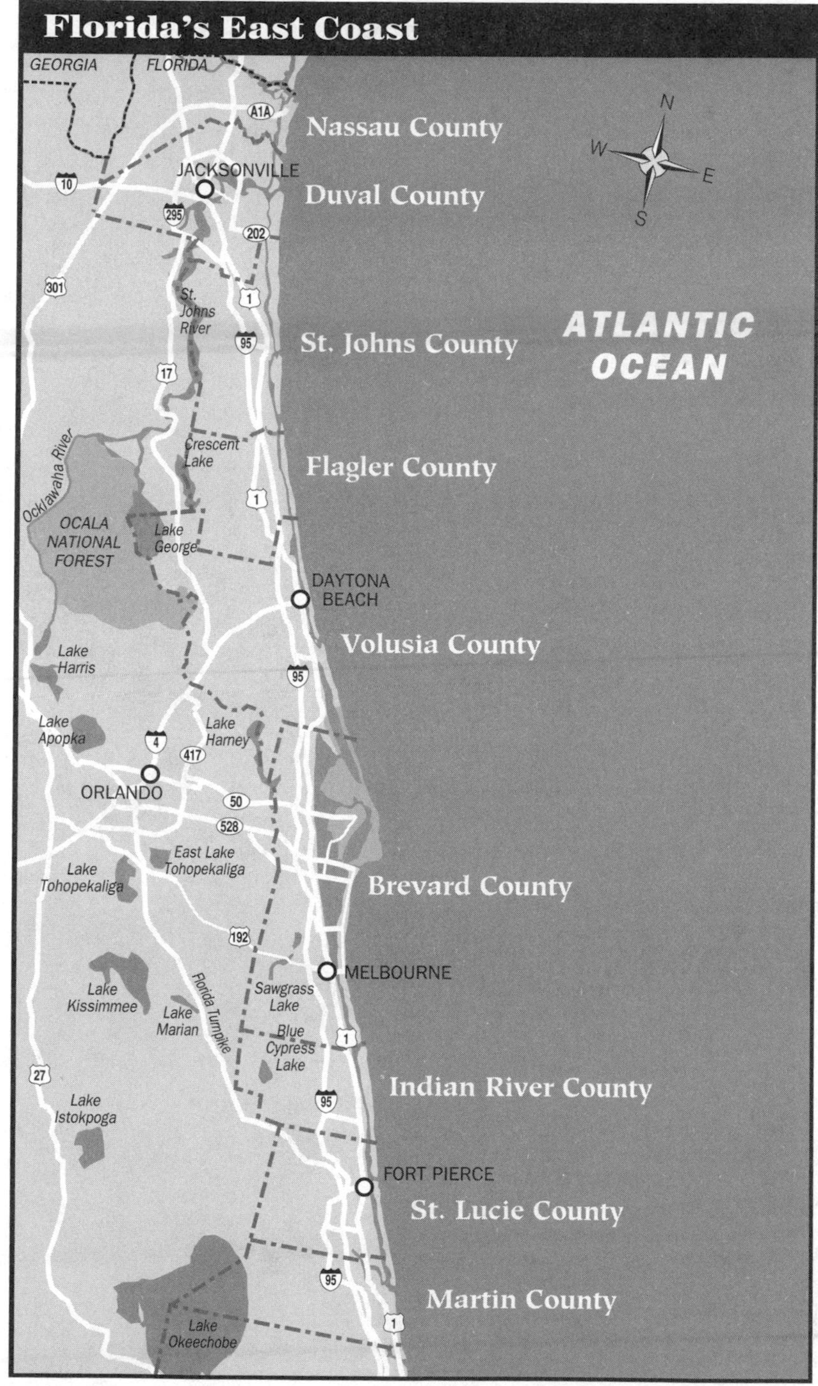
Florida's East Coast
GEORGIA
FLORIDA
A1A
Nassau County
JACKSONVILLE
10
295
Duval County
202
301
St. Johns River
1
95
St. Johns County
ATLANTIC OCEAN
17
Ocklawaha River
Crescent Lake
Flagler County
1
OCALA NATIONAL FOREST
Lake George
DAYTONA BEACH
Volusia County
Lake Harris
95
Lake Apopka
4
Lake Harney
417
ORLANDO
50
528
East Lake Tohopekaliga
Lake Tohopekaliga
Brevard County
192
MELBOURNE
Lake Kissimmee
Florida Turnpike
Sawgrass Lake
Lake Marian
Blue Cypress Lake
1
27
Indian River County
95
Lake Istokpoga
FORT PIERCE
St. Lucie County
95
Martin County
1
Lake Okeechobe
N
W
E
S

Nassau County

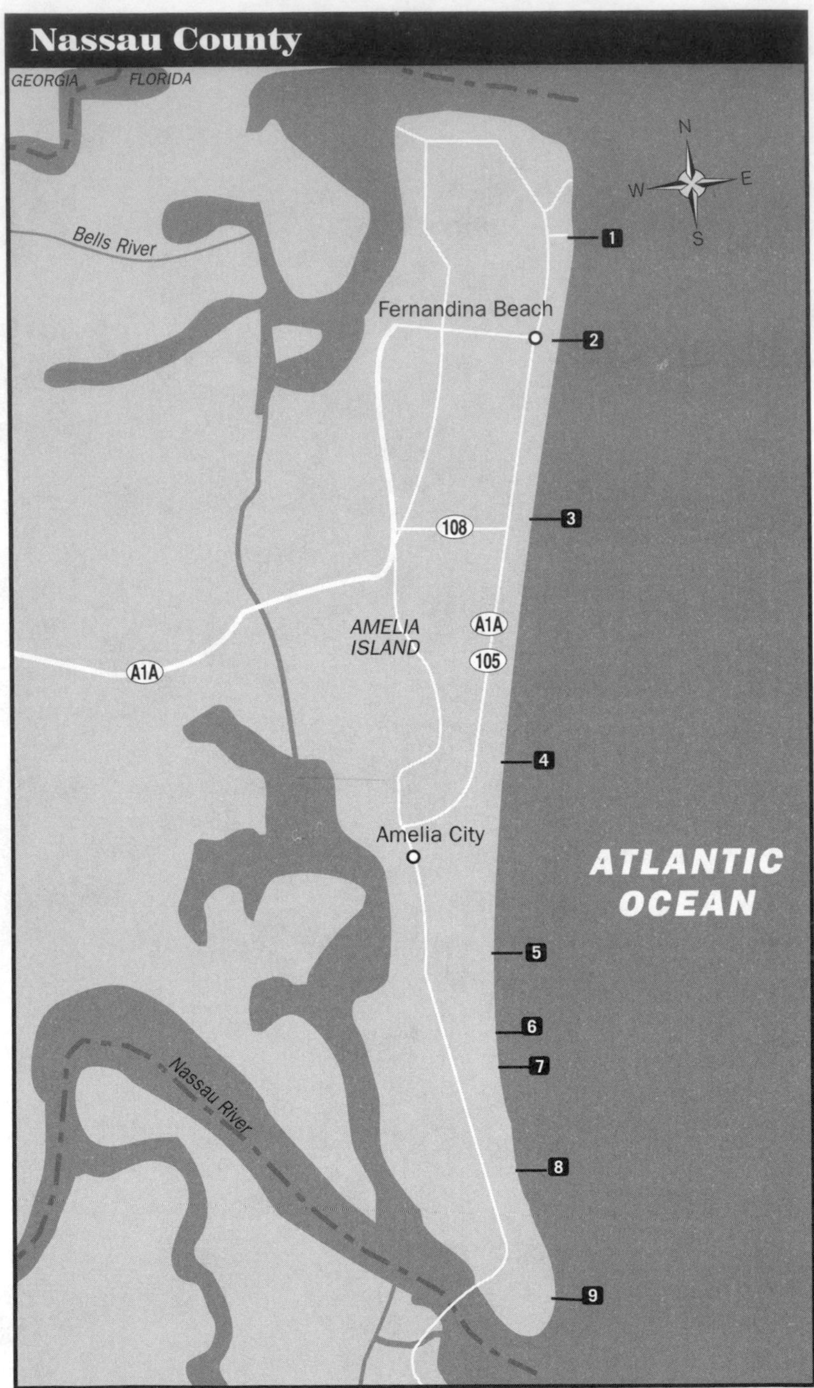

NASSAU COUNTY

Nassau County is pressed against the Georgia border. It is at the northeast tip of Florida and, therefore, the starting point of the state's plentiful beaches for huge numbers of travelers headed south along I-95. Amelia Island is coastal Nassau County in its entirety. The 13.5-mile island extends from Fort Clinch through the historical town of Fernandina Beach and down to Amelia Island Plantation, a resort leviathan. From the laid-back townsfolk to the geology of Amelia Island, this neck of the Florida coast exhibits traits of the state of Georgia. For one thing, the dunes are taller and more dramatic than those found on the rest of Florida's east coast.

Fort Clinch State Park

The first beach in Florida clinches the Sunshine State's unrivaled reputation for sandy shores. That beach—4,000 feet along the Atlantic Ocean, plus another 8,400 feet along the Cumberland Sound—can be found inside **Fort Clinch State Park**, just north of Fernandina Beach. One of the oldest of Florida's state parks, Fort Clinch embraces 1,121 acres of salt marsh, tidal estuaries, a coastal hardwood hammock (with oaks whose limbs are draped with Spanish moss), huge sand dunes, and 2.3 miles of ocean and sound beaches.

All of this bounty is centered around a pre–Civil War fortification that is still so remarkably intact that park rangers, dressed in period uniforms, offer regular programs to showcase the daily life of a Union garrison in 1864. Built in 1847, the fort was named for General Duncan Lamont Clinch, a hero of the Seminole War of the 1830s. In 1861, the fort was occupied by Confederate troops who abandoned it in 1862, when it was claimed by Union forces. Fort Clinch even played a minor role in World War II, as beach patrollers kept a lookout for invading Germans and a navigational beacon helped guide seaplanes home from training missions.

The park has an interesting history itself. The state of Florida purchased the abandoned fort, along with 256 acres, in 1935 and then began buying adjacent land as funds became available. They were the fortuitous beneficiaries of FDR's New Deal legislation in 1937, as the Civilian Conservation Corps built the initial hiking trails, roads, and facilities for what would become the state's showcase park the following year.

Today, the park has 62 campsites in two areas (on the Cumberland Sound and by the Intracoastal Waterway), a 2.5-mile hiking trail, restrooms, showers, a fishing pier, and a jetty that juts into the mouth of the sound. In addition to a breathtaking view of the south end of Georgia's Cumberland Island, the pier rewards eagle-eyed visitors with an occasional manatee spotting. We saw two of the sweet old sea cows during our long march out on the fishing pier on a bedazzling summer day. The pier runs a quarter mile from the parking lot to the water's edge and then extends a quarter mile further into the ocean.

Fort Clinch is a textbook case of a healthy barrier-island beach, with wide, hard-packed sand backed by fields of vegetation-covered dunes. (Interestingly enough, beach renourishment has never been necessary in Nassau County, although the first such project has tentatively been scheduled for 2003 or so.) No lifeguards are on duty at Fort Clinch but swimming isn't risky enough to keep the hundreds of people we saw out of the water. Families with young kids might want to point their flip-flops up to the north side of the jetty, where the sound's waveless and shallow water allows for per-

1 Fort Clinch State Park

Location: from Fernandina Beach, follow Atlantic Avenue (Highway A1A) north into the park

Parking/fees: $3.25 entrance fee per vehicle. An additional $1 per person (free for children under six) is charged for touring the fort.

Hours: 8 A.M. to sundown

Facilities: restrooms, picnic tables, showers, and a visitor center. There are 62 developed campsites in two areas (beach camping on the Cumberland Sound and river camping near the Intracoastal Waterway). Fees are $17 per night, plus $2 for hookups.

Contact: Fort Clinch State Park, 904/277-7274

MAP OF FLORIDA'S EAST COAST—PAGE 5

fectly safe swimming. The water is so clear that you can see the bottom for about a hundred yards from shore. You can also gaze across the sound to Cumberland Island, the sparsely inhabited Georgia barrier island and National Seashore that lies only a half mile north. If you want to see more of Cumberland Island, it can be visited via passenger ferry out of the Georgia port town of St. Marys.

With Fort Clinch State Park, the Florida coast sets a high standard for itself right off the bat. Happily, most of the other beaches along the so-called First Coast—from Fort Clinch to St. Augustine—sustain this level of excellence.

Contact Information
Fort Clinch State Park, 2601 Atlantic Avenue, Fernandina Beach, FL 32034; 904/277-7274; website: www.myflorida.com

Fernandina Beach

Fernandina Beach (pop. 10,890) is a charming, well-preserved city at the north end of Amelia Island, Florida's northernmost barrier island. That officially makes it Florida's first beach town. It also marks the beginning of the "First Coast," a chunk of Florida's northeast that is too often overlooked by vacationers who speed down I-95 toward South Florida. Just because it is the northernmost town on Florida's East Coast shouldn't deter you from putting Fernandina Beach on your itinerary. After all, it's still part of Florida and well south of such Deep South hotbeds as Savannah and Charleston. If you're looking for some storied history and an intact piece of the quickly vanishing "Old Florida," do not hesitate to detour off the traffic-choked interstate to check out Fernandina Beach for a few hours, a few days, or even longer.

Most notably, Fernandina Beach—and indeed, all of Amelia Island—is the only place in the United States to have been ruled by eight different entities. In addition to the flags of France, Spain, England, and the United States, a few off-brands have flown over this strategically situated island. The most short-lived was the "Patriots of Amelia Island," an anti-Spanish splinter group whose blue-and-white standard fluttered in the breeze for all of one day in 1812. As disarrayed as its early history was, Fernandina has—with the exception of 1861–1862, when the Confederate flag flew over Fort Clinch—flown the Stars and Stripes since 1821.

The federal occupation of the bustling port town brought an initial burst of prosperity after the Civil War. This segued into the Gilded Age (1875–1900), a real boom time for Fernandina Beach. Much of the town's wealth came from Florida's first cross-state railroad, completed in 1861, which ran from Fernandina to Cedar Key. That wealth was evident in the town's Victorian architecture. Two luxury hotels were built by the railroad, drawing wealthy guests from the north. Along Centre Street, near the natural harbor provided by the Amelia River, huge Victorian mansions were built by shipping magnates as year-round residences.

When Henry Flagler's East Coast Railway began to siphon wealthy tourists away to South Florida, Fernandina Beach relied on its fishing industry to bail it out of economic hard times. Specifically, the modern shrimping industry was founded in Fernandina Beach, with the first offshore shrimp trawlers pushing off in 1913. Shrimpers still dock at City Marina, which has the signal honor of being Florida's only marine welcome station. Shrimping was augmented by oyster harvesting and crabbing, which led to the construction of several canneries. The sweet Fernandina

MAP OF NASSAU COUNTY—PAGE 6

shrimp is still the unofficial town mascot. The unofficial town nuisance is its malodorous paper mills. Though they helped pull Fernandina out of the Great Depression, the belching mills don't do much to enhance the town's appeal in the present. The problem isn't just one of smell. In 1996, research indicated that ammonia discharges from the Rayonier Specialty Pulp Products mill appeared to be a primary cause of declining plankton species vital to the food chain in the Amelia River. "Because of the Rayonier plant and another company's paper mill, Nassau County consistently ranks among the worst counties in the United States for toxins going into waterways," according to an October 7, 1999, article in the *Florida Times-Union.*

On a more upbeat note, there's nothing shrimpy about the town's ambitious and ongoing restoration. A 50-square-block area, referred to as the Olde Town section, is a designated historic district in the National Register of Historic Places. A number of popular walking tours of the district, including a "Cemetery Crawl," are offered at the **Amelia Island Museum of History** (233 South 3rd Street, 904/261-7378). You can conduct your own guided walking tour with a brochure obtained at the Chamber of Commerce office, located inside the fully restored **1899 train depot** (102 Centre Street). The theme of preservation and renewal extends to the shopping district, where storefronts re-create the style of the previous century.

You'll happily discover that the town is not merely a cosmetic, dollhouse revival of glory days (although the New Age music piped into the downtown shopping district is a bit cloying). Fernandina Beach is a real working community. Much of it, away from the historic district, is low-key and residential, and the residents seem committed to keeping it that way.

It was all the more surprising, then, to learn that Fernandina Beach had developed a serious crack problem. Among the reasons is the lack of job opportunities. For one thing, the ongoing decline of shrimping as a viable occupation along the north Florida coast has left fewer than 150 small independent shrimpers working between Fernandina and Daytona beaches. Suddenly, unassuming Victorian Fernandina Beach found itself home to a bevy of crack dealers, some brazenly selling their wares on the street only blocks from the historic district. The hammer came down on February 2, 2000, when federal agents began serving warrants for cocaine traf-

❷ Main Beach

  4

Location: highway A1A (Fletcher Avenue) at Trout Street in Fernandina Beach
Parking/fees: free parking lots
Hours: 8 A.M.–9 P.M.
Facilities: lifeguards (seasonal), restrooms, picnic tables, a playground, and showers
Contact: Fernandina Beach Parks and Recreation Department, 904/277-7350

❸ South Fernandina Beach accesses

 3

Location: There are 21 beach accesses at street ends off South Fletcher Avenue (Highway A1A) between Main Beach and the south end of town.
Parking/fees: limited free street parking
Hours: 8 A.M.–9 P.M.
Facilities: none
Contact: For beach information, call the Fernandina Beach Parks and Recreation Department at 904/277-7350. Obtain permits for beach driving at the Nassau County Courthouse and some stores.

MAP OF FLORIDA'S EAST COAST—PAGE 5

ficking charges; ultimately, 31 dealers were imprisoned. The Nassau County Sheriff's office later arrested 45 more following its own investigation. In August, another 31 were nabbed in a big undercover bust. It's sad to think that crack dealers and not shrimp are being netted in quantity these days in Fernandina Beach, but it's a sign of the times and, hey, at least they're getting the bums off the street.

By and large, Fernandina Beach remains a pleasant surprise for those who venture by, offering great beaches in town and at Fort Clinch State Park, plus loads of Victoriana and charm in the Centre Street historic district.

Beaches

Fernandina's pristine beaches lie a mile from the center of town. Head east on Centre Street, which becomes Atlantic Avenue (at 8th Street) and ends at **Main Beach.** Because of its abundant parking and facilities, including four tall lifeguard stands and a grassy playground, the vast majority of **Fernandina Beach** visitors—especially those with children—gravitate to Main Beach. Ample free parking is provided at two large paved lots. Beside them are picnic areas, gazebos, restrooms, showers, and a boardwalk. While it's all the same long strand, running south from Fort Clinch State Park, the beach has thinned out a bit at Main Beach, augmented by riprap and a squat seawall. The sand is much shellier and uneven at Main Beach than at Fort Clinch, but the beach widens again as you move farther down Amelia Island. Though the beach park began to get a bit rundown in the Nineties, it has been refurbished nicely of late, and on the drawing board is a fishing pier and grass amphitheater—additions that, it is hoped, will make Main Beach more of a "community beach."

The "beach" part of the town name does not lie. From Main Beach down to the southern city limits sign, we clocked 4.5 miles of beach and counted 21 individual public accesses. Each is clearly marked with rectangular wooden signs. All are brought to you courtesy of the city of Fernandina Beach. Most of the northern accesses are for pedestrians only. At the south Fernandina Beach accesses, a limited number of free parking spaces (10 to 20) are provided. Surfing is not allowed at Main Beach, so board bums head down to the popular beach access at Sadler Road and Fletcher Avenue (Highway A1A), where the waves break better anyway.

Fernandina Beach has generally displayed foresight in its residential zoning, with homes built well behind the 40-foot-tall sand dunes. Most of the beach houses are modest in size, and some are appealingly eccentric. Two are shaped like miniature lighthouses.

Peter's Point is the most desirable of the beach accesses south of Main Beach. In addition to more of the same wide, walkable strand, it offers decent facilities (restrooms, showers, and picnic shelters). If the Main Beach crowds are too much, head down Amelia Island in this direction.

Shore Things

- **Ecotourism:** Kayak Amelia, 904/321-0697 or 888-30KAYAK.
- **Fishing charters:** Amelia Island Charter Boat Association, 904/261-2870.

4 Peter's Point

Location: south end of Fletcher Avenue (Highway A1A), just outside city limits
Parking/fees: free parking lots
Hours: none posted
Facilities: lifeguards (seasonal), restrooms, picnic tables, and showers
Contact: Nassau County Recreation Department, 904/321-5790

- **Lighthouse:** Amelia Island Lighthouse, 1/2 Lighthouse Circle, 904/261-3248.
- **Marina:** Fernandina Harbour Marina, 1 Front Street, 904/261-0355.
- **Pier:** Fort Clinch State Park, 2601 Atlantic Avenue, 904/277-7274.
- **Rainy-day attraction:** Amelia Island Museum of History, 233 South 3rd Street, 904/261-7378.
- **Shopping/browsing:** Centre Street (a.k.a. Historic Downtown Fernandina Beach)
- **Surf shop:** Pipeline Surf Shop, 2022 1st Avenue, 904/277-3717.
- **Vacation rentals:** Amelia Island Lodging Systems, 584 South Fletcher Avenue, 904/261-4148.

Bunking Down

You can make history a part of your stay in Fernandina Beach by choosing from among nearly a dozen bed-and-breakfast inns, some of which legitimately date from the Victorian era. Yesteryear is very much alive at the venerable **Amelia Island Williams House** (103 South 9th Street, 904/277-2328, $$$). The Williams House, which has four rooms to rent, has won numerous awards and been selected a "Top Inn of the Year" by *Country Inns* magazine. Built in 1856, it was bought three years later by Marcellus Williams, a railroad surveyor. He added a gingerbread-style porch in the 1880s, and not much has changed beyond that in over a century.

Pure Victoriana, inside and out, is available nearby at the five-room **Bailey House** (28 South 7th Street, 904/261-5390, $$). Built in 1895 by an agent for a steamship company, the Bailey House was one of the most elaborately constructed homes of its day, with many turrets, gables, and bay windows, plus period antiques, brass beds, and carved furniture.

While the above two inns are located in the historic district (a mile from the beach), **Elizabeth Pointe Lodge** is situated right behind the sand dunes (98 South Fletcher Avenue, 904/277-4851, $$$). The 25-unit lodge offers a full breakfast, and some rooms have kitchenettes.

Coastal Cuisine

On the culinary front, Fernandina Beach is famous for the shrimp its local fleet continues to haul from local waters, despite the struggles that dog small, independent shrimpers these days. The price of shrimp fluctuates according to catch size, but they are available all over town and usually served steamed in the shell with cocktail sauce and lemon. Nothing fancy, but when shrimp are this fresh, they don't need dressing up. If you don't mind peeling and eating, it's the way to go here.

In real estate, the catchphrase is "location, location, location," and **Brett's Waterway Cafe** (1 South Front Street, 904/261-2660, $$$) has the best location in town: at the foot of Centre Street in downtown Fernandina Beach, overlooking the harbor. Try coming as the sun is going down for a great view. It's a very happening place: noisy in a good way, with lots of interesting conversations and a happy mix of families, locals, tourists, and folks from Jacksonville who know a meal worth driving for. They feature the best in local seafood, such as out-of-this-world broiled Fernandina shrimp in a light tomato sauce over a bed of spinach. From appetizers to desserts, Brett's delivers the goods in a grand setting.

The **Marina Seafood Restaurant** (101 Centre Street, 904/261-5310, $$) is the hands-down favorite in town for seafood. It's not so much that it's fancy as that it's fresh. They serve fish all day long, from fish and eggs (with cheese grits!) in the morning to fisherman's platters at the dinner hour. Family owned and operated for

MAP OF FLORIDA'S EAST COAST—PAGE 5

a quarter century, they close at 9 P.M. If culinary sophistication is what you want, the **Beech Street Grill** (8th and Beech Streets, 904/277-3662, $$$) is a gourmet New American eatery in an old Victorian setting. They specialize in Cajun blackened and light Italian seafood preparations utilizing fresh herbs and sauces.

The **Down Under Restaurant** (Highway A1A, 904/261-1001, $$), family owned and operated since 1982, is a good place to go to partake of fresh, locally caught seafood. The name refers to its scenic location "down under" the Thomas J. Shave Bridge, which crosses the Amelia River.

The **Florida House Inn** (22 South 3rd Street, 904/261-3300, $$) serves home-style Southern cooking (fried chicken, BBQ

Where's the Beach?

Tales of beach renourishment, which begin right on the Florida border at Fernandina Beach and Amelia Island Plantation, will be a recurring theme in this book, since beach erosion has occurred all over Florida. A good measure of the "credit" has to go to the U.S. Army Corps of Engineers, whose engineered boondoggles—jetties, groins, seawalls, and other hardened structures—have often created the problem. The corps is responsible in another sense, as well. By damming rivers throughout the southeast, they've cut off the source of sediment to the beaches. Next time you wonder where all the sand that should be winding up on your favorite beach is hiding, look upstream toward the mountains: it's trapped behind a dam.

Real-estate builders and developers must bear some of the blame, too, since they've often destroyed or altered the dune structure in seaside communities in order to make it possible to live directly on the beach, which might seem like a nice idea but is, in actuality, a foolhardy one. Sand dunes are like bank accounts. The more money you have in the bank, the better you'll be able to weather a financial emergency. Likewise, the more sand that's banked into dunes, the more capable the beach will be of weathering hurricane and storm damage. If you destroy the primary and secondary dunes by flattening and building on them, all of that sand will not be there to serve as a buffer between land and ocean. If you have a clear and unobstructed view of the ocean, it has a clear and unobstructed path to you, too.

Moreover, we are in a period of global warming and sea-level rise, which means that a certain amount of beach will be lost every year because the ocean is advancing upon the land as polar ice caps melt. The average rate of sea-level rise has been about two millimeters per year, which means roughly one to three feet of beach width that is lost annually. To put an even more somber spin on the issue of beach development, we are emerging from a cycle of relatively low hurricane activity in the Atlantic Ocean. Consider all of the construction that has occurred during this relative break in the action over the last 30 years. Think of the endless millions in damage that have been caused by the big blows that have made landfall (Hurricanes Andrew, Hugo, and Opal, for starters). Imagine what lies ahead in a time of heightened hurricane activity.

Now, do you still want to live on the beach?

MAP OF NASSAU COUNTY—PAGE 6

pork, catfish, collards, biscuits, cornbread). The heaping platters and bowls back up their claim to give you "always all you care to eat." You might pay a bit more at the Florida House, but you get a more evocative setting: it's Florida's oldest hotel, dating back to 1857, and still operates as an 11-room bed-and-breakfast.

Night Moves

Simply by virtue of being Florida's oldest continuously operating bar, the **Palace Saloon** (117 Centre Street, 904/261-6320) is an interesting place to duck into while shopping 'n' shuffling through the historic district. Built in 1878, it thrived in the Gay '90s and continued to lure curious folks with its period appointments (hand-carved oak bar, brass rails, tin ceiling, murals) a century later. In fact, a lot of visitors began and ended their night moves right here. Sadly, an electrical fire gutted the Palace Saloon in February 1999, claiming the priceless 1907 wall murals and damaging the black mahogany bar. The Palace reopened three months later, but its restoration has taken much longer and is, in fact, ongoing as of this writing. Still, you can't keep a good bar down, and the Palace is slowly but surely being restored to its former glory. Even the murals depicting ships and pirates are being meticulously re-created.

In the historic district, we also like **O'Kane's** (318 Centre Street, 904/261-1000), a friendly Irish pub and eatery. Your best bet for finding rock and roll down by the beach is the ramshackle, dark, and beer-stained **Sliders** (1998 South Fletcher Avenue, 904/261-0954). Just avoid it on Disco Night. A decent place to spend your beachside evening is on the patio of **The Surf** (3199 South Fletcher Avenue, 904/261-5711), where breezes will serenade you between sets by (more than likely) a one-man band or a local DJ. Simple, serviceable food (smoked fish dip, seafood plates) can be ordered, and on a balmy evening with a big moon hung high, The Surf's wooden deck makes a fine place to knock back a brew or two. There's also a motel, cut from the plainest possible cloth, on the premises.

Contact Information

Amelia Island Tourist Development Council, 102 Centre Street, Fernandina Beach, FL 32035; 904/261-3248 or 800/2-AMELIA; website: www.ameliaisland.org

Map of Florida's East Coast—Page 5

Summer Beach

Summer Beach is an upscale resort development of roughly 80 private homes and condos and the Ritz-Carlton Amelia Island, at the south end of Fernandina Beach. It's just beyond the city limits, so the mailing address is Amelia Island and not Fernandina Beach. The layout is not dissimilar to its much larger neighbor, Amelia Island Plantation, which preceded it by a few decades. In addition to homes and condos, many of which are available for vacation rental, the property's commercial centerpiece is the Ritz-Carlton.

Bunking Down

We needn't go on about how bedazzled you'll be by the 445-unit **Ritz-Carlton Amelia Island** (4750 Amelia Island Parkway, 904/277-1100, $$$$) or how much you'll pay to stay here (rates range from $129 to $2,000 per night). Suffice it to say that it's earned AAA's rarely given five-star rating, that it has 1.5 miles of pristine Amelia Island beachfront, and that the property is an almost obscenely genteel paradise. It boasts of being the only mainland Ritz-Carlton tethered to a championship golf course. In addition to the 18-hole Golf Club of Amelia Island, other resort amenities include indoor/outdoor pools, tennis courts, a croquet lawn, pathways that meander over plush landscaped grounds, four on-premises restaurants... in short, the works.

Coastal Cuisine

The **Grill at the Ritz-Carlton** (4750 Amelia Island Parkway, 904/277-1100, $$$$) is the five-star culinary centerpiece at the Ritz, excelling in grilled steak and seafood. Do be aware that you won't get out of here for less than $60 a head, however.

Contact Information

Summer Beach Resort Central, 5000 Amelia Island Parkway, Amelia Island, FL 32034; 904/277-0905; website: www.summerbeach.com

5 Summer Beach

Location: This resort, which includes private homes and condos and the Ritz-Carlton Amelia Island, is accessed via turnoffs from Amelia Island Parkway (Highway A1A) just south of the Fernandina Beach city limits.

Parking/fees: Beaches and facilities are for the use of residents, registered guests, and their visitors only.

Hours: none posted

Facilities: concessions, restrooms, showers, and a visitor center

Contact: Summer Beach, 904/277-0905, or Ritz-Carlton Amelia Island, 904/277-1100

MAP OF NASSAU COUNTY—PAGE 6

American Beach

Though Southern bigots and greedy developers might argue otherwise, **American Beach** is aptly named. It is emblematic of a major aspect of American life and history: the African-American experience. It is proudly, defiantly, and somewhat angrily a black beach pressed between two sentinels of upscale white hegemony: the Ritz-Carlton Amelia Island and Amelia Island Plantation. Its appearance is almost shockingly poor compared to the marble-walled Ritz-Carlton and the villas of the neighboring "plantation." American Beach is, to all outward appearances, a down-on-its-heels place that developers have been angling to acquire, lot by lot, and turn into yet another soulless, gated resort for America's golfing gentry.

If you should happen to be driving down Highway A1A between Fernandina Beach and Amelia Island Plantation, you may spy a nondescript road sign that points east toward American Beach. If you are a tourist or passer-through, it is not a turn you'll wish to make unless you are morbidly curious about a historic seaside ghetto. If you are white, your presence in this tumble-down town of concrete-block bungalows in various states of decay and disarray will elicit raised eyebrows—that is, if anyone is even around to check you out.

American Beach used to come alive on weekends, when young blacks from the Jacksonville area headed up to party on the beach. Sometimes these parties got out of hand, and there have been confrontations with the authorities. As the result of a beefed-up police presence, however, the crowds have dwindled. In the summer of 2000, there were no crowds at all.

Access to American Beach is gained at the end of Lewis Street. Here stands a sign with a list of purportedly forbidden activities (e.g., "No Littering"). One item stands out, having been appended in a hand-drawn scrawl: "No Cops." We saw only two people during our sojourn through American Beach. One was a black kid on a go-cart who appeared to be tailgating us. We first picked him up at **Burney Park**, a Nassau County facility with picnic tables and a large parking lot that was completely empty on a beautiful summer day. Leaving the tortured matter of race relations and the war between the haves and the have-nots aside, we were impressed by Burney Park, with its big, bountiful dune bluffs and unspoiled beach. There was not a golf cart in sight. Only a go-cart.

The other figure we saw was a striking black woman whose long, unkempt, and apparently unwashed hair was gathered

❻ American Beach

Location: From Highway A1A five miles south of Fernandina Beach, turn east at the sign for American Beach. Follow signs to the beach.
Parking/fees: free street parking
Hours: none posted
Facilities: none
Contact: Nassau County Recreation Department, 904/321-5790; permits for beach driving: Nassau County Courthouse and some stores

❼ Burney Park

Location: From Highway A1A five miles south of Fernandina Beach, turn east at the sign for American Beach. Follow signs to the park.
Parking/fees: free parking lots
Hours: none posted
Facilities: restrooms, picnic tables, and showers
Contact: Nassau County Recreation Department, 904/321-5790

into a single elephant trunk-sized dreadlock. Eight-inch-long fingernails sprouted from her hands. This bizarre figure wandered between a squat house near the ocean and a Dumpster on the property that was covered with political bumper stickers. We circled around to have a closer look at the only ambulatory soul in American Beach but spun out of town when she began barking what we thought was some kind of reprimand at us.

Would that we had stuck around. Subsequent research turned up the information that her name is MaVynnee Betsch. She's a granddaughter of a cofounder of the Afro-American Insurance Company, an enormously successful Jacksonville-based firm started in 1901. (It has since been absorbed by a larger firm.) Afro-American purchased and founded American Beach back in the 1930s, which is why it's remained "in the family," so to speak, all these years. Betsch—known as the "Beach Lady" because of her tireless support for American Beach's preservation and recognition of its historic past—doesn't much care for or about money, choosing instead to live at and often literally on the beach. A former opera singer and a graduate of Oberlin College, she now patrols the town as its de facto guardian and conscience. She has not cut her hair or fingernails in years. And every word she says makes a hell of a lot of sense to us.

In fact, we'll give her the last word on American Beach. In 1995, there was another of the periodic flare-ups between the defiant citizens of American Beach and the white resort developers on either side of them. That year, the issue was the proposed development of 83 acres on the landward side of American Beach that had been acquired by Amelia Island Plantation. When the specter of yet another golf course surrounded by 60 or 70 "luxury single-family homes" appeared to be in the cards—this one right in American Beach's backyard—Betsch had this to say in the *Miami Herald:*

"I found [the attitude] insulting that we should be honored they were building a golf course next to us. I said to them: 'You should be honored to be living next to one of the most historic black communities in the South.'"

Contact Information

American Beach Property Owners Association, P.O. Box 6123, Fernandina Beach, FL 32035; 904/261-4396

MAP OF NASSAU COUNTY—PAGE 6

Amelia Island Plantation

If you like golf courses and beachfront condos, you might view Amelia Island Plantation (pop. 700) and its kindred developments in the area as better than what existed before. If, however, you are bothered by a pristine island's encroachment by people of means whose idea of communing with nature consists of an afternoon of golf, you might think it worse.

We do appreciate the atypical efforts at environmental preservation, or at least a respectful coexistence with nature, made by planners of Amelia Island Plantation, the island's developmental centerpiece. Moreover, we most definitely like certain aspects of Amelia Island Plantation—the word "plantation," with its evocation of slavery and subjugation in the Old South, not being one of them—and find it, in many respects, to be a model of how to develop without destroying the natural surroundings. The key concept is harmonious blending with nature, and while the principle has become incrementally compromised over time—there are now 54 holes of golf but fewer than seven miles of biking and nature trails—Amelia Island Plantation's claims of "environmental integrity" are not without merit.

Though advocates on both sides could carry on the golf course versus nature debate till they're green in the face, the fact remains that Amelia Island very nearly might have turned out looking like hell's half-acre had an enlightened developer named Charles Fraser not come along. The Union Carbide Corporation originally held title to the land upon which Amelia Island Plantation now sits. (That is, of course, after the Timucuan Indians, the flags of eight nations, and a now-vanished black community named Franklintown.) The chemical firm intended to strip-mine the land for potassium. Fortunately, the environmentally enlightened Fraser—whose Sea Pines Company had developed Hilton Head Island—purchased 900 acres and began looking for ways to design a resort community that would not unduly disturb the fragile barrier island ecology.

The plantation's overseers drafted a plan to protect salt marshes and oceanfront dunes while buffering waterways with strips of natural vegetation to minimize runoff from golf courses and habitations. Foot traffic was restricted to boardwalks. Covenants defining the restrictions and obligations of property owners were devised. Codified guidelines ensured that buildings were "aesthetically pleasing, functionally convenient, and part of the landscape design."

It's no coincidence that Amelia Island Plantation was plotted at the dawn of the 1970s, near the environmental awakening that found its most universal expression with the first Earth Day observance in April 1970. This broadly shared perspective began influencing the kinds of things people wanted to do and see on vacation. Fraser anticipated that people of means were beginning to desire more natural settings—not gaudy, silo-like monstrosities rising out of tree-strafed sandlots but taste-

8 Amelia Island Plantation

 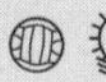

Location: From I-95, take Exit 129 (Highway A1A) into Fernandina Beach and continue south for seven miles, following signs to the resort.

Parking/fees: Beaches and facilities are for the use of residents, registered guests, and their visitors only.

Hours: none posted

Facilities: concessions, restrooms, showers, and a visitor center

Contact: Amelia Island Plantation, 904/261-6161 or 800/874-6878

The Geology of Amelia Island

Amelia Island is the name of the barrier island that presses against the Georgia border, separated from it by the St. Mary's River. Essentially, Amelia Island is coastal Nassau County. It is also the name of the largest resort development on the island, the 1,330-acre Amelia Island Plantation, which dominates its southern end, away from the working community of Fernandina Beach. In this chapter, we have broken down Amelia Island into Fort Clinch State Park, Fernandina Beach, Summer Beach, American Beach, and Amelia Island Plantation.

Geographically, Amelia Island and its neighbor to the south, Little Talbot Island (see separate entry), are the southernmost in the chain of barrier islands that begin with the Outer Banks in North Carolina. They have more in common with the Georgia "sea islands" than the rest of Florida's East Coast. The entire coast of Georgia consists of these sea islands—the "Golden Isle chain," by name—as do Amelia and Little Talbot Islands and parts of South Carolina's lower coast.

Sea islands are found at or near the head of the Georgia embayment, a wide arc described by the coastline from North Carolina to Florida. The embayment's head is subject to greater tidal exchange and lesser wave energy than the ends. At Amelia Island, for instance, the mean tidal range (i.e., the average difference between high and low tide) is more than two meters (i.e., over six feet). By comparison, the rest of Florida's east coast has a mean tidal range tide of one meter or less. Sea islands form along coastlines where the tidal range is 2–5 meters (which classifies them as "mesotidal").

The 2.1-meter tidal range found at the Georgia-Florida border allows inlets to form and remain open, creating barrier islands. As sand and sediment are transported by currents running parallel to the coast—a process known as "longshore drift"—their deflection by ebbing tides results in the buildup of deltas that emerge to form beach ridges at the tips. The upshot is that sea islands such as Amelia Island acquire a short, stubby appearance. They are known as "drumstick barriers," because their shape suggests that of chicken drumsticks. The sea islands' most prominent feature is an extensive, well-developed salt marsh on the inlet side. Between dunes and marshes, one encounters dense forests of palms, Southern magnolias, and magnificently gnarly live oaks draped with Spanish moss. What all this technical talk means to the average vacationer is that Amelia and Little Talbot are unique in Florida—and that you might want to put these often overlooked islands on your vacation itinerary if you're ever in the area.

ful condominium dwellings burrowed in the cooling shade of oak trees and sabal palms. At the same time, they also wanted the very best golf courses and tennis courts, as well as top-quality instructors.

In the nearly 30 years that have passed since the master plan was drafted, Amelia Island Plantation has stuck to the script pretty faithfully. The resort has increased its holdings by 430 acres, so that, at 1,330 acres, it is now nearly half again as large. To be sure, there is a lot more on the grounds than there was back when we first visited in the mid-1980s, and the general drift of late has more to do with earth-moving than Earth Day. But a general air of preservation continues to allow Amelia Island Plantation to rate a cut above the competition along Florida's grossly overbuilt East Coast. Here, you can at least see the forest and the trees—not to mention the beach.

Beaches

Amelia Island Plantation claims four miles of beach, which is quite an expanse. They have occasionally been forced to widen their eroding beach by trucking in sand, a process known as "beach renourishment." The sand used in such projects often doesn't match that which is naturally found on the beach. Thus, mixed in with Amelia's fine white sand is coarser, shelly material, evidence that the beach has been extended with sand dredged from elsewhere. Though it doesn't "feel" as right or look as natural as it should, there is a fine length of it at Amelia Island Plantation to walk, lie, or play on—that is, if you can tear yourself away from the tennis and golf (three 18-

Amelia Island's Recreational Scorecard

There's so much to do at Amelia Island and there are so many places to do it that we thought it would be easier on us (as writers) and you (as readers) simply to list them all, menu-style. Bear in mind that the resort occupies 1,330 acres, which is a significant chunk of real estate. Come with clubs, rackets, bikes, or whatever turns you on. The problem at Amelia Island Plantation isn't finding enough to do, it's finding enough time to do it all.

- **Beach activities**: Four miles of sandy ocean beach border Amelia Island Plantation.
- **Golf**: You'll find 54 holes of golf, including 36 holes designed by course architect Pete Dye and the 18-hole Long Point course, created by Tom Fazio. All are scenic and challenging, variously offering views of marsh, ocean, and deep woods. Seven of Amelia's 54 holes border the ocean—more than any other U.S. resort. A golf school is located at the Long Point course. Golf magazine rated Amelia one of the top 12 golf resorts in America.
- **Tennis**—The Racquet Park facility holds 27 tennis courts.
- **Workouts**: A full-service health and fitness center includes strength-training and cardiovascular machines; racquetball courts; aerobic and conditioning classes; a heated indoor-outdoor lap pool; Jacuzzis; and complete spa services ranging from manicure to massage.
- **Fishing and sailing**: Arrange expeditions at the Amelia Angler, where rods and fishing/crabbing gear are rented, and charter and sailing excursions can be booked. Freshwater fishing is available in lakes and lagoons stocked with bass and catfish. Surf casting is a cinch, especially if you're staying in an ocean-view or oceanfront villa.

hole courses), which are the resort's main recreational calling cards. If you're a beach person, one positive effect of all these other distractions is that you can easily find a spot where you'll literally have the beach to yourself.

Bunking Down

With the completion of the 250-unit **Amelia Inn** (Amelia Island Plantation, Highway A1A South, 904/261-6161, $$$$) and its opening in 1998, there are now more than 700 guest accommodations available at Amelia Island Plantation. These range from rooms at the inn (all of them oceanfront) to villas with up to three bedrooms. Villas range in age, decor, location (seaside, woods, marsh, golf course), and on and on. We've sampled a few of Amelia's villas over the years, most recently staying at a development called (appropriately for us) Beachwalker. The bedrooms were commodious, the appointments quite comfortable. We could get used to living like

- **Swimming:** There are 21 pools scattered about the property and one big ocean, as well.
- **Youth program:** Amelia has supervised youth programs that allow adults to get away and play their own games. The "Kids Campelia" program is offered on weekdays 8:30 a.m.–1 p.m. from early March to around Labor Day.
- **Nature tours:** The Plantation's full-time naturalist conducts informative ecotourist trips around the property.
- **Bicycling and jogging:** There are seven miles of biking and nature trails, not to mention lots of roads, around the property. Bikes rent for $5 an hour at Wheels 'n' Keels (904/261-6161, ext. 5427); also available for rental are baby joggers (strollers with mountain-bike wheels that can be pushed on the beach), golf carts (otherwise known as "island hoppers"), canoes, and more.
- **Paddleboats:** Sign up for hourly paddleboat rentals at Wheels 'n' Keels.
- **Shopping:** Well, this is a recreational activity, too, isn't it? Shopping burns up calories, takes up time, and thins the wallet, just like golf and tennis. An area known as the Village Shops is located just outside the gates of the Plantation. As you might expect, the shops tend to be upscale arts-and-crafts boutiques. On a practical note, stock up on food at the Village Market.

Having duly noted all of these things, it must be said that our favorite activity of all on Amelia Island is renting bikes and exploring the trails on the marsh side of the property. We recommend a ride out to Drummond Point and a stroll on its elevated boardwalk, which penetrates the pristine salt marsh. One night at around sundown, a big storm off in the distance streaked the heavens with jagged lightning and cast an eerie glow over the gray-green marsh. No offense to all the duffers and tennis bums, but you can't beat a bike or a hike when it comes to making contact with nature.

MAP OF NASSAU COUNTY—PAGE 6

this with no trouble at all.

If you're thinking of buying at Amelia Island Plantation, there are more than 900 villa units among 17 developments bearing names like "Piper Dunes," "Fairway Oaks," and "Sandcastles," all of them self-evidently describing their location. Villas at Amelia Island Plantation range in price from $100,000 to $500,000. If you want to book a vacation, you can do that, too. During peak season, which runs from mid-March to early May, a two-bedroom ocean-view villa goes for $555 a night. (That's roughly four times what they were when we visited in 1984.) If you're staying a week or longer, the nightly rate drops somewhat. You can save by booking a "resort view" (read: non-oceanfront) villa, where the in-season rate is $435 (less for a week or longer). During Amelia Island's low season, which spans the winter months—a contrast to the resorts of South Florida, where winter is peak season—you will get the best prices. Rooms at the inn go for between $130 and $335 per night. Finally, they offer package deals—centered around golf, tennis, and "romantic getaways"—that are worth asking about. New to the resort is the huge Spa at Amelia Island Plantation, reputed to be one of the largest in the Southeast.

Coastal Cuisine

As you'd expect of a gargantuan golf, beach, and tennis resort, there are all manner of places to wet your whistle at Amelia Island Plantation. The newly opened dining room at the **Amelia Inn** (Amelia Island Plantation, Highway A1A South, 904/321-5050, $$$$) specializes in upscale atmosphere and hearty food, simply but elegantly prepared from fresh ingredients. On any given night, you will find chophouse fare like beef tenderloin, veal chop, and free-range chicken counterpointed by seafood offerings of black grouper, red snapper, and yellowfin tuna. The fish are served seared, grilled, sautéed, or blackened.

The **Verandah** (Amelia Island Plantation, 904/321-5050, $$$)—our favorite on-premises eatery, refurbished in 1999—is a more price-conscious restaurant that does terrific things with seafood. Entrées we've tried in years past include blackened red snapper with crabmeat in ginger-herb sauce, grouper with lobster meat in herb-garlic sauce, and herb-crusted ahi with mango chili sauce.

Night Moves

While wandering around the grounds of the Amelia Island Plantation one night, we suddenly heard a siren go off, accompanied by a message delivered and repeated in an urgent, amplified robotic voice: "Island is being tampered with! Island is being tampered with!" We never figured out exactly what happened or who'd been "tampering" with the island, but this is the most excitement we've ever scared up after dark here. There's not much in the way of nightlife to be found beyond a civilized drink at the **Amelia Inn.** Best bet is the **Beach Club Sports Bar,** where you'll find pool tables and TV screens in profusion. But it is only open seasonally. If it's nightlife you want, head up the road to Fernandina Beach.

Contact Information

Amelia Island Plantation, 3000 First Coast Highway, Amelia Island, FL 32034; 888/261-6161; website: www.aipfl.com

Amelia Island State Park

After all the buildup at Fernandina Beach, Summer Beach, and Amelia Island Plantation, it's nice to find some wilderness acreage on the island. If you're a wild-beach type, **Amelia Island State Park**, eight miles south of Fernandina Beach along Highway A1A on Amelia Island, offers 200 acres on which to roam. Visitors can swim, fish, and ride horses on the beach. Lines can be cast from the shore or a mile-long fishing bridge extending into Nassau Sound, where the state record flounder was hauled in and redfish and speckled trout are common catches. **Kelly Seahorse Ranch** (7500 First Coast Highway, Amelia Island, 904/491-5166) serves the park with guided beach horseback rides that cost $35 and go out four times daily; call for information and reservations.

Contact Information

Amelia Island State Park, c/o Little Talbot Island State Park, 12157 Heckscher Drive, Jacksonville, FL 32226; 904/251-2320; website: www.myflorida.com

9 Amelia Island State Park

Location: eight miles south of Fernandina Beach along Highway A1A
Parking/fees: free parking lots
Hours: 8 A.M. to sunset
Facilities: restrooms
Contact: Talbot Islands GEOpark, 904/251-2320

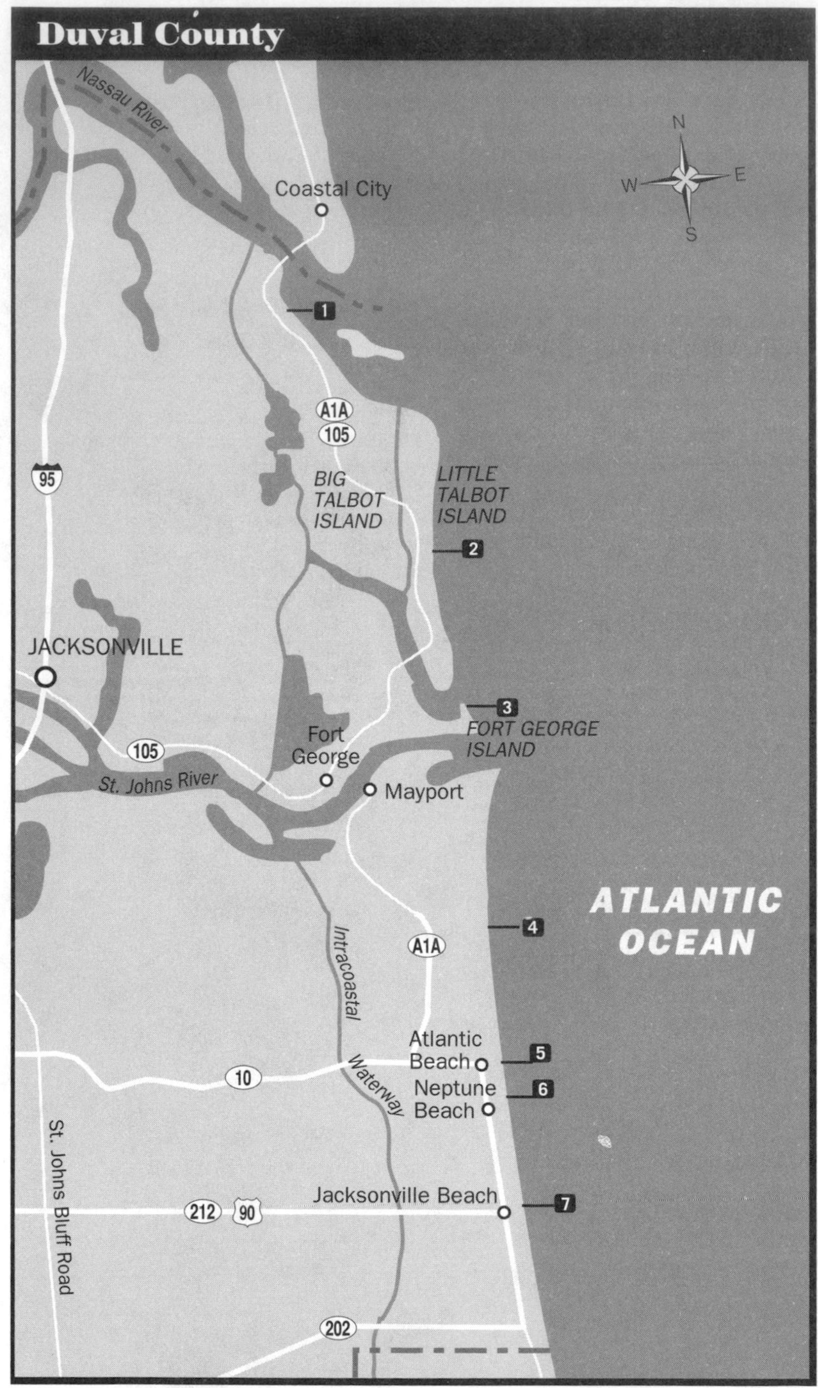
Duval County
Nassau River
Coastal City
N
W
E
S
1
A1A
105
95
BIG TALBOT ISLAND
LITTLE TALBOT ISLAND
2
JACKSONVILLE
3
FORT GEORGE ISLAND
Fort George
105
St. Johns River
Mayport
ATLANTIC OCEAN
4
A1A
Intracoastal Waterway
Atlantic Beach
5
Neptune Beach
6
10
St. Johns Bluff Road
Jacksonville Beach
7
212
90
202

Duval County

The county of Duval and the city of Jacksonville are essentially one and the same. The city expanded to the county borders in the late 1960s, making Jacksonville, at 841 square miles, the largest municipal land mass in the United States. Its vastness renders Jacksonville a kind of an endless blank slate that keeps filling with more people, businesses, bridges, developments, home teams, and, of course, traffic. You can still find glimmers of personality by the shoreline, 15 miles east of Jacksonville, where three struggling beach towns—Jacksonville Beach, Atlantic Beach, and Neptune Beach, collectively known as the "Jax Beaches"—recall parts of the Jersey Shore in their character and aspirations. The beach itself—16 miles in all, from the Talbot Islands to the Jax Beaches—is as wide and fine as they come.

Big Talbot Island State Park and Little Talbot Island State Park

In the northeast corner of Duval County, between Nassau Sound and Fort George Inlet, three islands lie side by side like lazy gators basking in the sun. They are, from north to south, Big Talbot, Long, and Little Talbot Islands. Highway A1A crosses all of them, though it just grazes Little Talbot Island, the gem in the chain from the perspective of beach access.

Bounded by Simpson Creek and Nassau Sound, **Big Talbot Island** is characterized by bluffs instead of dunes, and one descends to the beach by way of stairs. High tide comes to the base of the bluffs, and natural erosion causes oaks to topple seaward from time to time. The sand is dark, and the look of the island is wild. Big Talbot's proximity to Nassau Sound makes it great for fishing but not so good for shelling. If you want to lie out on a wide, breezy beach, you're better off heading down to Little Talbot Island, four miles south of Big Talbot's bluffs entrance. All the same, Big Talbot is worth a visit. Bring a fishing pole and/or boat to explore the teeming sound and tidal creeks. Also, hikers will want to keep an eye out for trailheads along Highway A1A as it crosses Big Talbot Island. Finally, an ecotourism firm known as Kayak Amelia leads paddling expeditions, some of which depart from Big Talbot Island.

Long Island lies between Big and Little Talbot Islands. Only its northern tip is exposed to Nassau Sound, so there is no beach out there. Mostly covered with maritime forest, this narrow island has lately become part of the state's expanding inventory of parkland.

Little Talbot Island is entirely preserved as a state park. Narrow and elongated, it is the southernmost barrier island in the extensive Golden Isles chain, which begins up at North Carolina's Outer Banks. Boardwalks at both ends of the Little Talbot Island lead to five miles of uncrowded beaches backed by a well-developed dune system. The island's midsection is a great place to get away from the crowds, if you're up for a hike from either access point in pursuit of solitude.

❶ Big Talbot Island State Park

Location: Along Highway A1A, at the south side of Nassau Sound, Big Talbot Island is between Amelia and Little Talbot Islands.

Parking/fees: $2 entrance fee per vehicle (honor system)

Hours: 8 A.M. to one hour before sunset

Facilities: restrooms

Contact: Talbot Islands GEOpark, 904/251-2320

❷ Little Talbot Island State Park

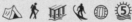

Location: 13 miles north of Jacksonville and seven miles south of Amelia Island, along Highway A1A.

Parking/fees: $3.25 entrance fee per vehicle. Camping fees March 1–October 31 are $15.75 per night (without hookups) and $17.88 (with hookups). The rates drop the rest of the year to $9 and $11, respectively.

Hours: 8 A.M. to sunset

Facilities: lifeguards (seasonal), restrooms, picnic tables, showers, and a visitor center

Contact: Talbot Islands GEOpark, 904/251-2320

Map of Florida's East Coast—Page 5

Little Talbot's beaches, having never been developed, are broader and healthier than those of Amelia Island. The whole island is worth exploring and appreciating. Seaward dunes are covered with sea oats and morning glory. Older, inland dune ridges support slash pines, red cedars, and cabbage palms. Grasses and sedges thrive in the interdune troughs. A coastal hammock thick with gnarly live oaks, Southern magnolia, and American holly occupies the northeast corner of the island. An unnamed nature trail, whose head is located just west of the ranger station, proceeds 2.4 miles through the hammock before ending on the beach. To complete a scenic loop, walk 1.7 miles south along the beach to the north boardwalk and then return via the boardwalk and park road.

The island's west side is a classic Southern sea island salt marsh of grass-covered flats interlaced with tidal creeks. The park's 40-site campground is located on the west side of the island, a short walk from the marsh's edge.

Contact Information

Little Talbot Island State Park, 12157 Heckscher Drive, Jacksonville, FL 32226; 904/251-2320; website: www.myflorida.com

Fort George Island

When Jacksonville city dwellers want to spend a day on the beach in a more natural setting than the exhaust-choked asphalt sprawl of Jacksonville Beach, they head up to Fort George Island. This triangular-shaped island lies over the St. Johns River from the naval town of Mayport. It is bounded on the east by the Fort George River, which separates it from Little Talbot Island, while the Intracoastal Waterway divides it from the swampy mainland. The island's drawing card is **Huguenot Park,** a city-run park bounded by ocean, inlet, and river. There are a couple of miles of beach out here that magically expand both in length and width at low tide. Fort George Island is far less urbanized than the Jax Beaches. You are likely to spy sand dollars and starfish on the beach at Huguenot Park, while it is unlikely you'd turn up either on Jacksonville Beach. By contrast to their dune-flattened city cousins, the dune fields at Huguenot are extensive, tall, and heavily vegetated.

Not surprisingly, Huguenot Park is popular with families, who bring the kids to fish, camp, or swim. One cause for concern is the area where the Fort George River meets the ocean, creating turbulent currents that led to drownings in the past. Lifeguards were introduced to the park in 1999, and they've had their hands full, making more than 40 water rescues in each season since their arrival. Families with young children might prefer to head to the calmer inlet side of the island. In addition to swimming and sunbathing, windsurfers carve

3 Huguenot Park

Location: on Fort George Island, east of Jacksonville. Take the Hecksher Drive exit off I-95, go east to Highway A1A, then north to the park.

Parking/fees: 50 cents per person entrance fee. Camping fees are $5.63 per night for tents and $7.88 for RVs; there are no hookups.

Hours: 8 A.M.–6 P.M. (8 P.M. in summer)

Facilities: concessions, lifeguards (seasonal), restrooms, picnic tables, and showers

Contact: Huguenot Park, 904/251-3335

MAP OF DUVAL COUNTY—PAGE 24

their way around the inlet. Bird-watchers train field glasses on the abundant avian life, including painted bunting. Anglers toss lines from beach, jetty, and riverbank. Many come early in the morning, stake out a prime location, and fish all day—a pleasant way to while away the hours. Three camping areas—by the inlet, on the river, and in the woodsy "middle ground"—offer a total of 88 sites in the park.

Because Huguenot's beach frontage is abundant and unspoiled, don't be surprised to find crowds of 5,000 or more on sunny weekends. The park is readily accessible from Jacksonville by taking the Mayport–Fort George Ferry ($3 per car, reachable via Highway A1A north of Mayport) or the Heckscher Drive exit off I-95. Beach access near an urban area doesn't get much cheaper than Huguenot's admission fee of 50 cents per person.

Contact Information

Huguenot Park, 10980 Heckscher Drive, Jacksonville, FL 32226; 904/251-3335

Jacksonville

Every time we roll through this resurgent Southern city, which is located 25 miles south of the Georgia border, along I-95 in northeast Florida, we're bowled over by the changes. For starters, Jacksonville (pop. 700,000) has the largest incorporated land area of any city in the United States, a whopping 841 square miles (almost twice the size of Los Angeles). With its population having increased by nearly 50 percent over the past decade—ranked 16th among U.S. cities—surely Jacksonville is worthy of a nickname like the Amazing Inflatable City. It is a headquarters for big business firms and insurance companies. Jacksonville's boomtown ways are reflected in the city boosters' trumpeting of its many amenities. Among these are a wealth of museums, including the Museum of Science and History ("MOSH," for short) and the Cummer Museum of Art & Gardens; a striking Edward Rouse–designed waterfront on the St. Johns River, anchored by a linear park and festival marketplace known as Jacksonville Landing; and the Jacksonville Jaguars. This hugely successful NFL franchise has marshaled a rabid fan base that amounts to a citywide pep rally. They play at Alltel Pavilion, near downtown Jacksonville, and tickets were a near impossibility for what became a disappointingly so-so 2000 season.

Jacksonville is, first and foremost, an aquatic city. The St. Johns River defines the city and its recreational prerogatives. If you live here, you almost can't get away with not having a boat. Enjoying a bottle of wine on the water at sunset, "tailboating" (the marine equivalent of a tailgate party) to a Jags game, trolling tidal creeks for redfish, kayaking around an estuary or out to an ocean sandbar—these are some of the recreational options that inspire Jacksonville natives to balance work with play in a way that coast-dwelling Californians, for instance, would understand completely.

One other aspect of life in the Jacksonville area that residents justifiably boast about is their beaches. Located 15 miles east of downtown (via Atlantic, Beach, or Butler Boulevard) is a trifecta of beach towns: Atlantic Beach, Neptune Beach, and Jacksonville Beach. They are collectively known as the "Jax Beaches." If downtown Jacksonville is all business, then the Jax Beaches are completely casual, as in flip-flops, cutoffs, jukeboxes, and cold beer. By contrast to much of Florida's overbuilt east

Map of Florida's East Coast—Page 5

coast, the Jax Beaches are in no mood to have their neighborhoods razed and replaced with condos and luxury hotels. Unpretentious and affordable, they remain a string of people's beach towns. In that sense, they are is much like the whole of Jacksonville: informal and neighborly, optimistic and engaging.

Contact Information

Jacksonville Convention and Visitors Bureau, 3 Independent Drive, Jacksonville, FL 32202; 904/798-9148; website: www.jaxcvb.com

Mayport

Mayport (pop. 2,781) is no Mayberry. It's a U.S. Navy port town, and Mayport Naval Station (commissioned in 1942) is the third largest such beast, in terms of personnel and vessels, in the United States. Really, the only reasons a visitor who doesn't have navy kin would detour to Mayport is to board the Mayport–Fort George Ferry or visit Kathryn Abbey Hanna Park. The ferry makes the half-mile passage across the St. Johns River in a matter of minutes, saving considerable miles and time for those headed from Jacksonville to Amelia Island or the parks of northern Duval County. It costs $3 per car; call 904/241-9969 for schedules and information. For a rundown on Hanna Park, read on.

Beaches

The stellar 450-acre **Kathryn Abbey Hanna Park**, run by the city of Jacksonville, is located just south of the Mayport Naval Station. Hanna Park offers free access to a gorgeous, lifeguarded 1.5-mile-long beach. The main draw, however, is the park's 20-mile network of hiking and biking trails.

The mountain-bike trails are maintained by local bike shops to be challenging, championship-level courses. The biking trails—about a half dozen of them, each two miles or so in length and bearing names like "Misery" and "Logjam"—ramble over the extensive park grounds, which include a 65-acre man-made lake and 293 campsites with full hookups. With an entrance fee of $1 a head—raised in early 1999 from 50 cents to a sawbuck by the Jacksonville city council over the strenuous objections of the mayor's office—Hanna Park is one of the best recreational bargains on the First Coast. It is a Rousseauian oasis of nature amid the blighted surroundings of Mayport's military sprawl.

Coastal Cuisine

Worth a detour, or right on your way if you're crossing the St. Johns River via the Mayport Ferry, is the unpretentious but excellent **Singleton's Seafood Shack** (4728 Ocean Street, 904/246-4442, $$). Specialties of the shack are steamed shrimp and rock shrimp, but you'll also find grouper, dolphin, snapper, flounder, and various other catches of the day on the ample menu. We feasted on fish dip, steamed

4 Kathryn Abbey Hanna Park

Location: 3.5 miles north of Jacksonville Beach, off Mayport Road, in Mayport

Parking/fees: $1 per head, ages six and up. Camping fees are $13 per RV and $10.13 per tent, with full hookups.

Hours: 8 A.M.–6 P.M. (8 P.M. in summer)

Facilities: concessions, lifeguards (seasonal), restrooms, picnic tables, showers, and a visitor center

Contact: Kathryn Abbey Hanna Park, 904/249-4700

shrimp, and blackened grouper one balmy late-winter afternoon after working up an appetite kayaking around the Timucuan Preserve with the gang at Kayak Amelia. We can scarcely imagine a better way to spend a weekend in the Jacksonville area than paddling the marsh and scarfing shrimp afterward. The floors at Singleton's are wooden, diners sit at unfancy picnic tables, the waitresses are busy but friendly, and the whole casual enterprise is a modest monument to seafood that bustles at lunch and dinner seven days a week. It's on the south bank of the river, only a block from the Mayport Ferry.

Contact Information

Kathryn Abbey Hanna Park, 500 Wonderwood Drive, Jacksonville, FL 32233; 904/249-4700

Atlantic Beach

The most immediately appealing of the three separate but contiguous communities that run along Jacksonville's oceanfront, Atlantic Beach (pop. 13,000) tries hard to be all things to all beachgoers. Most importantly, they've established a solid and dedicated year-round community with a clearly delineated "Town Center" of shops, restaurants, and nicely landscaped sidewalks. They also welcome outside visitors while keeping the resultant commercial zone, Atlantic Boulevard (State Route 10), free of low-end blight and upscale snobbery. In short, little Atlantic Beach (three square miles) has the right mix for a beach town, in our estimation.

Perhaps this relaxed posture derives from the town's resort history. Atlantic Beach was created in 1900, growing up around a depot of Henry Flagler's East Coast Railway. In 1901, Flagler built the Continental Hotel here. It was so staggeringly huge that its three-block verandah could hold 3,000 rocking chairs! In 1910, Atlantic Boulevard was laid down to connect this saltwater playground with Jacksonville. Today, it's still the town's main east-west thoroughfare, as well as its southern boundary (with Neptune Beach). Unlike standoffish Neptune, however, Atlantic has retained an open-arms policy to visitors. Come on down, y'all. FYI, *Tide Views* is a free local quarterly with all the pertinent local poop.

❺ Atlantic Beach

Location: Beach access points are located at eastern street ends north of Atlantic Boulevard.
Parking/fees: free street parking
Hours: none posted
Facilities: lifeguards (seasonal)
Contact: Atlantic Beach Recreation Department, 904/247-9828

Beaches

The town's newsletter, compiled by a well-meaning local booster, claims two miles of beachfront for **Atlantic Beach**, but our rented car's odometer gauged it at no more than one mile, and that's being generous. Running north from the main beach access at Atlantic Boulevard, there are additional public access points at each of the 15 street endings. As this is the most popular of the three "Jax Beaches," Atlantic Beach presents daytrippers with a major parking problem, as does neighboring Neptune Beach (but, oddly, not Jacksonville Beach, which has a lot more beach but a less desirable reputation). Some parking spots near the beach can be found on the streets, but they are snapped up quickly and relinquished rarely. A large pay lot is lo-

MAP OF FLORIDA'S EAST COAST—PAGE 5

cated between 18th and 19th Streets. Lifeguards are on duty at Atlantic Beach daily, from 8 A.M. to 6 P.M.

Bunking Down

The **Sea Turtle Inn** (1 Ocean Boulevard, 904/249-7402, $$) has the beach blanketed in Atlantic Beach, as it's the oldest oceanfront "inn" in town (actually, it's a high-rise). The Sea Turtle is also the largest hotel on the Jax Beaches, taking up a full city block and boasting 194 rooms. Other amenities: a swimming pool, a lounge, and an oceanfront restaurant/lounge. A major refurbishing of the property is in the works, as of this writing. Last but not least, staying at the Sea Turtle means you've got a coveted parking space in Atlantic Beach. Since it's located within walking distance of the best bars and restaurants, you have no reason to move the car, either.

Coastal Cuisine

It's rare to find a hot nightspot that also serves fine food, but such is the case at **Ragtime Tavern** (207 Atlantic Boulevard, 904/241-7877, $$$). A hint of New Orleans infuses a menu that's gloriously top-heavy with fresh Florida seafood. The grilled grouper (with roasted red pepper, rosemary, and lime aioli) and the charcoal-grilled seafood skewer are worthy of a certain large-girthed Louisiana chef with the surname Prudhomme. Ragtime is extremely popular, so be prepared to wait a while at one of its three bars. If the pangs get too loud, calm them with an order of Cajun-style popcorn shrimp.

Night Moves

Not only is Ragtime Tavern a top-notch restaurant, but once the plates are cleared this is the nightspot for yuppie party animals from the Jacksonville area. By the time we bailed out of the scene, we were forced to run a gauntlet of preppies in starched shirts, each with an imported beer in hand, fixed smile on face, perfect facial hair and tan, and a ready line of bar patter. (Overheard several years ago: "Did you see the *Seinfeld* where George went into that bar and . . . ?" And yada yada yada, all night long.) Outside, lined up alongside a theater rope with an usher letting in the horde a few at a time, an army of gorgeous, jewelry-bedecked and salon-coifed women wait their turn to run the same gauntlet we'd just escaped. Despite or maybe in addition to its meat-market rep, Ragtime does have an undeniable appeal. There are three full-service bars, each with its own seating and gathering area, plus decent live rock and roll on weekends. Ragtime has survived the coming and going of trends that have claimed lesser hotspots and even seems to grow a little bit yearly, as it gobbles up yet another adjacent storefront.

Contact Information

Jacksonville and the Beaches Chamber of Commerce and Visitor Center, 1101 Beach Boulevard, Jacksonville Beach, FL 32250; 904/249-3868.

Jacksonville and the Beaches Convention & Visitors Bureau, 201 East Adams Street, Jacksonville, FL 32202; 904/798-9111 or 800/733-2668; website: www.jaxcvb.com

Map of Duval County—Page 24

Neptune Beach

More residential than recreational, Neptune Beach (pop. 7,200) is caught between the rock of Atlantic Beach to the north and the hard place of Jacksonville Beach to the south. Clearly trying to hold both ends at bay, Neptune Beach has made obvious attempts to curb crowds, with speed bumps on side streets and virtually no public beach parking. The idea is to let the mostly year-round population enjoy its well-earned place in the sun. It seems to have worked. Established in 1931, originally as part of Jacksonville Beach, Neptune Beach is a nice enough small town that occupies only 2.5 square miles. Just don't plan a beach vacation around it.

Beaches

In **Neptune Beach**, the town's half-mile beachfront runs along North 1st Street, two blocks east of North 3rd Street (Highway A1A), which is the main north-south artery through all three of the Jax Beaches. Each of Neptune Beach's 23 streets ends with a public beach access onto the sand. Only two of these access points (Lemon and Hopkins Streets) have parking spaces, and those are limited. A few other free parking slots can be had along the sandy shoulder of a short one-way street along the ocean (Strand Street).

Lifeguards are on duty 9 A.M.–5 P.M. on weekdays, and 9 A.M.–7 P.M. on weekends in season.

6 Neptune Beach

Location: Beach access points are located at eastern street ends from Atlantic Boulevard south to Seagate Avenue.

Parking/fees: free limited street parking

Hours: none posted

Facilities: lifeguards (seasonal) and a shower

Contact: Neptune Beach Public Works Department, 904/270-2423

Bunking Down

There's little in the way of accommodations in Neptune Beach, with the exception of a serviceable oceanfront motel, the **Sea Horse** (120 Atlantic Boulevard, 904/246-2175), which is technically on Neptune's border with Atlantic Beach.

Coastal Cuisine

Art Deco American diner is the visual motif at the chrome-shiny **Sun Dog Diner** (207 Atlantic Boulevard, 904/241-8221, $$), while the food takes its cues from the tropics. Don't miss the brick-oven pizza or Italian specialties at **Mezza Luna Vagabondo Ristorante** (110 1st Street, 904/246-5100), either. And **Sliders** (218 1st Street, 904/246-0681) is the ultimate casual beach hangout in these parts. The food is affordable (a bulging seafood burrito goes for seven bucks) and save room for the signature dessert: "Florida Snowballs," ice cream rolled in coconut and covered with raspberry sauce.

Night Moves

Despite Neptune's penchant for privacy, some of the best watering holes in the Jax Beaches area are located here. **Sun Dog Diner** (207 Atlantic Boulevard, 904/241-8221) is a longtime favorite of the locals, who often stick around after dinner for the nightly live music. **Papa Joe's** (100 1st Street, 904/246-6406) is a less preppy version of Ragtime Tavern in Atlantic Beach. Another hangout beloved by locals is **Pete's Bar** (117 1st Street, 904/249-9158), "where the crowd is the entertainment."

Contact Information

Jacksonville and the Beaches Chamber of Commerce and Visitor Center, 1101 Beach Boulevard, Jacksonville Beach, FL

MAP OF FLORIDA'S EAST COAST—PAGE 5

32250; 904/249-3868.

Jacksonville and the Beaches Convention & Visitors Bureau, 201 East Adams Street, Jacksonville, FL 32202; 904/798-9111 or 800/733-2668; website: www.jaxcvb.com

Jacksonville Beach

By far the largest of the "Jax Beaches," Jacksonville Beach (pop. 24,000) has a lot going for it in terms of its sandy endowment. Unfortunately, the town has been stumbling along like a dragster stuck in beach sand for the past quarter century. As a result, it's a not-unfriendly but utterly nondescript oceanfront zone in which urban decay mingles with sporadic attempts at revitalization. Driving the beach along 1st Street, one passes a few unfancy eateries, benignly sloppy bars, dubious-looking businesses (gone, no doubt, when the lease runs out), and way too many boarded-up buildings and vacant, weedy lots for a town with so much doggone beach.

This isn't to suggest that Jax Beach—as it's known to everyone but cartographers—is exactly dangerous (although even the local newspaper has made reference to its "rowdy and lawless" reputation). However, the dilapidated condition undeniably hints, as it does on rundown parts of the Jersey Shore, that the area has seen better days. Of course, optimists will say that a renaissance is in the offing. They'll point with pride to a new City Hall and the Seahawk Pavilion, a gathering place for outdoor concerts and festivals where Beach Boulevard meets the ocean. Restaurants have been coming in, and some big new hotels have sprouted up or are on the drawing board. Existing hotels and motels tend to book up on summer weekends, as the area is popular with Georgians who really don't have too many beaches of their own. Meanwhile, Jacksonville natives beat a path down Atlantic and Beach Boulevards on the weekend to slather and sun themselves on Jax Beach's boundless strand.

The area does have its problems, including a homeless population that has had a deleterious effect on local business. Unkempt, smelly vagrants have been known to stare at and even snatch food off the plates of restaurant diners. Add this whiff of the unsavory to a beach town that services a large military population, and Jax Beach is not really operating from a position of strength to sell itself as a vacation destination. It's too far north on Florida's Atlantic coast to compete with the likes of Daytona, Cocoa, Vero, and the South Florida beaches. Moreover, it suffers some fundamental socioeconomic problems that will take more than a savvy marketing campaign to solve.

The first boom heard down this way was provided by Henry Flagler's East Coast Railway. The next stop down the line from Atlantic Beach was Pablo Beach (named for the San Pablo River, to the west), which became Jacksonville Beach in 1925. **Pablo Historical Park** (425 Beach Boulevard, 904/246-0093) goes into great detail about the area's past, and members of the Beaches Historical Society even offer guided tours of the remnants of the town's railroad origins. A thriving boardwalk developed in 1916, with dance halls, shooting galleries, boxing and wrestling matches, auto racing on the sand, and "other forms of entertainment" (read: games of chance). This scene flourished until the late 1950s, when gambling was chased out. Driving was allowed on the beach until the late 1970s, when it was sensibly banned within city limits.

Despite a less than auspicious first impression, Jacksonville Beach might well grow on you, as it has steadily grown over

MAP OF DUVAL COUNTY—PAGE 24

Nuts for Golf

People are going nuts over golf on the First Coast. Literally. In the past decade, what was once an unsurpassably intriguing piece of Old Florida—an enchanting mix of primordial swampland, palmetto-laden coastal habitat, and unhomogenized cracker culture—has become a place of second or even third homes to rich snowbirds in loudly colored pants scooting about carpets of manicured grass in motorized carts while waving obscenely expensive implements to swat around golf balls. Knocking a ball around a public course is one thing, but turning an entire stretch of coast into a private country club is quite another. Do you think we exaggerate?

There are nearly 50 resort, daily-fee access, private, and military courses on the First Coast, and 10 more in South Georgia, from St. Marys and Kingsland north to Brunswick. A golf-themed playland called the World Golf Village opened in May 1998 near St. Augustine. It is home to two golf courses (with more on the way), plus a hotel, convention center, retail shopping, and the World Golf Hall of Fame. The local spin doctor for the St. Johns County Visitors Bureau thinks that 500,000 is a "reasonable" estimate of the annual number of visitors who will pony up $21 per adult ($14 for kids!) to visit the Golf Hall of Fame, watch an IMAX movie, and have access to a putting course. By comparison, the venerable Baseball Hall of Fame in Cooperstown, New York, draws 330,000 visitors per year. Does he seriously think a bunch of gold-plated putters and such are going to become a bigger attraction than the wicked wood of Babe Ruth and Hank Aaron—especially at those prices?

the years on us. Certainly, it provides relief from the severely upscale affectations of Ponte Vedra Beach to the south or the parking headaches of Atlantic and Neptune Beaches. On a late Saturday afternoon when a rock band is playing on the deck at a beach bar or on a Sunday morning over a plate of fish and grits at Jacksonville Beach Fishing Pier, the place seems downright likable. There's a real warts-and-all beach-life feel about Jacksonville Beach that, in an odd sort of way, is preferable to the sort of soulless upscaling that has claimed so may other beach communities around the country. This is, after all, Lynyrd Skynyrd country. The Southern-rock legends came together in these parts, and their career is celebrated at the Freebird Cafe, which recently opened in Jacksonville Beach and is emblematic of the let-it-all-hang-out aesthetic that rules here.

Beaches

The beach along the trio of "Jax Beaches" extends for more than 100 blocks along 1st Street. It would be the envy of any in America, were it not for the area's perpetual economic problems. Because roughly 60 of those city blocks belong to **Jacksonville Beach**, the southernmost and most welcoming of the bunch, it has traditionally been the destination for the teeming multitudes. Though Atlantic and Neptune Beaches are part of the same lengthy strand, Jacksonville Beach boasts the widest beach of all. The hard-packed, blindingly white sand is backed by the remnants of sugary soft dunes. The most popular stretch of beach runs from around

A 15-year plan in St. Johns County calls for $1.5 billion in new construction. In addition to the Players Championship, held in Ponte Vedra Beach since 1977, the area will host the Liberty Mutual Legends of Golf, which permanently moved to the World Golf Village's "the Slammer and the Squire" course in 1999.

The local press—the institution whose responsibility it is to question dramatic and unchallenged societal transformations—has been one of the leading cheerleaders for this prodigious conversion of northeast Florida into one big golf resort. Here are some quotes taken verbatim from a puff piece found in the business section of the *Florida Times-Union,* Jacksonville's daily newspaper:

- A local golf club maker: "We have the perfect climate, great courses, the PGA Tour and now the World Golf Village [near St. Augustine] coming. It's a hotbed."
- A golf course developer: "I don't see any end to the possibilities."
- A golf pro, with absolutely no irony: "It's like traffic on Butler Boulevard—the golf industry just keeps coming and coming. This is a great time to be in the golf industry, from sales reps for manufacturers, to golf pros, superintendents and players."
- A real-estate developer: "The economic impact will be incredibly significant. Already it's enhancing the value of real estate along I-95 corridor. . . . Now we have to figure out how we're going to tie that into our marketing and piggyback off what they're doing. There's a lot of potential there."
- A local politico: "I think we're very lucky. We're in the middle of an industry that's going nuts. You can credit our climate, Tiger Woods or whatever you want, but people are getting involved. We're sitting on a rocket that's slowly exploding, and it will only get better."

Like we said, they've gone a little bit nuts over golf on the First Coast.

4th Avenue North down to 6th Avenue South, with Beach Boulevard the approximate midpoint. Twenty-five lifeguards are on duty on busy summer days. A beach renourishment in early 2001 saw half a million cubic yards of sand spread along 7.5 miles of thinning beach from Mayport down to Jacksonville Beach in what has been described as a minor tune-up—the first since 1996.

The town has provided beach-access points at the end of 64 avenues. Many of these accesses have a few free parking spaces by the beach, and if you don't luck into one of those, plenty of free parking can be found a block or so to the west. Jacksonville Beach is well maintained and patrolled by lifeguards from 10 A.M. to 5 P.M. daily. The 983-foot Jacksonville Beach Fishing Pier, at the end of 6th Avenue South, charges $3.50 per adult to fish ($5 more to rent a pole) and 75 cents to stroll the pier. The rickety

7 Jacksonville Beach

Location: Jax Beach's half-mile shorefront is accessible from the ends of 64 streets along its length. The heart of the beach area is at Beach Boulevard (U.S. 90/State Route 212) and the ocean.

Parking/fees: free street parking

Hours: none posted

Facilities: lifeguards (seasonal), restrooms, and showers

Contact: Jacksonville Beach Recreation Department, 904/247-6236

restaurant on the pier is a favorite spot for breakfast.

Shore Things

- **Dive shop:** Divers Supply, 9701 Beach Boulevard, 904/646-3828
- **Ecotourism:** Outdoor Adventures, 1625 Emerson Street, Jacksonville, 904/393-9030.
- **Fishing charters:** Monty's Marina Charter Fishing, 4378 Ocean Street, 904/246-7575.
- **Lighthouse:** American Lighthouse and Maritime Museum, 1011 North 3rd Street, 904/241-8845.
- **Marina:** Beach Marine, 2315 Beach Boulevard, 904/249-8200.
- **Pier:** Jacksonville Beach Fishing Pier, 3 6th Avenue South, 904/246-6001.
- **Rainy-day attraction:** Museum of Science and History, 1025 Museum Circle, 904/396-7062
- **Shopping/browsing:** Jacksonville Landing, 2 Independent Drive, Jacksonville, 904/353-1188.
- **Surf report:** 904/249-4452, 904/828-4848, or 904/241-0933.
- **Surf shops:** Hart's Surf Shop, 1019 South 3rd Street, 904/246-4451; Aqua East Surf Shop, 696 Atlantic Boulevard, 904/246-9744; and Sunrise Surf Shop, 834 Beach Boulevard, 904/241-0822.
- **Vacation rentals:** Seaside Realty, 1639 Beach Boulevard, 904/247-7000.

Bunking Down

In marked contrast to its outward appearance, Jax Beach tries hard to be accommodating. At least, it offers a lot of accommodations. The **Ramada Resort** (1201 North 1st Street, 904/241-5333, $$) used to be the oceanfront venue of choice. Though you can't argue with its location, the Ramada is beginning to show its age.

Days Inn Oceanfront (1031 South 1st Street, 904/249-7231) and **Comfort Inn Oceanfront** (1515 North 1st Street, 904/241-2311, $) have stolen some of Ramada's thunder. They are nicer, newer, cheaper, and have beach access and pools. Are you getting the idea that Jacksonville Beach is a Days Inn/Comfort Inn kind of beach town? Well, that's because it is. Both places offer just enough in the way of cleanliness and comfort so that you'll sleep well, but not so much that you'll be tempted to waste your day hanging around the room. Which is exactly how it should be at the beach.

Jacksonville Beach's top-of-the-line is the **Holiday Inn Sunspree Resort** (1617 North 1st Street, 904/249-9071, $$$). In addition to Holiday Inn's usual brand-name quality, especially in Florida, the Sunspree designation means modernized facilities and activity programs for kids. The key word here is "family"; they're pushing it all over Jacksonville Beach these days.

Coastal Cuisine

For breakfast or lunch, hit the **Beach Hut Cafe** (1281 South 3rd Street, 904/249-3516, $), which is good 'n' cheap and perennially popular, to boot. **The Loop** (14444 Beach Boulevard, 904/223-6611, $) is another local favorite for pizza, burgers, sandwiches, and hot dogs. (There's also a Loop on 3rd Street in Neptune Beach.) Best dinner honors belong to a pair of 1st Street eateries. **First Street Grille** (807 North 1st Street, 904/246-6555, $$$) serves grilled steaks and seafood with fresh seasonings; the ocean view is a bonus. Specialties of the eclectic menu include a Cajun-spiced sauteed red snapper and Pablo Beach shrimp. (Jacksonville Beach used to be known as Pablo Beach, and some old-timers still call it

MAP OF FLORIDA'S EAST COAST—PAGE 5

that.) The **Island Grille** (981 North 1st Street, 904/241-1881, $$$) features tropical seafood, fruits, and vegetables of Florida and the West Indies, as well as an ocean-facing deck.

Back toward town, on the west bank of the Intracoastal Waterway, **Marker 32** (14549 Beach Boulevard, 904/223-1534, $$$) offers casual ambience, sumptuous food, and a splendid setting. Fresh-fish specials might include cilantro-grilled tuna and pan-fried red snapper atop okra and tomatoes. Great service and a good wine list round out an exemplary dining experience. For a taste of Thai, a good friend and lifelong Jacksonville native turned us on to **Pattaya Thai** (10916 Atlantic Boulevard, 904/646-9506, $$) and **Old Siam** (1716 North 3rd Street, 904/247-7763, $$), where the spicy food is as sensational as their strip-mall locations are ordinary.

Night Moves

The red-faced locals, shaken and baked all day on the beach, are likely to hang out afterward at unpretentious bar/restaurants like **Buckets Baha Beach Club** (222 North Ocean Street, 904/246-7701). A good time is had by all, especially when local rock bands provide the soundtrack for the revelry in the upstairs nightclub. Another bar-restaurant combo that packs 'em in on the beach is **Manatee Ray's** (314 1st Avenue North, 904/241-3138), which serves food and drink with a Caribbean flair.

A great bar down in Key West, **Sloppy Joe's** (200 North 1st Street, 904/270-1767) has been franchised in Jax Beach, replete with the face of Ernest Hemingway on the logo. The ingredients are the same—relaxed atmosphere, cold beer, live music—but the chemistry misses the original's tropical pop. Maybe the Key West ambience just can't be transported as easily as the logo. The best beach sports bar is **R. P. McMurphy's** (798 South 3rd Street, 904/247-0196), named after the protagonist in Ken Kesey's *One Flew Over the Cuckoo's Nest*. A willing staff of Nurse Ratcheds dispense liquid medication from behind the bar.

Back in Jacksonville proper, **River City Brewing Company** (835 Museum Circle, 904/398-2299) produces a smashing lineup of home-brews (try the Pale Ale or English Porter) to go with its menu of seafood and bar food. The stunning view of downtown Jacksonville's skyline is all the more reason to come here at lunch or to watch the sun set.

Contact Information

Jacksonville and the Beaches Chamber of Commerce and Visitor Center, 1101 Beach Boulevard, Jacksonville Beach, FL 32250; 904/249-3868.

Jacksonville and the Beaches Convention & Visitors Bureau, 201 East Adams Street, Jacksonville, FL 32202; 904/798-9111 or 800/733-2668; website: www.jaxcvb.com

MAP OF DUVAL COUNTY—PAGE 24

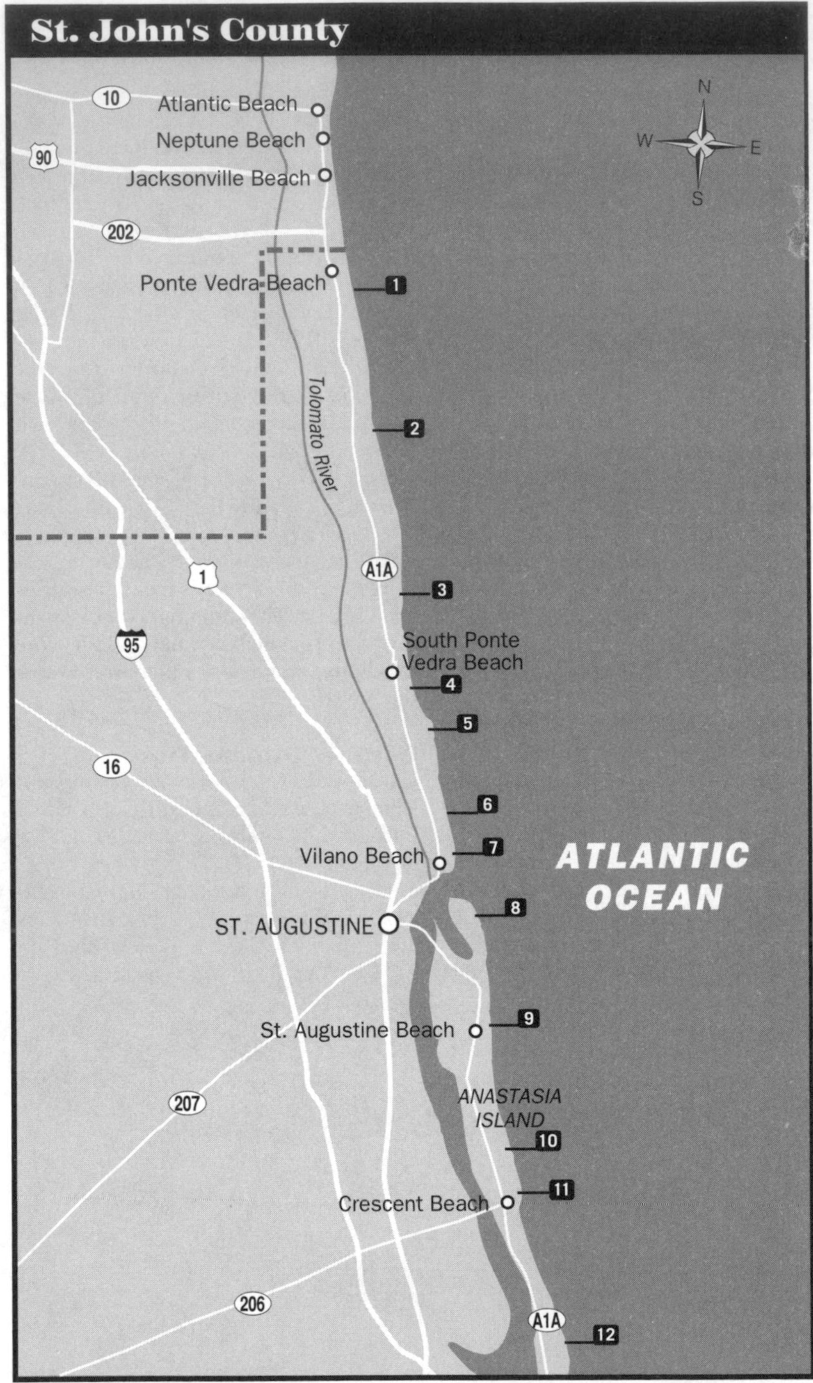
St. John's County
10
Atlantic Beach
Neptune Beach
90
Jacksonville Beach
202
Ponte Vedra Beach
1
Tolomato River
2
A1A
3
1
95
South Ponte
Vedra Beach
4
5
16
6
Vilano Beach
7
ATLANTIC
OCEAN
8
ST. AUGUSTINE
9
St. Augustine Beach
207
ANASTASIA
ISLAND
10
11
Crescent Beach
206
A1A
12
N
W
E
S

ST. JOHN'S COUNTY

St. Johns County is bordered by water—the Atlantic Ocean on the east, the St. Johns River on the west, and the Nassau and Matanzas Inlets to the north and south—and blessed with 24 miles of beaches. Its coastline varies from upscale (Ponte Vedra Beach) to unpretentious (Vilano Beach), from raw and wide (Guana River State Park) to narrowed to nothing (St. Augustine Beach). The historic centerpiece of the county is St. Augustine, which bills itself as "America's Oldest City," celebrating that fact with attractions trading on its colonial past. Still, St. Johns is very much attuned to the present, lately cultivating a dubiously upgraded image as a county of golf resorts and shopping malls.

Ponte Vedra Beach

Ponte Vedra Beach (pop. 25,000) is a world-class golf and tennis resort destination and an exclusive bedroom community for the executive class of Jacksonville, 20 miles to the northwest. Ponte Vedra often gets lumped in with the "Jax Beaches," but it's a decidedly different creature. Located in a separate county (St. Johns) from Jacksonville, Ponte Vedra is a world apart. Here, you will find the same emphasis on "golf course living" that's made Orange County, California, such a bastion of rock-ribbed Republicanism, although in this neck of what used to be woods they call it "country club values." Either way, it translates into an aggressive attempt to keep at arm's length anyone without a golf visor on his head or a briefcase in his hand.

As if to emphasize this point, Ponte Vedrans equip their beachfront mansions with security fences, serpentine walls, and shrubbery worthy of Dr. No and Goldfinger. Their residential subdevelopments are guarded via gated checkpoints. While this song and dance no doubt affords a measure of comfort and security to those who live here, it can be off-putting to those who come calling—even for a couple of veteran beach bums dropping in on an old friend who's lately sunk roots into these waterlogged soils. If nothing else, the rituals of the gated community surely limit one's options for being sociable and all but eliminate any hope of driving through out of mere curiosity.

For instance, while trying to locate the home of our friend, we became unwilling participants in a slapstick routine at one of these gated checkpoints. The boob in charge—a dead ringer for Floyd the barber in *The Andy Griffith Show*—opened the gate for us, but when we made to drive through, he quickly lowered it, nearly karate-chopping the hood of our rented car. Then he shouted at us, as though we were bloodthirsty Huns storming the ramparts of the virgin queen's castle: "Come back here!"

We put the car in reverse, returning to square one, and said, "But you opened the gate. . . ."

"I hit the wrong button!" he angrily retorted, as if this was somehow our fault.

He insisted on calling our party to obtain authorization for us, two obviously dangerous criminals, to enter the neighborhood. We gave him the name, and he promptly dialed two wrong numbers, holding us up for five minutes as he went through the painfully protracted process of explaining himself and then apologizing to each recipient of his wayward calls. Even after we wrote out the correct phone number for him, he misdialed it, necessitating another lengthy apology. On his next attempt, he finally managed to connect with our friend. Not content to be merely incompetent, he had to prove he was unobservant, too, as he announced us as "Mr. and Mrs. Park, here to see you." Though confused, our friend okayed our passage, and we were on our way.

Whoops, not so fast! The dunce at the guard gate still had to fill out our guest pass, a Magna Carta–sized document that had to be "displayed on the dashboard at all times." When the gate was raised, we burned rubber going through it, lest he shatter the windshield by lowering the gate again for no apparent reason.

While the name "Ponte Vedra Beach" may suggest ocean breezes and verdant stands of sea oats swaying atop sand dunes, most of the community lies west of Highway A1A, a good distance from the beach. Every available piece of real estate out that way is unnaturally, obsessively landscaped and contoured. Many of the beautiful residential developments were built on filled-in wetlands, created before the EPA put a stop to this environmental-

Map of Florida's East Coast—Page 5

ly destructive practice, and they derive their names from the very natural features they've supplanted (Marsh Landing, Old Palm Valley, etc.).

The biggest controversy in town during one of our visits was over the size of some beachfront houses that were pending zoning approval from the city and county. This proposed development—with the ridiculously self-inflated name "The Enclave" (there's already a development here called "The Plantation")—had some of the old-timer beachfront homeowners steamed. Their beef? These new homes wouldn't be big enough! There goes the neighborhood.

"This isn't like Daytona Beach," one owner huffed from behind his security fence. "There is a real residential feel here."

"This can't be permitted," they all vowed.

Hear, hear!

An inspection of the beachfront during a wicked nor'easter in late 2000 revealed waves lapping at the base of seawalls and splashing up on lawns, making homesteads at Ponte Vedra Beach seem not so terribly secure after all, guard gates or not.

Beaches

From the Duval County line to the south end of Ponte Vedra Beach is a distance of 6.5 miles, all of it fronted by a wide beach. However, as if sensing that it's not welcome, Highway A1A swerves inland requiring the oceanfront to be approached via a loop road for bluebloods only, Ponte Vedra Boulevard (State Route 203). Needless to add, the rabble are discouraged from entering here, too, attested to by the conspicuous lack of beach access along this stretch of asphalt. The exceptions are a trio of exclusive resorts (see "Bunking Down," below), the excessive tariffs for which include beach access, and one paved parking lot at the south end of State Route 203, just before it makes a 90-degree turn to reconnect with Highway A1A.

This has long been known as **Mickler's Landing** (though there's no sign to this effect) and only in recent years has a paved, visitor-friendly lot welcomed county residents who are in the know. A crossover affords access through thick, vegetation-covered dunes to a lovely beach with flat, hard-packed sand. Though this county-run park has no facilities, it's popular with local families and surfers who are otherwise fenced out of the sand for seven solid miles to the north. It's a crumb tossed at them by the Ponte Vedrans, shoehorned between gaudy mansions (and, no doubt, unenthusiastically). As if to add insult to the injury of near- total exclusivity, on our recent visit during a record-setting rainy season, the automatic sprinkler system for the mansion that abuts Mickler's Landing was flicking its spray into the wind, dousing everyone who used the public access trail to the beach.

Bunking Down

The centerpiece of Ponte Vedra Beach is Sawgrass, "an uncrowded resort community with a commitment to excellence." Its 4,800 acres offer three golf courses—including Pete Dye's "masterpiece," the Tournament Players Club—13 tennis courts, a wilderness preserve, the **Sawgrass Marriott Resort Inn** (1000 TPC Boulevard, 904/285-7777, $$$$), and the luxury Beach Club. The latter boasts an oasis pool

1 Mickler's Landing

Location: south end of Ponte Vedra Beach on Highway A1A
Parking/fees: free parking lot
Hours: October 1–April 30, 24 hours; May 1–September 30, 5 A.M.–10 P.M.
Facilities: Lifeguards (seasonal)
Contact: St. Johns County Recreation Department, 904/471-6616

MAP OF ST. JOHN'S COUNTY—PAGE 38

("an adult retreat with a poolside bar"), an Olympic-sized family pool, and a wading pool. Oddly, the beach itself is downplayed. In other words, Sawgrass has roped off one of the nicest beaches in northern Florida for its exclusive access, and yet visitors are encouraged to sit around swimming pools, nursing drinks while chinwagging about the good life. This all goes to prove a theory of ours: Much as youth can be said to be wasted on the young, some of the best beaches in America are wasted on the rich.

The **Lodge and Beach Club at Ponte Vedra Beach** (607 Ponte Vedra Boulevard, 904/273-9500, $$$$) is similar in tone to Sawgrass but not so intimidating. The 66 rooms and suites overlook the beach, set gracefully behind the dunes. The Mediterranean architecture and tasteful furnishings give it an air of relaxed elegance. Much more venerable elegance is available at the **Ponte Vedra Inn and Club** (200 Ponte Vedra Boulevard, 904/285-1111, $$$$), the first beach resort built here (in 1927). Again, golf and tennis are emphasized at both resorts, but the beach is right out back, as are swimming pools (three at the former, four at the latter). The bounty of beach rentals (chairs, umbrellas, cabanas, boogie boards, and kayaks) encourages visitors to immerse themselves in the ocean rather than ignore it.

Coastal Cuisine

For all its world-class affectations, Ponte Vedra Beach is oddly devoid of interesting or unique dining spots. The places

Henry Morrison Flagler

Henry Morrison Flagler (1830–1913) is remembered in these parts as the man who opened up Florida to travel and tourism. His handiwork is evident all over the state, from the luxury hotels and private mansions he constructed to his crowning achievement, the Florida East Coast Railway, which ran down the coast and out to Key West. The foundations that he laid for his railroad bridges between the Keys, which survived several hurricanes (though the tracks didn't), served as supports for the construction of the Overseas Highway.

Flagler made his millions as a cofounder of Standard Oil (a.k.a. Esso and later Exxon). John D. Rockefeller, Sr., was his partner in this and other enterprises. Flagler remained director of Standard Oil's board until two years before his death. A trip to Florida in 1878 filled him with dreams of possibilities for the state, which was then a swampy backwater. His vision for Florida's development recognized the need for a transportation network and hotel facilities. In the 1880s, he bought and combined several railways into the Florida East Coast Railway, offering service from Jacksonville and Daytona. But he didn't stop there.

In 1892, he began laying new track south from Daytona to Palm Beach and, ultimately, Miami. Towns along the route began to develop as Flagler's railroad opened them up to trade and tourism. Flagler also constructed luxury hotels in places like Palm Beach (The Breakers) and St. Augustine (the Ponce de León Hotel). In Palm Beach, The Breakers enticed the rich and famous down from the north to enjoy the balmy winters during America's Gilded Age. By 1896, Flagler's Florida East Coast Railway reached down to Biscayne Bay. Flagler was a prime mover in the development of Miami, dredging channels, paving

Map of Florida's East Coast—Page 5

touted by locals are dining areas found inside the **Marriott at Sawgrass Resort** (1000 TPC Boulevard, 904/285-7777): **Cafe on the Green** ($$) and the **Augustine Room** ($$$). The latter requires semiformal attire, which seems a little over the top at the beach. More interesting meals can be had seven miles north in Atlantic Beach or 20 miles south in St. Augustine.

Contact Information

Ponte Vedra Chamber of Commerce, Four Sawgrass Village, Suite 104F, Ponte Vedra Beach, FL 32082, 904/285-0666; website: www.pontevedra.org

Guana River State Park

One of Florida's newest and most farsighted acquisitions, Guana River State Park covers 2,400 acres. Stretching from the Intracoastal Waterway to the Atlantic Ocean, it offers public access to five miles of the finest beach in northern Florida. Nature programs are offered year-round and a visitor center is in the offing. This is the sort of beachfront development we can get behind!

Guana River affords plenty of unrestricted beach access, in marked contrast to Ponte Vedra and South Ponte Vedra Beaches. In addition to towering, thickly vege-

streets, laying power and water lines, and bankrolling the town's first newspaper. So central a figure was he in Miami's awakening that when the town incorporated in 1896, the residents wanted to name it Flagler. He declined the honor.

In 1905, Flagler undertook the last big push of his railway, extending it to Key West. Many thought the project an unattainable folly, and indeed its completion required engineering innovations, a workforce of 4,000, seven years of hard labor, and triumph over the numerous setbacks wrought by five hurricanes. The monetary incentive for linking the Keys with the mainland peninsula 128 miles away was to open up trade with Cuba and Latin America, particularly with the construction of the Panama Canal having been announced in 1905. Look at a map and it all makes sense: Key West is the United States' closest deepwater port to the canal. Flagler lived to see the project to completion, riding the first train into Key West in 1912. A year later he died at his palatial home, Whitehall, in Palm Beach.

Flagler's presence is still keenly felt in St. Augustine, most acutely in the splendid architecture of the old Ponce de León Hotel (now Flagler College, with a student body of 1,500) and the Memorial Presbyterian Church, built in tribute to his prematurely deceased daughter and grandchild. The spectacular church, which boasts a 150-foot dome copied from St. Marks Cathedral in Venice, is an Italian Renaissance–style masterpiece. We highly recommend a visit to Flagler College's tranquil courtyard to cool your heels. As you sit by its circular fountain, watching terra-cotta frogs gurgle water, try imagining the scene a century ago, when the wealthy took their ease at the Ponce de León Hotel during its brief but lively winter season (January through March). Those were different times, but some of the flavor of a less harried age still seeps through the nooks and crannies in and around St. Augustine.

MAP OF ST. JOHN'S COUNTY—PAGE 38

tated dunes and a long, primeval beach, the park contains a rich variety of habitat that attracts a diversity of wildlife, including more than 240 species of birds. Where there are birds, there are fish, and the Guana and Tolomato Rivers' tidal waters are teeming with them: redfish, bluefish, black drum, and flounder, as well as shrimp and blue crab. Judging from the number of lines we saw in the water, fishing is excellent at Guana Dam, too. In addition, anglers can fish freshwater Guana Lake for trout and striped bass. (Boats are restricted to 10 horsepower or less.) Nine miles of old service roads make for challenging mountain biking, and another 30 miles of trails offer excellent hiking through varied plant communities that include hardwood hammock, salt marsh, inland marsh, pine flatwoods, and scrub coastal strand.

Beaches

Guana River State Park maintains two official "beach use areas," known as North Beach and South Beach. (Before the park was established, the whole area was called North Beach.) They are three miles apart, with the state park's main entrance in the middle. Entrances and parking lots for all three areas are on the inlet (west) side of Highway A1A. To get acclimated, go to the main park entrance and obtain a brochure and directions. The fee at the beach parking lots is a modest $2 per car, self-paid on the honor system.

Each of the beach use areas has an ample paved lot with a few portable toilets—and that is the extent of the facilities. We offer only one word of warning. To reach the beach, you must dash across Highway A1A, at which point a wooden dune crossover will take you the rest of the way. Trust us; it's worth the sprint (though you should be mindful of traffic, especially if you're dragging kiddies). Here's a case study of a healthy beach, with three separate shelves of sand leading to a veritable mountain range of dunes, held in place by glistening sea oats, grasses and vines, sea grape, and a few squat palm trees. Though there are no lifeguards, the water gets packed with swimmers. An observation tower beside the boardwalk at the South Beach area affords stunning views of the wetlands to the west and miles of unbroken, undeveloped beach to the north and south.

If all that isn't enough for you, Guana River State Park marks the approximate location of Ponce de León's first landing and explorations. A newly unearthed account written by a Spanish historian in 1592 brought this fact to light.

2 Guana River State Park

Location: between Ponte Vedra Beach and St. Augustine on Highway A1A
Parking/fees: $2 per vehicle entrance fee
Hours: 8 A.M. to sundown
Facilities: restrooms
Contact: Guana River State Park, 904/825-5071

Contact Information

Guana River State Park, 2690 South Ponte Vedra Boulevard, Ponte Vedra Beach, FL 32082; 904/825-5071; website: www.myflorida.com

South Ponte Vedra Beach

The 10-mile drive south on Highway A1A from Ponte Vedra Beach to Vilano Beach is one of the nicest automotive excursions in Florida. It is a veritable tunnel of green created by grass- and scrub-covered dunes the size of small mountains (on the ocean side of Highway A1A) and by mangrove- and tree-thickened wetlands (on the inland side). Roughly five miles of this stretch passes through the community of South Ponte Vedra Beach. What development there is out here is more scaled down than Ponte Vedra Beach but equally exclusive.

Beaches

A few county-maintained beach accesses have been established through here, including a small lot and dune crossover at a Gate service station just over the southern boundary of Guana River State Park (which is why it is known as **Gate Station Beach**). **South Ponte Vedra Beach Recreation Area** is another barely developed access point (with a dirt lot and minimal facilities) to the same unspoiled stretch of orange coquina sand beach. **Usina Beach** is accessed in two places: at a ramp across from a private campground (North Beach Campground, popular with RVs) about three miles south of the state park and at a parking lot about a quarter mile south of the ramp in the 2900 block of Highway A1A. At the former, the ramp is open 5 A.M. until 10 P.M., but driving is impossible at high tide and unreasonable any other time. **McMulvie's Reef Restaurant** (4100 Coastal Highway, 904/824-8008, $$) sits next door, for those who'd rather sit it out altogether. At the latter, you'll find shaded picnic areas, fire rings, wooden stairwell accesses, and portable restrooms. A sign warns "No Loud Music Over 55 dB" and "Caution: Soft Sand and Strong Currents." The surf did look a little choppy, but the sand was wide and hard packed and the water was filled with swimmers.

❸ Gate Station Beach

Location: just below the southern boundary of Guana River State Park on Highway A1A
Parking/fees: free parking lot
Hours: October 1–April 30, 24 hours; May 1–September 30, 5 A.M.–10 P.M.
Facilities: none
Contact: St. Johns County Recreation Department, 904/471-6616

❹ South Ponte Vedra Beach Recreation Area

Location: 2.25 miles south of Guana River State Park on Highway A1A
Parking/fees: free parking lot
Hours: October 1–April 30, 24 hours; May 1–September 30, 5 A.M. –10 P.M.
Facilities: restrooms and picnic tables
Contact: St. Johns County Recreation Department, 904/471-6616

❺ Usina Beach

Location: four miles north of Vilano Beach on Highway A1A
Parking/fees: off-beach parking lot (free) or beach-driving exit ramp (beach permit required, obtainable at Surfside, Vilano Beach, Butler Beach, Crescent Beach, and Matanzas Beach toll booths)
Hours: October 1–April 30, 24 hours; May 1–September 30, 5 A.M.–10 P.M.
Facilities: restrooms
Contact: St. Johns County Recreation Department, 904/471-6616

MAP OF ST. JOHN'S COUNTY—PAGE 38

Contact Information
St. Johns County Visitors and Convention Bureau, 88 Riberia Street, Suite 400, St. Augustine, FL 32084; 800/653-2489; website: www.visitoldcity.com

Vilano Beach

Vilano Beach (pop. 1,000) is a little enclave of cracker heaven just north of St. Augustine. Since that small city has gradually been converted into what amounts to a giant historical theme park, some of its original residents no doubt got pushed into the margins, and Vilano Beach looks like where a lot of them landed. Save for the occasional two-story condo, gentrification has not yet found its way to this side of the Vilano Bridge. Instead, you'll find a scattering of motels and RV parks, a few good restaurants on the ocean and marshes, and a small surfing scene down on Vilano Beach, at the north end of the St. Augustine Inlet.

Beaches

The first thing we saw upon crossing Highway A1A from our motel to the beach was a pickup truck stuck in the sand, wheels furiously pumping their stiff green gallop in mute nostril agony. The ancient vehicle was piloted and occupied by what appeared to be kin to William Faulkner's Snopes family. None of them weighed less than 250 pounds. They'd burned out their transmission trying to get unstuck but only succeeded in digging themselves into a deeper crab hole. A good samaritan in a late-model Ford Bronco tried to haul them out of the sand to no avail. The hillbillies looked about helplessly, their fishing expedition having suddenly turned into an AAA emergency. If all the traction their collective weight was providing still couldn't get the vehicle moving, they were going to need a tow, for sure.

We tell this story only to discourage driving along the beach in **Vilano Beach**. It is allowed, for reasons that are unfathomable to us. The sand is coarser and softer than that found on driving beaches like Anastasia State Park (in St. Augustine Beach) or the mother of them all, Daytona Beach. Besides, this is a turtle-nesting beach, and the specter of jeeploads of yahoos bouncing around turtle nests is unconscionable, if the haz-

6 Surfside

Location: one-half mile north of the Vilano Beach entrance ramp on Highway A1A
Parking/fees: Off-beach parking lot (free) or on-beach parking and driving ($3 per day or $20 annually)
Hours: October 1–April 30, 24 hours; May 1–September 30, 5 A.M.–10 P.M.
Facilities: lifeguards (seasonal), restrooms, and a shower
Contact: St. Johns County Recreation Department, 904/471-6616

7 Vilano Beach

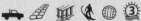

Location: two miles north of downtown St. Augustine, on Highway A1A just over the New Vilano Bridge at the end of Vilano Road
Parking/fees: off-beach parking lot (free) or on-beach parking and driving ($3 per day or $20 annually)
Hours: October 1–April 30, 24 hours; May 1–September 30, 5 A.M.–10 P.M.
Facilities: lifeguards (seasonal) and restrooms
Contact: St. Johns County Recreation Department, 904/471-6616

Map of Florida's East Coast—Page 5

ards of getting stuck weren't discouragement enough.

Vilano Beach is a high-energy beach with a sloping face and big waves crashing and chomping hungrily. Highway A1A sits right on the lip of the beach, and erosion would seem to be a constant worry. Most of the action, in terms of people, is down at the inlet, where public parking and access are provided. The waves are particularly good for skimboarding—kind of like surfing in reverse, in which a small board is tossed onto the wet sand of a receding wave and the skimboarder leaps on for a ride down the beach and up a wave face, where it briefly looks like he or she's surfing. We saw a healthy gaggle of skimboarders happily skimming away here. Another popular access point is at **Surfside**, a half mile north of the inlet. Otherwise, the dune crossovers you'll see leading onto the beach are private property.

Bunking Down

There are several modest places to stay on the beach at the inlet, including the affordable **Vilano Beach Motel** (50 Vilano Road, 904/829-2651, $$). They are friendly to surfers and families, and one brags of being American-owned and -operated. Up the road a mile or so, the **Ocean Sands Motel** (3465 North Highway A1A, 904/824-1112, $$) is the best Vilano Beach has to offer, a newish arrival with clean, comfortable rooms and free coffee and doughnuts in the morning. Guests get to use the Beachcomber Club's dune crossover to the beach, as well as a 1,000-foot pier that extends into the marshes bordering the Intracoastal Waterway. If you like fishing, Vilano Beach affords a gold mine of opportunity on both sides of the highway.

Coastal Cuisine

Fiddler's Green (2750 Anahma Drive, 904/824-8897, $$$) is a clubby beach establishment on a site formerly occupied by the historic Vilano Beach Casino, which burned in the 1930s. It's got a distinctive atmosphere and tasty fish, shellfish, and pasta dishes (e.g., shrimp Vilano with mushrooms, spinach, and three cheeses) brought to you by the folks who own Salt Water Cowboy's in St. Augustine.

Located at the end of a side road off Highway A1A, **Oscar's Old Florida Grill** (614 Euclid Avenue, 904/829-3794, $$) lists lazily in a picturesque setting beside a marsh. The atmosphere of Old Florida has been preserved in a classic cracker-style backcountry building with green-checked tablecloths and unfinished wood floors. You can dine inside or out on a deck overlooking the waterway. (We recommend the latter.) The menu consists of fresh local food from the surf and marsh. Those with adventurous palates may want to take on the "Swamp Thing," a platter consisting of frog legs, gator tail, and whole catfish. One of us had a house specialty, butternut grouper: a butter-marinated grouper fillet baked with pecan stuffing.

Night Moves

Head over the Usina Bridge into St. Augustine and then cross the Bridge of Lions to St. Augustine Beach for some real nightlife, if anything more than a drink or two at Fiddler's Green (see "Coastal Cuisine") isn't sufficient to quench your thirst.

Contact Information

St. Johns County Visitors and Convention Bureau, 88 Riberia Street, Suite 400, St. Augustine, FL 32084; 800/653-2489; website: www.visitoldcity.com

St. Augustine

St. Augustine (pop. 12,681) is a real puzzle. It is one of the more interesting, break-the-mold communities in Florida. There's a little bit of everything to be found here, the sum total of which is a mosaic of contradictory impressions. On the one hand, it is among the most historic communities in the nation, and there are endless informative and legitimate ways to explore its rich history. On the other, it is a virtual tourist theme park that assaults the enlightened traveler with bogus attractions, chintzy shops, and stop-and-go traffic. Beyond its appeal (or lack thereof) as a tourist destination, there is yet another side to this small city. It is something of a bohemian community, mixing a bit of New Orleans' festive, back-alley spirit with a shot of enlightened, Greenwich Village–style dropout culture. This side of St. Augustine was perhaps best expressed by a bumper sticker we saw affixed to an old van: "Plants and Animals Disappear to Make Room for Your Fat Ass." (One next to it read: "Strike a Blow for Justice—Punch an Attorney.") There are plenty of coffeehouses and more rare bookstores than you can wave a bookmark at, which is saying something for a town of modest dimensions that's otherwise preoccupied with herding tourists into wax museums and aboard trolley tours.

Nearly two million people a year visit St. Augustine. Essentially, you can find whatever kind of cultural niche you're looking for here, be it high, low, or somewhere in between. Your plan of attack on St. Augustine, as you survey the lengthy menu of attractions, boils down to one archetypal question: Would you rather tour the genteel Lightner Museum or hoof it through Ripley's Believe It or Not! with the madding crowd? If you prefer the latter option—well, you'll probably wind up having lunch at Hot Dogs of the World as well. St. Augustine is equipped to satisfy any appetite, with the only serious bugaboo being that traffic knots up into an unholy mess along the main thoroughfares.

We're told that the average length of stay by traveling families in St. Augustine is three days, which seems like a day too many to us. Most of the worthwhile sites can be adequately seen in a single day, if you start early and follow a reasonable itinerary with a few time-outs for fudge fixes and T-shirt browsing. Certainly, if you've come to Florida for the beaches, you will not find them in St. Augustine proper, which is bounded by two rivers and an inlet. If you're en route to points in southern or central Florida, St. Augustine makes an ideal place to spend the night, boasting an abundance of motels and good restaurants. On these counts, it beats the heck out of your average highway interchange. Even the sightseeing, though a mixed bag, is leagues more interesting than you'll find elsewhere in Florida.

For one thing, the town is a veritable museum of American history, having seen considerable bloodshed and flag hoisting over the centuries. St. Augustine claims to be "America's Oldest City," and indeed it is the oldest continuously settled city in America, dating back to the Spanish explorer Ponce de León's landing in 1513 and the town's founding by the Spanish admiral Pedro Menéndez de Avilés in 1565. Menéndez named the town for St. Augustine, upon whose feast day he sighted the coast. For the next two and a half centuries, with the exception of the British-occupied years 1763 through 1783, St. Augustine belonged to the Spanish. It has been part of the United States since 1821.

The unremitting cycles of fire, famine, disaster, and warfare in St. Augustine's past are appalling and make one grateful for the relatively peaceful present-day world in which we live. Along its way down the

Map of Florida's East Coast—Page 5

pockmarked highway of history, St. Augustine has earned the right to claim a lot of firsts. It was, as previously noted, the first European settlement in what is now America, having been founded a full 55 years before the Pilgrims' landing at Plymouth, Massachusetts. The first Catholic mass in America was conducted in St. Augustine, on September 8, 1565. The citrus industry was born here. It was the first planned city in North America. What, we wonder, would St. Augustine's original planners have made of it now, with its Pizza Huts and 7-Elevens, not to mention a Ramada Inn that sits squarely on the site of the continent's first orange grove? Ah, progress!

St. Augustine is the site of the oldest stone fort in the country, the Castillo de San Marcos. It is constructed of coquina, a rocklike substance built up from the calcified remains of billions of butterfly clams into a coral-type reef. The coquina was quarried by a chain gang of convicts and Native American slaves, and the edifice, which took 15 years to complete, proved an impregnable fortress that has withstood every attack upon it. The grand, gray solidity of the fort and other buildings made of coquina is one of the architectural high points of St. Augustine.

After centuries of hardship and an almost inconceivable record of violence and cruelty, it was only when oil magnate Henry Flagler took an interest in the east coast of Florida, and St. Augustine in particular, that the city began to enjoy any sort of refinement. An era of gracious living came to St. Augustine in the late 1800s and early 1900s, as wealthy northerners trekked down to stay at Flagler's Ponce de León Hotel and enjoy the subtropical clime

So You Want to Be a Gator Wrestler?

Alligators are the signature species of Florida, at least from a tourist's perspective. Everywhere one turns, an Indian village features a floor show involving squirming angry reptiles and their biped, Levis-wearing nemeses. That's right, gator wrasslin'. St. Augustine Alligator Farm is a rare exception to this tacky rule.

And yet, even as alligator-wrestling shows proliferate, the wrestler jobs are becoming harder to fill. The young Seminole Indians who used to fill all the positions are going to college or working at casinos, turning their backs on a proud heritage of lost fingers and hands. For the first time in memory, job openings are being publicly advertised and are open to non-Indians, male or female. The pay is $12/hour, with health benefits included.

Basic job description: sneak up behind a 250-pound flesh-eating reptile that has 80 razor-sharp teeth; grab tail of said beast; swing beast by tail in water to exhaust it; climb atop beast's back and yank its head violently backwards; politely acknowledge applause. Optional: keep hands out of beast's mouth.

Even with such seemingly irresistible enticements, the job postings have thus far gotten some nibbles from curiosity seekers but only a few serious, ahem, bites. When you lose your shirt at the Indian gaming establishments on your next trip down this way, you might want to keep this job option in mind. Your ticket home may be riding on your ability to wrassle. Our advice is to start practicing now on the family dog.

Map of St. John's County—Page 38

An Opinionated Guide to St. Augustine Attractions

We spent the better part of two days visiting many, if not most, of St. Augustine's laundry list of tourist attractions. To separate the wheat from the chaff, we've drawn up our own list of preferred sites (and one for those we didn't enjoy so much). We don't pretend to speak for all tourists and travelers. Some love the butter-laden fudge and saltwater taffy and tasteless T-shirts and tacky tourist traps, and more power to them. We enjoy such things ourselves, albeit ironically and in small doses, from time to time. Our idealized reader is reasonably well educated and curious, appreciates legitimate history and art, and casts a fairly jaundiced eye at the trivialization of culture and the insistent consumerist arm-twisting too often found in tourist towns. With that in mind, here we go:

Top Five Attractions in St. Augustine

1. **Castillo de San Marcos** (1 Castillo Drive, 904/829-6506, $4 admission)—The oldest masonry fort in the United States, constructed in 1695 from coquina, still looms impressively over old St. Augustine. The castle grounds make for great strolling, the aura of history is authentic, the exhibits are interesting and informative, and you can even have your picture taken with soldiers in Spanish military garb.
2. **Lightner Museum** (75 King Street, 904/824-2874, $5 admission)—Relics of the nineteenth century, including furnishings, costumes, housewares, and musical instruments, are on display. Not to be missed: the stained-glass room, featuring the work of Louis Comfort Tiffany. Civility and good taste survive at the Lightner, making the banality of the outside world fade, if only for a short while.
3. **Mission of Nombre de Díos** (27 Ocean Avenue, 904/824-2809, no charge)—St. Augustine, the first permanent Christian settlement in the United States, was founded on this site on September 8, 1565. On the grounds are a mission chapel and shrine, the 208-foot Great Cross, and some blessed peace from the downtown bustle. We bought St. Christopher's medals at the Mission Gift Shop, and they haven't failed us yet.

amid palm trees and orange groves. Neither as war-torn nor quite so rarefied these days, St. Augustine is a bustling tourist town in which you can study the relics and remnants of the past without having to worry about whizzing cannonballs, smoking muskets, or flaming tomahawks.

When you get to St. Augustine, head straight for the **Visitor Information Center** (10 Castillo Drive, 904/825-1000), where you can pick up maps and brochures and have questions answered. Traffic and parking in St. Augustine are a problem, so the large, inexpensive ($3 per day) lot at the information center is by far the best deal in town. It's within walking distance of downtown attractions, as well as train and trolley tour operators. If you've got time on your hands, stick around the information center to watch the 52-minute film *Dream of Empire,* about the city's history. If you're in a

Map of Florida's East Coast—Page 5

4. **St. Augustine Lighthouse and Museum** (81 Lighthouse Avenue, 904/829-0745, $4 admission)—Nautical exhibits, lighthouse lenses, and period artifacts are on display. A calf-burning, 219-stair climb leads up the lighthouse. You won't want to miss the view from the top.
5. **St. Augustine Alligator Farm** (Highway A1A South, 904/824-3337, $10.95 admission)—Not the typical alligator and pony show, this is an educational display of reptiles, tropical birds, and more, all on well-landscaped grounds that preserve the look of Old Florida. Best of all, there's not an alligator wrestler to be found, just naturalists who can give you the real lowdown on the world of reptiles.

Bottom Five Attractions in St. Augustine

1. **Fountain of Youth** (11 Magnolia Avenue, 904/829-3168, $4.75 admission)—The most bogus of St. Augustine tourist traps claims to be a "national archaeological park," but it is nothing quite as grand as that. It costs $4.75 to enter and sip from Ponce de León's "Fountain of Youth." What you get is a miserly plastic cup of sulfur water poured from a pitcher. Other on-site attractions: a pile of sticks meant to suggest an Indian "roasting spit" and a tacky gift shop where the same vile-tasting sulfur water is retailed for $1.99 a fifth.
2. **Oldest Wooden Schoolhouse** (14 St. George Street, 904/824-0192, $2 admission)—You will feel like donning the dunce cap on display after paying to tour this tiny museum.
3. **Museum of Weapons and Early American History** (81C King Street, 904/829-3727, $3.50 admission)—Guns, swords, rifles, pistols, muskets, and more fill this violence-themed museum.
4. **Zorayda Castle** (83 King Street, 904/824-3097, $5 admission)—The burning question about this one-tenth scale re-creation of a Moorish palace is, why? Highlights: a "sacred cat rug" and a mummy's foot.
5. **Ripley's Believe It or Not!** (19 San Marco Avenue, 904/824-1606, $9.95 admission for adults, $5.95 for kids 5–12)—Here's a spot for those with an appetite for the bizarre and little sense of, or interest in, the real history of St. Augustine.

hurry, at least watch the 12-minute capsule video on local attractions. If you're too pooped to hoof it around town, you have options. **Red Sightseeing Trains** (170 San Marco Avenue, 904/829-6545) offers package tours ranging from $17 to $42 per person that include a narrated train tour and various attractions. **St. Augustine Trolley Tours** (167 San Marco Avenue, 904/829-3800) sells passes that are good for riding around town all day long ($12 for adults, $5 for children ages 6–12); they dispense discounted attraction tickets as well.

Beaches

St. Augustine is bounded by two rivers (the San Sebastian and the Matanzas, which is also the Intracoastal Waterway) and the St. Augustine Inlet, so you won't find any beaches in town. But beaches abound only a bridge away: in Vilano

Believe It or Nuts!

The following are actual items on display at the Ripley's Believe It or Not! museum in St. Augustine, Florida. If you find yourself wondering why you would come to a historical community like St. Augustine to view such things, well, join the club. If you do pay the rather steep admission ($9.95 for adults, $5.95 for kids 5–12, and open every blessed day of the year), step right up—and don't avert your eyes. Among other things, you might see such sights as these:

- World's smallest domino set
- Degas' masterpiece *L'Absinthe,* rendered on 63 pieces of toast
- The Lord's Prayer engraved on a pinhead by a prison convict
- African vest made from human skin
- Recipe for soup made of human bones
- A manatee constructed from 1,700 soda cans
- Six-legged steer named Beauregard
- Articles found in a cow's stomach (string, nails, barbed wire)
- Wax replica of the world's tallest man, Robert Wadlow, who stood 8 feet 8 inches and weighed 490 pounds
- A model of the London Tower Bridge made out of 264,345 matchsticks

Here are a few additional "Believe It or Not" items culled from our own experiences around town:

- Believe It or Not, we actually heard a bedraggled tourist ask, "Is there a wax museum in the area?"
- Believe It or Not, a St. Augustine trolley guide informed us that the average length of stay for a family is three days!
- Believe It or Not, we'd had enough of the tourist attractions in three hours!
- Believe It or Not, you don't have to frequent the tourist traps to have a good time in St. Augustine! There's enough legitimate history to keep anyone occupied for at least a few days.

Beach, over the A1A North Bridge, and in St. Augustine Beach, over the Bridge of Lions (A1A South). They are described in separate entries for Vilano Beach and St. Augustine Beach.

Shore Things

- **Bike/skate rentals**: Sunshine Shop, 546 A1A South, St. Augustine Beach, 904/471-6899.
- **Dive shop**: Sea Hunt Scuba, 825 South Ponce de León Boulevard, 904/824-0831.
- **Ecotourism**: Victory II & III Scenic Cruise, Municipal Marina, 904/824-1806.
- **Fishing charters**: Conch House Marina Resort, 57 Comares Avenue, 904/829-8646.
- **Lighthouse**: St. Augustine Lighthouse,

81 Lighthouse Avenue, 904/829-0745.

- **Marina:** Municipal Marina, 111 Avenida Menéndez, 904/825-1026.
- **Pier:** St. Johns County Pier, 350 A1A Beach Boulevard, St. Augustine Beach, 904/461-0119.
- **Rainy-day attraction:** Lightner Museum, 75 King Street, 904/824-2874.
- **Shopping/browsing:** St. George Street, between Cathedral Place and Hypolita Street.
- **Surf shop:** Surf Station, 1020 Anastasia Boulevard, 904/471-4694 (store) and 904/471-1122 (surf report).
- **Vacation rentals:** Ocean Gallery, 4600 A1A South, St. Augustine Beach, 904/471-6663.

Bunking Down

St. Augustine is ruled by chain motels and hotels, which are clustered on or near San Marco Avenue, close to the downtown historic district, and along Anastasia Boulevard, over the Bridge of Lions in the direction of St. Augustine Beach. If you want to see the sights and soak up history, stay downtown. If you're toting kids and/or are watching your wallet, go for a recognizable name, like **Hampton Inn** (2050 North Ponce de León Boulevard, 904/829-1996, $$), the newest arrival in town and therefore a clean and safe bet. Some other dependably moderate motels, both in price and comfort afforded, are the **Holiday Inn Downtown** (1300 Ponce de León Boulevard, 904/824-3383, $$), the **Best Western Spanish Quarters Inn** (6 Castillo Drive, 904/824-4457, $$), and the **Ramada Inn** (116 San Marco Avenue, 904/824-4352, $$).

On a more upscale note, there are at least two dozen historic bed-and-breakfast inns in St. Augustine. For a brochure detailing them, write Historic Inns of St. Augustine, P.O. Box 5268, St. Augustine, FL 32084. Tops among them are the **Cedar House Inn** (79 Cedar Street, 904/829-0079, $$$), near the Lightner Museum, and **Casa de la Paz** (22 Avenida Menéndez, 904/829-2915, $$$), located on Matanzas Bay.

Coastal Cuisine

Several of the better restaurants in St. Augustine are located over the Bridge of Lions, on the north end of Anastasia Island, which is still part of St. Augustine. This side of Anastasia, incidentally, was not originally part of the island but was created in the 1920s by a man named Davis (who did a similar thing in Tampa) by extending the island with landfill. So while you may be on dry land, it's a man-made extension. Out here, motels, restaurants, and the odd surf shop line Anastasia Boulevard (Highway A1A) before you round a curve and begin paralleling the shore in St. Augustine Beach.

The **Gypsy Cab Company** (828 Anastasia Boulevard, 904/824-8244, $$$) is a healthy, cosmopolitan bistro that does creative things with fish, chicken, and beef. It's been around for many years and is a favorite of discriminating diners. You might find pepper-seared grouper in spicy Dijon sauce, flounder with white wine mustard, or something similarly intriguing on the changing menu.

Osteen's (205 Anastasia Boulevard, 904/829-6974, $$) is the place to go for fried shrimp; no one does it better, anywhere. The plump, perfectly breaded shrimp—listed as "Our Famous St. Augustine Fried Shrimp" on the menu—are served at lunch and dinner and are worth every penny ($9.95 for nine, $10.95 for 12). Squirt a few drops of Osteen's own sweet 'n' hot datil sauce (datil is a kind of pepper grown locally), and you'll be in shrimp heaven. Osteen's also does oysters, scallops, fish, catfish, crab, and clam strips, and they sell their bottled "Datil Squeezings" at the cash register.

Map of St. John's County—Page 38

Conch House Marina Resort (57 Comares Avenue, 904/829-8646, $$) is a one-stop full-service resort that includes a 23-unit motel, restaurant, lounge, 100-slip marina, sport-fishing charter, outfitter (Raging Watersports), sports bar, and gift shop. Alfresco dining on the Conch House's outdoor deck, with its thatched-roof dining huts and direct views onto the inlet, is the way to enjoy the Caribbean-themed menu. Try anything conchy, like cracked conch or conch fritters. The complex remains in the Ponce family of Minorcan bluebloods who founded St. Augustine. Yes, long before "the Fonz" came along, there was "the Ponce."

Speaking of St. Augustine, back in town there are dozens more options. A personal favorite is the **Raintree** (120 San Marco Avenue, 904/824-7211, $$$). Located in an exquisitely furnished old two-story home downtown, the Raintree will make you forget you're mere feet from busy San Marco Avenue. The menu is continental, with such dishes as veal Oscar (topped with asparagus, blue crab, and hollandaise) and brandy pepper steak (among the best filet mignons we've ever tasted), plus seafood specialties like grouper Raintree (sautéed in white wine, mushrooms, and cream). Once you've eaten here, you'll likely return with every visit to St. Augustine.

Night Moves

Over in the vicinity of St. George Street, you can wet your whistle at several English pub-type places. Two of the more frequented among them are the **Mill Top Tavern** (19 1/2 St. George Street, 904/829-2329) and the **White Lion Tavern** (20 Cuna Street, 904/829-2388). A popular gathering spot of long standing is **Scarlett O'Hara's** (70 Hypolita Street, 904/824-6535), a jazz-blues club and restaurant located in a two-story house. There are rocking chairs on Scarlett O'Hara's front porch, which just about sums up the low-key tenor of nightlife in downtown St. Augustine. Frankly, Scarlett, we just didn't give a damn and instead headed to St. Augustine Beach to fritter the night away.

Contact Information

St. Johns County Visitors and Convention Bureau, 88 Riberia Street, Suite 400, St. Augustine, FL 32084; 800/653-2489; website: www.visitoldcity.com

Anastasia State Park

Anastasia State Park, located on the northeast corner of Anastasia Island, features one of the finest beaches on the east coast of Florida—and certainly the finest in the "South Beaches" area of St. Johns County. The healthy width and condition of this beach, compared to the degraded condition of the beach behind the hotel resorts of St. Augustine Beach just over the park's southern border, is instructional as it dramatically demonstrates the negative impact that beach hardening and development can have on shoreline width. There is no beach at the north end of St. Augustine Beach, where waves slap against rock revetments, whereas there is an awesome beach on the undeveloped shoreline of Anastasia State Park. Take a good, close look; you'll never see a stronger argument against beach development in your life than the one on display here.

At Anastasia, a wide, fine-grained, hard-packed, table-flat, four-mile beach serves to allow cars to travel in both directions and park several rows deep. There is no charge, beyond the $3.25 park entrance fee, to drive on Anastasia Beach. Moreover, there's more to do at Anastasia in the way of outdoor recreation. A wooded,

Map of Florida's East Coast—Page 5

139-site campground borders the inlet. There's a great windsurfing spot, complete with parking lot and launch site, on the calmer inlet side. Surfboards, windsurfers, kayaks, and canoes are rented in the park at a concession operated by the Surf Station (904/471-4694), which also operates a complete surf shop immediately outside the park's gates. In addition to equipment rentals, the Surf Station offers instruction on board surfing and windsurfing.

Contact Information
Anastasia State Park, 1340A A1A South, St. Augustine, FL 32084; 904/461-2033; website: www.myflorida.com

8 Anastasia State Park

Location: St. Augustine Inlet, one mile east of downtown St. Augustine and directly north of St. Augustine Beach on Highway A1A
Parking/fees: $3.25 entrance fee per vehicle. Camping fees are $19.56 per night (with hookups) and $17.44 (without hookups) March 1–September 30; fees are $2 less per night October 1–February 28.
Hours: 8 A.M. to sundown
Facilities: concessions, lifeguards (seasonal), restrooms, picnic tables, and showers
Contact: Anastasia State Park, 904/461-2033

St. Augustine Beach

They really ought to think of shortening the name of St. Augustine Beach (pop. 4,320) to St. Augustine, because the distinction between the two adjacent communities is minimal. That is to say, there is no beach to speak of at St. Augustine Beach. There has been such dramatic narrowing of the beach behind the oceanfront hotels that they are now fighting a rearguard action—with boulders, riprap, and seawalls—just to keep from washing away. This is important to bear in mind, because if you come to St. Augustine Beach expecting a beach vacation, you may be sorely disappointed.

The situation is most alarming where the beach at Anastasia State Park, which is undeveloped and remains broad and healthy, meets the resort developments at the north end of St. Augustine Beach. Chain-link fences behind some of them, in fact, keep people from attempting to climb over the seawall onto the wave-battered rocks. The rock revetment runs from Anastasia State Park south to A Street. The situation improves as you move farther south, especially as you near the trio of county-maintained beaches that run from St. Augustine Beach to the county line.

Beaches
The bright light on the **St. Augustine Beach** scene, as far as sandy access to the ocean is concerned, is Anastasia State Park (see pages 54–55). The question in St. Augustine

9 St. Augustine Beach

Location: four miles south of downtown St. Augustine on Highway A1A. The main entrance point is at St. Johns County Pier, but there are numerous access points at street ends along the four-mile length of St. Augustine Beach.
Parking/fees: free street and lot parking
Hours: October 1–April 30, 24 hours; May 1–September 30, 5 A.M.–10 P.M.
Facilities: lifeguards (seasonal), restrooms, picnic tables, showers, and a visitor center
Contact: St. Johns County Recreation Department, 904/471-6616

Beach proper is, "What beach?" Beach erosion, which occurs due to the combined impact of natural conditions and man-made structures, has been noted out here as far back as the 1880s. If nothing else, they ought to forbid driving on the beach, which creates weak spots that worsen the erosion that occurs during storms and overwash. It would at least be a start. As it is, waves come right up to the wooden retaining fences. There is some thickly vegetated dune cover but precious little beach. About the best you can do is cast a line from St. Johns County Pier, which also is the site of a visitor center for the "South Beaches" area, where you can load up on maps, brochures, and local info, or wander up to Anastasia.

Bunking Down

The lodging situation out on St. Augustine Beach is certainly not hopeless, but without a beach, it may seem pointless to some visitors. The oceanfront hotels are literally in front of the ocean, facing a seawall bordered by chain-link fence and no beach. The safest bet may be the **Best Western Ocean Inn** (3955 A1A South, 904/471-8010, $$), on the side of the road opposite the water. Still, some remain undaunted in their desire to build upon the ocean. The newest entry in this high-stakes game is the spiffy mid-rise **Hampton Inn** (430 A1A Beach Blvd., 904/471-4000, $$), doing its best imitation of a Hilton. Its on-site amenities are the best on the ocean hereabouts (pool, Jacuzzi, fitness center, volleyball). Also on the ocean, and quite popular, is the **Holiday Inn** (860 A1A Beach Blvd., 904/471-2555, $$), which has a nice protected gazebo that overlooks the waves. An on-site sports bar can get raucous, depending on what team, rock band, or convention is staying at the motel.

Coastal Cuisine

If we could write a menu that expressed what we like most about food and unique dining experiences, it would resemble the menu at **Salt Water Cowboy's** (299 Dondanville Road, 904/471-2332, $$), two miles south of St. Augustine Beach. Everything about the place speaks to our sensibilities. The restaurant, started by a rugged Floridian whose nickname was "Cowboy," has been in business since 1964. The tin-roofed building, situated directly on the marsh, is a cracker's paradise. It looks more like an 1890s fish camp, with personal artifacts and weird photographs featuring gator carcasses on the wall. The wood floor was at one time the floor of the Jacksonville train station. Rustic willow furniture designed by a North Carolina craftsman occupies the plant-filled rooms, and large serpentine trees grow both inside and outside the restaurant, including some enormous live oaks. Salt Water Cowboy's has a no-reservation policy. Your stock portfolio and cell phone mean nothing here, podnuh; it's an egalitarian first come, first served. You come expecting to wait, so you sit out on the rambling wooden porch and knock back a drink while the sun sets over the marsh to the west. When you are seated, you will dine in either the Snake, Gator, or Hibiscus room.

Salt Water Cowboy's iced tea is served in mason jars. Delicious, cold, and not too sickly sweet, it is the perfect accompaniment to the spread of seafood laid out before you. The food is served either broiled or fried, and while it's all good, we'd steer you to the locally harvested oysters and shrimp in particular. If you have an adventurous palate, the Cowboy obliges with a bodacious Florida Cracker Combo appetizer, consisting of frog legs, cooter (soft-shell turtle), and alligator tail. Some entrées—chicken, catfish, steak, catch of the day, and "shrimp on a stick"—are also served blackened. You can even get chicken, shrimp, and ribs barbecued to a turn over an open pit. It's all too darn good, and if you have any room left they serve a key lime pie as tart and tasty as any you'll find this side of Key Largo.

Meanwhile, back at the beach, you will not go hungry. One of our favorite beachside haunts in Florida, the **Beachcomber** (2 A Street, 904/471-3744, $), will fill your belly and not empty your wallet. It's front and center on the beach, where A Street meets the ocean and everyone in town meets each other. Here, "proper attire" means only "shoes and shirt required after 5:30 P.M." The breakfast-lunch-and-dinner menu is surprisingly varied, from steamed shrimp and burgers to seafood specialties and dinner platters and salads. The prices are reasonable and the helpings plentiful. Parking is virtually impossible here—with a $175 towing fine—so the only way to visit the Beachcomber is when you are, uh, combing the beach.

Just up the street, the morning port of call and unofficial community bulletin board is **Stir It Up** (18 A Street, 904/461-4552). Even the roughest of morning-afters can be jumpstarted here with fruit smoothies and fresh roasted coffee blends. Diagonally across the street and fronting A1A is **Sharky's Shrimp Shack** (700 A1A, 904/461-9992), which offers "beachy casual ocean breeze dining" and 23 different preparations of fresh local shrimp from which to choose.

One curious place that came recommended but left us cold was **Dune's Cracker House** (641 A1A Beach Blvd., 904/461-5725, $$). It seemed to be mislabeled goods. This faux "cracker" house has a pretentious menu written in regal script, and the daily special when we visited was swordfish, not exactly a staple of the cracker diet. We did our best head-bobbing bucktooth leer and in a cornpone accent told the waitress, "No thankee ma'am" before backing out the faux cracker portico. More popular with the gourmands is **Hans' Beach House** (550 A1A South, 904/461-8446, $$$), which serves continental beef and seafood and has a line out the door. Reservation recommended on busy weekends.

Night Moves

St. Augustine Beach has always had the nightlife, as if St. Augustine, bowing under the awful weight of history, couldn't be bothered with such trifling. But that's the beauty of a beach town: all awareness of history gets washed away like a shoreline scoured clean by twice-daily tides, and the only thing that matters is the present. If *carpe diem* is the operative philosophy, then the best place to indulge footloose escapism in St. Augustine Beach is **Cafe Iguana** (321 A1A South, 904/471-7797), a restaurant that doubles as a jazz, blues, and dance club after the plates are cleared.

We gamely anted up the $2 cover and hung with the collegiate Gen X crowd in a kind of rave atmosphere in which a deejay spun manic dance tracks while a strobe light blinked its blinding semaphore signals. Coeds and whatever guys they could coerce onto the dance floor spun themselves dizzy to the crazy techno sounds. Some of the exhortations emanating from the speakers included: "Everybody put your hands in the air now" and "You got ta kick it" and "Jump jump jump jump jump jump." We watched watched watched for a while and then left left left, wondering whatever happened to real live rock and roll at the beach.

Contact Information

South Beaches Information Center, St. Johns County Pier, 350 A1A South, St. Augustine, FL 32084; 904/471-1596; website: www.visitoldcity.com

Map of St. John's County—Page 38

Crescent Beach

South of St. Augustine Beach, there's a small beach community (Crescent Beach) and a hat trick of beaches—Butler, Crescent, and Matanzas, by name. These three beaches run from St. Augustine Beach to the Matanzas Inlet, the southern boundary of St. Johns County.

Beaches

There are nine beach-access points between St. Augustine Beach and Fort Matanzas, which works out to about an access a mile. The beaches down this way are wide, white, and sufficiently hard packed to allow for beach driving (though we're not wild about the practice).

At **Frank B. Butler County Park**, a decent-sized park that extends from the ocean to the Intracoastal Waterway, you'll find beach access on the east side, a boat ramp into the Intracoastal on the west side, and picnic pavilions and restrooms on both sides. The first and second line of dunes are still intact and the beach is wide as a result.

Crescent Beach, a small beach community located on the south end of Anastasia Island, offers a glimpse at the magical lure of Old Florida. The central artery of Crescent Beach is SR206, which meets the ocean at a vehicular ramp that leads onto the beach. The appealing sun-baked cottages flare out from this point, north and south of the ramp. Located alongside the beach ramp is a wonderfully funky community landmark called **South Beach Grill** (45 Cubbidge Road, 904/471-8700, $), a two-story bar and restaurant that serves unbeatable food specials (wahoo for $7.95, half-pound steamed shrimp for $8.95) and, like the Beachcomber up in St. Augustine Beach, makes you feel instantly at home. They take care of their five-mile-long beach at Crescent Beach, too. An admirable dune revegetation project was just completed, and the healthy primary and secondary dune structure offers a stunning contrast to the thin strand on the overdeveloped coast to the north. The county maintains five street-end access points along Crescent Beach's five miles of shorefront, along with picnic tables, restrooms, showers, and lifeguards.

Down at the south end of the island, **Fort Matanzas National Monument** (8635 A1A South, 904/471-0116) stands sentry by the Matanzas Inlet. A free ferry from the mainland to Matanzas Island and its namesake eighteenth-century stone fort leaves every hour on the half hour from 9:30 A.M. to 4:30 P.M. The fort sits on Rattlesnake Island, which came by its name honestly and is one of the oldest historic sites in North America. *Matanzas,* in fact, means "slaughter," which is what occurred here in 1565. Though it lies on federal property, three-mile **Matanzas Beach** is maintained by St. Johns County. The beach is wonderfully natural and secluded, a real find. A separate access one-quarter mile south takes you via a wooden walk through a "living dune." One of the chief attractions at this end of Anastasia Island is fishing, judging from the number of an-

⑩ Frank B. Butler County Park

   ④

Location: two miles south of St. Augustine Beach on Highway A1A

Parking/fees: off-beach parking lot (free) or on-beach parking and driving ($3 per day or $20 annually)

Hours: October 1–April 30, 24 hours; May 1–September 30, 5 A.M.–10 P.M.

Facilities: lifeguards (seasonal), restrooms, picnic tables, and showers

Contact: St. Johns County Recreation Department, 904/471-6616

glers casting into the inlet from the Matanzas Bridge. Convoys of noisome Jet Skis careen their way back and forth, too. There ought to be a law, in our curmudgeonly estimation.

Bunking Down

If you're looking for beach, forget St. Augustine Beach. Instead, drive a few miles south to Crescent Beach and check out **Beacher's Lodge** (6970 A1A South, 904/471-8849, $$), where the rates are good and the dunes out back are high and healthy. Oceanfront rooms are king- and queen-bed suites with a sleeper sofa in the living area. You'll save a little more by staying on the ground floor because the dunes are tall enough to partially obscure the ocean view.

Contact Information

South Beaches Information Center, St. Johns County Pier, 350 A1A South, St. Augustine, FL 32084; 904/471-1596; website: www.visitoldcity.com

⓫ Crescent Beach

Location: three miles south of St. Augustine Beach on Highway A1A

Parking/fees: off-beach parking lot (free) or on-beach parking and driving ($3 per day or $20 annually)

Hours: October 1–April 30, 24 hours; May 1–September 30, 5 A.M. 10 P.M.

Facilities: lifeguards (seasonal), restrooms, picnic tables, and showers

Contact: St. Johns County Recreation Department, 904/471-6616

⓬ Matanzas Beach (Fort Matanzas National Monument)

Location: 7.5 miles south of St. Augustine Beach on Highway A1A

Parking/fees: off-beach parking lot (free) or on-beach parking and driving ($3 per day or $20 annually)

Hours: October 1–April 30, 24 hours; May 1–September 30, 5 A.M.–10 P.M.

Facilities: lifeguards (seasonal), restrooms, picnic tables, showers, and a visitor center

Contact: St. Johns County Recreation Department, 904/471-6616

MAP OF ST. JOHN'S COUNTY—PAGE 38

Alligators and Crocodiles

Both alligators and crocodiles are found in Florida, though gators are far more prevalent than true crocodiles. Here are some facts and figures about these aquatic predators, many of them gleaned from our visit to the St. Augustine Alligator Farm.

- There are 14 species of crocodiles and two species of alligators. The American alligator *(Alligator mississippiensis)* is the only native species. The rare Chinese alligator *(Alligator sinensis)* is endangered and perhaps extinct.
- The range for alligators and crocodiles overlaps only at the southern tip of Florida.
- An alligator has 80 teeth, all sharp, and its jaws can exert a biting force of 4,000 pounds per square inch (psi). A human's biting force is 200 psi.
- Both male and female alligators hiss; additionally, males roar loudly across long distances.
- The adult alligator diet consists of fish, small mammals, birds, and sometimes even deer and cattle. The crocodile mainly eats fish, mammals, waterfowl, and human beings.
- Alligators can reach a top speed of 25 mph in the water and 11 mph on land. To put it another way, they can run a five-and-a-half-minute mile. Can you?
- The number of crocodile-caused human deaths worldwide since the 1950s: 3,000.
- The number of alligator-caused deaths worldwide since the 1950s: Seven.
- The maximum sentence and fine for feeding a wild alligator in Florida: 30 days and $500.
- An adult alligator eats only 25 percent of its body weight yearly. Maybe there's something to be said for reptilian metabolism.
- How best to distinguish an alligator from a crocodile? If you can get close enough to tell, the fourth tooth on either side of a crocodile's lower jaw visibly projects outside the snout when the mouth is closed.
- Average length of an alligator: 6 to 12 feet. Maximum length: 19 feet.
- Alligators were trapped to near-extinction in this country, necessitating their placement on the endangered species list. Their subsequent recovery has been nothing short of remarkable, and limited hunting of them is permitted once again.
- Here is a harrowing account of what crocodiles do to their prey, excerpted from the *Encyclopedia Britannica:* "Crocodiles capture water animals in their jaws with a sideways movement of the muzzle. To catch land animals they remain motionless at the edge of a water hole from which the prey habitually drink, or they float passively in the water, resembling a drifting log. With a swift blow of the tail, they knock unsuspecting prey into the water. A number of crocodile species grip the legs of the victim in their jaws, then rotate themselves rapidly in the water, thus tearing the prey apart. When a crocodile cannot consume all of a victim at one time, it drags the carcass into its burrow."
- Crocodiles have the most highly developed of all reptilian brains. They exhibit curiosity (a sign of intelligence) and can even be tamed into pets, of sorts. Not in our households!

Summer Haven

At the south end of the bridge that goes over Matanzas Inlet, you'll notice that "Old Highway A1A" lurches toward the ocean while the real A1A continues south. If you want to see the Florida beach equivalent of Atlantis, pay heed and take the turn. Here, along this old washed-out road that riprap barely keeps traversible, sits an appealingly sleepy cottage colony called Summer Haven Beach. At the end of the road, where it spills jaggedly onto the beach, a hand-painted sign warns "YOUR GONNA GET STUK" *[sic]*. Surfers seem particularly drawn to Summer Haven, parking along Old A1A and hopping with their boards over the rip rap. Back out on the real A1A, take it south for a mile and you'll come to the other end of "Old Highway A1A" and another entry point into this lost summer colony. The road here is, if possible, even less inviting that the northern entry point, covered in sand drifts and barely accessible to the local residents. It is, in fact, so thin that cars cannot travel two abreast; out of deference to an approaching resident, we drove in reverse for a quarter mile to let him pass. One circular house is raised so high on stilts above the rising sand and water of the marsh that it looks like the Mothership from the funk group Parliament's stage show. Summer Haven used to be a summer haven for the DuPonts, Vanderbilts, Mellons, and their moneyed ilk.

Contact Information

South Beaches Information Center, St. Johns County Pier, 350 A1A South, St. Augustine, FL 32084; 904/471-1596; website: www.visitoldcity.com

MAP OF ST. JOHN'S COUNTY—PAGE 38

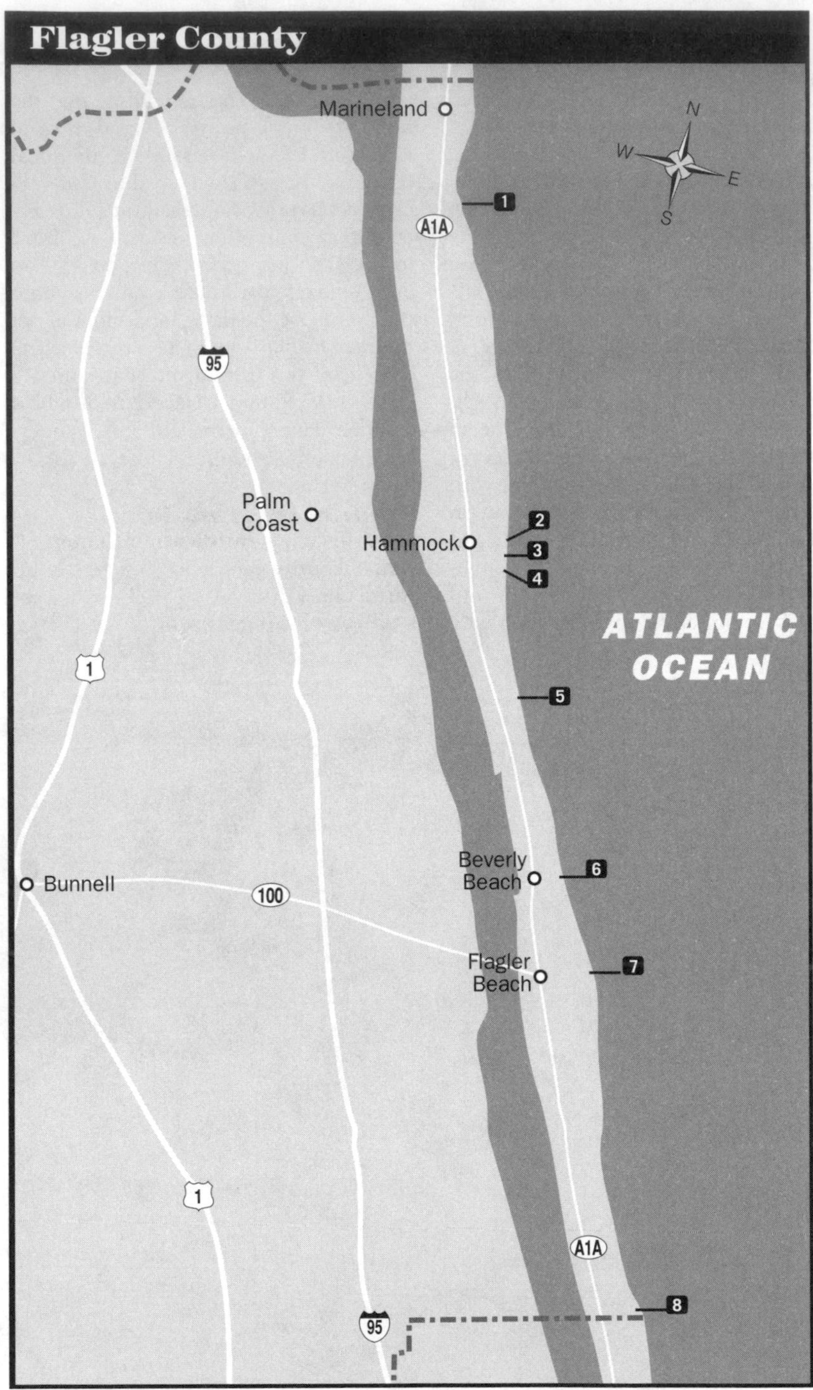
Flagler County
Marineland
N
W
E
S
1
A1A
95
Palm Coast
Hammock
2
3
4
ATLANTIC OCEAN
1
5
Beverly Beach
6
Bunnell
100
Flagler Beach
7
1
A1A
8
95

Flagler County

Flagler County is a less-traveled stretch of Highway A1A between the thriving tourist meccas of St. Augustine and Daytona Beach. Somehow the building frenzy that's afflicted so much of Florida has blown right by Flagler County, despite the fact that it claims 26 miles of fine beaches. With a population of only 45,000, the county—particularly the stretch from Painters Hill to Flagler Beach—markets itself as "the quiet side of Florida." The midcounty communities of Palm Coast and Hammock have fallen to architects of gated communities and golf-course designers. But how to explain Marineland, once Florida's biggest tourist attraction, now slowly going to seed? Or the authentically quaint, small-town feel of Flagler Beach? It's reassuring that places like these still exist in Florida.

Washington Oaks Gardens State Park

The 390 sublime acres of this lovely park were deeded to the state by its former owners. Located three miles south of Marineland, **Washington Oaks Gardens State Park** looks like much of coastal Florida did prior to European colonization. Great diversity is displayed within a brief distance here. At the ocean's edge, a "coquina beach" of fine orange coquina sand and rocks hosts a variety of shore-

Marineland: A Sunken Treasure

Marineland, an oceanarium up at the north end of Flagler County, used to be the world's most popular marine-oriented tourist attraction. However, the aging facility has not kept up with the times, heaving steadily lost ground to fizzier contemporary attractions like Sea World, Disney World, the Kennedy Space Center, the Daytona Speedway . . . and on and on. In 1996, Marineland Ocean Resort, Inc. bought the motel, marina, and campground surrounding the oceanarium, pledging a major refurbishment. A year later, they filed for bankruptcy protection. The oceanarium itself is owned by a separate organization, the Marineland Foundation, but the fates of the attraction and resort property are obviously intertwined. At least the University of Florida still maintains its Graduate School of Marine Biology (386/461-4000) here.

The sad part is that, though Marineland has been in business for more than 60 years, it barely remains afloat these days. What's most appealing about Marineland, at least from the vantage point of Highway A1A, is the very antiquated look of the place. It's like stepping back into the early 1950s. Maybe its salvation lies in playing up that fact to capitalize on the emerging spirit of retro chic. In fact, Marineland has been placed on the National Register of Historic Places. Lord knows there are more than enough sterile, eye-popping, postmodern, high-tech attractions zapping hoodwinked consumers at every turn as it is. Marineland's faded glory is kind of refreshing by comparison.

Even though Marineland is faltering, it remains the No. 1 tourist destination in Flagler County—which speaks volumes about Flagler County. Meanwhile, the dolphins continue to jump, though maybe not for joy. The same underwater film that was playing when we passed through 15 years ago—*Sea Dream*—still runs continuously in the Aquarius Theater. Underwater feedings, marine science displays, and an outdoor exhibit with sea lions, otters, and flamingos round out the watery fun. Marineland is open 9:30 AM–4:30 P.M. Wednesday through Sunday, offering a program of five shows twice daily. Admission is $12 for adults and $8 for kids age 3–11. For more information, contact Marineland of Florida, 9507 Oceanshore Boulevard, Marineland, FL 32086; 386/460-1275.

Marineland also offers a free public beach at 9610 Oceanshore Boulevard. A dirt lot allows access to an unusual rock formation that creates a beach of orange coquina sand, with lots of rock outcrops in the water. It's not exactly a prime vacation spot, though.

birds and marinelife, including crabs and starfish in the tidal pools and mussels and anemones glued to the rocks. Known as "the Rocks," about 0.4 miles of beach falls within park boundaries. The "rocks" are hardened outcrops of coquina sand, lovely sculptural formations. An informative display explains "Life on Beach Rocks." People come out here to sun themselves and study the unusual (and usually deserted) beach.

Moving inland from the beach, you proceed through a coastal scrub community (stunted vegetation that serves as habitat for the rare Florida scrub jay) to a coastal hammock community (live oak, hickory, magnolia) and, finally, to a tidal marsh bordering the Matanzas River.

A short nature trail winds through the hammock and along the river. The park's man-made gardens—whose cultivation dates from the mid-1800s—occupy a coastal swale awash in colorful flowers and exotic plants like the giant elephant's ear.

Dirt pathways wind through the oaks, their limbs overhung with Spanish moss, past a spring-fed pond and beautiful patches of roses, camellias, and azaleas. All in all, Washington Oaks Gardens is one of the most peaceful spots on Florida's east coast. It makes an ideal place for a picnic in a setting that's as picturesque as they come.

Contact Information

Washington Oaks Gardens State Park, 6400 North Ocean Boulevard, Palm Coast, FL 32137; 386/446-6780; website: www.myflorida.com

❶ Washington Oaks Gardens State Park

Location: three miles south of Marineland, along Highway A1A

Parking/fees: $3.25 entrance fee per vehicle ($2 for beach side only)

Hours: 8 A.M. to sundown

Facilities: restrooms, picnic tables, and a visitor center

Contact: Washington Oaks Gardens State Park, 904/446-6780

Palm Coast and Hammock

The midsection of Flagler County's coastline is going to the doglegs. That is to say, golf course living has staked its claim here, creating an entirely different climate than that found in the hangdog beach towns at the southern end of the county.

Palm Coast (pop. 18,677) bears the prefab look of a community that didn't even exist a quarter century ago. Rich and tony golf resorts, gated residential communities, and the fortress mentality of the cloistered rich are what you'll find in inland Palm Coast and coastal Hammock (pop. 600).

The premier development in these parts is Hammock Dunes ("A Private Oceanfront Golf Community"). You practically expect to hear "Also Sprach Zarathustra" rising to a crescendo as you approach

❷ Malacompra Beach Park

Location: at the end of Malacompra Road in Hammock

Parking/fees: free parking lot

Hours: 8 A.M.–10 P.M.

Facilities: restrooms

Contact: Flagler County Parks and Recreation Department, 904/437-7490

MAP OF FLAGLER COUNTY—PAGE 62

its sacred guard gates.

These are the sorts of places where golf courses are referred to in glossy brochures as "masterpieces." If so, then Tom Fazio, Jack Nicklaus, Gary Player, and Arnold Palmer are the Bach, Beethoven, Mozart, and Brahms of the links-minded set in Palm Coast.

The Hammock Dunes Toll Bridge (75 cents) connects Highway A1A with I-95 and Hammock with Palm Coast. Though the privatization of the shoreline goes against the grain, we will give them this much: the oceanfront development out here is low density, leaving lots of room for nature's manic tangle of trees, shrubs, and dune grasses, and a paved biking/jogging path runs for miles on the east side of Highway A1A.

One curious sociological phenomenon that we couldn't help but notice in Hammock was the palpable tension between the new gated, exclusionary "communities" being built here and the old spreads of trailer parks, RV campgrounds, flyblown motels, and biker bars along Highway A1A. You can see this dynamic most dramatically on 16th Street, where it courses three blocks to the ocean.

An earth-rattling upscale golf and condo development is being wedged in here, right alongside a real long-time community of mobile homes and salt box–style houses. One can't help but imagine that the resentment among the long-time residents who haven't sold out must be extreme. Either way, nature seems to be the big loser in Hammock, however this thing plays out culturally.

It's really a shame—and a black mark—that Flagler County has not done better by its long-time residents than to sell them out like this. You would think that they at least would try to buy some of this prime oceanfront land for their own park system before it's completely gone.

Beaches

There are three county beaches in Hammock. All have restrooms, wooden dune walkovers, a free parking lot, and no other facilities. From north to south, they are **Malacompra Beach Park, Old Salt Road Park**, and **Jungle Hut Road Park**; all are found at the ends of roads bearing those names.

Old Salt is not as rocky as Jungle Hut and Malacompra and would therefore be your best bet for a public beach in the immediate vicinity.

At Malacompra, a sign warns of "strong undercurrent. Swim at own risk." As if to reinforce the warning, a line of coastal scrub has been uprooted along the ocean's edge, and placed there, like battle corpses. On one visit we spied a sunbeaten, old salty dog perched atop the handrail of the crossover, smoking a ciggie butt and watching the waves. He's an endangered species in Flagler County, like the sea turtles.

3 Old Salt Road Park

Location: at the end of Old Salt Road in Hammock
Parking/fees: free parking lot
Hours: 8 A.M.–10 P.M.
Facilities: restrooms
Contact: Flagler County Parks and Recreation Department, 904/437-7490

4 Jungle Hut Road Park

Location: at the end of Jungle Hut Road in Hammock
Parking/fees: free parking lot
Hours: 8 A.M.–10 P.M.
Facilities: restrooms
Contact: Flagler County Parks and Recreation Department, 904/437-7490

MAP OF FLORIDA'S EAST COAST—PAGE 5

Bunking Down

It's not on the beach, but if you're coming to Palm Coast for golf, tennis, and/or boating on the Intracoastal—which is why most people come to this area—the **Harborside Inn at Palm Coast** (300 Clubhouse Drive, 386/445-3000, $$$) will fit the bill. We'll fall into line and play the numbers game: they've got an 80-slip marina, 18 tennis courts, four championship golf courses, and access to five miles of beach. And the prices are a lot less in Palm Coast than what you'd pay in Palm Beach and points south.

Contact Information

Flagler County Palm Coast Chamber of Commerce, Star Route Box 18-N, Bunnell, FL 32110; 386/437-0106; website: www.flaglerpcchamber.org

Painters Hill

Painters Hill (pop. 200) serves as a buffer between the upper-crust golf-course communities of Hammock and Palm Coast and the RV and trailer parks of Beverly Beach. Its chief feature, insofar as this book is concerned, is **Varn Beach Park**, a county-run oceanfront park with a free parking lot and dune walkovers that lead across healthy dunes to the orange sand beach. Varn is a little bit bigger than the trio of county beach accesses in neighboring Hammock. There's not much out here, but restrooms and showers are provided, and the relative peace and quiet is a decided bonus.

Contact Information

Flagler County Palm Coast Chamber of Commerce, Star Route Box 18-N, Bunnell, FL 32110; 386/437-0106; website: www.flaglerpcchamber.org

5 Varn Beach Park

Location: in Painters Hill, along Highway A1A

Parking/fees: free parking lot

Hours: 8 A.M.–10 P.M.

Facilities: restrooms and showers

Contact: Flagler County Parks and Recreation Department, 904/437-7490

MAP OF FLAGLER COUNTY—PAGE 62

Beverly Beach

Beverly Beach (pop. 322) is a hanging by its fingertips to Flagler County's coastline. It's an unappealing, rundown place where an RV campground sits directly across the road from a mobile home park—not exactly the most scenic sight you'll see on Highway A1A. But it is bound to be even less scenic when it is, inevitably, bought up and transformed into a millionaire's retreat. For now, the redeeming feature of **Beverly Beach** is a group of concrete picnic tables on the ocean side of the highway toward the south end of town, at which access can be gained to the two-mile strand of Beverly Beach, and the Shark House, Home of Sharky's Lounge, which hovers above the ocean and draws crowds from miles in either direction. But you can do better than that without going much farther by continuing south on Highway A1A to Gamble Rogers Memorial State Park.

6 Beverly Beach

Location: at the south end of Beverly Beach, on Highway A1A
Parking/fees: free parking lot
Hours: 8 A.M.–10 P.M.
Facilities: restrooms and picnic tables
Contact: Beverly Beach Town Hall, 904/439-6888

Contact Information

Flagler County Palm Coast Chamber of Commerce, Star Route Box 18-N, Bunnell, FL 32110; 386/437-0106; website: www.flaglerpcchamber.org

Flagler Beach

Flagler Beach (pop. 4,541) is, in many ways, the land that time forgot. They call it "the Peaceful Beach," but it's a peace engendered not by conscious choice but by a lack of interest or awareness from the outside world.

Flagler's squat cinder-block cottages, modest homes, and low-rent motor courts appear unchanged since the 1950s. Modernity has passed by this little town, which just celebrated its 75th birthday, giving it a kind of off-the-beaten-path charm.

Its beach runs for six miles along Highway A1A. The coast highway hugs the shoreline closely here, its shoulder practically on the edge of the short bluff that drops down to the beach. Numerous private dune crossovers lead to the beach, which is relatively narrow and somewhat steep in profile. The sand is a ruddy orange, colored by an unusual source: coquina, which comes from an offshore formation.

The town of Flagler Beach has been struggling almost from the beginning. Formerly named Ocean City and later renamed for oil, railroad, and tourism magnate Henry Flagler in 1923, the town was the site of the apparently magnificent four-story Flagler Beach Hotel, which thrived during the 1920s and died during the Depression.

If truth be told, Flagler Beach looks like it hasn't made great advances since the Depression. It's still holding on but hasn't exactly elevated its standing or kept pace with the rest of Florida's east coast beach towns. But that is not entirely a bad thing.

In town, there's the 844-foot Flagler Beach Pier ($2.75 to fish, 75 cents to walk out) and a lot of angle-in free parking in its vicinity. Lining the west side of Highway A1A are nondescript motels, restaurants whose specialties tend toward pizza, and a pretty cool-looking surf shop. The town doesn't project much character, but for those families who want nothing more from a vacation than a rented house or motel room with a beach across the road, it's probably fine. Still, we can't shake the feeling that Flagler Beach remains unfinished, a work-in-progress abandoned well shy of completion.

Beaches

Flagler Beach offers nothing more (or less) than a modest good time on an unpretentious Florida beach that has to rank as one of the state's most undiscovered coastal locales.

Free two-hour parking is available along Flagler Beach near the Flagler Beach Pier. A gray wooden boardwalk runs along the beach for a short distance. Families and surfers hoot and holler in the water. The break by the pier makes for the best surfing in the area, especially after a storm.

Interestingly, a public pool in nearby Palm Coast, the **Frieda Zamba Aquatic Complex** (4520 Belle Terre Parkway, 386/446-3453), bears the name of a famous local female surfer who still makes her home in Flagler Beach and can sometimes be seen riding the waves by the pier. Running for several miles along the length of the town are pull-offs for roadside parking and secluded access to the beach (no facilities).

Shore Things

- **Marina:** Flagler Bridge Marina, 131 Lehigh Avenue, 386/439-0081.
- **Pier:** Flagler Beach Pier, 215 South A1A, 386/439-3891.
- **Rainy-day attraction:** Marineland, 9507 Oceanshore Boulevard (Highway A1A), 386/471-1111.
- **Shopping/browsing:** Oceanshore Boulevard (Highway A1A) between Moody Boulevard (State Route 100) and South 7th Street.
- **Surf shop:** Z Wave Surf Shop, 400 South A1A, 386/439-9283.
- **Vacation rentals:** Palm Coast Home Realty, 296 Palm Coast Parkway, Palm Coast, 386/445-0777.

Bunking Down

Highway A1A is lined with small, old motels of late 1950s, early 1960s vintage. They're the kind of places that only a surfer—which is to say, someone oblivious to his or her surroundings or rarely in them—could love. There's one notable exception: **Topaz** (1234 South Oceanshore Boulevard, 386/439-3301, $$), a unique "motel, hotel, cafe, and porch" that's very well maintained. Its antique-filled parlor, including an authentic player piano, is a not-to-be-missed conversation piece. The buildings are white stucco with red doors and pipe roofing.

You can stay in the motel or the more quaintly done-up hotel section. Nightly rates range from an unbelievable $46 (for a motel room) up to $140 (for an antique-filled hotel room with Jacuzzi). You can

7 Flagler Beach

Location: The heart of Flagler Beach's six-mile municipal beach is at Moody Boulevard (State Route 100) and Oceanshore Boulevard (Highway A1A).
Parking/fees: free street parking
Hours: none posted
Facilities: lifeguards (seasonal), restrooms, and showers
Contact: Flagler Beach City Hall, 904/517-2000

MAP OF FLAGLER COUNTY—PAGE 62

even book a room for an entire month for a hard-to-beat $1,300—a bargain at any beach, on any coastline.

Of the less stylish lodgings, the two most appealing are **Whale Watch Motel** (2448 South A1A, 386/439-2545, $) and **Beach Front Motel** (1544 South A1A, 386/439-0089, $). Their names tell their tale.

Coastal Cuisine

The pickings are pretty plain in Flagler Beach. **Kings' Oceanside Restaurant & Patio Cafe** (500 North A1A, 386/439-9696, $$) sits directly across from the pier in a gray-shingled Cape Cod–style building. When we were there, the list of early-bird specials didn't include any seafood entrées (thumbs down), although they were offering a Buffalo-style fish fry on Friday nights (thumbs up).

Two miles south of town lies **High Tides at Snack Jack** (2805 South A1A, 386/439-4344, $$), a modest-looking seafood restaurant perched directly above the ocean. In the small, sandy parking lot is a sign (you've gotta be kidding) that says "Valet Parking."

Night Moves

The most promising place from the vantage point of Highway A1A is **Finnegan's Beachside Pub** (101 North A1A, 386/439-7755). You can't miss it: the mural outside depicts leprechauns on surfboards.

Contact Information

Flagler Beach Palm Coast Chamber of Commerce, P.O. Box 5, Flagler Beach, FL 32136; 386/439-0995; website: www.flaglerpcchamber.org

Gamble Rogers Memorial State Park

Gamble Rogers Memorial State Park is about 2.5 miles south of Highway A1A's junction with State Route 100 in Flagler Beach. Formerly known as first as Flagler Beach State Park, it has been a park since the state purchased it back in 1954. The 145-acre park makes the most of its relatively compact size. On the east side of Highway A1A are 34 oceanfront campsites and beach access. On the west side there are picnic areas, a boat basin on the Intracoastal Waterway, and a nature trail. The beach is markedly different from that of Daytona Beach to the south. Instead of being flat, broad, expansive, and white, it's reddish brown and narrow, with a steeper profile. The fishing is great on both the ocean side (pompano, bluefish, drum) and in the Intracoastal (speckled trout, redfish, flounder).

Contact Information

Gamble Rogers Memorial State Park, 3100 South A1A, Flagler Beach, FL 32136; 386/517-2086; website: www.myflorida.com

8 Gamble Rogers Memorial State Park

(4)

Location: 2.5 miles south of Flagler Beach, along Highway A1A

Parking/fees: $3.25 entrance fee per vehicle (main entrance, inland side), $2 entrance fee per vehicle (parking lots, beach side). Camping fees are $20.67 (with hookups) and $18.53 (without hookups).

Hours: 8 A.M. to sundown

Facilities: restrooms, picnic tables, and showers

Contact: Gamble Rogers Memorial State Park, 904/517-2086

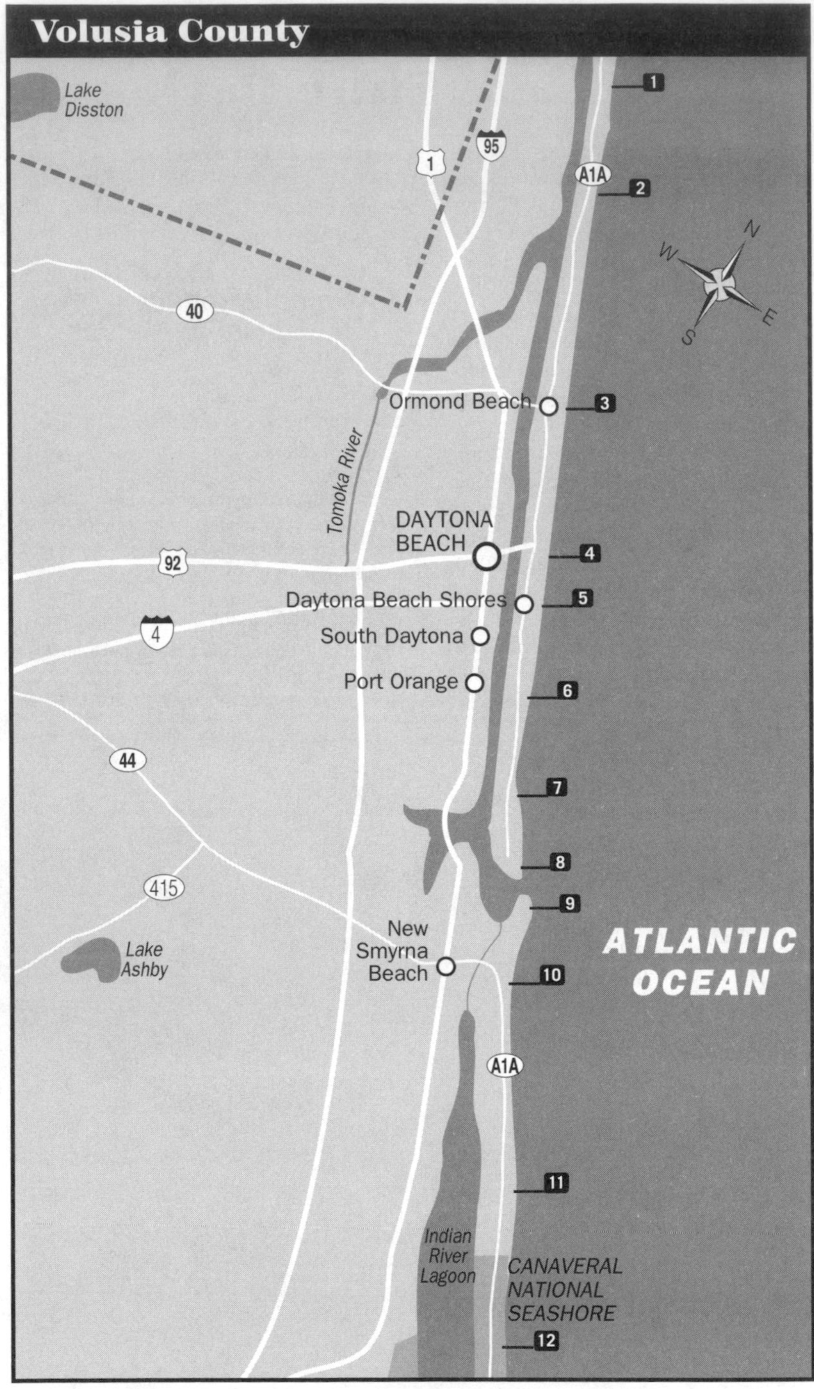
Volusia County
Lake Disston
1
95
1
A1A
2
N
W
E
S
40
Ormond Beach
3
Tomoka River
DAYTONA BEACH
4
92
Daytona Beach Shores
5
4
South Daytona
Port Orange
6
44
7
8
415
9
New Smyrna Beach
Lake Ashby
ATLANTIC OCEAN
10
A1A
11
Indian River Lagoon
CANAVERAL NATIONAL SEASHORE
12

VOLUSIA COUNTY

Volusia County is happily married to its beach, a 43-mile stretch of wide, hard-packed sand that fronts Ormond-by-the-Sea, Ormond Beach, Daytona Beach, Daytona Beach Shores, Ponce Inlet, New Smyrna Beach, and Bethune Beach. What makes the county unique is that 18 miles of beach from Ormond Beach to Ponce Inlet, plus another seven miles in New Smyrna Beach, are open to vehicular traffic (speed limit: 10 mph). Driving is a tradition here. Daytona and Ormond Beaches are the "Birthplace of Speed," referring to car races that once took place on the beach and now are held at the Daytona International Speedway. There's one more thing, besides cars and beachgoers, that moves across the sand: sea turtles. In their slow-going way, they're helping modify the character of Volusia County's beaches. The establishment of "natural conservation zones" has provided sea turtles with stretches of sand where they can nest in peace. As a consequence, life in Volusia County, while still motoring at a pleasurable velocity, has slowed to a more relaxed pace.

Ormond Beach and Ormond-by-the-Sea

Some folks tout New Smyrna Beach as the preferred alternative to the commercial crush of Daytona Beach, but that distinction might more reasonably go to these two affluent and pleasant neighboring communities to Daytona's immediate north. Ormond Beach (pop. 34,038) shares the title "Birthplace of Speed" with Daytona Beach because their adjoining beaches were the first in the country to allow automobile racing. Indeed, Daytona Beach picks up where Ormond leaves off: more of the same beach, more hotels and motels lining Highway A1A (and more of them). And yet Ormond Beach is a sizable and unique town in its own right, stretching west onto the mainland via State Route 40 (Granada Boulevard) and U.S. 1 (Dixie Highway).

Ormond Beach wears its size well, investing its considerable wealth in home improvements and public services that are the envy of other Volusia County towns. Ormond-by-the-Sea (pop. 14,328), on the other hand, is quieter and smaller, "an unincorporated residential community" that exists only on the barrier island east of the Halifax River. This sense of isolation is accentuated by its seemingly precarious location. The barrier island narrows to a thin point at the north end, which is the site of another crown jewel of Florida's state parks system, the North Peninsula State Park.

Ormond Beach acquired its legacy of wealth from John D. Rockefeller, whose former winter home, the **Casements** (25 Riverside Drive, 386/676-3216), has been beautifully restored. It is maintained as a free museum and cultural center noted for its Hungarian folk art and Boy Scout memorabilia. Other local residents have carried forward Rockefeller's moneyed legacy, most notably Ron Rice, president of Hawaiian Tropic tanning products, whose corporate headquarters and palatial home are found in Ormond Beach. You can't miss the latter, with its "RR" monogram on the iron fence along Oceanshore Boulevard. Rice has been a generous citizen, too, underwriting a lot of the cost to equip Volusia County's award-winning beach patrol.

One of the legends of the surfing world, Lisa Andersen, makes her home here, too. Winner of three consecutive world titles, Andersen has been described by *Surfing* magazine as "the mother of all champions . . . perhaps the most radical woman surfer of all time."

Ormond Beach is naturally blessed in other ways besides beaches. It's home to two interesting state parks, and while neither is located on the ocean, both offer unique natural settings. **Bulow Creek State Park** (3351 Old Dixie Highway, 386/677-4645) is centered around the 800-year-old Fairchild live oak tree, which serves as a monument to local preservationists. It has, according to the park brochure, "withstood Seminole Indian wars, developers, fires, and countless owners, each with his own vision of the land's purpose." A short hiking trail leads through a hammock of trees. Not far away are the ruins of the old Bulow Plantation,

1 North Peninsula State Park

Location: 10 miles north of Ormond Beach
Parking/fees: free parking lot
Hours: none posted
Facilities: none
Contact: Gamble Rogers Memorial State Park, 386/517-2086

MAP OF FLORIDA'S EAST COAST—PAGE 5

a former cotton, rice, sugar, and indigo plantation that is now a state historic site.

The other notable parkland is **Tomoka State Park** (2099 North Beach Street, 386/676-4050), located near the confluence of the Tomoka and Halifax Rivers. It is situated in an unusual live oak-filled hammock, once the site of a Timucuan Indian village called Nocoroco, which was cleared away, along with much of the forest, to make way for a plantation in the 1770s. Tomoka is now returning to its natural state. A tents-only campground on the river ($8 per night June 1 to January 31, $11 per night February 1 to May 31) affords access to the inland tidal waterways. Canoes are rented, and a guided canoe tour explores the old plantation ruins. There's also a short nature trail and even a sandy riverside beach at the north picnic area.

Beaches

The relative lack of development in Ormond-by-the-Sea has had positive consequences on its beachfront. With the possible exception of Lighthouse Point (down by Ponce Inlet), **Ormond-by-the-Sea** and neighboring **North Peninsula State Park** are home to the healthiest dune fields in all of Volusia County's 43 miles of beaches. North Peninsula is a 900-acre park created as part of a massive, multistate effort to save the endangered loggerhead sea turtle. It is primarily a nature preserve and refuge, which is to say that no parking is allowed along the road (there is a free lot along Highway A1A) and no dune crossovers are provided. However, you can hike north from Ormond-by-the-Sea (no vehicles allowed!) and have one of the most beautiful and secluded beaches—two miles in length—in central Florida all to yourself. An avuncular park ranger reported that couples stroll up and, under cover of dark, "do what young couples will do." For the less prurient-minded, the surf casting along this stretch of coast—for redfish, whitefish, and bluefish—is enough to make an angler's eyes well up with salt water. Fish get trapped inside the offshore bars, and fishers have a field day casting for them.

Ormond-by-the-Sea has 2.5 miles of beachfront, stretching from Essex Street (at the north) to Ocean Breeze Court (at the south), with 16 separate public beach accesses provided between these markers. **Ormond Beach** has a three-mile beach, running from Bosarvy Drive to Harvard Drive, with county-provided dune crossovers at 14 public beach accesses. Other dune crossovers are private, which explains their gates, locks, and makeshift

❷ Ormond-by-the-Sea

Location: The community's 2.5 miles of beach are located five miles north of Daytona Beach.
Parking/fees: free parking lot (Bicentennial) and numerous dune walkovers along Highway A1A
Hours: none posted
Facilities: lifeguards (seasonal), restrooms, picnic tables, and showers
Contact: Volusia County Beach Services, 386/239-7873

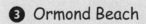

❸ Ormond Beach

Location: The community's three miles of beach adjoin the north end of Daytona Beach.
Parking/fees: $5 per day to park on the beach (free in December and January)
Hours: sunrise to sunset (autos only), 24 hours (pedestrians)
Facilities: concessions, lifeguards (seasonal), restrooms, picnic tables, and showers
Contact: Volusia County Beach Services, 386/239-7873

MAP OF VOLUSIA COUNTY—PAGE 72

Don't Get Ripped: The Lowdown on Rip Currents

Florida's beaches are a great place to be—there are none better, in our estimation—but a day at the beach is not entirely without hazards. Along Florida's east coast in general, and Volusia County in particular, you risk sunburn, jellyfish stings, and rip currents. While the sun's rays and jellyfish tentacles can hurt you, rip currents—also known as "riptides" and "runouts"—can kill. What's more, they are not freak occurrences, like hurricanes, but occur all too commonly. One Saturday in September 1997, for instance, "the runouts just erupted in the Core Area [of Daytona Beach]," according to Joe Wooden, deputy chief of the beach patrol. That day, Volusia County lifeguards made seven rescues. Three survivors required hospitalization, two of them were in critical condition, and one died the next day. That same afternoon, a surfer got bit by a shark down in New Smyrna Beach. Talk about a turndown day!

Statewide statistics bear this out. Between 1989 and 1999, Volusia County had 29 rip current deaths. Dade County, another popular east coast destination, led the state with 30. Rip currents do occur on the Gulf of Mexico, as evidenced by Bay County's (Panama City Beach) third place on the list, with 24 deaths.

appearances. There's even a roadside curiosity up here. Just inside the limits of Ormond-by-the-Sea is a battered old observation tower left over from World War II. It's the sole survivor of a series of towers that rimmed the coast from Florida to North Carolina. They were used to spot German U-boats in anticipation of a Nazi invasion of the U.S. mainland. This wasn't just paranoia. Artifacts of shipwrecked German subs have been found off the Outer Banks of North Carolina. While doing research for an earlier book, we met a lifelong resident of Ocracoke Island whose most vivid boyhood memory was of drowned Germans washing ashore.

The sand has a different texture and color up this way than it does in Daytona Beach. Its reddish brown hue comes from the wearing down of an offshore coquina reef and is most pronounced in the spring and summer. The particles are larger and therefore less easily packed. Occasionally, the beach requires renourishment after hard winter storms. It's a blessing in disguise, because the softer sand makes for more difficult beach driving. Even under the best conditions, only a small portion of Ormond Beach—near the intersection of Oceanshore Boulevard and State Route 40—can be driven, and all of Ormond-by-the-Sea's beach is off limits.

Shore Things

- **Bike/skate rentals:** The Bicycle Company, 201 East Granada Boulevard, 386/676-2453.
- **Ecotourism:** Tomoka State Park, 2099 North Beach Street, 386/676-4050.
- **Marina:** Aloha Marina, 231 Riverside Drive, Holly Hill, 386/255-2345.
- **Rainy-day attraction:** The Casements Cultural Center and Museum, 25 Riverside Drive, 386/676-3216.
- **Shopping/browsing:** Granada Cross-

Rip currents form as part of a cell-like circulation created when longshore currents moving in different directions converge in the surf zone and then turn seaward. Unevenness in wave height along a stretch of beach has been postulated as one reason such longshore currents form. Both sand and sediment are moved seaward by rip currents, and their deposition results in the formation of offshore bars. These currents can be 100 feet wide and stretch 1,000 feet into the water.

The strong pull of a rip current and the reflexive reaction of panicky swimmers who attempt to paddle against it create a recipe for disaster. The current's narrowness works to a cool-headed swimmer's advantage. If you swim parallel to shore instead of toward it, you should soon exit the pull of the rip current and can then return safely back to the beach. If you are caught in a rip current, don't panic. (Admittedly, this is easier said than done.) Call for help by waving your arms in the air, and then swim parallel to shore to extract yourself from the current. If you are within sight of a lifeguard tower on Volusia County's well-patrolled beaches, your chances of being rescued are excellent. In 1996, the beach patrol came to the assistance of more than 1,000 swimmers in distress.

As with sunburn, the danger posed by rip currents can be significantly reduced by taking a few precautions. As a general rule, it is safest to swim where the high-water mark is fairly even over a long stretch of sand. But your best advice is to swim with a friend and near a lifeguard tower and pay heed to warnings posted on it.

ings, Granada Boulevard, 386/677-0525.

- **Surf shop:** Sunrise Surf, 197 East Granada Boulevard, 386/677-6364.
- **Vacation rentals:** Ocean View Condominium Rental Group, 1350 Oceanshore Boulevard, 800/356-3409.

Bunking Down

Ormond Beach has a loyal following, in addition to inheriting the spillover from Daytona Beach during special events like Bike Week, Spring Break, and Race Weekends. Ormond has plenty of beachfront motels in which to house its guests. The huge flagship hotels are located at its southern end, near Daytona Beach, where Highway A1A is still referred to as Atlantic Avenue. The top choice, by general consensus, is the **Casa Del Mar Beach Resort** (621 South Atlantic Avenue, 386/672-4550, $$$), a three-star lodge run by the Staed family, the area's oldest hoteliers. A huge beachside pool deck and kitchen facilities in every room are pluses. Another beachside tower with similar amenities is the **Granada Inn** (51 South Atlantic Avenue, 386/672-7550, $$$). With these two fortresses booked solid—we foolishly arrived without reservations over a peak summer weekend—we got a perfectly fine oceanfront room at the **Quality Inn Oceanside** (251 South Atlantic Avenue, 386/672-8510, $$). All three hotels are located in a "transition zone," meaning that beach driving is allowed. So while the beach is plenty wide for everybody, watch out for vehicles on your way down to the water.

At the north end of Ormond Beach, the **Coral Sands Inn** (1009 Oceanshore Boulevard, 386/441-1831, $$$) offers a quieter alternative. There are 86 rooms in the main building and several seaside cottages on the spacious property, which also includes a pool and volleyball and badminton courts. All rooms have refrigerators, many have fully equipped kitchens. No cars are allowed on the beach here. Hallelujah.

MAP OF VOLUSIA COUNTY—PAGE 72

Coastal Cuisine

Though the community of Ormond Beach is more upscale than Daytona Beach, the cuisine is the same depressingly ordinary mix of franchises and unexceptional non-franchised restaurants. Up in Ormond-by-the-Sea, **Alfie's Restaurant** (1666 Oceanshore Boulevard, 386/441-7024, $) has won several "best breakfast in Volusia County" awards. You can eat your omelette while staring out to sea. They also serve lunch and dinner, including cheap early-bird specials from noon till six, with emphases on seafood, steak, and Italian dishes. If you want a really good dinner, however, head south to Ponce Inlet.

Night Moves

The "World Famous" **Iron Horse Saloon** (1068 North U.S. 1, 386/677-1550) is a biker bar whose main attraction is the Wall of Death, upon whose banked track revving Harley riders strut their stuff. This biker palace is located a good five miles from the beach, way out on Dixie Highway. You can call us a couple of Dixie Chickens, but we steered clear of the Iron Horse, pointing our wheels instead to **Billy's Tap Room** (58 East Granada Boulevard, 386/672-1910), which has the advantage of beach proximity. Plenty of folks head to **Rockin Ranch** (801 South Nova Road, 386/673-0386) for country line dancing 'til 2 A.M. nightly. The place won Best Nightclub in Daytona's *News-Journal*.

Contact Information

Ormond Beach Chamber of Commerce, 165 West Granada Boulevard, Ormond Beach, FL 32174; 386/677-3454; website: www.ormondchamber.com

Daytona Beach and Daytona Beach Shores

While it may seem strange that a city whose name is synonymous with sun, sand, surf, and speed is suffering from an identity crisis, this happens to be the case with Daytona Beach (pop. 64,138). However, unlike most beach communities that have been simultaneously blessed and cursed with international celebrity, Daytona is weathering a period of transition, in which it's trying to upgrade its image without driving away its steadiest customers, and doing it with foresight and common sense.

It helps to have something enviable to work with, and the Daytona Beach area has sandy assets in abundance: 23 miles of wide, hard-packed beaches, 18 miles of which are open to vehicular traffic. Beach driving is what originally gave the town its unique identity. It was a direct outgrowth of a legacy of car racing that took place on the sands of Volusia County—Ormond, Daytona, and New Smyrna Beaches—between 1903 and 1935. These days, the town's racing rituals are conducted and worshiped at the days-of-thunder cathedral known as the Daytona International Speedway, five miles inland.

Much talk has been made about reshaping Daytona as an ecotourist destination, a family destination, a historic stomping ground, and a place where the arts can flourish. Traces of all those things are already in place. Still, Daytona has a somewhat oversimplified worldwide reputation as a no-holds-barred party town to live down, and that seems to fly in the face of its newer, more rarefied self-image. In addition, any makeover it undertakes can only be so radical, since auto racing and beach driving, and the periodic influx of bikers (no matter how well-oiled with

MAP OF FLORIDA'S EAST COAST—PAGE 5

money) will necessarily have to remain a viable part of whatever new identity the community hopes to assume. It's the economy, stupid. But it's also a matter of striking the proper balance.

Among the oldest of Daytona's party-hearty traditions is Spring Break. A concerted effort has been made to "take the edge off Spring Break," in the euphemistic words of one town official. Almost to its detriment, Daytona Beach had become "sin"-onymous with this celebrated springtime college bacchanal, a sort of irreligious pilgrimage. So renowned is Daytona Beach as a mecca for misbehavior that for decades multiple layers of Spring Breakers have faithfully trekked here on various colleges' staggered mid-semester breaks. As the site of Black Spring Break, which coincides with the annual alumni reunion of Daytona's Bethune-Cookman College, Daytona has been an equal-opportunity playpen, too.

The sacraments of Spring Break include beer, sex, cars on the beach, rock and rap, more beer, gridlock, intense partying, even more beer, and possibly incarceration. The whole scene reached a crescendo of Caligula-like proportions when MTV got into the act in the mid-1980s. Broadcasting live from the sands of Daytona Beach each spring and then running the footage year-round, MTV gave the impression that the city was one gigantic Animal House by the sea. The collegiate crush peaked in 1989, when 400,000 kids showed up. There are about 20,000 hotel and motel rooms in and around Daytona Beach. Our pocket calculator tells us that works out to about, oh, 20 kids a room. The end result was chaotic gridlock and a worsening reputation as a tourist destination. In the words of one lifelong resident, "People thought we were a run-down party town."

Efforts to curb its lingering image as Spring Break central have met with mixed success, mainly because Daytona Beach approached this Herculean task with something less than autocratic zeal. Unlike Fort Lauderdale, which all but outlawed Spring Break—ran it out of town, in fact—Daytona Beach toned theirs down by emphasizing other aspects of the area, such as major-league baseball's spring training and NASCAR racing events. They even staged job fairs on the beach (presumably attracting those few collegians who could walk a straight line). While Spring Break remains a fact of life in Daytona Beach, it now draws about 200,000—about half the former inundation—and those are spaced out over a four- to six-week period (early March to Easter). Also, it no longer attracts the rowdiest core element. The wildest party animals now make their way to Panama City Beach, on Florida's Panhandle, which welcomes them with open cash registers.

In their place, Daytona Beach now courts bikers, er, "motorcycle enthusiasts." If this seems like an unlikely source of salvation for ailing city businesses, ponder that the biggest week on Daytona's calendar year now is Bike Week, held the first of March, when as many as 400,000 bikers arrive. Equally popular is Biketoberfest, a Halloween brewfest that caters to the Harley crowd and is more civilized than you might imagine. Who'd have thunk it? The image painted by local businesspeople is a far cry from the bikers depicted in Roger Corman flicks, where the town fathers had to hide their mothers and daughters, board up the windows, and oil the shotgun as leather-jacketed heathens roared down Main Street. As one motel owner put it, "I wish all our guests were as courteous and generous as the bikers. They're the biggest spenders and the best tippers. And the nicest people you'll ever want to deal with."

As if to reinforce this new image of motorcycling, the world's largest, sleekest, and most successful Harley-Davidson

MAP OF VOLUSIA COUNTY—PAGE 72

dealership is located in downtown Daytona. It's as stylish and neon laden as any Mercedes-Benz dealership in Bremen, Frankfurt, or Palm Beach. Think about it: anyone who can afford to drop 30 thou on a Harley isn't exactly an indigent outlaw. It may seem ironic, but room rates get jacked up for Bike Week and then fall again for Spring Break. "The hotels charge what the market will bear, and the kids don't have that kind of money," explained a Chamber of Commerce spokesman. All this biker boosterism notwithstanding, half a million bikers is half a million bikers, and every bar on Main Street caters to at least the affectations of that lifestyle. Rebel flags are much in demand and on display. There is little about this that suggests the "family vacationer" the city wants to court; nor can such an animal be found in the many adult video shops, titty bars, and tattoo parlors. And during Bike Week 2000, 16 people were killed in Daytona Beach.

Daytona Beach is filled with such paradoxes. Here are a few others:

- While tackiness abounds with attractions such as the World's Biggest Flea Market and Night of Wonder ("spectacular magic show!"), Daytona is also home to the **Southeast Museum of Photography** (Daytona Beach Community College, 1200 International Speedway Boulevard, 386/254-4475), **Bethune-Cookman College** (which has one of the world's richest collections related to African-American culture and history), and the **Museum of Arts and Sciences** (1040 Museum Boulevard, 386/255-0285). During one of our recent visits, the Museum of Arts and Sciences had on display both a room full of Picasso's handmade pottery and a remarkable exhibit on Florida's cracker culture.
- While some of the beachfront properties in the Core Area (the heart of Daytona Beach, between Seabreeze Boulevard and Silver Beach Avenue) are in need of repair or demolition, the historic "Old Daytona" district and the surrounding downtown have lately undergone a wholesale restoration.
- While towering new hotels and condos make their inevitable appearance along the shoreline, the overwhelming majority of accommodations in Daytona are modest, affordable, and family owned and operated.
- While too much mainland asphalt is devoted to cars, racing, and malls, the southern end of the barrier island, around Daytona Beach Shores (pop. 2,901) and Ponce Inlet, is thick with greenery, conservation land, and quiet residential areas. There's even a historic and beautifully preserved lighthouse. In 1997, Daytona Beach Shores received a $1.2 million state grant to purchase and develop an eco-park on beachfront property as a counterpoint to the encroachment of high-rises.

Make no mistake about it, though. Daytona Beach will always have a lived-in look, sound, and smell. Try as they might, the place also has pockets of genuine seediness and blight. Those are the occupational hazards of being a world-famous beach destination. It is a completely egalitarian town, attracting a mixed bag of people: Canadians and Cajuns, car nuts and tree huggers, hard-bodies and lard-asses, beehive hairdos and body piercers. Daytona is a funhouse mirror of society. As such, you can peer into it and find elements of stunning beauty as well as things of stultifying ugliness. Nothing will change or hide that fact. After all, you can't make a silk purse out of a sea cow's ear. But we love sea cows, and we like Daytona Beach just fine.

Beaches

From Ormond Beach to Ponce Inlet, the

unbroken stretch of ocean sands with **Daytona Beach** at the center runs for a kingly 23 miles. At low tide, the beach can be 500 feet wide (almost two football fields!). Such a sandy land grant can only accentuate the positive mood of all visitors. The most noticeable thing about the beach, besides its sheer size, is that vehicles, including RVs and trucks under 33 feet in length, are allowed on 18 of those 23 miles. The sand is comprised of ultrafine granules of quartz, with few rock or shell fragments, which results in a smooth, hard-packed surface.

So driveable are the sands of Daytona Beach that car races were first held on the beach in the early decades of the last century. The surviving legacy of that activity is that tourists and locals have been allowed to drive their cars on the sand, albeit at considerably reduced rates of speed (no faster than 10 mph), ever since. On sunny days over busy weekends, as many as 10,000 vehicles roam Daytona's beach at one time. The lowest tides occur during new moon phases, and the highest tides during full moons. During the latter "spring tides," the beach is sometimes shut down to wheeled traffic, especially when the full moon is accompanied by a rough winter storm. (For other rules and info regarding beach driving, see "Wheels on the Beach" sidebar, pages 90–91)

Besides driving, the beach here is great for walking, jogging, volleyball, surfing, and bicycling. (Bikes are not required to observe the rules that apply to cars.) Moreover, the swimming and bodysurfing at Daytona Beach are as good as it gets anywhere in Florida. Water temperatures climb as high as 84°F in the summer months, making for easy immersion and toasty wading and splashing. During outgoing tides, there are occasional problems with rip currents. We mention this only as a precaution and will quickly console you with the fact that the Volusia County Beach Patrol maintains a staff of 65 full-time and 180 part-time lifeguards in its towers. (For more on rip currents, see "Don't Get Ripped" sidebar, pages 76–77)

This eagle-eyed, cross-trained, and award-winning crew surveys 43 miles of shoreline in Volusia County, including Ormond Beach and New Smyrna Beach. In addition to the beach towers, they maintain five large substations, each equipped with an observation tower that allows for a long view of the beaches. Annually, they save thousands of swimmers. Given that as many as 200,000 people may be on the

4 Daytona Beach

Location: Five miles of beach, the heart of which is the Core Area, between Seabreeze Boulevard and Main Street
Parking/fees: $5 per day to park on the beach (free in December and January); free off-beach parking lots
Hours: sunrise to sunset (autos only), 24 hours (pedestrians)
Facilities: boardwalk, concessions, lifeguards, restrooms, picnic tables, and showers
Contact: Volusia County Beach Services, 386/239-7873

5 Daytona Beach Shores

Location: The 5.5 miles of beach are adjacent to the south end of Daytona Beach.
Parking/fees: $5 per day to park on the beach (free in December and January); free off-beach parking lots
Hours: sunrise to sunset (autos only), 24 hours (pedestrians)
Facilities: concessions, lifeguards, restrooms, picnic tables, and showers
Contact: Volusia County Beach Services, 386/239-7873

Map of Volusia County—Page 72

Daytona USA: A 250 MPH Tourist Trap

This sidebar is brought to you by Plax, Crest, Johnson & Johnson Mint Waxed Dental Floss, Listerine, Extra Strength Tylenol, Minute Maid Orange Juice, Folgers Instant Coffee, Dixie Crystals Sugar, Carnation Non-Dairy Creamer, and Bic Pens. We mention these products, which we used in that order one summer morning in Daytona, to place you in the proper mood for the ultra-commercialized Daytona USA. It is part museum, part shopping mall, and as complete a tourist trap as has ever been devised. It is, alas, "the Ultimate Motorsports Attraction."

It's a given that visitors to Daytona Beach will be driven by a need to immerse themselves in the lore of the sport. Almost as legendary as Daytona's wide, hard-packed beaches is its automotive subculture. If car racing can be said to be a religion, Daytona USA is its Chartres cathedral. The attraction is located in the shadows of Daytona International Speedway, which is racing's Elysian Fields. To further flog this metaphor, we proudly declare ourselves blasphemers and infidels.

Daytona USA is as rife with product placement as Washington, D.C., is with special interests. Let's not beat around the Busch. Daytona USA is a racing junkie's Lollapalooza—or, we should say, Logopalooza. Everywhere you look, there's a corporate logo. They're affixed to every square foot of every race car on display, stitched onto every square inch of clothing worn by every race car driver, and—most pertinent, from a tourist's perspective—plastered onto every conceivable surface upon which your eyes might fall, your feet might tread, or your butt might sit. They are draped from the rafters. They cling like mildew to the walls. They are attached to every TV monitor, loudspeaker, banner, stanchion, pole, beam, pipe, window, curtain, writing implement, brochure, turnstile, slot, door, handle, button, and knob. They are even emblazoned on your admission ticket.

Oh yes, despite massive corporate underwriting, you must pay to enter Daytona USA. And in the grand tradition of American tourist traps, you pay through the nose. It costs $12 per person to get in ($6 for children 6–12, free for kids five and under). This fee gains visitors admittance to the main building, half of whose space is devoted to a gift shop and video-game arcade where nothing is free and little is reasonably priced. Needless to add, the shop and arcade are packed, compared to the relatively humble exhibit area, which is what tourists ostensibly pay to see. A tram tour of the Speedway—the Advance Auto Parts Speedway Tour, to be precise—costs an additional $6. Already, we're up to $18.

Here's what you get for your money. In the main building, you learn about the early days of competitive motoring. It originated in 1902 atop the sandy beaches of Daytona and Ormond, earning them the moniker the "Birthplace of Speed." You also see, through vintage artifacts and display copy, how the sport developed into the big-time enterprise it is today.

You also have access to "interactive programs," on which you can pretend to be on a pit crew, interview a driver via computer, etc. These hands-on items are far and away the most popular part of the exhibit space. Thus, they're 10-deep with kids waiting their turn to twirl the bolts, so you can forget about taking your whack at the tire jack. Another factoid: A good pit crew can change all four tires, fill two tanks of gas, and tend to the biological needs of the driver in 20 seconds.

On the Speedway tram tour, you are driven slowly around one lap of the 2.5-mile track and given a viewing of the banked curves (their 31-degree incline requires a speed of at least 95 miles per hour to maintain control), the grandstands (seating capacity 100,000), and the infield (which can accommodate another 40,000). On this very track, the Daytona 500 is run every February, and seven other big races are staged here from October to March.

Our tram tour guide was given to well-practiced witticisms, as well as histrionic patter ("Forty-two gallons of 110-octane fuel would barely supply these voracious beasts for the first 100 miles!"). Were we to recommend anything at Daytona USA, it would be the tram tour. It's half as expensive and twice as entertaining as the museum. But please don't misinterpret that as an endorsement of Daytona USA.

Sorry to backfire on the sacred subject of racing, but we hate to see people pay through the nose to view such waste. By comparison, we spent a full day at the Kennedy Space Center, down by Cocoa Beach, which is a worthier attraction all the way around and blissfully logo free. It celebrates the most noble dreams and capabilities of humankind without the crassness of aggressive marketing. It also proves that an enlightened, democratic government is capable of mobilizing its populace for the common good of the entire planet.

By comparison, Daytona USA isn't much more than a reckless pastime. Collisions are common and fatal ones becoming more so. Two of NASCAR's stars, Kenny Irwin and Adam Petty, were killed in crashes in 2000. On February 18, 2001, the Daytona 500 was forever marred by the death of Dale Earnhardt, Sr. An aggressive driver who wore a black uniform and drove a black car (#3), Earnhardt was known as "the Intimidator." Hailed as "NASCAR's greatest driver," Earnhardt bumped or got bumped and slammed into the wall only a half mile from the finish line. He was cut from the wreckage and rushed to the hospital but never regained consciousness. According to NASCAR (though there is some dispute), his seatbelt failed during the crash, and he was not wearing a specially designed helmet that might have saved his neck from snapping. Death instantly conferred upon Earnhardt the status of a hero-martyr (candlelight vigils, comparisons to the day JFK died, etc.) that was completely at odds with his rough-and-tumble, win-at-all-costs image. And that was not the day's only collision. An earlier accident took out 21 cars—nearly half the field.

For those who relish this sort of thing, annual events include the Rolex 24 at Daytona, the Budweiser Shootout at Daytona, the Gatorade 125 Mile Qualifying Races, the Daytona 200 by Arai, the Florida Dodge Dealers 250, the Napa Auto Parts 300, the Pepsi 400, the AC Delco 200 Presented by Discount Auto Parts and the Discount Auto Parts 200 Presented by AC Delco. Then, of course, there's racing's premier event, the Daytona 500, which is free of corporate attachment. At least for now.

For race information, contact **Daytona International Speedway**, 1801 West International Speedway Boulevard, Daytona Beach, FL 32114; 386/254-2700 (general information) or 386/253-7223 (ticket office); website: www.daytonaintlspeedway.com. For attraction information, contact Daytona USA, 1801 West International Speedway Boulevard, Daytona Beach, FL 32114; 386/947-6800; website: www.daytonausa.com. Daytona USA is open daily except Christmas 9 A.M.–7 P.M.

beach at one time, more than a few of them having imbibed their share of "liquid courage" (booze), this is indeed an impressive and heroic feat.

Daytona Beach is popular with surfers, who ply their skills on either side of the Main Street Pier (but especially the north side). Surfers are mandated by ordinance to stay a minimum of 100 yards away from the pier's pilings. It ain't Waikiki, but when the surf's right, a steady diet of two-foot waves provides decent rides. The ramshackle 1,000-foot-long pier is a center of beach activity and a great place to cast a fishing line. The pier is open from 6 A.M. to 10 P.M. ($3.50 to fish, $1 to stroll). A sky tram offers a seagull's view of the entire scene from above, and a boardwalk runs along Daytona's Core Area (or "urban zone," as it has been designated).

An open-air band shell near the pier offers free weekly concerts during the summer, and is worth checking out for its architectural history, too. Built entirely of coquina rock in 1937, it's a stellar example of the good works done by the Civilian Conservation Corps. It won't be long before the neighborhood surrounding the band shell will be given a face-lift—in the form of the Ocean Walk Complex—and the beach around the pier will become off limits to cars. Also in the works are some massive off-site public parking projects, with shuttle bus service provided to the beaches. For day-trippers, this will mean a beach-access bonanza. For anyone staying at a motel along the beach, access is never a problem. Just roll out of bed or the chaise lounge and keep on rolling.

Between them, Daytona Beach and its southerly appendage, **Daytona Beach Shores**, account for nearly 11 miles of shoreline (claiming five and 5.5 miles, respectively). Daytona Beach is the wild and crazy beach town, dense with people, cars, and bars, while Daytona Beach Shores is, as they like to put it, "the quiet end of the world's most famous beach." That says pretty much all you need to know about the difference between the two adjacent communities and their beaches, and you can aim your car and beach blanket accordingly.

Finally, we must mention Beachwheels, a great innovation for beach patrons with disabilities. Invented by a member of the Volusia County Beach Patrol, they are wheelchairs with big, inflatable wheels designed for safe and comfortable travel in soft sand and shallow surf alike. They even have a fishing pole holder! Best of all, they can be used free of charge. Beachwheels are available at any of the Volusia County Beach Patrol's six lifeguard substations, from Ormond Beach to New Smyrna Beach. Call 386/253-0986 for more information.

Shore Things

- **Bike/skate rentals:** Bikesmith, 298 10th Street, 386/258-6550.
- **Dive shop:** Discover Diving Dive Center, 92 Dunlawton Avenue, 386/760-3483.
- **Ecotourism:** SHE Tours, 2652 Flowing Well Road, Deland, 386/734-7962.
- **Marina:** Halifax Harbor Marina and Park, 450 Basin Street, Daytona Beach, 386/253-0575.
- **Pier:** Main Street Pier, Main Street at Ocean Avenue, Daytona Beach, 386/253-1212. Sunglow Pier, 3701 South Atlantic Avenue, Daytona Beach Shores, 756-4219.
- **Rainy-day attraction:** Museum of Arts and Sciences, 1040 Museum Boulevard, Daytona Beach, 386/255-0285.
- **Shopping/browsing:** Seabreeze Boulevard, between Atlantic Avenue and the Intracoastal Waterway, Daytona Beach.
- **Surf shop:** Big Kahuna, 2739 North Atlantic Avenue, 386/677-6388 and 2540 South Atlantic Avenue, 386/322-1143.

MAP OF FLORIDA'S EAST COAST—PAGE 5

- **Vacation rentals:** Atlantic Properties, 3280 South Atlantic Avenue, Daytona Beach Shores, 386/756-6900.

Bunking Down

Because there are upward of 20,000 rooms in the area to be filled, Daytona Beach is a buyer's market much of the year. The exceptions to the rule—when rooms and campsites are scarce—are special-events weeks like the eight Race Weekends, Spring Break, Bike Week, and Biketoberfest. During the steamy peaks of summer, rooms along ocean-fronting Atlantic Avenue (Highway A1A) are advertised for as low as $25 and vacancy signs are abundant. (Of course, some of the more low-rent dives could offend the sensibilities of a corpse.)

Given a 20-mile stretch of motels from which to choose, it's nearly impossible to pick favorites. However, if you and your family want to be far from the madding crowds, you should stay somewhere other than the Core Area—the five-mile "urban zone" from Seabreeze Boulevard south to Silver Beach Avenue. This area is frequented by a younger crowd and is bisected by Main Street's corridor of bars and clubs. The revelry continues clear to the end of the street and right out over the ocean via the Main Street Pier, a great vantage point from which to survey beach partying in one of its definitive habitats. In short, it's a fun spot to visit, but not conducive to restful sleep.

South of the Core Area is the slightly more well-behaved Daytona Beach Shores, where a number of clean, well-lighted places can be found. Many of them are "Superior Small Lodgings," a designation created, rated, and overseen by the visitors bureau. These are "guaranteed high-quality places with no more than 50 rooms or units." (To receive a brochure describing the full roster of 53 Superior Small Lodgings in the Daytona area, call 800/854-1234.) Among all these worthy mom-and-pops, we were especially partial to the **Anchorage Beach Motel** (1901 South Atlantic Avenue, Daytona Beach Shores, 386/255-5394, $$), which has 22 oceanside rooms placed around a courtyard with a tropical garden and pool, and the **Ocean Court Motel** (2315 South Atlantic Avenue, Daytona Beach Shores, 386/253-8185, $$), a quiet, family-run and family-frequented place with a pool and a cookout area on the beach side. Most rooms have kitchens.

For those who don't want to be in such close quarters with other families, there are towering hotels in Daytona Beach Shores, the most reliable of which are the **Holiday Inn** (3209 South Atlantic Avenue, Daytona Beach Shores, 386/761-2050, $$) and the **Ramada Inn Surfside** (3125 South Atlantic Avenue, Daytona Beach Shores, 386/788-1000, $$). The **HoJo Inn** (2015 South Atlantic Avenue, Daytona Beach Shores, 386/255-2446, $) is a nicely downscaled oceanfront lodge with ocean-view rooms, kitchenettes and efficiencies, a pool, and steps down to the beach. The 10-story **Treasure Island Inn** (2025 South Atlantic Avenue, Daytona Beach Shores, 386/257-1950, $$) is a local institution and the flagship hotel of the five area hotels owned by the Staed family, whose name has long been associated with quality accommodations hereabouts. Their five properties are managed as Oceans Eleven Resorts; call 800/874-7420 for reservations and information.

At the northern boundary of the Core Area, the **Holiday Inn Sunspree Resort** (600 North Atlantic Avenue, Daytona Beach, 386/255-4471, $$) is a 323-room behemoth that boasts the area's largest pool deck, as well as a playground, fitness center, restaurant, lounge, and bar. If you're of the opinion that bigger is better, there's the 437-unit **Adam's Mark Resort** (100 North Atlantic Avenue, 386/254-8200, $$$), which dominates the landscape like a pyramid rising from the desert sands of

MAP OF VOLUSIA COUNTY—PAGE 72

Egypt. However, the motel was accused of racist policies by black college students, and the ensuing corporate dissembling left a lingering taste of ill will, which the chain is now trying to redress. Moving up Highway A1A toward Ormond Beach are a number of quality mom-and-pops. Among these we like the **Ocean Villa Motel** (828 North Atlantic Avenue, 386/252-4644, $). It has 38 units, many with kitchens, two pools, a water slide, back-door beach access, and a loyal clientele. It's more homey than fancy, which suits the folks who come back year after year just fine.

Arguably the nicest place to stay in the area is the **Hilton Oceanfront Resort** (2637 South Atlantic Ave., $$$, 386/767-7350), which offers all the amenities one could possibly need (pool, Jacuzzi, fitness center, beach) plus the sort of corporate cleanliness one expects of an upscale chain, but with the corporate ambience in check.

If you want a vacation that sounds like a game show prize—a week's lodging in a renowned Florida beach town for under $150—come to Daytona Beach after Labor Day. We're not promising the moon, nor a particularly memorable motel, but you will sleep comfortably, cheaply ($25/night), and right on the beach. Motel prices on the west side of A1A are slashed as low as $22/night. If you thought a Florida beach vacation was an unaffordable luxury, Daytona Beach says otherwise. After Labor Day is also a good time to visit because the water temperature is still as warm as high summer but the air temperature is not nearly so blisteringly hot.

Coastal Cuisine

At first glance, Daytona Beach seems a monument to culinary mediocrity: diners, grills, barbecue restaurants, "all U can eat" po-folks buffet troughs, a McDonald's every 10 blocks or so. Daytona's core clientele has certain very simple notions about what constitutes good food: large portions, preferably with free seconds, and all of it fried a golden brown. Nonetheless, we learned a new way to say grace at Daytona's Museum of Arts and Sciences, courtesy of an excellent exhibit called Cracker Culture in Florida History. "The Cracker Prayer" goes like this: "God, we thank you for all the food we got, especially the grits."

Indeed, hands folded, we uttered those words over our plates at **Aunt Catfish's on the River** (4009 Halifax Drive, Daytona Beach, 386/762-4768, $$), where we got our grits and a mess of other rib-tickling victuals done up in "Down South River Cooking" style (the culinary approach taken by Aunt Catfish). The "river" is the Halifax, which doubles as the Intracoastal Waterway through Ormond Beach and Daytona Beach, and the restaurant is located on its west bank, near Dunlawton Bridge (aka Port Orange Bridge), the southernmost of the six bridges that link Daytona's barrier island to the mainland.

At Aunt Catfish's, you are greeted, seated, and waited on by the sweetest bunch of belles this side of Petticoat Junction. (A typical salutation: "Hi, I'm Cousin Patty and I'll be your server.") The food is as fine as a covered-dish church supper down yonder in the Bible Belt, with all the trimmings and extra helpings. The signature dish is (duh) catfish, which is farm raised and served Cajun-grilled or lightly breaded and fried. We like the place so much we've returned several times, sampling the namesake catfish all three ways. We give Aunt Catfish's two very enthusiastic fins up. Along with your entrée, you get a choice of salad bar or hot bar. Take the hot bar, which features wonderfully sloppy coleslaw, baked beans, corn bread, and cheese grits. Another great touch is the sweetened iced tea served in mason jars (ask your "cousin" to leave the pitcher, because this stuff is addictive). We saved room for the key lime pie, which was made the right way: tart but not too rich, with a graham cracker crust.

Another good riverside haven, and not

quite as far off the beaten path as Aunt Catfish (which is officially in Port Orange) is **Park's Seafood** (951 North Beach Street, 386/258-7272, $$), a large, family-run, family-oriented restaurant. The nautical motif is in overdrive here, but the tableside aquarium adds to the friendliness of Park's, although we were briefly taken aback when, just as we were about to take a mouthful of delicious broiled grouper, a large fish stared forlornly at us from half a foot away. A full catfish or catch-of-the-day (gray sole when we visited) dinner will only run you $10, and the menu tops out with red snapper and broiled pompano for under $17. Meals are served with mullet dip and crackers, tomato-based seafood chowder, salad, and two side dishes. Indeed, a bargain.

Back at the beach, the **Ocean Deck** (127 South Ocean Avenue, 386/253-5224, $$) is the quintessential Daytona Beach bar and grill. A two-decked local institution for as long as anyone can remember (not to mention being ranked #1 on NASCAR's Top 10 list of "places to hang out"), Ocean Deck takes casual dining to an appealing extreme. You can wander in directly from off the beach downstairs or enjoy a bit more classy digs upstairs. Either way, you will have a lot of good company.

Right in the heart of Daytona Beach along the Seabreeze Boulevard bazaar, the **Oyster Pub** (555 Seabreeze Boulevard, 386/255-6348, $) is our perennial favorite for raw bivalves and cold brew. They have a decent lunch menu (seafood salads, sandwiches), but the drawing card all day and all of the night is their plump and juicy oysters.

A few words on Daytona Beach's restaurant scene as a whole. Given that 10 million visitors a year come through here—the great majority of them being bikers, college kids, NASCAR fans, and vacationing families—the restaurants tend to be more serviceable than memorable. Fast food, fried fisherman's platters, pancakes, Florida-style barbecue—this is the lay of the land along Atlantic Avenue. Get in your car, cruise the main drag, pick your trough, and belly up. For more (and better) area restaurants, look to Ponce Inlet.

Night Moves

It's important to note right up front that Daytona Beach has some of the most attractive women on the planet. The Beach Boys rave all summer long about California girls, but they obviously never spent any time in Daytona Beach or they would have written another verse singing its praises.

Women no doubt say the same thing about the guys on this sandy playground, which despite being marketed as a "family" beach also draws its fair share of singles—college kids, bikers, party animals, and other comminglers. That said, the nightlife of Daytona Beach is a well-oiled machine built for partying and centered around three distinct tracks: along Main Street and the Main Street Pier; along Seabreeze Boulevard; and in downtown Daytona (on the mainland), near the historic district. Each has, or has had, its own appeal.

At the moment, downtown has the appearance of an expensive failure, with For Sale and For Rent signs in many storefront windows. This is, no doubt, the price paid for aiming above Daytona Beach's core clientele of car freaks, bikers, teens, and blue-collar families from western Volusia County and beyond.

Downtown was where we once found the much touted but now defunct *Legends In Concert*, the very epitome of tourist-oriented nighttime entertainment upon which Daytona was hoping to bank. The theater where it took place was a beautiful Romanesque restoration that seemed slated to be the flagship of a downtown renaissance.

Legends In Concert was a Vegas show that featured uncannily accurate musical impersonations of famous performers—a wax museum with living, singing dummies, if you will. "Legends" included Little Richard, Tom Jones, Cher, the Blues Brothers (an impersonation of an impersonation), Michael Jackson, and Elvis Presley. Foreign tourists seemed to be the only people who ate this up or could afford the inflated cover charge.

Unable to resist such kitsch, we saw *Legends* play to a nearly empty house in midweek, and the atmosphere was as tense as any comedy club where the stand-up comic is bombing. Apparently, we saw it on its last legs because it was given the bums rush not long after that.

Legends may be gone, but we found its resurrected spirit at a free concert on the Adam's Mark pool deck during Biketoberfest 2000. It featured "Classic Rock All Stars," including "the original lead singers of Rare Earth, Iron Butterfly and Sugarloaf," plus members of Blues Image and Cannibal and the Headhunters. All on the same stage. At the same time. The thought of it sent chills down our spine.

The other two night districts, though always fun, are not for the faint of heart. The flavor of Main Street is best sampled at the **Boot Hill Saloon** (301 Main Street, 386/258-9506), a biker bar of the most benign kind. Their slogan says it all: "You're better off here than across the street." Boot Hill sits opposite an old cemetery. During Bike Week, of course, you can't get near the door, but any other time it's worth checking out for the ambience and live music. The Boot Hill T-shirt is one of Daytona's most popular and cherished souvenirs.

Just down the street is the **Bank & Blues Club** (701 Main Street, 386/257-9272), a nationally known blues venue. Across the street is **Full Moon Saloon** (700 Main Street, 386/257-8661), a rock and roll club with plenty of room to shake your moneymaker to live music.

No matter how hard they try to market "Historic Main Street" as a family entertainment Mecca, it's impossible to overlook its badass image. Frankly, nowhere we have ever been in the world has as hardcore a biker image as Main Street in Daytona Beach. Look at the names of the establishments: John's Rock and Ride, Dirty Harry's, Chopper World, Rat Hole, Harley Davidson, Tombstone, Badlands, Southern Comfort, Shotguns, Hot Leathers, Bikerstuff4Kids.com, Buckle and Hide, Beach Beauty Club. This is family fare? Manson Family fare, maybe. As one bumpersticker here aptly summed up the neighborhood: "American by Birth. Harley Rider by Choice."

Our favorite after-dark hangout is the Seabreeze corridor. That's because it's the home of one of our favorite bars in all of Florida, the **Oyster Pub** (555 Seabreeze Boulevard, 386/255-6348). You breathe a sigh of relief just entering its doors. They have a great jukebox; a relaxed, Cheers-like atmosphere; an enormous horseshoe-shaped bar; and multiple TV sets soundlessly broadcasting sporting events.

If you can hold out till midnight, the price of oysters drops to 25 cents apiece. Many's the night we've allowed our hunger pangs to expand to the witching hour, just to take advantage of this deal.

The friendliest folks in town frequent the Oyster Pub, too. Take it from us: this is a comfortable, casual town without the faddish, off-putting rituals of high-decibel discos and rave clubs. Good golly, you can even have friendly conversations with strangers here!

Directly across the street from the Oyster Pub is **Molly Brown's** (542 Seabreeze Boulevard, 255-5966), an adult strip club. In between sets, many of the dancers hang out at the Oyster Pub, where the atmosphere is a bit less intense. We watched one of these women drink a glass of iced tea. Her fingernails were so long that she nearly impaled herself every time she brought the glass up to her face. Look at it this way: the only difference between a place like Molly

Brown's and the Miss America Pageant is a few lousy square inches of cloth.

The two clubs that have made the biggest splash along Seabreeze are the **Baja Beach Club** (640 North Grandview Avenue, 386/248-3224) and **Razzle's** (611 Seabreeze Boulevard, 386/257-6236). The former bills itself as "America's most extreme party bar," a wild and excruciatingly loud complex that boasts seven separate bars and the outrageous come-on that "ladies drink free."

Razzle's bills itself as a "high-energy dance club," but to our ears it was a waking nightmare. For a $5 cover charge—paid to a surly bodybuilder who slapped the back of our hands with an ink stamp—we got assaulted with ear-throbbing contemporary "dance music" that's even worse than disco. It all sounds like a bad record with a skip in it. ("I wanna, wa-wa-wanna, wanna be-be-be yer lover, lov-lov-lover," on and on for 10 frigging minutes!) If this is, as the ad says, "the new club for the new Millennium," we're nostalgic for the Great Bronze Age.

Finally, one of the most enduring acts on the Daytona Beach scene is the Atlantic Ocean. This stalwart performer has been giving nightly shows for years that have literally had millions of fans stage diving long past midnight. There is no cover charge, of course, and now that cars can no longer drive on the beach past 7 P.M., it's safe to just sit back and dig the sound of the waves and the look of the moon rising overhead. (As many as 25 people used to get run over on the beach each year, most of them at night.) An equally relaxing experience, for those who have an itch to motor-vate (hey, it's Daytona!), is a moonlight drive along the west bank of the Halifax River. Riverside Drive is a palm-lined thoroughfare buffeted by breezes coming off the water. For our money, it beats the heck out of twitching spastically to the strains of "The Thong Song."

Contact Information

Daytona Beach Area Convention and Visitors Bureau, 126 East Orange Avenue, Daytona Beach, FL 32114; 386/255-0415 or 800/544-0415; website: www.daytonabeach.com

Daytona Beach Shores Chamber of Commerce, 3048 South Atlantic Avenue, Daytona Beach Shores, FL 32118; 386/761-7163; website: www.dbschamber.com

MAP OF VOLUSIA COUNTY—PAGE 72

Wheels on the Beach

As virtually everyone in the Western world is aware, you can drive on parts of Daytona, Ormond, and New Smyrna Beaches. Elsewhere in Florida, you can drive on selected beaches near St. Augustine and on Amelia Island. The only other beaches in America we've seen where people are legally allowed and physically able to drive their cars are Pismo Beach, California; Ocean Shores, Washington; and Long Beach Peninsula, Washington. But Daytona Beach is the best known of the bunch.

This unusual privilege is a curious holdover from the area's days as the Birthplace of Speed. Over the years, it has accrued the status of an inalienable right, up there with gun ownership, flag protection, and lawn watering. It was upon the wide, hard sands of Daytona and Ormond Beaches that the first racing cars were tested and, so the logic goes, anyone on wheels should be allowed to drive its hard-packed strand now. At present, 18 of the 23 miles of beach from Ormond Beach to Ponce Inlet are open to wheeled vehicles.

But, before you floor your car, motorcycle, or dune buggy in a due easterly direction, you might want to ponder "the Rules." They've changed a bit in recent years, beginning with the 1992 implementation of "natural conservation zones" created to protect endangered sea turtles. This gradual diminishing of driveable miles continued with the Habitat Conservation Plan, begun in 1996 to protect primary and secondary dune structure. The situation is slated to change even more dramatically as the vaunted Ocean Walk Complex is created in a formerly blighted "urban zone"—several blocks on either side of the Convention Center and the beachfront band shell. This will open even more of the busiest beaches to pedestrians only. That's the way, as Billy Preston once sang, God planned it.

Regardless of your viewpoint, the net result is that parts of the beach that were once open to vehicular traffic have been shut down. Guess what? Those wheel-free beach areas have now become popular and pleasurable havens for pedestrians, sunbathers, surfers, and swimmers, as well as sand dunes and sea turtles. The enviro-bashers—the loudest proponents of letting cars go where they will—never mention that when an area, such as a natural conservation zone at Daytona Beach, is protected for the benefit of an endangered species, all species including humans end up benefiting. End of sermon.

If you still want to drive on the beach, here are "the Rules":

- The beach is open to motorized traffic from 8 A.M. to 7 P.M., unless sand conditions are unusually soft and/or the beach has narrowed, usually because of a high tide, a big storm, or both. In such a scenario, the beach patrol will close the beach.
- There are between 25 and 30—the number varies according to season—marked entrance gates from north Volusia County (Ormond Beach) to south Volusia County (New Smyrna Beach).
- Vehicles for which entrance fees are required are cars, trucks (under 33 feet long only), motorcycles, vans, and RVs. Bicycles are allowed on the beach free of charge.
- The fee to enter the beach at designated gates is $5 per vehicle. This fee allows you unlimited entry all day long. Seasonal passes are available to nonresidents for $40.

- The speed limit is 10 miles per hour at all times.
- The beach has been divided into urban zones, transitional zones, and natural conservation zones. Driving is allowed in the first two zones and is illegal in the latter.
- The two designated urban zones are where "the concentration of people is the most intense most of the year." For this reason, sea turtle nesting is minimal. They are located on either side of Daytona Beach's Main Street Pier, from Zelda Boulevard down to Florida Shores Boulevard. Here, you can drive within 15 feet seaward of the dunes or seawalls.
- Transitional zones are located on either wing of the urban zones, plus the north end of New Smyrna Beach. Sea turtle nesting here is moderate, and you must drive no closer than 30 feet of the dunes or seawalls.
- Natural conservation zones are where dune habitats are largely intact and sea turtle nesting is highly concentrated. These areas are found north of Granada Boulevard on Ormond Beach; between Emilia Avenue and Beach Street on Daytona Beach; and south of 27th Avenue in New Smyrna Beach. The no-driving rule is strictly enforced in conservation zones (which are clearly marked), with a $500 fine for parking or operating any vehicle there.
- Park either facing the ocean or the dunes, but not parallel to the water. Those are "the Rules."

Most drivers on the beaches of Daytona are well behaved, coming to the beach to set up a base camp with their family or a group of friends. However, at or nearing high tide, these same folks often linger longer than they should. This leads to a common sight: a rental car being floored by a frantic driver unaccustomed to off-road conditions, which only digs them more deeply into the wet, soft sand. Soon they become dependent on the kindness of strangers to help push them out. The process is repeated 50 yards down the beach when the same driver gets stuck again. If you wait long enough—i.e., till the water is lapping at the hubcaps—the beach patrol will pull you out for free. On busy days in peak season, they extract as many as 200 stuck vehicles. Beyond having to be towed, you can do appalling damage to a car by bringing it to the beach for very long. Salt water, salt spray, and windblown sand will induce "dramatic rot," as one local put it, to a vehicle's underside. A three-year life span is normal for beach-driven vehicles.

While frantic, fishtailing drivers can be a comical sight, they can be downright dangerous under crowded conditions. At high tide in the urban zones, there's barely room to walk down to the water as it is. In years past, pedestrian fatalities were an all-too-common occurrence on the beaches of Daytona. Often alcohol was involved, with unwitting victims passed out in the sand or drivers practically passed out at the wheel. Rented big-wheeled buggies are driven particularly badly, usually by tubby tourists harking back to their go-cart days or beleaguered moms swatting at whining kids with one hand while trying to guide the unpredictable contraptions with the other. As one lifeguard put it to us, "They don't seem to have any conception of environmental impact or public safety."

While the issue of driving on the beach will always be a hot one in Daytona, the compromises that have already been made were unthinkable even a decade ago. As one veteran of the Volusia County Beach Patrol put it, "A lot of different agendas are in play here. I used to think a driving ban would never happen, but now I'd say the chances are about 50-50."

For up-to-date information on driving and beach conditions, call the Volusia County Beach Hotline at 386/239-7873 (Daytona Beach) or 386/423-3330 (New Smyrna Beach).

Wilbur-by-the-Sea and Ponce Inlet

While officially part of the Daytona Beach strand, occupying the southernmost chunk of its barrier island, Ponce Inlet (pop. 2,408) presents such a different profile that it demands to be handled separately. Locals even refer to it as the "Un-Daytona." Mostly residential homes (not condos), Ponce Inlet is also well endowed with a natural conservation zone, giving it a tropical, verdant seclusion. As recently as the late 1960s, Ponce Inlet was too far off the beaten path (and evacuation routes) to be worth anyone's while to develop. Nowadays, the property here is among the most coveted along the central Florida coast.

It's easy to see why. Developed later than much of the coast, Ponce Inlet has benefited from mistakes made elsewhere. As a result, low-density development and environmental restrictions have helped maintain its natural character and preserve those parts of the man-made Old Florida that were already out here. The most noteworthy example is the **Ponce de León Inlet Lighthouse**, which is open daily 10 A.M.–5 P.M. ($4 for adults, $1 for children under 11). Built in 1887, this 175-foot monolith of red brick and granite is the second tallest lighthouse in America. Shut down in 1970, the light was rekindled in 1982. Today, the on-site Museum of the Sea offers lessons in oceanography, navigation, and marine biology, and the Lighthouse Museum sheds light on the lives and labors of the keepers of the flame. You can also climb the steps to the top, which ought to earn you an extra order of hush puppies or conch fritters at one of several fine seafood restau-

6 Wilbur-by-the-Sea

Location: seven miles south of Daytona Beach
Parking/fees: $5 per day to enter and park on the beach via the Toronita Avenue approach (free in December and January); free off-beach parking lots
Hours: sunrise to sunset
Facilities: lifeguards and showers
Contact: Volusia County Beach Services, 386/239-7873

7 Ponce Inlet

Location: The 2.5 miles of beach are nine miles south of Daytona Beach.
Parking/fees: $5 per day to enter and park on the beach via the Beach Street approach (free in December and January); free off-beach parking lots
Hours: sunrise to sunset (autos only), 24 hours (pedestrians)
Facilities: concessions, lifeguards, restrooms, picnic tables, and showers
Contact: Volusia County Beach Services, 386/239-7873

8 Lighthouse Point Park and Recreation Area

Location: off Highway A1A in Ponce Inlet
Parking/fees: $3.50 entrance fee per vehicle; $20 annual pass
Hours: 6 A.M.–9 P.M.
Facilities: lifeguards (seasonal), restrooms, picnic tables, showers, and a visitor center
Contact: Lighthouse Point Park and Recreation Area, 386/756-7488

MAP OF FLORIDA'S EAST COAST—PAGE 5

rants in the immediate area. Any number of deep-sea sportfishing charters leave out of Ponce Inlet's harbor. A ban on netfishing within three miles of shore, enacted at mid-decade, has already paid dividends, allowing populations of shrimp and scallops (and the fish that feed on them) to bounce back.

Beaches

Wilbur-by-the-Sea is a small, mostly residential colony that serves as a zone of transition between Daytona Beach and **Ponce Inlet.** Wilbur's quiet beach can be vehicularly accessed via Toronita Avenue, and one can drive north all the way to Ormond Beach. The beach at Ponce Inlet is entered at Beach Street, but one can only drive south (because of the conservation zone) to the jetty at **Lighthouse Point Park and Recreation Area.** Four free off-beach parking lots and dune crossovers provide ways of parking and walking out to these communities' pleasant beaches.

The finest beach in Daytona Beach, in our opinion, used to be located along Ponce Inlet's Atlantic shoreline inside Lighthouse Point Park and Recreation Area, at the south end of Peninsula Drive. This is a state-owned but county-run facility that includes a jetty—from which the fishing is legendary—and an oceanfront pavilion and nature trails. The widest berm on any beach in Volusia County was found at Lighthouse Point, due in part to the creation of the natural conservation zones. Here also was one of the highest recorded concentrations of sea turtle nesting in the county. The surf was popular with surfers, though not quite as good as that on the south side of Ponce Inlet at Smyrna Dunes, in New Smyrna Beach.

All of this was true, that is, until 1999–2000, when the U.S. Army Corps of Engineers did a number on Lighthouse Point Park and Recreation Area. Their brilliant plan was to extend Ponce Inlet's North Jetty but not its South Jetty. As anyone with a high school science education could have told them, the prized, much-loved beach completely disappeared on the North Jetty. It is now replaced with riprap and rubble. Prior to this, it was one of the most popular beaches in Volusia County for families, because of the gentle, protected surf and because it's the only county-run beach park that allows dogs. A beach-hating sadist could not have performed a more devastating act than what the Corps' monkeying around ended up creating. Fixing us with a seen-it-all expression, the gatekeeper at the Lighthouse explained, "Any time the Corps of Engineers gets involved, you know what happens. . . Now they got crews out there full-time just to repair the damage the Corps has done."

Shore Things

- **Fishing charters:** Critter Fleet, Lighthouse Landing, 4940 South Peninsula Drive, 386/761-9271.
- **Lighthouse:** Ponce de León Inlet Lighthouse, 4931 South Peninsula Drive, 386/761-1821.
- **Marina:** Inlet Harbor Marina, 133 Inlet Harbor Road, 386/767-8755.

Coastal Cuisine

One of the most venerable meal tickets in the area is **Lighthouse Landing** (4940 South Peninsula Drive, 386/761-9271, $$), which bills itself as "the oldest restaurant on the East Coast." This ancient eatery is arrayed alongside the marina where the Critter Fleet, a deep-sea fishing fleet, docks. The casual setting enhances the dark, Old Florida ambience of the restaurant. Lighthouse Landing caters to an older crowd who've been coming here since Lawrence Welk was a young man.

MAP OF VOLUSIA COUNTY—PAGE 72

The bright new star of the Ponce dining scene is **Inlet Harbor Restaurant and Marina** (133 Inlet Harbor Road, 386/767-8755, $$). Opened in February 1997, it immediately began packing them in, with two-hour waits on weekends not uncommon. The wait is worth it and painless enough from the breezy vantage point of the patio bar, Riverdance, which has its own excellent appetizer menu featuring fresh shrimp, oysters, stone crab claws, conch fritters, and a wicked blackened "seafood burrito." The patio overlooks the blue-green inlet waters and their surrounding protected wetlands. If you get really impatient, stroll over to the marina and watch the fishing fleet unload their daily catch. The main menu at Inlet Harbor offers an assortment of fresh and simply prepared seafood, cooked to your choosing (grilled, fried, broiled, and blackened) at prices that won't bust a move on your wallet. We dug the Calypso crab cakes with spicy remoulade sauce and the Florida jumbo shrimp, which is their claim to fame.

Contact Information

Daytona Beach Area Convention and Visitors Bureau, 126 East Orange Avenue, Daytona Beach, FL 32114; 386/255-0415 or 800/544-0415; website: www.daytonabeach.com

New Smyrna Beach

Florida has its own homegrown beauties who rival any Valley Girl or Baywatch Babe. More enticingly, they have that sunny Southern capacity for friendliness, sans the airheadedness that brings most conversations in L.A. to a screeching halt within half a minute. We, in fact, talked to a great young woman in New Smyrna Beach (pop. 18,425), a mature and self-aware 20-year-old who is clearly sharp enough to make it anywhere she chooses. She has chosen to stay put in quiet, unprepossessing New Smyrna Beach, Daytona's southern neighbor. Although it shares Daytona's obsession for driving cars on the sand, New Smyrna would love to put more than an inlet's distance between itself and its much better-known neighbor.

"I've lived my entire life on New Smyrna Beach, but I have never been on Daytona Beach," she told us. "I've been over there, of course, but my feet have never actually touched the sand. I prefer the quiet stability here. I tried to move away once, to Virginia Beach, but that only lasted six days, and I came back home." She, like all locals, pronounces Smyrna not as it looks but with an extra syllable: "Sa-myrna."

There is obviously more to this town than initially meets the eye. In years past, what the eye met as it approached on U.S. 1 was a string of rickety motels, flyblown bait shops, and a few bucket-of-blood saloons. The beach at New Smyrna Beach is a 10-minute drive east via the Highway A1A causeway. Accommodations along the ocean were scarce, forcing anyone who didn't know better back to the inhospitable claptrap of U.S. 1.

The oceanfront at New Smyrna Beach has lately been opening itself to the tourist trade. That is, visitors no longer have to stay in places that time forgot in

9 Smyrna Dunes Park

Location: the north end of Peninsula Avenue in Smyrna Beach

Parking/fees: $3.50 entrance fee per vehicle

Hours: 6 A.M.–7 P.M. (8 P.M. in summer)

Facilities: restrooms, picnic tables, showers, and a visitor center

Contact: Smyrna Dunes Parks, 386/424-2935

order to enjoy the ample Smyrnan sands. They've been making up for lost time in this once-quiet haven, for better or worse. Not only has a second causeway bridge been built to the barrier island—the North Causeway, an extension of Flagler Avenue—but the length of New Smyrna's eight-mile beachfront has become a wall of high-rise condos and second homes for the part-time use of middle-class folks from Orlando.

Once the antithesis of Daytona, New Smyrna Beach has simply become a low-key alternative to a Daytona vacation. As a member of the Volusia County Beach Patrol told us, "On weekends and during special events, New Smyrna is just as packed as Daytona." This is not intended as a knock. We were, in fact, so impressed with the town's makeover that we stayed an extra day. But it is only fair to warn you that New Smyrna is no longer a quaint and quiet beach town.

The town's name originated with its founder, Dr. Andrew Turnbull, in 1876. He named New Smyrna Beach in honor of his wife, who came from Smyrna, in Asia Minor. Prior to European colonization, the area had been the longtime homeland of the Timucuan Indians. Juan Ponce de León landed somewhere in the vicinity in 1513 (thus the name Ponce Inlet). Interestingly, New Smyrna Beach has changed hands four times in its existence and, three times larger than Jamestown, was briefly the most lucrative of the British colonies in the New World.

Little of this local history has been preserved. For instance, the only Timucuan shell mound that wasn't used to pave the local roads can be found inside the Canaveral National Seashore. The roads have lately reached the saturation point, in terms of development. If they could only stop now and leave well enough alone, we'd certainly look forward to future visits to New Smyrna Beach.

Beaches

From Ponce Inlet at the north end of the barrier island to the Canaveral National Seashore entrance, **New Smyrna Beach** and its sister community of **Bethune Beach** are home to 13.2 miles of wide unbroken sand. Seven miles of that span, from Ponce Inlet to 27th Avenue, is a "transitional zone," which means beach driving and parking are allowed 30 feet seaward of the dunes or seawalls. South of 27th Avenue the beach is a "natural conservation zone," where no motorized vehicles are permitted. Even at peak season, the crush on Smyrna's beaches never quite achieves Daytona's intensity, but it's a popular and

⑩ New Smyrna Beach

Location: The 10 miles of beach are 20 miles south of Daytona Beach.
Parking/fees: $5 per day to park on the beach (free in December and January); free off-beach parking lots
Hours: sunrise to sunset (autos only), 24 hours (pedestrians)
Facilities: concessions, lifeguards, restrooms, picnic tables, and showers
Contact: Volusia County Beach Services, 386/239-7873

⑪ Bethune Beach

Location: at the south end of New Smyrna Beach and 10 miles south of Ponce Inlet
Parking/fees: free parking lot at Mary McCleod Bethune Park
Hours: 24 hours
Facilities: concessions, lifeguards, restrooms, picnic tables, and showers
Contact: Volusia County Beach Services, 386/239-7873

MAP OF VOLUSIA COUNTY—PAGE 72

busy beach all the same.

The best surfing spot in Volusia County is at the north end of New Smyrna Beach, on the south side of Ponce Inlet. The waves are said to peak two feet higher here than anywhere else in the county. This surfer's Shangri-la is accessed via **Smyrna Dunes Park**, located at the end of Peninsula Avenue. The county has leased this pristine, dune-covered acreage from the Coast Guard and created an intriguingly ad hoc park. Behind the shaded picnic area and shower facilities, a 1.5-mile boardwalk runs a loop out to and around Ponce Inlet, with two beach accesses provided en route. It's a blisteringly hot and dry hike, not a casual stroll, and there isn't a square inch of shade, so bring water and plan to stay on the beach for long enough to make it worth the trouble.

That said, it's worth every drop of sweat to get here for the view from the wetlands observation deck and for access to the inlet and a gorgeous, secluded beach. The only sour note to the view is an eyesore called Inlet Marina Villages, a brand-new condo abomination that should never have been allowed on the boundary of this natural parkland. As for the dunes, seldom have we seen such broad fields so dense with vegetation, including prickly pear cactus, sea oats, and railroad vine creeping along the sugar-white quartz sand. We also recommend hiking out here to watch the surfers. This tireless, dauntless, and usually penniless contingent will hike barefoot over the splintering boardwalk and sizzling asphalt with heavy boards in tow. In that respect, Smyrna Dunes is a lot like Trestles, a famous surf spot in San Clemente, California. Hopefully, places like Smyrna Dunes, with its inventive cross-jurisdictional partnership, will serve as templates for other beach communities who want to broaden public access.

South of Smyrna Dunes, Atlantic Avenue winds along to the stretch of beach most favored by locals. It is found at the end of Esther Street, just north of a 7-Eleven. You can park for free on the sandy shoulder, if you can find a spot. This area is called "The Wall," for the seawall over which you must hop (there's a makeshift ladder for the faint of heart) in order to gain beach access. Upon that seawall is a colorful, if somewhat faded, mural painted by local schoolchildren that depicts sea life and contains this plaintive and polite plea: "Save Our Oceans Please." On hot summer days, the beach just below the wall and for several hundred yards in either direction is packed with nubile bodies and cruised by cars enjoying the flesh parade.

The center of New Smyrna Beach's tourist activity is at the end of Flagler Avenue, where a concrete entrance ramp allows vehicular access onto the sand. From here south to 30th Avenue, beach access points are provided every three or four blocks and are marked by blue signs along Atlantic Avenue (Highway A1A). Parking is free but limited at most of these places. South of 27th Avenue, cars on the beach are nowhere to be found and neither are motels. Most of the beachgoers at this end of New Smyrna own units in the endless chain of condos. One break in that chain is Mary McCleod Bethune Park, in Bethune Beach, which derives its name from the great African-American educator who helped create Bethune-Cookman College in Daytona Beach. This county-run blufftop park has a picnic area and beach access.

Shore Things

- **Ecotourism**: Coastal Cruise Lines (at Sea Harvest Marina), 386/428-0201.
- **Fishing charters**: Captain J. B.'s Fish Camp, Highway A1A at Pompano Street, 386/427-5747.
- **Marina**: Sea Harvest Marina, South Atlantic Avenue, 386/428-0201.

- **Rainy-day attraction:** Atlantic Center for the Arts, 1414 Art Center Avenue, 386/427-6975.
- **Surf shop:** Inlet Charley's, 510 Flagler Avenue, 386/427-5674.
- **Vacation rentals:** Beachcomber Properties, 2705 South Atlantic Avenue, 386/427-3736.

Bunking Down

Condo-mania has gripped the beaches of New Smyrna. Unfortunately, they have almost screened out any other viable place to stay on the beach. The most obvious and appealing exception is the **Holiday Inn** (1401 South Atlantic Avenue, 386/426-0020, $$$), which directly overlooks the busiest part of New Smyrna's beach. Prices are a tad high, due to the town being a seller's market. But all units have fully equipped kitchens and ocean-view balconies, the pool is large, and the property is well maintained. The only other viable option is the **Oceania Beach Resort**, which has both a hotel (425 Atlantic Avenue, 386/427-4636, $$$) and a beach club (421 South Atlantic Avenue, 386/423-8400), the latter working like time-share condos.

Coastal Cuisine

Norwood's Seafood Restaurant (400 2nd Avenue, 386/428-4621, $$$) opened in 1946, in what was formerly a gas station, general store, mosquito control center, and piggy-bank factory. Now tastefully and unobtrusively set among a grove of palms and fruit trees, Norwood's hasn't lost its dedication to fresh seafood. In fact, they go through 2,000 pounds of fresh fish a week. The owners, Don and Helen Simmons, have spearheaded a remarkable menu makeover over the past decade, winning countless awards, including several from *Wine Spectator* for the 40-page wine list. Despite these sophisticated touches, Norwood's remains knee deep in tradition, exemplified by the beloved Aunt Bea, a server here for 30 years who now functions as an on-site goodwill ambassador.

After appetizers of wood-smoked trout and sun-dried tomato brochette, we had entrées of char-broiled grouper and golden tilefish. The tile was particularly memorable, a delicate whitefish topped with capers and salsa. We couldn't remember having had a better seafood dinner in the state of Florida. Non-fish eaters take note: Norwood's is also among the top 20 servers of Angus beef in the nation.

Though nothing in the vicinity can touch Norwood's for dinner, **Captain J.B.'s Fish Camp** (Highway A1A at Pompano Street, 386/427-5747, $$) is the one place you shouldn't miss for lunch. It's located in the community of Bethune Beach, seven miles south of Highway A1A's entrance onto the barrier island and close by the north entrance to Canaveral National Seashore. A ramshackle complex set along the Intracoastal Waterway, J.B.'s is indeed a fish camp, with guides for hire, a bait and tackle shop, and a dock out back near which a "resident manatee" hangs his snout. Better yet, this lovably sloppy eatery serves "Southern Seafood at Its Finest" inside a large porch cooled by ceiling fans.

At the entrance, a smiling stuffed alligator sits up on its tail (the Gator d'?), and there's also this notice: "Unattended Children Will Be Used As Crab Bait." Inside, you sit at picnic tables covered in butcher paper, flag down a hard-working waitress, and rattle off an order of conch fritters (loved 'em!) or any of a number of blackened specialties, including gator. While waiting for your order, wander about the place to admire the odd assortment of artifacts. Our steamed spiced shrimp and lightly fried oyster platter came out quickly and went down just as fast. They could never franchise a place like J.B.'s—"Where fun is legal"—because it's one of a kind. They sell some great T-shirts, too.

Night Moves

The old bucket-of-blood saloons out on Dixie Highway (U.S. 1) are still in business, boasting names like Fly Inn, Way Out Inn, and Last Resort, but a more appealing alternative has arrived on the scene. Called **Gilly's Pub 44** (State Route 44, 386/428-6523), it's a popular spot for rhinestone cowboys, sunburned tourists, wannabe bikers, and the real thing, too. Gilly's Pub 44, located in a strip mall west of the causeway bridge, derives its name and honky-tonk spirit from Mickey Gilley. It's not part of Gilley's chain (note the careful misspelling), which includes the Texas roadhouse where *Urban Cowboy* was filmed. We also heard about a place called the Cabbage Patch that occasionally features "coleslaw wrestling" (akin to mud wrestling and Jell-O wrestling), which packs the house. You're on your own with that one.

We preferred doing the "Flagler Crawl," a mug-hoisting tour of the several friendly pubs along Flagler Avenue, all located within earshot of the ocean and all within a three-block crawl of one another. There's nothing fancy about them, but they're a hell of a lot of fun. The following especially get our nod of approval: **Flagler Tavern** (414 Flagler Avenue, 386/426-2080) and **Traders** (317 Flagler Avenue, 386/428-9141).

Contact Information

Southeast Volusia Chamber of Commerce, 115 Canal Street, P.O. Box 129, New Smyrna Beach, FL 32069; 386/428-2449; website: www.sevchamber.com

Apollo Beach (Canaveral National Seashore)

The 33-mile length of Canaveral National Seashore is entered at the north end below New Smyrna Beach. A paved park road runs for seven miles along **Apollo Beach**, where you'll find five parking lots and four primitive campsites scattered alongside the beach. (Camping is permitted from November 1 through April 30 and costs nothing beyond the $5 daily entrance fee.) There's nothing much out here but beach, and lots of it. The big, shallow body of water behind the beach at Canaveral is called Mosquito Lagoon, so don't say you haven't been warned. A short trail at the south end of Apollo Beach, on the west side of the park road, leads to Eldora Hammock and the Eldora fishing piers, where you can cast into a tidal creek. There's also a boat launch on the lagoon side at Shipyard Island, just before the Canaveral National Seashore Visitor Information Center.

Canaveral's longest beach, Klondike Beach, is split evenly between Volusia and Brevard Counties. We cover it in greater detail in the write-up on Canaveral National Seashore in the next chapter.

Contact Information

Canaveral National Seashore, 308 Julia Street, Titusville, FL 32796; 321/267-1110; website: www.nps.gov/cana

12 Apollo Beach

Location: Canaveral National Seashore
Parking/fees: $5 entrance fee per car. There is no fee for camping beyond the daily entrance fee.
Hours: 6 A.M.–6 P.M.
Facilities: lifeguards (seasonal), restrooms, and a visitor center
Contact: Canaveral National Seashore, 386/428-3384

Making Waves in Ponce Inlet: Jet Skiers Versus Surfers

Perhaps a sign of how things have changed in New Smyrna Beach is that the local hot-button issue isn't pollution, crime, or vagrancy, but an all-too-familiar battle royale along the coast: Jet Skiers versus surfers. The argument against Jet Skis is persuasive. Not only are these "personal watercraft" expensive ($6,000), fast (up to 50 mph), and dangerous (the amphibious missiles weigh up to 100 pounds), but they also make a hellacious racket. Some of their operators, mostly inlanders with disposable income, reportedly enjoy taunting surfers. The primary access point to the ocean for Jet Skis along this stretch of Florida's coast is Ponce Inlet. As they come barreling out of the inlet's mouth, Jet Skis sometimes flare south too abruptly—they are mandated to stay 1,500 feet from shore—cutting directly into a great surfing zone known as Shark Shallows. Despite attempts by spin doctors of the personal watercraft industry to equate their use with the benign and nonpolluting sport of surfing, that is pure hogwash. As a result, surfers hate Jet Skiers, and we're none too fond of them ourselves.

A beach patrol supervisor told us, "Neither side are angels. There's a high testosterone level at work on both sides. It was bad enough when surfers fought each other over the pecking order for waves, but Jet Skis have just added fuel to the fire." Speaking of which, Jet Skis are notorious for their oily secretions.

Rather than let the conflict get out of hand, the county has gotten the two camps together to work out a compromise. They've also adopted a "one warning" policy for Jet Skiers, with a sizable fine awaiting those who are in violation a second time. It has worked to some degree, at least for now.

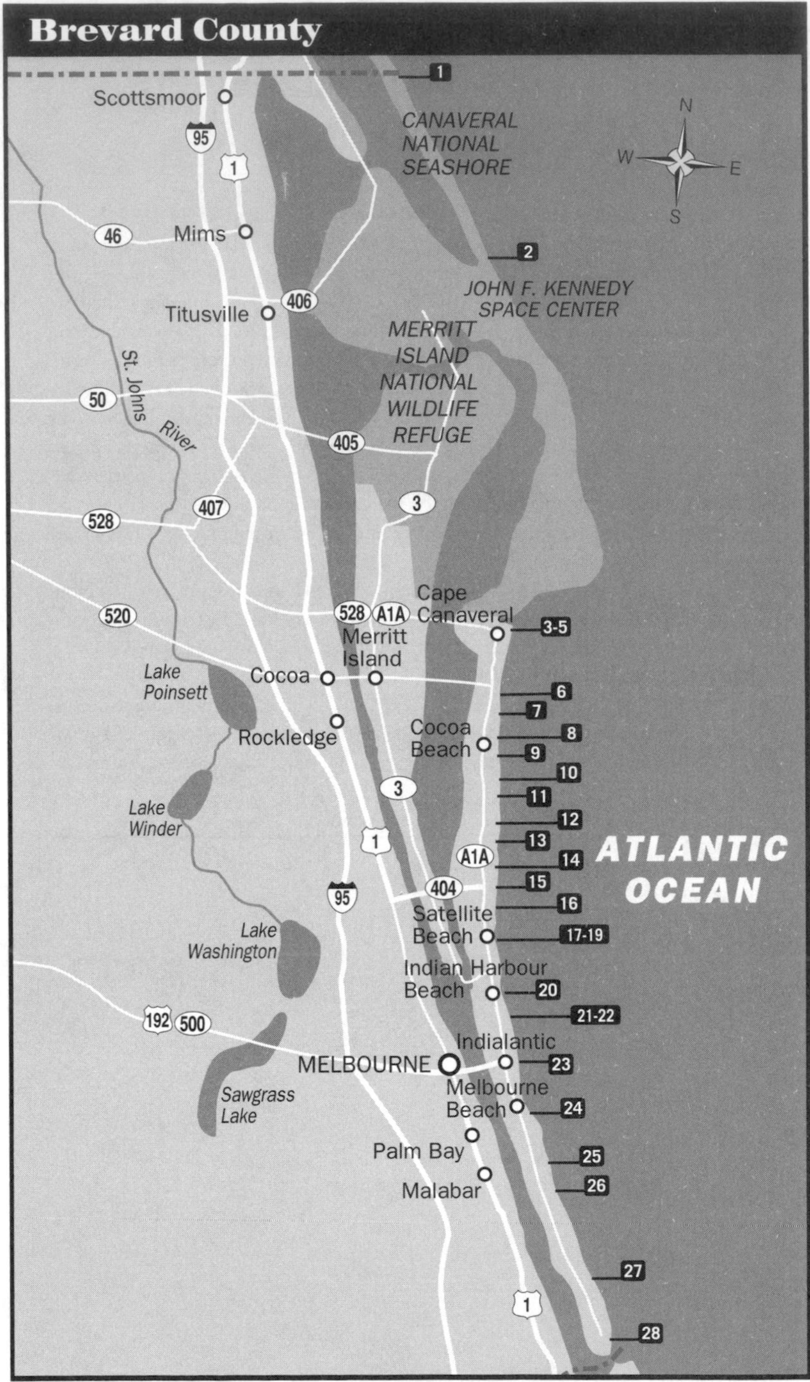
Brevard County
1
Scottsmoor
95
1
CANAVERAL NATIONAL SEASHORE
N
W
E
S
46
Mims
2
JOHN F. KENNEDY SPACE CENTER
406
Titusville
MERRITT ISLAND NATIONAL WILDLIFE REFUGE
St. Johns River
50
405
3
407
528
Cape Canaveral
520
528
A1A
Merritt Island
3-5
Lake Poinsett
Cocoa
6
7
Rockledge
Cocoa Beach
8
9
10
3
11
Lake Winder
12
13
1
A1A
14
ATLANTIC OCEAN
404
15
95
16
Lake Washington
Satellite Beach
17-19
Indian Harbour Beach
20
21-22
192
500
Indialantic
MELBOURNE
23
Sawgrass Lake
Melbourne Beach
24
Palm Bay
25
Malabar
26
27
1
28

BREVARD COUNTY

BREVARD COUNTY

America's space program began in 1961 when the first manned flight was sent into orbit from Cape Canaveral. The Kennedy Space Center—in north Brevard County, above Cocoa Beach—remains one of the top tourist draws in Florida. Yet there's more to "the Space Coast" than NASA's grand initiatives. The county claims 72 miles of sandy coastline—more than any other county in the state. They range from the isolation of Canaveral National Seashore to the surfable, sociable real estate of Cocoa Beach. South Brevard County is a lengthy stretch of contiguous small communities—including Satellite Beach, Indialantic, and Melbourne Beach—that ends at Sebastian Inlet, with the best surf in Florida.

The 33 miles of coast from Patrick Air Force Base to Sebastian Inlet is known collectively as South Brevard County Beaches. While the names of its incorporated towns and unincorporated hamlets change every few miles, the area shares an understated appeal, at least for the moment. Through most of this corridor, "Land For Sale" signs are jabbed into nearly every vacant lot on either side of Highway A1A. High-rise condominiums are noticeable beyond the borders of the many county beach parks and accesses.

Another decade down the road, it's anybody's guess what will be plopped down out here. For now, it's relatively quiet and mostly residential. The Old Florida beach ambience—mom-and-pop motels, local seafood joints, and watering holes—can still be found here and there, with the new-money imperatives of towering condos and gated communities encroaching on them step by step, acre by acre.

Some of the names encountered in south Brevard County don't yet appear on maps, and even the locals can't always tell you where one town ends and another begins. To add to the confusion, most of the businesses out this way are listed under the city of Melbourne, whose commercial umbrella keeps opening wider with each passing year. That's just the way it is out here. But the beaches are nice, and some of them are exceptional.

MAP OF FLORIDA'S EAST COAST—PAGE 5

Canaveral National Seashore

One of the longest and most gorgeous stretches of beach in the United States is Canaveral National Seashore. At the south end, the launching pads of Kennedy Space Center are visible from **Playalinda Beach** (although no one is allowed on the beach on launch days). To the west, the marshes and diked impoundments of Merritt Island National Wildlife Refuge, a safe harbor for migratory waterfowl, extend toward the distant horizon. Running north and south for 33 miles is a pristine, undefiled ribbon of sand and sea.

Canaveral, meaning "place of canes," is one of the oldest geographical names in America, originating with Ponce de León's claiming of the area for Spain in 1513. Canaveral and Merritt Island were originally set aside as a buffer zone for NASA's activities back in the 1950s. Today, the former is administered as a national seashore by the National Park Service, the latter as a national wildlife refuge by the U.S. Fish and Wildlife Service. Moreover, their mission goes far beyond abetting the space program. These preserves serve as

Merritt Island National Wildlife Refuge

Originally set aside as a buffer zone for NASA's operations at Cape Canaveral, Merritt Island has, quite frankly, gone to the birds—310 species of them, as a matter of fact. More endangered and threatened species of all kinds visit or make their home on Merritt Island than any other continental wildlife refuge. They include bald eagles, wood storks, Florida scrub jays, peregrine falcons, and brown pelicans, as well as manatees and sea turtles on the non-avian side. Then there's the inundation of nonendangered species. In winter, there may be as many as 70,000 migratory waterfowl on the refuge. There's a lot of room for them, too, as Merritt Island National Wildlife Refuge and Canaveral National Seashore, which adjoins it to the east, collectively preserve 239,000 acres of prime central Florida coast real estate.

The centerpiece of the refuge for those visitors who are passing through, either coming to or from the beaches of Canaveral National Seashore, is the Black Point Wildlife Drive. This unpaved, one-way road makes a six-mile circuit through piney flatwoods and along the edges of diked impoundments that serve as habitat for waterfowl. You'll want to move slowly along this road, stopping to sight bald-eagle nests or skinny ospreys spearing food from the water. Better yet, bring bikes and meander along the drive at ground level with the wildlife. Early morning and late afternoon are the best times for wildlife viewing, and the winter months are optimum in terms of bird numbers on the refuge. Linger a while and soak up some of nature's slower rhythms; you won't be sorry.

To get to Merritt Island National Wildlife Refuge from I-95, take Exit 80 (State Route 406). At its intersection with State Route 402, take that road east to the visitor information center or continue east on State Route 406 to Black Point Wildlife Drive.

For more information contact Merritt Island National Wildlife Refuge, P.O. Box 6504, Titusville, FL 32782; 321/861-0667; website: www.merrittisland.fws.gov.

MAP OF BREVARD COUNTY—PAGE 100

Playalinda Beach: Nude and Proud

Unlike liberated California, the state of Florida is not exactly chockablock with clothing-optional beaches. There are really very few of note: Haulover and South Beach in Miami Beach, which has more of an international clientele, are the exceptions that prove the rule. Then there's Playalinda Beach, part of Canaveral National Seashore in Brevard County. Unlike the decadence that is accepted as a fact of life down in Miami Beach, nudity still raises eyebrows up around Cocoa Beach. Consequently, Playalinda Beach—whose north end is frequented by swimmers and sunbathers who like to take it all off—has been something of a political hot potato with the Moral Majority.

The babble of voices, pro and con, has made the issue a cause célèbre from time to time. Here's the lay of the land: As often occurs on federally owned beaches, an area on the beach (usually remote) becomes known by word of mouth and force of habit as a nude beach. Up at Playalinda Beach, on Canaveral National Seashore, the bathing suits melt away at the north end of Lot No. 13, where the road that follows the beach for four miles gives out. North of dune crossover No. 13B is where the fun really begins. The line of demarcation is pretty sharp. On one side, you have fishermen, many clad from head to toe in jeans and T-shirts, happily casting away. On the other, you have people who aren't wearing a stitch, happily baring their privates to wind, sun, and water.

The situation grew heated in the early 1990s, when park superintendent Wendell Simpson cracked down on what he saw as "lewd and lascivious behavior." In 1993, he oversaw the arrest of more than 100 nudists on sex charges. When no federal and state laws held up in court, he worked in concert with the conservative, Arizona-based National Family Legal Foundation to implement a law at the local level banning nudity. Brevard County ordinance 95-21 makes it illegal to be nude or wear a thong bathing suit in public. Adding to the fire was a visit by a congressman who checked out the scene after receiving complaints from constituents and promptly pronounced himself offended.

The prime movers are busybodies of the sort who stick their noses in everyone else's business under the guise of policing morals. They often turn out to be the same breed of conservatives, paradoxically, who scream bloody murder whenever government attempts

vital habitat for numerous species—1,045 plant and 310 bird species—including 15 that are federally listed as endangered or threatened.

There are two entrances into Canaveral National Seashore. From the north end—below New Smyrna Beach, in Volusia County—access is gained at Apollo Beach (see page 98). From the south, via state routes 406 and 402—which cut across the Merritt Island National Wildlife Refuge, east of Titusville—Canaveral is entered at Playalinda Beach. A paved road runs along Playalinda Beach for four miles, with parking lots spaced at regular intervals. Nudity prevails at Playalinda, though not without controversy (see sidebar), north of parking area #13.

However, it's what lies at the road's end, between Apollo and Playalinda Beaches, that's most intriguing: a 24-mile stretch of isolated shoreline known as **Klondike Beach.** To get there, you'll have to walk south from Apollo or north from Playa-

to regulate and rein in corporate misbehavior. The nudists have continued disrobing, testing both the legality and enforceability of the prohibition. An exasperated park ranger to whom we spoke had this to say: "How can we enforce an ordinance like that when there's 40 miles of beach and maybe one ranger on duty, and he's got to worry about collecting entrance fees and any real crimes that might get committed? We've got more important things to do."

To which we can only add, folks, it's really no big deal. You truly have to go out of your way to be offended. We saw no orgies nor heard any talk of a sexual nature being made on the beach. Just a bunch of naked people in the sand, tanning areas of the flesh that normally don't see the light of day. On a warm summer Saturday, we witnessed approximately 100 nude sunbathers along about a mile's worth of beach. They were mainly clumped a short distance north of the No. 13B crossover and thereafter thinned out quickly. Statistically, 80 percent were men and 20 percent women. Most of the nude sunbathers appeared to be gay males. Maybe a third of the remainder were true naturists and the rest of them heterosexual couples. One spread-eagled guy with jewelry piercing his genitals did qualify as perverted by almost any measure of such things. Even so, as we've said, you'd really have to go out of your way to be offended by him or anyone else at Playalinda Beach, and it's really not worth the trouble. There's too much beach out here to let a little sliver of naturism at one end ruin your day.

Although the standoff continues, it's simmered down somewhat since park superintendent Simpson took a new assignment in 1997. The Brevard County ordinance banning beach nudity is still on the books but goes unenforced. Only four citations were issued in 1999, for instance. One of us felt compelled to break the law as a kind of statement of personal freedom. For those who have never tried it, swimming nude in the great, balmy Atlantic in summertime is indeed a liberating feeling—unless visions of stinging jellyfish and Portuguese man-of-wars begin playing through your mind, that is, at which point a swimsuit does seem practical. And what of sunburn in unfathomable places?

By and large, we side with the nudists of Playalinda Beach, as long as they remain discreet. (As discreet as one can be in public without clothing, that is.) As for those conservative naysayers who are ashamed of their bodies and everyone else's, we have one bit of advice: Tend your own garden.

linda. It owes its roadless isolation to the vast Mosquito Lagoon (see sidebar), which lies behind it. You really have to want to be here. But why wouldn't you? The beach is desolate and striking. Saw palmetto and Spanish bayonet rustle at the edge of short, sandy bluffs that drop to the beach. There's rarely another soul in sight. It seems ironic that on a particularly built-up stretch of Florida's east coast, between the speedway at Daytona and the space center at Cocoa, lies one of the longest and loveliest wilderness beaches in the lower 48 states.

Admission to Canaveral National Seashore is $5 per day, per vehicle; an annual pass is available for $28 per vehicle. Facilities are few: restrooms and drinking fountains at the visitor centers (which also feature informative exhibits on the area) and primitive toilets at parking lots along the beach. Boat docks to Mosquito Lagoon are located near the park's main information center, seven miles south of New Smyrna Beach on High-

Mosquito Lagoon

A few words about Mosquito Lagoon are in order. Running the length of Cape Canaveral National Seashore, it is the northernmost body of water in the 156-mile Indian River Lagoon. Mosquito Lagoon used to be the kind of place that drove folks buggy, being a haven for saltwater mosquitoes. Here's a statistic that'll make you itchy: At their most productive, the area's salt marshes are capable of producing a million mosquitoes per square yard per day! However, the conversion of 69,000 acres of salt marsh into diked freshwater impoundments has allowed for pest control on a grand scale. Lately, however, an effort has been under way to reverse alterations to the natural system by restoring the salt marsh and reconnecting the lagoon with the impoundments. Therefore, be sure to bring bug spray, as Mosquito Lagoon is again living up to its name. Bring your fishing pole, too. Mosquito Lagoon is a nationally renowned fishing spot. Catches include redfish and spotted trout. Clam and oyster beds also thrive in the shallows.

Abundant wildlife thrives around and in the lagoon, which supports an ecosystem of extremely high biological diversity. Among other things, 20 percent of the mangrove forests in the eastern United States are found here. The health of Mosquito Lagoon has become a hot issue. Threatened by various human-generated affronts—wastewater pumped into it by the communities of Edgewater and New Smyrna Beach, sediment-laden storm-water runoff from developments in the area, sea grass scarring by boat propellers, and bacterial contamination from leaking septic tanks—Mosquito Lagoon is a system out of balance. Remedial projects include the installation of sediment traps and the restoration of mangroves. Researchers at the University of Central Florida and the Harbor Branch Oceanographic Institution have been studying biodiversity and "biological fouling" in Mosquito Lagoon.

If you want to learn more about Mosquito Lagoon and its restoration, contact the Environmental Learning Center, 255 Live Oak Drive, Vero Beach, FL 32963; 561/589-5050; website: indian-river.fl.us/elc.

❶ Klondike Beach

Location: These 24 miles of wilderness beach, accessible only by foot, are located at the center of Canaveral National Seashore, between Apollo Beach (south end of Volusia County) and Playalinda Beach (north end of Brevard County).
Parking/fees: $5 per vehicle, per day, to enter Cape Canaveral National Seashore
Hours: 6 A.M.–6 P.M.
Facilities: none
Contact: Canaveral National Seashore, 321/267-1110

way A1A. Boat ramps to the lagoon are located at parking area #5 in the North District and at Eddy Creek. Bring a cooler with water and other beverages. In the blazing heat of summer, you will dehydrate quickly without frequent replenishment.

Contact Information

Canaveral National Seashore, 308 Julia Street, Titusville, FL 32796; 321/267-1110; website: www.nps.gov/cana. For information on surf conditions and launch closures at Playalinda Beach, call 321/867-2805.

Cape Canaveral

Cape Canaveral (pop. 8,900) lies east of Kennedy Space Center and above Cocoa Beach. It is so close to the latter that residential Cape Canaveral is practically indistinguishable from north Cocoa Beach. In fact, the two communities merge seamlessly, at least on the ocean. The character of Cape Canaveral is really shaped by Port Canaveral, off Highway A1A up at the north end. The port is an enormous complex of container ships, cruise ships, charter boats, storage facilities, docks, restaurants, and parks. Whether you're heading to the Bahamas aboard Canaveral Cruise Lines or merely want a seafood dinner on the waterfront, Port Canaveral is the busy, bustling heart of Cape Canaveral.

Beaches

Jetty Park is one of three parks run by the Port Authority. Its campground is close to the park's half-mile beach, which offers swell views of ships coming and going from the port. On the grounds are a bait-and-tackle shop and a 1,000-foot fishing pier; beach rentals and year-round lifeguards, too. All for a measly $3 per car entrance fee. Many improvements are currently underway, including upgrade of utilities, the bike path, signs, landscaping, a new entry building, and a rustic parking/general use area in the southeast corner.

Cape Canaveral also lays claim to peachy-keen **Cherie Down Park**, a charming seven-acre beachside park, plus public beach access via dune walkovers at about half a dozen spots along more than two miles of beach.

Bunking Down

"Location, location, location" is the catchphrase of the real-estate industry. With that in mind, we'll give you two choices in Cape Canaveral. If you want to be near Port Canaveral, book at the **Radisson Cape Canaveral Resort** (8701 Astronaut Boulevard, 321/784-0000, $$$). If you want to be on the beach, try the **Cape Winds Resort** (7400 Ridgewood Drive, 321/783-6226, $$$), a 67-unit "condo motel" that comes complete with tennis and basketball courts and free breakfast.

2 Playalinda Beach

Location: from I-95, take Exit 80 (State Route 406) at Titusville. After crossing the Indian River, take a right fork onto State Route 402 and continue east to the beach. From Cocoa Beach, take Highway A1A north to State Route 528 and proceed west to State Route 3. Follow State Route 3 north to State Route 402, then turn right (east) and proceed to the beach.
Parking/fees: $5 per vehicle, per day, to enter Cape Canaveral National Seashore
Hours: 6 A.M.–6 P.M.
Facilities: restrooms and a visitor center
Contact: Canaveral National Seashore, 321/267-1110

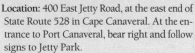

3 Jetty Park

Location: 400 East Jetty Road, at the east end of State Route 528 in Cape Canaveral. At the entrance to Port Canaveral, bear right and follow signs to Jetty Park.
Parking/fees: $3 per car entrance fee ($7 for RVs). Camping fees are $23–26 for RV sites and $19 for rustic tent sites
Hours: 24 hours
Facilities: concessions, lifeguards, restrooms, picnic tables, and showers
Contact: Jetty Park Campground, 321/783-7111

MAP OF BREVARD COUNTY—PAGE 100

Space Is the Place: A Quick Tour of Kennedy Space Center

The closest place to the moon in this world is the Kennedy Space Center, just above Port Canaveral on Florida's Space Coast. We've toured the complex a couple of times: in the mid-1980s, when we were not so impressed, and in the late '90s, when we were highly impressed by the quality of the tour and what we saw. In fact, we left the grounds dreaming the dream of every kid who grew up in the '60s of wanting to become an astronaut. It's a little late for us, but you can still blast off into that fantasy by visiting the Kennedy Space Center. It is the premier man-made attraction in all of Florida, beating Daytona USA and the Disney World colossus hands down. That is because it speaks eloquently to the most high-minded, transcendent strivings of the human species. We are talking about real-life miracles here.

The Kennedy Space Center is set a good distance from urban buildup, surrounded by the splendidly isolated acreage of Canaveral National Seashore and Merritt Island National Wildlife Refuge. Nearly three million people visit the space center yearly. The public obsession with the space program was driven home when we saw a 400-pound tourist in a polka-dot dress jog up to the counter at a Cocoa Beach motel lobby and blurt, "Is there going to be a space blast tonight? Is there going to be a rocket blast?"

If you were to relocate the United Nations inside Grand Central Station, you'd have an idea of the Kennedy Space Center Visitor Complex ticketing area, which teems with humanity chattering in many languages. Here's where you pay up and begin your tour. And when we say "pay up," we are not kidding. It pains us to report that admission fees at Kennedy Space Center have gone sky-high. Whereas a few years ago an adult could take a bus tour of the complex for $10, view an IMAX film for $6 and enjoy many exhibits in and around the Visitor Center for free, they are now charging an exorbitant single fee of $24 per adult ($15 for kids 3–11). It's good, they claim, for all tours, exhibits, and movies—except for the "historic tour" of the *Mercury, Gemini,* and *Apollo* launch pads. If you want to see those, the per-person charge leaps to $44! Oh, and the new "NASA Close Up" Tour, a more in-depth version of the general tour, costs an additional $20 per person. So does the guided "wildlife tour" of Merritt Island Wildlife Refuge.

Come early and plan on spending a big chunk of the day here, so that you leave feeling you got your money's worth. A family of four with kids who are older than 11 will ante up nearly $100 just to get in the door. Factor in another $80 to see the older

Coastal Cuisine

People head up to The Cove at Port Canaveral for dinner and nightlife. Ample servings of both can be had at a gigantic operation known as **Lloyd's Canaveral Feast** (610 Glen Creek Drive, 321/784-9031, $$), a combination seafood restaurant, indoor casino, and outdoor deck bar that's as large as some of the hangars at the Kennedy Space Center. **Rusty's Seafood & Oyster Bar** (628 Glen Creek Drive, 321/783-2033, $$) is casual and inexpensive, serving 25-cent oysters at happy hour (3 P.M.–6

launch pads or the "NASA Close Up" tour or the "KSC Wildlife Tour." Not to rock the spacecraft, but this smacks of rip-off. Since the space program is subsidized with American taxpayers' money, shouldn't we the people get to look it over without being pickpocketed? Shouldn't something as educational and historic as this be offered a bit more affordably, since it is part of our national heritage? Is the government aware of this gouging?

The Kennedy Space Center tour includes the Apollo/Saturn V Center (not to be missed!), the space shuttle launch pads, and a full-scale replica of the International Space Station Center. Two IMAX films—*The Dream Is Alive,* a space shuttle documentary, and *L5: First City in Space,* a fictional view of a future space settlement—play all day. The first of these is the one to see; it documents a shining moment in the domestic space program and contains outstanding footage of our little blue marble from the depths of space.

The Apollo/Saturn V Center is another must-see. The *Saturn V* rocket that launched *Apollo VIII* has been laid out across the length of the exhibit building, and its size—the very idea that this 363-foot and 6,200,000-pound behemoth overcame gravity and propelled a capsule into space—is enough to take your breath away. This it did with more horsepower (160,000,000 hp) than 8,000 starting fields in the Daytona 500. Then there's the Vehicle Assembly Building, a 525-foot-high building where these marvels are put together.

At the height of the Apollo program, the space center employed 3,000 workers. Here's another factlet: The average *Apollo* astronaut was 32 years old, 5 feet 10 inches tall, and weighed 164 pounds. By the way, wanna meet an astronaut? Every day of the year a real live astronaut takes questions from tour groups and reminisces about his or her adventures in space. It's a guaranteed thrill for kids of all ages—including baby boomers like us who grew up watching the space race.

If we recited all the facts thrown at us on the tour, we'd be well on our way toward writing another book. Suffice it to say that though you may suffer sticker shock from the hiked admission prices, you'll still have a wonderful time at the Kennedy Space Center. It is almost literally out of this world.

To get there from I-95 or U.S. 1, take State Route 405 east to NASA Parkway and follow signs to the Kennedy Space Center Visitor Complex. From Cocoa Beach, take State Route 520 north to State Route 528 west, then proceed north on State Route 3 to NASA Parkway and the visitor complex. Kennedy Space Center Visitor Complex is open daily, except Christmas and certain launch days, from 9 A.M. to dusk.

For more information contact the Kennedy Space Center Visitor Complex, Delaware North Park Services, Kennedy Space Center, FL 32899; 321/452-2121; website: www.ksc.nasa.gov.

P.M. daily) and a raft of dinner choices—sandwiches, fried seafood baskets, early-bird specials, and nightly deals on entrées like blackened grouper and mahimahi—for eight bucks or less. Wander around the cove and you'll find some other spots that serve grouper, oysters, beer and live music in casual surroundings. That's just the cut of this area's jib, mate.

Night Moves

The bar at Rusty's (see above) is a cool place to down beer and oysters. There's often live music, usually reggae, coming from at least a few other places on the water at the Cove at Port Canaveral. Just keep your antennae up as you stroll along, and duck inside when you hear something agreeable. Or keep walking and enjoy the bobbing vessels, as we did, if you don't.

Contact Information

Cocoa Beach Area Chamber of Commerce, 400 Fortenberry Road, Merritt Island, FL 32952; 321/459-2200; website: www.cocoabeachchamber.com

Space Coast Office of Tourism, 8810 Astronaut Boulevard, Suite 102, Cape Canaveral, FL 32920; 321/868-1126 or 800/93-OCEAN; website: www.spacecoast.com

❹ Cherie Down Park

Location: 8492 Ridgewood Avenue in Cape Canaveral
Parking/fees: free parking lot
Hours: 7 A.M. to dusk
Facilities: lifeguards (seasonal), restrooms, picnic tables, and showers
Contact: Brevard County Parks and Recreation Department (central service sector), 321/455-1380

❺ Cape Canaveral

Location: There are 2.3 miles of beaches, from Washington Avenue south to Wilson Avenue, off Ridgewood Avenue in Cape Canaveral.
Parking/fees: free street parking, plus free parking lots at the ends of Grant, Hayes, Garfield, Arthur, and Wilson Avenues
Hours: none posted
Facilities: none
Contact: Cape Canaveral Public Works Department, 321/868-1240

Cocoa Beach

Cocoa Beach (pop. 12,800) is indelibly linked to two things: the Kennedy Space Center and its world-class beach, which is not cocoa colored but a light golden brown of medium coarseness. This attachment to space and sand has prevented the town from developing much of a personality of its own. It doesn't really need to, because its accessibility to these attractions is a sufficient draw for the tourism that pumps everything up out here. Everything about Cocoa Beach seems aimed at striking the Golden Mean: the sand, food, motels, nightlife.

It's a family-friendly beach town whose selling point is affordability. The local tourist board boasts that the average price of a Cocoa Beach motel room is $47 per night. Given the kind of beach that it sits on, this is a real bargain. In fact, we'd argue that with Orlando only an hour away and the Kennedy Space Center just minutes away, it's sensible to make Cocoa Beach home base for your central Florida vacation. Think about it: you'll pay more to stay in landlocked Orlando, which doesn't have Cocoa's beach or cooling sea breezes—just Mickey Mouse's outstretched palm. Moreover, instead of the outstretched palm, Cocoa Beach has swaying palms, tree-lined neighborhoods, good traffic flow and an appealingly low-key demeanor. It is the proverbial golden mean of beach town.

Cocoa Beach first asserted its modest claim to fame when John F. Kennedy ignited the country with astronaut fever back in the early 1960s. His exact words: "Surely the opening vistas of space promise high costs and hardships, as well as high rewards. But Man in his quest for knowledge and progress is determined and cannot be deterred. For the eyes of the world now look into space, to the moon, and to the planets beyond." The luster and pizzazz of the space program helped bring to life an area that was otherwise known largely for citrus groves.

With NASA's burgeoning budget came an influx of professionals: engineers, designers, technicians, and assistants. Before the astronauts, Tom Wolfe wrote in *The Right Stuff*, "Cocoa Beach was the resort town for all the low-rent folks who couldn't afford the resort towns further south." In the wake of their arrival, however, "Cocoa Beach [began] to take on the raw excitement of a boom town and the manic and motley cast of characters that goes with it." Which is to say that it didn't change all that much, passing from a sleepy, low-rent resort town to one with

6 Cocoa Beach (north end)

Location: 1.5 miles of beach, from Harding Avenue south to Flagler Lane
Parking/fees: metered parking lots at the ends of Harding, Barlow, Mead, Pulsipher, and Winslow Avenues, and at the ends of Leon, Osceola, Gadsden, Marion, Palm, and Flagler Lanes
Hours: dawn till dusk
Facilities: none
Contact: Cocoa Beach Parks Department, 321/868-3274

7 Sheppard Park

Location: east end of State Route 520, off Ridgewood Avenue in Cocoa Beach
Parking/fees: $3 per vehicle entrance fee
Hours: dawn till dusk
Facilities: lifeguards (seasonal), restrooms, picnic tables, and showers
Contact: Cocoa Beach Parks Department, 321/868-3274

MAP OF BREVARD COUNTY—PAGE 100

a quicker pulse and a bit more money circulating through it.

What held true of Cocoa Beach in 1960 remains true today, to a great degree. Hemmed in by the Kennedy Space Center to the north and Patrick Air Force Base to the south, Cocoa Beach combines the nondescript personality of a military town with the nondescript personality of a just-folks beach town. Steady growth over the years has wrought miles of malls, restaurant rows, gas stations, and convenience marts, all jockeying to fill any available square footage. Along the ocean, you'll find a more or less unbroken wall of hotels, motels, and condos. Yet it's all a bit more pleasant in reality than this description makes it sound, especially on the oceanfront. Beachside parks, such as Lori Wilson Park, break up the monotony of buildings, and toward the south end of town Cocoa Beach takes on a more residential, neighborhood feeling, with beach access gained at street ends. One nice thing about Cocoa Beach is that traffic flow-through on the beach is discontinuous. This makes for a less traffic-choked beachfront and one with discrete pockets of activity, such as Cocoa Beach Pier. It is nowhere near the thundering racetrack you'll find up the road in Daytona Beach, for instance.

Finally, how can you not like a community that named one of its side streets after Major Anthony Nelson, the fictional astronaut of *I Dream of Jeannie* fame?

Beaches

Cocoa Beach is the most crowded stretch of Brevard County's long, unbroken beach strand, which runs from Port Canaveral to Sebastian Inlet. This is a quintessential American beach: green water and a wide, coarse-grained and sometimes steep brown-sand beach peopled with visitors of every race, creed, color, and swimsuit size. They tend to congregate most densely around the Cocoa Beach Pier, located on Atlantic and Meade avenues up toward the north end of town. Surfers ride the waves on either side of the pier. Kids splash and frolic. Parents repose on chaise lounges and surf chairs. The only thing missing from this picture is lifeguards. The lack of lifeguards around the populated pier seems an obvious demerit against Cocoa Beach, and one that should be addressed and remedied, because the beach itself is a treasure.

In addition to a vast beach strand accessible from street ends (useful if you're not staying on the ocean), four beachside parks offer free or inexpensive parking, restrooms, outdoor showers, and picnic tables. They are, from north to south, **Sheppard Park, Sidney Fischer Park, Lori Wilson Park** and **Robert P. Murkshe Memorial Park.** All but Murkshe post sea-

8 Sidney Fischer Park

Location: one-half mile south of State Route 520 on Highway A1A in Cocoa Beach
Parking/fees: $3 per vehicle entrance fee
Hours: dawn till dusk
Facilities: lifeguards (seasonal), restrooms, picnic tables, and showers
Contact: Cocoa Beach Parks Department, 321/868-3274

9 Lori Wilson Park

Location: 1500 North Atlantic Avenue (Highway A1A) in Cocoa Beach
Parking/fees: $1 per vehicle parking fee
Hours: 7 A.M. to dusk
Facilities: lifeguards (seasonal), restrooms, picnic tables, and showers
Contact: Brevard County Parks and Recreation Department (central service sector), 321/455-1380

sonal lifeguards as well. We are especially fond of the county-run Lori Wilson Park, at which a boardwalk nature trail winds through a patch of maritime forest.

Directly south of Lori Wilson is an area known as **Seacrest Beach.** It's more of Cocoa's abundant brown-sand beach, with ample parking a few blocks south of Lori Wilson along Tulip Avenue. Below this area, the east-west streets are numbered, the island thins a bit, and Highway A1A hugs the shore more closely. In South Cocoa Beach, below Highway A1A's intersection with Minuteman Causeway (State Route 520), the beach can be accessed via street ends from 4th Street north to 15th Street south. Down at this end, motels and commercial buildup gradually give way to a modest residential neighborhood where it's not unusual to find homes with pink flamingos staked into the front yards. The beaches themselves are narrower, but they're pleasantly uncrowded, being removed from the pierside bustle up at the north end. The island reaches its narrowest point around **South Cocoa/North Patrick Beach**, roughly from Olive Street south to 35th Street. The most popular spot along this strip is **Crescent Beach**, unsurprisingly located at the end of Crescent Beach Drive.

Incidentally, if you'd like to hear a prerecorded surf report, you've got your choice of three, each provided by a Cocoa Beach surf shop: **Ron Jon** (800/717-BEACH), **Quiet Flight** (321/783-6640), and **Natural Art** (321/784-2400). The concentration of surf shops in Cocoa Beach reflects the fact that the area offers some of the best surfing on the central Florida coast—especially at the Cocoa Beach Pier and down around Patrick Air Force Base and Sebastian Inlet in southern Brevard County.

Shore Things

- **Bike/skate rentals:** Ten Speed Drive Bicycle Center, 166 North Atlantic Avenue, 321/783-1196.
- **Ecotourism:** Funday Eco Tours, 1905 Atlantic Street, Melbourne, 321/725-0796.
- **Fishing charters:** Port Canaveral Sportfishing Charters, 626 Glen Creek Drive, Cape Canaveral, 321/784-6444.
- **Marina:** Cape Marina at Port Canaveral, 800 Scallop Drive, Cape Canaveral, 321/783-8410.
- **Pier:** Cocoa Beach Pier, 5240 North Atlantic Avenue, 321/783-7549.
- **Rainy-day attraction:** Kennedy Space Center, 321/452-2121.
- **Shopping/browsing:** Cocoa Village, U.S. 1 and State Route 520, Cocoa, 321/631-9075.
- **Surf shop:** Ron Jon Surf Shop, 4151 North Atlantic Avenue, 321/799-8820.
- **Vacation rentals:** Cocoa Beach Realty, 120 Canaveral Plaza, 321/783-4200.

Bunking Down

In keeping with its image as a no-frills plain-cloth kind of town, the upscaling of Cocoa Beach's oceanfront has been held to a minimum. What you have on the oceanfront are a lot of perfectly attractive, comfortable, and commodious chain hotels and motels. The Radissons, for instance, are down at Satellite Beach and up at Port Canaveral. Motels of the Days Inn, Comfort Inn, and Econo-Lodge class are plentiful in Cocoa Beach, however. And they are absolutely adequate for a stay at the beach. The Days Inn is an exemplar of that chain and perhaps the nicest place on Cocoa's oceanfront. It's certainly the best situated, being a few steps north of the pier and extending from the beach back a block and a half. The grounds are nicely landscaped with palm trees and tropical vegetation, and the property is

MAP OF BREVARD COUNTY—PAGE 100

well maintained. All things considered, it would be our first choice in Cocoa Beach.

Here's a rundown of lodging prices along the ocean, based on an informal survey of Cocoa Beach hotels and motels conducted while jogging along Ocean Beach Boulevard one hot July morning. This exercise in data collection gave us a legitimate excuse to duck into hotel lobbies for water breaks. We asked the price for a standard room, two persons, two beds, on a busy summer weekend:

- **Best Western Ocean Inn** (5500 North Atlantic Avenue, 321/784-2550, $89) is a half-block back from the beach and nets big savings.
- **Comfort Inn and Suites Resort** (3901 North Atlantic Avenue, 321/783-2221, $94) is right next door to Ron Jon Surf Shop!
- **Days Inn Oceanfront** (5600 North Atlantic Avenue, 321/783-7621, $152) has the best of all possible locations: on the beach, just up from the Cocoa Beach Pier.
- **Discovery Beach and Tennis Resort** (300 Barlow Avenue, 321/868-7777, $205) is a well-located older property with tennis courts atop its parking garage.
- **Hampton Inn** (3425 North Atlantic Avenue, 321/799-4099, $129) is the newest arrival in Cocoa Beach, and fairly gleams.
- **Hilton Oceanfront Cocoa Beach** (1550 North Atlantic Avenue, 321/799-0003, $139) is top-of-the-line in Cocoa Beach. It's seven stories tall and first-rate all the way, boasting a snazzy pool deck that opens onto a quiet sliver of beach. There is one downside: late check-in (4 P.M.), early check-out (11 A.M.).
- **Holiday Inn Cocoa Beach** (1300 North Atlantic Avenue, 321/783-2271, $109) is a gleaming, 500-unit compound sprawled across sizable landscaped grounds.
- **Doubletree** (2080 North Atlantic Avenue, 321/783-9222, $109) was formerly a Howard Johnson's Hotel. Now refurbished, it has rooms in both a plaza tower and a courtyard, plus a grand ocean observation deck.
- **Inn at Cocoa Beach** (4300 Ocean Beach Boulevard, 321/799-3460, $125) is a newish pink oceanfront beauty with the look of a hotel and the manner of a bed-and-breakfast.
- **Ocean Suites Hotel** (5500 Ocean Beach Boulevard, 321/784-4343, $89) is a bargain, and it's pierside to boot!

Bear in mind that prices fluctuate wildly according to what types of rooms are available, whether you booked in advance or are walking in off the street that day, discounts that may apply (AAA, AARP, hotel-club membership, website deals, coupons you may have picked up), and

⑩ Seacrest Beach

Location: south of Lori Wilson Park on North Atlantic Avenue (Highway A1A) in Cocoa Beach
Parking/fees: metered street parking on Ivy and Holly Avenues and a metered parking lot at the end of Tulip Avenue
Hours: dawn till dusk
Facilities: none
Contact: Cocoa Beach Parks Department, 321/868-3274

⑪ Cocoa Beach (south end)

Location: between North 4th Street and South 15th Street in Cocoa Beach
Parking/fees: metered street parking
Hours: dawn till dusk
Facilities: none
Contact: Cocoa Beach Parks Department, 321/868-3274

what the market will bear in a given season. That is to say, we do not claim this price list to be a firm and precise accounting of what you will pay at a given Cocoa Beach hotel or motel during your summertime stay. But it will be in the ballpark and at least provide a useful basis for comparison.

Bringing up the rear, in terms of price, is **Motel 6** (3701 North Atlantic Avenue, 321/783-3103). At $45 per night in summer. It is easily the best deal in Cocoa Beach, as the rooms are large, the appointments decent, and the location one street-width shy of the ocean. Moreover, it is only a few blocks south of Ron Jon Surf Shop (see Shore Things, above). What more do you want from a motel than a clean, comfortable room with a bed you can sleep on, a bearable bathroom with shower, and a TV that doesn't flicker like something that's been salvaged from a Salvation Army thrift shop? You get all the basics and a large courtyard pool at Motel 6, plus a major break on price. And they'll leave the light on for you.

Coastal Cuisine

We've got a couple favorite Cocoa Beach restaurants at the high end of the dining experience. They are relatively close together in what passes for "downtown" Cocoa Beach, near the middle of Atlantic Avenue (where "North" changes to "South").

First up is **Bernard's Surf** (2 South Atlantic Avenue, 321/783-2401, $$$$). This old reliable has been in business since 1948. Five decades of success in a fickle beach town is saying something. Bernard's itself has kept pace with changing times and tastes while sticking to the basics done well. Gone are the exotic menu items that made the restaurant a gourmet novelty in bygone decades—things like zebra and antelope steaks and various preparations of ants, grasshoppers, caterpillars, and (our ol' favorite) "chocolate-covered baby bees." As the U.S. Customs Service tightened up on importation of such comestibles, they were dropped from the menu.

We promise you won't miss dining on bees or ants when you've got such venerable standbys as Snapper à la Surf (baked red snapper topped with scallops, crabmeat, and a white sauce) and Grouper Française (a grouper fillet dusted with flour, dipped in egg wash, and served with a white wine butter sauce). They make a great, tangy Caesar salad from scratch at your table. For starters, be sure to try the Cajun gator tail, tasty little bites of tenderized alligator nuggets, or mushroom caps stuffed with crabmeat. There are a number of good dessert choices, but Bernard's flambés—peppered strawberries and bananas Foster—are irresistibly good. They're prepared tableside, and it's quite a show. They'll even set a cup of coffee, fortified with various liqueurs, on fire for you at meal's end.

Bernard's Surf is joined by two other on-premises eateries that appeal to different clienteles. **Fischer's Seafood Bar and Grill** (2 South Atlantic Avenue, 321/783-2401, $$$) is a meat-and-potatoes type room that projects a hearty, robust masculinity. **Rusty's Seafood & Oyster Bar** (2 South Atlantic Avenue, 321/783-2401, $$) is more casual and affordable. Waitresses clad in scanty Hooters-style ensembles

⓬ Robert P. Murkshe Memorial Park

Location: Highway A1A and South 16th Street in Cocoa Beach
Parking/fees: free parking lot
Hours: 7 A.M. till dusk
Facilities: restrooms, picnic tables, and showers
Contact: Brevard County Parks and Recreation Department (central service sector), 321/455-1380

bustle about the place. The Bernard's/Fischer's/Rusty's triplex covers all the bases in Cocoa Beach under one roof.

Then there's the **Mango Tree Inn** (118 North Atlantic Avenue, 321/799-0513, $$$$), a superlative restaurant set in an old home on Atlantic Avenue. The building has been added to over the years to accommodate the restaurant's growing clientele. Inside, the house is packed like a museum with artwork, aquariums, and greenery. The greenhouse effect continues outside into a lavish jungle of gardens. The owners, who cultivate orchids as a pastime, have turned Mango Tree's gardens into a world unto itself. The only thing missing is an actual mango tree; they grow well on nearby Merritt Island but, for some reason, don't take to Cocoa Beach.

As for the food, prepare to submit yourself to some of the most sophisticated and cosmopolitan cuisine outside a major urban center. It's all the more exceptional in Cocoa Beach, which otherwise tends toward fast-food shanties. Here's a meal actually savored by one of us, from start to finish: seared ahi with wasabi and teriyaki for an appetizer; seafood bisque; cornmeal-encrusted grouper with Dijon-hollandaise sauce; coffee with a shot of Godiva dark chocolate liqueur; and a large hunk of homemade key lime pie. That's what was served on one side of the table. On the other: an entrée-sized portion of Maryland-style lump crab cakes for an appetizer; salad with homemade vinaigrette dressing; seared filet mignon of tuna... ah, this is beginning to sound too much like bragging.

Like the restaurant itself, the food is beautifully presented. Piano music wafted throughout the restaurant on our last visit. When we cornered the old gent tickling the ivories between sets, he waxed poetic about the days of the big bands. An extensive wine list complements a delectable menu. You simply cannot go wrong at this gracious, romantic restaurant, which hits culinary heights as lofty as the atmospheric ones reached by rockets launched out of the Kennedy Space Center.

For a simpler seafood dinner (hold the atmosphere), there's **Florida's Seafood Bar & Grill** (480 West Cocoa Beach Causeway, 321/784-0892, $$), located on the FL 520 causeway between Cocoa and Cocoa Beach. We'd recommend the rock shrimp or one of their shrimp sampler platters that has rock shrimp as an option. Rock shrimp are spiny shelled shrimp that taste like lobster. Dip these tasty little suckers in butter and/or cocktail sauce. Their motto is "Where Shrimp Happens," but don't overlook the stone crab cakes and

13 South Cocoa/ North Patrick Beach

Location: between Olive Street (in south Cocoa Beach) and Patrick Drive (in North Patrick), on Highway A1A
Parking/fees: free parking lots at Fern Street, and free street parking at the end of Summer Street, Sunny Lane, between 26th and 35th Streets, and South Patrick and East Patrick Drives
Hours: dawn till dusk
Facilities: none
Contact: Cocoa Beach Parks Department, 321/868-3274

14 Crescent Beach

Location: Crescent Beach Drive at Highway A1A in South Cocoa
Parking/fees: free parking lot
Hours: dawn till dusk
Facilities: none
Contact: Cocoa Beach Parks Department, 321/868-3274

calico scallops, either. The atmosphere is pure Florida kitsch, with lots of burbling aquariums, nautical-themed wall murals, carved fish and birds, and a youthful wait staff.

Finally, there are four restaurants on the Cocoa Beach Pier, the most notable among them (for seafood lovers) being **Atlantic Ocean Grille** (401 Meade Avenue, 321/783-7549, $$).

Night Moves

We were a bit confused when a surfer dude hanging out at the Mango Tree Inn's bar started talking about "sleepy old Cocoa Beach" when we inquired about the nightlife. Wasn't this the "redneck Riviera" and the "surfing capital of the East Coast?" We had visions of *Animal House* by the sea, with hooting, hollering crowds knocking back longnecks while the mother of all wet T-shirt contests went on into the wee hours. He just smiled and tossed out a few suggestions, saying we might find a rock band here or a jazz trio there or a bit of a crowd up the road at this or that place. By God, he had the Cocoa Beach scene nailed. We searched for decent nightlife and pulled up an empty net.

In our futile search for something to do, Cocoa Beach's lack of personality surfaced with repeatedly disappointing encounters. Here's what transpired at several places we dropped by on consecutive weekend nights at summer's height. At the **Surfside Cafe** (211 East Cocoa Beach Causeway, 321/799-9977), an oceanfront lounge and eatery with two levels and an outdoor deck, we watched a Caucasian trio plod through Bob Marley's "No Woman, No Cry" to a sparse crowd as last call beckoned. At **Time Out Sports Bar** (1275 North Atlantic Avenue, 321/783-2252) on the second floor of the Econo-Lodge ("Where It's Ladies Nite Every Nite!"), another Bob Marley tune played as a seedy clientele shuffled around pool tables or stared glumly into drinks at the bar. The Marley song was "Buffalo Soldiers," and in its military spirit we beat a hasty retreat. At **Plum's Lounge** at the Holiday Inn (1300 North Atlantic Avenue, 321/783-2271), another three-quarters empty room was peopled with flush-faced middle-agers gamely attempting to rekindle lost adolescence to the familiar strains of beach music. At **Oh Shucks Seafood Bar** on the Cocoa Beach Pier (401 Meade Avenue, 321/783-4050), we'd earlier been part of a late-afternoon crowd noisily imbibing to a three-man reggae band and their tapes. But by nightfall, when we returned hoping for more of the same sort of action, Oh Shucks was closed. Oh, shucks!

Our luck turned when we impulsively decided to check out a place called **Lido Cabaret** (formerly Teasers, 104 Cleveland Avenue, 321/783-9317), on Highway A1A at the north end of Cocoa Beach. Which way it turned, we're still trying to figure out. You can probably surmise that this is not a milk bar or a Bible Belt bookstore. It is a strip club where beer and table dances are served to a crowd that is thirsty and horny in equal measure. What inspired us to visit was the parking lot, by far the fullest we'd seen in Cocoa Beach. It costs five bucks to get in. Then you really start flashing the cash for beer and lap dances, if you're so bold. Figure about four dollars apiece for the former and a buck a minute for the latter. It's a great way to deplete a paycheck in no time flat, and we saw all kinds of working stiffs doing just that. Let's just say that at Lido Cabaret, you won't lack for attention or titillation.

Memorable moment: the raw repartee of the deejay and lewd writhings of the dancers stopped for a brief intermission, during which it was announced that one of the dancers had recently given birth. The fulsome ballad "Butterfly Kisses" was played over the P.A. in honor of the blessed event. Somehow, the moment didn't seem as warm and fuzzy as it did incongruous. "Butterfly

Ron Jon Surf Shop

One thing you can do at Cocoa Beach that can be done nowhere else, aside from watching space shuttle launches at close range, is shop for surfwear in the middle of the night. If Cocoa Beach nightlife is pedestrian and disappointing, there's always Ron Jon Surf Shop (3850 South Banana River Boulevard, 321/799-8888 or 888/RJ-SURFS), which is open 24 hours a day, seven days a week, all year round. We've certainly availed ourselves of the opportunity to buy T-shirts at three in the morning. One time we even browsed the racks at Ron Jon's—would we lie to you?—during a hurricane. It was Hurricane Irene, which blew through on October 16, 1999. The store remained open, even as hotels and restaurants in the area lost electricity and roads flooded. While rain and wind pelted the windows, we calmly compared logoed T-shirts.

Located where the State Route 520 causeway meets Atlantic Avenue (A1A), Ron Jon is the Taj Mahal of surf shops. You simply can't miss it. A complex of buildings bathed in hot neon pink and turquoise, it dominates the landscape like nothing else in Cocoa Beach, including its tallest hotels. First, there's Ron Jon's "sports park," a combination sculpture garden and parking lot with towering life-size depictions of surfers frozen in the act of catching a monster wave. The main building is the cathedral, devoted to retailing a holy kingdom's worth of T-shirts, walking shorts, swimsuits, ball caps, and other apparel. Two other buildings rent and sell recreation equipment, from surfboards to Jet Skis, but the main show is the T-shirt emporium. At midnight on a Friday, Ron Jon's is likely to be doing more business than most nightclubs in Cocoa Beach.

Indeed, one cannot leave town without a shirt upon which the Ron Jon logo has been emblazoned. If you're a modest suburbanite, a three-button henley with a discreet Ron Jon logo will suffice. If you're a hip, urban-dwelling Gen X-er, a T-shirt with a huge glow-in-the-dark Ron Jon logo on the back is a must.

The irony is that if you're a real surfer and not just a gremmie or wannabe, you'll probably be found nowhere near Ron Jon. It's simply too big, too touristy. Surfers prefer more dedicated, less commercial shops run by members of the tribe: fellow board bums and board shapers. To them, a place like Ron Jon—52,000 square feet of clothing, souvenirs, and surfboards—is a tourists-only blasphemy. We're not quite so elitist about it, so we had a fine time browsing the racks at Ron Jon in the wee hours. They tend to go to places like **Quiet Flight Surfboards** (109 North Orlando Boulevard, 407/783-1530) and **Natural Art Surf Shop** (2370 South Atlantic Avenue, 407/783-0764).

A visit to Ron Jon can be entertaining, but it also must be noted that it's a little like historian Daniel Boorstin's definition of "celebrity" in his book *The Image*. Endless Ron Jon billboards line I-95, causing a visual blight second only to South of the Border's infamous roadside procession in the Carolinas. The Ron Jon logo is well known because it is well known. You simply must have a Ron Jon T-shirt because . . . you simply must. You know?

Incidentally, Ron Jon now has its own resorts: one in Orlando, one in Ormond Beach. This drives home the point that Ron Jon is not only a surf shop but a burgeoning commercial empire.

Kisses" at a strip club? Soon enough, the metallic din of rock and rap resumed, and the gals got back down to taking it all off. Business as usual, 24 hours a day.

Contact Information

Cocoa Beach Area Chamber of Commerce, 400 Fortenberry Road, Merritt Island, FL 32952; 321/459-2200; website: www.cocoabeachchamber.com

Space Coast Office of Tourism, 8810 Astronaut Boulevard, Suite 102, Cape Canaveral, FL 32920; 321/868-1126 or 800/93-OCEAN; website: www.space-coast.com

Patrick Air Force Base and South Patrick Shores

The first five miles of South Brevard's beaches fall under the stealthy wing of an air force base. From all outward appearances (read: staring enviously through iron fencing along the west side of Highway A1A), Patrick AFB (pop. 1,400) is the place to be stationed if you want to become a Top Gun. The grounds are as lush and well maintained as a country club, the housing neat and tidy, and the beach access is second to none for military bases in the United States.

South Patrick Shores is a nondescript community that serves partly as a commercial zone for residents of the air base. Some low-rise condominiums are going up, a small taste of sights to come farther south, but otherwise there are no accommodations, restaurants, or nightlife.

Beaches

Happily, civilians can enjoy a healthy measure of beach access at Patrick Air Force Base, too. Accesses are provided along the east side of Highway A1A in designated parking areas. Driving through, and you will find two large lots with dune walkovers north of the main gate, a smaller lot directly across from it, and two more large lots with dune walkovers south of it. One of the latter is near the "central gate," while the other is near the intersection of Highway A1A and State Route 404 (Pineda Causeway), the first of three causeways that connect South Brevard's beaches with the mainland.

All are free of charge and open to anybody, even those who protested the Vietnam War. We saw countless happy folks of all stripes, from seniors to surfers, hopping over the walkovers. The beaches are clean,

15 Seagull Park

Location: Sea Park Boulevard at Highway A1A in South Patrick Shores
Parking/fees: free parking lot
Hours: 7:30 A.M. to dusk
Facilities: picnic tables
Contact: Brevard County Parks and Recreation Department (south service sector), 321/952-4580

16 South Patrick Residents Association Park

Location: 1.5 miles south of Pineda Causeway (State Route 404) in South Patrick Shores
Parking/fees: free parking lot
Hours: dawn to dusk
Facilities: shower
Contact: Brevard County Parks and Recreation Department (south service sector), 321/952-4580

Map of Brevard County—Page 100

wide, and relatively safe, which is a good thing as there are no lifeguards or facilities. Locals refer to South Brevard as the "small wave capital of the East Coast," and the beach along Patrick Air Force Base is considered one of the three best areas for surfing these small waves. The other two are 5th Avenue Boardwalk (the name surfers have given to the boardwalk at James H. Nance Park) in Indialantic and the area by the north jetty at Sebastian Inlet.

Beach access in South Patrick Shores consists of small county-owned parks, including **Seagull Park** (1.6 acres) and **South Patrick Residents Association Park** (0.8 acres). They are, respectively, one mile and 1.5 miles south of the Highway A1A and State Route 404 intersection. Seagull Park has picnic shelters and is attractively landscaped with native plantings. Beyond its dune crossover, South Patrick Residents Association (S.P.R.A.) Park has an outdoor shower and a memorial to the space shuttle *Challenger.*

Satellite Beach

Appropriately named, Satellite Beach (pop. 10,275) has fired its retro rockets for development. It is the largest of South Brevard's beach towns and, for that reason, is the commercial hub. The town is soaring so high in the stratosphere of high finance that the oxygen supply appears to have been cut off to its brain. There are more *Saturn* rocket–sized cranes here, alongside countless oceanfront construction sites, than are found on all of Cape Canaveral. They hoist slabs of steel into place, prefab walls and balconies follow, then they hold the listing monstrosity up until the developers—often speculators with dubious associations—unload all the units. Strip malls, unimaginatively planned and mindlessly sprawling, run the length of the town on the opposite side of Highway A1A, creating a depressing tableau that is particularly off-putting on a sweltering summer day. The same cartoonish real-estate mistakes are being repeated here that were made in locales further south during the era of Reaganomics. And the same specious philosophy is at work: "Build it and they will come." By contrast, our philosophy is: "Leave it alone and they will thank you profusely a century from now."

17 Hightower Beach

Location: 4.5 miles south of Pineda Causeway (State Route 404) on Highway A1A in Satellite Beach
Parking/fees: free parking lot
Hours: dawn to dusk
Facilities: shower
Contact: Brevard County Parks and Recreation Department (south service sector), 321/952-4580

Beaches

Satellite Beach runs for two miles, with dune crossovers at street ends providing access to the town's generally narrow (especially at high tide) beach. The brown sand and warm, inviting water are good for the beach basics of sunbathing and swimming, but watch out for rocks in the water. The best beach-related reason to come to this built-up community is **Pelican Beach Park.** Located a few hundred yards north of the DeSoto Parkway and Highway A1A intersection, it's a county-owned, city-run park with ample free parking, two dune crossovers, picnic shelters and an observation tower. The beach was looking a little narrow and steep when we last passed through; in the previous edition, we noted that it was, by contrast, wide and hard packed, with "some of the only intact dune structure left in the area." The ocean giveth and the ocean taketh away.

The second best beach in the Satellite area is **Hightower Park**, a two-acre county beach up at the north end. There's little more than a small lot, outdoor shower, and dune walkover onto a narrow, sloping beach that's often deserted.

Coastal Cuisine

The only other reason to come to Satellite Beach is **Bunky's Seafood Grill and Raw Bar** (1390 A1A, 321/777-CLAM, $). This authentically funky and unpretentious eatery has been here for 20 years. It is exactly the sort of enterprise that all beach towns should be encouraging instead of foolish franchises. Reminiscent of the Oyster Pub in Daytona Beach, Bunky's is both a sports bar and a great place for cheap, fresh, and simply prepared seafood. One time, we pulled the trigger on the "38 Special": 38 plump, juicy, iced, raw Indian River oysters for $12.95. Those too squeamish for shellfish can take aim at fish sandwiches (the blackened wahoo is killer!), fish tacos, crab cakes, and other fresh, satisfying, and inexpensive fare. While you're here, look around: collegiate sports banners, race car memorabilia, and beer logos take up seemingly every available square inch of wall and ceiling space. Bunky's is also a friendly and popular late-night hangout, with weekly microbrew specials and sporting events playing on numerous television screens.

Contact Information

Melbourne/Palm Bay and the Beaches Convention and Visitors Bureau, 1005 East Strawbridge Avenue, Melbourne, FL 32901; 321/724-5400 or 800/771-9922; website: www.melpb-chamber.org

18 Satellite Beach

Location: between Grant Street and Palmetto Avenue, off Highway A1A in Satellite Beach
Parking/fees: free street parking at the ends of (from north to south) Grant Street, Park Lane, Ellwood Street, Cassia Boulevard, DeSoto Parkway, and Magellan, Sunrise, and Palmetto Avenues
Hours: dawn to dusk
Facilities: none
Contact: Satellite Beach Parks and Recreation Department, 321/773-6458

19 Pelican Beach Park

Location: 2.5 miles north of State Route 518 (Royal Palm Boulevard) on Highway A1A in Satellite Beach
Parking/fees: free parking lot
Hours: dawn to dusk
Facilities: restrooms, picnic tables, and showers
Contact: Satellite Beach Parks and Recreation Department, 321/773-6458

MAP OF BREVARD COUNTY—PAGE 100

Indian Harbour Beach

A marginally more palatable facsimile of Satellite Beach, Indian Harbour Beach (pop. 8,024) has one mile of oceanfront that is fast becoming indistinguishable from its larger neighbor. Like Satellite Beach, it is also home to a nice but small city-run facility, Richard G. Edgeton Bicentennial Park.

20 Richard G. Edgeton Bicentennial Park

Location: end of Ocean Dunes Drive, off Highway A1A in Indian Harbour Beach
Parking/fees: free parking lot
Hours: sunrise to 10 P.M.
Facilities: picnic tables and a shower
Contact: Indian Harbour Beach Parks and Recreation Department, 321/773-0552

Beaches

Located where Pine Tree Road meets Highway A1A, **Richard G. Edgeton Bicentennial Park** has a free parking lot (36 spaces), picnic tables and an outdoor shower. This sylvan park—an oasis of green amid a glut of development—has picnic tables, palm trees, volleyball nets, showers, and a broad wooden deck. Look north from the deck and you'll see all the visual evidence you'll ever need to argue against coastal development: a gross orange condo complex that hogs way too much of A1A in Indian Harbour Beach.

Contact Information

Melbourne/Palm Bay and the Beaches Convention and Visitors Bureau, 1005 East Strawbridge Avenue, Melbourne, FL 32901; 321/724-5400 or 800/771-9922; website: www.melpb-chamber.org

Canova Beach

Unincorporated Canova Beach (pop. 1,500) is listed in various local publications as being part of Indian Harbour Beach, Indialantic, Melbourne, and Melbourne Beach. It is also listed separately as Canova Beach, too. It is a viable vacation destination boasting ample oceanfront accommodations. It occupies only a half-mile-square parcel of oceanfront real estate, but they've gotten around that limitation by building up.

21 Canova Beach Park

Location: directly east of Melbourne, at the end of Eau Galle Causeway in Canova Beach
Parking/fees: $1 per vehicle entrance fee
Hours: 7:30 A.M. to dusk
Facilities: restrooms, picnic tables, and showers
Contact: Brevard County Parks and Recreation Department (south service sector), 321/952-4580

Beaches

Canova Beach has a small county-run beach facility, called **Canova Beach Park**, where Eau Galle Causeway (State Route 518) intersects Highway A1A. Parking costs $1 (self-pay). One caveat: Just beyond where the waves break is a rocky reef that would seem to present potential danger. No signs are posted and no lifeguards are on duty, so swim at your own risk. Erosion has narrowed the beach to the point that waves wash at the foot of the stairs. Up on the bluff, this green, clean park is large and nicely landscaped. A tantalizing tangle of a sea grape thicket provides a brief glimpse of what Florida's east coast once looked like from one end to the other.

Bunking Down

The **Holiday Inn Beach Resort** (2605 North A1A, 321/777-4100, $$) is actually the mainstay of Canova Beach. It is as relaxed a big resort as you will find on this part of the coast, with families happily frolicking around the pool and patio, which appear more popular than the beach below. The outside patio is a hot spot for unwinding and relaxing at the bar, which bills itself as the "best party on the beach." The live music is generally of the one-man-reggae-band ilk, replete with wacky names like Jamaican Me Crazy.

One place that sticks out like a sore thumb is the **Radisson Suite Hotel Oceanfront** (3101 North A1A, 321/773-0260, $$$), an absurdly huge building that dominates the landscape like the Vehicle Assembly Building at the Kennedy Space Center. Too off-putting for a vacation, it must be big with business travelers who are oblivious to this sort of thing, not knowing where they are half the time anyway. Canova, Cleveland, Canton, Cancún—what's the bloody difference?

Coastal Cuisine

The Holiday Inn's on-site restaurant, **Tropic Al's** (2605 North A1A, 321/777-4100, $$), offers a can't-beat-it seafood buffet on Fridays. The rest of the week, go to the **Flamingo Crab Co.** (Highway A1A and Eau Galle Causeway, 321/777-8069, $), located across the street from Canova Beach Park. Each night this restaurant and seafood market features an awesome special, such as all-you-can-eat grouper and shrimp on Tuesday. For an inexpensive happy-hour treat, hit the Flamingo from 4 P.M. to 6 P.M. daily, when raw oysters are two bits apiece.

Contact Information

Melbourne/Palm Bay and the Beaches Convention and Visitors Bureau, 1005 East Strawbridge Avenue, Melbourne, FL 32901; 321/724-5400 or 800/771-9922; website: www.melpb-chamber.org

Indialantic

Indialantic (pop. 3,000) is the most clearly defined and pleasant of the south Brevard County beach communities, occupying one compact and tidy square mile. Its backbone is the impressive-sounding 5th Avenue (State Route 500), which is actually an unassuming commercial zone that is anything but highfalutin or overpriced. It's all of five blocks long—the width of the barrier island. To give an idea of the quiet civility that awaits you in Indialantic, the town center boasts two decently stocked used bookshops. As for its oceanfront, Indialantic embraces 1.5 miles of beach whose understated appeal centers around two excellent parks. And there you have the town in a nutshell: grab a used paperback and head for the sand.

If you follow 5th Avenue westward, you'll hit Melbourne Causeway (State Route 500/U.S. 192), an east-west thoroughfare that brings beachgoers across the Indian River from "the Harbour City" of Melbourne, a burgeoning metropolis with a population of 70,000. Named after the first postmaster's home city in Australia back in the 1880s, Melbourne rode a wave of growth in the 1980s and 1990s generated by computer and electronics firms that relocated here. This apparently justified the need for an "international" airport, now said to be failing financially. While the area gained a host of big-city amenities, it's also gathered some of the

MAP OF BREVARD COUNTY—PAGE 100

concomitant problems. That includes an ungodly strip-mall sprawl that clings to U.S. 192 all the way out to I-95.

Beaches

Paradise Beach Park, south of the Eau Galle Causeway in Indialantic, is a nicely landscaped county park with a nominal self-pay entrance fee of $1. It is the largest county park of all, by the look of it, with endless parking lots stretching along A1A in the vicinity of Paradise Boulevard. It's also loaded with facilities: picnic shelters, volleyball nets, concession stand, lifeguards in season, and a bathhouse.

Conveniently located in the heart of Indialantic, where 5th Avenue dead-ends into Highway A1A, is **James H. Nance Park.** It's another huge park with zigzagging mazelike walkways. Ample metered parking (400 spaces) is available, and a concrete boardwalk runs along Wavecrest Avenue for Nance's half-mile length. At the north end of Nance Park is Bizarro's NY Pizza (!?), the perfect stop if you're a famished surfer with a hankering for a pizza slab.

Bunking Down

Since first staying here back in the early 1980s, we've been partial to the Sharrock Shores Resort, which changed owners and names in 1999 to **Tuckaway Shores Resort** (1441 South Miramar Avenue, 321/723-3355, $$), a reasonably priced complex with picture-window views of the churning ocean. Rooms have kitchenettes, refrigerators, sofas, and balconies, and are as comfortable as a beach house. Nice outdoor pool deck, too. Some folks rent rooms here by the week or month. It's located three-quarters of a mile south of 5th Avenue and Highway A1A.

Another sentimental favorite is the **Oceanside** (745 North A1A, 321/727-2723, $), the sort of well-tended mom-and-pop motel Florida's central coast used to have in abundance. There's a pool on the premises, and some of the efficiency units have full kitchens. Since bed-and-breakfasts are as rare in central Florida as ski slopes, the stately **Windemere Inn By the Sea** (745 Wavecrest Avenue, 321/728-9334, $$), a sunny, antique-filled guest home, is worth considering. At the other extreme, **Quality Suites** (1665 North A1A, 321/723-4222, $$$) is an ultramodern 10-story, twin-tower complex with 208 oceanfront suites, a pool, hot tub, sauna, exercise room, and complimentary "healthy attitude" breakfast.

Contact Information

Melbourne/Palm Bay and the Beaches Convention and Visitors Bureau, 1005 East Strawbridge Avenue, Melbourne, FL 32901; 321/724-5400 or 800/771-9922; website: www.melpb-chamber.org

22 Paradise Beach Park

Location: between Eau Galle Causeway (State Route 518) and Melbourne Causeway (State Route 516) at the north end of Indialantic
Parking/fees: $1 per vehicle entrance fee
Hours: 7 A.M. to dusk
Facilities: concessions, lifeguards (seasonal), restrooms, picnic tables, and showers
Contact: Brevard County Parks and Recreation Department (south service sector), 321/952-4580

23 James H. Nance Park

Location: end of 5th Avenue, off Highway A1A in Indialantic
Parking/fees: metered parking lot
Hours: dawn to 9 P.M.
Facilities: lifeguards (seasonal), restrooms, picnic tables, and showers
Contact: Indialantic Town Hall, 321/723-2242

"The Sea Turtle Preservation Society"

(sung to the tune of "The Village Green Preservation Society," by the Kinks)

We are the sea turtle preservation society
God bless loggerheads, leatherbacks, and Kemp's ridley
We are the condominium condemnation affiliate
Down with developers, realtors, and their advocates

(chorus)

Preserving the beaches for me and for you
Protecting sea turtles, water quality, too
What more can we do?

We use the beach bum surfing addict vernacular
God bless Surfrider and ocean waves spectacular
We are the Jet Ski elimination authority
Personal watercraft is offensive to the majority

(chorus)

Preserving the beaches for me and for you
Protecting sea turtles, water quality, too
What more can we do?

We are the raw oyster consumer consortium
Pass the cocktail sauce, horseradish, and lemon
We are the thong bikini appreciation society
God bless Ron Jon, Candy, Lexus, and Foxy

(chorus)

Preserving the beaches for me and for you
Protecting sea turtles, water quality, too
What more can we do?

(Note: If you want to contact the real Sea Turtle Preservation Society—yes, there actually is such an organization—it is located at 517 Ocean Avenue, Melbourne Beach, FL 32951; 321/676-1701.)

Melbourne Beach and Melbourne Shores

Melbourne Beach (pop. 3,300) and Melbourne Shores offer a bit of suburbia at the beach. The predominating development is residential, with a decided emphasis on middle-class values: S-shaped backstreets, sloped curbs, men with Weed Eaters and hedge trimmers prowling their lawns like big-game hunters, enormous SUVs parked in the driveways. These communities are not the least bit downtrodden, but neither are they exclusive. They're right down the middle of the road.

That is exactly where we found ourselves late one afternoon during a torrential summer rainstorm, the likes of which we'd never before seen. We were driving right down the middle of A1A, afraid to veer too close to either shoulder lest we be washed out to sea, afraid to stop because of the traffic on our tail. Adding to our fear of catastrophe was a glance at the map, which revealed how amazingly thin is the barrier island upon which these seemingly safe, tidy, and quiet communities sit. The strangest sight of all was a golf course being heavily watered by a sprinkler system while the mother of all monsoons flooded the fairways.

24 Ocean Avenue Park

Location: at the end of Ocean Avenue, off Highway A1A in Melbourne Beach
Parking/fees: free parking lot at Ocean Avenue and free street parking at the ends of A and B Streets and from 1st to 6th Avenues
Hours: 7:30 A.M. to dusk
Facilities: lifeguards (seasonal) and picnic tables
Contact: Brevard County Parks and Recreation Department (south service sector), 321/952-4580

Once the clouds passed—always within minutes in Florida on summer afternoons—we realized what a homey and appealing place Melbourne Beach really is. No wonder so many people have chosen to live here, trying to rein in attempts to convert it to a resort town.

Beaches

At one time, the beaches hereabouts were almost as wide as Daytona's, but Brevard County's beaches have thinned considerably, especially over the last few decades. The erosion is due to the construction of Port Canaveral, in Volusia County, back in the 1950s, whose jetties kept sand from "bypassing" the inlet and moving south to Brevard County's beaches, as had been the natural order of things. As a result, occasional renourishment of the beaches, at times on an emergency basis, has been necessary, especially in the Melbourne Beach/Indialantic area. A major beach renourishment project that will pile dredged sand onto beaches from Cape Canaveral in Volusia County south to Melbourne Beach in Volusia County. The cost in Volusia County alone will be $39 million. The renourishment of nearly 13 miles of thinning beaches in Brevard County began in November 2000.

There's plenty of public beach access out here to supply the needs of residents, tourists, and the weekend swarm that comes over from Melbourne. Pedestrian access, used mostly by town residents, is available at nine street endings, from B Street down to 6th Avenue. **Ocean Avenue Park**, a modest beachside playground with picnic tables and volleyball nets, is located at the east end of Ocean Avenue (Highway A1A). This provides some visual relief from the Breakers, a quarter mile of cheesy stucco condos that obscure a driver's view of the beach along A1A south of the little park.

More access is gained **Spesser Holland Park.** Located three miles south of Melbourne Causeway (State Route 500/U.S. 192), this lengthy beach park has north and south entrances, divided by a Patrick Air Force Base tracking station. Ample parking lots run for a quarter mile at each end, and pavilions and facilities are available at both. After all this, **Coconut Point Park,** a short distance south in Melbourne Shores, seems puny by comparison. There's restrooms, outdoor showers, and limited free parking, but the real appeal is botanical, as Coconut Point is set amid a pleasing tangle of sea grapes, saw palmettos, and short coconut palm trees.

Various parcels of beachfront in the Melbourne vicinity make up the Archie Carr National Wildlife Refuge, a protected habitat for sea turtles and other endangered species. The 20 miles of coastline between Melbourne Beach and Wabasso Beach (in Indian River County) is the most important nesting site for loggerhead turtles in the Western Hemisphere and second most important in the world. Astonishingly, 25 percent of all loggerheads and 35 percent of all green sea turtles in the United States nest on this brief stretch of shoreline. It was Dr. Archie Carr, a renowned ecologist and sea turtle expert at the University of Florida, whose research and advocacy led to the designation of a National Wildlife Refuge that now bears his name.

Attempting to save vital nesting habitat on what was still a relatively undisturbed coastline, Congress established the Archie Carr National Wildlife Refuge in 1991. It consists of discontinuous sections of the Melbourne-area coastline, with additional parcels being acquired as money becomes available. The refuge comprises only the beach and dune system, extending no further inland. These sandy shores are not only important nesting sites for sea turtles, but also provide habitat for the endangered Florida beach mouse. A couple of access points along its length are indicated by signs. Meanwhile, it remains a masterpiece in progress. When completely acquired, it will total 900 acres and 9.4 miles of coastline. If you want to do something on the turtles' behalf, contact your senator and representative and urge them to support increased funding for the Archie Carr National Wildlife Refuge.

Bunking Down

As in neighboring Indialantic, mom-and-pop motels rule the waves in Melbourne Beach. **Samperton's on the Atlantic** (3135 A1A, 321/951-8200, $) provides clean, comfortable, and unostentatious oceanfront rooms and efficiencies, as well as

25 Spesser Holland Park

Location: one-half mile south of Melbourne Beach, on Highway A1A
Parking/fees: $1 per vehicle entrance fee at both the north and south entrances
Hours: 7:30 A.M. to dusk
Facilities: lifeguards (seasonal), restrooms, picnic tables, and showers
Contact: Brevard County Parks and Recreation Department (south service sector), 321/952-4580

26 Coconut Point Park

Location: south of Melbourne Beach along Highway A1A
Parking/fees: free parking lot
Hours: 7:30 A.M. to dusk
Facilities: restrooms, picnic tables, and showers
Contact: Brevard County Parks and Recreation Department (south service sector), 321/952-4580

MAP OF BREVARD COUNTY—PAGE 100

claiming the best seafood restaurant in the area. Just down the road, **Sandy Shores Motel** (3455 A1A, 321/723-5586, $) offers much the same, though it's a bit more attractively decorated. The **Sea Dunes Resort** (5485 South A1A, $) offers rooms and efficiencies and has Loggerhead's Restaurant and Lounge on the premises. Moreover, Howard Hughes was alleged to be a frequent visitor. **Tiara by the Sea** (5815 A1A, 321/725-0525, $) may not be as diamond-studded as its name suggests, but it is on the ocean. A number of other motels and rental properties are available for the next eight miles as you approach Sebastian Inlet. None will ever be mistaken for the Ritz, but they'll do. In fact, their abundance makes this part of the coast something of a charming throwback to yesteryear.

Coastal Cuisine

Samperton's on the Atlantic (3135 A1A, 321/951-8200, $$) goes both ways with their cuisine, experimenting with creative dishes such as seared tuna in ginger sauce while also sticking to the basics. Fresh local catches like blackened grouper are simply and expertly prepared. The signature dish is a seafood sauté that includes shrimp, scallops, crab, scallions, and mushrooms in white wine sauce served over rice or pasta. The restaurant doesn't lie about being on the Atlantic, either. The view from the upstairs dining room is so close to the ocean that it's like being inside an aquarium. From this vantage point, we witnessed an awe-inspiring lightning storm. This natural fireworks display had every table of diners oohing and aahing.

A bit off the beaten track, overlooking the Indian River in Melbourne, is **Conchy Joe's Seafood Restaurant** (1477 Pineapple Avenue, 321/253-3131, $$), one of the area's old reliables. It's made to look like an Old Florida fish house, and it specializes in tried-and-true native Florida cuisine (gator tail, conch fritters, raw oysters), as well as Bahamian seafood dishes. Reggae and calypso bands play during the dinner hour. Conchy Joe's is open for lunch, too.

Night Moves

The center of attention for miles around is the **Sebastian Beach Inn** (7035 South A1A, 321/728-4311). Known as the "SBI," for short, it's a sprawling oceanfront restaurant, lounge, and live music venue. To make sure it stays in the public eye, the proprietor of the SBI produces a bimonthly called *The Real Paper,* distributed free everywhere. It's a quirky rag, abounding in misspellings, that consists primarily of rambling and often hilarious commentary (warning: libertarianism bordering on militia anarchism) on everything from the nude sunbathing controversy at Playalinda Beach to Allen Ginsberg's lasting significance.

Most pointedly, he justifiably hails his own on-site House of Bluez [*sic*], a spacious room where national acts (e.g., Steve Miller, Albert King) play on weekends. Live music of some kind, whether a national or local act or open-mike blues jam, goes on nearly every night of the week. The restaurant does a hefty dinnertime trade in prime rib and seafood. They also offer this guarantee: "If ya don't think dat our clam chowder is the best in the county, ya don't hafta pay fer it!" The SBI serves lunch and dinner. "We don't do breakfast," writes the owner, "cuz we're all sleepin' off the great time we had the night before partyin' at the SBI! Eat yer heart out." The SBI also hosts Saturday and Sunday "beach parties" (11 A.M.–9 P.M.) on the sands below its patio, replete with a "Jamaican Limbo contest." One of these shindigs was under way when we visited the SBI, which was packed with revelers. We couldn't help but notice this inscription on the motorcycle helmet of one guest: "Places to Go, People to Annoy." The SBI rocks so hard that no other place

MAP OF FLORIDA'S EAST COAST—PAGE 5

in the area even qualifies as competition.

A word of advice, directly from the SBI, about how not to get in trouble in South Brevard County: "DO NOT SPEED ON HWY A1A . . . PERIOD. . . . WATCH THE SIGNS AS THE SPEED LIMITS CHANGE FREQUENTLY . . . THEY MEAN IT, SO, OBEY THEM." Don't say you weren't warned.

And now for some rock and roll trivia about Melbourne. Did you know that the late Jim Morrison, charismatic vocalist with the Doors and self-styled "Lizard King," was born in this town? The son of Rear Admiral Steve Morrison (who was stationed here) and his wife Clara entered the world on September 8, 1943.

Contact Information

Melbourne/Palm Bay and the Beaches Convention and Visitors Bureau, 1005 East Strawbridge Avenue, Melbourne, FL 32901; 321/724-5400 or 800/771-9922; website: www.melpb-chamber.org

Floridana Beach and Sunnyland Beach

A land rush is on in these two communities between Melbourne Beach and Sebastian Inlet. Sunnyland Beach is winning, which is only to say that it resembles what Floridana Beach will look like before long. That is, a development called Aquarina Country Club—which bills itself as "ocean-to-river golf and tennis"—takes up virtually all of Sunnyland Beach (pop. 200). For now, Floridana Beach (pop. 200) is an unincorporated stretch of thickly vegetated hammock and coastal dunes, though "For Sale" signs are staked every few hundred yards.

Beaches

The only beach access around here is **Bonsteel Park.** It's county run, with free parking in a small dirt lot. No facilities, no lifeguards. Like the beaches north of here, the sand slopes dramatically to the water's edge and the waves crash hard and loud. It's easy to see why this part of Florida's coast is popular with surfers and less so with family vacationers. The El Dorado of surfing, East Coast–style, lies just a hair to the south of Bonsteel Park at Sebastian Inlet.

Contact Information

Melbourne/Palm Bay and the Beaches Convention and Visitors Bureau, 1005 East Strawbridge Avenue, Melbourne, FL 32901; 321/724-5400 or 800/771-9922; website: www.melpb-chamber.org

27 Bonsteel Park

Location: north of Sebastian Inlet in Floridana Beach, on Highway A1A
Parking/fees: free parking lot
Hours: 7:30 A.M. to dusk
Facilities: none
Contact: Brevard County Parks and Recreation Department (south service sector), 321/952-4580

Sebastian Inlet State Park

Sebastian Inlet is a watery playground for a stretch of coast that extends from Cocoa to Vero Beach. It is a man-made inlet that splits a long, narrow barrier island. What draws crowds to Sebastian Inlet is the great surfing and fishing, although many are simply content to drag coolers and folding chairs into the ankle-deep water of the lagoon on the north side. Straddling both sides of the inlet is **Sebastian Inlet State Park.** On the south side is a 51-unit campground and boat launch. On the north side: a fishing jetty, calm-water lagoon (for swimming), and surfing at what has been called "the best break in Florida."

When we passed through, the beach near the jetty was packed with boogie boarders. On this particular day, the waves were breaking close to shore, and they looked hazardous, particularly given the small children frolicking in the surf. Huge waves rose suddenly, crashed dramatically, and ran up a steeply sloping beach face. Their forceful backwash met incoming sets in a crashing torrent. Surfing is best on the north side of the inlet, right at and just north of the jetty, and is dangerous on the south side, where an area called "Monster Hole" poses hazards that include sharks, which enter the inlet on incoming tides in search of food.

Inlets are by definition high-energy areas, particularly in the vicinity of jetties that hold their mouths open for boat traffic. The tidal exchange through Sebastian Inlet is extreme. On an incoming tide, the water rushes with a speed and fury that stirs up stiff winds in its vicinity, making the inlet a pleasant place to stand around on a hot day. The best vantage point to enjoy these cooling blasts is on catwalks that run under the inlet bridge.

All totaled, Sebastian Inlet claims three miles of ocean beach. One of the more highly developed state parks in Florida, it offers concessions (food and drink, camping and fishing supplies, equipment rentals), a full-service marina, canoe and kayak rentals, ecotours (call 321/724-5424), and the McLarty Treasure Museum. The last of these is a museum that tells the story, via exhibits and recovered treasures, of a Spanish fleet that wrecked offshore in 1715. Laden with gold and silver from Mexico and Peru, much of its scattered treasure has remained on the ocean floor for more than two and a half centuries. Salvage operations began in earnest in the mid-1950s, and major finds have been made as recently as 1990. Hence, the nickname "Treasure Coast." The museum charges a separate admission on top of the park's entrance fee.

Outside the park, on U.S. 1 in the town of Sebastian, is Mel Fisher's Treasure Museum, housing another collection of Spanish artifacts unearthed from the same 1715 fleet's wreckage. Incidentally, Sebastian is also the site of the country's first national wildlife refuge: Pelican Island National Wildlife Refuge, founded in 1903 by President Theodore Roosevelt.

(28) Sebastian Inlet State Park (north side)

Location: north side of Sebastian Inlet, 18 miles south of Melbourne Beach, on Highway A1A
Parking/fees: $3.25 per vehicle entrance fee
Hours: 24 hours
Facilities: concessions, lifeguards (seasonal), restrooms, picnic tables, and showers
Contact: Sebastian Inlet State Park, 321/984-4852

Contact Information

Sebastian Inlet State Park, 9700 South A1A, Melbourne Beach, FL 32951; 321/984-4852. For camping reservations, call 561/589-9659; website: www.myflorida.com

MAP OF FLORIDA'S EAST COAST—PAGE 5

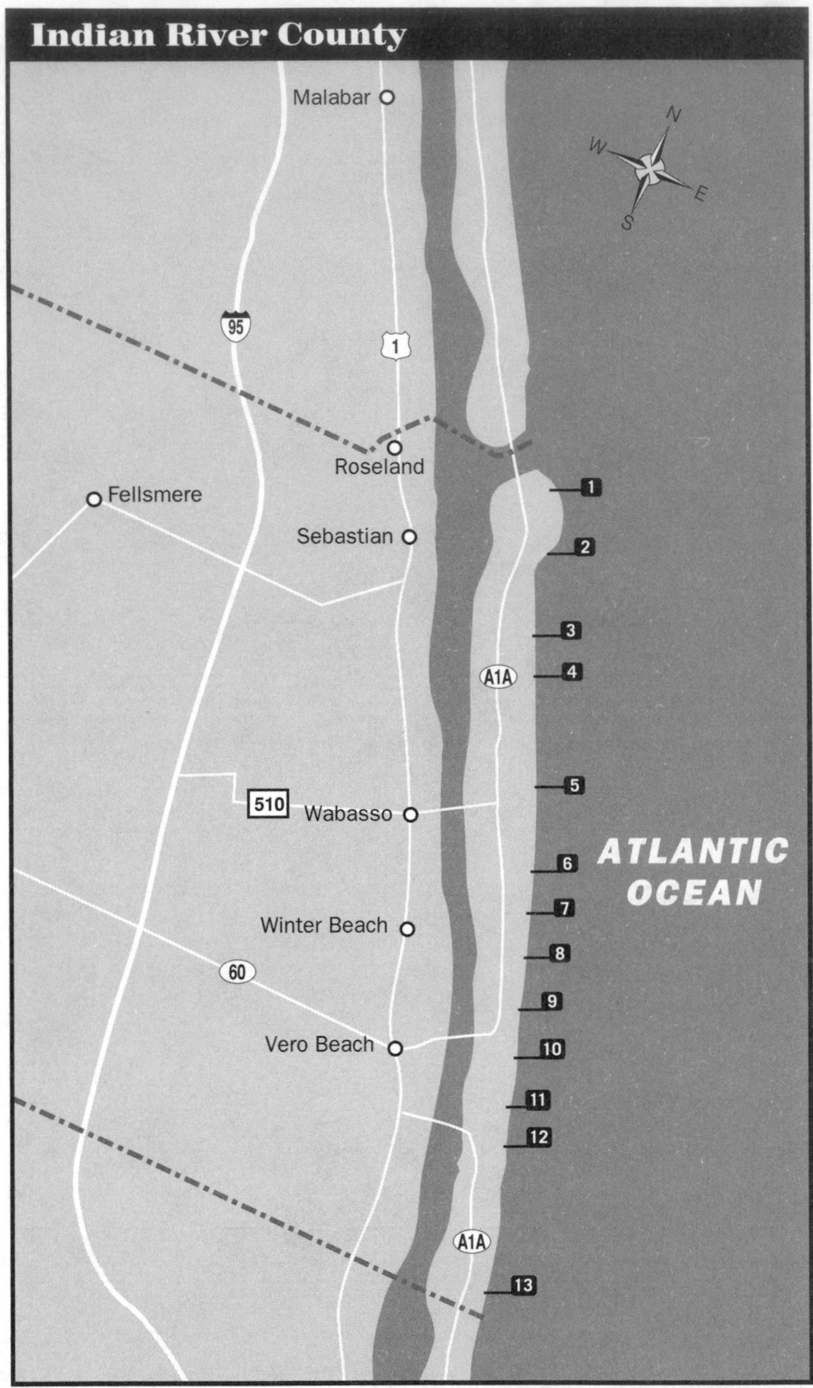
Indian River County
Malabar
N
W
E
S
95
1
Roseland
Fellsmere
Sebastian
1
2
3
4
A1A
5
510
Wabasso
ATLANTIC OCEAN
6
7
Winter Beach
8
60
9
Vero Beach
10
11
12
A1A
13

INDIAN RIVER COUNTY

Indian River County is renowned for Indian River fruit, a citrus crop that includes big, juicy oranges and grapefruits. There are also 29 miles of golden sand beaches on Orchid Island, the long, narrow barrier island bounded by the Indian River, Atlantic Ocean, Sebastian Inlet, and Fort Pierce Inlet. The only community of any size is Vero Beach. That leaves great stretches of untamed beach wilderness along A1A. When they call this the Treasure Coast, they're not just talking about sunken Spanish galleons. Especially at the north end, there are sizable beach parks—Golden Sands, Treasure Shores, Wabasso Beach—that rank among the best in Florida. Throughout much of the county, an offshore coquina reef tames the waves before they roll ashore.

North Indian River County

A magnificent series of beaches extends down Orchid Island from Sebastian Inlet down to Vero Beach. We cannot say enough good things about the number of them, the facilities provided, and the beaches themselves. **Sebastian Inlet State Park** is nearly evenly divided between Brevard and Indian River Counties, with Indian River County claiming 1.8 miles of the park's ocean frontage.

While Sebastian Inlet is covered in greater detail in Brevard County, we'll cursorily note its beach access here. A sandy, free lot is located a half mile south of the bridge. Though it lies on state park property, no entrance fee is charged to park and use the beach. A day-use fee is, however, charged to access the campground, marina, and jetties via the park road on the west side of Highway A1A, just south of the inlet bridge. Incidentally, one daily entrance fee gains access to both the north and south sides of Sebastian Inlet State Park.

Amber Sands Beach Park is a public beach access, with free parking and a dune walkover, located just below the southern boundary of the park. It lies along the thinnest part of the island, up at the north end of the county, where the arm of Orchid Island narrows to a fingerlet.

Located only a mile apart, **Treasure Shores Beach Park** and **Golden Sands Beach Park** are twin peas in the splendid pod of north county beaches. The grounds for both of these well-equipped seaside parks are meticulously maintained as veritable botanical gardens, teeming with colorful subtropical vegetation. A coarse-sand beach with a steep profile is backed by heavily vegetated dune ridges. If you look north, in the direction of Sebastian Inlet, the beach seems to stretch into an infinity of unbuilt-upon coastal wilderness. These county-run parks do post lots of "no's," though—no

❶ Sebastian Inlet State Park (south side)

Location: The entrance road to the campground, marina, and south jetty is on the south side of the inlet bridge. Beach access is one-half mile south of the inlet on Highway A1A.
Parking/fees: free parking lot at South Sebastian Beach. Entrance fee for developed areas of the park (campground, marina, jetty) is $3.25 per vehicle. Camping fees are $20.80 (with hookups) and $18.70 (without hookups).
Hours: 24 hours
Facilities: concessions, restrooms, picnic tables, and showers
Contact: Sebastian Inlet State Park, 561/589-9659

❷ Amber Sands Beach Park

Location: 4.4 miles north of the Wabasso Bridge (County Road 510), on Highway A1A
Parking/fees: free parking lot
Hours: sunrise to sunset
Facilities: none
Contact: Vero Beach–Indian River County Recreation Department, 561/567-2144

❸ Treasure Shores Beach Park

Location: 2.4 miles north of the Wabasso Bridge (County Road 510), on Highway A1A
Parking/fees: free parking lots
Hours: 8 A.M. to sunset
Facilities: lifeguards, restrooms, picnic tables, and showers
Contact: Treasure Shores Beach Park, 561/589-6411

scuba diving, no surfing, no fishing, etc.

Wabasso Beach Park is another awesome county-run coastal playground. It lies six miles north of Vero Beach, east of the mainland town of Wabasso and south of the tiny community of Orchid (pop. 150). Wabasso is a little stretch of sandy paradise as nice as any along Florida's east coast. A steep set of stairs leads down to a wide, kid-filled beach. We've seen boogie boarders and divers out in force on hot summer days, while more quiescent souls placidly repose in the shade of covered picnic areas and stare down on the action. Wabasso is a quintessential Florida beach park and gets a five-star thumbs-up from us.

We were urged by proudly possessive locals not to broadcast too loudly about the world-class beach at Wabasso, but the cat—or should we say mouse?—is already out of the bag. That is to say, the park abuts Disney's Vero Beach Resort at its south end.

Disney's first foray into the beach resort market was the result of a three-and-a-half-year search across Florida for the perfect location. (Incidentally, the resort is not really in Vero Beach but six miles north of it.) The fact that Disney chose this locale attests to how special Wabasso Beach is. Disney's Vero Beach Resort is a vacation ownership resort where rooms are also rented out as at a hotel. Make no mistake: you'll ante up dearly to play on the beach under the auspices of America's mouse. By contrast, at Wabasso Beach Park, you'll pay nothing to enjoy the same beach. Your call!

Moving south, two accesses situated in close proximity are **Sea Grape Beach Ac-**

4 Golden Sands Beach Park

Location: 1.4 miles north of the Wabasso Bridge (County Road 510), on Highway A1A
Parking/fees: free parking lots
Hours: 8 A.M. to sunset
Facilities: lifeguards, restrooms, picnic tables, and showers
Contact: Golden Sands Beach Park, 561/388-5483

5 Wabasso Beach Park

Location: east of the Wabasso Bridge (County Road 510), on Highway A1A
Parking/fees: free parking lots
Hours: 8 A.M. to sunset
Facilities: concessions, lifeguards, restrooms, picnic tables, and showers
Contact: Wabasso Beach Park, 561/589-8291

6 Sea Grape Beach Access

Location: 1.5 miles south of the Wabasso Bridge (County Road 510), on Highway A1A
Parking/fees: free parking lot
Hours: sunrise to sunset
Facilities: none
Contact: Vero Beach–Indian River County Recreation Department, 561/567-2144

7 Turtle Trail Beach Access

Location: north end of Indian River Shores, 2.3 miles south of the Wabasso Bridge (County Road 510), on Highway A1A
Parking/fees: free parking lot
Hours: sunrise to sunset
Facilities: none
Contact: Vero Beach–Indian River County Recreation Department, 561/567-2144

Indian River Fruit

The term "Indian River fruit" denotes the best that Florida has to offer in the way of oranges and grapefruits. This is true for several reasons:

1. The oak-hammock soil and underlying limestone are a rich storehouse of nutrients;
2. High annual rainfall (52 inches) makes for juicy, thin-skinned fruit;
3. Winters are sufficiently cool to trigger sugar production, which makes for sweet-tasting citrus. But Florida's balmier version of Old Man Winter seldom gets cold enough—most years, at least—to kill off the citrus crop.

The Indian River Citrus District extends from Daytona Beach south to West Palm Beach. Indian River County alone accounts for nearly one-third of the 220,000 acres under commercial cultivation. How good is Indian River fruit? Testing of citrus by the U.S. Department of Agriculture ranked Indian River citrus first in several categories, including juice content and peel thinness. Your own taste buds can confirm its supremacy by stopping at any of the grower/packers that sell to the public at stands on or near U.S. 1 in Indian River County, including the world-renowned Hale Groves (U.S. 1 at 4th Street, Vero Beach, 561/562-3653). Naval oranges are the most celebrated variety grown along the Indian River, but there are also wonderfully sweet red and white grapefruit, plus pineapple, Temple and Valencia oranges, tangerines, and tangelos.

If you would like to learn more about the citrus industry, a charming small museum in Vero Beach is devoted to the subject. The **Indian River Citrus Museum** (Heritage Center, 2140 14th Avenue, 561/770-2263) offers informative exhibits, tools, images, and artifacts that explore four centuries of citrus history in Florida.

cess and **Turtle Trail Beach Access.** Long, paved parking lots extend from Highway A1A to the dune crossover at each access. A tip of the beach visor to the Indian River County overseers who have set aside this pearl-like string of beach park access points before the developers who are working their way up from Indian River Shores further privatize the oceanfront with gated communities. Both Turtle Trail and Sea Grape are fine examples of nature held in public trust for the enjoyment of all, preserving bits and pieces of the fast disappearing Old Florida.

Contact Information

Indian River County Chamber of Commerce, 1216 21st Street, Vero Beach, FL 32960; 561/567-3491 or 800/338-2678, ext. 17802; website: www.vero-beach. fl.us/chamber

MAP OF FLORIDA'S EAST COAST—PAGE 5

Indian River Shores

Browsing through the annual edition of *Treasure Coast*—a glossy magazine for those looking to relocate or build second homes—we found everything that is developmentally problematic about the Florida coast in general, and Indian River County in particular, neatly and unironically summed up in one sentence: "In Vero Beach, Indian River Shores and the tiny town of Orchid, gated communities are winter residential retreats for the affluent." Now that we've told you all you need to know about Indian River Shores (pop. 2,640), an exclusive appendage of Vero Beach, we'll get straight to the only real thing worth writing about: its beachside park.

Tracking Station Beach, so named for the radar tracking station that adjoins the property, preserves the dense, almost blinding green vegetation that is the most striking feature of Florida's east coast when its ecology hasn't been altered or destroyed. A series of parking lots are surrounded by a tropical forest of sea grape and palm trees. A boardwalk crossover leads to a coarse, brown-sand beach backed by high, humpbacked dunes held in place by a healthy vegetative cover. When we last passed through, Tracking Station Beach was wearing the built-up profile of the summer beach as sizable breakers crashed ashore. It is the sort of semi-isolated spot where an inveterate beach lover could happily spend an entire day.

Contact Information

Indian River County Chamber of Commerce, 1216 21st Street, Vero Beach, FL 32960; 561/567-3491 or 800/338-2678, ext. 17802; website: www.vero-beach.fl.us/chamber

8 Tracking Station Beach

Location: one mile north of Beachland Avenue, on Highway A1A in Indian River Shores
Parking/fees: free parking lots
Hours: 8 A.M. to sunset
Facilities: lifeguards, restrooms, picnic tables, and showers
Contact: Tracking Station Beach, 561/231-2485

Vero Beach

Vero Beach (pop. 18,000) suffers from an identity crisis, insofar as tourism is concerned. Every other major town along Florida's east coast is associated with some activity or interest, be it recreational or historic, that instantly fixes it in people's minds. Cocoa Beach's calling card is Kennedy Space Center, while Daytona Beach has NASCAR racing, St. Augustine preserves early Colonial history, and Jacksonville claims pro football's joltin' Jaguars. To the south, Palm Beach, Fort Lauderdale, and Miami Beach collectively define the South Florida resort experience, and are known to one and all. As for Vero Beach, it's best known, if it's known at all, for being the center of Florida's citrus industry and the spring-training site for pro baseball's Los Angeles Dodgers. Now there's nothing wrong with Dodgertown or Indian River fruit (read the sidebars on pages 136 and 140), but they're hardly comparable to space-shuttle launches, the Daytona 500, or South Beach's flesh parade.

On previous visits, Vero Beach struck us as a pretty dull place geared toward a graying population of retirees. Maybe it's because we're a little older now ourselves, or maybe overbuilding and crime have dimmed South Florida's luster by comparison, but Vero Beach looks a lot more appealing these days. It is a charming, habitable small city boasting well-tended beachside parks, lovely older residential neighborhoods, and a modest tourist trade. The obvious demerit is, as it has been for decades, the severe beach erosion at the center of town, where Beachland Boulevard meets Ocean Drive. To combat the ocean's incursions, they've built seawalls (which is a virtual endgame in the progression of beach-hardening options). The beach regains a modest amount of width as you head away from Beachland Boulevard in either direction, and the town itself is a largely pleasant place that moves at a sea turtle's unhurried crawl.

Beaches

The beach at the heart of town is so eroded they should consider changing the town name from Vero Beach to just Vero. Besides saving five letters, it would be closer to the truth. The situation looked bad when we researched our first beach book in 1984 and is no better now. It's been this way for decades, and Hurricane Floyd, which glanced the Florida coast in September 1999, inflicted even more damage on Vero. At Sexton Plaza, where Beachland Boulevard meets the ocean, waves lap at the seawall. It is among the worst instances of beach erosion along a developed shoreline we've ever seen. North and south of Vero Beach's eroded center the beach reappears, though it's far from healthy. An offshore reef installed by the U.S. Army Corps of Engineers is supposed to help protect the shoreline. As with all Corps projects, *caveat emptor* applies.

Starting up north, **Jaycee Beach Park** is a grassy park with a big area for playing and picnicking (volleyball, playground equipment, covered picnic tables) and plenty of parking. A wooden boardwalk runs down the beach to some on-street parking in the vicinity of **Conn Beach**, which it adjoins. It's worth noting that all of the lifeguarded beaches in Vero Beach and Indian River County have a full complement of facilities—including playgrounds, picnic pavilions, and grills—and are exquisitely landscaped, to boot. Also worth noting: there is no public fishing pier in Vero Beach. One of the best bets for fishing in the Vero Beach area, aside from casting from the jetties and catwalks up at Sebastian Inlet State Park, is the "new" Barber Bridge, which has walkways from which people fish in the Indian River.

Humiston Park, which is three football fields south of Sexton Plaza, is another green, clean park that includes not just a beach but a grassy quadrangle. The beach, burdened by development on all sides, is backed by a seawall. It is narrow at low tide, virtually nonexistent at high tide, and just about as bad as Sexton Plaza overall. A

9 Jaycee Beach Park/Conn Beach

Location: Highway A1A at Mango Avenue in Vero Beach
Parking/fees: free parking lot
Hours: sunrise to sunset
Facilities: concessions, lifeguards, restrooms, picnic tables, and showers
Contact: Jaycee Beach Park, 561/231-0578

10 Humiston Park

Location: Ocean Drive at Easter Lily Lane, in Vero Beach
Parking/fees: free street and lot parking
Hours: sunrise to sunset
Facilities: concessions, lifeguards, restrooms, picnic tables, and showers
Contact: Humiston Park, 561/231-5790

MAP OF FLORIDA'S EAST COAST—PAGE 5

little retail area consisting of a deli, bakery, and convenience store gives the area a modest neighborhood feel.

Riomar Beach, located east of the intersection of Riomar and Ocean Drives, is a popular spot with surfers in Vero Beach. It's a private residential neighborhood, but there's a public beach accessway and limited street parking.

The pearl in the Vero Beach pendant is **South Beach Park.** South of town, Vero chills out, giving way to a modest complex of beach homes and small motels. It is a likable area in and of itself, but the beach earns an A. The city has provided parking for all comers, and the beach is a frolicker's delight. It's wider than you have any right to expect, given the erosion elsewhere in town. A mixed bag of young families, elderly retirees, and attractive bikini-clad singles—more than we ever expected to see in Vero Beach—crowds a markedly wide beach with clean, gleaming light-brown sand and emerald green waters. Walk along the beach a quarter-mile north of the entrance point, and you'll have a virtual in-town wilderness beach all to yourself. We believed that we'd somehow landed on Canaveral National Seashore or some other out-of-the-way place.

South Beach is yet another winner for Vero Beach and Indian River County. A tip of our Dodger-logoed ballcaps for providing public beach access at so many nicely designed parks. On top of everything, parking is free at South Beach and all the other city and county beach parks. Yahoo!

Shore Things

- **Bike/skate rentals:** Vero Beach Cycling and Fitness, 1865 14th Avenue, 561 /562-2781.
- **Dive shop:** Deep Six Dive & Watersports, 416 Miracle Mile, 561/562-2883.
- **Ecotourism:** Kayaks, Etc., 2626 U.S. 1, 561/794-9900.
- **Fishing charters:** Reel Fun Sportfishing Charters, 6165 60th Court, 561/569-6971.
- **Marina:** Grand Harbor Marina, 5510 North Harbor Village Drive, 561/770-4470.
- **Rainy-day attraction:** Indian River Citrus Museum, Heritage Center, 2140 14th Avenue, 561/770-2263.
- **Shopping/browsing:** Indian River Mall, 6200 20th Street, 561/770-9404.
- **Surf shop:** Inner Rhythm Surf and Sport, 2001 14th Avenue, 561/778-9038.
- **Vacation rentals:** Seaside Realty of Vero Beach, 3247 Ocean Drive, 561/231-7741.

Bunking Down

America loves an eccentric, and Vero Beach had a dandy. His name was Waldo Sexton, and he was an art collector, constructor, entrepreneur, and borderline nut case. He built three restaurants and one hotel here in the early 1900s. Their outlandishness is quite remarkable in a town this foursquare. His pièce de résistance was the **Driftwood Inn** (3150 Ocean Drive, 561/231-0550, $$$). Sexton was not a trained architect, but he designed the Driftwood with improvised verbal instructions. As its name suggests, the inn was constructed entirely from wood that washed ashore, and the rooms were decorated with whatever nautical bric-a-brac—ship bells, lanterns, cannons, boat parts—the sea coughed up. After it opened, Sexton continued to festoon the interior with artifacts obtained at estate auctions, flea markets, and his own world travels. Paintings, treasure chests, mastodon bones, ever more bells. . . . The Driftwood is a museum of the eclectic, unified only by its general nautical theme. The original Driftwood

Dodgertown

In 1997, the Los Angeles Dodgers celebrated the 50th season of spring training at their "Dodgertown" complex in Vero Beach. In a game that's not exactly known for loyalty or constancy—of all the players in major-league baseball, as of 1997, only five still played for the teams they'd been on 10 years earlier—this ongoing relationship between the Dodgers and Vero Beach is worth celebrating.

Of the 18 major-league baseball teams that train in Florida, the Dodgers' spring-training program is the one most grounded in tradition. The association with Vero dates back to 1948, when the team set up camp on the site of an old naval training station. Their loyalty to Vero Beach survived the franchise's relocation from Brooklyn to Los Angeles a decade later, and both team and town have been enamored of one another—though in the age of big money, those bonds have become stressed in recent years. Still, as of the 2001 exhibition season, the Dodgers remain the only West Coast team that trains in Florida.

The term "mystique" is often invoked by fans and players alike, and the ready accessibility of players to spectators in the casual environment at Dodgertown is cited as a big reason. The team has helped put Vero Beach on the map, such as it is. In the words of longtime Dodgers broadcaster Vin Scully, "I don't believe Vero Beach would be known anywhere outside of Vero Beach except for the presence of the Dodgers."

The Dodgers practice at Holman Stadium, which is part of the larger Dodgertown complex. Dodgertown also serves as home to a class-A minor-league team, the Vero Beach Dodgers. Football team practices and fantasy baseball camps are held here. There are six

Inn is intact, though it is now flanked by more modern lodgings and the whole complex has been renamed the Driftwood Resort.

There is also the **Holiday Inn Oceanfront** (3384 Ocean Drive, 561/231-2300, $$), which does indeed face the ocean but not a beach, thanks to erosion. Also along Ocean Drive, the main beachside thoroughfare in Vero Beach, are other upscale oceanfront resorts, such as the **Palm Court Resort** (3244 Ocean Drive, 561/231-2800, $$$), where you're invited to "rediscover Southern hospitality," and **Doubletree Guest Suites** (3500 Ocean Drive, 561/231-5666, $$$). Though these are all perfectly attractive properties, they're really going to have to do something about the beach in Vero Beach before they can truthfully market it as a place to come and enjoy the shore.

If you want to stay on a wide, healthy beach, either head south to the modestly appealing **Aquarius Oceanfront Resort** (1526 Ocean Drive, 561/231-5218, $), a clean, well-kept, and inexpensive motel located by Vero's marvelous South Beach Park, or drive north to **Disney's Vero Beach Resort** (9250 Island Grove Terrace, 561/234-2000, $$$$). At the latter, you'll pay upward of $165–305 a night for an ocean-view room next to Wabasso Beach Park; figure $60–70 more per night for a one-bedroom villa. They call it a "turn-of-the-century seaside inn," but at those prices, they must mean the year 2100. From our perspective, you'd have to be as daffy as Daffy Duck to part with that kind of money.

MAP OF FLORIDA'S EAST COAST—PAGE 5

practice fields, a conference center, housing, swimming pools, tennis courts, two golf courses, and a commercial citrus grove. But the springtime version of the summer game by the Los Angeles Dodgers is the biggest attraction at the 468-acre camp, whose centerpiece is Holman Stadium, where the lack of dugouts mean that players sit on benches, always visible and audible to those in the stands.

Players begin arriving at camp in mid-February and leave around the first of April. They play exhibition games with other major-league teams almost daily throughout the month of March, half of them away and half at Holman Stadium. Most games begin around 1 P.M. Once the major leaguers have vacated, the Vero Beach Dodgers launch a 140-game minor-league schedule that begins in early April and ends in early September. Tickets to major-league exhibition games are $12. Minor-league games are $4 for adults and $3 for kids ages 6–12. Entertainment doesn't come much cheaper than that.

In the late '90s, the Dodgers began scouting elsewhere for spring-training sites, with Las Vegas being the top contender. However, after much wrangling Florida governor Jeb Bush allocated funds in June 2000 to help the county of Indian River and the city of Vero Beach keep the Dodgers in Dodgertown. They're doing this by buying Dodgertown back from the Dodgers, making improvements to the facility and then leasing it back to the ball club. The deal will cost the city, county, and state about $20 million. So for now and hopefully forever, the Dodgers will continue to call Holman Stadium home when spring comes calling.

To find out more about spring training and game schedules for both the Los Angeles Dodgers and the Vero Beach Dodgers, contact Dodgertown, 4101 26th Street, Vero Beach, FL 32966. Call 561/569-4900 for information; or call 561/569-6858 for tickets, 9 A.M.–4 P.M. Tickets for the spring training season generally go on sale around February 3.

On the positive side, Disney's Vero Beach Resort is a great place to get away with the family, if money's no object. There are programs to occupy the kids, a jumbo heated pool with a two-story water slide, and, of course, a splendid beach right out the back door. They've made an effort to be nature friendly, the architecture blends in nicely, and it's two hours from Orlando (the further, the better, in our opinion). If a high-end Disney beach vacation appeals to your sensibilities, it is a very attractive property. Incidentally, Disney now also operates beach resorts in Key West and Hilton Head Island, South Carolina.

Coastal Cuisine

The **Ocean Grill** (1050 Sexton Plaza, 561/231-5409, $$$) overlooks the ocean across from the Holiday Inn at the end of Beachland Boulevard, a prime oceanfront location in Vero Beach. In fact, the location might be a little too good. In 1984, the Ocean Grill was washed into the sea by a vicious winter nor'easter. With it went a priceless collection of nautical bric-a-brac. According to one account, "It's old driftwood and European artifacts that decorated the popular bar were lost when the building collapsed into the sea." However, it's been rebuilt and still sways on pilings over the water, which just proves you can't keep a good restaurant down. Go for the seafood: broiled grouper, grilled swordfish, or the house specialty—Indian River crab fingers.

For another kind of dining experience that's also on the water—albeit the Intracoastal Waterway—point your car or boat to the **Riverside Cafe** (1 Beachland Boulevard, 561/234-5550, $$). To get there, follow signs from Beachland Boulevard just east of the New Merrill Barber Bridge to the restaurant's riverfront location, which is almost directly under the bridge. It's a great spot to watch the sun set in Vero Beach and observe cars and joggers crossing the gracefully arching bridge. With its open-air deck, divided into bar and restaurant areas, the Riverside is a pleasant place to nibble at bar food and listen to bar bands. They make a savory bowl of conch chowder, and the fish tostada—a nicely grilled slab of mahimahi served atop a cheesy tostada, with a mound of yellow rice and black beans on the side—is a stomach-filling entrée. Otherwise, the menu tends toward hearty appetizers such as baked stuffed oysters and Buffalo wings, basic items done decently and served in an archetypal Florida setting.

On the higher end, there's the **Black Pearl Brasserie** (2855 Ocean Drive, 561/234-7426, $$$$). It's so elegant you'd almost feel underdressed in a tuxedo—and forget about wearing that goofy Hawaiian shirt and Bermuda pants to dinner. Done up in dark and mauve tones, the dining room is a feast for the eyes, while the entrée creations are a feast pure and simple. Black Pearl concedes nothing in the way of gourmet excellence to the upscale brasseries of South Florida. Try the yellowtail snapper with lobster beurre blanc or blackened tuna with crab Creole. They do a great jerk-spiced dolphin and a Rockefeller-style fresh catch (pan roasted with spinach, bacon, and Pernod velouté). This is among our favorite restaurants between Jacksonville and Miami. The Black Pearl also has a location on the Indian River (4445 North Highway A1A, 561/234-4426, $$$$), to which a gourmet deli is appended.

Capt. Hiram's Restaurant (1606 Indian River Drive, 561/589-4345, $$$) is neither on the ocean nor in Vero Beach, but it's close enough for rock and roll. This multidimensional "fun complex" is built around a Key West-style restaurant on the banks of the Indian River in the town of Sebastian at the north end of Orchid Island. Seafood, including raw-bar items, is the house specialty at Capt. Hiram's. On the premises you'll also find a motel, two bars (Ramp Lounge and Sand Bar), both with seasonal entertainment, and a full-service marina. There's even a sand beach—albeit on the banks of the Indian River.

Night Moves

Coming to Vero Beach in search of nightlife is like going to Orlando in search

11 Riomar Beach

Location: Ocean Drive at Riomar Drive, south of the Riomar Country Club, in Vero Beach
Parking/fees: free street parking
Hours: sunrise to sunset
Facilities: nNone
Contact: Vero Beach Recreation Department, 561/231-4700

12 South Beach Park

Location: South Ocean Drive and East Causeway Boulevard (17th Street Bridge), in Vero Beach. South Beach Park can also be entered from the ends of Coquina, Flamevine, Jasmine, Pirate Cove, Sandpiper, and Turtle Cove Lanes, though no parking is available at these accesses
Parking/fees: free parking lots at South Ocean Drive and East Causeway Boulevard
Hours: sunrise to sunset
Facilities: lifeguards, restrooms, picnic tables, and showers
Contact: South Beach Park, 561/231-4700

of surfing opportunities. About the best you can hope for is a group with a name like the Landsharks playing reggae-inflected rock and roll at an outdoor tiki bar. We encountered this very band on the deck at the Riverside Cafe (see "Coastal Cuisine"). Their alternative-lite covers proved rousing to a table of elderly Swedish tourists, who bolted out of their seats and boogied around the premises as if they'd just won the lottery. America—what a wild and crazy place!

Contact Information

Indian River County Chamber of Commerce, 1216 21st Street, Vero Beach, FL 32960; 561/567-3491 or 800/338-2678, ext. 17802; website: www.vero-beach.f l.us/chamber

Round Island Park

Indian River County isn't as munificent with beach access south of Vero as it is in the northern part of the county. The only park south of Vero Beach with beach access is **Round Island Park,** which is mainly centered around the Indian River. There's not much in the way of facilities, but it's a welcome break in the wall of development and anglers love to toss a line from its shore.

Contact Information

Vero Beach–Indian River County Recreation Department, 1725 17th Avenue, Vero Beach, FL 32960; 561/567-2144

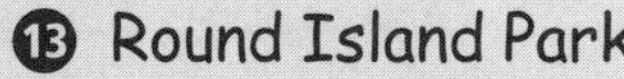

Location: Highway A1A at the St. Lucie County line
Parking/fees: free parking lot
Hours: sunrise to sunset
Facilities: restrooms, picnic tables, and showers
Contact: Vero Beach–Indian River County Recreation Department, 561/567-2144

MAP OF INDIAN RIVER COUNTY—PAGE 132

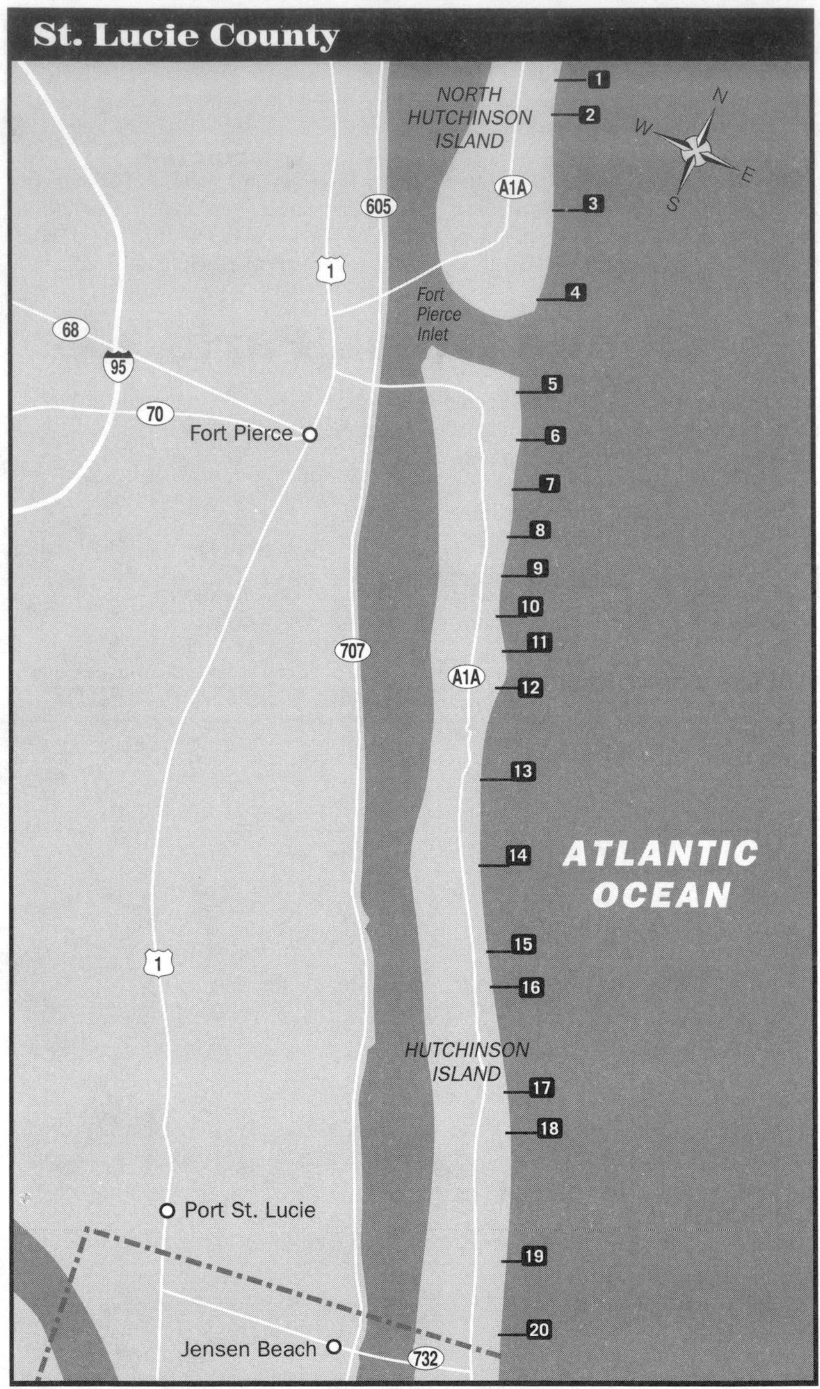
St. Lucie County
NORTH HUTCHINSON ISLAND
A1A
605
1
68
95
70
Fort Pierce Inlet
Fort Pierce
707
A1A
ATLANTIC OCEAN
1
HUTCHINSON ISLAND
Port St. Lucie
Jensen Beach
732
N
W
E
S
1
2
3
4
5
6
7
8
9
10
11
12
13
14
15
16
17
18
19
20

ST. LUCIE COUNTY

Putting a charitable spin on it, St. Lucie County offers visitors the full Taoist experience: the yin of the mainland and the yang of the beaches. We'll take the yang and leave the yin for the suffering hordes caught in traffic on U.S. 1 through the mainland Port St. Lucie/Fort Pierce corridor. The St. Lucie shoreline, especially Hutchinson Island between Fort Pierce and the Martin County line, is special. Of the county's 22 miles of ocean beaches, eight are publicly accessible, including splendid access points—Blind Creek and Middle Cove beaches, in particular—on land belonging to a nuclear generating plant.

North Hutchinson Island

First of all, let us make one thing perfectly unclear: North Hutchinson Island is also known as Orchid Island. Depending on which county you are in, the same island goes by different names. The south end belongs to St. Lucie County and is known as North Hutchinson Island, while the north end belongs to Indian River County and is known as Orchid Island. Confused? Join the club.

North Hutchinson Island is schizophrenic, being divided between wild, windswept beach parks and tall stands of condominiums. The thick buildup of 15-story condos, constructed with all the architectural imagination of college dormitories, runs for miles above Fort Pierce Inlet on North Hutchinson Island, blocking views of the ocean for those driving along Highway A1A. It seemed curious to us that at the height of summer, parking lots at these oceanfront fortresses were nearly empty. Ah, it's the absentee owner phenomenon! So, this is where all those absentee ballots came from! There would seem to be a certain injustice in permitting beach-facing condominiums to be built, thereby denying ocean views and beach access to others, when no one even lives in such places most of the time.

For stretches along Highway A1A on North Hutchinson Island, it's all towering condos on the ocean side and manufactured housing on the inland side, neither of them a pretty sight. The good news is that between Vero Beach and Fort Pierce Inlet, several superb beach parks and accesses have been emplaced between all the condos. They are (in order) **Avalon Beach**, **Bryn Mawr Beach**, and **Pepper Park**. Avalon Park is a state property with nothing much more than two entrance points, free lots, restrooms, and dune walkovers. You cross a broad meadow thick with beach grasses (a dune restoration in progress) to get to an unspoiled and usually deserted beach. The

❶ Avalon Beach

Location: 1.5 miles south of the Indian River County line along Highway A1A on North Hutchinson Island
Parking/fees: free parking lots
Hours: 8 A.M. to sunset
Facilities: restrooms
Contact: Fort Pierce Inlet State Park, 561/468-3985

❷ Bryn Mawr Beach

Location: two miles south of the Indian River County line along Highway A1A on North Hutchinson Island
Parking/fees: free parking lot
Hours: sunrise to sunset
Facilities: none
Contact: St. Lucie County Recreation Office, 561/462-1521

❸ Pepper Park

   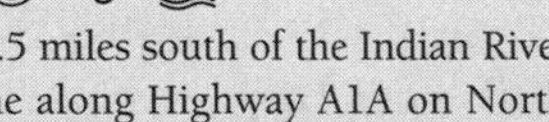

Location: 2.5 miles south of the Indian River County line along Highway A1A on North Hutchinson Island
Parking/fees: free parking lots
Hours: sunrise to sunset
Facilities: lifeguards (seasonal), restrooms, picnic tables, and showers
Contact: St. Lucie County Recreation Office, 561/462-1521

county has provided a parking lot and dune crossover to Bryn Mawr Beach, about a half-mile south of Avalon, and it's more of the beguiling same.

The gem of North Hutchinson Island is Pepper Park, a full-tilt boogie ocean-to-river park that's busting out with things to do and places to do them on. It's got volleyball, tennis, and basketball courts. On the lagoon side, there are boat docks and fishing piers. Picnic tables occupy a large, grassy quadrangle. There's also the intriguing Navy Frogman Museum (3300 North A1A, Pepper Park, 561/595-1570), devoted to those amphibious men in uniform who helped guard the coast from German U-boats during World War II. Best of all, there's nearly 2,000 feet of expansive, gently sloping beach at Pepper Park. The Fort Pierce Inlet jetties are visible to the south. All in all, this is a very inviting place that gets our highest commendations.

Contact Information
St. Lucie County Tourist Development Council, 2300 Virginia Avenue, Fort Pierce, FL 34982; 561/462-1535 or 800/344-8443; website: www.visitstluciefla.com

Fort Pierce Inlet State Park

The main attraction at the south end of the island is **Fort Pierce Inlet State Park**, a two-part park that consists of the north shore of Fort Pierce Inlet and Jack Island Preserve, a peninsula on the Indian River side of the island a mile and a half up Highway A1A. Good surf is occasionally kicked up at North Jetty Park when swells roll in from the north or northeast. On an ominously overcast day in October, we found a mile-long line of surfers out on the water here.

The swimming is fine all of the time on this lifeguarded beach. The sand is a natural brown-orange color, not at all like the mocha-colored fill south of the jetty, on Fort Pierce's beach. At Fort Pierce Inlet and Jack Island Preserve, trails wend their way through coastal plant communities—maritime hammock and mangrove wetlands, respectively—both of which are rarer than they ought to be these days. Bring a canoe and paddle around the mangrove swamp at Dynamite Point (so named for the Navy's Underwater Demolition Team, who drilled here during World War II), on the west side of the inlet. Also, be advised that the fishing is great on every flank of the park, from jetty to estuary.

Contact Information
Fort Pierce Inlet State Park, 905 Shorewinds Drive, Fort Pierce, FL 34949; 561/468-3985; website: www.myflorida.com

4 Fort Pierce Inlet State Park

Location: southern tip of North Hutchinson Island at the end of Shorewinds Drive
Parking/fees: $3.25 per vehicle entrance fee
Hours: 8 A.M. to sunset
Facilities: lifeguards (seasonal), restrooms, picnic tables, and showers
Contact: Fort Pierce Inlet State Park, 561/468-3985

Fort Pierce

As in Vero Beach, the main portion of Fort Pierce (pop. 38,401) is built on the west side of the Indian River, but Fort Pierce also crosses the river over to the north end of Hutchinson Island via Highway A1A. The area along the causeway and among the backwaters off the Intracoastal Waterway is a salty dog's mecca, with more vessels docked at the city's marinas than you'll find cars parked at a Wal-Mart during Sam's Birthday Bash. The central focus for all this activity is Fort Pierce Inlet, which allows boaters access to the inner harbor and several marinas. Docks line the inlet's mouth as well as the Intracoastal Waterway, and several motels and waterfront pubs service these boat people.

Other than that, the beach portion of Fort Pierce is generally low key and unpretentious—a throwback to another time and place, which is all the more amazing given the mad growth scenarios on the

Who Loves Lucie?

Judging from the recent growth spurt of cities west of Hutchinson Island, it might take the construction of another fort to protect the beaches of St. Lucie County from the mainland part of Fort Pierce and its landlocked neighbor, Port St. Lucie. The latter is the biggest culprit—at least Fort Pierce has tried to fix up its old downtown district and has added a Manatee Observation and Education Center—but both cities have been attracting hordes of people in recent decades, and we don't mean vacationers. These newcomers are mostly retirees who can't afford the luxury of aging down along the Gold Coast or suckers who've been taken in by apocryphal Florida real-estate come-ons.

How else to explain the following facts and figures, which translate to a visual blight that beggars the imagination: Port St. Lucie did not exist in 1961. Today, it is the blob-like home to 83,254 people, sprawled across 77 square miles (the third largest land area of any Florida city) of former swampland and pine savanna. From the perspective of U.S. 1, it's all sweltering asphalt as far as the eye can see.

Far sadder and more troubling is that fact that for whatever reason—poisoned drinking water from a municipal underground injection control well is being looked at as a possible cause—the incidence of rare brain and central nervous system cancers in children is abnormally high in Port St. Lucie, and health officials have been investigating. Of course, when we cited this information in an earlier edition—having read detailed reports in local, state and even national news media—we were accused of all sort of nefarious motives. The sitting mayor of Port St. Lucie labeled us "outside nuts," while a former mayor opined that we were "obviously suffering from cranial suffocation caused by rectal strangulation." (Huh?) A city councilman questioned our credibility as travel writers, and another said ours was a "fairy tale." In our opinion, after the bungled vote count in the presidential election of 2000, public officials in Florida would be well advised to avoid using terms like "fairy tale," "credibility" or (especially) "rectal."

What we didn't know was that soon before the first edition of our book appeared, a *New York Post* columnist—assigned for a month to the nearby Mets Spring Training camp—had

Map of Florida's East Coast—Page 5

mainland. In fact, with the exception of state and federal park land, no beachfront in Florida has changed less than Fort Pierce's since we began charting beaches in 1984. A string of green, clean beach parks and accesses only adds to the understated appeal.

Beaches

The beaches of Fort Pierce are good and have been improving. When we passed through in the mid-1980s, littering and lax enforcement had taken their toll on the sand. On our walks about the island, we found the vegetation-smashing tire tracks of joyriding Jeeps, as well as mounds of trash and tackle left behind by fishermen. All that has since changed for the better. **South Jetty Park**, located where Highway A1A meets the island in Fort Pierce, looks a bit more spruced up these days, though it too can get trashed on bad days. On our most recent visit, for example, wads of litter choked a dune restoration project. What kind of people would throw trash in a roped off dune restoration project area?

described Port St. Lucie as "a pathetic waste of map space" filled with "honky-tonk bars" and "briefly clad babes." Apparently, our less strident, fact-based observations struck the locals as piling on, which didn't minimize our shock at having the normally benign tourist council call our book "inaccurate" and "sad."

And then there were the spewings of the aptly named Joe Crankshaw, a writer for the *Stuart News* who devoted an entire column to our book—or, rather, his impressions of our book gleaned from the honking of local officials. His main beef about our "trashing" of Port St. Lucie was that the city has no beaches and, thus, should not be mentioned in our book. Then, he writes, "If they don't like the St. Lucie County beaches, it is just because they are too young [we wish!] and never knew the real Florida."

Sorry to burst this below-average Joe's bubble, but our writings were based on considerable time spent in Port St. Lucie (we have been passing through the area almost yearly since the early 1960s) and on Hutchinson Island. This shoot-from-the-hip hack, on the other hand, obviously never even thumbed through our book. If he had, it would have registered with him that we said many positive things about the beaches of St. Lucie County. We not only stand by everything we've previously written but suggest the elected and appointed leaders of St. Lucie County start paying heed to their own citizens, who have registered disparaging comments of their own about the county's growth patterns.

For example, this came from a lifelong native in response to the trashing of our book by the politicians: "I grew up here. I went to high school and college here . . . and I wonder where City Council members Bowen and Cernuto live? Are they blind? Do they not see all this destruction of property? The traffic is horrible. For them to say *[Florida Beaches]* is a fairy tale or misinformation—they're completely wrong. And when the authors of the book said 90% of the population of Port St. Lucie does not want to see all these strip malls, they're correct. No one does. Everywhere you turn, there's a new Publix, there's a new Lowe's. There no more land left. There's nothing. I think it's deplorable, and they need to wake up and see what Port St. Lucie is really like. It's not a beautiful city and it really does not have all that much to offer."

We repeat: Port St. Lucie is an overbuilt assembly line of brain-numbing franchised commerce that is best hurried through or avoided altogether.

The city-built facility is defined by a 1,200-foot rock and concrete jetty that juts into the Atlantic Ocean. Constructed to keep the inlet mouth open for boaters, the jetty and park were also designed with fishing and other forms of landlubbing fun in mind. Picnic tables are distributed around the parking area, with a fish-cleaning station at the center of the action. You can catch it, cut it up, and cook it right there on the barbecue grills. Best of all, just around the corner is a crescent-shaped beach that stretches for about a mile to the south. The beach and adjoining grounds are connected by a boardwalk and are cooled by constant breezes that blow off the churning waters of the inlet and jetty. Lifeguards are on duty from nine to five.

Between South Jetty Park and **South Beach Boardwalk** in Fort Pierce, there is a series of five dune walkovers—**St. Lucie Court/Avalon Avenue/Palm Haven/Porpoise Road/Gulfstream Avenue accesses**—that provides basic access to beachgoers (including those who live in the neighborhood but not on the beach). The walkovers are located at the ends of streets

5 South Jetty Park

Location: East end of Seaway Drive, off North Ocean Drive (Highway A1A) in Fort Pierce, on the south side of Fort Pierce Inlet
Parking/fees: free parking lot
Hours: sunrise to sunset
Facilities: lifeguards, restrooms, picnic tables, and showers
Contact: St. Lucie County Recreation Office, 561/462-1521

6 St. Lucie Court/Avalon Avenue/Palm Haven /Porpoise Road/ Gulfstream Avenue accesses

Location: Off South Ocean Drive (Highway A1A) between Fort Pierce Inlet and South Beach Boardwalk in Fort Pierce
Parking/fees: free limited street parking
Hours: sunrise to sunset
Facilities: none
Contact: St. Lucie County Recreation Office, 561/462-1521

7 South Beach Boardwalk

Location: One-quarter mile south of Gulfstream Avenue on South Ocean Drive (Highway A1A) in Fort Pierce
Parking/fees: free parking lot
Hours: sunrise to sunset
Facilities: lifeguards, restrooms, picnic tables, and showers
Contact: South Beach Boardwalk, 561/432-2355

8 Surfside Park/ Kimberly Bergalis Memorial Park

Location: One mile south of Fort Pierce Inlet, on South Ocean Drive (Highway A1A) in Fort Pierce
Parking/fees: free parking lots
Hours: sunrise to sunset
Facilities: lifeguards (seasonal), restrooms, picnic tables, and showers
Contact: St. Lucie County Recreation Office, 561/462-1521

Map of Florida's East Coast—Page 5

intersecting Highway A1A between Avalon and Gulfstream avenues.

The quarter-mile South Beach Boardwalk (in the 700 block of South Ocean Drive, aka Highway A1A) runs alongside a beach park that provides free parking, picnic areas, and lifeguard stands. Less than a half mile to the south, in the 1200 block of Highiway A1A, is another boardwalked beach, this one a side-by-side duo called **Surfside Park/Kimberly Bergalis Memorial Park**. The latter was named in memory of a local resident who contracted AIDS from her dentist and then spent her remaining days bravely speaking out for victims of the disease and petitioning for funds to research its cure. Although parking is limited, there's room for any spillover along Ocean Drive (Highway A1A). Lifeguards are on duty at the conjoined parks, which together account for about a quarter mile of sandy beach.

At all three of these parks, the sand is a chocolate color and is coarser than natural Florida beach sand. This fill was no doubt put here just before the current dune revegetation efforts got under way. Finally, small parking lots and dune crossovers (and nothing else) are provided at **Coconut Drive Park** and **Exchange Park**, at the south end of town.

Shore Things

- **Dive shop**: Dixie Divers, 1717 U.S. 1, 561/461-4488.
- **Ecotourism**: Turtle Walk, Florida Power & Light, 800/552-8440.
- **Fishing charters**: Grand Slam Fishing Center, 101 Seaway Drive, 561/466-6775.
- **Marina**: Harbortown Marina, 1936 Harbortown Drive, 561/466-0947.
- **Pier**: South Jetty Park, Fort Pierce Inlet, Seaway Drive at South Ocean Drive (Highway A1A).
- **Rainy-day attraction**: Harbor Branch Oceanographic Institution, 5600 U.S. 1 North, 561/465-2400.
- **Shopping/browsing**: Orange Blossom Mall, Okeechobee Road at Virginia Avenue, 561/466-5100.
- **Surf shop**: Deep Six Watersports, 521 North 4th Street, 561/465-4114.
- **Vacation rentals**: Ocean Village, 2400 South Ocean Drive, 561/489-6100.

Bunking Down

At the north end of Hutchinson Island, there's plenty of beach but precious few hotels or motels that lie on it. Most are located along Fort Pierce Inlet before Highway A1A makes a right-angle turn down the coastline. These unimpressive motels, along with strip malls and fast-food joints, serve the fishing and boating crowd. The names give away the game. One is called the **Dockside Inn** (1152 Seaway Drive, 561/461-4824, $), another, its name written in hot pink neon, is the **Angler Motel** (1172 Seaway Drive, 561/466-0131, $), and so on. The place closest to the beach—in fact, right on it where Highway A1A makes its southern turn—is the **Beachwood Motel** (110 South Ocean Drive, 561/467-0002, $), an age-old reliable that is in the process of being expanded. Nearby, but still a one-block walk from the water, is **Days Inn** (1920 Seaway Drive, 561/461-8737, $). It's a shrimp by this chain's standards, with only 32 units in a one-story structure, which is in desperate need of refurbishing.

The only oceanfront lodging really worth extolling on Fort Pierce's beach is **Ocean Village** (2400 South Ocean Drive, 561/489-6100, $$$). Located two miles south of the inlet, it offers beach access and is within walking distance of Green Turtle Beach. A condo complex that hugs the ocean for a mile, it occupies a small world within a world, offering a secure setting for quality living with an accent on recreation. It covers 120 acres and might be described as a miniature Amelia Island Plantation. On the grounds: a beach club, a beautiful swimming pool, a nine-hole golf course, tennis and racquetball courts, four high-rise residential towers, and rows of two-story villas lining the fairways. Like many such semiprivate places, Ocean Village is only partly open to the public. Individual units are rented out by the week or month when participating owners are not using them.

Coastal Cuisine

There's nothing much to recommend on the beach in Fort Pierce. **Harbortown Fish House** (1930 Harbortown Drive, Taylor Creek Marina, 561/461-8737, $$) seems the safest bet, though it's miles from the ocean and all over the map in terms of its menu, with Key West–style conch dishes cohabiting with New England clam chowder. Nearer the ocean is **Mangrove Mattie's** (1640 Seaway Drive, 561/466-1044, $$$), whose most salient feature is the lovely view of the inlet and the beach. Though Mattie serves fresh seafood, she sells it at inflated prices. This is Fort Pierce, not South Miami Beach. Most recently the featured entertainer was someone named Don Buffett. Jimmy's "wise guy" brother?

Contact Information

St. Lucie County Tourist Development Council, 2300 Virginia Avenue, Fort Pierce, FL 34982; 561/462-1535 or 800/344-8443; website: www.visitstluciefla.com

9 Coconut Drive Park

Location: South end of Surfside Drive on Blue Heron Avenue in Fort Pierce
Parking/fees: free parking lot
Hours: sunrise to sunset
Facilities: none
Contact: St. Lucie County Recreation Office, 561/462-1521

10 Exchange Park

Location: 2.25 miles south of Fort Pierce Inlet on South Ocean Drive (Highway A1A) in Fort Pierce
Parking/fees: free parking lot
Hours: sunrise to sunset
Facilities: none
Contact: St. Lucie County Recreation Office, 561/462-1521

Hutchinson Island

One of the most pleasant surprises of our Florida beachcombing was this 16-mile barrier island. Hutchinson Island encompasses parts of Fort Pierce and Jensen Beach, plus a whole lot in between. With the necessary exception of the fishing village atmosphere at the northern end (Fort Pierce's beachfront) and some motel accommodations where two southerly causeways (State Route 707A and Highway A1A) meet this thin strip of land, Hutchinson Island has pretty much been left to the natural elements. Mother Nature has, in fact, found a strange bedfellow out here in Florida Power & Light (FP&L), the electric utility that operates a nuclear plant at mid-island. For safety reasons and through creative land acquisition, FP&L owns a five-mile swath of undeveloped and thickly vegetated acreage that stretches from the ocean to the Indian River.

The Indian River watershed is hugely important to central Florida's agricultural, fishing, and tourist industries, as well as being a vital habitat for threatened and endangered sea turtle species and any number of delicious seafood items found on nearly every restaurant menu. Perhaps overcompensating for the PR woes of the much-maligned nuclear power industry, FP&L—whose Hutchinson Island plant has had its share of problems—has been a good steward of this land and the river watershed. They sponsor low-impact nighttime turtle walks, run a free and popular "Energy Encounter" program for the public, conduct outreach environmental programs for area schools, and have preserved a 400-acre freshwater cypress swamp (Barley Barber Swamp) in western Martin County. In short, FP&L has set the right example for the ecotourism market that Hutchinson Island badly wishes to cultivate. For these and other programs, call FP&L's Environmental Information Line at 800/552-8440.

Beaches

You'll find somewhere in the neighborhood of 20 public beach accesses on Hutchinson Island. This is the work of two counties (St. Lucie and Martin), among which the island has been divided, with the lion's share going to St. Lucie County. The maddening exception to the new low-impact, ecotourist spirit of Hutchinson Island is an unbroken line, four miles in length, of high-rise condominiums along the beach. This onslaught falls on the St. Lucie side of the county line.

Even with this false note, Hutchinson Island ranks among the top spots for secluded beaches in central Florida,

11 Green Turtle Beach/ John Brooks Park

Location: Just south of the Fort Pierce city limits along Highway A1A on Hutchinson Island
Parking/fees: free parking lot
Hours: sunrise to sunset
Facilities: none
Contact: St. Lucie County Recreation Office, 561/462-1521

12 Frederick Douglass Memorial Beach

Location: Four miles south of Fort Pierce Inlet, on Highway A1A
Parking/fees: free parking lot
Hours: sunrise to sunset
Facilities: lifeguards (seasonal), restrooms, picnic tables, and showers
Contact: St. Lucie County Recreation Office, 561/462-1521

comparing favorably with Canaveral National Seashore and north Indian River County. Our opinion on the matter is the result of hanging out on the island at some length (thanks to a broken-down rental car) and sampling its quieter charms. Like the sea turtles on their annual crawl ashore, we lumbered about the beaches of Hutchinson Island at a slow, unhurried pace, which allowed us to savor them properly. We recommend that you do so as well.

Here is what you will find, moving down Hutchinson Island from Fort Pierce to the Martin County line:

- **Green Turtle Beach/John Brooks Park:** This is another side-by-side beach park duo just outside the Fort Pierce city limits, albeit with no facilities and limited parking. What they do have a lot of is beach: a remarkable 8,600 feet of it, which translates to 1.6 miles of undeveloped shoreline.
- **Frederick Douglass Memorial Beach:** This St. Lucie County park is a fitting monument to a man who escaped slavery and then became one of its most articulate detractors, an orator of great power and a journalist and author of the first rank. The 1,000-foot beach is suitably grand, claiming the best seashell beds in the area and unblemished natural panoramic vistas. The park is also well maintained, with covered picnic areas, clean restrooms, and volleyball courts. Three Sundays a month, horseback riding is allowed. An old dune-buggy trail, now off-limits to

⓭ Middle Cove Beach Access

Location: Five miles south of Fort Pierce Inlet, on Highway A1A
Parking/fees: free parking lot
Hours: sunrise to sunset
Facilities: none
Contact: St. Lucie County Recreation Office, 561/462-1521

⓮ Blind Creek Beach

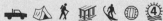

Location: Eight miles south of Fort Pierce Inlet, on Highway A1A
Parking/fees: free parking lot
Hours: sunrise to sunset
Facilities: none
Contact: St. Lucie County Recreation Office, 561/462-1521

⓯ Turtle Beach Nature Trail

Location: On property belonging to Florida Power & Light's St. Lucie Nuclear Power Plant, along Highway A1A on Hutchinson Island
Parking/fees: free parking lot
Hours: sunrise to sunset
Facilities: none
Contact: Florida Power & Light's Environmental Information Line, 800/552-8440

⓰ Walton Rocks Beach

Location: Directly south of the St. Lucie Nuclear Power Plant along Highway A1A on Hutchinson Island
Parking/fees: free parking lot
Hours: sunrise to sunset
Facilities: restrooms, picnic tables, and showers
Contact: St. Lucie County Recreation Office, 561/462-1521

Map of Florida's East Coast—Page 5

motorized vehicles, can be used by hikers and horseback riders.

- **Middle Cove Beach Access:** This St. Lucie County park is located 1.5 miles south of Frederick Douglass. You park in a small paved lot, then follow a dirt path to the beach. It is a short, pleasant stroll through a cover of tall grass and scrub pine, plus some of the dreaded Australian pine that is being slowly eradicated around Florida. The seclusion here is soul restoring and the beach itself is quite nearly perfect—gently tapered brownish-tan sand covered here and there with driftwood. The only drawback is that there are no facilities or lifeguards, but even that may be a blessing in disguise, as it renders this spot all the more enticing for those who want to feel like castaways on a fantasy Gilligan's Island.
- **Blind Creek Beach:** Two miles south of Middle Cove Beach, this beach access offers more of the same. A rutted road leads to a small parking lot, which in turn leads to a secluded beach with no facilities or lifeguards. It is unquestionably grand. The only question we had was about the name. Would drinking from the creek—given that it flows away from the spill tanks of FP&L's nuclear plant—render one sightless? In any case, the recent acquisition of a parcel by the county has extended the length of Blind Creek Beach to 835 feet. Now that's what we like to hear!
- **Turtle Beach Nature Trail:** This one-half-mile stroll through unusually thick

⓱ Herman's Bay Access

Location: 10 miles south of Fort Pierce Inlet, along Highway A1A on Hutchinson Island
Parking/fees: free parking lot
Hours: sunrise to sunset
Facilities: none
Contact: St. Lucie County Recreation Office, 561/462-1521

⓲ Normandy Beach Access

Location: 11 miles south of Fort Pierce Inlet, along Highway A1A on Hutchinson Island
Parking/fees: free parking lot
Hours: sunrise to sunset
Facilities: none
Contact: St. Lucie County Recreation Office, 561/462-1521

⓳ Dollman Park

Location: two miles north of the Jensen Beach Causeway, along Highway A1A on Hutchinson Island
Parking/fees: free parking lot
Hours: sunrise to sunset
Facilities: lifeguards, restrooms, and showers
Contact: St. Lucie County Recreation Office, 561/462-1521

⓴ Waveland Beach

Location: one mile north of the Martin County line along Highway A1A on Hutchinson Island
Parking/fees: free parking lot
Hours: sunrise to sunset
Facilities: lifeguards, restrooms, picnic tables, and showers
Contact: St. Lucie County Recreation Office, 561/462-1521

MAP OF ST. LUCIE COUNTY—PAGE 144

Doing the Turtle Walk

We don't just like sea turtles. We've fallen head over heels in love with them. Admittedly, they can't sing, dance, play, read, write, surf a wave, drive a car, cash a check, use a credit card or dunk a basketball. What they can do is show by determined example that what remains of the world's coastal habitat must be preserved, not just for their safety but for the salvation of humankind.

This is especially true in Florida, a greatly overdeveloped state that is home to an extraordinary and unrivaled array of animal and plant life. Using the same equation played out with dispiriting frequency all over the planet, the crush of human numbers in Florida has led to precipitous declines in the natural world and in some cases pushed certain species to the brink of extinction.

For sea turtles, this is particularly devastating. Two endangered species, the green turtle and the leatherback, make Florida their nesting area. So does the loggerhead turtle, a threatened species. Ninety percent of all sea turtle nesting in the United States occurs in Florida; most of it is done on Florida's east coast, with a smaller run on the Gulf Coast.

The highest concentration of nesting occurs between Volusia and Palm Beach Counties, and the peak locales are from South Brevard County to Indian River County. There, during egg-laying season (May through August) as many as 20,000 turtle nests are found, each with 100 eggs inside. While you're doing the math, you'll want to factor in some sad subtractions. For every 1,000 eggs that hatch (50 to 60 days later), only one sea turtle hatchling will survive to adulthood. The silver lining: For every hatchling that makes it to adulthood, life expectancy is as high as 80 years. Weights run to 400 pounds for loggerheads, greens, and Kemp's ridleys, and half a ton for leatherbacks.

Hutchinson Island has, in year's past, landed as many as 7,000 sea turtle nests, though numbers have been dwindling. Loggerhead nests totaled 5,030 in 1995; 3,920 in 1996; and 3,522 in 1997. The turtles' onshore stroll has been going on for 175 million years, since the first pregnant sea turtle waddled ashore on some isolated coastline to carefully dig a deep hole with her front legs, squat above it, and deposit an onslaught of eggs the size and shape of Ping-Pong balls. After securing the nest by covering it with sand, the mama turtle waddles back out to the ocean, never to see her brood. Only a few hours of a sea turtle's life are spent on land. Blink, and you'll miss it.

Turtle walks are intended to show respectful human beings this one blink in time. As

coastal habitat falls on the property of the nuclear facility and is marked by a sign on Highway A1A.

- **Walton Rocks Beach**: Located a half-mile south of the FP&L nuclear plant—and managed cooperatively by the county and the utility—Walton Rocks is reached via a dirt road that leads a quarter mile to a dirt parking lot. You can settle here or keep driving further to a second lot, with similar facilities (restroom, showers, picnic tables). From both places, you walk through a break in the healthy dunes, covered with sea oats and scrub pine, to find the same perfectly tan-colored sand as is found north of here. Living up to its name, Walton does have some rocks

such, they must be carefully regulated, limited to groups of 50, and led only by state-licensed marine biologists. On Hutchinson Island, these walks are conducted under the auspices of Florida Power & Light's Environmental Education Department. Sightings are not guaranteed, although they generally occur all but one or two nights a season. The epic struggle of sea turtles has had the positive effect of generating the near-unanimous sympathy of humans (with the exception of poachers, who are subhuman), engendering efforts to curb behavior that interferes with egg laying and hatching. However, it has also made turtles a loved-to-death tourist attraction, like puffins in Maine, otters in Monterey, and whales in Massachusetts.

As well-meaning as some folks may be, they are out of bounds should they wander onto the beach at night with flashlights, cameras, and beer coolers. In short, don't go out on your own. Flashes from cameras, headlights from cars, and even handheld flashlights startle skittish sea turtles and can also distract the hatchlings from making their seaward march from the nest two months later. They can be led in the wrong direction to be run over by cars—a needless tragedy. It's bad enough that raccoons and feral pigs raid the nests, shorebirds pluck the babes from the sand, and seabirds snatch them from the water. If a sea turtle is prevented from laying her eggs, she'll simply turn around, return to the ocean, and drop her load there, where it never hatches—another needless tragedy.

The goal of a turtle walk is to find a sea turtle clearly ready to lay her eggs, which is to say that a bucket-sized hole has been dug and she's squatting over it. These are spotted from a distance by biologists using infrared telescopes and binoculars. They patrol the beaches for three reasons: to rid them of human intruders, to count the number of nests laid by each species, and to spot a candidate for a turtle walk. When she's found, the news is radioed to the group, who are then quietly led by the guide. The group forms a semicircle at the turtle's head. Even noisy children are hushed into reverent awe by this extraordinary spectacle, the most moving aspect of which is the mother turtle's tears. As she squats and produces her progeny, tears flow unabated. She is not, however, weeping uncontrollably with joy or sadness. Her tear ducts simply keep her eyes from drying up while clearing them of sand and other debris.

Regardless, the sight of her tears makes watching this age-old ritual a humbling experience. You'll want to run home and hug your own mother.

Turtle walks are held in June and July, which are the prime months for turtle nesting activity. For reservations and information, call FP&L's Environmental Information Line at 800/552-8440, beginning in May.

in the water (known as "wormrock"), which makes the ocean vista more beautiful and evocative. Despite the hazards, Walton Rocks is popular with surfers. It's a good place to work on your moves as you negotiate the rocky waters. According to some surfers we spoke with who regularly ply these waters, the rocks form five tiers moving out from shore, each separated by about 15 feet of sand. At high tide, the water was only chest high, which they assured us was plenty safe for their purposes. And it is the second longest public beach in the county, running for six-tenths of a mile.

- **Herman's Bay and Normandy Beach Accesses:** At both south county sites

Club Med Sandpiper

Somewhere off of U.S. 1 in St. Lucie County, one can turn onto a road that leads to a semi-exotic playground a few miles away. Suddenly, the world is transformed from an all-American asphalt nightmare of retailing run amok to a European-style vacation oasis: Club Med Sandpiper. Here, the motto is "Life as it should be." This is one of only two Club Med resorts in the United States and the only one in Florida, which is why we are writing about it even though it's not on the beach. It is in Port St. Lucie, which lies west of the Indian River. But Club Med warrants inclusion as a vacation destination that's close to the beach and certainly evokes the spirit of fun in the sun. Besides, the resort runs shuttles to the beaches of Hutchinson Island for its sand-starved guests. And, since we were last there in 1998, the resort was closed for three months to complete a top to bottom overhaul. It enters the new millennium practically brand spanking new.

At Club Med, most every need—be it for lodging, food, or play (you pay separately for booze)—is taken care of with one daily price. They keep you hopping, too. Upon check-in, you are handed a printed sheet listing that day's activities. They occur hourly all day long and include such things as tennis and in-line skating lessons, as well as instruction on being a trapeze artist or bouncing up and down on a trampoline. There's never a dull moment at Club Med Sandpiper, which mainly draws European visitors who find it a safe harbor far from the carjackings and other acts of random violence that shape foreigners' perceptions of America. (And why not? These perceptions are true.) At Club Med, you play hard, eat well three times a day, snack between meals, and sometimes just relax by the pool (or pools: there are four of them). You can golf, water-ski, in-line skate, play tennis, aerobicize, do yoga, get massaged, lie in the sun, country line-dance, and more. An activities center for kiddies frees adults to make their own daytime whoopee.

you'll find free parking in a dirt lot and a smallish beach (100 feet) at each access that's covered with seaweed and driftwood. Both are used mostly by surfers. With all the other selections available, though, these spots don't rank at the top because of their unobstructed views of the wall of condos, all of which have self-important names like the Admiral, Atlantis, Oceana, and Regency Island. Oddly enough, on the inlet side, there's a tacky community comprised of mobile homes, squat houses, and boat docks, scattered like salmon croquettes upon the greased griddle of a landfill appropriately named Nettles Island.

- **Dollman Park:** This park, whose name may or may not have changed by the time you read this, has a sizable beach (1,850 feet), plus lifeguards, restrooms, and showers. Moreover, it is slated to grow in both acreage and facilities, so keep your eye on this one.
- **Waveland Beach:** This municipal park is located a mile north of the Jensen Beach Causeway (State Route 732). Hemmed in by condos on either side, this 320-foot beach tends to draw elderly condo dwellers and their visiting relations. Surfers flock here, too, though they're required to surf outside the lifeguarded area.

Map of Florida's East Coast—Page 5

At one time a playground for swinging singles, the Club Med chain now gears itself to families. Kids appear to outnumber adults at Club Med Sandpiper, and they scamper around as if they own the place. In a sense, they do. Which is to say if you're looking for a romantic retreat, Club Med Sandpiper might not be the best choice. If you're looking for a resort to bring the whole family, however, come on down. Europeans will feel right at home. And if you're from America, you'll feel as if you're in Europe. No passport necessary!

The villas on the property are Spanish styled, with terra-cotta tile floors and rattan furniture. They are casually elegant and very comfortable for lounging around. By the end of the day, after chasing balls around and gorging at the endless awesome cruise line-style buffet spreads, you might be tempted to chill out in your room. But before you turn in for the evening, be advised there is nightly entertainment, some of which is quite funny.

They happened to be holding a lip-synching competition when we were there. This wasn't just any old corner-bar karaoke, mind you, but elaborately costumed theatrical pantomimes of well-known songs by the Club Med staff. The audience registered yeas or nays for each performance by applauding. One group of dolled-up male staff members did a Broadway-worthy spoof of Queen's "Bohemian Rhapsody," which included a little impromptu theater: the guy wielding the cardboard bass actually fell off the stage in mid-song.

From here, it was on to Le Garage Discotheque for us, where a rainbow coalition of Europeans did their disco thing beneath spinning orbs that cast dizzying shards of light on the dance floor as pounding music blared from a high-tech sound system. As the character Dieter would say on the *Saturday Night Live* Eurodisco parody Sprockets, "And now we dance!"

Actually, we watched, which was just as much fun. It had been a long day, you see, and we were too tired to boogie-oogie-oogie.

For more information contact Club Med Sandpiper, 3500 Southeast Morningside Boulevard, Port St. Lucie, FL 34952; 561/335-4400. For reservations or information on Club Meds around the world, call 800/CLUB-MED or log on to www.clubmed.com

Finally, as an interesting side note, the county has prevailed over condo owners down in south St. Lucie County, providing a public access to the beach at the Islanda II condominium. It's mainly for people who live across the road and want a way to get to the beach, as is their God-given right. Putting this public easement in place required knocking down a wall blocking access to the beach. We'll be the first to champion any effort to let the walls fall in the name of public beach access.

Contact Information

St. Lucie County Tourist Development Council, 2300 Virginia Avenue, Fort Pierce, FL 34982; 561/462-1535 or 800/344-8443; website: www.visitstluciefla.com

MAP OF ST. LUCIE COUNTY—PAGE 144

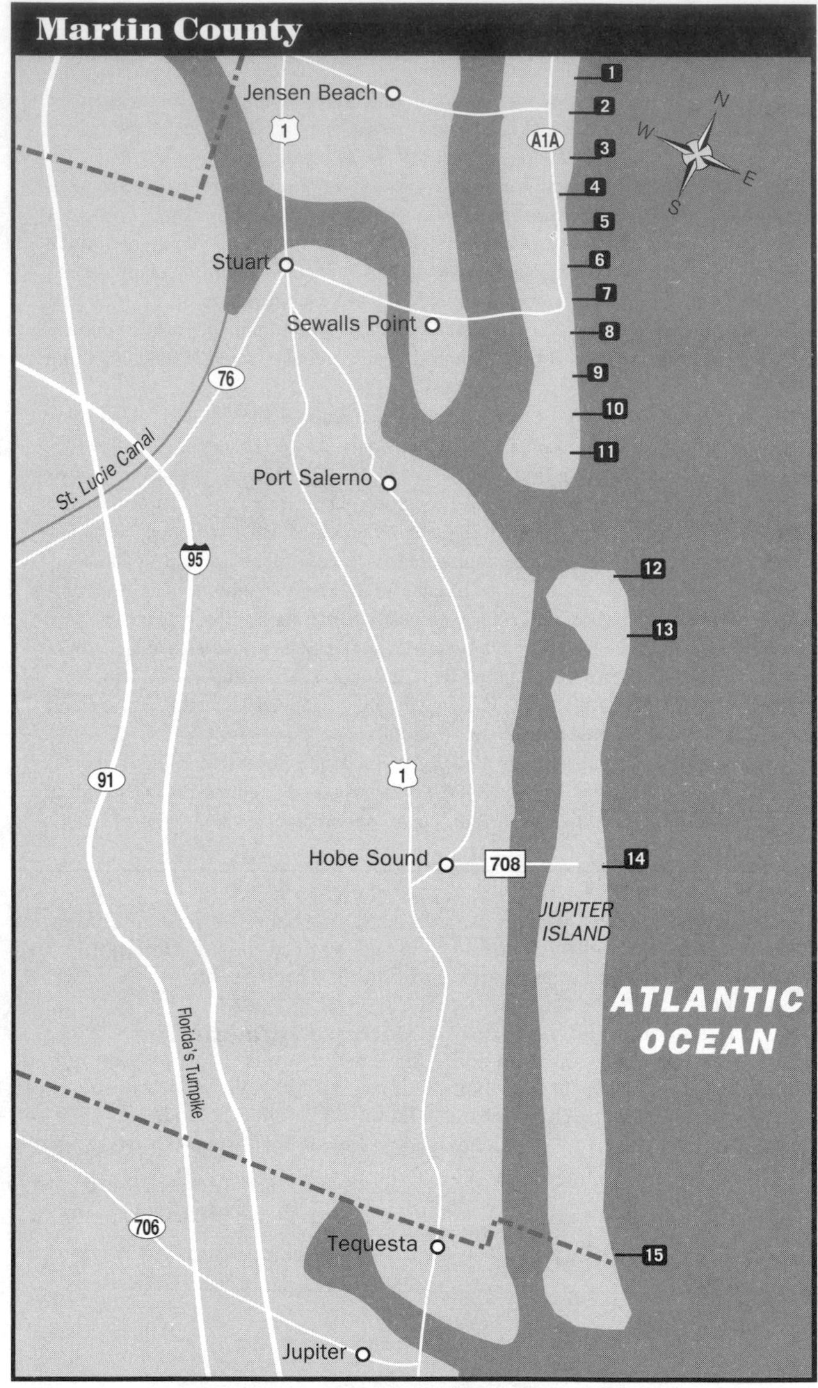

Martin County
Jensen Beach
1
A1A
Stuart
Sewalls Point
76
St. Lucie Canal
Port Salerno
95
91
1
Hobe Sound
708
JUPITER ISLAND
ATLANTIC OCEAN
Florida's Turnpike
706
Tequesta
Jupiter
N
S
E
W
1
2
3
4
5
6
7
8
9
10
11
12
13
14
15

MARTIN COUNTY

This hidden jewel of the Treasure Coast is an enlightened and farsighted county. Though small by comparison to its neighboring counties, Martin County is big on beaches, with almost 20 miles of ocean frontage. The county is an excellent steward of the south half of Hutchinson Island and most of Jupiter Island, a remarkably wild stretch of Atlantic shoreline. Martin County's beach parks are plentiful on Hutchinson Island. The state weighs in on Jupiter Island with St. Lucie Inlet Preserve State Park, while the federal government manages the magnificent Hobe Sound National Wildlife Refuge. These two preserves account for nearly seven continuous miles of wilderness beach that beg to be walked by nature-loving beachcombers.

Jensen Beach

The name "Jensen Beach" is somewhat misleading. Though the community is indeed known as Jensen Beach (pop. 15,000), most of it sits not on the beach but on the mainland, along a lovely riverfront. Still, the appeal of Jensen Beach is easy to understand, especially if you've driven south on U.S. 1 from Port St. Lucie and are in desperate need of some civilized relief. The larger part of Jensen Beach lies between U.S. 1 and the Indian River, west of Hutchinson Island in a unique landscape that rises to an ear-popping 85 feet above sea level—the highest point of land on Florida's east coast. The large historic district—one of Martin County's earliest settlements—is now the centerpiece of the riverfront community. Called Old Jensen Village, it's a pedestrian-friendly and antiquarian shopping district not unlike Fernandina Beach's refurbished Victorian downtown.

The town's initial wealth was made almost entirely from pineapples, which thrived on surrounding Indian River plantations, and from Henry Flagler's railroad, which arrived in 1894 to take those pineapples to the rest of the world. For the next decade, one million boxes of the prized fruit rolled out of Jensen each July. But a nematode infestation and increased freight fees brought that trade to a halt, in deference to a more modest fishing industry.

Hutchinson Island, due east via the State Route 732 Causeway (a.k.a. Jensen Beach Boulevard), was seemingly an afterthought in the old days, a good place to raise fruit and graze livestock, but too prone to hurricanes to be more than that. The first bridge, a mile-long wooden span, wasn't built until 1925. And, thankfully, a stampede didn't follow. The portion of Jensen Beach located on the barrier island is, in fact, one of the most pleasantly understated beachfronts on Florida's east coast.

Beaches

Glasscock Beach is up at the extreme north end of Martin County, between the county line and the Jensen Beach Causeway. Basically undeveloped, it's little more than a parking lot and dune walkovers leading out to a beautiful strip of beach wedged between residential developments. A few hundred yards farther south on Highway A1A is a second public access point for Glasscock, much larger and more accommodating than the one nestled right at the county's edge. It has a paved lot, four dune crossovers, outdoor showers but no restrooms. It is as close to a wilderness beach as you will find in south Florida.

Despite its early history of standoffishness, Jensen Beach is now madly in love

1 Glasscock Beach

Location: County Line Road and Highway A1A, just north of the Jensen Beach Causeway
Parking/fees: free parking lot
Hours: 24 hours
Facilities: none
Contact: Martin County Parks Department, 561/221-1418

2 Jensen Beach/ Sea Turtle Beach

Location: the intersection of Highway A1A and State Route 732 in Jensen Beach
Parking/fees: free parking lots
Hours: 24 hours
Facilities: concessions, lifeguards, restrooms, picnic tables, and showers
Contact: Martin County Parks Department, 561/221-1418

MAP OF FLORIDA'S EAST COAST—PAGE 5

with its beaches, and for good reason. The most recent valentine was a massive $11 million beach renourishment project in 1996. This combined effort of federal, state, and county governments led to a dramatic transformation of the 4.5-mile beachfront stretching from the southern tip of the island to just north of where State Route 732 enters it, near Sea Turtle Beach. The new sand—made up of soft, shelly, gray inlet dredge material—was added to the natural tan and brown beach sand, widening the strand in some places up to 120 feet. An attempt was made to hold the new combination in place with sea oat plantings, many of which have taken root in the interim. While it's always a losing battle to go toe to toe with nature at the shoreline, this effort has met with some success.

Sea Turtle Beach is the largest access point in **Jensen Beach**, and it is anything but folded up inside a shell. A brand-new beach park, Sea Turtle was combined with the venerable Jensen Beach access to form what is now called **Jensen Beach/Sea Turtle Beach.** It is located 300 yards north of the Holiday Inn, a local landmark. Parking is plentiful and free, and the amenities are generous, including concessions, a patio, boardwalk, volleyball courts, and lifeguards. The beach is 1,500 feet long, but the dredge sand hasn't mingled completely, making it too soft to jog in and even difficult to walk on at times. Surfing is allowed at the north end of the beach.

Heading south, the next beach access is **Bob Graham Beach**, a Martin County access point located a mile south of the Holiday Inn. Named for a former governor of Florida who was enlightened on envi-

3 Bob Graham Beach

 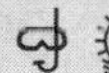 

Location: on Highway A1A, 0.7 miles south of Jensen Beach
Parking/fees: free parking lot
Hours: 24 hours
Facilities: none
Contact: Martin County Parks Department, 561/221-1418

4 Bryn Mawr Beach Access and Alex's Beach

Location: approximately one mile south of Jensen Beach on Highway A1A
Parking/fees: free parking lots
Hours: 24 hours
Facilities: none
Contact: Martin County Parks Department, 561/221-1418

5 Stokes Beach and Virginia Forest Access

Location: approximately 1.5 miles south of Jensen Beach on Highway A1A
Parking/fees: free parking lots
Hours: 24 hours
Facilities: none
Contact: Martin County Parks Department, 561/221-1418

6 Tiger Shores Access

Location: approximately two miles south of Jensen Beach on Highway A1A
Parking/fees: free parking lot
Hours: 24 hours
Facilities: none
Contact: Martin County Parks Department, 561/221-1418

MAP OF MARTIN COUNTY—PAGE 160

ronmental matters, Bob Graham Beach is nearly 2,000 feet long, and the texture of its sand is similar to Sea Turtle's. There's free limited parking (35 spaces) in a dirt lot, with no facilities or lifeguards. The next two access points, **Bryn Mawr Beach Access** and **Alex's Beach**, lie in close proximity on Highway A1A about a mile south of town. Another closely conjoined pair, **Stokes Beach** and **Virginia Forest Access**, are a half-mile farther south. Finally, there's **Tiger Shores Access**, located in the 1900 block of Highway A1A, another half mile or so down the highway. All are almost carbon copies of one another. Each has limited free parking in a dirt lot, with no facilities or lifeguards and about a hundred feet of beach. All of the beaches, from Bob Graham to Tiger Shores, are delightfully secluded and known for excellent surf casting. Of all the accesses above, only Sea Turtle is handicapped accessible.

Shore Things

- **Bike/skate rentals**: A-1 Bike Repair Sales & Rental, 4290 Northeast Indian River Drive, 561/334-5003.
- **Dive shop**: Deep Six Watersports, 3289 Northwest Federal Highway, 561/692-2747.
- **Ecotourism**: Tropical Visions, 600 West 1st Street, Stuart, 561/223-2097.
- **Fishing charters**: Free Jumper Charters, 555 Northeast Ocean Boulevard, Stuart, 561/283-7787.
- **Marina**: Boat House Marina, 3321 Northeast Indian River Drive, 561/334-1416; Finest Kind Marina, 3585 Southeast St. Lucie Boulevard, Port Salerno, 561/223-4110.
- **Rainy-day attraction**: Florida Oceanographic Society Coastal Science Center, 890 Northeast Ocean Boulevard, Stuart, 561/225-0505.
- **Shopping/browsing**: Old Jensen Village, Jensen Beach Boulevard, two blocks west of the Indian River.
- **Surf shop**: Sunrise Surf Shop, 11013 South A1A, Jensen Beach, 561/229-1722.
- **Vacation rentals**: Hutchinson Island By-the-Sea Realty, 10549 South Ocean Drive, 561/229-3394.

Bunking Down

The best and most relaxing place to stay on all of Hutchinson Island is the **Holiday Inn Oceanside** (3793 Northeast Ocean Boulevard, 561/225-3000, $$). Things are so relaxed at this two-winged, four-story complex (179 rooms, three suites) that an ambitious activities program sponsored by the manager failed to interest the guests even during the full houses of peak season. They seemed content to simply walk down the wooden steps to the beach with their lotions, umbrellas, chaise lounges, and paperbacks. The Holiday Inn offers access to three tennis courts, a pool, gym, game room, restaurant, and patio bar. The inn completed a $5 million renovation in January 2001.

The most unique place on the island is the **Hutchinson Inn** (9750 South Ocean Drive, 561/229-2000, $$), located three miles north of the Holiday Inn. (Technically, it's in St. Lucie County, but the mailing address is Jensen Beach. Yes, we're confused, too.) Somehow this 21-unit B&B-style beach motel has made a stylish stand against the encroaching no-man's-land of condos. The inn is a marriage between an old, expensively refurbished motel and a Cape Cod retreat. Chaise lounges surround a small swimming pool and spill over to the beautiful beach. The food is better here than at most seaside bed-and-breakfast inns, with fresh fruit and pastries in the morning and fresh cookies hand-delivered to the rooms at night.

The most exclusive place on the island is the **Indian River Plantation Beach Re-**

sort (555 Northeast Ocean Boulevard, 561/225-3700, $$$), located in Stuart. It is the largest single resort complex on the Treasure Coast. Located at the isolated southern stretch of Jensen Beach (the mailing address is Stuart), it started out as a gated, self-contained condominium but transformed itself into a haven for rich tourists, presumably when the units didn't sell. This "plantation" is now spread out over 200 ocean-to-riverfront acres that contain an 18-hole golf course, an "aqua range" (drive balls into a man-made lake), 13 tennis courts, four pools, and rental bikes and boats. The main hotel is a four-story luxury lodge with 200 units, but 126 Key West–style villas are also available for rent.

Coastal Cuisine

A number of fine restaurants and friendly pubs can be found in downtown Jensen Beach, both in the old village and along the riverfront. The two best seafood restaurants stand toe-to-toe along the latter. **Conchy Joe's** (3945 Northeast Indian River Drive, 561/334-1130, $$) serves native Florida and Bahamian preparations in a West Indian setting. The conch is served every which way it can be cooked, and house specialties include soft-shell crabs, seafood pasta, and grouper marsala. Reggae and calypso bands entertain late into the evening. **The Admiral's Table** (4000 Northeast Indian River Drive, 561/334-3080, $$) is less adventuresome though just as dedicated to fresh seafood. Both have glorious views of the Indian River.

Night Moves

If the luck of the draw brings you to Jensen Beach on a Thursday, you can partake of "Jammin' Jensen." This weekly affair starts at 5:30 P.M. in Old Jensen Village, the restored area two blocks west of the Indian River. Most of the bars offer live music and drink specials, while the restaurants cut deals on food and the shops remain open. Barring that, you can always quaff a brew at the **Jensen Beach Ale House** (3611 Northwest Federal Highway, 561/692-3111).

Contact Information

Jensen Beach Chamber of Commerce, 1910 Northeast Jensen Beach Boulevard, Jensen Beach, FL 34957; 561/334-3444; website: www.jensenchamber.com

Stuart

This unprepossessing and nicely restored town is located inland of Hutchinson Island, for the most part, though some of it spills onto the island's southern tip. Serving as the county seat, Stuart (pop. 13,846) has a legacy of enlightenment and individuality. One of the stops along Henry Flagler's East Coast Railway, it was originally called Potsdam. According to Star Glynis Grieser, a local historian:

"Soon after trains began stopping in Potsdam in 1894, some conductors took great delight in giving the name a peculiar cadence as they called it out. By inserting a long pause between the two syllables of Potsdam, the conductors were able to call more attention to the second syllable so that it sounded as though they were cursing loudly about the devil's kettle as they walked down the aisle of the passenger cars. Some passengers and residents found this offensive and began complaining. The town's new name is taken from the name of a Homer T. Stuart, a prominent resident."

Further proof of Stuart's good sense: In 1925, the town seceded from Palm Beach County in a dispute over taxes, leading to the creation of lovely and still relatively pristine Martin County. Stuart makes an appealing southern point of entry onto

Hutchinson Island. You might even want to stop and admire Riverwalk, a public pedestrian park along the St. Lucie River at its inland center. It's a pleasant place to catch a breath and a bite to eat before heading up and over the Highway A1A bridge to the island.

Still further proof of Stuart's good sense is evident in the community's response to a recently proposed leviathan development called SeaWind. It is a stupid attempt to build 7,000 houses at once near Stuart. Rather than offer our glancing opinion of SeaWind, we'll present this informed excerpt from a concerned local citizen's articulate letter to the editor of *The Stuart News:* "Piecemeal development might well produce a better result. It is virtually certain to do so if it is smaller, carefully controlled by the county commission, and carried out in response to demonstrated demand rather than ahead of any such demand in the hope of creating it. And as of now there is no demonstrated demand. There is no justification to dig up, sanitize, and pave over yet another bit of Florida in order to attract thousands of new residents and thus permanently alter the character of Stuart and Martin County. The SeaWind project is monstrous, both literally and figuratively. . . . Not all change is progress."

Already, there are more than a hundred golf courses along the Treasure Coast, which brings us to an astute assertion from a *Stuart News* columnist: "Golf courses ought to be banned as enemies of our environment. . . . To make a golf course you must cut down a lot of trees, reshape the terrain, alter natural drainage, and run off a lot of wildlife. After you've carved the fairways, built up the tees and greens, laid in sand traps and done all the groundwork, you have to build a clubhouse, cart storage, and acres of asphalt parking lots. To keep your course from looking bad you have to pump in millions of gallons of water—an increasingly valuable commodity in Florida—and pour on tons of pesticides and fertilizers. . . . Also, golf courses are restricted to the use of golfers. You can't just stroll happily about on them. Even golfers don't stroll along them." How true.

Stuart's southernmost toehold of Hutchinson Island is a real hidden treasure. Not only is it home to a stretch of unblemished oceanfront, but it also has two excellent museums and a science center within fallout distance of the waves. The first, **Gilberts Bar House of Refuge Museum** (301 Southeast MacArthur Boulevard, 561/225-1875), is the oldest standing structure in the county. This 1875 home is not, as the name suggests, a homey place to imbibe. The "bar" is shorthand for the sandbar upon which it sits, the millennial result of outwash from the St. Lucie River's mouth, which lies almost due west. The House of Refuge was once a recuperative refuge for shipwrecked sailors, presumably grounded by the sandbar and the turbulent waters off the St. Lucie Inlet two miles south. Now, it's a museum of marine artifacts and life-saving equipment, with an impressive seaquarium housed on the lower level.

Equally interesting is the nearby **Elliott Museum** (825 Northeast Ocean Boulevard, 561/225-1961), a Pepto Bismol–pink adobe-style mansion that houses quirky artifacts of Americana and invention history dating back to 1750. Its former owner, Sterling Elliott, was inventor of the stamp machine, a knot-tying device, and a four-wheeled bicycle that presaged the Stanley Steamer, a prototype for the gas-powered motorcar. Finally, the Florida Oceanographic Society has opened its **Coastal Science Center** along the inlet side of Hutchinson Island (890 Northeast Ocean Boulevard, 561/225-0505). While primarily a research center with a library and administrative offices, the 40-acre complex is also home to a new visitor center, with reef exhibits, touch tanks, and interactive computers. Nature trails along the river offer abundant photo ops.

MAP OF FLORIDA'S EAST COAST—PAGE 5

 Pigs Don't Golf

The new Florida of money and manners clashes with the old Florida of crackers and clutter all over the state, but never so amusingly as near Stuart. In the late 1990s, a subdivision of homes costing $300,000 and more, accompanied by a private golf course (called, not ironically, the Florida Club), was built next door to two pig farmers who've resided here all their lives. Now, the golfing newcomers are suing the pig-farming oldtimers over the smell and the noise created by their livestock. As farmer Paul Thompson told a *New York Times* reporter, "Who would choose to build a golf course next to a pig farm? Didn't they read the sign? It says 'pig farm,' not 'rose garden'. . . . And they say I'm crazy."

The farmers have only added fuel to the fire by insisting on playing country music to the pigs. As Thompson explained, "The music reduces stress and enhances the tenderness of the meat." It goes without saying that the farmers like country music, too. Both Martin and St. Lucie counties' sheriff's departments have determined that the pig farmers' music does not exceed the 60 decibels allowed in residential areas. Nonetheless, the golf club is pressing on with another civil lawsuit, which has inspired the farmers to set up a legal defense fund (yes, Pig Farmer Legal Defense Fund) and a website. Yes, it's www.pigfarmer.com. And while you're down this way, drop by the Pig Farm and say howdy. From the website: "Any day you can visit the Pig Farm and see the animals lying around listening to country music and getting fat!"

Beaches

Next door to the Elliott Museum, and sharing the same entrance road, is the town's real house of refuge, known as **Stuart Beach.** Like the other beach accesses in Martin County, Stuart Beach is clearly designated by a pale blue wooden sign with a wave logo. While it covers only a few acres, the park makes the absolute most of its location. There's ample free parking (260 spaces), restrooms, showers, a full-service concession (Moondoggies), nicely landscaped grounds, two basketball courts, a volleyball court, a sizable boardwalk and two lifeguard stands. Because of all this bounty, Stuart Beach is popular with everyone from baby-toting parents to surfboard-toting babes. There is, in fact, a minor surfer cult based in the Stuart area, for which this facility is the most accessible outlet.

Backed by a healthy dune structure held in place by sea grape, palms and railroad vine, the 1,200-foot strand of sand at Stuart Beach is shelly and gray colored (telltale signs of beach renourishment efforts), sloping steeply toward the water. Because of this and the presence of partially submerged rocks in the water lifeguards are ever vigilant here. The beach itself has lost a great deal of its width since the last time we visited; at high tide the water comes all the way up to the pylons of the boardwalk. The word on Stuart Beach from a surfer in the know: "decent on bigger swells but only surf here if you can't get a ride at the Rocks."

Speaking of "the Rocks," the locals have affixed unofficial names onto some of the county's numbered accesses, which may confuse anyone in search of real names and designations (there aren't any). Thus,

MAP OF MARTIN COUNTY—PAGE 160

what some call **Fletcher Beach**, the next beach a half-mile south of Stuart Beach (and a left turn at the Marriott Beach Resort, MacArthur Boulevard), others call Fletcher Strip and still others call "the Stairs" and the sign in front calls "Martin County Beach Access # 7." By any name, it has undeniable appeal. Here, you can swim, surf, snorkel, shell, and surfcast away from the larger crowds up at Stuart.

The next beach, a half-mile to the south, shares the entrance road for Gilbert's Bar Museum and House of Refuge. Dubbed **House of Refuge Beach**, this 2,100-foot strand is lovely to ponder, with sculptural orange outcrops jutting from the roiling waters and tidepools, but the water is not nearly as inviting as Stuart Beach. In fact, on our most recent visit in late 2000, the waves were crashing so hard on the shore that we could feel the ground shake under our feet from the parking area. Parking is free but limited to 25 spaces. No lifeguards are on duty. **Gilbert's Bar Museum and House of Refuge** is open 10 A.M.–4 P.M. daily ($4 for adults, $2 for kids), and it sits on the thinnest strip of land (the "bar") you are ever likely to find on any coast in the world.

Now, for "the Rocks." This is the beach that some people call **Chastain Access**, others call Sailfish Point, the parks department calls "Martin County Beach Access #8," but almost everyone calls the Rocks (not to be confused with Blowing Rocks Preserve on Jupiter Island to the

7 Stuart Beach

Location: MacArthur Boulevard at Highway A1A in Stuart
Parking/fees: free parking lots
Hours: 24 hours
Facilities: concessions, lifeguards, restrooms, picnic tables, and showers
Contact: Martin County Parks Department, 561/221-1418

8 Fletcher Beach

Location: approximately one-half mile south of Stuart Beach on Highway A1A
Parking/fees: free parking lot
Hours: 24 hours
Facilities: none
Contact: Martin County Parks Department, 561/221-1418

9 House of Refuge Beach

Location: One mile south of Stuart Beach on Highway A1A
Parking/fees: free parking lot; $4 per person to tour the Gilbert's Bar House of Refuge and Museum
Hours: 24 hours
Facilities: restrooms
Contact: Martin County Parks Department, 561/221-1418

10 Chastain Access (a.k.a. Stuart Rocks)

Location: between House of Refuge Beach and Bathtub Reef (St. Lucie Inlet) along Highway A1A on Hutchinson Island
Parking/fees: free parking lot
Hours: 24 hours
Facilities: restrooms and showers
Contact: Martin County Parks Department, 561/221-1418

south). Completely baffled yet? Okay, whatever name you choose, this beach access is located a few hundred yards south of House of Refuge Beach. It offers a by now familiar roll call in Martin County's seemingly unending bounty: a small parking lot, restrooms, showers and dune walkover onto a rockin', reefin' beach. As we walked from the jam-packed lot and through the dunes, we had to do a double take. Were we in Southern California? Weren't these 21 surfers lined up, nearly shoulder to shoulder, on the water on a rainy Wednesday in the off season, members of Tom Wolfe's fabled Pump House Gang?

Wrong again. In fact, this would have to be considered southern Florida's Steamer Lane, where the waves break directly onto rocks and everyone holds their breath as the surfers take their death-defying rides. This, we later learned, is "for pros only," where "north and northeast swells feed this hungry place" and one is forewarned to "watch out for the men in the brown suits" (i.e., sharks). It possesses "one of the best little breaks on the East Coast, which until the last 10 years had remained virtually unknown." The rocks are actually a sharp, jagged reef formation that runs right up to the shoreline and, at low tide, is only inches below the water surface. Suffice it to say, this is a "look but don't touch" sort of pleasure; it's fun to watch these bold souls do their thing, but nothing could get us into that water.

The complete opposite of "the Rocks" is the reef-protected haven known as **Bathtub Reef Beach Park**, less than a mile south, at the southern tip of Hutchinson Island. This gorgeous 1,000-foot-long beach sits behind an offshore coral reef created by honeycomb worms. Most reefs are made from coral polyps, but this one is built by the fluctuations of little worms. The reef itself covers 85 underwater acres and runs for 1.4 miles north. In the area between sand and reef—the stunning blue and green "bathtub"—snorkeling is excellent and the water is as safe as mother's milk for wading tots. Owing to this and the facilities—restrooms, showers, boardwalk, observation area, informative displays, two lifeguard towers, and 200 free parking spaces—Bathtub Reef is extremely popular with families.

Fishing is popular at St. Lucie Inlet, where the Indian River empties into the Atlantic Ocean. The best local purveyor of snorkeling equipment is **Dixie Divers** (1879 Southeast Federal Highway, 561/283-5588). If the Indian River looks as tempting to you as it did to us, **Tropical Visions** in downtown Stuart (600 West 1st Street, 223-2097) rents kayaks and conducts pontoon-boat tours of this vast watershed.

Bunking Down

Stuart is lacking in motel rooms at the beach—you'll have to go up to Jensen Beach for those—but it does have the appealing and unique **Harbor Front Inn** (310 Atlanta Avenue, 561/288-7289, $$), which is set on the west bank of the Indian River within walking distance of Stuart's historic downtown district. The main house (circa 1908) is made of Florida pine and cypress and has a number of pleasant and breezy guest rooms. Cottages with kitchens are also available, as is a home-cooked breakfast.

11 Bathtub Reef Beach Park

Location: south end of Hutchinson Island at the St. Lucie Inlet
Parking/fees: free parking lot
Hours: 24 hours
Facilities: lifeguards, restrooms, picnic tables, and showers
Contact: Martin County Parks Department, 561/221-1418

Coastal Cuisine

In downtown Stuart, we were partial to the **Jolly Sailor Pub** (1 West Osceola Street, 561/221-1111, $), which makes up for its less than exhilarating menu (pub grub of the Brit kind) with a comfortable dark-wood interior and a sunny patio. The best seafood restaurant downtown is the **Prawnbroker** (3754 Southeast Ocean Boulevard, 561/288-1222, $$), a fish market during the day and a creative spot at dinnertime, the menu being determined by whatever catches arrive that day. The best seafood restaurant in the area is **Fish Tales** (5042 U.S. 1, 561/288-5011, $$), featuring fresh seafood and Florida produce.

Contact Information

Stuart/Martin County Chamber of Commerce, 1650 South Kanner Highway, Stuart, FL 34994; 561/287-1088; website: www.goodnature.org

Port Salerno

As you head south on Dixie Highway (Highway A1A) from Stuart, you may not know it but, when you enter little Port Salerno, you are parallel to one of the most pristine wilderness beaches in Florida. It is located a mile and a half to the east, in St. Lucie Inlet State Preserve at the northern end of Jupiter Island. The reason you may not know it is because there is virtually no access to it from any road until you drive five miles south to Bridge Road (State Route 708), which leads over Hobe Sound onto the island. But low-key Port Salerno has a couple of waterfront parks worth singling out, especially for those towing a boat. The first is **Sand Spit Park** (a.k.a. Cove Road Park), off Highway A1A at the end of Cove Road. Here you will find a large, well-maintained park, with free parking and a boat launch into the Intracoastal Waterway. You can paddle a canoe or kayak (but no motorized boats) toward the north end of Jupiter Island and enjoy that pristine wilderness beach the rest of us car-bound folks will have to forego, at least on this trip. Lucky you.

Two miles farther south on A1A is **Seabranch State Preserve**, a low-key 919-acre sand pine scrub community, a rare enough habitat to be designated "globally imperiled." Indeed, anything within fallout range of Port St. Lucie is, by definition, imperiled. Seabranch was purchased through a public-private partnership but is overseen by the good folks who protect St Lucie Inlet Preserve State Park (see next entry). Seabranch provides habitat for gopher tortoise, eastern indigo snake, Florida scrub jay, bobcat, and Florida sandhill crane, as well as protected plant species like hand fern, Curtiss' milkweed, yellow bachelor button, and golden polypody. Hiking trails are in the process of being expanded; for now, there's a picnic area on the Intracoastal Waterway, with shorter nature trails and free limited parking.

Stop for the view, a chance to glimpse a bobcat on the run, or simply to stretch your legs in a natural setting, then head east over State Route 707 to Jupiter Island. Seabranch is open daily from 8 A.M. to dusk.

Contact Information

Stuart/Martin County Chamber of Commerce, 1650 South Kanner Highway, Stuart, FL 34994; 561/287-1088; website: www.goodnature.org

St. Lucie Inlet Preserve State Park

St. Lucie Inlet Preserve State Park ranks with the most beautiful beaches you've never visited in your life. Unless you have a boat or are willing to paddle a surfboard across the Indian River, you can't get to the preserve. It occupies the north end of Jupiter Island and is buffered from vehicular access by the Hobe Sound National Wildlife Refuge (see pages 172–173). If you have a boat, you're in luck, because there are 30 boat slips at the preserve's dock on the east side of the Indian River. From here, a 3,300-foot boardwalk leads across the island to the ocean. Nothing could be finer than its 2.7 miles of wide, untrammeled beach. Offshore is a reef tract, comprised of hard and soft corals, that occupies six square miles.

If you're looking for a place to launch your boat from the west bank of the Indian River, the state would like to oblige but its hands have been tied by petty politics. Originally, plans called for the construction of a dock in the small park at the end of Cove Road in Port Salerno, from which shuttle ferries and private boats could cross over to St. Lucie Inlet Preserve State Park. However, nervous local property owners, fearing God knows what, nipped that in the bud. As it stands, canoes and kayaks can launch from the boat ramp at Cove Road Park, but bigger boats are on their own and a state-run shuttle service is out for now.

Contact Information

St. Lucie Inlet Preserve State Park,16450 Southeast Federal Highway, Hobe Sound, FL 33455; (561) 744-7603; website: www.myflorida.com

12 St. Lucie Inlet Preserve State Park

Location: on the south side of the St. Lucie Inlet at the northern tip of Jupiter Island. The preserve is accessible by boat only.
Parking/fees: $2 per boat berthing fee
Hours: 8 A.M. to sunset
Facilities: restrooms and picnic tables
Contact: St. Lucie Inlet Preserve State Park, 561/744-7603

Hobe Sound National Wildlife Refuge

Hobe Sound National Wildlife Refuge encompasses 735 acres on Jupiter Island and 232 acres on the mainland in southern Martin County. It was created from private land donated by residents to the Nature Conservancy, which turned it over to the U.S. Fish and Wildlife Service. These precious acres represent a break in the action along the densely developed Treasure Coast. No doubt the sea turtles that come ashore along its 3.5-mile beach in heavy numbers from May to August regard its preservation as a break for them in their ritual nesting activities. Human visitors enjoy the refuge as well, parking in the lot at its southern boundary and walking out to the beach to swim, surf, surfcast, sunbathe, and comb for shells.

Not much else is allowed on the refuge; camping and picnicking are not permitted, and no roads penetrate its interior. No bikes, ATVs, or mopeds are allowed. Yet people are welcome to walk up the beach, and if you're of a mind for a lengthy wilderness-beach hike, a 13-mile round-trip will take you to the tip of St. Lucie Inlet State Preserve and back. "People do it every day," a refuge manager told us. The only way to get onto the refuge other than parking at the south end is by boating to Peck Lake Access Area, about 1.5 miles north. A dune crossover trail leads from the Indian River to the ocean at a point where the beach sees a whole lot less visitor use.

There are only portable restrooms in the way of facilities on the Jupiter Island tract. On the mainland tract, south of Bridge Road (County Road 708) off U.S. 1, an official visitor center also serves as headquarters for the Hobe Sound Nature Center. The latter is an environmental education organization that leads turtle walks in June and July and conducts trips to Merritt Island and other natural sites across the state. To reserve space on a turtle walk or get more information about outings and activities, call the **Hobe Sound Nature Center** at 561/546-2067. The mainland refuge headquarters, incidentally, is close to Jonathan Dickinson State Park (see sidebar, page 174), which preserves a vast tract of the same sand pine scrub ecosystem.

As for finding the main beach access point of the refuge, that's another matter. Unless you really know what you are doing, you will miss the chance to visit Hobe Sound National Wildlife Refuge. That is, you will mistake the access road to the refuge for a private road. Ignore the signs at its intersection with North Beach Road that say "Dead End" and "Designated for Golf Carts." This is a public road, and it runs for a mile and a half north from the entrance of Hobe Sound County Beach Park. The gall of moneyed Floridians who would, in effect, usurp a public road for their private use does not necessarily surprise us, but the failure of governing bodies, local and federal, not to make this clear to visitors is another matter. (Or, who knows, maybe there once

⑬ Hobe Sound National Wildlife Refuge

Location: From Hobe Sound, take Bridge Road (County Road 708) east until it ends at North Beach Road. Turn left and proceed 1.5 miles into the refuge parking lot.
Parking/fees: $5 parking fee per vehicle
Hours: sunrise to sunset
Facilities: restrooms and a visitor center (at the mainland tract)
Contact: Hobe Sound National Wildlife Refuge, 561/546-6141

was a huge sign announcing the refuge entrance that conveniently went missing.) Let us then offer the invitation that should be posted: "Welcome to Hobe National Wildlife Refuge."

Contact Information

Hobe Sound National Wildlife Refuge, 13640 Southeast Federal Highway, Hobe Sound, FL 33455; 561/546-6141; website: southeast.fws.gov/hobesound

Hobe Sound

The gold-plated community of Hobe Sound (pop. 14,825) is first prize for those seeking to make their home (or second or third home) on the Treasure Coast. The majority of the population is on the mainland, but the most rarefied and desirable part of the community lies on Jupiter Island. It is an exclusive place to live—even more so, it would seem, than Palm Beach. Delicately placed like a condor's egg in a gilded nest between Edenic nature preserves (Hobe Sound National Wildlife Refuge and Hobe Sound Nature Center), Hobe Sound's island enclave is so exclusive it's practically undetectable. Driving through the area, you catch glimpses of its golf courses and regal logo, but the ritzy subdevelopments are gated and its large estates sit at a distance from the roadway behind well-landscaped fortresses of greenery. In other words, if you have to ask how much it costs to live here, you can't afford it. Needless to add, not so much as a one-foot-wide easement to gain access to the beach is to be found in Hobe Sound's fortress-tight neighborhoods.

Beaches

The last gasp of public beach access in Martin County can be found at the eastern end of Bridge Road in Hobe Sound. It is the county's only beach holding on Jupiter Island. **Hobe Sound Beach** offers a sandy break in the reclusive privacy of the Hobe Sound area, complete with lifeguards and picnic pavilions. And it costs nothing to park here. Surfing is popular at the north end of the beach, as is surf casting. On the wall of the public restroom, we saw this message: "Hobe Sound locals do not like Mother F***ing Snowbirds. Love, HSL." A sign of the tension between fenced-out long-timers and billionaire beach hoarders?

Coastal Cuisine

A down-home respite from the country-club tenor of life in Hobe Sound, **Harry and the Natives** (Federal Highway, 561/546-3061, $) is an anomalous eatery at the intersection of Bridge Road and U.S. 1. It is rather like finding a Jimmy Buffett fan in full parrothead regalia downing margaritas at the opera house. The place is run by, and full of, characters. The menu is full of fictitious items (e.g., Marinated Beef Lips, fresh, frozen, or petrified for $14.25) and jokey asides ("New this year . . . indoor plumbing outside"). If you're on a budget, you can order "the Day Before Payday Peanut Butter & Jelly," but we'd urge you in-

⓮ Hobe Sound Beach

5

Location: from Hobe Sound, take Bridge Road (County Road 708) east until it ends at Jupiter Island

Parking/fees: free parking lot

Hours: 24 hours

Facilities: lifeguards, restrooms, picnic tables, and showers

Contact: Martin County Parks Department, 561/221-1418

Jonathan Dickinson State Park

This 11,328-acre park is one of South Florida's greatest natural treasures. While it is not on the beach, Dickinson is an easily accessible side trip from Jupiter Island. It offers eloquent commentary on the ocean-hugging estuaries that are the lifeblood of marine communities. With four hiking trails, 600 plant and 150 bird species, and access to the Loxahatchee River—Florida's only federally designated Wild and Scenic River—Dickinson is well worth your time. Located off U.S. 1 (Federal Highway) in Hobe Sound, the park charges a daily vehicle entrance fee of $3.25, while camping fees are $14 per night in summer and $16 in winter, plus $2 for electrical hookups.

Your first stop should be the Hobe Mountain Trail, an easy trek on an incline so gradual that the three flights up the observation tower at its end provide the most strenuous exercise. This 200-foot elevation passes for a "mountain" in Florida, much of which is barely above sea level. From atop the tower, a gaze eastward takes in the layers of land starting with the ocean, the barrier spit, the Intracoastal Waterway, and finally the sand pine scrub community—isolated pine islands within a sea of scrub, an ecosystem also known as Florida scrub. A placard reads: "This is Florida's oldest plant community and contains more rare and endangered plants and animals than any other area of the park. Originally, sand pine scrub extended to Miami, but due to development, this is the only large area of its kind left on the southeast coast of Florida."

On that sobering note, we drove three miles west to the main parking area and picked up the trailhead for the stunning Kitching Creek Trail, which piggybacks on the Wilson Creek Trail. Together, they provide an hour-long stroll that crosses two creeks and follows the shore of the Loxahatchee. The abundant plant life runs the gamut from cactus, scrub pine, and saw palmetto to lush ferns, flowers, and stunted turkey oaks, which shed leaves in the nonexistent Florida autumn. We had personal encounters with many animals, including raccoon, woodpeckers, hawks, lizards, deer, and fish that leaped from the brackish waters of Kitching Creek. The restful overlook's quiet is broken only by the plopping of acrobatic fish.

A longer hike is the 9.3-mile route that moves across the flat green horizon to the west, crossing Old Dixie Highway and the Florida East Coast Railway and passing by Trapper Nelson's Interpretive Site. This spot, on a high bank beside the river, is a tribute to the "wild man of the Loxahatchee" who lived here for almost 40 years, establishing his own nature sanctuary and wildlife zoo. The area remains virtually unchanged and is a must-see for urban children, who must be given the chance to appreciate nature before it disappears.

We regretted not having time to take the narrated boat "adventure" along the Loxahatchee waterway, which is home to alligators, manatees, and herons. The park contracts the waterway concession to reputable guides. Canoes can also be rented at reasonable prices for hours of family fun. For more information on tours and rentals, call 800/746-1466.

For more information contact Jonathan Dickinson State Park, 16450 Southeast Federal Highway, Hobe Sound, FL 33455; 561/744-9814; website: www.myflorida.com

MAP OF FLORIDA'S EAST COAST—PAGE 5

stead to dig a little deeper and ante up for a mahimahi sandwich. The Caribbean-style version is a sweet and spicy treat, but they also do it grilled or sautéed in basil butter.

Contact Information

Hobe Sound Chamber of Commerce, 8994 Southeast Bridge Road, Hobe Sound, FL 33455; 561/546-4724; website: www.hobesound.org

Blowing Rocks Preserve

The last glimpse of Martin County as you move south down Highway A1A is one to remember. It's the Nature Conservancy's **Blowing Rocks Preserve**, a mile-long stretch of coast that features a shallow limestone reef of the Anastasia formation just seaward of the sandy beach. This is part of the same lithified shelf of coquina that runs all the way from St. Augustine to Boca Raton, though the "blowing rocks" phenomenon is fairly unique. The rocky, unyielding, and unquarried coquina sits right in the surf zone. When breaking waves hit eroded blowholes in the reef, geysers of salt water spew skyward in explosive plumes, especially during unusually high tides or after a winter storm kicks up swell. On a big day, incoming waves can get blown upward of 50 feet.

People come not only to watch the spectacle but also to stroll the beach and snorkel around the reef. There are a scant 18 parking spaces at the preserve. There's no mandatory charge for parking, but a $3 donation is suggested and a collection tube is provided. Directly across Highway A1A from the beachside lot, on the Indian River side of the preserve, is the **Hawley Education Center**, a staffed facility with a small exhibit space, a butterfly garden, and a boardwalk along the Indian River Lagoon. It is open daily 9 A.M.–5 P.M.; free tours of the preserve are given Sunday at 11 A.M.

Contact Information

Blowing Rocks Preserve, 575 South Beach Road, Hobe Sound, FL 33455; 561/744-6668; website: www.tncflorida.org.

⑮ Blowing Rocks Preserve

Location: along Highway A1A in southern Martin County, just north of the Palm Beach County line
Parking/fees: suggested $3 donation
Hours: 9 A.M.–5 P.M.
Facilities: restrooms and a visitor center
Contact: Blowing Rocks Preserve, 561/744-6668

MAP OF MARTIN COUNTY—PAGE 160

South Florida

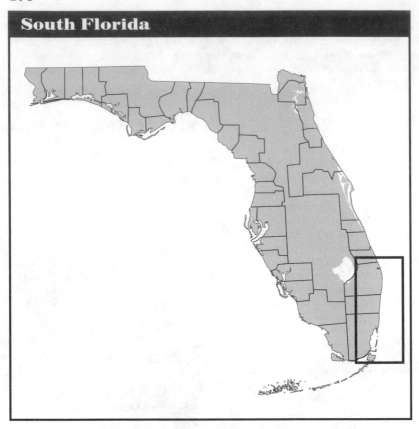

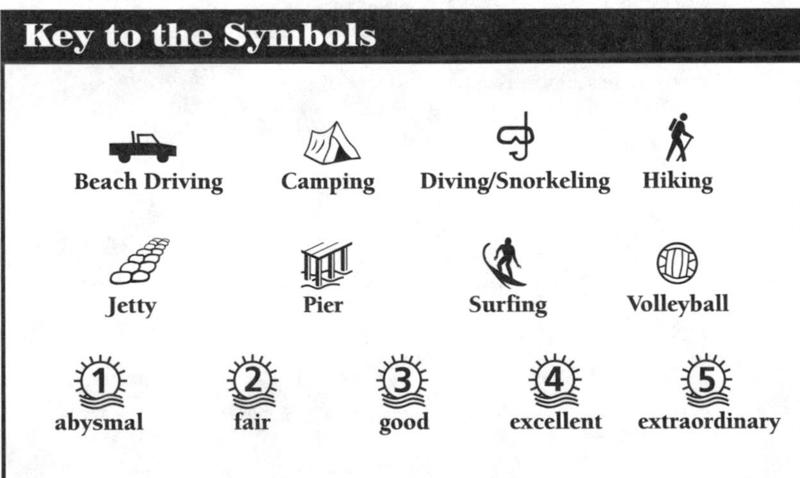

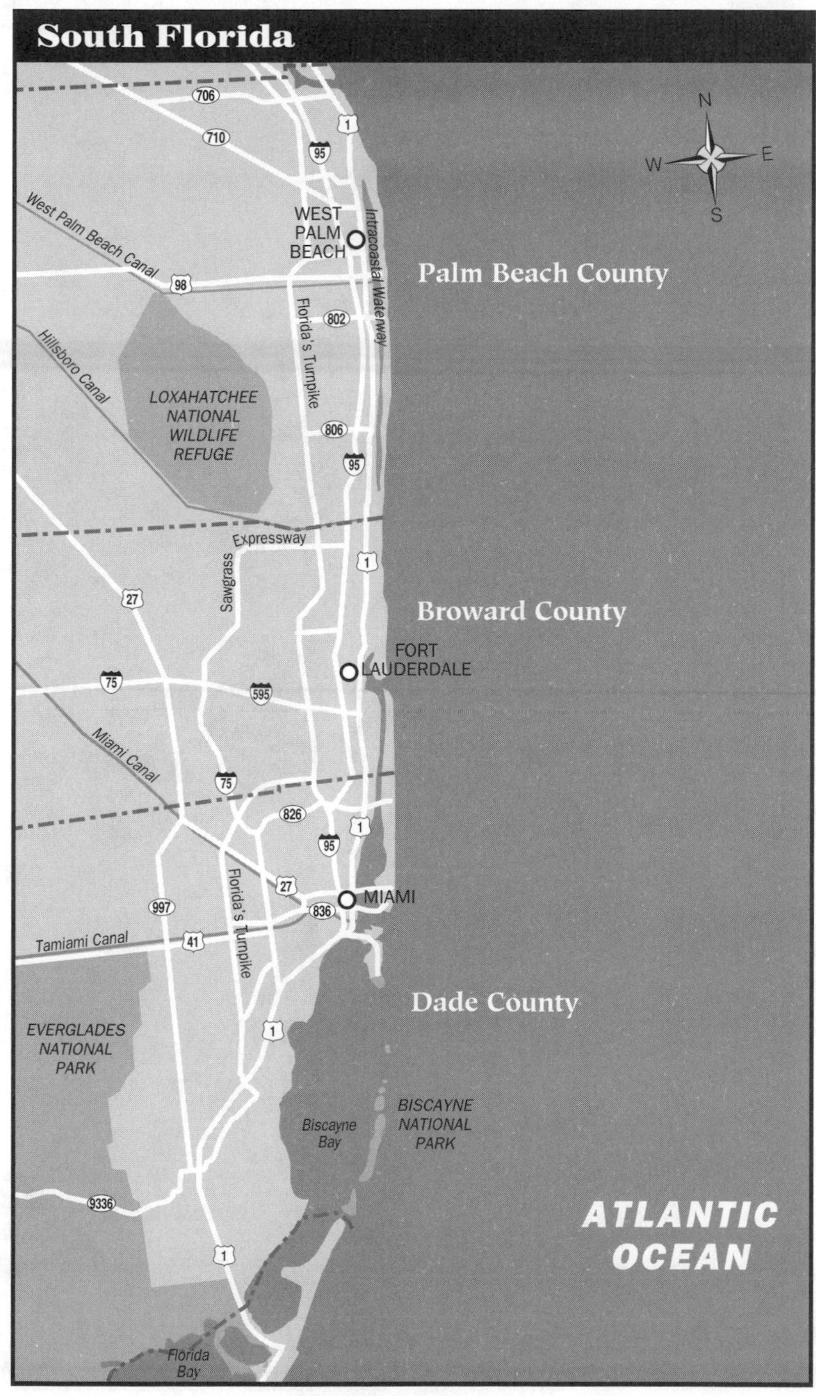
South Florida
N
E
S
W
706
710
1
95
West Palm Beach Canal
WEST
PALM
BEACH
Intracoastal Waterway
Palm Beach County
98
Florida's Turnpike
802
Hillsboro Canal
LOXAHATCHEE
NATIONAL
WILDLIFE
REFUGE
806
95
Expressway
1
Sawgrass
27
Broward County
FORT
LAUDERDALE
75
595
Miami Canal
75
826
1
95
27
MIAMI
997
836
Florida's Turnpike
Tamiami Canal
41
Dade County
1
EVERGLADES
NATIONAL
PARK
Biscayne
Bay
BISCAYNE
NATIONAL
PARK
9336
ATLANTIC
OCEAN
1
Florida
Bay

Palm Beach County

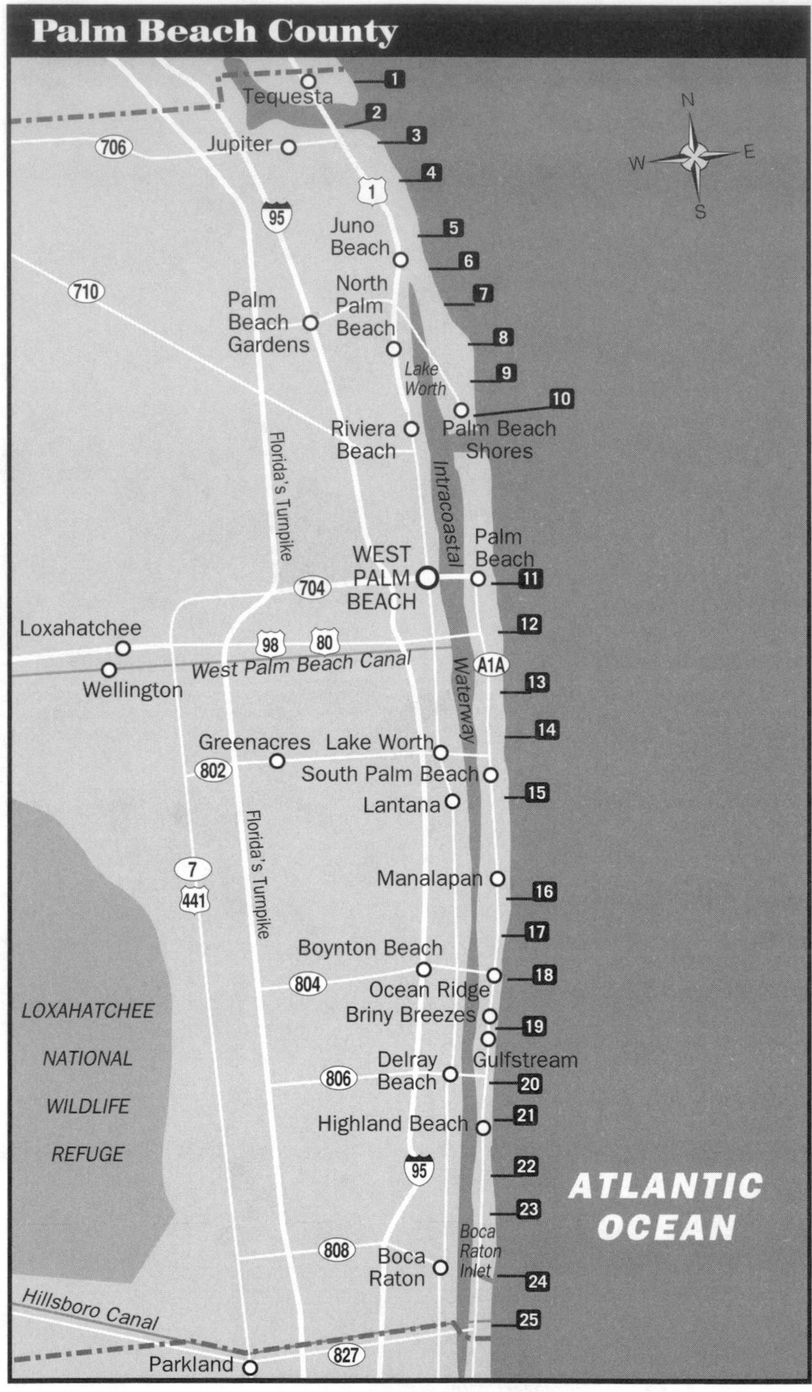

Palm Beach County

PALM BEACH COUNTY

Though it is now Florida's most populous county—and world famous as home of the butterfly ballot and hanging chad—Palm Beach was somehow missed by early Spanish conquistadors and explorers. Henry Flagler made up for the lost time when Palm Beach became the terminus of his railroad line and his personal home. This is a big county, occupying 2,000 square miles and stretching from the Everglades to the coast, which is kissed by the Gulf Stream—the closest that warm current swings toward land. Thanks to offshore breezes and the Gulf Stream's moderating effect, Palm Beach County's 47 miles of beaches are comfortable all year long. The city of Palm Beach is, true to its reputation, an epicenter of snobbery. Better beaches are located in less pretentious towns like Delray Beach and Singer Island. Even snooty Boca Raton had the uncommon foresight to buy up its beachfront in the 1970s, converting it into a string of lovely, contiguous beach parks.

MAP OF SOUTH FLORIDA—PAGE 177

Tequesta

As recently as 1955, the village of Tequesta was such a gnarly tangle of undeveloped subtropical vegetation that it was dismissed as being "just a jungle." Two years later, it was incorporated as a golf-course community around the Tequesta Country Club. Now, 40-odd years after that, Tequesta has a year-round population of 5,122 (which swells with second home-owning snowbirds in the winter), and it most definitely would no longer be mistaken for a jungle. Well-tended lawns have replaced the unruly splendor of nature in the raw. Its appeal is understandable. Most lots are waterfront, and the setting—along the north bank of the Loxahatchee River at Jupiter Inlet—couldn't be nicer.

Beaches

Almost all of Tequesta lies west of the Intracoastal Waterway, but here's one small sliver on Jupiter Island that belongs to the village. This is **Coral Cove Park**, a county-owned ocean-to-waterway playground that has 1,500 feet of ocean frontage, having recently expanded its beach through a Save Our Coasts program. Visitors walk through a lush sea grape hammock to the beach, where a lifeguard oversees the reef-filled waters and a set of colored flags offers fair warning to anyone prepared to dive in. The most jagged rocks protrude from the southern end of the beach; swimmers are advised to stay within 50 yards of shore. All in all, it's as placid a setting as one will find in Palm Beach County.

Contact Information

Jupiter/Tequesta/Juno Beach Chamber of Commerce, 800 North U.S. 1, Jupiter, FL 33477; 561/746-1111 or 800/616-7402; website: www.jupiterfl.org

1 Coral Cove Park

Location: State Route 707 at Highway A1A on Jupiter Island in Tequesta
Fees: free parking lot
Hours: sunrise to sunset
Facilities: lifeguards, restrooms, picnic tables, and showers
Contact: Palm Beach County Parks and Recreation Department, 561/966-6600

Jupiter

Three towns—Jupiter, Tequesta, and Juno Beach—lie together like peas in a pod along the coast in northern Palm Beach County. From the traveler's restricted vantage point of U.S. 1 (Federal Highway), there is nothing much to distinguish them from one another or the rest of the county. The same clutter of low-lying strip malls clings to this main drag, although an inordinate number of storefronts are vacant or going out of business, suggesting that the area has been rather optimistically overbuilt. That doesn't stop new construction on what empty lots remain, however. Dormlike condominiums and gated waterfront subdivisions dot the area, attesting to its desirability as one of the last coastal locales in South Florida that hasn't been completely "built out," to use the developer's lingo. But it's getting there.

Jupiter (pop. 30,925) is at the heart of a watery paradise that includes the Intracoastal Waterway, the Atlantic Ocean, Jupiter Inlet, and the Loxahatchee River (Florida's only federally designated Wild and Scenic River). There are more than a

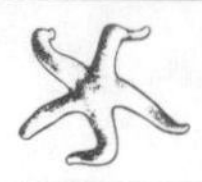

The Burt Reynolds Story

He is one of Florida's proudest sons, a former football hero at FSU who went on to become a movie star, sex symbol, and celebrity. Like Anita Bryant, Burt Reynolds is indelibly associated with the state. She had her singing voice and "Florida sunshine tree." He has his acting career and trademark mustache. Mostly associated with drive-in caliber entertainment like *Smokey and the Bandit* and *Cannonball Run,* Reynolds once jested, "My movies were the kind they show in prisons and airplanes, because nobody can leave." And yet he also worked in the critically acclaimed film *Deliverance*. Moving to TV, he played the lead character in *Evening Shade,* a '90s sitcom.

Reynolds' roots go deep into the sandy soils of north Palm Beach County. His father was chief of police in Riviera Beach. Though Reynolds found fame and fortune in Hollywood, he never lost touch with his home state, buying a ranch and starting a theater in Jupiter that bore his name. When he got hitched to busty, platinum-maned Loni Anderson in 1988, the ceremony was performed on the ranch.

Oddly enough, as we were passing through this very locale, national headlines were trumpeting the news that Reynolds, now 60, had declared bankruptcy. It was revealed in court that he'd accumulated $12.2 million in debts while leading a lifestyle that was costing him $116,000 a month. Among other things, he'd reportedly lost nearly $20 million investing in two Florida-based restaurant chains. Reynolds' financial unraveling came in the wake of his nasty public separation and divorce from Anderson. The sordid details of this unamicable parting made a splash in all the supermarket tabloids and even spilled over into mainstream magazines. He and she both made the rounds of tabloid talk shows while watching their misfortunes serve as comic fodder for late-night TV monologists and grist for the gutter press.

More dirt was dished about their private lives than the sleaziest voyeur needed to know. A tell-all memoir by Anderson portrayed Reynolds as "an abusive, pill-popping lout," in *People* magazine's shoot-from-the-hip summation. Such heapings of humiliation reduced Reynolds to abject self-pity. His nadir came during an appearance on *Good Morning America.* A purple scarf knotted around his neck, he spoke slowly with a clenched jaw and dazed expression, proposing in all seriousness that both he and Loni take lie-detector tests to see who was first unfaithful to whom.

hundred miles of various kinds of shoreline in the Jupiter area, making it a haven for boaters. On the north side of the Jupiter Inlet is Jupiter Beach Colony; on the south, Jupiter Beach Park, a large county-run facility. Standing sentry over it all is the fire-engine red **Jupiter Inlet Lighthouse**, a striking and historic tower. Built in 1860, it is the oldest standing structure in Palm Beach County. It can be climbed Sunday through Wednesday 10 A.M.–3:15 P.M. for $5, which seems a bit steep to us for a mere 105 steps. A small museum and gift shop are on the grounds.

At this point, you might be wondering how the town got the name Jupiter. The local Indians called themselves the Jobe, so Spanish settlers logically named the river after them. English settlers in the mid-eighteenth century misheard Jobe River

Bankruptcy was a particularly bitter pill for the macho Reynolds to swallow. Once America's biggest box-office draw, he'd been reduced to taking bit parts in low-budget made-for-TV and straight-to-video adventure flicks. Reynolds found himself in debt and not particularly in demand. And yet he bounced back like the old soldier he is, earning respectable notices for his acting in *Striptease* (a 1996 fiasco based on a Carl Hiaasen novel) and *Boogie Nights*. Released in 1997, the subject of the latter film was 1970s excess, appropriately built around the tumescent metaphor of the porno industry.

In April 1998, it was revealed that Reynolds' ranch in Jupiter was up for sale. Lawyers for Reynolds and his creditors haggled over his worth in order to determine what the latter might receive in the way of compensation. Our curiosity piqued, we called every business listing in Jupiter that had borne "Burt Reynolds" in its name to find out their status as Reynolds' titanic ego reeled from its collision with the iceberg of personal bankruptcy. Here's what we learned:

- **Burt Reynolds Ranch and Film Studio** — One listed number had been disconnected, while there was no answer at another. Formerly the site of the Burt Reynolds Museum (which no one will ever confuse with the Metropolitan Museum of Art), it had displayed movie props, memorabilia, and pictures. Also on the grounds: a petting zoo, feed store, and gift shop. We'd always wondered if you could get a souvenir mustache at the latter. Sadly, we'll never know.
- **Burt Reynolds Institute For Theatre Training** — Known as BRITT, for short, this was the place to come for seminars on such topics as the Stanislavsky Method in Action-Adventure Filmmaking, the Semiotics of High-Speed Car Crashes, and Deconstructing *Cannonball Run*. Again, the phone had been disconnected.
- **Burt Reynolds Jupiter Theatre** — Reynolds started the theater that bore his name in 1978 in an attempt to bring culture to Jupiter, calling it "the miracle at the truck stop." We've tried to imagine what the typical stage production might be—Shakespearean treatments of Reynolds' plebeian films, with titles such as *Romeo and the Bandit, A Midsummer Night's Drag Race,* or perhaps *Timon of Athens, Georgia.* The curtain fell on the theater that Burt built in 1989, but the facility reopened with new owners and a new name—the Jupiter Theatre—before finally folding in 1996.
- **Burt Reynolds East Park, Burt Reynolds West Park** — Eureka! The two parks named for Jupiter's proudest son still bear his name. They're located directly across from each other on U.S. 1, south of Jupiter Inlet. The Jupiter Chamber of Commerce is headquartered in the west park and the Florida History Center and Museum in the east.

as Jove River—Jove being the deity of Roman mythology, also known as Jupiter, who was the god of thunder and watcher of the skies. With a Jovian stroke, the name stuck to the inlet and the settlement at its mouth. In a more recent clap of Jovian might, the town of Jupiter has positioned itself to grow by another 50 percent almost literally overnight with the construction of an instant community known as Abacoa. This planned community is a behemoth with baseball at its core—specifically, a spring-training facility for major-league teams. In 1998, its first year of operation, the Montreal Expos and the St. Louis Cardinals both trained here. After the major leaguers split for the summer, the minor-league Jupiter Hammerheads take over the stadium.

Spring training is only the tip of the

sand dune at Abacoa, however. When completed according to its 20-year plan, this massive community will cover 2,055 acres. Six thousand homes will be built, joining a satellite college campus (the honors college of Florida Atlantic University), 400 acres' worth of shops and offices, three public schools, and an 18-hole golf course. We'd typically decry such an undertaking as overkill in an area that's already been developed to extremes, except for one extenuating factor: the project is the brainchild of architects Andres Duany and Elizabeth Plater-Zyberk, the dynamic duo who designed the exemplary community of Seaside on the Florida Panhandle (see pages 603–607). Abacoa, like Seaside, is being executed in the New Urbanism planning mode that seeks to reestablish the sense of community that is missing in so much of America. So go for it, we say, with the hope that the results at Abacoa are compatible with higher social and environmental goals.

Incidentally, the first of several legs in our beach travels undertaken specifically for this book began, oddly enough, in Jupiter. This was our starting point for a monthlong survey of South Florida, the three-county area that runs from Jupiter to Miami. We converged at Jupiter from our homes in North Carolina and Connecticut in early December. While the rest of the country was caught in an early-winter deep freeze, the midday mercury was perched at a near-perfect 78°F in sunny Jupiter. It sure didn't seem like December. (In South Florida, it never seems like December—or January, or February, for that matter.) The sight of a plastic snowman by the side of the road seemed hilariously incongruous to us. Christmas decorations adorned a few yards, no doubt belonging to recently arrived Northerners. Despite fleeting pangs of seasonal yearning and homesickness, we finally capitulated to the climate and said the heck with Christmas—let's work on a winter tan.

To that end, we detached ourselves from the congested inland corridors and headed out to Highway A1A. Florida's ocean highway runs beside the ocean from

❷ Dubois Park

Location: south side of the Jupiter Inlet on Dubois Road, in Jupiter
Parking/fees: free parking lot
Hours: sunrise to sunset
Facilities: lifeguards, restrooms, picnic tables, and showers
Contact: Dubois Park and Museum, 561/747-6639

❸ Jupiter Beach County Park

Location: 1375 Jupiter Beach Road, on the south side of the Jupiter Inlet
Parking/fees: free parking lot
Hours: sunrise to sunset
Facilities: lifeguards, restrooms, picnic tables, and showers
Contact: Palm Beach County Parks and Recreation Department, 561/966-6600

❹ Carlin Park

Location: 400 South Highway A1A, south of Indiantown Road in Jupiter
Parking/fees: free parking lot
Hours: sunrise to sunset
Facilities: concessions, lifeguards, restrooms, picnic tables, and showers
Contact: Palm Beach County Parks and Recreation Department, 561/966-6600

Jupiter Inlet to Juno Beach, providing a breezy, sight-filled ride that will lift the spirits any time of year.

Beaches

Taking it from the top, **Dubois Park** is a 30-acre site along the south shore of the Jupiter Inlet. It's got a guarded beach, a picnic ground, volleyball courts, a great view of the Jupiter Inlet Lighthouse on the opposite shore, access to a nearby fishing jetty, and the Dubois House Museum.

Dubois Park shares space on the same elongated barrier spit with **Jupiter Beach County Park**, a wide, 1,700-foot long beach that has been renourished in the recent past. Long rock jetties shelter the mouth of the inlet, south of which lies the flat, desertlike beach. A cluster of tall condos adjacent to the park provides a jarring visual note. Jupiter Beach is, however, a very pleasant place, a 50-acre facility with a children's play area, picnic area, grills, and showers. We saw people splashing in knee-deep water in a lagoon and walking a path that wraps around the inlet. We even had a conversation with a knot of friendly surfers who were about to brave the choppy surf. It seems that one of us writers and one of the surfers were coincidentally wearing the same T-shirt, which we'd both picked up at the 1996 U.S. surfing championship at Huntington Beach, California. They bade us adieu in minimalist surfer-speak—"Later on, dude," "Cool"—and we both went our separate waves. This knot of surfers in Jupiter is pretty tight knit, too; they have their own website (www.jupitersurf.com), on which they post photos of their moves, surf conditions, an Ocean Magic surf and sport shop, and a link to the local chapter to Surfrider Foundation USA.

Next up is **Carlin Park**, also in Jupiter, a 118-acre county-run facility with large parking lots on either side of Highway A1A, as well as a snack bar, children's play area, picnic pavilions, and amphitheater. Shakespeare by the Sea was in progress and *Macbeth* the featured play when we passed through. Zounds! Real culture at the beach—what a concept! Particularly appealing at Carlin Park are the sheltered picnic tables that lie behind windbreaks formed by palms, pines, shrubs, and tall dune grasses. Some folks were sunning themselves back here rather than brave the windy beach. The beach itself is narrow, with dune grasses gamely attempting to hold the eroding sand in place, along its 3,000-foot frontage. Carlin Park lies on the downdrift side of the Jupiter Inlet, meaning that longshore transport of sand is interrupted by the inlet jetties, starving the beaches to the south and necessitating that expensive process euphemistically known as renourishment.

Shore Things

- **Bike/skate rentals**: J-Town Bicycle, 126 Center Street, 561/575-2453.
- **Dive shop**: Seafari Dive & Surf, 75 East Indiantown Road, 561/747-6115.
- **Ecotourism**: Canoe Outfitters of Florida, 4100 West Indiantown Road, 561/746-7053.
- **Fishing charters**: Waterdog Sportfishing Charters, 1095 North Highway A1A, 561/744-5932.
- **Lighthouse**: Jupiter Inlet Lighthouse, Capt. Armour's Way (U.S. 1 and Beach Road), 561/747-8380.
- **Marina**: Jupiter Hills Lighthouse Marina, 18261 U.S. 1, 561/744-0727.
- **Rainy-day attraction**: Marinelife Center, 1200 U.S. 1, Juno Beach, 561/627-8280.
- **Shopping/browsing**: Loggerhead Plaza, 1225 U.S. 1, Juno Beach, 561/627-2702.
- **Surf shop**: Seafari Dive and Surf Shop, 75 East Indiantown Road, 561/747-6115.

Sea Lice: A Pain in the Swimsuit

Swimming in Palm Beach County has its hazards. These include rip currents, rocks in the surf (emplaced to stabilize the eroding beaches), Portuguese man-of-wars, and sea lice. The last of these is more irritating than hazardous, but it's enough to affect the tourist economy. You see, microscopic sea lice are a real pain in the butt—and anywhere else they happen to bite an unsuspecting swimmer. Think of them as the mosquitoes of the sea. Actually, they are the juvenile form of the thimble jellyfish. Their bite is bothersome at least and, at worst, can leave susceptible victims feeling poorly for days with mild nausea, fever, sleeplessness, and discomfort. The scourge—which also goes by the name "seabather's eruption"—is bad enough to discourage visitors from returning to the beach, according to a Juno Beach lifeguard. In an outbreak area, one in every four swimmers is likely to contract the dermatitis.

Peak season for sea lice runs from April through July. The good news is that the number of these creatures appears to wax and wane on a long-term cycle, and that after a long, lousy decade, they appear to be abating. This may mean that the pestilence is abating and that swimmers may have one less thing to worry about at the beach—at least until the next locust-like inundation comes along. Hopefully, that will be several editions of *Florida Beaches* in the future. In the meantime, if you do encounter sea lice, treatment of the ensuing dermatitis includes taking an antihistamine (such as diphenhydramine) for the itching and applying an over-the-counter 0.5% hydrocortisone cream to the rash.

SOUTH FLORIDA

- **Vacation rentals:** Oceanside Reality of Jupiter, 725 North A1A, 561/746-7476.

Bunking Down

There are no resorts directly on the ocean and few even close to it in Jupiter and Juno Beach. The **Jupiter Beach Resort** (5 North A1A, 561/746-2511, $$$) is the notable exception. Lying directly on the ocean, this nine-story white wonder is easily the resort of first choice in northern Palm Beach County. You'll pay around $115 a night in the off-season and three times that during the winter to enjoy a two-bedroom oceanfront room. The resort offers a battalion of amenities: heated pool, balconies, fitness center, access to nearby golf and tennis facilities, and outstanding on-premises restaurants. Frankly, we'd rather stay here than at The Breakers in Palm Beach. For one thing, they have a beach in a natural setting with a thick buffer of vegetation between the resort and the water.

If $360–400 a night for an oceanfront room in the high season is beyond your budget, try the **Wellesley Inn** (34 Fisherman's Wharf, 561/575-7201, $), which offers clean, serviceable accommodations on the west bank of the Intracoastal Waterway at the back of a restaurant/shopping center complex. The beach is less than a mile away, and you'll save a bundle, which you can spend on crab dinners.

Coastal Cuisine

They've got a bad case of the crabs in Jupiter. For some reason, they're really keen on Maryland-style crab houses down here, even though the Chesapeake Bay blue crabs that form the basis for this cuisine come from about a thousand miles to the north. In any event, three crab houses—**Jupiter Crab Company** (1511 North Old Dixie Highway, 561/747-8300, $$$$), the **Crab House** (1065 North A1A, 561/744-1300, $$$), and **Charley's Crab** (1000 North U.S. 1, 561/744-4710, $$$)—sit on or near the Jupiter Inlet in close proximity. Our advice would be to order the freshest Floridian catch of the day—black grouper, red snapper, or whatever—and leave the Maryland crabs, the North Atlantic salmon, the Maine lobster, and the Canadian scallops to others, unless you've just got to have 'em. At the Crab House, you can book a postprandial cruise of the Intracoastal Waterway aboard the *Manatee Queen* (561/744-2191).

The Jupiter Beach Resort has an award-winning restaurant, **Sinclair's Ocean Grill** (5 North A1A, 561/745-7120, $$$), that's both semiformal and semi-affordable, with entrées running in the $12–24 range. All the on-premises restaurants at the resort are serviced by the main kitchen, so quality is assured throughout.

Night Moves

You can bend an elbow in Jupiter at any number of hospitable taverns, including **Duffy's Drafthouse** (185 East Indiantown Road, 561/743-4405) and the **Jupiter Ale House** (126 Center Street, 561/746-6720). If you're staying at the **Jupiter Beach Resort** (5 North A1A, 561/746-2511), they've got a lounge with live music Wednesday through Sunday and live music beside the humongous heated pool on weekends.

Contact Information

Jupiter/Tequesta/Juno Beach Chamber of Commerce, 800 North U.S. 1, Jupiter, FL 33477; 561/746-1111 or 800/616-7402; website: www.jupiterfl.org

Juno Beach

This town of 2,903 is the only one of the trio in northernmost Palm Beach County that has "beach" in its name. In fact, most of the town does exist between the Intracoastal Waterway and the ocean. It's a pretty serene, low-key place, given the general bustle and boom surrounding this growing, populous county's beachside communities. That makes it all the harder to believe that Juno Beach was at one time the county seat of Dade County. That's right, Dade County, which at one time encompassed 7,200 square miles. Juno enjoyed its day in the sun during the 1890s, then the honor was passed along to burgeoning Miami, and Dade County was subsequently subdivided. Today, Juno's a

5 Juno Beach Park

Location: 14775 Highway A1A in Juno Beach
Parking/fees: free parking lot
Hours: sunrise to sunset
Facilities: concessions, lifeguards, restrooms, picnic tables, and showers
Contact: Palm Beach County Parks and Recreation Department, 561/966-6600

6 Loggerhead Park

Location: 1200 U.S. 1 in Juno Beach
Parking/fees: free parking lot
Hours: sunrise to sunset
Facilities: lifeguards (seasonal), restrooms, picnic tables, showers, and a visitor center (Marine Life Center)
Contact: Palm Beach County Parks and Recreation Department, 561/966-6600

MAP OF PALM BEACH COUNTY—PAGE 178

no-frills beach town with the usual South Florida mix of single-family homes and high-rises, with the former creating a pleasant small-town aura and the latter countering with an incongruous air of anonymity.

Beaches

The county-run beaches of northern Palm Beach County are nicely landscaped and well maintained, with lifeguard stands, ample parking, and decent facilities. The only thing that is missing, really, is a beach wide enough to do much of anything on. At tiny **Juno Beach Park,** for instance, high tide laps at the base of the lifeguard stand, which itself is pressed against a sandy bluff, above which lies Highway A1A. So it goes in Palm Beach County, where the irresistible force of the ocean combines with the erosive power of upcoast jetties and the various harden-

Rubes With a View II

A long, wave-lashed beach has never failed to induce in us feelings of humility, awe, and joy. When such magisterial settings are defiled by other humans—in the form of pollution, littering, poaching, or recklessly piloting Jet Skis within earshot of beachgoers—we find our tempers sorely tested. By now, it should be clear we're not the world's most reverent guys, never wasting an opportunity to focus our dyspepsia upon instances of human folly at the beach. Our displeasure doesn't end with witnessing defilement of the outdoors, either. Once the Jet Skis' racket has abated and the beer cans have been left in the sand, beach boors head to waterfront restaurants to put on the feed bag, occasioning a further display of bad manners. We observe the behavior of such rubes with both amusement and mortification.

One of the peculiar quirks of this ill-bred animal is the way a group of them can sit at the most enviable table in a scenic restaurant and turn their collective backs on the view. It happens all the time. We would be content to let it slide if it weren't for the fact that these people call attention to their ignorance and often ruin a magical evening for those around them.

The worst case we've ever witnessed occurred in Northern California at a cliffside dining room offering an unrivaled view of a rocky headland. Hence, we wrote our first screed on the subject, "Rubes With a View," in our book *California Beaches* (Foghorn Press, 1999). Not to be outdone, Florida has yielded its own bumper crop of candidates for this book's award to those least deserving of a good seat in a waterfront restaurant. In South Florida, your typical contender is a cranky senior citizen whining about how a restaurant "thinks it can get away without serving shrimp scampi." This line, or one like it, is usually the prelude to a long-winded litany of complaints about the food, service, table, and weather.

However, that kind of talk is child's play compared to what we overheard one night at a dockside restaurant in northern Palm Beach County. We'd been seated at a table so close to the placid, light-dappled surface of the Intracoastal Waterway we could have reached down and plucked our own dinner from the water. It was the last night of one leg of our Florida beach travels. We were exhausted but content, quietly appreciative of the wa-

ing schemes (seawalls, bulkheads) man has planted in its path to create a recipe for severe beach narrowing. Juno Beach has, according to local surfers, "one of the county's most consistent breaks." Surfers have dubbed the beach here "Double Roads," a reference to the fact that Highway A1A and U.S. 1 run parallel and close by one another through town. Their latest victory, courtesy the generous county parks and recreation department, is the privilege of surfing off 990-foot Juno Pier, an agreement worked out by calmly sitting down with the fishermen and lifeguards. All in all, an enlightened place, this Juno Beach.

Loggerhead Park boasts both a beach and an environmental education mission: informing the public about loggerhead turtles and other ocean dwellers via kid-friendly exhibits at the Marinelife Center. The

tery view and willing to let the setting wrap itself around our road-weary psyches.

Suddenly, the scene was disturbed by the arrival of a party of four from Ohio, seated at the next table within earshot and arm's reach. This waddling herd immediately began swapping jokes. One after another, mirthless and tedious tales gushed forth in round-robin fashion. Their semiautomatic expelling of punchlines was interrupted only by the arrival of servers to pour drinks, take orders, and deliver food.

Each joke was more offensive than the one that preceded it. Even more surprising was the fact that every member of the party was over 40—certainly old enough to know better, one would think. The younger couple were the son and daughter-in-law of the elders, both of whom were in their 70s. The son wore a V-necked sweater vest. His wife sported a garish "USA" sweatshirt, with each of the three letters loudly outlined in glitter. The unstaunched, uncauterized flow of bad taste sent us into a despairing tailspin that culminated with us muttering under our breaths, "I'd gladly trade a hundred human beings for one healthy manatee."

Meanwhile, all tables within a 10-yard radius of the rube clan from Ohio were held hostage by their flapping jaws. It's a mystery to us why no one told them to pipe down. Here's an unappetizing sampling of what we heard that night:

"So anyways, he takes it out and starts whacking it against the bedpost, see, and his wife sez, 'Izzat you, Justin?' You see, she tinks it's de udder guy."

"Oh, he's got about 20 or 30 of them as good as that. . . . You gotta do the one about the stuttering dog, Bob. Come on . . . do the dog!"

"There was this Amish couple, see, and they wuz robbed by a highwayman. . . ." (The Amish? Come on, leave the Amish out of this.)

"And the gynecologist sez, 'Can I numb that fer ya?' And then he goes, 'Num num num num num' . . . get it? . . .'Num num num num num' . . . get it?"

In between these assaults on common decency and the natural setting, the older woman—a crow-faced, beady-eyed, small-minded harridan—began whispering asides about "the blacks," in particular how "the blacks are taking over all the major cities." In a lovingly supportive gesture, her son added, "You're right, ma, they'll just as soon kill ya as lookit ya. . . . I won't even go near Chicago anymore."

The behavior of these rubes was rawer than any oysters we'd enjoyed before their untimely arrival. Our revenge upon them and anyone like them is to report the scene as accurately as we can. We hope that neither you nor we must ever sit near their like again.

MAP OF PALM BEACH COUNTY—PAGE 178

park also has a bike path, nature trail, tennis courts, and play area. Not that a sensible adult would need to be told otherwise, but just in case you had any ideas, the penalties for molesting nesting loggerheads run up to $20,000. They take their loggerheads seriously here in South Florida, as well they should. The center is open 10 A.M.–4 P.M. Tuesday through Saturday; noon–3 P.M. Sunday (free, donations appreciated).

Snowbirds, take note: On a typical early-December afternoon in Juno Beach, the water temperature was an inviting 76°F. Offshore, we saw windsurfers carving back and forth. Inshore, people sunned themselves on the narrow beach at the base of the stairs leading down from the roadway.

Bunking Down

A few chain motels repose a block or two back from the ocean in Juno Beach. Actually, the **Holiday Inn Express** (13950 U.S. 1, 561/626-1531, $$) is a mere half-block from the beach at the intersection of Federal Highway (U.S. 1) and Donald Ross Boulevard. And that's as close as you'll get in Juno Beach.

Contact Information

Jupiter/Tequesta/Juno Beach Chamber of Commerce, 800 North U.S. 1, Jupiter, FL 33477; 561/746-1111 or 800/616-7402; website: www.jupiterfl.org.

John D. MacArthur Beach State Park

John D. MacArthur Beach State Park is named for its benefactor, who donated nearly 800 acres of land and a two-mile undeveloped beachfront to the state. It is a green haven for humans, as well as a popular nesting spot for loggerhead turtles. The park has been intelligently planned to optimize access while minimizing impact on its four ecosystems: beach, reef, mangrove estuary, and hardwood hammock. There's one hiking trail among 225 acres of uplands. A 1,600-foot wooden boardwalk traverses Lake Worth Cove en route to the beach, which is reached via your pick of four wooden walkways that climb over but don't disturb the dune vegetation. Numbered stops on the trails are keyed to informative brochures. On a casual stroll, we saw herons, ibis, roseate spoonbills, and ospreys, as well as acres of mangrove, cabbage palms, and gumbo-limbo. On the trail through the back dune area, we came upon spider webs so thick that walking into them would have created natural shower caps on our heads. More than 150 bird species have been sighted at MacArthur, and a helpful brochure lists them all, if you're of a mind to keep track.

At the beach, two warnings are posted: "No Lifeguard on Duty—Swim at Your Own Risk" and "Caution: Bottom May Contain Submerged Rocks." We dove right in, though, encountering neither rocks nor

7 John D. MacArthur Beach State Park

Location: 2.5 miles north of Riviera Beach, on Highway A1A
Parking/fees: $3.25 per vehicle entrance fee
Hours: 8 A.M. to sunset
Facilities: restrooms and a visitor center
Contact: John D. MacArthur Beach State Park, 561/624-6950

risks. We were, however, bothered by some tenacious mosquitoes, so come armed with insect repellent. Bugs aside, John D. MacArthur Beach State Park is a magical setting with some of the last unbuilt-upon beach wilderness in South Florida.

A shuttle cart offers regular service from the parking area to the dune walkovers. We hopped aboard and had a spirited discussion with our driver about (of all things) Luddites. "Wouldn't it be great," he mused, "to have the technology of today with the values of the '40s. It's people who kill off nature, not machines." While we've heard that unconvincing argument elsewhere (with regard to handguns), it was nice to strike up an intelligent debate with a genial stranger for a change.

Contact Information

John D. MacArthur Beach State Park, 10900 State Route 703 (Highway A1A), North Palm Beach, FL 33408; 561/624-6950; website: www.myflorida.com

Singer Island: Riviera Beach and Palm Beach Shores

Singer Island has always occupied a special place in our hearts for having been the winter watering hole of the late Frederick Exley, a writer with whom we've been smitten since college. In *Pages from a Cold Island*—the second volume of his celebrated trilogy of memoirs—he paints an appealing picture of the island from the vantage point of a barstool. Passing the downtime occasioned by his massive writer's block with the island's fishermen, fry cooks, barkeeps, dropouts, and other assorted dreamers, Exley comes off as a beery Socrates warding off his "private malaise" by hanging around people he liked. So smitten is he with Singer Island that he actually experiences physical pain when he must cross the bridge onto the mainland sprawl of Riviera Beach (pop. 29,020) to shop for essentials.

Some of the spirit that Exley celebrated still remains, though one must look hard to find it. Without question, the toothbrush-shaped island—which includes the community of Palm Beach Shores (pop. 1,037) at its southern tip—puts on fewer airs than its neighbors to the north and south, offering some relief from their fortress-type atmosphere. While Singer can be reached by two access points—PGA Boulevard at the north and Blue Heron Boulevard at the south—its best foot is put forward at the north end, where one is immediately welcomed by the outer fringes of John D. MacArthur Beach State Park, a miraculous preserve of subtropical coastal habitat that once covered all of South Florida.

From MacArthur Park south, alas, Singer Island has begun to take on the look of its neighbors, riven with indistinguishable high-rises, each given a fancified name (Martinique II, Corniche, Cote d'Azur, Eastpointe). Most are eerily empty in the off-season, as if a neutron bomb had struck them. John D. MacDonald, Florida's great mystery writer, may have had Singer Island in mind when he wrote his terrifying thriller *Condominium*. (Now there's a good South Florida beach read!)

Even so, Singer Island is cheerfully accommodating, relative to its Palm Beach neighbors. At the island's central point is a pleasant, unpretentious business district anchored by Ocean Mall and a generous swath of lifeguarded beach. That warmth is not illusory. If one believes the local literature, the warm waters of the Gulf Stream approach nearer to land at Singer Island than at any other spot in North

MAP OF PALM BEACH COUNTY—PAGE 178

America. As a result, the temperature varies only slightly. Night and day, winter and summer, Tuesday and Saturday, the mercury hovers at an average of 76°F. In the hot summer months, while inland areas are baking at 100°F and high humidity, Singer is a not unpleasant 86°F, and the cooling breezes make the scorching sun bearable.

Singer Island is, by the way, noted for sportfishing, with deep-sea expeditions for dolphin, sailfish, wahoo, and shark available at local marinas. Scenic waterway cruises also leave from **Sailfish Marina** (98 Lake Drive, 561/844-1724). Taking the cruising theme one step further, Phil Foster Park—a pea-shaped landfill island located beneath the Riviera Bridge at Blue Heron Boulevard—is the launching point for an *Island Queen Riverboat* cruise in a genuine 150-seat Mississippi River paddle wheeler. The cruise goes to and from Palm Beach, offering a scenic means of surveying lifestyles of the rich and famous from offshore. They also offer a number of themed dinner/dance cruises through *Star of Palm Beach;* call 561/848-STAR for information and reservations. Nearby, accessible only by boat from the Intracoastal Waterway is 87-acre Peanut Island, a special facility run by the county that has a fishing pier, boat dock, 18 boat slips, 20 camp sites. Also here is the Palm Beach Maritime Museum and Kennedy Bunker.

With a free public beach, a peerless state park, and a nod of approval from Fred Exley, a beach lover would be hard pressed to top Singer Island. The inland portion of Riviera Beach is a different kettle of fish. Most of this city of 30,000 lies across Blue Heron Bridge on the mainland. It is even less inviting now than when Exley dreaded having to make provisioning trips there. Moving down Federal Highway (U.S. 1), fast-food stands and suburban mall sprawl give way to unbroken miles of boarded up storefronts, cracked sidewalks, pawnshops, and a plague of cheerless, decrepit businesses with names like the Cheer Food Market and Onan: the Generator People (say what?). The smell of petty crime wafts along this corridor from Riviera Beach to West Palm Beach. Yecch.

Beaches

At the north end of Riviera Beach's stake on Singer Island, **Ocean Reef Park** harbors an offshore reef popular with snorkelers, as well as a 700-foot beach. It's a block north of the private Palm Beach Racquet Club on Ocean Boulevard (Highway A1A). The main public beach on Singer Island is **Riviera Beach Municipal Beach,** which has a thousand feet of lifeguarded beach. It is claimed to be the widest public beach on the Gold Coast. That isn't quite the boast it may first appear to be, as the beaches south

8 Ocean Reef Park

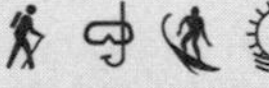

Location: near Bimini Lane at Ocean Boulevard (Highway A1A) on Singer Island
Parking/fees: free parking lot
Hours: sunrise to sunset
Facilities: lifeguards, restrooms, picnic tables, and showers
Contact: Palm Beach County Parks and Recreation Department, 561/966-6600

9 Riviera Beach Municipal Beach

Location: Blue Heron Boulevard at Ocean Drive, beside Ocean Mall on Singer Island
Parking/fees: metered parking lot
Hours: sunrise to sunset
Facilities: lifeguards, restrooms, picnic tables, and showers
Contact: Riviera Beach Municipal Beach, 561/845-4079

MAP OF SOUTH FLORIDA—PAGE 177

and north are often narrow and erosion prone, and this one has been artificially widened by trucking in sand.

Riviera Beach Municipal Beach is easily found by following Ocean Avenue (Highway A1A) to the large parking area in front of Ocean Mall. (Incidentally, Highway A1A exits the island at this point via Blue Heron Boulevard.) On these replenished and bulldozed sands, volleyball courts contribute to the look and feel of a typical Southern California beach during peak season. The professional volleyball circuit makes a tournament stop here. This beachside park also offers a boardwalk, children's play area, and sheltered picnic tables. It's no good for snorkeling because of the sandy bottom, but it's a fine beach for swimming.

Much of the remaining oceanfront down to Lake Worth Inlet belongs to Palm Beach Shores. This uptight community attempts to restrict beach access to residents only. To park here, you must (1) live here and (2) obtain a beach sticker for your car at Town Hall. Of course, you can always walk down the sand from Riviera Beach with no problem. **Palm Beach Shores Park** has a lovely beach, make no mistake, with a boardwalk running beside it, plus benches for the weary or contemplative and a playground for the kiddies. Too bad they're not of a mind to share their bounty with others. Surfers ignore the edicts by simply walking with their boards from Riviera Beach, because the surf off the Pump House has "long rights."

Shore Things

- **Dive shop:** Dive USA, 1201 North Ocean Boulevard, 561/844-5100.
- **Ecotourism:** Adventure Times Kayaking, 1372 North Killian Drive, Lake Park, 561/881-7218.
- **Fishing charters:** Sailfish Marina Resort, 98 Lake Drive, Palm Beach Shores, 561/844-1724.
- **Marina:** Sailfish Marina, 98 Lake Drive, 561/844-1724.
- **Rainy-day attraction:** South Florida Science Museum, 4801 Dreher Trail North, West Palm Beach, 561/832-1988.
- **Shopping/browsing:** Ocean Mall, Ocean Boulevard at Blue Heron Boulevard.
- **Surf shop:** Island Watersports, Ocean Mall, 2501 North Ocean Boulevard, 561/844-6983.
- **Vacation rentals:** Home Property Management, 4360 Northlake Boulevard, Palm Beach Shores, 561/624-4663.

Bunking Down

Hidden among the towering condos and luxury resort hotels are a few quintessential beach motels that have somehow survived the trend toward verticality. The **Island Beach Resort** (3100 North Ocean Boulevard, 561/848-6810, $$) and **Tahiti on the Ocean** (3920 North Ocean Boulevard, 561/848-9764, $$) are both adequate and affordable, by Gold Coast standards. The latter, for instance, offers oceanfront rooms for around $100 a night during the winter high season.

10 Palm Beach Shores Park

Location: along Ocean Avenue from Bamboo Road to Lake Worth Inlet in Palm Beach Shores

Parking/fees: Parking is restricted to Palm Beach Shores residents displaying beach stickers, obtainable at Town Hall (247 Edwards Lane) for a $10 annual fee. On July 1st of every year—and only on this day—beach stickers are sold to nonresidents at a cost of $100 for 10 stickers.

Hours: sunrise to sunset

Facilities: lifeguards, restrooms, picnic tables, and showers

Contact: Palm Beach Shores Town Hall, 561/844-3457

For a few dollars more, chain motel franchises are abundant, including the **Best Western Seaspray Inn** (123 Ocean Avenue, 561/844-0233, $$$) and the **Days Inn Oceanfront Resort** (2700 North Ocean Boulevard, 561/848-8661, $$$). A bit more upscale and pricey are the **Radisson Resort Singer Island** (3200 North Ocean Boulevard, 561/842-6171, $$$) and the **Holiday Inn Sunspree Resort** (3700 North Ocean Boulevard, 561/848-3888, $$$). At the latter, conveniently located a quarter mile north of Ocean Mall and Riviera Beach Municipal Beach, in-season rates range from $144 to $169 for a double room.

At the top end of the scale—and right off the scale, in terms of price—is the **Embassy Suites Resort Hotel** (181 Ocean Avenue, 561/863-4000, $$$$), which is on the Palm Beach Shores end of the island. An oceanfront room with two beds runs—gulp!—$309 per night in February. We could make that kind of money go a lot further than one night at the beach.

Coastal Cuisine

You'll not go hungry on Singer Island, but it's not exactly a hotbed of haute cuisine. There are restaurants with gourmet pretensions at some of the luxury hotels, but you're better off pointing your sail to the local marinas. Both Sailfish and Buccaneer marinas in Palm Beach Shores have popular seafood restaurants—the **Buccaneer Restaurant & Lounge** (142 Lake Drive, 561/844-3477, $$$$) and the **Sailfish Marina Restaurant** (90 Lake Drive, 561/848-1492, $$$)—which feature fresh catches hauled in daily from beyond their windows. You will find some of the friendliest nightlife on the island here, too.

Night Moves

The liveliest scene on Singer Island is at **Oceans Eleven** (2603 North Ocean Boulevard, 561/840-1812), beside the beach at the north end of Ocean Mall. Any watering hole named after a film by the Rat Pack (Frank, Sammy, and Dino) has got the right idea when it comes to boozy fun. A burger-and-wings joint with seemingly dozens of TVs tuned in to sporting events, they feature an outdoor deck upstairs and claim to have the world's longest happy hour: "all day and all night." Well, not quite. They're open 11 A.M.–5 A.M.—long enough to keep any party animal well lubricated, with a few hours off to rest up for the next bout.

Contact Information

Singer Island Business Association, 1211 The Plaza, Singer Island, FL 33404; 561/842-2477; website: www.singerislandflorida.com

The Golf Coast

Golf is another of the secular religions practiced by moneyed pilgrims in Palm Beach County, which has the highest concentration of golf courses in Florida. There are more than 150 of them, according to the Palm Beach County Tourist Development Council. Florida, in turn, has more than a thousand golf courses—the most of any state in the nation—covering a combined ground area of over 312 square miles. Nearly every environmental law on the books would have been violated had most existing courses been built in the past decade. Wetlands were drained and filled, mangrove forests razed, and chemicals dumped onto the courses (and, via storm runoff, into watersheds). Prodigious quantities of chemicals are needed to fertilize and maintain these unnatural spaces. In humid climates like Florida's, up to nine pounds of herbicide, fungicide, and insecticide are sprayed and spread per acre each year. That's three times the rate used by the most chemically dependent agribusiness.

Water-quality analyst Richard Klein, one of the foremost authorities on the environmental impact of large-scale development, works for and with citizens who oppose shopping malls, housing developments, and golf courses in their communities. When he was asked by *Sierra* magazine to name the least desirable location for a golf course, he responded, "Near a water source in a sandy area with a shallow water table."

That basically describes the entire state of Florida.

In recent years, vigilant citizens and tougher environmental regulations have forced golf-course developers and maintenance crews to clean up their act to some degree. Less intrusive strategies are now employed in course construction, parts of courses are allowed to remain in a natural state (isn't it odd to say that about the outdoors?), and alternatives to pesticides are being developed and tried. Even so, the powerful U.S. golf industry—whose annual gross receipts run about $64 billion a year, with upward of 16,000 courses in operation and a new course opening somewhere every day—remains environmentally culpable. For one thing, golf courses cover 2.4 million acres in the U.S., and $8 billion in chemicals and equipment are spent annually to maintain them.

Scientists argue that environmental issues associated with golf-course management and construction are such that essential research on runoff and sediment in golf watersheds must be conducted. Ironically, Florida's course designers and developers are now using ecological buzzwords and playing up their natural settings. One new course in Palm Beach County calls attention to "the surrounding native Florida terrain, with its wetlands and abundance of wildlife." Needless to say, if you truly appreciated wetlands and wildlife, you would probably be hiking or kayaking, not golfing.

SOUTH FLORIDA

Palm Beach

Lest you be tempted to swallow the myth that Palm Beach is one big oceanside playground where drop-dead specimens parade in the sand and poutily soak up the sun's rays all day long, we are here to inform you otherwise. That is because the truth of the matter is that, depending on the vigilance of sand renourishment and the not always kind winter storms, Palm Beach is often more palm than beach.

On our last visit, though, in late 2000, we were pleasantly surprised by the latest bounty of replacement sand here. A major renourishment done in 1997 seems to have at least stabilized the beach in the main part of the town. On previous visits, we found most of the sand was gone with the wind or, more accurately, the sea, and the only sound we heard was the relentless pounding of ocean upon seawall in front of zealously guarded and gated private real estate.

Part of the Palm Beach myth is accurate. It is a hedonistic place where the rich lead lives of self-indulgent ease and luxury. The prevailing attitude can best be expressed by a sight we saw one afternoon in front of the Breakers. Two head-turning rich girls in a red Corvette came cruising up the long driveway that leads to a turnaround in front of the venerable resort. They wheeled to a stop beside the Florentine fountain, then took turns photographing each other striking nonchalant poses atop the car's hood, splayed out with the posh resort as a backdrop as if to say, "All this is mine, baby!"

Palm Beach is synonymous with money, privacy, and the opportunities for decadence afforded by the zealous hoarding of both. Hunter S. Thompson captured it perfectly when, while covering the debauched Roxanne Pulitzer divorce trial for *Rolling Stone* in 1984, he wrote the following of Palm Beach: "It is the ultimate residential community, a lush sand bar lined with palm trees and mansions on the Gold Coast of Florida—millionaires and old people, an elaborately protected colony for the seriously rich, a very small island and a very small world."

The term "Palm Beach" is indivorceable from the word "socialite." Just for fun, we searched the online archives of the *Miami Herald* for the phrase "Palm Beach socialite" and came up with 212 articles. Many bore headlines like these: "Millionaire Charged in Wife's '87 Murder, but Ex-Palm Beach Suspect Missing," "Palm Beach Socialite a Suspect in Daughters' Kidnapping," "Jewelry Missing, Police Hint Robber May Have Killed Palm Beach Socialite." And on and on.

Since it sits beside an ocean that periodically can't be used, the resorts tend to focus on golf, tennis, and shopping. The game of golf is an obsession down here because it can be played all year long, thanks to Florida's warm, comfy climate. There are 150 golf courses in Palm Beach County—more than any other county in a state with the most courses of any in the whole country.

Odds are you're not coming to Palm Beach for the traditional family beach vacation anyway. The town is primarily a winter playground for the wealthy, who jet down from places like New York, Newport, Nantucket, Martha's Vineyard, et al., when cold weather begins blowing in. Its reputation as an enclave of high society is a drawing card that's used to pump up Palm Beach County tourism on the theory that people like to be around money. What they don't tell you is that an outsider stands less chance of penetrating the social whirl than the domestic help. And outside of the winter season (December–-April), Palm Beach is honest-to-God not happening.

Palm Beach is actually a rather small place, with a year-round population of

9,710 that swells to 25,000 in winter. The community's provenance as a hideout for the wealthy dates back to Henry Flagler—yes, him again—and his construction of two resort hotels in the 1890s and a splendid private mansion, Whitehall, in 1901. A gift to his third wife, Mary Lily Kenan, Whitehall is now open to the public as the **Henry Morrison Flagler Museum** ($8 for adults, $3 for children 6–12, closed Monday). It has variously been referred to as the Taj Mahal of the South, the San Simeon of the East, and the most magnificent private residence in the nation. Each room in this immense marble mansion was designed and furnished after a different period: Italian Renaissance, French Renaissance, Louis XIV, Louis XV, Louis XVI. We fantasized a room decorated in early garage-rock: Louie, Louie.

We can't help but think that Flagler would be pleased with the look of Palm Beach today. In a delightful turn of phrase, the historic WPA *Guide to Florida* drolly had this to say about Palm Beach in the '30s: "Its habitués constitute a fragment of international society seeking June in January and the pleasures afforded by right of social prestige and heavy purse." In all essential aspects, the town has little changed since those words were written. The streets and "vias" of Palm Beach remain lined with private mansions hidden from view by huge, boxlike hedges trimmed with geometrical precision. God knows what goes on behind those hedges. Beyond the torn curtain that afforded glimpses of sordid goings-on in that world during the Roxanne Pulitzer divorce and William Kennedy Smith rape trials, we'll never know. Nor do we really care to.

Before moving on to beaches, we'll make cursory mention of West Palm Beach, which lies on the mainland side of the Intracoastal Waterway. In terms of population it is nearly eight times as large as Palm Beach (and about that many times less glamorous). It is a city of malls, girdled by freeways. It is the multicultural mix that Palm Beach decidedly is not. It is where thousands of voters who cried foul during the presidential electoral circus of 2000 live. It is the voice seldom heard on Worth Avenue and, apparently, in Washington, D.C.

There are other communities with the words "Palm Beach" in them, too: North Palm Beach, South Palm Beach, Palm Beach Gardens, Palm Beach Shores, yada yada yada. They, too, are home to voters snared in the butterfly ballot net of 2000.

Gradually, it sinks in that the Palm Beaches are a scaled-down, East Coast version of Southern California, specifically Los Angeles. If West Palm Beach is downtown L.A., then Palm Beach is Beverly Hills. Various other towns (Riviera Beach, Lantana, Lake Worth, the other Palm Beaches) are arrayed around it. One travels great distances on highways and bridges to get from point to point. It all adds up to a bulging, spread-out mass of civilization that is utterly dependent on the automobile. In the emphasis on wealth and living well beneath the bright and sometimes blinding sun, the Palm Beaches evoke all the rewards and frustrations that make the City of Angels tick so maniacally.

Beaches

The town of Palm Beach built its reputation on the bank accounts and bloodlines

⓫ Midtown Beach

Location: east end of Worth Avenue at South Ocean Boulevard (Highway A1A) in Palm Beach
Parking/fees: metered street parking
Hours: sunrise to sunset
Facilities: lifeguards and showers
Contact: Midtown Beach, 561/838-5483

of the rich and famous whose walled estates contribute to the air of chilly inaccessibility. You would be led to believe that Palm Beach is a five-karat diamond in a gold setting, but if it's beaches you're looking for, the bauble is costume jewelry. South Beach in Miami is much more cosmopolitan, hip and alive—and the beach is no mirage down there.

A short little sand-colored wall runs along much of the oceanfront in Palm Beach, discouraging public access. That said, there is one public beach in Palm Beach proper. **Midtown Beach** is located where Worth Avenue meets South Ocean Blvd. (A1A). The public beach extends for half a mile, a quarter-mile of which is lifeguarded. There's nothing much out here in the way of facilities besides a public shower, not even a lousy restroom, which says everything you need to know about Palm Beach's grudging provision of public access. Adding to the sense of exclusion, the beach is closed 8 P.M.–8 A.M. Yes, closed. Metered parking is available along A1A ($1 per hour), but one gets the distinct feeling that one is much more welcome strolling Worth Avenue, which functions as the de facto beach in the sense that it is here that visitors get soaked (see sidebar).

There are two other beach parks on the south end of Palm Beach: **Phipps Ocean Park** is a quarter-mile municipal guarded beach with a natural dune line but a rocky, narrow shoreline. **Richard G. Kreusler Park** is a tiny (450 feet) lifeguarded county beach that lies close to Lake Worth. The latter boasts a small artificial reef for diving and snorkeling fun. While none of these spots is worth rattling your jewelry about, they are all that opulent Palm Beach has to offer.

The entire stretch of coast from Palm Beach to Boynton Beach can be viewed as the East Coast's answer to the 17-Mile Drive in Pebble Beach, California. Driving Ocean Boulelvard (A1A) in search of hassle-free beach access is as forbidding as entering a Worth Avenue boutique with no wallet, a squadron of hungry salesclerks on the prowl, and no other customers in sight. There are no shoulders beside the road, so you can't pull over to get your bearings or drink in all the architectural ego gratification on view. The beach is gated off for the private pleasure of multimillionaires who live here part-time or upscale sorts who keep way stations in high-rises with names like "the Patrician." There are no utilitarian businesses to speak of, though poodle groomers and plastic surgeons hang their shingles. Everything seems designed to keep visitors moving along. We found ourselves wondering, as we did in Pebble Beach, why they even bother with the pretense of a public road.

⓬ Phipps Ocean Park

Location: 1.5 miles north of Lake Worth Beach, on the south end of Palm Beach
Parking/fees: metered parking lot
Hours: sunrise to sunset
Facilities: lifeguards, restrooms, picnic tables, and showers
Contact: Phipps Ocean Park, 561/585-9203

⓭ Richard G. Kreusler Park

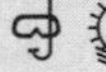 

Location: One-half mile north of Lake Worth Beach, at the south end of Palm Beach
Parking/fees: metered parking (25 cents for 15 minutes)
Hours: sunrise to sunset
Facilities: lifeguards, restrooms, picnic tables, and showers
Contact: Palm Beach County Parks and Recreation Department, 561/966-6600

Fairway to Heaven

(set to the tune of "Stairway to Heaven")

There's a place at the shore
Where the lots are for sale
'Cause they're building a fairway to heaven.
It's a tenet unspoken
That the laws will be broken
With a bribe they'll be draining the wetlands.

Ooh-ooh ooh, ooh-ooh ooh-ooh
And they're building a fairway to heaven.

There's a man on the course
Spraying pesticides and worse
The environment's taking a beating.
But the trees and the brook
Have no way to say, "Look,
We're filing a suit for mistreatment."

Ooh, it makes us wonder.
Yeah, it makes us wonder.

There's a feeling I get
When I hook to the left
And my caddie goes quietly hunting.
He's the best ever seen
At finding balls lost in trees
Improving lies while the others aren't looking.

Ooh, it makes us wonder.
Yeah, it makes us wonder.

And it's whispered anon
When the coast lots are gone
The developers will start moving inland.
When the rising sea comes
Swamping home, course, and club
Mother Nature will bellow with laughter.

If there's a rustling in your hedgerow
Don't make a scene, no
It's just a sea turtle laying eggs there
There's nowhere else to lay
Her beach eroded away
The fairway lies on the shore's sad edge.

Ooh, and it makes us wonder.
Yes, it makes us wonder.

Our anger's seething when we can't go
Down to the seashore
Tall condos block all the access
Dear politician can you hear the wind blow
And did you know
Your silly lies have made an awful mess

And as we drive down A1A
Past guarded gates and green fairways
Money talks loudest, they all say
But why did it turn out this way?
How could this paradise be sold
To those who hoarded all the gold
Who tear down dunes and build seawalls
Wear lime-green pants and chase golf balls
While their wives stalk shopping malls?

And they think they've found the fairway to heaven.

SOUTH FLORIDA

Shore Things

- **Bike/skate rentals:** Palm Beach Bicycle Trail Shop, 223 Sunrise Avenue, 561/659-4583.
- **Boat cruise:** Atlantic Coastal Cruises, 900 East Heron Boulevard, West Palm Beach, 561/848-7827.
- **Dive shop:** Ocean Sports Scuba Center, 1736 South Congress Avenue, West Palm Beach, 561/641-1144.

MAP OF PALM BEACH COUNTY—PAGE 178

- **Ecotourism:** Okeeheelee Nature Center, Okeeheelee Park, West Palm Beach, 561/233-1400.
- **Marina:** Palm Beach Yacht Club and Marina, 800 North Flagler Drive, West Palm Beach, 561/655-1944.
- **Pier:** Lake Worth Municipal Pier, 10 South Ocean Boulevard, Lake Worth, 561/533-7367.
- **Rainy-day attraction:** Henry Morrison Flagler Museum (a.k.a. Whitehall), Coconut Row and Whitehall Way, 561/655-2833.
- **Shopping/browsing:** Worth Avenue, 561/659-6909.
- **Surf shop:** Palm Beach Boys Club, 309-A South County Road, 561/832-3596.
- **Vacation rentals:** Paulette Koch, 328 Royal Poinciana Plaza, 561/655-9081.

Bunking Down

The Breakers (1 South County Road, 561/655-6611, $$$$) is the most venerable resort in Palm Beach and maybe all of Florida. Built in the Italian Renaissance style by Henry Flagler, The Breakers celebrated its centennial in 1996. A little remedial history: Flagler's first Palm Beach hotel was not The Breakers but the Royal Poinciana, on Lake Worth. He enlarged a winter home that sat on oceanfront property he'd purchased to serve as an overflow for the Royal Poinciana, calling his new hotel the Palm Beach Inn and opening its doors to the public in 1896. In 1901, he renamed it The Breakers. At the time, it was the only oceanfront hotel south of Daytona Beach, incredible as that may seem.

You will indeed hear breakers all right at The Breakers. They break right on the seawall that protects the 100-year-old fortress from the pounding might of the ocean. It is almost too close to the beach. Since you cannot, for all practical purposes, swim or sun by the ocean, despite The Breakers' claim to a half mile of ocean frontage, they've provided a beach club with a huge heated pool, vast deck area with chaise lounges for sunning, and a poolside bar and restaurant. There are two golf courses and 14 tennis courts on the premises. They also provide activities, which on an average day might include tennis clinics, fly-fishing, water aerobics, and a Worth Avenue shopping trip.

Unless you're attending a convention and your employer is picking up the tab, you will probably pay dearly to stay at this 572-room, five-star hotel. At the extreme low end, a "standard superior" room runs around $260 during the low season (mid-May through October) and climbs to $405 during the high season (early January through mid-May). An oceanfront suite will set you back $555–840 a night.

Like all posh resorts that are described with such words as "venerable" and "grand," you sometimes feel like a walled-in captive going broke in high style. Beyond the room you'll be sleeping in, the nightly tariff entitles you to nothing else, and you'll wind up dropping all kinds of loot on food and incidentals. The on-premise restaurants are expensive (e.g., entrées run from $24 to $36 at the Flagler Steakhouse). It costs to use the fitness room ($35 per person for a full day, dropping to $15 after 4:30 P.M.). It costs $16 per night to valet-park your car. Beach and pool cabanas run around $175 per day, in season. The charge for 18 holes of golf is $50–100. (Incidentally, the lately renovated Breakers Ocean Course is the oldest golf course in the state of Florida, dating back to 1897.) There are valets and bellhops to be tipped. And, of course, on-site stores vend everything from Breakers-logoed merchandise to Steuben glassware.

Admittedly, part of the thrill of staying at The Breakers is getting to say you stayed at The Breakers. The rooms are quite commodious, the result of the resort's recent $100 million makeover. Ours was airy and

They Deserve Each Other

The wealthy old snobs of Palm Beach, exhausted from doing nothing all day, have really worked themselves up into a lather in recent years. Because the surrounding county is the second-fastest growing in the state, some of the nouveau riche riff-raff have begun settling in their palm-swaddled enclave. Among the sorts of people who've moved to Palm Beach are high-tech millionaires, investment bankers, architects, and celebrities. (No writers, though.)

The old-timers not only don't like the newer, younger people—partly on general principles (they are not "like us")—they also really don't like this new breed's propensity for showing off with gaudy, obscenely expensive, mansion-sized houses. An oil billionaire, for example, who wanted to enclose his second-story porch was recently taken to court by one old neighbor complaining that this would obstruct his ocean view. Similar beefs about size of houses and extent of renovations have also ended up in court of late, prompting the town to hire consultants to study the "Big House Problem." Their conclusions, detailed in a report to the town, were that zoning issues in Palm Beach have become "increasingly fractious and divisive, causing citizens to turn against one another." Also: "The town is faced with a paradoxical demand from citizens. 'Don't let them build any more big monster houses, and don't get in my way when I want to add rooms to my own house'."

In his coffee-table book, *Palm Beach Houses* (a staple of all self-respecting homeowners here), Robert A.M. Stern writes, "Without the magic of architecture, real estate is just so much land." No single sentence sums up the disconnect from reality and nature that the moneyed classes exude, especially here in the epicenter of snobbery. They deserve each other, the old and the new.

light, with coral walls and coordinated comforters and draperies done in a riotously flowered pattern. Our oceanfront room had sliding glass doors that we left open to be serenaded by the churning sea. As for the public spaces, there are attractions like the Tapestry Bar, a cocktail bar adjoining the Florentine Dining Room, which is bedecked with priceless 16th- and 17th-century tapestries collected by Flagler. However, more guests spend their time gaping at the hallway photo portfolio of celebrity patrons—among them, Heather Locklear, Loni Anderson, Donald Trump, and Sally Jessy Raphael. Of all the celebs pictured, only Robin Williams looked the least bit human.

The other five-star/five-diamond resort in Palm Beach is the **Four Seasons Ocean Grand** (2800 South Ocean Boulevard, 561/582-2800, $$$$). Though it's five miles south of Worth Avenue, the Ocean Grand falls within the Palm Beach city limits. (The same cannot be said of the Ritz-Carlton Palm Beach, which is in Manalapan.) The Ocean Grand, which opened for business in 1990, was Palm Beach's first major new hotel in nearly 40 years. A typically fortress-like construction, it's a veritable bank vault encircled by palm trees. The restaurant is so self-smitten that it calls itself simply "The Restaurant."

More down to earth (and to our liking) is the **Heart of Palm Beach Hotel** (160 Royal Palm Way, 561/655-5600,

SOUTH FLORIDA

Worth Avenue: Shops Without End, Amen

The romance of Old Palm Beach, the fresh look of couture fashion, the bloom of bougainvillea tumbling over arched doorways and tiled stone stairways. This is Worth Avenue, the heart of the Island, an international street of dreams and dramatic encounters . . . Go ahead, take a long walk on Worth Avenue. Have a tall tropical drink, fill your arms with shiny designer shopping bags, and give yourself a day or two of the really good life. After all, this is Palm Beach.

—from "*Worth Avenue Adventure,*" an article in a local magazine devoted to shopping

If, as has been suggested, shopping in Palm Beach is a religion, then it is most similar to the Latin High Mass. The emphasis is on high, as in if you gotta ask the price, you can't afford it. As it is in the cathedral, if you are at all uncertain about the rituals, please remain seated or kneeling suppliantly in your pew.

When it comes to the worship of shopping, we are defiant infidels. But, because we believe in trying anything once, we offer the following list of items, prices, and observations culled from a window-shopping spree along Worth Avenue in Palm Beach, the Fifth Avenue of the south. We ducked into and quickly back out of a goodly number of Worth Avenue's 250 posh businesses.

Our original idea had been to book an adventure tour of the Wild and Scenic Loxahatchee River in nearby Jonathan Dickinson State Park and then embark on a Worth Avenue shopping excursion, comparing and contrasting the two experiences (à la Bill McKibben's *The Age of Missing Information*). Though we sadly missed the river tour due to a tight schedule and uncooperative weather, we pressed ahead with our Worth Avenue adventure. Each of us took one side of the street and worked his way up the sidewalk, dressed in our best wrinkled clothes. Here is some of what we found:

- Asian straw handbag that, we were told, "the ladies love because they don't scratch their silk dresses." Don't you hate it when that happens?
- "Bandstand Bears": xylophone-playing bears as tacky as anything found on the Jersey Shore.
- "Crocodile diaries" made from the skin of this tropical reptile for $2,000 and up.
- Estée Lauder SPF 25 suntan lotion for $15 more than anyone should have to pay for an over-the-counter ointment.
- Facsimile of a 1925 Christofle's tea set, for $3,125, with the notation that it "includes a real coffee pot." At that price, it ought to include a house call from Juan Valdez bearing sacks of the world's finest coffee beans.

MAP OF SOUTH FLORIDA—PAGE 177

- "French Country" Louis XVI daybed for $6,400.
- Fur coats for men (enough said).
- Ghastly life-sized bronze sculptures of kids playing ball, skipping rope, or swinging on a rope.
- Gold-mesh belt with inlaid "baroque" stones (and you'll be baroque after you finish paying for it).
- Grace Kelly handbags that started at $4,500. Their steep price was attributed by the perky saleswoman to "craftsmanship. . . . They are made partly by hand. I was lucky enough to see one of the purses being made in Paris last year."
- Hand-carved wooden handbags.
- Hippo tusk carving for $6,500. When we asked its vintage, we were told "twentieth century." This is presumably a code for "very recently," meaning that endangered-species laws have probably been violated.
- "King of the Road," a miniature jeep Hummer replica that "proves to be an enjoyable way to navigate both suburbia and the wilderness."
- Limited-edition prints of polo players, setting suns, boats bobbing on water, etc.
- Needle-sharp glass-heeled snakeskin shoes.
- Photographs of estates for sale in the windows of real-estate offices. Overheard: "Look, honey, we can own our own private island!"
- Puke-gold, panty-thin golf shirt for $425.
- Short note in the handwriting of Sigmund Freud—who had a thing or two to say about the libidinous underpinnings of spending—for $9,500.
- Signed photograph of "Golden Bear and the King" (Jack Nicklaus and Arnie Palmer) for $1,800.
- Silver Mongolian elephant bookends for $17,500.
- Sixty milliliters of "limited edition" Champs Elysées by Guerlain Eau de Parfum Spray for Women, "contained in a beautiful 82-year-old Baccarat crystal bottle," for $975.
- Unpriced counter check of Marilyn Monroe's, made out for the amount of $8.22 and noted as being "for drugs."
- Window display of mannequins affecting snobbish poses with long, jewel-encrusted cigarette holders extending from their pressed wood lips.

For some reason, we were attracted to a metal bottle opener in the shape of a horse's ass that was hanging by a nail in one shop's window display. Upon removing it, the unexpectedly heavy and clunky item fell from its perch, knocking over some

continued on next page

Worth Avenue: Shops Without End, Amen

continued from previous page

fancy picture frames, which, in turn, fell upon some pricey ornaments, which sent several other glimmering baubles spilling down upon the display case. A hush fell over the shop, bringing in its wake a buttoned-down old gentleman with sun-leathered skin and a fake British accent. Sizing up the situation (i.e., nothing was broken), he took the opportunity to lessen the tension. Affecting a studied calm, he told one of his "favorite shopping anecdotes along these lines."

Briefly, it goes like this: a rich matron walks into a Fifth Avenue galleria, goes straight to an Etruscan vase on a pedestal, removes it to have a closer look, and promptly drops it on the floor. "Not to worry," she reassures the horrified sales staff, "I wasn't hurt." Jeeves was still chuckling at his rusty wit-nugget as we hurriedly took our leave.

By local ordinance, the word "sale" cannot appear in the window of any shop on Worth Avenue. There's even a "chief code compliance officer" whose job it is to see that this and many other downscaling tendencies are discouraged. This, of course, only encourages Worth Avenue shopkeepers to further inflate their prices.

If Worth Avenue doesn't sate your shopping addiction or completely deplete your bank account, we discovered in our Worth Avenue Adventure brochure that "Palm Beach–style" shopping can be done at nine other local malls, each of which has between 125 and 200 stores. Each is variously described as "exclusive," "world-class," "world-renowned," "out of the ordinary," and "truly in a class of its own." But the most shameless advertising come-on has to be the following: "Forget the beach—south Florida's newest hot spot is Mizner Park." This is, of course, just another upscale boutique- and gallery-filled shopping mall along Federal Highway (U.S. 1) in nearby Boca Raton.

We, of course, think just the opposite. Forget the shops! The only hot spot in any oceanfront town is the beach. Period.

$$$), an attractive, coral-colored stucco hostelry in the European style that is conveniently situated within easy walking distance of both Midtown Beach and Worth Avenue. Rooms are spacious, the staff is helpful, and the location is ideal. And there is no charge to park your car on the premises. Why should you be charged for parking a car when you're already paying for a room?

The **Brazilian Court Hotel** (301 Australian Avenue, 561/655-7740, $$$) is another old reliable that prizes casual elegance over ostentation. It has 134 rooms, a swimming pool, a restaurant (the Chancellor Grill Room), and a cocktail lounge. Their summer rates are a bargain, by Palm Beach standards.

If you want to stay in Palm Beach on the cheap, or relatively so, there's a **Howard Johnson** (2870 South Ocean Boulevard, 561/586-6542, $$) along the Intracoastal Waterway at the south end of town, very near the Four Seasons

Ocean Grand. Finally, as a general rule of thumb, you can get a room in Palm Beach during the low summer season for about $100, but that same room will triple or quadruple in price when winter rolls around and the trunks of the well-to-do begin arriving.

Coastal Cuisine

Testa's (221 Royal Poinciana Way, 561/832-0992, $$$$) has been in business for three-quarters of a century. The food and atmosphere are unpretentious and high quality. It is an indoor-outdoor restaurant that mercifully lacks the air of snootiness that hangs over Palm Beach like a suffocating fog. The lunch menu offers a good selection of salads (i.e., a seared tuna Caesar or poached salmon with sliced tomatoes and buffalo mozzarella), while dinner focuses on seafood and steaks, with fresh catches running in the $18 to $22 range. Of all the chichi eateries that line the north side of Royal Poinciana Way for several blocks, Testa's is the most inviting. And the outdoor patio makes a great place to dine while watching the passing Palm Beach parade.

The best location belongs to **Charley's Crab** (456 South Ocean Boulevard, 561/659-1500, $$$$). Unlike any other restaurant or retail establishment in Palm Beach, Charley's sits right on Highway A1A, as close to the beach as a crab hole. We found the food to be serviceable, though not good enough to merit any sort of rave. Our paella was bland, the grilled snapper just so-so. But it lies directly across from the beach in a quiet corner of Palm Beach along South Ocean Boulevard, and atmosphere and location do count for something. Surfers, for one, consider Charley's a landmark.

Here are some other suggestions from Palm Beach's upscale bounty:

- **Bice Ristorante** (313 1/2 Worth Avenue, 561/835-1600, $$$$) serves up Italian cuisine.
- **Cafe L'Europe** (331 South County Road, 561/655-4020, $$$$) serves up French fare.
- **Casablanca Cafe Americain** (101 North County Road, 561/655-1115, $$$) provides Mediterranean meals.
- **Chuck and Harold's** (207 Royal Poinciana Way, 561/659-1440, $$$$) and **Ta-Boo** (221 Worth Avenue, 561/835-3500, $$$$) are two places to see-and-be-seen.
- **Hamburger Haven** (314 South County Road, 561/655-5277, $) and **Green's Pharmacy** (151 North County Road, 561/832-4443, $) are good bets for a cheap lunch.

Night Moves

In a town where one of the jumpingest spots is called **Ta-Boo** (221 Worth Avenue, 561/835-3500)—a Worth Avenue restaurant that doubles as a bar and disco—you can be certain the nightlife is racy, bold, and fraught with decadence. A comely young, blonde ingenue holding fast to the tailored blazer of a wealthy, older male consort is a common sight around here. The music to which these odd couples dance is from another time, another place, ranging from big-band jazz to *Saturday Night Fever*–era Bee Gees. Vocalist/songwriter Bryan Ferry would have a field day decoding this scene. Writer Cleveland Amory certainly did.

They'd both ironically enjoy the tragically hip goings-on at **Au Bar** (336 Royal Poinciana Way, 561/832-4800), which is where Will and Ted were hanging out the night that . . . ah, but that's ancient history now. It's a popular bar and disco with curious tourists and native bon vivants alike, so ante up the cover charge and let the champagne flow. Other necessary stops on the Palm Beach party trolley: **E.R. Bradley's Saloon** (111 Bradley Place, 561/833-3520), **Chuck and Harold's** (207 Royal Poinciana Way, 561/659-1440), and

MAP OF PALM BEACH COUNTY—PAGE 178

The Breakers (1 South County Road, 561/655-6611), which offer the only ocean-view public bars in town.

Contact Information

Chamber of Commerce of the Palm Beaches, 45 Coconut Row, Palm Beach, FL 33840; 561/655-3282; website: www.palmbeaches.com

Palm Beach County Convention and Visitors Bureau, 1555 Palm Lakes Boulevard, Suite 204, West Palm Beach, FL 33401; 561/233-3000; website: www.palmbeachfl.com

Lake Worth

The town of Lake Worth (pop. 31,209) is a thick grid of residential and commercial streets south of Palm Beach, extending westward from the Intracoastal Waterway. It seems to be a kind of clubhouse for the retirees who flock here and play at one of the 15 golf courses within a tee shot of the city limits. The town was founded by immigrating Chicagoans in the 1870s. In keeping with the explosion of numbers all over South Florida, Lake Worth's population has tripled since the 1950s. Since we're really only concerned with the coast, we'll leave it at that and move out to Lake Worth's one window on the ocean.

Beaches

While Lake Worth is almost entirely inland from Palm Beach's barrier island, it does retain a toehold on the oceanfront via the **Lake Worth Municipal Beach**, Casino, and Municipal Fishing Pier. This inauspicious beach park is accessed via Highway A1A at Lake Avenue (State Route 802 extended).

Into this 1,200-foot-long public park are squeezed a "developed beach" (read: seasonally buttressed with dredge sand), lifeguards, a pool (at the casino), shuffleboard courts, a picnic area, grills, and a 1,300-foot fishing pier. On the latter sits a modest, rusty, and windblown eatery. This complex was built in 1922, rebuilt in 1947, and seems to have been unimproved since. A one-way entrance road leads to metered parking (25 cents for 15 minutes). Access to the pier costs 50 cents (for walkers) and $2.50 (if you're fishing).

The scene always seemed to be fishing for something that had clearly eluded it, until now. Lake Worth Municipal Beach has never looked better. The sand is golden and clean, the tiki huts on the beach are as inviting as the blue-green water or the friendly chatter at Benny's on the Beach, a genial outdoor bar near the pier entrance. One caveat for tiny tots: there's a steep drop-off in the water just a few feet from shore.

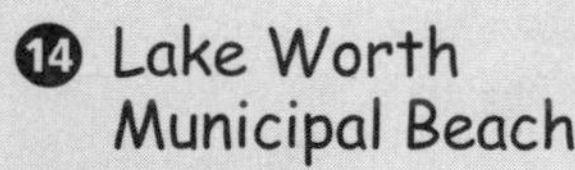

Location: 10 South Ocean Boulevard in Lake Worth, due east of Lake Worth Road

Parking/fees: metered parking ($1 per hour) by the beach or token lot ($2 per day) on the west side of Highway A1A

Hours: 6 A.M. to midnight

Facilities: concessions, lifeguards, restrooms, picnic tables, and showers

Contact: Lake Worth Municipal Beach, 561/533-7367

Bunking Down

The **Beachcomber Motel** (3024 South Ocean Boulevard, South Palm Beach, FL 33480, 561/585-4646, $$) offers a rare option to those with more limited budgets. At just less than $100 per night year round, this low-key, likeable establishment qualifies as a bargain among the Palm Beaches.

Contact Information
Greater Lake Worth Chamber of Commerce, 811 Lucerne Avenue, Lake Worth, FL 33460; 561/582-4401; website: www.lwchamber.com

Valet Boys

A car pulls up to the front door of a resort. Before the vehicle has come to a stop, it is pounced upon by bustling young strangers. Jogging over from a stand by the corner of the entrance is an earnest young man from among a clump of them attired in Bermuda shorts and golf shirts tagged with the resort's corporate logo. As the valet breathlessly sprints toward the vehicle from the front, a bellman comes rattling along at the rear, pushing a bronze-plated contraption for hauling luggage. You really don't want to deal with either of these pesky factotums but are caught off-guard by their haste and zeal. With somewhat less enthusiasm than you'd muster for a highway patrolman who's asked to see your license and registration, you obediently hand over the keys and pop open the trunk. Next thing you know you're standing in a vast hotel lobby without car or luggage, dazed and confused, wondering what happened.

Unless you're us, that is. A long time ago, we developed ways of thwarting valet boys and bellmen. If that means parking a half mile away and furtively dragging a metric ton of luggage up ten flights of back stairwells, we will do so. We initially approach a resort with trepidation, scouting to see if contact with the front-door service staff can be avoided or minimized. This is because we see no reason why able-bodied humans, many of whom have driven hundreds of miles, cannot pilot their own car the final few feet to a parking space or carry their luggage a short distance across a lobby if they so desire.

All of the scrambling around by valets and bellhops is well and good for handicapped or elderly visitors, who may require this service, or the well-to-do, who expect it. For those of us who can live without luggage handlers and teenage drivers, however, it is completely unnecessary and somewhat maddening—doubly so when you hear the screeching of brakes and squealing of tires as your car disappears around a corner into an underground garage.

Take it from us: Don't be afraid to decline unwanted assistance with luggage, and always ask if self-parking is an alternative. You have nothing to lose but your unease. And you'll save money, too.

Map of Palm Beach County—Page 178

South Palm Beach, Lantana, and Manalapan

The same privatizing of beaches seen at Lake Worth continues south into the adjacent towns of South Palm Beach (pop. 17,500), Lantana (pop. 8,776), and Manalapan (pop. 317). All retain discernible, though mostly private, footholds on the beach. Incidentally, tabloid newspaper addicts may be interested to learn that Lantana is home to the *National Enquirer.*

The exclusive community of Manalapan (median income: $90,000) picks up where Lantana ends and raises the stakes even higher. The narrow spit upon which the sprawling estates of Manalapan perch is so thin in places that a reasonably well-struck chip shot would carry from the sand trap of the tiny beach in front of their palaces to the water hazard of the Intracoastal Waterway. So much pricey real estate piled atop so fragile a foundation!

Here's a "fun fact" about Manalapan from the local historian: "Manalapan, founded in 1931 by Commodore Harold Vanderbilt—scion of one of America's wealthiest families—prefers its low-key gentility to the noisy social scene of Palm Beach." We can just see the noses being raised in the air like drawbridges.

15 Lantana Municipal Beach

Location: Ocean Avenue (State Route 812) at Ocean Boulevard (Highway A1A) in Lantana
Parking/fees: metered parking lot for nonresidents and unmetered free parking area for residents displaying beach stickers ($6 annually per vehicle). Beach stickers are available to nonresidents for $100 per year per vehicle
Hours: sunrise to sunset
Facilities: concessions, lifeguards, restrooms, picnic tables, and showers
Contact: Lantana Municipal Beach, 561/540-5731

Beaches

Lantana Municipal Beach is a six-acre complex up where Ocean Avenue (State Route 812) meets Ocean Boulevard (Highway A1A). The south end of its metered parking lot is adjacent to the loading dock at the Ritz-Carlton Palm Beach. Lantana's public beach is a similar sort of sop to the non-oceanfront-dwelling public as at Lake Worth, albeit less seedy. There's a lifeguard station and a beach of modest width made more appealing by sea grape–gripped dunes. In addition, the park has a restaurant, a souvenir shop, a volleyball court, a playground, and an offshore reef.

Bunking Down

Though South Palm Beach is only one-tenth of a square mile in size, it is filled to bursting with high-rise condos. The lone exception is the **Palm Beach Hawaiian Ocean Inn** (3550 South Ocean Boulevard, 561/582-5631, $$). Fronted by an appealingly kitschy tiki-roofed office, the Palm Beach Hawaiian is a modest two-story structure that rambles from Highway A1A down to the water. The rooms are clean and unpretentious, and the price is affordable. The Aloha Room on the premises provides a great spot from which to survey the world over a morning cup of coffee. This hotel/restaurant/tiki bar complex is the only commercial enterprise allowed in South Palm Beach, having been grandfathered in because it was already here when the town incorporated in 1955. As such, it offers a welcome break in a great wall of condominiums. We're cheered to see something so authentic and unchanged by time survive intact. We raise our hollowed-out, rum-filled pineapples in salute to the Palm Beach Hawaiian Ocean Inn.

You don't have to travel very far—not much more than a couple miles down Highway A1A—to go from one extreme in accommodations to another. By contrast to the low-lying, low-key, and low-price Palm Beach Hawaiian, the **Ritz-Carlton Palm Beach** (100 South Ocean Boulevard, 561/533-6000, $$$$) swaddles its guests in marble and marvels. A six-story resort that boasts a five-star rating from AAA and four on-premises restaurants, it is a typically top-of-the-line operation for a chain that puts on the Ritz from the second you hand over car keys to the valet till you check out. The hallways are lined with original artwork, bathed in the amber glow cast by chandeliers. The palm-filled grounds out back feature a spacious pool deck and easy access to the beach. The rooms are simply but elegantly decorated with French Provincial furnishings. You will pay dearly for cosseting of this kind—roughly $300–600 per night in season—in these pricey environs. After all, making it and spending it is the name of the game in Palm Beach.

Contact Information

Greater Lantana Chamber of Commerce, 212 Iris Avenue, Lantana, FL 33462; 561/585-8664; website: www.geocities.com/lantanachamber

Boynton Beach, Ocean Ridge, Briny Breezes, and Gulfstream

The city of Boynton Beach (pop. 55,483) was named for Civil War officer Nathan South Boynton. As for the "beach" part, Boynton Beach is oddly misnamed. None of the town lies east of the Intracoastal Waterway. Out by the ocean along Highway A1A you'll find Ocean Ridge (pop. 1,658), a small, exclusive community that once was part of Boynton Beach but spun off on its own. In order to do so, the wealthy Ocean Ridge residents made the town of Boynton Beach an offer they couldn't refuse: they paid off the debt-plagued community's sewer and water bonds during the Depression.

To make matters in the present more confusing, the Boynton Beach Oceanfront Park, though located in Ocean Ridge, does in fact belong to Boynton Beach. So, to answer your question as to whether Boynton Beach extends out to the beach—well, it does and it doesn't.

Recreationally, the Boynton Beach area is of more interest to fishermen than to beachcombers. The South Lake Worth Inlet connects Lake Worth with the ocean, providing access to a couple of the East Coast's best fishing holes, dubbed Kingfish Circle and Sailfish Alley. But Boynton Beach and the rest of south Palm Beach County may well be of most interest to golfers. As a local publication put it, intending praise and not irony, "At first

16 Ocean Inlet Park

3

Location: south side of the South Lake Worth Inlet, at the end of North Ocean Boulevard in Ocean Ridge
Parking/fees: free parking lot
Hours: 24 hours
Facilities: concessions, lifeguards, restrooms, picnic tables, and showers
Contact: Palm Beach County Parks and Recreation Department, 561/966-6600

Map of Palm Beach County—Page 178

glance, South County looks like a collection of golf courses, plus a little room for people." We'll play up the irony, though, by noting that they've tipped their hand with more candor than may have been intended. By the way, have you ever heard of a city so large that has made such a negligible impression on the general consciousness? It is essentially South Florida residential sprawl, albeit of a more friendly, less snooty character than is found in neighboring Boca Raton or any of the upscale Palm Beaches.

Ocean Ridge, by contrast, is a luxury condo community that keeps its upper lip stiff and its building codes as flexible as the law will allow. We'll note a news item we saw while passing through. A mansion-in-progress was being held up by those pesky ordinances against destroying sand dunes. The project's architectural engineer told the town commissioners that "we will not disturb the dune any more than we would have to" in constructing a pool deck and crossover to the ocean that would fall beyond the mandated line for beachfront construction. The easement was granted by the pliable local board, and the mansion was on its way. Among its amenities: 10 bathrooms, five guest bedrooms, three baths, three "powder rooms," a game room, wine room, music room, and "grand hall." The initial buzz was that Oprah Winfrey had purchased the lot, which she vehemently denied. The *National Enquirer* will no doubt keep abreast of this story.

Then there's Briny Breezes (pop. 400) and Gulfstream (pop. 714)—two more dots on the map with evocative names that claim a sliver of oceanfront. While president, the elder George Bush once took a fishing vacation in Gulfstream, a visit which briefly put the town on the map, probably for the first time since its incorporation in 1926. As for Briny Breezes, what can you say about a township that occupies one-fourth of a square mile in toto, almost all of which is a trailer park (albeit a quiet, well-tended one)?

Beaches

On the south side of the South Lake Worth Inlet, which separates Ocean Ridge from Manalapan, is **Ocean Inlet Park**, which offers marina facilities on the Intracoastal side. While it's best for fishing and surfing, families will be pleased to discover a 600-

17 Ocean Ridge Hammock Park

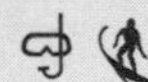 

Location: between Ocean Inlet Park and Boynton Beach Oceanfront Park on Highway A1A in Ocean Ridge; look for the small lot on the east side of the road

Parking/fees: free parking lot

Hours: sunrise to sunset

Facilities: none

Contact: Palm Beach County Parks and Recreation Department, 561/966-6600

18 Boynton Beach Oceanfront Park

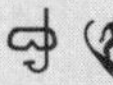  

Location: Just north of Ocean Avenue on Highway A1A in Ocean Ridge

Parking/fees: free parking lot for local residents with beach permits, obtainable for $20 from the Department of Citizen's Services in Boynton Beach City Hall. A $10 per vehicle entrance fee for nonresidents November 1–April 14; $5 per vehicle entrance fee for nonresidents April 15–October 31

Hours: sunrise to sunset

Facilities: concessions, lifeguards, restrooms, picnic tables, and showers

Contact: Boynton Beach Leisure Services, 561/375-6225; recording on beach conditions, 561/734-7989

foot lifeguarded beach, picnic tables, and a playground. The county sheriff's office is right next door, too, in case any spin-the-bottle games get out of hand. A short distance south of here is **Ocean Ridge Hammock Park**, essentially a nature preserve and the newest unit in the galaxy of county parks. It consists of a small roadside parking lot (28 spaces) and a pathway across the dunes to the beach. It's a fairly splendid escape from the Palm Beach hustle and bustle.

Boynton Beach Oceanfront Park, a gated public access, isn't very well marked (watch for the blue sign on the ocean side of A1A). It's free to locals with permits (which cost $20 annually) but charges outsiders a stiff $10 per car per day to park. Thus, it is effectively a locals-only beach, and the locals are welcome to it. This is not said in disrespect. It's an okay spot with a healthy plateau of sea oats giving way to dwarf sea grape on the dunes. It's got year-round lifeguards, plus a concession stand, barbecue grills, and picnic areas, as well as a playground and basketball court. The formerly sand-starved beach—having been deprived, no doubt, by the groins to the north—has recently been renourished by the U.S. Army Corps of Engineers and is now 300 feet wider.

All the same, if you don't live in Boynton Beach, then you don't need to pay a daily ten-spot at Oceanfront Park when Delray Beach, a free and easy beach town, lies just down the road. Besides, free beach access can be had at Ocean Ridge Hammock Park and **Gulfstream County Park**, which lie due north and south, respectively. Gulfstream is an attractive 6.37-acre park with plenty of free parking, a boardwalk that leads through a coastal pine and sea-grape hammock to the picnic area, playground, and 600-foot-long beach. A popular snorkeling reef lies just south of the lifeguarded area. Signs caution about underwater rocks, but the large number of families that we saw on a recent visit suggested the relative safety of the location.

Contact Information

Greater Boynton Beach Chamber of Commerce, 639 East Ocean Avenue, Suite 108, Boynton Beach, FL 33435; 561/732-9501; website: www.boyntonbeach.org

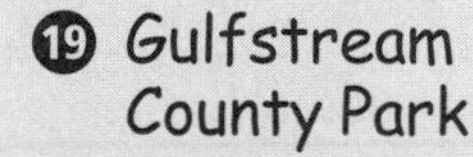

Location: .7 miles south of Woolbright Road on Highway A1A in Gulfstream
Parking/fees: free parking lot
Hours: sunrise to sunset
Facilities: lifeguards, restrooms, picnic tables, and showers
Contact: Palm Beach County Parks and Recreation Department, 561/966-6600

MAP OF PALM BEACH COUNTY—PAGE 178

Delray Beach

From a sensible traveler's perspective, Delray Beach is the light at the end of Palm Beach's tunnel of moneyed self-absorption. For beach lovers, it's the pot of golden sand at the end of the asphalt rainbow. It is a quintessential South Florida beach town in the best sense of the word. All oceanfront communities should be similarly blessed with natural bounty and enlightened citizenry.

While Delray Beach has been a resort community for many decades, in recent years the reliable base of senior citizens has headed off to other communities or the great beyond. Delray is still extremely senior friendly, but more college kids, young families, and DINKS (dual income, no kids) have moved here, taking advantage of the town's affordability, relaxed appeal, and enviable beaches. Due to this influx, Delray's population has reached 53,589, but the numbers are tastefully accommodated and a common-sense approach is evident. *Florida Trend* magazine declared it the best-run town in the state.

During peak season, Delray Beach gets wild but not crazy. The renovated downtown, with its Old School Square, gives off a homey village feel. Delray takes its name from a suburb of Detroit. The original plots were sold through advertisements in Michigan newspapers in the 1890s. A century later, we'd compare it to Capitola, California, another town of comparable dimensions on the West Coast that is both well mannered and fun, with a touch of unpretentiously arty gentility to balance out the beach craziness. They haven't commercialized the beachfront at Delray as has been done elsewhere. Moreover, it is a safe, well-patrolled stretch of sand. A couple can take a moonlight walk without fear of violent crime. Though Delray Beach lies only 45 miles north of Miami, its residents and visitors live in comparative tranquillity.

One of Delray's most unique attractions is the **Morikami Museum and Japanese Gardens** (4000 Morikami Park Road, 561/495-0233). Located three miles west of town via Linton Boulevard, it's a living tribute to a pocket of Japanese settlers who came to the area in the early 1900s to establish the Yamato Colony, an agricultural community. Their plan was to farm tropical plants, but the commune didn't pan out. However, one tenacious pilgrim, George Sukeji Morikami, eventually grew rich from his pineapple plantation. He donated the 200-acre property to the town in the '70s, along with its meticulous gardens, water-

20 Delray Beach Public Beach

   5

Location: one-half mile in either direction along Ocean Boulevard (Highway A1A) from its intersection with Atlantic Avenue in Delray Beach

Parking/fees: metered street parking

Hours: 24 hours (except no beach parking north of Atlantic Avenue 11 P.M.–5 A.M.)

Facilities: concessions, lifeguards, restrooms, and showers

Contact: Delray Beach Public Beach, 561/243-7352; recording on beach conditions, 561/272-3224

21 Atlantic Dunes Park

   4

Location: 1.5 miles south of Atlantic Boulevard, in Delray Beach

Parking/fees: metered street parking

Hours: 24 hours

Facilities: lifeguards, restrooms, and showers

Contact: Delray Beach Parks and Recreation Department, 561/243-7260; recording on beach conditions, 561/272-3224

falls, bonsai trees, nature trail, and Japanese cultural artifacts. Strict adherence to customs extends to visitors, who are asked to remove their shoes before entering.

Beaches

What does Delray do so well to gain the unabashed praise of a couple of jaded beach bums? Let us count the ways:

- Public access to the main beach—where Atlantic Avenue meets Ocean Boulevard (Highway A1A)—is a breeze, with more than a mile of metered parking (20 minutes for 25 cents). This lengthy strand is called **Delray Beach Public Beach**. The city also maintains **Atlantic Dunes Park**, which lies 1.5 miles south of Atlantic Avenue, via a leasing arrangement with Palm Beach County. It's a small beach with one lifeguard stand and metered parking.
- Getting onto the beach is safe and easy, and the dunes remain protected. Numerous clearly designated access points—three dozen in all, with a public shower at every one—lead over vegetated dunes to the beach.
- Delray Beach's overseers have successfully segmented activities on the city beach to ensure that swimmers don't get whacked by surfboards and sunbathers don't get bonked by errant Frisbees. There are designated areas for recreation, swimming and sunbathing, volleyball, boat launching, and snorkeling and diving. On the snorkeling front, the remnants of a 1902 shipwreck lie a few hundred yards offshore at the south end of Delray Beach.
- An able contingent of EMT-trained and U.S. Lifeguard Association–certified guards patrols the main beach from several towers. The Delray lifeguards are legendary, having won several contests in national competitions, including a gold medal in "line pull rescue." They recently placed fourth in the nation overall. With a staff of 29 competing against teams of 500 or so from Los Angeles, Delaware, and the Jersey Shore, that is an amazing feat.
- A local lifeguard told us that a window between the Bahamian Islands allows swell to come through unimpeded here, making for a rare stretch of decent surf along this length of coast.
- The Gulf Stream swings within one and three miles of Delray Beach, depending on seasonal fluctuations. This proximity, coupled with the lack of a pier and all of the water-fouling crap it generates, makes for warm, clear, sparkling waters all year long.
- Three good, cheap spots to eat, drink, and be merry sit directly across Ocean Boulevard (Highway A1A) from the beach, reinforcing the town's sensible, anti-uptight philosophy of fun.

Shore Things

- **Bike/skate rentals**: A1A Bike Rentals, 1155 East Atlantic Avenue, 561/243-2453.
- **Dive shop**: Force E, 660 Linton Boulevard, 561/276-0666.
- **Ecotourism**: Gumbo Limbo Environmental Complex, 1801 North Ocean Boulevard, Boca Raton, 561/338-1473.
- **Fishing charters**: Delray Charters, 946 Seasage Drive, 561/265-3367.
- **Marina**: Ocean Inlet Marina, 9600 North Ocean Boulevard, Ocean Ridge, 561/966-6646.
- **Rainy-day attraction**: Morikami Museum, 4000 Morikami Park Road, 561/495-0233.
- **Shopping/browsing**: Downtown Delray Beach, along Atlantic Avenue (State

MAP OF PALM BEACH COUNTY—PAGE 178

Route 806), a half mile east of Ocean Boulevard (Highway A1A).

- **Surf shop:** Funboards Watersports Center, Seagate Hotel and Beach Club, 400 South Ocean Boulevard, 561/272-3036.
- **Vacation rentals:** Sea Aire Villas, 1715 South Ocean Boulevard, 561/276-7491.

Bunking Down

There are a few high-styled accommodations in Delray, most notably the **Delray Beach Marriott** (10 North Ocean Boulevard, 561/274-3211, $$$$). This new arrival took over from the Holiday Inn that formerly occupied the site. A new building has been added to the refurbished old one, and the location couldn't be more choice: Atlantic Avenue at Ocean Boulevard (Highway A1A).

Otherwise, the adjacent city of Boca Raton more than amply fills the luxury niche. In fact, the two towns make a nice counterpoint, being more companions than competitors. The spirit of Delray Beach is best preserved in the low-scaled motels and rental apartments that abound on and near the beach. The **Bermuda Inn** (64 South Ocean Boulevard, 561/276-5288, $) is typical of the pleasantly unfancy lodgings that are available. Its 20 units include motel rooms and apartments, and the ocean is well within view from the dry side of Highway A1A. There's a small pool on the premises. As the sunbaked, gold-chained proprietor said, "You don't get lost in the shuffle here." The Bermuda is located next door to Boston's at the Beach, a fun and occasionally raucous beach bar. Talk about convenience!

The **Sea Aire** (1715 South Ocean Boulevard, 561/276-7491, $) is a similar kettle of fish: villas and apartments, each with a kitchen. Book early at both because they are popular with a regular clientele. The **Colony Hotel** (525 East Atlantic Avenue, 561/276-4123, $$) is a holdover from the days of the senior influx. This lovely, three-story wooden structure (circa 1926) lies a few blocks up Atlantic Avenue from the beach. Even if you don't stay here, the Colony's rattan-dominated lobby is worth a gander. If you do—and it is only open in peak season (January–April)—breakfast and dinner come with the room tariff, and you get a crack at a shuffleboard tournament championship.

At the more secluded south end of town near Highland Beach, **Wright by the Sea** (1901 South Ocean Boulevard, 561/278-3355) is the sort of low-scale non-franchise motel we wish was in every beach town in Florida.

Coastal Cuisine

A sign of Delray's enlightenment hit us as we drove down Atlantic Avenue to the beach. We noticed that a venerable and appealing diner called **Doc's All-American** (10 North Swinton Avenue, 561/278-3627, $) was holding its own, despite the presence of a Dunkin' Donuts a block away. It never ceases to amaze us that, given these two choices so close at hand, anyone would ever choose to frequent a franchise. To treat symptoms of fast-food hunger pangs, we prescribe Doc's and an hour's rest on the beach before swimming.

On the ocean, the two obvious choices are **Boston's at the Beach** (40 South Ocean Boulevard, 561/278-3364, $$) and **6 South** (6 South Ocean Boulevard, 561/278-7878, $$), both of which have airy outdoor patios that catch the ocean breezes wafting across the highway. These are also the hottest nightspots. You can grab lunch or dinner at either of these places—we had a perfectly adequate Caesar salad and blackened swordfish at Boston's. If you're feeling up for something a little more gourmet, just two blocks from the beach, along East Atlantic Avenue, are two of the most acclaimed new restaurants in southern Palm Beach County. **Thirty Two East** (32 East Atlantic Avenue, 561/276-7868, $$$) has a retro feel but contemporary creativity in entrées like sauteed hog snapper with brown caper butter and spaghetti squash, and cumin-encrusted tuna with avocado salsa. The other is **Dakota 624** (270 East Atlantic Avenue, 561/274-6244, $$$), which also has the sort of retro-martini-bar look, but transcends that affectation with inventive fare and wall-to-wall beautiful people.

Night Moves

Where there's interesting nightlife, we'll write about it, but we won't force the issue when there's only the blare of dance clubs or the tinkling of ivories in a piano bar to report. We'd just as soon get a good night's sleep. But Delray Beach kept us up way past our bedtime, because it's the most happening place in Palm Beach County. Delray's best live music venue is the **Back Room** (16 East Atlantic Avenue, 561/243-9110), which books local and national acts for reasonable cover charges (under $10). During the week we were in the area, the Back Room hosted a respectable lineup that included John Mayall and NRBQ, among others. The ambience is as ramshackle and unpretentious as, well, the music of NRBQ itself. Sofas line the walls, there's a small dance area, and only beer and wine are sold.

On the beachfront, it's double your pleasure, double your fun at **Boston's at the Beach** (40 South Ocean Boulevard, 561/278-3364) and **6 South** (6 South Ocean Boulevard, 561/278-7878). They are only a few doors apart, and there is much spillover between them (as well as a pleasant sandwich deli).

Boston's dresses up in all things Beantown. Its walls are covered with signed photos of Carl "Yaz" Yastrzemski, Bobby Orr's hockey sticks, and street signs for Yawkey Way and Landsdowne (the road behind "the Green Monster," the infamous left field wall at Fenway Park). But Boston's is more than just another themed sports bar (a type of venue we've come to abhor). It is a place where people interface giddily at the lengthy happy hour (4 P.M.–8 P.M.) and stick around for the occasional live music. Monday at Boston's is legendary, with Reggae Night featuring a house band that includes one of Delray Beach's veteran lifeguards.

6 South offers lighter, taped musical fare—inoffensive jazz, folk, and lite rock that function more as aural wallpaper—but it, too, is more than a lounge. It's an amazingly designed place with a round concrete bar, a tiled alligator above the bar, and neon and exposed metal adorning the premises. An open front patio beckons the sea breezes. There's even a sushi bar at 6 South.

Boston's and 6 South, it goes without saying, also offer the enticement and opportunity of a midnight stroll on the public beach across the street.

Contact Information

Greater Delray Beach Chamber of Commerce, 64 Southeast 5th Avenue, Delray Beach, FL 33483; 561/278-0424; website: www.delraybeach.com

MAP OF PALM BEACH COUNTY—PAGE 178

Highland Beach

Though there's nothing much a nonresident can do here—i.e., go to the beach or even book a room (with one exception)—we feel duty bound to mention Highland Beach. It is a town of 3,477 with as much ocean frontage as Delray Beach and Boca Raton, neither of which allowed so solid a walling off of its major resource. It lies between them on Highway A1A, and though it's a seemingly hidden community of private homes and estates, it does make for a scenic ride through an area that retains at least the vestigial look of Old Florida. Interestingly, the only commercial property in Highland Beach is the **Holiday Inn** (2809 South Ocean Boulevard, at least 278-6241, $$$), which sits directly on the beach up toward the Delray side of town.

Contact Information

Palm Beach County Convention and Visitors Bureau, 1555 Palm Lakes Boulevard, Suite 204, West Palm Beach, FL 33401; 561/233-3000; website: www.palmbeachfl.com

Boca Raton

The name of the town is Boca Raton, but we have taken to calling it Boca Right On! That is because the town deserves a hearty "right on" for the good things it's done on behalf of its beachfront. Before the real-estate land grab and condo-building boom began in earnest, Boca Raton (pop. 70,000) had the uncommon foresight to purchase its oceanfront. It did this with bond money raised via referendums dating back to the early 1970s. It has been money well spent. The beaches belong to the residents of Boca Raton. Not coincidentally, the paved bike trail that parallels Highway A1A all the way from Boca Raton to Delray Beach is as pleasant and green a passage as you're likely to find anywhere in South Florida.

Boca Raton is a diamond-studded link in the chain of bulging, burgeoning cities that are quickly growing together into the giant coastal metropolis of South Florida. Boca is the last gasp of Palm Beach–style chic before you cross into Broward County's less gilded sphere of influence via Deerfield Beach and Pompano Beach. Boca Raton is a riches-to-rags-to-riches story. Established by renowned Florida architect Addison Mizner—the gentleman largely responsible for the Mediterranean style with which the state is identified—Boca Raton went from glamourville in the 1920s to ghost town in the '30s with the collapse of the stock market. A classic failed city, Boca Raton's population had declined to less than 1,000 by the early '50s. Now it is 70 times that, having benefited from the real-estate boom that has resounded all over South Florida in recent decades.

Despite the incoming tide of wealthy retirees and nouveau riche boomers who have washed ashore, Boca Raton is not a very warm or interesting place, especially if you're outside the social whirl. It is a city without much history, having been virtually rebuilt and repopulated since the 1970s. The inland thoroughfares are jammed with cars and lined with fancy Italian restaurants and upscale malls. Along Highway A1A, however, Boca Raton shows a completely different side of itself, having demonstrated rare good judgment in allocating revenue to the most proactive use a coastal community can devote itself: beach acquisition and preservation.

Beaches

Virtually the entirety of Boca Raton's beach belongs to the municipality. From Spanish

River south to Palmetto Park Road, it's all city-owned beach. We were told by an elderly gatekeeper that Boca claims title to more beach (five miles' worth) than any other municipality in the United States. But unless you live in Boca Raton, in which case you're entitled to use the three beach parks for a $27 annual fee, it will cost dearly to park at the beach. The charge for nonresidents is $8 per car on weekdays and $10 on weekends and holidays. That is a fairly stiff tariff merely to gain beach access, and it means there is essentially no place where those who don't live here can use the beaches of Boca without paying.

The money no doubt goes to fund not only the usual maintenance costs but also the renourishing of the beaches, which is an ongoing concern. Yes, although the beachfront parks of Boca Raton are lovely, complete with lighted boardwalks and picnic tables and gazebos that overlook the ocean, the beach itself can get pretty skimpy. The strand that runs from Spanish River down to South Beach Park was narrow in 1996, when we saw dump trucks depositing loads of coarse fill-sand on the beach while bulldozers flattened them. To be honest, it looked more like midwestern sod than beach sand. Four years later, Boca's beach strand looked much healthier and we enjoyed a pleasant early-fall swim at South Beach Park after a six-mile run along Boca Raton's beach-paralleling asphalt walkway.

We highly commend the city of Boca Raton for not succumbing to the blight of condos and private estates that makes so much of the county seem like a walled fortress. The parks themselves, stretching a few hundred yards from the ocean to the Intracoastal Waterway, preserve the coastal hammock communities that existed before these barrier islands were descended upon by European settlers and their condo-raising descendants. The beachside jungle is thick with coconut palms, sea grape, and saw palmetto. The coastal hammock on the Intracoastal side begins with mangroves at the water's edge and then becomes a rain forest–like area of tall trees—predominantly cabbage palms, mastics, pigeon plum, and paradise tree (see the sidebar on the Gumbo Limbo Nature Center on page 219).

Boca's beachfront is broken into the following units, from north to south: **Spanish River Park**, **Red Reef Park**, and **South Beach Park**. Red Reef boasts a man-made offshore reef. The Boca Raton Artificial

22 Spanish River Park

  4

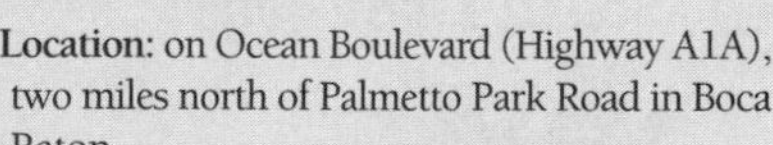

Location: on Ocean Boulevard (Highway A1A), two miles north of Palmetto Park Road in Boca Raton

Parking/fees: free for Boca Raton residents with beach permits ($27 per vehicle annually); $8 per car for nonresidents ($10 on weekends)

Hours: 8 A.M. to sunset

Facilities: lifeguards, restrooms, picnic tables, and showers

Contact: Boca Raton Parks and Recreation Department, 561/393-7810

23 Red Reef Park

  3

Location: on Ocean Boulevard (Highway A1A), one mile north of Palmetto Park Road in Boca Raton

Parking/fees: free for Boca Raton residents with beach permits ($27 per vehicle annually); $8 per car for nonresidents ($10 on weekends)

Hours: 8 A.M.–10 P.M.

Facilities: lifeguards, restrooms, picnic tables, showers, and a visitor center at Gumbo Limbo Nature Center

Contact: Boca Raton Parks and Recreation Department, 561/393-7810

Reef was constructed in 1988 and consists of six reef "modules." Each reef comprises 25 limestone boulders weighing upward of five tons apiece and arranged in two layers. In all, there are 600 tons of limestone. So far, it seems to be taking, as some 95 fish species and 76 invertebrate species have been cataloged on the reef. Let's hear it for biodiversity! Red Reef also has an executive golf course attached to it, though for the life of us it's not clear why one is needed here.

There's an especially nice boardwalk at Red Reef and a neat little nature trail at Spanish Bay. At South Beach Pavilion, a no-fee overlook with a few parking spaces that lies where Palmetto Park Road dead-ends into Highway A1A, folks turn out early to grab a seat and contemplate the dawn's early light or bring a bagged lunch at midday to this special spot. It's something of a community gathering place, and you see all kinds, from old men working crossword puzzles to rawboned young surfers discussing the waves kicked up by a storm system somewhere out in the Caribbean a few days ago.

The last link in Boca's beach chain is **South Inlet Park**, which lies just south of Camino Real Bridge. It's is an okay place to park a beach blanket, though not the best Boca has to offer on that count. The real calling card at South Inlet is Buck's Cave, a wormrock outcropping with caves beneath a protruding shelf that's a great snorkeling spot.

24 South Beach Park

  3

Location: Ocean Boulevard (Highway A1A) at Northeast 4th Street in Boca Raton
Parking/fees: free for Boca Raton residents with beach permits ($27 per vehicle annually); $7 per car for nonresidents ($9 on weekends)
Hours: 8 A.M. to sunset
Facilities: lifeguards, restrooms, picnic tables and showers
Contact: Boca Raton Parks and Recreation Department, 561/393-7810

Bunking Down

The best resort in Boca is the **Boca Raton Resort & Club** (501 East Camino Real, 561/447-3000, $$$$), a Gold Coast grande dame that was originally designed and built by Addison Mizner as the Cloisters back in the mid-1920s. With its beveled French doors, Romanesque archways, Oriental rugs, Venetian lobby, and Spanish oil paintings, it's no wonder Mizner went bankrupt and skipped town (prompting the name change). In addition to the original Cloisters, the resort encompasses the Boca Raton Beach Club, the Boca Country Club, and the hot-pink, 27-story Tower—963 rooms in all—plus dining options that run from a rooftop restaurant in the Tower to the more atmospheric and formal Cathedral Dining Room in the Cloisters.

To enter the grounds of the Boca Raton Resort is like being transported to an earlier time when the world moved more slowly to the easy rustling of Floridian breezes. Set in a residential neighborhood, it is a huge but largely hidden (from the street) wonder. The rooms are inviting and classy without being ostentatious, and the beds are as comfortable as any we've encountered. On

25 South Inlet Park

   3

Location: along the south side of the Boca Inlet, on Highway A1A in Boca Raton
Parking/fees: $2 per car ($4 on weekends)
Hours: sunrise to sunset
Facilities: lifeguards, restrooms, picnic tables, and showers
Contact: Palm Beach County Parks and Recreation Department, 561/966-6600

MAP OF SOUTH FLORIDA—PAGE 177

Gumbo Limbo Nature Center

It started as the dream of a high-school science teacher who wanted a place to educate and expose young minds to the biological wonders of Old Florida. It grew to become a reality through the combined efforts of the city of Boca Raton, the Palm Beach County School Board, and Florida Atlantic University. Inside the main building at the Gumbo Limbo Nature Center in Boca Raton are exhibits about the flora and fauna of the Florida coast. Can't-miss winners for the kids include huge sea turtle shells and alligator skulls. Computers allow youngsters to call up a particular class of coastal plants and animals and get a brief rundown on their physical characteristics. Fact-filled murals and cases bring this world to life in ways that are interesting to laypeople, beach bums, and schoolchildren alike.

From the main building, a left turn goes out to a boardwalk trail through the coastal hammock. Proceeding straight to the Intracoastal Waterway brings you to the underwater tanks—saltwater basins that harbor sharks, loggerhead turtles, and other live specimens. Beginning on the right side of the building, the North Trail passes a butterfly garden, a bird blind, grass flats, and mangroves. The Coastal Hammock Trail winds through a peaceful forest whose calm is interrupted only by the chirping of songbirds and lapping of water against the mangrove-lined shores of the Intracoastal Waterway. The word "hammock" derives from a Native American term meaning "shady place." It is a unique environment in that the microclimate found on the narrow strip of land between ocean and estuary allows for plant species that are otherwise found only in the tropics.

Our favorite among the many tree species native to the hammock is the strangler fig. Its roots propagate near the bases of tree trunks. Using the host tree for structure and support, the strangler fig grows upward by encircling and eventually "strangling" the host. It is nature's equivalent of the sleeper hold employed by some professional wrestlers. The site of two trees bound together in twisting, turning agony, parasite and host desperately arching skyward for light, offers mute testimony to nature's struggle for survival using ingenious adaptive techniques.

The literal high point of the Coastal Hammock Trail is the 40-foot observation tower, which protrudes above the top of the canopy. Only the green crowns of the trees are visible. As is the case in the Amazonian rain forest, all the photosynthetic action occurs in the canopy. Below is a sunless void with little understory or ground cover. Up on top lies a whole other world, as becomes clear from the observation tower. The only thing taller than the tree tops is the outline of distant condos. And to think all of Florida's coastline once looked like this.

Gumbo Limbo Nature Center is an incredible facility that should be visited by all. Best of all, it is free and open daily 9 A.M.–4 P.M. (except Sunday, when it opens at noon). It sure beats a wasted day spent haunting strip malls along Federal Highway.

For more information, contact Gumbo Limbo Nature Center, 1801 North Ocean Boulevard, Boca Raton, FL 33432; 561/338-1473; website: www.ns1.fau.edu/gumbo.

the premises you can savor the incredible landscaping and architecture from a bench on a covered walkway. Inside, you can admire the furnishings or bone up on your Mizneriana, particularly the curious tale of Addison Mizner and his pet monkey, which is documented in words and pictures. He was, apparently, the Michael Jackson of his day in that he was rarely seen without his pet spider monkey, Johnnie Brown. The two were inseparable and when death did them part, the monkey was buried at Via Mizner in Palm Beach.

What you'll find at the Boca Raton Resort, above and beyond the commodious surroundings, is something subtler than can be seen with the naked eye. It's the way that old money does things, and has done thing for many decades, in Florida.

The **Radisson Bridge Resort** (999 East Camino Real, 561/368-9500, $$$), an 11-story hotel bathed in "Boca pink," sits beside the bridge where Camino Real crosses the Intracoastal Waterway. The units, especially the two-room suites, are large enough to make guests feel at home. Many overlook the Intracoastal Waterway and the ocean. From the Radisson, you can easily walk to the beach at South Inlet Park or head north along the bike path that parallels Ocean Boulevard (Highway A1A) all the way to Delray Beach.

The **Ocean Lodge** (531 North Ocean Boulevard, 561/395-7772, $$) is cut from plainer cloth, but it's a clean, affordable, and quiet small motel directly across the road from the beach. In that regard, it is fairly unique in Boca Raton. Even the Boca Raton Resort & Club doesn't have such ready beach access. Each room has two double beds and a dining area. Room rates range $50–100, depending on the time of year, and weekly rates are offered as well.

Coastal Cuisine

By and large, the dining scene in Boca Raton is elegant, formal, and pricey. There's little out on the beach, but gourmet French and Italian restaurants abound along Federal Highway (U.S. 1), Palmetto Park Road, and other inland corridors. All aim at offering an upscale (read: expensive) dining experience. For Italian, try **Ecco** (499 South Federal Highway, 561/338-8780, $$$$), **Josephine's** (5700 North Federal Highway, 561/988-0668, $$$) and—especially worth singling out, given this book's orientation toward all things oceanic—**Nick's Italian Fishery** (One Boca Place, 2255 Glades Road, 561/994-2201, $$$). At Nick's, go for the freshest catch of the day, grilled over oak. For French cuisine, the top contenders for your gold card's attention are **La Vieille Maison** (770 East Palmetto Park Road, 561/391-6701, $$$$) and **Marcel's** (1 Ocean Boulevard, 561/362-9911, $$$). We'd recommend snapper with fresh herbs at the former and shrimp with curry and saffron at the latter. And that's just a sampling; many more fine continental eateries are sprinkled around Boca Raton like Godiva chocolates.

Incidentally, if you happen to be in town at midweek, **Carmen's Top of the Bridge Restaurant** at the Radisson Bridge Resort (999 East Camino Real, 561/368-9500, $$$) puts out a bountiful seafood buffet on Tuesday for $22.95. We gorged ourselves senseless on raw oysters, steamed shrimp, and crab legs—and that's just for starters—on top of which you get to order a seafood entrée. We are not the sort to high-five each other, especially over food, but we were doing just that at Carmen's, which offers not only good food but also a great view from the top.

Boca Raton is stuffed to the gills with fine restaurants of every ethnic description. Oddly, though, there aren't many decent eateries whose focus is fresh Florida seafood. That's all the more reason to go to **Mido's Japanese Restaurant** (508 Viaduct de Palmas, 561/361-9683, $$). For $7.95 at lunch, they'll lay out a healthy and sizable serving of sushi. There are other lunch specials, too, but the sushi is one of the best bargains in Boca.

MAP OF SOUTH FLORIDA—PAGE 177

Night Moves

Not being the party animals we used to be, we proceed cautiously when it comes to poking around the nightlife of South Florida. These days, we much prefer rising at dawn to hike on a deserted beach than hanging out till dawn in some decibel-plagued dance club. In the process, we've spared ourselves a lot of loud, robotic music, ringing ears, and painful hangovers.

We have noticed that the Boca hotspots we've begrudgingly written about in years and editions past—i.e., Club Boca and Egoiste—have shut down. The once-popular Club Boca has been reincarnated as **Radius** (7000 West Palmetto Park Road, 561/989-9946) and is hyped as Boca's "hottest networking spot." Beyond that, nightspots come and go in Boca Raton with alarming frequency, and your best bet for signs of life after dark is a place that bears the wonderfully appropriate name **Gatsby's** (5970 Southwest 18th Street, 561/393-3900). If you're into cigars, martinis, big-screen TVs, and chatter, Gatsby's is the ticket.

Contact Information

Greater Boca Raton Chamber of Commerce, 1800 North Dixie Highway, Boca Raton, FL 33432; 561/395-4433; website: www.bocaratonchamber.com

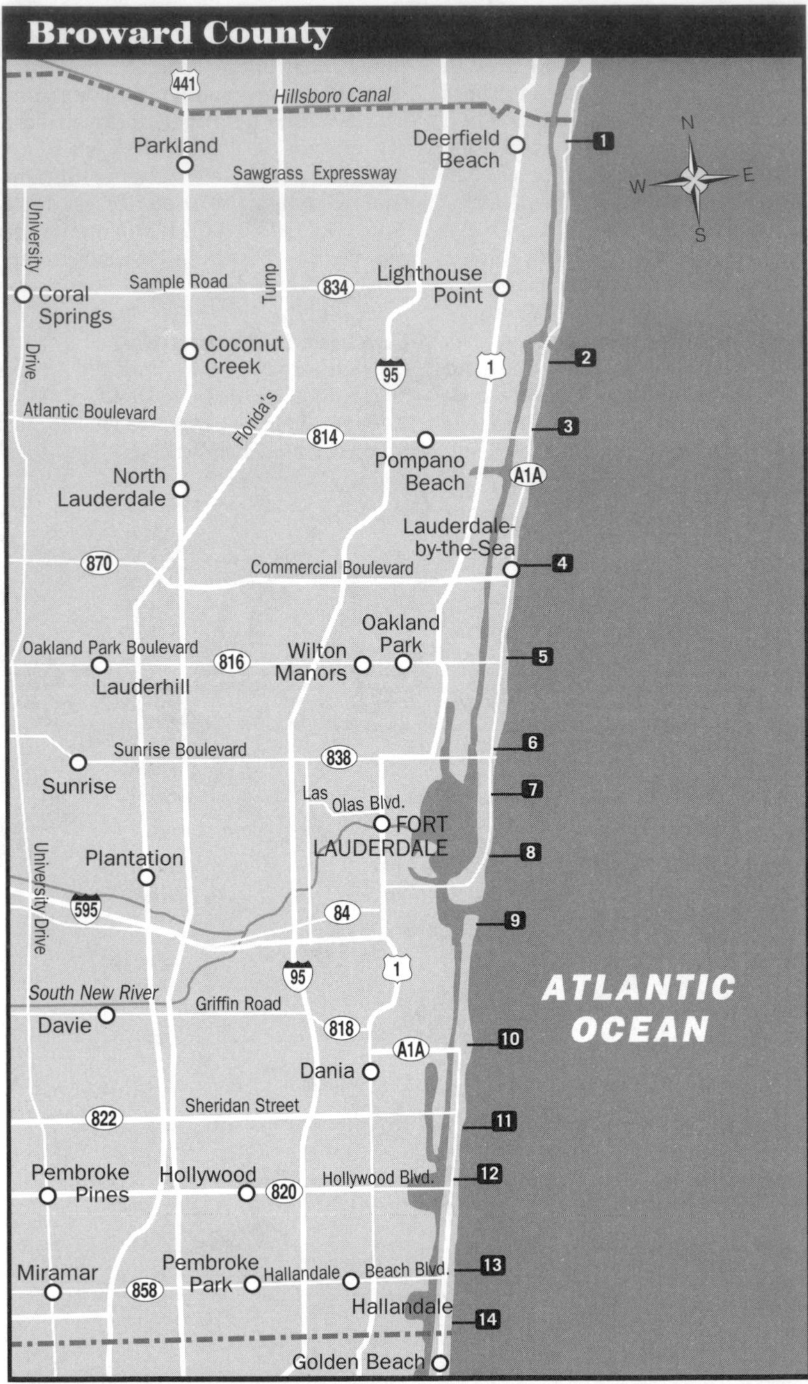
Broward County
441
Hillsboro Canal
Parkland
Deerfield Beach
Sawgrass Expressway
1
N
W
E
S
University Drive
Sample Road
Turnp
834
Lighthouse Point
Coral Springs
Coconut Creek
95
1
2
Atlantic Boulevard
Florida's
3
814
Pompano Beach
North Lauderdale
A1A
Lauderdale-by-the-Sea
870
Commercial Boulevard
4
Oakland Park
Oakland Park Boulevard
816
Wilton Manors
5
Lauderhill
6
Sunrise Boulevard
838
Sunrise
7
Las Olas Blvd.
FORT LAUDERDALE
Plantation
8
University Drive
595
84
9
95
1
South New River
Griffin Road
ATLANTIC OCEAN
Davie
818
A1A
10
Dania
Sheridan Street
822
11
Pembroke Pines
Hollywood
820
Hollywood Blvd.
12
Miramar
Pembroke Park
Hallandale
Beach Blvd.
13
858
Hallandale
14
Golden Beach

South Florida

Broward County

Broward County combines the best of Palm Beach County's affluence and Dade County's excitement while moderating those neighboring counties' worst traits (elitism and crime, respectively). There are 23 miles of coastline in Broward County, which also pushes west to include a half-million acres of Everglades. Fort Lauderdale serves to anchor it all. With its 165 miles of canals, gleaming streets, understated wealth, exceptional restaurants, and a peerless oceanfront, Lauderdale is a class act all the way. The communities north of Lauderdale are a varied lot, ranging from modestly charming Deerfield Beach to bustling, condo-filled Pompano Beach to the low-slung Jersey Shore feel of Lauderdale by the Sea. A trio of beach communities in south Broward County—Dania Beach, Hollywood, and Hallandale—appeals to an older retired crowd and harks back to an earlier time. But there's action to be had here, too: jai alai in Dania Beach, greyhound racing in Hollywood, and horse racing in Hallandale.

Deerfield Beach

Deerfield Beach (pop. 51,269) occupies the space between Boca Raton and Pompano Beach like a low-lying valley between outbreaks of mountainous condos. It is also considerably less frantic than Pompano Beach and Fort Lauderdale, its Broward County neighbors. Deerfield Beach hugs Highway A1A, which makes a few 90-degree turns through town, briefly running east-west along 2nd Street. This is where the town center, such as it is, can be found.

Along A1A's S-curve sits a newish wooden pier, a handful of casual bar/restaurants, a clump of beachwear shops, and a Howard Johnson hotel. One of the shops is Wings, a franchise chain of beachwear shops that can be found approximately every six feet in a bona fide beach town. We stocked up on sunscreen and "Deerfield Beach" T-shirts, and it felt like summer as we hoofed it over to the warm sand nearby. It was, in fact, mid-December. Ah, Florida.

People-watching around Deerfield Beach yields a gamut of ages and types, from old folks who gather on the boardwalk and make small talk about their condos to young families with children straining at the leash to the ubiquitous European travelers looking for sun and fun in South Florida. Unlike Fort Lauderdale and Miami, you feel out of range of citified dangers and distractions in Deerfield Beach. Unlike Palm Beach and Boca Raton, you don't sense the oppressive hand of big money, either. Deerfield Beach is, like Delray Beach, a modest and likable beach town.

That said, pro-development forces have been working to convert Deerfield into another link in what may someday be an unbroken wall of condos and hotel towers extending the length of South Florida. In 1998, former Deerfield Beach mayor Jean Robb busily waged a PR campaign opposing construction of a proposed seven-story luxury hotel called the Deerfield Ocean Grand. "We like to say we're the most underrated and beautiful beach in South Florida, but they're trying to change all that," she told us. "They're planning to build some monstrosity on our beach. They want to destroy the main beach parking lot and fire station and give it to some developer to put in a 260-room hotel."

That's just the half of it: there'd also be town houses, 16,000 square feet of retail space, 666 parking spaces (an oddly apropos number), and a pavilion and amphitheater. The townsfolk got riled enough to form a grassroots "Save Our Beach" committee and to protest the proposal to the county commission. It must've worked, because two years later there is no Deerfield Ocean Grand—just the same handful of big beachfront hotels that have been here for years (Howard Johnson, Embassy Suites) and many smaller ones.

To be fair, there was another side to this argument, cogently and sensibly made to us by a local lifeguard (of all the atypical pro-development boosters), as the Deerfield Ocean Grand looked to be a pretty classy facility that might well have enhanced and enriched the community. While we're all for slow growth and even no growth in towns that can avoid others' bad example, it is shortsighted to simply be a knee-jerk naysayer all the time, as some projects can brighten a blighted area. But Deerfield Beach is not exactly blighted, just low-key, and we wish the preservationists well in this and future battles. For now, it remains a neat, unassuming little beach town at a bend in the road.

Beaches

Deerfield's renourished beach is flat and broad, especially by the pier. We saw bulldozer tracks all over the beach—maybe not exactly what Mother Nature intended, but it's got to be done down here in South

MAP OF SOUTH FLORIDA—PAGE 177

Florida. Cheers to whoever is responsible for the grassy greenbelt and wide wooden boardwalk that runs along the beach. The **Deerfield Public Beach** extends for one mile, with the center of the action being the 900-foot Deerfield Beach International Fishing Pier. (What makes a fishing pier "international"? Is it the fish that swim up from the Caribbean?)

The beach is informally divided into three areas: north of the pier ("North Beach"); from the pier south to a beach-hogging yellow monster called the Cove Beach Club ("Main Beach"), and south of the Cove ("South Beach"). North Beach draws a young, recreation-minded crowd of surfers and volleyball players. South Beach is where you go to escape the numbers. Main Beach is a happy medium between old and young, stoked and laid-back.

Metered public parking spaces ($1 per hour, 7 A.M.–7 P.M.) line the beachfront. The boardwalk is nicely landscaped, with tiki huts, gazebos, and benches affording shelter from the sun and a vantage point to gaze out to sea. People stare as if mesmerized by the sight—and well they should be. Concessioners rent cabanas, beach chairs, and umbrellas for about $15.

Bunking Down

The twin towers on Deerfield Beach are the **Howard Johnson Plaza Resort** (2096 Northeast 2nd Street, 954/428-2850, $$$) and the **Embassy Suites Deerfield Beach Resort** (950 Southeast 20th Avenue, 954/426-0478, $$$$). The 30-year-old Howard Johnson is at the center of the action, which means it's only a steps away from a fish dinner at Flanigan's and a leisurely stroll on the pier.

Embassy Suites lies about a half mile south on a quieter stretch of Highway A1A. Its suites are roomy and comfortable. A huge pool sits in the middle of an attractive whitewashed courtyard. The beach is just across the road, making it easy to pop from pool to ocean and back again, which we did one warm December morning. A free evening cocktail hour and a prepared breakfast come with the room charge, which is not inexpensive ($219–349 per night in winter, $109–189 in summer, and somewhere in between the rest of the year).

Less vertically commanding but no less accessible to the ocean are a couple of so-called beach clubs—**Berkshire Beach Club** (500 North Highway A1A, 954/428-1000, $$$) and **Rettger Resort Beach Club** (100 Northeast 20th Terrace, 954/427-7900, $$$)—where a room will set you back roughly $100–200 a night, depending on the time of year.

Beyond the high-rise sentinels and the "beach clubs," an endless string of modest, one- and two-story mom-and-pop places lines Highway A1A. They are variously identified as "motel apartments," "efficiencies," and "resort motels," the idea being that you can either check in overnight or book a longer stay. All bear idyllic names like Golden Sands, Sea Fare, Emerald Seas, and Tropic Isle, and they offer a serious break on price, if Embassy Suites and Howard Johnson are out of range. For instance, a week's stay at the **Tropic Isle** (370 South A1A, 954/427-

1 Deerfield Public Beach

   4

Location: north and south of the Deerfield Beach International Fishing Pier, which is located at the east end of 2nd Street (Highway A1A) in Deerfield Beach

Parking/fees: metered street parking

Hours: 6 A.M.–11 P.M.

Facilities: concessions, lifeguards, restrooms, picnic tables, and showers

Contact: Deerfield Beach Parks and Recreation Department, 954/480-4412; taped beach report, 954/480-4413

1000, $$) will set you back $500–700 in season, which works out to $100 or less per night. When business is slow, these places are a downright steal, with some rooms going for as little as $268 a week, or $38.29 per night. Who says the beach life is unaffordable?

Coastal Cuisine

A couple of casual spots occupy the curve where Highway A1A crooks its arm in the vicinity of the pier. The **Whale's Rib Raw Bar and Restaurant** (2031 Northeast 2nd Street, 954/421-8880, $$) offers everything from take-out sandwiches to baked mahimahi and seared garlic pepper tuna, with full dinners running around $12.

A few steps away is **Flanigan's Hi-Tide Seafood Bar** (2041 Northeast 2nd Street, 954/427-9304, $$), whose specialty is fresh Florida mahimahi sandwiches or fried "fingers" at lunch, and blackened, fried, sautéed, broiled, or grilled fillets at dinner. If you don't want to leave your room at Embassy Suites, the on-premises restaurant **Cagney's Crabhouse** (950 Southeast 20th Avenue, 954/426-0478, $$$) specializes in seafood and Florida regional cuisine.

Night Moves

The north-south Federal Highway (U.S. 1) corridor slices through the contiguous cities of Deerfield Beach, Pompano Beach, and Fort Lauderdale about a mile inland from the beach, offering endless places to eat, drink, and shop for clothes, toiletries, office supplies, tires, and guns. It is always irritating to navigate this clogged stretch of asphalt, with its unending congestion, bad driving, and outbreaks of road rage that result in flashing blue lights at accident scenes with greater frequency than would seem statistically possible.

The fact is, basic needs for shelter, food, and nightlife can be met on the beach side of Deerfield Beach without having to cross the Hillsboro Boulevard bridge. Saunter over to either of the aforementioned eateries (Whale's Rib, Flanigan's) for beer or booze and raw ones, or amble into one of the hotel bars for a civilized gin and tonic. If you're staying at the Embassy Suites, drinks are free for two hours nightly. By the way, **Big Daddy's Liquor Store** adjoins Flanigan's—same address, different phone number (954/427-3920). Best of all, once parked and checked in, you don't need a car to get around Deerfield's compact beachside commercial district.

Contact Information

Greater Deerfield Beach Chamber of Commerce, 1601 East Hillsboro Boulevard, Deerfield Beach, FL 33441; 954/427-1050; website: www.deerfieldchamber.com

Hillsboro Beach

Hillsboro Beach (pop. 1,756) is a ritzy residential community between Deerfield Beach and Pompano Beach, along Hillsboro Mile (Highway A1A). It's located almost entirely on the seaward side of Highway A1A along a stretch of beach modestly referred to as "Millionaire Mile." In addition to municipal autonomy, Hillsboro Beach has 30 luxury condominiums and a private marina going for or against it, depending on how you feel about beachfront privatization. It's similar to Highland Beach, up in adjacent Palm Beach County, in that it lacks much commercial business—with one notable exception, the Seabonay Beach Resort.

Bunking Down

The **Seabonay Beach Resort** (1159 Hillsboro Mile, 954/427-2525, $$) is a six-story "apartment hotel" comprising standard hotel rooms and one- and two-bedroom units with full cooking facilities, a pool deck, exercise room, and more. It's perfect for couples or families who want a relaxing vacation right on the Gold Coast without being in the thick of its congestion and clamor.

Contact Information

Greater Fort Lauderdale Convention and Visitors Bureau, 1850 Eller Drive, Suite 303, Fort Lauderdale, FL 33316; 954/765-4466 or 800/22SUNNY; website: www.sunny.com

Pompano Beach

Pompano Beach (pop. 74,400) is Fort Lauderdale without class and charisma. The two cities bear roughly the same relationship as Oakland and San Francisco, to draw a West Coast parallel. Along Highway A1A, Pompano Beach is an unappealing wall of faded resorts and condos that resemble public-housing projects. It's worse along Federal Highway (U.S. 1), an endless procession of stores and signs. Strip malls and strip clubs are found in profusion. It's a land of franchises and megastores, a blown-up version of the way towns all over America have come to look these days.

The 17 square miles that make up Pompano Beach used to be farmland, but it's been a long time since anything but condos and shopping malls have sprouted from its asphalt acreage. It was incorporated as the inland town of Pompano (after the fish) in 1906 and then expanded in 1947, annexing 3.5 miles of beach to become Pompano Beach. In addition to its plague of condos and surfeit of malls, latter-day Pompano Beach exists to serve the prurient interests of Broward County, offering a concentration of adult-oriented nightclubs along Federal Highway (U.S. 1). A more appealing side of the community exists at Hillsboro Inlet and Lighthouse Point, site of the scenic Hillsboro Lighthouse and yacht marinas.

Fishing is a big draw to Pompano Beach. Not for nothing is the town named after a particularly tasty catch. The waters off South Florida teem with more than 400 kinds of fish, and fishing charters can be booked in the marinas at Hillsboro Inlet. Popular catches include king mackerel, tarpon, snook, dolphin, sailfish, cobia, and the namesake pompano. The town calls itself the "Sportfishing Capital of the World," which beats the "XXX Nightclub Capital of South Florida," although both titles are fairly accurate.

Beaches

The city maintains **Pompano Public Beach**, which runs for three-fifths of a mile along Pompano Beach Boulevard, extend-

MAP OF BROWARD COUNTY—PAGE 222

Naked Came the Strangers

Okay, we're going to tell the truth, the whole truth, and nothing but the truth. We went to a strip club in Pompano Beach one night. Make that a "nude cabaret." It sounds more respectable. Real businessmen swarm to these places in suits and ties, so they've got to be respectable. It seemed like the thing to do, being that there are so many of them in South Florida and that the parking lots are often full, or close to it. As longtime travel writers and nightlife enthusiasts (whose enthusiasm, to be honest, has dimmed somewhat in recent years), we felt duty bound to check it out.

The place we went to was called—well, the name's not important, since they all offer more or less the same experience. Let's just say it's way the heck up Federal Highway in Pompano Beach. We chose this establishment from among the bounty of nude cabarets in Broward County based on the size of the place and the fact that it didn't look too honky tonk from the outside. Sometimes they refer to these vaguely upscale strip joints, invariably outlined in purple neon, as "gentlemen's clubs," which is stretching credibility but allows the clientele to feel better about patronizing them.

In any case, we pushed open the enormous doors and were greeted by a gal who cheerfully chirped, "Hi, guys," as if to reassure us that being here was perfectly normal and to put us at ease for the ambushing of our wallets that was to follow. We paid the five-buck cover and were escorted to a table, choosing not to sit ringside but unobtrusively positioned at a corner table a row back from the action. "Ooh, the girls are going to pin you in here when they come around," giggled our hostess, who was wearing a thong bikini bottom.

What we found was not an obvious place of depravity but rather a kind of secular house of worship. The female form was only the most visible object of adoration. Also being celebrated in this ritual of controlled hedonism were sports, rock and roll, alcohol, and money—all the things that keep America merrily bopping down the road toward its brainless unraveling. Maintaining the veneer of faux gentility was a bouncer who circulated around the club in a black tuxedo, looking every inch a dapper fool. Everything was as controlled as a sterilized plant where computer chips are made. And the atmosphere was equally surreal.

The strip club we patronized was a warehouse-sized place with a giant, elevated dance floor in the center where girls took turns bumping and grinding to excruciatingly loud, redundant music. At each corner a transparent pole containing a bubbling column of water served as a prop for the dancers to frolic on. A huge, theater-size TV screen occupied

ing north from its intersection with Atlantic Boulevard. Its golden sands include Pompano Beach Municipal Pier, which juts a fifth of a mile into the ocean and is open around the clock. Surfing is allowed north of the pier. In addition, Pompano Beach provides access points at roughly a dozen street ends along the beach, from Northeast 10th Street down to Southeast 8th Street. A particularly hot surfing break can be found at Southeast 2nd Street.

Up toward Hillsboro Inlet, at Northeast 16th Street and North Ocean Boulevard (Highway A1A), is **North Ocean Park.** On this non-lifeguarded beach, you're allowed to launch wind-driven, non-motorized

one wall, tuned to a sporting event with the sound off.

We were bugged and bothered from the second we sat down. Cocktail waitresses circled the joint, forcing drinks on patrons at 30-second intervals—"You guys okay?" "You doin' alright here?" "Can I get you another?" "Need anything?" "Another round?"—while trying to spirit away half-full glasses from the table so already self-conscious voyeurs would be further shamed into handing over another $6 (plus tip) for a bottled beer. The desperate dupes sitting ringside were continuously seduced into tipping the dancers, who'd wander over and gyrate in their faces, for which display a dollar got stuffed inside a garter. Each woman did a four-song turn on the stage, during which she disrobed in increments, song by song: first clothed; then stripped to lingerie; next, off came the top; and finally, she was completely bare. By the end of each brief shift, a dancer's garter would be bursting with wadded bills, flapping like miniature green guidons.

Between turns onstage, dancers made the rounds of the floor hawking table dances. This led to some awkward exchanges. A pair of dancers wandered over to our table, introducing themselves and shaking our hands as if we were peers at a corporate mixer. The blond wore a skimpy red vinyl outfit, her raven-haired partner a short, diaphanous dress. They offered us a "double deal"—"Just ten bucks, apiece, guys"—which we declined with all the dignity we could muster. Like car salesmen, they wouldn't take no for an answer. We could feel their moist heat as they leaned in to close the deal. "Later," we promised, "after we've had a few more." Since we were drinking club soda, this was simply a ruse to get them to move on. "Okay," they giggled. "We'll be back later to take your wallets!"

The music that got pumped over the sound system was predictably repellent—pulverizing heavy metal segueing into mind-numbing electronic dance music ("body-body-body, ooh baby I want your body, oh"). The deejay would perform his carny-barker routine in an unctuous, nasal voice, announcing the dancers' entrances and exits like the emcee at a Paris fashion show: "Let's hear it for Lola, guys. And now Bianca is approaching the main stage while Candy moves to cage number one."

The truth is, there's more silicone in these dancers' heaving chests than in Silicon Valley. You might as well rename Federal Highway, which is lined with strip joints, Silicon Alley. After an hour or so of watching assembly-line disrobing and robotic dancing while fending off Comanche-style raids on our cash holdings, we concluded that the whole setup is more about the aphrodisiac of money than sex; that the dancers probably hold the gawkers in the highest contempt (and vice versa); and that the whole spectacle is a sad, soulless, and ultimately sexless charade.

watercraft such as Hobie Cats. If you want to launch the noisy stuff—i.e., Jet Skis and Waverunners—that can be done on the Intracoastal Waterway at Alsdorf Park, on the Northeast 14th Street Causeway. Offshore, they've sunk 20 freighters to create a massive artificial reef that's a haven for fish and fishermen.

Bunking Down

Sandwiched between all the oceanfront high-rises in Pompano Beach are some brand-name hotels and mom-and-pop motels. By the look of it, certain of the latter will not survive the current economic downturn. On the positive side, **Howard Johnson Plaza Resort** (9 North Pompano

Beach Boulevard, 954/781-1300, $$) is right in the heart of the action, where Atlantic Avenue meets Pompano Beach Boulevard. There's also a **Holiday Inn** (1350 South Ocean Boulevard, 954/941-7300, $$$) with rooms on the Atlantic Ocean and the Spanish River. Scuba diving and snorkeling equipment can be rented, and there's a dock on the river. The **Best Western Beachcomber** (1200 South Ocean Boulevard, 954/941-7830, $$), a recent arrival, offers resort amenities, such as a 300-foot private beach, at motel prices. Its neighbor is a **Sheraton Four Points Hotel** (1208 South Ocean Boulevard, 954/782-5300, $$$), which at least gives this end of Pompano Beach a reassuring corporate hotel presence. At the low end, you can just about name your price at some of the less stellar motels in Pompano Beach, of which there are many. Just drive the main thoroughfares and look for signs of desperation.

Coastal Cuisine

Pompano Beach doesn't have much luster of its own, so it basks in the reflected glow of Fort Lauderdale and other better-tended, better-looking communities in Broward County. Accordingly, it isn't exactly the bastion of haute cuisine that Fort Lauderdale can rightly claim to be, tending to places with names like **Chez Porky's** (105 Southwest 6th Street, 954/946-5590, $$) or novelty restaurants like the **Speed Cafe** (2401 Northeast 15th Street, 954/783-3488, $$), where you dine on wings and beef while seated inside custom cars. Other names we love drawn from the Pompano Beach dining scene: Red's Backwoods BBQ, Ronnie B's Taste of 50's, the Briny Irish Pub, Bru's Room Wing 'N' Ribs, and the East Coast Burrito Factory. Are you beginning to get the picture?

Having said that, there are first-class meals to be had in Pompano Beach at **Darrel & Oliver's Cafe Maxx** (2601 East Atlantic Boulevard, 954/782-0606, $$$$) and **Joe's Riverside Grill** (125 North Riverside Drive, 954/941-2499, $$$). And anyone visiting South Florida absolutely has to take a meal at **Cap's Place Island Restaurant** (2765 Northeast 28th Court, 954/941-0418, $$$).

One of the oldest restaurants in South Florida, having served Old Florida–style cuisine before it became necessary to call it that, Cap's is accessible only by a boat that shuttles diners from a dock in Lighthouse Point (at the aforementioned address) out to Cap's island locale. Specialties include fresh hearts of palm salad and local sea-food (grouper chowder and smoked mahi-mahi). They're open for dinner seven days a week, starting at 5:30 P.M. Curiously, Cap's

2 North Ocean Park

Location: Northeast 16th Street and North Ocean Boulevard (Highway A1A)
Parking/fees: limited metered parking
Hours: sunrise to sunset
Facilities: restrooms, picnic tables, and showers
Contact: Pompano Beach Parks and Recreation Department, 954/786-4111; taped beach report, 954/786-4005

3 Pompano Public Beach

Location: 10 North Pompano Beach Boulevard, at Atlantic Avenue in Pompano Beach
Parking/fees: metered parking lot
Hours: sunrise to sunset
Facilities: concessions, lifeguards, restrooms, picnic tables, and showers
Contact: Pompano Beach Parks and Recreation Department, 954/786-4111; taped beach report, 954/786-4005

MAP OF SOUTH FLORIDA—PAGE 177

Place is the only restaurant in Florida that harvests and serves its own hearts of palm, which are taken from the Florida state tree, the sabal palm. They'll bring out a Saran-wrapped heart of palm for you to look at, and they'll tell the story of when and how they're harvested. (For every palm they take from their tract near Lake Okeechobee, they replant two.) Truth to tell, it's not exactly delicious, offering texture more than taste. What is delicious are the seafood entrée items. Our recommendation: the sautéed seafood platter ($23.95). The restaurant is fashioned to look like a cracker house: tin roof, wood walls, and cozy, low-ceilinged rooms. It's been around since 1928 and has hosted presidents (JFK, FDR) and statesmen like Winston Churchill.

Night Moves

Duplicate bridge is very popular among those who live in Pompano's high-rise communities. We read that in the *Hi-Riser*, a local publication that serves "the condominium communities of Fort Lauderdale and Pompano Beach." If you want something a little livelier than an evening of cards, hit the highway—Federal Highway (U.S. 1), that is. For a more detailed accounting of Pompano Beach after dark, we herewith refer you to "Naked Came the Strangers" (see sidebar on pages 228–229).

Contact Information

Greater Pompano Beach Chamber of Commerce, 2200 East Atlantic Boulevard, Pompano Beach, FL 33064; 954/941-2940; website: www.pompanobeachchamber.com

Lauderdale by the Sea

Lauderdale by the Sea (pop. 3,800) has the funky look and feel of a Jersey Shore beach town. We intend that as praise. By comparison to the high-rise drabness of Pompano Beach, Lauderdale by the Sea's down-to-earth bustle is refreshing. Pompano seemingly has no height restrictions while Lauderdale by the Sea enforces severe ones. As a result, Pompano is all high-towered condos and Lauderdale by the Sea is low-to-the-ground motels and shops. In other words, the latter looks like an unretouched, old-fashioned beach town—which is just the way we like 'em.

The heart of Lauderdale by the Sea—better known in local's shorthand as L-B-T-S—is the intersection of North Ocean Boulevard (Highway A1A) and Commercial Boulevard. Single-story restaurants and shops proliferate in the vicinity. One real curiosity is Anglin's Pier. It is the only privately owned pier on Florida's east coast. Built by the government as a lookout for German U-boats during World War II, it was then deeded to the landowner after the war. It's priced the same as the public piers: $3 for anglers, $1 for sightseers. They catch snapper, snook, mackerel, cobia, and grouper here. There's a pretty remarkable picture of one guy who landed a 1,040-pound hammerhead shark from the pier in 1965. Talk about catch of the day!

Beaches

The mile-long **Lauderdale by the Sea Public Beach** is steep and drops off quickly. A healthy stand of palms gives it a tropical, suitably beachy look. There's a real mix of people here: families, bikers, locals, out-of-towners, etc. We kept flashing on beaches up north, like Old Orchard Beach, Maine, and Seaside Heights, New Jersey. The proximity of stores and restaurants to the beach gives the area a feeling of immediacy and vigor. A reef that lies 100 yards offshore is a draw to snorkelers and divers. The only thing that is missing from this otherwise perfect picture is lifeguards.

Bunking Down

There are a lot of modest "resort motels" and "apartment motels" in Lauderdale by the Sea, where rooms can be had for under $100 a night in season and plummet to $25–35 per night out of season. Even the more upscale resorts, such as **Lauderdale by the Sea Beach Resort** (4660 North Ocean Drive, 954/776-5660, $$), **Costa del Sol Resort** (4220 El Mar Drive, 954/776-6900, $$), and **Villas by the Sea Resort and Beach Club** (4456 El Mar Drive, 954/772-3550, $$), have fairly toned-down prices, by Gold Coast standards.

Coastal Cuisine

The **Aruba Beach Cafe** (1 East Commercial Boulevard, 954/776-0001, $$) is the prime beachside perch in Lauderdale by the Sea.

4 Lauderdale by the Sea Public Beach

Location: east end of Commercial Boulevard in Lauderdale by the Sea
Parking/fees: metered street parking
Hours: 24 hours
Facilities: concessions, picnic tables, and showers
Contact: Lauderdale by the Sea Public Works Department, 954/776-0576

It's larger than it looks from the street, as there are several bars and dining rooms on the premises. It's a great place for lunch, happy-hour drinks, or even dinner. Among the starters, try ahi sashimi, Bahamian conch fritters, or Caribbean lobster salad. For an entrée, go for the blackened trio or fresh catch (which was grouper and swordfish during our last visit).

Adding to the non-corporate charm of this bustling beach town is the **Pier Coffee Shop** (Anglin's Pier, 2 Commercial Boulevard, 954/776-1690, $), which has been in business for over 30 years. The grub won't win any notices from *Gourmet* magazine, but you can't beat the view and authentically funky ambience. Tourists generally ask for the open-air booths, while locals sit inside. Wherever you sit, you'll enjoy a long view of the Atlantic Ocean with your coffee and eggs.

While in the area, grab a glass of fresh-squeezed juice at **Mack's Groves** (4405 North Ocean Drive, 954/776-0910, $). It's the perfect tonic on a hot day at the beach.

Night Moves

Head to the Aruba Beach Cafe (see "Coastal Cuisine") and start in on the tropical drinks. You can't go wrong with a Mango Madness or Caribbean Iced Tea, which beats its Long Island cousin hands-down.

Contact Information

Lauderdale by the Sea Chamber of Commerce, 4201 North Ocean Drive, Lauderdale by the Sea, FL 33308; 954/776-1000 or 800/699-6764; website: www.lbts.com

Fort Lauderdale

The password is "billions." Fort Lauderdale (pop. 150,000) has sunk and is sinking literally thousands of millions into "tourism investment" as part of its dramatic and ongoing transformation from a former Spring Break mecca and party town of great renown to a year-round upscale vacation and convention destination. The refurbishing of its beachfront and other parts of the city is evident everywhere you go. The fruits of these labors are evident in the fact that it now attracts nearly seven million visitors a year and was voted *Money* magazine's "best big city in America to live" in July 1996.

On the beach, the city appears to imitating the glitzy Art Deco upscaling that's made South Miami Beach such a success story. No longer does the city court or tolerate balcony-diving Spring Breakers and aimless teen cruisers who made Fort Lauderdale's beach a kind of Sunset Strip by the sea in decades past. Local police began cracking down on the annual collegiate booze and fertility rituals in 1986, and Spring Break was virtually eliminated after that. These days, Fort Lauderdale courts upscale tourists: foreigners, families, and singles who are likely to spend money without making trouble. The beach makeover really began in earnest with the passage of a bed tax in 1991 to fund redevelopment along the Central Beach area.

The "new" Fort Lauderdale's refined and redefined ambience is best expressed by a neon tube embedded into the wall that runs along the beach. It changes colors from green to yellow to blue to fuchsia. You don't find this sort of thing on your average public beach. On the other side of Atlantic Boulevard is Beach Place, a 100,000-square-foot complex of shops and restaurants where you can get drinks and/or dinner at a faux Irish pub, a faux piano bar, a faux Key West restaurant, a faux Louisiana Cajun hangout, and so on. This is where Fort Lauderdale has become Faux Lauderdale, to some extent. That's not entirely a bad thing, since Beach Place is a safe, clean alternative to the brawling mobs that used to prowl the Strip.

Fort Lauderdale is defined by the ocean and a network of inland canals that have earned it the nickname "the Venice of America." There are 165 miles of canals in Fort Lauderdale and 300 total miles of them in Broward County. Frequent late-afternoon thunderstorms clear the air and cleanse the streets. So much water pumping through the city's aortic passageways makes decay seem impossible (the real Venice notwithstanding). To extend the physiological metaphor, this is a robust municipality whose vital signs include chic malls and specialty shops; more restaurants per capita (2,500 in all) than any other American city; a mind-numbing 42,000 yachts lashed to docks in front of huge homes or berthed in the hundred or so marinas in the area; and impeccably manicured yards heavily landscaped with citrus trees and colorful tropical flora.

Fort Lauderdale was not heavily settled until the end of the nineteenth century. Named for Major William Lauderdale, it served as a fortification, built in 1838, against the Seminole Indians. It was then settled by fishermen and farmers in the 1890s and became a full-fledged township with its incorporation in 1911. With the opening up of South Florida to travel and tourism, Fort Lauderdale became a thriving resort whose permanent population also grew steadily after World War II. There is no mystery to Fort Lauderdale's appeal. It's summed up in one word: weather. The average year-round temperature is a near-perfect 75.4°F, and the mercury has never exceeded 100°F, thanks to those moderating sea breezes. Here's a statistic to ponder on some cold, gray day back home: Fort Lauderdale boasts 3,000 hours of sunshine per year.

MAP OF BROWARD COUNTY—PAGE 222

Obviously, somebody is getting the word. In 1999, tourist visitation surpassed 6.7 million and tourist expenditures topped $3.8 billion—record numbers in both cases. One regrettable aspect of the city's upscaling, however, is its recent adoption of the catchphrase "Positively Posh," which smacks of nose-thumbing Palm Beach–style elitism. We grew up loving Fort Lauderdale not because of its snooty airs but its natural beauty and accessibility to all. We have no affinity for the "international jet set" or pitches aimed at them. Just get a whiff of this fulsome prose from the local convention and visitors bureau: "Cars are not the only indication that Greater Fort Lauderdale has come of age as a positively posh vacation destination. Hundreds of private jets, costing as much as $30 million apiece, fly into three airports catering to private aircrafts [*sic*] each day so owners can be whisked away to their 150-foot+ seagoing yachts tied up at their fabulous waterfront mansions or docked at the Bahia Mar Marina, home of the world's largest annual international boat show, or one of the many exclusive marinas in the area." Why should this waste of fuel and resources by monied hyper-consumers be touted or even tolerated? We urge those dispensing Greater Fort Lauderdale's tourist P.R. to dispense with the "Positively Posh" approach and get back to promoting the city as a clean, civilized community with a splendid beachfront.

In addition to a four-mile municipal beach, there's a glut of attractions in and around Fort Lauderdale. These include Riverwalk, a 1.5-mile "linear park" that runs along the banks of the New River, and Las Olas Boulevard, a close-by area of cafés and chichi boutiques. On the zoological front, **Butterfly World** (3600 West Sample Road, Coconut Creek, 954/977-4400) teems with myriad winged wonders in a rain-forest setting of flowers and gardens, while **Flamingo Gardens** (3750 Flamingo Road, Davie, 954/473-2955) showcases the flightless pink wonders, as well as alligators, in a subtropical forest setting. History and architecture buffs will want to check out **Stranahan House** (335 East Olas Boulevard, 954/524-4736), a tiny riverside domicile that belonged to Fort Lauderdale's founder. Art aficionados will enjoy the savvy, sophisticated exhibits and collections at the **Fort Lauderdale Museum of Art** (1 East Las Olas Boulevard, 954/463-5184), now occupying an impressive new facility. Then there's the ***Jungle Queen*** (801 Seabreeze Boulevard, 954/462-5596), a must-do boat trip around

5 Fort Lauderdale City Beach (north area)

Location: Oakland Park Boulevard south to Northeast 20th Street along North Atlantic Boulevard in Fort Lauderdale

Parking/fees: metered street parking

Hours: 24 hours

Facilities: lifeguards and showers

Contact: Fort Lauderdale City Beach Lifeguard Office, 954/468-1595

6 Hugh Taylor Birch State Park

Location: sunrise Boulevard at Atlantic Boulevard (Highway A1A) in Fort Lauderdale

Parking/fees: $3.25 per vehicle entrance fee; $1 entrance fee per bicycle rider, or walk-in visitor. Free street parking along Highway A1A as well

Hours: 8 A.M. to sunset (9 A.M.–5 P.M. on the beach)

Facilities: lifeguards, restrooms, picnic tables, showers, and a visitor center

Contact: Hugh Taylor Birch State Park, 954/564-4521

the city's canals and waterways past the spectacular winter domiciles of the wealthy to a Seminole Indian village where the great spectator sport of alligator wrestling is demonstrated. It has been around as long as we have. Maybe longer.

That's just the tip of the palm tree. There are gambling cruises, gondola tours, golf courses (72 of them in Broward County), the Swimming Hall of Fame, the Fort Lauderdale Historical Museum, and the Seminole Indian Casino and Bingo. Take our advice: call 800/22SUNNY right now and they'll send you an information package that will lay it all out in greater detail. There's lots more to do in Fort Lauderdale than hang out on the beach, as fine a beach as it is. You really can't lose by coming here. We've been coming back for decades.

As you can probably tell, we're keen on Fort Lauderdale, especially compared to Miami. At various times on our Florida travels, we'll ask ourselves a litmus-test question to gauge our overall feeling for a community: "Could we live in this place?" Miami rates a firm "no way," while Fort Lauderdale gets two very enthusiastic thumbs up.

Beaches

Fort Lauderdale City Beach runs for four miles along Highway A1A, from the southern border with Lauderdale by the Sea down to Port Everglades. Angle-in beach parking is free for several miles along Highway A1A, but spaces fill up quickly and the early birds get these highly desirable spots. There's also a large municipal parking lot near Las Olas Boulevard at Highway A1A toward the south end of the beach, which costs $6 per day, plus parking on lots and streets inland from the beach.

The renourished beach is plenty wide and, as is typical of beaches where the dune system has been disturbed, basically flat from the surf zone to the sidewalk. Short palms line the beach along Highway A1A; many of the taller ones succumbed to blight back in the 1980s. It is a visually appealing beach, being that the city of Fort Lauderdale had the foresight to forbid development on the ocean side of Atlantic Boulevard. The view of the ocean adds a refreshing note, conveying the feeling of being in a vibrant beach town that respects its greatest asset and has left it open and accessible. Fort Lauderdale's beaches were certified in 2000 for environmental quality and public safety by a the Clean Beaches Council, a national organization, as part of its "Blue Wave"

7 Fort Lauderdale City Beach (central area)

Location: sunrise Boulevard south to Las Olas Boulevard, along North Ocean Boulevard (Highway A1A) in Fort Lauderdale
Parking/fees: free street parking
Hours: 24 hours
Facilities: lifeguards and showers
Contact: Fort Lauderdale City Beach Lifeguard Office, 954/468-1595

8 Fort Lauderdale City Beach (south area)

Location: Las Olas Boulevard south to Port Everglades along South Ocean Boulevard (Highway A1A) in Fort Lauderdale
Parking/fees: $6 per day parking lot (Las Olas Boulevard at Ocean Boulevard) by the beach, plus metered street parking and lot in the area
Hours: 24 hours
Facilities: concessions, lifeguards, restrooms, picnic tables, and showers
Contact: Fort Lauderdale City Beach Lifeguard Office, 954/468-1595

MAP OF BROWARD COUNTY—PAGE 222

The Death of Fun on Fort Lauderdale's Strip

Spring Break and Fort Lauderdale are no longer on speaking terms, but the memories of many wild years on Fort Lauderdale Beach linger unforgettably, like the image of a fat college kid diving into a barside pool for laughs while a foul-mouthed deejay eggs him on and hundreds of lubricated yahoos cheer loudly. Or the spectacle of a drink-befuddled coed shedding her inhibitions as she competes in a wet T-shirt contest. Or the sight of a frat boy watering the shrubs on A1A, oblivious to the milling crowds.

It's very different today on Fort Lauderdale's Strip, the stretch of beach along Atlantic Boulevard (A1A) between Sunrise and Las Olas Boulevards. Those who have refashioned the town's image don't even like to hear it referred to as the Strip—too many echoes of the bad old days when Fort Lauderdale was out of control. While they have succeeded in dramatically transforming the beach's look and image, they may have gone too far. Fort Lauderdale's Strip, whatever else you might say about it, at least had a discernible soul back in its salad days. With its funky bars, mom-and-pop motels, and T-shirt shops, the Strip had the down-to-earth feel of a democratized beach accessible to all, regardless of means. Now it is rather too genteel and affected, casting its neon rainbow upon people who think nothing of dropping $120 on dinner for two. They market the town as being "Positively Posh." That is a far cry from the days when Fort Lauderdale was known as "Party Town U.S.A."

The change came suddenly. Up until the mid-1980s, Fort Lauderdale willingly courted Spring Break, which drew upward of 350,000 winter-weary collegiate revelers from as far away as Maine and Michigan between February and April. The rites of spring had been practiced on the sands of Fort Lauderdale as far back as the 1930s. Yet only after *Time* magazine publicized the annual migration in 1959—with an article in which a lass explained the allure with a soon-to-be-famous catchphrase, "This is where the boys are"—did collegians begin to descend en masse. In 1960, the beach flick *Where the Boys Are* became a box-office hit—thanks in part to the sultry title tune sung by the film's costar, Connie Francis—and the spotlight shone even more brightly on Fort Lauderdale. In its wake, the Spring Break crowd doubled to an estimated 50,000. A street riot erupted in 1961 between bottle-throwing collegians and authorities. Elvis Presley turned up in Fort Lauderdale in March 1964 to film scenes for *Girl Happy*, a cash-in film about the Spring Break phenomenon whose soundtrack included such Elvis-sung lowlights as "Fort Lauderdale Chamber of Commerce" and "Do the Clam."

The political turmoil of the Vietnam era put a damper on Spring Break, or at least gave it a more urgent, hippiefied edge: rock bands playing in the sand, braless hippie chicks and acres of bikinis, head shops and the potent aroma of pot smoke and burning incense. It was a Woodstock-era sense of community on the beach amid the tensions of the Vietnam era, witnessed and enjoyed by one of us yearly from the early 1960s through the mid-1970s.

After the body blows suffered by Spring Break owing to war, gas crisis, and recession, the ritual rebounded spectacularly in the late 1970s. By 1977, more than 100,000 packed Fort Lauderdale Beach, spending in excess of $35 million. A sequel to *Where the Boys Are* was filmed in 1983 as Spring Break accelerated to the point of inundation and excess. "There aren't any rules here," a security guard at the Holiday Inn Oceanside, a veritable riot house during Spring Break, told the *Miami Herald.* "We don't care how many people they stick in the room or what they do as long as the door is closed." By this time, the most famous bar on the strip, the Button—located by the Holiday Inn Oceanside—boasted of dispensing three-quarters of a million beers during Spring Break. Meanwhile, some residents and community leaders openly complained that the rites of spring ran counter to the city's best interests.

The watershed year for revelry was 1985. A record 350,000 collegians completely overwhelmed the streets of Fort Lauderdale. By now, Spring Break had degenerated to a Roman orgy, at least in some quarters. The scene at the Button was notably one of debauchery. According to the *Miami Herald,* "The sweaty hordes, periodically hosed down by Button bartenders, watched or participated in contests that involved nudity, masturbation, beer enemas, drinking urine, and simulated oral sex onstage." One of the deejay ringleaders was sentenced to 18 months in jail for promoting obscenity and actually served 90 days. The bar was fined $25,000 and ordered shut down for 60 days.

In the wake of such antics, the town clamped down hard on Spring Break in 1986. The collegiate crowd, expecting to run wild in the streets as usual, instead found a beefed-up police force ready to throw them in jail. More than 2,200 people were arrested during Spring Break '86, mostly on charges of disorderly conduct or violating a new ordinance against carrying open containers. A wall erected along the Strip separated sidewalk pedestrians from drivers on Atlantic Boulevard, eliminating the possibility that a drunk might wander into the street and pass out on your car hood. Capacity limits were enforced in hotels and bars. The fun appeared to be setting in Fort Lauderdale, and some bar owners and shopkeepers griped about police-state tactics and the effect of negative publicity on the Spring Break economy, which sustained many businesses on the Strip.

Before you get too misty-eyed over the demise of erotic banana-eating contests, consider that seven collegians died in Florida over Spring Break in 1986. Most were drunken balcony-divers. The city of Fort Lauderdale thereupon made a conscious decision to send Spring Break packing, and Daytona Beach eagerly picked up the beat. By 1989, Spring Break had been effectively driven from Fort Lauderdale, with a paltry 20,000 showing up that year.

"Fort Lauderdale is no longer the current Spring Break haven, and it will never be that Spring Break haven again," declared the executive director of the Broward County Tourist Development Council. The nail officially got pounded in the coffin of Spring Break when the Holiday Inn Oceanside and the Button were razed in the early '90s to make way for a parking lot. Even Daytona Beach eventually lost its appetite for hosting Spring Break for many of the same reasons that Fort Lauderdale shooed it away, and today the rites of spring are headquartered in Panama City Beach, on Florida's Panhandle.

MAP OF BROWARD COUNTY—PAGE 222

campaign. Only five of Florida's East Coast beach communities, all of them in Broward County, have applied for and been granted certification. The others are Deerfield Beach, Pompano Beach, Dania Beach, and Hollywood.

We've taken many morning jogs along Fort Lauderdale's beach. We've hung out at its bars till the early morning hours, too. At all times, especially since they've chased away the youthful cruisers and ambulatory lowlifes who used to haunt "the Strip," it is a pleasant place to be—one of the premier municipal beaches in the country.

The heart of Fort Lauderdale City Beach is along Atlantic Boulevard between Sunrise and Las Olas Boulevards. Areas to the north and south—up by Oakland Park Boulevard and down toward Port Everglades, respectively—are less dense with beachgoers. The beach is widest and most deserted (an ideal combination) by the jetties at Port Everglades. Parking and access are difficult unless you live in one of the condos that tower over the harbor, so the best bet is to park up around Las Olas and walk down to Harbor Beach. That is, if you want to get away from the crowds. We like people-watching, however, and Fort Lauderdale City Beach is an eyeful when packed.

In addition to its exemplary municipal beach, Fort Lauderdale has the added advantage of green space between the ocean and the Intracoastal Waterway along at least a portion of Atlantic Boulevard near Sunrise. **Hugh Taylor Birch State Park** preserves a corner of Old Florida in the form of a coastal hammock. It's used by walkers, joggers, in-line skaters, bicyclists, and nature lovers who come to recreate and sightsee on an unspoiled tract right in the heart of the city. It also creates a convenient opportunity to park and cross Atlantic Boulevard to the beach via a pedestrian underpass. The small (400 feet) strip of beach in front of the state park is overseen by the city, which is paid to provide lifeguard services, so all the usual city beach rules are in force here. That means no surfing while lifeguards are on duty (9 A.M.–5 P.M.).

On the south side of Sunrise Boulevard, just down from Hugh Taylor, is **Bonnet House** (900 North Birch Road, 954/563-5393), a 35-acre estate that formerly belonged to a couple of Floridian artists. The grounds and mansion have been preserved and can be toured Wednesday–Sunday ($9 for adults, $7 for children under 18). The stretch of beach in front of Bonnet House, known as Bonnet Beach, is a good place to get away from crowds in the Central Beach area while still being close to the Strip.

Shore Things

- **Bike/skate rentals:** Skate Shack, 2939 East Las Olas Boulevard, 954/768-9020.
- **Boat cruise:** Jungle Queen, Bahia Mar Marina, 801 Seabreeze Boulevard, Fort Lauderdale, 954/462-5596.
- **Dive shop:** Lauderdale Diver, Fort Lauderdale, 1334 Southeast 17th Street, 954/467-2822.
- **Ecotourism:** Anne Kolb Nature Center, West Lake Park, 751 Sheridan Street, Hollywood, 954/926-2415.
- **Fishing charters:** Fish Lauderdale, Fort Lauderdale, 954/764-8723.
- **Lighthouse:** Hillsboro Inlet Lighthouse, Hillsboro Inlet, Pompano Beach.
- **Marina:** Bahia Mar Marina, 801 Seabreeze Boulevard, Fort Lauderdale, 954/764-2233.
- **Pier:** Anglin's Pier, 2 Commercial Boulevard, Lauderdale by the Sea, 954/776-1690.
- **Rainy-day attraction:** Museum of Discovery and Science & Blockbuster 3D IMAX Theater, 401 Southwest 2nd Street, 954/467-6637.

MAP OF SOUTH FLORIDA—PAGE 177

- **Shopping/browsing:** Galleria Mall, 2414 East Sunrise Boulevard, Fort Lauderdale, 954/564-1015.
- **Surf shop:** Obsession Watersports, 1804 East Sunrise Boulevard, Fort Lauderdale, 954/467-0057.
- **Vacation rentals:** Beach Condos, 3300 East Oakland Park Boulevard, Fort Lauderdale, 954/564-1633.

Bunking Down

Just in case you're wondering, the average daily room rate in Fort Lauderdale came to $84.53 in the most recent year for which a figure was available. Of course, you'll pay more than that to stay on the beach. Basically, the prime oceanfront hotels on Fort Lauderdale's beach can be found along a two-mile stretch between Sunrise and Las Olas Boulevards.

The Sheraton chain claims two of the more prized locations in this desirable stretch, which is where most of the fun and the action can be found. The two Sheratons are known as the **Yankee Trader** (321 North Atlantic Boulevard, 954/467-1111, $$$) and the **Yankee Clipper** (1140 Seabreeze Boulevard, 954/524-5551, $$$). The former is in the thick of things at the beach's hopping midsection, while the latter sits directly on the beach farther south. If you're wondering how it can get away with that placement given the ordinance against building on the beach, the explanation is history. Sheraton's Yankee Clipper has sat on this spot for over four decades and was, in fact, the first oceanfront hotel in Lauderdale to be open year-round.

Don't worry that you'll be stuck in 40-year-old rooms at the Yankee Clipper, however. It's been refurbished and kept modern, and the rooms and appointments are first-rate. The hotel is like a miniature city, consisting of four towers and more than 500 rooms. There are pools all over the place. The main one has a poolside bar right off the beach. A concessionaire at the pool bar rents beach equipment—cabanas, chairs, boogie boards, and so on—and can arrange for more serious equipment rentals, like Waverunners and Jet Skis. They can even set you up for a parasailing adventure. The cost: $50 to go 300 feet in the air, $60 to go 600 feet in the air. Looks like a lot of fun from the vantage point of the shore, where we watched enviously, vowing to try it later on in the Keys. Both the Yankee Clipper and the Yankee Trader offer comparably cushy accommodations, book-ending Fort Lauderdale City Beach with nearly a thousand rooms between them.

Other beachfront hotels of the upscale chain variety can be found grouped together at the south end of the beach. These include the **Doubletree Oceanfront Hotel** (440 Seabreeze Boulevard, 954/524-8733, $$$), **Radisson Bahia Mar Beach Resort** (801 Seabreeze Boulevard, 954/764-2233, $$$), and **Marriott's Harbor Beach Resort** (3030 Holiday Drive, 954/525-4000, $$$$).

Toward the north end are the dependable middle-rank chain hotels: **Howard Johnson Ocean Edge** (700 North Atlantic Boulevard, 954/563-2451, $$), **Ramada Sea Club Resort** (619 North Atlantic Boulevard, 954/564-3211, $$$), and **Holiday Inn Fort Lauderdale Beach Galleria** (999 North Atlantic Boulevard, 954/563-5961, $$$). For location, right on Sunrise and Atlantic Boulevard, the Holiday Inn can't be beat. Its proximity to the beach, Hugh Taylor Birch State Park, and Galleria Mall makes it an ideal vacation base. The only downside is that the shops and bars directly behind it have grown a little seedy. Incidentally, the infamous Holiday Inn Oceanside, which functioned as a veritable Spring Break riot house and the site of the Button, the notorious and ribald party palace, exists no longer. It is, alas, a parking lot.

Affixed to Beach Place and rising

behind it is **Marriott's Beach Place Towers** (21 South Atlantic Boulevard, 954/525-4440, $$$$). The words "luxury," "exclusive," and "premium" are invoked a lot in describing this property, but we'd opt for "antiseptic" and "overpriced" instead, as it really seems as disconnected from the true let-it-hang-out experience of a beach vacation as you can get, despite the ready proximity.

Along the middle of the beach is a transitional mélange of small mom-and-pop motels (with rates as low as $35 a night in season) and new faux Art Deco hotels that charge a premium for their tony facades. The mom-and-pops are no doubt an endangered species as the upscaling mandate shifts into overdrive, and the sights and sounds of construction all along Atlantic Boulevard would seem to affirm that their days are numbered. That's not to say what's going up in their place is necessarily an improvement.

A couple of new arrivals have all their South Beach wannabe moves together, practically screaming "Art Deco" in an area that, to our knowledge, has no such history. There's something even more wrong with this picture: at ground level are Dunkin' Donuts, Baskin-Robbins, and McDonald's, lending an air of sugary, grease-soaked cheeseburger malaise to the whole affected enterprise.

If you'd prefer to stay off the beach, we'd recommend the **Riverside Hotel** (620 East Las Olas Boulevard, 954/467-0671, $$$$), located on the New River near the shops of Las Olas. The rooms and grounds are understated and elegant, and the dining room is one of the finest in Fort Lauderdale. Moreover, the beach is just a short drive east along Las Olas.

Coastal Cuisine

For an authentically fun dining experience as opposed to a mere meal, you can do no better than **15th Street Fisheries** (1900 Southeast 15th Street, 954/763-2777, $$$). The restaurant overlooks the water from the 15th Street Marina. Inside, it is adorned with the accoutrements of a working fishery. The host greets you by saying "We're glad you're here," and buttons worn by the wait staff reiterate the message. It's a friendly, bustling place where you're truly made to feel welcome. And the freshest seafood from Florida and elsewhere is served in creative, appetizing ways. You make your selections from a large blackboard menu carted to your table by a server who explains the choices and answers questions. Favorite items are highlighted with stars. From our perspective, the stars of the 15th Street Fisheries' menu include filet mignon of yellowfin tuna, a thick center cut which is marinated in a soy-ginger sauce and grilled (rare to medium-rare is best), and snapper sautéed in white wine, ginger, garlic, and soy and topped with scallions.

You can't go wrong with the simple preparations of the fresh catches that are local to Florida: mahimahi, snapper, and tuna. Among the appetizers, the house specialty is flying fish, which are flash-fried tableside and are sweet and tasty. Indeed, there is so much that is good on the menu at 15th Street Fisheries that you'll want to return again and again to try it all.

Shula's on the Beach (321 North Atlantic Boulevard, 954/355-4000, $$$$) is a recent arrival, having opened in November 1996 as part of Sheraton's Yankee Trader Resort. Like the several other Shula's that preceded it, steaks are their mainstay; indeed, they are rated among the very best steak houses in America. But this particular location has an expanded menu and a classy continental ambience that break the mold. In addition to the trusty steaks, there are a lot of good surf items to complement the turf on the menu. You can select from an array of fresh fish and such specialties as char-grilled Florida lobster, which we'd highly recommend.

The preparations bear a Cuban flair,

with fruit salsas and black beans being common accompaniments. Desserts include a lighter-than-air flourless chocolate cake and a frozen tropical fruit soufflé. All in all, if you're a football fan-cum-gourmet partial to training-table fare—you know, high-quality meat and potatoes—you won't be disappointed. We'd especially recommend the 24-ounce porterhouse steak, a thick, juicy slab of tasty Black Angus that would sate the heartiest carnivore.

Shula's joins a couple of other class acts in the area, including **East City Grille** (505 North Atlantic Avenue, 954/565-5569, $$$$) and **Mark's Las Olas** (1032 East Las Olas Boulevard, 954/463-1000, $$$$). A good "view" restaurant serving an eclectic menu of well-prepared dishes is **Yesterday's** (3001 East Oakland Park Boulevard, 954/561-4400, $$$), whose large dining room overlooks the Intracoastal Waterway. If you don't mind eating well before the sun sets, they have a cost-effective list of early-bird specials.

On the other side of the bridge is **Shooter's** (3003 Northeast 32nd Avenue, 954/566-2855, $$), a great hangout for downing drinks and watching boats that has a huge, affordable menu ranging from pizza to pasta and burgers to grilled grouper. Shooter's rocks and rolls like the wake from a Cigarette boat, so don't be surprised if you have to wait for a table, even during midweek.

We've also enjoyed excellent seafood dinners at the **Sea Watch** (6002 North Ocean Boulevard, 954/781-2200, $$) and the **Old Florida Seafood House** (1414 Northeast 26th Street, 954/566-1044, $$). The former is located right on the ocean in north Lauderdale, while the latter is situated in an old shopping center in an area known as Wilton Manors. Among the best seafood entrées we've ever had is stuffed Florida lobster, available at the Old Florida Seafood House and other restaurants around town at certain times of the year if harvesting is permitted. (The lobsters' numbers have been way down, thanks to overfishing.)

The Florida lobster tastes nothing like its Maine cousin. It's tender, almost flaky like a fish. For one thing, it lacks claws. It is very good, and in some ways we like it better than its more popular New England counterpart. When it's stuffed with scallops, crabmeat, and light breading, you'll be in warmwater lobster heaven.

In terms of freshwater fish, we'd be remiss not to mention **Catfish Dewey's** (4003 North Andrews Avenue, 954/566-5333, $$), a funky joint that serves up Southern-style home cookin' for about as cheap as you could hope to eat in Fort Lauderdale. Their all-you-can-eat specials, including fried catfish, are hard to beat. Catfish, hush puppies, cole slaw, sweet tea—Southerners like ourselves are in hog heaven at Catfish Dewey's, which also serves humongous quantities of ocean seafood at reasonable prices. And the local color—they get all kinds out here, and all seem to be in a boisterous good humor—comes free of charge.

At the other extreme is **Indigo** (620 East Olas Boulevard, 954/467-0045), in the Riverside Hotel. This is an extremely genteel hotel restaurant where the culinary emphasis is Southeast Asia. The room has been modeled after the Singapore Officers Club. The national dish of Bali, coconut-grilled chicken, is a specialty. We can highly commend the sesame-crusted rare tuna with wasabi, soy, coconut rice, and snow peas. Nasi Goreng is a gigantic bowl of Indian fried rice with chicken, shrimp, and pork—enough for two. Everything is good here, and the mingling of flavors borders on the sensual.

Another favorite Lauderdale restaurant of ours—there are so many—is **Bistro Double U** (3355 Northeast 33rd Street, 954/561-8789, $$$$). Located on a shop-lined side street that tourists rarely get to, this exceptional bistro is owned by two Germans,

MAP OF BROWARD COUNTY—PAGE 222

Uli and Udo (ergo "Double U"). The restaurant has been designed with precise Germanic attention to functionality: spotless and utilitarian, with complex dishes rendered by an extremely orderly kitchen that makes it all look simple. "What we do in this restaurant is 'eclectic,'" laughs chef Udo Mueller. "That's what they say in the papers." We were fortunate enough to get a cooking demonstration from the maestro, who prepared prosciutto-wrapped scallops, a salad with two dressings (white balsamic vinaigrette and curried tomato), a hearty portobello-mushroom risotto, and a brandied pumpkin pie for dessert. You'll drop about a $100 on dinner for two here and not regret it one bit.

At this point, we're slightly flustered, because the Fort Lauderdale restaurant scene is so extensive. An entire book could be written about dining out in Fort Lauderdale, and it would have to be updated a couple times a year since the scene is so changeable, with old restaurants folding and new ones coming along all the time. With all the evolution on the beachfront, the pace of change has accelerated even more furiously in recent years. There are now 3,500 restaurants in Broward County, most of them in the Fort Lauderdale metropolitan area. Suffice it to say that you cannot and will not go hungry in Fort Lauderdale—unless indecision drives you to starvation, that is.

Night Moves

Nighttime is the right time in Fort Lauderdale. If you can't have fun in Fort Lauderdale after dark, you can't have fun, period. The club scene here is not the most original in the world, we must admit, borrowing liberally from Southern California and South Miami Beach. But it is lively and it does go late—as late as 4:30 A.M. If you're a night owl, you'll be hooting and hollering. You can get your ya-ya's out under a neon rainbow that goes down only when the sun comes up.

The most libidinous party spot in town that isn't a bona fide strip joint is a surf bar-cum-dance club called **Baja Beach Club** (3339 North Federal Highway, 954/563-7889). It's just a few moves shy of being an out-and-out orgy, with bartenders simulating sex acts while serving shooters with names like Blow Job (Kahlua, Bailey's, whipped cream), Leg Spreader (vodka, Peach Schnapps, cranberry juice), and 1-800-ME-NASTY (151, Rumpleminze, Jagermeister). If you haven't by now turned the page in disgust, we'll continue with a blow-by-blow description of a night out at Baja. You pay a cover ($7 on weekends), walk upstairs, and enter a world that is like an X-rated pinball game with all the buzzers going off at once.

The motif seems to be an East Coast surfer dude's conception of a Southern California beach bar, juiced up with a lot of incongruous dance club affectations. While the end result is about as inauthentic as it is loud, the hybrid does have a certain crazy logic to it. Whatever they're doing here seems to work: people shed their inhibitions and get down like party maniacs.

Girls in bikinis that appear to be made of dental floss dispense drinks at portable stations. How can you refuse to buy a Corona when a nubile blonde Playmate-of-the-Month candidate wearing barely more than a smile is doing the asking? They're referred to as "beer tub girls," in case you're wondering. One in particular left us slack jawed and speechless. On a scale from one to 10, she was a 12. Not to be outdone are the guys, who appear to be clones of the SoCal surf punk icon: billowy, bottle-blond Fabio-style hair, well-toned pecs, and washboard abs, stripped down to bike pants.

Girls and guys in various states of undress circulate about the noisy, multi-level club with $3 shots in fluorescent test tubes. Behind the bars, the bartenders cavort even more lewdly than the mixologists in that unintentionally hilarious Tom Cruise flick

Cocktail. Typically they wear little more than cutoff jeans, with their first names scrawled on their chest. Now and then they strip to their boxers, stick cone-shaped pieces of papers in the fly, and set fire to them, thrusting their pelvises over the bar to allow girls to light cigarettes. On occasion one will stop mixing drinks and recline on the bar, covering his torso in whipped cream while female patrons suck it off with straws. We couldn't make this stuff up.

They don't miss a dirty trick at Baja. Patrons are strapped inside a gyroscope contraption and spun around. Off in one corner, stress massages are given and handmade jewelry is sold. A raised platform is reserved for those who want to shake their booty for all the world to see. The music is a nonstop blare of high-energy dance music and hard rock, ranging from Cheap Trick to Metallica, with the occasional campy bone tossed to the crowd, such as "YMCA," which invariably ups the energy level to an arm-waving crescendo. Baja can best be described as a three-ring circus, with Fellini, Rabelais, and Larry Flynt as ringleaders. If you want to blow it all out, Baja is the place to come. It's the end of the world as we know it—but we feel fine.

One thing we'll say for South Florida: Multiculturalism is a way of life, with the races and ethnicities easily intermingling on the streets and in the clubs. The under-30 crowd seems refreshingly color blind. No matter the color of your skin or country of origin, age, gender, or the language you speak, you'll fit right in, because everyone's a freak in this subtropical urban melting pot.

Take **Bermuda Triangle** (219 South Atlantic Boulevard, 954/779-2544), for instance. That is where we wound up one evening around 2 A.M. with what seemed like every insomniac in South Florida. Bermuda Triangle is right by the beach on Atlantic Boulevard at Las Olas Boulevard. Its main ballroom is so huge that a crowd of a few thousand can mill around with room to spare. The band we heard one night rotated lead singers—first a black male, then a Latino female, and finally a dreadlocked Jamaican bloke. There may have been more who came out later, for all we know. The music reflects and appeals to pan-ethnic tastes.

From our roaming around South Florida in general and places like Bermuda Triangle in particular, we've detected the emergence of a hybrid, polyglot culture that has progressed beyond racial divides to de facto equality. If people choose to party together on their own time, they must want to be together, and we'll happily raise our glasses to more scenarios like the ones we saw at Bermuda Triangle and other clubs around Fort Lauderdale. By the way, Bermuda Triangle stays open until 4 A.M. on weekends. The official capacity is 1,877, and upward of 4,000 might pass through on a given evening.

This just scratches the surface of Fort Lauderdale nightlife. If you're looking for something on the Intracoastal, try **Shooter's** (3003 Northeast 32nd Avenue, 954/566-2855) or **Yesterday's** (3001 East Oakland Park Boulevard, 954/561-4400), restaurants with lively bar scenes that sit on the east and west side of the waterway, respectively, off Oakland Park Boulevard. Shooter's is particularly busy. There are other bars close by in this under-the-bridge area, too. Park on the street, but be sure to stuff the meter (it's enforced 24 hours) and cruise from one joint to another, as we have done on many occasions. Our rambles through this area have yielded everything from free hot dogs at a sports bar during Monday Night Football to a riotous New Year's Eve at Shooter's, with wildly lit boats parked four deep on the Intracoastal and wait staff gamely hopping from one boat to the next with drink and food orders.

Squeeze (2 South New River Drive W, 954/522-2151) is an alternative-oriented club, while the **Poor House** (110 Southwest 3rd Avenue, 954/522-5145) doles out the blues. Back on the beach, places like the **Elbo Room** (241 North Atlantic Boulevard, 954/463-4615), the **Quarterdeck** (1541 Cordova Road, 954/524-6163), and **Sloop John B** (239 South Atlantic Boulevard, 954/463-3633) rock loudly into the wee hours. You might hear anything from a bar band playing "Mustang Sally" to a deejay spinning rave, trance, techno, hip-hop, or whatever else is fresh. Just case the joints (they're all within a few blocks of each other) till you hear something you like and then wander in for a while. One thing's for certain: The sun may set but the fun never stops in Fort Lauderdale.

Contact Information

Greater Fort Lauderdale Chamber of Commerce, 512 Northeast 3rd Avenue, Fort Lauderdale, FL 33301; 954/462-6000; website: www.ftlchamber.com

Greater Fort Lauderdale Convention and Visitors Bureau, 1850 Eller Drive, Suite 303, Fort Lauderdale, FL 33316; 954/765-4466 or 800/22SUNNY; website: www.sunny.com

John U. Lloyd Beach State Park

John U. Lloyd Beach State Park is a sizable barrier-island beach with a lot of unlovely civilization lying over its proverbial shoulder. Strolling the beach or fishing from the jetty at its tip keeps you mindful of that fact as planes streak in to nearby Fort Lauderdale International Airport and the sound of vehicular traffic and industrial noise at Port Everglades intrudes upon the calm. It makes for a weird real-life collage, with New Florida superimposed upon Old Florida.

> **9 John U. Lloyd Beach State Park**
>
> 
>
> **Location:** north end of North Ocean Boulevard, a quarter mile north of Dania Beach Boulevard, in Dania
> **Parking/fees:** $4 entrance fee per vehicle ($2 for single driver and car)
> **Hours:** 8 A.M. to sunset
> **Facilities:** concessions, lifeguards, restrooms, picnic tables, and showers
> **Contact:** John U. Lloyd Beach State Park, 954/923-2833

The 2.3-mile beach fronts emerald Atlantic waters, behind which lie a tidal creek, coastal hammock, and mangrove swamp. The beach looks like the sort of fantasy isle on whose shores you'd hope to land if your ship went down in the South Pacific. A nature trail loops around the island's densely forested interior. While it is a lovely and instructional walk, the Barrier Island Trail tends to disappear underfoot in an obscuring carpet of Australian pine needles and sea grape leaves, so pay attention or you might lose your way.

Up at the north end, a rock jetty is hugely popular with anglers. From here you look over the inlet that serves as the entranceway to Port Everglades, with the south end of Fort Lauderdale City Beach visible directly across the water. If you hang out for any time at all, you'll likely see a huge freighter being escorted into port by tugboats.

Students of wetlands may be interested in the man-made red mangrove swamp on the west side of the park, which is a mitigation site for acreage destroyed during the expansion of Port Everglades in the late 1980s. Manatees live in the waterways and sea turtles nest on the beaches. Lloyd is a vital sliver of vanishing South Florida habitat for these endangered creatures.

The 250-acre park houses a concession stand (Coco's Cafe), where food and drink are sold. Canoes and kayaks are rented at another close-by site. The entrance fee at Lloyd is $4 per car ($2 if there's a single occupant). It is money well spent if you're looking to find an oasis of calm in the midst of citified cacophony.

Contact Information

John U. Lloyd Beach State Park, 6503 North Ocean Drive, Dania Beach, FL 33004; 954/923-2833; website: www.myflorida.com

Dania Beach

Dania Beach, Hollywood, and Hallandale Beach are a winning trifecta of communities that escape some of the worst aspects of the South Florida megalopolis. They lie off to the side of the manic I-95 corridor, literally nestled between Fort Lauderdale and Miami like undisturbed loggerhead turtle nests.

Dania Beach (pop. 18,500) claims the novelty of having been the first incorporated city in Broward County. In some respects, little has changed here in the last 30 years but the name. Apparently desirous of the imprimatur conferred by the magical word "beach," the community of Dania officially became Dania Beach in November 1998. They promote it as "a dynamic waterfront community," but that's really a stretch. Largely a quiet community of older citizens, it is also the home of Dania Jai Lai, where this gambling sport—touted as the world's fastest—is played. Interestingly, Florida Atlantic University's Institute for Ocean and System Engineering is located on the Intracoastal Waterway in Dania Beach at a place called "Sea Tech." More to the point of this book, Dania Beach is home of John U. Lloyd Beach State Park (see section in this chapter), nearly two and a half miles of pristine barrier island that ranks with Florida's finest, as well as its own modestly likable city beach.

Beaches

Dania Beach, located at the end of Dania Beach Boulevard, has gotten a facelift in the last couple of years. The old wooden pier has been replaced with a concrete pier. They've been sewing wild oats—sea oats, that is—to help build up the dune structure. The beach has been renourished and widened. Access for the elderly has been improved with the addition of ramps to the beach. Dania Beach boasts a pleasant and attractive public beach that draws elderly locals and a public pier that attracts rabid anglers. Fishing insomniacs also love Dania Pier, since it never closes.

Bunking Down

Small, nonfranchised motels along U.S. 1

10 Dania Beach

Location: Dania Beach Boulevard at Beach Road (Highway A1A) in Dania

Parking/fees: metered parking lot. Residents can purchase a $15 annual parking sticker at Dania City Hall cashier's window.

Hours: sunrise to 10 P.M.

Facilities: concessions, lifeguards, restrooms, picnic tables, and showers

Contact: City of Dania Parks and Recreation Department, 954/921-8700, ext. 370

are what you'll find in Dania Beach, which despite its unassuming charm is probably not the first place that would enter our minds to book a Florida beach vacation. Places like the **Dania Beach Hotel** (180 East Dania Beach Boulevard, 954/923-5895, $) and the **Blue Ocean Motel** (480 East Dania Beach Boulevard, 954/921-2775, $) are unfancy but affordable.

Coastal Cuisine

We walked into the **Fish Grill** (103 East Dania Beach Boulevard, 954/923-1001, $$) knowing nothing more about it than there sure were a lot of cars in the parking lot. Plenty of bodies packed the lobby, too, waiting to be seated in the dining rooms. We soon found out why. Between 4 P.M. and 7 P.M., two can eat for $18.95. The list of eligible entrées included swordfish, flounder, strip steak, and about two dozen other entrées. The Fish Grill specializes in charcoal-grilled seafood, and this is definitely the way to go. Skewered, chargrilled swordfish and sea bass are particularly good. The early-bird deal also includes soup or salad, vegetable, drink, and dessert. It's a real bargain in these parts, and real fine food, too—especially if you let them grill some fish for you.

Contact Information

Dania Beach Chamber of Commerce, 102 West Dania Beach Boulevard, Dania Beach, FL 33004; 954/926-2323; website: www.greaterdania.org

Hollywood

Though it pales in comparison to the publicity routinely heaped upon its more famous neighbors, Hollywood (pop. 127,600) is a full-fledged city with five miles of sandy beach. It boasts a two-mile beach walkway (called the "Broadwalk"), and roughly 50 street-end public beach accesses. It is a great beach and, from the perspective of the outside world, a well-kept secret.

Maybe it's the name that throws people off. Hollywood evokes long avenues of fantasy and wealth, swimming pools, movie stars, scandals, decadence, and cellular phones. Florida's Hollywood is a different scene altogether. It does have the long avenue—namely, Hollywood Boulevard. It was the first thing built by John W. Young, a California land speculator who initially planned the city as a resort for the rich. This palm-lined chariot track ends at the Hollywood Beach Resort Hotel, which he intended as the castle that would house his glittering Gatsbys. But, after an initial burst of popularity, Hollywood fell from favor, playing second fiddle to its glitzier neighbors, Miami Beach and Fort Lauderdale. In recent decades, Hollywood seems to have fallen off the maps of American beachgoers altogether.

This is too bad, because Hollywood is an understated, appealing city with low-density residences, lots of open space, and a neighborly feel to it (though Hollywood does deal with the ravages of the drug trade, like its larger neighbors). Few attempts have been made to give Hollywood a designer makeover, as pro-development forces have met stiff resistance from those who would maintain the status quo. Lately, the debate appears to be taking on a more heated urgency as Hollywood has gone fishing for a facelift. Certain projects, such as the razing and rebuilding of the old Diplomat Hotel, have turned out splendidly. Others, such as Diamond on the Beach, have been foundering for years. It was hoped that Diamond on the Beach—a hotel, shopping, and parking project to be built on the city of Hollywood's beachfront Casino property—would become the hub in the revitalization of the Central Beach area. But after

MAP OF SOUTH FLORIDA—PAGE 177

years of bickering and legal battling, Diamond on the Beach remains on the drawing board. Leasing public land to private developers so that they may construct a for-profit luxury hotel and retail shopping arcade seems to us to be a pretty a sorry way to manage the environment.

A few things do strike us as, well, odd. The population breakdown, for instance. Hollywood is an old city, 58 percent of whose population is over 45. This tells us that the young are inevitably born to run when they come of age. Also, this sizable city does not even have its own daily newspaper, relying on the *Miami Herald* and Fort Lauderdale's *Sun-Sentinel* for its daily dose of bad news and goings-on in its own backyard. There is something distinctly ostrich-like about Hollywood.

This suspicion was corroborated rather zealously by a local businessman on the Broadwalk. The city, he explained, is run by an entrenched older establishment who are way behind the times. The Broadwalk is jokingly referred to as the "Deathwalk" by younger townspeople. And the beach is considered a "No Beach," as in, "No, you can't do this" and "No, you can't do that."

He recounted a tale about two young Germans who'd inquired, in broken English, where they might sunbathe topless. He told them to drop their tops behind a nearby dune, where they'd be discreetly out of sight of families and those who might take offense. All went well until they entered the water. Some old fogey got bent out of shape (probably had an erotic thought for the first time in decades), and the cops were called. Words were exchanged with the fräuleins. Bikini tops were donned. All was safe in Hollywood once again.

"This beach hasn't changed in 30 years!" the fellow concluded in frustration. This, of course, is not altogether a bad thing, from our perspective. There are beach towns on both coasts that would happily cut a deal with the devil to be like they were 30 years ago, before the beach-defiling big-bucks developers got hold of them. Hollywood, even now, is anything but paralyzing. In fact, the beachfront was a delight to our sore eyes. Most of the motels are mom-and-pops, located right behind the dunes with easy access to an egalitarian beach. We couldn't have asked for much more than what greeted us on a recent day: a perfect cloudless afternoon; a wide, sparsely inhabited beach; and cheap eats, cheap thrills, and cheap novelty postcards.

Other nationalities have taken notice. Canadians love Hollywood. During Florida's blistering summers, a good chunk of South America shows up in Hollywood for a winter respite. Some friendly dreadlocked Jamaicans were hanging around the Central Beach bandshell, and we bantered with them about the laid-back appeal and multiethnic makeup of Hollywood Beach.

A local lifeguard told us that Hollywood is "on the brink of making some big changes." The debate that has been raging of late pits advocates of change against those who would maintain the status quo. As much as the restless young would like to see Hollywood become a more vibrant place, the evolution ought to proceed slowly and surely so as not to screw up the many blessings they already enjoy—whether they realize it or not.

Beaches

Hollywood Beach runs for roughly six miles, from Balboa Street to the Hallandale border. Just turn down any street in town and you're bound to find a way onto the beach. Metered street parking (25 cents for 15 minutes) is the name of the game, though there are fee parking garages in the area. One is on Johnson Street, which is at the center of the Hollywood Beach scene. Lifeguards are stationed along the 2.5-mile Broadwalk, which runs from Sheridan Street (at North Ocean Park) south. This asphalt promenade is so wide (27 feet) that lines demarcating lanes have been painted on it.

MAP OF BROWARD COUNTY—PAGE 222

Informally, **Hollywood Beach** is broken down into "north," "central," and "south" areas. North Beach is the most pristine, with fewer condos and a more natural look. Central Beach is the site of the Broadwalk, with its shops, restaurants and watering holes. South Beach is more built up, with motels and condos. Surfing is

Detonating the Population Bomb in Florida

That explosion you just heard was the population bomb. The fuse on the bomb was lit years ago, when Florida's population began swelling during the winter with part-time "snowbirds" from up North. But the bomb didn't really explode until the 1990s.

Curiously, Hurricane Andrew, which struck South Florida on August 23, 1992, and did $14 billion worth of damage, did not reverse this trend. It did not even slow it down. If anything, the migration went into overdrive. This is true for two reasons. First, the federal government paid to rebuild much of the coastal development destroyed by Andrew through its "emergency relief" program. Secondly, the state of Florida has taken nearly a decade to draft a new building code, after learning that 40 percent percent of Andrew's damage was preventable with proper construction and inspection. In yet another example of how citizens don't matter as much as campaign supporters, the state code was drafted to be acceptable to business interests—the real estate and construction industries—as well as pro-business governor and presidential helpmate Jeb Bush. Consequently, the code is generally regarded as a joke to activists.

According to census figures, Florida is growing at a rate of 750 people per day. As a result, the state loses 450 acres of forest, destroys 328 acres of farmland, and depletes its water supply by another 110,000 gallons every single day. Though many counties pay lip service to implementing "growth plans," the state's current population of 15 million is projected to top 90 million in 100 years. That, of course, assumes the planet can survive another century like the last one.

In late summer 2000, *USA Today* released figures about the population boom along the Atlantic coast and Gulf of Mexico between 1990 and 1998. Included among the stats is the astonishing fact that one in seven Americans (41 million) live in a county on the Atlantic or Gulf coasts. No county in Florida lost population during the last decade. To get more specific:

- Broward County added 140,891 residents, an 18 percent increase.
- Palm Beach County added 118,781, a 23 percent increase.
- Pasco County added 56,360 residents, a 32 percent increase.
- Lee County added 53,471 residents, a 19 percent increase.
- Sarasota County added 38,438 residents, a 33 percent increase.
- Collier County added 36,188 residents, a 29 percent increase.
- Hernando County added 31,772 residents, a 33 percent increase.
- St. Johns County added 30,044 residents, a 35 percent increase.
- Manatee County added 26,887 residents, a 36 percent increase.
- Flagler County added 19,472 residents, a 33 percent increase.

Map of South Florida—Page 177

permitted between up north by Frankl and Meade Streets and on the south end between Georgia Street and Azalea Terrace. Boaters can launch nonmotorized craft here as well. Three reefs lie offshore at distances of a hundred yards, one-half mile, and one and a half miles.

While the scene resembles the friendlier aspects of the Jersey Shore, it is also afflicted with, as stated above, a "No Beach" mentality. While the list of things one is forbidden to do is long, most of it is commonsensical (no guns, no fighting, no funeral pyres, no macarena dancing on Sunday). Some items, however, make little sense at all. Take, for example, the ban on in-line skating and bicycling from December 15 to April 15. What are they thinking? Presumably, this is the dictate of Hollywood's atrophied city council.

If you're coming for a full day, the best bet is to park at **North Beach Park**, a county-run facility at the north end of the Broadwalk. You can wander the beach or Broadwalk from here without worrying about pumping quarters into a meter. The beach itself belongs to the city of Hollywood, while the foliage and park grounds belong to the county. This 56-acre park has a picnic area with grills and a paved bike path.

A short distance inland, along the east bank of the Intracoastal Waterway, is a diamond off the beach called West Lake Park. This is one of the largest urban parks we've ever seen, occupying 1,500 acres and boasting a lake with a 2.5-mile shoreline. West Lake Park has hiking trails, the ecotourism-minded Anne Kolb Nature Center, boat rentals, and a vast expanse of lovely green acres as far as the eye can see.

Bunking Down

One of the stars in Hollywood is the **Holiday Inn Sunspree Resort** (2711 South Ocean Drive, 954/923-8700, $$$). In recent years, the Sunspree has undergone a $7 million facelift, and the cheerful, lively staff makes a striking counterpoint to the dowdy dictates of City Hall. The reasonable room tariff includes access to a large swimming pool, health club, and the beach right out back.

You also have the option of stepping back into the Hollywood of yesteryear by staying at the **Hollywood Beach Resort Hotel** (101 North Ocean Drive, 954/921-0990, $$), the crown jewel of the city's first incarnation as a resort. Built in 1925, and modeled along the Mediterranean lines of Addison Mizner's Palm Beach digs, the Hollywood Beach Resort Hotel quick-

⓫ North Beach Park

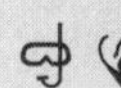  

Location: 3501 North Ocean Drive (Highway A1A), at the east end of Sheridan Street in Hollywood
Parking/fees: $5 entrance fee per vehicle on weekends ($3 after 2 P.M.); $3 entrance fee per vehicle on weekdays ($2 after 2 P.M.)
Hours: 8 A.M.–7:30 P.M. (6 P.M. after time change to EST)
Facilities: concessions, lifeguards, restrooms, picnic tables, and showers
Contact: North Beach Park, 954/926-2444

⓬ Hollywood Beach

Location: Hollywood Beach runs for 4.5 miles along Ocean Drive (Highway A1A) from Balboa Street to the Hallandale border. The central area is where Johnson Street meets the Broadwalk.
Parking/fees: metered street parking and fee parking garages at Hollywood Boulevard and Johnson Street
Hours: 24 hours
Facilities: concessions, lifeguards, restrooms, picnic tables, and showers
Contact: Hollywood Beach Safety Department, 954/921-3423

ly became a winter playground for status-conscious northerners. While its fortunes have ebbed and flowed with the world's economy (it has always been popular with an international clientele), the place is putting its best foot forward these days.

The Diplomat Hotel, for decades the "crown jewel of Hollywood Beach," closed its doors in 1991. The building stood idle for nearly a decade and was demolished in April 2000. However, they're building an all-new **Diplomat Resort Tower** (3355 South Ocean Drive, 954/457-2000, $$$$) on the same site. Scheduled to open in early 2002, the 39-story Diplomat will have 1,000 rooms, making it the largest and tallest hotel in Broward County. Giant outdoor pools, five restaurants in the hotel, and a retail shopping area behind it (with ten more restaurants) will make the Diplomat Resort Tower a city within a city.

That's not all there is to the Diplomat story. In addition to the beachside tower, there's the **Diplomat Resort and Country Club** (501 Diplomat Parkway, Hallendale Beach, 954/457-2000, $$$$), a golf resort and world-class spa on the Intracoastal Waterway, about a mile inland. This part of the Diplomat complex is open now, and if golf is your bag or a spa treatment is foremost on your agenda, you should definitely check out this property. The Plumbers and Pipefitters Pension Fund owns the entire Diplomat operation, so if nothing else you can rest assured that the showers and toilets will work. The two parts of the Diplomat Resort will be linked by a shuttle system, making it easy to get to the beach from the country club (and vice versa).

Coastal Cuisine

When a city's chamber of commerce includes a Burger King and an IHOP among its lists of recommended restaurants—as is the case in Hollywood—you have no reason to expect culinary wonders. Hollywood is indeed rife with mediocrity on the food front, and we wondered if this might be partly owing to so many fixed-income, bargain-desperate natives and visitors. Still, if you look hard enough, a decent meal might come your way.

Several seafood emporiums occupy the west side of North Ocean Drive (Highway A1A), overhanging the Intracoastal Waterway. They are institutional-sized facilities, catering simultaneously to the boating, dining, and party-cruising crowds. The dining halls are like banquet rooms that accentuate the waterfront setting. We snagged a decent seafood platter at **Martha's Tropical Grille** (6024 North Ocean Drive, 954/923-5444, $$), a second-floor dining room that's locally famous for its Floridian and Caribbean cuisine and its Sunday brunches. There's also a supper club with a different menu on the ground level, where tourists can follow their broiled snapper with dancing to swingin' sounds.

Night Moves

Only curiosity would bring us out to Hollywood Beach after dark. We were fascinated by the number of ethnic pubs down by the water. At the Johnson Street access, for instance, we came upon the **12 O'Clock High Lounge** (314 Johnson Street, 954/921-4938), which featured the musical talents of one Pierre Poirier. Just down from there was **Frenchie's Cafe** (300 Johnson Street, 954/923-7228), with an all-Gallic menu. Many street ends along the Hollywood Beach Broadwalk offer cozy saloons that cater to a particular clientele. For coffeehouse aficionados, two gathering places in close proximity are **Now Art Cafe** (1820 South Young Circle, 954/922-0506) and **Cafe Latte** (1840 South Young Circle, 954/926-6644).

Contact Information

Greater Hollywood Chamber of Commerce, 330 North Federal Highway, Hollywood, FL 33020; 954/923-4000 or 800/231-5562; website: www.hollywoodchamber.org

MAP OF SOUTH FLORIDA—PAGE 177

Hallandale Beach

The last sand bunker in Broward County belongs to Hallandale Beach (pop. 31,500). This spot was formerly known as Hallandale, with the "Beach" having officially been added to the town name in November 2000. While Dania Beach has jai alai and Hollywood is Florida's greyhound racing capital, Hallandale Beach is home to **Gulfstream Park** (901 South Federal Highway, 954/456-1515), where the horses run. The Florida Derby and other race events are held here from mid-January to early May. Lately, Hallandale Beach is an under-construction madhouse along the beachfront, with construction dust, noise, and inconvenience intruding upon the calm as condo towers go up. The most visually striking thing about Hallandale is its water tower, a rainbow-hued structure that resembles a teed-up golf ball. Since you couldn't miss this landmark if you tried, you won't miss Hallandale Beach's public beach, either, because its parking lot is located at the base of the colorful tower.

Beaches

Hallandale City Beach is a two-part affair. The north and south ends are each 300 feet long, with another football field's worth of private property separating them. **North Beach** is located where Hallandale Beach Boulevard meets Ocean Drive (Highway A1A) at the water tower. The lot's 140 metered parking spaces form an "L" around a great little outdoor bar, the Beachside Cafe. It's really a hut with a tentlike extension, serving everything from fast food to fish dinners (alcoholic beverages, too). Its sunbaked simplicity is a snapshot of what fun used to be like in South Florida. Five walkways carry you from a picnic area and playground over the healthy dunes. A lifeguard stand oversees the scene. Chairs, cabanas, and umbrellas can be rented. **South Beach** offers more of the same, the main difference being that the food concession is more rudimentary—a trailer that dispenses basic fare like burgers, chips, and sodas.

Contact Information

Hallandale Beach Chamber of Commerce, 1117 East Hallandale Beach Boulevard, Hallandale Beach, FL 33009; 954/454-0541; website: www.ci.hallandale.fl.us

⓭ Hallandale Beach (North Beach)

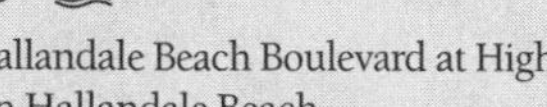

Location: Hallandale Beach Boulevard at Highway A1A, in Hallandale Beach
Parking/fees: metered parking lot
Hours: 6 A.M.–10 P.M.
Facilities: concessions, lifeguards, restrooms, picnic tables, and showers
Contact: Hallandale Parks and Recreation Department, 954/457-1452

⓮ Hallandale Beach (South Beach)

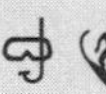  

Location: just south of Hallandale Beach Boulevard, along Highway A1A in Hallandale Beach
Parking/fees: metered parking lot (75 cents per hour)
Hours: 6 A.M.–10 P.M.
Facilities: concessions, lifeguards, restrooms, picnic tables, and showers
Contact: Hallandale Parks and Recreation Department, 954/457-1452

Miami/Dade County

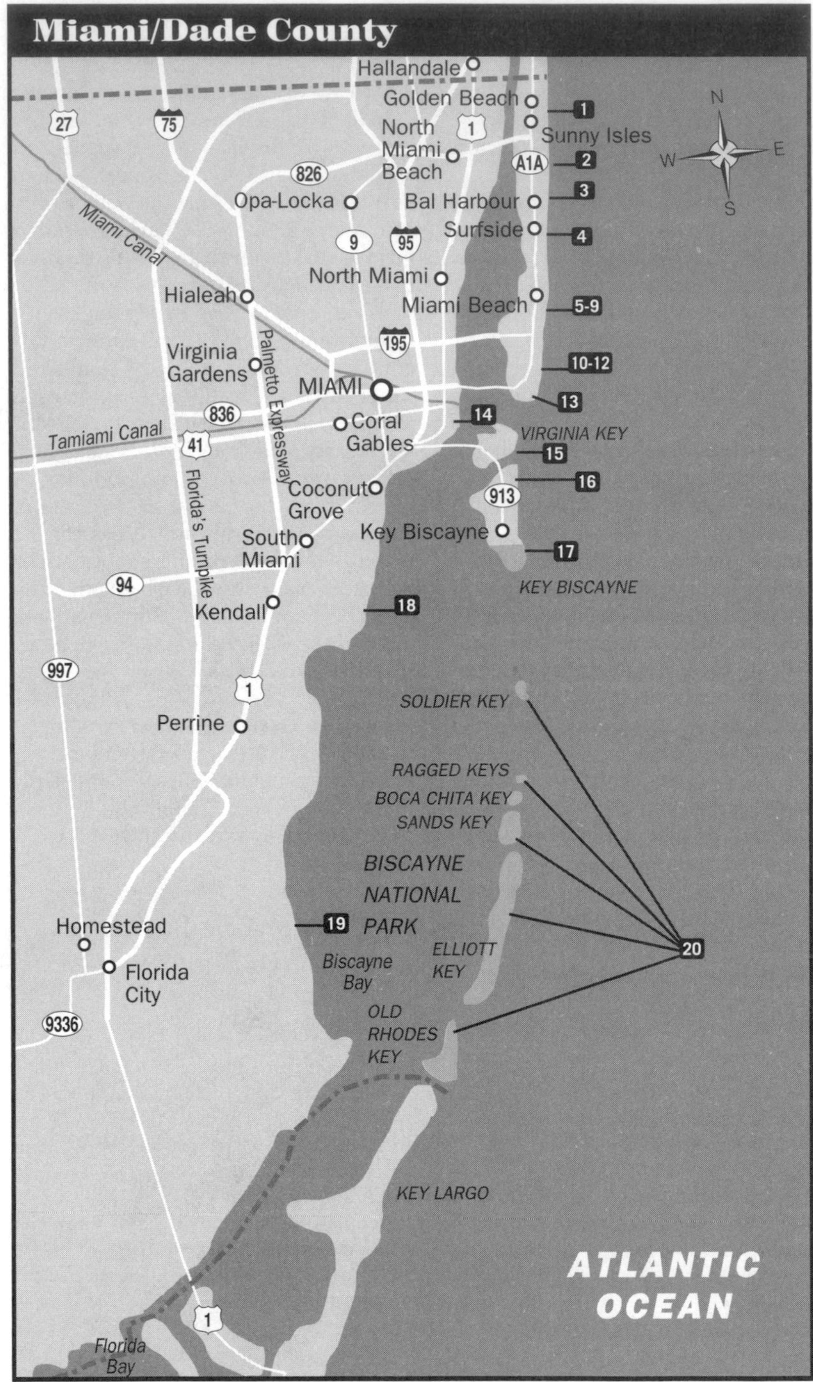

Hallandale
Golden Beach
North Miami Beach
Sunny Isles
Opa-Locka
Bal Harbour
Surfside
North Miami
Miami Canal
Hialeah
Miami Beach
Virginia Gardens
Palmetto Expressway
MIAMI
Coral Gables
Tamiami Canal
Florida's Turnpike
VIRGINIA KEY
Coconut Grove
South Miami
Key Biscayne
KEY BISCAYNE
Kendall
Perrine
SOLDIER KEY
RAGGED KEYS
BOCA CHITA KEY
SANDS KEY
BISCAYNE NATIONAL PARK
Homestead
Florida City
Biscayne Bay
ELLIOTT KEY
OLD RHODES KEY
KEY LARGO
ATLANTIC OCEAN
Florida Bay
N
S
E
W
27
75
1
826
A1A
9
95
195
836
41
913
94
997
9336
1
2
3
4
5-9
10-12
13
14
15
16
17
18
19
20

Miami/Dade County

MIAMI/DADE COUNTY

The county of Dade and the city of Miami have been much in the news these past few years as they lurch from one crisis to another. More than any other American metropolis, the fuel that powers Miami consists of equal parts controversy and catastrophe. Miami's woes are all the more reason to make your way east via any number of causeways onto Dade County's exceptional array of beaches. From Sunny Isles Beach and Surfside in the north to the southernmost tip of Key Biscayne, Dade has more than 20 miles of ocean frontage. Admittedly, it's not always paradise by the sea. Sure, there's scarcely a break in the oceanfront skyline, traffic on Collins Avenue is as dependably hellacious as an afternoon thunderstorm, and the beach is as artificial as a plastic flamingo. Oddly enough, that is all part of Miami Beach's peculiar charm. Nowadays, Miami Beach is a major player in Florida's tourist economy. The locus for much of the attention is that international hotbed of sun, sand, sin, and revelry known as South Beach.

MAP OF SOUTH FLORIDA—PAGE 177

Golden Beach

The first barnacle on Dade County's oceanfront hull is Golden Beach, a wealthy residential municipality within the Greater Miami sprawl, 11 miles north of Miami Beach, near the Broward County line on Highway A1A (Ocean Boulevard). Golden Beach (pop. 845), stretching from Haulover Park to 194th Street, picks up the same sandy beach left off by Hallandale (in southern Broward County), although it's lacking in the latter's friendliness. One reason for Golden Beach's sour mood may be that the community was embroiled in and ultimately lost a protracted legal battle with neighboring Sunny Isles Beach and Miami Beach.

Actually, the town's real nemesis is the U.S. Army Corps of Engineers, and it has every right to be steamed over the latter's dredging of the ocean floor 1.5 miles off their shoreline. Opponents were concerned that the process would damage, if not destroy, sensitive coral reefs nearby. Golden Beach contended that the Corps ignored the hired experts (a trademark of the Corps at the shore). The imbroglio was referred to as "South Florida's first big sand war." A three-year federal court battle ended in late 1996 when a U.S. district court judge ruled that the Corps could proceed. Golden Beach filed for another injunction but it was denied in February 1997, and the dredging began the following month. A dredge the size of a football field worked night and day for two months, pumping sand down to Sunny Isles Beach and Miami Beach's eroded shores. More than 700,000 cubic yards of sand were taken from a site two miles offshore from Golden Beach.

While we side with grumpy Golden Beach on this one, we can't help but wonder whether their concern for the environment was motivated by anything more than self-interest. Would they, in other words, have been as concerned if some

Condo Names We'd Like to See

From Jupiter to Miami, South Florida's Gold Coast is a domino line of high-rises, many of whose units are part-time residences (i.e., empty nine months a year). While they all look depressingly similar to our nature-loving eyes, they desperately try to distinguish themselves from their neighbors by putting on airs with a rogue's gallery of fancy names. Since construction of these monoliths never ends, no matter how bottomed-out the market gets, we propose the following names for the high-rises and "luxury communities" of tomorrow:

- Captains Folly
- Checkpointe
- Chicanery
- Dune Eraser
- Eau de Nerve
- The Effrontery
- Egrets Regret
- Eroding Sands
- Fools Caprice
- Greased Palms
- Hubris Harbour
- L'Arrogance
- Loggerheads Demise
- Looters Retreat
- Mortgage Deux
- Nature's End
- Royale Paine
- Silos By The Sea
- Swindler's List
- Titanique
- Uneasy Winds
- Valet Halla
- Vanishing Acres
- Wronged Terns

MAP OF MIAMI/DADE COUNTY—PAGE 252

other beach community's sand banks were siphoned (and coral reef destroyed) to pump up their own sagging shoreline? What is needed, obviously, is a sane approach to coastal development and beach renourishment so that communities are not pitted against one another, with coral reefs and other natural systems being the ultimate losers.

In October 2000, Golden Beach was tossed a bone of sorts when the town was offered an artificial reef as compensation for all of the sand that had been dredged and placed elsewhere.

Beaches

The unfriendly spirit of Golden Beach is expressed in signs that read: "Private Beach. Residents Only." With the open, accessible beaches of Hollywood and Miami Beach close by, Golden Beach has nothing to offer visitors but an unspoken directive to move along. In short, there is no public beach access in Golden Beach. Well, perhaps in response to constant complaints, they've added four public parking spaces to Tweedle Park, near the south end of town ($1.25 per hour). Other than that niggardly gesture, there are no easements, no right-of-way, no access, nada. From end to end, the town is private property. You have to live here or be visiting someone who does to legally get onto the beach. For this reason, we find some sort of karmic comeuppance in the fact that the state has been stealing Golden Beach's offshore sand to pump up the beaches elsewhere. At least the public is welcome on those renourished beaches.

Contact Information

Florida Gold Coast Chamber of Commerce, 1100 Kane Concourse, Suite 210, Bal Harbour, FL 33154; 305/866-6020; website: www.flgoldcoastcc.org

Sunny Isles Beach

Sunny Isles Beach (pop. 14,329)—formerly just Sunny Isles and now considering an even more radical name change to Aventura Beach—is the most visitor friendly of the pack of oceanfront communities in north Dade County. It is a safer, slower alternative to the frenetic pace down in Miami Beach. What it mainly has to offer the touring public are hotels and motels—a bevy of them, from single-story dinghies to towering dreadnoughts. Sunny Isles Beach draws visitors from all over the world. A local accommodations guide lists the languages spoken ("translation services available") at each hotel and motel. These include: Arabic, Bengali, Bulgarian, Cantonese, Catalan, Chinese, Creole, Czech, Dutch, Finnish, French, French-Canadian (yes, a separate listing), German, Greek, Hebrew, Hindi, Hungarian, Italian, Japanese, Korean, Mandarin, Polish, Portuguese, Russian, Serbo-Croatian, Spanish, Swedish, Tagalog, Ukrainian, Urdu, and Yiddish.

We couldn't help but wonder how many calls they've had to translate Tagalog lately. Oh yes, English is spoken here, as well.

1 Sunny Isles Beach

Location: Sunny Isles Causeway (State Route 826) and Collins Avenue
Parking/fees: metered parking lot
Hours: 24 hours
Facilities: lifeguards, restrooms, and showers
Contact: Sunny Isles City Hall, 305/947-3912

Grin and Bare It: The Naked Truth About Nude Beaches in Florida

Nude beaches are an endless source of titillation, offering both the hope of copping a peek at a hot bod and the guilt of doing so and having to face one's God in the morning. There is nothing titillating about nude beaches for honest-to-god "naturists," though. They just want to be left alone. The best way to do that is to find a secluded spot and to simply be discreet. This works well almost everywhere but Florida, where millions of tourists trample upon nearly every sandy nook and cranny of the state and where the terrain (unlike California) does not provide rocky, cliff-bordered coves where privacy and seclusion can be easily gained.

In Florida, it seems, no nudes is good nudes. It is difficult here to get naked without getting in trouble. As one naturist put it, "If you want to go nude, you have to be plain-out choosy and careful. Though a number of beaches around the state have earned a reputation as skinny-dipping beaches, one by one, they have been, shall we say, redressed by local law."

However, a real honest to goodness subculture of nudity at the beach does exist in Florida. The "clothing optional" epicenter is, oddly enough, in the most populous corridor: the northernmost part of North Miami Beach. At the north end of Haulover Beach (10800 Collins Ave.), one can skinny-dip or expose naked flesh to the sun's rays legally and without fear or disfavor. During National Nude Week each July, Florida's flesh-tivities are held at Haulover. In March, the annual Tropical Pig Roast is held here too. (Oh, behave!)

Another, albeit unofficial hot spot for nude sunbathing in the Miami area is South Beach, where the gawking is better than at Haulover. At least that has been our experience.

Other beaches in Florida where nudity is tolerated or permitted, as long as participants are discreet—well, as discreet as one can be without clothes—include the following:

- Guana River State Park (below Ponte Vedra Beach)
- Playalinda Beach (above Cocoa Beach, at Canaveral National Seashore)
- Blind Creek Beach (near Jensen Beach)
- Boca Chica Beach (near Key West)
- St. George Island (east end of Gulf Beach Drive)
- St. Vincent National Wildlife Refuge (offshore from Apalachicola)
- Navarre Beach (Eglin Air Force Base, on the Panhandle)
- Santa Rosa Beach (a unit of Gulf Islands National Seashore, east of Pensacola Beach)
- Fort Pickens (just west of Pensacola Beach, also part of Gulf Islands National Seashore)
- Perdido Key (Gulf Islands National Seashore, near Alabama state line)

For more information, contact the South Florida Free Beaches/Florida Naturist Association, P.O. Box 530306, Miami Shores, FL 33153; website: www.sffb.com

Beaches

On the beach is where you want to be in Sunny Isles Beach, because this town has five miles' worth. Some of it has been replenished in recent years from sand dredged offshore of neighboring Golden Beach. **Sunny Isles Beach** is located near the intersection of Sunny Isles Causeway (State Route 826) and Highway A1A, and it stretches from 194th to Bayview Court.

Renourishing South Florida's Eroded Beaches

The largest beach restoration project in history was conducted along Miami Beach from 1977 to 1982 by the U.S. Army Corps of Engineers, which placed 14.5 million cubic yards of sand on 9.3 miles of shore to create a new beach the width of a football field. The bill for the project was $60 million. Each year, more than 200,000 cubic yards are required to maintain the beach at its desired width. The euphemism for this procedure is "beach renourishment." Even though the unprecedented investment might appear worth it from a cost-benefit perspective—the benefit being tourist-generated revenue—in fact the cost is quickly becoming prohibitive. Moreover, the supply of sand is dwindling. Florida has come close to depleting its own offshore sandbanks for purposes of beach renourishment. Already, Dade and Broward Counties have effectively consumed all the usable sand that can be dredged from their offshore banks. When last we checked, they were hungrily eyeing the Bahamas as a source of sand.

Though nature can do spectacular damage on occasion, it's usually of a kind that heals itself over time. The root causes of the severe beach erosion along the East Coast of the U.S., especially in South Florida, are human generated. The principal culprits are the flattening of dunes and dune vegetation for oceanfront developments; the erection of seawalls to protect homes and condos built too close to the water; and the construction of groins and jetties to hold inlets, harbors, and beaches in place. Blockage of the natural flow of sand with the currents (a process known as "longshore transport") caused by these structures results in eroded beaches on the downdrift side. Being that it lies at the very bottom of the state, Miami Beach is downdrift of everything: all the inlets, jetties, groins, seawalls, and condos from Fernandina Beach on south. That's 372 miles of arrested sand flow. No wonder Miami lost its beach.

Initially, Miami's renourished beach stuck around long enough to be judged a success.

Newport Pier, located at the Newport Beachside Crowne Plaza Resort (a Holiday Inn operation), is the center of fishing and surfing activity in the area.

In terms of access, parking, and expansiveness, **Haulover Beach** is the preferable choice. This county park is located in the 10800 block of Collins Avenue. At the Haulover Marine Center, you can charter a full or half day of drift and bottom fishing in search of snapper, yellowtail, mackerel, and grouper. Everything about the park is, uh, fishy. Haulover acquired its name from an early fisherman in the area, a man named Baker who would regularly haul his sponge boat from Biscayne Bay over the thickly wooded dunes to the ocean at this spot. The practice was adopted by succeeding generations of fishermen. "Baker's Haulover" appears on maps as early as 1823.

More recently, Haulover Beach has been the subject of controversy, centering around nude sunbathing. Haulover became wildly popular as a clothing-optional beach, and the benignly tolerant county had no objection to the revenue brought in by the fee-paying naturists. However, when their naked bums began overwhelming the beach, a hue and cry ensued. The solution arrived at was reasonable and fair. Up at

Before the infusion, waves were literally lapping at the lower floors of resort hotels, which tried fending off the ocean with unsightly stone groins. All the new sand was a consoling sight for sore eyes. Subsequently, dune plantings have been made, which have helped stabilize the renourished beaches. A wooden boardwalk runs along and above the dunes, offering more public access points to the beach than just about any coastal community we've ever seen. The result is one of the happier transformations of a beach profile in the world. And yet there have been setbacks, such as Hurricane Andrew (1992) and Tropical Storm Gordon (1994).

Due to losses from storms and the normal rate of erosion here at the south end of the state, maintaining a healthy-looking beach requires eternal vigilance and intermittent renourishment. In 1995, local politicians who went begging for more funds to beef up the beaches pointed to a 15-block stretch of Miami Beach, between 32nd and 47th Streets, so thoroughly eroded that lifeguards could no longer drive their emergency vehicles along the beach. And on and on it goes, with the beach gobbling up sand—and public funds to replace it—on a regular cycle that will have to end someday when both run out. The most sensible strategy, though no one wants to hear it, would be to stop renourishing and let nature take its course. Coastal geologist Orrin Pilkey, whose studies are the bane of the development community, proposes that threatened oceanfront dwellings be razed or relocated to allow the shoreline to "roll back" as it would naturally, maintaining its width as it moved inland.

John Yeend, a South Florida coastal engineer, concurs: "To continue to restore the beaches by dredging sand from offshore is going to be, in the long run, a losing battle," he told the *Miami Herald* in 1984. "Long-term, people are going to have to consider abandoning the shore areas."

Meanwhile, the renourished Miami Beach strand remains a healthy width. It's even too wide in places for some who gripe of having to hike so far across the hot sand to get to the water. A decade from now, beachgoers who are able to complain of the same inconvenience should consider themselves lucky.

the north end, out of view of families and others who might be offended, an 800-yard stretch of Haulover's 1.3-mile beach has been partitioned off for those who want to sun and swim in the buff. The scene is a bit seedy, if truth be told. It gets self-sorted into gay and hetero sections (heavy on the former), and the beach seems to be more like a daytime extension of the prurient goings-on in the darker corners of South Beach clubland than an innocent gathering of enlightened naturists. Down by the inlet at the south end of the beach is a jetty, which draws anglers and surfers.

One of the many lures to Sunny Isles Beach, besides the fishing, is the diving sites. In the offshore waters, divers can explore four artificial reefs—wrecks deposited between 1985 and 1991 to encourage the formation of coral-reef communities. For specifics on location and rules, call the Metro-Dade Department of Environmental Resources Management at 305/375-DERM.

Shore Things

- **Ecotourism**: Urban Trails Kayak, Haulover Beach, 10800 Collins Avenue, 305/947-1302.

- **Fishing charters:** Blue Waters Fishing Charters, 16300 Collins Avenue, Sunny Isles Beach, 305/944-4531.
- **Dive shop:** Diving Locker, 223 Sunny Isles Boulevard, Sunny Isles Beach, 305/947-6025.
- **Marina:** Haulover Marine Center, 10800 Collins Avenue, Sunny Isles Beach, 305/945-3934.
- **Pier:** Newport Pier, Newport Beachside Crowne Plaza Resort, 16701 Collins Avenue, Sunny Isles Beach, 305/949-1300, ext.1266.
- **Rainy-day attraction:** Museum of Contemporary Art, 770 Northeast 125th Street, North Miami, 305/893-6211.
- **Shopping/browsing:** Bal Harbour Shops, 9700 Collins Avenue, Bal Harbour, 305/866-0311.
- **Vacation rentals:** Sunny Isles Beach Resort Association, 17100 Collins Avenue, Suite 217, Sunny Isles Beach, 305/947-5826.

Bunking Down

Among the more interesting aspects of Sunny Isles Beach are the oddball architectural touches found at some of the old motels and motor courts that still thrive among the sleek, faceless high-rises. In front of the **Sahara Beach Club Motel** (18335 Collins Avenue, 305/931-8335, $), for example, are sculptured camels. Two enormous mermaids hold up the front of the **Blue Mist Resort Motel** (19111 Collins Avenue, 305/932-1000, $). Anyone intrigued by roadside oddities ought to check out Sunny Isles Beach. It's a living history exhibit chronicling the wave of tourism that trickled up here in the wake of Miami Beach's explosion as a vacation mecca in the first half of the 20th century.

A good way to secure a room in one of the many beachfront motels is by contacting the **Sunny Isles Beach Resort Association** (17100 Collins Avenue, 305/947-5826). There are Taj Mahals of faded glory like the **Marco Polo Resort Hotel** (19201 Collins Avenue, 305/932-2233, $$$), a 550-room leviathan with restaurants, nightclubs, and a shopping arcade. Not to be outdone, the tropically festooned **Newport Beachside Crowne Plaza Resort** (16701 Collins Avenue, 305/949-1300, $$$), a high-end Holiday Inn, has its own pier, plus restaurants, a deli, pub, club, and more. Wherever you wind up, the proliferation of rooms in the 50-plus motels makes this town a buyer's market. While it was snowing up north one recent December (pre-Christmas, of course), we found rooms going for $29 a night in Sunny Isles Beach at places that, while hardly palaces, were by no means dives, either.

Coastal Cuisine

A sentimental favorite of long standing is **Wolfie Cohen's Rascal House** (172nd Street at Collins Avenue, 305/947-4581, $$). For over 40 years, this hefty home of Manhattan-style delicatessen gourmandizing has sat in the heart of motel row, overwhelming diners with more than 400 menu items, from seafood to stuffed cabbage. The pièce de résistance is its famous corned beef sandwich, an "eating experience" piled higher than the proverbial condo. How popular is it? Well, one em-

2 Haulover Beach

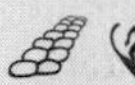

Location: 10800 Collins Avenue, in North Miami Beach
Parking/fees: $3.50 per vehicle entrance fee
Hours: sunrise to sunset
Facilities: concessions, lifeguards, restrooms, picnic tables, and showers
Contact: Haulover Beach Park, 305/947-3525

ployee does nothing but carve corned beef all day long at his own station. If you can eat an entire sandwich in a single sitting, you should immediately point your feet in the direction of the nearest gym to do some hardcore calorie-burning penance. Half a corned-beef sandwich is a filling meal, and the rest can be lugged back to home or hotel room for later. They provide metal bowls full of accompaniments—mostly pickles, slaw, and such. The menu at Wolfie's is vast and extensive, the company is colorful (oy, you've never heard such kvetching!), and the joint never closes.

Night Moves

For those who believe gold chains never went out of style, the disco at the Marco Polo Resort Hotel is called (we kid you not) the **Swingers Lounge** (19201 Collins Avenue, 305/932-2233). Virtually all the action is in the big hotels. The bar at the Thunderbird is called the **Birdcage** (18401 Collins Avenue, 305/931-7700). There are dinner shows, dinner buffets, and dinner theater. It's much like what you'd find at hotels on the Jersey Shore, combining Atlantic City and Cape May with the "Sixth Borough" ambience of South Florida.

Contact Information

Sunny Isles Beach Resort Association, 17100 Collins Avenue, Suite 208, Sunny Isles Beach, FL 33160; 305/947-5826; website: www.sunnyislesfla.com

Bal Harbour Village and Surfside

On the south side of Haulover Inlet are a pair of pleasant municipalities just above Miami Beach's frantic orbit. Bal Harbour (pop. 3,231), which stretches from 96th Street to Haulover Inlet, is the tonier of the two, with its "world famous" Bal Harbour Shops, located at Collins Avenue and 96th Street. If you get weak in the knees at the word "elegance," Bal Harbour is your kind of shopping mecca. Founded in 1915, the mall is located one block off the ocean and boasts dozens of the "world's most elite shops," including Saks, Nieman-Marcus, Cartier, Tiffany, Chanel, Armani, Dior, Versace, and other Italian-surnamed designer outlets. Bal Harbour profited from Miami Beach's spell of hard times, pre–Art Deco renaissance. Now glamorous shopping is back in South Beach—on Lincoln Boulevard, to be exact—so the Bal Harbour Shops have been facing formidable competition.

Surfside (pop. 4,331), which stretches from 96th Street to 87th Terrace, is homey and residential, more a suburb of Miami Beach than a resort destination.

Beaches

Bal Harbour is all of three-tenths of a mile long, and it provides beach access at either end: under the Haulover Bridge (102nd Street), where there's a metered lot, and at 96th Street, where there's a fee parking lot attached to the Sheraton. On good wave days, surfers fill the Haulover Bridge parking lot. The town had its beach renourished in the summer of 1998. A walking/jogging path extends from one end of **Bal Harbour** to another (all of six blocks!), and **Surfside** picks up the baton with its own beachside walkway. Public access in this similarly small-scale town extends from 96th Street down to 88th Street. At 87th Terrace, extending south from Surfside's boundary with Miami Beach, the most remarkable bounty in Greater Miami greets you at North Shore Open Space Park (see Miami Beach). Best of all, Surfside provides access to a lifeguarded beach. The lifeguard stand at 93rd Street and Collins Avenue, behind the community center, is the other nice place to congregate in Surfside. The lapping blue-green waters off Bal Harbour and Surfside are safe and unthreatening, even to small children.

Bunking Down

The **Sheraton Bal Harbour Beach Resort** (9701 Collins Avenue, 305/865-7511, $$$$) and **Sea View Hotel** (9909 Collins Avenue, 305/866-4441, $$$$) are pricey but well placed. The Sea View has been around for more than 50 years and is a European-style high-rise hostelry in the grand tradition. You'll pay $235–320 a night to stay here in season (mid-December through mid-April) and $165–245 the rest of the year. The Sheraton is a 16-story, 642-room contemporary monster breaching vertical space between the beach and the Bal Harbour Shops. It's got everything: easy access to the beach and shopping, three restaurants, spa and health club, and $12 million "fantasy poolscape." It's also got a price tag that starts at $305 a night in season. Yeow.

On the more affordable side, **Baymar Ocean Resort** (9401 Collins Avenue, 305/866-5446, $$) is a well-tended three-story motel with a 300-foot beach, palm-fringed courtyard, and pool a few blocks south of Bal Harbour in Surfside. You'll only pay $125 a night for an oceanfront room in season. Such a bargain!

Contact Information

Florida Gold Coast Chamber of Commerce, 1100 Kane Concourse, Suite 210, Bal Harbour, FL 33154; 305/866-6020; website: www.village.bal-harbour.fl.us

Surfside Tourist Board, 9301 Collins Avenue, Surfside, FL 33154; 305/864-0722; website: www.town.surfside.fl.us

3 Bal Harbour

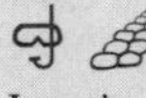

Location: along Collins Avenue between 102nd and 96th Streets in Bal Harbour, with access points at both ends

Parking/fees: metered parking lot under the Haulover Bridge at 102nd Street and Collins Avenue. Fee parking at the Bal Harbour Shops and Sheraton Bal Harbour, at 96th Street and Collins Avenue.

Hours: 24 hours

Facilities: none

Contact: Bal Harbour Town Hall, 305/866-4633

4 Surfside

Location: at street ends between 96th and 88th Streets in Surfside

Parking/Parking/fees: metered street parking

Hours: 24 hours

Facilities: lifeguards, restrooms, and showers

Contact: Surfside Town Hall, 305/861-4863

Miami Beach and Miami

Though the words "Greater" and "Miami" seem to go together, like "gator" and "hungry," we would like to make one thing perfectly clear: Miami Beach (pop. 96,000) and Miami (pop. 400,000) are two different cities—technically, legally, and practically. Then there's this entity known as "Greater Miami," home to 2.1 million people, more than 60 cultural groups, the busiest cruise-ship harbor in the world, and one of the busiest airports in North America. How busy is Miami International Airport? It is claimed that of the nearly 10 million visitors annually to Greater Miami, 93 percent of them arrive by air and only 7 percent by car, boat, or train. Moreover, 55 percent of them are foreign visitors. No wonder Miami often feels as if it's not really a part of the United States It is more of a stateless international community than your typical America city.

In fact, "Greater Miami" is often referred to as the "city of the Americas." It is a fascinating polyglot of multi-ethnic neighborhoods like Coral Gables, Little Havana, Little Haiti, Hialeah, Biscayne Park, Bayside, and North Miami. That Miami is beyond the scope of this book and, after the Elian Gonzalez debacle and the December 2000 "white riot" at the Dade County Courthouse, which cut short a legal recount of presidential ballots, that Miami is beyond the comprehension of these authors, too. Some of Miami's neighborhoods and businesses (i.e., Bad Boyz Bail Bonds) are enough to make you want to catch the next flight home. Miami Beach, by contrast, will seduce you into sticking around.

We lump Miami and Miami Beach together under one heading because in order to visit the beach, you have to pass through the city. This is especially true if you're an international traveler; the airport is nestled in the thicket of Miami's westward sprawl, which stretches all the way to the Everglades. Obviously, logistical snags and Miami vice notwithstanding, the area can be an enjoyable and relaxing place from the perspective of the beaches, 15 miles of which are located in the Greater Miami area.

In an earlier book, we wrote, "In Miami, life whirls on all around you, on overhead freeways and Metrorails, inside fast cars and secured buildings, metamorphosing by the moment into 'the city of the future.' Will the future be horrible, tolerable or utopian? It's anybody's guess." That was in 1986. When we wrote that, the now world-heralded transformation of South Beach's Art Deco District was in its nascent stages. An old photo shows one of us curiously combing through a pile of blue, pink, and yellow commodes piled up on the porch of a property undergoing renovation. Presumably, those very toilet seats are now attached to the rear ends of wealthy tourists in any number of beautifully refurbished hotels. Bravo, we say. Miami Beach deserves commendation for its good works and good looks.

Miami, the city, is another matter. You can pick up the *Miami Herald* nearly every day and find some freakishly heinous crime (e.g., a man carrying his wife's head in a grocery sack) described in gory detail. In fact, a former *Herald* reporter, Edna Buchanan, has become a best-selling mystery novelist just by turning her experiences on the police beat into fiction, and this same high-crime-in-the-urbanized-tropics is a staple of other best-selling crime chroniclers, including John D. MacDonald, Elmore Leonard, Carl Hiaasen, and Charles Williford. It may also explain the off-kilter humor of Dave Barry, another *Herald* staffer. Beyond the endless waves of crime (remember the early-1990s carjacking epidemic?), Miami practically ceased to exist in 1996. At that time, the papers were filled with news about the city of Miami declaring itself insolvent and

Doing the Art Deco Dance in Miami Beach

As we were browsing the flamingo salt-and-pepper shakers at the Art Deco Welcome Center gift shop in Miami Beach, we struck up a conversation with the brassy, elderly woman behind the counter. "I'm a newcomer," she rasped. "I've only been here 68 years." She reminisced, without prompting, about the good old days in Miami in the 1930s: "We used to go to the movies and walk. Everything was walking. Those were wonderful days." An old love song from the bygone big-band days played on the radio, and she hummed along. "I knew the lady who wrote that," our cashier remarked. "Her husband was killed in the war. 'I'll Never Smile Again,' it was called."

Those days of war and upheaval are long gone, and life is good again in Miami Beach. In a way, it's a lot like it was in the pre-war days, as old things are now revered and even fashionable. Take the Art Deco architectural renaissance, which helped lift Miami from a morass of crime and poverty and turn it into one of the liveliest and most fashionable communities in the world.

We are actually just biding time in the gift shop as we wait to hook up with George Neery, a legendary local who served as executive director of the Miami Art Deco Design Preservation League from 1990 to 1997. He leads us on a brisk, informative walking tour of the Art Deco district, and we gain a richer appreciation of this style of architecture and the way it's defined and revived the area. He starts out by noting that there's nothing original about Miami Beach. The palms are imported from Panama. The beach is artificial, having been created with sand trucked in from elsewhere. Even the people aren't original. Everyone comes to Miami Beach from somewhere else.

As America's first vacation playground, the island gave people something to do with two

turning its fate over to the state of Florida. This came only months after Miami celebrated its centennial with a presidential visit and hurrahs about being "the city of the Americas."

Since the fiscal crisis, several top city officials were indicted, a $68 million budget deficit was uncovered, and the director of the Port of Miami resigned when it was learned he was using city money to make purchases at Victoria's Secret and other places having nothing to do with official business. The results of one mayoral election were overturned after a recount found massive voter fraud. In another story with profound political implications, Alex Penelas, the county mayor and most powerful Democrat in Miami/Dade County, oddly went missing during the 2000 presidential campaign. Had he supported Al Gore, enough voters would have paid attention that there would have been no need of recounts in Florida. But the Elian Gonzalez case, and the anti-Clinton/Gore sentiment it stirred up in Miami's Cuban community, made a political no-show of Penelas and cost Gore the election. Penelas wouldn't even intervene to allow a legal recount of votes to proceed in Dade County after myriad anomalies and undercounts were turned up.

Beyond the endless political travails,

new things that they'd acquired: disposable money and time. The first buildings, in fact, were constructed on the bayside, because oceanfront property had no value. People didn't know what to do with or on a beach, but they learned quickly.

The style known as Art Deco—an Anglicization of the French *arts décoratifs*—defined the way Miami was built 1929–1942. It caught on in the wake of the 1925 Paris Exhibition, whose formal name was the "1925 Exposition Internationale des Arts Décoratifs et Industriels Modernes." The modernist movement came together with Mediterranean Revival architecture—a Spanish influence that surfaced at the Pan American Exposition in San Diego—on the breezy shores of Miami.

The idea was to give Miami Beach—which was essentially being created out of whole cloth to serve the leisure interests of suddenly prosperous Americans—a modern look that was also whimsical and fun. They wanted to help people forget where they had come from (and would have to return to). Some of the design elements were inspired by the rounded corners and nautical details (e.g. portholes) of large cruise ships, which were becoming streamlined and speedy—much like American culture. There were lots of ornamental elements, too: finials, faux window boxes, "eyebrows," friezes, ziggurats.

What began as a whimsy has turned out to be an architectural legacy that defines the look and feel of Miami Beach. The Miami Art Deco Design Preservation League, which was founded in 1976, is a force in the community, and they want the 1,200 Art Deco buildings in Miami Beach to be regarded "like the pyramids," according to Neery. "We want people to come back here in a hundred years and see them here." And so the league members have agitated, protested, and fought for buildings and, by extension, for a legacy.

Neery notes with pride that architects are more important than lawyers in Miami Beach. They may be more effective than lawyers, too, when it comes to preserving Miami Beach in the style to which it has become accustomed. "We're like bees," he says. "You don't want to get the hive riled."

Miami remains a dependable hotbed of stories about assaults and homicides. These aren't just tales of druglords warring on ghetto streets, either. Consider the rash of news stories during just one three-day period in early 2001. Gus Boulis, the multimillionaire founder of Miami Subs and SunCruz casinos, was gunned down in his car during an execution-style street hit on February 6, 2001. His well-planned homicide "fits right in to our rich and bloody history," said a defense attorney who leads crime-scene tours of South Florida for profit as a side business. A day later—no problem rustling up news in this town!—Miami Mayor Joe Carollo was charged with domestic battery and spent a night in jail after allegedly assaulting his wife. Like a bad penny, Miami resident O.J. Simpson also turned up on the police blotter. On February 9th, the former multiple-murder defendant pleaded not guilty to charges of misdemeanor battery and felony burglary of an occupied vehicle stemming from a road-rage incident the previous December.

Rewinding back to July 1997, South Beach's most famous part-time resident, designer Gianni Versace, was shot to death in front of his Ocean Drive mansion by gay serial killer Andrew Cunanan. "Let me assure you that Miami Beach and Dade

MAP OF MIAMI/DADE COUNTY—PAGE 252

County are safe," said county Mayor Penelas, but his words rang hollow. If this were true, the TV show *Miami Vice* would have been a plotless failure. To be fair, however, latter-day Miami Beach—and, in particular, the lower third known as South Beach, which runs from 21st Street to South Pointe Park—is more spice than vice, and the beach itself is an international sensation. In fact, the whole of South Beach virtually defines the term "multiculturalism." It is as exotic a human exposition as the tropical reefs off the Florida Keys are a repository of colorful sea creatures.

One major reason for South Beach's resurgence has been the renovation of the Art Deco District (see sidebar), within which some 800 buildings are now listed on the National Register of Historic Places. It has allowed Miami Beach to reconnect with its glory days of the early 20th century as a Tropical Deco resort paradise. Miami Beach also benefits from its broad-minded acceptance of all people, regardless of race, creed, sexual persuasion, and ability to dance the macarena. In this sense, it is a true melting pot—with the sun providing the heat—that's blended, assimilated, and color blind. In short, it is a functioning blueprint for a more internationalist world that, not coincidentally, knows how to throw a great party, too.

Beaches

By way of orientation, Miami Beach runs from 87th Terrace down to the jetties at South Pointe Park. From Miami, three bridges cross Biscayne Bay to the barrier island. From north to south these are I-195 (Julia Tuttle Causeway), which ends at 41st Street in Miami Beach; the Venetian Causeway, a toll road that ends at 23rd Street; and I-395 (MacArthur Causeway), which ends at 5th Street. If you're heading to South Beach ("SoBe" for short)—home of the Art Deco District, the most popular and accessible beaches, and the hottest

5 North Shore Open Space Park

Location: Collins Avenue between 79th and 87th Streets in Miami Beach
Parking/fees: metered street parking, plus $1 entrance fee per person
Hours: 7 A.M.–8 P.M.
Facilities: lifeguards, restrooms, picnic tables, and showers
Contact: North Shore Open Space Park, 305/993-2032

6 72nd Street Beach

Location: 72nd Street at Collins Avenue in Miami Beach
Parking/fees: metered parking lot at 72nd and 73rd Streets between Collins and Washington Avenues in Miami Beach
Hours: 5 A.M. to midnight
Facilities: lifeguards, restrooms, and showers
Contact: Miami Beach Parks and Recreation Department, 305/673-7730, or Miami Beach Patrol, 305/673-7714

7 64th Street Beach

Location: 64th Street at Collins Avenue in Miami Beach
Parking/fees: metered parking lot
Hours: 5 A.M. to midnight
Facilities: lifeguards, restrooms, and showers
Contact: Miami Beach Parks and Recreation Department, 305/673-7730, or Miami Beach Patrol, 305/673-7714

nightlife this side of Manhattan—you're well advised to park at one of municipal garages found between Collins and Washington Avenues on 7th, 8th, 10th, 12th, 13th, and 17th Streets. You will otherwise drive in endless bumper-to-bumper traffic with only lucky drivers snagging a spot on the street. These garages cost a reasonable $1 per hour; moreover, they're safe and even attractively landscaped. If you do park on the street, the meters cost $1 per hour as well.

Within Miami Beach's borders, there are lifeguard stands at the following street ends (from north to south): 83rd, 81st, 79th, 74th, 72nd, 64th, 53rd, 46th, 35th, 29th, 21st, 17th, 14th, 13th, 12th, 10th, 8th, 6th, and 1st. The first three stands listed fall within the boundaries of **North Shore Open Space Park.** Running from 87th Terrace to 79th Street, this is one of the more delightful surprises in the Miami area. Originally set aside as an open space in 1972, its 40 acres have been batted like a volleyball between the state and the city of Miami Beach. At one time a state park, it is currently leased to the city by the state. Who knows or cares who runs it as long as they continue to maintain the attractive landscaping (lots of shade and picnic areas) and dune walkovers. The entrance fee is a princely $1 per person, and you will be treated like a king by Mother Nature. A bike/pedestrian path runs through the park. In the heart of high-rise heaven, it's a slice of seclusion and quiet—what a treat!

From 79th Street south to 21st Street—roughly, the northern boundary of South Beach—Miami Beach is one long strand used mainly by guests at the wall-to-wall high-rise condos and hotels that line this route. Unless you're a lodger at one of these places, it's tough to find a spot to leave your car. Collins Avenue can be an adventure to navigate even without having to keep an eye out for parking. However, there are metered parking lots by the beach at 72nd, 64th, 53rd, 46th, 35th, and 21st Streets, plus restrooms and showers at all of them except 35th Street. A boardwalk runs between 46th and 21st Streets—an area known as "mid-beach"—

8 53rd Street Beach

Location: 53rd Street at Collins Avenue in Miami Beach
Parking/fees: metered parking lot
Hours: 5 A.M. to midnight
Facilities: lifeguards, restrooms, and showers
Contact: Miami Beach Parks and Recreation Department, 305/673-7730, or Miami Beach Patrol, 305/673-7714

9 46th Street Beach

Location: 46th Street at Collins Avenue in Miami Beach
Parking/fees: metered parking lot
Hours: 5 A.M. to midnight
Facilities: lifeguards, restrooms, and showers
Contact: Miami Beach Parks and Recreation Department, 305/673-7730, or Miami Beach Patrol, 305/673-7714

10 35th Street Beach

Location: 35th Street at Collins Avenue in Miami Beach
Parking/fees: metered parking lot
Hours: 5 A.M. to midnight
Facilities: lifeguards and showers
Contact: Miami Beach Parks and Recreation Department, 305/673-7730, or Miami Beach Patrol, 305/673-7714

and parking lots can be found at either end. There's also a municipal parking garage at 42nd Street.

South Beach, where 40 percent of Miami Beach's population resides, is an altogether different story. It says yes to parking and just about everything else, too. Anything goes (and comes off) along the stretch of South Beach from 17th to 5th Streets. Sights along the beach include completely nude sunbathing (though sunbathers are legally supposed to go no further than toplessness), as well as thong bathing suits that make a mockery of the word "clothed." As we overheard one amazed and amused tourist say, "I've seen more cloth on a necktie!" We strolled as casually and unobtrusively as possible along South Beach. The scene that greeted us was right out of an old *National Geographic* pictorial about Tahiti. Gorgeous lotion-lathered European and Hispanic women lounged unabashedly in the buff. Gay men sat cross-legged, knees touching knees, conversing intently while staring into each other's eyes.

Within these boundaries falls **Lummus Park** (officially 5th–14th Streets), a breathtakingly wide stretch of sand backed by palm trees and "chickees" (those thatch-roofed, umbrella-shaped, shade-giving huts), colorful snack shacks, lifeguard stations, and a curvaceous walking, biking, and in-line skating trail. You haven't lived until you've jogged along South Beach hereabouts, ogling all the other joggers and models. By the way, the ocean water is warm, relatively clear, and almost wavelessly calm, though there's a slight drop-off about ten feet from shore. After the drop-off, though, the bottom levels out and the water depth remains about chest high for several hundred feet into the ocean. A recent relaxing swim took us further out to sea than we've ever been with the water depth still not over our heads. A family's sense of security is further enhanced by the presence of 17 lifeguard stations between 79th Street and South Pointe Park. Play areas are set back from the water for the kiddies, though it's hard to imagine

⓫ 21st Street Beach

Location: 21st Street at Collins Avenue in Miami Beach
Parking/fees: metered parking lot
Hours: 5 A.M. to midnight
Facilities: lifeguards, restrooms, and showers
Contact: Miami Beach Parks and Recreation Department, 305/673-7730, or Miami Beach Patrol, 305/673-7714

⓬ Lummus Park

Location: Ocean Drive, between 5th and 15th Streets in Miami Beach
Parking/fees: fee parking lot and metered street parking
Hours: 5 A.M. to midnight
Facilities: concessions, lifeguards, restrooms, and showers
Contact: Miami Beach Parks and Recreation Department, 305/673-7730, or Miami Beach Patrol, 305/673-7714

⓭ South Pointe Park

Location: along Washington Avenue between 1st and 5th Streets, at the southern tip of Miami Beach
Parking/fees: metered parking lots
Hours: 5 A.M. to midnight
Facilities: concessions, lifeguards, restrooms, picnic tables, and showers
Contact: South Pointe Park, 305/673-7224

MAP OF SOUTH FLORIDA—PAGE 177

a kid growing bored with the beach and ocean. Look sharp around 8th Street for the Asher sculptures next to a popular shaded pavilion (unofficially known as Asher Beach), a donation to Miami Beach from the people of Israel.

South Pointe Park runs from 5th Street to a municipal fishing pier at the bottom of the barrier island, overlooking the shipping channel and Fisher Island. The park offers lifeguards, showers, picnic shelters, concessions, a playground, a lighted pier, an exercise course, and a restaurant, **Smith & Wollensky** (1 Washington Avenue, 673-1708, $$$$), that specializes in steaks and chops. Because it is less trendy than the heart of the SoBe bazaar, you will see fewer bulging thongs here. The one bulging thing you will see is the ill-advised (and much-despised) construction of The Towers. The Towers are not just a visual blight. Their construction threatens to reconfigure the shoreline and, thus, change the wave patterns here. Since South Pointe has one of the finest wave breaks in south Florida, you can imagine

Cruise Blues

Since Miami is the busiest cruise-ship port in North America, a word to the wise is in order. The multibillion-dollar cruise industry claims it's cleaning up its act after years of flaunting national and international laws. This is because federal authorities are finally monitoring the previously hands-off industry. In 1999, for example, Miami-based Royal Caribbean pled guilty to 21 felony counts involving environmental crimes. Because this was a plea bargain, the actual number of violations was far higher. Royal Caribbean agreed to pay $18 million in fines for illegally dumping wastewater and hazardous waste in six U.S. jurisdictions, lying to the Coast Guard, and falsifying waste-discharge records.

While some companies are making efforts to right past wrongs, the cruise industry as a whole is still polluting the oceans and even the air, provoking one federal investigator to characterize it as a "culture of crime." Alaska and California have strengthened state laws and oversight of the cruise industry, but Florida has not. Though many cruise lines maintain Miami as home base, they actually sail under the flags of countries like Liberia, which have virtually no environmental standards. There are, in fact, 17 foreign-registered cruise lines that operate out of South Florida, and this may be the aspect of cruise industry venality that most rankles us. It directly affects the quality of beach experiences one can have in South Florida when the beaches are closed due to pollution from offshore sources. More indirectly, it affects one's beach enjoyment when pollution clouds visibility for divers in and around the Keys while suffocating coral reefs. We find ourselves asking how can companies that routinely spoil our waters and that abuse and overwork underpaid staff in clear violation of our labor laws be allowed to retain headquarters on American soil? Why aren't they forced to clean up their act or get out of our country?

To date, Congress has done little more than administer a tongue lashing (by Senator John McCain). Meanwhile, travelers are clamoring to climb aboard, and cruise-industry profits have never been higher. The key to any change in the status quo rests with the customers. To them, we respectfully suggest booking only with lines that are registered under the American flag, as they are duty bound to follow American laws.

The Wolfsonian

One of the most fascinating and unusual museums in the United States, the Wolfsonian, can be found in the heart of South Beach's Art Deco District. While its location inside a reverently restored Mediterranean-style building—formerly a storage company—nicely augments the museum's devotion to the decorative arts, the Wolfsonian is much more than a collection of pastel bathroom tiles and sculpted peacock feathers. The decorative arts are, in fact, only one facet of the 70,000-item collection. It is also a research and educational center, affiliated with Florida International University. It's committed to the history, restoration, and appreciation of the decorative arts, design, architecture, advertising, transportation, world fairs, and political propaganda from 1885 to 1945 in Europe and the Americas. Indeed, it's hard to say exactly what the Wolfsonian is, which is what makes it so endlessly fascinating and unusual.

Perhaps the uniting element of the place is that objects in the collection were typically very much ahead of their time. That is, they were created not as elitist objects to be hoarded, hidden, and envied by the rich and famous but mass-produced with the explicit intention of persuading or altering the perceptions of large numbers of people. Thus, the title of the museum-generated *Journal of Decorative and Propaganda Arts* is oddly accurate. Still confused? Okay, here are some of the sorts of items on view at any given time in the changing exhibitions and semipermanent installations: furniture, industrial design, glass, ceramics, metalwork, government-funded artwork, war recruitment posters, books, works on paper, ephemera, paintings, sculpture, propaganda pamphlets, tourist brochures (yes!), and advertising graphics.

The eclectic nature of this collection reflects the tastes of the institution's founder, Mitchell Wolfson, Jr. Upon opening the museum to the public in 1995 (the research center opened in 1993), Wolfson announced, "This is a movement, a crusade, and a mission, and we're all zealots. . . . Objects contain powerful information, and we have to learn to read them." By "propaganda," Wolfson means the sixteenth-century sense of the word, which is when the Catholic Church coined that Latinate term to denote the "propagation of the faith" (as Malcolm X would later say, by any means necessary). All of Wolfson's objects, in that sense, propagate the ideals of their times.

The Wolfsonian collection is, if nothing else, a rewarding visual delight not unlike the surrounding neighborhood of restored Art Deco and Mediterranean architecture. At the risk of sounding propagandistic, we'll end by saying a visit to Miami Beach is incomplete without a visit to the Wolfsonian. The museum is open every day except Wednesday. Hours are 11 A.M.–6 P.M. (11 A.M.–9 P.M. on Thursday and noon–5 P.M. on Sunday). Admission is $5 for adults and $3.50 for seniors, students with ID, and children ages 6–12.

For more information contact the Wolfsonian, 1001 Washington Avenue, Miami Beach, FL 33139; 305/531-1001.

how the surfers, or anyone who loves beaches, feel about The Towers.

Incidentally, vileness of a more tangible sort washed ashore on Miami Beach in June 2000 when construction workers ruptured a sewer line, sending millions of gallons of nasty stuff into the ocean and causing the beaches to close for nearly two weeks. Gloriously, they reopened on the Fourth of July. Sadly, another round of pollution—an oil spill this time—desecrated the South Florida beaches again in August 2000. In March 2001, another ruptured sewage pipe poured 12 million gallons of raw human waste into the bay, closing all area beaches yet again.

A final word about South Beach. A broad, flat apron of sand separates the sidewalk bazaar along Ocean Drive from the water's edge. It really is a hike to the beach—so much so that to refer to the hotels and restaurants along Ocean Drive as "oceanfront" is stretching things a bit. The beach isn't even the principal preoccupation of those who flock to Miami Beach. They come here for the social whirl, and often Ocean Drive is far more crowded than the beach across the street, even on the nicest days.

Shore Things

- **Bike/skate rentals:** Spokes, 601 5th Street, Miami Beach, 305/672-2550; Skate 2000, 1200 Ocean Boulevard, Miami Beach, 305/538-8282.
- **Boat cruise:** Carnival Cruise Lines, 3655 Northwest 87th Avenue, 305/599-2200, Miami.
- **Dive shop:** South Beach Divers, 850 Washington Avenue, Miami Beach. 305/531-6110.
- **Ecotourism:** Mangrove Coast Kayaks and Tours, 5794 Commerce Lane, South Miami, 305/663-3364.
- **Fishing charters:** Reward Fishing Fleet, Miami Beach Marina, 300 Alton Road, 305/372-9470.
- **Lighthouse:** Key Biscayne Lighthouse, Bill Baggs Cape Florida State Park, Key Biscayne, 305/361-5811.
- **Marina:** Miami Beach Marina, 300 Alton Road, Miami Beach, 305/673-6000.
- **Pier:** South Pointe Park, 1 Washington Avenue, 305/673-7224.
- **Rainy-day attraction:** Miami Seaquarium, 4400 Rickenbacker Causeway, Key Biscayne, 305/361-5705.
- **Shopping/browsing:** Lincoln Road Mall (16th Street from Collins Avenue to Alton Road), Miami Beach; CocoWalk, 3015 Grand Avenue, Coconut Grove.
- **Surf shop:** X-Isle Surf Shop, 437 Washington Avenue, Miami Beach, 305/673-5900.
- **Vacation rentals:** The Vacation Store, 820 Washington Avenue, Miami Beach, 305/532-1516.

Bunking Down

Do not stay in Miami, period. Cross the causeway bridge, pay the extra bucks, and stay somewhere along the 9.3 miles of oceanfront in Miami Beach. We'll spare you the gory details, but suffice it to say Miami is filled with vice, and tourists are sitting ducks for it. While robberies are down from the legendary days of the early 1990s, you're better off being safe than sorry by avoiding it. Miami is reportedly home to more pawnshops than New York City, all of which are ready customers for that expensive Nikon around your neck or Rolex around your wrist. We saw this unsavory side of Miami one evening when we ill-advisedly stayed at a hotel near Bayside (a crumbling mall facing an ugly, churning industrial port). The hotel was incompetently run, the building was decayed, the rooms were overpriced and malodorous, and the bedspreads had holes in them. And this was a name-brand chain hotel! Adding insult to injury, we were charged an extra $9 to park in an unsafe lot surrounded by urban blight. Furthermore, they levy a 12.5 percent room tax. It amazes us that Miami, which hosts millions of tourists a year, perpetually teeters on the edge of bankruptcy. Where does all the money go?

Over by the ocean, we've always found safe, affordable accommodations in the midtown area of Miami Beach (within fallout of the Fontainebleau, in the 4000 block of Collins Avenue) and in the less frenetic northern Dade County communities of Surfside, Bal Harbour, and Sunny Isles Beach (see separate writeups). Each has its own appeal, and all are about as safe as it gets in the Miami area.

Still, if you really want to sample the Art Deco dance of South Beach, you simply must book a room in the Deco District. In this roughly ten-by-four-block area you will find more than 800 Art Deco buildings and 200 Mediterranean revival structures—including the late Gianni Versace's lavish 1930 mansion, at 1116 Ocean Drive—that have been restored since the preservation campaign began in the 1970s. The most desirable Deco hotels line Ocean Drive between 5th and 14th Streets, but you must have a high tolerance for the endless party on the sidewalks below. Before naming names, one small disclaimer. With the exception of the **Clay Hotel and Hostel International** (1438 Washington Avenue, 305/534-2988, $) and a few less trendy hotels beyond the Deco District's borders, it's not cheap to stay in South Beach. One of the non-trendies is the **Claremont Hotel** (1700 Collins Avenue, 305/538-4661, $). From the outside, it looks Deco-esque, with a pink-and-beige pattern on a Bauhaus-style three-story building, but inside it's clean, comfortable, functional, and utterly unaffected.

Among the more reliable of the more "pure" Art Deco lodges is the **Colony Hotel** (736 Ocean Drive, 305/673-0088, $$$). You can't miss its distinctive neon-rimmed pastel-blue entrance. Inside, it's all sleek marble and sharp angles, with a popular club and restaurant (Colony Bistro) on the premises and continental breakfast included with each of the 36 rooms. Two blocks off the bustle of the oceanfront—but fully embracing its spirit—is **Hotel Astor** (956 Washington Avenue, 305/531-8081, $$$), which appears as venerable as its name. Greeting all who enter is a stunning lobby paneled in an olive-green and black pattern that only a Deco-phile could love. Built in 1936 and meticulously restored in recent years, the Astor has 41 rooms and a pricey though much-ballyhooed restaurant, the **Astor Place Bar and Grill**, (305/672-7217, $$$$).

Combining luxury and enviable beach access is the aptly named **Ocean Front Hotel** (1230–1238 Ocean Drive, 305/672-2579, $$$), a Mediterranean-style complex that luxuriously overlooks the ocean for an entire block at the north end of the Art Deco District, near the similarly decked-out Versace mansion. Restored to 1930s splendor, the Ocean Front suggests the setting of a Somerset Maugham story. Fittingly, a breezily casual French restaurant, **Les Deux Fontaines** (1230 Ocean Drive, 305/672-7278, $$$$), is on the premises.

Other delectable Deco palaces are the **Marlin** (1200 Collins Avenue, 305/604-5063, $$$$), the **Tides** (1220 Ocean Drive, 604-5070, $$$$), and the **Essex House** (1001 Collins Avenue, 305/534-2700, $$$). The Marlin is a fancy fish, a remodeled hostelry on the site of a former crack house. It might best be described as austere and techno. With its severe lines and liberal use of burnished metal, it is as utilitarian as a website. There's a recording studio in the basement and a sunken bar off the lobby. How expensive is it? Hey, they wouldn't even tell us the price! If money's no object, dive right in. The Tides is an example of the newest trend in South Beach architecture: monochromaticism, which is not to say monotonous. There's something appealing about the sandy color and pebbly texture of this 45-room, three-restaurant monolith, where a deluxe oceanfront room runs $350–475 per night. Classic and simple in architecture and decor, the Tides is the largest hotel on Ocean Drive. Done up in mauves and browns, the Essex House looks like a ship rising from the dry dock of Collins Avenue. Rooms are cleanly, sparely appointed, and rates reasonable, by South Beach Art Deco standards. Even if you don't stay at one of these places, by all means drop by for a drink. Each has its own look, history, character, and appeal.

If your sole reason for coming to Miami Beach is to party, **The Clevelander** (1020 Ocean Dr., 305/531-3485, $$) is the place to dump your bags and let it all hang out. Its outdoor poolside bar is party central on the beach, but the rooms are actually quite nice and reasonably priced (for Miami Beach). As a friend told us, "The only disappointment was the fact that more expensive oceanfront rooms do not have balconies, so they are not a significant advantage over any other room in the place." So save yourself some money and avoid some noise in the bargain by booking a non-oceanfront room.

Even if you're just mildly curious, you can still spend some enjoyable hours strolling the district, admiring the architectural wonders and the civic spirit that helped rejuvenate them. The **Miami Design Preservation League** operates a beachfront welcome center (1001 Ocean Drive, 305/672-2014, open 11 A.M.–6 P.M. daily), and the Miami Beach Visitors Bureau has an information kiosk in the pedestrian mall at Lincoln Road and Washington Avenue, if you want to arm yourself with maps and literature before your stroll.

Since we brought up the name, we should give you the goods on the **Fontainebleau Hilton** (4441 Collins Avenue, 305/538-2000, $$$$), the monolithic resort dedicated to high rollers. Like its Vegas cousins, the Fontainebleau is lavishly tacky, with an ocean-sized swimming pool shaped like a tropical lagoon only a few hundred feet from the actual ocean. Be sure to wear your sunglasses inside to protect your eyes from the gleam of all the gold chains, Gucci loafers, and polar-white capped teeth.

Speaking of high-rises, South Beach is watching its stock and its skyline soar. The Ritz, Radisson, and Loews are all opening new venues here. Of the three, our favorite is the **Loews Miami Beach Hotel** (1601 Collins Avenue, 305/604-1601, $$$$), a cut above the others because they've used the St. Moritz, a neighboring historic hotel from the 1920s, which they also own, as their architectural template. As a result—at least from the beach—the Loews doesn't look nearly as imposing as its 18 stories. And it probably will seem downright quaint as the never-ending monolithic high-rise construction begins to dwarf any and everything outside of the Art Deco district. The Loews, by the way, has a fabulous lobby bar and an incredible pool deck with a lively social scene. Everything about the Loews is oversized and dressed to impress. Having seen every oceanfront hotel and resort in America, we don't impress easily at this point, but the Loews blew us away.

Coastal Cuisine

The catch of the day in South Beach is **A Fish Called Avalon** (700 Ocean Drive, 305/532-1727, $$$), which has been serving some of the tastiest, most innovative seafood on the beach since 1989. It was opened by Gerry Quinn, an Irishman who had the chutzpah, before moving to Miami Beach, to open an Irish restaurant in Paris—our kind of guy. Its specialties include Bang Bang Shrimp: fat prawns cooked in a spicy, curry-based marinade and drizzled with a cooling mint sauce. It has won multiple "Taste of the Beach" awards from *South Florida Gourmet*. Popular entrées include Caribbean snapper, marinated in curry-based spices, served

MAP OF MIAMI/DADE COUNTY—PAGE 252

on black-bean salsa and topped with a cooling orange sauce. Chilean sea bass is poetry on a plate: pan-seared quickly and served with a red and yellow pepper purée. The superbly cooked food is just one of the many appeals of A Fish Called Avalon. Others include the cordial staff, live Latin-guitar accompaniment and, of course, the wonderful setting overlooking the passing parade on Ocean Drive. If you find it too humid or loud on the patio, head to the indoor dining room, whose art-filled decor makes for a memorable setting and meal. Top off your dinner experience with Guava Cheesecake, and then walk it off by entering the swarm along Ocean Avenue. Incidentally, A Fish Called Avalon is attached to a hotel called **Avalon** (700 Ocean Drive, 305/538-0133, $$$). Actually, it's the Avalon Majestic, comprising two separate and adjacent small Deco hotels. The smallish rooms are merely adequate; it's the location you'll be crowing about—and paying for.

Given the volatile state of Miami's economy and the speed with which restaurants go in and out of business, we felt it advisable to stick with tried and true restaurants that have survived for awhile. First on our—and everyone's—list is **Joe's Stone Crab** (see "Eat at Joe's" sidebar). We've also had good meals at a franchise restaurant called the **Crab House** (1551 79th Street Causeway, 305/868-7085, $$$). Located on a small key between Miami Beach and Miami, the Crab House has an appealingly informal atmosphere. How could it be otherwise when the dining experience is so wonderfully messy? Tables are

Eat at Joe's

Joe's Stone Crab restaurant (227 Biscayne Street, 305/673-0365, $$$) runs an ad in local papers that says more than a mouthful: "Before SoBe, Joe be." Established in 1913, Joe's has never looked back. This South Beach institution, located at the very southern tip of Miami Beach's barrier island, hasn't sacrificed an ounce of quality in its trend-resistant fare: fresh seafood that's simply prepared, with excellent service, no reservations needed or accepted. Needless to add, Joe's is extremely popular; an hour wait is not uncommon.

Joe's specializes in a native delicacy, the stone crab, which swims in the warm waters off Florida's Gulf Coast. They're like nothing you've ever eaten. For one thing, you eat only the claw. One claw per crab, in fact, is all the state allows commercial crabbers to harvest. The stone crab is protected under a law that prevents anything more than temporary capture during a brief season. The nets scoop them up, the crab is grabbed and the crusher claw twisted off, and the amputated crustacean is then tossed back overboard. The claws regenerate, like starfish arms.

At Joe's the claws are boiled and served cold, with drawn butter and a spicy mustard sauce. Each claw is a natural work of art bearing the texture of fine china, colored ivory and rose with a black border. The taste is more subtle than the familiar Chesapeake blue crab, and the claws provide an ample portion of delicate, tasty crabmeat. You can fill yourself on four stone crab claws. Seriously!

At Joe's the tuxedoed waiters (don't worry; diners can wear whatever they want) engage customers in solicitous patter. We lucked into Ozzie, an old surfer with the comically gruff

covered with newspaper in the manner of a Chesapeake Bay crab house, and standard operating gear includes a wooden mallet, a nutcracker, buckets for discards, and lots of moist towelettes for periodic cleanups. Stone crabs and garlic crabs are the house specialties. The latter are blue crabs seasoned and steamed with loads of garlic. They also serve a superb seafood bisque and a sublime key lime pie.

One enduring South Beach institution at the low end of the scale is **The News Cafe** (800 Ocean Drive, 305/531-0392, $$). It's open 24 hours a day but is best enjoyed over a platter of eggs and a mug of coffee, with a newspaper propped up in front of you. Though the food is average (at least ours was), the atmosphere is unique, with a newsroom motif, stocked magazine rack, and view of the goings-on along the sidewalk and beach. If you just want a simple, decent sandwich sans hype, try **La Sandwicherie** (229 14th Street, 305/532-8934, $).

The rest of Miami Beach's cuisine follows—and sometimes starts—national trends. Generally speaking, Thai and Italian are the rage as of this writing, but Cuban, Spanish, and Latin are the most authentically native and the least likely to go out of style. As mentioned, the restaurant scene in SoBe is highly competitive and therefore fluctuates like the stock market. To get a handle on the latest, hottest, and hippest spots, pick up a copy of *New Times,* a free alternative weekly that provides annotated and opinionated restaurant reviews. These are among the most desirable and seemingly most durable spots:

• **BANG** (1516 Washington Avenue,

demeanor of Dan Aykroyd, who has been at Joe's for 10 years. He offered, "Whatever I can do to make you happy, let me know." When we riposted, "A back rub might be nice," he parried, without missing a beat, "I'll give you a Miami back rub. Get up and face the wall over there, and I'll pat you down, then put on the handcuffs." Many other fresh seafood items are offered, along with the wit. On one recent visit, we had an excellent grilled pompano and the cold seafood platter—a great deal including stone crabs, Florida lobster, and large shrimp. Side dishes are à la carte but large enough to feed two diners.

One change has taken place at Joe's in the last decade, and it's not necessarily for the better. They've added a sleek, expensive back bar (thus shrinking the waiting area) and an annex where logoed merchandise and mail orders can be purchased. This unbridled commerce undercuts the old atmosphere, but it may just be a case of Joe trying to keep up with the Joneses (and the Margaritavilles and Planet Hollywoods). The surrounding area, once a dilapidated no-man's-land of ramshackle huts and dumps, is now home to "another Portofino development," a building so obnoxiously tall, wide, mirrored, and against the grain of Joe's that you understand why regulars complain. (We overheard one veteran waitress agreeing with a customer cawing about the changes.) They'll have more to bicker about next time though, because another lot next to Joe's has been cleared for an equally monolithic construction. You wonder if the island won't eventually sink under the combined weight of the buildings and the egos of the men who build them.

In the meantime, you can still feast on stone crabs at Joe's, as well as the world's best coleslaw and hash brown potatoes. While the menu is long and tempting, the trio of stone crabs, coleslaw, and hash browns is a classic. If you order just as we've instructed, your old-time waiter will likely cock an eyebrow and smile as if to say, "Ah, a regular."

305/531-2361, $$$$) has a hip New York cousin, BOOM.

- **Booking Table Cafe** (728 Ocean Drive, 305/672-3476, $$$) is known for seafood and beautiful people.
- **Lareo's on the Beach** (820 Ocean Drive, 305/532-9577, $$$), launched by local diva Gloria Estefan, is stylish and Cuban.
- **Maiko** (1255 Washington Avenue, 305/531-6369, $$$) serves up superlative sushi and sashimi.
- **Mark's South Beach** (1120 Collins Avenue, 305/604-9050, $$$$), which opened in March 2000, is already garnering raves for changing-daily menus and wine pairings.
- **Nemo** (100 Collins Avenue, 305/532-4550, $$$$) is très chic with New American cuisine and an open kitchen.
- **Starfish** (1427 West Avenue, 305/673-1717, $$$$) is rising star that shines with fresh, creative seafood items.
- **Wish** (801 Collins Avenue, 305/674-9474, $$$$) boasts a lush fountain court setting and gourmet seafood on the plates.

Night Moves

On repeated visits to the area, we've noticed that the choices in South Beach fall to extremes: either hellish goth-rock dungeons or discotheques specializing in deejayed electronic club music. In South Beach, the Deco begat the disco (or vice versa) and there's no escaping it, whether synth driven, salsa powered, or deejay mixed. Much of this dance music is marketed to a gay clientele (i.e., prison-fortress clubs with names like Hombre). South Miami nightspots, gay and straight alike, often go by one-word minimalist names. The roll call of primo SoBe clubs and bars, extant and defunct, includes Vivid, Touch, Opium, Crobar, Level, Bash, Amnesia, Kremlin, Liquid, and Twist. There are often celebrity owners, such as The Artist (formerly known as Prince), who opened Glam Slam in 1994 and partied there like it was 1999, though it only lasted until 1996. Glam Slam reopened Prince-lessly, under new ownership, in 1997 and promptly closed again. So it goes in Miami Beach.

For dance-club aficionados, the scene in South Beach is as hot as it gets. God knows we tried to get into the groove, to bust a move on the trendiest night life South Beach has to offer. We dutifully made the rounds of Washington Street, between 5th and 15th streets, stopping at every party palace to ponder the possibilities. Each was like a stage setting for a futurist play about the fascist takeover of the entertainment industry: Behind the obligatory velvet rope, a small committee of formally attired minions waited, one of whom had the sort of physique and grim smile that suggests severe corporeal punishment should you get out of line. You are slowly surveyed by this mute contingent—head to toe, toe back up to head—as you, in turn, survey the cryptic runes that pass for the club's name or logo, as well as the darkened windows, black curtains, and glimpse of cat-house red or mausoleum black of the club's interior. Your inquisitiveness does not enter into the transaction. If you are deemed suitable, the velvet rope is briefly detached from one pole, and you are waved forward. You have earned the privilege of paying a cover charge that averages $20 to gain access to taped or turntable-spun music, overpriced drinks, and smug attitude for the rest of the evening. Haggling over the cover charge is not permitted; it is also a clear indication that you are not suited for this establishment.

After perusing several of these similar Washington Street scenes, we found that only **Club Madonna** (1527 Washington St., 305/534-2000), a strip joint specializing in "European friction dances," held any appeal for us. This may only have been because the three lithesome spike-heeled, mini-skirted honeys waving us inside seemed glad we were alive. And they were democratic in their solicitations, inviting all comers to the friction dance, no matter how ugly, shabby, or unhip. Yet, eschewing even the temptation of a friction dance, we continued down Washington Street to find a club desperate enough to let us inside its velvet rope for no cover charge whatsoever. It was at this point that we understood a certain amount of mystique about these places needs to be created out on the sidewalk, because you would not want to set foot inside if you know how empty the charade truly is.

The music runs to mind-numbing loud rap and Eurodisco dance remixes built around exhortations like "Put your hands in the air" or "Get on your feet" or "Shake your booty" or "Check yo ass," which are repeated more times than Bill Withers sings "I know" in "Ain't No Sunshine." Draft beer costs $4 for Dixie Cup–sized domestic horse piss; even a thimble of club soda, nearly all ice, is $4. The bartenders are as surly as the patrons, and the whole soulless scene makes you want to holler, toss a stool over the bar, and leave. Even when there are no cover charges, which is the case at some of the lower-rung joints, these places are ripoffs.

If you really must go to one of these clubs, the best by far is **Level** (1235 Washington Street, 305/532-1525). They were celebrating and reliving the Studio 54 era on the night we visited, replete with guest appearances by disco diva Thelma Houston, parade floats with characters dressed like Miss Liberty and Austin Powers, transvestites in cowgirl outfits shaking their booties, and, of course, a line that stretched two blocks. Similarly packed, frenetic scenes are found at **Crobar** (1445 Washington St., 305/531-8225) and **320** (320 Lincoln Road, 305/531-2800). Liquid, among the hippest clubs of all, was liquidated in 2000 when its owner, Chris Paciello, was charged by the FBI with robbery, racketeering, and murder. It turns out that the well-liked Paciello had a shady past in Staten Island as an associate of the Bonanno crime family prior to his relocation to Miami Beach and reinvention as a mover and shaker (and friend of Madonna) on the SoBe scene. He has been called "the most celebrated club owner in Miami Beach since Al Capone."

Like a strutting peacock, the Miami Beach club scene is entirely too infatuated with itself. Peel away the surface glitter, and there is something distinctly unsavory, insular, and overrated about the vaunted nightlife. In any case, hanging out with the glitterati in dance clubs is really not our cup of tea at this point in life's rich pageant. Rather than wait for hours to catch glimpses of fashion robots, Bond-girl wannabes, dapper yuppie playboys, aging bon vivants, and gaudily costumed Eurotrash, we simply returned to Ocean Drive, where there's real fun to be had at the open-air bars and on the egalitarian sidewalks. In fact, we advise all like-minded, disco-averse people to begin and end their night moves on Ocean Drive. You really can't go wrong.

The best place to begin and end a night of carousing in SoBe is the **Clevelander** (1020 Ocean Dr., 305/531-3485), one of the great beach bars and hotels in the solar system. The party space is built around an outdoor pool that adds a splashy quality to proceedings at the five separate bars. Live music is provided by bands who mix disco, funk, R&B, and rock and roll. There's a large pool of musicians to draw from in the area, what with the music program at the University of Miami turning them out in profusion. We've noticed that people seem friendlier in open, life-affirming environments like the Clevelander than at the trendy Dracula's dens on Washington Street. Any night is good at the Clevelander, and no cover is charged. A few doors down, and just as inviting, is the Latino-flavored **Mango's Tropical Café**

MAP OF MIAMI/DADE COUNTY—PAGE 252

Little Havana: The Cuban Community in Miami

Tony Wagner has been living in Little Havana since the early 1960s, when he was just a boy. He was born and raised in Cuba, where his father worked for the government until Fidel Castro's Communist revolution upended life in that island nation and sent families like the Wagners fleeing. Wagner, who gave us a guided tour of Little Havana, remembers the suddenness of their uprooting, and the hurt is still visible in his eyes after four decades. "The Cuban experience is a very particular and painful experience," he said with a smile that conveyed the opposite of a smile. Many of those who left rather than endure life under Castro landed in Miami, where an immigrant community of exiled Cubans took root as "Little Havana." They replaced what had been a poor neighborhood of elderly Jewish retirees.

Little Havana made national news in 1999 when "little Elian Gonzalez"—that is how he was identified in the round-the-clock press coverage on CNN and other networks, as if "little" were part of his name—lived here with relatives. Gonzalez had been rescued at sea by a resident of Little Havana after the capsizing of a rickety raft transporting him, his mother, her boyfriend, and others to the United States from Cuba. It was a miracle that he survived, but that was just the beginning of a long and torturous legal battle to keep his Cuban father from taking him home. The Cuban community in Miami wanted him to stay in the U.S., while his dad, the immigration service, attorney general Janet Reno, and Fidel Castro believed the law held that the father's wishes should prevail. It played out over a period of months and was the biggest story out of Florida until the Election 2000 fiasco.

The Elian Gonzalez story might have died down, but the passions it stirred in Little Havana didn't. In fact, there is a direct link between Gonzalez and the Election 2000 fiasco. The position of the Clinton administration, which sided with attorney general Reno in urging that the boy be reunited with his father and returned to Cuba, so enraged the Cuban

(900 Ocean Dr., 305/673-4422), an indoor-outdoor club that was as packed as any place we've ever seen. The operative exclamations were "Whoooo!" and "Ariba!" Mango's is a hell of a lot of fun, regardless of what language you speak.

When you want to take a break or get away from the blare in Miami Beach, try the "coffee music bar" **Spec's** (501 Collins Avenue, 305/534-3667). Spec's is a megastore that retails CDs, tapes, and videos, but you can also buy a large mug of caffeinated high-test and wander among the stock. Spec's has glommed onto a great gimmick by offering an alternative to hanging out in dance clubs, where the blaring beats will make you deaf (and dumb). The **News Café** (800 Ocean Drive) is also good anytime for an evening-ending Irish coffee or an morning, eye-opening cup of java. The most original of all alternative hangouts is the **Laundry Bar** (721 North Lincoln Lane, 305/531-7700), a laundromat and lounge whose motto is "Get sloshed while your clothes get washed."

The final rule of thumb on South Beach night moves: the bars on Ocean Drive fill up around 10 P.M., and the dance clubs on Washington Street don't really start hop-

community in Miami that they switched their allegiances and voted for George Bush—this despite the fact that Al Gore parted ways with Clinton on this issue and held that Elian should stay. When we visited Little Havana in December 2000, pro-Bush signs (and none for Gore) were staked about Little Havana. The lingering association with Clinton hurt Gore in Little Havana, and their votes provided the slim-to-none difference that pushed Bush to apparent victory in Florida—and, therefore, the nation.

Today, Little Havana (or "Calle Ocho") is undergoing a modest renaissance. The neighborhood informally runs from 37th to 8th Avenues, and is solidly Cuban from 27th to 8th Avenues. As a matter of definition, the Historic District runs from 17th to 8th Avenues. It is a lively bazaar. Maximo Gomez Park, a city park without so much as a square foot of greenery, provides tables and shelter where Cuban gentlemen play dominos and smoke cigars. You can hear the clicking of domino tiles and hearty laughter competing with street noise and the overhead sounds of jets taking off. (Little Havana is directly in the flight pattern for Miami International Airport.)

Moving along, we entered a cantina called Cafe Panza. In one room, Cuban men rolled dice while smoke curled from the ever-present cigars pressed between their lips. Over by the bar, curing hams hung overhead. In the back room, Cuban art—colorful, zesty, and surprisingly cubist in orientation, with a definite debt owed to Picasso—hung on the walls. Who would've thought you'd find Cuban cubism on the walls of a cantina in Little Havana?

It is these kinds of surprises that makes the area so delightful. Directly across the street is Bode & Moore, one of the most celebrated small cigar makers in the world. Shops like this one are everywhere in Little Havana, which teems with the sights and sounds of Cuban culture. Wagner looks around before responding to a question about how many here would head to Cuba if Castro were removed or died.

"What are we going to do, go back and start over?" he asks rhetorically. "This is who we are now. We will stay here. This will be an extension of Cuba and vice versa. Rather than look at it negatively, like some people do in different parts of the country, I think it will make this nation a lot stronger. It is good for us as a people because we are more enculturated and have better diversity. We're Calle Ocho. We're international."

SOUTH FLORIDA

ping until midnight, Club Madonna lists its hours as running from "6 P.M. to Sex A.M." Part of the reason for the late hours is that it is often sticky, hot, and humid until well after 10 P.M. on South Beach. On one recent late-fall trip, when the leaves and temperatures were dropping everywhere else, we were mopping our brows in Miami Beach as the temperature hung steady at 87°F while the humidity topped 95 percent—at 11 P.M.!

If you don't dig bars or clubs, you can still enjoy the nightlife of South Beach simply by watching the show on the sidewalk. Several evenings of South Beach voyeurism cost us nothing but the spare change we handed the vagrants who flowed by, attached like remora fish to the belly of the Saturday night schooling of sharks along Ocean Drive. On a busy night you'll see sexy women in spiked heels, dolled-up guys with heavily oiled hair, a sweater-clad iguana on a leash, Aristotle Onassis lookalikes, Jackie O. clones, and an occasional homeless person. Women hawk cigars. Many of the restaurants display plastic replicas of their entrées on plates—an unusual sight, to say the least. They're hard to miss, since the bistros along Ocean Drive have usurped the pub-

MAP OF MIAMI/DADE COUNTY—PAGE 252

lic's right-of-way as part of their dining area. Thus, you find yourself in the awkward position of shuffling within inches of diners trying to enjoy their meals. In SoBe, for this and other reasons, we sometimes feel like strangers in a strange land. But at least we're amused strangers, most of the time.

Just in case you were wondering whether any of the beautiful people ever connect with one another in a conjugal way, there's a regular column in a local coffee table magazine for the rich and restless called "Sex on South Beach." Sample excerpt from a column when we were last in town: "While discussing IPOs and the new Joop! Collection, I somehow remember working in the fact that I hate to be called 'Babie' [*sic*] or 'Honey'. . . ." As Joe South sang a long time ago, "These are not my people. . . ."

Contact Information

Greater Miami Convention and Visitors

Another German with a Master Plan

Overlooking the entrance to the Port of Miami—at the very southern tip of Miami Beach's barrier island—the Portofino Tower is a 44-story monstrosity that was the brainchild of a brash, flamboyant German named Thomas Kramer. This entrepreneur arrived in Miami Beach in the early 1990s, his personal wealth inflated by canny speculation on East German properties, the values of which skyrocketed after reunification, as well as a marriage (now an ex-marriage) to a wealthy heiress. Kramer quickly earned a reputation as a party animal with a propensity for high-rolling real-estate deals. His amoral acquisitiveness is best summed up by the name of a trendy nightclub he opened, Hell, which just as quickly developed a reputation for discriminating against gays. With an ethically challenged zoning board doing his bidding, Kramer was able to buy up all available property in South Pointe, the former ghetto along the southern shore of the Port of Miami's entrance channel. He then used the term "Master Plan"—apparently not apprehending the terrible irony of those words to the ears of the sizable Jewish community in South Florida—to describe his intention of building a replica of Portofino, an Italian Riviera resort.

Unbelievably, the cash-strapped city of Miami gave him $11.4 million and allowed him to erect some of the tallest residential buildings south of Manhattan, despite a zealous campaign by South Pointe residents and against their outraged objections. Well, Kramer got his tower built—from any angle it looks like the architectural equivalent of an obscene gesture—but his wife divorced him, and his ex-in-laws have sued him, charging misappropriation of $145 million of their money. He was also given the highest fine ever levied by the federal government against an individual for illegal campaign donations. In April 2000, a Swiss court ordered Kramer to pay $91 million to his ex-in-laws. By late 2000, Kramer was still involved in South Pointe real estate ventures. The ultimate sign of Kramer's inveterate decadence: Against the complaints of energy conservationists, he installed an air conditioner to cool the backyard of his $1.8 million mansion on posh Star Island. Yes, you read correctly—an outdoor air conditioner.

Bureau, 701 Brickell Avenue, Suite 2700, Miami, FL 33131; 305/539-3000 or 800/283-2707; website: www.miamiandbeaches.com

Miami Beach Visitor Information Center, 1920 Meridian Avenue, Miami Beach, FL 33139; 305/672-1270; website: www.miamibeachchamber.com

Fisher Island

Because this private island off the southern tip of Miami Beach (across Government Cut Inlet) has frontage on the Atlantic Ocean, we are duty bound to include it here. With that said, Fisher Island (pop. 400) is beyond the means of most travelers and can only be reached via boat. Nonetheless, it is a beautiful 216-acre enclave of palm-caressed wealth dominated by the Mediterranean-style mansion of the late William K. Vanderbilt II, who obtained the island in 1925 from Carl Fisher (creator of Miami Beach) by trading him, even up, a 250-foot yacht. Surely it was the best deal any interloper has made since the purchase of Manhattan for a cache of beads and trinkets.

Fisher Island has 400 residents who have paid anywhere from $600,000 to $6 million for their condo or villa space—mostly part-timers from Brazil, Germany, Italy, France, and Russia. The island has a mile-long sand-fringed beach. The unusually white sand on Fisher Island was brought here from the Bahamas. There are no facilities and no lifeguards.

The karmic payback? Fisher Island is upwind from a sewage treatment plant on Virginia Key.

Bunking Down

The only way the public can recreate on the beach here is to stay at the posh, 60-room **Inn at Fisher Island** (1 Fisher Island Drive, Fisher Island, 305/535-6020, $$$$), which is part of the private Fisher Island Club.

Contact Information

Inn at Fisher Island, 1 Fisher Island Drive, Fisher Island, FL 33109; 305/535-6020; website: www.fisherisland-florida.com

Key Biscayne and Virginia Key

These two keys in a pod, separated only by a man-made cut, offer a less harried alternative to the shores of Miami Beach. There is neither the concentration of neon-scripted outdoor cafés and Art Deco hotels that one finds in South Miami Beach nor the density of high-rise condos that run like an unbroken wall in north Miami Beach. Instead, Key Biscayne pop. 9,700) is upscale, low key, and casually elegant, while Virginia Key is largely uninhabited.

The village of Key Biscayne's high-end real estate draws an "affluent mix of international and domestic buyers" who think nothing of dropping a million or so on a second home. Bounded by the Atlantic Ocean and Biscayne Bay on its sides and by 1,800 combined acres of parkland at its ends, Key Biscayne does make an idyllic hideaway. It's a veritable paradise for watersports enthusiasts, offering everything from exceptional windsurfing and sailing on Biscayne Bay (the U.S. Olympic sailing team trained here) to snorkeling and scuba diving among the wrecks and reefs offshore. Tennis and golf bums will find plenty to do on the island, too. Though the presence of money out here is as thick as the briny, humid air, Key Biscayne offers some of the greatest riches in the form of sizable swaths of undeveloped shoreline that are accessible to all.

Beaches

Considering their size, Key Biscayne and Virginia Key are generously seeded with beach parks facing the Atlantic Ocean. Starting on Virginia Key, or actually before it, is **Hobie Beach.** It lies on the north side of Rickenbacker Causeway and is a terrific spot to learn how to windsurf. Picnic tables, sailboat rentals, and concessions can also be found at this unguarded bayside beach.

Virginia Key Beach has had a checkered history, having been closed since from January 1997 to September 1999—and, as of this writing in July 2001, closed again— by the financially strapped city of Miami. To its eternal misfortune, Virginia Key Beach falls within Miami city limits; it is the city's only public beach. In order to save operating costs of $112,000 a year (while facing a budget deficit of $68 million and possible bankruptcy), Miami elected to shut down one of the few things it has going for it: a lovely public beach park and a great windsurfing spot. During its downtime, the park went from being a haven for families, windsurfers, and bird-watchers to a hangout for homeless derelicts and drunks who left behind broken bottles and garbage. Guess who got stuck with the cost of cleanup? The city of Miami! Access to Virginia Key Beach, when and if it is open, costs $3 per car for Miami residents and $5 per car for nonresidents. The beach entrance sits across from the Miami Seaquarium and next to the city's yard-waste management facility.

Out on Key Biscayne, **Crandon Park** and **Bill Baggs Cape Florida State Park** boast 2.3 and 1.5 miles of sandy shore, respectively. That's nearly four miles of public beach on one small key! Crandon is among the very finest beaches in South Florida and certainly tops in the Miami area. The lifeguarded beach is of a healthy width and gently slopes off as you enter the water, making it relatively safe for children. The sand is soft and free of shells, broken glass, and litter. We took an early-evening stroll along the beach at Crandon Park, and it occurred to us as the sun disappeared and the distant city skyline lit up that this was one of the few places in Miami where one could feel safe walking after dark. Incidentally, the Biscayne Na-

⓮ Hobie Beach

Location: along Rickenbacker Causeway between the mainland and Virginia Key
Parking/fees: free parking along the causeway
Hours: sunrise to sunset
Facilities: concessions, restrooms, picnic tables, and showers
Contact: Miami Parks and Recreation Department, 305/416-1313

⓯ Virginia Key Beach

Location: Rickenbacker Causeway, on Virginia Key between the mainland and Key Biscayne
Parking/fees: for Miami residents, $3 per vehicle and $1 for walk-ins; for nonresidents, $5 per vehicle and $3 for walk-ins
Hours: Virginia Key Beach has been closed periodically since 1997, due to budgetary problems and restoration efforts. As of mid-summer 2001, it was closed again but with the promise that "it will soon reopen to the public."
Facilities: concessions, lifeguards, restrooms, picnic tables, and showers
Contact: Miami-Dade Parks, 305/755-7800

MAP OF SOUTH FLORIDA—PAGE 177

Yes Virginia Key, There was a Sandy Claws

In the annals of American racism, Virginia Key stands out as a shining exception to the black exclusionary rule. As Dade County's only beach for black people, it provided an alternative to the Jim Crow laws of the Deep South. Though the large black population in Miami had helped build and service the whites-only resorts of the 1920s and 1930s, they were not allowed on the sands of Key Biscayne and Miami Beach. As Pulitzer-winning reporter Rick Bragg put it, "Think what it was like to live beside such cool beauty and not be able to stick a toe in it. For the people who did most of the heavy lifting in this utopia, it was a tropical paradise with a padlock." However, partly in response to the brave and tireless service rendered the nation by black soldiers in World War II, county leaders in 1945 designated this then-deserted 1,000-acre barrier island as a public beach for black people.

Until 1947, when a bridge was built, blacks took a ferry over from the mouth of the Miami River. Cottages and small motels were built, and for two decades Virginia Key became a hotspot of African-American culture. Black families and church groups viewed it as a safe haven, and well-known black entertainers and athletes made it a regular port of call while in the area. By the mid-1960s, the civil rights movement opened other beaches in the area to African-Americans, even while a hurricane wiped out most of the structures. Since then, however, Virginia Key has gone to seed as the clueless and often corrupt Miami government has neglected one of the nicest remaining unspoiled beaches in South Florida—and the city of Miami's only beach holding, since Miami and Miami Beach are distinct municipal entities.

Not for long, though. Word is out that the city is thinking of leasing the island to developers, who want to build condos, resorts, and "entertainment venues." In short, they want Virginia Key to echo the same mindless high-rise sprawl that runs in a nearly unbroken line up the Gold Coast. The black community is understandably upset, as they want a civil-rights monument and park erected here. Environmental and outdoor-recreation proponents are also outraged at being ignored by city government. They want what has miraculously become a wildlife sanctuary—purely by default, not proactive policy—to stay that way. The endangered manatee has found Virginia Key to its liking, as has a diverse bird population.

The smart and honorable way to go would be to let nature take its course, to celebrate this vital piece of African-American history, and to allow Virginia Key to return to its shining incarnation as a symbol of accessibility and hope. Though it appears that a Civil Rights Museum will be built at Virginia Key Beach, it doesn't take an Alan Greenspan to forecast what will likely happen elsewhere on Virginia Key. This is, after all, Miami. Look for more condos built with mysterious infusions of foreign cash, gated communities, exorbitantly priced convention hotels, etc. As Hunter Thompson put it years ago in his rephrasing of Ernest Hemingway, the scum also rises. In Miami, that is not likely to change anytime soon.

MAP OF MIAMI/DADE COUNTY—PAGE 252

ture Center, an ecotourism enterprise based in Crandon Park, takes tour groups out on snorkeling trips; call 305/361-8097 for information and reservations.

The north end of Key Biscayne belongs to Bill Baggs Cape Florida State Park. This used to be one of the loveliest and least spoiled coastal environments in Greater Miami until a hurricane came along and wrecked it. Hurricane Andrew, which leveled the town of Homestead to the south, did a thoroughly destructive job at Bill Baggs as well, clearing the park of vegetation. When we called shortly after the 1992 hurricane, we were told there was no point in visiting because there was nothing left to see. If the story ended there, it would be a sad testimony to nature's destructive might. Instead, we have a much happier tale to relate about nature's indomitable will to recover, especially with a human-assisted push in the right direction. What a difference a decade makes! The regeneration has been nothing short of amazing. While it will take years for the trees to attain pre-hurricane heights, the tropical-hammock thickets are dense and buzzing with life once again. In an odd sort of way, Andrew did the park a favor. By leveling all the non-native Australian pines, it gave park naturalists a chance to start from scratch with native vegetation. Now the park truly looks like nature intended it.

The east-facing beaches of Key Biscayne and Virginia Key, incidentally, collect a lot of the ocean's photosynthetic debris. Seaweed washes up on the beach and accumulates in bale-sized mounds along the high-tide line. They're bulldozed into piles and hauled off on the beach in front of the Sonesta Beach Resort but pile up along the more natural beaches elsewhere on the two keys. Their brown, beardlike accumulations tend to attract insects, especially at dusk.

Bunking Down

Aside from private condos, there are only a handful of places for the public to stay on the beach in Key Biscayne, but they are superlative luxury accommodations. One is the elegant **Sonesta Beach Resort** (350 Ocean Drive, 305/361-2021, $$$$). A warning: You may grow so comfortable here you might find it hard to leave. We certainly didn't, happily slouching around in hammocks slung between palm trees on the beach. The Sonesta has a big, breezy beach that's swept clean of seaweed each morning. Cabanas, beach chairs, hammocks, palm trees, a big blue Olympic pool the size of a small lake, the requisite poolside tiki bar, huge circular Jacuzzi, and even a setup at one end of the pool where you can play water basketball—what more could you want from life than this?

16 Crandon Park

Location: 4000 Crandon Boulevard, at the north end of Key Biscayne
Parking/fees: $3.50 per vehicle entrance fee
Hours: 8 A.M.–7 P.M.
Facilities: concessions, lifeguards, restrooms, picnic tables, and showers
Contact: Crandon Park, 305/361-5421

17 Bill Baggs Cape Florida State Park

Location: 1200 South Crandon Park Boulevard, at the south end of Key Biscayne
Parking/fees: $4 entrance fee per vehicle
Hours: 8 A.M. to sunset
Facilities: concessions, lifeguards, restrooms, picnic tables, and showers
Contact: Bill Baggs Cape Florida State Park, 305/361-5811

MAP OF SOUTH FLORIDA—PAGE 177

One-Man Blands

Some might argue that rock and roll has been on a downward spiral since the 1980s, the decade during which MTV came on the air, CDs replaced vinyl, the drinking age was raised from 18 to 21 (excluding college kids from bars and clubs), and rap, heavy metal, grunge, techno, and teenybopper pop became the lingua franca of pop culture. We are devoted rock-hounds of longstanding, having both worked as music journalists. One of our great pleasures in researching beach books has been going out at night to find that the heart of rock and roll is still beating. We have heard plenty of good bands playing for appreciative audiences at the beach.

However, we must admit that lately the heart of rock and roll—especially of the live, organic variety—may be in need of bypass surgery. There are several reasons for this clogging of the musical arteries. First, fewer people go out at night. Second, dance music, hip-hop, and various other popular strains are mostly electronic in nature, rendering "real" musicians obsolete. Deejays and turntables have taken the place of performing bands. Third, many places that once booked rock and roll bands have adopted a cost-cutting alternative: the one-man band. These are individuals who come armed with taped or computer-programmed music, to which they sing and sometimes play along on guitar or keyboard. It is basically glorified karaoke.

We've heard one-man bands everywhere in Florida. They serenade happy-hour drinkers with mild fare at beachside tiki bars. (One more version of "Margaritaville" and we're taking hostages.) They rumble through the Chuck Berry, Bob Seger, and Stevie Ray Vaughan songbooks at bars that cater to a rock and blues crowd. They pump up middle-aged Rogaine users with Motown retreads. They soothe dinner audiences with Lou Rawls and Julio Iglesias. They cause booties to shake to the songs of Ricky Martin and Enrique Iglesias. They even perform country music this way. We saw one grizzled old codger with a notebook computer sing "All My Ex's Live in Texas" at a bar in out-of-the-way Cedar Key. It doesn't get any weirder than that.

One-man bands have become the kudzu of the Florida club scene. These individuals have an arsenal of tunes available at the push of a button, and bland, malleable voices suited to any occasion. Meanwhile, live rock and roll is getting crowded out of the picture. It's enough to make a beach bum teary.

Hey, mister, does your computer know "I'm So Lonesome I Could Cry"?

The hotel itself is opulent, its walls adorned with paintings collected by the Sonesta family, well-known patrons of the arts who stock their Sonesta Hotels from a collection numbering 6,000 original art works. The Sonesta Beach Resort survived Hurricane Andrew, although the trail of sand deposited by the storm extended up onto the pool area and into the lobby. More than $20 million was spent in restoration. The same cannot be claimed of the neighboring Sheraton, which was destroyed by the hurricane and never rebuilt.

For a long time, the Sonesta was the only game in town for upscale travelers, many of them well-to-do Latin Americans. Now there is a new arrival, the **Ritz-Carlton Key Biscayne** (415 Grand Bay Drive,

Cuckoo for CocoWalk

Coconut Grove is not on the ocean, and it has no beaches (or coconuts or groves, come to think of it), but it qualifies for honorable mention in our book. Located along Biscayne Bay, just south of Rickenbacker Causeway (which crosses over to Key Biscayne), Coconut Grove has an eccentric if decidedly upscale appeal that draws the city's party animals and tourists in equal numbers. There is also said to be a budding "hippie community" in the Grove that's been vocal about the encroachment of mall consciousness upon what was formerly a funky and diverse neighborhood. This anti-stylish clan hangs out at lovely Peacock Park, just a few blocks from CocoWalk.

The "village" of Coconut Grove was settled by Bahamian seamen and later solidified by yacht designer Ralph Munroe, whose eccentric waterfront home, the **Barnacle** (circa 1891), has been preserved as a state historic site (3485 Main Highway, 305/448-9449) open Friday–Sunday. Nearby is **Vizcaya** (3251 South Miami Avenue, 305/579-2708), a turn-of-the-century Italian Renaissance mansion that's the city of Miami's show palace. Vizcaya has hosted the pope and the queen and probably even Prince. You can't miss this 70-room "palace" on the bayfront. Across from Vizcaya are the lush grounds of the **Museum of Science and Space Transit Planetarium** (3280 South Miami Avenue, 305/854-4247). This venerable palace of wisdom has been popular since 1949, offering 140 hands-on exhibits and shows that are, well, heavenly.

Okay, these are all places you should visit in Coconut Grove. Most people, however, think of "the Grove" as a shopping opportunity and a place to see and be seen. The epicenter for this narcissism is CocoWalk, an airy, three-tiered, mostly outdoor mall that was built in 1990 and has not known a quiet moment since. After visiting this place and then pondering the millions of money-toting tourists who visit the area each year, we wondered how Miami could possibly have gone bankrupt in 1996.

We visited CocoWalk on a busy Friday night. Judging from the friendly, unbridled frenzy at Hooters, Dan Marino's Sports Bar, the Baja Beach Club, and Cafe Tu Tu Tango, it must have been a tough work week in Miami. So much steam was being blown off that even

305/365-9575, $$$$), which is one of the hottest properties in South Florida. A modest, more affordable contrast to the Ritz and Sonesta is offered by the **Silver Sands Beach Resort** (301 Ocean Drive, 305/361-5441, $$$), whose flowering, plant-filled courtyard and 56 single-story units make it a lot closer to the original look of the casual Old Florida than its towering neighbors.

Coastal Cuisine

The Sonesta Beach Resort has three on-premises restaurant: the **Purple Dolphin** (350 Ocean Drive, 305/361-2021, $$$$), which specializes in fine dining and offers a Friday-night seafood buffet for $29; **Two Dragons** (350 Ocean Drive, 305/361-2021, $$$), which serves Chinese and Thai items, as well as an extensive menu of sushi (try the Dragon Roll: eel, crab, avocado, and mango); and the casual **Jasmine Cafe** (350 Ocean Drive, 305/361-2021, $). The menu here is short and sweet, including soup, sandwiches, and lighter fare such as grilled shrimp quesadillas served with home-

the cops were smiling in wonder. We retreated, briefly, to a Borders Books, quaffing a reviving cup of java before rejoining the fray. We met a Jamaican lawyer for the Justice Department named Paula, who'd only recently moved to Miami after having lived in Washington, D.C. (hated it) and San Francisco (loved it). She wasn't yet sure how she felt about Miami, but she did aver that "it is completely different from any city in America." And she really liked the Grove, which she compared to "a more friendly Georgetown." Just a few blocks away from CocoWalk, she insisted, the area was so quiet and neighborly she wouldn't consider living anywhere else during her year-long assignment in Miami.

Meanwhile, back on the streets, suburban kids were cruising bumper-to-bumper in sleek cars that throbbed so loudly with the blare of hip-hop and Latino music that the very tailpipes were rattling. Those pretty young thangs who were not in cars were on the street, dressed to thrill from the racks of the nearby Gap, Banana Republic, and Victoria's Secret. It was a scene right out of *American Graffiti,* albeit sanitized by the mercantile mind-set and corporate logos of the upscale chain stores.

Planet Hollywood is capitalism's flagship, or so we thought before poking our noses inside the one at Coconut Grove (3390 Mary Street, 305/445-7277). The brainchild of box-office buffoons Bruce, Demi, Arnold, and Sly, it holds down an entire block next door to CocoWalk. In case you've never made the plunge, Planet Hollywood is a monument to spending and bad taste. Ghastly wax dummies hang suspended in agonized poses from the ceilings, while TV monitors pump out previews for the newest batch of movies at the 16-screen cinema next door. The sound system booms with moronic music and sound effects. Then there's the wallet-busting "Merch Shop," which are the words that hang, in sanitized neon, above a high-priced tourist trinket trough. The Planet Hollywood logo is grafted onto such indispensable "merch" as appliquéd sweatshirts (from $45), leather jackets (from $325), varsity jackets ($225), "Celebrity Edition IV T-shirts" ($21), and so on, all the way down to Planet Hollywood boxer shorts ($15). We are only too happy to report that on a perfectly breezy and busy Friday night, Planet Hollywood was less than half full. The upstairs had been roped off entirely, and we saw not one single solitary person march up to the Merch Shop. May people all over the planet be so enlightened.

made guacamole and salsa. Try the conch chowder, a cumin-spiced concoction that takes a more Cuban approach to the soup than you'll typically find farther down on the Keys.

Contact Information

Key Biscayne Chamber of Commerce, 87 West McIntire, Key Biscayne, FL 33133; 305/361-5207; website: www.keybiscaynechamber.org

MAP OF MIAMI/DADE COUNTY—PAGE 252

Matheson Hammock County Park

South Dade County is beachless and mucky, but there are a couple parks with swimming areas along Biscayne Bay. One of them is **Matheson Hammock County Park**, which lies south of Coconut Grove and east of Kendall. Constructed by the Civilian Conservation Corps in the 1930s, it is the oldest park in Dade County. Between the lushly vegetated grounds and the view of the Miami skyline and Key Biscayne across the bay, Matheson Hammock occupies a scenic corner of South Dade. As improbable as it sounds, there is even a sandy swimming beach here.

18 Matheson Hammock County Park

Location: 9610 Old Cutler Road in South Coral Gables
Parking/fees: $3.50 entrance fee per vehicle
Hours: 6 A.M. to sunset
Facilities: concessions, lifeguards, restrooms, picnic tables, and showers
Contact: Matheson Hammock County Park, 305/666-6979

Though the sand has been trucked in, it's a nice illusion and definitely more fun to recreate on than the grayish soil that lines the bay. The swimming area is a natural lagoon that has been enclosed to form a tidal-fed "atoll pool." Triathletes train here, finding the park a nice place to run and the atoll pool a great place to swim laps. Mainly, though, it's a family-oriented park, with a picnic area and the lifeguarded lagoon. There's even an alfresco restaurant, the **Redfish Grill** (open 5 P.M.–10 P.M. nightly), that's run by the owners of a fancy Coral Gables restaurant called Christy's. County parks don't get much nicer than this!

Homestead

You might recall Homestead (pop. 28,000) as the headline-making city that was nearly wiped off the map by Hurricane Andrew in 1992. It was the costliest natural disaster up to that point in U.S. history, and Homestead took a direct hit. Since then the city has rebuilt and is still on the rebound. Homestead Air Reserve Base, which was slated for decommissioning, has a new lease on life as the proposed site of a commercial airport for Miami, although environmental issues have proved to be a sticking point. Seemingly trying to become South Florida's answer to Daytona, Homestead has a new motorsports complex whose grandstand (capacity: 65,000) can hold more than twice the population of Homestead. If an ear-splitting car race in the heat and humidity of swampy South

19 Homestead Bayfront Park

Location: east end of Canal Drive (S.W. 328th Street) in Homestead
Parking/fees: $3.50 entrance fee per vehicle
Hours: 6 A.M. to sunset
Facilities: concessions, lifeguards, restrooms, picnic tables, and showers
Contact: Homestead Bayfront Park, 305/230-3034

Florida sounds appealing, then Homestead is your kind of town. For most travelers, however, Homestead is bypassed with dispatch en route to or from the Keys.

Beaches

Homestead Bayfront Park, like Matheson Hammock County Park, features an "atoll pool": an enclosed saltwater lagoon fed by tidal exchange, with a sandy shoreline. Located eight miles east of Homestead, this popular and well-equipped county park is adjacent to the visitor center for Biscayne National Park.

Contact Information

Greater Homestead/Florida City Chamber of Commerce, 43 North Krome Avenue, Homestead, FL 33030; 305/247-2332; website: www.chamberinaction.com

Biscayne National Park

Biscayne National Park plays second fiddler crab to its better-known neighbor, Everglades National Park. One reason for this may be that 97 percent of its 181,500 acres are underwater. The park has been in existence since 1968, and yet it remains something of a well-guarded secret, at least by comparison to the Everglades and John Pennekamp Coral Reef State Park on Key Largo. Mostly, it's visited by pleasure boaters, divers, snorkelers, and anglers. Within the park boundaries, which run from the south end of Miami to Key Largo, are 41 keys. There are also mangrove forests, living coral reefs, and 25 miles of mainland shoreline. We took the snorkeling trip, which lasts all afternoon. Pray for a calm, wave-free day; we did not get one and were made seasick by all the rocking and rolling not in the boat but as we bobbed around in the water. The ride out to whatever reef the guide decides to visit that day is a good way to see the bay, and the snorkeling sights are colorful as long as the water hasn't been stirred up by waves and currents. You might ask about conditions before making the long trip out here and plunking down your $30.

The point of entry for landlubbers is the Convoy Point Visitor Center, on Biscayne Bay. You can pick up literature and check out exhibits at the newly constructed visitor center or picnic on the grounds. There's really not much else to do on the mainland, which is why you'll want to take a boat trip. Daily trips include a glass-bottomed boat tour at 10 A.M. ($19.95 for adults, $12.95 for children under 12) and a snorkeling excursion at 1:30 P.M. ($29.95). Scuba-diving trips ($44.95) depart at 8:30 A.M. on weekends, as long as six or more sign up. Arrangements for boat transportation to and from Elliott and Boca Chita Keys ($24.95 round-trip) can be made through the park concessionaire, which also rents canoes ($8 per hour), kayaks ($16 per hour), and scuba gear. For information and reservations, call 305/230-1100.

Free campgrounds are located on both Elliott Key and Boca Chita Keys, which lie about eight and 10 miles offshore, respectively. (Note: A $15 fee is charged for

20 Biscayne National Park

Location: The Convoy Point Visitor Center at the east end of Canal Drive (S.W. 328th Street), nine miles east of Homestead

Parking/fees: free

Hours: 8:30 A.M.–5 P.M.

Facilities: concessions, restrooms, picnic tables, showers, and a visitor center

Contact: Biscayne National Park, 305/230-7275

MAP OF MIAMI/DADE COUNTY—PAGE 252

docking personal boats at both islands.) Elliott is 11 miles long and one mile wide, with a ranger station at the harbor and a hiking trail that runs along its coral spine. Boca Chita is small and round, a little puffball of a key by comparison. Both islands have restrooms, picnic areas, and boat docks. Elliott has showers and drinking water, to boot. While there are no sand beaches in the park, there's a grassy one on Elliott Key. (Hey, in the Keys, you take what you can get.)

Boca Chita Key was reopened to the public in December 1996 after having been closed for more than three years by Hurricane Andrew. Biscayne National Park was ground zero for the devastating storm, which killed about 90 percent of the mature red mangroves. However, the park's recovery in the intervening years has indeed been impressive. Come out and discover for yourself!

Contact Information

Biscayne National Park, 9700 Southwest 328th Street, P.O. Box 1369 Homestead, FL 33090; 305/230-7275; website: www.nps.gov/bisc

MAP OF SOUTH FLORIDA—PAGE 177

Get Thee Behind Me, Miami

At its southern end Miami dribbles on and on with seemingly no end in sight. If you're headed to the Keys and have decided that U.S. 1 is the straightest line between two points, you will become entrapped for what seems like forever inside a hamster wheel of redundant roadside commerce. By the time you've reached the relatively unblemished Overseas Highway and are cruising to the Keys, you will feel sullied and exhausted, as if you've run some sort of gauntlet. U.S. 1 out of Miami is a cow pie of capitalism so shoddy you might briefly flirt with the notion that even Castro's brand of dictatorial communism couldn't yield results much worse than this. And you will not want to gaze on another American flag anytime soon.

Some of the largest flags ever fabricated, joined by countless smaller flags arrayed in mind-numbing rows, fly over car dealerships along this blighted stretch of highway. The enormity of their wind-whipped furls is matched only by the transparent gall of those who have hoisted Old Glory in these parts. There is an implied yet spurious relationship between the size and numbers of flags and the patriotic intent of the dealerships. The tautology goes like this: We fly more and bigger American flags, therefore we are a more trustworthy place to buy a Japanese car. A further irony rests in the fact that this parading of the red, white, and blue occurs deep in South Florida, a land swollen with illegal immigrants, drug runners, welfare cheats, pawnshop brokers trading in stolen goods, and people who can't speak a word of English.

But flags are the least of the assorted horrors along this drive. You are dragged—as if in slow motion, thanks to all the stoplights and congestion—past mile after droning mile of seedy commerce that worsens as you plunge into the belly of the beast. It all starts at the end of I-95 in South Miami, where traffic is dumped onto U.S. 1. At this point, it is like any other bad case of suburban sprawl, thick with the sort of franchised mediocrity that makes every American city look more or less identical and almost negates the whole point of traveling anymore.

Still, we derived a measure of comfort from passing recognizable franchise names, even if they were of the Kentucky Fried Chicken and Miami Subs ilk. It did not last long as we proceeded farther south on U.S. 1, where the landscape deteriorates into a tawdry diorama of adult video shops, bail bondsmen, no-tell motels, gas stations, convenience stores, filthy fast-food stands, weed-choked lots, abandoned businesses, and the absurd spectacle of heavy machinery ravaging the countryside to erect more pointless enterprise on the very rim of the suffering Everglades.

Our advice is to go out of your way to avoid U.S. 1 out of Miami by taking Florida's Turnpike. This route, which swings west of the city, adds mileage but saves considerable time and will spare you the sort of red-faced diatribes that were erupting in our car.

The Keys

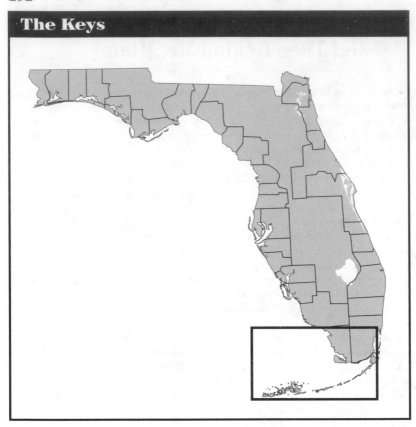

Key to the Symbols

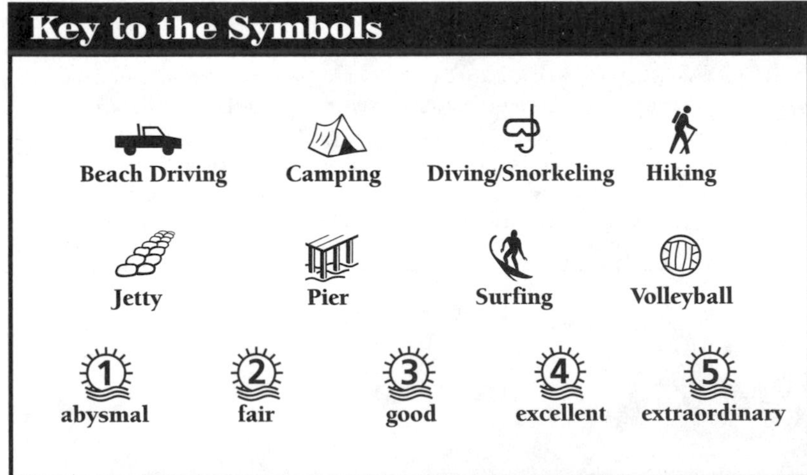

The Keys

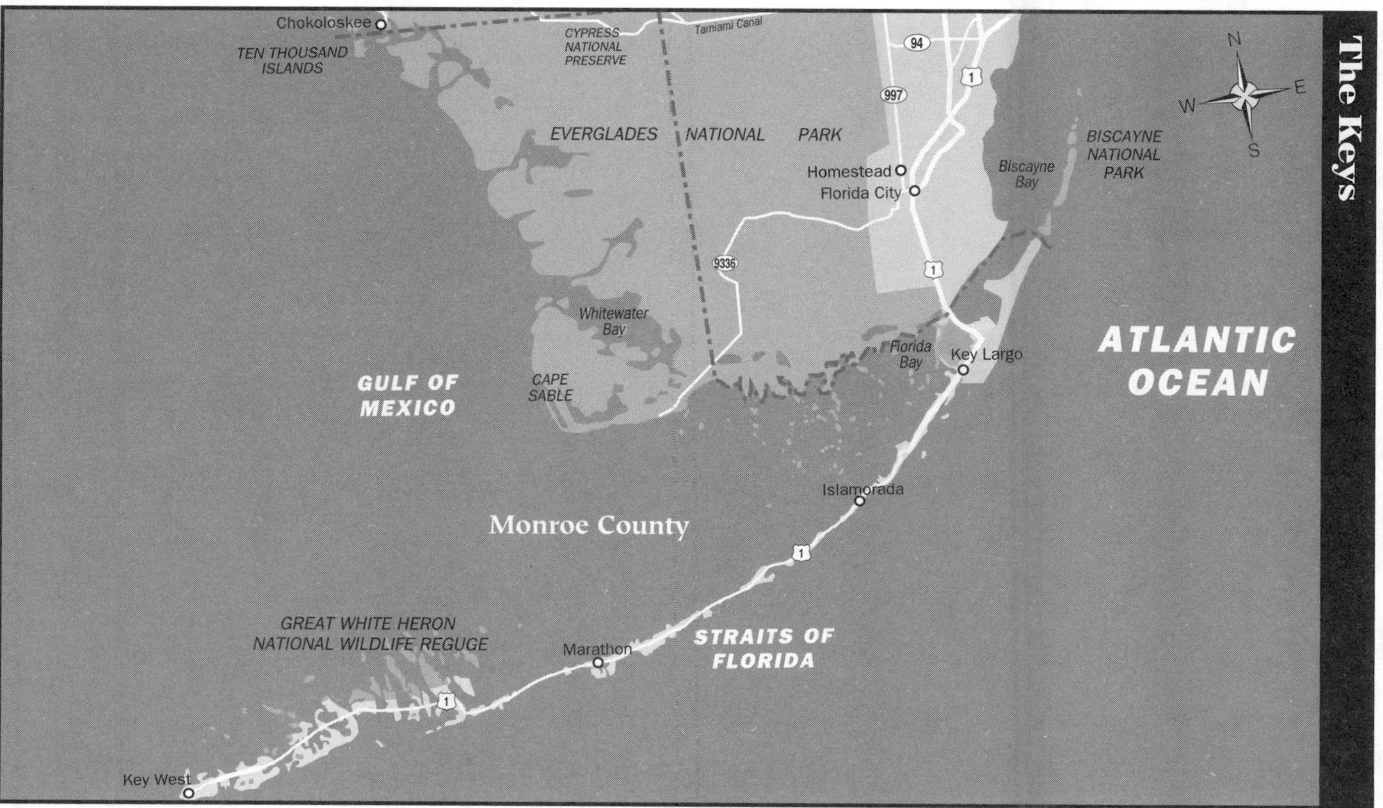
Chokoloskee
TEN THOUSAND ISLANDS
CYPRESS NATIONAL PRESERVE
Tamiami Canal
94
1
997
EVERGLADES NATIONAL PARK
N
W
E
S
BISCAYNE NATIONAL PARK
Biscayne Bay
Homestead
Florida City
9336
Whitewater Bay
Florida Bay
Key Largo
ATLANTIC OCEAN
GULF OF MEXICO
CAPE SABLE
Islamorada
Monroe County
GREAT WHITE HERON NATIONAL WILDLIFE REGUGE
Marathon
STRAITS OF FLORIDA
Key West

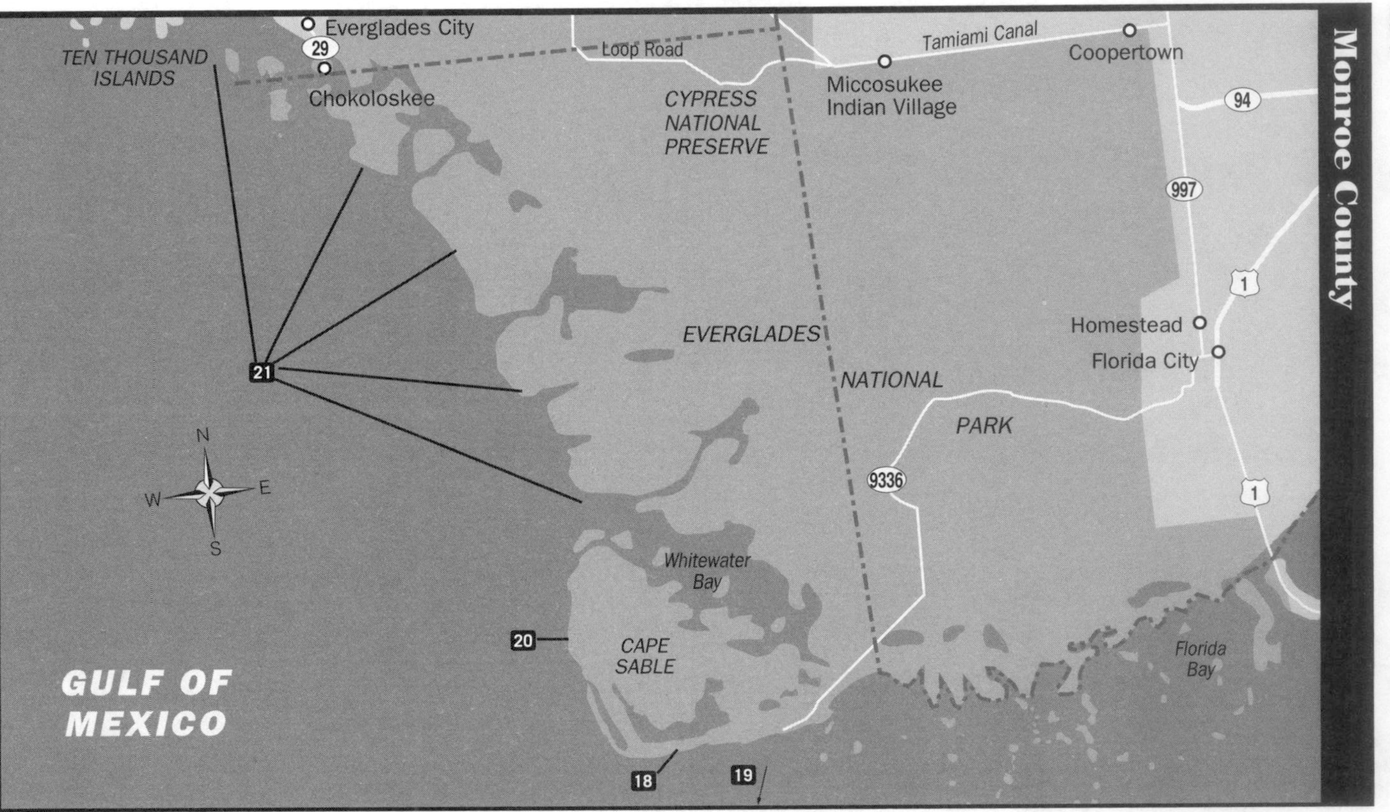
Monroe County
TEN THOUSAND ISLANDS
Everglades City
29
Chokoloskee
Loop Road
CYPRESS NATIONAL PRESERVE
Miccosukee Indian Village
Tamiami Canal
Coopertown
94
997
1
Homestead
Florida City
EVERGLADES
NATIONAL
PARK
9336
1
21
N
E
W
S
Whitewater Bay
20
CAPE SABLE
Florida Bay
GULF OF MEXICO
18
19

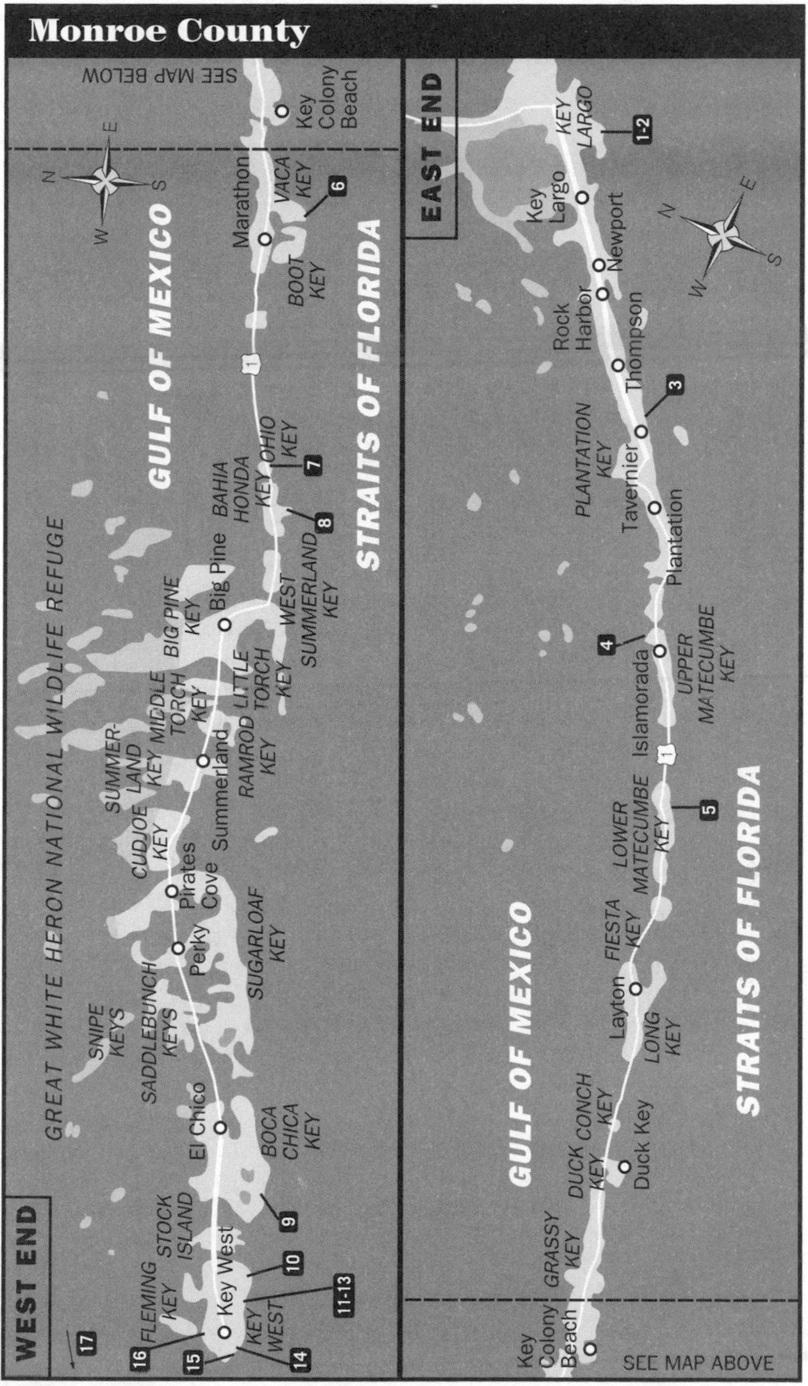

Monroe County

WEST END
GREAT WHITE HERON NATIONAL WILDLIFE REFUGE
GULF OF MEXICO
STRAITS OF FLORIDA
SEE MAP BELOW
17
16 FLEMING KEY
15
14 KEY WEST
Key West
11-13
10
STOCK ISLAND
9
El Chico
BOCA CHICA KEY
SNIPE KEYS
SADDLEBUNCH KEYS
Perky
SUGARLOAF KEY
Pirates Cove
CUDJOE KEY
SUMMERLAND KEY
Summerland
RAMROD KEY
MIDDLE TORCH KEY
LITTLE TORCH KEY
BIG PINE KEY
Big Pine
WEST SUMMERLAND KEY
BAHIA HONDA KEY
8
OHIO KEY
7
1
BOOT KEY
Marathon
VACA KEY
6
Key Colony Beach

EAST END
GULF OF MEXICO
STRAITS OF FLORIDA
SEE MAP ABOVE
Key Colony Beach
GRASSY KEY
DUCK KEY
Duck Key
CONCH KEY
LONG KEY
Layton
FIESTA KEY
LOWER MATECUMBE KEY
5
1
Islamorada
UPPER MATECUMBE KEY
4
Plantation
Tavernier
PLANTATION KEY
3
Thompson
Rock Harbor
Newport
Key Largo
KEY LARGO
1-2

MONROE COUNTY

MAP OF THE KEYS—PAGE 293

To lovers of land's end, Monroe County is an endlessly fascinating finale for the East Coast. The county embraces the Everglades and the Florida Keys, both environmentally sensitive areas. Most of the 1.5-million-acre Everglades National Park falls inside Monroe County. The Keys extend for 108 miles from the mainland in a southwesterly direction, closer at road's end in Key West to Havana than Miami. Though sand beaches are few and far between, several world-class exceptions are scattered between Marathon and Key West: Bahia Honda State Park (on Bahia Honda Key), Anne's Beach (on Lower Matecumbe Key), and Sombrero Beach (in Marathon). The Keys have given birth to a laid-back way of life that finds its culmination in Key West, home base for the "Conch Republic" and as close to the tropics as America gets.

MAP OF MONROE COUNTY—PAGES 294 & 295

Key Largo

Key Largo (pop. 11,336) is the northernmost and largest of the Florida Keys, 30 miles in length from stem to stern. Yes, maritime metaphors are appropriate here, because most vacation activities are done from a boat: fishing, diving, snorkeling, cruising. Beaches are in relatively short supply on Key Largo. Still, enough points of historical and natural interest—and some genuine curiosities—can be found to justify a stopover. And, if you come here to fully explore the wonders of John Pennekamp Coral Reef State Park, you'll want to hole up on Key Largo for a few days.

The most obvious curiosity about Key Largo is its fixation with Humphrey Bogart. This obsession originated with the 1948 movie *Key Largo,* which, obviously, derived its name from local geography. Beyond that, the Bogie connection is tenuous at best. With the exception of a few interior scenes filmed inside the Caribbean Club (MM 104.5), Key Largo was made on a soundstage in Hollywood, and Bogie himself never set foot on the Keys. Nonetheless, the biggest town on the key, Rock Harbor, changed its name to Key Largo—presumably in hopes of translating Hollywood celebrity into tourist dollars. (If you look closely, you will still find a sign for Rock Harbor on U.S. 1).

While this is harmless and diverting enough, it would be nice if Key Largo expended some of this same energy restoring other parts of town to a more nostalgic, if not idyllic, condition. For instance, the concept of zoning seems nonexistent, judging from the unending line of fast-food franchises and the scattershot development that finds an adult video shop next to a boat-propeller shop next to a fruit stand next to a church next to a T-shirt emporium next to a shell shop. Incredibly enough, Key Largo remains unincorporated, which explains the unregulated (and unconscionable) sprawl. By the way, be especially wary of shell shops. They take whatever they legally can from the Keys and import precious coral and shells from other parts of the world where the environmental laws are lax, at best. Unsuspecting tourists buy this ecological plunder like they would saltwater taffy, giving it nary a second thought.

While this may seem like carping, it does have some connection to Key Largo's most prominent drawing card, John Pennekamp Coral Reef State Park. The living reefs off Key Largo have been under assault from tanker wrecks, oil spills, agricultural runoff, coral poachers, and prop dredge from myriad small boats. Swinish boaters even dump trash overboard, which sinks or washes ashore; we have seen detritus along the shoreline like you wouldn't believe. Several divers have told us that underwater visibility has declined dramatically in recent years among the reefs of the Keys. A management plan for the Florida Keys National Marine Sanctuary was implemented in 1997, and we hope it will help turn the tide.

Key Largo gets a lot of mileage out of calling itself the "Dive Capital of the World." Established in 1960, Pennekamp was the nation's first undersea preserve. The Key Largo National Marine Sanctuary was created in 1975. As part of the Florida Keys National Marine Sanctuary, Key Largo lays claim to six Sanctuary Preservation Areas, where fishing of all kinds—even with a hook and line—is prohibited. Other popular dive sites in the area include Molasses Reef and French Reef, with its underwater caves. Kayaking the waters of Florida Bay is an eco-friendly way to find some quietude away from the crowds.

Key Largo, like all of the Florida Keys, has become a destination resort—and, for retirees, destination of last resort—for the wealthy. This is unfortunate in that the late-

MAP OF THE KEYS—PAGE 293

ly arrived builders of trophy homes in the Keys have been displacing those of more modest means who have called the area home for much of a lifetime. In short, natives are being priced out of their own communities by rich, retiring doctors from New Jersey and the like. We're not writing an editorial about social injustice but simply stating facts, which in all likelihood will not pertain if you're coming here just to vacation. Despite all the complications and kinks in the social matrix, the fact remains

Highway to the Keys

U.S. 1 runs the 108-mile length of the Florday Keys, from Key Largo to Key West. Technically, however, it all begins in Florida City, below Homestead at the eastern boundary of Everglades National Park, where U.S. 1 officially becomes the Overseas Highway. The first mile marker (MM 126) is encountered here, and those numbers decrease as you make your way west down the Keys. The final mile marker (MM 0) is at the corner of Whitehead and Fleming Streets in Key West. On these narrow keys, mile markers function as addresses and directions. Often, the words "oceanside" or "bayside" will be included, as in "Harry Harris County Park, MM 92.5 oceanside."

Although you travel west-southwest on the Overseas Highway, the Keys are spoken of as being north or south of one another. So why, then, do they call it Key West? Because this particular key originally bore the Spanish name Cayo Hueso ("bone island"), which got misheard by English-speaking ears as Key West. It's actually a pretty accurate name, when you look at the map. (Besides, "Key South" doesn't have quite the same ring.) Another bit of nomenclature: "Upper Keys" refers to the stretch from Key Largo to Islamorada. "Lower Keys" extends from the western foot of the 7 Mile Bridge (Little Duck Key) to Stock Island. The "Middle Keys" include everything in between, with the town of Marathon as the hub. Key West stands alone at the end of the road, an entity unto itself.

More than 800 islands make up the 180-mile chain of Florida Keys. They extend from Biscayne Bay to the Dry Tortugas, although only the stretch from Key Largo to Key West is bridged. The Keys range in size from tiny mangrove islands to the sizable likes of Key Largo and Big Pine Key (the two largest). A total of 42 bridges cross the Keys, ranging in length from 37 feet (Harris Gap, in the Lower Keys) to 35,716 feet (7 Mile Bridge, which actually falls 1,244 feet shy of seven miles). Average elevations on the Keys are between two and six feet above sea level, with the highest point at 18 feet, at Lignumvitae Key. These limestone spines are the remnants of coral reefs that died when sea level dropped during the last ice age. Most keys are so narrow you can see the Straits of Florida out of one eye and Florida Bay from the other.

It was the unsinkable Henry Morrison Flagler who hatched the idea of linking the seemingly unbridgeable Keys by extending his Florida East Coast Railway from Homestead to Key West. Despite the project's cost, in terms of expense and human lives, the cross-Keys railroad was completed in seven years, with Flagler triumphantly riding into Key West in 1912 (only to die a few months later). His railroad survived until the raging hurricane of September 2, 1935, which destroyed the tracks. However, the pilings survived, and the Overseas Highway (U.S. 1) was built atop them.

that here is nothing like the sight of mist rising off Florida Bay in the early morning in Key Largo. Rise before the sun to do something water related, and you can't go wrong.

Beaches

It's a given that you're not really coming to the Keys for the beaches, because they are few and far between. Offshore coral reefs intercept the waves, so there's no physical mechanism for transporting sand shoreward to build up a beach. Having said that, you will find several beaches on Key Largo, but they're man made. Two of them, **Cannon Beach** and **Far Beach**, are in John Pennekamp Coral Reef State Park. Cannon Beach is a small sliver of sand that features a replica of a seventeenth-century shipwreck, located 130 feet off shore, which attracts tropical fish and snorkelers. Swimming in the balmy waters is fine, but you really must pack snorkeling gear or you'll miss the best Cannon Beach has to offer. Far Beach, a short hop down Largo Sound, is the prettier site, lined with coconut palms that afford some shade.

Harry Harris County Park completes Key Largo's trio of faux sand beaches. It has a little something for everyone, from ballplayers (baseball fields, basketball courts) to boaters (two boat ramps, which are the best landings on the ocean between Miami and Key West) to beachgoers (an enclosed tidal pool that's about as wide as a football field). There's also a large picnic area and children's playground. Wilkinson's Point is an interesting coral outcrop that extends about 100 yards into the water. On the north side, you can wander into the three-foot shallows of Florida Bay (wear shoes). It is a well-guarded fact that this is one of the best bonefishing areas around, and you don't even have to be in a boat to take advantage of it. County residents don't have to pay to use the park. Nonresidents are charged $5 on weekends and holidays but can enter for free at all other times.

Shore Things

- **Bike/skate rentals:** Key Largo Bikes, MM 99, 305/451-1910.
- **Boat cruise:** Key Largo Princess, MM 100, 305/451-4655.
- **Dive shop:** Silent World Dive Center, MM 103.2, 305/451-3252.
- **Ecotourism:** Florida Bay Outfitters, MM 104, 305/451-3018.
- **Fishing charters:** Bluewater World, MM 100.5, 305/451-2511.

1 Cannon Beach

Location: John Pennekamp Coral Reef State Park, off U.S. 1 at MM 102.5 in Key Largo
Parking/fees: $2.50 per person per vehicle for first two visitors; 50 cents apiece for all others. Camping fees are $23.69 per night (without hookups) and $25.84 (with hookups).
Hours: 8 A.M. to sunset
Facilities: concessions, restrooms, picnic tables, showers, and a visitor center
Contact: John Pennekamp Coral Reef State Park, 305/451-1202

2 Far Beach

Location: John Pennekamp Coral Reef State Park, off U.S. 1 at MM 102.5 in Key Largo
Parking/fees: $2.50 per person per vehicle for first two visitors; 50 cents apiece for all others. Camping fees are $23.69 per night (without hookups) and $25.84 (with hookups).
Hours: 8 A.M. to sunset
Facilities: concessions, restrooms, picnic tables, showers, and a visitor center
Contact: John Pennekamp Coral Reef State Park, 305/451-1202

- **Marina:** Marina del Mar, MM 100, 305/451-4107.
- **Rainy-day attraction:** Maritime Museum of the Florida Keys, MM 102.5, 305/451-6444.
- **Shopping/browsing:** Tavernier Towne Shopping Center, MM 91.2.
- **Vacation rentals:** Loveland Realty, 103300 Overseas Highway, 305/451-5055.

Bunking Down

Westin Beach Resort Key Largo (MM 97, 305/852-5553, $$$$) is as unobtrusive as any four-story hotel can be, set among a 12-acre buttonwood grove that insinuates itself nicely into the visitor's consciousness. An on-premises restaurant/lounge called Treetops looks directly into the upper limbs of the native greenery. Located on Florida Bay, the resort, formerly part of the Sheraton chain, has benefited greatly from the change of ownership, with a wholesale facelift and upgrading of facilities (not that it was a ghetto before the change, mind you). There's a nice little bayside beach out back, with a waveless swimming area that's great for kids and a volleyball net set up in the water. Watersports adventures (parasailing, water-skiing, windsurfing, sailing, and more) can be arranged at the on-site marina. One of the best features is the pool area, where there's an ample-sized swimming pool for adults (no kids allowed) and another for families. A waterfall and beautiful murals divide the pools, the white noise generated by the former affording road-weary adults a respite from screaming kids. A nature trail through the buttonwood grove is a grace note to one of the more intelligently designed resorts we've encountered in our coastal wanderings.

Other interesting accommodations can be found in the area, none more intriguing than an underwater inn (you read correctly) named **Jules' Undersea Lodge** (MM 103.2, 50 Shorelane Drive, 305/451-2353, $$$$). Jules' carries scuba mania to new, er, depths—30 feet below sea level, to be exact. Originally an undersea research lab off the coast of Puerto Rico, the lodge was purchased by two seasoned divers who wanted to maintain an entrepreneurial attachment to their first love. A special "Luxury Aquanaut" package features a chef who swims into the cruise-ship-sized room (with TV, phone, etc.) to cook a meal on the premises.

Another original is **Amy Slate's Amoray Dive Resort** (MM 104, 305/451-3595, $$), which offers special packages that include an underwater wedding. Visitors also book ecotours, courses in underwater photography, reef ecology, fish identification, and night diving at the Amoray. Rooms are adequate, and one- and two-bedroom apartments with fully equipped kitchens are also available.

One more local curiosity is the **Holiday Inn** (MM 103.4, 305/451-2121, $$$), notable for its unabashedly friendly service and the fact that the boat used in the 1952 film *The African Queen* is docked on the premises. The hotel's restaurant? Bogie's Cafe, natch! The hotel has its own marina and will assist in booking watery expedi-

3 Harry Harris County Park

Location: east Beach Road at MM 92.5 in Tavernier, at the south end of Key Largo
Parking/fees: free to county residents at all times. Nonresidents pay $5 per person on weekends and holidays, and nothing at other times. A $10 fee for use of the boat ramps is charged.
Hours: 7:30 A.M. to sunset
Facilities: concessions, restrooms, picnic tables, and showers
Contact: Monroe County Department of Parks and Beaches, 305/295-4385

John Pennekamp Coral Reef State Park

This underwater park's 150 square miles of protected ocean waters are home to a coral reef, mangrove swamps, and sea grass beds. The visual delights of the coral reef—not unlike a drugless LSD trip—can be appreciated in several ways. You take a glass-bottomed boat tour that heads to Molasses Reef ($18 for adults, $10 for kids ages 3–12, free for children 3 and under; offered at 9:15 A.M., 12:15 P.M., and 3 P.M.). Alternatively, they offer a 2.5-hour snorkeling tour ($25.95 for adults, $20.95 for kids under 18, plus $5 to rent masks, fins, and snorkels; offered at 9 A.M., noon, and 3 P.M.) that gets to the reef via motorboat and allows 90 minutes of snorkeling. The sailing and snorkeling tour ($31.95 for adults, $26.95 for kids under 18; offered at 9 A.M. and 1:30 P.M.) makes the trip via catamaran, which is more relaxing. The round-trip takes 90 minutes longer, for a total tour time of four hours. Reservations for all tours are strongly recommended.

Scuba tours leave from the dive shop ($39 per person; offered at 9:30 A.M. and 1:30 P.M.). Participants must be certified divers. Certification can be gained through scuba courses taught on-site. PADI certification takes 3–4 days and costs $450; not a bad way to spend a vacation. For a briefer taste of diving thrills, try the Scuba Resort Course ("Begin at 9 A.M., be diving by 2 P.M."), which costs $160 and includes two reef dives. You can also rent a power boat at the marina and take off on your own adventures.

Pennekamp is part of the only living coral reef in the lower 48 states. The reef, which extends three miles offshore, took thousands of years to form. The coral creature—a small, fleshy polyp—secretes a limestone home around itself, attaching to other coral dwellings. The result is a reef that's home to 40 types of coral, 600 species of fish, and an assortment of other marine life: Florida spiny lobsters, sea turtles, crabs, shrimp, and more. This underwater wonderland has been likened to a tropical rain forest.

The park is open daily from 8 A.M. to dusk, though the visitor center closes at 5 P.M. Admission is $5 for a car with two occupants ($2.50 if you're alone), plus 50 cents for each additional person. If you're arriving via bike or on foot, the charge is $1.50. The main attraction at the visitor center is the 30,000-gallon saltwater aquarium, and there are also exhibits and films on the reef ecosystem. A 47-site campground surrounds a pond behind the marina. Hiking paths explore the mangroves and uplands. A 2.5-mile canoe trail follows a channel through the mangroves. Canoes and kayaks can be rented at the marina, as can seacycles, Hobies, viewing rafts, and bumper boats. Pennekamp even provides man-made beaches. Across the highway is the private **Maritime Museum of the Florida Keys** (MM 102.5, 305/451-6444). It is devoted to underwater archaeology—how shipwrecks are located, surveyed, and preserved—and kids will enjoy its reconstruction of a shipwreck site.

For more information contact John Pennekamp Coral Reef State Park, MM 102.5, Key Largo, FL 33037; 305/451-1202; website: www.pennekamppark.com. For tour information and reservations, call the Pennekamp Park Concession at 305/451-1621.

tions. A casino boat departs from the marina. Off-season rates of under $80 are a steal for the Keys.

Coastal Cuisine

Key Largo's dining scene seems to be, at first glance, a bad (stomach) acid trip of fast-food joints. The glowing familiarity of their signs and artificially bright interiors must entice enough unadventurous tourists to support the full smorgasbord of them represented here. Ah, but there are alternatives to their useless ilk. The newest venue for "Floribbean" cooking is **Gus' Grille**, located in the Marriott Key Largo Bay Beach Resort (MM 103.8, 305/453-0000, $$$). Off the beaten track a bit and even more creative is **Flamingo Seafood Bar and Grill** (MM 106.5, 45 Garden Cove Drive, 305/451-8022, $$$).

Less pricey local hangouts are **Mrs. Mac's Kitchen** (MM 99.4, 305/451-3722, $$) and **Crack'd Conch** (MM 105, 305/451-0732, $$). Mrs. Mac's is a likably ramshackle eatery that's gamely holding its own against the reef of franchises encroaching from all sides. Peeling wood paneling is covered with license plates, slogans, and snapshots of loyal customers, and the food is as homey as its interior. After all, the founder named Mrs. Mac's for his mom, whose homemade chili, conch chowder, and meat loaf are the signature dishes. (Before 1976, it was another local institution called Jerry and Dee's.) You'll definitely want to check out the Thursday through Saturday "Seafood Sensation": huge portions of delicious, simply prepared fish, fritters, crab, and shrimp for under $10. Crack'd Conch has been a landmark in the Upper Keys for years, a weatherbeaten but solid seafood house that serves reliable fare and large helpings.

Similar in friendly atmosphere, attentive wait staff, and solid reputation is the **Fish House Restaurant** (MM 102, 305/451-4665, $$), which has the added attraction of a fresh seafood market on the premises. We can think of no sweeter visual experience, outside of an art museum, than staring at fresh fillets of fish on beds of ice. Fresh catches usually include mahimahi, yellowtail, and snapper, and the way to go from among several preparation options is pan sauteed. They dip the fillet in egg wash, sauté it in lemon and butter, and finish with a splash of sherry. Another good choice is the "Matecumbe" style, in which a fillet is baked with tomatoes, shallots, capers, basil, olive oil, and lemon juice. They make a good key lime pie, to boot.

Night Moves

Key Largo is no Key West, but there's still a viable nightlife. Take **Coconuts** (MM 100, 305/453-9794), for instance. Located at the Marina del Mar Resort, it's a triple-threat restaurant, outdoor bar, and indoor nightclub. Tuesday night is Blues Night, which brings in talent from all over the country. Wednesday through Saturday is given over to Top Forty dancing. Live music and cool drinks are also on tap at **Zappie's** (MM 100, 305/451-0531) and the **Caribbean Club** (MM 104, 305/451-9970).

For an authentic Keys dive bar, find your way to the **Mandalay Marina and Tiki Bar** (80 East 2nd Street, 305/852-5450), which lies at the end of the road on the gulf side of Key Largo. It's unfancy as hell, full of local color and a clientele that looks like a Jimmy Buffett song come to life. In fact, we heard a Jimmy Buffett song performed—warbled badly, in actuality—by a local duo here. This is the place to come if you want to soak up the native ambience in all its ragged glory. You'll see all kinds of cheeseburgers in paradise downing beer and swapping boat stories.

Contact Information

Key Largo Chamber of Commerce, 106000 Overseas Highway, Key Largo, FL 33037; 305/451-4726 or 800/822-1088; website: www.floridakeys

Islamorada

This is our favorite of the more populous Keys between Miami and Key West, mainly because it best embodies and preserves the laid-back Keys lifestyle. Islamorada (pop. 7,639), which occupies much of Upper Matecumbe Key, projects the relaxed air of a fishing village first and foremost. For whatever reason, Islamorada's restaurants and resorts do a better job of grasping the essence of what the Keys are about than Key Largo, Marathon, and the increasingly boutique- and condo-lined streets of Key West.

Islamorada was the first key to be colonized by European settlers: 50 Anglo-Bahamian conchs who established a community on Matecumbe Key. They built the first church and schoolhouse on the Keys around the turn of the century. All their hard work came to an untimely end when a devastating hurricane destroyed the community on Labor Day 1935. A graveyard for these pioneers, many of whom were among the 423 who perished in the hurricane, can be found on the grounds of Cheeca Lodge, near the swimming pool. It is noted with a historical marker. A larger monument to hurricane victims sits on the Overseas Highway.

Islamorada justifiably markets itself as "the Sportfishing Capital of the World," boasting the largest charter fleet in the Keys (350 separate listings in the local phone book), as well as the world's greatest number of resident fishing vessels per square mile. Deep-sea and backcountry charters, as well as boat rentals, can be arranged at marinas in the vicinity, including **Bud 'n' Mary's** (MM 79.8, 305/664-2461) and **Papa Joe's** (MM 79.7, 305/664-5005), which are opposite each other on the ocean and bay, respectively. Also check out the action at Whale Harbor Bridge, which separates Upper Matecumbe Key (on which the town of Islamorada sits) from Windley Key. You'd have to be the world's unluckiest angler not to catch something from a boat or bridge, for the waters surrounding the Keys are the largest breeding and feeding grounds in the world. The Atlantic Ocean meets the Gulf of Mexico here, with the Gulf Stream acting as an incubator.

The town of Islamorada takes its name from two Spanish words, *islas moradas*, which translates as "purple island." It was so christened by Spanish explorers for the violet sea snails that covered the shore once upon a time. A small town on a medium-sized key, Islamorada is a relaxing place to cast a line and unwind.

4 Upper Matecumbe County Park

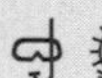

Location: behind the Islamorada Public Library, at MM 81.5 on bayside
Parking/fees: free parking lot
Hours: 7:30 A.M. to sunset
Facilities: restrooms, picnic tables, and showers
Contact: Monroe County Department of Parks and Beaches, 305/295-4385

Beaches

Sand beaches are a precious and rare commodity out on the spiny keys, and Islamorada is no exception. Private resorts, such as Cheeca Lodge, have their own man-made beaches and sandy lagoons, but Islamorada is otherwise devoid of them-with one quasi-exception on the bayside. That is **Upper Matecumbe County Park,** located behind the local library. It's not much more than a picnic and playground for the locals. People do swim in the bay, although it's not encouraged because the tidal currents can be swift.

MAP OF THE KEYS—PAGE 293

Port Bougainville: Entering the Twilight Zone

Come with us on a surreal side trip at the north end of Key Largo. This is a section of the Keys often missed by vacationers speeding on and off them via U.S. 1. Not so long ago, State Route 905 was slated to become the main boulevard for a city known as Port Bougainville. All of the land had been purchased, lots platted, plans approved. In short, the deal was done. Port Bougainville would have been the largest development in the history of the Keys, with the building of 2,800 condos, two 300-room hotels, and yacht marinas. But then environmentalists fought and banks foreclosed on it, and Port Bougainville was history.

The happy ending is that conservation groups, including the Friends of the Everglades, rescued the area at the last minute, and now this vital green buffer and estuary belongs to the state, which purchased its 431 acres for $22.8 million in 1988. The site is now a ruins being reclaimed by nature. If you're passing through, take the eye-opening drive along State Route 905 north from its junction with U.S. 1 on Key Largo. At various intervals you can see where the streets of this phantom burg had been laid out and where the vacation homes of the wealthy were going to be plopped among them. Some human habitations predating Port Bougainville still exist out here, but they take up only the tip of Key Largo. State Route 905, in fact, dead-ends at the gated tower of a private development, just past signs for the Ocean Reef Club and Key Largo Angler's Club.

Port Bougainville's unraveling is the good news from our side trip into the Twilight Zone. The bad news begins two miles back down State Route 905, where it junctions with Card Sound Road (State Route 905A), which courses over Card Sound from the mainland. This is a less-traveled, alternative way of entering and exiting the Keys. We now know why. What should be a pleasurable, scenic drive is instead an aesthetic nightmare that traverses one of the ugliest side pockets in the state of Florida. You do not want to break down out here. From its origin at U.S. 1 just south of Homestead to the toll bridge at Card Sound, the road is blighted by human degradation.

The sparsely settled area on both sides of State Route 905A is choked with garbage. The roadside is not just littered but aggressively attacked by trash, as if it had been blown there with fire hoses. The few human habitations are flyblown hovels, their residents glowering at passing cars as if daring passengers to provoke them with eye contact so they can go for their guns. Sure enough, a local news item during one of our visits related the tale of some gun-toting ne'er-do-well's attempt to shoot his way back into his ex-girlfriend's mobile home and, presumably, her heart.

Bunking Down

Cheeca Lodge (P.O. Box 527, MM 82, 305/664-4651, $$$$) is an "environmentally friendly" resort situated near the Hurricane Monument on the oceanside of Islamorada. We note the monument because the lodge's own sign is not much larger than a bumper sticker. That principle of understatement extends to the resort, where nature is allowed to play the starring role and side shows are held to a minimum. Okay, there is a par-three golf course that might better have been left a tropical hammock. But much of the grounds have been left in a natural state. Guests can wander along a nature trail and gain an education along the way by reading about the plants and trees on the numbered trail guide. As a side note, part of the emerging environmental awareness in Florida is learning the difference between native and nonnative (a.k.a. "exotic") species. Problematic exotics include familiar trees like the Australian pine, a tenacious grower that crowds out other species and, worse, blows over easily in a hurricane or big storm.

But back to Cheeca Lodge, where we're trying to decide whether to sit by the large, bathtub-warm pool, beside the saltwater lagoon, on the sand beach, or away from the action to the left of the pier. Chaise lounges line the property at all of these sites. Cheeca Lodge overlooks a blue million miles of ocean. The Tennessee Reef Lighthouse is visible off in the distance. We became more relaxed here more quickly than at any other stop in our Florida travels. Even the beds seemed unusually comfortable. The blue-and-white lodge reposes gracefully among swaying coconut palms and royal poincianas. They have an excellent kids program (Camp Cheeca) and two on-premises restaurants, so there's no excuse to leave once you've checked in. Just chill out and let the laid-back aura of the Keys overtake you.

If Cheeca Lodge, where rooms go for upward of $350 a night in season, is a bit beyond your means, Islamorada is chock full of places to stay at different price points, including other full-service resorts with private beaches such as the **Chesapeake Resort** (P.O. Box 909, MM 83.5, 305/664-4662, $$$) and the **Plantation Yacht Harbor Resort** (87000 U.S. 1, MM 87, 305/852-2381, $$). **Hampton Inn** (MM 80, 305/664-0073, $$$), the upper-middle-caliber chain hotel that's been making a big push in Florida, is a relatively recent arrival on Islamorada. Located on the ocean, this Hampton has got a pro dive shop, boat ramp, and daily scuba trips. There's also a glut of decidedly modest "resort" motels where rooms can be had for under $100 a night (and easily half that out of season), if you're not particular about where you lay your head. And, let's face it, most fishermen aren't.

Coastal Cuisine

Atlantic's Edge (at Cheeca Lodge, MM 82, 305/664-4651, $$$$) offers a stunning, glassed-in lookout over the ocean. It is the best interior view of open water in the Keys, being something akin to standing on the bow of a ship. The outdoor **Ocean Terrace** (also on the Cheeca premises, 305/664-4651) is more casual and affordable. At both restaurants, they will cook the catch of the day—either yours or theirs—in myriad ways. Ocean Terrace will cook yours or theirs (for a few dollars more) as follows: crusted with onions or plantains, jerk grilled, braised, baked, or steamed. Atlantic's Edge will cook yours or theirs in all the ways previously listed, plus à la nage, meunière, steamed, or blackened.

There are other good restaurants on Islamorada. If you want the freshest possible catch, priced reasonably and served in a casual setting among a crowd heavily tilted toward locals, make your way to the **Islamorada Fish Company** (81532 Overseas Highway, 305/664-9271, $$). Be forewarned that pelicans will be eyeballing your meal from nearby perches on the outdoor deck. They are envious for good reason. Seafood is served by the basket here: tenderized deep-fried conch; catch of the day (mahimahi, snapper, cobia) served fried, grilled, Cajun spiced, or teriyaki marinated; and more. Preparations and presentation are uncomplicated, which is fitting since seafood this fresh doesn't need much more than a squeeze of lemon. Out of necessity, they use wooden clothespins at the Islamorada Fish Company to keep money and napkins from blowing off the tables and into the water.

You might also check out the two of the more down-home seafood eateries in the Keys, the **Green Turtle Inn** (MM 81.5, 305/664-9031, $$), which has been in business since 1947, and **Papa Joe's Landmark Restaurant** (MM 79.7, 305/664-8109), built in 1937 and ready to cook your own catch for you.

Night Moves

Woody's (MM 82, 305/664-4335) is the place to go in Islamorada if you're in the mood to rock out. In addition to being an Italian restaurant (some of the best pizza on the Keys), it's a low-slung joint that gets raucous to the sound of a house band that goes by the name (we kid you not) Big Dick and the Erections. That should tell you all you need to know. Party hard, dude.

Contact Information

Islamorada Chamber of Commerce, P.O. Box 915, MM 82.6, Islamorada, FL 33036; 305/664-4503 or 800/322-5397; website: www.islamoradachamber.com

Lignumvitae Key Botanical State Park

The entirety of this 365-acre key, located one mile north of Lower Matecumbe Key in Florida Bay, is a botanical state park, and visitation is restricted to ranger-guided tours. You can't get here by car, but it is accessible by boat. Guided tours are given daily, except Tuesday and Wednesday, at 10 A.M. and 2 P.M. The official tour-boat concessionaire is **Robbie's Marina** (MM 77.5, Islamorada, 305/664-9814). Show up at Robbie's at least a half hour before tour time to catch the boat over to Lignumvitae Key, which costs $15 per person. Reservations are accepted but usually not necessary. The tour itself costs $1 per person.

Lignumvitae Key is unique for its altitude (at 18 feet, the highest in the Keys) and vegetation. It's basically the same stand of tropical species that once flourished all over the Upper Keys before man bridged the keys and reshaped the landscape. Thus, one of the last surviving stands of tropical virgin forest is preserved here. Lignumvitae ("tree of life") is the Latin name for a small blue-flowered tree with wood so dense it doesn't float. This small key is the last place in the Western Hemisphere it is known to grow. Other trees found in Lignumvitae's crazy tangle include gumbo-limbo, mastic, strangler fig, poisonwood, and pigeon plum. When you come out here, try to imagine what the rest of the Keys must have looked like when such forests covered them.

Contact Information

Lignumvitae Key State Botanical Park, P.O. Box 1052, Islamorada, FL 33036; 305/664-2540; website: www.myflorida.com

Indian Key Historic State Park

This tiny 10-acre key three quarters of a mile southeast of Islamorada is reachable by boat only, but was nearly blown off the map by Hurricane Georges in 1998. The historic state park located here remained closed for more than two years as repairs were made, reopening in early 2001. Indian Key was inhabited by Native Americans for thousands of years prior to the arrival of Spanish colonists in the 16th century. In the 18th century, the key became a haven for wreckers (who salvaged what they could from boats that ran aground on the reefs) and pirates (who plundered merchant vessels negotiating the Straits of Florida). Surprising as it may seem, Indian Key was at one time the most populous settlement between Jacksonville and Key West and served as the seat of Dade County. A hotel, general store, shops, wharves, and warehouses were built. Naturalist John James Audubon sketched birds here, and noted botanist Dr. Henry Perrine, especially curious about hemp(!), conducted experiments with nonnative species. Perrine was killed here on August 7, 1840, during the second Seminole War.

Rich in history, Indian Key has preserved ruins, a restored boat dock, trails, and an observation tower (but no restrooms). Guided tours are led daily, except Tuesday and Wednesday, at 9 A.M. and 1 P.M. The official tour-boat concessionaire is **Robbie's Marina** (MM 77.5, Islamorada, 305/664-9814). Show up at Robbie's at least a half hour before tour time to catch the boat over to Indian Key, which costs $15 per person. Reservations are accepted but usually not necessary. The tour itself costs $1 per person.

Contact Information

Indian Key Historic State Park, P.O. Box 1052, Islamorada, FL 33036; 305/664-2540; website: www.myflorida.com

THE KEYS

Anne's Beach

Anne's Beach, located on Lower Matecumbe Key, is one of the real treasures of the Florida Keys. It is the second best beach in the Keys (*numero uno* being Bahia Honda State Park). Two entrance ramps are situated about half a mile apart along the ocean side of U.S. 1. Follow the signs for Anne's Beach and park for free, barely a whisper off the road. The beach is nearly two miles long and made up of hard-packed sand. At its hardest, it has a claylike consistency. Walk in either direction and you will soon have a section of the beach to yourself.

If you don't want to traipse the wet sand, a recently constructed wooden walkway runs above the tidal wetlands and dunes beneath a canopy of young trees. Several covered picnic areas have been built along the boardwalk, each with steps leading down to the water. The

5 Anne's Beach

Location: eight miles west of Islamorada, at MM 73.5 on Lower Matecumbe Key
Parking/fees: free parking lots
Hours: 7:30 A.M. to sunset
Facilities: restrooms and picnic tables
Contact: Monroe County Department of Parks and Beaches, 305/295-4385

walkway parallels the beach for a quarter mile, ending at the inlet that separates Upper and Lower Matecumbe Key. Across the inlet is a marina called Caloosa Cove. Anne's Beach was known to locals for many years as Caloosa Beach. The beach is calm, waveless. The most exciting activity is to shuffle along in knee-deep water and admire the critters at your feet and the birds wading contentedly just out of arm's reach. We had the unique experience of finding—sadly, among a thicket of litter we tried to clear from the mangrove roots—a message in a bottle. It was not from Sting. It was from a native of Melbourne, Florida, who wrote: "I am seven years old. I am now in Key West. If you find this, please write me. Signed, Toni Arjemi." We've done you one better, Toni. We've written about you in our book.

Anne's Beach was named for Anne Eaton. According to a plaque on a stone monument, Eaton "lived on this island for many years and dedicated herself to maintaining the beauty and serenity of these Keys. Anne helped bring this park to life." Would that there were more folks like her in this world.

Long Key

Spaniards originally named this key Cayo Vivora ("Rattlesnake Key") for its serpent-like shape. Long Key, located 10 miles west of Islamorada at MM 70, is the site of a state park and the town of Layton (population 200). Zane Grey, renowned author of Westerns, was one of Layton's most familiar faces. Henry Flagler built his Long Key Fishing Club here. The first of 42 bridges on Flagler's Key West Extension Railroad, in fact, was constructed at Long Key. Both Flagler's fishing club and cross-Keys railway thrived from 1912 to 1935. Then came the cataclysmic hurricane of 1935, which obliterated the railroad, whose supports later served as foundations for the Overseas Highway (U.S. 1).

Much of the south end of the island is occupied by Long Key State Park. Visitors can hike, canoe a watery trail, or camp by the ocean in the 965-acre park, which turned 30 in 1999. The most unique feature is the Long Key Canoe Trail, a mile-long paddle around a tidal lake rimmed with mangroves. Canoe rentals are cheap ($4 per hour) and the paddling is easy, especially if you time it so that you're on the water at high tide and the winds are calm. At low tide, the pool is only a few inches deep in some places, so you might wind up portaging the canoe over the shallows while birds stare as if you've lost your mind, as happened to us. The basin is filled with birdlife, including graceful egrets and long-beaked pelicans. The canoe trail is lined with numbered markers that correspond to items on a trail guide picked up at the front kiosk when you sign in.

Being hearty outdoors types, we followed our canoe adventure with a hike on the Golden Orb Trail. The trail is named for a spider that is common in these parts. The female of the species is huge and slings massive icky-sticky webs straight out of science fiction in the trees overhead. The males, by contrast, are inconspicuous. This well-maintained trail encompasses a variety of ecological zones in close proximity between ocean and bay, including a tropical hardwood hammock and an area where only scrubby, stunted trees will grow. The trail also crosses over patches of tarry, anaerobic muck from which red and black mangroves rise via prop roots. Flaring off the Golden Orb Trail, arrayed along a boardwalk that runs beside the ocean, are primitive campsites that cost $8 per night. It's a real steal, if you don't mind lugging your gear a couple hundred feet. More developed sites lie along the park road beneath the shade of gumbo-limbo and other tropical trees, close to the beach. You'll pay more for these ($25.84 per night with electricity, $23.69 without), but look at it like this: the cost of camping at Long Key is about what you'd spend on taxes alone at an upscale Keys resort.

This is, by the way, a beachless key. You can stroll the shoreline or wade out in the shallows. But you will not find on Long Key a sandy, swimmable beach like those at Bahia Honda Key or Anne's Beach. Just so you know.

Contact Information

Long Key State Park, MM 67.5, P.O. Box 776, Long Key, FL 33001; 305/664-4815; website: www.myflorida.com

Duck Key

Duck Key, located between Long and Grassy Keys at MM 61, sprang to life as a gleam in the eye of Bryan Newkirk, a mining baron and real estate agent who bought the key sight unseen in 1953. Wanting to turn it into a West Indian–style resort with a yacht basin and residential community, he built his own bridge to this small key, which lies to the side of the string of keys connected by the Overseas Highway. Though Newkirk's son (who directed the development) died of polio in 1955 and the resort changed hands several times thereafter, Hawk's Cay managed to stay afloat over the decades. Now firmly established as a full-service resort, Hawk's Cay is today something like the "complete island community" that Newkirk originally envisioned.

Beaches

The beach at Hawk's Cay, which is the only one the public can get to (and then only by booking at the resort), is typical of those you'll find on the grounds of resorts on the Upper Keys—to wit, a quarter inch of kitty litter sprinkled atop a hard coral spine and raked into neat furrows by groundskeepers early each morning. These are not the sort of beaches you'd write home about, but you take what you can get out here, and it's better than nothing.

Bunking Down

Now this is what we call a resort. **Hawk's Cay** (MM 61, 305/743-7000, $$$$) provides so many things to do in such an environmentally respectful setting that it rates as one of the premier resorts in the Keys. Where to start? First, the rooms are large and high ceilinged. As a reminder of the old days, bathroom doors are solid wood with crystal doorknobs, and they stick a little. A library and game room are down at ground level. In addition to burping video games on which galaxies are conquered, the game room has a Ping Pong table at which one of us showed the other how the game is meant to be played.

Step outside and check out the pool, a large heated rectangle surrounded by comfortably padded chaise lounges. It is here that we saw an amusing animal blooper: a seagull skimming the surface of the pool, claws dragging water, in the hope that it might come away with a fish. The pool is the centerpiece of the outdoor courtyard, which also includes two Jacuzzis and a large saltwater lagoon with chickees and more chaise lounges. The pool and lagoon look out on the Long Key Bridge, a 2.5-mile span that bridge-building visionary Henry Flagler pronounced his favorite.

Another lagoon serves as a staging area for Hawk's Cay's Dolphin Discovery Program. For $90, guests will learn about and swim among these marine mammals, which many scientists believe are as highly evolved as humans. The fun doesn't end at the porpoise pool. There's more: snorkeling, fishing, tennis, volleyball, a fitness trail, boating, parasailing, scuba diving, sunset cruises, ecology tours. Nightly room rates run $235–385 in season (Christmas through late April) and $195–235 the rest of the year.

Coastal Cuisine

On-premises restaurants at Hawk's Cay range from the casual poolside **Cantina** to **Waters Edge**, where a waterfront view is served with your steak or seafood. At the **Palm Terrace**, a daily breakfast buffet looks to be a good deal if you're hungry, as you can load your plate from a heaping presentation of fresh fruit, pastries, and hot items extending from one end of the room to another.

Contact Information

Hawk's Cay Resort, MM 61, Duck Key, FL 33050; 305/743-7000 or 800/432-2242; website: www.hawkscay.com

Grassy Key

Located two miles east of Marathon, this key is home to the **Dolphin Research Center** (MM 59, 305/289-1121), formerly Flipper's Sea School (yes, that Flipper). Marine mammals are studied and cared for here, and interactive programs are open to the public, including Dolphin Encounter (a lecture and "playful, structured swim session" among the dolphins for $125). As you might imagine, these are extremely popular and fill up quickly; call 305/289-0002 for information and reservations. You can make a reservation for a given half-month (say, September 1–14) as early as a month before the first date in that period (August 1, in this case). Should you be really flush with funds, another $75 will net you a video of your dolphin encounter. These prices would even have Flipper flipping out.

One of the Keys' favorite fishing resorts, **Rainbow Bend** (MM 58, 305/929-1505, $$$), is located on Grassy Key in a hurry-up-and-slow-down setting reminiscent of the way things used to be on the Keys. Also on Grassy Key is a beloved diner called the **Grassy Key Dairy Bar** (MM 58.5, 305/743-3816, $). It doesn't look like much from the front, and locals don't care a whit if tourists pass it by—a sure sign there's something worthwhile cooking inside.

Contact Information

Greater Marathon Chamber of Commerce, 12222 Overseas Highway, MM 48.7, Marathon, FL 33050; 305/743-5417 or 800/262-7284; website: www.floridakeys marathon.com

Marathon and Key Colony Beach

The big news in Marathon was its incorporation as a city in November 2000. The vote was overwhelmingly in favor of incorporation, the citizens of Marathon obviously desiring a greater say in their own destiny. Ironically, Key Largo voted at the same time by an almost reverse margin of two to one against incorporation. Go figure.

Marathon is the second largest city on the Keys. Its year-round population is 10,387, but the figure doubles in season. If Key West is the more populous Sodom at the end of the Overseas Highway, then Marathon must be the Gomorrah of the Middle Keys. In the bright light of day, it's as messy as can be. At night, it's a nonstop party beneath a neon rainbow as sunbaked Jimmy Buffett lookalikes argue the relative merits of boat engines. To be fair, Marathon is a vital commercial corridor for those scattered among the numerous keys between Islamorada and Big Pine Key (the last town of any size before Key West). It is also home to the sleek new Marathon Airport.

The city of Marathon stretches from Crawl Key (MM 57) to the foot of the majestic 7 Mile Bridge (MM 47). It came by its name as the result of Henry Flagler's quixotic attempt to build the "railroad that went to sea." A base camp for hundreds of railroad workers was set up here in 1908. The grueling work of building the 7 Mile Bridge provoked one overwhelmed laborer to bemoan the "marathon effort" still ahead if they were going to push all the way to Key West before the venerable Flagler croaked. They succeeded, Flagler rode into town triumphantly on his train, and the name Marathon stuck.

The fate of Marathon prior to incorporation has largely been overseen by county commissioners involved in the real-estate trade. One member of this brainless trust had the nerve to pooh-pooh local tree-huggers who were bent out of shape by the razing of an ancient stand of 25-foot gumbo-limbo trees by a developer. "You can refoliate things so fast in Florida," she offered cavalierly, "it'll make your hair fall out" (a fate we wish upon her alone).

All of this makes Marathon's cluttered appearance inevitable. Every fast-food chain imaginable has an outlet along the Overseas Highway through Marathon. Their gaudy logos and touting billboards are particularly jarring in this otherwise magical setting, like a series of blows to the head. We had to wonder why anyone would frequent these redundant grease pits when fresh seafood is available at any number of affordable, locally owned, non-franchised outlets.

Still, if you stick around long enough, you will grow entranced by Marathon and maybe even have your soul ensnared by the place. True, Marathon does not possess the blue, green, and red vistas of a postcard vision, but once the sun starts to fall upon your brow and the boats return to port, the town and the keys it spreads across take on a certain subtropical charm. If you commandeer a chaise lounge at one of Marathon's resort encampments or a barstool at one of its many watering holes, the town begins to make a lot more sense than it does from the sweltering vantage point of the highway.

In Marathon, people find sanctuary from stormy or stale lives on the mainland. One tanned and bearded barkeep we met ditched his businessman's life in Denver ("I got stupid and got respectable . . . don't know what got into me."). He now dreams of living rent free on a boat. "And in the evening," he rhapsodized, "I can float to any bar on the island." Another fellow left Detroit—where he'd worked for 18 years as a rivethead for General Motors—after a family tragedy. Now he toils in a restaurant kitchen. After a year of scrubbing plates and pounding conch into edible submission, his face glows with a ruddy contentment we saw all over the Keys. Still another man retired as a schoolteacher in Kansas and came here to write a book. After six years the book remains unwritten, but "there's still time, there's always more time."

Marathon, for many local residents, means fishing. Period. Visitors come here on extended leave from winters in the north for the pleasure of taking to the sea in boats hired out for fishing the waters of the Gulf Stream ("wider than a thousand Mississippi Rivers") or Florida Bay. The lure of big game fish—marlin, sailfish, wahoo, tuna—is irresistible. Among the reefs close to shore, they fish for grouper and yellowtail snapper. From the bridges and shore, they stalk tarpon and snook. Divers comb the reefs of the Middle Keys, which are less crowded than those of Key Largo. If you're interested in seeing the underwater world, local dive shops offer certification and instruction.

If you don't dig angling and/or diving, chances are you will keep on trucking out of town over the 7 Mile Bridge. And that's too bad, because Marathon has hidden charms that make it worth braking for at least a little while. Among the literature distributed by the local chamber is a helpful list of "50 Free Things to Do in the Marathon Area." One such activity that we would encourage the adventurous to try is "Walk, bike, skate, or jog on the old 7 Mile Bridge—breathe some really fresh air (1.9 miles each way)." While on your stroll, "observe the fantastic array of sea life from the comfort of the bridge. See tarpon, sharks, stingrays, and more. The morning is the best time."

We will end this discussion by throwing some of the aforementioned commissioner's own words back in her face. In a separate story from the gumbo-limbo massacre, she could be heard chastising tourists who visit the Middle Keys. (Like "big government," tourists make an easy target for curmudgeonly locals.) "This is our backyard," she snorted. "This is where we live. Treat it like it was your home, realizing you are our guests."

No, you treat your own hometown better than you have been, and appreciative visitors will follow suit. In other words, lead by example.

Beaches

Beginning at Crawl Key, at the north end of Marathon, signs point to a sandy beach at the end of an unnamed road off the highway. It's called Valhalla Beach, and it's home to the **Valhalla Beach Motel** (MM 56, 305/289-0616, $), which rents totally unstylish but serviceable efficiencies by the night or week. It would seem the perfect way to enjoy this secluded side pocket. By the way, the so-called sand beach is actually along a tidal creek—but as we've said elsewhere, you take what beaches you get in the Keys and are grateful for them.

A couple of off-highway detours lead to bona fide beaches right on the ocean. Just past MM 54 is a community called Key Colony Beach. To get to it, turn south on Key Colony Beach Causeway. While you never actually leave land, you are entering what was formerly Shelter Key, a filled-in mangrove swamp. It is also Key Colony Beach, which incorporated long before Marathon. The irony is that it is much smaller than Marathon, with a population of only 1,084. Undoubtedly, the municipal oversight that comes with incorporation is one reason Key Colony Beach looks so enviably pleasant. The beach is an ocean-fronting, pearly white stretch of sand, all privately owned. In order to sample its charms, you must check into one of several motels along its length. The beach is dainty but clean, and the wave activity is a bit more brisk than on the beaches of the Upper Keys. An added enticement on Shelter Key is the nine-hole, par-three Key Colony Public Golf Course, which has been squeezed in among the houses.

The second detour in Marathon leads to **Sombrero Beach.** To get there, turn east on Sombrero Beach Boulevard, just past the ancient K-Mart at MM 50. You'll drive for about two miles through a congested but well-tended residential area. At the end of this tunnel of real estate is the bright white sand of Sombrero Beach. This is a perfect little curve of hard-packed sand—real sand, not pumped-in filler. The beach continues around a bend, where it turns into a hardened reef, then picks up with a few more tiny pockets of sand, upon which solitary souls contentedly snooze. The adjoining park is a recreational bonanza, with a baseball field, a kids' playground, picnic tables, restrooms, shelters, and even a jug filled with a chemical that removes any tar that might get on your feet. By the way, conch collecting is not allowed, no matter how tempting, and the fines can reach $500.

A third detour, onto 20th Street (a.k.a. Boot Key Boulevard) at MM 48, is decidedly less pleasant. The street carries you over a drawbridge onto Boot Key (see section in this chapter). This mysterious key has a healthy chunk of ocean frontage, but you'll be too bummed out by the garbage dumped here to want to stick around any longer than it takes to U-turn and head back over the bridge.

6 Sombrero Beach

Location: Sombrero Beach Road in Marathon
Parking/fees: free parking lots
Hours: 7:30 A.M. to sunset
Facilities: restrooms, picnic tables, and showers
Contact: Monroe County Department of Parks and Beaches, 305/295-4385

Incidentally, you may encounter printed references to a Chamber of Commerce Beach. It's supposedly on the bayside at the end of 33rd Street, next to the Marathon Yacht Club. The Marathon Chamber of Commerce used to occupy a small building by the turnoff, which is how it got its name. The name persists, but there's no beach to speak of and no reason to come looking.

Finally, at MM 54, on what is called Fat Deer Key, turn onto Coco Plum Drive to find an entirely residential beach condo community possessing the upscale manners of Key Colony Beach but lacking the public accommodations. The beach here is long but entirely private. We just wanted you to lay eyes on the most anomalous sight in the Keys—a 15-story condominium development called Bonefish Towers. Who allowed this boneheaded eyesore out here?

Shore Things

- **Bike/skate rentals:** SK8 America, 3890 Overseas Highway, 305/743-5206.
- **Boat cruise:** Hootman Sunset Sails, Banana Bay Marina, MM 49, 305/289-1433.
- **Dive shop:** Capt. Hook's Marina and Dive Center, MM 53, 305/743-2444.
- **Ecotourism:** Marathon Kayak Resources, 19 Sombrero Boulevard, 305/743-0561.
- **Fishing charters:** Marathon Guides Association, P.O. Box 50065, Marathon, FL 33050, 800/262-7284.
- **Marina:** Banana Bay Resort Marina, MM 49.5, 305/743-3648.
- **Pier:** Old 7 Mile Bridge (world's longest fishing pier!), MM 47.
- **Rainy-day attraction:** Museum of Natural History of the Florida Keys, MM 50, 305/743-9100.

Museum of Natural History of the Florida Keys

If you have a spare hour or so, stop by the Museum of Natural History of the Florida Keys (MM 50, 305/743-9100). Located at Crane Point Hammock in Marathon, they've been one of the lone voices for responsible appreciation and preservation of the ecosystems that make the Keys special. They've also preserved what they can of the artifacts of the pre-Columbian cultures that inhabited these islands. Naturally, they must touch on the mystique of pirates, smugglers, and wreckers, but this lore is intelligently presented. Other attractions on the 63.5-acre preserve include a coral reef, an underwater cave, touch tanks, a saltwater lagoon, a tropical aquarium and terrarium, and one of the last stands of virgin tropical palm hammock in South Florida.

- **Shopping/browsing:** Gulfside Village, MM 50.
- **Vacation rentals:** Land & Sea Vacations, 5701 Overseas Highway, 305/743-6494.

Bunking Down

Key Colony Beach is a well-mannered, almost secret society of homes, condominiums, and beach resorts. Commendable motel choices out here include the **Key Colony Inn** (700 West Ocean Drive, 305/743-0100, $$) and the **Continental Inn** (MM 53.6, 305/289-0101, $$). They are affordable during the off-season and a minor luxury during the choicer months (mid-December to mid-April). Both are clean and quiet.

Another top-notch choice that comes with real sand is the **Coco Plum Beach & Tennis Club** (109 Cocoplum Drive, MM 54.5, 305/743-0240, $$$$), where the amenities (private beach, tennis courts, heated pool, sundeck, Jacuzzi) and roomy villas don't come cheaply (upward of $2,100 a week in season). At the opposite end of the price scale, yet clean, comfortable, quiet, and attractive, is the **Hidden Harbor Motel** (2396 Overseas Highway, MM 48.5, 305/743-5376, $). It's on the bayside, where its private marina has a boat slip for every room.

Of course, there are numerous places to stay along the Overseas Highway spanning the keys that make up Marathon, including the **Banana Bay Resort** (MM 49.5, 305/743-5500, $$), which has its own marina and watersports center, and **Hampton Inn & Suites** (1688 Overseas Highway, 305/743-9009, $$$), a sparkling gulfside property that has its own dive center. There are dozens of others, many of them unfancy and cheap. The Greater Marathon Chamber of Commerce will be only too happy to help you book a room. Stop by their office at MM 53.

Coastal Cuisine

If you're not into fishing, surely you're into eating fish. If so, Marathon (like Islamorada) is your meal ticket. For lunch or dinner, you can choose between two of our favorite seaside eateries anywhere in America, Herbie's Raw Bar and the 7 Mile Grill. From the outside, **Herbie's Raw Bar** (MM 50.5, 305/743-6373, $$) is not much to look at, but looks are always deceiving in the Keys. Herbie's is a triple-threat wonder, with an outdoor restaurant, indoor bar, and screened-in dining/drinking area.

On our numerous visits here, we've feasted on ice-cold raw oysters, piping-hot conch chowder, autumn salad (a house specialty), conch fritters, grouper fingers, cracked conch, crab and shrimp salad, and fresh catch of the day, prepared in whatever manner the wait staff suggests. The best bet for first-timers might be the blackened catch. At all hours, you'll see locals here, quaffing frosty mugs in between hired boating expeditions. The friendliest sort of interaction imaginable between tourists and locals goes on at Herbie's.

The **7 Mile Grill** (MM 47, 305/743-4481, $$) is a must visit, too. Hit it to fortify yourself before tackling the formidable bridge that looms just beyond its outside dining area. You can't do much better than this low-key "grill" in the way of local color and cuisine. Again, order whatever is freshest. While waiting for your meal, scout the premises. It's a true Keys institution, with snapshots of happy local families and fishermen, stuffed fish on the walls, beer cans along the ceiling, and novelty bumper stickers and placards that boast goofy slogans like "Sometimes I Wake Up Grumpy. Sometimes I Just Let Him Sleep." Other signs—"English for Florida" and "Give Me A Break, I Live Here"—are an indication of the local hot-button issues. Then there's the grub: rock-ribbed seafood prepared wonderfully, with interesting side dishes like rice and beans (goes great with grouper). Finally, the key lime pie at the 7 Mile Grill is, quite simply, the best we've ever had. Everyone claims to make the best, of course, but the 7 Mile

Key Lime Pie

In every port of call on the Florida coast, we make it a point to order key lime pie when we see it on a menu. We even ask for it when it's not listed, just in case there has been some tragic oversight at the menu printing plant. Why? Because we agree with food writer Craig Claiborne, who once said, "If I were asked to name the greatest of all regional American desserts, my answer might very well be key lime pie." Ours most certainly would be, if a Floridian were to ask the question.

The basic ingredient of this pie is, of course, the key lime *(Citrus aurantifolia)*, which takes its name from the Florida Keys, where key lime trees grow well in the chalky, rocky soil. This variety of lime differs greatly from the garden-variety lime most commonly found in grocery stores *(Citrus latifolia)*. For one thing, key lime trees have thorns. For another, the fruit is much smaller and rounder, the rinds are a splotchy brownish yellow, and the pulp is more acidic, which explains the widely admired and unmistakably tart taste.

Ah, but here's the rub. Actually, several rubs. First of all, the key lime is not native to the Florida Keys, having been brought over from Asia in the early days of European exploration of the Caribbean. It's true that groves of these miniature limes were established on the Keys in the 1800s and flourished, but they're no longer commercially grown there. Today, most cultivated key limes are grown near Homestead and in Mexico and Guatemala.

Regardless of its origins, the key lime makes a delectable pie, and it is prepared at its simplest and best in the Florida Keys. While the fruit didn't originate in the Keys, the pie sure as heck did, deriving from the introduction to the local population of Borden's canned condensed milk in 1856. Because there were no cows to produce fresh milk and no highways

Grill backs up the boast with numerous awards and the evidence of your own taste buds. It's a sliver of tart, tangy perfection that makes you want to shout "hallelujah!" when you're done. For some reason, the place is closed on Wednesday and Thursday, so plan accordingly.

Just south of the 7 Mile Grill is **Porky's** (MM 47.5, 305/289-2065, $$), another local institution with much the same ambience but a different specialty: barbecue. Don't even get us started singing the praises of barbecue. That's a whole other book! Yet another favorite is the **Cracked Conch Cafe** (MM 50, 305/743-2233, $$). They raise their own conch on a farm (thus, not depleting the reef's sanctuary) and serve it every which way but bad. A shady mahogany tree outside makes for a great setting for a quick cup of coffee, too.

Slightly more upscale dining can be had at **The Quay** (MM 54, 305/289-1810, $$$), which—like Herbie's and the 7 Mile Grill—overlooks Florida Bay, making for great sunsets if not exactly "fine dining with the freshest seafood in the Keys" (with Maine lobster on the menu, this seems a dubious claim). The Quay's real selling point is its raw bar, housed in a separate wooden hut down by the water. Served ice cold, the oysters are out of this world.

Night Moves

If the sun hasn't completely sapped your energy by day's end, you can run out the rest of your line at one of Marathon's many waterside lounges. Admittedly, Marathon will never be able to boast of the unbri-

or railroads to ship it to them, the locals relied on condensed milk. It seemed only natural to combine the cheek-puckeringly sour taste of key limes with the gooey sweetness of sweetened condensed milk.

The classic recipe for key lime pie is really quite simple. mix four egg yolks, a half-cup of key lime juice (about 10–12 key limes), and a can of sweetened condensed milk. Pour into a graham-cracker pie shell and bake for 15 minutes at 350°F. No cheating allowed. No green food coloring (real key lime juice is a dull yellow). No whipped cream. No gelatin. If you can't lay hands on key limes back home in Des Moines, regular limes can be substituted, but it won't be quite the same. If you must dress the pie up a bit, making a meringue of the leftover egg whites is the most legitimate variation. Beat the four leftover egg whites with a half-teaspoon of cream of tartar till foamy, then gradually add one-third cup confectioners' sugar and continue beating until stiff peaks form. Spread the meringue over the bottom layer, then bake as instructed before.

Because ordering key lime pie comes as naturally to us as breathing, and because restaurants all over the state reflexively insist that their version is Florida's best, we've compiled a list of our favorites. (Feel free to submit suggestions of your own.) We don't pretend this is an exhaustive list, just one that reflects our own tastings. It should come as no surprise that the best key lime pie was served in the Florida Keys at one of the most unassuming places.

1. 7 Mile Grill, Marathon
2. Manny and Isa's, Upper Matecumbe Key
3. Blond Giraffe, Key West
4. White Lion Cafe, Homestead
5. Joe's Stone Crab, Miami Beach
6. Mangrove Mama's, Sugarloaf Key
7. That Place on 98, Eastpoint
8. Crow's Nest, Venice
9. Ophelia's By the Bay, Siesta Key
10. Sea Critters Cafe, Pass-a-Grille

dled outrageousness of Key West, nor would its inhabitants wish to. The general tenor of nightlife in Marathon consists of sunset-watching happy hours, with local musicians playing "sunset music" as people chatter and sip beer or multicolored drinks.

Outrigger's Sports Bar and Brew Pub (MM 49.5, 305/743-5755) is about as wild as it gets in Marathon, with happy hours, deejays and/or live entertainment, bikini contests, wings specials, etc. Outrigger's is among the liveliest spots between Miami and Key West. For a quieter night out, angle over to **Angler's Lounge** (MM 48, 305/743-9018), located at the Faro Blanco Resort on the bayside. It has a happy hour, a dart board, and generally restrained music.

The Brass Monkey (MM 50, 305/743-4028), located by the K-Mart Plaza, is the local rock and roll hangout of long standing. We partied hardy here back in 1984, and live bands are still flogging classic rock till 3 A.M. nightly.

Contact Information

Greater Marathon Chamber of Commerce, 12222 Overseas Highway, MM 48.7, Marathon, FL 33050; 305/743-5417 or 800/262-7284; website: www.floridakeysmarathon.com

Boot Key

The Middle Keys put their worst foot forward on the mysterious Boot Key. It is, from all appearances, the favorite illegal trash dump for the Keys' government-flaunting residents. It is also another piece of evidence that they cannot properly care for these islands. Boot Key is a large, mostly uninhabited, and highly vegetated island that fronts the Atlantic Ocean for a long stretch. Instead of becoming the cleaned-up public treasure it ought to be, it has been reduced to a Hades of fast-food wrappers and abandoned machinery. Apparently, hundreds of live-aboard boaters—free spirits who dock at Boot Key Harbor, where they live like animals and answer to no laws—have created all kinds of problems out here.

For the curious, turn onto 20th Street (MM 48) in Marathon and continue out to the key. An anomalous ultramodern drawbridge leads over an inlet to Boot Key, which at first looks like a tree-covered refuge. Then the roadside flotsam hits your field of vision: rusted file cabinets, a pile of truck tires, bloated trash bags, and, finally, a heap of old kitchen appliances barricading the road. There's no development to speak of on Boot Key, but there is a beach—according to maps of the area, at least. Fascinated by the utter squalor, we pressed on, squeezing our car between a break in the appliances.

After fumbling among the litter-choked brush for a while, we gave up. Everywhere we roamed in the Keys, we came upon similar mounds of trash along the shore, where it gathers into shockingly large clumps. We turned the car around in a pock-marked driveway near the ocean. A scrawny cat crossed our path, and beyond it we could make out several inhospitable-looking shacks, the flotsam from which covered the ground for yards in every direction.

Ironically, prior to trekking over to Boot Key, we'd just gotten an earful from some bad-tempered local outside the Chamber of Commerce, who was telling us that the government ought to "just get the hell on out of here and let us run the place the way we know how." With all due respect, we beg to differ, offering Boot Key as our case against self-governance.

On the way off Boot Key, we glanced into the bridge tender's hut at the center of the bridge. He was sound asleep, slumped on his stool. Could there have been a more appropriate metaphor for Boot Key? More to the point, why don't they crack down on encroachment and illegal dumping here? Why aren't the derelicts who've defiantly set up a militia-style boot camp on Boot Key sent packing? In short, what in the Sam Hill is going on?

A bad situation got worse in 2000 when they couldn't find the money to pay the bridge tender. The newly formed city of Marathon squabbled with the county of Monroe over who should, um, foot the bill for the Boot Key bridge. In October 2000, they finally agreed to split the expense. Leading up to this was the earnest offer by a Monroe County commissioner to do it himself. "I'm going to learn how to be a bridge tender!" swore George Neugent, sounding as gung-ho as Gomer Pyle. He couldn't have been any worse than the dozing gatekeeper we'd seen. But really, is this any way to run a city, a county, a key?

Contact Information

Greater Marathon Chamber of Commerce, 12222 Overseas Highway, MM 48.7, Marathon, FL 33050; 305/743-5417 or 800/262-7284; website: www.floridakeys marathon.com

Pigeon Key

This small key lies 2.2 miles west of Marathon. The original cross-Keys bridge (7 Mile Bridge) passes through it, and that's how you'll get there now: by walking, jogging, biking, skating, in-line skating, or break-dancing over the old bridge. Cars, however, are not allowed. Alternatively, a shuttle bus makes seven daily trips over from the Pigeon Key Visitors Center on Knight's Key (a small key at the foot of the 7 Mile Bridge), leaving hourly between 10 A.M. and 4 P.M. The combined shuttle and visitor fee is $7 for adults and $4 for students.

Between 1908 and 1935, Pigeon Key served as a base camp for railroad workers, and historical buildings from those times survive. Since the days of railroad construction, Pigeon Key has been home to the U.S. Navy, a fishing camp, and the University of Miami's Institute of Marine Science. The Pigeon Key Foundation maintains it as a research and education center; it's even affiliated with the Mote Marine Laboratory in Sarasota. An afternoon spent on Pigeon Key will reward visitors in search of a more natural Keys environment and/or a slice of Keys history.

Contact Information

Pigeon Key Foundation, MM 48, P.O. Box 500130, Marathon, FL 33050; 305/289-0025; website: www.pigeonkey.org

Little Duck Key and Ohio Key

These two small, adjacent keys lie on the far side of the 7 Mile Bridge from Marathon, Little Duck Key at MM 40 and Ohio Key at MM 39. Having made the crossing, you are now officially in the Lower Keys. Little Duck Key is the site of the oceanside **Veterans Memorial Park** (formerly Duck Key County Park), where you'll find picnic tables, grills, and a concession stand, in addition to basic facilities and a bit of beach.

Ohio Key (a.k.a. Sunshine Key) is home to a 400-site camping resort spread out over 75 acres. Far from roughing it at the **Sunshine Key Camping Resort** (38801 Overseas Highway, MM 39, 305/872-2217, $), you'll find yourself surrounded by stores, grills, game rooms, laundry facilities, tennis and shuffleboard courts, a marina, a fishing pier, and a beach.

7 Veterans Memorial Park

Location: west end of 7 Mile Bridge, at MM 40 on Little Duck Key
Parking/fees: free parking lot
Hours: 7:30 A.M. to sunset
Facilities: restrooms, picnic tables, and showers
Contact: Monroe County Department of Parks and Beaches, 305/295-4385

Contact Information

Lower Keys Chamber of Commerce, MM 31, P. O. Drawer 430511, Big Pine Key, FL 33043; 305/872-2411 or 800/872-3722; website: www.lowerkeyschamber.com

Bahia Honda State Park

The pearl of Keys beaches can be found at the popular Bahia Honda State Park, which takes up the entirety of Bahia Honda Key (at MM 36.5) and a small island at the southwest end of the park. It is the southernmost site in Florida's state park system, and one of the highlights of the Keys—especially since natural sand beaches are otherwise in such short supply on these coral-spined islands. In addition, one of the largest remaining stands of the threatened silver palm tree can be found at Bahia Honda. Gumbo-limbo and yellow satinwood thrive here as well. These are not your typical mainland species, being native to subtropical islands.

A trek along the beach toward the south end of the park will bring you to the foot of the old Bahia Honda Bridge, the last remnant of Henry Flagler's Overseas Railroad. This magnificent two-tiered structure spans Bahia Honda Channel, the deepest in the Keys and one that is subject to the strongest cross currents. In order to traverse what seemed to be a bottomless depth here (*bahía honda* means "deep bay" in Spanish), the bridge's mammoth pylons were built higher than any along the 100-mile stretch of Flagler's route. This mile-long crossing was more difficult to build than the 7 Mile Bridge. Today, the abandoned bridge makes for an eerie sight. Divers love exploring the rich underwater life here, but one should only attempt this deep and treacherous dive with a seasoned pro.

Bahia Honda offers some of the finest camping we've ever seen on or near the beach. Nestled among a thick hammock, these sites make an inviting spot to drop anchor. There are two camping areas by the ocean and a smaller one on the bayside, totaling 80 sites (and costing $19 per night). Alternatively, a half dozen two-bedroom cabins that accommodate up to eight people can be rented for $110 nightly (dropping to $85 from mid-September through mid-December). Reservations are accepted up to a year in advance. A 19-slip marina and dive shop (305/872-3210) are at the south end of the park. Gear can be rented and excursions booked—everything from snorkeling to parasailing, kayaks to powerboats—all year long.

Beaches

At 2.5 miles, Bahia Honda is the longest natural sand beach on the Keys. Two named beaches make up **Bahia Honda State Park.** Loggerhead Beach, located by the concessions at the south end of the park, is small and protected. Sandspur Beach is long with shallow sandbars extending seaward for a great distance. Wide it is not—10 yards at most—but the sand is pearly white and easy to trek. Periodically, the beach gets covered with thick mats of seaweed that wash ashore, accumulating at the high-tide line. This helps build up the dunes, and the park wisely lets nature take its course, leaving well enough alone.

Depending on the tide, you can wade out as far as 100 yards from shore on the soft sand bottom without even reaching your knees. The crystal-clear blue-green water turns a darker brown where it greets the line of underwater aquatic vegetation at this point. One fisherman we saw was about a thousand feet offshore and the water had yet to reach his waist. Kayaking is a popular pastime here, as these buoyant vessels don't displace much water and therefore don't scrape bottom at low tide. Kayaks can be rented by the hour ($10 for a single, $20 for a double).

Contact Information

Bahia Honda State Park, 36850 Overseas Highway, Big Pine Key, FL 33043; 305/872-2353; website: www.myflorida.com

8 Bahia Honda State Park

Location: MM 36.5 on Bahia Honda Key

Parking/fees: $2.50 entrance fee for car and driver, plus $2.50 for first passenger and 50 cents for each additional passenger. Camping fees are $23.69 (without electricity) and $25.84 (with electricity), plus a $2.24 surcharge for waterfront sites.

Hours: 8 A.M. to sunset

Facilities: concessions, restrooms, picnic tables, showers, and a visitor center

Contact: Bahia Honda State Park, 305/872-2353

THE KEYS

West Summerland Key

National Boy and Girl Scout Camps, and little else, are located on this small key located at MM 34 on the Overseas Highway (U.S. 1).

Contact Information

Lower Keys Chamber of Commerce, MM 31, P. O. Drawer 430511, Big Pine Key, FL 33043; 305/872-2411 or 800/872-3722; website: www.lowerkeyschamber.com

Big Pine Key

Big Pine Key is the unofficial hub and welcome center of the Lower Keys, situated 25 miles north of Key West, at MM 29 on the Overseas Highway (U.S. 1). It is also the home to 5,000 human beings and roughly 800 key deer. It is the second largest of the Florida Keys in terms of land area (two by eight miles) and is fast becoming one of the most populous as well. That is because it is attracting a lot of the spillover from Key West, which is effectively built out. That may be good news for Century 21, but it is terrible news for the endangered key deer, a stunted subspecies of the Virginia white-tailed deer that stands barely two feet tall at the shoulder. Two-thirds of the estimated population of key deer in the world live on Big Pine Key, and the rest are scattered on smaller keys. These little dears all too frequently become road kill, the victims of traffic zooming to and from Key West, even though the speed limit drops to 35 mph on Big Pine Key. As you well know, no one obeys the speed limit anymore and all too few give a hoot about nature. A suggestion: Why not construct an elevated roadway over Big Pine Key for through traffic?

From the perspective of the Overseas Highway, Big Pine Key is just another bit of roadside blight en route to Key West. From the perspective of the key deer, however, it is a sanctuary (or is supposed to be). The island runs on a north-west axis and is much longer than the east-west crossing by the Overseas Highway might suggest to the casual traveler. Despite the ever-present danger posed by the highway, much of the island is a wildlife refuge out of range of U.S. 1. All the same, your vigilant attention when driving across Big Pine Key—particularly in the early morning hours and at dusk, when key deer forage—is humbly requested by the caretakers of the Key Deer National Wildlife Refuge and two wildlife-loving beach bums. Within the refuge is a spot called the Blue Hole: a borrow pit dug out in railroad days that now serves as home to alligators, turtles, and fish. An observation tower offers a safe place for humans to study the reptiles.

The unabated key-deer carnage makes the little white lie that opens the tourist brochure for Big Pine Key all the more specious. "These Lower Keys are by far the most unspoiled little islands in America," it reads. With a shopping center, Century 21 signs the size of schooners, and residential areas that swell to the very borders of the Key Deer National Wildlife Refuge, this is a dubious claim. However, Big Pine Key's burgeoning growth has been dealt a serious blow by a moratorium on new construction. This, of course, has exacerbated tensions between environmentalists and the developers/property owners of Big Pine Key. The latter typically grumble about federal bureaucrats cramping their style. Too bad, you know? After all, Big Pine Key is one of the last refuges for not only key deer but Caribbean pines, both of which are endangered. So slow down when you cross Big Pine Key and enjoy the scenery—and perhaps the sight of a scampering, dog-sized key deer.

It was estimated in the summer of 2000 that conservation efforts have allowed the key deer population on Big Pine Key and No-Name Key to grow to 800. (That's from a low of 50 key deer in the 1940s.) Of course, that bit of good news led to stepped-up calls to rescind the building moratorium and blather about "meeting the needs of both deer and people." There are already 5,000 residents crowded onto Big Pine Key. Enough is enough. Leave something for nature, for a change.

Bunking Down

If you do happen to be staying over, chances are it's because you're fishing or

MAP OF THE KEYS—PAGE 293

taking a dive trip to Looe Key. Accommodations are limited and consist mainly of RV parks (plenty of those!) and rustic fishing camps, such as **Big Pine Key Fishing Lodge** (MM 33, 33000 Overseas Highway, 305/872-2351, $), which rents efficiencies and RV and tent sites, and the evocatively named **Old Wooden Bridge Fishing Camp** (MM 31.5, 1791 Bogie Drive, 305/872-2241, $), which has its own bait shop and private fishing bridge. There's also the modest **Big Pine Key Resort Motel** (MM 30.5, 30725 Overseas Highway, 305/872-9090, $).

Coastal Cuisine

What is something called the Baltimore Oyster House doing on Big Pine Key?

Fishing the Florida Keys

In the Florida Keys, fishing is as automatic an activity as breathing. Many anglers head to the Keys in winter to cast for bonefish, tarpon, and other gamefish found in the mangrove-studded "backcountry" of Florida Bay. In the open ocean, sailfish, mackerel, kingfish, and more are taken from November through March. Here is the lowdown on the primary fish species you're likely to cast for and catch in the Keys:

Bonefish — This fighting fish is pursued for sport only, since it is inedible. It is caught in the shallows from a poled boat or with waders, using crab or shrimp as bait cast in the bonefish's direction.

Grouper — Black grouper is unbeatable on the table, and the other types are delicious, too. Troll the bottom with cut or live bait. Unfortunately, they've been overfished, and the Nassau grouper is being considered for endangered species status.

Mahimahi (a.k.a. dolphinfish) — A superb eating fish, this iridescent, multicolored beauty is a surface dweller that schools beneath sea grass mats in summer.

Sailfish — This leaping billfish has a raised dorsal fin that looks like a sail and a sword-like upper jaw. It's another desirable wall hanging best returned to the tropical waters it calls home.

Snapper — Comes in many varieties: red (tasty but depleted), yellowtail (a favorite on sushi menus), gray, mangrove, mutton, etc. They're hard to land but worth the effort.

Snook — A gamefish found beneath bridges and around jetties, snook is a good, stealthy fighter, though its taking is strictly regulated (if not outright prohibited) in Florida; check the latest regulations.

Tarpon — Its scales gleam like newly minted silver dollars. A leaping game fish that makes a coveted trophy, the tarpon is, happily, more often turned loose by anglers to leap some more.

Fishing tournaments are conducted throughout the year on the Keys. For information on places, dates, fees, rules, and awards, write Florida Keys Fishing Tournaments, P.O. Box 420358, Summerland Key, FL 33042.

And now a word on behalf of the species threatened by overfishing. For those who are fishing the Keys—or anywhere in Florida, for that matter—bear in mind that the following are overfished and in precipitous decline: bluefish, grouper, mackerel, marlin, snapper, swordfish, and tuna.

Ditto Bagel Island Cafe? Domino's Pizza? Captain Anne's Sports Bar? Are we back in Miami? Closer to the spirit and locale of the Florida Keys is **Montego Bay Food & Spirits** (MM 30.2, 305/872-3009, $$), where you can at least order some seafood dishes. In general, however, the restaurants on Big Pine Key are as misconceived and out of place as the residential development that threatens the key deer.

Night Moves

The **No Name Pub** (Watson Boulevard, 305/872-9115) is the most popular hangout in the area, "a nice place if you can find it." It's a beer garden and pizza joint located just before the No Name Bridge over Bogie Channel. That's not to say it's easy to find. From the stoplight at MM 31 on the Overseas Highway (U.S. 1), turn onto Key Deer Boulevard. Continue to Watson Boulevard; turn right. Bear left at a fork in the road, cross a bridge and you'll find the No Name Pub in a yellow house at the foot of the No Name Bridge. Its history dates back to 1936, making it refreshingly authentic, at the least.

Contact Information

Lower Keys Chamber of Commerce, MM 31, P.O. Drawer 430511, Big Pine Key, FL 33043; 305/872-2411 or 800/872-3722; website: www.lowerkeyschamber.com

Looe Key

Looe Key lies seven miles southeast of Big Pine Key in the Straits of Florida, and is reachable by boat only. The attraction is a coral reef that offers unsurpassed snorkeling and diving. Some claim it to be the most spectacular living reef in North America. It's been a national marine sanctuary since 1981 and isn't really a key but a reef, named for a British frigate, H.M.S. *Looe,* that sank here in 1744. The reef skirts the edge of the Gulf Stream, and the warm waters and varying depths help produce the diversity of life forms in this surreal coral garden. Diving and snorkeling trips can be arranged at outfitters all over the Lower Keys, such as **Strike Zone Charters** (MM 29.5, Big Pine Key, 305/872-9863) and the **Looe Key Reef Resort and Dive Center** (MM 27.5, Ramrod Key, 305/872-2215).

Contact Information

Lower Keys Chamber of Commerce, MM 31, P.O. Drawer 430511, Big Pine Key, FL 33043; 305/872-2411 or 800/872-3722; website: www.lowerkeyschamber.com

Little Torch Key

Named for the torchwood tree, Little Torch Key can be found one mile south of Big Pine Key at MM 28 on the Overseas Highway (U.S. 1). It is home to three small resorts, including the **Dolphin Resort & Marina** (MM 28.5, 305/872-2685, $$), whose roll call of "beds, boats, bait, beer" sounds like just the ticket. A cut above your average Keys roadside "resort"—which is, more often than not, a glorified motor court (and that's okay, too)—the Dolphin has some neat cottages and bungalows hidden among the greenery of this overlooked key.

Contact Information

Lower Keys Chamber of Commerce, MM 31, P.O. Drawer 430511, Big Pine Key, FL 33043; 305/872-2411 or 800/872-3722; website: www.lowerkeyschamber.com

MAP OF THE KEYS—PAGE 293

Ramrod Key

Ramrod is the name of a ship that wrecked against a reef just off this key, which is two miles south of Big Pine Key at MM 27 on the Overseas Highway (U.S. 1). You'll find a complete resort on the north end of Ramrod Key. **Looe Key Reef Resort and Dive Center** (MM 27.5, Ramrod Key, 305/872-2215) has it all: motel, restaurant, dive shop, swimming pool, tiki bar, gas station, convenience store. Room rates are about as cheap as you'll find in the Keys ($75–90 a night). The motel is perfectly adequate, and the dive shop rules.

Contact Information

Lower Keys Chamber of Commerce, MM 31, P.O. Drawer 430511, Big Pine Key, FL 33043; 305/872-2411 or 800/872-3722; website: www.lowerkeyschamber.com

Summerland Key and Cudjoe Key

There's little reason to stop on these largely residential islands between Big Pine Key and Key West on the Overseas Highway (U.S. 1) at MM 26 (Summerland Key) and MM 23 (Cudjoe Key), unless you're renting a home for a month or more. They go for around $2,500 a month, on average. (For a list of seasonal rentals, contact **Action Keys Realty**, MM 24.8, P.O. Box 421063, 305/745-1323.) Summerland Key rates an airstrip and post office. Cudjoe Key earned a footnote from us in an earlier book for having pioneered a new low in real-estate mongering: the "condominium trailer park."

Contact Information

Lower Keys Chamber of Commerce, MM 31, P.O. Drawer 430511, Big Pine Key, FL 33043; 305/872-2411 or 800/872-3722; website: www.lowerkeyschamber.com

Sugarloaf Key

This ear-shaped island at MM 20 is receiving some of the developmental backwash that floats 15 miles east from Key West. The island harbors a few communities and developments, including the town of Perky, renowned for its bat tower(!). Incidentally, Sugarloaf Key is followed by the Saddlebunch Keys, a grouping of small, uninhabited keys that are numbered one through five.

Bunking Down

Sugarloaf Key has its share of things to offer travelers other than bridges to and from Key West. There's **Sugarloaf Lodge** (MM 17, P.O. Box 440148, 305/745-3211, $$), a "complete vacation resort" with 55 waterfront rooms, restaurant, tiki bar, pool, tennis courts, miniature golf, and shuffleboard. There's even a marina and an airstrip! Rooms run $125 in season (December 19 through April 30) and $75 the rest of the year. RVers who like to fish frequent a popular oceanfront KOA campground, the **Sugarloaf Key Resort** (MM 20, P.O. Box 420469, 305/745-3549, $).

Contact Information

Lower Keys Chamber of Commerce, MM 31, P.O. Drawer 430511, Big Pine Key, FL 33043; 305/872-2411 or 800/872-3722; website: www.lowerkeyschamber.com

Big Coppitt Key and Boca Chica Key

Boca Chica ("little mouth") has been the site of a U.S. naval air station since 1941. Big Coppitt is mainly inhabited by service families from the naval facility. That might suffice by way of description for this book's purposes, but there is a county beach out here. **Boca Chica Beach** is reachable by exiting the Overseas Highway at MM 10, where State Route 941 (Old State Route 4A) runs alongside the ocean. At its end is a county-maintained beach about a quarter-mile long where you'll find not much more than patches of sand and a few refuse containers. But it is a pet-friendly beach, so bring your canine out here for a longer romp on the beach than he or she will ever be allowed in Key West.

9 Boca Chica Beach

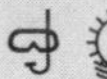

Location: from U.S. 1 at MM 10 on Big Coppitt Key, follow State Route 941 (Old State Route 4A) to the beach
Parking/fees: free parking lot
Hours: 7:30 A.M. to sunset
Facilities: none
Contact: Monroe County Department of Parks and Beaches, 305/295-4385

Contact Information

Lower Keys Chamber of Commerce, MM 31, P.O. Drawer 430511, Big Pine Key, FL 33043; 305/872-2411 or 800/872-3722; website: www.lowerkeyschamber.com

Key West

The road ends here. Key West (pop. 28,000) is the southernmost tip of the tail on the American land mass, being truly isolated from the mainland by 42 bridges and a hundred miles of narrow keys that barely poke above sea level. Most people who trek out here find Key West to be a worthwhile pot of gold at the end of U.S. 1's asphalt rainbow (whose terminus in downtown Key West is duly noted). Perhaps it is the tropical setting that makes Key West so appealing; though it falls shy of the tropics by 30 miles, that is just a technicality. As it is in any far-flung province, especially those in equatorial climes, the rules that are in force in general society are more relaxed down here. In fact, they almost don't apply at all. People simply do not judge or ask questions in Key West. That is why it is such a celebrated enclave for gays and why it has historically attracted pirates, rumrunners, offbeat literati, dope smugglers, and outlaws of every imaginable stripe.

Of course, all is not coconut milk and mangrove honey in Key West. With the steady influx of tourists and its reshaping by developers has come a certain loss of intimacy. Although Ernest Hemingway was once quoted as saying, "I like Key West because people don't stare at me on the street," he'd undoubtedly find himself a harried celebrity were he to stroll around today. Since the mid-1980s, a lot of changes have come to Key West. Take Duval Street, along the miracle mile between Truman and Front Streets, which is now wall-to-wall with stores and bars that must depress the citizens of the Conch Republic. There's been a bloodless invasion of Key West by well-worn franchise names that have been branded into the American psyche. Worse, cruise ships now disgorge tourists by the hundreds at Mallory Square to prowl the downtown streets on souvenir-hunting junkets. As a result, Key West appears to be vying for the title of T-shirt capital of America, competing with the low-rent likes of Venice Beach, Myrtle Beach, and Fisherman's Wharf in San Francisco.

Seemingly every third storefront peddles T-shirts, with racks of rock-bottom come-ons. But that's not even the worst affront on Duval Street. Adult video stores and strip clubs exist, not in profusion but just enough to register an uncomfortable impression. Hired touts hector milling tourists with verbal and printed come-ons, crisply snapping the topmost sheet against the stack before thrusting it into people's disinterested hands while clucking, "Check it out." Surely, there is something they can do about this affront, which combines the worst of Manhattan and New Orleans. Of late, they seem to be trying, as the current mayor is spearheading an effort to make Key West "the cleanest little city in America." Well, good luck. Considering Key West's renegade history, they've got their work cut out for them. Somewhere between irredeemable sleaze and an antiseptic makeover, though, there has to be a happy medium.

At the other extreme, Key West has become occupied and encircled by a fortress of upscale condominiums and hotels that block sunsets and water views in a town where these things were once available to one and all, regardless of means. The battle for Key West's soul is driven by the fact that tourism pumps more than a billion dollars a year into the economy of the Florida Keys. This bending in the direction of money is one reason that getting to Mallory Square, Key West's sacred spot of sunset-watching, has become tantamount to negotiating an obstacle course. The area in its vicinity is perpetually under construction. The streets and lots adjacent to Mallory Square were torn up when we last passed through, much as they have been on visits we've made as far back as 1984. Don't try entering Mallory Square by walking along the waterfront just north of it; the businesses there don't allow passers-through, so one must enter from Tifts Alley, off Front Street. Such obstacles had us wondering just whose town is it, anyway.

If everything we've written about Key West implies that it can be a hassle to get around and that it's choked with tourists, tawdry dives, and a roll call of franchises depressingly similar to that found in every other American city, that much is indeed all too true. But it's equally true that Key West retains its essential character despite the encroachments. There's still enough that's unique and individualistic about the place to make it worth visiting, albeit with a healthy skepticism and a wary eye.

Take the rites of sunset-watching at Mallory Square, for instance. After maneuvering our way around the yuppie-tourist bars and past earth-moving equipment, we found ourselves on a concrete walkway along the waterfront. Many of the same characters from years past were still out working the crowd at sunset, doing stupid human tricks and passing the hat. A guy dressed like Uncle Sam—a good-natured soul who's a little off his noggin—handed out his $22 bills and explained their numerological significance, even invoking Dennis Rodman's name to confused tourists. A long-haired, sun-bronzed Key West lifer did a high-wire balancing act while playing the crowd like a Vegas-savvy pro so that they'd fill his overturned hat with tips. One lanky fellow in a hard hat and red jumpsuit inhaled fire and then belched a big plume of it. A kilt-clad Scotsman with an incongruously deep tan blew Christmas tunes on his bagpipes, filling the warm tropical air with familiar melodies. It did not seem like the holiday season, though it was late December. It never feels like Christmas—or winter, for that matter—in Key West. That's why people come here.

Sunset arrived at 5:42 P.M. on this particular evening. At that very moment, the sun slipped behind a narrow bank of clouds just above the horizon. This sunset was particularly riveting, as the bright orange rays it cast across the heavens focused and intensified with each passing moment into a brilliant red the color of holly berries. After sunset, the heavens glowed a clear metallic blue-orange that lingered for a while, as did the crowd on Mallory Square. At that sacred moment, street performers and chattering observers alike were reduced to an appreciative silence by the solar spectacle, which no human feat—be it tightrope walking or condo erecting—could possibly top. The crowd, unified at this one glorious moment, quickly dispersed into their various worlds—some to $200 hotel rooms, some to ramshackle houses tucked on side streets, and some to pricey dinners at fancy restaurants, while others (many others, we might add) set off on a Duval Street pub crawl that would last into the wee hours, until that point at which the sun prepared to rise over Key West for yet another day of revelry.

Tourists, locals, snowbirds, and jet-setters converge uneasily and somewhat comically out here at land's end. Each clique comes with its own set of expectations and designs on the place. Sometimes it's hard to tell hosts from parasites. Out at the intersection of South and Whitehead Streets, for instance, tourists line up to take pictures beside the painted buoy that identifies this spot as the southernmost point in the continental United States. It's a pilgrimage and photo op you simply must make, having come this far. Thus, Southernmost Point draws hordes of tourists and handfuls of locals availing themselves of a chance to cadge tips. We watched one weather-beaten opportunist work the crowd, offering to snap pictures of the tourists with their own cameras. It's a win-win situation. The beaming Middle American couple gets to show the folks back home a snapshot of themselves beside the buoy, while the local—a character from a Jimmy Buffett song come to life—pockets a buck or two. Only in Key West.

At the end of the road, people tend to get a little more surreal and devil-may-care. It can be something as incongruous as the distant sound of Bob Dylan's protest songs being performed by Duval Street folksingers to tourists wearing flip-flops and Hawaiian shirts. Everything is topsy-turvy and carnivalesque. When Key West is alive, there is something in the blueness of the sky, the emerald of the water, the salt tang in the air, the crazy quilt of people, the endless singing, whistling, shouting, parading, and drinking that tells you this is it. This is land's end.

Beaches

Don't let anyone tell you Key West is not a beach town. People tried to tell us Key West is not a beach town. They're almost paranoid on that point, particularly the hotel owners, who tell of having to endure tirades from disappointed families and couples who have come to Key West expecting a standard Florida beach vacation. Hotel lobbies are littered with beleaguered concierges who have had their heads chewed off by angry guests demanding to know "where's the beach?"

After combing the island's perimeter, we would like to counter the prevailing wisdom by asserting in no uncertain terms that Key West is indeed a beach town. You've just got to know where to look. For starters, don't book downtown if being near the beach is part of your agenda. There are beaches along the south-facing side of Key West, running for about three miles from where South Roosevelt Boulevard (Highway A1A) makes a 90-degree turn in the vicinity of Key West International Airport all the way down to Fort Zachary Taylor.

Smathers Beach is the longest stretch of beach, running along South Roosevelt for about three-fifths of a mile. It is a man-made beach that's widest around Atlantic Avenue, narrowing as you move away from town and eventually dwindling to nothing but waves slapping the seawall that protects the road by the airport. There's plenty of free parking on Highway A1A and a bit of a seaside bazaar in progress, with people dealing their wares out of vans. You can rent Hobie Cats, sailboards, and snorkeling gear; buy ice cream, sandwiches, and cool drinks; purchase seashells (don't even think about it!); or snag a beach chair and umbrella for the day. The snorkeling off Smathers Beach is great, so dive in and enjoy the reefer madness, which is among

10 Smathers Beach

   ④

Location: along South Roosevelt Boulevard (Highway A1A) in Key West
Parking/fees: metered street parking
Hours: 7 A.M.–11 P.M.
Facilities: concessions, restrooms, picnic tables, and showers
Contact: Key West Parks Department, 305/292-8190

11 C.B. Harvey Rest Beach Park

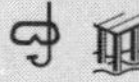  ④

Location: along Atlantic Boulevard between Smathers Beach and Higgs Beach in Key West
Parking/fees: free parking lot at Sunny McCoy Indigenous Park
Hours: 7:30 A.M.–11 P.M.
Facilities: picnic tables and restrooms
Contact: Key West Parks Department, 305/292-8190

the best off any beach in the United States.

The next two beaches are along Atlantic Avenue, which takes over from Highway A1A in following the beachfront. **C.B. Harvey Rest Beach Park** (formerly just Rest Beach) and **Clarence South Higgs Memorial Beach** are adjacent and indivisible. Rest Beach has picnic tables, a sunbathing dock and nothing more, but you can park across the road at McCoy Park, which has all the other necessary facilities. Higgs Beach is amply endowed with amenities, including a restaurant, showers, and tennis and volleyball courts. Both are festive beaches. Colorful sails, covered picnic tables, dense stands of shady palms, a paved bike path, and a beachside cafe make this a wonderful spot for gathering rays and cooling off in the water. Colorful characters cruise past on bikes and mopeds or streak by in a blur on in-line skates. A mixed crowd of gays, families, Europeans, oldsters, yuppies, and hippies congregate in an environment that embodies Key West at its relaxed, catholic, and tolerant best. If it's true, as the saying goes, that "it takes all kinds," then you'll find what it takes on these beaches.

A couple of sights stand out in our minds. There's the guy whose belly is as enormous as his bathing suit is tiny, walking a tiny, ratlike dog on a leash. They are repeatedly stopped by women who purr, "Oh, he's so cute." Then there's the hippie couple who are living out of their van, performing morning ablutions at a public shower while a Grateful Dead tape plays and their kerchief-clad animal companion observes it all with wagging tail and panting tongue. A wooden pier goes out for a ways and then gives way to a stretch of pier pilings. Those in the know refer to this, indelicately, as the "dick dock." Gays in thong bikinis sun themselves out here like seals on rocks. The only woman we saw out on the dock looked European and probably didn't know any better. The scene on the sand, by contrast, is more heterogeneous (read: heterosexual).

A fence divides Higgs Beach from the private beach in front of Marriott's Casa Marina Resort, a stretch of sand and beach chairs known as Kokomo Beach. Farther west, at the end of Vernon Avenue, is a very small beach known as **Dog Beach** that's popular with pet-owning locals. Unless you're traveling with Fido, it's of no use or consequence to tourists. **South Beach** is a small swath of sand and hard-bottom beach a block away from the "Southernmost Point" marker. **South Beach Restaurant** (1405 Duval Street, 305/294-2727, $$) is part of the landscape on this city beach—the southernmost public beach in the U.S., for those keeping track of such facts.

Fort Taylor Beach, at the Zachary Taylor State Historic Site, is the final ocean-fac-

⓬ Clarence South Higgs Memorial Beach

Location: West end of Atlantic Boulevard (Highway A1A) in Key West
Parking/fees: free street and lot parking
Hours: 7:30 A.M.–11 P.M.
Facilities: concessions, restrooms, picnic tables, and showers
Contact: Monroe County Department of Parks and Beaches, 305/295-4385

⓭ Dog Beach

Location: South end of Vernon Avenue in Key West
Parking/fees: Limited free street parking
Hours: 7:30 A.M.–11 P.M.
Facilities: none
Contact: Key West Parks Department, 305/292-8190

Map of The Keys—Page 293

ing public beach in Key West's procession of them. It is a good beach, albeit difficult to maneuver around (necessitating a lot of gingerly scrambling over the reef until the water deepens), and a great sunset-watching spot—arguably even better than Mallory Square, though it lacks the entertaining diversion of crowds and street theater. As a final footnote offered only out of a pathological need to be comprehensive, there is one public beach on the gulf side of Key West. Known as **Simonton Street Beach**, it is located downtown, a few blocks east of Mallory Square. Facilities are very limited; however, you will find a boat ramp and public restroom. The beach is less than ideal for swimming.

To summarize, Key West is a beach town after all. Just realize that beaches aren't the primary focus of the Key West experience. Having said this, we must add a disturbing footnote. The beaches of Key West have become fouled in recent years with untreated sewage spewing from an ancient treatment plant. Elevated levels of fecal coliform (bacteria found in human waste, and an indicator of other viruses and parasites) and enterroccus (an effluent-based bacteria that causes gastrointestinal problems) have resulted in beach warnings and closures in Key West. The crap has even drifted out to the Dry Tortugas, where a health advisory had to be posted on the beach at Fort Jefferson

They are working to modernize the sewage treatment facility in Key West, but that is still a few years off. In the meantime, visitors will take cold comfort from the mayor's less than reassuring observation, "The fact is that people can still use the beaches. We just advise them not to go into the water." It's hard to believe that a smallish key in open water has fouled itself so thoroughly. In addition, some of the canals on the Keys have become polluted, and at least one was found to contain live infectious viruses, including those that cause polio and viral meningitis. Moreover, not only has Key West been subjected to fecal contamination. In 1999, two beaches in

14 South Beach

Location: south end of Duval Street in Key West
Parking/fees: metered street parking
Hours: 7:30 A.M.–11 P.M.
Facilities: concessions, picnic tables, and restrooms
Contact: Key West Parks Department, 305/292-8190

15 Fort Taylor Beach

Location: Fort Zachary Taylor Historic Site, south end of Southard Street in Key West
Parking/fees: $2.50 entrance fee for car and driver, plus $2.50 for first passenger and 50 cents for each additional passenger. Pedestrian fee is $1.50 per person.
Hours: 8 A.M. to sunset
Facilities: restrooms, picnic tables, showers, and a visitor center
Contact: Fort Zachary Taylor State Historic Site, 305/292-6713

16 Simonton Street Beach

Location: north end of Simonton Street, on the bayside in downtown Key West
Parking/fees: metered parking lot
Hours: 7:30 A.M.–11 P.M.
Facilities: restrooms
Contact: Key West Parks Department, 305/292-8190

Marathon (Coco Plum and Curry Hammock) and one in Tavernier (Harry Harris Park) flunked late-summer water quality tests. The good news is that the state of Florida has stepped up water-quality testing on the beaches of South Florida, and that an effort is underway to modernize waste treatment plants in the Florida Keys. Still, the beaches were under health alerts as of this writing in the summer of 2001. For the latest information, call 305/293-1653 from the Keys and 877/892-9585 outside them.

Shore Things

- **Bike/skate rentals:** Sun-N-Fun, 925 Duval Street, 305/295-6686.
- **Boat cruise:** Sunny Days Sunset and Snorkel Trips, 201 Elizabeth Street, 305/296-5556.
- **Dive shop:** Subtropic Dive Center, 1605 North Roosevelt Boulevard, 305/296-9914.
- **Ecotourism:** Reef Relief Environmental Center and Store, 201 William Street, 305/294-3100.
- **Fishing charters:** Key West Fishing Guides, 800/497-5998.
- **Lighthouse:** Key West Lighthouse and Museum, 938 Whitehead Street, 305/294-0012.
- **Marina:** A&B Marina, 700 Front Street, 305/294-2535.
- **Pier:** White Street Pier, C.B. Harvey Rest Beach Park.
- **Rainy-day attraction:** Hemingway House, 907 Whitehead Street, 305/294-1575.
- **Shopping/browsing:** Mallory Square, 1 Whitehead Street, 305/296-4557.
- **Vacation rentals:** Rent Key West Vacations, 1107 Truman Avenue, 305/294-0990.

Bunking Down

Marriott's Casa Marina Resort (1500 Reynolds Street, 305/296-3535, $$$$) is rife with history that dates back to its formal opening on New Year's Eve 1921. It was yet another of railroad and resort magnate Henry Flagler's posh hotels, intended as his pièce de résistance as a resort. Although he never lived to see it completed, he'd no doubt be happy to learn that the on-premises restaurant is named Henry's. Casa Marina thrived until World War II, when it was commandeered for Navy housing. Since Marriott took it over in 1978, by which point the Spanish Renaissance–style resort had fallen into disrepair, Casa Marina has been made over and spruced up, but the aura of history and high times hasn't been lost in the process. The lobby remains impressive, with its high ceilings, dark wood, and comfortable chairs conferring an understated elegance. The rooms are well appointed and comfortable in a somewhat more relaxed mode than the corporate hotel-chain norm. Try to get an ocean-view room. If you leave the sliding doors open and the air-conditioning off, you'll be lulled to a heavenly slumber by waves and sea breezes.

The best part of all is the spectacular pool and beach area. There are several pools and a large Jacuzzi in the palm-shaded courtyard. A few steps farther lies Kokomo Beach, where a cabana attendant will set you up with lounge chair, towels, and little table. This is the perfect place to cultivate a tan and further dog-ear the pages of the latest opus by Mary Higgins Clark or Tom Clancy. As is the case at the city and county beaches, there's a short pier you can walk out on, at the end of which stairs lead into the water. This is to spare you a filleting closer to shore on the shallow, wickedly sharp and knobby reef. Equipment is rented and suntan oil sold from a beachside hut.

Out on South Roosevelt Boulevard,

across from Smathers Beach, you've got three choices. In order of ascending ritziness and cost, they are the **Key Wester Resort Motel** (3675 South Roosevelt Boulevard, 305/296-5671, $$), the **Best Western Key Ambassador Resort Motel** (3755 South Roosevelt Boulevard, 305/296-3500, $$$), and the **Sheraton Suites Key West** (2001 South Roosevelt Boulevard, 305/292-9800, $$$$). The Sheraton is the only one that faces Smathers Beach at its prime south end, where there's a bonafide beach. Sheraton ("Key West's only all-suite resort") offers the choicest digs if you want to stay on the beach in Key West, though this upscale corporate lodge doesn't exactly project the native joie de vivre.

In downtown Key West, near the intersection of Duval and Front Streets, lodgings include the **Hyatt Key West** (601 Front Street, 305/296-9900, $$$$), whose tropically landscaped acreage rambles down to the gulf's edge, and the **Crowne Plaza La Concha** (430 Duval Street, 305/296-2991, $$$), a restored property that's positioned in the center of the Duval Street bazaar. Both are steps away from Mallory Square, the Conch Train tour's departure point, and the hottest bars and restaurants.

Okay. That is a sampling of the choices from among the flotilla of corporate giants that have streamed into Key West in the relatively recent past. At the other extreme, there are a host of funkier choices more in keeping with the spirit of the tropics and Key West's reputation as a haven for nonconformists escaping the mainland rat race. Many of the more low-key motels and guest houses are a bit frayed around the edges. It's the sun, the moisture, the tropics. It's okay. Unless you're hopelessly phobic with a fear of decay, there's no commandment saying you must plop down $200 a night for a perfectly sterile hotel room in Key West when you might find something for a third as much in a comfortably funky motel or "resort." An upstairs shutter may need a coat of paint and the air conditioner might groan like an ailing sea cow, but it's nothing to get freaked out about.

A lot of Key West's more modest properties lie along Truman Avenue in the "Old Town" area, including such old-timers as **Key Lime Village** (727 Truman Avenue, 305/294-6222, $). Seemingly frozen in time, it appears to have changed not a whit over the years (and, without dating ourselves, we stayed here many years ago). Painted a sun-faded greenish yellow, like the namesake key lime, and hidden among a short forest of stunted trees, this "village" is a series of cottages distributed randomly around the property. A well-shaded pool and lounging area is set off in a corner. In addition to a real break on price, with many cottages going for under $100 a night in season, you are a short stroll from the heart of town. And you'll ooh and aah over the grounds, an enchantingly tropical tangle of key lime trees and dense, shady greenery.

Key West is also well suited to the guest house and bed-and-breakfast craze. It's got the old buildings, the distinctive architecture, the history, and the personality to be an "inn" kind of town. A classic high-end Key West bed-and-breakfast is the **Curry Mansion Inn** (511 Carolina Street, 305/294-5349, $$$), the circa-1855 Victorian home of Florida's first millionaire, William Curry. Another is **Eden House** (1015 Fleming Street, 305/296-6868, $$), a surprisingly affordable guest house. Built in 1924, it's got a bit of literary/bohemian history lurking in its past. Eden House remains an archetypal Key West hostelry, boasting clean and simple rooms with ceiling fans, plus a pool and garden café.

If you want assistance in booking a place to stay—be it hotel, motel, bed-and-breakfast, guest home, or whatever—call **Key West Reservations** (635 United Street,

305/293-9815), a free reservations service for Key West and the other keys.

Coastal Cuisine

They do exquisite things with fish at **Nicola Seafood Restaurant** (601 Front Street, 305/296-9900, $$$$) in the Hyatt Key West Resort and Marina. Using Bahamian and native Florida ingredients, the chef prepares the dishes with a continental flair. Barbados tuna is an enormous tuna steak that has been marinated in orange-soy sauce, grilled medium rare, and placed atop a heap of shredded vegetables and crispy grilled onions. Plantain-crusted black grouper is sautéed and surrounded with a pineapple-pepper salsa. Grated sweet potato coats a prime fillet of yellowtail snapper, which is sautéed till the exterior is crisp. Baked Florida lobster tail comes with a seafood stuffing that includes scallops and shrimp. Appetizers include a shrimp cocktail that's prepared like a margarita, with the shrimp marinated in lime and served in a glass with a salted rim. Among the salads, the blackened Caribbean scallop Caesar salad is a winner. The conch chowder is delicious: the conch tender, the soup spicy.

Duval Street is lined with restaurants that ostentatiously cater to the tourist trade. A closer look will ferret out smaller places that have been given the locals' seal of approval. **Camille's** (703 1/2 Duval Street, 305/296-4811, $$) is a perfect example. It looks something like a British tearoom crossed with a tropical diner. There are 10 tables and a counter with stools. A giant stuffed toucan sits in a perch by the window. The menu is creative and generally healthy, including garden veggie burgers and omelettes filled with shrimp, sun-dried tomatoes, and such. At lunch a grilled snapper sandwich is topped with pepper-jack cheese and shitake mushroom salsa. Yum! Dinner usually includes two fish (mahimahi, snapper, and/or cobia), plus prime rib for the carnivores and some creative entrées by the French chef. Camille's is beloved by locals and those fortunate tourists who stumble onto it.

At the **Rooftop Cafe** (310 Front Street, 305/294-2042, $$$), you can either sit on a balcony overlooking the Mallory Square shopping district or inside beneath whirling fans. The food and ceremony are more elaborate than at Camille's, but it's worth it for the privilege of dining alfresco from a perch above the downtown bazaar. Three meals a day are served, and the top entrées are grilled mahimahi with macadamia nuts, brown butter, and fresh mango, and crab and shrimp cakes. The latter dish won the establishment a Florida "master chef" award. The key lime pie is among the best in Key West. Close by is a Key West landmark, **Pier House** (1 Duval Street, 305/294-9541, $$$$), a casually classy gulfside resort with splendid guest rooms and suites, plus one of the best-known restaurants in town. At Pier House, get anything made with conch (sausage, fritters, chowder), expect a first-class array of fresh fish entrées, and finish it all off with a slab of key lime pie prepared frozen or chilled.

Affluent and upscale present-day Key West also boasts a lot of high-priced, chichi restaurants that are, if not exactly beyond our means, then certainly beyond our threshold of interest in a town this funky and low to the ground. If you want to drop a bundle, that's your business, but in these laid-back environs we prefer cheeseburgers in paradise to rack of lamb. And they serve a mean cheeseburger at Sloppy Joe's, which is our next stop. Read on.

Night Moves

Having been away from Key West for some time, we began a long evening getting reacquainted by ducking our heads into **Sloppy Joe's** (201 Duval Street, 305/294-5717), just to make sure it was still there. To our great relief, it was alive and rocking. The idea of a world without Sloppy Joe's is unthinkable. It is the Plymouth Rock of watering holes on the East Coast.

Then we began making our way up Duval Street. Planning a night on the town in Key West is a simple matter. You walk up one side of Duval Street and then back down the other, keeping an ear cocked to the music spilling out of the bars. If it sounds good and the place is hopping, stop in for a drink or two. Then move on to the next place. Simple as that. Just don't be afraid to call a cab home when the evening's over, or have a designated driver in your party. Having issued that public service announcement, we'll now move on to Key West's endless block party.

One bit of bad news: As is the case all over Florida, club owners have opted to save money by booking one-man bands. A one-man band is a sad parody of a real flesh-and-blood group. An individual pushes buttons, triggering prerecorded accompaniment to his/her own guitar or keyboard playing and singing. It is a sort of listless, half-assed approximation of rock and roll that's enough to depress anyone raised on the real thing. One guy we heard at a Key West bar was a decent guitar player with a convincing growl, but he was tackling the likes of Chuck Berry and Creedence Clearwater Revival in this bogus format. After recovering from the shock of seeing how automation has tainted the nightlife even in a freewheeling town like Key West, we swiftly strode past bars whenever we heard a one-man band. What a fraudulent crock of shit.

One more bit of bad news: **Hard Rock Cafe** (313 Duval Street, 305/293-0230) opened in Key West late in 1996. **Planet Hollywood** is just down the street (108 Duval Street, 305/295-0003). Adjoining all the franchised hot spots are "merchandise shops" that sell T-shirts and other logoed paraphernalia that announce to the world that you have drunk beer there. Hard Rock Cafe is the chain that elevated merchandising to a lucrative and now mandatory side business in this country. In Key West, Hard Rock Cafe has a merch shop. So does **Hog's Breath Saloon** (400 Front Street, 305/292-2032), a restaurant/saloon franchise that's unaffiliated with Clint Eastwood's identically named operation out in Carmel, California. Even good old Sloppy Joe's now sells logoed merch at an on-premises shop.

Despite all the crass merchandising, people manage to have a good time in Key West by force of will. There are so many bars and nightclubs—some serve food, others just drinks—that you are bound to find something that suits you sooner or later. There are gay clubs with darkened interiors, prisonlike bars on the windows, and electronic dance beats streaming from the premises. Casually trendy hangouts like Hog's Breath attract swinging yuppies and boat people. Old reliable saloons like the **Bull and Whistle** (224 Duval Street, 305/296-4545) and **Captain Tony's Saloon** (428 Greene Street, 305/294-1838) can be counted on to hire singers who hoarsely belt blues, folk, and rock year after year. Tourists head to Jimmy Buffett's original **Margaritaville Cafe** (500 Duval Street, 305/292-1435), while locals gravitate to seriously fun and funky hideaways like the **Green Parrot** (601 Whitehead Street, 305/294-6133). Trendy restaurant/bars look down on the action from second-story decks along Duval. Finally, there is Sloppy Joe's, open 9 A.M.–4 A.M. every blessed day.

After wandering the Duval Street bazaar for hours, we reentered Sloppy Joe's feeling ambivalent about the nightlife—not only in Key West, but everywhere. That is to say, it seems to us that clubs and bars are no longer places where people have genuine experiences. Instead, they are served scripted evocations of genuine experiences, from fake '50s retro to fake '60s coffeehouses to fake '70s discos. There are

The Conch Republic

In the Florida Keys, you will frequently hear references to an entity called the Conch Republic. Put it in the same category as the Monkey Wrench Gang. More an absurdist state of mind than a government, the Conch Republic is a by-product of the pirate/smuggler/loose-cannon mentality that has pervaded the Keys since the arrival of the white man and the quick disappearance of the Calusa Indians. One of the most lucrative ways early whites and Bahamians (known as "Conchs") made their money in the early 1800s was by "wrecking," the practice of luring ships onto the reefs with strategically placed lanterns and then waiting until the bounty (and the drowned bodies) washed ashore.

Nowadays, the Conch Republic is part legacy, part macho-buccaneer fantasy, and part tourist-trap-souvenir mentality. It has been embraced by pirate wannabes whose idea of rebellion is drinking 10 margaritas while attending a Jimmy Buffett concert with a stuffed parrot on their heads. Buffett's huge success as a musician has helped fuel the mythology. The precipitating event that led to the official name "Conch Republic" was an April 1982 federal Border Patrol roadblock set up on U.S. 1, just before entering the Keys from mainland Florida. The intention was to check cars for drugs and illegal aliens. The result was widespread unrest among residents of the Keys, sick of the delays at the Soviet-style checkpoint.

The Lexington and Concord of the Conch Republic occurred at Mallory Square in Key West on April 23, 1982, when hundreds of protesters symbolically seceded from the United States and then quickly surrendered, requesting $1 billion in "foreign aid" from the state. Their secession/surrender charade was followed by a weeklong party. What was wacky then is obnoxious now, as the Conch Republic has become the nom de guerre of renegades who've tried to sabotage the work of the National Oceanographic and Atmospheric Administration, the Nature Conservancy, and a coalition of state and federal politicians.

Loosely affiliated with the "property rights" and "wise use" movements, the Conchs have succeeded in polluting the air with propaganda about how environmentalists and big government are taking over their corner of the world. The antigovernment strain runs deep in the psyche of the Conch Republic, which kids itself into thinking it's the last bastion of rugged individualism in America—a sort of laid-back, rum-stoked version of the Montana Freemen. The cluttered roadsides and littered shorelines along the Keys offer silent testimony to their inability to care for that which they claim as their birthright.

fake biker bars, fake British pubs, fake Caribbean-themed hangouts, and plenty of places to serve the gold card–carrying yuppie, who is by definition a kind of fake human being.

Upon walking into Sloppy Joe's, we weren't exactly soothed by what we saw at first. It was Miller Lite night. There on the stage was an unctuous dude who spoke in an adenoidal whine. He goaded the crowd into dancing to retro disco tunes. They played KC & the Sunshine Band, Donna Summer, and that unspeakable song with the chorus "push push in the bush." The dancing was awful: robotic, stiff-limbed Europeans

The long and short of it is that the latter-day Conchs—they've assumed this identity for themselves—are not taking care of the Keys, yet they defiantly oppose intervention for the protection and restoration of this treasure. In the November 1996 elections, for example, Monroe County's voters rejected by a 55 to 45 margin Referendum No. 4 ("Shall we have a Florida Keys National Marine Sanctuary?"). The following vignette, taken from a local weekly called the *Keys Advertiser,* is typical of what passes for democracy down here. It seems that one brave local woman stood up in a public meeting before the election to voice her opinion about those who would vote no on the referendum. "The no vote is due to the pirate mentality in the Keys," she challenged the room. "Don't expect those who are destroying the reef to vote for the sanctuary. The Keys belong to the nation, not just the residents of the county."

She was, of course, roundly booed by the conch heads. We give her a belated standing ovation, and recognition is also due U.S. Representative Peter Deutsch, who put his job on the line by supporting the sanctuary. We also challenge the disgruntled denizens of Monroe County to come up with something more viable than local referendums and rhetoric about the "will of the people." The idea that the health of the Keys' priceless coral reefs would become snagged on the shoals of a local referendum is, well, conky indeed.

And, indeed, it hasn't. Despite all their saber-rattling theatrics, the Florida Keys National Marine Sanctuary was established by an act of Congress in 1990, but because two-thirds of its 2,800 square miles fall in Florida waters, approval from the state was needed. On January 28, 1997, despite the fact that Monroe County voters had rejected the sanctuary in the 1996 elections, a management plan for the sanctuary was approved and adopted by the late Florida Governor Lawton Chiles and his cabinet. Its provisions went into effect that July. They included closing 19 small areas of the Keys to fishing and establishing rules to curb reckless boating. In addition, channel markings have been improved, sea grass beds have received enhanced protection, and scientific studies of the dying reefs have been undertaken. It all sounds eminently reasonable to us.

Meanwhile, the reef crisis worsens. According to *Mother Jones,* "Between 1996 and 1997, the incidence of coral disease in the Florida Keys increased by 292 percent." On the bright side, at the National Oceans Conference—held in Monterey, California, in June 1998—President Clinton pledged unprecedented support for efforts to restore the coral reefs of the Florida Keys. His concrete proposals made a lot more sense than anything heard from the Keys separatists, which amounted to little more than the blowing of hot air into a conch.

So what's left of the Conch Republic? Every April, they celebrate "the independent and eccentric spirit of Key West" with 10 days of birthday revelry: "drag" races involving female impersonators, mock sea battles, and so forth. The Annual Conch Republic Independence Celebration turns 20 in 2002.

stumbling about the floor, rednecks in cowboy hats who'd studied one too many line-dancing videos, four-eyed nerds of every possible waist size who were painfully lacking in natural rhythm. Their spastic writhing elicited patronizing exhortations from the emcee, who'd occasionally fling Miller Lite T-shirts into the crowd. "You gotta dance if you want a shirt," he growled, looking like the sort of loser who hadn't shaken his own gangly booty since the high-school prom. Glowering at the other end of the stage was an enormous bouncer who bore a striking resemblance to Attila the Hun—shaved head, thick handlebar mustache

Map of Monroe County—Pages 294 & 295

—and carried a big nightstick. When an occasional rock and roll song such as "19th Nervous Breakdown" sneaked into the disco frenzy, the crowd vacated the dance floor as if Attila the Bouncer had cut the cheese.

At this point we were ready to leave, but then, wonder of wonders, a rock and roll band took the stage. They were called Calabash, and they came from Cleveland. (Cleveland rocks!) There were four musicians: guitars, bass, and drums, the classic rock lineup. They opened with "All Right Now," by Free. It was real rock and roll, the kind you feel in your chest. The crowd morphed before our very eyes. Instead of gyrating goofily to disco bilge, they began moving unaffectedly to the beat. Meanwhile, Calabash was cutting up onstage, attacking each other with a plastic barracuda and musically tripping one another up for laughs. It was the tightest sort of shambles, a spontaneous breath of fresh air in a suffocating world of programmed dance beats. They played songs by the Doors ("L.A. Woman"), the Rolling Stones ("You Can't Always Get What You Want"), and the Who ("My Generation"). Sloppy Joe's began pulsing like the gloriously sloppy rock and roll club we've always known it to be. We left feeling recharged by the three-chord grandeur of a bar band that meant what they played. And we were relieved to find out that live rock and roll still rules at Sloppy Joe's.

Moral of the story: Though Duval Street has largely sold its soul to the corporate franchise mentality, essential elements of Key West nightlife are unchanged, if you know where to look. At its off-kilter best, Key West remains unpretentious, wide open, ribald, wild—in short, tickled to be on the festive edge of the tropics at the very end of the civilized world.

Contact Information

Key West Chamber of Commerce, 402 Wall Street (Old Mallory Square), Key West, FL 33040; 305/294-2587 or 800/LAST-KEY; website: www.keywestchamber.org

Dry Tortugas National Park

The road may come to an end in Key West, but America dribbles on a bit longer. A clump of seven keys that lie 70 miles west of Key West make up **Dry Tortugas National Park** (formerly Fort Jefferson National Monument). These islands were discovered in 1513 by Juan Ponce de León, who named them "Las Tortugas" for the proliferation of sea turtles. The name was amended to Dry Tortugas due to the complete lack of fresh water.

They've been an interesting part of American history—a site of pirate activity and shipwrecks, lighthouses, a fort (Jefferson, a strategic 19th-century coastal fortification, on Garden Key), a naval fueling station, a seaplane base—as well as haven for migratory birds and the remarkable diversity of life attracted to the submerged coral reefs and sea grass beds. Some pronounce the snorkeling here the best in North America.

17 Garden Key (Dry Tortugas National Park)

 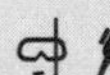  5

Location: Dry Tortugas National Park
Parking/fees: $3 camping fee
Hours: 8 A.M. to sunset
Facilities: concessions, restrooms, picnic tables, and a visitor center
Contact: Dry Tortugas National Park, c/o Everglades National Park, 305/242-7700

Franklin Roosevelt had the foresight to designate the keys and underwater ecosystem a national monument in 1935. Most of what is now a 64,700-acre national park is underwater, with the seven small exposed coral reefs collectively amounting to only 39 acres of land. Despite their remoteness, the Dry Tortugas are receiving more visitors every year and more, some believe, than they can handle. In fact, you could say there's a run on the place. Visitation tripled during the 1990s, with 50,000 people descending annually on the dry islands, and soared to 100,000 in 2000. This inundation has created concern about reef preservation, fish populations, and the rare seabirds that pass through.

Primary activities are swimming, diving, snorkeling, fishing (a Florida saltwater fishing license is required), and bird-watching (especially on Bush Key, a nesting area for sooty and noddy terns that's closed to the public from April through September). Camping is allowed on Garden Key for $3 at 13 sites overlooking the white-sand beach, plus a group site that accommodates up to 40 people. On the grounds are picnic tables, grills, and toilets, but no sinks, showers, or phones. All supplies, including fresh water, must be brought over and refuse must be removed on departure. The park is open daily from 8 A.M. to dusk.

The main point of debarkation in the Dry Tortugas is Garden Key, 68 miles west of Key West, where Fort Jefferson is located and a national park ranger is on duty. Other than by personal boat, there are two ways to get here from Key West—by ferry (roughly 2–3 hours each way) or seaplane (40 minutes). **Seaplanes of Key West** (3471 South Roosevelt Boulevard, Key West, 800/950-2359) provides four-hour half-day and eight-hour full-day trips ($179 and $305 per adult, respectively) to the Dry Tortugas. Boat services include the **Yankee Freedom Dry Tortugas Ferry** (Lands End Marina, 240 Margaret Street, Key West, 800/926-5332), which leaves at 8 A.M. and returns at 6:30 P.M. The cost is $85 for adults ($55 for children) and includes breakfast, lunch, snorkel gear, and a 45-minute tour of Fort Jefferson. The high-speed catamaran ***Fast Cat II*** (Elizabeth and Green Streets, Key West, 305/292-6100 or 800/236-7937) makes the passage in two hours and allows you four and a half hours at Fort Jefferson. A round-trip ticket costs $85 for adults ($55 for children), leaving daily at 8 A.M. and returning by 6 P.M. Try to make reservations at least a day ahead of time.

Contact Information

Dry Tortugas National Park, Box 6208, Key West, FL 33041; 305/242-7700; website: www.nps.gov/drto

Everglades National Park

This is a park that boggles the imagination: a 50-mile-wide stream creeping almost imperceptibly through a 1.5-million acre freshwater marsh (the world's largest) in a state that is home to more endangered species than any other except Hawaii. Among the endangered species that live primarily in the Everglades: the Florida panther (down to an inbred population of perhaps 50–75), American crocodile (400), snail kite (1,500), Cape Sable seaside sparrow (4,000), Everglades mink, white ibis, and indigo snake. Above and beyond these rare creatures, the Everglades is home to 1,000 plant and 120 tree species, 600 fish and reptile species, and 350 bird and 40 mammal species.

The national park that bears the name Everglades, founded in 1947, covers only 12 percent of the Everglades' watershed. It is essentially a slow-moving river whose headwater is Lake Okeechobee and whose mouth is Florida Bay. Water moves across a bed of porous limestone at a depth ranging from a few inches to six feet. Mainly, the Everglades consists of vast fields of saw grass dotted with islands of tropical hardwoods known as hammocks. It serves as an ideal habitat for alligators and bird life. Until people took time to understand its hydrology and ecology, it was thought of as worthless swampland to be plundered. Because of developmental pressure, pollution, and the withdrawal of water, the Everglades is considered the most imperiled of the 336 properties in the national park system.

For our purposes, we'll use the death of the woman who wrote the book on the Everglades as our springboard. Her name was Marjory Stoneman Douglas. She died May 14, 1998, at age 108, in the Coconut Grove cottage where she'd lived for more than 70 years. Her book, *The Everglades: River of Grass* (1947), was the gauntlet hurled at the feet of nature's despoilers in South Florida. Much as the books of Rachel Carson did a decade later, hers served as a wake-up call for the nascent environmental movement. When *River of Grass* became an instant best-seller, it helped change the public perception of swamps in general and the Everglades in particular.

Some of the things Mrs. Douglas warned about—draining, dredging, and paving over wetlands, development, channelization—are still going on, and the Everglades' subtropical watershed has shrunk to less than one-sixth of its original 13,000 square miles. It has been strangled by 1,400 miles of levees and canals and polluted from the runoff of 700,000 acres of sugarcane farms, as well as the crush from east and west of the suburbs. More than 70 percent of the flows into the Everglades

18 Clubhouse Beach (Everglades National Park)

Location: from the main park headquarters, 12 miles southwest of Homestead on State Route 9336, continue southwest along State Route 9336 for 38 miles to the Flamingo Visitor Center; from there, hike west for 7.5 miles along the Coastal Prairie Trail to Clubhouse Beach.

Parking/fees: $10 entrance fee per vehicle; $5 entrance fee for pedestrians or bicyclists. A boat fee of $5 per powerboat and $3 per canoe or kayak is charged. Campers pay $10 for a wilderness camping permit.

Hours: 24 hours (Everglades National Park) and 9:30 A.M.–4:30 P.M. (Flamingo Visitor Center), with extended visitor-center hours in season

Facilities: none

Contact: Flamingo Visitor Center in Everglades National Park, 941/695-2945

have been diverted by agriculture and development. Populations of wading birds have plummeted by as much as 95 percent. The Everglades took 19 million years for nature to create and about a century for mankind to very nearly destroy.

The frightening prospect of losing America's most unique natural habitat finally motivated President Bill Clinton to protect what remains by buying 50,000 acres of surrounding farmland (sugar plantations that have been the beneficiary of federal tax-break boondoggles), a deal finalized in December 1997. Much of what's been lost in the Everglades is irreplaceable, and the job of restoration that lies ahead is formidable. To that end, the Clinton administration and the Army Corps of Engineers pushed an ambitious $7.8 billion plan for "replumbing" South Florida. Aiming at the restoration of the Everglades ecosystem, the plan consists of 68 projects to be implemented over the next half-century. The park's gravest threat, according to some scientists, is the melaleuca, an introduced Australian tree that's spread like kudzu throughout the Everglades. Already it's turned half a million acres of open sawgrass prairie into a dense forest with practically zero biodiversity.

The main points of entry into this vast park are Homestead in the east, and Everglades City in the west. The main visitor center and park headquarters lies 11 miles west of Homestead and 45 miles southwest of Miami along State Route 9336. The Gulf Coast Visitor Center, in Everglades City, is located on State Route 29, four miles south of the Tamiami Trail (U.S. 41), which forms the northern park boundary. Another point of entry on the park's periphery is the Shark Valley Visitor Center, located on the Tamiami Trail (U.S. 41) about halfway between Miami and Everglades City. Admission to the park is $10 per vehicle (good for seven days) or $5 per person on bike, motorcycle, or foot. Activities include canoeing, kayaking, self-guided hiking, airboat rides, and tram tours. There is camping at Long Pine Key (108 sites, seven miles west of park headquarters on Route 9336) and Flamingo (234 sites, just west of the Flamingo Visitor Center). A third campground, Chekika (northwest of Homestead), is out of commission, pending repairs from damage sustained during Hurricane Irene in 1999. However, it reopened for day-use only in December 2000. The fee at Flamingo and Long Pine Key campgrounds is $14 per night; call (800) 365-CAMP for reservations.

As a footnote, when asked on her 100th birthday whether the Everglades would survive, Marjory Stoneman Douglas said, "I'm neither an optimist nor a pessimist. I say it's got to be done." Former president

⑲ Carl Ross Key (Everglades National Park)

  ④

Location: from the main park headquarters, 12 miles southwest of Homestead on State Route 9336, continue southwest along State Route 9336 for 38 miles to the Flamingo Visitor Center; from there, Carl Ross Key is accessible by boat only. Consulting nautical maps and tide charts, leave the marina at the visitor center and proceed south for approximately 10 miles to Carl Ross Key.

Parking/fees: $10 entrance fee per vehicle; $5 entrance fee for pedestrians or bicyclists. A boat fee of $5 per powerboat and $3 per canoe or kayak is charged. Campers pay $10 for a wilderness camping permit.

Hours: 24 hours (Everglades National Park) and 9:30 A.M.–4:30 P.M. (Flamingo Visitor Center), with extended visitor-center hours in season

Facilities: none

Contact: Flamingo Visitor Center in Everglades National Park, 941/695-2945

Bill Clinton took a big step toward beginning the process by signing the Everglades Restoration Act on December 11, 2000—barely a month before he left office. Should the Comprehensive Everglades Restoration Plan turn out to be a success, it will be one of his greatest legacies.

Beaches

Strange or incidental as it may seem, beaches exist on Cape Sable and numerous small keys facing the Gulf of Mexico along the national park's western flank. One of the most interesting and out-of-the-way areas in the Everglades is the Flamingo Visitor Center, which lies at the end of State Route 9336, nearly 40 miles southwest of the main visitor center and park headquarters. At Flamingo you'll find a lodge, restaurant, marina, picnic ground, and the 7.5-mile Coastal Prairie Trail, which leads to **Clubhouse Beach**. Unfortunately, it's a narrow mud beach that even a ranger describes as "pretty nasty . . . not a very good place." Sometimes there's a bit of sand accumulation, but storm-driven waves regularly wash it away. In the stormy winter months, Clubhouse Beach can remain underwater much of the time. You can camp along the beach, but with big, hungry clouds of mosquitoes making life miserable, why would you want to? The skeeters are so bad out here that it's difficult to breathe during the day because of the bug cloud, and visitors are advised to wear long-sleeved shirts and head

20 Cape Sable (Everglades National Park)

Location: from the main park headquarters, 12 miles southwest of Homestead on State Route 9336, continue southwest along State Route 9336 for 38 miles to the Flamingo Visitor Center; from there, Cape Sable is accessible by boat only. Consulting nautical charts, leave the marina at the visitor center and proceed due west along the shoreline for 10 miles to Cape Sable.

Parking/fees: $10 entrance fee per vehicle; $5 entrance fee for pedestrians or bicyclists. A boat fee of $5 per powerboat and $3 per canoe or kayak is charged. Campers pay $10 for a wilderness camping permit.

Hours: 24 hours (Everglades National Park) and 9:30 A.M.–4:30 P.M. (Flamingo Visitor Center), with extended visitor-center hours in season

Facilities: none

Contact: Flamingo Visitor Center in Everglades National Park, 941/695-2945

21 Gulf Coast Keys (Everglades National Park)

Location: from Naples, proceed east on U.S. 41 (Tamiami Trail) for 25 miles, then turn south on State Route 29 and follow for three miles into Everglades City; the Gulf Coast Visitor Center for Everglades National Park is along State Route 29 on the south side of town. There is a public boat ramp at the visitor center and many private ones in Everglades City. Consult nautical charts and tide tables before departing for offshore keys. The most popular and accessible keys along the Gulf Coast within Everglades National Park are, from south to north, Highland Beach, Pavilion, Rabbit, Picnic, and Tiger Keys. There are, however, numerous other smaller keys along this part of the coast, which is known as the Ten Thousand Islands.

Parking/fees: $10 entrance fee per vehicle; $5 entrance fee for pedestrians or bicyclists. A boat fee of $5 per powerboat and $3 per canoe or kayak is charged. Campers pay $10 for a wilderness camping permit.

Hours: 24 hours (Everglades National Park) and 9 A.M.–5 P.M. (Gulf Coast Visitor Center)

Facilities: restrooms (on Rabbit, Picnic, and Pavilion Keys)

Contact: Gulf Coast Visitor Center in Everglades National Park, 941/695-3311

nets. And if you're thinking of going swimming, be forewarned that the shallow waters of Florida Bay are filled with stingrays and lemon sharks. It all sounds like a setting for the next installment of *Survivor.*

This area of the park is much more hospitable to boaters than landlubbers. Because mosquitoes don't fly out over open water, you can escape them pretty quickly from the Flamingo Marina. About 10 miles offshore is **Carl Ross Key**, where there's a primitive campground and a smallish beach. In 1960, Hurricane Donna split the key in two, causing neighboring Sandy Key to form. You're not allowed on Sandy Key, but you can watch roseate spoonbills and other birds attracted to it from Carl Ross Key.

The real jewel out here is **Cape Sable**: a 15-mile cape, much of whose length is shell beach. Camping is allowed at three beach areas (East, Middle, and Northwest Cape). Wilderness camping permits are obtainable at the Flamingo Visitor Center and cost $10 per stay for between one and six people. To get to Cape Sable, which is accessible only by water, exit the marina and head 10 miles due west along the shoreline. This is an especially scenic trip to make via canoe or kayak (which can be rented at the marina). Powerboats must swing away from the shoreline because of shallows; consult nautical charts and tide tables before setting out.

If you would like more information about boat and tram tours; powerboat, kayak, and canoe rentals; and the lodge, restaurant, and store at the Flamingo Visitor Center, contact the **Flamingo Lodge, Marina & Outpost Resort**, Flamingo, FL 33034; 941/695-3101.

On the **Gulf Coast Keys** of Everglades National Park, boaters will discover no fewer than 15 isolated keys with sandy, gulf-facing beaches on which to camp, fish, and sunbathe. Mainly, people beach their boats, wade out, and cast lines into the Gulf of Mexico. Of the 15 camp-able keys, the following are the most notable: Highland Beach (a.k.a. McLaughlin Key), Pavilion Key, Rabbit Key, Picnic Key, and Tiger Key. Pavilion is the largest and best known, with a mile-long beach. Highland has the biggest beach. Rabbit Key reveals a nice sand spit at medium-to-low tide. Camping on all the gulf keys is primitive, but there are portable toilets at Rabbit, Pavilion, and Picnic Keys.

The number of campers at each key is restricted, and that limit is often reached between November and April. Eighty percent of the campers on these keys are canoeists and kayakers; the rest are anglers in powerboats. There's a boat ramp at the Gulf Coast Visitor Center in Everglades City, a small town whose economy is driven by tourism and recreational fishing. It is a destination place, not a drive-through place; you come here specifically to be here. There are no facilities along the coast between Everglades City and Flamingo, a distance of 100 miles. It is, in other words, a 100 percent self-sustaining wilderness area that's yours for the enjoying.

The area offshore of Everglades City is evocatively known as the Ten Thousand Islands. From the Gulf Coast Visitor Center, a concessionaire leads 90-minute boat tours ($13 per adult); call 941/695-2591 for information and reservations. Wildlife you're likely to spot on the offshore islands includes wading birds (herons, ibises), manatees, and bottle-nosed dolphins.

Contact Information

Everglades National Park Headquarters, Ernest F. Coe Visitor Center, 40001 State Route 9336, Homestead, FL 33034; 305/242-7700; website: www.nps.gov/ever

Flamingo Visitor Center, Everglades National Park, Flamingo, FL 33034; 941/695-2945

Gulf Coast Visitor Center, Everglades National Park, State Route 29, P.O. Box 130, Everglades City, FL 33929; 941/695-3941

Waist Deep in the Big Muddy Everglades

How much does Michael David Cushing like mucking about in the Everglades? Let's put it this way: he passed up tickets to the University of Miami vs. Florida State football game on a beautiful Saturday in October to lead a pair of beach bums through one of the watery "strands" along U.S. 41 in Everglades National Park. Instead of watching what turned out to be one of the great upset victories of the 2000 season (Miami won), he took the plunge into sometimes chest-deep tannic water to show us the great natural beauty of the Everglades.

If being chest deep in swamp water filled with alligators and water moccasins—not to mention mosquitoes and giant golden orb weaver spiders in the air—sounds like your worst nightmare, you might be surprised to learn that it was actually a pleasant traipse through nature in the raw. Yes, there are gators, but they congregate in the deeper, fish-rich man-made canals beside the highway. Moreover, they don't want to be around you any more than you want to be around them, so if they are in the swamp it won't be anywhere near a bunch of rustling, muck-about humans. Ditto with the snakes. Cushing claims in all his years of wandering never to have seen a snake or gator at close range. As for the spiders, you just have to walk around their formidable webs. Sometimes, as the guide, he'll reluctantly knock down a web in order to allow a group of nervous humans to pass, commenting to the spider, "That will give you something to do this afternoon."

Cushing is the owner-operator of Dragonfly Expeditions, a Coral Gables-based outfitter that leads walking tours of the Everglades, as well as longer eco-tours to the Caribbean and South America. He got interested in "mucking about" in the wild after being sent to Jamaica to help build some infrastructure as part of a college project in adventure travel, cultural outreach, and personal growth. He is a knowledgeable guide whose low-key disposition helps allay any fears one might have about swamp critters. In truth, one quickly and happily discovers that the soggy "strands" of the Everglades are some of the most pleasant places in South Florida. By contrast to all the negative images that swamps evoke in the popular mind—dark, dank, smelly places that harbor dangerous creatures, human criminals, and malevolent spirits—the swamp is a sweet-smelling arboretum of beautiful flowers, dappled sunlight, and water that is clear and clean. It is one of the coolest places to be on a hot day. While the rest of South Florida was sweltering in 90°F temperatures beneath a blazing sun, we were cool and comfortable in the swamp.

The water was waist deep for much of the two-hour walk. The initial plunge might take some aback, but after a minute or two you get used to it and indeed enjoy slogging about like a swamp fox. Along the way, Cushing regales you with facts about the Everglades and its current health (or lack thereof). Water flow into the 'glades is only one-tenth of what it used to be, thanks to altered hydrology and human withdrawals in places like Miami (which used to be part of the Everglades). There were once numerous varieties of snails, which would hang from the trees, sedges, and grasses by the thousands. They're mostly all gone, many species sadly extinct. Alligators, which lie out in the warm asphalt highway to thermo-regulate their cold-blooded selves, often get run over by speeding motorists, their carcasses laughingly referred to as "speed bumps." There's no question that the Everglades—an ecosystem unique in its design, function, and scope—has been taken to the brink of ruin by human impact. At the same time, a massive effort is underway to repair the damage. How successful it will be, given the continuing population growth of South Florida, remains to be seen.

Walking the 'glades with an expert like Cushing will go a long way toward disavowing you of any lingering fears about swamps, and in fact introduce you to a hidden world of beauty and delight amid the towering bald cypress. It is a far preferable way to experience the Everglades than an airboat tour. The boats are horribly loud (you are given toilet paper to stuff in your ears) and make a mess of the 'glades grasses as they pass over them. Moreover, you only get to see the "sawgrass prairie" areas of the Everglades and not the hidden depths of the tree-filled swamps. Finally, the airboat operators bait the gullible gators with marshmallows, which is a crass manipulation of nature to please hoodwinked, clueless tourists. If you want to know the real Everglades, you really need to go mucking about in the swamp.

For more information on day hikes and overnight trips to the Everglades, contact Dragonfly Expeditions, 1825 Ponce de Leon Boulevard (#369), Coral Gables, FL 33134; 305/774-9019 or 888/992-6337.

ida's West Coast

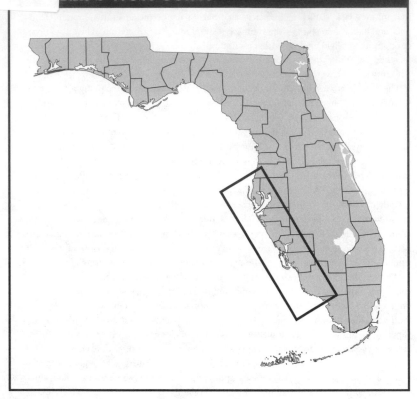

Key to the Symbols

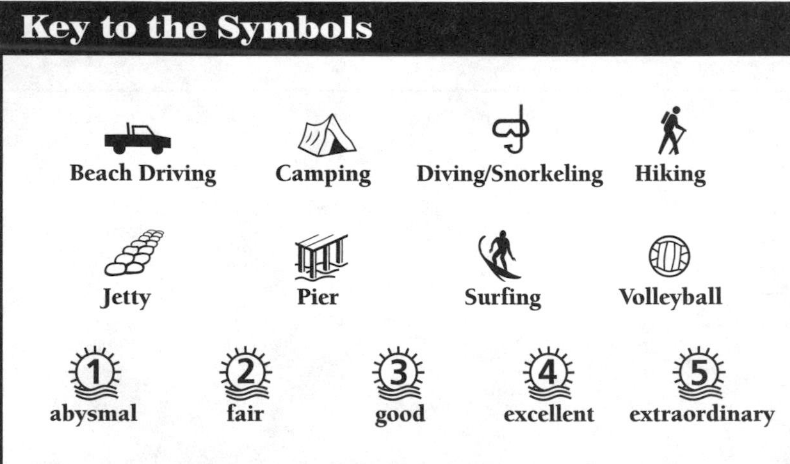

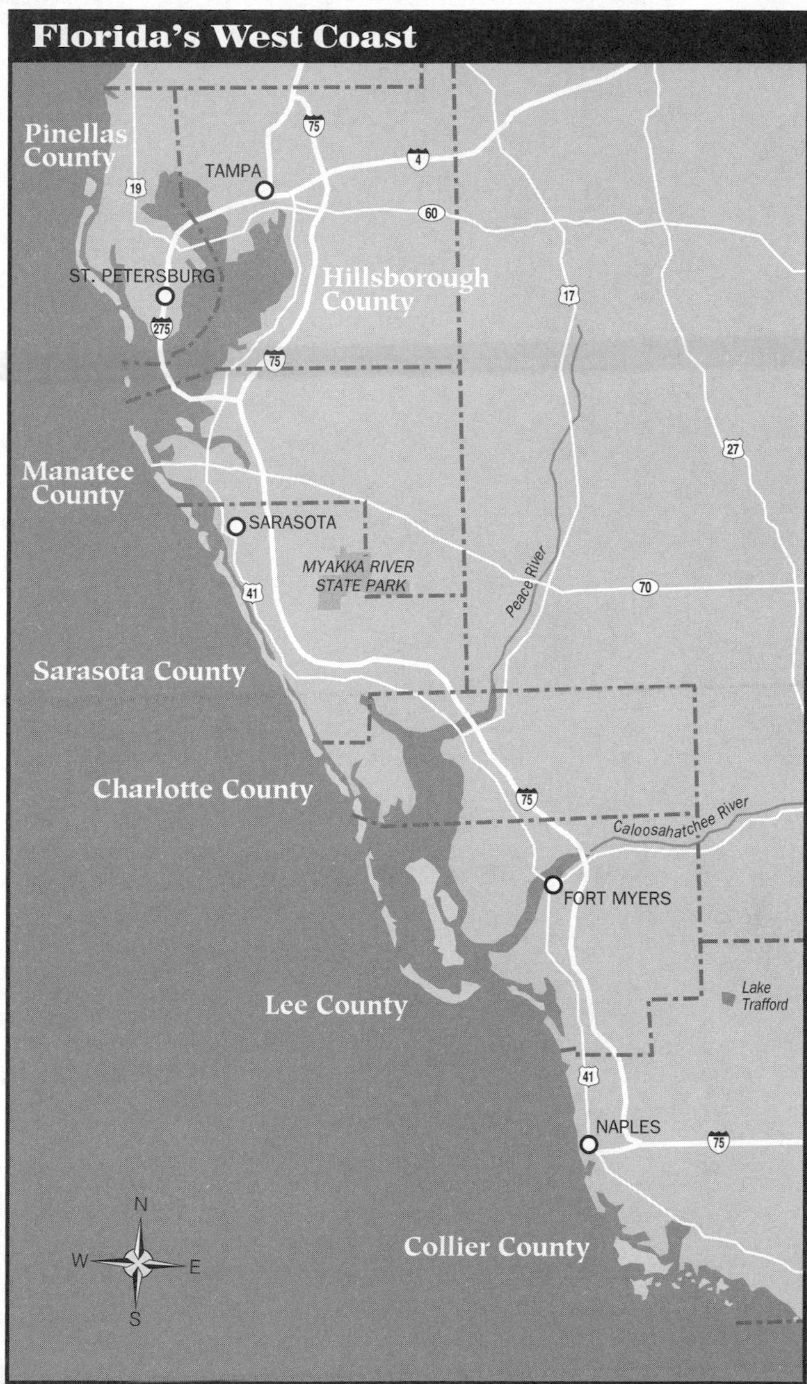

Florida's West Coast
Pinellas County
TAMPA
ST. PETERSBURG
Hillsborough County
Manatee County
SARASOTA
MYAKKA RIVER STATE PARK
Peace River
Sarasota County
Charlotte County
Caloosahatchee River
FORT MYERS
Lake Trafford
Lee County
NAPLES
Collier County
75
4
19
60
17
275
27
41
70
N
W
E
S

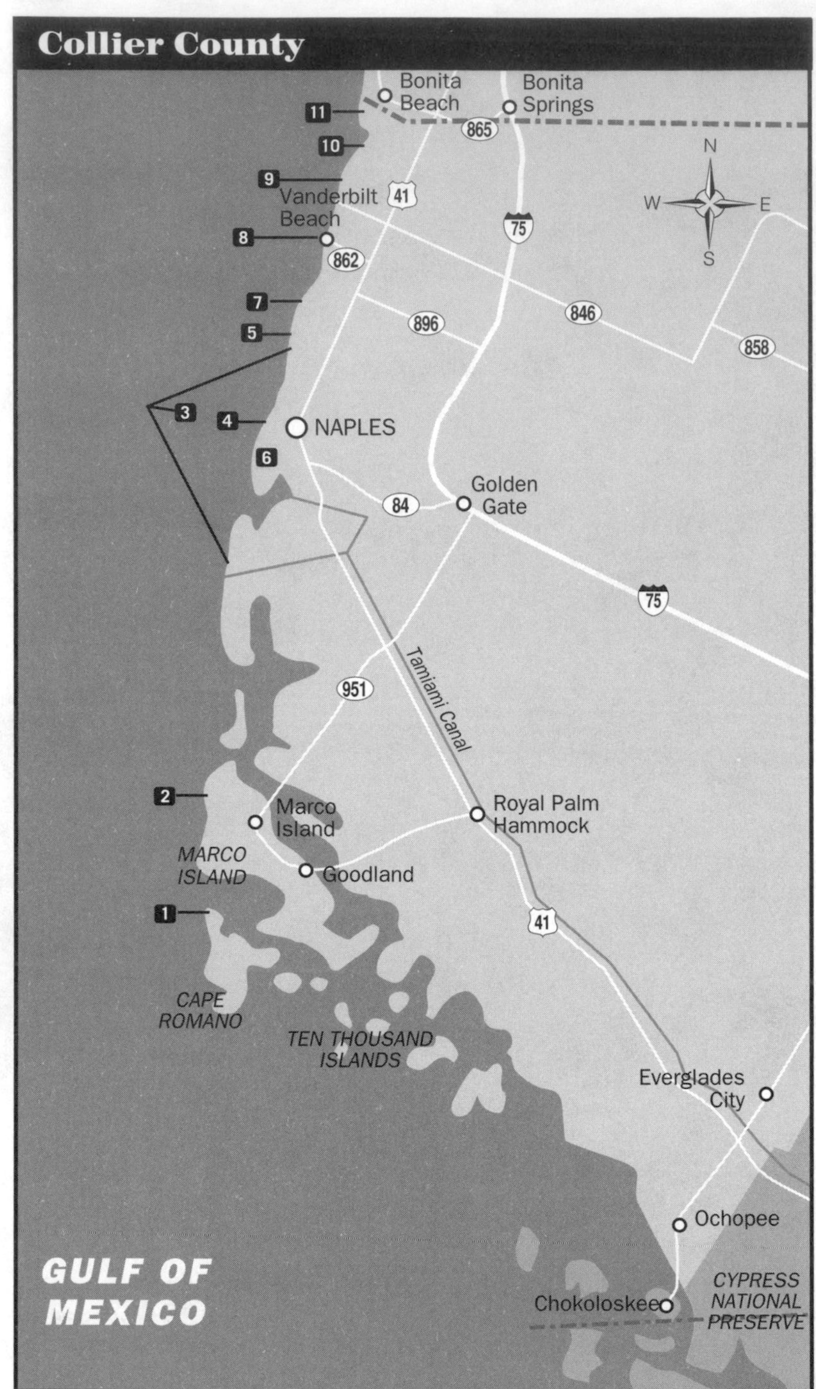
Collier County
Bonita Beach
Bonita Springs
865
N
W
E
S
9
Vanderbilt Beach
41
75
8
862
7
5
896
846
858
3
4
NAPLES
6
Golden Gate
84
75
Tamiami Canal
951
2
Marco Island
Royal Palm Hammock
MARCO ISLAND
Goodland
1
41
CAPE ROMANO
TEN THOUSAND ISLANDS
Everglades City
Ochopee
GULF OF MEXICO
Chokoloskee
CYPRESS NATIONAL PRESERVE
11
10

Collier County

Collier is the second largest county in Florida, and the good news is that more than 70 percent of its land area is under preservation. However, most of the preserves are inland, while much of the county's beachfront has been overdeveloped. The construction is particularly thick on Marco Island, the largest of southwest Florida's Ten Thousand Islands. Until the late 1960s, Marco was a secluded paradise, but it was bought and built up to the point its skyline rivals Miami's. Nearby Naples is far more appealing and one of the most attractive cities in Florida. Its lovely beachfront is a model of public access. Elsewhere, Collier County has given the green light to development, and unincorporated high-growth areas like Pelican Bay and Vanderbilt Beach resume the gauntlet of skyscraping real estate along the Gulf of Mexico. Fortunately, Delnor-Wiggins Pass State Park and Barefoot Beach County Park salvage a decent stretch of Collier County's north coast for birds and beachgoers.

Cape Romano and Kice Island

If you've got a boat and some time, there's a pair of idyllic islands located due south of Marco Island, directly across Caxambas Pass. Cape Romano and Kice Island are, for all intents and purposes, one island separated only by a now-closed pass. Together, they comprise a beachfront that looks to be at least as long as Marco's. If you stand on the jetty in front of the Cape Marco development and look south, you can see a gorgeous white stretch of sand called Morgan Beach beckoning all would-be Gilligans away from overbuilt Marco Island. In reality, it is probably visited by more sea turtles than human beings and is purported to be a place where you can remove your swimsuit with impunity.

Contact Information

Rookery Bay National Estuarine Research Reserve, 10 Shell Island Road, Naples, FL 33962; 941/775-8845; website: www.inlet.geol.sc.edu/RKB

Marco Island

A wide chasm exists between what your five senses tell you about Marco Island (pop. 15,000) and what you may hear or read about the place before you arrive. Not unlike the "credibility gap" of the Nixon and Reagan years, this chasm is equal parts wishful thinking and outright misrepresentation. Speaking of those two ex-presidents, Marco Island—the southwesternmost developed barrier island in Florida, and the largest of the Ten Thousand Islands—would probably be their idea of heaven: golf courses, real-estate deals, and total gatekept exclusivity. Marco indeed functions as something of a preview of the afterlife for affluent retired seniors, who clog the roadways with their wide-bodied, gas-guzzling Monte Carlos, Caddies, and Benzes. For us, Marco Island looked more like a paradise gone tragically wrong—a beautiful three-mile-long, 100-yard-wide beach that's about as hard to crash as Frank Sinatra's funeral.

The thick, slick local media packet tells an entirely different story. Its contents hail the "timeless beauty" and "unspoiled beaches" of "Florida's best-kept secret." They call Marco Island "secluded," claim that it is "carefully planned" and "rich in diversity," and assert that it makes you ask questions like "How can people living outdoors be so invisible?" After two days of fruitlessly looking for a secluded and carefully planned slice of anything on Marco Island, we found ourselves asking different questions.

Among them: How could such a beautiful and remote barrier island wind up covered by two unbroken miles of high-rise buildings? How could this have happened since the 1980s, when the lessons of coastal overdevelopment were already common knowledge? Why wasn't the Deltona Corporation, who did most of the construction, regulated more vigilantly by state and county governments? Why does the Marco Island Beach Association (MIBA), which oversees all aspects of beaches and "beautification," not protest the continued walling off of the beach, as with the Cape Marco project (see "Cape Marco on the Gulf" sidebar, page 354)? Furthermore, why should beach access be claimed by people who don't even live here most of the year? Why do local residents have to pay to use the beach? How could two private golf clubs be allowed on the island while not a single hole exists for public use? When will inviolable laws be made to protect other coastal communities from being Marco Island-ed to death by foreign and out-of-state investors who seldom lay eyes on their so-called properties?

The answers to these questions come in varying flavors and theories, all of which we heard from people who live in the surrounding area. The most plausible one is this: Collier County decided to make Marco Island its golden goose. That is, they allowed the coast to be walled off by the Deltona Corporation, which barnstormed into town and began buying up property in the 1960s. The tradeoff for the county was the tax windfall from part-time residents who would, they presumed, not need much in the way of county services and facilities. Thus, their attitude was to relax principles of conscientious development and just let 'er rip. Sure enough, Marco Island acquired a skyline that puts us more in mind of Manhattan Island than the "secluded" southwest coast of Florida.

From a 1988 article in the *Miami Herald,* entitled "Developer Deltona, Buyers Dispute Claims Over Lots at Marco Island": "Russell and Beverly Albright felt crushed in 1976 when they found out that the $14,000 Marco Island dream property they bought from Deltona Corp. was an undeveloped chunk of wetlands." We had the opposite reaction when we first laid eyes on Marco Island in the mid-1990s. We would have been overjoyed to see wetlands and a natural environment. Instead we were confronted with an incongruous block of high-rises on an island that was out in the middle of nowhere (and should've been allowed to stay that way).

If you can set aside the lingering image of Marco Island as a sardine-packed cavalcade of condos—and it takes a mighty effort, if you're disgusted by crass development—there are a few spots where some of the island's original charm survives. Foremost is Olde Marco Village. There is nothing old or historic about Olde Marco Village. It is simply the middle-class residential area that was here before Deltona entered the picture. Today, it affords a glimpse at how comfy-cozy the place must have seemed to the original residents and retirees who had the good fortune to be here. Away from the high-rise Himalayas on the ocean, Marco Island has a sort of watery charm. Its backstreet residential areas are coursed by man-made canals. A drive around this part of Marco Island gives one the unmistakable sensation of being in the middle of a huge golf course, with lots of water hazards.

The local newspaper, the *Marco Eagle* is a puff sheet for the business community, featuring upbeat stories on new construction techniques. A running scorecard on the number of condominium units sold mimics the way some papers feature weather news on their cover. The chart is called "Marco Island Market Indicators," and it includes the dollar amount brought in by each real-estate transaction. It's a disgrace to honest community journalism.

One interesting bit of archaeology on Marco was the discovery of a carved wooden figure of a half-man, half-panther. (The Florida panther, an endangered species, is purportedly making a tentative comeback hereabouts.) The carved figure was claimed, in one local brochure, to "date back to A.D. 700–1450." (How's that for precise archeological dating?) Naturally, the figure is long gone, allegedly to the Smithsonian, but gold replicas of the icon—cutely called "the Marco Cat"—are on sale at myriad gift shops. The relic's disappearance and reincarnation as a souvenir trinket makes a fitting allegory for what has happened to this once quiet, lovely, and unspoiled island.

Beaches

Just as it's hard for a rich man to enter the gates of heaven, it's hard for a poor visitor to get at the beaches of Marco Island. While public accesses are provided at

South Marco Beach and Tigertail Beach, they are almost begrudgingly offered. Take the **South Marco Beach Access**, for example. Collier County has wrested a small walkway between high-rises for the public to gain passage onto the beach (a condominium complex named Apollo is your best landmark), but the parking area is two blocks away, on Swallow Avenue, and costs $3. (You feed dollar bills to a vending machine and place the receipt on your dashboard.) The beach is wide, flat, and expansive, but the proximity to these hideous buildings is oppressive, and the beach itself ends a few hundred yards to the south at the point where a development called Cape Marco, a towering architectural eyesore, blots out the very sky.

Tigertail Beach County Park, at the north end of the island, is way cooler and more appealing. For the same $3 fee you get access to a much less developed beach encompassing 2,500 linear feet of open sand. Moreover, there are full facilities—a picnic area and pleasant seaside eatery (Todd's); rentals of cabanas, kayaks, paddleboats, sailboats, windsurfing gear, and beach chairs; 32 acres of parkland; and the freedom to roam north along the beach to the end of the three-mile barrier island.

Bunking Down

The tone of Marco Island is set by the resort hotels on its beachfront. There's not a single mom-and-pop among them. Every building along the ocean seems to adhere to a strict architectural dress code: tall, ramrod-stiff fortresses with men in white uniforms skittering about, ready to put on the squeeze for services you never knew you wanted or needed.

Marriott's Marco Island Resort and Golf Club (400 South Collier Boulevard, 941/394-2511, $$$$) is, to quote the late Frank Sinatra, "A-Number One, top of the heap." That is to say, it's the largest (735 rooms) and most luxurious convention resort on the Gulf Coast. Here, you can honor your Inner CEO with an entire city's worth of amenities and an army of happy minions ready to cater to your every whim. Every minute of your stay at the Marriott will be choreographed by the staff, if you so choose, and you never even have to leave the premises. The pool here is a work of art, and beach access is the best of any property on the island.

Among the activities in a typical week: adult tennis clinics and tournaments, catamaran rides, "bead it" tutorials, tanning tips,

❶ South Marco Beach Access

Location: Parking is along Swallow Avenue, at the south end of Marco Island. Beach access is gained via a pathway between condominiums two blocks away
Parking/fees: $3 entrance fee per vehicle; free for Collier County residents with a beach parking permit (obtainable at Naples City Hall)
Hours: sunrise to sunset
Facilities: none
Contact: Collier County Parks and Recreation Department, 941/353-0404

❷ Tigertail Beach County Park

Location: from Collier Avenue on Marco Island, turn onto Kendall Drive and continue to Hernando Drive. Turn left and proceed to Tigertail Beach
Parking/fees: $3 entrance fee per vehicle; free for Collier County residents with a beach parking permit (obtainable at Naples City Hall)
Hours: sunrise to sunset
Facilities: concessions, restrooms, picnic tables, and showers
Contact: Tigertail Beach County Park, 941/642-8414

a "Ping-Pong toss across" competition, scuba diving, sailing seminars, scavenger hunts, shelling, body toning, aqua-slimnastics, tropical drink recipe classes, basketball shootarounds, bike tours, Skittle counting contests, and the "live Hermit Crabby 500." Each of these, of course, costs extra, with 18 holes of golf (off premises) running $100 in peak season and $35–75 the rest of the year. All activities at this enormous complex are really icing on the cake, with the pool area and beach being sufficiently entrancing to keep most folks happily occupied. They do a ton of convention business here. Families traveling without corporate pretext can expect to pay $150–325 a night, depending on time of year, with the first three months of the year being the most expensive and the late summer months (especially August) the least.

Other corporate sentinels—the **Hilton Beach Resort** (560 South Collier Boulevard, 941/394-5000, $$$$) and **Radisson Suites Beach Resort** (600 South Collier Boulevard, 941/394-4100, $$$$)—are represented on Marco Island's skyline, but Marriott's is, in our opinion, the choicest pleasure dome on the island. The only alternative to the high-rises is the **Paramount Suite and Hotel Beach Club** (901 South Collier Boulevard, 941/394-8860, $$$), located across the street from the beach. While staying here requires a short walk to the beach access at South Marco, you don't have to pay the day-use charge at the public lot. The Paramount offers a low-key contrast (only 52 rooms and four stories) to Marco's condomania. A pool and racquetball courts are on the premises.

With all the condo units available on Marco Island, many of them unoccupied much of the year, you could go the rental route. Here are a few local agencies specializing in vacation rentals: **Marco Beach Rentals** (1000 North Collier Boulevard, 941/642-5400) and **Marco Island Vacation Properties** (647 North Collier Boulevard, 941/393-2121).

Coastal Cuisine

For all its high-class manners, Marco Island has a culinary reputation about one step up from convention food. This makes **Cafe De Marco** (244 Palm Street, 941/394-6262, $$$) an even more pleasant surprise than it would normally be. Located in "Olde Marco"—specifically, in the Port of Marco Shopping Village—Cafe De Marco is the finest restaurant on the island. Our dinner started with oysters Oscar (baked with crabmeat gratinée sauce and bread crumbs) and ended with peanut butter pie. For entrées, one of us tried pasta originale (seafood, mushrooms, onions, and peppers, served with lobster sauce over linguine), and the other opted for grouper fresca (a hefty fillet simmered with garlic, butter, wine, shrimp, mushrooms, shallots, sun-dried tomatoes, carrots, and peppers). We declared both dishes victors in this culinary contest. All fresh fish selections can be prepared "de Marco" (with mushrooms, shallots, garlic butter, and bread crumbs) or any other way your palate desires. Cafe De Marco ranks among our favorite restaurants in Southwest Florida. As for dessert—well, the peanut butter pie is another story entirely (see below).

Night Moves

Whenever we asked about Marco Island's nightlife, we'd get an earful about lounge pianists and lite jazz. Boring. We also kept hearing about some guy who had been wowing the locals with dead-on impersonations of "everyone from Tony Bennett to Elvis." We fully intended to check him out, if only to indulge our appetite for cheesy entertainers. But, alas, a piece of peanut butter pie at Cafe De Marco got in the way.

This amazing concoction of peanut butter, chocolate chips, whipped cream, and chocolate sauce looked like a replica of a Marco Island high-rise. The more you pick at it, the larger it seems to grow. We guarantee that after devouring an anvil-like

Cape Marco on the Gulf

If one were searching for an *Exxon Valdez*–like symbol for what is wrong with Marco Island, one need look no further than Cape Marco on the Gulf. Indeed, one can see no farther than Cape Marco on the Gulf, because this monstrous development on the southernmost tip of Marco Island blocks the view of the shoreline for miles around. A complex of four sky-scraping condominiums with two more on the way, Cape Marco is set on 30 acres and hogs 1,200 feet of beachfront. What is here is enough to give anyone who isn't making money off it a case of the heebie-jeebies. So was the ludicrously sophisticated tone affected by its developers when describing the amenities of the "most prestigious site" on the island. Here are a few select descriptions intended to attract what the salesperson with whom we spoke referred to as the "right people":

- "majestic entrance"
- "meticulously designed aquascapes"
- "charm and grace of the Spanish Mediterranean architecture"
- "luxuriously appointed"
- "casual elegance"
- "breathtaking"
- "white sugar sands grace the shores"

While seeking more information on this monstrosity and its permitting, we learned that owners of many units at Cape Marco have never set foot in them. Instead, they rent them out for as much as $6,000 a month, realizing annual profits of up to $30,000, after expenses. No doubt the absentee owners are grateful for the Reagan-era tax breaks that made such speculation not only possible but lucrative.

Units at Cozumel—a 24-story building at the bottom of the island—started at $990,000 for a two-bedroom-and-den configuration. Too steep? Hardly. It sold out! The Antarami-

slab of peanut butter pie at Cafe De Marco, the only "getting down" you'll be doing tonight is a groan-filled belly flop onto your bed. It was more difficult to drive after eating a piece of this brain-fogging pie than if we'd knocked back several Manhattans on an empty stomach. It took a designated driver—the one in our party who had the sense to order key lime pie—to navigate the car back to the hotel. Suffice it to say that we were sound asleep by 10 P.M. on a Saturday night, which caused us to miss both the nightclub impersonator and the jungle golf course we'd intended to play. The peanut butter pie is delicious beyond words, but unless you'll be sharing it with another person or two, please do as Nancy Reagan advised and "just say no."

Contact Information

Marco Island Chamber of Commerce, 1102 North Collier Boulevard, Marco Island, FL 34145; 941/394-7549; website: www.marco-island-florida.com

an Development Corporation, headed by Australian Jack Antaramian, is responsible for Cape Marco. Their mouthpiece in the marketing department elaborated: "Our biggest challenge, once we got through the permitting process, was to design buildings that speak to the market. What the customer is buying is the beach, and the view is never going to get old." The view of the beach is almost too good, as the ocean appears to be encroaching on certain of the Cape Marco towers. "Most of our buyers are between 55 and 60, retired or semiretired," the marketer continued. "Many have more than one home."

In 1999, by a 5–1 vote, the pliable Republican city councilors of Marco Island approved a request by Antaramian to increase the height of one of his proposed buildings (Corozol) from 20 to 24 stories. That is despite the fact that city staff recommended against it because it would detract from the island's "small-town atmosphere." We applaud the sentiment, but Marco Island is about as small-town as the Bronx. The gall of these profit-blinded cretins reached a zenith with this statement by Antaramian's lawyer: "If you look up and down the beach, you have a kind of saw-tooth effect. That's part of the charm of Marco Island." This guy's good. They should hire him to do PR for Riker's Island!

The rest of the story played out something like this. All four of the existing buildings at Cape Marco on the Gulf sold out completely and now belong to the units' owners. In January 2000, with two more 24-story condos yet to be built at Cape Marco, Antaramian denied rumors that he intended to sell all his Marco Island holdings to Watermark Communities Inc. Then, in August, he did just that. Included in the transaction was a retail shopping center on Smokehouse Bay, a project put on hold after a manatee protection group protested the proposed docks and boat slips. The unfinished site has been referred to as "Marco's Stonehenge."

Incidentally, they did get one fact right in their description of this speculative fantasy world. They boast that Marco Island was "once the home to conquistadors and pirates." Not much has changed on that count. Pirates still plunder the island. They just happen to wear suits and ties these days.

Naples

If Marco Island is the Miami Beach of Florida's southwest coast, then Naples is its Fort Lauderdale. Naples is neatly trimmed lawns, squeaky-clean streets, and upscale strip malls. Naples is golf courses and galleries and high-end clothiers and hundred-shop mall/marketplaces on or near the water. Naples is canals and yachts and carefree living (for those who can afford it) on gulf and bay. There's even a touch of Palm Beach's Worth Avenue along Naples' 5th Avenue and 3rd Street shopping districts, both of which have been revitalized and improved over the past half-decade. Oh yes, Naples also claims to be home to "the only true Teddy Bear Museum in the United States." (How we despise those faux teddy bear museums!)

All the comparisons with South Florida have an actual basis in fact, as Naples has become something of an escape hatch for those who cannot abide the high-stress, high-crime lifestyle that has overwhelmed that distressed corner of the state. Here's a statistic to ponder: In one recent year, the Relocation Crime Lab Index—a relative gauge of crime, based on statistics in 500 American cities, with a rating of 100 being exactly average—was 392 in Miami (no surprise there!) and only 53 in Naples. The number of permanent residents gives no indication of how greatly Naples swells with the seasonal influx from wintering northerners. Peak season runs from Christmas through April. The Naples area claims the largest percentage of vacation-property owners in the country, according to *USA Today*, which means that it's largely a land of second homes.

The city of Naples proper is long and narrow, bounded by the Gulf of Mexico on the west and Tamiami Trail (U.S. 41) on the east. However, the city only technically ends there, as development continues and even accelerates beyond the city limits in unincorporated areas of Collier County, which are less restrictive of growth and development. The permanent year-round population of Naples is only 22,000, but when you figure in all the adjoining unincorporated communities that press up against it, the metropolitan area to which it serves as a hub is much larger, claiming a significant chunk of the county's population of 220,000.

Behind the facade of "luxury living" that Naples presents to the world, there are clashes between developers and environmentalists (but more often between developers and local citizens who want well enough left alone). Environmental interests are represented by The Conservancy, an enlightened advocacy group that does its best to preserve what remains of the subtropical ecosystems in Southwest Florida in general and Collier County in particular. This corner of the state has witnessed an extraordinary growth spurt in the last two decades. Between 1980 and 1990, Naples grew by an 77 percent, giving it the dubious distinction of being the fastest growing metropolitan area in the United States. Between 1990 and 2000, it grew by 64 percent.

They call Naples "the golf capital of the world," noting that Collier County has more golf courses per capita than almost any other area of the country. This is not a good thing. The relatively sudden impact of roughly 60 golf courses (with 20 more on the drawing board) and endless subdevelopments is bound to exact a toll on the environment. The feisty Conservancy has taken on Deltona, at one time Florida's biggest developer, over Marco Island and neighboring Horr's Island. They're involved in preserving nesting habitat for endangered loggerhead turtles. Yes, sea turtles do come ashore on the Gulf Coast, though not in as great numbers as on Florida's ocean-facing beaches. It is estimated that between 900 and 1,500 sea turtle nests are laid each year in Collier County, so there is a real interest in preserving them. Inland from the beaches, if you want to check out what the area looked like before construction crews descended on Collier County, head to **Corkscrew Swamp Sanctuary** (375 Sanctuary Road, 941/348-9151), an Audubon Society preserve northeast of town that harbors the largest subtropical old-growth bald cypress forest in the entire world. It is an untouched oasis that makes one pine for the good old days of 500-year-old trees and hooting birds. To get there, take I-75 north to Exit 17, then follow Imokalee Road (FL 846) 20 miles east to Sanctuary Road, which leads into the preserve. Corkscrew Swamp Sanctuary is open daily from 8 A.M.–5 P.M.; admission is $8 for adults, $3 for children, and free for kids under six.

Despite its rapid growth, the city of Naples has employed a modicum of urban planning—making it an anomaly among cities in South Florida—and the abundance of wealth means attractive homes and neighborhoods. Moreover, the town periodically imposes building moratoriums, and height limitations apply. This is why the really tall towers, such as the Ritz-Carlton Naples, fall outside the city limits

MAP OF FLORIDA'S WEST COAST—PAGE 347

in places like Vanderbilt Beach, which serves as an alternative staging area for developmental sprawl.

The best news about Naples has to do with the way it's handled its beaches. Many east-west streets in the heart of town end at the gulf as public accesses, with metered parking and a walkway onto the beach. Now, that is urban planning in the public interest. Combine this with the romantic, strollable Naples Pier (on the Gulf of Mexico) and City Dock (on the Bay of Naples), and you've got a recipe for a town that's almost too good to be true.

We said "almost." We already mentioned mounting population and environmental issues. The other negative factor is that they drive like maniacs in and around Naples. Tamiami Trail (U.S. 41) is a six-lane demolition derby whose contestants include pickup truck renegades changing lanes with reckless abandon and nearsighted, cotton-haired old ladies who nervously wheel whale-sized Cadillacs out of parking lots into traffic, leaving it to other drivers to scatter in their wake. To make matters worse, stoplights stay red for what seems like forever. In terms of traffic woes, U.S. 41 in Naples is reminiscent of the Miami/Fort Lauderdale metroplex. In many other respects, however, Naples is a privileged world apart.

Beaches

Within the heart of Naples, the beachfront is mostly quiet and residential, and nearly every east-west street that intersects Gulf Shore Boulevard ends at the beach with metered parking (25 cents for 20 minutes) and public access. It's simple: you pull into a space, pop in your quarters, step through a break in the shrubbery, and you're on the beach. If you live here, the deal's even better: slap a beach parking sticker on your bumper (available at Naples City Hall to full-time county residents or those who pay property taxes), and you're entitled to park anywhere in town for free. Though there isn't any remaining dune structure on Naples Beach, at least they're covering their assets by seeding the back-beach area with dune grasses. The beach itself is of a decent width and flat as a pancake, bearing the usual imprint of tire marks from equipment used to clean it up and iron it out in the morning, like Zambonis at hockey games.

Naples Beach encompasses the sandy whole of Naples, with public access at street ends from 33rd Avenue South all the way up to the north end of town, just below Clam Pass County Park. Gulf Shore Boulevard parallels the gulf for most of the beach's 5.5-mile length. Down at the

3 Naples Beach

Location: West ends of streets from 33rd Avenue South to Park Shore Drive in Naples
Parking/fees: metered street parking; free for Collier County residents with a beach parking permit (obtainable at Naples City Hall)
Hours: 8 A.M.–11 P.M.
Facilities: none
Contact: Naples Community Services, 941/434-4687

4 Naples Municipal Beach and Pier

Location: 12th Avenue South at Gulf Shore Boulevard South in Naples
Parking/fees: metered street and lot parking; free for Collier County residents with a beach parking permit (obtainable at Naples City Hall)
Hours: 24 hours
Facilities: concessions, restrooms, picnic tables, and showers
Contact: Naples Pier, 941/434-4696

south end, below 21st Avenue South, Gordon Drive fronts the gulf. **Naples Municipal Beach and Pier** is located at by a palm-fringed, brick-tiled circle (at 12th Avenue South) in the kind of neighborhood where you don't have to fear walking around after dark. There is no charge to use Naples Pier; we've paid to walk or fish on many a pier that would give their pilings to look half this nice. The lights on the pier are atmospheric, making for a setting as conducive to romance as fishing. The pier itself never closes, while the snack bar and bait shop are open till 5 P.M. daily.

In the middle of Naples' municipal beach lies **Lowdermilk Park**, a seaside playground equipped with picnic tables, gazebos, a play area, volleyball courts, and concessions. Lowdermilk is located a few miles north of Naples Pier at the west end of Banyan Boulevard. As with the street-end accesses, all you have to do to enjoy Lowdermilk Park is keep a parking meter satisfied with quarters.

Up at Naples' north end, the development gets more exclusive and vertical, and beach access is less abundant. Fear not; there are still ways to get to the beach. First of all, there's a 25-space access along **Gulf Shore Boulevard North**, near the west end of Seagate Drive; no facilities, but good beach access. The real gem in north Naples, however, is **Clam Pass County Park**. To get there, head west along Seagate Drive, continuing straight where it makes a sudden swing to the left (just past Crayton Road). You will soon come to a fork in the road, which presents a conundrum. Bear left and you'll find yourself in Clam Pass County Park, where you can spend a day at the beach for $3. Bear right and you'll be hoisted upward into the rarefied air of the Registry Resort, where you can spend one day and night at the beach for around $300.

5 Lowdermilk Park

Location: West end of Banyan Boulevard, at Gulf Shore Boulevard North in Naples
Parking/fees: metered parking lot; free for Collier County residents with a beach parking permit (obtainable at Naples City Hall)
Hours: sunrise to sunset
Facilities: concessions, restrooms, picnic tables, and showers
Contact: Naples Community Services, 941/434-4687

6 North Gulf Shore Boulevard Beach

Location: Gulf Shore Boulevard North near west end of Seagate Drive, in Naples
Parking/fees: $3 entrance fee per vehicle; free for Collier County residents with a beach parking permit (obtainable at Naples City Hall)
Hours: sunrise to sunset
Facilities: none
Contact: Collier County Parks and Recreation Department, 941/353-0404

7 Clam Pass County Park

Location: From Tamiami Trail (U.S. 41), head west on Seagate Drive to intersection with Crayton Road; from here, follow signs to Clam Pass County Park
Parking/fees: $3 entrance fee per vehicle; free for Collier County residents with a beach parking permit (obtainable at Naples City Hall)
Hours: sunrise to sunset
Facilities: concessions, restrooms, picnic tables, and showers
Contact: Collier County Parks and Recreation Department, 941/353-0404

We took the $3 option and went to Clam Pass, where we were as happy as clams to stroll the three-quarter-mile wooden boardwalk that leads out to the beach. If you don't want to hike that distance, a tram will shuttle you there in about six minutes. It's a great spot for non-motorized fun, as kayaks, canoes, and sailboards are rented on-site. The 35-acre park includes a thick mangrove forest, a tidal bay humming with birds and wildlife, and a beach that runs for three-fifths of a mile. Best of all, it's never crowded.

Shore Things

- **Bike/skate rentals:** Bike Route, 655 Tamiami Trail North, 941/262-8373.
- **Boat cruise:** Naples Princess, 1001 10th Avenue South, 941/649-2275.
- **Dive shop:** Scubadventures, 971 Creech Road, 941/434-7477.
- **Ecotourism:** Corkscrew Swamp Sanctuary, 375 Sanctuary Road, 941/348-9151.
- **Fishing charters:** Fish Finder, Inc., 179 South Bay Drive, 941/597-2063.
- **Marina:** Naples Marina and Boating Center, 475 North Road, 941/643-3666.
- **Pier:** Naples Pier, 12th Avenue South at Gulf Shore Boulevard South, 941/434-3696.
- **Rainy-day attraction:** Conservancy Nature Center, 1450 Merrihue Drive, 941/262-0304.
- **Shopping/browsing:** 3rd Street South, between 14th Avenue South and Broad Avenue South, 941/649-6707.
- **Surf shop:** Board Room Surf Shop, 4910 Tamiami Trail North, 941/649-4484.
- **Vacation rentals:** Naples Marco Vacation Accommodations, 3757 Tamiami Trail North, 941/261-7577.

Bunking Down

The **Naples Beach Hotel and Golf Club** (851 Gulf Shore Boulevard North, 941/261-2222, $$$) is a sprawling resort located near the center of town. Surprisingly, given that proximity, they occupy a significant expanse of land, on which is an 18-hole golf course, six Har-Tru tennis courts, and several buildings that offer various levels of accommodations. We stayed in the main building, a five-story salmon-colored beachside hotel. The rooms are done in interesting color combinations. The walls in our room, for instance, were painted lavender. Instead of the impressionistic, Hallmark card renderings of beach scenes typically found in corporate hotels, the artwork consists of stunning black-and-white photographs of nature scenes along the Gulf of Mexico by nationally renowned photographer Clyde Butcher (who lives up in Fort Myers). A back door with a porthole opens onto a small balcony overlooking the gulf. The downstairs lobby is an enormous hub for the bustling complex, where it's hard not to find something to do. Kids are especially well taken care of at the Naples Beach Hotel, which ranks among the top family resorts in the world. The resort offers creature comforts within friendly and human-scaled parameters.

The **Registry Resort** (475 Seagate Drive, 941/597-3232, $$$$) and the **Ritz-Carlton Naples** (280 Vanderbilt Beach Road, 941/598-3000, $$$$), by contrast, offer corporate plushing in an arid five-star environment. To our jaded senses, these Italian-marble monuments to arrogance completely miss the concept of what it means to be at the beach. The charges to stay here are ludicrously inflated, and their institutional facades are depressing examples of corporate ego run amok. What such grandiose entombments are all about is (business)man's relationship to the natural world he presumes to conquer. The Registrys and Ritz-Carltons of the world overwhelm the landscape they pretend to celebrate, brazenly asserting dominion and superiority. At the other extreme, such as downtown Naples or nearby Sanibel and Captiva Islands, one discerns a willingness to defer to the natural world with grateful humility. The idea is not to subdue or even eradicate nature but to blend in and harmonize. That, in a nutshell, is our own philosophy of how to develop along the beach or any natural environment, for that matter.

Note: Room rates at all the upper-crust resorts drop from June through September, when you can snag what passes for a deal for around $130 a room. It's twice and even three times that amount at the Ritz-Carlton and the Registry the rest of the year. If you're traveling on a budget, try the **Wellesley Inn** (1555 5th Avenue South, 941/793-4646, $$) or the **Best Western Naples Inn** (2329 9th Street North, 941/261-1148, $$). Both are modern, well kept, nicely landscaped, accessible to shopping areas, and only half a mile or so from the beach. Moreover, you can take the money you save by staying here and eat like kings and queens in princely Naples.

Coastal Cuisine

The **Dock at Crayton Cove** (842 12th Avenue South, 941/263-9940, $$$) overlooks the Bay of Naples from the historic City Dock. The relaxed air within starts with the two brothers who own and run the place, Vin and Phil Depasquale. They amble around their lair in faded Hawaiian shirts and Dockers like two beach boys who just happened to wander in. But don't let their casual demeanor fool you. They are sticklers for quality at the Dock, and they're constantly coming up with new ways to prepare seafood. When we passed through, they'd just begun debuting some new dishes that tasted like winners to us: grilled tuna steak served atop spinach and mushrooms with a tangy ceviche marinade, and grouper fingers rolled in crushed pecans, lightly fried, and served with a brown demiglace. There's always grilled mahimahi and tuna, plus such palate pleasers as sautéed red snapper in a sweet and sour sauce of coconut, pineapple, jalapeños, and scallions. If you want something lighter, grouper Rueben resembles the namesake sandwich, except for the substitution of fish for corned beef.

If you're wandering around the Old Marine Marketplace at Tin City, the former hub of Naples' fishing industry, drop in on the Dock at Crayton Cove's sister operation, the **Riverwalk Fish & Ale House** (1200 5th Avenue South, 941/263-2734, $$$). It's housed in an old clam- and oyster-processing plant. The menu is more casual and family oriented, featuring items like grouper and chips, fried shrimp, and a surf-and-turf combo.

As one might expect in a moneyed community like Naples, there is a decided emphasis on fine dining. Some of the more popular spots in town that boast high-end cuisine (and tabs to match) include **St. George and the Dragon** (936 5th Avenue South, 941/262-6546, $$$$), which serves hearty surf-and-turf fare in a stately, nautical-themed atmosphere (jackets required); **Michael's Cafe** (2950 Tamiami Trail North, 941/434-2550, $$$$), specializing in fine European and New American cuisine; and **Villa Pescatore** (8920 Tamiami Trail North, 941/597-8119, $$$$), whose name translates from the Italian as "house of fish" and whose char-grilled catch of the day is especially commended.

If you're angling for fish in a more family-friendly environment, try **Grouper House** (396 Goodlette Road South, 941/263-4900, $$$), bearing in mind that the grouper is the king of fish on the Gulf Coast, and **Kelly's Fish House** (1302 5th Avenue South, 941/774-0494, $$$), which has been serving seafood in its riverfront location since 1952. We could go on listing restaurants till the groupers come home, because there's no end of them in Naples.

MAP OF FLORIDA'S WEST COAST—PAGE 347

We haven't been so exhausted by all the culinary research we've had to do since Fort Lauderdale. Seriously.

Night Moves

Among the hottest spots on the southwest Gulf Coast is **Revel** (475 Seagate Drive, 941/597-3232), the aptly named nightclub at the Registry Resort. It is a dress-up-and-disco kind of place that nets glitteringly turned-out night swimmers from all over. Not to be outdone is the Ritz-Carlton, whose on-premises nightclub, authoritatively named **The Club** (280 Vanderbilt Beach Road, 941/598-3300), is another gathering place for those willing to pay a five-buck cover to shake their booties in an upscale, prom-night atmosphere.

One of Naples' most popular nightspots, **Hurricane Jane's** (2023 Davis Boulevard, 941/732-8400), stands apart from the resort hotel pack, which is a plus in our book. On a lower-key note, the Naples Beach Hotel has a poolside bar that's kind of fun, especially on Sunday nights, when they bring in bands and throw a pool party that attracts locals and guests alike. The best part of all is there's no cover.

If you'd rather pub-crawl than put on the ritz, there are places to do that, too. None of them is as rustic as they pretend to be, but the beer's cold and it beats the plastic revelry at Revel. All of them serve lunch and dinner and have live music on Thursday, Friday, and Saturday. From south to north:

- **Old Naples Pub** (255 13th Avenue South, 941/649-8200) lies in "historic Old Naples" and features soup, salads, and lite piano accompaniment.
- **Old Florida Pub & Brewery** (1948 9th Street North, 941/403-3536) claims to be Naples' first "mini-microbrewery" . . . does that make it a brew pub for Munchkins?
- **Village Pub** (4360 Gulf Shore Boulevard North, 941/262-2707) serves pizza and pub food, displays maritime memorabilia, and features an Irish guitarist/humorist to further the illusion of chillier climes.
- **Backstage Tap & Grill** (5355 Tamiami Trail North, 941/598-1300) is a "jazzy little spot" that serves breakfast, lunch, and dinner in a waterside mall setting.

Contact Information

Naples Area Chamber of Commerce, 3620 Tamiami Trail North, Naples, FL 34103; 941/262-6376; website: www.naples chamber.org

Vanderbilt Beach

Vanderbilt Beach (pop. 15,000) is in unincorporated north Collier County, an area that likes to attach itself to Naples, obtaining cachet by proximity. Though the city of Naples ends just below Clam Pass County Park, the area including Vanderbilt Beach and extending up to the Lee County line is referred to as "North Naples." Be advised it is nothing like Naples. The roads to the coast are crowded; construction and congestion are endemic; and gulf views are restricted to those who can get past the guard gates. The tallest resort hotels in the area, the Registry and the Ritz-Carlton (see "Bunking Down" in the Naples listing), actually lie outside the Naples city limits. That doesn't prevent the latter from somewhat disingenuously referring to itself as the Ritz-Carlton Naples (shades of the state's east coast, where the Ritz-Carlton Palm Beach is really in Manalapan).

Beaches

Both money and sand have been pumped into Vanderbilt Beach, a locale

8 Vanderbilt Beach County Park

Location: The west end of Vanderbilt Beach Road (State Route 862) in Vanderbilt Beach
Parking/fees: $3 entrance fee per vehicle; free for Collier County residents with a beach parking permit (obtainable at Naples City Hall)
Hours: sunrise to sunset
Facilities: concessions, restrooms, picnic tables, and showers
Contact: Collier County Parks and Recreation Department, 941/353-0404

where the erosion potential ranges from high to extreme. Beach access is about all you get for your $3 parking fee at **Vanderbilt Beach County Park**, located at the west end of Vanderbilt Beach Road, near the Ritz-Carlton. You'll get more beach for your money (and less development crowding it) at nearby Delnor-Wiggins Pass State Park and Barefoot Beach Preserve.

Contact Information

Naples Area Chamber of Commerce, 3620 Tamiami Trail North, Naples, FL 34103; 941/262-6376; website: www.naples chamber.org

Delnor-Wiggins Pass State Park

One of the Gulf Coast's most alluring beaches lies between Vanderbilt Beach and Wiggins Pass, where the Cocohatchee River empties into the Gulf of Mexico. The lushly vegetated park occupies the north end of a barrier island. The back of the island is a mangrove forest crisscrossed with tidal creeks, while sea oats

9 Delnor-Wiggins Pass State Park

Location: North of Vanderbilt Beach at the west end of County Road 846 (Bluebill Avenue/Immokalee Road)
Parking/fees: $4 entrance fee per vehicle with up to eight occupants; $2 for car and driver only. $1 per bicyclist or pedestrian
Hours: 8 A.M. to sunset
Facilities: lifeguards, restrooms, picnic tables, and showers
Contact: Delnor-Wiggins Pass State Park, 941/597-6196

and cabbage palms line the low-lying open beach. The fine-textured, white-sand beach at **Delnor-Wiggins Pass State Park** can be accessed from five parking areas that run from the south entrance up to Wiggins Pass. Each lot has its own bathhouse. A boardwalk leads out to the pass, which is a great place to fish and the only spot where fishing is permitted. There's also an observation tower from whose summit one can survey 360 degrees of natural splendor.

Delnor-Wiggins' only drawback has to do with the fact that swift currents in the vicinity of Wiggins Pass make for hazardous swimming at that end. The fact that the park has the only lifeguard stand in Collier County is cause for both comfort and concern, so swim carefully.

Contact Information

Delnor-Wiggins Pass State Park, 1110 Gulf Shore Drive North, Naples, FL 34108; 941/597-6196; website: www.myflorida .com

Map of Florida's West Coast—Page 347

Barefoot Beach

Barefoot Beach is a two-part beach: a large preserve and a small access. **Barefoot Beach County Park** is where you want to go. To get there, you'll drive for a few miles through a stand of condos as thick as jungle bamboo, but it's worth putting up with speed bumps and signs telling you to stay on the main road. At the end of Lely Barefoot Road is 342 acres of dense tropical hammock, mangrove swamp, and open-sand beach.

Barefoot Beach County Park is as healthy and natural a stretch of coast as exists in Collier County. The beach runs for 1.5 miles, extending south to Wiggins Pass, well beyond where the road ends. A boardwalk meanders through the hammock and out to the beach. Facilities include a learning center, where lectures on such topics as shells, fossils, and artifacts are given from time to time. Exhibits on sea turtles and shorebirds make apparent the need for habitat preservation and left us wondering how developments such as those we passed through to get here were allowed to happen. The protected gopher tortoise makes its home in the hammock. Out on the beach, sea oats anchor low-lying dunes. Don't worry, they haven't been bulldozed away. The dunes are just smaller on this part of the coast, owing to less favorable conditions for dune formation having to do with wind and waves (or lack thereof).

Barefoot Beach Access, which lies several miles north of the park, is little more than a parking lot and walkway to the beach. It lies at the end of Bonita Beach Road, smack-dab on the Lee County line. Parking costs $3 at both Barefoots. The beach at the access is fine and the parking (100 spaces) is ample. However, your three sawbucks are better spent letting nature entrance you at Barefoot Beach County Park.

Contact Information

Barefoot Beach County Park, Lely Beach Boulevard, Naples, FL 33963; 941/353-0404; website: www.co.collier.fl.us/parks

⑩ Barefoot Beach County Park

Location: from Bonita Beach Road, turn south on Lely Beach Boulevard and drive approximately two miles into the park

Parking/fees: $3 entrance fee per vehicle; free for Collier County residents with a beach parking permit (obtainable at Naples City Hall)

Hours: 8 A.M. to sunset

Facilities: concessions, restrooms, picnic tables, showers, and a visitor center

Contact: Collier County Parks and Recreation Department, 941/353-0404

⑪ Barefoot Beach Access

Location: from Bonita Beach Road, turn south on Lely Beach Boulevard and look for the parking lot just inside the Collier County line

Parking/fees: $3 entrance fee per vehicle; free for Collier County residents with a beach parking permit (obtainable at Naples City Hall)

Hours: 8 A.M. to sunset

Facilities: none

Contact: Collier County Parks and Recreation Department, 941/353-0404

MAP OF COLLIER COUNTY—PAGE 348

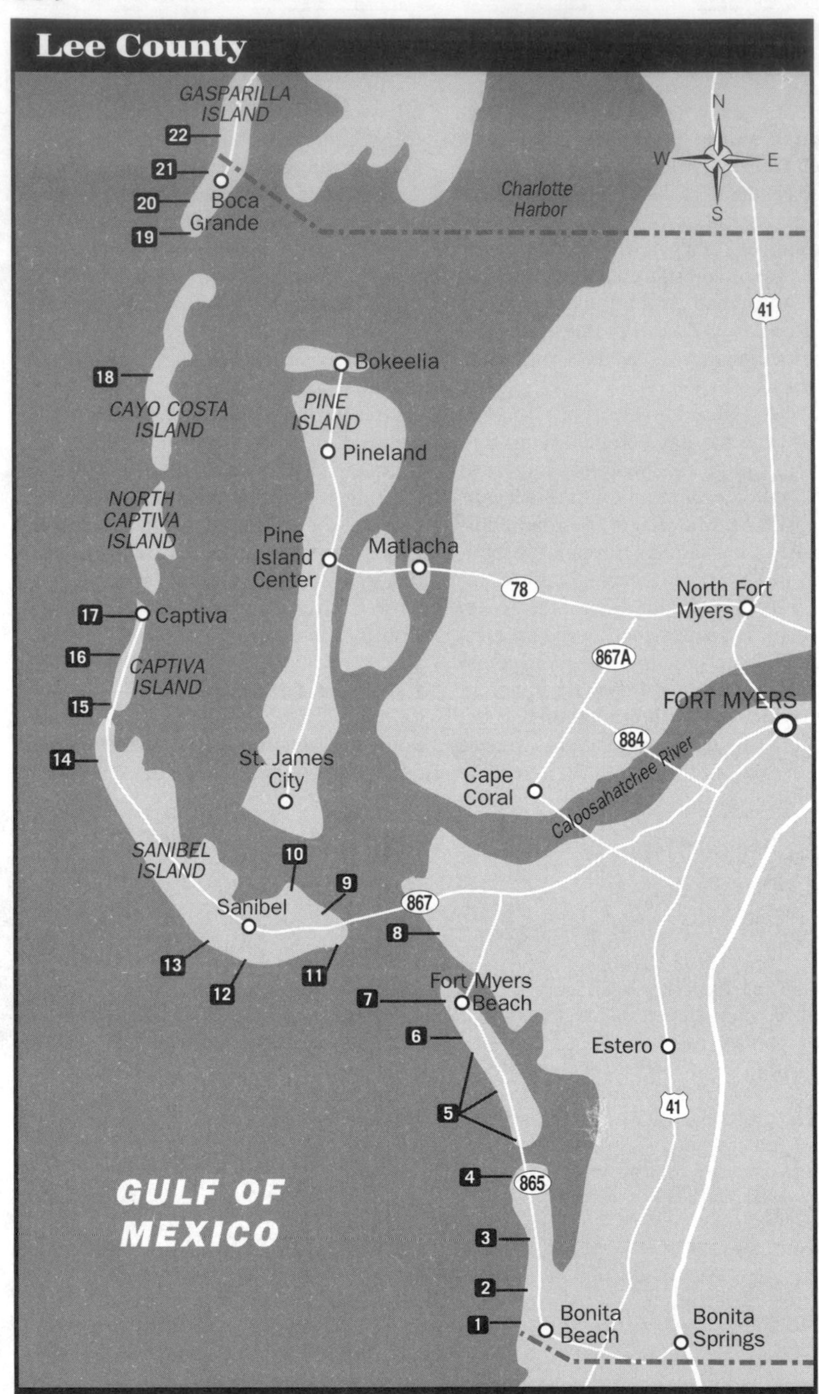
Lee County
GASPARILLA ISLAND
22
21
20
Boca Grande
19
Charlotte Harbor
N
W
E
S
41
18
Bokeelia
CAYO COSTA ISLAND
PINE ISLAND
Pineland
NORTH CAPTIVA ISLAND
Pine Island Center
Matlacha
78
North Fort Myers
17
Captiva
16
CAPTIVA ISLAND
867A
15
FORT MYERS
884
14
St. James City
Cape Coral
Caloosahatchee River
SANIBEL ISLAND
10
9
Sanibel
867
8
13
12
11
Fort Myers Beach
7
6
Estero
41
5
4
865
GULF OF MEXICO
3
2
1
Bonita Beach
Bonita Springs

Lee County

LEE COUNTY

Lee County is a model of how to develop the beaches to suit all kinds of tastes and income levels while minimally disturbing the natural environment. Among Lee County's 52 miles of sandy beaches are some of the finest in the state, from the standpoint of seclusion (Cayo Costa, the Captiva Islands), perennial popularity (Fort Myers Beach), and brilliantly planned combinations of the two (Sanibel Island, Boca Grande). Many of these beaches are renowned for their prodigious supply of seashells and sharks' teeth. A separate chapter could be written on Lee County's "inland coast," an appealing mix of islands (Pine, Little Pine, San Carlos), wilderness keys, and towns (Cape Coral, Bokeelia) that we regrettably omitted in order to stay focused on the gulf beaches.

MAP OF FLORIDA'S WEST COAST—PAGE 347

Bonita Beach

This small coastal community, which is technically part of Bonita Springs is a very low-key version of Fort Myers Beach, its accommodating neighbor to the north. For years, in fact, it has operated as a sort of less harried alternative to the latter, with its selling point being a more homey pace. Bonita Beach seems to take its tone from a county-wide ordinance we saw posted here (but not elsewhere): from May 1 to October 31 no one is allowed to shine lights on the beach, in deference to egg-laying sea turtles.

There are more than shelly gulf beaches for nature lovers to explore, including inland swamps (the Audubon Society's Corkscrew Swamp Sanctuary lies due east of Bonita Springs in Charlotte County; see Naples writeup) and the Estero River. One spot of surpassingly strange historical interest is **Koreshan State Historic Site.** It's located eight miles north of Bonita Springs, in the town of Estero (U.S. 41 at Corkscrew Road, 941/992-0311). Here you'll find the reconstructed village of the Koreshans, a bizarre religious sect who migrated here from Chicago in 1894. Led by one Dr. Cyrus Reed Teed, they believed that "the earth was a hollow sphere with the sun in the center and life existing on the inside surface of the sphere." Teed and his followers hoped to found a "new Jerusalem" in Estero that would eventually swell to 10 million followers of "Koreshanity" (which rhymes with "insanity"). In fact, the last four surviving members of this nut-house sect deeded the land to the state in 1961. It just goes to prove that madmen and willing followers are ubiquitous throughout history, which is mildly reassuring amidst the onslaught of them in modern times.

Beaches

As far as providing public beach access goes, Lee County is among the most proactive in all of Florida. We counted at least 10 "Lee County Beach Access" signs along **Bonita Beach's** three-mile length, and there are more than 40 of them in all throughout coastal Lee County—and that's in addition to the bona fide beach parks. The accesses range from six-foot-wide easements between private properties to 50-foot walkways with some parking spaces. All of the accesses lead to the same wide, clean beach, providing those who crave seclusion with an unexpected bonanza, given that you're in the middle of a resort town.

From the south, the fun begins with

❶ Bonita Beach Park

Location: west end of Bonita Beach Boulevard (County Road 865) at 27950 Hickory Boulevard in Bonita Beach
Parking/fees: metered parking lot (free if you display a beach sticker, obtainable for $35 at the Bonita Springs Recreation Center)
Hours: 8 A.M. to sunset
Facilities: concession, restrooms, picnic tables, and showers
Contact: Bonita Beach Park, 941/495-5811

❷ Bonita Beach Public Accesses

Location: 10 public accesses along Hickory Boulevard (County Road 865) north of Bonita Beach Park
Parking/fees: free parking lots at several accesses; pedestrian easements only at others
Hours: 8 A.M. to sunset
Facilities: none
Contact: Lee County Department of Parks and Recreation, 941/461-7400

MAP OF LEE COUNTY—PAGE 364

Bonita Beach Park, at the west end of Bonita Beach Boulevard. The park has been renovated, with an added picnic area, bathhouse, and volleyball courts. Parking is limited, with the 75 cents per hour fee paid via a machine that's easier to use than an ATM. (This looks to be the wave of the beach-parking future.) Both beaches are near enough to motels, cafés, and condos to keep you from feeling like a shipwrecked South Sea adventurer, but far enough away to let you daydream about the possibility. About two miles north of Bonita Beach Park is **Little Hickory Island Beach Park**, a small county-run facility that shares the same long, semisecluded beach.

Bunking Down

Two appealing resort motels are located almost diagonally from one another. The aptly named **Beach House Motel** (26106 Hickory Boulevard, 941/992-2644, $) is directly on the beach (just south of Little Hickory Island Beach Park). The units, from efficiencies and motel rooms to one- and two-bedroom apartments, are spread among eight detached two-story houses. Across the road is the **Bonita Beach Resort Motel** (26395 Hickory Boulevard, 941/992-2137, $). A similar range of accommodations is offered, but the complex stretches all the way to the bayside (actually, Hogue Channel). Numerous motel-owned docks along the waterway allow for a multitude of boating options. Neither place is fancy, but that very lack of pretension explains Bonita Beach's longtime appeal. Look at it this way: nesting sea turtles know a good beach when they see one.

Will that appeal remain intact for the foreseeable future as development works its way toward Bonita Beach from north and south? Well, we can't say for sure, but we suspect the worst. To rephrase Bob Dylan, something's happening in Bonita Beach, and neither we nor Mr. Jones know what it is. But here's a dead giveaway: Almost every other house along Hickory Boulevard (County Road 865) has a For Sale sign out front.

3 Little Hickory Island Beach Park

Location: two miles north of Bonita Beach Boulevard on Hickory Boulevard (County Road 865)

Parking/fees: metered parking lot (free if you display a beach sticker, obtainable for $35 at the Bonita Springs Recreation Center)

Hours: 8 A.M. to sunset

Facilities: restrooms, picnic tables, and showers

Contact: Lee County Department of Parks and Recreation, 941/461-7400

Contact Information

Bonita Springs Area Chamber of Commerce, 25071 Chamber of Commerce Drive, Bonita Springs, FL 34135; 941/992-2943; website: www.bonitaspringschamber.com

MAP OF FLORIDA'S WEST COAST—PAGE 347

Lovers Key State Park

The entrance to **Lovers Key State Park** sits on Black Island, the barrier island immediately south of Fort Myers Beach's Estero Island. With the triad of Lovers Key, Inner Key, and Carl E. Johnson County Park now under state ownership, the park has swelled to 712 acres. Lovers Key provides a unique glimpse at an entire ecosystem—beaches, estuaries, wetlands—that is on the comeback trail after having been subjected to invasion by nonnative species and disturbance by dredge-and-fill activities.

The beaches are some of the wildest and most visually arresting on this part of the coast. We aren't the first to notice; a national survey ranked them sixth among the beaches on the Gulf of Mexico. The modest entrance fee includes easy access via tram shuttle to the isolated beach at the park's south portion, on the far side of Oyster Bay. It's a scenic, meditative ten-minute ride ending at a wide beach with nature trails that wind back through the surrounding wetlands. Large, family reunion–sized picnic pavilions are provided, offering a semblance of privacy. Alternatively, you can walk out to the beach at the park's midsection. Two long wooden walkways proceed from the parking area over the mangrove-choked estuaries onto Inner Key and then Lovers Key, a pearly-white beach covered with shells and driftwood. No lifeguard is on duty, and signs warn "Swim at your own risk," though the water doesn't look particularly dangerous. People come here to boat (there are boat and canoe launches for easy access to the Gulf of Mexico and Estero Bay). Casting for trout and redfish and cast-netting for mullet are popular fishing activities.

There are a few picnic tables on the beach (no grills), but the real appeal of Lovers Key is its seclusion. With its gray, skeletal driftwood formations and open horizon, the beaches here are somewhat reminiscent of isolated spots in the Pacific Northwest. Bring your camera and prepare to spend at least half a day tramping the wild and secluded shoreline. Visitors facilities were completed in 1997, and the incorporation of the formerly county-run Carl E. Johnson Park into Lovers Key State Park was celebrated with a dedication ceremony in June 1998.

Contact Information

Lovers Key State Park, 8700 Estero Boulevard, Fort Myers Beach, FL 33931; 941/463-4588; website: www.myflorida.com

4 Lovers Key State Park

Location: entrance on Black Island, between Bonita Beach and Fort Myers Beach on County Road 865

Parking/fees: $4 entrance fee per vehicle with up to eight occupants; $2 for car and driver only; $1 per bicyclist or walker

Hours: 8 A.M. to sunset

Facilities: restrooms, picnic tables, and showers

Contact: Lovers Key State Park, 941/463-4588

Fort Myers Beach

Fort Myers Beach (pop. 9,300) is a rare specimen along the southwest Florida coast, a quintessential fun and funky beach town with few affectations. The visual experience of arriving on Estero Island—the seven-mile-long barrier island on which the town sits—recalls the best of the Jersey Shore, and we mean this as a compliment. That is to say, Fort Myers Beach is utterly unconscious of style, and this is part of its charm. From the north, you enter on San Carlos Boulevard (County Road 865) over the dizzying Sky Bridge and are suddenly air-dropped into a hustling, bustling epicenter of fun, featuring a long public pier, sun-baked motels, and low-key bungalows stretching for miles along Estero Boulevard, the main drag.

While you can also access the island from the less harried south end, the important thing to remember is that you are entering a pretension-free fun zone. You will not see people puttering about in golf carts, sipping wine or picking at platters of brie. You will instead find jukeboxes blaring Lynyrd Skynyrd, beer served in ice-cold pitchers, and sun-reddened revelers suddenly and unabashedly shouting "Yahoo!" or "Yee-haw!" These are the playful exclamations of folks "commonly referred to as having red body parts just below their heads," according to a local fact sheet. The editor of the *Beach Bulletin*, a local publication, bragged that he had written a song called "I Can't Love You 'Cause Your Dog Drank My Beer." Being Northern by birth but Southern by the grace of God (to quote a boast often affixed to pickup-truck bumpers south of the Mason-Dixon line), we found ourselves right at home in Fort Myers Beach.

That's the just-folks image of Fort Myers Beach some killjoys would like to see toned down and perhaps even sent packing. This wave was ushered in by the town's incorporation in 1995, which triggered $2.3 million in county funds earmarked for "improvement projects." While home rule is, of course, a good thing, it has made some local entrepreneurs lose sight of what a nice place they already have. The feeling we got during our most recent visit was something out of Mark Twain's "The Man That Corrupted Hadleyburg," with people madly trying to make a silk purse out of Fort Myers Beach's perfectly fine sow's ear. Getting rid of wet T-shirt nights and the crowd to whom they cater is one thing, but replacing them with traffic-snarling upscale hotels at the foot of Sky Bridge is not necessarily an improvement.

Because Fort Myers Beach has a long history of providing the sloppy and affordable fun desired by generations of vacationers—both native Floridians and beach-starved families from the Upper Midwest—it seems only natural that the town would suffer from stereotyping. One local Donald Trump wannabe—a "commercial lender" who came carpetbagging from Boston—was quoted as saying, "You're seeing more and more normal people." Normal, you rightfully ask, what is that? Well, this clone of "the Donald" continues, "People with families. They're not all Jimmy Buffett and Robinson Crusoe types. The number of toothless, tattooed yahoos is going down."

We're sorry, but a few toothless renegades are not a good reason to give a decent town an upscale reaming. As menacing as certain Robinson Crusoes can be after some pitchers of beer, we'll take 10 of them over any one "commercial lender" or self-proclaimed "normal" person any day of the week. Defining standards of normalcy smacks of fascism, and there's already enough economic fascism in Florida without adding the specter of some sort of moneyed Aryan prototype to the picture. Why even try? Fort Myers Beach,

MAP OF FLORIDA'S WEST COAST—PAGE 347

like a happy-go-lucky nephew, is seated at the gulfside banquet between two well-mannered, if politically opposed, great aunts: Marco Island and Sanibel-Captiva. To our way of thinking, it is the perfect just-folks alternative to both places. Not that we don't revere Sanibel and Captiva Islands, but sometimes we like to kick back and howl at the sunset with the rest of the pack. You can do that at Fort Myers Beach and not get arrested. At least for now.

You can do lots of other things here, too. Fort Myers Beach is a gulfside relative of the inland city of Fort Myers (which, with a population of 47,000, is five times as large). The beach community has traditionally championed what one local called "ticky tackiness," while the big city to the east promotes itself as the "City of Palms." Fort Myers lined its streets with them and its pockets with the mounting revenue from unregulated suburban sprawl. Fort Myers Beach, on the other hand, was allowed to become a combination family haven and redneck Riviera, happily going about its business of pleasing the yokels, even if this meant occasionally lapsing into uncouth behavior. Despite the airs put on by the City of Palms, the yokels out on the beach have shown way more foresight by instituting a height limit on buildings and making sure to keep the beaches of Estero Island, which is 75–100 yards wide at certain points, open to all.

With county funds from their newly incorporated status, Fort Myers Beach has spruced up Times Square, the popular grid of streets at the island's north end, where most of the big-time partying is done. They've also begun shoring up public access points with attractive and clearly marked signs, as well as cleaning the beaches of seaweed and storm-generated scum, which can at times be an aesthetic problem. These are improvements worth making.

The best news is that Fort Myers Beach hasn't yet gone too far toward gentrifying its appealing funkiness out of existence. That is, it's still an affordable alternative to Sanibel and Marco Islands, and the old regular vacationers—including many loyal families who trek down from the Midwestern states for their week or two at the beach—return annually in droves. Despite some of the worst traffic jams you'll find in any beach community, there's much to like about Fort Myers Beach. We just hope they don't lose their enviably abnormal soul to the money-driven pursuit of "normalcy" in the process.

Beaches

The sandy beaches here are as wide open as the town's attitude toward visitors. Fort Myers Beach is the most popular vacation destination in Lee County, and it's easy to see why. Most of Estero Island's barrier beach is as spacious as it is inviting, enduring an occasional renourishment project to keep it that way. **Fort Myers Beach Public Accesses,** from Flamingo Avenue north to Avenue A, are easy to find and use. On our numerous drives along Estero Boulevard, we counted 30 clearly marked signs over a five-mile span—a noble effort to provide ample public access. Some of the signs merely mark where an easement has been provided for pedes-

5 Fort Myers Beach Public Accesses

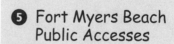

Location: numerous beach access points along Estero Boulevard between Flamingo Avenue and Avenue A in Fort Myers Beach
Parking/fees: metered or pay parking lots
Hours: 24 hours
Facilities: none
Contact: Lee County Department of Parks and Recreation, 941/461-7400

MAP OF LEE COUNTY—PAGE 364

trian traffic, while other signs sport a large P, which designates free parking. Hurry, though, because the spaces are limited.

Indeed, parking is by far the biggest hang-up in Fort Myers Beach, as traffic in peak season (January through Easter) is one long standstill on the two-lane main drag at certain times of day. That's when the year-round population of 15,000 swells to over 40,000. Estero Island is liberally dotted with motels and you can just park your car wherever you check in and walk or bike around town. You can also catch a free ride with the LeeTrans shuttle service, whose buses sport eye-catching manatee logos on their sides. (Call 941/275-8726 for more information.)

While the beach in most places along the island is wide, that distance is cut in half in front of those older houses or lodgings that have man-made seawalls in front of them. Intended to hold the beach in place, these walls and groins have had the opposite effect. In fact, the beaches on either side of them are wider. The sand in the widest, unwalled areas is of a powdered-sugar texture nearest the dunes and hard-packed by the water. While the blinding white powdery sand seems inviting to anyone with a beach blanket, we've noticed here, as in other places along the southwest coast, that it makes more sense to rent a cabana or lounge chair for the day, because your hours on the beach will be far more comfortable.

At various unpredictable times of year, huge storms out in the gulf will churn up a mess of seaweed and microscopic vegetation (no, not red tide, although that infrequently makes its devastating presence felt, too) that accumulates in spongy red-brown masses and off-gases an olfactory stench. The rich birdlife along Estero Island digs it, though, as it attracts bite-sized sea animals. We spent an entire morning enjoying the daredevil aerial show provided by the gulls and pelicans, as well as the more dignified ballet of the herons and ibises, some of which are the size of wild turkeys. The former dive-bomb the water, crashing headlong into the surf and disappearing from view, only to resurface seconds later with some squirming varmint in their beaks. The latter stand stock still until the moment of truth, at which point they duck their big bills delicately into the water, as if dipping into a fondue dish, and pull away with their gourmet sushi.

The beach along Estero Island invites strolling, an experience made all the more pleasant by the sight of numerous benches along the way, each with the message "Enjoy and Share." While the beach is pretty much unbroken for the entire length

6 Lynn Hall Memorial Park

Location: 950 Estero Boulevard, beside Fort Myers Beach Pier
Parking/fees: metered parking lot
Hours: 7 A.M.–10 P.M. (gates open 24 hours)
Facilities: concessions, restrooms, picnic tables, and showers
Contact: Lynn Hall Memorial Park, 941/463-1116

7 Bowditch Point Regional Park

Location: 50 Estero Boulevard, at north end of Estero Island, above Fort Myers Beach
Parking/fees: free parking lot at Main Street Park in Fort Myers Beach. Free trolley service from Main Street Park to Bowditch Point Regional Park.
Hours: 8:30 A.M. to sunset
Facilities: restrooms, picnic tables, and showers
Contact: Bowditch Regional Park, 941/463-1116

of the island, segments of it are designated by various names. The area around the public pier is called **Lynn Hall Memorial Park**, which stretches into nicely landscaped grounds to the north, dotted with benches and picnic tables. Bathhouses and restrooms for beachgoers are located here, too. Parking is at metered lots (75 cents an hour) that are closely monitored by the gendarmes. A block away are the rollicking shops and pubs of Times Square. The centerpiece, Fort Myers Beach Pier (informally known as Pelican Pier), is a pleasantly ramshackle affair popular with, yes, pelicans, who stand around so stiffly on the ledges that you think they're wooden carvings. Signs posted along the pier give step-by-step instructions on how to remove a fish hook from an accidentally snagged pelican.

Just south of the pier is the most popular section of Fort Myers Beach. Along what's called Motel Row, the sociable beach is lined with volleyball nets, blaring radios, and even the occasional surfer, with plenty of mingling between unattached members of the opposite sex. Yet another sign that we were in a quintessential beach town: people appeared willing and indeed happy to make one another's acquaintance. Just for the record, it sometimes seems as if there's an unofficial contest in progress to see who can wear the smallest bikini in public.

At the northern tip of Estero Island is **Bowditch Point Regional Park**, located where Estero Boulevard dead-ends at a traffic circle. A truly inviting location that's free of charge, the 17-acre park is inaccessible to cars, with only a few parking spaces for the handicapped. No hang-up, really, if you walk up from the pier, ride a bike (plenty of bike racks are provided), or catch the free LeeTrans shuttle bus from Main Street Park in Fort Myers Beach, which ends its circular route right at Bowditch Point. Picnic areas and grills are provided, as is a short hiking trail. The beach bends around the barrier island, which is anorexically thin at this point. You can see all the way over to Sanibel at the tip here, an exciting vista unblemished by high-rises.

Shore Things

- **Bike/skate rental:** Fun Rentals, 1901 Estero Boulevard, 941/463-8844.
- **Boat cruise:** Playtime Cruises, 7225 Estero Boulevard, 941/463-9700.
- **Dive shop:** Seahorse Scuba, 17849 San Carlos Boulevard, 941/454-3111.
- **Ecotourism:** Estero River Canoe Outfitters, 20991 South Tamiami Trail, Estero, FL 33928, 941/992-4050.
- **Fishing charters:** DS Charters, Deebold Marina, 18500 San Carlos Boulevard, 941/466-3525.
- **Marina:** Fort Myers Beach Marina, 703 Fisherman's Wharf, 941/463-9552.
- **Pier:** Fort Myers Beach Pier (a.k.a. Pelican Pier), Estero Boulevard at San Carlos Boulevard, 941/765-9700.
- **Rainy-day attraction:** Marine Science Center, Ostego Bay Foundation, 718 Fisherman's Wharf, 941/765-8101.
- **Shopping/browsing:** Times Square, Estero Boulevard at San Carlos Boulevard.
- **Surf Shop:** West Coast Surf Shop, 1035 Estero Boulevard, 941/463-1989.
- **Vacation Rentals:** Bluebill Properties, 2670 Estero Boulevard, 941/ 463-1141.

Bunking Down

A prolonged fight in the mid-1990s over approval for a proposed multi-story convention center and hotel was dubbed "the last straw" by a local activist. Well, as these things go, the last straw was drawn and it was the activists who lost. The brand-new 12-story **DiamondHead Beach Resort**

MAP OF LEE COUNTY—PAGE 364

(2000 Estero Boulevard, 941/765-7654, $$$) is an atypical vacation budget-buster in otherwise affordable Fort Myers Beach. Beachfront rooms here go for $175–285 a night, depending on time of year (with Christmas through April being the high season in these parts). It's quite the tony resort, but the concept of "refined luxury," with rarefied prices to match, seems a little out of place here, although it is rather over-optimistically referred to as "the anchor for the main-street district." Not in our book.

For unpretentious seaside hideaways, you can do no better than the **Outrigger Beach Resort** (6200 Estero Boulevard, 941/463-3131, $$). This four-story, 144-unit motel complex reaches out toward the heart of Estero Island's main beach, as if trying to embrace the sunset. The staff is down-home friendly, the pace is relaxed, and the tiki bar beside the pool is the best perch in town from which to view the sunset. The Outrigger is also the obvious choice for tightly budgeted families looking for a bargain that doesn't cut corners to provide it.

While both a café and restaurant are on the premises—and Charley Brown's is across the street—the homey rooms come with full kitchens, implements, and enough dinnerware for five. The Outrigger has been serving up unmatched hospitality since 1964, and guests return each year at exactly the same time, many coming from the Midwest, where a bargain's a bargain and a handshake is more morally binding than a contract. Even the locals come here at the end of the day to partake of the friendly patter at the tiki bar. When the red disc makes that final plunge, someone bleats a long, sustained note on a horn, and the gathered throng applauds enthusiastically. The Thursday wine-and-cheese social is legendary among regular guests.

From our perspective as beach bums, we were happy to learn that for once the sign in front of a motel ("Look No Further. We Have the Best Beach!") doesn't lie. The beach just beyond the enormous sundeck is the widest on Estero Island, the sand powdery and white, and the water safe and warm. It is also far enough south of the pier to be considered off the beaten track.

Two excellent Best Westerns are located at the northern end of this island's ample beach. One is the **Best Western Beach Resort** (684 Estero Boulevard, 941/463-6000, $$$), a five-story motel that runs for 450 feet along the beach. Every room is beachfront, and each comes with a balcony, kitchenette, and continental breakfast. Guests are also within easy strolling distance of the city pier and the bars and restaurants of Times Square. The **Best Western Pink Shell Beach Resort** (275 Estero Boulevard, 941/463-6181, $$$$) is a full-service resort. Not only does it cover 12 palm-laden acres and stretch out along 1,500 feet of white barrier sand, the Pink Shell offers three pools, tennis, volleyball, shuffleboard, water sports, boat rentals, and supervised children's activities. Plus, it offers easy access to the beach at Bowditch Point Regional Park.

If you want assistance in booking your beach vacation here, contact **Beach Accommodations** (1335 Santos Road, 941/765-1998 or 877/232-2448). They'll help set you up with a motel room, cottage, condo or home at this central reservation center for Fort Myers Beach. It's a great service and completely free.

Coastal Cuisine

A longtime local resident claims the biggest problem with restaurants in Fort Myers Beach is consistency—that is, getting the same quality with each visit. The one place we heard nary a negative word about in that department was **Charley Brown's** (6225 Estero Boulevard, 941/463-6660, $$$). From the outside, it looks like a nondescript old steak house, but inside it lightens up considerably with numerous saltwater aquariums and a garden atmosphere. Most important, the seafood is fresh, and the salad bar ranks among the best in these parts. Charley's has been in business for over 20 years, and though it's part of a national chain of no great distinction, this location is popular enough with locals that the parking lot is always full at dinnertime.

Snug Harbour (645 San Carlos Boulevard, 941/463-8077, $$) and the **Gulfshore** (1270 Estero Boulevard, 941/463-9551, $$) are two waterfront restaurants that also get thumbs-up for their fresh local seafood. The former is on the bayside, under Big Sky Bridge, and the latter overlooks the gulf. Each offers dinner specials for the value-conscious (check local papers for coupons). Snug Harbour has the added visual bonus of dolphins playing in the waters outside its windows. Finally, a raw bar, home-brewed beer, and seafood menu, can be found at **Smokin' Oyster Brewery** (340 Old San Carlos Boulevard, 941/463-3474, $$).

Night Moves

For those who dig draft beer and loud jukebox music, the Times Square area still earns its reputation for unbridled nighttime fun, though it seldom gets out of bounds any more. The most appealing places we ducked into were **Pete's Time Out** (1005 Estero Boulevard, 941/463-5900) and **Top O' Mast Lounge** (1028 Estero Boulevard, 941/463-9424). The latter appeared to attract the rowdiest clientele. To be perfectly honest, the **Tiki Bar** (Outrigger Beach Resort, 6200 Estero Boulevard, 941/463-3131) was more our speed, offering a friendly crowd at sunset. After the Tiki Bar shuts down post-sunset (around 7 P.M.), the **Junkanoo Beach Bar** (3040 Estero Boulevard, 941/463-2600) picks up the spillover and runs with the party concept until the wee hours. The Junkanoo even starts its "party that never ends" earlier, with a happy hour that begins at 2 P.M.!

It did not escape our notice that a large contingent of Europeans find Fort Myers Beach to their liking. This makes sense, as it's the most affordable place on the southwest coast. Germans flock here, a fact corroborated not only by the sizable German-American community in the town of Cape Coral to the north but also by a unique nightspot in Fort Myers Beach called **Dusseldorf's on the Beach** (1113 Estero Boulevard, 941/463-5251). It's a cozy *Biergarten* with over 120 imported beers, including eight on tap. Live polka music is offered Wednesday, Friday, and Saturday nights. Roll out the barrel!

Finally, though the toothless, tattooed Robinson Crusoes have been forbidden their wet T-shirt nights in Fort Myers Beach, the "normal people" have their very own playboy palace in **Hooters** (1600 Estero Boulevard, 941/463-6033). This restaurant chain, whose name is a double entendre for . . . well, you know . . . has built its reputation on attiring waitresses in confining T-shirts and skimpy shorts. If this tawdry titillation represents an improvement over the good old days, we'll eat a stuffed owl.

Contact Information

Fort Myers Beach Chamber of Commerce, 17200 San Carlos Boulevard, Fort Myers Beach, FL 33931; 941/454-7500 or 800/782-9283; website: www.fortmyersbeach.org

Bunch Beach

The county maintains an off-the-beaten-path bay beach to which few tourists find their way, while the road to it gets lined with locals' vehicles on weekends. Located on the mainland between Estero and Sanibel Islands, there's nothing more to **Bunch Beach** than a boat launch and a few trash cans that collect beer bottles and picnic remains. Sociable locals bring their dogs, boats, fishing poles, and volleyball nets, then set up and have a good time. If this sounds like a recipe for trouble, a county park official claims, "We've never had any problems or complaints." It's not the kind of beach you'd go out of your way to see, but if you live in the area, it's a viable alternative to the parking problems in Fort Myers Beach and the toll bridge over to Sanibel Island. It is also allegedly a gay gathering place at the south end.

8 Bunch Beach

Location: from Fort Myers Beach, proceed north on San Carlos Road (County Road 865), then west on Summerlin Road (County Road 869); turn south on John Morris Road and follow to beach
Parking/fees: free parking lot
Hours: 8 A.M. to sunset
Facilities: none
Contact: Lee County Department of Parks and Recreation, 941/461-7400

Sanibel Island

If American beaches were awarded the equivalent of Oscars, Sanibel Island's mantel would be lined with gold statuettes in the following categories: Best Beach for Shelling, Most Sensibly Developed Beach, and Best Supporting Estuary. It would also be nominated for Best Special Effects (those sunsets!) and Best Soundtrack. In addition to bird and nature sounds, the latter would surely include what would seem to be the Sanibel natives' theme song, Billy Joel's "I Love You Just the Way You Are."

The reason for Sanibel Island's success is that the beach, island, and back bay are given starring roles, and human intruders in the natural environment are relegated to the status of extras who have been respectfully directed to maintain a low profile. In practical terms, what this means is that you enter the island via a series of causeways, leaving the bustling mainland world of Fort Myers behind. Once on the island, you're in a kind of Emersonian paradise where nature rules—or is at least treated as an equal—and restaurants, stores, and strip malls occupy buildings that blend in with rather than obliterate the environment. There are no garish signs lunging for the consumer jugular. Development has been held in check on Sanibel Island (pop. 6,000) through a series of ordinances and regulations that limit building heights (three stories maximum) and impose minimum setbacks from the water's edge. We were told that you have to jump through more hoops than a circus tiger to get building permits. They like to refer to themselves as the "anti–Miami Beach."

All of this oversight is still not enough, some of Sanibel's hard-liners will tell you. One of them put it like this: "If you saw what Sanibel Island looked like 20 years ago compared with the way it is today, you'd say it's gone to hell in a handbag. At the same time, when you look at the rest of Florida's coastline, it seems like a fairly idyllic place to be." Indeed, it is. In addition to being built low to the ground, which gives the trees a distinct height advantage, the island has been outfitted with 25 miles of bike trails—asphalt pathways for cyclists, skaters, joggers, and walkers that parallel the main roads. A free trolley system and cheap bike rentals mean you can put the car keys away once you've parked at a hotel or rental property. This can be a real boon to those visiting during the high season, from Christmas to Easter, when roads get choked to capacity with residents, vacationers, and daytripping inlanders.

Sanibel's first line of defense against traffic is its toll bridge. As motorists approach the island via the Sanibel Causeway, they stop to pay a $3 toll before crossing the first of three bridges. Even though the bridges have long since been paid for, the toll is still levied to minimize the number of cars crowding onto the island. Think of it as a cover charge, but instead of getting into a nightclub, you're allowed onto an island. Many who live here believe that $3 is not enough to staunch the flow of traffic, so there is always talk of raising it. However, the bridge toll remains $3, as it has since it first opened. Incidentally, annual or semi-annual stickers that greatly reduce the tariff are obtainable. Even if you're only on Sanibel/Captiva for a few weeks, this can be a

Damn That Traffic Jam

We found ourselves caught in the mother of all traffic jams while trying to leave Sanibel Island one balmy December afternoon. The period between Thanksgiving and Christmas is one of the slowest times of year for tourism in South Florida. However, we encountered what seemed to us like substantial traffic everywhere we went during this alleged lull in the action. Nevertheless, this would-be down time is when they undertake road repairs in South Florida, and the toll bridge to Sanibel was being worked on. This construction project left only one lane open and caused huge backups in both directions. No sooner had we braked to a halt near the rear of a two-mile line of traffic when there came a sickening series of screeches and thuds, followed by a billowing cloud of blue-gray smoke about a 100 yards behind us.

A speeding lawn-care truck full of chattering, preoccupied workers had rounded a curve and come upon the line of stalled vehicles too late to avoid a collision. Five cars were crushed like accordions and seven people sent to the hospital (none injured very seriously). If we'd left the island two minutes later, we would surely have been among the parties with physical injuries and wrecked cars. To make a bad situation worse, emergency rescue vehicles were slow in getting to the scene because of the tie-up in both directions. It made us think.

Specifically, it made us think that the almighty automobile—guzzler of non-renewable fossil fuel, polluter of the air we breathe, destroyer of the ozone layer, and veritable daily death trap in overcrowded South Florida—is an almighty headache for which radical, progressive alternatives are needed. If you're planning on coming to South Florida during the high season—roughly Christmas through Easter—be aware that traffic does crawl and accidents are commonplace. There's got to be a better way.

End of sermon, and thank God we're still around to deliver it.

MAP OF LEE COUNTY—PAGE 364

cost-effective purchase. (Call the LeeWay Service Center at 941/931-0100 for more information.)

Sanibel's history, at least that part of it preceding its bridging to the mainland, makes a relatively short story. First, there were Calusa Indians, dating back to around 500 B.C.; then came Spanish conquistadors in the 1500s. Homesteaders farmed tomatoes, citrus, and coconuts in the 1800s. The Sanibel Lighthouse was built in 1884 to ensure safe passage around the island to mainland ports. Ferries brought the well-to-do onto the island enclave from the 1920s onward, including such luminaries as President Theodore Roosevelt and the Lindberghs. One regular visitor, political cartoonist Jay "Ding" Darling—who displayed an uncommonly activist environmental awareness in his work for the time—argued for the island's preservation. A 5,000-acre national wildlife refuge on the island's north side bears his name in recognition of his farsighted efforts (see sidebar, page 380).

The developmental floodgates opened when the three-mile causeway connecting Sanibel to the mainland opened in 1963. However, the island's slow-growth, preservationist philosophy was already in place, and the worst environmental affronts have been held at bay, so to speak. About half the island's acreage is wildlife preserve. Showy hibiscus, feathery casuarinas, swaying coconut palms, and fragrant citrus blossoms are more visible features of the Sanibel landscape than the semi-hidden shopping centers along Periwinkle Way. Environmental blight is less a concern on Sanibel Island than traffic tie-ups. If you can minimize your use of the automobile—getting around on bicycles, trolleys, your own two feet, or just staying on property—your visit to Sanibel Island will be considerably more enjoyable. Learning to chill out on this warm subtropical island is the key.

Here's the lay of the land. Exiting the causeway, you'll find a chamber of commerce stocked with the latest literature and helpful attendants in a houselike setting on your immediate right. The causeway road soon meets Periwinkle Way, where most of the island's restaurants and shopping centers are located. A left turn carries traffic out to the island's quiet east end, home to the Sanibel Lighthouse, Lighthouse Beach Park, and a T-shaped public pier. Turn right and you'll enter the bustling commercial heart of Sanibel Island. Periwinkle Way ends at Tarpon Bay Road. A left turn on Tarpon Bay Road will lead you to Gulf Drive, whose "East," "West," and "Middle" portions delineate the island's beach-facing south side. This is

9 Causeway Islands

Location: along Sanibel Causeway (State Route 867) between the mainland and Sanibel Island
Parking/fees: free parking lots
Hours: sunrise to sunset
Facilities: restrooms, picnic tables, and showers
Contact: City of Sanibel Parks and Recreation Department, 941/472-9075

10 Dixie Beach

Location: On Sanibel Island, follow Periwinkle Way to Lindrin Road, turn right and continue for three miles to Dixie Beach Road. Turn right and follow for one mile to beach.
Parking/fees: A (resident) or B (nonresident) parking permit required; these can be purchased at the Sanibel Police Department
Hours: sunrise to sunset
Facilities: picnic tables
Contact: City of Sanibel Parks and Recreation Department, 941/472-9075

where most of the hotels, motels, resorts, and rental properties are located. If you turn right on Tarpon Bay Road from Periwinkle Way, it soon hooks up with Sanibel-Captiva Road ("San-Cap," in local shorthand), which runs along the bay side of the island. It leads out to J.N. "Ding" Darling National Wildlife Refuge and over to Captiva Island. On our latest visit, Sanibel and Captiva Islands appear to have been joined with the closing of the pass between them.

Our final words of wisdom regarding the Sanibel-Captiva experience are these: take it easy and let nature do all the heavy lifting.

Beaches

The lovely beaches of Sanibel Island run for 14 miles along its south face. Shelling is one of the biggest draws to Sanibel's beaches, with solitude on a well-preserved island finishing a close second. Sanibel has been deemed the best site for shell collecting in America and third best in the world (see "Seashellology 101," pages 382–383). The endless piles of shells washing ashore leads to a sort of Catch-22. The preponderance of shelly material—from wholly preserved specimens to jagged shell fragments—makes walking barefoot on the beach uncomfortable. But if you wear shoes, you'll wind up crushing precious little shells with every step. The solution is to buy a pair of soft-soled, slipper-type "shelling shoes," which are perfect for strolling Sanibel's shelly beaches.

Sunset on Sanibel Island is observed with less ritual than on Key West. People informally assemble on the beach. Some congregate up at the east end of Captiva Island, just over the bridge from Sanibel. There are no performing freaks cadging spare change and nothing to divert your attention from the solar spectacle as it unfolds over the gulf. Shore birds turn out to observe the setting sun, too. They line up at the surf's edge, long lines of them, staring out to the horizon as the sun slips into the gulf. Sundown colors the sky with fiery corals and electric blue-greens—a solar signature unique to the skies of South Florida. It's enough to make a nature-attuned soul weak in the knees.

If you're booked at any of the hotels or resorts along Gulf Drive, you will have instant backdoor beach access. If not, there are four public beaches scattered along Sanibel Island's gulf side. They generally get better, in terms of beach quality and isolation, from east to west. At the eastern tip is **Lighthouse Beach Park,** home of the still-operative Sanibel Lighthouse (a.k.a. Point Ybel Light), a refurbished concrete pier and Lighthouse Beach. The city of Sanibel is currently negotiating with the U.S. Coast Guard to acquire the light-

⓫ Lighthouse Beach Park

Location: east end of Periwinkle Way at the tip of Sanibel Island
Parking/fees: metered parking lot
Hours: sunrise to sunset
Facilities: concessions, restrooms, and picnic tables
Contact: City of Sanibel Parks and Recreation Department, 941/472-9075

⓬ Gulfside City Park (a.k.a. Algiers Beach)

Location: from Sanibel Island, take Periwinkle Way to Casa Ybel Road; follow to Algiers and turn south till it ends at Middle Gulf Drive
Parking/fees: metered parking lot
Hours: sunrise to sunset
Facilities: restrooms and picnic tables
Contact: City of Sanibel Parks and Recreation Department, 941/472-9075

J.N. "Ding" Darling National Wildlife Refuge

The natural centerpiece of Sanibel Island is the J.N. "Ding" Darling National Wildlife Refuge (hereafter referred to as "Ding Darling"), more than 6,000 acres of wet and wild acres of open water, mangrove swamps, and brackish and freshwater marshes. The animal life seems positively giddy to have so much pristine habitat. They squawk and shout their approval all over the refuge till you think you've landed in nature's equivalent of a loony bin. But that's nature in the raw: howling, ecstatic, exclamatory. There's a lot of it on display at Ding Darling.

Ironically, the entire habitat was nearly destroyed by reckless human uses during the nineteenth century and the first half of the twentieth. Restoration began with its establishment as a refuge in 1945. It was named after political cartoonist Jay Norwood "Ding" Darling, an early environmentalist who assailed human misuse and overconsumption, and was specifically interested in this island's preservation.

Facilities on the refuge include a visitor center, a boardwalk trail, two observation towers, alligator-viewing platforms, a canoe trail, and a five-mile wildlife drive. The latter can be driven, biked, hiked, or toured via tram. (Tram tours leave at 10:30 A.M. and 2:00 P.M. every day but Friday; they cost $8 and take two hours.) We came on rented bikes, taking the dirt loop slowly so as to savor every sighting. Early morning and late afternoon are prime times for wildlife sightings (and the light's optimum for photography, too). Some 291 bird species have been inventoried on the refuge. We saw long-necked black anhingas and pink-feathered roeseate spoonbills. We saw graceful white egrets and ibises stalking the shal-

house. Currents at this end of the island are strong, so it's not the best beach for swimming, and the lack of lifeguarding means it's particularly ill advised to bring children here.

The mid-island beach parks, **Gulfside City Park** and **Tarpon Bay Road Beach** are more conveniently situated. The latter is large, busy, and popular, and its size makes it the likeliest spot to nab a parking space. Up at the west end is **Bowman's Beach**, the most remote of the public beaches. It is also the best for shell-collecting and sunset-watching. The beach is impressively wide along the accreting spit at Sanibel's west end, so you're in for an altogether pleasant hike of about a quarter-mile from the parking lot to the gulf. En route, you'll see a lot of nature: birds plummeting for dinner or staring at the gulf, plus tropical plantings. You'll walk through zones of beach grasses and shrubs, pines, wetlands, a canal, picnic tables shaded by sea grapes and pines, and finally the open beach. The sand is soft and

13 Tarpon Bay Road Beach

Location: Tarpon Bay Road at West Gulf Drive on Sanibel Island
Hours: sunrise to sunset
Parking/fees: metered parking lot
Facilities: restrooms and picnic tables
Contact: City of Sanibel Parks and Recreation Department, 941/472-9075

MAP OF FLORIDA'S WEST COAST—PAGE 347

lows on spindly legs. We saw a red-shouldered hawk peering down pensively from a snag. We saw, and we saw, and we saw, and you should, too.

We also paddled the refuge. The concessionaire for equipment rentals and guided tours at Ding Darling is **Tarpon Bay Recreation** (900 Tarpon Bay Road, 941/472-8900), an excellent one-stop outfitter of bikes, canoes, kayaks, and fishing equipment. They're open 8 A.M.–5 P.M. daily in season (8 A.M.–4 P.M. in summer). You can rent a kayak or canoe and explore the refuge on your own or take a guided tour. These include a 10:30 A.M. trail tour and a 4:15 P.M. birding trip that returns at sunset.

We took the two-hour trail tour along a tidal creek ($25 for adults, $12.50 for kids under 12), learning along the way about the estuarine ecosystem from our informed naturalist guide. We were admittedly novices, insofar as paddling two-man kayaks is concerned. There was a little confusion on our part about how to negotiate turns. The oarsman in the rear is supposed to back-paddle on one side while the one up front rows forward from the other. Instead, we both furiously paddled forward—from the left side if we wanted to turn right, and from the right if we wanted to turn left. All this did was accelerate our kayak as we crashed into mangrove prop roots, embankments, oyster reefs, and whatever other obstructions lay in our path. In the end, though, we proved that brute force can sometimes trump finesse. Heaving, rowing, and grunting with all our might, we came from the back of the pack, beating a German couple by a hair to become the first boat ashore. We climbed out of our boats, exultant, victorious, and wet as manatees, much to the amusement of our guide. All in a day's play.

Admission onto the refuge is $5 per vehicle. A site-specific pass costing $12 is good for admission into Ding Darling for a whole year. For $15, you can purchase a Duck Stamp that's good for entry into any National Wildlife Refuge from July 1 through the following June 30.

For more information, contact J.N. "Ding" Darling National Wildlife Refuge, 1 Wildlife Drive, Sanibel, FL 33957; 941/472-1100; website: www.dingdarling.fws.gov.

fine until you near the surf zone, where the sloping sand is full of shell fragment and whole shells. Parking at all four gulf beaches is 75 cents an hour, which is inserted in a machine that issues a sticker that must be displayed on the vehicle's dashboard. Enforcement personnel are on the premises and you will be ticketed if your time expires. Trust us on this point: we saw the traffic cops lying in wait for those who neglected to pay up. It's very much worth it, as Bowman's Beach is among the top beaches in Florida.

A few more notes about Sanibel beaches. There's one bay beach on the north shore called **Dixie Beach,** which lies at the end of Dixie Beach Road, off Periwinkle Way. It's a bayside beach in the middle of a subdivision that's used mainly by residents. There's not much beach area and not much reason to come here. Also, beachside parks—complete with restrooms, picnic tables, and showers—are found on the **Causeway Islands** (two

 Bowman's Beach

Location: from Sanibel Island, proceed north on Sanibel-Captiva Road to Bowman's Beach Road, then turn south and follow to beach.
Parking/fees: metered parking lot
Hours: sunrise to sunset
Facilities: restrooms, picnic tables, and showers
Contact: City of Sanibel Parks and Recreation Department, 941/472-9075

small islands crossed en route to Sanibel). Windsurfers and anglers flock to these palm-shaded islands.

Shore Things

- **Bike/skate rentals:** Bikes, Boats and Beach Stuff, 1711 Periwinkle Way, 941/472-2169 and 2427 Periwinkle Way, 941/472-8717; Finnimore's Cycle Shop, 2353 Periwinkle Way, 941/472-5577.
- **Boat cruise:** Sanibel Island Cruise Line, 941/472-5799; Captiva Cruises, 941/472-5300.
- **Ecotourism:** Tarpon Bay Recreation, 900 Tarpon Bay Road, 941/472-8900.
- **Fishing charters:** Santiva Saltwater Fishing Team, 6211 Starling Way, 941/472-4701.
- **Lighthouse:** Sanibel Lighthouse, Lighthouse Park, Periwinkle Way (east end).
- **Marina:** Sanibel Marina, 634 North Yachtsman Drive, 941/472-2531.
- **Pier:** Sanibel Pier, Lighthouse Beach Park, Periwinkle Way (east end).
- **Rainy-day attraction:** Bailey-Matthews Shell Museum, 3075 Sanibel-Captiva Road, 941/395-2233; Sanibel Historical Museum, 950 Dunlop Road, 941/472-4648.
- **Shopping/browsing:** Bailey's Shopping Center, Periwinkle Way at Tarpon Bay Road, 941/472-1516.
- **Surf shop:** Yolo Surf Shop, 11534 Andy Rosse Lane, Captiva, 941/472-1296.
- **Vacation rentals:** Reservation Central, 695 Tarpon Bay Road, Suite 1, 941/395-3682 and 800/290-6920.

Seashellology 101

Sanibel and its neighboring islands (Captiva, North Captiva, Cayo Costa) are recognized as the best locale for shell collecting in the United States. That is no idle hype spun by an overeager chamber of commerce. Shells wash ashore on these islands in incomprehensible mounds that accumulate on the beach, causing otherwise sane people to walk around for hours in a hunched-over position known as the "Sanibel stoop." The reason is that Sanibel, instead of paralleling the mainland as most barrier islands do, extends outward in a perpendicular direction, acting as a scoop to haul in a bounty of shells. In addition, the absence of inshore reefs allows shells to roll in with the tides.

Shells are deposited by waves and tide in parallel strips, with each one representing a different scenario in the unending physical dialogue between land and water. There are bands for the most recent high and low tides. They're also at the mean high tide line, at lines marking spring tides (occurring when the sun and moon line up, reinforcing each other's tidal pull), and at the very back of the beach, where storm surges occasionally penetrate. It's easier to walk between bands than on them, although these shell heaps serve as convenient benches for watching the sunset.

Seashells are the calcified homes of soft-bodied mollusks, which secrete a liquid that hardens around them. Some 275 shell types wash ashore on Sanibel Island. Some common finds include lightning whelks, the Florida horse conch (the state shell), cockles, coquinas, cones, pens, olives, augurs, tulip mussels, top shells, scallops, and sand dollars. A few harder-to-

FLORIDA'S WEST COAST

Bunking Down

Hotels and resorts line Gulf Drive. They're a decided cut above what you'll generally find at the beach, even though they don't tower over the beach, as is typically the case. The feeling is Old Florida personified, recalling a more placid era when people would take their ease at beach cottages, bungalows, and motor courts that existed in humble concert with the environment.

There are any number of choices on Sanibel's resort row, from brand names like **Best Western** (3287 West Gulf Drive, 941/472-1700, $$$$) and **Holiday Inn** (1231 Middle Gulf Drive, 941/472-4123, $$$$) to non-franchised charmers that draw a loyal, long-term clientele, such as **Song of the Sea** (863 East Gulf Drive, 941/472-2200, $$$$) and the congenial, long-lived **Island Inn** (3111 West Gulf Drive, 941/472-1561, $$$$), which celebrated its centennial in 1995. Paradise doesn't come cheaply, and rates at the above-mentioned resorts generally begin at $180 a night in season (and drop by about a third out of season).

A favorite of ours is the **West Wind Inn** (3345 West Gulf Drive, 941/472-1541, $$$$). For one thing, it has a great location, being the westernmost beachside lodge on Sanibel Island. Up at this quiet, unhurried end of Sanibel, birds greatly outnumber beachcombers. The comfortable, decorous rooms at the West Wind have sliding glass doors that face a heated pool in the center courtyard. Also on premises: Billy's Bikes, a bike- and boat-rental operation, and the Normandie, a decent restaurant. The island trolley stops here, too. The best perk of all is the proximity to the beach, just steps away down a short path. This is truly a place to relax and kick back. However much stress

find ones are the Sanibel drillia, yellow Florida spiny jewel boxes, and a few kinds of tellins, one found in sand (great tellin), another on mudflats (rose petal tellin). The brass ring for Sanibel shell collectors is the lovely, speckled junonia, which is very rare—so much so, in fact, that whoever finds one gets his or her picture in the local paper.

Given Sanibel's seashell obsession, it's fitting that the only museum in the United States devoted exclusively to shells of the world is on the island. Nearly a third of the 10,000 kinds of shells that have been identified worldwide are on display at the **Bailey-Matthews Shell Museum** (3075 Sanibel-Captiva Road, 941/395-2233), which opened in 1995. If you want to learn all there is to know about shells and their habitat, the museum is open 10 A.M.–4 P.M., Tuesday through Sunday. Admission is $5 for adults, $3 for children 8–16, and free for kids under eight.

If you do go shell-collecting on Sanibel or the adjacent islands, never, but never, take a live specimen. If the shell moves, however slowly, or if it appears to be occupied, leave it alone. Here is the official Sheller's Code, presumably to be repeated with one hand over your heart while the other holds a conch shell aloft:

"We realize that mollusks are part of our precious national wildlife resources, therefore

1. We will make every effort to protect and preserve them, not only for our own future enjoyment but for the benefit of generations to come;
2. We will leave every shelling spot as undisturbed as possible;
3. We will leave behind damaged and juvenile specimens so that they will live to multiply;
4. We will not collect live egg cases unless they are to be used for scientific study;
5. We will never 'clean out' a colony of shells;
6. We will practice and promote these conservation rules in every way possible."

you've brought to Sanibel Island, it will begin exiting your pores as soon as you check in and especially if you minimize your use of the automobile.

Coastal Cuisine

McT's Shrimp House (1523 Periwinkle Way, 941/472-3161, $$$) is a bit of a misnomer. Sure, they have shrimp, but the extensive menu also includes artful preparations of locally caught grouper, snapper, and mahimahi. There's steamed and Cajun-style gulf shrimp (doused in a peppery sauce) or steamed rock shrimp. If you're undecided and have a large appetite, order an all-you-can-eat platter of all three. The rock shrimp have a spiny shell and are best dipped in melted butter. The seafood is on display for all to see behind the counter at the front of the restaurant. Even if it weren't, McT's does such a steady business that the constant turnover guarantees freshness. For dessert, try the Famous Sanibel Mud Pie (Oreos, fudge, ice cream, and more piled on in decadent layers); just make sure there's a gastroenterologist available on short notice.

Another popular seafood outlet is the **Timbers Restaurant & Fish Market** (703 Tarpon Bay Rd., 941/473-3128, $$), a perennial winner in local "Best Seafood" polls ("Best Steak" polls, too). Canvas umbrellas, nautical artifacts, and murals make the large, ski lodge–like dining area seem more intimate. The house specialty is "crunchy grouper" and "crunchy shrimp," a tasty preparation that involves rolling the seafood in crushed cereal crumbs. Fresh catch can be prepared to your specs, too, though chargrilled or broiled with garlic butter sounds simplest and best to us. The Timbers serves only dinner, but a fish market on the premises opens daily at noon.

Another Sanibel Island favorite is the **Lazy Flamingo** (1036 Periwinkle Way, 941/472-6939, $$), an unfancy eatery popular with locals and tourists alike. They have a good raw bar that turns out fresh, ice-cold oysters on the half shell. They also smoke fish. Our lunchtime appetizer of smoked mahimahi, rolled in blackening spices and accompanied by cocktail sauce and crackers, was first rate. They do good things with grouper, too. The **Jacaranda** (1223 Periwinkle Way, 941/472-1771, $$$) specializes in Sanibel seafood in an alfresco setting (live entertainment nightly, too).

Night Moves

We went looking for some action on Sanibel, albeit halfheartedly, reserving our energy for an early morning kayaking adventure on the waters of Ding Darling National Wildlife Refuge. Even on a Monday night at the height of the NFL season, only a handful of Sanibel Island stragglers bothered to take advantage of the "Monday night madness" that turns so many sports bars into raving palaces of beer foam, hot wings, and hooting, high-fiving maniacs. A lot of the restaurants and resorts have bars on the premises, including **Crocodial's** [*sic*] **Pool Bar** (Sundial Resort, 1451 Middle Gulf Drive, 941/472-4151) and **Delfini's Pool Bar** (Sanibel Inn, 937 East Gulf Drive, 941/472-3181). But the ones most often cited for pub-crawlers are **Lazy Flamingo I** (6520 Pine Avenue, 941/472-5353); **Lazy Flamingo II** (1036 Periwinkle Way, 941/472-6939); and **McT's Tavern** (1523 Periwinkle Way, 941/472-3161).

For more sophisticated tastes, Sanibel is home to two theatrical venues. The Pirate Playhouse Company offers seasonal productions at the **J. Howard Wood Theatre** (2200 Periwinkle Way, 941/472-0006). Resident professional performers at the **Old Schoolhouse Theater** (1905 Periwinkle Way, 941/472-6862) offer a regular choice of musical theatre and comedy, including a musical version of *Dracula*.

Contact Information

Sanibel-Captiva Islands Chamber of Commerce, 1159 Causeway Road, P.O. Box 166, Sanibel, FL 33957; 941/472-1080; website: www.sanibel-captiva.org

MAP OF FLORIDA'S WEST COAST—PAGE 347

Sanibel-Captiva Conservation Foundation

The preservation of open space is fast becoming a nationwide concern as suburban sprawl and real-estate speculation shortsightedly gobble tract after tract of land along the outer fringes of every American community. In Florida, the land-grab capital of the world, the issue is more pressing, as the state must balance its need to accommodate a nonstop swarm of visitors and the desire on the part of those who live here to keep their towns from becoming the next Miami or Marco Island.

On Sanibel and the Captiva Islands, the mission to preserve land has reached nearly religious dimensions. Not only does this reflect the progressive bent of the locals, but it's the imperative and commonsensical desire of area merchants, too. That is, people come to these parts—and, frankly, pay the extra tariff—precisely because the landscape has been kept as natural and uncluttered as is possible, and because they're sick of all the other once lovely beach communities that don't share this view.

While it's not true that economic and environmental needs can always be met, they converge as snugly as is possible on Sanibel and the Captivas. Much of the credit for that goes to farsighted organizations like the Sanibel-Captiva Conservation Foundation. Since its inception in the wake of the rampant real-estate speculation and overbuilding of the Reagan era, the foundation has secured over 1,500 acres.

The foundation doesn't just acquire land, either. They clear it of invasive and non-indigenous plants, allowing native vegetation to fill the gaps. This new habitat provides food, shelter, and room to roam for native species of birds, mammals, insects, and marine life. The most crucial project undertaken by the foundation is the securing of the Sanibel River, which is fed only by rain and allows the island to attract a much more diverse assortment of wildlife than most barrier islands (including the Captivas).

The work of the foundation is subtle, but it's there if you know what to look for. For a quick environmental education, drop by the foundation's Nature Center on Sanibel-Captiva Road. Admission is $3 for adults and free for kids under 17. On the premises are four miles of self-guided hiking trails, educational exhibits, a butterfly house, a nature shop, and a native plant nursery. Guided walks (including beach walks), boat trips, programs, and activities are conducted. If you like what you see, become a member and donate some money to the land acquisition fund. That way you can return to the islands knowing you had some hand in their preservation.

For more information, contact Sanibel-Captiva Conservation Foundation, 3333 Sanibel-Captiva Road, Sanibel, FL 33957; 941/472-2329; website: www.sccf.org.

Captiva Island

There are few nicer fates in the world than to be held captive on Captiva Island or be stranded on North Captiva Island. They are both slender, sparsely populated, and densely wooded barrier islands that assume a sudden south-to-north trajectory off the west coast of the better-known Sanibel Island. All three islands are part of the Charlotte Barrier Chain, which has historically ranged between five and eight islands, depending on how many passes have opened or closed. Captiva is six miles long and North Captiva, four and a half. Both are covered with an icing of beach that runs along their west coasts.

Captiva Island (pop. 300) is connected via bridge from Sanibel Island, while North Captiva can only be reached by boat or small airplane. The two Captivas were carved from one in 1926, when a hurricane split them. The name "Captiva" is alleged to have derived from pirate Jose Gaspar, who would hold wealthy young women for ransom on then undivided La Isla de Las Cautivas ("the island of captive women"). Once you've crossed the bridge onto Captiva, you'll drive for a few miles before any sort of human habitation becomes evident. Homes and rental villas are scattered among the sea grape, palm, and oak trees, but they are all but invisible from the road. You'll want to keep both hands on the wheel because the road on Captiva has some hairpin turns.

After a couple of days on any of these islands—Sanibel and the two Captivas—you will be asking yourself why wherever it is you come from can't be this intelligently planned, zoned, and respectful of nature. The reacquaintance with nature and reverence for solitude are the greatest gifts these islands bestow on visitors. When one returns home, the first impulse is to join a local land trust and begin haunting town meetings. No more Marco Islands!

Captiva Island offers all kinds of noncommercial activities for the family. Biking is the biggie, and that is understandable since the highest elevation on any of the islands is 14 feet. Be careful, especially along Captiva's curves. Beach bikes and more can be rented at **Jim's Rentals** (11534 Andy Rosse Lane, 941/472-1296). The teeming waters of Pine Island Sound Aquatic Preserve can be explored by kayak via **Wildside Adventures** (11401 Andy Rosse Lane, 941/395-2925), at McCarthy's Marina. This full-service outlet offers guided natural history and sea-life tours, as well as kayak rentals for do-it-yourselfers. Finally, for a mellower time, the **Captiva Memorial Library** (11560 Chapin Lane, 941/472-2133) is worth a visit, not just for the collections—lots of books on shells, birds, wildlife, conservation, and Floridiana—but also for its proximity to the **Chapel by the Sea** (11580 Chapin Lane, 941/472-1646). This ancient landmark and its lovely cemetery are inspiring reminders of the early inhabitants of the island. Both lie at the end of Wiles Road.

Beaches

A continuous beach runs the six-mile length of Captiva's west coast, with public access points dispersed along its length. Because the beach runs south to north, subtle differences in shell and sand distribution and wave formation distinguish it from the beaches along Sanibel, which lies on an east-west axis. For one thing, the surf is rougher and wavier on Captiva, and at the south end, near Blind Pass, swimming is discouraged due to a nasty undertow. The beach on Captiva has, in fact, been worn down by strong currents, and in recent years the local government has spent $3 million dumping sand on it, an expensive process euphemistically referred to as "beach renourishment."

To enjoy Captiva's beach, it helps to get

MAP OF FLORIDA'S WEST COAST—PAGE 347

here early in the day in order to claim one of the limited parking spaces. The first beach access, **Turner Beach**, is located just over the bridge from Sanibel. On our most recent visit, Blind Pass, the inlet between the islands, had shoaled up completely, temporarily making one island of Sanibel and Captiva. Storms may well open the pass again. A tiny dirt lot allows access to the beach and inlet. There's great fishing by the bridge and sunset-watching on the beach, but strong currents make swimming hazardous. Restrooms are provided, but that's all.

There are several other beach accesses in town, but these are right of ways only for pedestrians, and no parking is provided. For instance, at the end of Andy Rosse Lane, beside the popular Mucky Duck pub and restaurant, you can walk out to the beach, but don't try leaving your car here. Signs warn, "Cars Will Be Towed" and "$32 Fine for Parking on Roadside."

At the north end of Captiva Road, left of where it dead-ends at the gate to South Seas Plantation, is **Captiva Beach**. This is the most popular access on the island (not that there's much competition), and the free lot has been enlarged to accommodate more vehicles. Still, it fills quickly, and out-of-luck day-trippers will find themselves heading back to Sanibel if they can't snag a spot here. Although this is in keeping with the islands' noble attempt to limit cars, it sometimes resembles an argument with a vegetarian who's wearing a leather belt and shoes when you consider that all of Captiva residents own and drive cars, too.

Regardless, Captiva's six-mile beach is a stunning place to spend a day or pass a week. The sand is wide and slightly grayer than Sanibel's, with a largely intact dune structure and small groves of trees that grow right up to the sand. The misty, unblemished vistas in either direction beg to be combed for shells or the timeless experience of wandering the wild setting, as we are wont to do. Since lifeguards are not provided, it's best to swim with a group or within sight of companions.

The 2.5 miles of beach at the north end of Captiva Island fall within the boundaries of the private South Seas Resort. However, anyone can legally roam the beach (below the mean high-tide line, that is) by walking up from public accesses south of here.

Captiva Island is part of a barrier-island chain that also includes Sanibel, North Captiva, Cayo Costa, Cabbage Key, and Gasparilla Islands. If you want to explore the less-developed outer islands, you can either rent a boat from a local marina or have them ferry you over and back. For instance, **Jensen's Twin Palms Marina** (15107 Captiva Drive, 941/472-5800) will take parties of up to six to North Captiva Island and back for $105. Call ahead for reservations and to arrange dropoff and

15 Turner Beach

Location: at Blind Pass, just over the bridge onto Captiva Island on gulf side
Parking/fees: metered parking lot
Hours: sunrise to sunset
Facilities: restrooms
Contact: City of Sanibel Parks and Recreation Department, 941/472-9075

16 Captiva Beach

Location: end of Captiva Drive on Captiva Island
Parking/fees: free parking lot
Hours: 8 A.M. to sunset
Facilities: restrooms
Contact: Lee County Department of Parks and Recreation, 941/461-7400

pickup times on the island. Jensen's also services Cayo Costa Island ($125 round-trip), Cabbage Key ($135 round-trip), and Gasparilla Island ($225 round-trip). They are located about three miles north of the Blind Pass bridge.

Bunking Down

You can solve the beach-access dilemma on Captiva's north half by staying at the **South Seas Resort and Yacht Harbor** (5400 Plantation Road, 941/472-5111, $$$$). This upper-crust establishment has a variety of accommodations—600 units in all—ranging from hotel rooms to two- and three-bedroom villas, and it covers the range of wants for the leisure set: 21 tennis courts, a nine-hole golf course, 18 swimming pools, planned activities, boat rentals, water sports, three restaurants, a cocktail lounge, and the aura of gated security. In peak season (February–April) a three-bedroom Seabreeze Villa goes for $670 a night. In the low season (June–September) a bayside hotel room goes for $100 a night. Price-wise, those are the extremes at South Seas Resort, and the off-season rate is a great bargain. Though it's not in our nature to lavish fulsome praise on high-end venues, we found South Seas Resort to be as congenial as they come, with very few add-ons to the bills and an attentive but not overly solicitous staff. In addition to the amenities above, a biking trail and nature center are on the property, and attempts have been made to remain as low-impact as possible (for one thing, no building is taller than two stories). It is also possible to book cruises to North Captiva and Cayo Costa Islands from the marina here.

As for less frilly lodgings, the best (and almost only) place is **'Tween Waters Inn** (P.O. Box 249, 941/472-5161, $$), located mid-island on Captiva Drive. It's on the beach, providing a great jumping-off spot to wander in either direction and sparing you parking headaches. As a bonus, it's home to the Old Captiva House, the island's award-winning continental restaurant. It also has the No-See-Um Lounge, named for the microscopic bugs that plague Southern climes. The 'Tween Waters Marina is also part of the complex.

Other than these two choices, cottage and villa rentals are the way to go for visits of a week or more. And why not? Captiva requires at least a week to get all the kinks out of your soul. Rentals may be made via any number of companies, including **Helen Thomas Realty** (P.O. Box 1090, Captiva, FL 33924, 941/472-6669). **Priscilla Murphy Realty** (1019 Periwinkle Way, Sanibel, FL 33957, 941/472-1511) is more centrally connected, covering Sanibel, Captiva, and Fort Myers Beach like a beach blanket. In general, weekly rentals range in summer from $500 for a cottage or duplex to $2,000 for a beachfront house with an occupancy of six. At winter's peak, prices rise to $1,000 for cottages/duplexes to $3,500 for beach homes.

Coastal Cuisine

It's a rule of thumb that the farther from the mainland one travels, the higher the cost of eating out. Captiva is no different. Using this metaphor as a yardstick, the restaurant farthest away is **Chadwick's** (5400 Plantation Road, 941/472-5111, $$$$), at the entrance to South Seas Plantation. Still, if one brings an appetite and a tolerance for lounge entertainment, Chadwick's offers a decent seafood buffet.

Captiva offers a number of casual lunch or dinner options, including the **Village Cafe** (14970 Captiva Drive, 941/472-1956, $$) and the **Green Flash** (15183 Captiva Drive, 941/472-3337, $$), so named for the last glint of sunset that occasionally flashes an eerie green glow on the horizon.

For a truly memorable dinner, head to the heart of Captiva, near the intersection of Andy Rosse Lane and Captiva Drive. Here, two intriguing places offer striking variations on the art of dining. The first is the **Captiva Art Cafe** (11506 Andy

Rosse Lane, 941/395-1142, $$$), which features Mediterranean cuisine (tapas, ensaladas) and fresh seafood (grouper, yellowfin tuna) amid a gallery of fine original artwork. The second restaurant is, well, second to none in the realm of wackiness. This is the **Bubble Room** (15001 Captiva Drive, 941/472-5558, $$$), a place that has to be seen to be believed. The servers are called "Bubble Scouts" and they sport Boy Scout uniforms and silly hats. The tables are actually museum display cases filled with nostalgic gewgaws (Monopoly game money, old records, baseball cards, shoelaces, water pistols). The walls are covered with enough quirky memorabilia to keep necks craning throughout a meal. Oh yes, the food: ample portions of local seafood, baskets of "Bubble Bread" and sticky buns, and the best desserts on the island. (Oddly, they won't allow you to come here just for dessert and coffee.) There's a special game menu and game room for the kids, who dig this place. That's the double-edged sword here: If your inner kittycat is not up to cuteness and kitsch beyond compare, then you may want to consider less kooky cuisine.

Night Moves

The Mucky Duck (11546 Andy Rosse Lane, 941/472-3434) is a pub-like place for after-dinner yucks. Though it's a restaurant, the fare is of the fish 'n' chips and Super Frankfurter variety. The main selling point is its assortment of sturdy draft beers (Bass, Harp, Guinness, John Courage, Pilsner Urquell) and the prime location (a dart's toss from the Gulf of Mexico). Alternatively, there's the **Crow's Nest Lounge** at the 'Tween Waters Inn (15951 Captiva Drive, 941/472-5161).

Contact Information

Sanibel-Captiva Islands Chamber of Commerce, P.O. Box 166, 1159 Causeway Road, Sanibel, FL 33957; 941/472-1080; website: www.sanibel-captiva.org

North Captiva Island

On North Captiva Island, habitation is limited to the north end, along Captiva Pass, the inlet separating it from Cabbage Key and Cayo Costa. The sheltered bay that sits in the crook of land to the east of the pass is called Safety Harbor. This is where passenger boats dock, and that is how most visitors arrive on **North Captiva Island.** If the logistics for spending a day here can be ironed out, visitors have four miles of wonderfully secluded beaches to wander. The state of Florida owns 350 acres of North Captiva, a mid-island parcel that runs from beach to bay. There's nothing out here for the public—no docks, no facilities of any kind—and they don't exactly encourage visitation. These North Captiva holdings are considered part of the Barrier Islands GEOpark, administered through Cayo Costa Island State Park.

Passenger service to North Captiva Island can be arranged through **Island Charters Water Transport** on Pine Island (Mattson Marine, Pineland Marina, 941/283-2008). Also North Captiva can

⑰ North Captiva Island

Location: between Captiva Island and Cayo Costa Island; accessible via private boat or passenger ferry from Captiva Island, Pine Island, and Boca Grande
Parking/fees: no parking or fees
Hours: 8 A.M. to sunset
Facilities: none
Contact: Cayo Costa Island State Park c/o Barrier Islands GEOpark, 941/964-0375

be accessed via a 10-minute boat or water-taxi ride from Captiva Island; contact local marinas for boat-rental or ferry fees.

Only 6,000 people a year set foot on North Captiva. There are cars, no hotels, and no grocery stores. There are, however, a handful of restaurants, and many of the private homes on the island are part of a "rental pool" administered by the North Captiva Island Club Resort. Hey, you could have a three-bedroom house on a semi-secluded, semi-tropical island paradise for $1,500 a week. You'd pay no less for a single room with two beds at a fancy hotel on the mainland.

Contact Information

North Captiva Island Club Resort, P.O. Box 1000, Pineland, FL 33945; 941/395-1001 or 800/576-7343

Cayo Costa Island State Park

Just above North Captiva Island is an unblemished jewel known as Cayo Costa Island. Measuring 7.5 miles long by one mile wide and accessible only by boat, **Cayo Costa Island State Park** is the least-visited park in the Florida State Park system. Owing to its seven miles of blindingly white and mostly deserted gulf beach, it has earned the nickname "Florida's Tahiti." While no naked women will swim out to greet your boat, the natural wonders of Cayo Costa more than compensate. These include acres of pine forest, oak-palm hammock, and mangrove swamps, plus abundant birdlife, including bald eagles in the spring. Hiking opportunities abound, both along the shore and on a nature trail in the wooded area. There are regular ranger-led turtle and shelling walks, as well as Calusa and Indian history talks. The island offers the best snorkeling and shelling in southwest Florida.

18 Cayo Costa Island State Park

Location: Between North Captiva Island and Gasparilla Island; accessible via private boat or passenger ferry from Captiva Island and Boca Grande

Parking/fees: $2 entrance fee per family, 50 cents per person fee to ride tram from bayside to gulfside. Fees for overnight stay are $13 per campsite and $20 per cabin, plus tax.

Hours: 8 A.M. to sunset

Facilities: restrooms, picnic tables, and showers

Contact: Cayo Costa Island State Park c/o Barrier Islands GEOpark, 941/964-0375

For those who plan ahead, cabins are available for rent ($20 per night), and primitive tent camping is also allowed ($13 per night), but only in a designated area at the north end of the island. There are 30 campsites and 12 cabins, and they book quickly. Reservations are accepted up to 11 months in advance. If you're planning on coming between Thanksgiving and Easter, book at least eight months ahead. Cabins sleep up to six. There's no electricity, and there are cold-water showers only; visitors must bring all necessary supplies. Restrooms, showers, and grills are provided.

The lure for most visitors, especially during the winter months, is the shelling, with over 400 species of shells found on the Cayo Costa beaches. The highest concentration is found at the northern tip of the island, along Johnson Shoals. Because shells are piled high and foot traffic is low, such hard-to-find species as murises, nautiluses, and spiny jewel boxes can be picked up in mint condition.

The state owns most of this island, which is accessible only by private boat and passenger ferry. Cayo Costa is served by ferries from seven locations: Pine Island, Boca Grande, Sanibel, Captiva, Punta Gorda, Fort Myers, and Burnt Store. (Yes, Burnt Store.) As an alternative, outlets on Sanibel and Captiva rent boats by the day. If you have a modest-sized party, an all-day motorboat rental is cheaper than a monitored group tour, and chances are the trip will be more exciting. The biggest boat rental outlet is **Port Sanibel Marina** (941/472-8443), on the Sanibel Causeway. The lowest rates (or so they claim) are at **Castaways Marina** (941/472-1112), on the Sanibel Island side of the bridge over Blind Pass. They also rent canoes and kayaks. These are especially good for exploring the nooks and crannies of the mangrove swamp on the bayside of Cayo Costa, which, conveniently, is where the island's dock is located. For a 50-cent charge, a tractor-pulled open-air tram spirits visitors across the island from bay to beach.

Contact Information

Cayo Costa Island State Park, c/o Barrier Islands GEOpark, P.O. Box 1150, Boca Grande, FL 33921; 941/964-0375; website: www.myflorida.com

Boca Grande

Boca Grande (pronounced "grand," with a silent "e") is like no other beach town in Florida. It is so casual, relaxed, and unpretentious that after one day spent walking its streets, lying out on its beaches, and talking to its natives, we felt as at ease here as we did in our hometowns. It's rare in communities with prime coastal real estate that the tenor of life is set by the townspeople and not the big-money barons whose projects are typically rubber-stamped by pliable, shortsighted commissioners' boards of governance (who typically work in real estate or business). But that's how it goes in Boca Grande, where Carl Sandburg's "The People, Yes!" could be the unofficial town poem.

Oh, sure, there are condo developments at the north end, where a small chunk of Gasparilla Island extends into Charlotte County, which is a horse of an entirely different color. But most of the town of Boca Grande, which occupies almost all of five-mile-long Gasparilla Island (named for pirate Jose Gaspar), manages to preserve an unhurried character that has been its calling card since the 1920s. The preferred mode of transportation among natives is golf carts, because they're quiet and easy to get around in. Back in the 1980s, the good folks of Boca Grande banded together and built a bike path that extends the length of the island. The "downtown" area of this narrow, five-block-wide community is not exactly bustling. It preserves the much-vaunted but rarely experienced Old Florida feel. Typical is the Temptation ("the Temp," for short), a down-home restaurant and unofficial community center that has been doing business on this spot for half a century.

In the words of a woman who's been living here since the '60s—talking with us while taking drags off a cigarette and watching the waves break from her golf cart—Boca Grande is "a sleepy little island" that changes slowly and incrementally. She also claims that its 1,700 residents are "one big happy family." Despite its history as a getaway for the wealthy—the usual suspects, including du Ponts, Astors, and Eastmans, who'd stay at the Gasparilla Inn and grow so charmed by the island that they'd build homes on it—not everyone who lives here is rich and retired. Boca Grande has something of the feel and look of a New England fishing village. For a glimpse at the town's back pages, check out two old yet still-functioning marinas—Whidden's and Miller's—at the south end of the island, on the bay near 1st Street.

The only real hassle worth complaining about in Boca Grande is the $3.50 bridge fee one must pay to enter the island. Built in 1958, the entrance bridges and the land at the north end were, until recently, privately owned by the Gaspar family. They were bought out a few years back, and the bridge is now maintained by the Gasparilla Bridge Authority. If $3.50 seems a lot to pay and you're making the trip with some frequency, discounted passes are available.

In the spring, this sleepy little community wakes up for an annual tarpon run. In fact, Boca Grande, which modestly eschews attention and accolades in every other way, proudly bills itself as the tarpon-fishing capital of the world. Fishing for 200-pound tarpon and golfing at the Gasparilla Inn are two reasons people with deep pockets come to Boca Grande, but we'd suggest a third incentive: peace and quiet.

Beaches

The sand on Gasparilla Island is powdery white, with mounds of coarse, shelly material here and there. The beach is relatively narrow and diminishes to nothing in those places where landowners (such as the town's several "beach clubs") have built seawalls, which prevent the beach's landward retreat.

Almost all of Boca Grande's public beaches—certainly all the ones worth seeing—are located at the bottom end of the island, where a discontinuous group of five accesses are collectively referred to as **Gasparilla Island State Park.** There's parking at each of the accesses, which extend from the island's tip to just south of the village. They are, from south to north, Lighthouse Beach, Dunes, Sea Wall, Sea Grape, and Sand Spur. Of the latter four, **Sand Spur Beach** offers the most in the way of parking and facilities: restrooms and picnic tables, plus the most swimmable of Gasparilla Island's beaches.

The most interesting vantage point is

19 Lighthouse Beach Park

Location: south end of Gasparilla Island, at Boca Grande Lighthouse
Parking/fees: $2 per vehicle parking fee
Hours: 8 A.M. to sunset
Facilities: restrooms, picnic tables, and a visitor center
Contact: Barrier Islands GEOpark, 941/964-0375

20 Gasparilla Island State Park

Location: three parking areas (Dunes, Sea Wall, Sea Grape) along Gulf Boulevard on the southern end of Gasparilla Island
Parking/fees: $2 per vehicle parking fee
Hours: 8 A.M. to sunset
Facilities: restrooms
Contact: Barrier Islands GEOpark, 941/964-0375

21 Sand Spur Beach

Location: Gulf Boulevard between Wheeler and 1st Streets in Boca Grande
Parking/fees: $2 per vehicle parking fee
Hours: 8 A.M. to sunset
Facilities: picnic tables and restrooms
Contact: Barrier Islands GEOpark, 941/964-0375

MAP OF FLORIDA'S WEST COAST—PAGE 347

Lighthouse Beach Park, which looks across Boca Grande Pass to Cayo Costa Island. The pass is the main inlet into the bay, and tarpon use it as an expressway to blue crabs, upon which they feast and fatten themselves in the spring and summer. En route to their waiting smorgasbord in seafood-rich Charlotte Harbor, these glittering silver wonders are snatched from the waters of the pass by anglers looking to hook a trophy. The "world's richest" tarpon tournament is held each July. (Call the Boca Grande Chamber of Commerce for dates and entrance fees.) Fortunately, the vast majority of hooked tarpon are released, causing only stressful delays and not death to the fighting fish.

Also at this southernmost beach are the 1890 Boca Grande Lighthouse, some huge oil-storage tanks, and a clump of old Coast Guard buildings that now serve as headquarters for the Barrier Islands GEOpark, a collection of island parks managed by the state, including Cayo Costa, Gasparilla Island and Don Pedro Island state parks. The oldest building on Gasparilla Island, the lighthouse still serves as a U.S. Coast Guard light and as a museum of local history (open Wednesday through Saturday 10 A.M.–4 P.M.). Surfcasting by the lighthouse is good, judging from the five-pound grouper we saw a screaming woman reel in seconds after casting her line. Swimming, though, is hazardous because of strong currents through the pass. We heard the unutterably sad story of children who drowned here when their parents weren't looking. As a general rule, inlets are not good or safe places for swimming.

In town, at the west end of 5th Street, a public parking lot sits beside a seawall. Boca Grande's seawalls have been around "as long as I've been coming here," according to a local with 30 years under her belt. The beach takes a beating, and with the seawall blocking its retreat, there is no beach—just rocks and the violent slapping of waves on concrete. Periodically, they renourish the beach, but it's all for naught, vanishing once again in a season or two. You can cast a line from the seawall, but forget about swimming or sunning on the beach, because there is none. **Boca Grande Public Beach Accesses** are found between 7th and 19th Streets, indicated by signs at the head of each street. Some of these street-end accesses offer half a dozen or so parking spots.

In early 2001, they were floating another renourishment scheme. This one was more ambitious than the patchwork projects of years past. Nearly three miles of beach would be extended 150–200 feet with sand from an offshore bar. The price tag of the project would be $11 million, with beachfront property owners picking up less than 10 percent of the tab (such a deal!). Valid concerns were raised by state officials about ecological ramifications and the impact and effectiveness of limestone boulder groins and an offshore breakwater to protect the artificial beach. We wish them the best of luck, but it all sounds like another case of dumping huge sums of money down a bottomless crabhole to us.

22 Boca Grande Public Beach Accesses

Location: public beach accesses located at certain street ends between 7th and 19th Streets in Boca Grande; the streets with accesses are identified with signs at their intersections with Gulf Boulevard
Parking/fees: free limited street parking at certain access points only
Hours: sunrise to sunset
Facilities: none
Contact: Lee County Department of Parks and Recreation, 941/461-7400

Shore Things

- **Bike/skate rentals:** Island Bike n' Beach, 333 Park Avenue, 941/964-0711.
- **Boat cruise:** Boca Boat Cruises and Charters, Uncle Henry's Marina Resort, 5800 Gasparilla Road, 888/416-2628.
- **Ecotourism:** Grande Tours, 12571 Placida Road, Placida, 941/697-8825.
- **Fishing charters:** Boca Grande Fishing Guides Association, 800/667-1612.
- **Lighthouse:** Boca Grande Lighthouse, Lighthouse Point Park, 941/964-0375.
- **Marina:** Millers Marina, 220 Harbor Drive, 964-2232; Whidden's Marina, 190 East 1st Street, 941/964-2878.
- **Pier:** Gasparilla Pier (railroad trestle turned public pier at north end of island).
- **Rainy-day attraction:** Old Theatre Mall (theater, art gallery, restaurants).
- **Shopping/browsing:** Railroad Depot and Railroad Plaza, 4th Street between Park and East Avenues.
- **Vacation rentals:** Boca Grande Real Estate, 430 West 4th Street, 941/964-0338 or 800/881-2622.

Bunking Down

The **Gasparilla Inn** (Palm Avenue and 5h Street, 941/964-2201, $$$$) is a magnet for those serious about getting away from it all. This yellow clapboard wonder is so unpretentiously situated in its bayside neighborhood that we weren't positive we were entering a public inn at all. There's not even a sign out front. An air of casual exclusivity permeates its rooms and cottages. It's not on the beach, but it's not far from the public beaches. The 18-hole, par-72 golf course out back is the only one on the island. So entrenched in an inflexible code of traditions is the Gasparilla Inn that ex-President George Bush (not Dubya, but his daddy) was denied use of the golf course when he was staying on the island because it's strictly reserved for members and guests. During the "social season" (mid-December through mid-April) rates run $170–240 a night per person and are based on the full American plan, with three meals included. During the "tarpon season" (mid-April through mid-June) they drop by roughly a third.

For something a little less snooty, the **Anchor Inn** (450 East 4th Street, 941/262-4674, $$$) is a four-room inn occupying a restored cracker home. There's a swimming pool and courtyard festooned with tropical plantings on-premises. Weekly room rates run $1,100–1,600 in winter and drop by almost half ($600–850) between mid-July and mid-December.

Coastal Cuisine

The Temptation (350 Park Avenue, 941/964-2610, $$$$) is an old reliable whose atmosphere is almost as palatable as the salads and fried seafood that make up the bulk of the menu. It recently celebrated its 50th anniversary. "We wear it well, don't we?" bragged the woman who filled our water glasses. It's sort of an informal community center, with the mostly retired clientele gathering to sup on grilled shrimp salad, fried oysters, grouper fingers, and so forth. Lunch is a relative bargain at $6.95 and up, but nothing comes cheaply at dinner, where entrées run in the $19–27 range. Under the same roof is the Caribbean Room, a darkened bar festooned with ornaments and bric-a-brac that serves more island-oriented fare at somewhat more moderate prices.

Other seafood spots of longstanding are **PJ's Seagrille** (321 Park Avenue, 941/964-0806, $$$$) and the **Pink Elephant** (491 Bayou Avenue, 941/964-0100, $$$). Neither is inexpensive, though the latter is a little ritzier (good wine list) and more ballyhooed.

Loons on a Limb (3rd Street and East

MAP OF FLORIDA'S WEST COAST—PAGE 347

Railroad Avenue, 941/964-0155, $$$$), is the place to head for hearty breakfasts and brunches, which are served till 11:30 A.M. daily. Finally, your stay is not complete without homemade ice cream at the **Loose Caboose** (4th Street and Park Avenue, 941/964-0440, $), which also dispenses soup, sandwiches, and more from the Railroad Depot.

Night Moves

If you're younger and friskier than Boca Grande's demographic median, head to **South Beach** (777 Gulf Boulevard, 941/964-0765), a bar and grill with lime-green decor and colorful fish on the wall. You can hoist a tall draft Guinness and order dinner from a menu that includes the usual bar food staples (wings, steamed shrimp) as well as entrées in the $16–20 range, such as crispy grouper Gaspar and stuffed shrimp South Beach. From either the indoor bar and dining room or alfresco patio, you can gaze across the sands of South Beach to the gulf. It is the ideal spot on Gasparilla Island to quaff a tall, cool one at sunset, and you may even want to stick around after the sun disappears.

Contact Information

Boca Grande Chamber of Commerce, 5800 Gasparilla Road, P.O. Box 704, Boca Grande, FL 33921; 941/964-0568; website: www.bocagrandechamber.com

MAP OF LEE COUNTY—PAGE 364

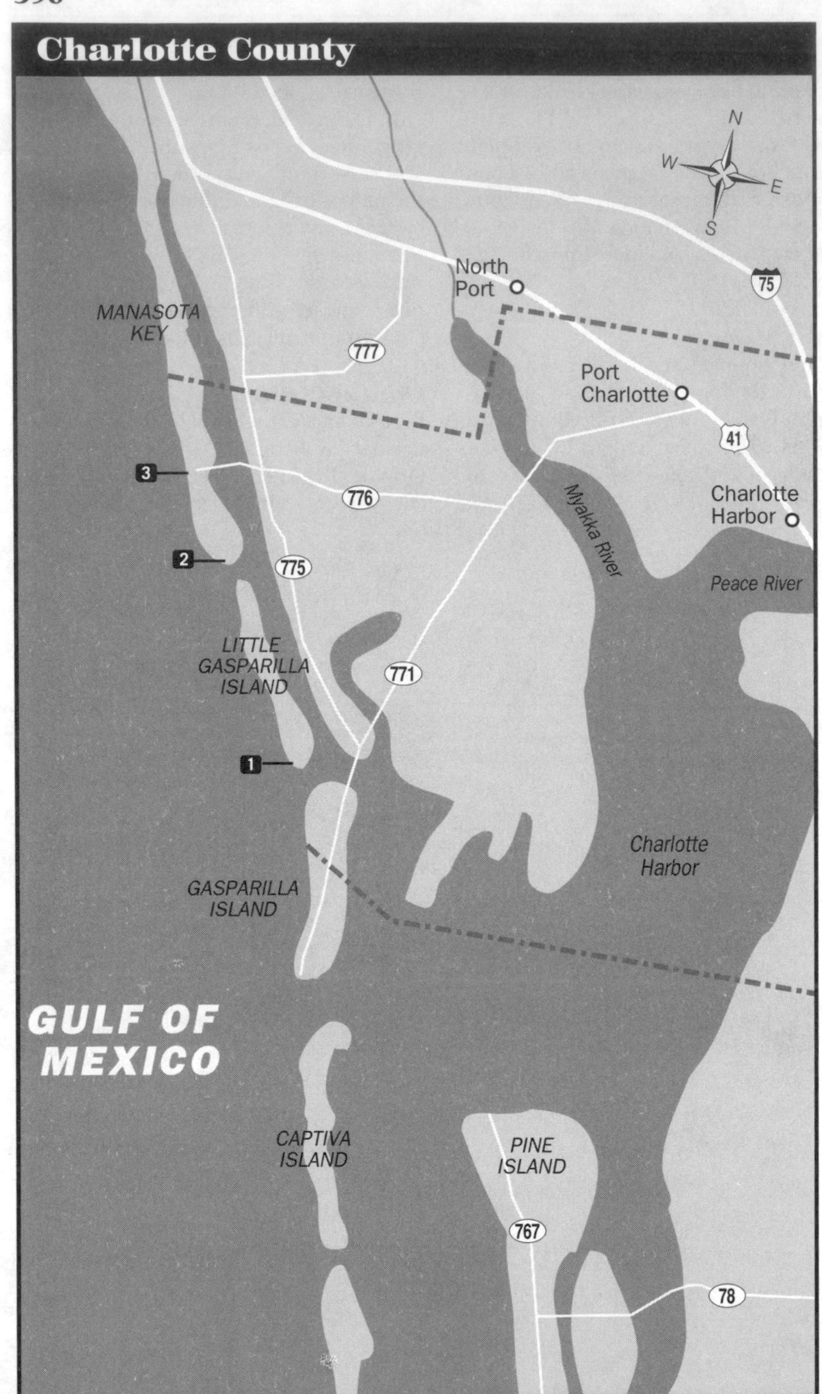
Charlotte County
N
W
E
S
North Port
75
MANASOTA KEY
777
Port Charlotte
41
3
776
Myakka River
Charlotte Harbor
2
775
Peace River
LITTLE GASPARILLA ISLAND
771
1
Charlotte Harbor
GASPARILLA ISLAND
GULF OF MEXICO
CAPTIVA ISLAND
PINE ISLAND
767
78

Charlotte County

Only 17 miles long, Charlotte County has more than 120 miles of tidal coastline, most of it along Charlotte Harbor, a favorite anchoring spot for anglers. The county's prodigious history includes landfalls by Ponce de León and Hernando de Soto, and its name derives from King George III's wife, Charlotte Sophia. Despite the illustrious background, Charlotte County has done little to build on it, especially in the management of its coast. There's just one county beach park—Chadwick Park, in Englewood Beach—and it's in need of a facelift. The state of Florida has managed to jimmy together some beach holdings as part of its Barrier Islands GEOpark. The mainland towns, specifically Englewood, exhibit an unappealing roadside sprawl common to counties without any sort of guiding vision.

Little Gasparilla Island, Don Pedro Island, Knight Island, and Palm Island

What's in a name? If, as Gertrude Stein suggests, a rose is a rose is a rose, then Little Gasparilla Island is a bouquet of hybrids. Not that long ago, this barrier island—stretching for seven miles, from Gasparilla Pass to Stump Pass—comprised four islands. Now, through natural sand movement and human intervention, the islands have been grafted together. Due mostly to the dredging of the Intracoastal Waterway, the narrow inlets that once separated the islands—Little Gasparilla, Don Pedro, Knight, and Palm (sometimes mangrove-covered Thornton Key is included in the lineup)—filled with sand. This created one thin sliver of land that still retains its separate identities.

Thus, we nominate Little Gasparilla Island as an overall name, because it's already a known quantity. But then, we heard that some folks on Little Gasparilla would be horrified to be associated with upscale snowbirds on Palm Island, at the northern end. Because it's part of the same barrier system that created Sanibel, Captiva, North Captiva, Cayo Costa, and Gasparilla Islands to the south, this island is blessed with a sublime combination of wide, hard-packed sand and uncrowded seclusion. Unlike on Sanibel, Captiva, and Gasparilla Islands, car traffic is virtually nonexistent on Little Gasparilla Island because no bridge joins it to the mainland, though there's a barge ferry for residents on the south end. The primary modes of transportation are golf cart, moped, and bicycle. This automatically limits the whims and priorities of the usual beach vacationer. We should all be so lucky. The utter carelessness afforded by car-lessness can be a grand thing indeed.

So far, so good. But this rose has some thorns, too. The main one, to be expected when three government entities (county, state, federal) try to lay out a comprehensive plan for four conjoined yet separate islands, is that everything is ad hoc and nothing makes much sense. For instance, Don Pedro Island State Park, near the south end of the barrier island, is a buried treasure in the state park system that no visitor will quite know what to make of. Like Cayo Costa State Park, it can only be accessed by private boat, because there's no longer any ferry service. (Passengers used to be able to cross for $5, but the service was terminated.)

Moreover, you can't bike to Don Pedro from the north end of the island without illegally crossing the private property of two developers who loathe each other. (One built a fence and wall to force the other to hire private barges to bring his construction supplies.) The law, of course, allows you to hike along the beach below the mean high-tide line, but that is the only way to get from Palm Island Resort to Don Pedro Island State Park—unless you think like us, that is. We rode our rented bikes as far south as we could through the

1 Don Pedro Island State Park

Location: south end of Little Gasparilla Island, accessible via private boat
Parking/fees: $2 per boat docking fee
Hours: 8 A.M. to sunset
Facilities: restrooms and picnic tables
Contact: Barrier Islands GEOpark, 941/964-0375

private domains of Bocilla Bay and the Preserve at Don Pedro (the two adjacent developments owned by the bickering developers). Then we cut through their properties to the beach, stashed our bikes behind a sand dune (bikes are forbidden on the beach), and walked the half mile down to the park.

Ideally, there would be none of this construction on such a fragile island to begin with. But we live in a compromised world, so we took Little Gasparilla Island as we found it. And we generally found it to our liking. In fact, the tiny communities of homes on Knight Island were the sorts of places where hermits such as ourselves would love to spend our dotage. What's frustrating is that after seeing the intelligent planning employed on (Big) Gasparilla Island—at least the Boca Grande part of it, inside the Lee County line—we expected more from Little Gasparilla Island.

Beaches

Of the seven miles of beach on Little Gasparilla Island, six are virtually inaccessible to anyone other than owners or renters of private homes or guests at the Palm Island Resort at the northern end. The island's 1.3 miles of purely public beachfront belong to **Don Pedro Island State Park**, at the south end. Thus, Don Pedro is accessible only by boat but is worth the trip.

The park stretches from the bayside to the beachside and was purchased by the state in 1989. It has a white-sand beach with interesting deposits of shells and driftwood, as well as stunning, elevated sand dunes. You tie your boat up on the bayside dock, pay the $2 dockage fee, then cross the boardwalk to the gulf beach. Facilities include restrooms and picnic pavilions, as well as an on-site ranger, but no lifeguard. "What's wrong with this beach?" a beaming Ranger Rick Storsberg rhetorically asked on the day we visited. "What more could people want?!" Well, maybe 30 more acres that Charlotte County let get away (see "Cowards of the County," sidebar page 400).

Bunking Down

The place to stay on Little Gasparilla Island is **Palm Island Resort** (7092 Placida Road, Cape Haze, 941/697-4800, $$$$), a vacation complex and real-estate venture that fronts the Gulf of Mexico for two miles. At the resort, 160 privately owned one- to three-bedroom villas are rented out to vacationers. It isn't cheap; daily rates run around $200–300. Still, you can get a two-bedroom gulf-view villa for less than $1,500 a week between late April and mid-December.

Because of its relative inaccessibility and low-key nature, crowds are nonexistent even at the height of the season. The white sand has been eaten away by erosion in recent years. In fact, a $1.3 million renourishment project was undertaken in 1994, and a seawall was unwisely added in front of a small parcel of homes in 1997. Still, Palm Island makes a fine spot to recline on a chaise lounge, if you're looking to get away from it all.

Until 1998, cars were not allowed on Palm Island. Now your car, luggage, groceries, and whatever else you want to bring come over on the car barge from Placida. (The car ferry is located at the end of Panama Boulevard, off County Road 775 just north of Johnny Leverock's Seafood House and the Gulfwind Marina.) The resort's reception area moved from the mainland to the island, too. We're not sure if all the changes are signs of progress or regress, but Palm Island struck us as an appealingly secluded place with ample amenities and activities, including five swimming pools, 11 tennis courts, bike rentals, a children's play area, and, of course, an inviting beach.

The tract that Palm Island occupies was purchased in 1980 by Garfield Beckstead, the man who rescued Useppa Island (east of Cayo Costa) in 1976. After

Cowards of the County

Charlotte County has seriously shortchanged its citizens and done a disservice to all future visitors to this area. With a little courage and foresight, they could have acquired one of the nicest remaining tracts of unbuilt-upon barrier island beach in Florida. As it is, the county owns only an eroding little strip up at Englewood Beach. By their cowardly actions, they lost a gorgeous 30-acre gulf-to-bay tract on Little Gasparilla Island that would have adjoined Don Pedro Island State Park. The story of how they let what should have been a treasure to future generations slip through their swinish fingers is a shining example of local politics at its most myopic.

All of the circumnavigation required to get around on Little Gasparilla Island and the maze of private development that has marred its appeal could have been avoided had the Charlotte County Board of Commissioners cast a simple, logical vote in 1996. A plot of land known as the Preserve at Don Pedro, now under development, could have truly been preserved for a song. That song? Try "Bargain," by the Who. The owner of the parcel, who really wanted to sell to the county, had significantly discounted his asking price. After the state kicked in grant money, Charlotte County's contribution toward the purchase of a tract appraised at $5 million would have been a mere $450,000. (This in a county with a $328 million annual budget.) The Don Pedro project was ranked second on a list of more than 40 such projects from all over Florida, and the state bent over backward to accommodate the hemming and hawing of the county commissioners.

"Bargain," however, was not the tune they chose to sing. Instead, the cowards of Charlotte County sang "I Can't Explain." That is to say, after dragging their feet on the matter for two years they voted not to vote on the issue as a final deadline approached. The names of the commissioners who voted to tank the Don Pedro purchase—offered in the spirit of the adage "those who forget history are doomed to repeat it"—are Adam Cummings, Max Farrell, and Michael Youssef. The very day after their vote-not-to-vote, land movers, cranes, and tractors were out at the Preserve, knocking down trees and plotting out lots. Thanks to these three stooges, Little Gasparilla Island will forever remain a confusing hodgepodge of real-estate speculation that could have been a case study in the enlightened multiple-use planning of an unbridged barrier island.

That is not to impugn all of Charlotte County's commissioners. Two of them who sat on the board that voted it down were staunchly in favor of the Don Pedro purchase. Moreover, there's a real hero in Charlotte County politics whose name is Joe Tringali. The efforts of this former three-term commissioner led to the state's acquisition of the 133 acres that now make up Don Pedro Island State Park. With all this in mind, we suggest that the more reality-attuned county residents join together and sing "Won't Get Fooled Again," paying more attention to whom they put in office when election time rolls around.

We'll leave the last word to Jack Alexander, a local columnist who summed it up like this: "Politicians can be so dumb. And our County Commission could be in the *Guinness Book of Records* under 'Dumbest.'"

studying the natural gifts of Palm Island—his new name for this chunk of Knight Island (justified, as there are plenty of palm trees)—he reportedly reduced the number of planned homesites by half. As it now stands, Palm Island Resort is more than halfway to buildout, at which point there will be 500 dwellings. Still, that's probably too much construction on a shifting island where desperate measures like seawalls have already been undertaken.

For the time being, a balance between nature and human habitations seems to have been struck. For instance, an early morning jog from Palm Island's villas to Stump Point (part of the 7,667-acre Cape Haze Aquatic Preserve) presented a living lab of marine ecology: live sea urchins, starfish, and sand dollars, fish leaping in the pass, silent lagoons, and driftwood-studded beaches. For 10 minutes, an egret stared us down from a limb. It cleaned its feathers, surveyed the gulf, and waited for breakfast to appear in the teeming waters, where manatees are often spotted.

Coastal Cuisine

At Palm Island Resort, unless you've brought groceries from the mainland, you are a fish in a barrel. There's nowhere to go for a meal other than their **Rum Bay Restaurant** (Palm Island Resort, 941/697-0566, $$$). The menu is top-heavy with glorified bar fare, and the food is adequate at best. Rum Bay is much more appealing as a place to hoist a drink at sunset or after dinner before taking a moonlit stroll back to the bungalow. All villas at Palm Island come with fully equipped kitchens, so you might want to hit the Food Lion or Publix in Englewood before ferrying over. While you're shopping for groceries, drop by the video store, too.

Contact Information

Englewood Area Chamber of Commerce, 601 South Indiana Avenue, Englewood, FL 34223; 941/474-5511 or 800/603-7198; website: www.englewoodchamber.com

Manasota Key (south end)

The beaches of Charlotte County's portion of Manasota Key fall within the town limits of Englewood (pop. 51,000). Most of Englewood, like neighboring Grove City and Lemon Pass, sprawls on the mainland in an unplanned, unzoned string of homes, malls, and businesses that stretches for five miles on County Road 775 and County Road 776. These towns are the commercial centers for the numerous gated private condo developments that dot the shoreline of Lemon Bay. If the signs staked in nearly every vacant lot along this corridor are any indication, more strip malls, Eckerd drugstores, franchised restaurants, Wal-Marts, car dealers, and mellifluously named developments are on the way. It's business as usual in Charlotte County, where business and real estate transactions are apparently the only things that matter. Charlotte County has the most elderly population of any county in Florida, and that explains a lot. The median age for the entire state of Florida is 39.2 years; in Charlotte County, it's 53. To say it's lacking in vitality or vision is an understatement.

To get to Englewood Beach from County Road 776 in Englewood, turn west on Beach Road, which leads over a drawbridge (below is Lemon Bay and the Gulf Intracoastal Waterway) and onto a short causeway. Englewood Beach is a modest improvement over Englewood. The first thing you encounter on this thin barrier spit is Chadwick Park, site of Englewood Public Beach. Turn left and you'll be headed to a state-owned sliver of beach known

The Folly of Federal Flood Insurance

As we passed through Charlotte County, we heard a recurrent chorus of voices bemoaning the fate of the coast. The general consensus was that the county had shot itself in the foot with its beach planning. (Indeed, that was the most printable of the comments we heard.) Nowhere is this more obvious than on Manasota Key, which has a secluded charm in spots but could offer much more than that. As one ecotourism guide bluntly put it, "If they did away with federal flood insurance, we could save these barrier islands."

Federal flood insurance is a government program available to coastal home owners who would, for good reason, not be able to get insurance elsewhere. While it was originally intended to help victims of natural disasters like hurricanes and tsunamis, it has turned into welfare for the wealthy and a windfall for the real-estate industry. It is a program administered by the Federal Emergency Management Agency (FEMA).

Despite the fact that virtually no one would purchase beachfront property if federal flood insurance weren't available, local real-estate developers and zoning boards flout federal government guidelines. The feds, for example, prescribe setbacks for homesites—a suggested minimum distance from the high-tide line on which to build safely. But these are routinely ignored, with numerous homes failing to meet federal flood guidelines. The situation is hardly unique to Charlotte County. Up in Manatee County, for instance, county officials claimed to lack the manpower to enforce guidelines. And why should a developer, homeowner, or local government worry about it anyway, if the rest of us are going to wind up paying to rebuild, via a federal flood insurance bailout, after storms wash away beachfront constructions?

as Stump Pass Beach (formerly Port Charlotte State Park). Turn right and you'll soon enter Sarasota County's portion of Manasota Key, with its more appealing temperament and better beach parks (see next chapter).

2 Stump Pass Beach

Location: south end of Manasota Key Road, on Manasota Key
Parking/fees: free parking lot
Hours: 8 A.M. to sunset
Facilities: restrooms
Contact: Barrier Islands GEOpark, 941/964-0375

At the south end, the yin and yang of Manasota Key becomes evident. Manasota Key Road ends at Stump Pass Beach, part of the state-owned string of coastal parklands known as Barrier Islands GEOpark. The good news is that more parking spaces have lately been added. (There used to be just four.) The contrast between the unblemished state park and the cinderblock Weston's Resort next to it could not be more stark. Step into the pine and mangrove canopy of the park, and you are instantly calmed. From this natural habitat, you venture onto the beach, which stretches for a mile down to Stump Pass. By con-

What an inefficient way to do business! Especially now, when it has been proven how ill-advised it is to build on vulnerable barrier islands. The captain of a boat that services the islands said it best. Referring to the resort that employs him, he said, "Hell, this place shouldn't even be here."

In July 2000, *USA Today* ran a series of in-depth articles on America's coastal migration. Some of the startling facts:

- 41 million Americans (one in seven) live in a county on the Atlantic Ocean or the Gulf of Mexico. This population growth rate surpasses the rest of the country by 15 percent (and that includes California, with its 1,200-mile coastline and rapid population growth).
- From 1970 until 1994, an unusually small number of major hurricanes struck the Atlantic or Gulf Coasts. Since 1995, hurricane activity has increased dramatically, and 1999 actually set a record for the most "violent" hurricanes in any year since meteorological records have been kept. The likelihood of a "killer hurricane" is increasing at a time when more people are in harm's way in coastal flood zones.
- The federal government (read: American taxpayer) spends $10 million a year just on emergency evacuations from coastal flood zones.

Here's the kicker: American taxpayers will, unless the laws are changed, foot the bill for these folks who built their houses in the sand. By 2030, the cost of property damage to hurricanes on the Atlantic and Gulf Coasts is expected to top $50 billion a year (compared to $5 billion now). Are we really prepared to underwrite such selfish shortsightedness?

This is not some paranoid fiction but is based on data accepted by all parties. Even FEMA estimates that 30,000 single-family homes and condominiums within 500 feet of the Atlantic and Gulf Coasts will be under water in 30 years, based on conservative projections that sea-level rise will swamp an average of two linear feet of beach per year. In Florida, where most of the state is barely above sea level to begin with, the rising tide is expected to consume 1,000 feet of coast in some regions during this same time period.

trast, Weston's is set atop a cracked seawall with no beach to speak of in front of it. What we saw was in dire need of overhaul: paint peeling, concrete chipping, a fence rusting and falling away.

The rest of Englewood Beach wears a similarly downtrodden look. Even Englewood Public Beach, at Chadwick Park—Charlotte County's only county-run beach on the gulf—has severe erosion problems, and the only thing that keeps it operative are some disbursements from the Land and Water Conservation Fund, a federal program that offers matching funds to states for land conservation, open-space protection, and parks and recreation. A local journalist likened the park to a "neglected old car." What a pathetic showing, in a county filled with beaches!

3 Englewood Public Beach

Location: Beach Road (County Road 776) at Manasota Key Road, in Englewood
Parking/fees: $1 parking fee per vehicle
Hours: 6 A.M.–11 P.M.
Facilities: concessions, restrooms, picnic tables, and showers
Contact: Chadwick Park, 941/473-1018

MAP OF CHARLOTTE COUNTY—PAGE 396

Beaches

At the south end of the island, **Stump Pass Beach** offers a secluded, mile-long beach. The sand is gray-black and spongy—part of the **Englewood Beach** strand that has had to be renourished with dredge material. There's no entrance fee, and virtually no facilities beyond restrooms. One good way to visit is by bicycle, using the racks provided.

Chadwick Park is another spongy, mile-long beach that has full facilities and is within walking distance of shops, restaurants, and bars. No one under the age of 50 or a weight of 200 pounds was present the day we visited. Typical of Charlotte County, it's not clear what one must pay to visit the park. Parking is supposedly a dollar a day. A sign said to pay at the meters, but the meters had been removed. Didn't Bob Dylan write a song about this?

Bunking Down

There are few motels worth recommending in Englewood Beach, and there's one (Weston's Resort) we wouldn't recommend to Saddam Hussein. The best bet on Manasota Key is a vacation home, condo, or villa rental. One caveat: At the north end of the key, in Sarasota County, local regulations require a minimum one-month rental. Therefore, any weekly rentals on Manasota Key must be done on the Charlotte County side of the line. Try **Surfside Realty** (1271 Beach Road, Englewood, 941/473-4050).

Contact Information

Englewood Area Chamber of Commerce, 601 South Indiana Avenue, Englewood, FL 34223; 941/474-5511 or 800/603-7198; website: www.englewoodchamber.com

MAP OF FLORIDA'S WEST COAST—PAGE 347

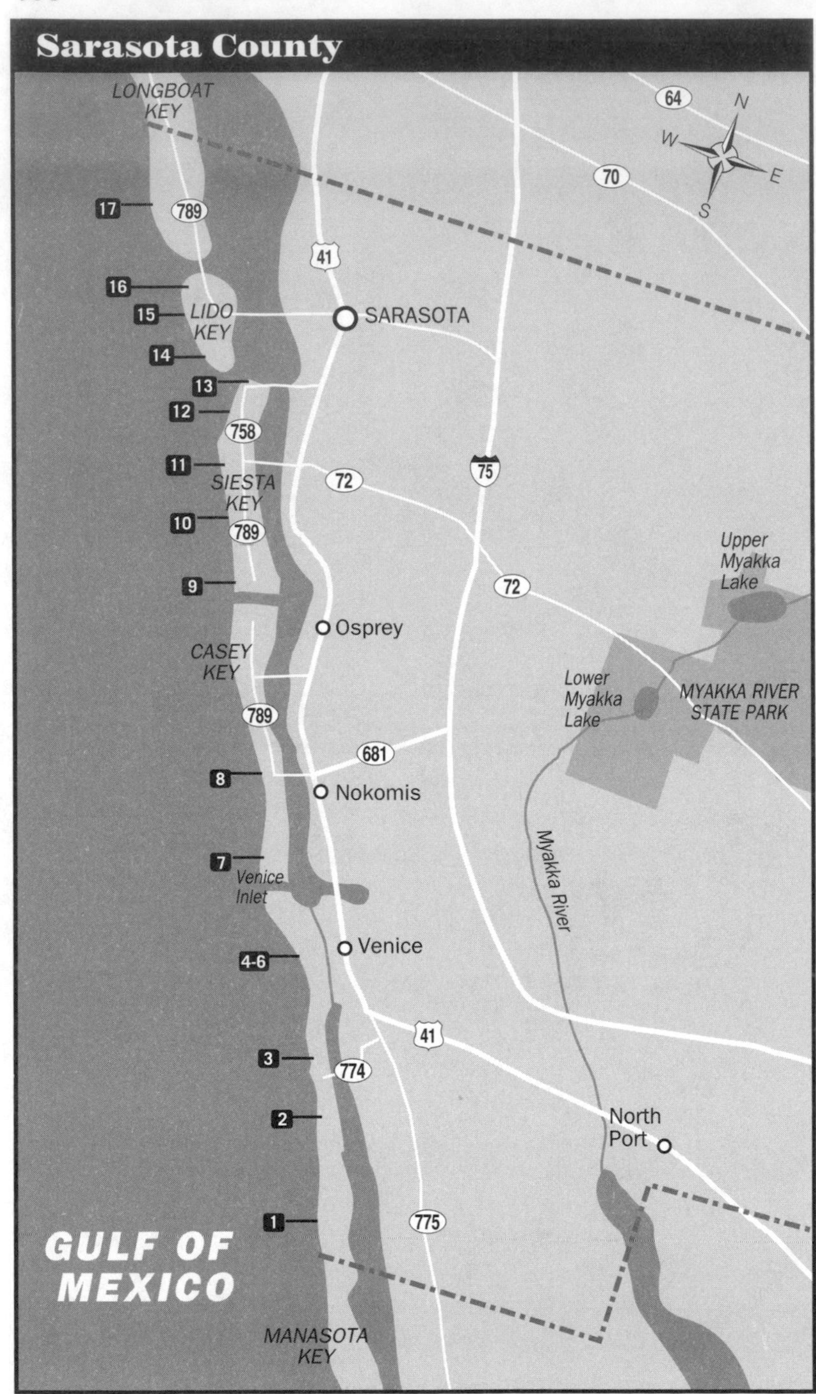
Sarasota County
LONGBOAT KEY
64
N
W
E
S
70
17
789
41
16
LIDO KEY
15
SARASOTA
14
13
12
758
11
75
SIESTA KEY
72
10
789
Upper Myakka Lake
9
72
Osprey
CASEY KEY
Lower Myakka Lake
MYAKKA RIVER STATE PARK
789
681
8
Nokomis
Myakka River
7
Venice Inlet
Venice
4-6
41
3
774
2
North Port
1
775
GULF OF MEXICO
MANASOTA KEY

Sarasota County

Sarasota County claims north Manasota Key, and it's a huge improvement over the Charlotte County–owned south end. Above it lies the well-mannered harbor town of Venice, which takes architectural cues from the more famous canal city in Italy. One of Florida's better-kept secrets, Venice also has miles of wide, renourished beaches. North of Venice are the Old Florida havens of Nokomis and Osprey, as well as the lush exclusivity of Casey Key. Then comes Siesta Key, whose sand has been judged the best in the world. Nearby Sarasota—the most cultured city on the gulf and maybe all of Florida—is connected to the coast via Ringling Causeway, which leads to St. Armands and Lido Keys. Out here are beachfront hotels and the glitz of St. Armands Circle, with its shops, restaurants, and nightspots. The only sour note in Sarasota County's coastal fantasia is Longboat Key, which exhibits all the snobbiness of a private country club.

Manasota Key (north end)

Manasota Key improves dramatically as you move north from Englewood Beach, exiting Charlotte County. (In this case, parting is not such sweet sorrow.) "Interval ownership" villas and mobile home parks are replaced by single-family homes and unadulterated nature. Trees form a canopy over the road. From here on out, it's clear sailing. You're officially in Sarasota County.

Beaches

The first park in Sarasota County is **Blind Pass Beach** (a.k.a. Middle Beach), a 60-acre public preserve located a mile north of the Charlotte County line. Here, the gulf-hugging road swerves dramatically and the barrier spit grows so thin that visitors park on the bayside and walk over to the beach. It's an exceptionally clean and modern facility, with a wild and healthy beach that stretches for over half a mile (no lifeguards). Also, next to the parking lot is a nature trail dedicated to Frederick Duesberg (1910–89). This winding sawdust-covered trail offers a peek at the fragile bayside habitat that remains out here, ending at a quiet lagoon. Fishing and kayaking are popular pastimes on the many coves nestled along the bayshore. In the vicinity of Blind Pass the island is pretty fragile, and the road often has to be closed during nasty storms.

Another attractive, free county facility, **Manasota Beach**, lies 1.5 miles above Blind Pass, at the north end of Manasota Key. This 14-acre park includes 1,400 feet of gulf beach, as well as a boat ramp and dock on the bayside. There are year-round lifeguards here, among the first we'd seen on the entire southwest coast thus far. One caveat: Manasota Key is not an island, per se, because it connects with Venice to the north. But since the road doesn't extend to Venice, the key is island-like. In other words, you have to leave the key at Manasota Beach, via State Route 776, to get to Venice.

Bunking Down

Toward the remote north end of Manasota Key is the **Seafarer Beach Motel** (8520 Manasota Key Road, 941/474-4388, $$), a small—eight rooms and four efficiency apartments—mom-and-pop motor court that possesses low-key charm. Most rates here are by the week, but daily rates are offered in the off-season.

Contact Information

Venice Area Chamber of Commerce, 257 Tamiami Trail North, Venice, FL 34285; 941/488-2236. website: www.venicechamber.com

❶ Blind Pass Beach

Location: one mile north of the Charlotte County line, at 6725 Manasota Key Road, on Manasota Key
Parking/fees: free parking lot
Hours: 6 A.M.–11 P.M.
Facilities: restrooms, picnic tables, and showers
Contact: Sarasota County Parks and Recreation Department, 941/316-1172

❷ Manasota Beach

Location: north end of Manasota Key, at the west end of Manasota Beach Road
Parking/fees: free parking lots
Hours: 6 A.M.–11 P.M.
Facilities: lifeguards, restrooms, picnic tables, and showers
Contact: Sarasota County Parks and Recreation Department, 941/316-1172

Map of Florida's West Coast—Page 347

Venice

Venice, Florida, could not be more different from Venice, California, if it tried. And yet each of these popular, canal-filled beach towns—loosely based upon the more famous Italian model—appeals to beach lovers in its own way. California's Venice is a fast-paced human parade that's equal parts freak show and *Baywatch* episode. In Florida's Venice, if the human parade were moving any slower it would be going backwards.

Venice is an incorporated community with a population of about 17,000; the greater Venice area, which also includes the surrounding communities of South Venice, Nokomis, Laurel, and Osprey, totals 84,000. This is the heart of AARP country, which means a lot of early-bird specials are served nightly at local restaurants. It also means that Venice and its neighboring communities are comfortably non-trendy and almost completely devoid of yuppie affectations. The thematic emphasis is on rock-solid hometown America. Venice is the sum total of all the middle-American towns these retirees left behind in order to enjoy their golden years in the Florida sun. Since we're closer to AARP membership than we are to a *Teen Beat* subscription, we'll just wish you many happy, sun-filled days, dear Venetians. You deserve your well-earned peace and quiet.

From its inception, Venice was endowed with understated appeal. It fell within the borders of a 140,000-acre purchase of "wild Florida frontier land" by Mrs. Bertha Palmer, an heiress from Chicago who used her dead husband's fortune to build an elegant winter residence ("the Oaks") in nearby Osprey. She also used her influence to have the railroad extended to Venice. A New York physician named Fred Albee chugged into the picture soon thereafter, promoting a new "master-planned community." With railroad money backing him, Albee set to work creating what he saw as a congenial mix of farming, industry, housing, commerce, and recreation, all the while establishing a Northern Italian architectural theme. In 1927, Venice was incorporated. Throughout its history it has tried adhering to tasteful growth rather than slipshod sprawl, and the local preservation league is particularly strong. One caveat: Car traffic often snarls in downtown Venice, due to a combination of too many timid drivers in barge-sized cars and too few drawbridges crossing the Intracoastal Waterway.

Naturally, this well-mannered and neatly manicured community is not in the market for party animals. As if to underscore that point, beachfront accommodations are at a bare minimum, bars are tame, and the primary recreational vehicles are golf carts and yachts. The latter bob in the town's harbor, from whose ends extend massive jetties. Venice is blessed with nearly five miles of beach (including several exceptional beach parks), a sturdy fishing pier, jetties that are popular with fishers and bird-watchers, and pleasant year-round weather.

Beaches

The beaches of Venice are renowned for sharks' teeth. You will find references to them all over the area. The shark's tooth is a major part of the town's marketing cam-

❸ Casperson Park

Location: south of Venice Airport, on Harbor Drive in Venice
Parking/fees: free parking lots
Hours: 6 A.M.–9 P.M.
Facilities: restrooms, picnic tables, and showers
Contact: Sarasota County Parks and Recreation Department, 941/316-1172

paign. To drive the point home, shark-adorned T-shirts proclaim Venice "The Sharks Tooth Capital of the World." There's no need to freak out about shark attacks, though, because the teeth that wash up are the fossilized remnants of a massive shark burial ground located several miles offshore in a deep trench where they mysteriously go to die.

Of more concern than sharks, at least to the locals, is the fragility of the town's beaches. In 1996, Venice undertook an ambitious and expensive engineering project, renourishing and expanding a 3.3-mile stretch of beach with dredge from an offshore sandbar. This strand, from **Casperson Park** north to the harbor mouth, is a fine piece of work, but the $64 million question (literally) is, will it stay put? For now, the locals are so smitten with "the new beach" that they prefer it to North Jetty Park, where they used to go in droves. It is, in some places, nearly a football field wide, and the beach largely maintained its width during the first few winters after the renourishment project. The sand has a crunchy texture due to shell and rock fragments, and it is spongy near the water. Moreover, the new sand has made scavenging for sharks' teeth difficult. "Since the renourishment of Venice Beach, I have been unable to find teeth there," lamented a shark's-tooth collector. But there's room for just about everybody now, and three tall lifeguard stands provide year-round protection.

The renourished beach begins at the south end of Venice, in Casperson Park. It is another outstanding Sarasota County facility with ample free parking and nearly two miles of beachfront (no lifeguards this far down, however). A well-marked nature trail runs through 177 acres of coastal hammock, tidal flats, and mangrove forests, offering peaceful diversion from the waves. Despite its popularity, Casperson is large enough to offer isolation—just walk south toward Manasota Key, two miles away—as well as a gorgeous, unpeopled setting. Casperson, like all of Venice's beaches south of the harbor jetties, has experienced erosion problems. Scattered rocks in the water are a

4 Brohard Park

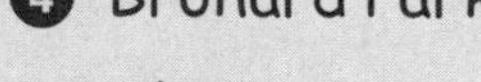

Location: in Venice, near the Venice Fishing Pier
Parking/fees: free parking lot
Hours: 6 A.M.–9 P.M.
Facilities: concessions, restrooms, picnic tables, and showers
Contact: Sarasota County Parks and Recreation Department, 941/316-1172

5 Service Club Park

Location: adjoining Brohard Beach at the north end, on Harbor Drive in Venice
Parking/fees: free parking lot
Hours: 6 A.M.–9 P.M.
Facilities: restrooms, picnic tables, and showers
Contact: Sarasota County Parks and Recreation Department, 941/316-1172

6 Venice Municipal Beach

Location: west end of Venice Avenue, in Venice
Parking/fees: free parking lot
Hours: 6 A.M.–9 P.M.
Facilities: concessions, lifeguards, restrooms, picnic tables, and showers
Contact: Sarasota County Parks and Recreation Department, 941/316-1172

testament to the failed groins that preceded the latest renourishment project. The light gray sand is a giveaway to its origins as dredge material.

Moving north along Harbor Drive, we were impressed with the extent of natural habitat left intact in Venice. Both sides of the road are covered with sand dunes, some of the errant sand spilling onto the asphalt-like snowdrifts. Up by the Venice Fishing Pier is **Brohard Park**, a city-owned, county-maintained beach with a dirt lot, basic facilities, snack bar, and bait shop. The beach beside the 740-foot pier is industrial-strength dredge fill, dark gray and dropping sharply to the surf zone where waves cut terraces into it. The Venice pier is popular with anglers and strollers, who are charged a nominal fee ($1 for adults, 50 cents for kids) to roam its length. A popular pierside restaurant and hangout, Sharky's at the Pier, completes the picture. Brohard Park claims nearly a mile of shoreline and includes a subunit called **Service Club Park**, which has its own parking lot, restrooms, picnic area, playground, and dune walkovers.

From the pier, Venice's beachfront stretches two miles north to the jetties. **Venice Municipal Beach**, a publicly accessible 875-foot strand, is located where Venice Avenue intersects Harbor Drive, 1.4 miles north of the pier. Just offshore is a reef with large fossil deposits that are swarmed over by divers. The stretch from the pier to Venice Beach is combed by hopeful beachgoers looking for the allegedly ubiquitous shark teeth. (We didn't see any.)

You can also get out to the water's edge at South Jetty, on the harbor at the north end of Venice. There is no public beach, but the jetty area is used for strolling, jetty fishing, or watching pelicans swoop along the man-made waterway. We offer the beaches on the south and north side of the harbor jetties as a case study in the dynamics of jetty-caused beach erosion. Stand on the south, downdrift side of the jetties and look north toward North Jetty Park. Over there, the coast sticks out a couple hundred yards farther into the gulf, and the sand is powdery, white, and natural. North Jetty has no need for the sort of renourishment done on the sand-starved beaches south of the harbor. You don't have to be a coastal engineer to realize the jetties have profoundly reshaped Venice's beaches—and, correspondingly, its future.

Shore Things

- **Bike/skate rentals:** Louie's Bicycles, 1580 Tamiami Trail South, North Port, 941/423-2613.
- **Boat cruise:** Seven Seas Yacht Charters, 2216 Lakeshore Drive, Nokomis, 941/966-6017.
- **Dive shop:** Scuba Quest, 2357 Tamiami Trail South, Venice, 941/497-5985.
- **Ecotourism:** Myakka Wildlife Tours, Myakka River State Park, State Route 72 (nine miles east of I-75, via Exit 37), 941/365-0100.
- **Fishing charters:** Gaona Sportfishing Charters, 505 Tamiami Trail North, Venice, 941/488-2311.
- **Pier:** Venice Fishing Pier, 1600 Harbor Drive South, Venice, 941/488-1456.
- **Marina:** Crow's Nest Marina, 1968 Tarpon Center Drive, Venice, 941/484-7661.
- **Rainy-day attraction:** Historic Spanish Point, 337 North Tamiami Trail, Osprey, 941/966-5214.
- **Shopping/browsing:** Historic downtown Venice, along Venice, Tampa and Miami avenues.
- **Surf shop:** V-Town Surf & Skate, 101 West Venice Avenue #15, 941/488-3896.
- **Vacation rentals:** Heritage Vacation Rentals, 101 West Venice Avenue, Suite 5, Venice, 941/488-9141.

MAP OF SARASOTA COUNTY—PAGE 406

Bunking Down

There are only two motels near the beach at Venice. They are the **Best Western Sandbar Beach Resort** (811 Esplanade North, 941/488-2251, $$$$) and the **Inn at the Beach Resort** (101 The Esplanade, 941/484-8471, $$$). The former is directly on the beach, the latter a block off it. Both are clean and better than average but more pricey than one would expect in modest Venice, which is hardly a beach-lover's mecca. At the Best Western, for instance, a two-bedroom gulf-view efficiency goes for $229 a night in season. The plethora of chain motels on U.S. 41 bypass, three miles west of the gulf, are a budget-conscious alternative. But, our rule of thumb in the entire south Sarasota County area is to avoid any motel with a Tamiami Trail address.

Coastal Cuisine

For our money, the best place in Venice is topside at the **Crow's Nest Marina Restaurant and Tavern** (1968 Tarpon Center Drive, 941/484-9551, $$$). This airy,

Red Tide Rising

Red tide is the name given to an aquatic-driven biological phenomenon that typically occurs in the summer months, mostly along the Gulf of Mexico and only in sporadic bursts. As if to punish the two of us for our myriad sins—perhaps for never having read a Tom Clancy novel—a relatively mild red-tide outbreak occurred later than usual in the year (November), just as we entered the Venice area. This outbreak blanketed the beaches from Venice Inlet south to Captiva Island, with deposits of dead fish, crabs, and other shelly critters festooned in brown straps of seaweed. The smell was bad enough to floor Hulk Hogan, but the worst aspect of red tide is that the microscopic toxin that causes all this carnage becomes airborne via sea spray and wind.

Exposure to this malevolent mist can cause watering eyes, sore throats, coughing, wheezing, sneezing, and headache. Though swimming in waters infested with red tide is ill advised and unpleasant, it won't kill you. More damaging is the effect red tide has on local fishing and aquaculture, often necessitating temporary bans on oysters, clams, mussels, and scallops.

These outbreaks are the work of dinoflagellates, one-celled organisms *(Gymnodinium breve)* that propel themselves with whiplike tails, as we observed through a microscope at the Mote Marine Aquarium, up near Sarasota. The "red" refers to the reddish brown pigment produced when the dinoflagellates bloom into their toxic stage, at which point their cells burst, releasing a poison that's washed landward by the tides. The initial burst occurs 10–40 miles offshore. As it moves toward land, smaller sea animals are most susceptible to its poison.

Though marine biologists know the mechanism by which the poisons are released, they still don't know why the process is initiated. Educated guesses point to the usual suspect: human-generated pollution. Sewage runoff and other pollutants upset the chemical balance in the waters through which the *Gymnodinium* tumble, perhaps setting off devastating red tides as a defense mechanism. It is so commonplace that a red tide hotline (941/492-3156) has been set up; call for the latest conditions.

MAP OF FLORIDA'S WEST COAST—PAGE 347

relaxing two-story restaurant overlooks the yacht harbor on the south side of the inlet. It's top-notch in quality but downplays yachting-class snobbery. We whiled away an entire evening here, basking in the nautical decor and excellent food. Before and after-dinner drinks are nursed downstairs, where lighter fare is available. Exquisitely prepared fresh seafood is served in the galley upstairs.

By all means climb the mast to the Crow's Nest's main dining room, where entrées are consistently interesting without going overboard. We started with an excellent seafood bisque that was tangy, robust, and liberally stocked with shrimp, crabmeat, and fish. Suggested and affordable wines are appended to the various entrée descriptions. Grouper Key Largo is a worthy signature dish, a generous portion of fresh grouper accompanied by succulent scallops, shrimp, and chunks of crabmeat. It is served over wild rice with a tureen of hollandaise sauce (tip that sucker over!). Another excellent choice is pan-seared pompano, served over a delicious risotto, flavored with applewood bacon and doused in a caper mushroom sauce. How about pan-seared medallions of monkfish, shrimp, and scallops with pesto garlic butter? If you've got any room for dessert, the Crow's Nest key lime pie could compete with that served at all but a few restaurants in the Florida Keys.

Night Moves

We were given the lowdown by a lovely 20-something waitress who was born and raised in Venice. "After midnight, Venice is done," was her summary statement. The large retiree population and self-policing good manners allow for only so much rocking and rolling after sundown. The leader of the pack is **Sharky's at the Pier** (1600 Harbor Drive South, 941/488-1456). Live music is offered nightly, Wednesday through Sunday, and it's a mix of rock, blues, and reggae, with a "calypso party" every Sunday evening. The outside patio is a great place to watch the sun go down and enjoy a frozen drink (a "deck delight"), but there's a limit: "for safety's sake," you are allowed only two frozen drinks on the patio. The **Crow's Nest Tavern** (1968 Tarpon Center Drive, 941/484-9551), downstairs from the aforementioned restaurant, attracts whatever youngish Venetians are wont to party after the dinner plates have been cleared. Boogie nights bigger than these require a drive north to Sarasota, where the action is hotter and heavier.

Contact Information

Venice Area Chamber of Commerce, 257 Tamiami Trail North, Venice, FL 34285; 941/488-2236; website: www.venicechamber.com

Nokomis and Casey Key

Entering Casey Key at the town of Nokomis (pop. 3,500) via Albee Road (State Route 789), you are embraced by vestiges of Old Florida. Development in unincorporated Nokomis tends toward low-key homes and small motels. Nokomis Beach is conveniently located where Albee Road meets the water, at Casey Key Road. Half a mile south, the key gives out at North Jetty Park.

Just about everything north of the jetty is residential, and the scale moves dramatically upward as you travel in that direction. Casey Key Road is a winding, bending, and at times breathtakingly thin and scenic thoroughfare. The homes here offer lovely if ostentatious displays of wealth, not unlike Palm Beach. (One longtime area resident explained, "Casey Key is for people with money who want to show it off, but they're stuck with that road way out there.") Reportedly, some celebrities own homes out here, and John Gotti once owned the walled, gated fortress at the very north end of the key. The need to maintain appearances keeps a small city of laborers gainfully employed, as crews of painters, plasterers, gardeners, and landscapers work on homesites at nearly every bend in the road.

Beaches

The best beach in the Venice area is **North Jetty Park**, which lies across the harbor from Venice at the south end of Casey Key. The park has a lot to offer: nearly a thousand feet of wide, breezy beach; bay and gulf access; excellent fishing from the jetty; and viable surfing where the waves curl around the end of the jetty. At various times of year and under certain conditions (e.g., a good south swell), North Jetty is one of the best surfing spots on the Gulf of Mexico. This Sarasota County park is partly underwritten by National Park Service funds, and it is money well spent. Lifeguards are on duty year-round. Volleyball, horseshoe courts, and concessions are on the premises.

Nokomis Beach is Sarasota County's oldest public beach. The unvarnished, weathered wood benches would seem to affirm this. The table-flat white-sand gulf beach at this 22-acre recreation area runs for a third of a mile. Popular with families, Nokomis Beach has ample free parking in large gravel lots, picnic pavilions, restrooms, outdoor showers, a snack bar, and lifeguards. A boat ramp is available on the Intracoastal Waterway.

At the north end of Casey Key is Palmer Point Beach. Before Midnight

7 North Jetty Park

Location: at the south end of Casey Key, at Venice Inlet
Parking/fees: free parking lot
Hours: 6 A.M.–11 P.M.
Facilities: concessions, lifeguards, restrooms, picnic tables, and showers
Contact: Sarasota County Parks and Recreation Department, 941/316-1172

8 Nokomis Beach

Location: Albee Road (State Route 789) at Casey Key Road
Parking/fees: free parking lot
Hours: 6 A.M.–11 P.M.
Facilities: lifeguards, restrooms, picnic tables, and showers
Contact: Sarasota County Parks and Recreation Department, 941/316-1172

Map of Florida's West Coast—Page 347

Pass was closed by local property owners in 1983 after passage of a county ordinance permitting them to do so, Palmer Point was the northern tip of a barrier island. Now it's connected to Siesta Key, although no through road connects Casey and Siesta Keys. Rumors abound as to how the inlet closure took place, and none of them are savory. Regardless, the beach at Palmer Point is a pristine and secluded spot, with 2,400 feet of gulf beach to wander, more often than not by yourself. You're also on your own in that there are no facilities or lifeguards. For what it's worth, John Gotti lived near here before he took up more permanent lodgings at a federal penitentiary with a less striking view.

Bunking Down

Very little in the way of traditional beach accommodations can be found out this way, but beach-facing suites are available at the irresistibly named **Suntan Terrace Beach Resort** (117 Casey Key Road, Nokomis, 941/484-7110, $$) and **Gulf Sands Beach Apartments** (433 Casey Key Road, 941/488-7272, $$). Rooms in a more traditional mode are found further north at **Gulf Surf Resort Motel** (3905 Casey Key Road, 941/966-2669, $$$).

Contact Information

Venice Area Chamber of Commerce, 257 Tamiami Trail North, Venice, FL 34285; 941/488-2236; website: www.venicechamber.com

Siesta Key

Siesta Key (pop. 12,000) is split down the middle, literally and figuratively. The beaches are divided by an outcrop known as Point of Rocks. North of it, the constituent sand is powdery, white, and nearly 100 percent pure quartz in content. To the south, the sand is composed of shellier material. Likewise, the community is divided into two distinct halves, with the line of demarcation being Stickney Point Road. Turn right at the light, and there's a dense concentration of commercial activity with buildup and hubbub. Turn left, and a quieter, laidback, less harried stretch of shoreline unfolds. The community is further divided in its opinions on the reopening of Midnight Pass (see sidebar, page 419), as well as other developmental and environmental issues. Fortunately for all, however, the residents of Siesta Key are largely in agreement about the kind of place they want their island to be: an unpretentious albeit upscale escape from reality that preserves an appealingly unhurried character.

On the plus side, Siesta Key claims some of the finest sand beaches in the state of Florida, if not the world. Eight miles in length, the key extends from what used to be Midnight Pass up to Big Pass (which separates it from Lido Key, at the north end). Siesta Key won the Great International White Sand Beach Challenge, held in 1987. Conducted by no less august a scientific body than the Woods Hole Oceanographic Institution, Siesta Key beat out 29 other entries because of the floury, undefiled composition of its sand. Beyond the professional commendations its sand has received, there's a discernible village character and way of life to be found on Siesta Key.

We feel obliged to warn about one thing, however. On long, narrow keys like Siesta where only one main artery (Midnight Pass Road, in this case) runs its length, come prepared for heavy traffic. It's bumper to bumper in season and just plain bad the rest of the year. Incidentally, the whole concept of seasonality is dissolving as Siesta Key's fame spreads far and wide. We visited the island during what was reputed to be one of the slowest times of the year (the week after Halloween) and still hit more than a few traffic jams north of Stickney Point Road. Basically, snowbirds and Europeans come during the high season, while native Floridians make vacation getaways here the rest of the year. That's another way of saying it's always busy. With award-winning beaches, 50 miles of canals and waterways, and prime fishing opportunities—bridge fishing, surf casting, deep-sea trolling—it's no wonder Siesta Key is popular all year round.

There are two ways on and off the island: State Route 72 (Stickney Point Road) at its midsection and State Route 758 (Higel Avenue/Siesta Drive) at the northern "village" end of the island. Siesta and the other keys within easy reach of Sarasota—Casey, Lido, St. Armands, and Longboat—are celebrity-studded places. The rich and famous maintain part- and even full-time residences on these isles. Some of the names we heard bandied about on our last pass through Siesta Key include Michael Jordan (who played minor-league baseball in Sarasota), Tom Selleck, Jerry Wexler (famed producer for Atlantic Records), Brian Johnston (vocalist for hard rockers AC/DC), and Paul Reubens (Pee Wee Herman) and his parents. We even heard that Tom Cruise and Nicole Kidman roosted here in happier times. No doubt other celebs are ensconced behind tropical privacy hedges. Siesta Key is the kind of place that draws them like a magnet, because of its beautiful setting far from the stampeding paparazzi and nosy public. Besides, you won't find prettier sunsets over the water anywhere this side of Malibu.

Beaches

Siesta Key became welded to Casey Key in 1983 with the man-made closing of Midnight Pass. It is, however, separated from Lido Key to the north by Big Pass. Since Siesta Key falls in Sarasota County, the public is well taken care of with beaches. The beaches on Siesta Key, though markedly different in character, are winners from tip to tip. The main beach accesses—i.e., those with parking lots and facilities—are Turtle Beach and Siesta Key Public Beach. Between them is the not terribly accessible Crescent Beach. A string of beach accesses lies north of Siesta Key Public Beach, off Beach Road and Ocean Boulevard. One last access can be found at Siesta Key's extreme north end, by Shell Road at Big Pass.

Turtle Beach is a generous marvel of preservation on the public's behalf. A spur road runs along the beach for about a quarter mile, offering ample public parking. Turtle Beach is more narrow and sloping than Siesta, and the sand is coarser, browner, and shellier. That is precisely why turtles nest here—they can dig holes in the soft, mounded sand—and how the beach got its name. The writer Joy Williams has expounded on this beach, having owned land around here

9 Palmer Point Beach

Location: On Casey Key; walk south for half a mile from Turtle Beach on Siesta Key
Parking/fees: free parking lot at Turtle Beach
Hours: 6 A.M.–11 P.M.
Facilities: none
Contact: Sarasota County Parks and Recreation Department, 941/316-1172

10 Turtle Beach

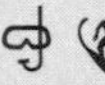  

Location: south end of Siesta Key
Parking/fees: free parking lots
Hours: 6 A.M.–11 P.M.
Facilities: restrooms, picnic tables, and showers
Contact: Sarasota County Parks and Recreation Department, 941/316-1172

MAP OF FLORIDA'S WEST COAST—PAGE 347

that she preserved through a conservation easement. Her essay about Turtle Beach and Siesta Key, "One Acre," is contained in her book *Ill Nature*. It is a primer on Florida real estate that should be read by anyone who loves the state's natural habitat. About the condos of Turtle Beach, she writes:

"The turtles still come to nest, and the volunteers who stake and guard the nests are grateful—they practically weep with gratitude—when the condo dwellers keep their lights out during the hatching weeks so as not to confuse the infant turtles in their late night search for the softly luminous sea. But usually the condo dwellers don't keep their lights out. They might accommodate the request were they there, but they are seldom there. The lights are controlled by timers and burn bright and long. The condos are investments, mostly, not homes. Like the lands they've consumed, they're cold commodities. When land is developed, it ceases being land. It becomes covered, sealed, its own grave."

That said, Turtle Beach is less crowded than Siesta Key Public Beach, and from it you can walk south to **Palmer Point Beach**, where Midnight Pass formerly separated Siesta and Casey Keys. Along the way, you will spy abundant birdlife. We came upon a great blue heron at the surf's edge. It appeared to be as tall as us and was staring out over the gulf with a quizzical expression. We are not used to encountering human being–sized creatures on the beach. When it took off, flapping its enormous wings, it resembled an old World War II biplane.

Above an outcrop known as Point of Rocks, the beach sand changes in composition from shell-based to quartz. At this point, the coastline describes a pronounced curve—hence the name **Crescent Beach**. Located at Siesta Key's midsection, this 2.5-mile beach can be reached from two public access points: Point of Rocks, at the west end of Point of Rocks Road, and Stickney Point, at the west end of Stickney Point Road. Both are off Midnight Pass Road, which runs the length of the island. The only problem is parking, which is limited to a few spaces on the roadside. Those in the know park at Crescent Market (on the east side of Midnight Pass Road) and walk onto the beach in the vicinity of the Surfrider Motel. The best scuba diving and snorkeling in the Sarasota area is at Point of Rocks, with its nearshore reef formation.

Siesta Key Public Beach is a three-quarter-mile swath of sand on the north half of the island. They don't make 'em any nicer than this. Consisting mostly of quartz crystals, the sand is fine grained, white, and therefore highly reflective. This means that

⓫ Crescent Beach

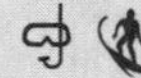

Location: Siesta Key
Parking/fees: free limited parking at the west ends of Point of Rocks Road and Stickney Point Road
Hours: 6 A.M.–11 P.M.
Facilities: none
Contact: Sarasota County Parks and Recreation Department, 941/316-1172

⓬ Siesta Key Public Beach

Location: south end of Beach Road, on Siesta Key
Parking/fees: free parking lot
Hours: 6 A.M.–11 P.M.
Facilities: concessions, lifeguards, restrooms, picnic tables, and showers
Contact: Sarasota County Parks and Recreation Department, 941/316-1172

you won't singe your feet when walking across it on a hot day. It actually feels kind of cool, even in the scorching heat of high summer. There is a downside: because so thoroughly it reflects the sun's rays, it's easy to get sunburned, so slather on the suntan lotion. Also, because it is fine grained, it is also hard packed, so you might wish to bring a beach chair or a chaise lounge for comfort's sake.

At Siesta Key Public Beach you'll find a full complement of facilities, including showers, a shaded picnic area, and a beachside café. A glorified grease pit, the café serves its purpose of assuaging hunger pangs and also provides some unintentional hilarity in the form of winged predators. It is the only restaurant we've ever seen where the counter help hands you a fried shrimp basket and then tenders the warning, "Watch out for the birds, sir." Hungry seabirds perch on the beams above diners' heads, waiting to pounce on any untended grub. We saw them lurking and heard their shrieking. Alfred Hitchcock would no doubt have been delighted by the spectacle. In addition to all that's been mentioned, there are benches, green space, volleyball nets, and lifeguard stands that are staffed year-round. The place has such a pleasant vibe about it that we almost joined a clutch of vegan belly dancers who were gyrating wildly around a group of dreadlocked conga thumpers participating in a good, old-fashioned Ra-worshipping Sunday afternoon drum circle.

Beach lovers should not miss an opportunity to spend time on Siesta Beach or Turtle Beach. The one thing they have in common is the green, inviting water of the gulf. But otherwise they offer strikingly different beach experiences on the same small island. Don't discount the residential north end of the island, either. Though parking is limited, the cluster of public beach accesses off Beach Road and Ocean Boulevard afford entrée onto a less congested and no less beautiful stretch of Siesta Key's award-winning beach.

⓭ Siesta Key (north accesses)

Location: nine beach accesses at the north end of Siesta Key, off Beach Road and Ocean Boulevard; beginning at the north end of Siesta Beach and moving up to Big Pass, these numbered accesses are as follows: Avenida del Mare (No. 11), Calle del Invierno (No. 10), Plaza de las Palmas (Nos. 8 and 9), Calle de la Siesta (No. 7), Ocean Boulevard, (No. 5), Avenida Navarra (No. 4), Avenida Messina (No. 2) and Shell Road (No. 1)
Parking/fees: free limited street parking
Hours: 6 A.M.–11 P.M.
Facilities: none
Contact: Sarasota County Parks and Recreation Department, 941/316-1172

Shore Things

- **Bike/skate rentals:** Siesta Sports Rentals, 6551 Midnight Pass Road, South Bridge Mall, Siesta Key, 941/346-1797.
- **Boat cruise:** Siesta Parasail and Dolphin Tours, 1249 Stickney Point Road, Siesta Key, 941/349-1900.
- **Dive shop:** Dolphin Dive Center, 6018 South Tamiami Trail, Sarasota, 941/924-2785.
- **Ecotourism:** Sweetwater Kayaks, 5263 Ocean Boulevard, Siesta Key, 941/346-1179.
- **Fishing charters:** CB's Saltwater Outfitters, 1249 Stickney Point Road, Siesta Key, 941/349-4400.
- **Marina:** Siesta Key Marina, 1265 Old Stickney Point Road, Siesta Key, 941/349-8880.

MAP OF FLORIDA'S WEST COAST—PAGE 347

Open Midnight Pass!

As we noted in the main text of this chapter, Siesta Key is split down the middle in all kinds of ways: the character of its north and south ends, the sand composition of its beaches, and public opinion surrounding Midnight Pass. This small inlet used to separate Siesta Key from Casey Key, but the two islands are now joined at the hip, so to speak, thanks to the county's decision to fill in and close Midnight Pass. The reasons they did so are not altogether convincing. As we understand it, some homeowners at the south end were worried about their swimming pools, which were subsiding in the saturated sands in the vicinity of the pass. Caving in to the argument of declining property values and imminent risk to private property, the county brought in the bulldozers and the inlet was closed.

This was a shame, because it created a great distance, roughly 30 miles, between inlets—all the way from Stump Pass, at the south end of Manasota Key, up to Big Pass, which divides Siesta and Lido Keys. That's a long way between breaks, and a bay can get pretty polluted without the regular flushing provided by tidal inflow and outflow. The closing of Midnight Pass has contributed to the decline in water quality of Little Sarasota Bay, which is studded with mangrove islands that are bird sanctuaries. The waters are also home to a few wandering manatees from time to time, and some prize fish, including the odd tarpon, have been caught right off the bayside docks of Siesta Key. But the water quality is, make no mistake, suffering. Tamper with nature at your own peril.

Now a vocal grassroots group wants to see Midnight Pass reopened. It wouldn't take a lot, frankly, to make it happen. A channel used by boaters nearly reaches the water now, stopping at the foot of the dunes by Palmer Point. The waterway is used by kayakers and small boaters who come to the end, carry their vessel over the dunes, and launch in the ocean. A few sticks of dynamite, and—*voilà!*—instant inlet. The positives, it seems to us, would outweigh the negatives, the main benefit being that the tides would once again flush the bay twice daily. Oddly enough, some environmental organizations oppose its reopening. Their argument is that the ecological balance that has formed since the pass's closure in 1983 would be thrown out of kilter. Moreover, the unbuilt-upon, pristine public beach that exists at Palmer Point would vanish with the pass's reopening.

All sorts of pro and con arguments can be made, depending upon which side of the pass you live on and what the ensuing changes in the beaches would do to your property (i.e., accretion or erosion). For reasons that involve property values, economic issues, and the environment on Siesta and Casey Keys, the future of Midnight Pass is the hot-button issue in these parts. In a larger sense, it's symbolic of the types of decisions that lay ahead for all coastal communities that wish to balance environmental well-being with economic growth. Finally, the fact that Midnight Pass was closed in the first place is a sad commentary on the sort of influence wielded by those with money and clout. The issue is far from settled, but we'll cast our vote right now: Open Midnight Pass!

MAP OF SARASOTA COUNTY—PAGE 406

- **Rainy-day attraction:** John and Mable Ringling Museum of Art, 5401 Bay Shore Road, Sarasota, 941/359-5700.
- **Shopping/browsing:** St. Armands Circle, St. Armands Key, Sarasota, 941/388-1554.
- **Surf shop:** Village Surf Shop, 149 Avenida Messina, Siesta Key, 941/346-7873.
- **Vacation rentals:** Siesta Key Realty, 5111 Ocean Boulevard, 941/349-8900.

Bunking Down

Down at the less harried south end, there's a little masterpiece of an inn on the bayside. From the street, you'd never guess about the world-within-a-world that lurks behind the modest facade of the **Turtle Beach Resort** (9049 Midnight Pass Road, 941/349-4554, $$$$). An enterprising couple, Gail and Dave Rubinfeld, have transformed what used to be an old fish camp into one of coastal Florida's most unique and appealing getaways. They're up to 10 units, ranging from studios to two-bedroom charmers. Each unit is individually decorated to reflect a different region or theme (e.g., "Country French," "Victorian," "Montego Bay").

We stayed in the "Key West," which evokes tropical surroundings with its flowered rattan furnishings and airy, casual feel. Each unit has full kitchen facilities and a private outdoor patio with hot tub. There's a pool on the premises, a dock with a paddleboat for guests, and one of the best restaurants in the whole of Florida (Ophelia's) next door. Turtle Beach is only a few short steps across the road. The inn is popular with all sorts of people, from honeymooners to vacationing families with pets. Seven-day minimum stays are imposed in the winter high season.

Most folks who come to Siesta Key stay for a week or two. To get the lowdown on rental properties, write the Chamber of Commerce for their latest visitor's guide. The high season on Siesta Key runs from mid-December through the end of April; thereafter, prices drop by about a third. There's only one chain motel on the island—the **Best Western Siesta Beach Resort** (5311 Ocean Boulevard, 941/349-3211, $$$)—and even that is a chain in name only. With its kitchenettes and apartment-style units, it is more in keeping with the beach-apartment standard in Siesta Key.

You'll find a number of places clustered at mid-island by Crescent Beach on Sara Sea Circle, including **Captiva Beach Resort** (6772 Sara Sea Circle, 941/349-4131, $$$) and **Sara Sea Inn at the Beach** (6760 Sara Sea Circle, 941/349-3244, $$$); both have about 20 units, a heated pool, and easy beach access.

Coastal Cuisine

Ophelia's by the Bay (9105 Midnight Pass Road, 941/349-2212, $$$$) has got it all: setting (overlooking Sarasota Bay, with its bird-filled mangrove islands), food (creative preparations made from the freshest ingredients), and atmosphere (casual, rarefied elegance). The dimly lit dining room, done in rich mauves and browns, is suitably romantic, but we'd recommend the outdoor deck if you're inclined toward alfresco dining, mainly because the view is sublime and the breezes refreshing. For an appetizer, try smoked trout with potato pancake, which has a subtle and mild flavor, or ask for a popular off-menu item, Szechuan tuna, which also comes in an entrée-sized portion. Generous hunks of pepper-coated, sushi-grade tuna are flash fried and served with noodles, soy-sherry sauce, and wasabi. Entrées include the ever-popular cedar-roasted salmon: a thick fillet of Atlantic salmon baked on a cedar plank. The fish develops a crisp, dark exterior and sweet, moist interior that picks up sublime nuances and accents from the wood.

The printed menu changes daily but might also include something like baked red snapper crusted with dried, finely chopped black olives. You'll want to try dessert, too: Ophelia's crème brulee is one of the richest served anywhere and moved some fussy foreign diners seated near us to exclamations usually reserved for the conclusion of operatic arias. You, too, will be singing the praises of Ophelia's and shouting "Encore!"

Of course, there's plenty of culinary action on an island as cosmopolitan as Siesta Key. The **Summerhouse** (6101 Midnight Pass Road, 941/349-1100, $$$$) is the key's other great continental restaurant. For casual "Cali-Florida" seafood dining on the water, point your sail toward **Coasters** (1500 Stickney Point Road, 941/923-4848, $$$) at the east end of South Bridge. The **Siesta Fish Market** (221 Garden Lane, 941/349-2602, $$) is a rustic "Old Florida"–style seafood house. Then there's the **Wildflower Restaurant** (5218 Ocean Boulevard, 941/349-1758, $$) for vegetarian and healthy seafood dishes, the **Broken Egg** (210 Avenida Medera, 941/346-2750, $) for breakfast . . . and that should get you started. Don't forget that virtually all motels, resorts, and rental properties on Siesta Key come with kitchens, so you can always toss a line from North Bridge (one of the best fishing spots on the Gulf Coast) and hook your own dinner.

Night Moves

The night moves to a relatively restrained beat on Siesta Key. Most folks inclined to go out after dark head into Sarasota for an evening of jazz, opera, or dance music. Incidentally, an internationally popular subgenre of spliced, diced, and sampled hip-hop comes right out of Sarasota's local scene, so if you want to experience it in its native surroundings, head to a dance club like **In Extremis** (204 Sarasota Quay, 941/954-2008). Actually, anyplace advertising a deejay on its marquee (for example, "DJ Madness," which was one of the handles we saw) will do for getting down. This isn't exactly our idea of a good time, but it's plenty of other people's, so pump up the volume.

Closer to home on Siesta Key, you might scare up some live music and a buzzing crowd at the **Beach Club** (5151 Ocean Boulevard, 941/349-6311). It's located in Siesta Village and open every blessed night of the year.

Contact Information

Siesta Key Chamber of Commerce, 5100-B Ocean Boulevard, Siesta Key, FL 34242; 941/349-3800 or 888/837-3969; website: www.siestakeychamber.com

MAP OF SARASOTA COUNTY—PAGE 406

Sarasota

At the risk of sounding like the nose-in-the-air snobs that we're not—*Beverly Hillbillies* and *Sanford and Son* reruns are our ideas of a good time—Sarasota (pop. 52,000) is something we never thought we'd see on the Gulf Coast of Florida: a genuine cultural capital. Located 60 miles south of Tampa and five miles west of I-75 (Exits 34 through 40), it also serves as a welcome mat to the superb beaches on the barrier islands of Siesta and Lido Keys. In fact, we strained our noggins to think of a city of comparable size in any state that offers so much in the way of history, art, and contemplative wonders. Sarasota has museums, bookshops, colleges, and world-class opera houses, concert halls, and theaters. What's more, it's got beaches, inland parks, aquariums, and historic sites within easy reach.

Sarasota is a veritable three-ring circus of culture, taking its cue from the Ringling family, who got the caravan rolling in 1927. That was the year John and Charles moved the Ringling Brothers and Barnum & Bailey Circus here from Bridgeport, Connecticut. John and wife Mable built their remarkable home and museums (see sidebar "Step Right Up," this chapter), and numerous other wor-

Step Right Up: The Ringling Museums

Whereas much of Florida is a figurative zoo, Sarasota is more like a circus. Seriously. When John and Charles Ringling relocated their world-renowned Ringling Brothers and Barnum & Bailey Circus here in 1927, they inaugurated a tradition of circus mania that continues to this day. Currently, 15 separate circus companies are headquartered in Sarasota County, the largest concentration of big-top artists in the world. To show its support, the community lovingly maintains the Sarasota Circus Hall of Fame, inducting new members each year. The names of these immortals are etched upon a gigantic bronze circus wheel in the middle of St. Armands Circle, at the end of Ringling Causeway on St. Armands Key.

This lush park was originally intended to be the entranceway to the Ringling Brothers' dream resort of Lido Beach. They never completed the resort, but the park is now a beautiful tribute to the marquee names of the circus world (Clyde Beatty, the Wallendas, Gunther Gebel-Williams, Lillian Leitzel, Emmett Kelly) and the lesser known (the Nerveless Nocks, Loyal-Repensky Troupe, "Captain" Curtis, La Norma, Franz Unus). The great Gebel-Williams died at his home in Venice, Florida, on July 19, 2001. R.I.P., Gunther.

Meanwhile, over on the mainland, the John and Mable Ringling Museum of Art and Circus Museum offers an earthly afterlife to circus artifacts. This is no roadside tourist trap—a fact that becomes obvious as you approach the ornate Italian Renaissance–style structure and catch your first gander of the 66-acre complex, replete with a world-class rose garden. An intriguingly eccentric and intelligent man, Ringling wasn't a miser like P.T. Barnum. (Bar-

thy venues followed their lead. Top among these is the **FSU Center for the Performing Arts** (5555 North Tamiami Trail, 941/351-8000), home of the Sarasota Ballet and the award-winning Asolo Theatre Company, whose interior reconstructs a 1903 Scottish opera house. There's also the **Ringling Museum of Art** (5401 Bayshore Road, 941/351-1660), the **Sarasota Opera Association** (61 North Pineapple Avenue, 941/366-8450), and the **Florida West Coast Symphony** (Beatrice Friedman Symphony Center, 709 North Tamiami Trail, 941/943-4252). The centerpiece of Sarasota's bayfront is the city-owned **Van Wezel Performing Arts Hall** (777 North Tamiami Trail, 941/953-3366), a stunning facility whose wholesale renovation was completed in October 2000.

In addition to these attractions, Sarasota is the springtime home of the Cincinnati Reds and the winter home—actually, from December to June—of the Sarasota Kennel Club, which hosts greyhound racing. It is the jumping-off point to Florida's largest state park, Myakka River State Park, and home of the Selby Botanical Garden. Finally, the Sarasota area is a mecca to anyone interested in archaeology, with three prehistoric sites of enduring interest close by: Spanish Point, Little Salt Springs, and Warm Mineral Springs.

The best way to get a handle on Sara-

num's last words: "How were the receipts at Madison Square Garden today?") Inspired by the East Coast manses of Henry Flagler and John D. Rockefeller, as well as that of Henry Plant of nearby Tampa, Ringling built a multifaceted paradise in Sarasota.

The Circus Museum is just one part of the tour. To get to it requires passing through an impressive art museum. This high-ceilinged, parquet-floored palace houses enough old Dutch masters, Madonnas, angels, Christ childs, and grim-visaged popes to outfit a national gallery. Also in the collection is a monumentally scaled series of works by Peter Paul Rubens. Just outside the art museum is a meditative sculpture garden, and beyond that the celebrated rose garden.

The Circus Museum turns out to be an exceptionally honest, understated, and eclectic tribute to what seems like a lost world now. The working calliopes—in their day, known by fundamentalist fuddy-duddies as "the Devil's whistle"—draw you like Sirens, making it easy to see how they might have lured runaways to the circus in the days before television, rock music, Nintendo, and nose piercing. It's all here: beautiful posters and prints, documentary photographs, equipment (including the human cannonball's cannon), circus wagons that look like prototypes for Ken Kesey's Merry Prankster bus, and Emmett Kelly's Weary Willie suit (a precursor of Johnny Rotten's wardrobe).

Then there's the Cà d'Zan ("House of John"), the Ringling's 30-room terra-cotta mansion, an extravagant bayfront residence built to suggest Mable's two favorite pieces of architecture, the Doge's Palace in Venice and the Old Madison Square Garden. Finally, of course, there's a café and gift shops. The reasonable admission fee ($9 for adults, free for children under 12) includes access to the art museum, courtyard, rose garden, circus museum, and Cà d'Zan. The Ringling complex is open daily 10 A.M.–5:30 P.M.

For more information, contact John and Mable Ringling Museum of Art, 5401 Bay Shore Road, Sarasota, FL 34243; 941/359-5700; website: www.ringling.org.

sota's many attractions is to contact the Sarasota Convention and Visitors Bureau in advance or drop by on the way into town. Ask for a copy of "Sarasota Over My Shoulder," an informative brochure published by the Department of Historical Resources. The only downside to all this cultural capital is that you can get happily hung up on the mainland and forget to cross the bridges to the beaches. Don't let this happen to you. In fact, make like a human cannonball and blast yourself toward the beach over the road named for the man himself, John Ringling Causeway (State Route 789).

Contact Information

Greater Sarasota Chamber of Commerce, 1819 Main Street, Suite 240, Sarasota, FL 34236; 941/955-8187; website: www.sarasotachamber.org or www.sarasota.com

Sarasota Convention and Visitors Bureau, 655 North Tamiami Trail, Sarasota, FL 34236; 941/957-1877 or 800/522-9799; website: www.sarasotafl.org

Lido Beach, Lido Key, and St. Armands Key

First, a clarification. Lido Beach is not an incorporated town but part of the city of Sarasota. It lies on Lido Key, a three-mile gulf-fronting key located just north of Siesta Key. The configuration of the two neighboring keys is fairly similar. Though only half as long as Siesta Key, Lido shares the same preponderance of soft, powdery white sand in roughly the same configuration: wide at the north end of the key, thinning as you move south. To get to Lido Key from mainland Sarasota, head west on Ringling Causeway (State Route 780). En route, you'll cross three smaller keys: in order, Bird Key, Coon Key, and St. Armands Key. The last of these is a compact, Chicken McNugget–shaped key enfolded on three sides by the protective embrace of Lido Key. Your arrival on St. Armands is heralded by the glittery spectacle of St. Armands Circle, an upscale shopping district that one local described to us as "our Rodeo Drive."

Happily, St. Armands Circle is not nearly so off putting and exclusive as Rodeo Drive in Beverly Hills or Worth Avenue in Palm Beach, to which it bears only a dim resemblance. Instead, it is a lively, accessible, and not completely snooty shopping area that's something like CocoWalk, in the Miami suburb of Coconut Grove. Initially the centerpiece of John Ringling's dream resort community, St. Armands Circle is a lushly landscaped traffic circle and park, with side streets flaring off it like spokes. Each street is home to a strip of upscale boutiques and gift shops, many of which have daffy-sounding names—Soft as a Grape, To Die For!, Wet Noses, Tommy Bahama, Ted E. Bear Shop—that subliminally soften the damage you'll wind up doing to the vacation budget. While these stores have their undeniable appeal to a certain class of shoppers, we were amused by the fact that our pressing quest for something practical—a spool of masking tape to seal a box of materials for mailing home—among the 120 or so shops was unsuccessful. For that, we had to drive back over to Sarasota.

For us, the most important side street off St. Armands Circle is the one that leads to Lido Beach. It's located halfway around the circle from where you entered via Ringling Causeway (it is, in fact, the continuation of Ringling Boulevard). Barely a quarter mile away, Lido Beach offers a welcome, low-key counterpoint to the gauntlet of rampant consumerism you just exited on St. Armands Key. Here

MAP OF FLORIDA'S WEST COAST—PAGE 347

is an almost nondescript beach strip running the length of Ben Franklin Drive. It is public-access heaven for beachgoers out here, with free ample parking, very little commercial buildup, and not much of an artificial identity at all. This is not a complaint. Indeed, if you hit Lido Beach at the right time, you'll have a wide, wonderful swath of beach all to yourself. Given the crowds and traffic on Siesta Key and the almost fascistic exclusivity of Longboat Key to the north, Lido Beach strikes a happy medium.

Beaches

The gulf-facing coast of Lido Key—a 2.5-mile stretch from Big Sarasota Pass to New Pass—is one long, uninterrupted beach, and it's delightfully isolated in places. In fact, given the large sums exchanging hands on St. Armands Circle, it is somewhat surprising to find Lido Beach relatively free of condos, high-rises, and the other types of development normally attracted to beaches proximate to a metropolitan area. But before you hail Sarasota to loudly for keeping gentrification at bay, this piece of news: construction began in early 2001 on an 11-story Ritz-Carlton beach club, which joins a 13-story Radisson Lido Beach Resort hotel tower. The $80 million Ritz-Carlton is set to open in late 2001.

The good news in all this is that the county owns 6,740 linear feet (about 1.3 miles) of gulf beach frontage on Lido Key. A trio of county beach parks starts at Big Pass with **South Lido Beach**, a 100-acre nature preserve with a small (640 feet) gulf beach and a much larger stretch of shoreline along Big Pass (3,500 feet). There are two park entrances: a north one facing Sarasota Bay and a south one on Lido Beach. Within each park section is a nature trail. The Northern Nature Trail explores a coastal ridge, mangrove swamp, and tidal swamp forest. The shorter Southern Nature Trail runs along a sandy-soiled coastal ridge that's thick with Australian pine. A highly competitive tree that shades out other species, this exotic is high on the list of species targeted for removal in Flori-

⓮ South Lido Beach

Location: south end of Ben Franklin Drive, at the southern tip of Lido Key
Parking/fees: free parking lot
Hours: 6 A.M. to sunset
Facilities: lifeguards (seasonal), restrooms, picnic tables, and showers
Contact: Sarasota County Parks and Recreation Department, 941/316-1172

⓯ Lido Beach

Location: 400 Ben Franklin Drive, a half-mile southwest of St. Armands Circle at Lido Beach
Parking/fees: free parking lot
Hours: 6 A.M. to sunset
Facilities: concessions, lifeguards, restrooms, picnic tables, and showers
Contact: Sarasota County Parks and Recreation Department, 941/316-1172

⓰ North Lido Beach

Location: from St. Armands Circle, follow John Ringling Boulevard west to Lido Key, then turn right on North Polk Drive and proceed to North Lido Beach Park
Parking/fees: free parking lot
Hours: 6 A.M. to sunset
Facilities: none
Contact: Sarasota County Parks and Recreation Department, 941/316-1172

Mote Marine Aquarium and Laboratory

The Sarasota area tosses a lot of tantalizing, unique, and non-Disneyesque attractions your way. If you're staying at least a week, many are well worth checking out, including the Ringling Museum, Spanish Point, Selby Botanical Garden, Myakka River Excursions, and even the newly expanded Jungle Gardens. If, however, your schedule is tight or you just don't want to spend a vacation madly scrambling for diversions when there's a chaise lounge in the sand with your name on it, one place should nonetheless be a required stop for any visit here: Mote Marine Aquarium and Laboratory.

There are several reasons for this, not the least of which is that Mote Lab is located close to the beach, off the northeast corner of St. Armands Key on man-made City Island. More important, Mote comprises both a museum and a research lab that brings visitors as close to the coastal ecosystem as they can get without a wet suit and snorkel. Upon entering the aquarium, you're greeted by a tiger shark jaw over whose four rows of razor-sharp teeth you're invited to run your finger. Sharks, you learn, are flirting with the endangered species list, and one of Mote's programs has been to tag sharks in order to study their dwindling numbers and keep them from being needlessly slaughtered.

It is worth noting that, to prepare for their opening presidential and vice presidential debates with George W. Bush and Dick Cheney in October 2000, Al Gore and Joe Lieberman set up their base camp at Mote Lab, spending most of their time studying shark behavior. Given the result of the election and the post-election chaos in Florida, perhaps they should have spent some time studying the eel, as well.

The centerpieces of the aquarium are a 135,000-gallon shark tank and a touch tank at which kids can handle various species and learn from the helpful staff. At Mote, they're working to restock shark and other fish species in the oceans and gulf, especially

da. In addition, the northern unit has a canoe trail that winds along mangrove-lined waterways. South Lido Park offers a lot to the nature enthusiast, so eat your Wheaties and head out here. If you're planning on swimming, be advised that currents near the pass can be swift, so stick to marked areas only.

The main beach is called, simply, **Lido Beach**, and it's located half a mile southwest of St. Armands Circle on Ben Franklin Drive. The park claims over 3,100 feet of beachfront and an enormous free parking lot. There's metered parking along Ben Franklin Drive to handle any spillover. Also at Lido Beach: a snack bar, a gift shop, restrooms, showers, a playground, beach rentals, and a 25-meter heated swimming pool with diving board. Lifeguards are on duty year-round. The beach itself suffers erosion problems, eloquently demonstrated by the sight of naked, forlorn palms standing in wet sand. The groins that line the shallows along the central part of the key are another giveaway. A beach renourishment project along the entirety of Lido Key was begun in 1997, and the city has been petitioning the state for funds (to the tune of roughly $600,000 per year) to keep it fortified for the next half-century. This does not bode well either for beaches or budgets. There's

Map of Florida's West Coast—Page 347

those whose vital grasslands habitat is disappearing, thus robbing them of the first stage of their life cycle. All told, 200 live marine species are on display. They come in every shape and size, from spiny lobsters, balloonfish, and cowfish to urchins, sturgeons, barracudas, and octopuses. (Pop quiz: How many hearts does an octopus have?) Admission to Mote Marine Aquarium is $8 for adults, $6 for students ages 4–17, and free for kids under 4. It's open from 10 A.M.–5 P.M. daily. (Answer to pop quiz: An octopus has three hearts.)

The other building here that's open to the public is the Marine Mammal Visitor Center, which has tanks full of dolphins, manatees, and whales. This facility takes in and rehabilitates large injured sea animals (everything from porpoises to sea turtles). The center also works to find aquaculture solutions to environmental disasters. For example, most of the caviar that's sold comes from a criminal black market and is stolen from nearly extinct sturgeon. (Just say no to caviar). The main attraction at the center is a pair of manatees who bob together inseparably in their tank, subsisting on Romaine lettuce and other vegetarian fare. Their grocery bill for the week is $1,163. But they don't know that.

Based out of the same facility is **Sarasota Bay Explorers** (941/388-4200), an ecocruise operation that leads "sea life encounter trips." They leave every weekday at 4 P.M., and there are 11 A.M. and 1 P.M. cruises as well on weekends, barring inclement weather or rough seas. This two-hour educational outing cruises Sarasota and Robert Bays, exploring grass flats and mangrove islands for close encounters with dolphins, manatees, pelicans, herons, ibises, egrets, ospreys, eagles, and more. Binoculars are provided.

In the same spirit and just down the block is **Pelican Man's Bird Sanctuary** (1708 Ken Thompson Parkway, 941/388-4444), which does for our injured winged friends what Mote does for wounded ocean dwellers. This "open-air home and rehabilitation center" welcomes visitors, and admission is free.

For more information contact the Mote Marine Aquarium and Laboratory, 1600 Ken Thompson Parkway, Sarasota, FL 34236; 941/388-2451 or 800/691-MOTE; website: www.marinelab.sarasota.fl.us.

even talk of emplacing gigantic limestone groins to hold the beach in place. This is not good.

A quarter-mile northwest of St. Armands Circle is **North Lido Beach**, a 77-acre beachfront preserve located at the end of the road (but not the end of the key). There's a whopping 3,000 feet of shore at North Lido, which is more secluded than Lido Beach, though parking is practically nil. There are no lifeguards or facilities. Basically, it's been kept in a wild state for the birds and the beachcombers who want to escape the crowds. Nude sunbathing was allowed here well into the 1980s. Chances are that it still goes on, though it is now technically illegal. Currents here can be dangerous, so maybe nude sunbathing is the safest activity after all.

Shore Things

- **Bike/skate rentals**: Pedal 'n' Wheels, 2881 Clark Road, 941/922-0481; Flamingo Coast RollerBlade, St. Armands Circle, 941/388-1889.
- **Boat cruise**: The Enterprise, Marina Jack's, 2 Marina Plaza, 941/951-1833.
- **Dive shop**: Dolphin Dive Center, 6018 South Tamiami Trail, 941/924-2785.

- **Ecotourism:** Sarasota Bay Explorers, Mote Marina, 1600 Ken Thompson Parkway, 941/388-4200.
- **Fishing charters:** Flying Fish Fleet, Marina Jack's, 2 Marina Plaza, 941/366-3373.
- **Marina:** Gulfwind Marine, 1601 Ken Thompson Parkway, 941/388-4411.
- **Pier:** New Pass Fishing Pier, Ken Thompson Parkway, 941/316-1172.
- **Rainy-day attraction:** Mote Marine Aquarium and Laboratory, 1600 Ken Thompson Parkway, 941/388-4441.
- **Shopping/browsing:** St. Armands Circle, St. Armands Key, 941/388-1554.
- **Surf shop:** One World, 6245 Clark Center Avenue, 941/925-0007.
- **Vacation rentals:** Lido Vacation Rentals, 528 South Polk Drive, 941/388-1004.

Bunking Down

A block of hotels perch directly on Lido Beach. All are located along Ben Franklin Drive southwest of St. Armands Circle. They offer resort-style amenities, with pools, lounges, and restaurants. The beach is uniformly wide, white, and breezy in front of all three. In ascending order of appeal, they are **Harley Sandcastle** (1540 Ben Franklin Drive, 941/388-2181, $$$), the **Holiday Inn–Lido Beach** (233 Ben Franklin Drive, 941/388-5555, $$$), and the **Radisson Lido Key Beach Resort** (700 Ben Franklin Drive, 941/388-2161, $$$). The last of these is the newest, which gives it an edge up on the older properties on the island. You'll pay in the vicinity of $185 a night at the Radisson in season. God knows what the tariff will be at the Ritz-Carlton, mentioned earlier, when it's completed.

Coastal Cuisine

St. Armands Circle is a tamer version of Miami's Coconut Grove. While the tone is decidedly upscale, it is not dominated by huge flagship shops or faddish food and entertainment emporiums like Planet Hollywood. Instead, a large number of unique shops and eateries can be found here, making for pleasurable evening strolls. Suffice to say there's a whole lotta window shoppin' goin' on. Morning strollers are in for a treat, because they'll luck into **Morty's Bagel Cafe** (24 South Boulevard of Presidents, 941/388-3811, $), just a block from **Barnie's Coffee & Tea Co.** (382 St. Armands Circle, 941/388-1195, $). The former turns out bagels as good as any in Brooklyn, while the latter serves eye-opening cups of java, donating a portion of their profits to Habitat for Humanity. Speaking of socially responsible businesses, two doors down is **Ben & Jerry's** (372 St. Armands Circle, 941/388-5226, $).

For dinner, we drifted to the most hailed of the local eateries, **Columbia Restaurant** (411 St. Armands Circle, 941/388-3987, $$$). The Columbia originated in Tampa's Ybor City in 1905, and the St. Armands Circle location is one of its limited number of affiliates, having opened for business in 1959. The Columbia serves Cuban dishes, including a paella and arroz con pollo to die for. This is a must-stop on St. Armands Circle. We also heard commendations for **Chef Caldwell's** (20 Adams Drive South, 941/388-5400, $$$$), whose signature dishes are grilled venison, roasted duckling, and pecan-crusted snapper.

Night Moves

The outdoor patio at **Cha Cha Coconuts** (417 St. Armands Circle, 941/388-3300)—next door to the Columbia Restaurant on the northeast quadrant of St. Armands Circle—is about as wild as it gets on St. Armands Key. Even on a Friday night, the partying we witnessed was not enough to scare off the elderly couples contentedly strolling the sidewalks below the mayhem. All in all, this is a civilized place to visit at night. Seldom is heard a discouraging word, and blaring rap and mindless dance beats are but minimally encountered.

Taking our cue from St. Armands, we headed into Sarasota and spent a pleasant evening browsing **Main Bookshop** (1962 Main Street, 941/366-7653), which is open until 11 P.M. seven days a week. This place is a monster, with the largest selection of "remainders" (out-of-print books for rock-bottom prices) outside of New York City, plus hundreds of thousands of new books, posters, prints, free coffee, and reading areas. We tip our beach visors to any independent shop that can stand toe to toe with the corporate mega-chains.

Contact Information

Greater Sarasota Chamber of Commerce, 1819 Main Street, Suite 240, Sarasota, FL 34236; 941/955-8187; website: www.sarasotachamber.org or www.sarasota.com

Sarasota Convention and Visitors Bureau, 655 North Tamiami Trail, Sarasota, FL 34236; 941/957-1877 or 800/522-9799; website: www.sarasotafl.org

Longboat Key (south end)

The honest truth is that Longboat Key (pop. 8,000) is an island without soul or personality. What you see is exactly what you get—a sterile, manufactured paradise on the gulf for those who can afford the real estate. At one time Longboat Key had a history and a certain island quaintness based upon those who'd lived or visited for generations, but today it projects all the welcoming warmth and charm of a bank lobby. The tropical greenery is in place, as is typical of privatized hideaways on Florida's various coasts, but it's so obsessively tended and preternaturally lush that it exists in almost brazen disharmony with the landscape it is meant to decorate. The local landscaping services apparently work overtime trimming hedges into perfectly shaped silos and meatballs. A thicket of greenery embowers the premises of homes and condos so densely from the roadway as to create an impenetrable wall. There's nothing aesthetically generous or remotely artful in these horticultural presentations, which instead convey an obsessive demand for privacy that practically screams, "Stay off my property!"

Longboat Key managed to survive the first half of the 20th century as a quiet fishing village. John Ringling made an attempt to construct a resort at the south end of the island in the 1930s, but he abandoned the golf course and hotel in midstream. Groundwork for a serious developmental makeover began when the Arvida corporation began buying up land, including Ringling's holdings, in the late 1950s. Arvida, one of the big (earth) movers and shakers on the Florida development scene, is largely responsible for what has happened on Longboat Key. At one time, there wasn't much more than ranch-style vacation homes and "sandspur" lots (i.e., vacant tracts covered with prickly sandspurs). Arvida patched together enough plats and implemented a developmental game plan that consisted mainly of scraping off the natural surroundings and erecting private homes and condo complexes for buyers with deep pockets. It's well known that condo units on Florida's coasts often belong to absentee owners. Typically, these are the kinds of people with multiple residences scattered around the planet. So few people owning so much real estate that blocks beach views and access for the many who deserve better—that is the coast of Florida in general and Longboat Key in particular.

To be fair, there are discernible differences between opposing ends of the 11-mile island, which is almost evenly

MAP OF SARASOTA COUNTY—PAGE 406

The Wrong People Have All the Money

We're lounging poolside at an upscale beach resort somewhere on the coast of Florida. No need divulging the name and location, or even which coast it's on, since the experience could happen anywhere. We've stuck this next to Longboat Key because this 12-mile island typifies the phenomenon we are about to address. Bear in mind, however, this rant is not about a particular place but is a general commentary on the way that wealth behaves and is courted at the beach.

The high-rise building behind the pool and Jacuzzi where we're hanging out has all the architectural charm of an armory. Everything about it encourages isolation, in the profoundest existential sense of the word. There is no real sense of celebration and few opportunities for interacting, just a block of well-furnished concrete cells in which those who can afford the stiff tariff ($350 or more per night in season) loll around, sleeping and watching TV and running up the tab by golfing or partaking of the in-room "convenience bar." You even pay at such places for the privilege of lying on the beach. A cabana setup—basically, a chaise lounge and umbrella—can set you back $20 a day, plus tip to the attendant.

That's another place they get you time and again, the "plus tip" part of any service rendered, no matter how trifling or unnecessary: getting a bath towel, having luggage toted to your room (even if you'd rather do it yourself), having your car parked by a mandatory valet "service" (translation: paying strangers to strip your car's gears). Think of such resort stays in these terms: You'll spend several days' wages to gain access to a room for roughly 16 hours. America's economy is kept healthy by this sort of racket.

The resort tower where these dark thoughts are flooding our heads blocks views of and access to the beach to all but those who are staying here. It is as if all the hotels and condos are saying, "Not only can't you afford to vacation on this beach, we're not even going to allow you to look at it." It goes without saying that non-guests cannot cross the property to the beach, encountering an off-putting maze of guard gates, fences, manned checkpoints, winding pathways, and signs warning them off the property. Legally, the beach is public property seaward of the mean high-tide line. It belongs to everybody, and everybody has a right to be on it. The trick is crossing the private property to get to the public property. Hence, the need for public beach access, which is well served by some counties and communities and virtually nonexistent in others.

All this is passing through our minds as we stand a few feet away from the Jacuzzi, weighing the merits of mingling with strangers in a giant outdoor bathtub. We realize with a sinking feeling that we have nothing in common with any of them. There are eight people in the Jacuzzi. Half are grossly overweight men with highballs in their hands. They have not actually been on the beach, which is all of 50 feet away, during their entire stay, and this is their first lungful of fresh air following a full eight hours of business conventioneering. The others are yuppie couples gossiping about the pending divorce of some friends: "Poor ol' Rob, he's gonna feel like he's been robbed when Julie's done with him—ha! ha! ha!"

At the poolside tiki bar, a well-heeled young couple stares wordlessly at each other—not out of rapture but from a lack of anything meaningful to say. A pair of $300 designer sunglasses (we know, because we heard him quote the price) dangles from a cord around his neck as he sips numbly on a frozen drink immortalized in a Jimmy Buffett song. She's staring goofily into the middle distance, her lips—a marvel of the plastic surgeon's art—strained into an unnatural smile. A few old folks are tromping around, dripping wet in baggy swimsuits, muttering grumpily about where and when they'll have dinner. The cabana clerk begins breaking down the setups on the beach. On the patio, a waitress sets up tables for the dinner hour. The sun is setting and the sky is beautiful, but the human landscape in the shadow of this gray building is unbearably depressing.

Several questions haunt us constantly in our travels around the beaches of America: Who are the beaches for? Do the people who have access to the most desirable of the beaches really deserve the exclusivity that wealth and income purchases? Shouldn't the best things about a democracy—especially equality of access to the grandest natural features of the very land itself—be available to all?

Some hours have passed, and we're eating dinner in a restaurant to which we'd been tipped off by some locals. A foursome walks in: two couples dripping money and self-importance. In fact, it quickly becomes apparent they've got more money than sense. Before the waiter can get a word out, one of the women blurts, "Ya got any salmon?" With all the available choices of native species plucked fresh from local waters, she wants salmon, flown in from the other side of the continent. Her jowly husband peers over his bifocals and scowls, to no one in particular, "I ought to get broiled. Know it's better for you. But I don't like broiled. Always shrinks up to nothing." Once the orders are placed and menus collected, the big-mouthed patriarch avails himself of a reserve of tasteless, unfunny, and tired jokes about the Clintons. When we leave, he's still at it, huffing and puffing, full of hot air and fried seafood.

No sooner have we returned to our room in the high-priced resort when there's a knock at the door. It's a maid armed with a rose and some chocolates offering "turndown service." If you've never stayed in an expensive hotel, then try to imagine the following, represented to the overpaying guest as a "service." A chambermaid stealthily enters your room like the tooth fairy, often when you're out to dinner, and turns down the sheets, thereby making it infinitely easier for you to get into bed. Oh, and a chocolate wafer is placed atop the pillow. In our case, as this is a very upscale resort, she's brought a fresh flower as well. We're best friends but we don't exchange flowers. We turn her away, politely declining the proffered turndown and the rose. "No thanks," one of us blubbers, flustered at having to explain such matters to a non-English-speaking maid, "I'm here with my pal."

Our final thoughts before turning in have to do with soap—specifically what a waste of soap there is in this place. Large plastic-wrapped scented imported soaps made of the finest ingredients are stationed at every sink and tub (which number six in all at our two-bedroom condo). What happens to the 95 percent of the bar that isn't used? Isn't there a better way—say, refillable tanks of liquid soap, which would cut down on packaging and eliminate the wasteful discarding of countless bars of barely used soap?

Really, the larger point that's driven home to us by day's end—after surveying wasteful extravagance and unconscionable charges at a place we could never afford to stay were we not writing a book—is that the wrong people have all the money. One of the things that makes them wrong, in our view, is the presumption that a beach can be owned.

divided between Sarasota County (south end) and Manatee County (north end). The south end is old-fogey land, where Reagan-era "I got mine"-ism is the reigning philosophy and uptightness reaches a starchy crescendo. The north end is marginally more residential and younger (read: yuppie), a bit more attuned to history and nature, although there's not much left to preserve on either count. The north-enders refer to themselves as the "village idiots," because they're wild and crazy liberals compared to the sour-faced, golf club-toting, Mylanta-chugging sorts down south.

What bothers us most about Longboat Key is the relative lack of beach access and facilities for those who don't own or rent property here. Basically, the condo architecture is boring, the beaches hard to get at, and the general vibe unfriendly. That's not to say you can't have a good time if you arrive with family or friends, doing things that people traveling together like to do for rest and relaxation. The beach is white and fine, the gulf inviting. In addition, a 10-mile bike path runs the length of the island, paralleling Gulf of Mexico Drive. But there's something inexplicably generic about Longboat Key, and you have to bring your good times with you because they don't exist here. The island lacks the just-folks conviviality that ideally makes going to the beach fun for one and all. To our eyes, which have seen every ocean and gulf beach in the continental United States, Longboat Key is lacking in any quality that might captivate the spirit as completely as it assaults the pocketbook. It's as uptight as the Hamptons, but even that wealthy Long Island enclave can justly boast of having wide, beautiful, and publicly accessible beaches. The same cannot be said of Longboat Key.

Okay, enough bashing. We'll just leave off by saying there are better vacation spots worth touting in both of the counties that claim a share of Longboat Key. Ultimately, this island is an uptight expression of wealth, luxury, entitlement, and the urge to conquer and claim the best that nature has to offer.

17 Longboat Key accesses (south end)

Location: beach accesses with parking located at 3055 (near Neptune Avenue), 3174 (across from Buttonwood Plaza), 3400 (near the Sea Horse Restaurant) and 3500 (near Long View Drive) Gulf of Mexico Drive on Longboat Key; in addition, there is a county-owned access at Triton Avenue
Parking/fees: free parking lots
Hours: 5 A.M.–11 P.M.
Facilities: none
Contact: Longboat Key Public Works Department, 941/316-1966

Beaches

All other quibbles aside, the city of **Longboat Key** does offer a grudging shore of public beach access. On the Sarasota County side of the line, accesses are provided every quarter mile between 3000 and 3500 Gulf of Mexico Drive. There are four such parcels, each offering free parking lots with between 19 and 54 parking spaces. Each has a wood-chip parking lot and access to a wide, white-sand beach. It's an undeniably nice beach that's part of the same string of sugar-sand keys that include Siesta, Lido, and Anna Maria, with the main difference being that there are no public facilities—not a restroom, water fountain, or even a lousy garden hose to rinse off your feet—at any of Longboat's accesses. Therefore, you're probably better off crossing the bridge onto Anna Maria Island, where you'll immediately find yourself at Coquina Beach, a broad, white, healthy, and inviting public park covered in more detail in the Manatee County chapter.

Ultimately, it's hard to shake the feeling that you're not really wanted on Longboat Key unless you're an owner or paying guest. The beach and ocean are hidden from view of the road along much of Longboat Key, with the exception of one beach-hugging stretch at its midsection. Surfers refer to the area as "Lookout," because it's the one place you can look out at the gulf from the road to gauge the surf. However, the beach views here are spoiled by a plague of signs spiked into the sand that read "Private Property." So you must keep shuffling along, lest you threaten the security of their gilded enclave. The good news is that getting off the island will make both you (the would-be visitor) and the cranky property owners of Longboat Key (the reluctant hosts) happy.

It should be noted that there are a couple of commendable city parks on the bay side of Longboat Key: Quick Point Nature Preserve, a tidal lagoon and mangrove wetland at the island's south end, and John M. Duarante Community Park, which preserves a sliver of coastal hammock up at the north end.

Bunking Down

If you're not renting for a week or two, there are several resort hotels on the island, with the best beachside locations belonging to the **Holiday Inn and Suites of Longboat Key** (4949 Gulf of Mexico Drive, 941/383-3771, $$$$) and the **Longboat key Hilton** (4711 Gulf of Mexico Drive, 941/383-2451, $$$$). We will give the overseers of Longboat Key this much credit: They've done a great job of minimizing signage with restrictive ordinances. No sign can be more than four feet tall, and neon is forbidden. This contributes to the anonymity of the island in a positive way; that is, hotel, motel, restaurant, bar, and store signs do not assault the senses. We wish only that in addition to this commonsense aesthetic there was something more along the lines of "welcome" than "go away" projected on this highly privatized island.

Without question, the top-of-the-line resort is the **Resort at Longboat Key** Club (301 Gulf of Mexico Drive, 941/383-8821, $$$$). It is located at the extreme south end of Longboat Key, on the site of what used to be land owned by John Ringling. He built a Ritz-Carlton on this spot in the 1930s, lavishly appointed with chandeliers and brass fixtures in the pursuit of his dream for a luxury resort by the sea. Unfortunately, Ringling's dream was dashed by the Depression, and the hotel was abandoned shy of completion. The "Ghost Hotel," as it was called by locals, stood for 30 years until its demolition in 1963. To this day, many Sarasotans who came of age in the '50s can spin yarns of adolescent misdeeds committed in and on the grounds of the Ghost Hotel.

Where once an old, unused hotel stood, however, now there are six suite-filled towers, three restaurants, 36 tennis courts, and 45 holes of golf. If Dad is a golf nut, Mom likes tennis, and the kids just want to splash around a pool, the whole kit and caboodle will be happy at the Longboat Key Club. The buildings may seem a bit impersonal from the outside, but inside well-appointed suites offer all the comforts of home: roomy rooms, balconies, and extras like robes, coffeemakers, and TVs everywhere you turn. Guest rooms run $325–410 in the high season (late January through late April) and drop to $160–275 in the summer months. The replenished beach at the Longboat Key Club, which lies half a mile north of New Pass Bridge, is a wide, white ribbon and the cabanas look inviting. Nothing could be finer than a day spent gazing on the gulf from a cabana with a dog-eared book and a cool drink. Who needs golf when you've got gulf?

Coastal Cuisine

One slice of life as it used to be on Longboat Key can be found by turning onto

Broadway where it meets Gulf of Mexico Drive (State Route 789) at a Chevron station on the island's far north end. Off the main road, low-slung bungalows and normal-looking yards impart a whiff of yesteryear. Supposedly three of the original "Whitney Beach cottages" still stand near the water in this small area. Two waterfront restaurants preserve the real ambience of Longboat Key (as opposed to the contrived aura at developments like L'Ambience, where condo units start at $600,000).

The oldest seafood restaurant in Manatee County, **Moore's Stone Crab** (800 Broadway Street, 941/383-1748, $$$) is a gray, weathered structure that specializes in stone crab claws in season. When we last passed through, stone crab dinners were going for $22, while jumbos were fetching $40. The menu lists all sorts of seafood, but for a good sampling try "The One and Only Longboat Platter," which includes fried shrimp, oysters, scallops, fish fingers, and seafood chowder. You can dock your boat at Moore's. The glassed-in dining room overlooks the dock, which serves as a perch for pelicans and seagulls. There are lots of waterbirds hanging around, so bring your camera. When it comes to good seafood, 50 perching pelicans can't be wrong, right?

Euphemia Haye (5540 Gulf of Mexico Drive, 941/383-3633, $$$$) sets the standard for fine dining on Longboat Key with a continental menu spanning everything from fresh seafood to roast duckling. We're partial to the **Mar Vista** (760 Broadway Street, 941/383-2391, $$$), which looks like an old bait shack because that's exactly what it is. The ceilings are low and studded with grubstake. At lunch you can get a grilled grouper Reuben ($10) or a Caesar salad topped with fresh shrimp and crabmeat ($11). At dinner, the chef works his sorcery on an array of made-from-scratch sauces that adorn such dishes as triggerfish Kyoto (a sautéed fillet served with palm hearts, shitake mushrooms, and soy-sherry butter). Also recommended is the sesame tuna, which is pan seared and served with a pungent ginger wasabi soy sauce. If you've just got a yen for seafood simply prepared, go for the steamer pots.

Night Moves

Most of the night moves on Longboat Key are made by befuddled sea turtles looking to lay eggs on narrowing beaches of what was for thousands of years their private property.

Contact Information

Longboat Key Chamber of Commerce, 6854 Gulf of Mexico Drive, Longboat Key, FL 34228; 941/383-2466; website: www.longboatkeychamber.com

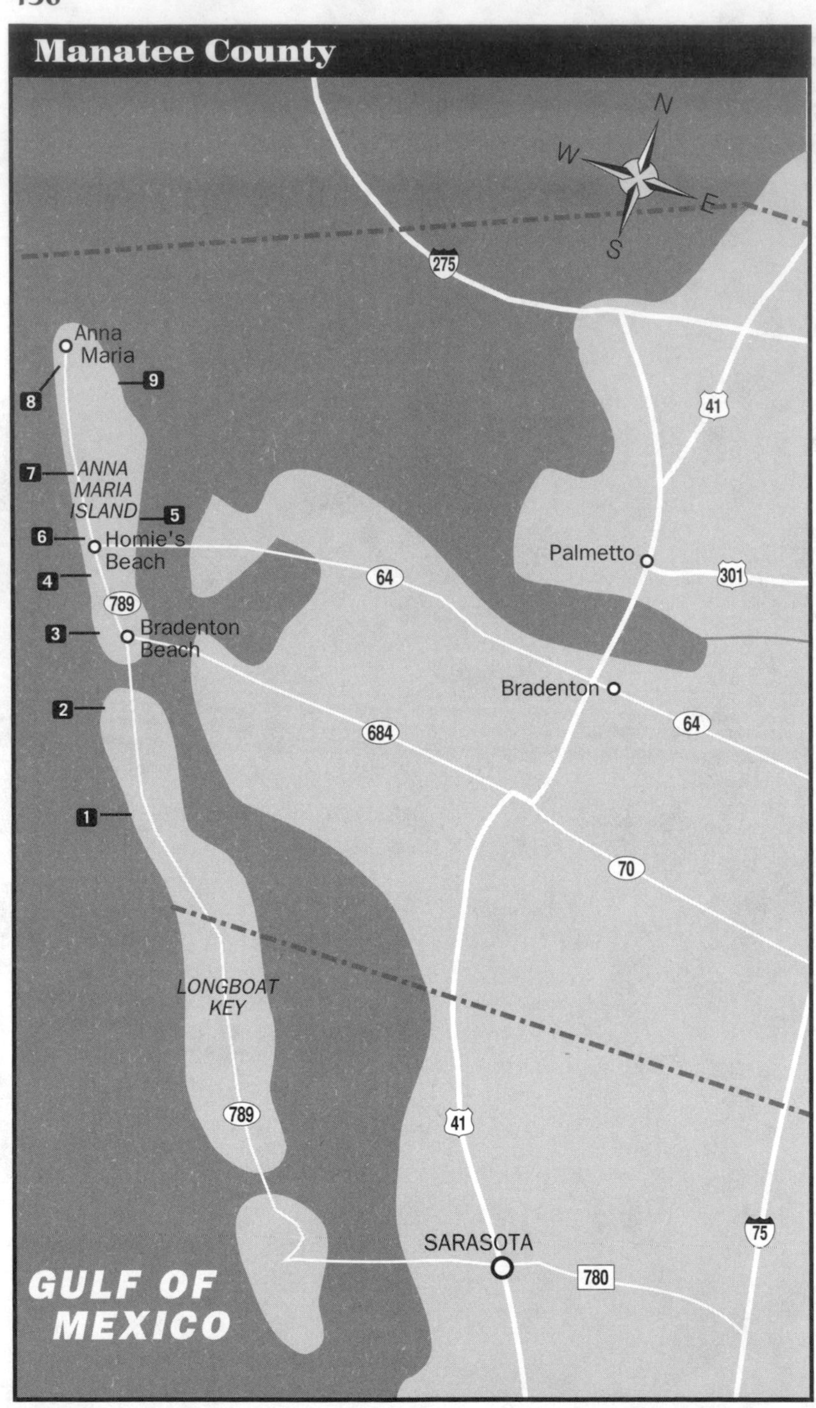

Manatee County
N
W
E
S
275
Anna
Maria
9
8
41
7
ANNA
MARIA
ISLAND
5
6
Homie's
Beach
Palmetto
4
64
301
789
3
Bradenton
Beach
Bradenton
2
684
64
1
70
LONGBOAT
KEY
789
41
75
SARASOTA
780
GULF OF
MEXICO

Manatee County

Manatee County's coastline consists only of the north half of Longboat Key and all of 7.5-mile-long Anna Maria Island. Anna Maria Island is home to a trio of old-fashioned, family-oriented beach communities—Bradenton Beach, Holmes Beach, and Anna Maria—that are the vacationer's equivalent of comfort foods. It's impossible not to like them, if you've got any feeling for the beach life and the Old Florida sensibility, not to mention white sands and golden sunsets. The county is named for the beloved sea mammal, who is a frequent visitor to its waterways. Spotting manatees is the Gulf Coast equivalent of whale-watching, and the Manatee County Parks and Recreation Department lists 15 manatee watch areas.

Longboat Key (north end)

Longboat Key (pop. 8,000) is equally shared between Sarasota and Manatee counties. We're guessing that joint custody was instituted so no one county would have to look after the arrogant whole. In any case, Longboat Key is an entity unto itself that bears little resemblance to the rest of either county's extremely likable coastlines. While the 11-mile key falls within two counties, it is one municipality, and therefore the write-ups in the Sarasota County chapter will serve to cover the entirety of Longboat Key. However, the one category that it does make sense to break out separately is beaches, so we've done that below. One observation: While much of Longboat Key is all but impenetrable to an unwealthy outsider, the village area along Broadway Street up at the north end (in Manatee County) does contain vestiges of a humbler past and is worth a look-see, just to catch a glimpse of what once was and still should have been.

Beaches

A string of public beach accesses will get you onto the sand on the Manatee County side of Longboat Key, and one provides a point of entry to the hooked spit at the extreme north end known as Beer Can Island (named for what got left behind when people came out here to party). The accesses with parking lots are on Gulf of Mexico Drive near Atlas Street (50 spaces), Gulfside Road (50 spaces), and Broadway Street (50 spaces). **Beer Can Island** is reachable from a lot at North Shore Road (26 spaces). The beach runs for half a mile up to Longboat Pass. There are no facilities—not so much as a portable toilet—at any of the access points, leaving us wondering what kind of day at the beach they want you to have.

Contact Information

Longboat Key Chamber of Commerce, 6854 Gulf of Mexico Drive, Longboat Key, FL 34228; 941/383-2466; website: www.longboatkeychamber.com

❶ Longboat Key accesses (north end)

Location: Beach accesses with parking are located on Gulf of Mexico Drive at Atlas Street, Gulfside Road, and Broadway Street on Longboat Key. In addition, there are beach-access easements (no parking) on Gulf of Mexico Drive at the Longboat Key Hilton, 6677 Gulf of Mexico Drive, Beachwalk, and Coral/Seabreeze Avenues
Parking/fees: free parking lots
Hours: 5 A.M.–11 P.M.
Facilities: none
Contact: City of Longboat Key Public Works Department, 941/316-1966

❷ Beer Can Island

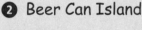

Location: North Shore Road, off Gulf of Mexico Drive on Longboat Key
Parking/fees: free parking lot
Hours: 5 A.M.–11 P.M.
Facilities: none
Contact: City of Longboat Key Public Works Department, 941/316-1966

Anna Maria Island: Bradenton Beach, Holmes Beach, and Anna Maria

Anna Maria Island is the Cinderella who didn't get invited to the developers' black-tie ball down on Longboat Key, and she hasn't regretted the snub one bit. She is, in fact, looking prettier and more dignified than her sister key with each passing season. For starters, most of this 7.5-mile barrier island is accessible to the beach-going public, from Coquina Beach through Holmes Beach. (The community of Anna Maria, at the north end, is a tougher nut to crack.) No, this is not a nature sanctuary or a national seashore but a fully developed, family-friendly island. However, the growth here has been intelligently overseen, beginning with a concerted effort 30 years ago to enact a master plan and stick to it. That plan includes a building height limit of three stories and a laissez-faire attitude toward Mother Nature. That is, the coastline hasn't been dramatically tampered with or built on. The result is a sandy, low-key paradise that anyone would be proud to call home—or a home away from home.

Two bridges—Cortez (State Route 684) and the Palma Sola Causeway (State Route 64)—connect Anna Maria Island to the mainland city of Bradenton. At the south end, Gulf Drive (State Route 789) joins the island with Longboat Key. Here you'll find Coquina Beach, which runs along Gulf Drive for a mile. A tree-lined beach lies on the west side of the road, and undeveloped natural habitat flourishes on the east. As if that weren't reason enough to visit, this stretch of Florida's west coast once set a Guinness record for the most consecutive sunny days: 768 in a row. That's more than two years' worth!

Anna Maria Island comprises three relaxed, unpretentious, and contiguous communities. From south to north, they are Bradenton Beach (pop. 1,700), Holmes Beach (pop. 5,000), and Anna Maria (pop. 1,800), and all share a few characteristics. The low-scale development common to them was based on need and not rampant real-estate speculation, and the towns that slowly grew here exhibit a funky, sunbaked character (hand-painted murals, slapdash houses, screened-in porches, nonfranchised businesses) and a lived-in authenticity that can't be faked. Rather, it has evolved naturally over generations as locals and loyal visitors have developed a congenial common ground. They are the sort of unaffected beach towns we loved when we were kids. We strongly feel that people still want communities and experiences like these when they go on vacation today, not the overpriced and highly privatized beaches of Longboat Key and Marco Island.

Because Anna Maria Island has tried to surmount the slippery slope of social class, room and board are affordable, and much of its low-key, low-to-the-ground real estate is located within easy walking distance of the beach. Of the three towns, Anna Maria is the quietest and most residential, making it a great place to rent a vacation home or villa. Holmes Beach is the largest, with roughly 5,000 year-round residents and three miles of beach that is easily accessible from a plethora of street ends. Bradenton Beach has sunk the deepest taproot, centered around the renovated Bradenton City Pier (circa 1921). At this bayside complex, you can stroll and fish for free or sit on one of the many benches after polishing off a chili cheese dog basket.The three towns collectively impart a reigning philosophy of come one, come all and don't worry, be happy.

MAP OF MANATEE COUNTY—PAGE 436

Beaches

Because there are no gated gulf-front communities or horizon-obscuring high-rises on Anna Maria Island, the beach is part of every visitor's daily reality and a constant reminder of why people rescue two weeks from their stress-filled lives to come here. The beachfront is fairly consistent, with powdery white sand (renourished in 1993 and due again in 2001) backed by anchoring vegetation, including tree breaks, that runs the length of the key. Public access, as noted, is no problem on Anna Maria Island except in the town of Anna Maria itself. Three county-run, gulf-facing beach parks (Coquina, Cortez, and Manatee) provide the facilities you may need for an all-day visit if the beach isn't right out the back door of wherever it is you're staying. Working from south to north, the beaches of Anna Maria Island are as follows:

- **Coquina Beach** — This popular Manatee County park has both gulf beach and bayfront boating access. Even the sprawling, free parking area evinces an enlightened touch—it's not asphalt, but a mixture of shell, rock, dirt, and sand. Picnic tables run the length of the park; they're set behind the healthy sand dunes under a canopy of Australian pines. There's a playground for kids as well as a designated safe swimming area that's lifeguarded. (Signs warn of a steep dropoff in the water.) You'll also find a full complement of visitor facilities, including a café and concession kiosk at which beach chairs and umbrellas can be rented. The coquina shell beach is white, hard-packed, and wide, and it runs for a mile along the Gulf of Mexico.
- **Cortez Beach** — Another popular Manatee County park, Cortez picks up at the north end of Coquina and proceeds into the center of Bradenton Beach, running from 5th to 13th Streets. A continuation of the same ample beach, Cortez has the bonus of being within walking distance of town restaurants, shops, and bars. It's also the site of a primo surf spot known as Three Piers—

❸ Coquina Beach

Location: south end of Anna Maria Island, off Gulf Drive (State Route 789)
Parking/fees: free parking lot
Hours: sunrise to sunset
Facilities: concessions, lifeguards, restrooms, picnic tables, and showers
Contact: Manatee County Parks and Recreation Department, 941/742-5923

❹ Cortez Beach

Location: between 5th and 13th Streets, off Gulf Drive in Bradenton Beach
Parking/fees: free parking lot
Hours: sunrise to sunset
Facilities: lifeguards, restrooms, picnic tables, and showers
Contact: Manatee County Parks and Recreation Department, 941/742-5923

❺ Palma Sola Causeway

Location: along both sides and at both ends of the Palma Sola Causeway (Manatee Avenue/State Route 64), which links Bradenton and Anna Maria Island, entering the latter at Holmes Beach
Parking/fees: free parking lots
Hours: sunrise to sunset
Facilities: restrooms and picnic tables
Contact: Manatee County Parks and Recreation Department, 941/742-5923

MAP OF FLORIDA'S WEST COAST—PAGE 347

which aren't really piers but erosion groins. You're not supposed to swim or surf around them, but signs to that effect get taken down almost as quickly as they're put up.

- **Palma Sola Causeway** — Bayside beaches line the Palma Sola Causeway (Manatee Avenue/State Route 64), the northernmost of the two causeways linking Bradenton with Anna Maria Island. Facilities include restrooms, picnic tables, boat ramps, and sandy bay beaches.
- **Manatee Beach** — This full-service park is located at the west end of Manatee Avenue in Holmes Beach, making it one of the most popular year-round spots on Anna Maria Island. Officially, it's on 40th Street, which is the extension of State Route 64, the main road over from Bradenton. There's free parking in a sprawling dirt and shell lot, as well as lifeguards, volleyball nets, and one of the coolest beach cafés going (see Coastal Cuisine). At the center of the beach is an erosion-control groin, which either works well or is unnecessary because the sand is wide and soft here, offering plenty of room for all comers. The Holmes Beach Pier anchors the action here. Interestingly, the surf on the south side of Tampa Bay is better than on the north, because the water's deeper so the waves pick up more juice. In fact, Anna Maria Island has been called "the surfing epicenter south of Tampa."
- **Holmes Beach** — Access to nearly three miles of beach is gained via street ends from 28th to 72nd Streets, plus the named streets above 72nd up to White Avenue (which divides Holmes Beach from Anna Maria). No public facilities or lifeguards, though.
- **Anna Maria Beach** — The beach on the island's gulf-facing north end is pedestrian accessible via dune walkovers at residential street ends, but there are neither facilities nor parking spaces. Your best bet is to park at the public lot by the post office at Spring Avenue and Gulf Drive, then walk west on Spring Avenue to the beach. A shore break at the south end of Anna Maria,

6 Manatee Beach

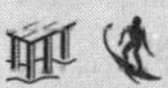  

Location: 40th Street and Gulf Drive in Holmes Beach
Parking/fees: free parking lot
Hours: sunrise to sunset
Facilities: concessions, lifeguards, restrooms, picnic tables, and showers
Contact: Manatee County Parks and Recreation Department, 941/742-5923

7 Holmes Beach

Location: Street ends between Beach Drive and 27th Street, off Gulf Drive in Holmes Beach
Parking/fees: free street parking
Hours: sunrise to sunset
Facilities: none
Contact: Holmes Beach Public Works Department, 941/778-6633

8 Anna Maria Beach

Location: West ends of streets from White Avenue north to Bean Point in Anna Maria
Parking/fees: free parking lot at Spring Avenue and Gulf Drive; no parking allowed on residential side streets that end at the beach
Hours: sunrise to sunset
Facilities: none
Contact: Anna Maria Public Works Department, 941/778-7092

in the vicinity of Beach and White Avenues, is another good surf spot on Anna Maria Island when the waves are cooperating.

- **Anna Maria Bayfront Park** — Located on Bay Boulevard, this county park features 1,000 feet of beach on Tampa Bay. Parking, picnic shelters, and restrooms are available. Anna Maria City Pier is located just south of the park, on Pine Avenue at Bay Boulevard.

Shore Things

- **Bike/skate rentals:** Island Rental Service, 3214 East Bay Drive, Bradenton Beach, 941/778-1472.
- **Boat cruise:** Lo-Seas II, 5501 Marina Drive, Holmes Beach, 941/778-1977.
- **Dive shop:** Sea Trek, 105 7th Street North, Bradenton Beach, 941/779-1506.
- **Ecotourism:** Oceanbound Kayak Shop, 605-A Manatee Avenue, Holmes Beach, 941/778-5883.
- **Fishing charters:** Dolphin Dream Charters, 306-A 58th Street, Holmes Beach, 941/778-4498.
- **Marina:** Bradenton Beach Marina, 402 Church Avenue, Bradenton Beach, 941/778-2288.

9 Anna Maria Bayfront Park

Location: Off Bay Boulevard along Tampa Bay in Anna Maria
Parking/fees: free parking lot
Hours: sunrise to sunset
Facilities: Restrooms and picnic tables
Contact: Manatee County Parks and Recreation Department, 941/742-5923

- **Pier:** Bradenton Beach Pier, east end of Bridge Street, Bradenton Beach; Holmes Beach Pier, west end of Manatee Avenue in Holmes Beach; Anna Maria City Pier, Pine Avenue at Bay Boulevard in Anna Maria.
- **Rainy-day attraction:** Anna Maria Island Museum, 402 Pine Avenue, Anna Maria, 941/778-0492.
- **Shopping/browsing:** Bridge Street, Bradenton Beach.
- **Surf shop:** West Coast Surf Shop, 3902 Gulf Drive, Holmes Beach, 941/778-1001.
- **Vacation rentals:** Mike Norman Realty, 3101 Gulf Drive, Holmes Beach, 941/778-6696.

Bunking Down

Anna Maria Island is the sort of haven you'll want to drop anchor at for a week or longer, so a house, villa, or apartment rental is the way to go here. Rates generally range from $500 weekly for an efficiency to $1,700 weekly for a nice gulf-front house. If you write the Anna Maria Island Chamber of Commerce, your mailbox will soon be bowing under the weight of lodging-related brochures and catalogs.

A number of small motels and inns hang shingles on the island, mostly in Bradenton Beach. Two that caught our eye were the 12-unit **Queen's Gate** (1101 Gulf Drive, Bradenton Beach, 941/778-7153, $$), which is a cut above the island norm without being pretentious about it, and the 36-unit **Catalina Beach Resort** (1325 Gulf Drive North, Bradenton Beach, 941/778-6611, $). The latter is an "apartment motel" where most rentals are by the week, though some rooms can be had by the night. Often shuffleboard courts are attached to the various "beach clubs" and "resorts," which is a tipoff to the drowsy tenor of life on Anna Maria Island.

MAP OF FLORIDA'S WEST COAST—PAGE 347

For those in search of a brand-name motel, you're not going to find much more than the 54-unit **Econo Lodge Surfside** (2502 Gulf Drive North, Bradenton Beach, 941/778-6671, $). A touch of sophistication is available at **Harrington House** (5626 Gulf Drive, Holmes Beach, 941/778-5444, $$$), a beachside bed-and-breakfast. Built in 1925, this three-story coquina-block structure has been lavishly and lovingly preserved.

Coastal Cuisine

You can stuff yourself silly on Anna Maria Island. Take our favorite beach dive, **Cafe on the Beach**, located at Manatee Beach (4000 Gulf Drive, Holmes Beach, 941/778-0784, $). We saw people who were the size of manatees taking advantage of a daily all-you-can-eat pancake breakfast special. The place gets equally packed on Friday nights for the all-you-can-eat fish fry with live musical entertainment.

The best beachfront cuisine is at the **Beach Bistro** (6600 Gulf Drive, Holmes Beach, 941/778-6444, $$$$), which is a sit-down restaurant with linen tablecloths, rose-filled bud vases, and romantic sunset views. It routinely wins awards and raves from *Wine Spectator, Zagat Survey* and *Florida Trend*. It has been decreed "one of Florida's top 20 restaurants" and is said to have "the best food on the Gulf Coast." Consider just a few of the entrée selections in the seafood category: Andrea's Floribbean grouper (crusted with coconut and cashews, pan-seared and oven-finished, drizzled with red pepper papaya jam) and their "famous" Bistro bouillabaisse (lobster, shrimp, shellfish, squid, and fish poached in a "killer broth." Now for the tough part: the grouper is $28.95, the bouillabaisse $34.95.

Bistro Land's End (10101 Gulf Drive, Anna Maria, 941/779-2444) is less pricey and more casual than Beach Bistro.

For a considerably less expensive bite, hit the **Sandbar** (100 Spring Avenue, Anna Maria, 941/778-0444, $$), a popular gulf-front dining spot. The lunch menu features a wide selection of sandwiches, salads, and entrées. The seafood penne pasta and tuna tropic salads hit the spot with us, especially as they were accompanied by a visual side dish of foaming waves slamming on the riprap just beyond the patio.

Another unique waterfront setting for lunch is **Anna Maria Oyster Bar** (100 Bay Boulevard South, Anna Maria, 941/778-0475, $), a longtime favorite. Located at the end of 750-foot Anna Maria City Pier, just south of Anna Maria Bayfront Park, it offers a fresh grouper sandwich that will tickle your gills, plus the namesake oysters. The view of Passage and Egmont Keys and Sunshine Skyway off in the distance is a further enticement.

At the **Beachhouse** (200 Gulf Drive North, Bradenton Beach, 941/779-2222, $$), you'll swear you can hear the heartbeat of America. It's family dining in an airy wooden building with picture windows that frame the beautiful sunsets. Beachnut grouper is the signature dish at the Beachhouse, and for good reason: it's prepared with a nut crust, citrus-ginger sauce, and fruit salsa garnish. Scampi Anna Maria finishes a respectable second.

Night Moves

Key West Willy's (107 Gulf Drive South, Bradenton Beach, 941/778-7272) and the **Surfside Cafe** (5340-F Gulf Drive North, Holmes Beach, 941/779-1320) are the best bets for those who want to hang out and knock back a friendly drink after dark. As for the rest of you, it's shuffleboard or shuffle off to bed.

Contact Information

Anna Maria Island Chamber of Commerce, 5337 Gulf Drive North, Holmes Beach, FL 34217; 941/778-1541; website: www.annamariaislandchamber.org

MAP OF MANATEE COUNTY—PAGE 436

Hillsborough County

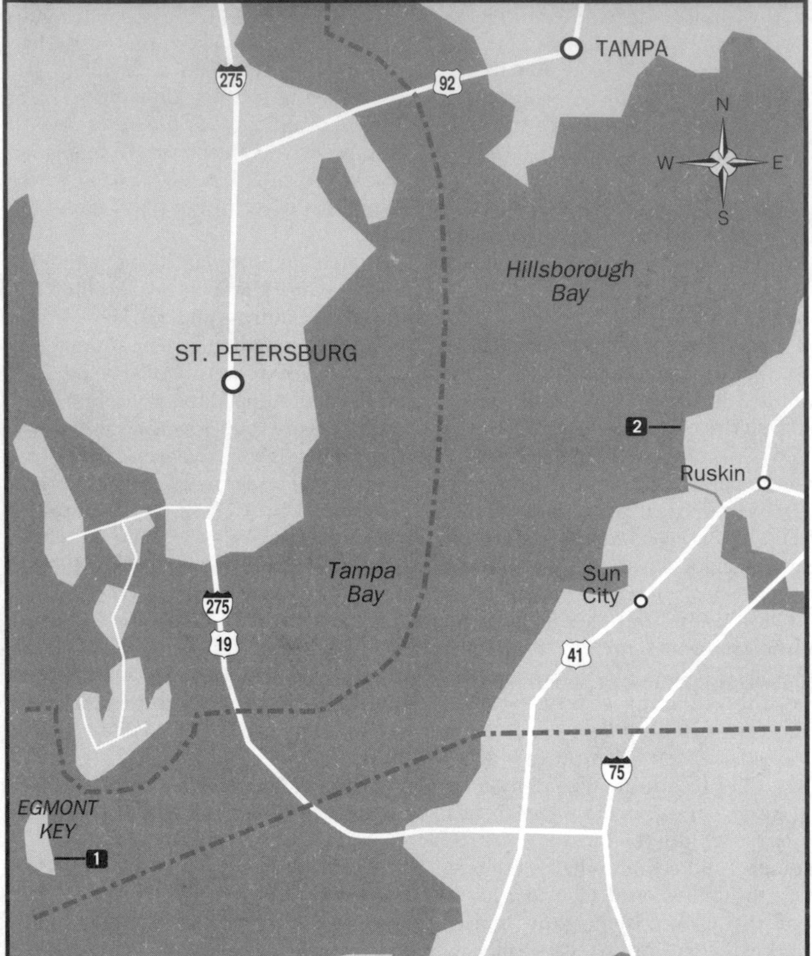

TAMPA
275
92
N
W
E
S
Hillsborough Bay
ST. PETERSBURG
2
Ruskin
Tampa Bay
Sun City
275
19
41
75
EGMONT KEY
1
BRADENTON
41
GULF OF MEXICO

Hillsborough County

Hillsborough County is crowned by the booming city of Tampa. Florida's fourth largest city, Tampa has grown up and out with a tower-filled downtown and a quainter, more sociable area of red-brick streets known as Ybor City. But there's practically nothing in the way of gulf-facing sand beaches in Hillsborough County, which is why this is the second shortest chapter in *Florida Beaches.* The only reason we include it is Egmont Key. Look at a map. Manatee County extends to the tip of Anna Maria Island, while Pinellas County presses down below St. Petersburg. In between lies Egmont Key, a straggler that somehow fell to Hillsborough County. The Tampa and Tampa Bay metropolitan area are beyond our scope. For more information, contact the Tampa Bay Convention and Visitors Bureau, 400 North Tampa Street, Suite 2800, Tampa, FL 33602; 813/222-2753 or 800/448-2672; website: www.thcva.com

Egmont Key

Egmont Key has a lot of history buried in its past, especially the 1800s, for a place that's now so deserted. Because of its location at the mouth of Tampa Bay, this was the site of the first lighthouse on the west coast of Florida, built in 1848. The key was a holding camp for Seminole Indians during the third Seminole War, from which point they were shipped out to Oklahoma. Union forces captured the key during the Civil War. Then, during the Spanish-American War of 1898, Fort Dade was built here to protect Tampa. The fort never saw much action, though it grew into a city of 300 residents and 70 buildings until being decommissioned in 1923. There's not much left of those days but ruins, as most of what was out here broke down, burned up, or got vandalized over the decades.

Today, Egmont Key is a combination state park, nature preserve, and historic site. The 380-acre key falls inside a narrow sliver of Hillsborough County, between Sarasota and Pinellas Counties. Egmont Key was delegated to Hillsborough County back in the 1920s to placate the Tampa Bay Pilots Association, so they wouldn't have to cross into different counties (and incur extra charges) when sailing up the bay and into port at Tampa.

Egmont Key lies two miles north of Anna Maria Island and two miles south of Fort De Soto Park. It was, until recent years the site of the only manned lighthouse in the United States. The lighthouse is still standing and operative; it's just unmanned these days. The key's lone full-time resident is the park ranger.

Egmont Key State Park has a 1.5-mile-long beach as pristine as any on Florida's west coast. It's also one of the best dive sites in the area, because some now-submerged armament bunkers from its military days serve as reefs, attracting tropical fish. Egmont Key is notable for having the densest population of gopher tortoises in the world. "They're almost a pain in the butt," jokes a ranger. "You can't take a step without having to move them out of the way." The fauna is typical of Gulf Coast barrier islands: sabal palms, red cedars, and so on.

There's no charge to come onto Egmont Key beyond what you'll pay to take a cruise boat, if you're not piloting your own. There's no dockage, either, so you'll have to anchor off the beach. Nor are there facilities of any kind, even restrooms.

Half a dozen excursion boat operators lead trips to Egmont Key from Anna Maria Island, Sand Key, and the Tampa–St. Pete area. One recommended to us is **Hubbard's Sea Adventures** (Johns Pass Village, Madeira Beach, 727/398-6577). Among

❶ Egmont Key State Park

Location: between Anna Maria Island and Fort De Soto Park, at the mouth of Tampa Bay, the key is accessible by boat only.
Parking/fees: free
Hours: 8 A.M. to sunset
Facilities: none
Contact: Gulf Islands GEOpark, 727/469-5942

❷ E.G. Simmons Park

Location: 19th Street NW, off U.S. 41 in south Hillsborough County
Parking/fees: free parking lot
Hours: 8 A.M.–6 P.M.
Facilities: restrooms, picnic tables, and showers
Contact: E.G. Simmons Park, 813/671-7655

FLORIDA'S WEST COAST

MAP OF FLORIDA'S WEST COAST—PAGE 347

the many cruises they offer in the area is a six-hour snorkeling trip to Egmont Key, departing at 10:30 A.M. on Wednesday, Friday, and Sunday. The cost is $29.95 for adults and $19.95 for kids under 12.

Contact Information

Egmont Key State Park, c/o Gulf Islands GEOpark, 1 Causeway Boulevard, Dunedin, FL; 727/469-5942; website: www.myflorida.com

Apollo Beach

We're a sucker for any town that has "beach" in its name, so when we saw Apollo Beach on a map of the Tampa area, we decided to check it out. It's on the shore of Tampa Bay and not the Gulf of Mexico, so we should have left well enough alone since our specified beat is sandy beaches along the ocean or gulf. But then we found out there's a Surfside Avenue in Apollo Beach, so it sounded beachier by the minute.

We needn't have bothered. Apollo Beach (pop. 6,025) looks to be a floundering attempt at a retirement resort community. There is precious little beach in evidence at Apollo Beach. Indeed, waves were rudely slapping a seawall at the base of the **Ramada Bayside Inn and Resort** (6414 Surfside Boulevard, 813/645-3271, $$). So we snapped a few shots, looked around at the unsold lots, and went on our way.

Happily, we found cause for celebration a few miles south of Apollo Beach, at **E.G. Simmons Park**, also off U.S. 41 (via Northwest 19th Avenue). This lovely, shaded, and extensive 469-acre county park has a boat launch, fishing piers, a campground, picnic areas, and a public beach.

Contact Information

Apollo Beach Chamber of Commerce, 6432 U.S. 41 North, Apollo Beach, FL 33572; 813/645-1366; website: www.apollobeachchamber.com

FLORIDA'S WEST COAST

MAP OF HILLSBOROUGH COUNTY—PAGE 444

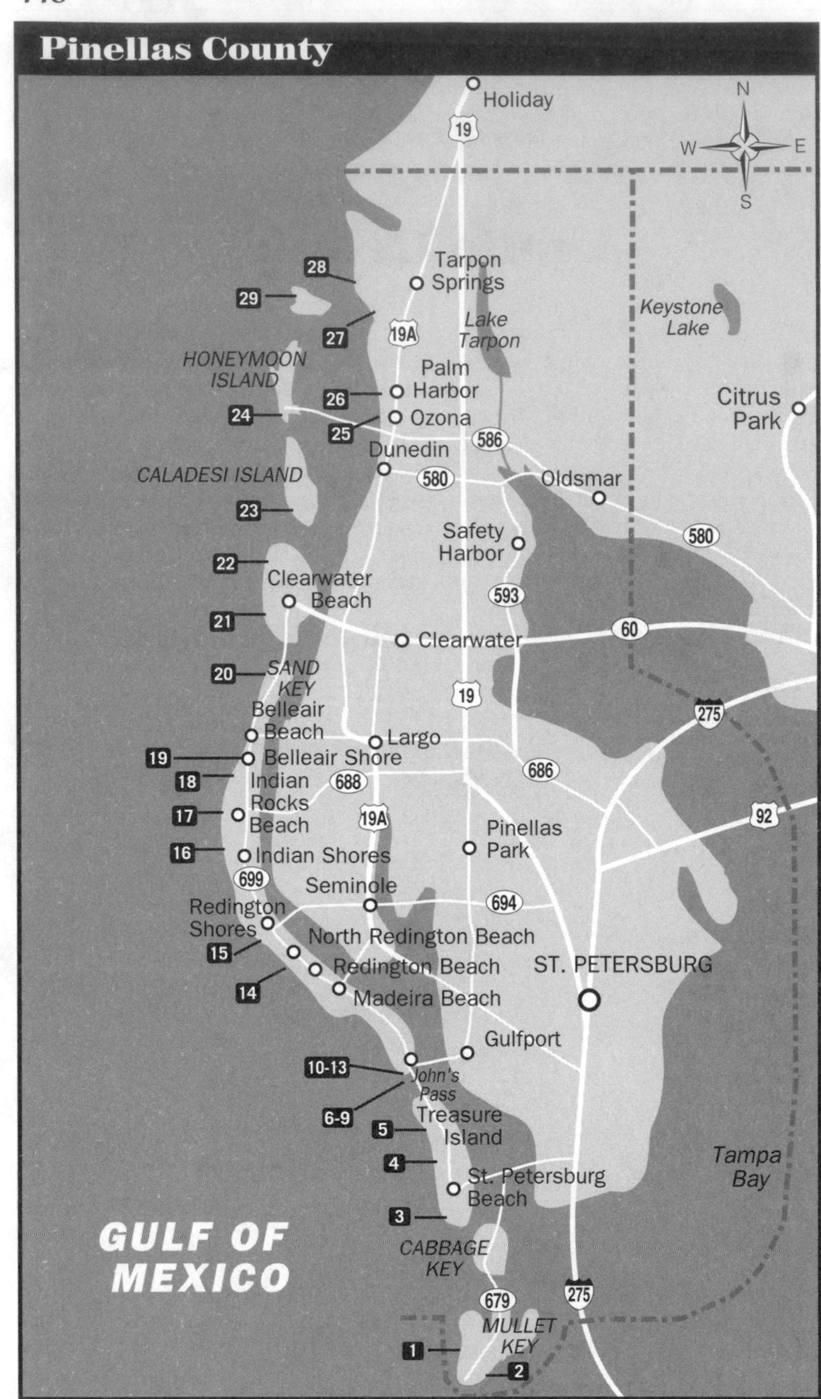
Pinellas County
N
W
E
S
Holiday
19
Tarpon Springs
Lake Tarpon
Keystone Lake
19A
HONEYMOON ISLAND
Palm Harbor
Ozona
586
Dunedin
Citrus Park
CALADESI ISLAND
580
Oldsmar
Safety Harbor
Clearwater Beach
593
Clearwater
60
SAND KEY
Belleair Beach
Largo
Belleair Shore
Indian Rocks Beach
688
686
275
92
Pinellas Park
Indian Shores
699
Seminole
694
Redington Shores
North Redington Beach
Redington Beach
Madeira Beach
ST. PETERSBURG
Gulfport
John's Pass
Treasure Island
St. Petersburg Beach
Tampa Bay
GULF OF MEXICO
CABBAGE KEY
679
MULLET KEY
1
2
3
4
5
6-9
10-13
14
15
16
17
18
19
20
21
22
23
24
25
26
27
28
29

Pinellas County

PINELLAS COUNTY

Pinellas is the fourth most populous county in Florida and the second smallest in terms of land area. Putting these facts together yields another statistic: with more than 3,000 residents per square mile, Pinellas is Florida's most densely populated county. Its principal cities, St. Petersburg and Clearwater, merge with Tampa and many smaller communities to make up the Tampa Bay metropolitan area, which has a total population of 2.3 million. Fortunately, Pinellas has 28 miles of beaches strung along a barrier-island chain that runs from Mullet Key (below St. Petersburg) to Anclote Key (above Tarpon Springs). In between, this beach-blessed county includes St. Pete Beach, Treasure Island, Sand Key, and Clearwater Beach. In addition, Caladesi Island and Honeymoon Island—two prize jewels in the state park system—lie west of the soundside city of Dunedin.

MAP OF FLORIDA'S WEST COAST—PAGE 347

Fort De Soto Park

South of St. Petersburg lies an island in the bay that should have every resident of Pinellas County, as well as the odd non-native who finds his or her way out here, jumping for joy. The island—actually a series of connected keys—is entirely given over to Fort De Soto Park. To get there, take the Pinellas Bayway (State Route 682) to State Route 679 and follow south for six miles to the park. En route, you will cross another island, Tierra Madre. For a mere 85 cents in road tolls, the nature-filled, 900-acre wonderland at Fort De Soto Park is yours to enjoy.

They call it a county park, but it is larger than some counties. It is not one key but five, with V-shaped Mullet Key being the main stem and four smaller ones flaring off it. Where to go first on this oddly shaped island, with its arm-like keys? The camping area, which comprises 235 sites, occupies St. Christopher Key, off to the right where the road enters the island from the mainland. Bayside campsites enjoy a picture-perfect setting of tall, tropical plants and shrubs, offering cooling shade and a perfectly framed window on the bay. Campsites are intended for county residents, but unclaimed sites can be used by nonresidents. It's all first come, first serve, with no advance reservations.

Massive picnic shelters have been erected at the **North Beach** and **East Beach** areas. They can be reserved ahead of time, or you and your group can simply show up and take a table at any that haven't previously been claimed. The tables beneath each shelter, and the shelters themselves, seem endless in number. If anyone ever wanted to set a Guinness record for the world's largest picnic, Fort De Soto Park would be the place to do it. (To reserve picnic shelters, call 727/866-2484.)

The fort is named for Hernando de Soto, who sortied through the area with his Spanish exploration ships in the late 1530s, claiming the west coast of Florida in the name of the mother country. This portended the extermination of the Tocobaga Indians, who had peacefully resided here until the gold-seeking conquistadors showed up and set about their slaughter. The fort named for de Soto sits at the north end of the island, near the refreshment stand and souvenir shop. The

1 North Beach (Fort De Soto Park)

Location: From St. Petersburg, take the Pinellas Bayway (State Route 682) to State Route 679 and follow it south to the park for six miles. Turn right at park headquarters and follow to North Beach parking area.

Parking/fees: 85¢ per vehicle in road tolls en route to the park

Hours: sunrise to sunset

Facilities: concessions, restrooms, picnic tables, showers, and a visitor center

Contact: Fort De Soto Park, 727/866-2484

2 East Beach (Fort De Soto Park)

Location: From St. Petersburg, take the Pinellas Bayway (State Route 682) to State Route 679 and follow it south to the park for six miles. Turn left at park headquarters and follow to East Beach parking area.

Parking/fees: 85¢ per vehicle in road tolls en route to the park

Hours: sunrise to sunset

Facilities: concessions, restrooms, picnic tables, showers, and a visitor center

Contact: Fort De Soto Park, 727/866-2484

latter is a nest of cheap trinkets not worth rummaging; it is the only false note sounded at Fort De Soto Park.

Beaches

Advisories against swimming are posted on North Beach ("No Swimming, Dangerous Currents"), which faces the Gulf of Mexico. Instead, people stroll and sun themselves on its endless deserted expanse. Rumors of nude sunbathing abound, and the beach is so enormous that proscriptions against disrobing would be tough to enforce. East Beach is the designated swimming beach at Fort De Soto Park, and its still waters are inviting. Facilities at East Beach are more compact than at North Beach and include picnic shelters, restrooms, and a less dauntingly vast swath of sand. The St. Petersburg Skyway is visible from its shoreline.

Beaches aren't really the calling card at Fort De Soto; it's the totality of nature and the ample space to beat the crowd that make the trip worth the trouble. The park's ribbon-like miles of paved pathways are ideal for biking and in-line skating, and many visitors come equipped to do just that. They also fish from a 500-foot bay pier and a 1,000-foot gulf pier.

On your way to Fort De Soto Park you'll pass through Tierra Verde, which has marinas and restaurants. Among them are the perennially popular **Fort De Soto Joe's Seafood Wharf** (200 Madonna Boulevard, 727/867-8710, $$). It's right on the water, and the glass walls and polyurethane wood interior make you feel as if you're aboard a boat. Early-bird dinners (noon–6 P.M.) are priced fairly, and plates arrive amply filled. One afternoon we early birds ordered identical dinners: blackened mahimahi with sautéed vegetables, real mashed potatoes, and Caesar salad for only $7.95.

Contact Information

Fort De Soto Park, 3500 Pinellas Bayway South, Tierra Verde, FL 33715; 727/866-2484; website: www.fortdesoto.com

Pass-a-Grille

Pass-a-Grille (pop. 1,500) is a small community affixed to the southern end of St. Pete Beach like a barnacle on the hull of a big ship. Technically, it's part of the municipality of St. Pete Beach and has been for 40 years, but it feels like a different community altogether, so we're singling it out for special praise. There's more than initially meets the eye in Pass-a-Grille. In fact, one of the best beaches along the whole splendid stretch from St. Pete Beach to Clearwater can be found in this unassuming area. There are no high-rises, and the community—the first established town on Florida's Gulf Coast—is a National Historic District.

Pass-a-Grille Beach

Location: between 1st and 21st Avenues, off Gulf Way in Pass-a-Grille, south of St. Pete Beach
Parking/fees: metered street parking
Hours: sunrise to sunset
Facilities: concessions, restrooms, and showers
Contact: St. Pete Beach Parks Department, 727/367-2735

Pass-a-Grille is separated from St. Pete Beach by the Don Cesar Resort, which acts as a princely pink sentinel protecting the low-key neighborhoods of Pass-a-Grille from the commercial buildup of St. Pete Beach. The homes in Pass-a-Grille are attractive but not ostentatious,

MAP OF FLORIDA'S WEST COAST—PAGE 347

the yards well landscaped but not overdone. Within its modest borders, something of an idyllic lifestyle beside the gulf appears to have been cultivated. To top it off, the quaint **Gulf Beaches Historical Museum** (115 10th Avenue, 727/360-2491), with its collection of island lore and artifacts, is located here. It's open Thursday and Saturday from 10 A.M. to 4 P.M. and Sunday from 1 P.M. to 4 P.M.; admission is free.

Beaches

Pass-a-Grille Beach is a five-star winner if ever we've seen one. There is a lot of beach, the sand is white and powdery, and the emerald gulf is warm and inviting. In fact, Pass-a-Grille is much wider than St. Pete Beach. Best of all, there's easy and ample access. Angle-in metered parking (25 cents for 15 minutes) runs for 20 splendid beach-hugging blocks, from 21st to 1st Avenues, all of it mercifully unblocked by homes, hotels, or condos. So bring your quarters, beach blanket, suntan lotion, coolers, and paperback, and pass a day at Pass-a-Grille.

Bunking Down

The affordable, well-situated **Island's End Resort** (1 Pass-a-Grille Way, 727/360-5023, $$) offers six rooms at the very southern tip of Pass-a-Grille. The comfortable, homey **Inn on the Beach** (1401 Gulf Way, 727/360-8844, $$) overlooks Pass-a-Grille Beach, offering airy rooms with a beachy feel that are done up in brass, wicker, and ceramic tile.

You can also stay at the **Keystone** (801 Gulf Way, 727/360-1313, $), a clean, well-kept 30-unit motel that sits on the opposite corner from the Hurricane Restaurant and is, in fact, affiliated with that mammoth restaurant and entertainment complex. Read on.

Coastal Cuisine

Pass-a-Grille boasts a number of bistros and cafés where you can get a bite on or near the water. For a relaxed, reasonably priced dining experience, **Sea Critters Café** (2007 Pass-a-Grille Way, 727/360-3706, $$) is the freshest catch in south St. Pete. The owner proudly dubs himself "a local beach bum born and raised on the beach." He's also enamored of all things Key Westerly, including bizarre artifacts, bric-a-brac, Jimmy Buffett's music and "Duval Street key lime pie." He calls his restaurant's relaxing ambience "Key West attitude with no change in latitude." We wave all four of our flip-flops in appreciation of his well-executed fixation.

The smoked portobello mushroom and salmon appetizer had us squawking like Parrotheads at a Buffett concert. The smoked amberjack dip is another excellent opener, as all smoking is done on the premises. Signature dishes include Tortugas coconut shrimp (a.k.a. "human bait"), Hemingway pasta, and grouper. Without question, grouper is the way to go here: grilled, blackened, jerk, pretzel-crusted, fried, charcoal-grilled, and more. (Our advice: go for the "Bubba size," and get it char-grilled.) A post-prandial tradition at Sea Critters is the feeding of a thick, squirming school of sea catfish with buckets of bread. The owner has prepared a hilarious manual on "how to properly feed catfish."

Also excellent in the area is the **Hurricane Seafood Restaurant** (807 Gulf Way, 727/360-9558, $$$). It's a dining and entertainment multiplex, with a downstairs café, outdoor deck, and second-floor, Caribbean-themed operation called Stormy's. Grilled black grouper is what made Hurricane famous, and they'll likely have other fresh catches on the menu as well. Breakfast, lunch, and dinner are served daily. Try to catch sunset here on a nice afternoon (hint: they're almost always nice). There's docking for those arriving by boat.

MAP OF PINELLAS COUNTY—PAGE 448

Night Moves

Hurricane's (807 Gulf Way, 727/360-9558) offers three places and ways to celebrate: Stormy's, an upstairs restaurant that turns into a dance club at 10 P.M.; the Keys Club, a piano bar where single-malt Scotch and martinis are sipped while gazing at tropical fish suspended from the ceiling; and the Hurricane Watch Rooftop Deck, where you can drink in the 360-degree view while imbibing a Hurricane Rum Runner or some frozen libation with a wacky name. Call the main number, which offers prerecorded listings of dinner and drink specials, as well as what time to catch the sunset.

Contact Information

Gulf Beaches of Tampa Bay Chamber of Commerce, 6990 Gulf Boulevard, St. Pete Beach, FL 33706; 727/360-6957 or 800/944-1847; website: www.gulfbeaches-tampabay.com

St. Pete Beach

No, it is not St. Petersburg Beach. Yes, St. Pete Beach is correct. Back in 1994, the name was officially changed to what people had informally been calling it for decades. St. Pete Beach (pop. 9,700) is the autonomous barrier-island community adjacent to the major city of St. Petersburg (pop. 266,767). The small city on the beach and the big city by the bay are joined by two causeways: Pinellas Bayway (at the south end) and Pasadena Avenue. Technically known as Long Key, though that name is rarely used, St. Pete Beach runs for seven miles from Pass-a-Grille (see separate write-up) to Blind Pass, which separates it from Treasure Island.

With the exception of cool, calm, and collected Pass-a-Grille, St. Pete Beach has been built up in herky-jerky fashion, lacking evidence of zoning and planning strategies, not to mention green space or sufficient public beach access. It's not a bad place by any means, but they could have done a lot more with it. It's also somewhat snoozy and slow-going—more like Sunny Isles than Miami Beach, to draw an east coast parallel. This appraisal was confirmed by Nils, a fuzz-faced kid wielding the scoop at an ice-cream parlor we ducked into. He characterized St. Pete Beach as a place to come and "take a load off, man."

Though affixed to the Tampa–St. Pete metroplex, St. Pete Beach does not feel like a big-city beach. It's well-stocked with hotels, motels, and restaurants (mostly franchised), plus the occasional sports bar and 7-Eleven, but it is not a wild and crazy strip of revving cars and jammed sidewalks by a long shot. St. Pete Beach doesn't have much personality, and about the best thing you can say about it is that it is generally unthreatening.

The high season starts just before Christmas and continues through March. During the spell, you might see a smattering of Spring Breaking collegians, but you are more likely to spy kids traveling with families.

Much of the tourism comes from overseas. Traditionally, St. Pete Beach has been a favored destination for vacationing Midwesterners, but it's become a major resort for British tourists, too. They flock here in droves throughout the winter months. So pervasive is their presence that you will find any number of British-style pubs serving British-style pub food (they crossed the ocean to eat more of that gruel?) along Gulf Boulevard. Newspaper and gift shops carry the dreadful British tabloids (the *Sun*, the *Mirror*), all dishing out gossip on the latest rumor or the scandal du jour. One of the styling salons in St. Pete Beach is called "British Hairways."

In a sense, St. Pete Beach has become an American version of the Brits' "holiday camps," except that the gulf waters are generally balmy and the town itself is not rundown. In *Kingdom by the Sea,* Paul Theroux described the scene in Blackpool, a popular seaside resort: "[V]acationers sitting under a dark sky with their shirts off, sleeping with their mouths open, emitting hog whimpers. They were waiting for the sun to shine, but the forecast was rain for the next five months." It's no wonder they love Florida.

Between international visitors—principally Britons, but also Germans and Canadians—and snowbirds from the North and Midwest, St. Pete Beach gets most crowded from late December through early May. However, as was pointed out to us repeatedly throughout Florida, the whole concept of seasonality is dissolving. The coastal communities have learned that when the vacationers and part-timers head home, that's the time to pull in convention business.

When we visited St. Pete Beach one November, which should have been the least busy of all months, our resort was running at full occupancy. Hearing some strange calliope music, we opened a ballroom door and spied 500 elderly women who were wearing fezzes while clapping, hooting, and singing. And they say Spring Breakers get out of hand!

Incidentally, the 11-mile Sunshine Skyway (I-275) that connects St. Petersburg with Manatee County to the south provides access to a pair of fishing piers worth knowing about. North Pier (on the St. Petersburg side) is a quarter mile long. South Pier (Manatee County side, near Rubonia) is 1.5 miles long, making it the longest fishing pier in the world. These piers are actually remnants of the old Skyway Bridge, and you can still drive out on them to park and fish.

At its highest point, the "new" 4.1-mile Sunshine Skyway Bridge rises to a height of 19 stories above Tampa Bay, making it the largest cable suspension bridge in the Western Hemisphere. Driving across it is like taking an amusement park ride.

Beaches

The beach along St. Pete Beach is renourished, wide, and long. If you're staying at one of the hotels, motels, or resorts on the beach side, you'll have instant access to the gulf, with its bejeweled waters, soft white sand, and heart-stopping sunsets. However, the Gulf Boulevard strip along St. Pete Beach is fairly miserly with public access, given the size of the inland metropolitan area it's serving. There's metered parking in two places: mid-island, off Gulf Boulevard between 44th and 50th Avenues, and

❹ St. Pete Beach Access

Location: 4700 Gulf Boulevard in St. Pete Beach
Parking/fees: metered parking lot
Hours: sunrise to sunset
Facilities: concessions, restrooms, picnic tables, and showers
Contact: St. Pete Beach Access, 727/866-2484

❺ Upham Beach

Location: between 66th and 70th Avenues, off Beach Plaza at the north end of St. Pete Beach
Parking/fees: metered parking lot
Hours: sunrise to sunset
Facilities: restrooms and showers
Contact: St. Pete Beach Parks Department, 727/367-2735

toward the north end, off Beach Plaza between 66th and 70th Avenues. The former is known as **St. Pete Beach Access** and the latter, more favored by locals, **Upham Beach**. Neither is as nice as the beach at Pass-a-Grille (see separate write-up), just south of the Don Cesar, which would be our first choice.

Shore Things

- **Bike/skate rentals:** Beach Cyclist Sports Center, 7517 Blind Pass Road, 727/367-5001.
- **Boat cruise:** Captain Anderson Cruises, 3400 Pasadena Avenue South, 727/367-7804.
- **Dive shop:** Treasure Island Divers, 111 108th Avenue, Treasure Island, 727/360-3483.
- **Ecotourism:** Shell Island Cruises, Captain Mike's Watersports, Dolphin Beach Resort, 4900 Gulf Boulevard, 727/360-1053.
- **Fishing charters:** Florida Deep Sea Fishing, 4737 Gulf Boulevard, 727/360-2082.
- **Lighthouse:** Egmont Key Lighthouse, Egmont Key, 727/893-2627.
- **Marina:** Blind Pass Marina, 9555 Blind Pass Road, 727/360-4281.
- **Piers:** Merry Pier, 801 Pass-a-Grille Way, Pass-a-Grille, 727/360-6606; St. Petersburg Pier, 2nd Avenue East at Tampa Bay, 727/821-6164.
- **Rainy-day attraction:** Salvador Dalí Museum, 1000 3rd Street South, St. Petersburg, 727/823-3767.
- **Shopping/browsing:** Dolphin Village, 4600 Gulf Boulevard.
- **Surf shop:** Aguera Wind and Surf Shop, 4665 Gulf Boulevard, 727/360-3783.
- **Vacation rentals:** Gulf Bay Realty, 9815 Gulf Boulevard, 727/360-6969.

Bunking Down

The **Don Cesar** (3400 Gulf Boulevard, 727/360-1881, $$$$) rises at the south end of St. Pete Beach like a pink-stucco Taj Mahal. This neo-Mediterranean edifice houses one of Florida's premier resorts. It is first class all the way, with an air of unpretentiousness that makes vacationing here a real treat. Particularly pleasurable is the outdoor pool deck, with its several huge pools, Jacuzzis, and poolside bars, where blenders work overtime mixing frozen drinks. A quick plunge in the gulf, followed by a warm soak in the Jacuzzi, is especially refreshing during the cooler months. You could lay on the deck and look up at the architecture of the uniquely rouged Don Cesar for hours. It's also a splendid perch for watching the sun do its nightly slow fade.

Everything you could possibly want, including restaurants, fitness center, spa, and gift shops, is on-premises. We'd only quibble with the $7 per adult "resort charge," which is levied to cover such things as local phone calls and use of the on-site spa, which should rightly come with the $250–300 nightly room fee. We were also not too terribly psyched by the minibar between our beds, which visibly displayed a row of candy bars. There's something tacky about looking at a vending machine in a pricey resort hotel room.

St. Pete Beach's other tower of vacation power is the **Tradewinds Resort** (5500 Gulf Boulevard, 727/367-6461, $$$), a resort so large it's like a small city—one with its own faux reggae theme song whose key line goes, "You got that Tradewinds feelin'!" This place is huge, occupying 18 acres of gulfside real estate. Its several towers contain 577 hotel rooms and suites. All feel like real living quarters, as they come with coffeemakers and refrigerators. If you get a room facing west—and it's worth the extra money—sunsets over the gulf can be savored from the balcony.

Tradewinds has so many amenities and so much to do that space prohibits listing it all. Among the most unique features is the quarter-mile waterway that loops around the property, which can be toured via paddleboat or gondola. Designed with families in mind, Tradewinds has a supervised children's program, KONK (Kids Only, No Kidding!) that will free up time for big kids to pursue their own playtime activities. Tradewinds is so oversized that it's worth studying a map of the grounds before you set out from your room. Just for starters: four heated swimming pools, a fitness club, a body works salon, nine restaurants and bars—and let's not forget the hefty slice of beach that lies directly on the Gulf of Mexico.

Beyond these two St. Pete Beach sentinels, Gulf Boulevard is lined with motels and hotels of every description, condition, and price range. **Alden Beach Resort** (5900 Gulf Boulevard, 727/360-7081, $$$) is a well-maintained mid-rise alternative to the corporate towers that have blossomed on all sides. The resort actually occupies nine buildings and offers a broad choice of accommodations and prices. You can book everything from a basic no-frills hotel room to a large two-bedroom, two-bath apartment overlooking the gulf. The suites are comfortable, and two large swimming pools on the premises are inviting. So are shuffleboard courts and instant access to the wide, powder-sand beach out back.

Coastal Cuisine

A long-lived favorite on St. Pete Beach, Silas Dent's, burned down in the mid-1990s and got rebuilt as **Silas Steakhouse** (5501 Gulf Boulevard, 727/360-6961, $$$). It continues to please old-timers and tourists by the galleon-load with its steaks and seafood. Though it is regularly awarded for serving "the best prime rib on the beach," we like it because it was named after a grubby, beloved beachcomber-cum-folk hero who lived on nearby Tierra Verde.

If you're slumming for Southern-style comfort food, **Caldwell's Bar-B-Q & Grill** (7081 Gulf Boulevard, 727/363-6313, $$) has been serving ribs, chicken, beef brisket, pulled pork, and a whole lot more on Gulf Boulevard since 1950 (though they sat out much of the 1990s, reopening in 1997). The food is hearty and inexpensive, ranging from barbecue platters to prime rib, barbecue ribs, and seafood combo dinners that run in the $11.95 to $13.95 range. Being Southern-bred barbecue hounds, we felt right at home here.

Mostly, this is a town whose culinary pulse-beat tends toward chicken wings and grouper sandwiches. If you want something upscale, the **Maritana Grille at the Don Cesar Resort** (3400 Gulf Boulevard, 727/360-1881, $$$$) will oblige with creative and adventurous cuisine from chef Eric Neri. The general culinary approach is "Floribbean," but the menu might lead anywhere: from jerk-grilled prawns with banana papaya chutney to wood-grilled beef tenderloin with tomato confit, portobello mushrooms, and truffle oil.

"If you lock yourself into a dominant style of cooking, you won't go very far," Neri stated at a cooking demonstration we were fortunate enough to attend. He'll only state a general emphasis on all things Floridian: nice light flavors, colors, presentations. Along those lines, how does a warm lobster quesadilla served with a fruity dipping sauce stung with a hint of habanero pepper sound? Well, it tastes even better. Believe it or not, more money is generated at the Don Cesar by its kitchens than the room charges. If you've ever eaten here, that claim is not hard to digest at all.

At another extreme, the **Internet**

MAP OF PINELLAS COUNTY—PAGE 448

Outpost Café (7400 Gulf Boulevard, 727/813-360-7806, $) serves as a way station for international travelers as well as a great place to start the day. They serve fresh blends of coffee and home-made muffins so moist they render you temporarily tongue-tied. Opened in 1997, it has caught on with visitors from Europe (where cyber cafés are as plentiful as sports bars here) and is gradually winning local converts. All in all, it's a civilized alternative to fast food or "family restaurant" spreads. And, who knows, you might meet some budding Brigitte Bardot or Gérard Dépardieu on whom you can try out your broken high-school French. There are eight terminals in a comfortable living room–style setting; an Internet hookup costs $2 per 15 minutes.

Night Moves

Follow the bouncing crowd to the sports bars of St. Pete Beach, where one can guzzle beer to the sight of bodies being blocked, checked, tackled, and carried off the field. The theme of this sports-crazy area—home to pro football's Tampa Bay Buccaneers and major-league baseball's Devil Rays, and host of the 2000 Super Bowl—is mined in clubs like the ever-popular **Undertow** (3850 Gulf Boulevard, 727/360-1748) and **Players** (6200 Gulf Boulevard, 727/367-1902). The latter is a multi-room retreat in the St. Pete Beach Days Inn with lots of TVs tuned in to sporting events and a modest menu of decently prepared bar food. Their fine blackened-grouper sandwich helped make the sorry football game we watched here one night easier to swallow. Our alma mater, the University of North Carolina, got positively shellacked by Florida State, which at least made the bar crowd happy.

As an alternative to sports bars, hit the Corey Avenue Historic Shopping District, where a renovated old movie house called the **Beach Theatre** (350 Corey Avenue, 727/360-6697) screens art movies and independent productions you won't likely see at a 12-screen suburban multiplex.

Contact Information

Gulf Beaches of Tampa Bay Chamber of Commerce, 6990 Gulf Boulevard, St. Pete Beach, FL 33706; 727/360-6957 or 800/944-1847; website: www.gulfbeaches-tampabay.com

Treasure Island and Sunset Beach

St. Pete Beach looks downright understated compared to Treasure Island (pop. 7,500), which takes the concept of family fun to illogical extremes. It is a jammed-to-the-max vacationland of eccentrically named and oddly shaped motels, goofy golf courses, amusement parks, strip malls, beachwear emporiums, hot-dog huts, ice-cream stands, souvenir shops, convenience stores, gas stations, restaurants, bars, and still more convenience stores.

The island's resort destiny commenced in 1915 with the construction of the Coney Island, its first hotel. Beginning in the 1950s, the mangroves bordering the inland side of Treasure Island were destroyed and filled in to create developments with names like Capri Isle and Isle of Palms. They really put the pedal to the metal in the 1970s. Today, Treasure Island is described by its boosters as a "mature, built-out city," though "overbuilt" is more like it.

The island derives its name from rumors that a Spanish galleon sank nearby in the early 1700s and still lies buried offshore. Treasure Island's swashbuckling motif is carried to absurd extremes by its motels, which include the Sea Chest, the Jolly Roger, the Buccaneer, the Swashbuckler, and the Treasure Chest. The real treasure on this 3.5-mile island is the beach, which you can't see from Gulf Boulevard for all the motels, hotels, and condos. Once you're splayed out on it, however, you'll turn from a stressed-out road warrior to a happy landlubber.

At the less harried south end, reachable via West Gulf Boulevard, Sunset Beach is cloistered away from the mayhem. Sunset Beach is to Treasure Island what Pass-a-Grille is to St. Pete Beach: i.e., a quiet stretch of residences and rental apartments that maintains its low-key island character by virtue of its isolation from the main drag. Also like Pass-a-Grille, it once enjoyed small-town autonomy until 1955. In that year, the island communities of Sunset Beach, Boca Ciega, Treasure Island, and Sunshine Beach banded together to incorporate as the city of Treasure Island.

Beaches

Like Miami Beach, Treasure Island has been artificially buttressed and is now so wide in places it seems almost unfair to the rest of the world. The beach here is touted as "the largest white sand beach on the Gulf Coast" and "the widest beach on the Pinellas Suncoast." Isn't it cheating that Treasure Island has achieved its spectacular width not as a result of natural processes but because of human-engineered beach renourishment? In any case, it took us not seconds but minutes to casually stroll from the edge of Treasure Island Beach to the gulf's edge. It looks more like a glaring white desert than a beach.

At the island's southernmost tip, in the community of Sunset Beach, **Treasure Island Park** looks directly across Blind Pass at Upham Beach in St. Pete Beach. A public boardwalk extends for three-fifths of a mile over the dunes and along the pass. It's a great spot for sunset-watching (not for nothing is the community called Sunset Beach). Free parking is available but there are no facilities. Treasure Island additionally boasts 45 dune walkovers at street ends from 77th to 127th Avenues. The access at 120th Avenue is a little more substantial than the street-end walkovers found elsewhere on Treasure Island, and what had been metered parking in a lot next to the Ramada Inn is now free.

Pinellas County operates **Treasure Island Beach Access**, the island's main public beach, up around 100th Avenue. There are free parking facilities, showers, and drinking fountains, and benches line a cement jogging/biking path that runs for a mile or so, ending at the Holiday Inn. The city of St. Petersburg maintains **St. Petersburg Municipal Beach** on Treasure Island, directly across the street from the

6 Treasure Island Park

Location: south end of West Gulf Boulevard, in Sunset Beach on Treasure Island
Parking/fees: free parking lot
Hours: 5 A.M.–1 A.M.
Facilities: none
Contact: Treasure Island Parks Department, 727/360-3278

7 Treasure Island Beach Access

Location: 100th Avenue and Gulf Boulevard, on Treasure Island
Parking/fees: free parking lot
Hours: 5 A.M.–1 A.M.
Facilities: restrooms and showers
Contact: Pinellas County Parks Department, 727/464-3347

MAP OF PINELLAS COUNTY—PAGE 448

Howard Johnson, at 112th Avenue and Gulf Boulevard. Full facilities, including a snack bar, are available, as are ten volleyball courts. Parking costs 50 cents per hour in a large metered lot.

Bunking Down

Top of the heap on Treasure Island is the **Bilmar Beach Resort** (10650 Gulf Boulevard, 727/360-5531, $$), a massive complex located front and center on 550 feet of beach. Prices are moderate, in keeping with the family-friendly tenor of Treasure Island, and units come in a variety of shapes and sizes. Most have refrigerators and breakfast nooks. The Bilmar also has a pair of popular nightspots on the premises, the Beach Bar Cafe and the Grog Shoppe.

Next door to the Bilmar is the **Thunderbird Beach Resort** (10700 Gulf Boulevard, 727/367-1961, $$) with the most spectacular neon sign in the area. You can't miss it. Of the accommodations bearing swashbuckling names, the **Buccaneer Beach Resort Motel** (10800 Gulf Boulevard, 727/367-1908, $) is the most presentable, and the rates qualify as a bargain. Then there's the aforementioned **Holiday Inn** (11908 Gulf Boulevard, 727/367-2761, $$$) and **Howard Johnson** (11125 Gulf Boulevard, 727/360-6971, $$), which offer dependably clean and comfortable rooms.

Coastal Cuisine

Sturgeon General's Warning: Portion size and low prices dictate the popularity of restaurants on Treasure Island, with pancake houses, hot-dog huts, and all-you-can-eat seafood buffets ruling the scene. Happily, you can bypass the mediocrity and head up to **Gators on the Pass** (12754 Kingfish Drive, 727/367-8951, $$), a colossal restaurant/nightclub complex (capacity 900) along Kingfish Wharf. The menu is about as large as the premises, ranging from ribs and chicken to grouper and mahimahi. The seafood chowder and gumbo are homemade from 60-year-old recipes, and the you-peel-'em shrimp can't be beat.

One of our favorite places in the area requires an eastward bridge-hopping over Pasadena Avenue (a.k.a. St. Pete Beach Causeway) into South Pasadena. Here, you will find **Ted Peters Famous Smoked Fish** (1350 Pasadena Avenue South, 727/381-7931, $$), which has been serving the St. Petersburg area for nearly 50 years. Fish are smoked from four to six hours in wire mesh racks suspended over smoldering beds of Florida red oak coals. You sit on bar stools or picnic tables on an outdoor patio and flag down one of the friendly waitresses. While mullet is not always the public's fish of choice (some consider it worthwhile only as

8 St. Petersburg Municipal Beach

Location: 112th Avenue at Gulf Boulevard, on Treasure Island
Parking/fees: metered parking lot
Hours: 5 A.M.–1 A.M.
Facilities: concessions, restrooms, picnic tables, and showers
Contact: St. Petersburg Department of Leisure Services, 727/893-7335

9 120th Avenue Access

Location: 120th Avenue at Gulf Boulevard, on Treasure Island
Parking/fees: free parking lot
Hours: 5 A.M.–1 A.M.
Facilities: none
Contact: Treasure Island Parks Department, 727/360-3278

MAP OF FLORIDA'S WEST COAST—PAGE 347

"You're Not Going Swimming, Are You?"

When we visited Florida's West Coast two consecutive years for late fall and early winter research trips, the waters of the gulf were still highly swimmable and comfortable. The average water temperature along the southern Gulf Coast in November hovered around 78°F—balmy to our grateful bodies, which knew that back home, people were wearing overcoats and raking leaves. But to our surprise, the Florida natives along this stretch of the coast claimed the waters were too cold for them to swim.

"We're used to the summertime, when the gulf is in the high eighties, low nineties," said a ranger along one of the coastal state parks. "When it gets below 80, it's too cold for us." We heard this refrain over and over. A smile, a shake of the head: too chilly for us blood-thinned natives.

On Treasure Island, we were treated like freaks for climbing into the water. As one of us approached the gulf, the male half of a strolling couple stopped to ask, "You're not going swimming, are you?"

"That's what I intended to do." What, was there a problem: sting rays? red tide?

"God bless you," he said. "You're a better man than I. Yesterday, I went fishing and waded up to my waist, and it was so cold my bowels haven't been the same since."

Oh, come on. We're hardly the Hardy boys when it comes to braving frigid waters. At 72°, the gulf waters off Treasure Island felt eminently swimmable on this warm, sun-dappled afternoon. We'd describe it as "refreshing." They described it as just too damn cold.

The water-temperature rating scale below will hold true for most people.

85°F Uncomfortably hot
80–85°F Bathwater warm
75–80°F Perfect temperature—stay in all day!
70–75°F Refreshingly cool
65–70°F Uncomfortably cool
60–65°F Intolerably cold
60°F Hypothermia (wetsuits only!)

bait fish), we highly recommend the smoked mullet at Ted Peters, a house specialty. Also, mouth watering is the smoked Spanish mackerel and the salmon. We prefer the smoked platter, which includes the whole fish, to the smoked fish spread, which is more like tuna salad.

Two blocks east of Ted's is **Florida Orange Groves and Winery** (1500 Pasadena Avenue South, 727/347-4025), which offers cold, fresh-squeezed orange juice. This is, of course, Florida's signature drink, but it's a more elusive a purchase in the Sunshine State than you might imagine, so pull over here and purchase a jug of liquid gold while you have the chance. This is some killer OJ . . . and we don't mean the allegedly murderous ex-jock, either (who currently resides in Miami and was, in fact, charged with assault in a road-rage incident there in December 2000). But that's neither here nor there. Also sold at

Florida Orange Groves and Winery are key lime wine, orange wine, watermelon wine, and grapefruit wine. Can you imagine the hangover from the latter?

Night Moves

Action central for nightlife at the south end of Treasure Island is at **Beach Nutts Bar and Grill** (9600 West Gulf Boulevard, 727/367-7427) and the **Seabreeze** (9546 West Gulf Boulevard, 727/360-1398), two bars that share a dirt parking lot and ownership. Officially, they are located just inside the otherwise quiet and cozy community of Sunset Beach. Both are appealingly funky places with a rowdy but friendly clientele and a decent bar menu (peel-and-eat shrimp, burgers, grouper sandwich).

The more immediately appealing of the two, Beach Nutts is elevated above and over the beach like an enormous lifeguard tower or tree fort. The higher elevation seems to allow for more generous sea breezes, too. Don't be put off by the occasional line of Harleys out front or the sudden rumble of a hog revving its engine. This is as happy a mix as you'll find of people who wouldn't normally be seen together: young yuppies, old regulars, beach nuts, sports nuts, bikers, surfers, rockers.

Live music is provided most nights by bands that have names like Naked People and Driving Blind, and classic FM rock blares the rest of the time. On a good night, there's no better beach bar in all of Florida than Beach Nutts. It's the sort of place you'd legitimately expect to find, but rarely do, in any self-respecting beach town.

The Seabreeze has pool tables right on the beach, which was a first for us. If you lose your shirt, you just go for a swim, right? They, too, have live music, mostly solo strummers.

Up north, it's all happening at **Gators on the Pass** (12754 Kingfish Drive, 727/367-8951), which boasts "the world's largest waterfront bar." Tuesday is devoted to swing music; the rest of the time, they rock and roll all night (and party every day). In addition to live music, a menu of microbrews, and a nonsmoking bar, Gators works the sports-bar angle, with 28 televisions tuned into whatever gamut of games is on, especially anything Bucs-related. Here's a plan for an action-packed evening, if you're up to it: start with a sunset dinner at Gators, then stroll the boardwalk to the gambling boats that depart from John's Pass and wager some of your hard-earned cash, and finally return to dry land for a rock and roll nightcap at Gators.

There's a bonafide nighttime subculture for European travelers in lounges affixed to the larger beach resorts. One night, we popped into the **Grog Shoppe** (10650 Gulf Boulevard, 727/360-5531) at the Bilmar Resort for a look-see. Between songs the burly singer asked, without irony, "Are there any Americans here?" As it turned out, we were the only American customers. As he went around the room, each table of patrons called out their country of origin: "Deutschland! Wales! Scotland! England! Canada!"

Contact Information

Gulf Beaches of Tampa Bay Chamber of Commerce, 6990 Gulf Boulevard, St. Pete Beach, FL 33706; 727/360-6957 or 800/944-1847; website: www.gulfbeaches-tampabay.com

Madeira Beach

First, a word is in order about Sand Key, which encompasses Madeira Beach and seven other communities. Sand Key extends for "14 miles of heaven" between John's Pass and Clearwater Pass. The towns along this barrier-island charm bracelet are collectively marketed as the Gulf Beaches on Sand Key.

There's a little something for everybody out here: hotels and motels for tourists, beach parks for mainland daytrippers, condos and single-family homes for those who have sunk roots into the sand. If you look closely, parts of Sand Key look unchanged from the 1950s: little L-shaped cottage courts and mom-and-pop motels, worlds within worlds right off the main road. The very fact that in the 21st century you can pull into a place like the Wit's End Motel or the Sea Fever Motel or any of dozens of other hidden charmers like them is encouraging to those of us who fret it's all been scrubbed away by developmental prerogatives.

A varied lot of communities is strung out along Sand Key with barely a break in the action. From south to north, they are: by name: Madeira Beach, Redington Beach, North Redington Beach, Redington Shores, Indian Shores, Indian Rocks Beach, Belleair Shore, and Belleair Beach. They range in character from tourist-friendly beach towns to quieter residential communities.

At one time, Madeira Beach was nothing more or less than a fun and funky beach town. While Treasure Island was adopted by teeming teen hordes from St. Petersburg, Madeira Beach became the favorite haunt of the young and restless from Tampa, who lovingly dubbed it "Mad Beach." Then the condo brigade grabbed a chunk of the community chest and since then, to paraphrase Paul Revere and the Raiders, kicks just keep getting harder to find. As the cost of living rose, the marginal group-house tribes were elbowed out, and the town opened its floodgates to tourists, more of whom now come from Europe and Canada than from Tampa.

Even with all the changes, Mad Beach is still a fun though slightly less funky beach town. Bits and pieces of the old Mad Beach spirit still exist, rearing its head in subtle, unexpected ways. For example, we fell into conversation with a friendly, long-haired chap manning the counter at a Gulf Boulevard convenience store. Half an hour later, we'd discussed the entire recorded catalogs of Lou Reed ("Lou changed my life," he offered), John Cale, Nico, and the New York Dolls. We then visited Mad Music, a nearby hangout for alternative rockers that dispenses guitars and amps plus independent recordings, fanzines,

⑩ John's Pass Beach and Park

Location: On Gulf Boulevard at 129th Avenue in Madeira Beach
Parking/fees: metered parking lot
Hours: sunrise to midnight
Facilities: restrooms, picnic tables, and showers
Contact: Madeira Beach Public Works Department, 727/391-1611

⑪ Kitty Stewart Park

Location: Gulf Boulevard at 143rd Avenue in Madeira Beach
Parking/fees: metered parking lot
Hours: sunrise to midnight
Facilities: picnic table and a shower
Contact: Madeira Beach Public Works Department, 727/391-1611

comics, and rock and roll collectibles. Next door is Mad Beach Surf Shop, a mainstay of the beach scene.

The town of Madeira Beach has a population of 4,225, and those who don't make their living servicing tourists are engaged in commercial fishing out of John's Pass. Madeira's mayor boasts, "More grouper is brought into John's Pass than any other place in the state." Seafood is celebrated each October with a three-day festival at John's Pass Village—the commercial hub of Madeira Beach—that draws over 100,000 people.

Beaches

Beginning at John's Pass, on the southern end of Sand Key, and stretching for 2.5 miles, the beach at Madeira is a dazzling white strand that is not quite as wide as Treasure Island's. Just over the bridge from Treasure Island, necessitating a quick turn toward the Gulf, is **John's Pass Beach and Park**, where the fishing is reportedly excellent, a judgment that would seem to be confirmed by a capped jetty filled with anglers. Dune walkovers lead to 500 feet of beachfront, but as is the Gulf Coast norm, there are no lifeguards. Heading north along Gulf Boulevard, beach access is provided at numerous street ends. Parking is catch-as-catch-can. From south to north, access points are located at 129th through 137th Avenues, plus 141st, 142nd, and 148th Avenues, and the end of Bayshore Drive.

Pinellas County's Park Department oversees the **Madeira Beach Access**, which is not the best of their parks. A sign warns of "No Loitering on Beach," making us wonder, what isn't loitering on a beach? Metered parking is available here ($1 per hour). The beach is thinning in places, with remnants of wooden piers and groins in the water. Beach rentals are reasonably priced: $2 an hour or $7 all day for a double chaise lounge. There are restrooms and showers but no lifeguards.

At 144rd Avenue and Gulf Drive, just south of the county access, is **Kitty Stewart Park**, a small beach turnout with eight parking spaces and a single picnic shelter. At the north end of Madeira Beach is **Archibald Memorial Beach**, a city-run park with concessions and facilities.

⓬ Madeira Beach Access

 2

Location: Gulf Boulevard at 144th Avenue in Madeira Beach
Parking/fees: metered parking lot
Hours: 7 A.M. to sunset
Facilities: concessions, restrooms, and showers
Contact: Pinellas County Parks Department, 727/464-3347

Shore Things

- **Boat cruise:** Europa Sea Kruz, 150 153rd Avenue #202, 727/393-2885.
- **Dive shop:** Madeira Beach Dive Center, 13237 Gulf Boulevard, 727/392-4423.
- **Ecotourism:** Hubbard's Sea Adventures, 150 John's Pass Boardwalk, 727/393-1947.

⓭ Archibald Memorial Beach

Location: Gulf Boulevard and Municipal Drive at 153rd Avenue in Madeira Beach
Parking/fees: metered parking lot
Hours: sunrise to midnight
Facilities: concessions, restrooms, picnic tables, and shower
Contact: Madeira Beach Public Works Department, 727/391-1611

MAP OF FLORIDA'S WEST COAST—PAGE 347

- **Fishing charters:** Snug Harbor Charter Service, 13625 Gulf Boulevard, 727/398-7470.
- **Marina:** Hubbard's Marina, 150 John's Pass Boardwalk, 727/393-0167.
- **Pier:** Pelican Pier, John's Pass Village, 727/399-9633.
- **Rainy-day attractions:** Book Nook, 15029 Madeira Way, 727/392-8541, and Mad Music, 13107 Gulf Boulevard, 727/393-9663.
- **Shopping/browsing:** John's Pass Village and Boardwalk, 150 128th Avenue, 727/397-1571.
- **Surf shop:** Mad Beach Surf Shop, 13111 Gulf Boulevard, 727/397-3249; surf report, 727/398-7873.
- **Vacation rentals:** Travel Resort Services, 13030 Gulf Boulevard, 727/393-2534.

Bunking Down

The **Shoreline Island Resort Motel** (Gulf Boulevard, 727/397-6641, $$) is an "exclusively all-adult" motel, with all guests and visitors required to be over the age of 21. For the prurient-minded, "adult" does not mean what you're thinking. La-Z-Boy recliners, not heart-shaped tubs, are provided with each room, and the emphasis here is on peace and quiet. The Shoreline is a clean and polite five-building complex with hands-on service from the same family who has owned and operated it for the past 30 years. Four of the buildings are right on the gulf, opening onto 400 feet of beach.

In Mad Beach, you'd expect to find a place called the **Wits End Motel** (13600 Gulf Boulevard, 727/391-6739, $). Name aside, this motel's beachfront location, heated pool, fully equipped efficiency apartments, and reasonable rates will actually help restore your sanity. The king of the beachfront for families ("kids eat free") is the **Holiday Inn** (15208 Gulf Boulevard, 727/392-2275, $$). Situated right on the beach, they have tennis and volleyball courts, a restaurant, sports bar, and heated pool. We spent a memorable evening on barstools at the poolside tiki bar listening to honeymooning Aussies get progressively louder with each can of brew they ingested. Meantime, as the sun went down the sky took on a rosy hue, matching the ruddy faces of those knocking 'em back at the tiki bar.

Coastal Cuisine

Madeira Beach primarily caters to undiscriminating palates of American families who want more, more, more. If you're on the hunt for seafood, **Johnny Leverock's Seafood House** (565 150th Avenue, 727/393-0459, $$) is a gulfside chain with a firm foothold in these parts. Just be sure to order the fresh fish prepared as simply as possible (char-grilled or blackened). Otherwise you'll be ordering off a menu that isn't much different from that of any inland Red Lobster franchise.

Up at John's Pass Village, the **Friendly Fisherman** (150 128th Avenue, 727/391-6025, $$) serves waterfront views along with breakfast, lunch, and dinner. It's a family-friendly place where food is served at wooden tables, many of which overlook the marina. For broiled, fried, or char-grilled grouper brought in fresh right off the adjacent docks, the Friendly Fisherman will do just fine. A "captain's platter" of gulf-caught grouper, shrimp, and scallops goes for a thoroughly reasonable $13.95.

Night Moves

Some of our best night moves were made on the miniature golf courses, of which there are several in the area, each more ludicrously landscaped than the last. Our favorite was **Smugglers Cove** (15395 Gulf

Boulevard, 727/398-7008), a clean, well-lit course of 18 interesting holes that reward skill as often as dumb luck. Obviously, the pirate motif is a recurring theme. One hole takes place on a shipwrecked galleon's deck, and another runs alongside a lagoon filled with live alligators. During one memorable round between the two of us (beach bum vs. beach bum), the score was tied as we went to the last hole. It was a tricky spiraling sucker that forced us to confront the age-old question: Play it safe or go for broke? One of us played it safe and won. The other went for broke and lost the game. Lost poorly, in fact. Words were exchanged.

Contact Information

Gulf Beaches on Sand Key Chamber of Commerce, 501 150th Avenue, Madeira Beach, FL 33708; 727/391-7373 or 800/944-1847; website: www.usa-chamber.com/gulf-beaches

Redington Beach, North Redington Beach, and Redington Shores

Between them, the three towns of Redington Beach (pop. 1,600), North Redington Beach (pop. 1,100), and Redington Shores (pop. 2,700) hold sway over four miles of beachfront. "Hold sway" is a fairly accurate description, as these are mostly single-family bedroom communities whose beaches are utilized primarily by residents (especially in Redington Beach, which is as uptight as they come). The grip loosens the farther north you go, with Redington Shores being the most visitor friendly of the three. In fact, it goes out of its way, relatively speaking, to attract an esoteric mix of vacationers, especially in the summer when travelers from Canada, England, France, Germany, Italy, and Denmark beat a path here. No, our eyes weren't deceiving us when we spied a Danish-American restaurant along Gulf Boulevard. "Danish lobster tails," anyone?

Beaches

The beach is within walking distance of most homes in these three communities, which is great if you live here. Otherwise,

14 North Redington Beach/Redington Shores accesses

Location: various street-end accesses in North Redington Beach and Redington Shores
Parking/fees: limited free street parking
Hours: sunrise to sunset
Facilities: none
Contact: Redington Shores Town Hall, 727/397-5538

15 Redington Shores Beach Access

Location: Gulf Boulevard at 182nd Avenue in Redington Shores
Parking/fees: free parking lot
Hours: 7 A.M. to sunset
Facilities: restrooms and showers
Contact: Pinellas County Parks Department, 727/464-3347

MAP OF FLORIDA'S WEST COAST—PAGE 347

you can just about forget about it, especially in Redington Beach, which has absolutely no public beach access. **North Redington Beach** has public access with spotty parking at various street ends. Among them, 171st and 173rd Avenues have lots. **Redington Shores** also has street-end accesses, beginning at 175th Avenue and continuing up to 184th Avenue. **Redington Shores Beach Access**, at 182nd Street, offers ample free parking and an extremely wide beach, but in the water just offshore are exposed rocks, a section of which has been roped off for swimmers' protection.

Bunking Down

Each of the 125 rooms at the **North Redington Beach Hilton Resort** (17120 Gulf Boulevard, 727/391-4000, $$$) has a balcony overlooking the gulf. You'll pay for the privilege ($160 and up a night in season), but this six-story property is one of the nicer corporate lodges on Sand Key. A dining room and lounge are located on the premises. Some of the smaller gulf-front properties, such as the three-story **Sandalwood Beach Resort** (17100 Gulf Boulevard, 727/397-5541, $$), offer a considerable break on price in homier surroundings. If you're looking to lay in at a condo, try **Suncoast Resort Rentals** (16401 Gulf Boulevard, 727/393-3425).

Coastal Cuisine

Shells Seafood Restaurant (17855 Gulf Boulevard, 727/393-8990, $$) is a Florida chain that rises above the pedestrian franchised norm. Shells has won top honors among locals for nearly a decade for their "casual seafood" and big helpings. While some of the menu is given over to the obligatory fried platters—hey, this is a family restaurant—Shells also has some excellent seafood pasta dishes and an array of fresh fish, which they'll char-grill or blacken. They're open for lunch and dinner. FYI, there's also a Shells in St. Pete Beach (6300 Gulf Florida, 727/360-0889, $$).

In addition to other seafood restaurants, North Redington Beach boasts a real anomaly for this middlebrow stretch of the Gulf Coast: a continental restaurant, the **Wine Cellar** (17037 Gulf Boulevard, 727/393-3491, $$$). If you're wearying of fried seafood, it's an option. The newest, most popular entry on the seafood scene is **Ballyhoo Grill** (16699 Gulf Boulevard, North Redington Beach, 727/320-0536), which is part of a regional chain, like Shells and Leverock's.

Night Moves

The **Friendly Tavern** (18121 Gulf Boulevard, 727/393-4470) in Redington Shores has been around for half a century, and the name of the place pretty much tells you why. A broad selection of foreign beers adds to the, ahem, brew-ha-ha. They sell food, too, including fresh shrimp steamed in beer. Finally, they boast of being "the original Gulf Coast home of laser karaoke."

Contact Information

Gulf Beaches on Sand Key Chamber of Commerce, 501 150th Avenue, Madeira Beach, FL 33708; 727/391-7373 or 800/944-1847; website: www.usa-chamber.com/gulf-beaches

Indian Shores and Indian Rocks Beach

The most congenial of the Sand Key communities, Indian Shores and Indian Rocks Beach are populated with a mix of year-round residents, regular seasonal visitors, and vacationers from all over the map. Indian Shores (pop. 1,400) is justifiably proud of its five-story height limit on buildings and its wide-open beaches, which host a popular "Taste of the Beaches" fair each May. Likewise, Indian Rocks Beach (pop. 4,200) has three miles of beaches whose welcoming spirit is as warm as the gulf waters. To add to the communities' appeal, creative local entrepreneurs cater to the needs of one and all. The conspicuous absence of fast-food franchises and corporate logos offers a lesson from which all beach towns could take a cue.

Beaches

As you might expect in towns that roll out the welcome mat so unhesitatingly, public access to the five miles of shoreline in Indian Shores and Indian Rocks Beach is quite generous. There are accesses, with limited free parking, at the west ends of 20 out of 27 avenues in **Indian Rocks Beach.** Most also have outdoor showers and trash receptacles (but no restrooms).

⑯ Indian Rocks Beach accesses (south)

Location: west ends of avenues in Indian Rocks Beach
Parking/fees: free limited street parking
Hours: 6 A.M.–11 P.M.
Facilities: picnic tables and showers
Contact: Indian Rocks Beach Public Works Department, 727/595-6889

Pinellas County oversees two excellent beach parks here, too. One is **Tiki Gardens–Indian Shores**, which has public parking on the east side of Gulf Boulevard (50 cents per hour, self-pay), but you must cross this busy thoroughfare to get to the beach. Luckily, the button on the pedestrian signal at the crosswalk has a hair trigger, so you don't have to wait long for it to bring cars to a halt before crossing. The beach itself is worth the extra footsteps, with a healthy strip of white sand backed by a few intact dunes.

The other county park is **Indian Rocks**

⑰ Tiki Gardens-Indian Shores

Location: 19601 Gulf Boulevard in Indian Shores
Parking/fees: metered parking lot
Hours: 7 A.M. to sunset
Facilities: restrooms and showers
Contact: Pinellas County Parks Department, 727/464-3347

⑱ Indian Rocks Beach Access (north)

Location: 1700 Gulf Boulevard in Indian Rocks Beach
Parking/fees: free parking lot
Hours: 7 A.M. to sunset
Facilities: restrooms and showers
Contact: Pinellas County Parks Department, 727/464-3347

Beach Access, where the gulfside parking is free, but the sand is thinner, grayer, and shellier than at Indian Shores. There are restrooms and showers at both county accesses, but no lifeguards. The beaches of Indian Shores have been renourished in recent years, an obvious attempt to keep visitors happy and to encourage their return.

Shore Things

- **Bike/skate rentals:** Bikers America, 19709 Gulf Boulevard, Indian Shores, 727/593-0665.
- **Boat cruise:** Starlite Princess, Hamlin's Landing, Indian Rocks Beach, 727/595-1212.
- **Dive shop:** Indian Rocks Tackle/West Florida Scuba, 1301 North Gulf Boulevard, Indian Rocks Beach, 727/595-3196.
- **Ecotourism:** Suncoast Seabird Sanctuary, 18328 Gulf Boulevard, Indian Shores, 727/391-6211.
- **Fishing charters:** Hamlin's Landing, 401 2nd Street East, Indian Rocks Beach, 727/595-9484.
- **Marina:** Redington Shores Marina, 17811 Gulf Boulevard, 727/391-1954.
- **Pier:** Redington Long Pier, 17490 Gulf Boulevard, Redington Shores, 727/391-9398.
- **Rainy-day attraction:** Indian Rocks Area Historical Museum, 1507 Bay Palm Boulevard, Indian Rocks Beach, 727/593-3861.
- **Vacation rentals:** Gulfside Properties, 2215 Gulf Boulevard, Indian Rocks Beach, 727/517-7722.

Bunking Down

The lodgings here are geared for vacation-length visits, with weekly and monthly rentals the norm. Two nice but unglamorous "apartment motels" are located directly on the gulf, offering similar amenities. **Holiday Isle Apartments** (2200 North Gulf Boulevard, Indian Rocks Beach, 727/596-3488, $$) has full kitchens in each of its 22 rooms. The **Sea Resort Motel** (102 Gulf Boulevard, Indian Rocks Beach, 727/595-0461, $) is less expensive and has refrigerators and microwaves in its 29 rooms.

Coastal Cuisine

"Don't Worry, Be Crabby!" is the motto of **Crabby Bill's Old-Time Oyster Bar** (412 1st Street, 727/595-4825, $$), a wild and wacky family seafood restaurant in Indian Rocks Beach. The fun starts when you walk in the door, where you're greeted by a woman in a crab headdress at whose heels stalks Crabbo the Clown. Her job is to lead you to one of the long picnic tables strewn about this spacious room, and then to encourage total strangers to scoot around to make room for you. His job is to lead the packed house in foot-stomping, hand-clapping singalongs, and if you're not ready for prime-time *Romper Room* action, you might want to eat elsewhere. Of course, since this is the best seafood place for miles around, you must eat here and you will enjoy it!

Crabby Bill's, in fact, fondly recalled memories of Maine clambakes we've attended and smokehouses we've visited in the Pacific Northwest. You order from the menu on your paper placemat or off the handwritten signs listing "today's specials" that cover the walls. The prices are reasonable, the seafood is fresh, and the portions are huge and hearty. Crabs are obviously the specialty here. But how could we resist one pound of grilled yellowfin tuna for under $12?

The dining experience is not unlike a giant family reunion, with people shouting, chatting, staring enviously at other diners' portions, and offering order suggestions of their own. One friendly man proffered an unsolicited forkful of his own food to us in order to demonstrate just how good his selection was. Forget Woodstock, we'll take Crabby Bill's! There are four other Crabby Bill's in the area, but this is the original and still the best. The others are franchised knockoffs that own rights to the name. The Indian Rocks Beach location is, in fact, the only Crabby Bill's still run by Bill himself.

Guppy's (1701 Gulf Boulevard, Indian Rocks Beach, 727/593-2032, $$) is a stylish but unpretentious restaurant serving lunch and dinner across the street from Indian Rocks Beach Access. The menu offers interesting variations on old standards, like a smoked salmon sandwich on pita that was so delicious it was sad to see it disappear. The same could be said for the Jamaican jerk grouper with pineapple salsa. We vowed to try the grouper fajitas the next time through. You can sit outside, on a patio that overlooks the boulevard and beach, or inside, away from the car noises.

One of the more expensive restaurants on Sand Key, the **Salt Rock Grill** (19325 Gulf Boulevard, 727/593-7625, $$$$), merits its tariffs with an upscale, art-filled interior and a menu of surf-and-turf preparations pit-grilled over citrus and oak embers. If you're looking to splurge, the Salt Rock Grill is the place to do it.

Night Moves

Along the stretch of coast between St. Pete Beach and Sand Key, the preponderance of pubs can sometimes make you feel as if you've been dropped by cosmic transporter into Merry Olde England. Actually, it's the other way around, as many Britons make the trip to Florida's West Coast for sun 'n' fun of a sort they rarely get back home. You could design a pub crawl that began down in St. Pete Beach and ended in Indian Rocks Beach at the **Red Lion Pub** (1407 Gulf Boulevard, 727/596-5411) or the draft house known as, simply, **The Pub** (20025 Gulf Boulevard, 727/595-3172). Cheers, mate! Two other popular pubs are **Mahuffer's**, a.k.a. Sloppy John's (19201 Gulf Boulevard, Indian Shores, 727/596-0226) and **J.D.'s** (125 Gulf Boulevard North, Indian Rocks Beach, 727/595-1320).

Contact Information

Gulf Beaches on Sand Key Chamber of Commerce, 501 150th Avenue, Madeira Beach, FL 33708; 727/391-7373 or 800/944-1847; website: www.usa-chamber.com/gulf-beaches

MAP OF FLORIDA'S WEST COAST—PAGE 347

Suncoast Seabird Sanctuary

The largest wild bird hospital in the United States, Suncoast Seabird Sanctuary, is located in Indian Shores. This rescue, rehabilitative, and rerelease facility is an uplifting place to visit—for birds and humans. At full capacity, the Suncoast is haven for more than 500 birds, with as many as 20 new avian patients arriving each day. Most of the birds have been injured—either directly or indirectly—by humans. The main sources of injury are fish hooks and monofilament fishing lines, which can cause so much damage to birds that, even when recovered from their wounds, some cannot be re-released into the wild. Other injuries are caused by flying into power lines and windows or ingesting pesticides and other pollutants.

However they fall, the birds are quickly diagnosed, treated, and put through an extensive recuperative process. The ultimate goal is to reacclimate each bird to the outdoors in an aviary with others of its species. The public is invited and encouraged to view the aviary, treatment rooms, and facilities, where the staff have pioneered new techniques in avian medicine, including safe anesthesia regimens, prosthetic feet, artificial bills, and the successful captive breeding of Eastern brown pelicans.

It all started on December 3, 1971, when zoologist Ralph Heath, Jr. came upon a wounded cormorant walking in a daze alongside Gulf Boulevard. He took the bird in, named him Maynard, and fixed his wing. The feathers really started flying as word of Maynard's rescue made the rounds. Wounded birds started showing up at Heath's doorstep, and he couldn't turn them away. He opened the sanctuary soon thereafter and runs it to this day. Money is raised completely by donations, and much of the work is done by volunteers. Do yourself and your kids a favor and make Suncoast Seabird Sanctuary part of your vacation itinerary. It's enough to make anyone's spirit take wing.

For more information contact Suncoast Seabird Sanctuary, 18328 Gulf Boulevard, Indian Shores, FL 34635; 727/391-6211; website: www.webcoast.com/SeaBird.

Belleair Shore and Belleair Beach

The two Belleairs are almost all residential, and their tone is one of strident privacy. This astonishing boast about Belleair Shore (pop. 75) was found in a local publication: "No commercial activity is sanctioned within the town." We also encountered this telling summary statement about Belleair Beach: "Beaches in the community are public [note: this is a matter of state law, not community largesse], but access is private." In short, these are year-round bedroom communities for overpaid executives who commute to the neighboring cities of Tampa, St. Petersburg, and Clearwater. They got theirs, and they want you and yours nowhere near them.

In the fall of 2000, the mayor of Belleair Beach (pop. 2,080) resigned from office. He had been involved in a money laundering scheme, and his criminal trial was deadlocked. Rather than face another trial, he confessed to stealing $250,000. His fellow citizens raced to his defense as a "man of honor" in hopes of averting prison time for their mayor of 12 years. We can't help but marvel at the great gulf in this country when it comes to white- collar and blue-collar crime. The mayor of Belleair Beach makes off with a quarter mil, and his punishment is that he's forced to resign. Some poor shmuck robs a 7-Eleven for $200 and he's branded as society's scourge and tossed in the slammer for 25 years.

⓳ Belleair Beach accesses

Location: 7th, 13th, 19th, and Morgan Streets in Belleair Beach
Parking/fees: free limited street parking
Hours: 7 A.M. to sunset
Facilities: none
Contact: Belleair Beach Public Works Department, 727/595-4646

Beaches

Beach accesses exist at the ends of 7th, 13th, 19th, and Morgan Streets in **Belleair Beach**. There is limited parking near the accesses, "as required by Florida state law," as was pointed out to us by a seemingly reluctant city administrator. In other words, the Belleair communities provide the public with no more than they legally must.

Bunking Down

Belleair Beach Resort (2040 Gulf Boulevard, 800/780-1696, $$$) offers apartments, efficiencies, and a few rooms at weekly and monthly rates (even nightly, when available). A heated pool and barbecue grills are on the premises. There are no other resorts or motels in either community, and what few condo rentals exist are generally let out on a seasonal basis only.

Contact Information

Gulf Beaches on Sand Key Chamber of Commerce, 501 150th Avenue, Madeira Beach, FL 33708; 727/391-7373 or 800/944-1847; website: www.usa-chamber.com/gulf-beaches

Sand Key County Park

All 14 miles of barrier island between Clearwater Pass and John's Pass is known as Sand Key, but something weird happens somewhere just north of Indian Rocks Beach. The transition is as surreal as anything at the Salvador Dalí Museum in St. Petersburg. You leave a calm, relaxed environment that's welcoming to all and enter the fortress mentality of a Tehran or the Gaza Strip. This is a land of security gates, horizon-obstructing monoliths, steamrollers, speed bumps, cranes, fences, and barricades. What has occurred to engender such rampant paranoia and reckless overdevelopment at the north end of Sand Key? The towering condos at the north end of the island, a sliver that technically belongs to the city of Clearwater, are the architectural equivalent of

⓴ Sand Key County Park

Location: north end of Gulf Boulevard on Sand Key, at Clearwater Pass
Parking/fees: metered parking lots
Hours: 7 A.M. to sunset
Facilities: concessions, lifeguards, restrooms, picnic tables, and showers
Contact: Sand Key County Park, 727/595-7677

a row of extended middle fingers.

Fortunately, Sand Key is crowned at its tip by **Sand Key County Park**, one of the prize jewels in the Pinellas County chain. One of the finest beach parks on the Gulf Coast, Sand Key boasts an extraordinarily white, shelly sand beach that is among the widest we have ever laid our beach towels on. It runs for a full mile on the south side of Clearwater Pass. Sand Key County Park regularly makes the experts' best beaches lists, and it is easy to see why. Parking is metered (75 cents per hour) and abundant (nearly 800 spaces). Lifeguards, which are otherwise rarer than gulls' teeth on the Gulf Coast, are on duty year-round. Full facilities are found here, as are cabana rentals and even a playground for the kiddies. The park occupies 90 wide, wonderful acres, 25 of which have been added due to natural accretion since the original purchase of 65 acres back in the mid-1970s. The park's intact dunes and native vegetation evoke what the whole of Sand Key must have looked like at one time in the not-so-distant past.

Contact Information

Sand Key County Park, 1060 Gulf Boulevard, Clearwater Beach, FL 34630; 727/595-7677; website: www.pinellascounty.org/park/sand_key_park

Clearwater Beach

By comparison to the more colorful and down-to-earth communities strewn along Sand Key, Clearwater Beach (pop. 110,000) is grievously overbuilt and commercialized. Mausoleum-like towers dominate much of the gulfside skyline along Clearwater Beach (not to mention that part of Sand Key onto which Clearwater spills over). Meanwhile, older motels and efficiencies cut from plainer cloth cower in the shadows, set back like bleacher seats far from the home plate of the Gulf of Mexico. Lacking any sort of middle ground, the combination of exclusive beachside resorts and humbler hostelries relegated to the shadows creates its own forms of class-warfare pathology, and all hell breaks loose when cruisers, boozers, and losers hit town to blow off steam.

Maybe we just hit town at a bad time, but we didn't feel particularly safe strolling the streets of Clearwater Beach one rowdy Saturday night, even with all the traffic on the streets (or maybe because of it). Here are some random images that stuck in our minds. As a soundtrack, imagine the loudest, crudest gangsta rap blaring from a string of vehicles cruising Gulfview Boulevard, the main drag. The chest-rattling decibels block out all other sounds, including the rustling of breezes in the palm trees that any sane person would prefer to hear. The screech of peeling rubber punctuates the chaos. A carload of white suburban gangsta wannabes piloting someone's dad's fancy ride slows in our vicinity, and one of the occupants hurls an insult… something to do with a pair of socks one of us is wearing. Jolted by the gratuitous asininity of the remark, we stop in our tracks, not knowing whether to laugh out loud or drag the little creeps out of the car for a richly deserved ass whipping.

A block up the street, we happen upon a scene of aimless delinquency in the parking lot of a convenience store and gas station, where every shaven-headed no-account for miles around has congregated to strike surly poses against cars and to curse, smoke, spit, glower, shout insults, hatch schemes, plot revenge, and shamble around the property like petty criminals. In other words, they're up to no good. We're no naïfs when it comes to urban delinquency, having lived in New York

MAP OF PINELLAS COUNTY—PAGE 448

City and Washington, D.C. But this beats anything we've ever seen on the Lower East Side for bad vibes, so we moved on after a few moments of studying the squalid goings-on at close range.

As we shuffle off, spasms of profanity are blaring out of a cruising Benz whose chassis is outlined in purple neon. We then wander into a place that has been recommended to us as being one of the livelier hangouts on the beach. The act that is performing instantly has us doubled up with laughter. Two women dressed in getups straight out of *Star Trek: The Next Generation* are accompanied by a pair of blown-dry replicants flipping buttons on synthesizers. The music is programmed and execrable, people are dancing like dizzy robots, and we're laughing just to keep from crying. Back on the street, Clearwater Beach is lit up like a pinball machine with all the flippers, bumpers, buzzers, and balls revving in an orgy of sound and motion. We decide to call it a night.

Given this urban tableau, we could only shake our heads upon reading this line from the "Official Visitors Guide": "Clearwater is very safe, very affordable, and much more quiet and calm than other, more prominent destinations." We beg to differ. Basically, although we found some things to like about about Clearwater Beach—the north end of the beach in particular—the community as a whole seems dispossessed of its past and somewhat out of control.

Matters get worse over Memorial Causeway in downtown Clearwater, where uniformed members of the Church of Scientology, which is headquartered here, walk the streets. The cultish secrecy and authoritarian tactics of this religious sect adds another level of bizarreness to Clearwater's social gridlock. Scientologists hit town in 1975, armed with a plan to "take control of the city," according to a *New York Times* article based on records seized in an FBI raid. Their efforts to take over Clearwater were downright diabolical: "Government and community organizations were infiltrated by Scientology members. Plans were undertaken to discredit and silence critics. A fake hit-and-run accident was staged in 1976 to try to ruin the political career of the mayor. A Scientologist infiltrated the local newspaper."

The historic Fort Harrison Hotel in downtown Clearwater, furtively purchased by Scientologists hiding behind the name of a dummy corporation, serves as their headquarters. Even though they're a major presence in Clearwater, often blamed by locals for their downtown's decline, we could not find one reference to Scientology in the voluminous literature generated by the Greater Clearwater Chamber of Commerce. Both the Scientologists and the city that serves as their unwilling host remain wary of one another.

Clearwater was a very different place many centuries ago. The Native Americans who lived in the area called it Pocatopaug ("clear water") for the freshwater springs that bubbled up along shore. Conquering Spaniards forced the Indians to move inland, and the area languished until the construction of Fort Harrison in 1841 on the bluffs overlooking Clearwater Harbor. In 1880, Clearwater became a resort community with the construction of the Orange Bluff Hotel, followed by the Seaview and Belleview Hotels. The Belleview still does business as the **Belleview Mido Resort Hotel** (25 Belleview Boulevard, 727/442-6171, $$$), a golf resort on the Intracoastal Waterway that claims to be the largest occupied wooden structure in the world.

In the present, Clearwater Beach bustles without exhibiting much identifiable personality. We will give them credit for trying to improve. On our last visit, we were stopped on the pier by a well-dressed gent with a clipboard who was soliciting visitors' opinions of the beach for an independent survey. We suggested reining in development, which has already had too much say in the Clearwater area in general and at the beach in particular. He allowed that the town was concerned most about traffic and overdevelopment. So why does all the building continue?

Beaches

We'll be the first to admit that appearances can be deceiving and that **Clearwater Beach** merits a second look. In our first edition, we had little kind to say about it. Subsequent visits have led us to revise our opinion somewhat, at least of the beach itself. Initially, Clearwater Beach looks to be dominated by high-rise hotels placed perilously close to the gulf and choked by traffic, construction, and congestion, and indeed this is true at the south end. Hotel towers practically sit in the surf, desperately trying to hold what little beach they have in place with groins. But from about the Adams Mark on up, a pleasant change in appearance and amenities makes this one of the better municipal beaches on Florida's West Coast.

For a mile or so, the table-flat, talcum powder–soft sands of Clearwater Beach provide ample space for public recreation. The beach itself is a fetching crescent as white as a gull's wing. It runs north from Clearwater Pass for 1.3 miles. Not only is there plenty of sand to go around, but they've been generous with parking, too. Metered lots (25 cents per 15 minutes) and a gated pay lot ($1.50 per hour) run beside the ocean. Whatever else one might find wrong with all of Clearwater and parts of Clearwater Beach, they've redeemed themselves in the area of public beach access. Moreover, it's lifeguarded year-round, which is a rarity on the gulf.

The centerpiece of Clearwater Beach is a concrete pier that juts into the gulf. Clearwater puts its best foot forward at Pier 60, across from Clearwater Marina where Causeway and Gulf Boulevards meet. There's plenty of activity—fishing, shops, restaurants, beach concessions—on and around the pier. Inspired by the sunset-watching ritual at Mallory Square in Key West, Clearwater Beach launched a similar late-afternoon rite here in 1995. Called "Sunsets at Pier 60," it features a similar cast of characters (clowns, jugglers, tightrope and stilt walkers, singers and musicians), vying for spare change as the sun shuts its weary eye. The gathering lasts two hours before and after sunset. For more information on this "nightly festival of fun for the whole family," call 727/449-1036.

At the foot of the pier are well-maintained picnic shelters, shaded playground equipment, and open-air public restrooms. You see a little bit of everything on the beach: oldsters reposing in the shade of the pier with mass-market paperbacks; tourist families taking a break from their Mickey Mouse vacation in Orlando; teenage kids showing how little they can get away with wearing in public; and oodles of Aussies and Brits enjoying a seaside holiday in the States.

Evidence of the British presence is everywhere but especially at the numerous British-themed "pubs" that make these tourists feel right at home (as if you should feel right at home when you're traveling). In Clearwater Beach, you can knock back a pint and toss darts with the lads, as far-fetched as that sounds. The

21 Clearwater Beach

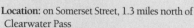

Location: on Somerset Street, 1.3 miles north of Clearwater Pass
Parking/fees: fee parking lots ($1 per hour)
Hours: 24 hours
Facilities: concessions, lifeguards, picnic tables, restrooms, and showers
Contact: Clearwater Beach Lifeguard Station, 727/462-6963

European influx occurs mostly in the winter months, while American tourists and Clearwater-area locals crowd beaches in the summertime, when school is out and the water is warm.

A cautionary note: as nice as the north side of Clearwater Beach may be, signs of developmental mayhem are looming. On our last visit, cranes were preparing to erect what looked to be another towering edifice beside the gulf—a resort hotel or luxury condo, undoubtedly. A letter to the editor printed in the *Clearwater Times* (dated September 27, 2000) put it perfectly: "Enough is enough! I have had it with the hypocrisy demonstrated by the Clearwater mayor and city commission, chastising everyone who disagrees with them while courting developers as if they were the second coming." We agree that it is time to put on the brakes in Clearwater Beach.

The other named beach on the island is **North Clearwater Beach** (a.k.a. North Beach), which runs along Mandalay Avenue north of Acacia Street. Up at this quieter, more residential end of the island, beach access can be gained from numerous street ends, but parking is a near impossibility.

22 North Clearwater Beach (a.k.a. North Beach)

Location: along Mandalay Avenue, from Acacia Street north to the end of Clearwater Beach Island
Parking/fees: free limited street parking
Hours: 24 hours
Facilities: none
Contact: Clearwater Beach Lifeguard Station, 727/462-6963

Shore Things

- **Bike/skate rentals:** Fritz's Skate Shop, 700 Cleveland Street, 727/445-1954.
- **Boat cruise:** Dolphin Encounter, Clearwater Beach Marina, 727/442-7433.
- **Dive shop:** Dive Clearwater, 25 Causeway Boulevard, 727/443-6731.
- **Ecotourism:** Gulf Coast Kayak Center, 400 Mandalay Avenue, 727/446-3343.
- **Fishing charters:** Queen Fleet Deep Sea Fishing, 836 Island Way, 727/446-7666.
- **Marina:** Clearwater Municipal Marina, 25 Causeway Boulevard, 727/462-6954.
- **Pier:** Pier 60, Causeway Boulevard and Gulfview Boulevard, 727/462-6466.
- **Rainy-day attraction:** Clearwater Marine Museum, 249 Windward Passage, 727/447-0980.
- **Shopping/browsing:** Countryside Mall, U.S. 19 and State Route 580, 727/796-1079.
- **Surf shop:** Mandalay Surf Company, 499 Mandalay Avenue, 727/443-3884.
- **Vacation rentals:** Clearwater Beach Real Estate, 1390 Gulf Boulevard, 727/593-2300.

Bunking Down

While touring the oceanside community of Monterey, California, we came upon a Doubletree Inn plopped in the middle of town in a most intrusive way. Our host, a local resident, complained that its positioning "short-circuited the flow of energy in the community," thereby altering its personality for the worse. "I don't know how to explain it," he said, fumbling for words, but we knew exactly what he meant.

The same observation can be made of Clearwater Beach, except that instead of just one, there are many circuit breakers.

Their presence suggests that the community just can't say no to development, placing non-quantifiable considerations such as aesthetic appeal, quality of life, and a community's right to access and open space behind the grab for corporate dollars. We say this not because we categorically dislike high-rises on the beach but because Clearwater Beach is so thoroughly saturated with them, both on the north side of Clearwater Pass and the northern sliver of Sand Key onto which Clearwater's developmental tentacles extend like an aggressive form of brain cancer.

At the upper end, you've got your choice of such high-rises as the **Hilton Clearwater Beach Resort** (400 Mandalay Avenue, 727/461-3222, $$$$), the **Radisson Sand Key** (1201 Gulf Boulevard, 727/596-1100, $$$$), **Adam's Mark Caribbean Gulf Resort** (430 South Gulfview Boulevard, 727/443-5714, $$$$), and the **Holiday Inn Sunspree Resort** (715 South Gulfview Boulevard, 727/447-9566, $$$). They're all roughly the same height, price, and appearance (to wit: tall, high, and impersonal). They're all upscale and commodious, of course, with the problem being the extent to which they dominate the shoreline to the detriment of all that isn't directly situated on the beach. For instance, the 425-room Hilton offers "ten acres of sandy white beach" while the Holiday Inn claims "1000 feet of private white sandy beach." How'd they acquire so much of the shoreline, and shouldn't Clearwater worry about providing its growing population with greater access?

A smaller and slightly less expensive option is the **Best Western Sea Wake Inn** (691 South Gulfview Boulevard, 727/443-7652, $$$). If you're really light in the wallet, cruise the glut of nonfranchised motels set back from the beach. Blocks of modest lodgings from another era recoil in the shadow of the corporate big boys.

Coastal Cuisine

Done up in orange and coral tones, **Frenchy's Rockaway Grill** (7 Rockaway Street, 727/446-4844, $$) is a great place for a full dinner, lite bite, a brew at sunset, or whatever. This beachside bistro is a friendly, bustling place where you might hear an acoustic guitarist (as we did) tackling everything from Van Morrison to Jimi Hendrix. There are fish on the walls—ceramic, ocean-themed murals—and fish on the plates. The house specialty is crabmeat-stuffed grouper with hollandaise sauce. They also prepare everything from chicken and pork to fish and shrimp in a sweet, piquant jerk sauce. Frenchy's lies at one end of a metered public parking lot—and the meters are enforced until one every morning, so pay heed. Incidentally, the original **Frenchy's Cafe** (41 Baymont Street, 727/446-3607, $$) is close by, on the bay side. They're known for an award-winning grouper sandwich.

Seafood and Sunsets at Julie's (351 South Gulfview Boulevard, 727/441-2548, $$) is an anomaly on Clearwater Beach: a nonfranchised eatery that's modest, unassuming, and very fairly priced. You can eat for $10 or less, choosing from dinners that include grilled mahimahi and stuffed flounder. Fresh fish specials are posted and reasonable, too, such as a grilled red snapper atop black beans and rice that was just $11 on our last visit. The decor is yellowish, the ambience marginally New Agey, the food hearty and wholesome, and the tab absurdly reasonable. The only drawback is the desserts, which are just average and come from a bakery.

Leverock's Seafood House (551 Gulf Boulevard, 727/446-5884, $$) has the best location: by the foot of the bridge over Clearwater Pass, where the setting and view are pretty splendid. A large operation that's part of a Florida-based chain, Leverock's has a number of rooms, plus an outdoor dining area. However, the food is pretty ordinary, or at least our meal was, with the selection comparable to that of any Red Lobster you might find in Nebraska. Yet it's so popular that people often wait—and wait happily—for tables. To us, Leverock's takes too little advantage of fresh Florida catches and ingredients. But maybe that's the appeal, to native Floridians at least (i.e., they want something else for a change). To each his own. At least the view and the drinks are worthwhile.

By contrast, the seafood buffet at **Shephard's Restaurant and Lounge** (641 South Gulfview Boulevard, 727/441-6875, $$$) was groaning with peel 'n' eat shrimp, crawfish, crab legs, baked grouper, stuffed flounder, and other delights from the sea. The buffet costs $16.95 per person, and if a mountainous display of fresh seafood served seven nights a week sounds like a winner, hustle on over. You might wind up doing the hustle afterward, too, as Shephard's changes into a dance club geared toward live Top Forty sounds after the plates are cleared. Incidentally, Shephard's also operates a 40-unit gulfside resort, complete with huge heated pool and waterfront tiki bar. Like the restaurant, **Shephard's Beach Resort** (601–619 South Gulfview Boulevard, 727/442-5107, $$) boasts eminently reasonable rates and a great location.

Night Moves

All we wanted was a place to watch Monday Night Football. A sports bar, in short. First, we tried the **Adams Mark** (430 South Gulfview Boulevard, 727/443-5714). After figuring out how and where to park, we fumbled our way to the lobby (there is nothing intuitive the layout of these resort fortresses) and asked the whereabouts of the hotel bar, where a trio was performing covers of soft, alternative-rock hits. A savvy bellman sent us off to the **Hilton** (400 Mandalay Avenue, 727/461-3222), whose lounge was showing the game.

Another series of wrong turns ensued as we tried to figure out where parking was permissible, which gates rose and which didn't, etc. After locating a parking space in the labyrinthine lot, we were directed to the lobby by a young bellman with stripes on his impressive-looking uniform. There were about 25 dead souls strewn among the tables at Coasters Lounge and a terrible game (Eagles versus 49ers) unfolding on a multitude of screens. With multiple screens visible from many angles, we realized how vaguely psychedelic a sports bar can be. Quickly losing concentration and interest, we only hung around till halftime, when logoed paraphernalia (ballcaps, T-shirts) got raffled off. We didn't win a thing. In fact, the entire evening made us feel like losers.

We would've been better off if we'd just pointed our wheels in the direction of the **Beach Bar & Grill** (454 Mandalay Avenue, 727/446-8866), a down-to-earth hangout with live bands that is much closer to our idea of a good time.

Contact Information

Clearwater Beach Chamber of Commerce, 100 Coronado Drive, Clearwater, FL 33767; 727/447-7600 or 888/799-3199; website: www.beachchamber.com

Dunedin

Two beach bums rolled into a small town along the west coast of Florida one picture-perfect afternoon. They spied tidy homes and an attractive harbor, then glanced down a Main Street so innocuously safe and well tended that they could have been in Kansas. In actuality, somewhere between the height of their expectations and the depth of their fears, they found themselves in . . . the Twilight Zone.

Things are not quite as they seem in placid Dunedin (pop. 37,500), it occurred to us in our admittedly brief passage through the area (located four miles north of Clearwater, on U.S. 19A). Along its Main Street, we passed a series of arty, upscale restaurants and antique shops dispensing such knickknacks as a carving of a weeping sailor. Despite this seemingly high-end exterior, we were rattled by what we heard and saw while strolling its few blocks. First, a store owner stood in the sidewalk, puffing on a cigarette while complaining bitterly about business to a coworker and announcing his intention to "get the hell out." Then, while walking to Dunedin's tiny **Historical Society Museum** (349 Main Street, 727/736-1176), we ran into some sort of ethnically mixed gang, laughing and signifying a little too loudly. Next, our footsteps were dogged by three skateboard punks, wool caps pulled over their ears in 80°F weather, who disturbed the peace with repeated attempts to noisily leap and ride along the cement ledge beside a monument to some local hero.

More offense was provided by 1470 West, a glitzy gay discotheque that posted flyers describing its nightly promotions on the front window. Tonight was "Undie Monday,"" and revelers were encouraged to "screw your nut into someone else's bolt." The grace note to all this strangeness was provided during a sunset walk out onto Dunedin's fishing pier. We passed a gay male costumed like the construction worker in the Village People. He loudly began singing cabaret music to himself, punctuated with comments like, "You're late" and "You'll be sorry," and finally, "I'm leaving now . . . bye-bye."

We can't fix the exact parameters, but Dunedin exists somewhere between divinity and depravity. The town boasts Scottish immigrants among its founders (hence the name "Dunedin," derived from the city of Edinburgh). It was, at one time, a major seaport that boasted the largest fleet of sailing vessels in Florida. It is the oldest town south of Cedar Key. Each spring, Dunedin's roots come to life with the Highland Games, a celebration of all things Scottish.

Dunedin lies due north of Clearwater, facing St. Joseph Sound. It is blocked from direct gulf frontage by Caladesi and Honeymoon Islands. In fact, the best thing about Dunedin is that it serves as a jumping-off point, via the Dunedin Causeway, to Honeymoon Island and Caladesi Island State Parks. A lot of its appeal also derives from the calm-water harborage it offers. There's a small, attractive waterside park down by the harbor, located where U.S. 19A makes a series of perpendicular turns. People fish off the T-shaped dock, and sunset photo ops are the order of the day. A few steps away from the water, a brick facade announces the entrance to Main Street, which is outwardly spruced up but . . . well, we described what we saw and heard, and will leave it at that.

Beaches

Two pristine west coast barrier islands—one completely uninhabited (Caladesi) and one only partially built up (Honeymoon)—lie but a bridge away from Dunedin. A separate writeup on these island state parks follows.

Bunking Down

True to its name, the four-story **Inn on the Bay** (1420 Bayshore Boulevard,

727/734-7689, $$) directly overlooks the bay. Waterfront rooms have balconies from which one can watch incomparable Gulf Coast sunsets. Rooms are spacious and comfortably furnished with kitchenettes that include small refrigerators, coffeemakers, plates and dishes, and a sink. Just off the fourth-floor lobby is a restaurant, the Dolphin's Smile, and at ground level, a poolside tiki bar. You can't get closer to the water than this, and you're only a hop, skip, and a jump from the causeway to Honeymoon and Caladesi Islands.

Coastal Cuisine

Sea Sea Riders (221 Main Street, 727/734-1445, $$), which takes its name from an old soul song recorded by Mitch Ryder and Elvis Presley, sits beside U.S. 19A at Dunedin's harborfront park. It looks more like a house than a restaurant, and indeed the building it occupies is an Old Florida cracker home dating from 1916. This is the place for fresh seafood in the Dunedin area.

Night Moves

Returning from an evening spent chasing nightlife in Clearwater Beach, we thought we'd spin by **1470 West** (325 Main Street, 727/736-5483), described earlier, to see how "Undie Monday" was progressing. From our moving car we peered into the open front door, from which came blaring, shrieking disco-diva music. The number of decibels was greater than the number of patrons. A block up Main Street, **Skip's Place** (371 Main Street, 727/734-9151) was packed with locals in a friendlier, less hysterical corner-bar setting.

Lest we forget, Dunedin is the springtime home of the Toronto Blue Jays. They play at **Dunedin Stadium** (311 Douglas Avenue, 727/733-0429). In fact, they signed a deal that will keep them there till 2017.

Contact Information

Dunedin Chamber of Commerce, 301 Main Street, Dunedin, FL 34698; 727/733-3197; website: www.dunedin-fl.com

Caladesi Island State Park and Honeymoon Island State Park

A graceful, arching span leads over the Gulf Intracoastal Waterway to Honeymoon Island. First, the bad news: at the island's east end is a block of retirement condos. However, these give way soon enough to unblemished nature. Pay the $4 per car entrance fee at the gate, and you're off and running on this lobster-shaped island. Your choices of destinations and activities at **Honeymoon Island State Park** include:

- A two-mile sand spit along a roadless, gulf-facing beach, upon which you can walk your way to splendid isolation.
- Hiking trails on an arm of the island shielded by the spit, where you can birdwatch and study the abundant plant life, including the dominant Florida slash pine, the regal-looking sabal palm (the Florida state tree), the low-to-the-ground saw palmetto, and more than 200 other species.
- Picnicking possibilities at large, well-landscaped areas on the gulf and sound sides of the island. They've even provided volleyball nets in the picnic and play areas, so you can bump, set, and spike in as nice a setting as one could ask for.

Caladesi Island State Park offers all that and less. This uninhabited island is reachable by private boat or passenger ferry from Honeymoon Island ($7 round-trip for adults, $3.50 for children 4–12, and free for kids under four). There's a bayside marina with 99 slips, if you're piloting your own craft out to Caladesi Island. A park entrance fee of $3.25 per private boat is charged. At or near the ferry landing are a concession stand, wooden bathhouses, shaded picnic areas, boardwalk nature trails, and a playground. Boardwalks cross the island from the marina to the gulf, where the sand is as fluffy, white, and fine as flour. With 3.5 miles of beach, it's possible to find your own sandy strip on which to spend a perfect day at Caladesi Island State Park. We took a long, unforgettable walk to the end of the island and back with only shorebirds for company.

For more ferry information, call the **Caladesi Connection** at 727/734-5263. For reservations (accepted but not required) and schedules (which vary according to time of year), call 727/734-1501. Ferries run seven days a week, weather permitting, generally from 10 A.M. to 5 P.M. In order to regulate crowding, they'll tell you that the maximum stay on the island is four hours, but this is hardly an enforceable rule, so follow your conscience. Overnight boat camping is permitted—on a first-come, first-served basis at a cost of $8 per night. Tent camping is prohibited on the island, which closes at sundown.

Out on the beach, you might want to grab a beach setup: two chaise lounges and an umbrella, already plunked in the sand where the boardwalk meets the beach, for $5 an hour or $15 for a four-hour "day." The more appealing alternative is to create some distance between yourself and your fellow beachgoers by walking down the beach. Solitude is easily gained out here. Caladesi's white sand and emerald gulf waters regularly earn high marks on "best beaches" listings, and we'd rate it up there ourselves.

Contact Information

Gulf Islands GEOpark, 1 Causeway Boulevard, Dunedin, FL 34698; 727/469-5918; website: www.myflorida.com

23 Caladesi Island State Park

Location: due south of Caladesi Island; reachable by passenger ferry or private boat only
Parking/fees: $4 per vehicle entrance fee on Honeymoon Island, plus a $7 per adult round-trip ferry charge ($3.50 for children 4–12, free for kids 3 and under) from Honeymoon Island to Caladesi Island. If you're boating to Caladesi Island, a $3.25 per boat entrance fee is charged at the dock. If you're staying overnight, an additional $8 docking fee is charged.
Hours: 8 A.M. to sunset
Facilities: concessions, restrooms, picnic tables, and showers
Contact: Gulf Islands GEOpark, 727/469-5918

24 Honeymoon Island State Park

Location: from U.S. 19A on the north end of Dunedin, turn west onto Dunedin Causeway (State Route 586/Curlew Road) and follow onto island
Parking/fees: $4 per vehicle entrance fee ($2 for car and driver only)
Hours: 8 A.M. to sunset
Facilities: concessions, restrooms, picnic tables, and showers
Contact: Gulf Islands GEOpark, 727/469-5918

MAP OF PINELLAS COUNTY—PAGE 448

Ozona, Palm Harbor, and Crystal Beach

Between Dunedin and Tarpon Springs, a trio of retirement communities are arrayed along U.S. 19A. They are, from south to north, Ozona, Palm Harbor, and Crystal Beach. The beaches around here are pretty small potatoes, so the recreational focus is on fishing piers and boat ramps rather than on swimming and sunning. For instance, there's really not much more to Crystal Beach (pop. 1,000), once you escape the congested morass of U.S. 19A, than the church, a youth center, town hall, post office, a few small businesses, and the people who quietly live here. Ozona (pop. 2,000) is a bit larger and Palm Harbor (pop. 80,000) a lot larger. In fact, for such a young and still-unincorporated community, Palm Harbor is soaking up population like a sponge. It is comparable in that respect to Port St. Lucie on Florida's east coast, and that is not a compliment.

Beaches

Palm Harbor has a gulfside park named for one **H.L. "Pop" Stansell.** This pleasantly wooded park's five acres include a pier, boat ramp, and three picnic shelters. The Pinellas County Recreation Trail passes within a block of it. As for the beach—well, it's just a short strip with more mud than sand in evidence.

Ozona doesn't have a beach, but it does have the **Ozona Beach Grill** (315 Orange Street, 727/781-5100, $), which will do if you want to duck in for a bite after having searched in vain for beaches out here.

Though its enticing name would seem to suggest white sand and clear water, the reality of **Crystal Beach** is a bit more down to earth. The actual beach is only 150 feet long, and it sits behind Crystal Beach Community Church, at the west end of Crystal Beach Avenue. While the beach affords the church a perfect setting for its regular sunset services, the rest of us might be better off heading south to Caladesi or Honeymoon Islands to worship sun and sand. Still, it's a public beach, located at the west end of Crystal Beach Avenue (two blocks off U.S. 19A) and is easily accessible from the Pinellas County Recreation Trail, which snakes its way through town. The beach (which has no facilities) is adjacent to Live Oak City Park, a community park.

Bunking Down

A resort the size of an entire town can be found in Palm Harbor. The **Westin Innisbrook Resort** (36750 U.S. 19 North, Palm Harbor, 727/942-2000, $$$$) is one

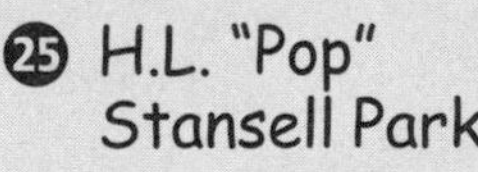

Location: from U.S. 19A in Palm Harbor, turn west on Florida Avenue and proceed to park.
Parking/fees: free parking lot
Hours: sunrise to sunset
Facilities: restrooms and picnic tables
Contact: Palm Harbor Recreation and Parks Department, 727/785-9862

26 Crystal Beach

Location: Crystal Beach Avenue at South Gulf Road in Crystal Beach
Parking/fees: free parking lot
Hours: sunrise to sunset
Facilities: none
Contact: Crystal Beach Community Church, 727/784-8222

Pinellas County Recreation Trail

Not since encountering the South Bay Bicycle Trail, which runs for 26 miles along the beaches of Los Angeles County, have we seen a paved pathway to match the Pinellas County Recreation Trail. It is a 33.7-mile wonder that runs from 34th Street in St. Petersburg to U.S. 19A in Tarpon Springs, passing through the communities of Seminole, Largo, Clearwater, and Dunedin as well. Walkers, joggers, in-line skaters, and bicyclists all use the trail, much of which, in a rails-to-trails conversion, occupies the site of an old railroad line. We first crossed its path, so to speak, in Dunedin, where it passes through the center of town. The trail makes a spectacular overpass of U.S. 19A north of Dunedin, near the causeway to Honeymoon Island. The section of the Pinellas Trail from here to Crystal Beach swings closest to the gulf.

We salute the county for allocating resources toward such an ambitious project, which benefits the many who use it and is a better use of tax dollars than yet another road-construction project. Other counties around Florida would do well to emulate the Pinellas County Parks Department, which has generously attended to the recreational needs of its residents by seeding the county with splendid beachside parks and this magnificent recreation trail.

The free "Guidebook to the Pinellas Trail" comes with detailed maps and en route listings of parks, restaurants, pay phones, bike shops, convenience stores, and places of interest (including osprey-nesting platforms!). Toward the end of an explanatory note, the publication casually observes, "Of course, all guidebooks are obsolete by the time you read them." Gulp!

For more information, contact the Pinellas County Planning Department, 14 South Fort Harrison Avenue, Clearwater, FL 34616; 727/464-4751; website: www.co.pinellas.fl.us/BCC/trailgd.

of the premier sports resorts in the nation, placing a special emphasis on golf. There are four golf courses here, including the celebrated Copperhead course, home to the annual Tampa Bay Classic (a PGA Tour event). In addition to 72 holes of championship golf, the 1,000-acre resort has 11 tennis courts, six swimming pools (including the Loch Ness Monster pool, a veritable water park in itself), and even a wildlife preserve. Seven hundred guest suites are arrayed in 28 golf course–hugging lodges. Six restaurants, including a world-class steakhouse, are arrayed about the grounds. The Gulf of Mexico is close by, but this leafy resort in the rolling hills of north Pinellas County is really more about golf than gulf. A recent arrival is the Ironman Institute, which provides medically based comprehensive health assessments and designs fitness program based on the results. Particularly popular is the day-long "health enhancement exam."

Contact Information

Greater Palm Harbor Area Chamber Of Commerce, 32845 U.S.19 North, Suite 210, Palm Harbor, FL 34684; 727/784-4287; website: www.palmharborcc.org

Tarpon Springs

Tarpon Springs (pop. 20,600) is not a beach town, per se, but it has a storied relationship with the Gulf of Mexico and its related estuaries. Water is the defining element of this small city. Tarpon Springs is dissected by the Anclote River, several bayous, bays, and lakes, and is bordered by the Gulf of Mexico. In all, there are 50 miles of waterfront, lending credence to the occasional boast that it is the "Venice of the South." As it is, the town's name is a bit of a misnomer. There are no springs in Tarpon Springs. The name originated with a chance remark made by a landowner's daughters in the late 1800s. She saw fish jumping in the bayous and said, "Look at those tarpon spring!" Nowadays you can see manatees spring, as they've begun showing up in the waters of beautiful Spring Bayou in recent years.

The town center of Tarpon Springs is two miles from the coast, where Tarpon Avenue (State Route 582) meets Pinellas Avenue U.S. 19A. The renovated historic district—a reminder of when the area was a winter haven for wealthy Northerners—is a pleasant place to stroll and browse the shops. The top attraction, however, is the Sponge Docks, a quarter mile north of the historic district on Dodecanese Boulevard. The docks occupy the south bank of the Anclote River, where a community of Greek sponge divers plies their trade.

27 Sunset Beach

Location: west end of Gulf Road in Tarpon Springs

Parking/fees: free parking lot

Hours: sunrise to 10 P.M.

Facilities: restrooms and picnic tables

Contact: Tarpon Springs Parks Department, 727/942-5610

It may seem hard to believe, but at one time sponging was the largest industry in Florida. When the wealthy settlers left town for more southerly climes, Tarpon Springs began sponging off its pure and pristine waters. A booming sponge collecting industry took root in 1905, eventually earning Tarpon Springs the title "Sponge Capital of the World." Greek immigrants were particularly skilled at this grueling trade, a throwback to the time when the original Greek Olympic Games featured a competition for "excellence in skin diving to gather sponges." Plying this trade requires donning heavy diving suits, lead-weighted belts, and metal diving bells straight out of a Jules Verne novel, all as a prelude to prying live sponges from the gulf's bottom with small rakes. By the mid-1940s, pollution, overharvesting, and a devastating sponge blight killed the trade, and the town declined along with it.

Today, Tarpon Springs has been revived by seafaring of all kinds, including a more modest sponge fishing industry and a shrimping fleet. The industry's rehabilitation is the direct result of environmental standards put into place in the 1960s and enforced to this day. There are roughly 20 active spongers working out of Tarpon Springs today, and they've had to resort to importing them from Greece since so few locals take up the occupation. It's a rough way to make a living. You work against currents at depths of 30 to 60 feet for two or three hours at a time. You may be gone for several weeks and venture as far as a hundred miles offshore. Out of 5,000 species of sponges, only five have commercial value. Sponge harvests remain low because of pollution in the gulf and shrimp boats that rake the bottom, destroying the sponges.

"It's real, it's a way of life," we were told by George Billiris, a sponge merchant and former sponge diver. "It's not something cooked up to entertain tourists." We asked this garrulous old Greek gentleman if he still dives himself. "No, I'm too busy," he said. "But next summer I'm going to get all the old divers together. There's six of us. Wait—no, five. The count changes every year. Anyway, we're going out on a dive for two weeks. The last hurrah."

Half-hour boat cruises that include a sponge-diving exhibition are conducted from the docks ($5 for adults, $2 for children 12 and under). You will learn, among other things, that a sponge diver wears 172 pounds worth of gear and must walk at a 45-degree angle against the underwater currents. At the gift shops beside the docks, you can buy a natural wool sponge for around $10. Once you've tried it, you will never want to clean yourself with anything else.

Beaches

The word "beach" doesn't often come up in connection with Tarpon Springs. However, the town is home to the northernmost of Pinellas County's beach parks, Fred H. Howard Park and Beach. The park is a bit hard to find but worth the quest. A byzantine set of turns is required from U.S.19A. Start by heading west on State Route 880 (Klosterman Road) and then follow the signs. You'll eventually pass beneath Spanish moss–draped oaks along Sunset Drive, and as a beach bum, you'll find no cause for celebration just yet. While the 150-acre Fred H. Howard Park is a nice spot for a shaded picnic, a beach is nowhere to be seen.

Lo and behold, a causeway suddenly appears, leading west for a mile out to a little palm-lined island in the gulf that materializes like some kind of optical illusion. It's a beach! And a more substantial one than you might expect. Moreover, there's ample free parking and facilities at **Fred H. Howard Beach**. Windsurfers are particularly smitten with the park, sailing the breezy waters between this tiny island and the mainland. It is claimed that nearly two million people a year visit the Park and Beach.

Just south of Howard Park, at the west end of Gulf Road, is the town-run **Sunset Beach**. A favorite with locals, it's more popular as a picnic area (with 15 shelters) and boat launch than a beach, though it does have a swimming area.

Shore Things

- **Bike/skate rentals:** Outdoor Gear, 212 East Tarpon Avenue, 727/943-0937.
- **Boat cruise:** St. Nicholas Boat Line, 693 Dodecanese Boulevard, 727/942-6425.
- **Dive shop:** Tarpon Sports & Scuba, 39322 U.S.19A North, 727/937-8201.
- **Ecotourism:** Island Wind Tours, Tarpon Springs Sponge Docks, 600 Dodecanese Boulevard, 727/934-0606.
- **Fishing charters:** Lazy Bones Sport Fishing Charters, 408 Riverside Drive, City Slip # 7, 727/920-4846.
- **Lighthouse:** Anclote Lighthouse, Anclote Key State Park, 727/469-5942.
- **Marina:** Port Tarpon Marina, Marker 39, 531 Anclote Road, 727/937-2200.

28 Fred H. Howard Park and Beach

Location: from U.S. 19A in Tarpon Springs, turn west on State Route 880 (Klosterman Road) and follow signs to the park at 1700 Sunset Drive
Parking/fees: free parking lots
Hours: 7 A.M. to sunset
Facilities: restrooms, picnic tables, and showers
Contact: Fred H. Howard Park and Beach, 727/937-4938

- **Pier:** Sunset Beach, Gulf Road, 727/942-5610.
- **Rainy-day attraction:** Coral Sea Aquarium, 850 Dodecanese Boulevard, 727/938-5378.
- **Shopping/browsing:** Sponge Exchange, 735 Dodecanese Boulevard, 727/934-9262.
- **Vacation rentals:** Coastal Bay Real Estate, 638 East Tarpon Avenue, 727/938-2270.

Bunking Down

Most of the motels in Tarpon Springs are located on U.S. 19A. Trust us; you do not want to stay on U.S. 19A. Located in the historic district is the **Spring Bayou Inn Bed & Breakfast** (32 West Tarpon Avenue, 727/938-9333, $$), a converted turn-of-the-century home with five rooms. It overlooks Spring Bayou, and a prettier spot you could not wish to see.

Coastal Cuisine

Even if you don't swim, windsurf, or work on your tan in Tarpon Springs, you should definitely sponge a meal here. How often do you get to eat authentic Greek food? Excellent Greek restaurants can be found in the blocks surrounding the sponge docks. Our favorite is **Mykonos Mayerion** (628 Dodecanese Boulevard, 727/934-4306, $$). The food is as good as it is inexpensive. You can feast on things like Greek-style shrimp (with lemon, garlic, and oregano), lemon baked potatoes, and incredible stuffed grape leaves. A pan-fried fontanel cheese appetizer comes out sizzling, especially when they squeeze lemons all over it just prior to placing the platter in front of you. The Greek salad, so tangy and healthful, is another must-order. Ditto the pan-fried fish of the day. You cannot order wrong or go away hungry here.

The largest restaurant in Tarpon Springs—indeed, one of the largest in all of Florida—is **Louis Pappas' Riverside Restaurant** (10 West Dodecanese Boulevard, 727/937-5101, $$). They seat around 1,000 and serve seafood "fresh from the docks," including Grouper 3rd Generation (dipped in a sauce of lemon, garlic, and mustard, then floured and fried), Octopus Greek Style (broiled in lemon and olive oil), and Kalamarakia (fried baby squid). The prices are right, to boot, with entrées running in the $8.95 to $11.95 range. For a lighter bite, the best bakery in town is the **Parthenon Pastry Shop** (751 Dodecanese Boulevard, 727/938-7709, $).

Contact Information

Greater Tarpon Springs Chamber of Commerce, 11 East Orange Street, Tarpon Springs, FL 34689; 727/937-6109; website: www.tarponsprings.com

Anclote Key State Park

Anclote Key is the northernmost of a string of barrier islands that includes the more accessible Honeymoon and Caladesi Islands. Because there is no access by road or state-run ferry to Anclote Key, this four-mile long island seldom gets mentioned as frequently as the other islands do. Yet the entirety of its western shoreline is one long, secluded beach, backed by healthy dunes that are held in place by sea oats. "If you like a completely natural beach, this is the place," a ranger at Caladesi told us, and he wasn't just whistling Dixie. There's even an old lighthouse at the southern end of the island, a decommissioned Coast Guard beacon dating from 1886 that is in the process of being restored by a local organization.

Anclote Key lies three miles off the coast of Tarpon Springs, and you must get out there on your own. Boats can be rented in Tarpon Springs, and regular cruises head over there. (Try **Island Wind Tours,** 600 Dodecanese Boulevard, 727/934-0606.) The only other problem, if it can be called that, is that there are no facilities, no running water, and no ranger on duty. At one time, the state built a boardwalk over the dunes and put up picnic tables, but vandals destroyed them and used the pieces for firewood. "We're too short of manpower to keep an eye on everything," said the Caladesi ranger, "so there's no more boardwalk or picnic tables." Primitive camping is allowed. Most campers plop their gear down on the beach, which is the best place to escape the mosquitoes.

Contact Information

Anclote Key State Park, c/o Gulf Islands GEOpark, 1 Causeway Boulevard, Dunedin, FL 34698; 727/469-5918; website: www.myflorida.com

29 Anclote Key State Park

Location: three miles west of Tarpon Springs, in the Gulf of Mexico
Parking/fees: none
Hours: 8 A.M. to Sunset
Facilities: none
Contact: Gulf Islands GEOpark, 727/469-5918

The Nature Coast / Big Bend

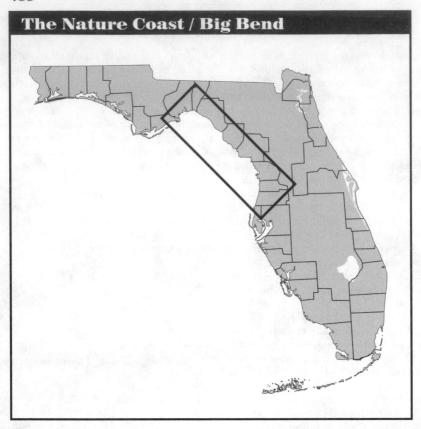

Key to the Symbols

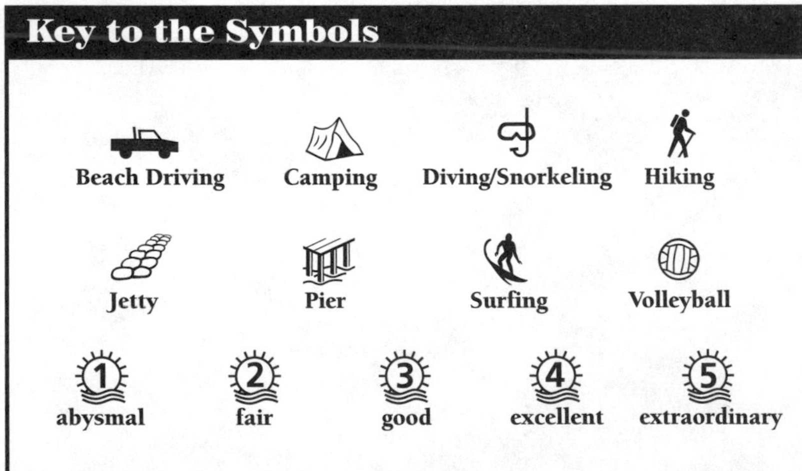

The Nature Coast / Big Bend
TALLAHASSEE
APALACHICOLA NAT'L FOREST
10
319
Aucilla River
19
27
98
27
OSCEOLA NATIONAL FOREST
Jefferson County
Wakulla County
75
19
98
Taylor County
GAINESVILLE
Suwannee River
Dixie County
24
Levy County
Lake Rousseau
Lake Apopka
Citrus County
WITHLACOOCHEE STATE FOREST
CHASSAHOWITZKA NAT'L WILDLIFE REFUGE
GULF OF MEXICO
19
Hernando County
Pasco County
41
75
Lake Tarpon
N
W
E
S
TAMPA
275
92
ST. PETERSBURG

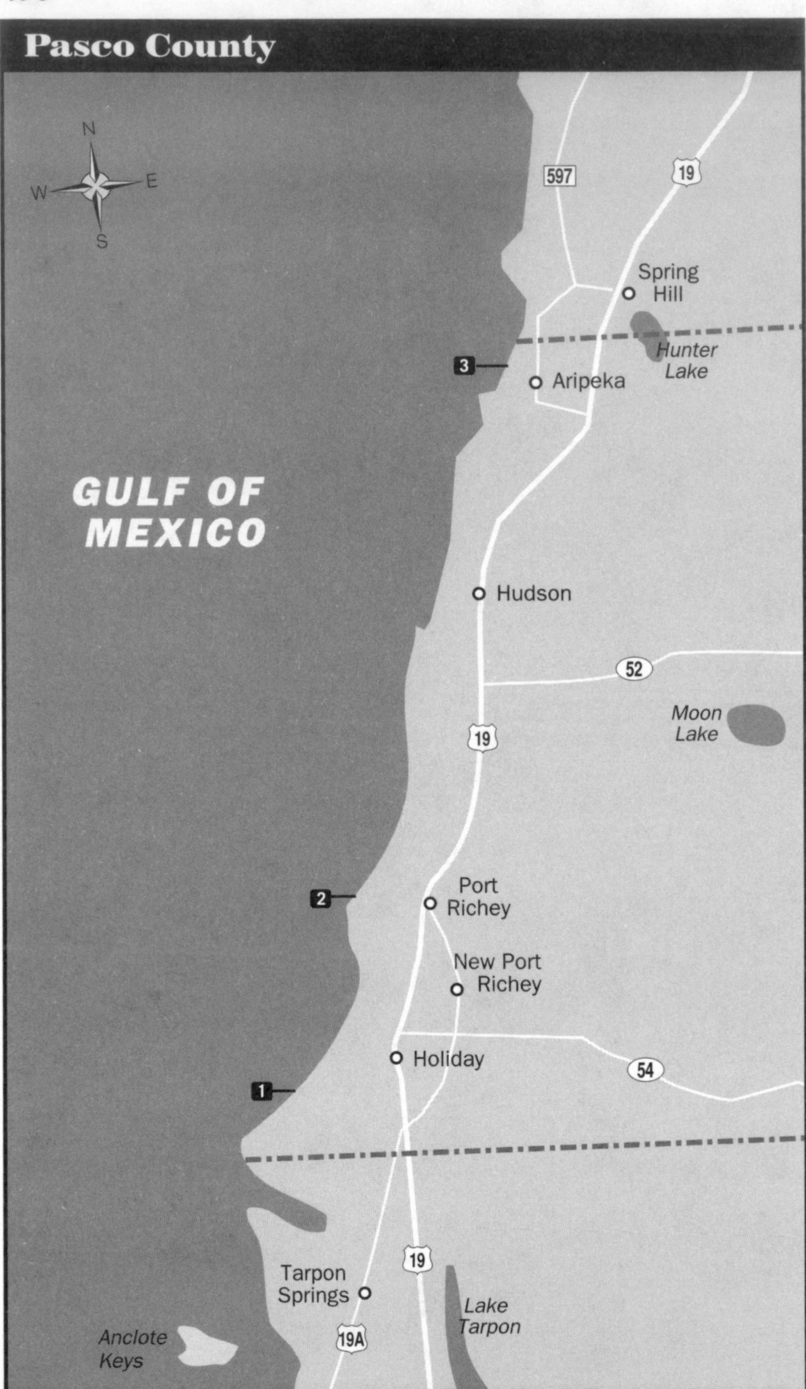

Pasco County
N
E
S
W
597
19
Spring Hill
Hunter Lake
3
Aripeka
GULF OF MEXICO
Hudson
52
Moon Lake
19
2
Port Richey
New Port Richey
Holiday
54
1
19
Tarpon Springs
Lake Tarpon
Anclote Keys
19A

Pasco County

We dutifully explored Pasco County's 15 miles of gulf coastline, grateful for any excuse to turn off U.S. 19, even if we turned up mostly dead ends in the way of sand beaches. There are exceptions: several small beaches exist at county parks off the beaten track in Holiday, Hudson, and Port Richey. For the most part, however, Pasco is one county you'll want to pass through en route to points north or south. It is bisected by the grossly overbuilt U.S. 19 corridor, with its endless blight of strip malls and fast-food franchises. After having to negotiate this wretched and hazardous stretch of four-lane blacktop several times in the course of our travels, we decided that the hard-rock band AC/DC must have had U.S. 19 in mind when they recorded the song "Highway to Hell."

Holiday, New Port Richey, and Port Richey

You've heard of "the real Florida," which is the motto of the state park system in its preservation efforts. U.S. 19 through Pasco and Hernando counties might be described as the surreal Florida. It stands alone among all our travels on both coasts of the United States as the most unremitting and overbuilt thoroughfare of franchised commerce in existence. In particular, Pasco County is the ugliest coastal county in the state of Florida because of it. For at least 25 miles the strip-mall sprawl and man-made devastation of the landscape are daunting to navigate and depressing to behold. Moreover, it obscures any differences that might otherwise distinguish Holiday (pop. 20,000) from Hudson or Port Richey (pop. 2,700) from New Port Richey (pop. 15,000).

We wish we could offer an alternate route or strategy for combating Pasco County, but U.S. 19 is the only way through this

The Nature Coast

North of Tarpon Springs, the Florida coast undergoes its most dramatic transformation. It does a disappearing act, of sorts, and the object of this "now you see it, now you don't" routine is sand. It's there in snow-white abundance at Clearwater Beach and Caladesi Island and then virtually disappears. The human population recedes as well, which is why the area has been dubbed "the Nature Coast." Geographically, it lies along the broad, curving interior elbow whereby the north-south axis of Florida's Lower Peninsula gives way to the east-west orientation of the Panhandle. For this reason, the area is also referred to as the "Big Bend."

The Nature Coast/Big Bend area is a region where, in many places, wildlife greatly outnumber real-estate agents and golfers. It comprises eight gulf-fronting counties: Pasco, Hernando, Citrus, Levy, Dixie, Taylor, Jefferson, and Wakulla. Though it hugs nearly 200 miles of shoreline along the Gulf of Mexico, the Nature Coast is not known for its beaches. At least in terms of locales accessible by car, by bike, or on foot (as opposed to unbridged offshore keys), the sandy backdrop that one associates with a Florida vacation does not reappear until St. George Island in Franklin County. In fact, the book *Florida's Sandy Beaches: An Access Guide*—which purports to be the official word on the subject (but hasn't been updated since its publication in 1985)—completely omits all eight counties.

That is not to say there are no sand beaches along the Nature Coast, just that they're relatively rare, generally small in size, and almost always overlooked. Hence, our self-imposed challenge: to scour for sand beaches along the Nature Coast. And scour we did. Responding to our queries about the region's beaches in advance of our travels, a local official provided a refreshingly honest assessment: "There are no great beaches between Panama City on the north coast all the way down to Clearwater. The entire coastline abuts on relatively shallow water—only 40 feet deep 40 miles from shore. No big wave wash to scour

mess. How could such a monstrous defiling of what was once an appealingly isolated corner of the state been allowed to happen? It makes a mockery of the term "Nature Coast," as nature has been sent packing to make way for more retail sprawl, housing subdivisions, and golf courses than you can shake a five-iron at. They euphemistically refer to the mind-set that has allowed this to happen as "a progressive business climate." The end result of their reckless permissiveness is that nature, the only real asset they can claim, has taken a beating out here. In place of unmolested acreage upon which black bears and Florida panthers should be roaming you'll find an endless, redundant procession of Eckerd's, Wal-Mart, McDonald's, Taco Bell—in short, all the prime suspects in the franchised dimming of the American mind.

So take a sedative or an antidepressant, drive with both hands firmly on the wheel, place some soothing music in your car stereo, and motor through this blight as best you can. No stopping for cheeseburgers or tacos.

Beaches

A quieter bit of yin to U.S. 19's loudmouthed yang is offered at a trio of coun-

the bottom. We also have barrier islands ranging out to three miles, hence a mucky bottom at low tide. White sand beaches, yes, but a lousy bottom."

While the Nature Coast is the sort of place slogan-makers like to call "a land that time forgot," it is not time but the hurry-scurry modern would that has passed it by, for the most part. There are exceptions: Pasco and Hernando Counties, along the U.S. 19 corridor, are as blighted by commerce and unchecked growth as any big-city beltway. But by and large, the Nature Coast offers vast acreage of what has otherwise become a vanishing commodity in Florida: a condo-less sanctuary of peace and quiet where nature reigns.

It is impossible to mention all of the natural sights, parklands, and preserves within the entire region, but here are some highlights:

- Anclote Key State Preserve
- Apalachicola National Forest
- Cedar Key Scrub State Preserve
- Cedar Keys National Wildlife Refuge,
- Chassahowitzka National Wildlife Refuge
- Crystal River
- Homosassa Springs
- Kings Bay
- Lower Suwannee National Wildlife Refuge
- Manatee Springs
- St. Marks Wildlife Refuge
- Waccasassa Bay State Preserve
- Wakulla Springs

In all, the Nature Coast claims 980,000 acres of land that have been set aside for conservation or recreation, and it is home to at least 19 endangered or threatened animal species. For once, even the wildlife would agree that this neck of the woods deserves to be called by the name given it by humans, the Nature Coast.

MAP OF PASCO COUNTY—PAGE 490

ty parks in southwest Pasco County. First up is **Anclote River Park**, on the mouth of the Anclote River at the west end of Bailey's Bluff Road in Holiday. Boaters and fishers will have a good time out here, but the real surprise is the sandy strip of beach that is lifeguarded all summer long.

Neighboring Anclote Gulf Park lacks a beach but is worth mentioning because it has a fishing pier that's often swamped with happy anglers. Both parks have a picnic area and playground. Port Richey (as opposed to "New" Port Richey, the rapidly growing community that lies inland) claims **Robert K. Rees Park**, which also has a small but natural strip of sandy beach, boardwalk, and seasonal lifeguards, plus canoe access to the gulf. Lifeguards are rare along the west coast of Florida, where there are broad, sandy beaches and real waves to worry about. It's odd indeed that Pasco County should have not one but three lifeguarded county beach parks.

Contact Information

West Pasco Chamber of Commerce, 5443 Main Street, New Port Richey, FL 34652; 727/842-7651; website: www.westpasco.com

❶ Anclote River Park

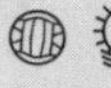

Location: west end of Bailey's Bluff Road in Holiday
Parking/fees: free parking
Hours: sunrise to sunset
Facilities: concessions, lifeguards (seasonal), restrooms, picnic tables, and showers
Contact: Pasco County Parks and Recreation Department, 727/929-1260

❷ Robert K. Rees Park

Location: at the west end of Green Key Road in Port Richey
Parking/fees: free parking lot
Hours: sunrise to sunset
Facilities: concessions, lifeguards (seasonal), restrooms, and picnic tables
Contact: Pasco County Parks and Recreation Department, 727/929-1260

Hudson and Aripeka

A brief but welcome respite from U.S. 19's mindless sprawl is offered in northwest Pasco County, where a smaller state road forks off toward the coast while U.S. 19 swings a bit inland. This wonderful blue highway is called Old Dixie Highway (State Route 595), and it does indeed lead into the heart of an older Florida shaped by cracker houses, coastal scenery, and pristine wetlands.

Beaches

One mile west of U.S. 19 via Clark Street in Hudson (pop. 35,000) is **Robert J. Strickland Memorial Park** (a.k.a. Hudson Beach). This end of Hudson has a resort atmosphere and fronts a highly appealing sand beach. It is, to say the least, a surprise to find such a quiet, clean, and inviting beach attached to so cankerous a county. The beach is small, but the sand is pearly white and fairly wide, leading to slippery-bottomed, waveless water. (Watch out for oyster shells and rocks.) Full facilities, including picnic shelters and lifeguards, can be found here. Parking is free and ample. The beach is bounded by a boardwalk, and you can get a good view of the surrounding area from the pavilion. This popular park gets especially crowded on warm days. The neighborhood itself has a homey atmosphere and looks to have been around a lot longer than the retail clutter out on U.S. 19.

Five miles north, on Old Dixie Highway, is Aripeka (pop. 1,000), an unincorporated town that shares the same zip code as Hudson. It has a sandy coastline, fish camp, and rundown marina. Signs that urged us to "Beware of Dog" were willingly heeded.

Bunking Down

A more than adequate beachfront motel and a perfectly pleasant seaside restaurant sit side by side along the gulf in Hudson. The former is the **Inn on the Gulf** (6330 Clark Street, 727/868-5623, $$) and the latter is **Sam's Hudson Beach Snack Bar** (see below). On an offbeat note, **Gulf Coast Resort** (13220 Houston Avenue, 727/868-1061, $) is an "RV nudist park on 40 wooded acres." Imagine the human manatees on display!

Coastal Cuisine

Sam's (6325 Clark Street, 727/868-1971, $) is a "snack bar"—meaning you eat at picnic tables under an open-air pavilion—with an extensive menu that's heavy on seafood items. Their specialties: shrimp, oysters, and clams.

Contact Information

West Pasco Chamber of Commerce, 5443 Main Street, New Port Richey, FL 34652; 727/842-7651; website: www.westpasco.com

3 Robert J. Strickland Memorial Park (a.k.a. Hudson Beach)

Location: at the west end of Clark Street in Hudson
Parking/fees: free parking lots
Hours: sunrise to sunset
Facilities: concessions, lifeguards (seasonal), restrooms, picnic tables, and showers
Contact: Pasco County Parks and Recreation Department at 727/929-1260

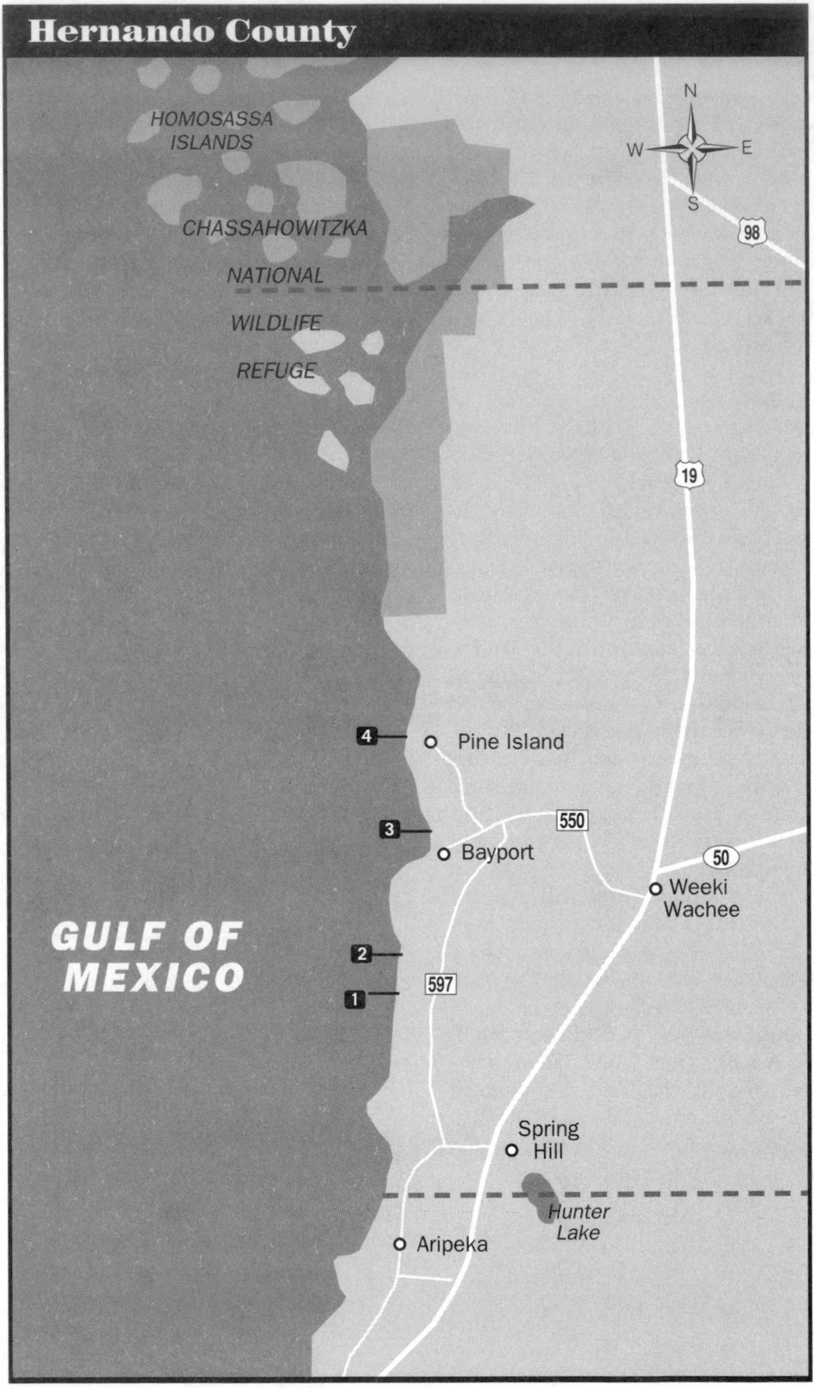

Hernando County

HOMOSASSA ISLANDS
CHASSAHOWITZKA NATIONAL WILDLIFE REFUGE
N
W
E
S
98
19
4
Pine Island
3
550
Bayport
50
Weeki Wachee
GULF OF MEXICO
2
597
1
Spring Hill
Hunter Lake
Aripeka

Hernando County

In its expansive state forest and the swamps along its meandering rivers, the Withlacoochee and the Weeki Wachee, Hernando County lives up to its claim of being "the heart of the Nature Coast." But it is growing too fast, with the population having shot up by 62 percent in 10 years, and the main artery (U.S. 19) is an unrelieved eyesore of congestion and traffic, as it is in neighboring Pasco County. Relief can be found along state and county backroads that loop closer to the coast, where you'll find glimpses of Old Florida at Bayport and Pine Island. Both are worth a peek, though neither is exactly worth building a vacation around. The rest of the county's 15 miles of coastline falls inside the virtually inaccessible Chassahowitzka Swamp.

Hernando Beach

Proceeding north on Old Dixie Highway (County Road 595) from Pasco County, you will cross the Hernando County line. While County Road 595 loops back out to U.S. 19, another county road, Shoal Line Boulevard (County Road 597), runs along the Gulf Coast to Hernando Beach (pop. 2,000). This waterfront community consists of a sizable spread of homes built along an extensive series of canals, docks, marinas, seawalls, and a muddy, shelly, and rocky shore. It's a veritable suburbia, with boat slips instead of two-car garages, but little in the way of vacation amenities.

Beaches

There are no sand beaches in Hernando Beach, but the county operates four small parks in the area, three of which have beaches. Running from south to north, the first is **Hernando Beach Park.** Despite the name, it's at least a mile from the Gulf of Mexico, but it's a very attractive and large (135 acres) park with lots of trees and native vegetation. Hernando Beach Park is ideal for young kids, with an extensive playground, restrooms, sturdy observation tower, and safe swimming area on an artificial beach along Jenkins Creek. Across the road is Jenkins Creek Park, a small parcel with a fishing pier and boat launch for canoes and small powerboats.

About a mile north is **Rogers Park,** which has a boat launch into a manatee-frequented area of the Weeki Wachee River, as well as restrooms, picnic tables, an artificial beach, and the friendliest group of ducks we ever encountered. One even tried to get in our car. An admission fee of $2 is charged in summer only.

Bunking Down

Aside from the chain motels on U.S. 19 and I-75, there's the **Hernando Beach Motel** (4291 Shoal Line Boulevard, 352/596-2527, $). It's nothing fancy, mind you, but if you're coming down to fish or get away from it all, it will fit the bill just fine. The motel's 14 units range from one-bedroom efficiencies with full kitchen and bath to two-bedroom, two-bath condos.

Coastal Cuisine

Just across the river from Rogers Park is an inviting seafood, steak, and rib house called **Otters** (5386 Darlene Street, Weeki Wachee, 352/597-9551, $$), set inside a rambling brown wooden house. The belting of Frank Sinatra provides an interesting counterpoint to the quacking of ducks across the Frances Carlisle Bridge.

1 Hernando Beach Park

Location: 6400 Shoal Line Road (County Road 597), a mile west of Hernando Beach on Jenkins Creek
Parking/fees: free parking lot
Hours: sunrise to sunset
Facilities: restrooms, picnic tables, and showers
Contact: Hernando County Parks and Recreation Department at 352/754-4031

2 Rogers Park

Location: 7244 Shoal Line Boulevard (County Road 597), on the Weeki Wachee River, five miles west of Weeki Wachee
Parking/fees: $2 per vehicle entrance fee
Hours: sunrise to sunset
Facilities: concessions, lifeguards (seasonal), restrooms, picnic tables, and showers
Contact: Hernando County Parks and Recreation Department, 352/754-4031

Contact Information
Greater Hernando County Chamber of Commerce, East Fort Dade Avenue, Brooksville, FL 34601; 352/796-0697; website: www.hernandochamber.com

Hernando County Tourist Development, 16110 Aviation Loop Drive, Brooksville, FL 34609; 352/754-4405 or 800/601-4580; website: www.co.hernando.fl.us/tourdev

Bayport and Pine Island

The historic town of Bayport (pop. 232) is located at the mouth of the Weeki Wachee River. Because of this prime location, it was Hernando County's major port before the Gulf Coast railroads went into service in 1885. Some of the old vernacular architecture is still intact and some is collapsing along the side of Cortez Boulevard (County Road 550), which links Bayport and neighboring Pine Island (pop. 421) with U.S. 19, seven miles east.

The drive through this area is an unbridled delight, with Spanish moss draping down from the oak limbs and wetlands spreading in all directions. Think of it as Florida's Mont-Saint-Michel, because during winter storms parts of the roadway are under water at high tide, and on the lowest tides, you can walk out almost a mile from shore. A gale the locals call the "No Name Storm" badly tore up the area in 1993, and many residents had to be evacuated by helicopter and boat.

Beaches
Cortez Boulevard ends in Bayport at **Bayport Park**, a small gulfside county park with two boat ramps, a fishing pier, and picnic pavilion, but no beach to speak of. A few miles north, the silver lining of 1993's "No Name Storm" can be seen on Pine Island. The turnoff to Pine Island, County Road 495, is located two miles east of Bayport, off Cortez Boulevard (County Road 595). You will scarcely believe your eyes when you reach the end of this serpentine road, two miles of wetlands and mudflats later.

Welcome to **Alfred A. McKethan Pine Island Park.** It's as nice and unexpected a surprise as any beachcomber could hope for on the Nature Coast. Since that dastardly storm, sharp new facilities have been built here, including restrooms, pavilions, a play area, volleyball nets, and a beach café with an improbably extensive and interesting menu. The beach is built around a three-acre point of land, with sand

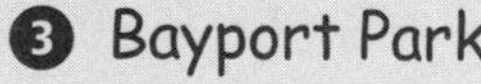

Location: west end of Cortez Boulevard (County Road 550), in Bayport
Parking/fees: free parking lot
Hours: sunrise to sunset
Facilities: restrooms and picnic tables
Contact: Hernando County Parks and Recreation Department, 352/54-4031

4 Alfred A. McKethan Pine Island Park

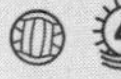

Location: on Pine Island Drive, at the west end of County Road 495, eight miles northwest of Weeki Wachee
Parking/fees: $2 per vehicle entrance fee
Hours: sunrise to sunset
Facilities: concessions, lifeguards (seasonal), restrooms, picnic tables, and showers
Contact: Hernando County Parks and Recreation Department, 352/754-4031

trucked in and spread inside a seawall that's backed by a row of palm trees. Two lifeguard stands overlook the swimming area. If you blinked, you could swear you were on Clearwater Beach.

Contact Information

Greater Hernando County Chamber of Commerce, East Fort Dade Avenue, Brooksville, FL 34601; 352/796-0697; website: www.hernandochamber.com

Hernando County Tourist Development, 16110 Aviation Loop Drive, Brooksville, FL 34609; 352/754-4405 or 800/601-4580; website: www.co.hernando.fl.us/tourdev

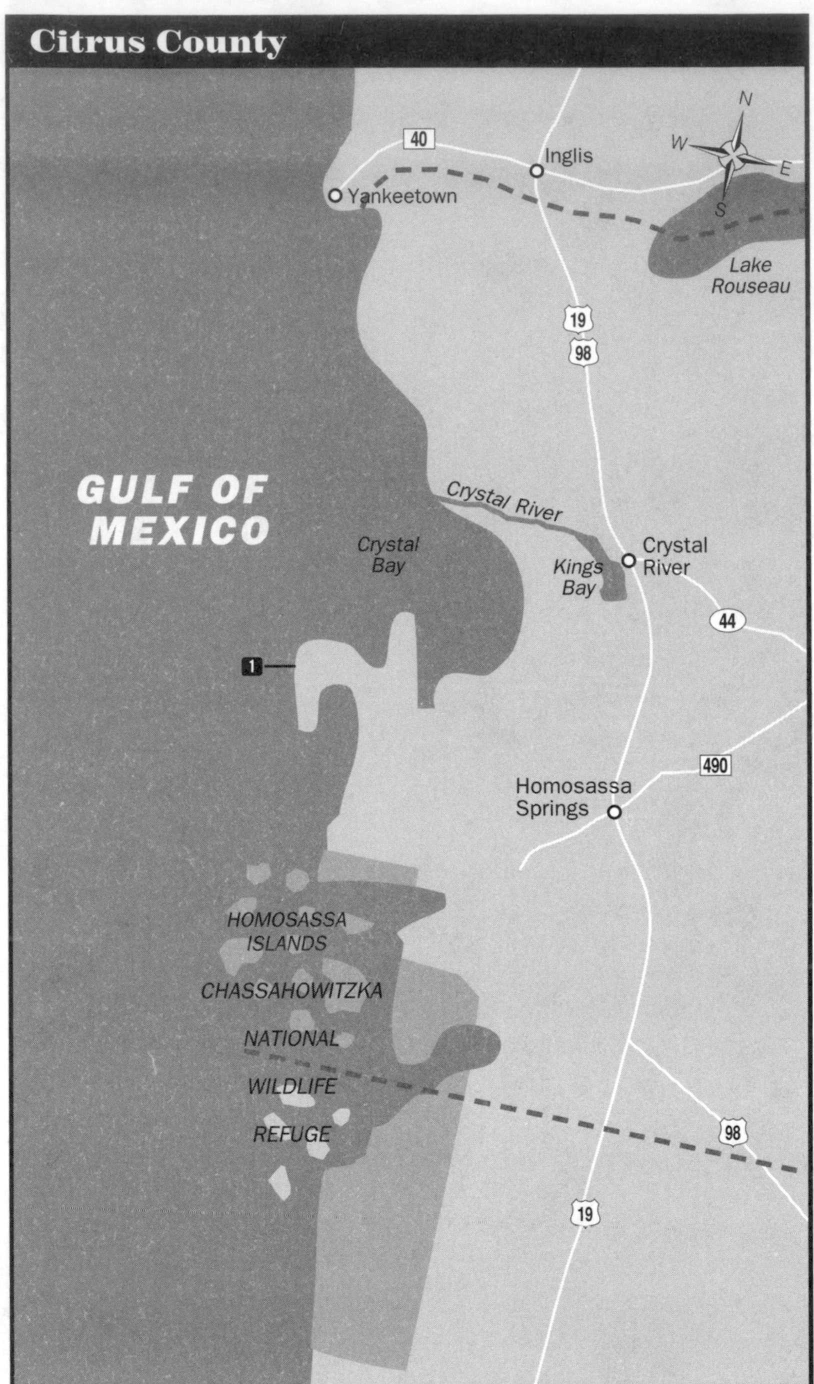
Citrus County
N
W
E
S
40
Inglis
Yankeetown
Lake
Rouseau
19
98
GULF OF
MEXICO
Crystal River
Crystal
Bay
Kings
Bay
Crystal
River
44
1
490
Homosassa
Springs
HOMOSASSA
ISLANDS
CHASSAHOWITZKA
NATIONAL
WILDLIFE
REFUGE
98
19

Citrus County

Citrus County declares itself "Mother Nature's Theme Park." With one-third of the county's land area under preservation, they are justified in this boast. Citrus County claims seven pristine rivers, numerous lakes, a state forest, and Chassahowitzka National Wildlife Refuge, a monumental tract of coastal wetlands. However, beaches are almost nonexistent and only one, Fort Island Gulf Beach, is worth mentioning. People instead come to Citrus County to commune with nature—especially the manatees who are drawn to its pure, spring-fed rivers. The springs from Crystal River north to the Suwannee River are among the finest snorkeling spots in the world, and the fishing is good enough to make an old slugger like Ted Williams retire here.

Chassahowitzka National Wildlife Refuge and Crystal River National Wildlife Refuge

The Nature Coast earns its name partly through the extraordinary confluence of four National Wildlife Refuges (Chassahowitzka, Crystal River, Lower Suwannee, and Cedar Keys) in adjacent counties (Citrus, Levy). As most ecotourists know, National Wildlife Refuges are federally owned conservation lands managed by the U.S. Fish and Wildlife Service. They have been set aside to protect habitat and to ensure that future generations will have wildlife and wilderness to enjoy.

There are currently more than 540 refuges in the United States, encompassing more than 92 million acres and providing haven for 200 endangered or threatened species. The state of Florida is fortunate to have 16 refuges, most of which are vital wintering grounds for waterfowl and other migrating birds. They also delineate boundaries for the never-ending development that otherwise threatens to turn Florida into a gigantic asphalt sprawl.

The coastal wetlands that this system of refuges protects along the Nature Coast are prodigious and endlessly fascinating. Chassahowitzka National Wildlife Refuge is located southwest of Homosassa, sprawling across southern Citrus County and northern Hernando County, and is accessible via the Chassahowitzka River Campground and Recreation Area at the west end of Miss Maggie Drive (County Road 480).

The refuge covers 30,500 acres of bays, creeks, estuaries, brackish marshes, fringing hardwood swamps and mangrove islands. It stretches along a mostly inaccessible coastline, from the Homosassa River down to Raccoon Point, below the mouth of the Chassahowitzka River. Refuge headquarters can be found on U.S. 19, a mile north of the Citrus County line. The refuge itself is accessible by boat only, and the idea is to largely keep it that way in order to preserve the unspoiled estuarine habitat.

However, the Citrus County Parks and Recreation Department, through a lease arrangement with a Florida state agency (Southwest Florida Management District), maintains the Chassahowitzka River Campground and Recreation Area within the refuge. To get there from U.S. 19, turn west onto County Road 480 (Miss Maggie Drive) and follow for 1.7 miles until it ends at the river.

Day-use facilities include a boat ramp, canoe and kayak rentals, and a stellar location near the natural springs. A parking fee of $1.50 per vehicle, plus an additional 50 cents for a trailer, is charged. You won't find a better campground on the Gulf Coast than the 92-siter at Chassahowitzka River. There are primitive tent sites ($14 per night) and ones with water and electric hookups ($16 per night).

Because most of the land surface in the refuge is mudflats and salt marsh, there are no hiking trails. About 250 species of birds, 50 species of reptiles and amphibians, and 25 species of mammals can be found here. Fishing is allowed in the pure, spring-fed creeks that sluice through the wetlands.

By comparison, Crystal River National Wildlife Refuge is a shrimp, embracing a mere 46 acres of islands in Kings Bay. But it's an extraordinarily important habitat for the manatee. The protection of this species was the sole reason the refuge was established.

The area, with its many natural springs pumping 600 million gallons of water daily, is the most significant warm-water refugium for the beleaguered mammal. (Oddly enough, outputs of warmed water from power plants along the Florida coast also serve as important manatee refuges.) Approximately one-fourth of the nation's manatees congregate in Kings Bay, which is why its refuge islands are so critical to the preservation of this endangered species.

Commercial marinas and dive shops are located along the shore of Kings Bay, mainly at the end of Kings Bay Drive and Paradise Road. Diving, snorkeling, and swimming are the activities of choice, while fishing is prohibited on the refuge. Peak time for manatee viewing is December to March. To learn more about the manatee in advance of a visit here, check out the Manatee Education Center at Homosassa Springs State Wildlife Park, seven miles south of Crystal River on U.S. 19.

Contact Information

Chassahowitzka and Crystal River National Wildlife Refuges, 1502 Southeast Kings Bay Drive, Crystal River, FL 34429; 352/563-2088; website: www.chassahowitzka.fws.gov or website: www.crystalriver.fws.gov

Chassahowitzka River Campground and Recreation Area, 8600 West Miss Maggie Drive, Homosassa, FL 34446; 352/382-2200

Homosassa Springs and Homosassa

The flotsam from U.S. 19 begins thinning out in Citrus County, which pays more than lip service to the natural wonders over which it is entrusted. Much of that responsibility, of course, has been taken out of Citrus County's hands by the Chassahowitzka National Wildlife Refuge and the Withlacoochee State Forest. Without lifting a finger, in fact, Citrus County has had fully one-third of its 682 square miles set aside as federal, state, or county conservation land and, as a result, it is a vital home to 12 endangered species, including the Florida black bear, the manatee, the scrub jay, the peregrine falcon, and the Southern bald eagle.

If you can ignore the human presence elsewhere in Citrus County, you'll be rewarded with uniquely fascinating destinations among the coastal backroads. For instance, this self-proclaimed "soul of the Nature Coast" and "Mother Nature's theme park" is home to Native American archaeological sites dating back 10,000 years, historic remnants of the Spanish and pioneer presences, and a number of truly remarkable natural springs where manatees can be clearly and closely observed in their natural habitat. A few towns are worth visiting, as well. Homosassa, Homosassa Springs, and Crystal River have close ties with the coast, including tarpon fishing in the offshore gulf waters, diving and snorkeling in spring-fed rivers, and prodigious bird-watching in the coastal wetlands. There's even one legitimate sand beach.

Just south of Crystal River, the towns of Homosassa Springs (on U.S. 19/98, at Couty Road 490) and Homosassa (three miles west of Homosassa Springs, near the Gulf of Mexico) each have enticing points of interest. In Homosassa (pop. 2,100), six acres at Yulee Sugar Mill Ruins State Historic Site (352/795-3817) are all that remain of a 7,000-acre sugar plantation run by David Levy Yulee, who later became Florida's first U.S. Senator. The mill

MAP OF CITRUS COUNTY—PAGE 502

This lovely 180-acre nature park was initially preserved not by the state but by the good citizens of Citrus County, who did not want to see one of its last large parcels of private acreage auctioned off and turned into more of the subdivided morass that's creeping up from Hernando and Pasco Counties. They bought the land and deeded it in the early 1990s to the state, which set about its gradual restoration—pending funding, which was slow to come—and refurbishment into a wildlife park.

Homosassa Springs State Wildlife Park is designed along the lines of a high-class alligator farm. You walk a 1.1-mile loop around the park and gaze at caged critters—flamingos, hawks, bald eagles, alligators, and so forth—some of which are recovering from injuries in the wild. You will never get closer to a bald eagle or a crested caracara then at Homosassa Springs. The biggest thrill, and a sad spectacle in its own way, are the cages harboring a Florida black bear, a bobcat, and the king of them all, the endangered Florida panther. The remaining population of Florida panthers in the wild is estimated to be down to 50 in the wild, and the surviving members of the species are not genetically healthy.

The majestic panther needs room to roam, but there's very little room left in Florida, where developmental sprawl has invaded nearly every nook and cranny of the state. The Florida panther that bides his time in this cage seems sulky and withdrawn, and who can blame him? In the wild, these fleet, stealthy animals are rarely spied by human eyes. Here, the caged panther is on display to any lumbering tourist with a point-and-shoot wanting a souvenir of a nearly vanquished species. We couldn't resist studying the majestic creature ourselves, just as he couldn't resist studying with hungry eyes the flamingos across the

has been partially restored, and a self-guided tour gives you a glimpse of the pioneering spirit hereabouts. The park is off Yulee Drive in Homosassa, three miles west of U.S. 19. In Homosassa Springs (pop. 6,300), the attraction is a state wildlife park (see Homosassa Springs State Wildlife Park sidebar, this chapter).

In terms of water-based recreation, many come to Homosassa to snorkel and dive among the spring-fed rivers and associated caves carved into the underlying limestone. Guided airboat and excursion-boat tours, as well as boat rentals for do-it-yourselfers, are available in Homosassa and Crystal River. Inland, in eastern Citrus County, the 57-mile Withlacoochee State Trail is a rails-to-trails conversion that follows the course of the Withlacoochee River from Trilby (in northern Pasco County) to Citrus Springs (in northern Citrus County).

Coastal Cuisine

The most popular restaurant in Citrus County—actually, two restaurants in one—is **KC Crump Restaurant and Ramshackle Cafe on the River** (11210 West Halls River Road, 352/628-1500, $$). This converted 1870s fishing lodge overlooking the Homosassa River is a well-established favorite.

We wove our way out on backroads to Old Homosassa after soliciting recom-

trail. What could he be thinking? We'll never know. But one thing's for sure: something as precious as a Florida panther deserves every effort at preservation. If it goes extinct, a piece of our own humanity and self-worth will die right along with it.

In addition to the birds, the bear, and the panther, manatee sightings are guaranteed here. It's one of the only places in the world where manatees may be observed at close range 365 days a year. From an underwater observatory into which visitors descend by stairs, you can watch manatees (who look like fleshy submarines) as they swim around warm natural springs in which they feed and live. The park also has a museum, children's education center, and about a half-day's worth of exhibits and activities. Your visit begins with a relaxing, narrated trip by pontoon boat up a shallow creek to the west visitor center, where the trail and animal exhibits are located. You can also drive up to this west entrance, but it's much more fun to park at the east entrance (on U.S. 19, adjacent to the Ramada Inn) and take the boat ride.

En route, you pass beneath a canopy of wetlands-tolerant tree species: sweetgum, red maple, bayberry, sweet bay, longleaf pine, and magnolia, plus the handful of bald cypress that weren't cut down for the pencil factory that used to operate nearby. Their overhanging boughs provide cooling shade during the ride. Overhead, you'll spy the occasional golden orb spider, a giant (as spiders go) whose volleyball-net-size webs are a wonder of nature. Dragonflies buzz beside the boat. Indeed the whole adventure is a glimpse at Florida's vanishing natural heritage.

The park entrance and visitor center are located on U.S. 19 in Homosassa Springs. Homosassa Springs State Wildlife Park is open daily from 9 A.M. to 5:30 P.M. The last ticket is sold at 4:30 P.M., but it's recommended you get here by 1 P.M. in order to fully enjoy the programs. Admission costs $7.95 per adult ($6.75 with an AAA or AARP card) and $4.95 for kids 3–12.

For more information, contact Homosassa Springs State Wildlife Park, 4150 South Suncoast Boulevard, Homosassa, FL 34446; 352/628-5343; website: www.myflorida.com

mendations for good seafood in the area. Everyone sent us to **Charlie Brown's Crab House** (5297 South Cherokee Way, 352/621-5080, $$), which specializes in Florida hard-shell blue crabs served Chesapeake Bay style—which is to say spiced and steamed. The house specialty is garlic crabs, which are wok fried in whole garlic, spices, and oil. Moved by the backwater bayou ambience, we tried the blackened catfish, but really anything is good here, be it grouper fingers or gator tail. Lunch specials, served from 11 A.M.–4 p.m., are a bargain. If you're famished at the dinner hour and want something other than a crab feast, try Charlie's seafood combo, a mound of fish, shrimp, scallops, and oysters for $15.95. As an added bonus, you get to gaze out the windows onto Monkey Island, an actual island that is prowled by playful squirrel and spider monkeys.

Contact Information

Homosassa Springs Area Chamber of Commerce, 3495 South Suncoast Boulevard (U.S. 19), Homosassa Springs, FL 34448; 352/628-2666; website: www.homosassachamber.com

MAP OF CITRUS COUNTY—PAGE 502

Ozello

Out in the middle of a sliced-and-diced watery nowhere of mangrove islands and teeming marshlands is Ozello (pop. 200). County Road 494 (Ozello Trail) wends its way out to Ozello from U.S. 19. Out by the Gulf of Mexico is Ozello Community Park, which boasts a boat ramp, fishing pier, and picnic tables, but no beach to speak of. If you're seeking cracker ambience and victuals, be sure to stop at **Peck's Old Port Cove** (139 North Ozello Trail, 352/795-2806, $$). The locally harvested crab and fish are especially recommended.

Contact Information

Homosassa Springs Area Chamber of Commerce, 3495 South Suncoast Boulevard (U.S. 19), Homosassa Springs, FL 34448; 352/628-2666; website: www.homosassachamber.com

Crystal River

Crystal River (pop. 4,200) is the second largest incorporated town in Citrus County (Inverness, the county seat, is first) and the largest on the coast. The town bills itself as "Where Man and Manatee Play," which is, perhaps, an unintentional koan. If man is playing with manatee, this is not good. If man and manatee are playing separately, this is probably good. If man is playing too close to manatee, this is potentially tragic. We've heard and witnessed too many tales about bone-headed human behavior around this endangered species to swallow the idea that man and manatee can somehow exist in "harmony." For instance, we saw one unsupervised lad of seven who would not be satisfied until he had actually ridden on the back of a manatee. But that pales in comparison to reckless boaters who inflict injury and even death upon these gentle sea mammals, which now number a mere 3,276 in the United States.

Crystal River attracts manatees because of its warm springs. Manatees cannot tolerate water temperatures below 68°F, and the millions of gallons of water issuing daily from thermal springs along the Citrus County coast are a constant, year-round 72°F. The town lies east of Kings Bay, which is fed by Florida's second largest springhead and is connected, via the Crystal River, to the Gulf of Mexico. To say Kings Bay is teeming with life is putting it mildly. With its steady, comfy water temperature and glassine pure water, Kings Bay is the most popular nesting area in the state for the West Indian manatee.

The land area along the north bank of the Crystal River was so vibrant with life that the original pre-Columbian inhabitants constructed a series of religious temples, shrines, and mounds in homage. Three different peoples lived here, beginning about 200 B.C.—first the Indians of the Deptford culture, then the Weedon Island culture (A.D. 300–900), and finally the Safety Harbor culture. The Safety Harbor gang was here in 1539 when Hernando de Soto, smitten with gold fever, stumbled upon

❶ Fort Island Gulf Beach

Location: nine miles west of U.S. 19 via Fort Island Turnpike, in Crystal River
Parking/fees: free parking lot
Hours: sunrise to sunset
Facilities: lifeguard (seasonal), restrooms, picnic tables, and showers
Contact: Citrus County Parks and Recreation Department, 352/795-2202

them. These mysteries can be explored in depth at the **Crystal River State Archaeological Site** (3400 North Museum Point, 352/795-3817). The visitor center here contains artifacts of all these cultures, and park personnel can answer any questions after you've taken a self-guided tour of the grounds. The park entrance is two miles north of Crystal River on U.S. 19.

One curious note about the local citrus crop of Citrus County: Originally, this area was dominated by David Yulee's sugar plantation, but a major freeze in 1894 sent the citrus industry even farther south, where it remains today. One of Florida's oldest citrus varietals, the "Homosassa orange," is still grown hereabouts, but don't expect to find roadside stands dispensing fresh-squeezed orange juice, as is so common on the East Coast of Florida. We were disappointed to learn that fresh-squeezed OJ is going the way of the manatee, as it's too much trouble for local farmers to produce. A few scattered places along the highway sell citrus by the bag, however.

Beaches

There's a real sand beach in Crystal River called **Fort Island Gulf Beach.** From U.S. 19 in Crystal River, head west on Fort Island Turnpike for nine miles until it ends at the water. The drive goes through a nature preserve with nothing but open horizons and bird sounds to lull and serenade you. The beach at Fort Island is crescent shaped, with soft brown sand and no waves. It's safe, snug, and protected, with lifeguards on duty in the summer months. Parking, picnic tables, some sheltered pavilions, restrooms, and a boat launch are provided.

Shore Things

- **Bike/skate rentals:** Suncoast Bicycles, 471 Northeast 1st Terrace, Crystal River, 352/795-0018.
- **Boat cruise:** Crystal River Manatee Dive & Tour, 267 Northwest 3rd Street, Crystal River, 352/795-1333.
- **Dive shop:** American Pro Diving Center, 821 Southeast U.S.19, Crystal River, 352/563-0041.
- **Ecotourism:** Homosassa Springs State Wildlife Park, 4150 South Suncoast Boulevard, Homosassa, 352/628-5343.
- **Fishing charters:** Homosassa Fishing Guides Association, Homosassa, 352/795-7302.
- **Marina:** Twin Rivers Marina, 2880 North Seabreeze Point, Crystal River, 352/795-3552.
- **Rainy-day attraction:** Crystal River State Archaeological Site and Museum, 3400 North Museum Point, Crystal River, 352/795-3817.
- **Shopping/browsing:** Heritage Village, North Citrus Avenue, Crystal River, 352/795-8630.
- **Vacation rentals:** Greenbriar Rentals, 2432 North Essex Avenue, Hernando, FL 34442, 352/746-5921 or 888/446-5921.

Bunking Down

As this area gets hip to the ecotourism concept, more and more motels and marinas around Kings Bay and along Crystal River offer guided manatee-viewing tours, diving and fishing treks, and canoe/kayak rentals. One of best places to lay over in the area is **Best Western Crystal River Resort** (614 Northwest U.S. 19, 352/795-3171, $$), which is right on Kings Bay. Its 114 rooms blend nicely into the natural landscape, and the nearby waters are easily accessed via the on-site dive shop and marina, where motorized and nonmotorized boats of all kinds can be rented. For landlubbers, the bay can be vicariously enjoyed from the tiki bar.

Humanity and Huge Manatees

The most damning indictment that can be levied on mankind occurs whenever a species goes extinct due to human behavior. There is no excuse—and, to our minds, no permission or forgiveness granted in the "Good Book" or anywhere else—for destroying creation and explaining it away as a kind of manifest destiny: to wit, that some poor species just got in the way of our economic activity and development, and our recklessly burgeoning numbers.

One of the more visible species that is teetering on the brink in Florida is the West Indian manatee. This gentle giant inhabits the waters along the Florida coast, including estuaries, bays, canals, and rivers. The average adult manatee is 10 feet long and weighs 1,000 pounds, although they can grow as large as 13 feet and weigh as much as 3,000 pounds. These gray-brown, submarine-shaped herbivores forage for plant material in shallow waters. Being mammals, they must breathe air, and they break the surface to do so every three to five minutes.

It takes a long time for manatees to reproduce. Males reach sexual maturity at nine years and females at five; the gestation period is 13 months. Manatees can live to 60 years of age or longer, though they rarely do in Florida. That is because they are massacred by boat propellers, drowned in canal locks and flood control structures, strangled in crab trap lines, choked to death by ingested fish hooks and monofilament line, and sometimes deliberately harassed, injured, and even killed by sadistic vandals.

Manatees are tracked by marine biologists who actually identify individuals by the pattern of boat-prop scars on their backs. The current population of manatees in the U.S., according to a 2001 aerial survey, is around 3,276. That is a good number, given the

Coastal Cuisine

Adjacent to the Best Western in Crystal River (see "Bunking Down") is **Crackers Bar & Grill** (502 Northwest 6th Street, 352/795-3999, $$), a beef-and-seafood kind of place with a full bar.

Contact Information

Nature Coast Chamber of Commerce, 28 Northwest U.S. 19, Crystal River, FL 34428, 352/795-3149; website: www.citrusdirectory.com

BIG BEND

alarming mortality rates in recent years. In the first three months of 1996, for example, 210 manatees died (nearly a tenth of their population!), including 120 that perished along Florida's lower southwest coast due to a "mysterious infection." The manatees were succumbing to pneumonia, but the source of infection wasn't really all that mysterious. The culprit was human-generated pollution washed into waterways during a particularly heavy spell of winter rains that year. Some 83 manatees died in one 23-day period along the short stretch of coast from Venice to Naples.

In order to save the species, a code of conduct is in order. Manatees are legally protected by the Marine Mammal Protection Act of 1972, the Endangered Species Act of 1973, and the Florida Manatee Sanctuary Act of 1978. The Save the Manatee Club, an advocacy organization cofounded by singer Jimmy Buffett, is working to raise public awareness (see address below). Beyond that, it's up to each individual to act responsibly in order to ensure that the manatee's numbers can be raised and the population stabilized.

Here are some rules of the road regarding human interactions with manatees:

- Do not enter designated manatee sanctuaries for any reason.
- Do not pursue, corner, or follow a manatee while swimming or diving.
- Do not disturb a resting manatee.
- Do not attempt to feed or give water to manatees.
- Do not ride, poke, prod, grab, or otherwise disturb a manatee at any time.
- Do not separate a manatee calf from its mother or any single manatee from a group.
- Do observe idle, slow-speed, caution, no entry, and safe operation zones when boating.
- Do use snorkeling gear, and not scuba gear, when attempting to observe manatees.
- Do stay out of seagrass beds, which are prime manatee habitats.

For more information, contact the Save the Manatee Club, 500 North Maitland Avenue, Maitland, FL 32751; 407/539-0990; website: www.savethemanatee.org.

Levy County

Bronson
Otter Creek
River
Waccasassa
Inglis
Yankeetown
Waccasassa Bay
Chiefland
MANATEE SPRINGS STATE PARK
Suwannee River
Cedar Key
CEDAR KEYS
GULF OF MEXICO

Levy County

Florida begins turning a corner at Levy County as the southern peninsula gives way to the Panhandle. Levy County would appear to be the state's elbow. To the south, the unassuming community of Yankeetown nestles beside the bucolic Withlacoochee River. At the center is Cedar Key, a likeable and bohemian island community surrounded by prodigious natural beauty and extensive preserves. These include the Waccasassa Bay Preserve State Park, Cedar Key Scrub State Reserve, Cedar Keys National Wildlife Refuge, and Lower Suwannee National Wildlife Refuge. Both Cedar Key and Yankeetown have sandy beaches, but you must be forgiving in your conception of what constitutes a beach. If you're up for an adventure and have access to a boat, the offshore islands of Cedar Keys National Wildlife Refuge, especially Atsena Otie and Seahorse Key, are ringed with sandy beaches.

Yankeetown

In the South, the old historical saw "George Washington Slept Here" has been changed to "Elvis Presley Played Here." In Yankeetown (pop. 600), oddly enough, that rebel yell is true. The King took up temporary residence here in July and August of 1961 while filming an otherwise forgettable movie called *Follow That Dream*. To commemorate that historic occasion, the road connecting Yankeetown to the main drag of U.S. 19/98 is known as Follow That Dream Parkway. More prosaically, it is County Road 40. The 6.5-mile drive out County Road 40 struts through hundreds of acres of unspoiled tidal flats and wetlands, with islands in the distance.

Yankeetown gets its name not from the New York Yankees (à la "Dodgertown," the L.A. baseball franchise's spring-training complex on the East Coast) but from the Northerners who began coming here in the 1920s. Today, the community is a scattering of modest dwellings in a woodsy, watery setting. The Withlacoochee River empties into the Gulf of Mexico here, and vast, Everglades-style stands of grasses extend into the gulf. The town landmark is the Izaak Walton Lodge, named for the seventeenth-century author of *The Compleat Angler*, a Briton who never set foot in Florida. Yankeetown is a slowed-down vision of the way Florida used to be. In fact, we've heard that locals have been buying up property so they can keep it that way. More power to 'em.

❶ Yankeetown Park (a.k.a. Vassey Creek Park)

Location: west end of County Road 40 in Yankeetown
Parking/fees: free parking lot
Hours: sunrise to sunset
Facilities: restrooms and picnic tables
Contact: Levy County Mosquito Control Department, 352/486-5127

BIG BEND

Beaches

Near the end of Follow That Dream Parkway is **Yankeetown Park** (a.k.a. Vassey Creek Park), which offers teeming bird and marine life, pleasant isolation, ripples for waves, and a crescent-shaped swath of sand. Just around the corner, at the very end of County Road 40, is Levy County Boat Ramp, a launching site that affords access to the grass flats where the fishing, we were told, is excellent. If you're an angler, "follow that dream" out to Yankeetown, because you won't be disappointed.

Bunking Down

The **Izaak Walton Lodge** (6301 Riverside Drive, 352/447-2311, $) is a still-functioning, 75-year-old lodge that rents out guest rooms, suites, and villas. Rooms are inexpensive, but the building (a two-story wood lodge with a gigantic limestone fireplace) is priceless. The area can be explored via bike and canoe, which are available at the lodge, but many come instead for the fishing. Boat rentals and guided trips can be arranged.

Coastal Cuisine

The gourmet dining room at the Izaak Walton Lodge is called **The Compleat Angler** (6301 Riverside Drive, 352/447-2311, $$$), after the classic text on fishing by the lodge's namesake. The food is prepared with more flair than one might expect to find in a place as humbly removed from an urbanized setting as Yankeetown. Specialties include surf (such items as red snapper topped with crabmeat and béarnaise sauce, or Cajun oysters and scallops) and turf (steak au poivre, chateaubriand). The breakfast menu might include seafood omelettes or eggs Benedict. It's almost too good to be believed.

Contact Information
Withlacoochee Gulf Area Chamber of Commerce, 167 County Road 40, P.O. Box 427, Yankeetown, FL 34449; 352/447-3383

Cedar Key

Cedar Key calls itself the "gem of the Nature Coast," a not unfair self-appraisal. It is several things in one: a working fishing community, an artists colony, a historic village (settled in the 1840s), an archaeological site, a grouping of islands, and a state of mind somewhere between Downeast Maine and Greenwich Village. One of the more articulate waitresses we met in town even went so far as to liken Cedar Key, with its tight-knit year-round population of 1,000 and genial eccentricities, to the Big Sur community of the 1960s. That may be overstating the case a bit, but it is easy to see how such happy thoughts might arise.

Good vibes begin even as you approach Cedar Key on State Route 24. The final 20 miles cut through Cedar Key Scrub State Reserve, an unbroken natural habitat that is free of rusted trailers, burnt-out junkyards, and trash heaps. So this is the Nature Coast, you find yourself nodding in approval. The highway ends in the town of Cedar Key, which unfolds around a small circular point, like a coastal Maine village. (We were, in fact, struck by the resemblance of Cedar Key to Stonington, Maine.) The fishing docks of Cedar Key are built around a circular cul-de-sac, with the grid of the village behind them like a ball nestled snugly in a catcher's mitt. Keeping things perfectly simple, the streets in the village's grid are numbered (1st, 2nd, 3rd, etc.) and lettered (A, B, C, etc.). As one local pundit put it, "Cedar Key is very laid-back, quiet, no tall buildings, one grocery store, one gas station, one policeman on duty, and no crime."

But Cedar Key is more than the town that bears its name. It is also a grouping of more than 100 different keys ranging in size from one acre to 165 acres. There is, in fact, no Cedar Key, per se. The town itself occupies Way Key, the largest of the hundred islands. The first settlement hereabouts was on Atsena Otie Key (the Creek Indian name for "Cedar Island"), which can be seen directly offshore from the docks in the village. Thirteen of the islands make up Cedar Keys National Wildlife Refuge, set aside by President Herbert Hoover in 1929. The outermost, Seahorse Key, was added to the refuge by President Roosevelt in 1936 and is now a world-renowned bird sanctuary as well as the highest point of land on the gulf coast, with a sand ridge that rises 52 feet. Seahorse Key is the site of a pre–Civil War lighthouse that's now used by the University of Florida.

All this talk of cedar refers to the red cedar forests that once blanketed most of the islands. The wood was cherished by the Native Americans for many purposes, but the white settlers, beginning in 1855, used it mainly in the thriving pencil trade. Eberhard Faber bought land and built a factory here to take advantage of the timber boom, which went bust by 1900 when all the trees were gone. Two notable enterprises came to a much more glorious end here. The first was the trans-Florida railroad, which linked Cedar Key to Fernandina Beach in 1861. The second was the naturalist John Muir's marathon trek from Wisconsin, chronicled in the classic *A Thousand-Mile Walk to the Gulf* (1867). Muir may have even inspired the

MAP OF LEVY COUNTY—PAGE 512

town's nickname when he wrote, "Today I reached the sea and many gems of tiny islets called keys."

Another enterprise, indicative of the independent spirit that had developed by the 1890s, came to a crashing halt when railroad baron Henry Plant plotted to extend his gulf coast railway through here. He was impolitely told to go packing. Not only did Cedar Key refuse to become a station stop on his potentially lucrative line, but they also wouldn't even let his supply boats dock in their harbor. For a closer look at the area's fascinating history, two local museums cover events dating back to pre-Columbian times. They are the **Cedar Key State Museum** (170 Museum Drive, 352/543-5350, open Thursday through Monday) and the **Cedar Key Historical Society** (2nd Street, 352/543-5549, open daily). Both museums charge $1 for admission.

Despite some inevitable encroachment of nouveaux riches—e.g., a few condos on stilts—Cedar Key stubbornly retains its edge. Fishing is the one thing that touches everyone's life, including visitors who reap the bounty at local restaurants. The quirky local paper, the *Cedar Key Beacon,* is filled with tide tables and fishing reports, tips, and news. Many Beacon stories offer Cedar Key legend and lore, and all the local wits seem to have weekly columns. Funny and eccentric, these are required reading for visitors. One female columnist, for example, offers this unimpeachable observation about men, with their macho need to cast lines as though they'd entered an Olympic discus throwing event: "I mean, if you're already 40 miles out from land, it stands to reason that it's just as deep right next to the boat as it is if you try to use up the entire reel of line. But, if you honestly believe that it's deeper 500 yards away, why not just pull the boat over another 500 yards?"

Fishing fanatics, naturalists, birdwatchers, painters, photographers, and we two beach bums have all been smitten with Cedar Key. It should be added that Cedar Key is a popular weekend getaway for people who live in relatively big cities like Tallahassee (the state capital) and Gainesville (the university town that lies due north on State Route 24).

Regardless of what draws you to this area, it is like coastal Maine in another important regard: the bestowing of "local" status. "You are a local if your grandparents were born here," said one longtime resident. Local or not, you will feel at home on Cedar Key.

Beaches

Cedar Key doesn't need a beach to sell itself to us, because we're hooked on this place. To sell itself to others, perhaps, there's a small and tidy manmade beach at **Cedar Key City Park**, located on the corner of 2nd and Dock Streets. Frankly, this little patch of hard-packed sand is the least of Cedar Key's charms and nothing to get excited about. Picnic pavilions, parking, and restrooms are provided. On the

❷ Cedar Key City Park

Location: 2nd and Dock Streets, in Cedar Key
Parking/fees: free parking lot
Hours: sunrise to 10 P.M.
Facilities: restrooms, picnic tables, and a shower
Contact: Cedar Key City Hall, 352/543-5132

❸ Sand Spit Park

Location: 1st and G Streets in Cedar Key
Parking/fees: free street parking
Hours: 24 hours
Facilities: none
Contact: Cedar Key City Hall, 352/543-5132

west side of town, at G and 1st Streets, a small natural sand beach called **Sand Spit Park** is where locals sometimes go to watch sunset or collect sand dollars. There's also a public pier at the west end of Dock Street.

The real beach miracles occur offshore, on keys like Atsena Otie and Seahorse, which are part of Cedar Keys National Wildlife Refuge (see section in this chapter). At Atsena Otie, a secluded key one half-mile offshore, a hard-packed sand beach faces the gulf. Unless you have access to a boat, the only way to get there is via **Island Hopper Boat Tours and Rentals** (City Marina, 352/543-5904). This rental, cruise, and ferry service operates at the main dock in Cedar Key, next to the Seabreeze Restaurant. They will drop you off on Atsena Otie and pick you up later in

Manatee Springs State Park

This state park is not on the coast, but it's not far from it (23 miles, to be exact). And since it attracts manatees from the ocean, there's a tangential connection with the subject of our book. We love these giant, gentle sea cows and support all efforts to preserve their endangered numbers, so we've herewith included Manatee Springs. The central focus of the park is an underground spring that pumps a staggering 117 million gallons of fresh water daily. That's 81,250 gallons a minute! The water that issues from the limestone aquifer is a constant 72°F. In winter, the run between the spring and the Suwannee River is a favorite hangout of manatees, who come to warm themselves. We saw three of them—two adults and a juvenile—swimming around Manatee Springs one cool November morning. They surfaced frequently, noisily exhaling and then inhaling through their snouts, and then they dove and swam some more.

Most park visitors quietly and appreciately observed the manatees' comings and goings, but an older couple—one in a kayak, the other loudly flapping around in diving gear—chased the poor manatees all over the place. Does nature not ever know a moment's peace from the reckless intrusions of human beings? Canoes are rented at Manatee Springs, and many visitors bring diving equipment so they can have close encounters with manatees. Yet there's a long and winding boardwalk, bordered by a cypress-gum swamp, that follows the spring run out and into the Suwannee River. This vantage point is really about as close as a respectful human observer needs to get to the endangered manatees. Think about it: would you want hordes of nosy manatees chasing you around a heated pool?

Facilities at Manatee Springs include 86 campsites and a picnic area at the head of the spring run. There are nine miles of hiking trails in the park, too, including the North End Trail and the Sink Trail. Manatee Springs State Park is, in short, another jewel in the impressive necklace of state parks that, as they like to say, preserve more of the real Florida. To get there, take U.S. 19/98 north just past Chiefland and proceed west on County Road 320 for six miles.

For more information, contact Manatee Springs State Park, 11650 Northwest 115th Street, Chiefland, FL 32626; 352/493-6072; website: www.myflorida.com

MAP OF LEVY COUNTY—PAGE 512

the day. They also conduct several daily cruises to the many offshore keys.

Shore Things

- **Boat cruise:** Cedar Key Island Hopper, City Marina, Cedar Key, 352/543-5904.
- **Dive shop:** Aztec Dive Center, 1005 Northwest 19th Avenue, Chiefland, 352/493-9656.
- **Ecotourism:** Atsena Otie Key, Cedar Keys National Wildlife Refuge, 352/493-0238.
- **Fishing charters:** Native Sons Charters, 352/543-9930.
- **Kayak Rentals:** Cedar Key Kayaks, 3rd Street Dock, Cedar Key, 352/543-9437.
- **Marina:** Norwood Marina, 12780 State Route 24, Cedar Key, 352/543-6148.
- **Pier:** Cedar Key Public Fishing Pier, Dock Street (west end), Cedar Key
- **Rainy-day attraction:** Cedar Key Historical Museum, State Route 24 and 2nd Street, Cedar Key, 352/543-5549.
- **Shopping/browsing:** Cedar Key Historic District, Cedar Key.
- **Vacation rentals:** Island Place, 1st and C Streets, P.O. Box 687, Cedar Key, 352/543-5307.

Bunking Down

For such a secluded place, Cedar Key has a surprisingly wide array of accommodations, including the mom-and-pop-style **Faraway Inn** (3rd and G Streets, P.O. Box 370, 352/543-5330, $), the historic (circa 1861) **Island Hotel** (2nd and B Streets, P.O. Box 460, 352/543-5111, $$$), and the meticulously restored, oak-shaded Victorian home (circa 1880) that is now **Cedar Key Bed & Breakfast** (3rd and F Streets, P.O. Box 700, 352/543-9000, $$). Beyond that, there are assorted townhouses, cottages, and campgrounds. Contact the **Cedar Key Chamber of Commerce** (480 2nd Street, 352/543-5600; website: www.cedarkey.org) for an illustrated booklet of available places to stay.

One of the nicest compromises between modern comfort and the laid-back look of yesteryear is **Island Place** (1st and C Streets, P.O. Box 687, 352/543-5307, $$). Its tastefully constructed three-story wood villas have the privacy, personality, and comfort of someone's home, because that's exactly what they are: the second homes of folks who rent them out when they're not around themselves. A swimming pool and Jacuzzi are on the premises, and the docks are just down the street, as is everything else in town.

Cedar Cove Beach and Yacht Club (10 East 2nd Street, P.O. Box 837, 352/543-5332, $$) is the closest thing to a beachfront motel on Cedar Key. It sits beside Cedar Key City Park and has a pool, Jacuzzi, sauna, fitness room, restaurant, and bar on the premises. The "yacht club" is an odd affectation, though. What yachts? And why would anyone want a yacht on Cedar Key?

Coastal Cuisine

Fishing is king in the pristine offshore waters, and every day brings in a royal catch of grouper, yellowtail, redfish, flounder, mackerel, croaker, and mullet. Much of the bounty is catchable by surfcasting or dangling a line right off the village docks. The shallow, protein-rich waters near shore are also ideal for oysters and clams. A local specialty is farm-raised Cedar Key cherrystone clams, which are as tender and tasty as their Long Island cousins. Other favorites include heart of palm salad, smoked mullet, stone crab claws, blue crabs, and soft-shell crabs.

Before diving into the feast, we solicited opinions of two waterfront seafood restaurants from locals. The reviews were typically succinct. Of one place, we were smilingly told, "I don't want to say anything against it" (which, of course, spoke volumes). About another place, we were told, "I don't eat there. That ought to tell you something." We won't name names but the restaurants in question are conspicuous by their absence here.

One place we did light upon, the **Seabreeze** (520 Dock Street, 352/543-5738, $$), was a breath of fresh air on the seafood scene. From its upstairs dining room, overlooking the water, we were pleasantly surprised by the mullet and cherrystone clam dinners. Served with drawn butter, the clams were small, tasty, and fresh. As for mullet, they are those giddy fish you often see leaping above the surface of the water. They are netted, not hooked, and used mostly for bait, but they also make for good eating (though some consider the lowly baitfish unworthy of human consumption). A bit more gamy and rich than most fish, mullet are also small and bony, so appoint one of your party to be the designated Heimlich maneuver provider. Seabreeze serves its mullet rolled in meal, then fried and accompanied with coleslaw and baked potato. By meal's end you'll be leaping giddily, too.

Two local favorites for breakfast are the **Red Luck Cafe** (Cedar Key Dock, 352/543-6840, $) and **Cook's** (2nd and B Streets, 352/543-5548, $). The dining room at the **Island Hotel** (2nd and B Streets, 352/543-5111, $$$) is unanimously hailed as the gourmet seafood restaurant of choice and is the original source for much of what is considered local cuisine on Cedar Key. The hotel is listed on the National Register of Historic Places. Dating back to 1861, it's one of the few structures that survived the hurricane of 1896, which basically wiped out the town. An Island Hotel dining experience is steeped in local tradition, utilizing some of the earliest known recipes for smoked mullet, poached and broiled seafood, and heart of palm salad.

Night Moves

After your peanut butter pie plate has been cleared upstairs at the **Seabreeze**, mosey downstairs to the lounge and pass some time. On the night we visited, a bewhiskered country gentleman sang along with music uploaded to the house P.A. via a laptop computer, which sat conspicuously on a chair beside him. The irony struck us hard. We could not have been in a more out-of-the-way place, and yet we were being entertained by cyber-country karaoke. One minute he was importuning, "Take the ribbons from your hair," and the next he was crooning, "All my ex's live in Texas."

On weekends, a sober night is possible at the **Yellow Door Coffee Shop** (511 2nd Street, 352/543-8008), which is open Thursday through Monday and serves ice cream, yogurt, and homemade baked goods.

Contact Information

Cedar Key Chamber of Commerce, 480 2nd Street, P.O. Box 610, Cedar Key, FL 32625; 352/543-5600; website: www.cedarkey.org

MAP OF LEVY COUNTY—PAGE 512

Waccasassa Bay Preserve State Park and Cedar Key Scrub State Reserve

Nearly all of the coast between Yankeetown and Cedar Key falls within the confines of the 32,128-acre **Waccasassa Bay Preserve State Park**, which is home to the northernmost mangrove forest in the United States. Two-thirds of the acreage is salt marsh or mud-bottomed, serpentine tidal creeks (over 100 of the latter!), which are the liver and kidneys of the natural world. Large as it is, this preserve is but a sliver of the gulf hammock that used to cover the state in pre-development times.

While access to Waccasassa Bay is limited, the rewards are unsurpassed for fishers, photographers, bird-watchers, and campers. Primitive campsites on the Waccasassa River are accessible by canoe or kayak. Canoe access is available on State Route 326 at the Waccasassa River in Gulf Hammock and on County Road 40A at Covass Creek near Yankeetown. The preserve can also be entered from Cedar Key. Certain activities are restricted in certain seasons. Call in advance of your visit for details.

Adjacent to Waccasassa Bay Preserve State Park is the **Cedar Key Scrub State Reserve** (on State Route 24), which comprises 5,028 acres of pine flatwoods and sand pine scrub, fringed by salt marsh. Because it is a state reserve (and not a preserve), hunting is permitted on a limited basis from September through mid-November. There's also fishing, hiking, and canoeing to be done here, but no camping.

Contact Information

Waccasassa Bay Preserve State Park and Cedar Key Scrub State Reserve, P.O. Box 187, Cedar Key, FL 32625; 352/543-5567; website: www.myflorida.com

Cedar Keys National Wildlife Refuge and Lower Suwannee National Wildlife Refuge

Cedar Keys National Wildlife Refuge comprises 13 islands offshore from the town of Cedar Key. These islands in the gulf have sand beaches and no habitations on them, save for an inoperative lighthouse on Seahorse Key (which today is run by the University of Florida as a marine research and environmental education center). The islands can be visited by private boat or commercial operation such as Island Hopper Boat Tours out of Cedar Key. The public is allowed on the beaches but not the island interiors. In the case of Seahorse Key, the entire island is off limits during bird-nesting season, which runs from March 1 through June 30. Seahorse Key is particularly notable to beach hounds in that it is a gigantic sand dune with a central ridge that rises to a height of 52 feet—barely a dimple anywhere else in the country, but the highest elevation on Florida's West Coast.

The one exception to the rules regarding visitation is the latest acquisition, Atsena Otie Key. This formerly inhabited (the last homes were removed a century ago) and now marvelously isolated key came perilously close to being developed as recently as 1996. The state, in the form of the

Map of Big Bend—Page 489

Suwannee River Water Management District, came to the rescue in 1997, purchasing the island for $3 million. Now it is owned by the state and managed as part of Cedar Keys National Wildlife Refuge. The island has a short nature trail, educational kiosks, and a dock.

Atsena Otie lies a half-mile offshore from Cedar Key. Visitors can walk among the ruins of two cedar mills, both of which were destroyed in a devastating 1896 hurricane. Drawbacks to visitation are snakes (especially cottonmouths) and mosquitoes, which can be hellish in the warmer months. The best time to visit Atsena Otie Key is during the cooler winter months.

The Lower Suwannee National Wildlife Refuge protects 52,000 acres in the watershed of the lower Suwannee River. It is home to such endangered and threatened species as the bald eagle, the eastern indigo snake, the manatee, and the gulf sturgeon, plus three species of sea turtles. In addition, 250 bird species have been identified as residents or visitors. A boardwalked trail leads out to the Suwannee River. Thirty miles of refuge roads are open to vehicles, and many more miles of old logging roads can be explored on foot or by bike.

Contact Information

Cedar Keys and Lower Suwannee National Wildlife Refuges, Route 1, Box 1193C, Chiefland, FL 32626, 352/493-0238; website: www.fws.gov/r4swe/ckshpage (Cedar Keys) and website: www.fws.gov/r4swe (Lower Suwannee)

4 Cedar Keys National Wildlife Refuge

Location: the refuge consists of 13 islands in the Gulf of Mexico offshore of Cedar Key, including Atsena Otie, Seahorse, Snake, and North Keys

Parking/fees: accessible by boat only; free day use

Hours: beaches on the various Cedar Keys are open to the public from sunrise to sunset. The islands' interiors are closed to the public at all times. In addition, the entirety of Seahorse Key is closed to the public March 1–June 30.

Facilities: restroom (Atsena Otie Key) and a visitor center (10 miles west of Chiefland, on County Road 347)

Contact: Cedar Keys National Wildlife Refuge at 352/493-0238

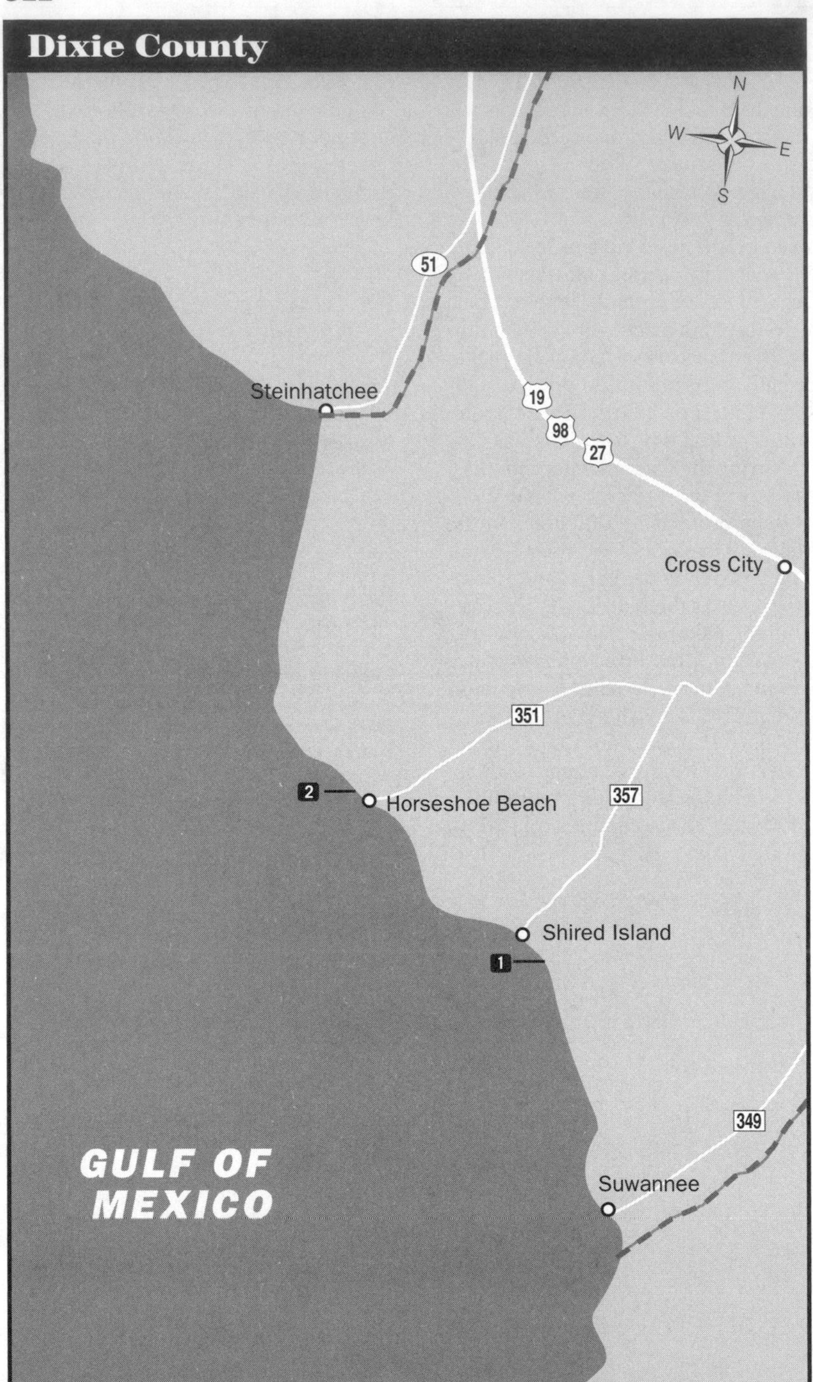
Dixie County
N
W
E
S
51
Steinhatchee
19
98
27
Cross City
351
2
Horseshoe Beach
357
Shired Island
1
349
Suwannee
GULF OF
MEXICO

Dixie County

Dixie County is bounded by the Suwannee and Steinhatchee Rivers and the Gulf of Mexico. It is great in size (704 square miles) but small in population (14,000 residents). It is peaceful and serene on the gulf—that is, when you can find roads leading to it from the main highway (U.S. 19/27/98). You won't find many beaches in this out-of-the-way county along Florida's Big Bend. Between the county parks at Shired Island and Horseshoe Beach, there's about enough sand to fill a child's sandbox. Making up for their lack are the excellent fishing and appealing natural setting, not to mention the splendid isolation that comes from being in the proverbial middle of nowhere.

Suwannee

You've heard of the song "Old Folks at Home," which goes, "Way down upon the Suwannee River"? Well, you can't get any farther down the Suwannee River than Suwannee (pop. 300), a fishing village at the mouth of this wide, wild, and wonderful waterway. If you're a disciple of blue highways, as we are, you'll love the 23-mile scenic drive down County Road 349 from U.S. 19/27/98 in Old Town to Suwannee.

The Suwannee is a slow-moving blackwater river that seems to define the meandering pace of life in the Deep South—and to embody much of its tantalizing mystery as well. The river gets its start up in the Okefenokee Swamp, curling through remote parts of north-central Florida before emptying into the Gulf of Mexico in two places: East Pass and West Pass. The village of Suwannee lies on the West Pass, where it empties into the Gulf of Mexico. The village is a fisherman's haven, offering opportunities for freshwater fishing in the river and saltwater fishing in the gulf.

Bunking Down

Lots of folks with a yen to cast a line drop anchor at places like **Bill's Motel and Fish Camp** (County Road 349, 352/542-7086, $) or the area's several RV parks.

Coastal Cuisine

You can break bread on Suwannee's waterfront at **Salt Creek Shellfish Company** (County Road 349, 352/542-7072, $$) and the **Suwannee Cafe** (Corbin Street, 352/542-0500, $).

Contact Information

Suwannee River Chamber of Commerce, P.O. Box 518, Old Town, FL 32860; 352/542-2000

Shired Island County Park

Shired Island County Park is adjacent to the Shired Island unit of Lower Suwannee National Wildlife Refuge, west of the Suwannee River on the Gulf of Mexico. To get there, take County Road 351 out of Cross City. The turn off U.S. 19/27/98 isn't well marked, but use the Ace Hardware store on the northwest corner of the intersection as your landmark. Follow County Road 351 for about eight miles, than take County Road 357, a left fork, another 12 miles to Shired Island (which is properly pronounced "shared"). En route you will pass flyblown trailers and squished critters in the roadbed. The charred, flattened remnants of a small boat lay in a canal beside the road. (This is how rural folks live in their beloved "country.") The pavement gives out and the road simply ends with no warning, but if you take a right turn just before the dead end, identified by a pair of beat-to-shit Dumpsters (one of which bears the following graffiti: "Horseshoe Boys Make Better Lovers"), you will find yourself at Shired Island County Park.

1 Shired Island County Park

Location: at the end of County Road 357, 20 miles south of Cross City

Parking/fees: free parking lot. Camping fees are $14 per night for RVs and $8 per night for tents

Hours: 24 hours

Facilities: restrooms, picnic tables, and showers

Contact: Dixie County Coordinator, 352/498-1240

Beaches

The word "park" is used rather loosely at Shired Island, as it more closely resembles a gypsy encampment. Modest RVs are scattered about the property. We're told there's a 14-day limit on camping, but some of the RVs looked as though they had been planted here since the Reconstruction. The smoke streaming from wood fires filled our nostrils, but we saw no humans stirring. It was a tad eerie, if truth be told. But there is a beach here, a real sand beach with a small stand of cabbage palms along the shore, and beaches are as rare as sharks' teeth along Big Bend. We took a picture, dipped our toes in the water, and were happy to leave, just as those who were silently studying us from their trailers were no doubt happy to have us leave. Again, fishing is the operative concept along this stretch of coast. There's a boat ramp on the federal side of Shired Island, and bank fishing is popular among anglers.

Contact Information

Dixie County Chamber of Commerce, Evans Square, U.S. 19, P.O. Box 547, Cross City, FL 32628; 352/498-5454. website: www.dixiecounty.org

Horseshoe Beach

Don't come looking for a beach in Horseshoe Beach (pop. 300). This town at the end of the road looks like a developer's dream that was aborted shy of what is known as a "buildout." Some nice-looking weathered-wood houses perch atop cinderblock stilts here. There's even an unusual house that looks like a big boat hoisted onto dry land. The road into Horseshoe Beach gives out at an asphalt circle. We turned off the car's engine and listened to the gulf waters lap against the rocks. On this gray day, we stared into an elemental tableau of water and sky. Out in the water sits a string of small, forested keys. No doubt they'd be fun to explore, if you had a boat. In all other respects, Horseshoe Beach reminded us of Shelter Cove on the northern California coast: in a word, isolated. Despite the presence of a marina, a dry dock facility, and canals backing up to homes, Horseshoe Beach looked like deadsville to us.

Beaches

Horseshoe Beach itself has only the merest sliver of sand at **Butler and Douglas County Park.** You can park your RV or plunk your tent down here, and there are picnic pavilions, a boat ramp, and indoor showers as well. Fishing is the raison d'être out here, as you are literally surrounded by water on three sides: two canals and a bay (named Horseshoe Cove). Folks also take scallops from the water in season.

Coastal Cuisine

If you should ever find yourself in Horseshoe Beach with an appetite (hey, stranger things have happened), you might duck into the **Crimson Crest Restaurant** (Main

2 Butler and Douglas County Park

  1

Location: at the end of 4th Avenue West in Horseshoe Beach

Parking/fees: free parking lot. Camping fees are $14 per night for RVs and $8 per night for tents

Hours: 24 hours

Facilities: restrooms, picnic tables, and showers

Contact: Dixie County Coordinator, 352/498-1240

Street, 352/498-0005, $). This humble house of home cooking serves a seafood buffet from 5 P.M. to 9 P.M. on weekends. Beyond that, you're really and truly on your own out here.

Contact Information

Dixie County Chamber of Commerce, P.O. Box 547, Evans Square, Highway 19, Cross City, FL 32628; 352/498-5454

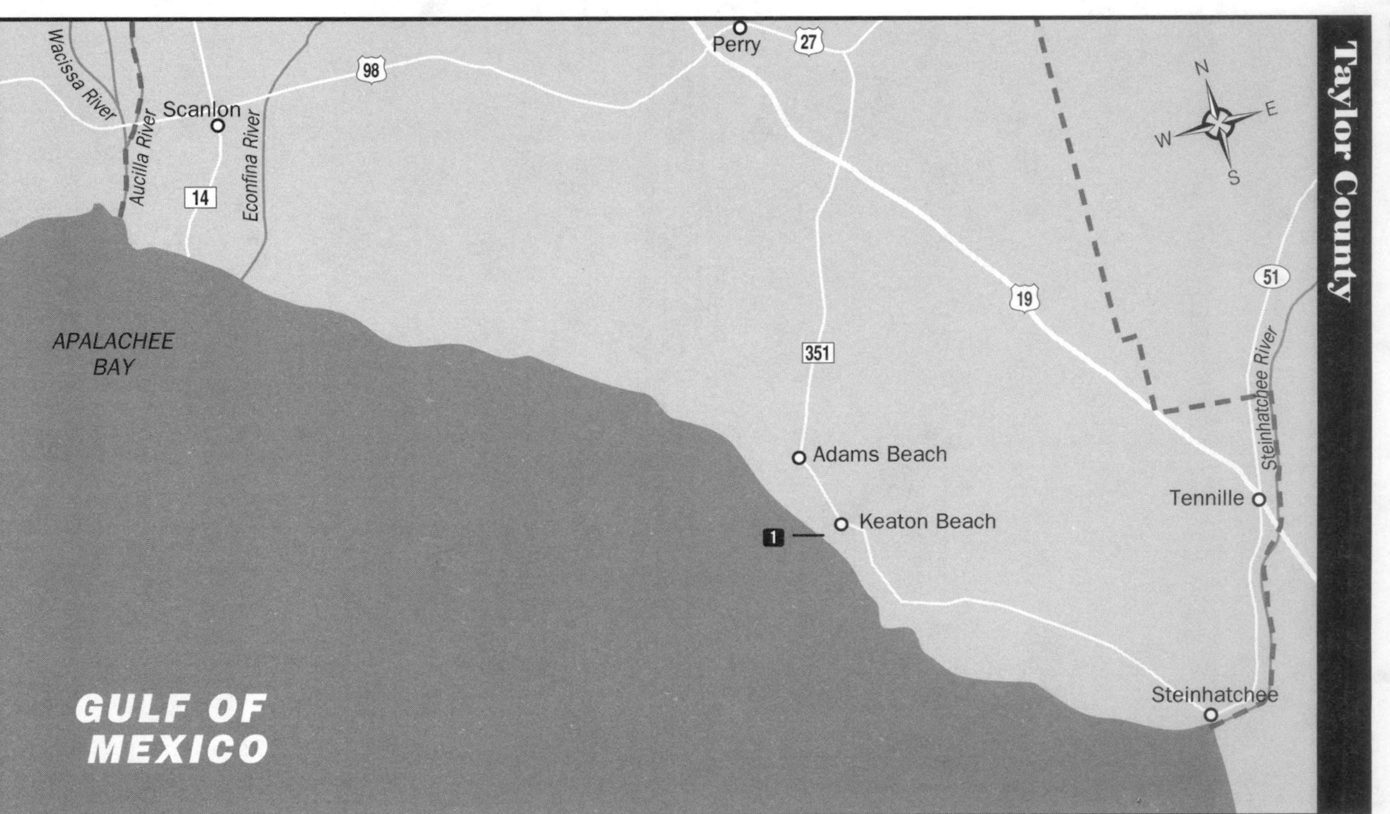

Taylor County
N
E
S
W
Wacissa River
Aucilla River
Scanlon
Econfina River
14
98
Perry
27
19
351
51
Steinhatchee River
Adams Beach
Keaton Beach
1
Tennille
Steinhatchee
APALACHEE BAY
GULF OF MEXICO

Taylor County

Taylor County's 60 miles of coastline is the longest in the state, but it has only one accessible sand beach: Hodges Park, in Keaton Beach. A lack of beaches shouldn't discourage anyone from visiting this sparsely populated county. A great number of rivers and creeks course through Taylor County, including the Steinhatchee, Econfina, and Aucilla. People explore Taylor County's waterways in canoes, kayaks, and even houseboats. There's great fishing, with winter runs of trout and redfish drawing gaggles of anglers, and nearshore fishing in grass flats keeping them occupied in spring and fall. Scalloping and crabbing are popular, too. Taylor County refers to itself as the "Forest Capital" of Florida, and 90 percent of its land is covered by trees. The Forest Capital State Museum in Perry celebrates this fact.

Steinhatchee

If you're traveling north up the coast, advance notice of this fishing community at the mouth of the Steinhatchee River is served in the nearby town of Jena, just over the Dixie County line. The turnoff along County Road 361 to Steinhatchee (steen-HATCH-ee) is announced by 30 or so small signs plugged into the earth. The town itself (pop. 800) is more pleasant than this initial assault portends. It is oriented toward boating and fishing (but not beaching), with a modest clump of commercial enterprises aimed at the angler, like the full-service **River Haven Marina** (State Route 51, 352/498-0709).

Steinhatchee is a self-described fishing village. Fish camps are everywhere, so come armed with rod and reel and RV. There are no beaches, but people head here in summer to go scalloping in Deadman's Bay, and all year-round to catch speckled trout, Spanish mackerel, redfish, and flounder in the saltwater flats of the gulf. The old bridge over to Jena now serves as a fishing pier and gets packed when redfish run up the Steinhatchee River. The river is a beautiful sight, with an attractive overview offered from the County Road 361 bridge. It looks like the sort of place Charles Kuralt would have ferreted out for his Sunday-morning *Eye on America,* with the sounds of lapping water and laughing gulls audible as the camera holds steady on the peaceful river and forested fringe.

Bunking Down

One of the nicest places to stay in northwest Florida is **Steinhatchee Landing** (State Route 51, 352/498-3513, $$), a collection of 20 cottages, many of them done in the cracker style of architecture (wood frames, tin roofs, open porches) and strewn around an attractive property on the river. A modern all-suites motel a half-mile downriver, the **Steinhatchee River Inn** (State Route 51, 352/498-4049, $), is run by the same owner. These properties, both of which have swimming pools, are the highest-quality accommodations in Steinhatchee, but there are perfectly acceptable and less expensive alternatives geared toward the everyday angler, such as the **Ideal Fish Camp and Motel** (114 Riverside Drive SE, 352/498-3877, $).

Coastal Cuisine

If you haven't managed to catch your own dinner, drop in on **Roy's** (State Route 51 at County Road 361, 352/498-5000,$$), whose glassed-in dining room looks out on the river and its grassy wetlands. Local seafood—including scallops, shrimp, oysters, mullet, and blue crab—is served in entrée-sized portions that range from $8 to $11. Check out the roof of the place for your best recommendation: 50,000 seagulls can't be wrong!

Contact Information

Perry-Taylor County Chamber of Commerce, 428 North Jefferson Street, Perry, FL 32347; 850/584-5366; website: www.perry.gulfnet.com/chamber

Big Bend Wildlife Management Area

Feeling adventurous, we followed a sign to Dallus Creek Landing, part of the Tidal Swamp Unit of the **Big Bend Wildlife Management Area**, a State of Florida gameland. Sandy roads lead into the refuge, with hunters' check-in stations located at the head of several of them, along County Road 361 between Steinhatchee and Keaton Beach. We rumbled our rental car along four miles of backroads before reaching a dead end at a picnic area and boat landing that overlooks a breathtaking marsh. Along the way, we noticed the varied tree species—oaks, maple, ash, gum, and other hardwoods meeting subtropical palms—which suggested an area of ecological overlap. That is to say, we were near the northern range of palm trees and southern range of certain hardwoods, which coexist hereabouts in a kind of patchwork. Spanish moss drapes the limbs of live oaks, and towering coconut palms jut high above the forest canopy.

Another area worth visiting on the same reserve is Hagens Cove, which offers a boat landing and a way into the gulf. Like Dallus Creek Landing, it has no beach, but it's a good crabbing and scalloping area that features a boat ramp, picnic area, and a wildlife observation tower. Camping is available by permit at both Dallus Creek Landing and Hagens Cove (see "Contact Information" below), though it is prohibited from November 1 through January 15.

Contact Information

Big Bend Wildlife Management Area, 663 Plantation Road, Perry, FL 32347; 850/838-1306; website: www.myflorida.com

Keaton Beach

Here's another window on the gulf located in the middle of nowhere. If you're up for investigating what lies at the end of the road out where the road narrows and the population thins, by all means mosey down County Road 361 for a look-see. Keaton Beach (pop. 500) is one of those places that appeals to the sort of person who wishes to be as far away from crowds as possible. The ghost-town look of Keaton Beach is typical of the small villages along Florida's rural Big Bend, where the beachless gulf is lined with houses of weathered wood perched upon tall cinderblock stilts. Some lots sit on canals.

At first glance, you might think they were dug in the hopeful expectation of a building boom that never materialized. The real story dates back to 1993, with a ferocious storm that rose up in the middle of the night and basically washed Keaton Beach and neighboring Dekle Beach off the map. Referred to as the "No Name Storm," it was not a hurricane per se but packed winds clocked at 110 mph, which is stronger than many hurricanes. A 25-foot storm surge that residents describe as coming ashore like a tidal wave completely swamped Taylor County's unsuspecting coastal towns. Moreover, the surge inundated low-lying areas as far as a mile inland.

Eleven people were killed in the Keaton Beach and Dekle Beach area, and survivors tell horrific stories of having to climb up roof-mounted TV antennas with their babies to keep from being washed away. A plaque commemorating the dead has been erected at the Keaton Beach hot-dog stand. The No Name Storm probably set back

MAP OF TAYLOR COUNTY—PAGE 528

the pace of development out here by decades. There used to be three or four good restaurants and motels in Keaton Beach. Now, there's just one of each. And so nature has seen to it, in its indifferent and inevitable way, that the Nature Coast remains as nature intended it.

Beaches

To our unsuspecting and incredulous eyes, there is a sand beach in Keaton Beach. Is it worth making a long detour off U.S. 19 through the wilds of Taylor County? We'll leave it to you to make that call. At the end of the road that winds its way through sleepy Keaton Beach, we found ourselves at Hodges Park. To our amazement, there was a real sand beach. These things are not supposed to exist along the inner crook of Florida, where the West Coast makes its big bend into the Panhandle. The eight counties of the Nature Coast/Big Bend area are not even mentioned in *Florida's Sandy Beaches: An Access Guide,* which was compiled with the aid of the Florida Division of Beaches and Shores and the Division of Coastal Zone Management. Yet we found bona fide sand beaches in the unlikeliest places in nearly every one of those counties, Keaton Beach among them.

At **Hodges Park**, you'll find cement picnic shelters, restrooms, and a sand beach that runs for a couple hundred yards. It's bounded at one end by a rock jetty that protects Keaton Beach's marina, at the mouth of Blue Creek. Bird life is abundant out here, and we felt like interlopers on a stretch of sandy shore that belonged to our winged friends. All the same, we walked the length of the beach several times in amazement and appreciation. What a nice surprise.

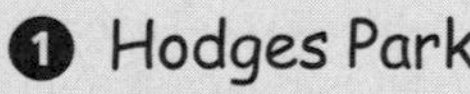

Location: Keaton Beach Drive, in Keaton Beach
Parking/fees: free parking lot
Hours: sunrise to sunset
Facilities: restrooms and picnic tables
Contact: Taylor County Public Works Department, 352/838-3528

BIG BEND

Bunking Down

For reasons noted above, the pickin's out here are slim, but you might try **Keaton Beach Marina, Motel, and Cottages** (County Road 361, 850/578-2897, $) or contact **Beach Realty** (Route 2, Box 165, 850/578-2039), which handles vacation rentals by the weekend, week, or month along this isolated stretch of the Gulf Coast. Otherwise, camping is king in Keaton Beach and Steinhatchee.

Coastal Cuisine

Keaton Beach Hot Dogs (21215 Keaton Beach Drive, 850/578-2675, $) has served commoners and kings—well, presidents, at least, if their claim to have Jimmy Carter's signature in their guest book can be believed. They've also got signatures from residents of all 50 states and many foreign countries as well. We're not talking haute cuisine here—basically hot dogs and whatever else they feel like fixing, which can range from catfish to Salisbury steak.

Night Moves

A short distance north of Keaton Beach, near the junction of County Road 361 and Adams Beach Road, sat Joe's Video, which was offering an unbeatable deal: rent two videos, get one free. The only problem was that Joe's had gone out of business. Its windows were bashed in and had been long since abandoned. A sign on the same road pointed to something called the "Haunted Hayride," and we dutifully followed it to a driveway where we saw a funky-looking truck with "Haunted Hayride" spray-painted on its side. But it was three weeks after

Halloween, so we figured the Haunted Hayride was through for the year and they just hadn't taken the sign down. Ah, so much for night life in Keaton Beach.

Contact Information

Perry-Taylor County Chamber of Commerce, 428 North Jefferson Street, Perry, FL 32347; 850/584-5366; website: www.perry.gulfnet.com/chamber

Dekle Beach

Dekle Beach (pop. 200; pronounced "DEE-kle") is an eerily quiet community of homes on stilts three miles north of Keaton Beach. It doesn't show up on every map of Florida, but a road sign along County Road 361 clearly points to it. Being devotees of backroads and blue highways, we followed the arrow to the water. There, a smattering of homes, maybe two blocks deep, faces the gulf. You might think it's just another no-go development started by some Hekyll, Dekle, Jekyll, or Hyde. But the real culprit was 1993's No Name Storm (see Keaton Beach for a fuller account), which devastated the town.

Some of the surviving or rebuilt homes out here are nice vacation dwellings of weathered wood, hoisted high on cinderblock leggings, while others are dumpy-looking ground-level boxes. Eagles Nest, a rebuilt five-house resort that sits directly on the water, boasts a private fishing pier that extends a quarter mile into the gulf. Some neighboring dwellings are fronted only by pilings: the remnants of docks that collapsed, no doubt, in the ferocious storm. Our proudest find, near the asphalt circle where Dekle Beach comes to an end, was a postage stamp–sized sand beach.

Bunking Down

The aforementioned **Eagles Nest** (Route 2, Box 18, 850/584-7666, $$) comprises five houses arrayed around the gulf and a canal. The homes are rented by the day, week, or month. At $500 or so per week for a two-bedroom, two-bathroom home, it's a steal, but only if you're into isolation, fishing, sunsets, and the like. (Sounds good to us!) You might also call **Beach Realty** (Route 2, Box 165, Keaton Beach, 850/578-2039) about other vacation rentals in Dekle Beach.

Contact Information

Perry-Taylor County Chamber of Commerce, 428 North Jefferson Street, Perry, FL 32347; 850/584-5366; website: www.perry.gulfnet.com/chamber

MAP OF TAYLOR COUNTY—PAGE 528

Adams Beach

There's an intriguing dot on the map labeled Adams Beach, located three miles north of Dekle Beach. But unlike the neighboring communities of Keaton Beach and Dekle Beach—intriguing dots on the map that exist in reality—we could locate hide nor hair of Adams Beach. In short, Adams Beach appears to be a figment of some mapmaker's imagination. Maybe it's a Stephen King–type conjuring that comes to life only at Halloween, visited by the horror merchants behind the Haunted Hayride (see "Night Moves" under Keaton Beach). Confounding the mystery is the cryptic notation about Adams Beach, in a brochure about Florida's "hidden coast," that "cows often wade here."

The truth of the matter is that what small settlement did exist here got wiped out by a hurricane in the 1950s. Not only is there no formal community of Adams Beach left, but there is no beach at the place where Adams Beach is supposed to be. Our best guess is that what gets called Adams Beach today is just a cluster of dwellings at the end of dirt roads off County Road 361, bearing the names of those who live on them (e.g., Dennis Howell Road).

We did find Adams Beach Road, a short spur at a 90-degree bend in County Road 361. This dead-end blacktop leads to a physical barrier at the Gulf of Mexico, at the foot of which lies an assortment of broken beer bottles and other signs of illicit partying after dark. If you were, for some reason (blind drunkenness, perhaps), to shoot past the barrier, your car would wind up in a mudflat. At least you'd have a nice view of the gulf while waiting for the tow truck to arrive.

Contact Information

Perry-Taylor County Chamber of Commerce, 428 North Jefferson Street, Perry, FL 32347; 850/584-5366; website: www.perry.gulfnet.com/chamber

Econfina River State Park and Aucilla River State Canoe Trail

The Econfina (eco-FEEN-a) and Aucilla (aw-SILL-la) are two highly canoeable rivers in northwest Taylor County. Econfina River State Park encompasses 3,377 acres of forest, salt marsh, and pine flatland. This land forms part of the state's park system of canoe trails. To get to the Econfina, take U.S. 98 west from Perry for 20 miles, turn south on State Route 14, and follow this to the river. To get to the Aucilla, proceed west on U.S. 98 from its intersection with State Route 14. Take the first left after Cabbage Grove Road onto an unmarked road and follow the boat ramp signs to the river. For a map and information about put-ins, contact the state park (see below) and ask for a brochure entitled "Historic Big Bend Saltwater Paddling Trail."

Bunking Down

There are campsites, motel rooms, condo rentals, and a swimming pool at **Econfina on the Gulf** (Route 1, Box 255, Perry, 850/584-2135, $), which also has a seafood restaurant open on weekends and some weekdays.

Both rivers are located in northwest Taylor County. To get to the Econfina, take U.S. 98 west from Perry for 20 miles, then turn south on State Route 14 and follow to the river. To get to the Aucilla, proceed west on U.S. 98 from its intersection with State Route 14. Take the first left after Cabbage Grove Road onto an unmarked road and follow the boat ramp signs to the river.

Contact Information

Econfina River State Park, 1022 DeSoto Park Drive, Tallahassee, FL 32301; 850/922-6077; website: www.myflorida.com

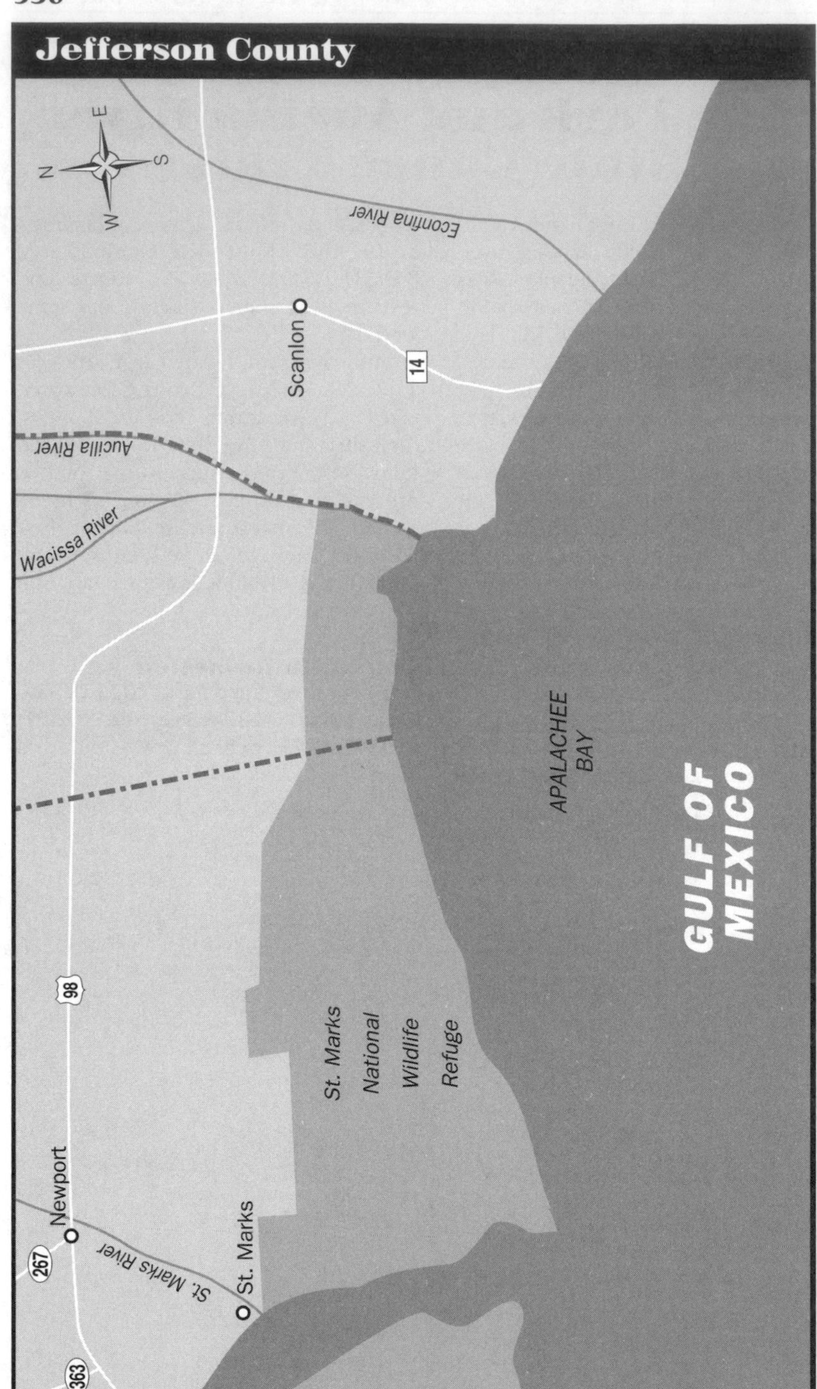
Jefferson County
N
E
S
W
Econfina River
Scanlon
14
Aucilla River
Wacissa River
APALACHEE BAY
GULF OF MEXICO
98
St. Marks National Wildlife Refuge
Newport
267
St. Marks
St. Marks River
363

Jefferson County

Jefferson County is the only county in Florida that touches both Georgia and the Gulf of Mexico. It is unique among in this book in the brevity of its coastline. There are neither roads leading to it nor beaches on it. Shaped like the state of Vermont, the county is widest (24 miles) along the Georgia line and narrowest (six miles) at the Gulf of Mexico. Its coastline lies at the head of Apalachee Bay. U.S. 98 passes through southern Jefferson County. Everything between the highway and the gulf, amounting to 9,000 acres, belongs to St. Marks National Wildlife Refuge. Most of Jefferson County is forest and marshland. At 235 feet in elevation, its county seat, Monticello, is one of the highest points in Florida.

Aucilla River, Wacissa River, and St. Marks National Wildlife Refuge

First, a confession. We didn't initially include Jefferson County in our list of Florida's coastal counties for this book, an omission explained by the fact that most maps don't make it crystal clear that the county extends down to the gulf. In fact, we were driving west along U.S. 98, negotiating the Big Bend between Keaton Beach and Shell Point, when a sign telling us we'd just entered Jefferson County made us do a double take.

Well, even if we had excluded Jefferson County, *Florida Beaches* wouldn't have been much poorer for its omission. The bottom end of the county, south of U.S. 98 to the Gulf of Mexico, belongs to St. Marks National Wildlife Refuge (see the section on Wakulla County), but there's not much to be done out here recreationally and no ready access to the gulf. Even the refuge-provided boat ramp on the Aucilla River, which divides Jefferson and Taylor Counties, is on the Taylor side.

A portion of the Florida National Scenic Trail does cross U.S. 98 in Jefferson County, in addition to passing through the county's refuge lands. Jefferson is mainly a watery wonderland of rivers—the dark, tannic Aucilla and the clear, spring-fed Wacissa, two canoeable rivers that meet at Nutall Rise, and the St. Marks, which skirts the county's western edge before flowing into Wakulla County.

Contact Information

Jefferson County Planning Department, P.O. Box 1069, Monticello, FL 32345; 850/342-0223; website: www.co.jefferson.fl.us

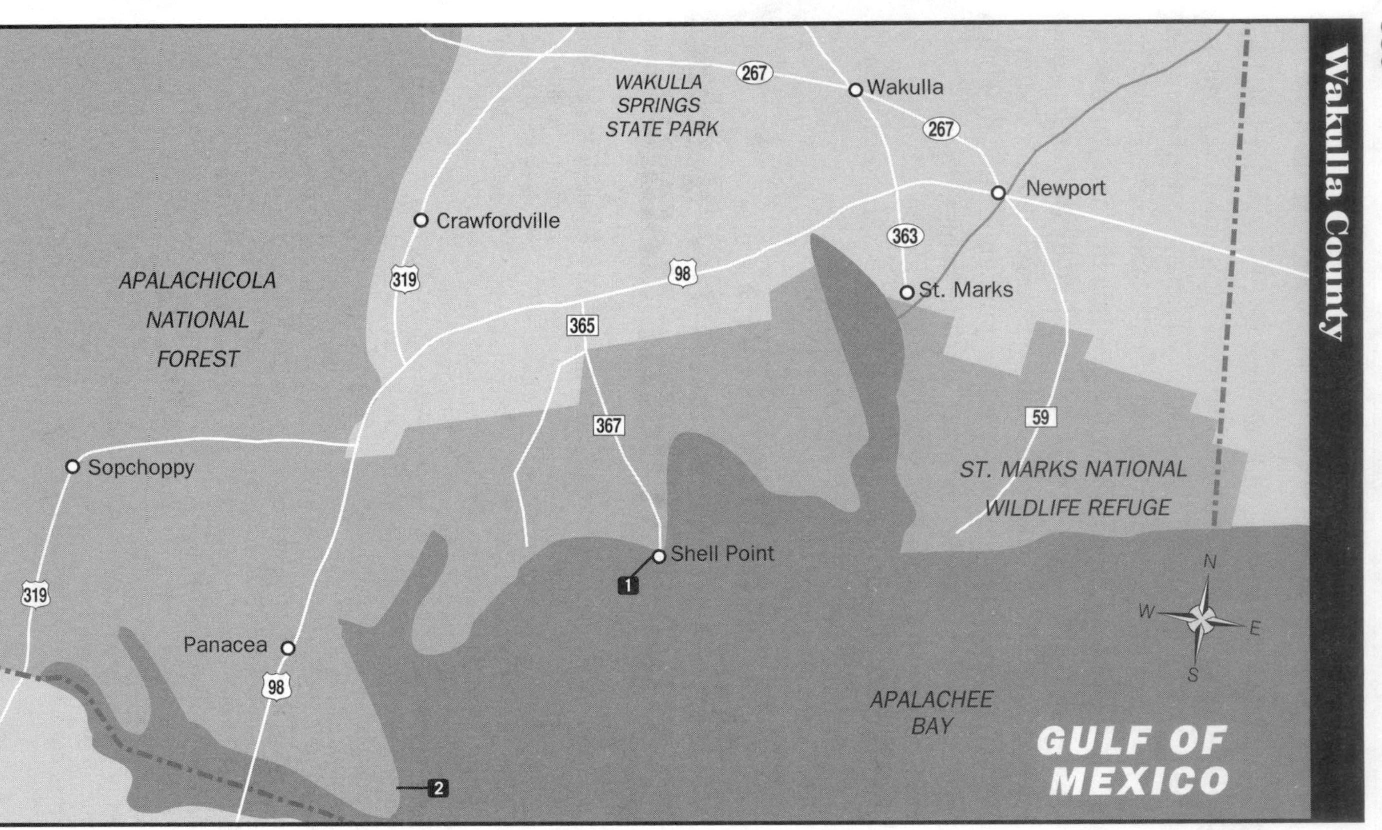
Wakulla County
WAKULLA
SPRINGS
STATE PARK
267
Wakulla
267
Newport
Crawfordville
363
319
98
St. Marks
APALACHICOLA
NATIONAL
FOREST
365
367
59
Sopchoppy
ST. MARKS NATIONAL
WILDLIFE REFUGE
Shell Point
1
N
W
E
S
319
Panacea
98
APALACHEE
BAY
GULF OF
MEXICO
2

Wakulla County

It's hard to believe a county this rural lies so close to Tallahassee, the state capital and a bustling city of 130,000. By comparison, Wakulla County has only 19,000 residents. Much of the land is owned by the federal government. Both Apalachicola National Forest and St. Marks National Wildlife Refuge occupy vast tracts, and Wakulla Springs State Park claims 3,000 acres. Four rivers run through the county—the St. Marks, Sopchoppy, Ochlockonee, and Wakulla. There's plenty of good hiking in Wakulla County. The 16-mile Tallahassee–St. Marks Historical Railroad State Trail runs from the capital to the St. Marks River, and the Florida National Scenic Trail—a 1,300-mile work in progress—crosses the county. Beachgoers have only a few county-owned slivers at Shell Point and Mash Island Park, but anglers who love flats fishing are right at home here.

Newport

The tiny community of Newport (pop. 30), which we saw spelled as both one and two words, is situated 20 miles south of Tallahassee on U.S. 98 at the St. Marks River. It also marks the point at which you've officially rounded Florida's Big Bend. That is to say, you've left the massive peninsular part of the state, and it is a westerly shot across the Panhandle to Pensacola. Aside from this geographical fact, there's really not much to say about Newport except that early in the last century it was the fifth largest city in Florida (with a population of 1,500). Now it's not much larger than a crawdad mound, serving mostly as the gateway to St. Marks National Wildlife Refuge (see below). Newport is also the home of a popular riverside oyster bar. If you're into colorful, offbeat places, Ouzts' makes a good introduction to the sort of funky eateries strewn along U.S. 98 from Newport to the Alabama border.

Coastal Cuisine

If you're attracted to local color, not bothered by curious and/or defiant stares, and like cold beer and oysters, **Ouzts' Too** (7996 U.S. 98, 850/925-6448, $) is the real deal. It's also something of a phoenix. After having burned to the ground in January 2000, the long-lived Ouzts' Oyster Bar was rebuilt and reopened as Ouzts' Too. It just goes to prove you can't keep down a good honky-tonk oyster bar. It is a rather colorful place, sitting on the west bank of the St. Marks River. It is also living proof that the Cajun influence in cooking, drinking, and music-making is not just confined to the bayous of Louisiana. That influence can be found not only along the brief coasts of Mississippi and Alabama but all across Florida's Panhandle. At Ouzts', which has been around since 1969, they'll shuck a dozen of the coldest, freshest Apalachee Bay oysters you'll find anywhere. They're known for smoked mullet, bacon-wrapped shrimp, and shrimp pie, too. Ouzts' also rents canoes, which can be paddled to such attractions as Natural Bridge (seven miles upriver) or the community of St. Marks (three miles downriver).

The regulars at Ouzts' are a cigarette-smoking, beer-guzzling, hell-yessing band of bikers, brigands, and buccaneers. This roadhouse can get pretty wild after dark, judging from the posted snapshots and the scurvy characters we saw hanging around at lunchtime a few years back. One enormous, overalls-clad fellow seemed to be a magician of sorts, making longneck Budweisers disappear faster than you can say "one more for the road." Then he unleashed an incoherent monologue punctuated with fits of snuffling laughter before taking his leave.

We overheard the following dialogue between waitress and customer:

"I saw them dogs were tied up outside and I thought, 'Oh God, they've had them another knock-down drag-out.'"

"What the hell you mumblin' about?"

"Nothin'," said the waitress, resuming her chores behind the bar.

A mustachioed river rat, perhaps intending to taunt us citified carpetbaggers, started ragging on New York: "Heck, we could take these oysters up to New York City and git four times what we git for a dozen down here," he said, chuckling at the absurdity of Northerners. Little did he know that we'uns, Southern by the grace of God, weren't all that put off by his putdowns.

The coup de grâce was provided by a bushy-bearded fellow who, glued to a barstool, fixed us with an unnerving stare.

He was typical of ornery locals who try to rattle outsiders for sport. But we're used to that and didn't take the bait. Instead, we minded our own business and enjoyed the bivalves and brew.

Contact Information
Wakulla County Chamber of Commerce, 23 High Drive, P.O. Box 598, Crawfordville, FL 32326; 850/926-1848; www.tfn.net/~wakullac

St. Marks National Wildlife Refuge

Parkland-studded Wakulla County gets high marks for land preservation. Much of its land—68,000 wild acres of marsh, open water, diked impoundments and slash pine-palmetto forest, plus 31,000 acres of open water in Apalachee Bay—belongs to St. Marks National Wildlife Refuge. Forty miles of the Florida National Scenic Trail pass through here, and another 36 miles of trails cross the refuge, extending into its wild interior or circling ponds and impoundments close to the roadway.

Located at the head of Apalachee Bay, the refuge takes its name from the St. Marks River, which empties into the Gulf of Mexico on refuge land. The visitor center and most accessible part of the refuge lie 20 miles south of Tallahassee, along County Road 59. The visitor center should be your first stop. Orient yourself, ask questions, and collect maps, trail guides, and a checklist of birds sighted on the refuge. Behind the visitor center is Plum Orchard Pond Trail, which skirts a pond and swamp via path and boardwalk. Along the way you'll spy a variety of tree species—pines, palms, and hardwoods grow here—and some scintillating natural sights.

At the end of County Road 59 (11 miles from the U.S. 98 turnoff in Newport) is St. Marks Lighthouse. The present structure dates from 1866, when the 1842 original was rebuilt after being blown up during the Civil War. The tower is crowned by a red top housing an electric lamp that can be seen for 15 miles. If you've traveled all the way out here, the 80-foot-tall lighthouse is a mandatory photo opportunity. Next to it is a wildlife viewing stand. Close by is an impoundment with a levee mounded around it. On one side of the levee is the Gulf of Mexico; on the other, a pond filled with native and migratory birds. We saw all kinds of great and graceful winged wonders out here: wood ducks, cormorants, egrets, herons, ibises. Nearly 300 bird species have been identified on the refuge. Alligators were visible, too, sunning themselves on the banks.

Although you can't camp on the refuge unless you're a through hiker on the Florida National Scenic Trail, opportunities for outdoor recreation are abundant. They include hiking, picnicking, bird-watching, wildlife observation, boating, fishing, crabbing, and hunting.

Beaches

Always intrepid when it comes to tracking down sand beaches, we spread out a giant map of Wakulla County and looked for any road that might lead to a beach. Most of Wakulla County's coast is saltwater marsh, so we weren't hopeful. Still, Wakulla Beach Road looked promising, so we turned off U.S. 98 and proceeded four miles down a sandy, mildly rutted road through St. Marks National Wildlife Refuge. We passed pickup trucks and camouflaged hunters carrying bows and arrows, tracking hapless critters through the woods. Soon we were at the muddy end of the road, face

Map of Wakulla County—Page 538

to face with a flock of scurrying fiddler crabs. We won't stretch credibility by calling it a beach, but there is a 24-hour boat launch here, and it is yet another open window on the wide, wonderful gulf.

Contact Information
St. Marks National Wildlife Refuge, 1255 Lighthouse Road, P.O. Box 68, St. Marks, FL 32355; 850/925-6121; www.saintmarks.fws.gov

Wakulla Springs State Park

Wakulla Springs State Park and Lodge are located 15 miles south of Tallahassee and seven miles northwest of Newport on State Route 267, and are well worth the inland detour off U.S. 98. The natural feature from which the park takes its name is one of the deepest and largest freshwater springs in the world. Water flows out of the ground through the limestone aquifer at the rate of 600,000 gallons per minute. There's a swimming beach by the marina at the spring's headwaters, as well as a dive tower from which one can jump into pure, limpid waters. We found the dive tower rules interesting and unusual enough to warrant repeating, having never seen anything quite like them:

- No jumping while boats are near tower.
- Only two persons may jump at a time.
- No swimming over the spring.
- No jumping from the rails.
- No gainers, inwards, or handstands.

Park admission costs $3.25 per vehicle. Tours via both glass-bottom boat and ordinary pontoon boats depart hourly and cost $4.50 per adult ($2.25 for kids under 12). Wildlife can be viewed on the shore, plants and marine life in the water. Overlooking the spring-fed lake is the park's man-made centerpiece, **Wakulla Springs Lodge** (550 Wakulla Park Drive, 850/224-5950, $$). This august old building was constructed in 1937 by entrepreneur and railroad magnate Edward Ball. Its 27 rooms are appointed with marble floors and antique furnishings. Rooms run from $69 to $90 a night.

In the lobby is an enormous Plexiglas case in which a giant alligator known as Old Joe is interred. Old Joe was known in these parts as "the most photographed wild alligator in existence" until some criminals killed him in 1966. A $5,000 reward was offered, but the perpetrators were never caught. A sign above the case of this 12-foot reptile says it all: "This is Old Joe's one and only cage."

A network of trails crisscrosses the 3,000-acre forest surrounding the lodge and springs. If you are going to lay over in Wakulla County, Wakulla Springs Lodge is the best and practically the only place to stay (save for Shell Point Resort). We recommend it highly.

Contact Information
Wakulla Springs State Park, 550 Wakulla Park Drive, Wakulla Springs, FL 32305; 850/922-3632; www.myflorida.com

Shell Point

Shell Point (pop. 300) occupies a knob of land extending into the gulf at about the county's coastal midsection. Most of Wakulla County, including its coastline, is taken up by St. Marks National Wildlife Refuge and Apalachicola National Forest. However, out on this tip—which includes the small communities of Shell Point, Live Point, and Oyster Bay—private homes line the gulf and Shell Point Resort lies at the end of the road. It's not the bustling, thriving place evoked by the word "resort" but is instead another unexpected hideaway along the Forgotten Coast.

Beaches

Shell Point Beach is a sandy/muddy tidal flat along a calmwater stretch of the gulf at the head of Apalachee Bay. Along the beach, a concrete seawall protects the modest homes scattered along its length. It wasn't much use in 1998, when Hurricane Georges drove a four-foot wall of water onshore, damaging a lot of the ground-level homes. The county maintains a small beach park on this narrow, sandy shore—one of two sand beaches in all of Wakulla County.

Bunking Down

Shell Point Resort is a triple-threat operation that includes a marina, motel, and restaurant. You can berth your boat at the Shell Point Marina, satiate your seafood cravings at Shell Point Restaurant, or bunk down at the **Shell Point Motel** (1541 Shell Point Road, 850/926-7163, $). The motel is an extremely modest place—cinderblock walls, dropped acoustic-tile ceiling, mattresses that crackle when you move on them—that's comparable to a Motel 6. In other words, you'll get a clean room for a fair price, and that is exactly what the anglers who come here are angling for. Save for the lodge at Wakulla Springs State Park, there are virtually no other places to stay in Wakulla County, unless you're camping like a bear in the woods.

Coastal Cuisine

It doesn't look like much from the outside, but the **Shell Point Restaurant** (1541 Shell Point Road, 850/926-7161, $$) puts on a hell of a spread when it comes to seafood. In the words of an overexcited elderly gentleman, exclaiming between mouthfuls, "I've been coming here for 13 years, and the food is better than ever!" This same gourmand also announced, "I've fallen in love four times tonight!" We watched as he danced with the hostess and waitress to ragtime numbers performed by the house pianist. Some guys have all the luck!

On one wall is a mural with a tarpon leaping from the water; on another, a painting of St. Marks Lighthouse. At Shell Point Restaurant, they'll broil or fry just about any seafood item you can name—grouper, mullet, shrimp, oysters, and such—with a slightly spicy Cajun breading. If the seafood platter happens to be on special, by all means go for it, especially if you're packing an appetite. This

❶ Shell Point Beach

Location: From U.S. 98 (Coastal Highway) east of Medart, turn south on Spring Creek Highway (County Road 365), then follow for 1.5 miles. At a fork in the road, take the left fork (Shell Point Road/County Road 367) and follow until it ends at Shell Point Beach.
Parking/fees: free parking lot
Hours: sunrise to sunset
Facilities: restrooms, picnic tables, and showers
Contact: Wakulla County Parks and Recreation Department, 850/926-7227

MAP OF WAKULLA COUNTY—PAGE 538

multi-plate extravaganza includes fried oysters, scallops, grouper, and Alaskan snow crab legs, plus salad, potato, and dessert. We waddled away sated and happy, wondering how our fellow diner had any energy left to dance.

Night Moves

Across the marina from the Shell Point Restaurant glow the unmistakable outlines of neon beer logos. If you've got the inclination or need for a drink, just follow the hot pinks and purples to the tavern beside the marina at the end of the road. We, on the other hand, were too stuffed to even wander over and check out its name, instead returning to the Shell Point Motel to belly-flop on the crackling mattresses.

Contact Information

Wakulla County Chamber of Commerce, 23 High Drive, P.O. Box 598, Crawfordville, FL 32326; 850/926-1848; www.tfn.net/~wakullac

Panacea

The town of Panacea (pop. 1,200), located at a point where U.S. 98 runs a direct north-south axis, isn't quite the cure-all for body and spirit that its name promises. Still, it's a haven for retirees and a home for working fishermen. You will find a handful of seafood eateries by the side of the road and one noteworthy attraction that plays to the interests of this book: the **Gulf Specimen Marine Laboratory** (300 Clark Drive, 850/984-5297). The lab's specimen tanks present an array of bizarre and beautiful underwater life forms found in the Gulf of Mexico, from jellyfish to hermit crabs, sharks to stingrays. Admission is $4.50 for adults and $2 for children under 12, and the museum is open seven days a week.

❷ Mash Island Park

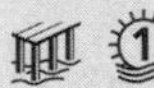

Location: from Panacea, take U.S. 98 south for three miles, then turn west on Mashes Sands Road (County Road 372) and follow two miles to the park

Parking/fees: free parking lot

Hours: sunrise to sunset

Facilities: restrooms and picnic tables

Contact: Wakulla County Parks and Recreation Department, 850/926-7227

Beaches

Mash Island Park is located southwest of Panacea on Ochlockonee Bay. Or at least there used to be a beach, until the hurricanes of '98 (especially Georges) severely eroded it. Because of its shallow water, it's a nice place for children to swim. There's also a formidable fishing pier. As for the fate of the missing beach, "we're working on it," a county parks administrator promised.

Coastal Cuisine

They likes to eat in this part of the state, and what they likes to eat is seafood. The **Harbor House** (107 Mississippi Avenue, 850/984-2758, $$) has a great broiled seafood platter and a quiet, civilized atmosphere. A little spicier, in terms of food and setting, is **Angelo's Seafood Restaurant** (U.S. 98, 850/984-5168, $$), which features raw oysters, heads-on shrimp, and seafood Creole.

Contact Information

Wakulla County Chamber of Commerce, 23 High Drive, P.O. Box 598, Crawfordville, FL 32326; (850/926-1848; www.tfn.net/~wakullac

MAP OF BIG BEND—PAGE 489

The Panhandle

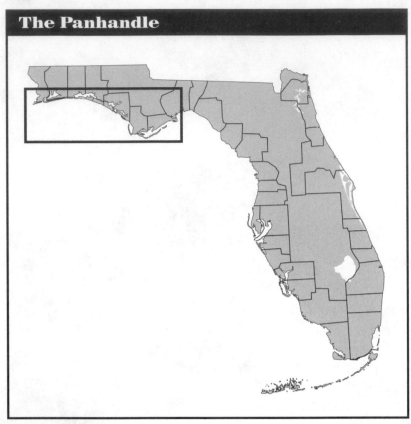

Key to the Symbols

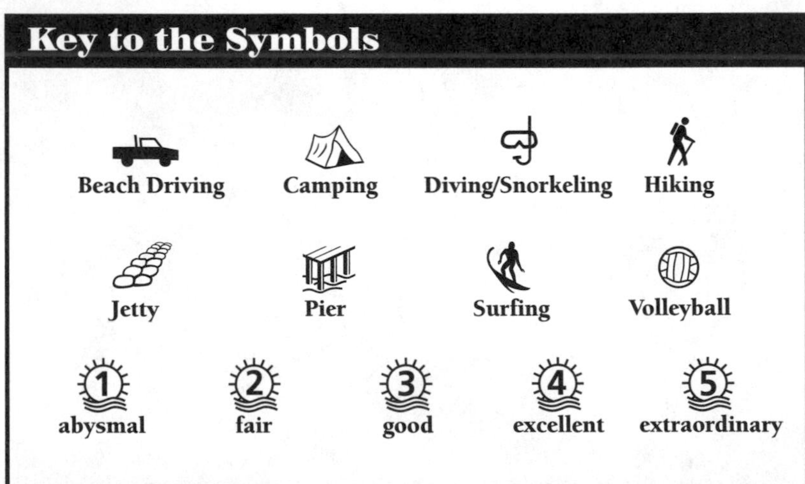

The Panhandle

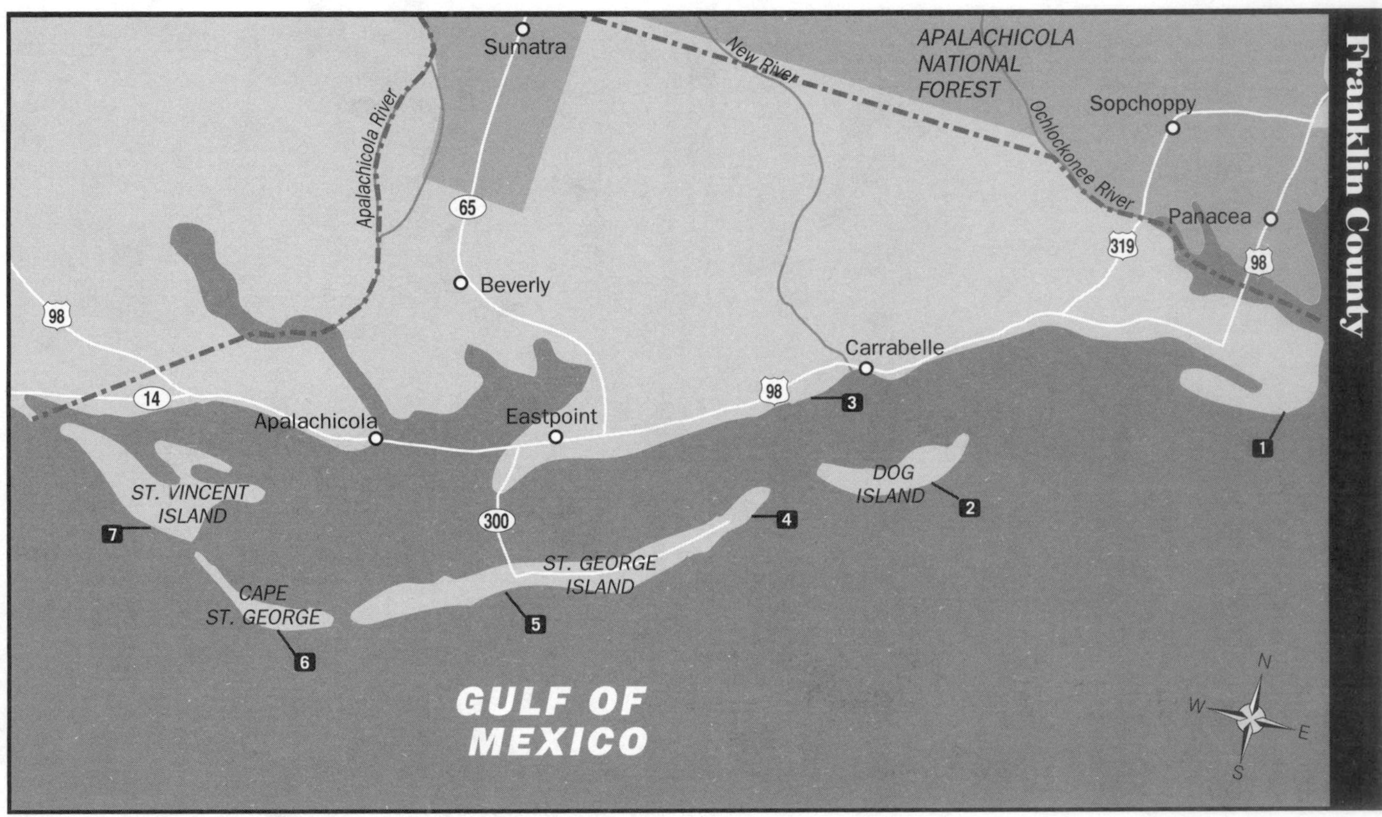
Franklin County
Sumatra
Apalachicola River
New River
APALACHICOLA
NATIONAL
FOREST
Sopchoppy
Ochlockonee River
Panacea
319
98
65
Beverly
98
14
Apalachicola
Eastpoint
Carrabelle
98
3
1
DOG
ISLAND
2
4
300
ST. VINCENT
ISLAND
7
ST. GEORGE
ISLAND
5
CAPE
ST. GEORGE
6
GULF OF
MEXICO
N
W
E
S

FRANKLIN COUNTY

Franklin County has the best of both worlds: great, sandy Panhandle beaches and the appealing isolation of the Nature Coast/Big Bend counties. Franklin County is large in size (545 square miles) but small in population (under 11,000). They like to call it "Florida's Final Frontier" and "the Forgotten Coast," Franklin County claims 60 miles of sandy coastline on its four barrier islands: Dog, St. George, Little St. George, and St. Vincent. Fortunately, preservationists have beat developers to most of it. St. George Island is the exception, though much of its east end is a state park. On the mainland, there's the extremely ingratiating town of Apalachicola, long famous for its oysters and lately gaining attention for its inns and restaurants. Apalachicola is also the home of the county's one traffic light: a blinker located downtown. If you come to Franklin County, you might want to heed the blinking light's reminder to stop and relax.

Alligator Point

At the east end of Franklin County, a peninsular knob of land juts into Apalachee Bay. It looks from the map like a barrier island that has been welded to the mainland at one end, with the thinnest sliver of sand extending westward from it into the bay. The turnoff from U.S. 98 to **Alligator Point** (pop. 100) lies just south of a bridge that crosses the Ochlockonee River. The bridge is an impressive edifice spanning a beautiful waterway, and it's worth your undivided attention. If you spy a trailer parked at the west end where they're selling boiled peanuts—a Southern tradition that makes a salty, soggy snack—by all means buy a bag.

So what's out here? For one thing, a lot of private homes plopped on a peninsular sliver that looks to be eroding. It's worth the drive just to witness firsthand how inappropriate certain kinds of construction can be on a dynamic, shifting barrier-spit environment. At one point along its midsection, the stilt-like pilings on which homes have been built are practically standing in water, and beach erosion has exposed their concrete moorings. There are no houses along one stretch, where storms such as 1998's Hurricane Earl appear to have razed the place. On the backside, road signs warn of flooding, and it's obvious that storm overwash is a not-infrequent hazard.

❶ Alligator Point

Location: scattered accesses along County Road 370 at Alligator Point
Parking/fees: free street parking
Hours: sunrise to sunset
Facilities: none
Contact: Franklin County Parks and Services Department, 850/927-2111

Bunking Down

Most of the construction at Alligator Point is ill-advisedly located on the west side of the island, along the narrow peninsular spit. It's not our idea of a day at the beach, but if you want to rent a house at Alligator Point, contact **Coastal Shores Realty** (53 Coastal Highway, Crawfordville, FL 32327; 850/984-5800). Many folks come out to Alligator Point to camp at **Alligator Point KOA** (County Road 370, 850/349-2525) or to use the facilities at **Alligator Point Marina** (3461 County Road 370, 850/349-2511), a large, full-service marina, bait shop, restaurant, and lounge at the west end.

Contact Information

Carrabelle Area Chamber of Commerce, U.S. 98 (Carrabelle Mini Mall), P.O. Drawer DD, Carrabelle, FL 32322; 850/697-2585; website: www.carrabelle.org

Lanark Village

Lanark Village (pop. 1,000) used to be the site of Camp Gordon Johnson, an army base where personnel were trained for amphibious assaults. In fact, some of those who passed through Camp Gordon landed on the beaches of France during the now-legendary D-Day invasion. They practiced by staging landings on nearby Dog Island. Since 1996, there's been an annual three-day reunion of veterans who served at Camp Gordon. A new feature is the **Camp Gordon Johnson Museum**, located in a small house on 4th Street. It's open from 1000 hours till 1400 hours (that's 10 A.M. to 2 P.M. to you civies) on Saturday.

The camp existed for three years, then a

developer came in and replaced the tarpaper barracks with rows of concrete ground-floor condos that stand to this day. Mainly, they're occupied by retirees. Lanark Village was advertised in big-city newspapers across the Midwest back in the 1950s, so most of its residents are from Chicago, Wisconsin, Pennsylvania, and so forth. For someone desiring a quiet, convivial place to retire, Lanark (LAN-ark) Village practically sells itself. A lot of folks come down to visit a friend or relative and wind up liking it so much they stay.

This quiet, likable gulfside community between Alligator Point and Carrabelle on U.S. 98 has its own post office, fire department, boat club, and six-hole golf course. Lanark residents also have a community center where they congregate to drink coffee, swap stories, and gossip. Some apartments are available for rental and occasionally come up for sale. There are no beaches in serene Lanark, and seemingly no one under retirement age, either. "That's what we need, younger people to get involved," asserted the septuagenarian president of the Lanark Village Association. We think it's fine just the way it is.

Contact Information

Carrabelle Area Chamber of Commerce, U.S. 98 (Carrabelle Mini Mall), P.O. Drawer DD, Carrabelle, FL 32322; 850/697-2585; website: www.carrabelle.org

Carrabelle and Carrabelle Beach

Carrabelle (pop. 2,000) calls itself "the pearl of the Panhandle," and with its watery setting, that is no idle boast. Its south side faces St. George Sound, on the Gulf of Mexico. On the west side, it is bounded by the Carrabelle River, formed by the confluence of the Crooked and New Rivers. Carrabelle is a small town that hasn't changed much in the last half century. According to a resident who's been around that long, it hasn't changed at all. No wonder they call it the Forgotten Coast.

Carrabelle is the sort of town that never misses an opportunity to trumpet its novelty tourist attraction: "the World's Smallest Police Station," which is located inside a phone booth. Mostly, Carrabelle is populated by those who work the water—fishers, shrimpers, oystermen—and those who have come to retire on its quiet shores. There are a good number of docks and marinas at which one can charter a fishing boat. It is the logical place to begin or end a trip down the Gulf Coast. The real appeal of Carrabelle is the location on the water, the absence of a high-powered tourist industry, and the air of honest community that it's able to project as a result.

Beaches

Just west of town is **Carrabelle Beach**, a lengthy strand that gets a little larger each time another storm chews away more trees and highway roadbed to uncover the underlying sand. The beach has, thanks to Hurricanes Opal and Earl, already doubled in length to about 3.5 miles. At

2 Carrabelle Beach

Location: one mile west of Carrabelle on U.S. 98
Parking/fees: free parking lot
Hours: sunrise to sunset
Facilities: restrooms and picnic tables
Contact: Florida Department of Transportation (District 3), 850/697-3838

MAP OF FRANKLIN COUNTY—PAGE 548

this rate, it won't be long before the 13-mile stretch from Carrabelle to Eastpoint is all beach. Of course, this will necessitate relocating parts of U.S. 98 (Coastal Highway), which takes a beating each time another storm chomps at it. The underreported Hurricane Earl, with its 110 mph winds and storm surge, really did a number on the highway, one lane of which had to be closed while repairs were made.

Carrabelle Beach runs directly along U.S. 98, and provides free parking, restrooms, and concrete picnic tables. A boardwalk leads to the beach. There's not much in the way of action on this laid-back beach. Just bring your chair, towel, and book, and prepare to spend a good, old-fashioned day at the beach.

Bunking Down

Island View Inn (1714 U.S. 98 East, 850/697-2050, $) benefits from its location on the gulf, where it looks out on St. George and Dog Islands. There are cottages (with and without full kitchens), free boat slips for guests, boat rentals, an RV park, and two fishing piers. The atmosphere is friendly and the attitude down-home. In their own words, "We love fishin' and bluegrass pickin'." Yahoo!

A modest step up the lodgings ladder is the **Moorings** (1000 U.S. 98, 850/697-2800, $), which is still plenty cheap ($55–65 per night). It's also a marina-motel combo, offering excursions to Dog Island as well as docking services for those piloting their own boats. Directly across from Carrabelle Beach is a 48-site campground called **Sting Ray Station RV Park** (U.S. 98, P.O. Box 929, 850/697-2638, $). You couldn't ask for a nicer location.

Coastal Cuisine

Julia Mae's (U.S. 98, 850/697-3791, $$) enjoys a worldwide reputation for its down-home cooking, particularly the seafood chowders and fresh-fish preparations conjured by the restaurant's legendary namesake. Though Julia Mae herself is retired, the restaurant hasn't missed a beat. In a town that hauls in a daily bounty of seafood, you really can't go wrong anywhere you sit down to eat. A couple of other local favorites are the **Shrimp House** (201 West 11th Street, 850/697-2098, $$) and **Harry's Georgian Restaurant** (113 St. James Avenue NW, 850/697-3400, $$).

Night Moves

During our admittedly brief passage through Carrabelle, we couldn't help but notice the number of bars and lounges, some open and others out of business. Among the former is **Harry's Bar and Lounge** (306 Marine Street, 850/697-9982), located downtown. Hey, if you worked on the water all day, wrestling with shrimp nets, crab traps, and oyster bars, wouldn't you want to knock back a tall cool one when you hit dry land?

Contact Information

Carrabelle Area Chamber of Commerce, U.S. 98 (Carrabelle Mini Mall), P.O. Drawer DD, Carrabelle, FL 32322; 850/697-2585; website: www.carrabelle.org

Dog Island

Long, narrow, and sandy barrier islands begin reappearing on the Panhandle side of the Big Bend around Franklin County. The first east-west barrier of any size is Dog Island (pop. 12), which lies 3.5 miles offshore and is seven miles long. There are no bridges to the island, which has insured that it remains relatively undeveloped. Some 1,100 acres have been set aside as the Jeff Lewis Wilderness Preserve, with the Nature Conservancy and the Barrier Island Trust involved (though not always amicably) in their acquisition and management.

Around a hundred small homes dot the island, with the late Florida governor Lawton Chiles among the landowners. There is one small inn and no stores on Dog Island, necessitating provisioning trips to the mainland via private boat or ferry. (To inquire about ferry schedules or to charter a private run over, call Captain Raymond Williams at 850/657-3434.) The soothing sounds of the surf, the seasonal comings and goings of 270 bird species, and an isolated beach on which to swim, shell, surfcast, or meditate make Dog Island an untrammeled paradise.

Beaches

Six miles of white-sand beach run along **Dog Island**'s south side. An area of sand dunes rising to heights of 50 feet is referred to as "the mountains." Inland are freshwater marshes and stands of live oak and slash pine. Hiking trails crisscross the preserve. Anyone who would say "there is not much to do" out here really means "there is no place to shop or watch TV." In other words, they have no love for or grounding in the real world of nature.

Bunking Down

A perfect getaway can be had by tossing a line into the gulf, landing a redfish for dinner, and cooking it in your room at the **Pelican Inn** (Dog Island, 850/697-4728, $$). Built in the '60s and grandfathered in as the only commercial structure on Dog Island, the inn has eight efficiency apartments with sliding glass doors that face the gulf. It's almost what's not available that's most appealing. The Pelican Inn has no TVs or VCRs and just one cellular phone in case of emergency. There are not many places left where you can have that kind of experience. The mailing address for the Pelican Inn is P.O. Box 123, Apalachicola, FL 32329.

Contact Information

Carrabelle Area Chamber of Commerce, U.S. 98 (Carrabelle Mini Mall), P.O. Drawer DD, Carrabelle, FL 32322; 850/697-2585; website: www.carabelle.org

❸ Dog Island

Location: 3.5 miles south of Carrabelle in the Gulf of Mexico
Parking/fees: no parking; free day use of beach
Hours: sunrise to sunset
Facilities: none
Contact: Northwest Florida Chapter of the Nature Conservancy, 850/643-2756

St. George Island

St. George Island (pop. 1,000) was the first serious stretch of sand reachable by road and bridge we'd laid eyes on since leaving the Clearwater area on Florida's West Coast. The "road and bridge" provision, of course, excludes Dog Island (see separate entry), which lies just east of St. George Island and is reachable by boat only. The mainland approach to St. George Island is the town of Eastpoint, which is basically one long seafood-offloading dock. The four-mile ride out to St. George Island along State Route 300 is a real dipsy-doodle: part roller-coaster bridge, part causeway crossing man-made keys nearly at sea level. On the east side of the bridge lies St. George Sound; on the west side, Apalachicola Bay. Wonderfully plump oysters, tasty small calico scallops, and serious eating fish like grouper, redfish, mackerel, and flounder are plucked from these teeming gulf and bay waters.

St. George Island is long and narrow, oriented northeast to southwest. The island is roughly 20 miles in length, with nine miles at the eastern end preserved as St. George Island State Park. From the point where the causeway meets the island at its midsection, it is four miles to the state park guard station. Four miles of paved road continue into the park, and four miles of dirt road lie beyond that. The state park is the natural treasure and saving grace of St. George Island, which is otherwise succumbing to willy-nilly development.

It is a lovely island, many of whose natural features remain intact, but it is in the process of a transition that can only portend more of the sorts of things that make havens like this one less appealing: more houses, more traffic, more people (which is to say, more people who can afford it). Ultimately, there will be fewer uncrowded beaches and less of the backside habitat that made the island attractive in the first place. One piece of tourist literature had the audacity to claim, "Strict building codes and low-density zoning regulations have preserved the beauty of St. George." Yeah, and voting in Florida is as smooth as a pair of silk drawers. Those who are plotting St. George's future would do well to study the story of the goose that laid the golden egg.

We were struck by several ironies during our time on the island. First of all, signs warn of penalties as high as $1,000 for disturbing sea oats or $500 for riding vehicles on the dunes. Yet it is perfectly legal for earth-moving equipment to raze the dunes, vegetation and all, in order to put up another vacation home. On an otherwise peaceful Saturday, we saw lots being flattened and heard the whirring of band saws as home construction proceeded apace. Another irony: while looking for a place to mail postcards, we were told there was not a post office or even a street-corner mailbox on the island. "Put your mail in the private mailbox outside one of the real-estate offices and raise the flag," we were told by a convenience-store clerk. "That's what everyone else does." Let us get this straight: developers more or less get to do anything they want on St. George, yet the island lacks a mailbox so that some fiction about its isolation from the ways of the mainland world can be preserved. Where is the sense in any of this?

The best evidence of folly at work on St. George greets the eye upon one's arrival on the island. Directly on the beach sits a stunningly ugly row of narrow, vertical shotgun cottages. Pressed as close together as New York City brownstones, painted in loud colors, they act as a wall to obstruct views of the beach. One other note: at the west end of the island, the road gives out at a private development, St. George Plantation, with a guard gate. The real affront here is that boaters cannot launch from the west end of St. George Island and cross the man-made channel to Little St. George Island. Fording this brief cut is the simplest way to get there, but boaters must instead take a different approach. Lot by lot, gate by gate, and dollar by dollar, St. George Island is under siege. Since it is being developed rather late in the game, you might think they would have learned from mistakes made during the big-bucks building boom that brought many island environments to their knees.

Okay, enough bashing of St. George Island. We're only pointing all this out because there's still much that's good about the island and much left to preserve. At present, the island's year-round residents number 1,000, but that is growing every year. Many visitors come from Tallahassee and Atlanta. Typically, they vacation here and like it so much they build a second home, which they then rent out through a local realtor in the summer months. During quieter times of year, they live here themselves, subsidizing their mortgage with summer rental income. Thus, in the summer you see lots of families on the island. Many of the rental homes have four or five bedrooms and sleep from eight to ten people, so families share a rental for a one- or two-week vacation. Here are a few sample home names and weekly prices, for your information (and amusement): Loafer's Glory ($1,225 summer, $695 winter), Stairway to Heaven ($1,175 summer, $655 winter), Beachy Keen ($1,095 summer, $595 winter). In general, weekly beach-house rentals run about $1,110 to $1,200 in summer and $600 to $700 in winter. This is the reverse of the scenario in South Florida, where winter is the high season.

You'd be hard pressed to find a nicer place to kick back and relax than St. George Island. We just hope that prudent reins are applied to growth and development so that it remains that way.

Beaches

First, a factlet: the tallest spot in Franklin County is a 55-foot sand dune on St. George Island. Ride along St. George Island via bicycle, as we did for its entire paved length, and you'll appreciate the ground-level view of the dunes. They are more substantial, for obvious reasons, in St. George Island State Park than on the inhabited parts of the island. Not to beat a dead horse, but just compare the high, humpbacked dunes in the state park with the modest mounds along Gorrie Drive.

The beaches of St. George Island are wide and fine, brownish-white, and gently sloping across a broad berm. A ridge of small, mostly whole shells identifies the high-tide line. The water temperature out here on the Panhandle explains why late fall and winter is a down time, compared to peninsular south Florida. The gulf cools precipitously after September, bottoming out at around 60 unswimmable degrees from December through February. It warms up quickly in March and hits a peak around 80°F for much of the summer. This is a great beach for hiking, and these are great beach roads for biking. (For cheap bike rentals, drop by Island Adventures, on East Gulf Drive.)

St. George Island State Park is the island's natural highlight. A couple of miles past the entrance station is a large parking lot and a wooden pavilion with showers and picnic tables that faces the beach. The same complement of facilities

4 St. George Island State Park

Location: from the south end of Bryant Patton Causeway (State Route 300) on St. George Island, turn east on Gulf Drive and follow the road four miles to the park entrance

Parking/fees: $4 per vehicle entrance fee. Camping fees are $10 per night with full hookups and $8 without

Hours: 8 A.M. to sunset

Facilities: restrooms, picnic tables, and showers

Contact: St. George Island State Park, 850/927-2111

5 St. George Island Public Beach

Location: on St. George Island at Bryant Patton Causeway (State Route 300) and West Gorrie Drive

Parking/fees: free parking lot

Hours: 24 hours

Facilities: restrooms and picnic tables

Contact: Franklin County Planning Department, 850/653-9783

is repeated a few miles farther down. A campground on the Apalachicola Bay side of the island comes with full hookups. Alternatively, backpackers can hike a 2.5-mile trail through pine flatwoods from the developed campground out to Gap Point, where primitive camping is permitted.

St. George Island Public Beach is located where the causeway meets the island. There's a free parking lot but no visitor facilities even though they've been long promised and are long overdue. Mother Nature has done her part, providing an ample strand that stretches for miles in either direction.

Shore Things

- **Bike/skate rentals:** Island Adventures, 115 East Gulf Drive, St. George Island, 850/927-3655.
- **Boat cruise:** Governor Stone, 268 Water Street, Apalachicola, 850/653-8700.
- **Dive shop:** Captain Black's Dive Center, U.S. 98, Port St. Joe, 850/229-6332.
- **Ecotourism:** Jeanni's Journeys, 240 East 3rd Street, 850/927-3259.
- **Fishing charters:** Rockfish Charters, 925 East Gulf Drive, St. George Island, 850/927-3839.
- **Lighthouse:** Cape St. George Lighthouse, Little St. George Island.
- **Marina:** Rainbow Marina, 123 Water Street, Apalachicola, 850/653-8139.
- **Pier:** "Think of St. George Island as a massive fishing pier jutting five miles out into the Gulf of Mexico across one of the most productive estuaries in the world."—John B. Spohrer, Jr., *Fish St. George Island,* Florida.
- **Rainy day attraction:** Apalachicola National Estuarine Research Reserve, 261 7th Street, Apalachicola, 850/653-8063.
- **Shopping/browsing:** Avenue D and Commerce Street, Apalachicola.
- **Vacation rentals:** Collins Vacation Rentals, 60 East Gulf Beach Drive, St. George Island, 850/927-2900 or 800/423-7418; and Prudential Resort Realty, 123 West Gulf Drive, St. George Island, 850/927-2666 or 800/332-5196.

Bunking Down

St. George Island is geared to the rental of vacation homes for stays of one or more weeks. During the high summer season, you will pay between $600 and $2,000 a week for a vacation rental, depending on size, amenities, and location, location, location. They all have evocative names like Sea Spell, Serendipity, Island Dream, and A Bit of Paradise. Would you be surprised to learn that one of largest, most lavishly appointed and expensive is called Doctor's Orders? A broad selection of rental properties is handled by Collins and Prudential (see Shore Things, above).

Motels are few and far between, except for the **Buccaneer** (160 West Gorrie Drive, 850/927-2585, $$), a rather plain-looking but serviceable leviathan that looks like it drifted up from Treasure Island on Florida's West Coast. It's smack-dab on the beach at the end of the causeway. The rooms are simply furnished and cleanly kept.

There is one more option: the **St. George Inn** (135 Franklin Boulevard, 850/927-2903, $$). More appealing than a motel and less expensive than a house rental, the inn is a fine place to lay over on the island—quiet and civilized yet only a block away from the beach. It is a white Victorian three-story, trimmed in blue with wraparound porches. The rooms in this elegant wooden wonder—which feels more like a rambling hotel than a bed-and-breakfast—are homey and well appointed. TVs are ingeniously stashed in built-in cabinets over the closet, with doors that shut to hide the idiot box (which we closed pronto).

We Dream of Jeanni

If you've got the bug to see what lies beyond the horizon, give Jeanni McMillan a ring. She is the impresario behind Journeys of St. George Island (a.k.a. Jeanni's Journeys), an ecotourism outfit based on St. George Island that specializes in boat trips to the surrounding barrier islands and waterways. Jeanni leads her journeys from March 5 through December 31. Destinations include Little St. George Island, St. Vincent National Wildlife Refuge, and Dog Island. She also leads trips up the Apalachicola River and to Owl Creek, in Apalachicola National Forest.

She'll take you fishing, crabbing, oystering, or shelling. You can opt for motorized boat trips or paddle a kayak or canoe. Not everything is geared to adults. She'll teach kids how to make sand sculptures on the beach, and there are "kids-only trips." Her prices are very reasonable, given the time, equipment, and expertise involved. A three-hour guided boat trip (e.g., "oyster adventure," "birding cruise") for up to six people costs $200. Half-day (four- or five-hour) trips to Little St. George Island run $250. All-day trips to Dog Island or St. Vincent Island are $375. Kayak and canoe paddles of a half day ($50 per person) and full day ($75 per person) go everywhere: St. Vincent, Little St. George, blackwater creeks, you name it. Moreover, Jeanni's knowledge of the area is vast and her enthusiasm genuine.

For more information, contact Journeys of St. George Island, 240 East 3rd Street, St. George Island, FL 32328; 850/927-3259; website: www.sgislandjourneys.com.

Coastal Cuisine

Set sail for the **Oyster Cove** (201 East Pine Street, 850/927-2600, $$$), located on the sound side of the island and out of the way. Ascend the stairs, be seated, and start your culinary adventure with a bowl of Louisiana seafood gumbo, a thickened stew made from homemade roux. Oysters St. George make a good appetizer, pairing local scallops with a topping of herbs, garlic, and parmesan. Of all the cheeses, parmesan complements baked oysters the best; something about the taste and texture works to perfection.

Chef Nathan Montgomery's namesake dish, A.J. Montgomery, consists of amberjack with tomatoes and artichoke hearts in a light wine sauce thickened with caraway and served atop angel-hair pasta. Also highly recommended is the Chef's Combo: baby gulf shrimp, sweet calico scallops, and chunks of grouper sautéed in "sauce divine" (mushrooms, green onions, garlic, parmesan, butter, and white wine). If they're in season, stone crab claws and Florida lobster will turn up on the menu. One special platter we snagged comprised a broiled half-lobster, succulent and tender stone crab claws, and a portobello mushroom stuffed with a mixture of minced mahimahi and three cheeses. Top it all off with key lime pie.

Another commendable island eatery is **Finni's Grill & Bar** (40 West Gorrie Drive, 850/927-3340, $$$), which has a beach-facing outdoor deck and an indoor dining room. The emphasis is on seafood, with signature dishes including curry shrimp kabobs and grouper jalamango (a spicy grilled fillet served with tropical fruits as a chutney-style accompaniment). If you want something other than seafood for a change, try the chicken St. George, which is grilled and served with roasted bananas, black beans, and rice.

Just off the island, in Eastpoint, is another noteworthy seafood restaurant, **That Place on 98** (500 U.S. 98, 850/670-9899, $$). Facing St. George Bay, they serve chilled oysters on the half shell, fried oysters with mustard-horseradish sauce, oysters Rockefeller, and "Oysters 98" (bacon, parmesan, mozzarella, garlic, onions, Worcestershire sauce). There are great fish sandwiches at lunch and seafood platters at dinner. And their key lime pie, balancing sweetness and tartness, is among the best you'll ever taste this side of the Keys. By the way, try to get a table on the weathered-wood deck. The tangy gulf breezes will complement your meal perfectly.

Night Moves

It is generally quiet out here. Most of the commercial buildup is located within a few blocks in either direction of the causeway's end. If you want to knock one back at happy hour, sunset, or bedtime, try **Finni's Grill & Bar** (40 West Gorrie Drive, 850/927-3340). A stone's throw away, if you really feel like making a pub crawl, is the **Blue Parrot Oceanfront Cafe** (68 West Gorrie Drive, 850/927-2987). They've got great drinks and terrific grouper sandwiches too, best enjoyed on the outdoor deck. Then there's **Harry A's Porch Club and Oyster Bar** (10 West Bayshore Drive, 850/927-9810), the island's oldest tavern and a popular spot to down oysters, sandwiches, and suds.

However, being a family island that doesn't even have a mailbox, St. George is basically not oriented to wild and woolly goings-on.

Contact Information

Apalachicola Bay Chamber of Commerce, 99 Market Street, Apalachicola, FL 32320; 850/653-9419; website: www.baynavigator.com/chamber

Little St. George Island (Cape St. George State Reserve)

St. George Island used to be 29 miles long until 1954, when the Army Corps of Engineers cut a channel west of center to allow boats to get out into the Gulf of Mexico more quickly. Now St. George is smaller (20 miles long), but he has a son, Little St. George Island (nine miles long). Separating the two islands is a man-made pass, known as Bob Sikes Cut. Unfortunately, you cannot cross the pass from big St. George Island unless you're a property owner or guest at St. George Plantation, an extensive private development that hoards the west end of St. George Island. How could this have been allowed to happen?

That's the bad news. The good news is that Little St. George Island, a part of the Apalachicola National Estuarine Research Reserve (one of 27 such reserves in the nation), is completely undeveloped. The island is jointly funded and managed by the National Oceanographic and Atmospheric Administration, a federal agency, and the Department of Environmental Pro-

6 Little St. George Island

Location: due west of St. George Island
Parking/fees: no parking or fees; public docking available at Government Dock
Hours: 24 hours
Facilities: none
Contact: Apalachicola Estuarine National Research Reserve, 850/653-8063

tection, a state agency. The reserve operates a visitor center in Apalachicola and an administrative and research facility in Eastpoint. Drop by the Apalachicola office, which has exhibits and conducts environmental educational programs.

Little St. George Island is open to the public for swimming, fishing, bird-watching, and hiking. Primitive camping is permitted at either end; all they ask is that you call the office with the date and number of people and let them explain a few rules. Foremost among the rules is that fires can only be built on the beach, and no live wood can be cut. There's a public dock on the island, but the recent spate of hurricanes has severed it from the shore. "It wasn't connected to the land the last time we checked," according to a reserve spokesperson. You might just have to anchor offshore and wade in, and if you're camping on the east or west end of the island, this may be the best alternative anyway.

The midsection of the boomerang-shaped island juts out at Cape St. George. Three lighthouses have occupied the island since the first was constructed in 1833. Hurricanes subjected the latest lighthouse (dating from 1852) to severe erosion, resulting in it becoming non-operational. It actually listed off-center by 10 degrees. You've heard of the Leaning Tower of Pisa? This was the leaning lighthouse of Florida—until, that is, a quarter million dollars were raised by the Cape St. George Lighthouse Society to right the light. It has been moved back to perpendicular and is no longer in any danger of falling over.

Beaches

The Beaches Are Moving is the title of a controversial but well-researched and well-reasoned book written by Duke University geologist Orrin Pilkey. His proposition—that barrier islands are unstable landforms that should not be subjected to intensive development—is unpopular with developers and the network of profiteers who support them. Of course, his premise makes perfect sense if you examine the situation objectively. The proof in Pilkey's pudding can be seen at **Little St. George Island**, whose beach has shifted 400 yards north, at the rate of about 10 feet a year, in little more than a century. Can you imagine losing that much of your lawn on an annual basis?

The beach nonetheless runs for nine lovely, unbuilt-on miles. The only problem is residual damage done in the 1960s to dune ridges, which were flattened during military training exercises when simulated amphibious assaults were carried out on Little St. George Island. Thanks, Uncle Sam!

Contact Information

Apalachicola National Estuarine Research Reserve, 261 7th Street, Apalachicola, FL 32320; 850/653-8063; website: www.ocrm.nos.noaa.gov/nerr/reserves/nerrapalachicola

Apalachicola

We fell in love with this scenic and unassuming small town, nestled 75 miles west of Tallahassee and 65 miles east of Panama City on U.S. 98. Apalachicola (pop. 2,800) is situated on the west bank of the Apalachicola River, where it empties into Apalachicola Bay. We were impressed by the low-key working waterfront along Water Street, which in any other town would be heralded with an ostentatious "Old Town" designation, and by the historic downtown area. The town is the home of the annual Florida Seafood Festival, held the first weekend in November, and for good reason: there is no fresher seafood than that plucked from the bayous, bay, sound, and gulf surrounding Apalachicola. In fact, 90 percent of the bivalves harvested commercially in the state of Florida come from the Apalachicola Bay.

There is only one traffic light in Franklin County: a blinking red light in downtown Apalachicola. There are few fast-food franchises, leaving you free to pick from any number of wonderful hometown restaurants. Just don't come to Apalachicola looking for sand beaches. Those are found on close-by islands: Dog, St. George, Little St. George, and St. Vincent (from east to west). Do come to Apalachicola as a jumping-off point for fishing trips or island exploration. By all means spend a night at one of the restored bed-and-breakfasts and enjoy a seafood dinner or two. You might just be tempted to stick around for good. While you're in town, tune in 100.5 FM ("Oyster Radio"), which is the most eclectic and entertaining rock station in the whole of Florida.

Local history can be explored on foot with a map of landmarks (available at inns, restaurants, and the chamber of commerce). At various times, lumber, cotton, and shipping have contributed to Apalachicola's fortunes. Today, it's seafood that drives the economy, and they're generating revenue from tourism of late, as well. Deservedly so, in our opinion.

Bunking Down

Apalachicola is ideally suited to inns. Its old homes are sprawling and architecturally distinguished, and its natural setting is conducive to rocking away an afternoon on the verandah. The pale yellow **Coombs House** (80 6th Street, 850/653-9199, $$), a classic example of steamboat gothic architecture, has been meticulously restored so that its dark-toned hardwoods (black cedar, tiger oak) gleam with the muted opulence of a bygone area. Each room has been furnished differently by owner Lynn Wilson, an antiques collector and a doyen among Florida's interior designers. Everything about the inn is lavish, but the rates are surprisingly reasonable.

Another hostelry worth touting is the **Gibson Inn** (57 Market Street, 850/653-2191, $). This tin-roofed, three-story Victorian dates from 1907. Entering the lobby, you feel as if you've stepped into the past. Reposing on the wraparound porch, you'll become convinced that time is standing still. In this insanely sped-up world, that is no small pleasure. Once you've adjusted to the slowed-down pace, you'll appreciate the wisdom of a local who explained, "Sitting on the porch of the Gibson in a rocker, watching the world go by . . . that is what Apalachicola is all about." In addition to 31 rooms and room rates that are a steal, ranging from $75 to$125 per night, the Gibson Inn has a first-rate dining room offering surf (oyster, shrimp, and grouper with a Cajun twist) and turf (oven-roasted prime rib).

The **Apalachicola River Inn** (123 Water Street, 850/653-8139, $) is part of a complex that also includes a marina and restaurant. The color scheme is pink and the modest motel-style rooms all face the river. Best of all, it adjoins Boss Oyster (see "Coastal Cuisine").

Coastal Cuisine

The oysters in Apalachicola are plucked from the waters of the bay using old harvesting techniques. They're plumper, thicker shelled, and tastier than those found elsewhere. Surgeon General's warnings aside, we love raw oysters, and Apalachicola's are the best. **Boss Oyster** (123 Water Street, 850/633-9364, $$) is the be-all and end-all of oyster bars. They prepare the bivalve in so many ways that it takes a stapled eight-page menu to describe them all. Other seafood delicacies are offered—steamed blue crabs, double-battered Boss Buffalo Shrimp, po' boys, smoked fish dip, and a belly-busting Golden Fried Seafood Platter that serves two—but oysters are Boss' pride and joy.

How do they prepare them? Let us count the ways: raw, with cocktail sauce, or steamed, with melted butter, or baked and served with a multitude of accompaniments. There's Oysters Max (parmesan cheese, capers, garlic, herbs), Oysters Captain Jack (bacon, jalapenos, Colby cheese, hot sauce), Oysters Bienville (shrimp, mushrooms, garlic, cheddar), Oysters Monterray [*sic*] (blue crab, sherry, Monterey jack), Oysters Diana (olives, feta, garlic, herbs) . . . the list goes on and on. Moreover, they encourage you to submit your own ideas for toppings: "See your name on the menu. . . . Become famous!"

If you're undecided, try a Boss Oyster Combo, which allows diners to order a dozen oysters three different ways (your choice). They also make a wicked Snickers cheesecake and an authentic key lime pie. On your way out, grab a T-shirt, which features renderings of a bivalve and Boss Oyster's motto: "Shut up and shuck!"

A huge bound higher up the culinary totem pole, in terms of atmosphere and sophistication, is **Chef Eddie's Magnolia Grill** (133 U.S. 98, 850/653-8000, $$$$),

Refrigerator Magnate: The John Gorrie Story

A little-known fact: the scientific basis for modern refrigeration and air conditioning was largely pioneered in Apalachicola. The inventor was John Gorrie (1803–55), a South Carolina–born and New York–trained physician who began looking for a way to cool down yellow fever and malaria patients. Using a system of pumps, coils, and tanks, he devised an apparatus that produced bricks of ice. He called his invention the "ice machine." In 1851, he was granted the first U.S. patent for mechanical refrigeration. His research eventually led to the invention of the air conditioner by Willis Haviland Carrier, for which Carrier was granted a patent in 1906.

Gorrie's ice machine, which directly and indirectly made daily life in the sultry South more bearable, is celebrated at John Gorrie Museum State Park in Apalachicola. Gorrie never profited from his invention, whose widespread promulgation was opposed by (of all things) the ice lobby: i.e., those who cut, sold, stored, and shipped block ice from the wintry north to other parts of the country. The museum is open from 9 A.M. to 5 P.M., Thursday through Monday. This is one place where the overused exclamation "cool" really applies.

For more information, contact John Gorrie Museum State Park, 6th Street and Avenue D, Apalachicola, FL 32320; 850/653-9347; website: www.myflorida.com.

where the menu tends toward rich or hearty sauces (béarnaise, bordelaise, lobster) adorning lamb, quail, filet mignon, and whatever's fresh at the fish market. One of chef Eddie Cass's best-known dishes is the Ponchartrain: sauteed mahimahi topped with shrimp, artichokes, almonds, and a cream scampi sauce.

Tamara's Floridita Cafe (17 Avenue East, 850/653-4111, $$) is owned by a Venezuelan woman who's come to Apalachicola with some exceptional recipes. Pecan-crusted grouper with jalapeno cream sauce and margarita chicken with honey tequila glaze are two of the more memorable preparations. Her dense key lime pie is a worthy departure from the traditional preparation. Paintings of musicians (James Brown, Alberta Hunter) line the walls, and the restaurant is located downtown, within easy walking distance of the inns of Apalachicola.

A huge bound back down to earth will deposit you at the door of **The Hut** (U.S. 98 W, 850/653-9410, $$), a beloved hole-in-the-wall that does seafood and steaks at prices that will make you smile. The Friday lunch special (a spread of fried seafood) is legendary. Another longtime (since 1903) local favorite is the **Apalachicola Seafood Grill** (100 Market Street, 850/653-9510, $$), which lures tourists with the bait "the world's largest fried fish sandwich." They also have a huge selection of fresh seafood to go with their friendly atmosphere. And you can't miss it: it's on the corner of Market Street and Avenue E, near the only traffic light in Franklin County.

Bottom line: you really can't go wrong eating seafood anywhere in the vicinity of Apalachicola Bay.

Contact Information

Apalachicola Bay Chamber of Commerce, 99 Market Street, Apalachicola, FL 32320; 850/653-9419; website: www.baynavigator.com/chamber

St. Vincent Island National Wildlife Refuge

At 12,358 acres, St. Vincent Island is five times as large as Little St. George Island. It appears to be shaped like a conch shell: wide on its east and south faces, the island tapers to a point at its northwest end. The shape and dimensions of St. Vincent are explained by the fact it lies at the western end of a barrier-island chain in which sand moves in a westerly direction. Because it's at the terminus of a sand cell, a series of parallel dune ridges have built up over the millennia, some reaching elevations of 35 feet (which is tall in these parts).

The island is notable for its varied inland habitats, including freshwater lakes, oak hammocks, and upland pine forests. For much of the last century it was a private game preserve, stocked with exotic fauna ranging from sambar deer to zebras. The Nature Conservancy purchased the island in 1968, and the federal government bought it from the conservancy, at which point it became St. Vincent Island National

7 St. Vincent Island National Wildlife Refuge

Location: six miles offshore from the mouth of the Apalachicola River
Parking/fees: no parking or fees; no public docking
Hours: sunrise to sunset
Facilities: none
Contact: St. Vincent National Wildlife Refuge, 850/653-8808

Wildlife Refuge. Because of the size and diversity of its habitats and the endangered and threatened species it attracts (sea turtles, indigo snakes, wood storks, peregrine falcons, bald eagles), St. Vincent Island is one of the most unique coastal locales in all of Florida. In the 1990s, endangered red wolves were introduced to the island.

St. Vincent is open for visitation during daylight hours. It is closed only during public hunts (for white-tailed and sambar deer, wild pigs, and raccoon), which take place over four-day periods in November, December, and January. Camping is prohibited, but 80 miles of sand roads crisscrossing the island are used as hiking trails. We paddled over to the island via kayak and had a wonderful time poking around with our guide from **Broke-a-Toe's Outdoor Supplies and Services** (Indian Pass, Cape San Blas, 850/229-9283). On the bay side of the island, he took us to a site where pottery shards dating back 4,000 years are often turn up. Even we, who could not find a penny in a wishing well, turned up a couple of pottery pieces. He also showed us "the spaces"—watery chutes on the bayside into which Native Americans chased fish and then blocked their exit.

Private operators ferry visitors over and back from the mainland for a nominal fee. **St. Vincent Island Shuttle Services** (850/229-1065) charges $10 for adults and $7 for children under 10 for dropoff and pickup. They also rent bikes to adults only for exploring the island ($25 per bike and ferry trip). They operate during daylight hours and ask that you call ahead before coming. The shuttle departs from Indian Pass Boat Launch, at the end of Indian Pass Road (County Road 30-B). If you've got your own boat, be advised that there are no public docking facilities on St. Vincent Island.

Beaches

Strange as it sounds, given its 14 miles of isolated beaches, swimming is among the least popular activities on **St. Vincent Island National Wildlife Refuge**. The beach is found on the south side of the island, but the gulf water isn't as pure and appealing as it is on St. George Island because it doesn't get the twice-daily tidal flushing that occurs through the passes flanking St. George. Moreover, hurricane-engendered erosion has narrowed St. Vincent's beaches, which have retreated in places to the point where there are tree stumps in the surf zone. So while the island as a whole rates highly, its beaches aren't its primary asset.

Contact Information

St. Vincent National Wildlife Refuge, P.O. Box 447, Apalachicola, FL 32329; 850/653-88081; southeast.fws.gov/stvincent

Map of Franklin County—Page 548

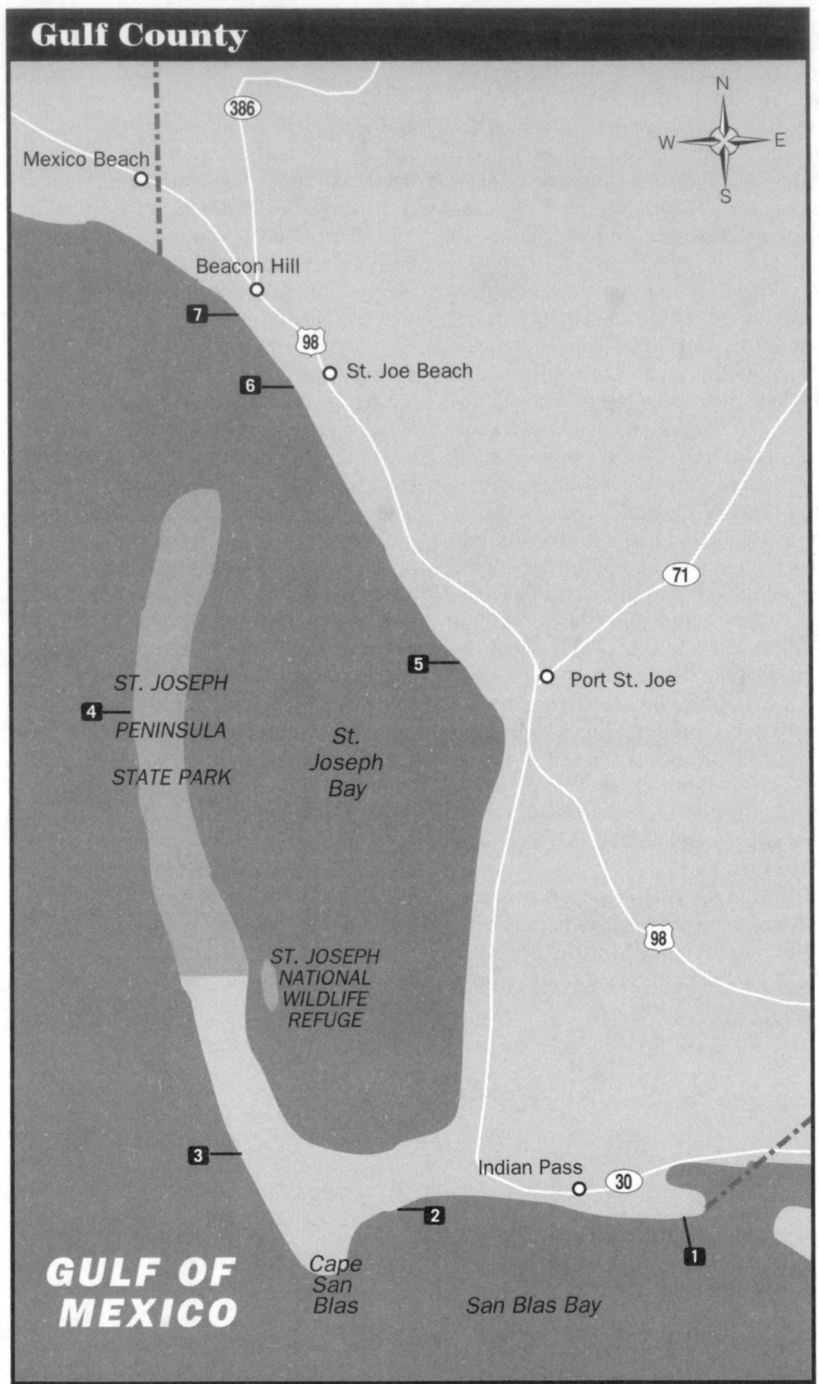
Gulf County
386
N
W
E
S
Mexico Beach
Beacon Hill
7
98
St. Joe Beach
6
71
5
Port St. Joe
ST. JOSEPH
4
PENINSULA
STATE PARK
St.
Joseph
Bay
98
ST. JOSEPH
NATIONAL
WILDLIFE
REFUGE
3
Indian Pass
30
2
1
GULF OF
MEXICO
Cape
San
Blas
San Blas Bay

GULF COUNTY

Gulf County is a rural county with a population of barely 14,000. There are only two towns of any size: Wewahitchka (pop. 1,800), in the swampy interior, and Port St. Joe (pop. 4,500), on the shore of St. Joseph Bay. It is the sort of county that, for lack of alternatives, gets stuck with the kind of industry most other places turn away. The most prominent structures in Port St. Joe are its chemical plant and paper mill. Gulf County puts its best face forward at Cape San Blas and St. Joseph Peninsula, where a couple of attractive county beaches (Salinas and Cape Palms) and an exceptional state park (St. Joseph Peninsula) preserve a good stretch of the hilly dunes and sugar-sand beaches. Moreover, the smaller peninsula at Indian Pass is an undiscovered gem.

Indian Pass

Indian Pass (pop. 850) is one of the better-kept secrets along the Forgotten Coast. It's an actual pass, as well as the name of a small community in remote southeast Gulf County. It's tucked along a scenic loop road that exits U.S. 98/County Road 30 near Apalachicola and rejoins it at Port St. Joe. Whereas most folks head out to Cape San Blas and St. Joseph Peninsula, the road less traveled—in this case, County Road 30-B—runs east from County Road 30 along Indian Peninsula, inside of which is Indian Lagoon. The tip of Indian Peninsula practically touches the west side of St. Vincent Island; between them is Indian Pass. Some of the better-quality oysters in an area that's renowned for them come out of the bay around here.

Indian Pass is more secluded than Cape San Blas, which is to say there are fewer vacation homes out this way and under a thousand year-round residents. There are also a few campgrounds and boat launches. The biggest news to come out of Indian Pass lately was the sighting of a giant, iguana-like creature by a reliable ecotourism guide, Tom Brocato, and a couple of nervous customers.

❶ Indian Pass

Location: from U.S. 98/County Road 30, turn east on County Road 30-B and follow for two miles to Indian Pass

Parking/fees: free parking lot. Beach driving requires a permit, available for $15 per year for county property holders and $150 for non-property holders. Call the Gulf County Tax Collector, 850/229-6116 for more information.

Hours: sunrise to sunset

Facilities: none

Contact: Gulf County Planning and Building Department, 850/229-8944

Brocato told us the story: "It was an eight-foot black reptile. It rose out of the water, undulating and red-eyed, with a serpent's head, and it looked mean. The tail came out of the water, and it was pointed. . . . We all thought we saw teeth, and they were not cow teeth—they were shredding teeth."

It turned out to be a marine iguana that had been imported from South America and kept as a "pet" until it escaped. The story goes that it was eventually caught and sold to a zoo.

Beaches

Curiously, the controversial practice of beach driving—which is hell on the beach and the critters that live on and under it—is permitted along Indian Peninsula and part of Cape San Blas. There are two designated beach entrance/exit points at **Indian Pass** and three on Cape San Blas. A permit is needed to drive on the beach. It can be obtained at the office of the Gulf County Tax Collector for a fee of $15 per year for property holders and $150 for everyone else. Wisely, driving on the beach is forbidden at dusk during turtle-nesting season.

The beach along Indian Peninsula is more for anglers and amblers than swimmers. The bay bottom is more silty than sandy, and the water is more occluded than that found off St. George Island and St. Joseph Peninsula. It's not polluted, however, and once you're a few hundred yards offshore, it's clear as a bell again.

Coastal Cuisine

We found a joint worth crowing about out in the middle of nowhere. **Indian Pass Raw Bar** (8391 State Route C-30, 850/227-1670, $) is the place to go for some of the freshest and best-tasting oysters on the Panhandle, which is to say in the entire United States. Funky and weather-beaten with barely decipherable lettering, it looks like a country store from the outside. Indeed it was a gas station and convenience store many years ago. Inside, in an unfancy room with a bar and some tables, they serve raw oysters ($4.50/dozen), baked oysters, shrimp, and crabs, plus beer, wine, and soft drinks to wash it all down.

Contact Information

Gulf County Chamber of Commerce, 104 West 4th Street, Port St. Joe, FL 32457; 850/227-1223; website: www.homtown.com/gulfco

Cape San Blas

Viewed on a map, Cape San Blas and the peninsula that shoots up from it look like an arm that's been bent at the elbow. The undulating shoreline at the southern end of St. Joseph Bay is the bulging biceps. Cape San Blas is the crooked elbow protruding into the Gulf of Mexico. The long forearm, bent slightly inward at its wrist-like tip, is St. Joseph Peninsula. The peninsula extends for about 20 miles, enclosing St. Joseph Bay and protecting the mainland town of Port St. Joe. Severe beach erosion is evident just inside the elbow of the cape, which has necessitated shoring up from road crews.

Does the gulf want to open an inlet and make a barrier island of St. Joseph Peninsula? Only the next major hurricane knows for sure, but we'll offer this word to the wise: the area where the peninsula flares off from Cape San Blas is the most highly erodable section of coastline in the state of Florida. A total of 1,600 feet of width has been lost in the last 80 years, and erosion occurs at the rate of 36 feet per year. Moreover, the federal government is not subsidizing any new programs of beach renourishment, and the state of Florida won't underwrite renourishment, either, in areas where there is limited beach access, such as Cape San Blas and the St. Joseph Peninsula. In other words, buy or build out here at your peril.

Vacation homes and condos are sited all along the skinny peninsula, though stores and restaurants are few and far between. The dunes, particularly at the western third of the island—protected as St. Joseph Peninsula State Park (see separate writeup)—are formidable. Cape San Blas, with its treacherous offshore shoals, has been the site of five lighthouses, three of which have been destroyed by storms and encroaching waters. The latest was con-

2 Salinas Park

Location: on County Road 30-E (Cape San Blas Road), a quarter mile west of its intersection with County Road 30, on Cape San Blas
Parking/fees: free parking lot
Hours: sunrise to sunset
Facilities: restrooms, showers and picnic tables
Contact: Gulf County Planning and Building Department, 850/229-8944

3 Cape Palms Park

Location: five miles northwest of Cape San Blas on St. Joseph Peninsula, via County Road 30-E (Cape San Blas Road)
Parking/fees: free parking lot
Hours: sunrise to sunset
Facilities: restrooms, picnic tables and showers
Contact: Gulf County Planning and Building Department, 850/229-8944

MAP OF GULF COUNTY—PAGE 564

structed in 1885 and made to be moved, which is good because the shifting sands necessitated its relocation inland in 1918. In the lighthouse's history, one can discern the wisdom of the biblical warning against building one's house on sand.

Beaches

The white ribbon of sandy beach along the gulf side looks almost like it's been dusted with frost. The longest and healthiest stretch of public beach is at St. Joseph Peninsula State Park. Beyond that, the county has provided two beach parks, one near Cape San Blas (Salinas Park) and one halfway between the cape and the state park entrance station (Cape Palms Park). **Salinas Park** faces south along a wide, accreting beach. Boardwalks lead over the dunes to the usually uncrowded beach; a gazebo sits atop the tallest dune. Facilities at Salinas include picnic tables and a playground, with the only sour note being that they've been the frequent target of vandals.

Cape Palms Park offers a parking area and boardwalk to the beach along the peninsula's midsection. The park has had much added to it in recent years, including a covered pavilion and picnic tables, a playground, grills, showers, and landscaping. The improvements have been considerable, and the county is to be commended.

Contact Information

Gulf County Chamber of Commerce, 104 West 4th Street, Port St. Joe, FL 32457; 850/227-1223; website: www.homtown.com/gulfco

St. Joseph Peninsula State Park

St. Joseph Peninsula State Park occupies the upper half of a lengthy spit, protruding northwesterly from Cape San Blas. This undefiled park is out of the way of any major population centers (Tallahassee is 75 miles distant) and therefore truly merits its claim of isolation. Statistics reveal just how easy it is to find quietude out here. There are nine miles of gulf beach, 10 miles of bayshore, and 2,516 acres of parkland, much of it consisting of hardy sandpine scrub and pine flatwoods. An area at the north end, unviolated by roads, is a designated wilderness preserve. From the park road's end to the tip of the peninsula is 7.5 hikeable miles. You can easily find a remote spot on the beach and fish, swim, and sunbathe to your heart's content. Kayaking and scalloping are popular on the bayside. Bird-watchers know St. Joseph Peninsula as a prime location for sighting hawks—especially the sharp-shinned hawk—during their fall migration. All told, 209 bird species have been catalogued on the peninsula. Monarch butterflies pass through en route to Mexican wintering sites, too. Mammals include deer, foxes, skunks, and bobcats.

Beaches

Four boardwalks and an access path from the cabin area lead onto the state park's ample white-sand beach. Several boardwalks got chewed up pretty badly by Hurricane Earl in 1998 but have since been repaired. As for the dunes . . . well, they were in the process of recovering from damage inflicted by Hurricane Opal in 1995 when Earl meted out more punishment. On average, they lost three feet of elevation and from 20 to 40 percent of their size. Many of the stabilizing sea oats planted in the wake of Opal were taken out as well. The beach itself has narrowed in some places and widened in others. Even though the beach and dunes have been adversely impacted by this recent spate of hurricanes—a sad reality that is true all over the Panhandle—they are still lovely to look at and play on. Time, of course, will heal all wounds.

Bunking Down

Eight furnished cabins on the bayside bearing names like "Starfish," "Trout," "Conch," and "Snapper" are available for rental ($55–70 per night, depending on the time of year), and 119 campsites with hookups are located in two areas on the gulf side of the spit. Primitive camping can also be done by hiking out on the wilderness preserve. The cabins blend in with the landscape, and they're a cut above the typical rustic-to-dilapidated state-park lodgings. A recent renovation has spruced them up considerably. Cabin and camping reservations are accepted up to 11 months in advance; call the park well ahead of time, as they book quickly.

Contact Information

St. Joseph Peninsula State Park, 8899 Cape San Blas Road, Port St. Joe, FL 32456; 850/227-1327; website: www.myflorida.com

4 St. Joseph Peninsula State Park

Location: west end of St. Joseph Peninsula, via County Road 30-E (Cape San Blas Road)

Parking/fees: $3.25 per vehicle entrance fee. Camping fees in the two developed campgrounds are $16–18 per night March 1–September 15, $8–10 per night September 16–February 28. Primitive camping in the wilderness area is $3 per night for adults, $1 for kids under 16. Cabins rentals are $70 per night March 1–September 15 (minimum five-night stay) and $55 per night September 15–February 28 (minimum two-night stay).

Hours: 8 A.M. to sunset

Facilities: concessions, lifeguards, picnic tables, restrooms, and showers

Contact: St. Joseph Peninsula State Park, 850/227-1327

Port St. Joe

We've included mention of Port St. Joe (pop. 4,500) more as a biohazard warning than for any relevance it has to this book as a coastal destination. Port St. Joe lies along the inner shoreline of St. Joseph Bay, serving as a gateway to Cape San Blas and St. Joseph Peninsula. It's the only town of any size along Gulf County's coast. Aside from this, Port St. Joe is an undistinguished and downright ugly community that is better passed through than lingered over. In much the same spirit that has resulted in such PR handles as "the Nature Coast" and "the Forgotten Coast," inspiration visited us in the form of a nickname for the area between Port St. Joe and Panama City: "the Chemical Coast."

Arizona Chemical, a subsidiary of International Paper, has mammoth industrial operations on the waterfront in Port St. Joe. The stench from the smokestack emissions will have you holding your nose

5 Frank Pate Park

Location: south end of 5th Street in Port St. Joe

Parking/fees: free parking lot

Hours: 24 hours

Facilities: restrooms and picnic tables

Contact: Port St. Joe City Hall, 850/229-8261

while crossing the bridge in or out of town. Rundown shacks list within sight of the dark, satanic mills. Along the road is an auto parts store next to a Chevron next to a Subway next to a (insert franchise name here). It's just another good ol' all-American eyesore, with the worst aspects of industry and franchising sucking the life out of what surely must have been an appealing and unbothered stretch of the Gulf Coast once upon a time.

Except to patronize some of the water-oriented bayside businesses (see "Shore Things"), since there are precious few of them on Cape San Blas, you're best advised to make your time in Port St. Joe as brief as possible. There is one bright spot: a large new marina, with 120 wet slips and charter boats, can only improve the town's lot.

Beaches

Frank Pate Park, at the south end of 5th Street on St. Joseph Bay, has a boat ramp and a fishing pier, plus tennis courts, a picnic area, and a playground. There's a bit of sand on the shore, but few (if any) swim in the bay.

Shore Things

- **Dive shop:** Captain Black's Dive Center, 301 Monument Avenue (U.S. 98), Port St. Joe, 850/229-6330.
- **Ecotourism:** Broke-a-Toe's Outdoor Services and Supplies, 7155 Leeward Street, Cape San Blas, 850/229-9283.
- **Fishing charters:** Bay Charters, 308 13th Street, Port St. Joe, 850/229-1086.
- **Lighthouse:** Cape San Blas Lighthouse, Cape San Blas.
- **Marina:** Port St. Joe Marina, 340 West 1st Street, Port St. Joe, 850/227-9393.
- **Pier:** Frank Pate Park, 5th Street at Monument Avenue (U.S. 98), Port St. Joe.
- **Rainy-day attraction:** Constitution Convention State Museum, 200 Allen Memorial Way, Port St. Joe, 850/229-8029.
- **Vacation rentals:** Gulf Coast Vacation Rentals, 2010 Highway C-30, Port St. Joe, 800/451-2349.

Contact Information

Gulf County Chamber of Commerce, 104 West 4th Street, Port St. Joe, FL 32457; 850/227-1223; website: www.hometown.com/gulfco

St. Joe Beach and Beacon Hill

Proceed northwest from Port St. Joe along U.S. 98 through St. Joe Beach and Beacon Hill (combined pop. 1,150), and you'll find yourself entering a new time zone. The line demarcating the Eastern and Central time zones falls between Beacon Hill and Mexico Beach, in Bay County. Election-night controversy was engendered in November 2000 when TV networks, vying to be the first to call the state of Florida for Bush or Gore, did so before the polls had closed on the western side of the time zone line. In so doing, they essentially disenfranchised Panhandle-dwelling voters.

A sandy shore reappears on the mainland as the protective influence of the outlying St. Joseph Peninsula disappears. Most of St. Joe Beach consists of new, boxlike two-story houses that block the view of the gulf from the road and are situated precariously close to the water. Some of the homes in Beacon Hill look like they've been around forever, while others appear to have popped up overnight, such as the plague of connected units painted in garish colors that line the gulf side of U.S. 98 at the east end of town.

Beaches

Access is catch-as-catch-can in **St. Joe Beach**, where any lot that doesn't have a home on it serves as an impromptu easement onto the beach. Pull onto the shoulder and follow the trails that have been blazed to the beach; everyone else does. **Beacon Hill Community Park** is a nearly new park whose facilities are located on the inland side of U.S. 98, atop the dune ridge where the Beacon Hill Lighthouse aids navigation into St. Joseph Bay. The park is mainly oriented toward baseball/softball games and picnicking, but it does have a boardwalk leading out to the gulf.

Contact Information

Gulf County Chamber of Commerce, 104 West 4th Street, Port St. Joe, FL 32457; 850/227-1223; website: www.hometown.com/gulfco

6 St. Joe Beach

Location: various trails lead to the beach from pulloffs along U.S. 98 in St. Joe Beach.
Parking/fees: free roadside parking
Hours: sunrise to sunset
Facilities: none
Contact: Gulf County Planning and Building Department, 850/229-8944

7 Beacon Hill Community Park

Location: on U.S. 98 in Beacon Hill, by the Beacon Hill Lighthouse
Parking/fees: free parking lot
Hours: sunrise to sunset
Facilities: restrooms and picnic tables
Contact: Gulf County Planning and Building Department, 850/229-8944

MAP OF GULF COUNTY—PAGE 564

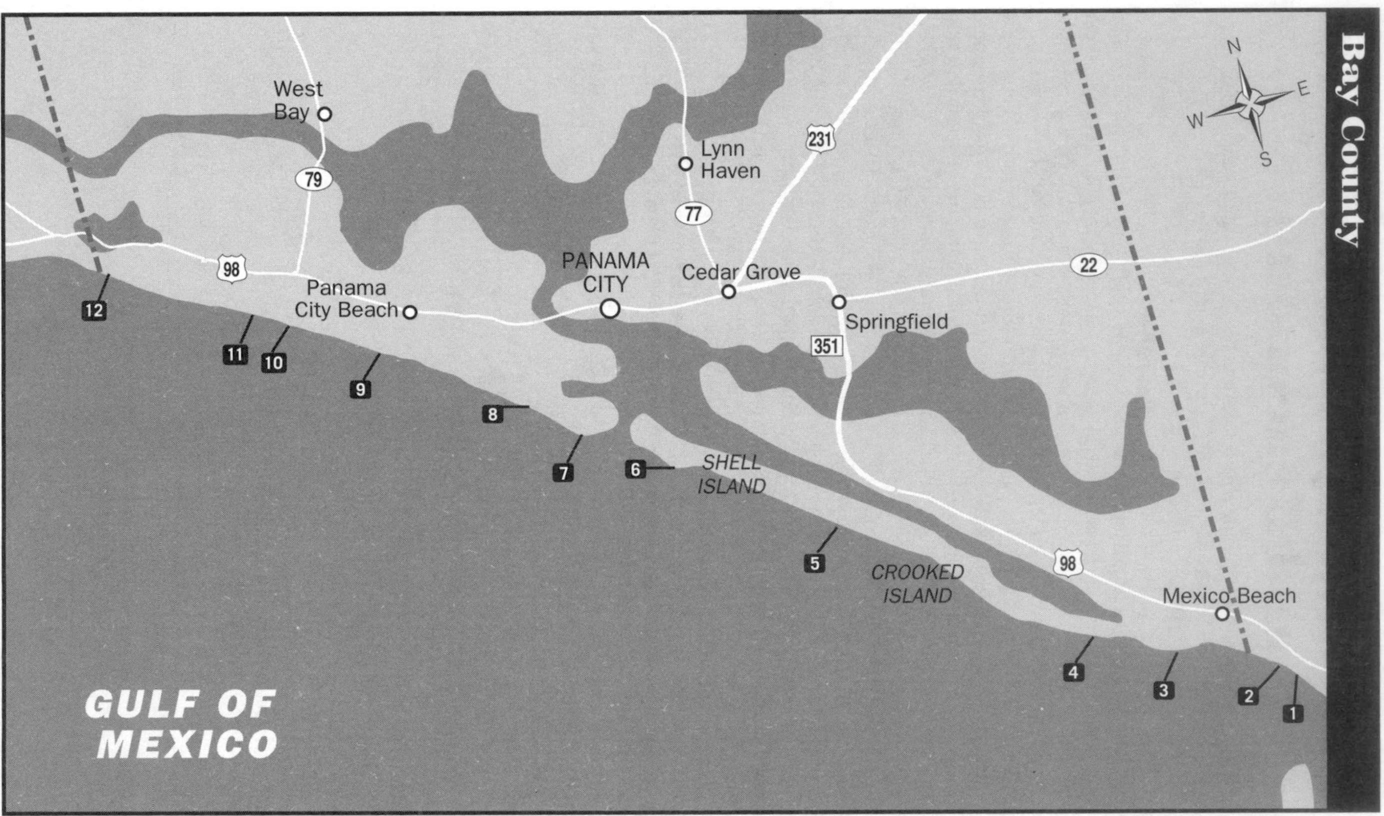
Bay County
N
E
W
S
West Bay
Lynn Haven
231
79
77
PANAMA CITY
Cedar Grove
22
98
Panama City Beach
Springfield
351
12
11
10
9
8
7
6
SHELL ISLAND
5
CROOKED ISLAND
98
Mexico Beach
4
3
2
1
GULF OF MEXICO

BAY COUNTY

Bay County takes its name from St. Andrews Bay, a serpentine body of water that stretches 10 miles inland and 25 miles from east to west. Bay County's main claim to fame is Panama City Beach, whose bleached-white sands and emerald waters have made it home to collegiate Spring Break since 1990 and a family-friendly vacation mecca much of the rest of the year. "PCB" dominates the county's coast, stretching for 26 miles across a sandy peninsula that nearly hooks up with another lengthy peninsula, the lately conjoined Shell and Crooked Islands, to the east. Although Crooked Island is part of Tyndall Air Force Base, its deserted beaches are provisionally open to the public. Mexico Beach, at the county's east end, is the last gasp along Florida's Forgotten Coast. In the middle of Bay County is the busy port and military town of Panama City, which is the antithesis of—and not to be confused with—Panama City Beach.

Mexico Beach

As we entered Mexico Beach from the east on U.S. 98, we realized that we were nearing the end of the Forgotten Coast. Mexico Beach (pop. 1,300) isn't exactly forgotten, nor is it very memorable. It's just a linear, no-frills beach town that serves as a small-scale, low-density foreshadowing of what's to come in Panama City Beach. They like to refer to themselves as "the quiet alternative." Like PCB, Mexico Beach attracts a faithful following. Unlike PCB, the wave of new condo construction that has gone overboard there has only trickled into east Bay County—so far, at least. The majority of existing homes in Mexico Beach are faded, candy-colored box-like structures that evoke happy memories of vacations in the Old Florida mold. Some have faded too much, however, and are in need of fixing up.

The biggest culprit, in terms of inflicting damage, was Hurricane Opal in 1995. Opal devastated most of the town on the gulf side of U.S. 98. Proving the old adage that those who forget history are condemned to repeat it, the majority of Mexico Beach's post-hurricane construction has been—you guessed it!—on the gulf side of the road. Why not just paint a target on the back door? The east end of Mexico Beach is more appealing, because the development is on the inland side of the highway, neither obstructing views of the splendid white sand beaches nor destroying the dune cover.

Mexico Beach would seem to have more in common with the Forgotten Coast counties to the east than the rest of Bay County, of which it is a part. Mexico Beach is closely aligned with the Gulf County communities of Beacon Hill and St. Joe Beach, which it adjoins. It appears to have been adopted by Gulf County, even though it is in a different county and time zone.

Beaches

One thing Mexico Beach does well is provide public access to its 3.5 miles of sparkling beaches. A couple of small beach parks, **Wayside Park** (at 7th Street) and **Sunset Park** (at 19th Street), are sited at

❶ Wayside Park

Location: 7th Street and U.S. 98 in Mexico beach
Parking/Fees: free parking lot
Hours: sunrise to sunset
Facilities: restrooms and showers
Contact: Mexico Beach Town Hall, 850/648-5700

❷ Sunset Park (a.k.a. El Governor Park)

Location: 19th Street and U.S. 98 in Mexico Beach
Parking/fees: free parking lot
Hours: sunrise to sunset
Facilities: concessions, restrooms, picnic tables, and showers
Contact: Mexico Beach Town Hall, 850/648-5700

❸ Canal Park

Location: 37th Street at U.S. 98 in Mexico Beach
Parking/fees: free parking lot
Hours: sunrise to sunset
Facilities: concessions, restrooms, picnic tables, and showers
Contact: Mexico Beach Town Hall, 850/648-5700

the east and middle parts of town, respectively. Sunset Park is next to El Governor Motel and was, until recently, called El Governor Park. At the west end of town is **Canal Park**, which includes the Mexico Beach Pier (at the foot of 37th Street). Additionally, four dune walkovers are strewn along the town's three-mile length. Parking is free at all the parks and accessways, and the beach is within easy walking distance of the town's businesses. Mexico Beach is a kid-friendly beach, as the tail end of St. Joseph Peninsula intercepts and tames the waves, leaving Mexico Beach's shoreline calm and undertow free.

Bunking Down

The most arresting structure in Mexico Beach is **El Governor Motel** (U.S. 98, P.O. Box 13325, 850/648-5757, $), a five-story gulfside motel that looms like the Empire State Building in this otherwise low-to-the-ground community. Cut from plain cloth and boasting an outdoor pool and bar, El Governor sits so close to the gulf that it looks like it could topple forward into it during the next big blow. More mannerly is the **Driftwood Inn** (U.S. 98, P.O. Box 13447, 850/648-5126, $$), a two-story Victorian bed-and-breakfast that's also on the beach side. Other than that, there are rental properties (try **Mexico Beach Harmon Realty**, 1432 U.S. 98, 850/239-4959) and a trio of RV parks.

Coastal Cuisine

The **Toucan Restaurant and Oyster Bar** (812 U.S. 98, 850/648-3010, $$) was destroyed by Hurricane Opal in '95 but has been rebuilt bigger and better than ever, with two outdoor decks and an indoor dining room. The cuisine is finer than you'd have any reason to expect in Mexico Beach, including such entrée offerings as tequila lime chicken, salmon in a bag, and local oysters.

Contact Information

Mexico Beach Community Development Council, P.O. Box 13382, Mexico Beach, FL 32410; 850/648-8196 or 888/723-2546; website: www.mexicobeach.com/cdc

Tyndall Air Force Base

Twenty-five miles of Panhandle real estate between Mexico Beach and Panama City is claimed by the massive Tyndall Air Force Base. It's a city in its own right, with 21,000 personnel associated with the base, whose mission is "air superiority for F-15 Eagle pilots" (i.e., top guns). As you pass through Tyndall on U.S. 98, signs beside the road serve notice to all would-be Saddam Husseins: "Global Power. Global Reach. For America."

Tyndall's military mission does not completely exclude the public from enjoying the land it occupies. On the 12-mile-long peninsula that stretches to the west, bounded by East Bay and St. Andrews Bay, roads and boardwalks can be used by hikers and mountain bikers. Moreover, the beach along Crooked Island, which juts into the Gulf of Mexico, is open to the public most of the time, provided you can flash the necessary passes. To obtain a map and a recreational permit for hiking, biking, or beaching, you must register at the Natural Resources Office. We've detailed the necessary bureaucratic hurdles below.

Beaches

Give it up for Uncle Sam, y'all. Crooked Island, upward of 10 miles of deserted barrier island that adjoins Shell Island to the west, is accessible to the public, albeit with restrictions. To wit, you must obtain a recreational pass at the Natural Resources Office, and to obtain a recreational pass, you must first get a gate pass from the Vis-

MAP OF BAY COUNTY—PAGE 572

itor Center. Sound confusing? Well shape up, soldier, here's the drill. Gate passes are obtained at the visitor center, located by the entrance gate at Sabre Drive. To get there from Panama City, head east on U.S. 98, then turn onto the base at Sabre Drive. Vehicle registration is required for a gate pass, which must be shown anytime you enter a gated area.

With your gate pass in hand, proceed to the Natural Resources Office. To get there from the visitor center, go through the Sabre Drive gate and then take the first left (Dejarnette Road) and park at the only building on the right. The Natural Resources Office will issue a recreational pass, which is good for the entire year. You must provide a picture ID, vehicle registration, and proof of car insurance (for liability reasons).

With the requisite passes in hand, you can now make an amphibious assault on the beach. There are two access points: **Crooked Island East** at the east end, and **Tyndall Beach** (a.k.a. Crooked Island West) at the west end. The unmarked access road to Crooked Island East lies at the eastern border of the base, near the city limits of Mexico Beach. Do have a recreational pass on your person, because the military police will ticket you otherwise. Don't bring your dog. Don't leave litter on the beach, either. Litter is a big problem out here. What kind of anti-patriotic oaf would litter the beaches of a U.S. Air Force base that was kind enough to let them play out here?

Tyndall Beach is accessible from the west side of the base, near Panama City. To get there, turn south onto the base from the main gate (Florida Avenue), located at the first stoplight on U.S. 98 east of Panama City, over the Dupont Bridge. Once inside the main gate, take the first left and the next right, then turn right at the third stop sign and follow the road out to the beach. There's a boardwalk and pavilion with a restroom and shower. Interestingly, the pass between Crooked Island and Shell Island has closed, making one continuous island where once there were two. Hurricane Opal initiated the closure in 1995, and Hurricane Earl sealed the deal in 1998.

A final note: public access is granted under normal peacetime conditions. When the military is in a state of high alert, recre-

4 Crooked Island East

Location: from U.S. 98, turn south onto the easternmost access road within the boundaries of Tyndall Air Force Base, just west of Mexico Beach

Parking/fees: free parking lot

Hours: sunrise to sunset (Note: sometimes the area is completely off limits to the public; check the marquees as you enter Tyndall AFB or call the Natural Resources Office for the latest information.)

Facilities: restrooms, picnic tables, and showers

Contact: Natural Resources Office on Tyndall Air Force Base, 850/283-2641

5 Tyndall Beach (a.k.a. Crooked Island West)

Location: Enter the main gate (Florida Avenue) at Tyndall Air Force Base. Take the first left and the next right, then turn right at the third stop sign and proceed to the beach.

Parking/fees: free parking lot

Hours: sunrise to sunset (Note: sometimes the area is completely off limits to the public; check the marquees as you enter Tyndall AFB or call the Natural Resources Office for the latest information.)

Facilities: restrooms and showers

Contact: Natural Resources Office on Tyndall Air Force Base, 850/283-2641

Look Out Joe, Here Comes Arvida

Outside of its coastal strip, a shockingly huge portion of Bay County is owned by a single corporation. The Jacksonville-based St. Joe Company is far and away the largest private landowner in the state of Florida, with 1.2 million acres. Most of it is Panhandle timberland, though they also own five miles of prime coastal real estate. Its holdings in Florida amount to an area the size of the state of Delaware. St. Joe is an old industrial company (founded in 1936) involved in timber and paper. Lately, it has also decided to become a modern real-estate company. To that end, St. Joe lured Peter Rummell, the former head of the Disney empire's "Imagineering Group," to become its new CEO in 1996. A year later, St. Joe acquired a controlling interest in Arvida, the mammoth, Boca Raton–based developer. The idea was to pair St. Joe's huge landholdings with Arvida's expertise at developing large-scale residential projects.

Florida's Panhandle, east of Destin, is still relatively undeveloped, while the rest of the state's coastline (with the exception of the virtually beachless Big Bend counties) has been maxed out. With investors and developers hungrily eyeing this last frontier like birds of prey circling road kill, you can just imagine what's in the cards. Already, St. Joe/Arvida is planning massive residential communities for the 800 acres it owns on the Panhandle coast. The only reason they're not galloping faster is the permitting process, which they estimate will hold up groundbreaking ceremonies for as long as to two years.

In other words, hold on tight, because the Forgotten Coast is about to be remembered all too well. After approval from Governor Jeb Bush in 2000, some $139 million in road projects will be undertaken in Bay County, mostly in furtherance of economic development objectives. U.S. 98 will be four-laned through the whole county, as will stretches of State Route 77 and State Route 79. Some of the locals are none too pleased with the big plans their county commissioners and various developers have drawn up. "People in rural Bay County have been fighting the illegal annexation of their community for years with no help from the Bay County Commission," complained a letter-writer to the *Panama City News-Herald* in September 2000. Isn't that always the way it seems to go?

ational passes are not granted. The status of public access is stated on marquees as you enter the base, and you can call ahead before visiting, too. For detailed information on public recreation and access on Tyndall Air Force Base, call the Natural Resources Office at 850/283-2641.

Contact Information

Tyndall Air Force Base, Panama City, FL 32403; 850/283-1113; website: www.tyndall.af.mil

St. Andrews State Park

It's really no mystery why St. Andrews **State Park** is the most popular and highly rated beach in the area. Not only is the beach here and on adjoining Shell Island breathtakingly beautiful, but the spacious park (1,260 acres) includes a lake, marshlands, two hiking trails, and full facilities for camping (176 sites), swimming, fishing (including gulf and bay piers, rock jetties, and a boat ramp), picnicking, snorkeling, canoeing, kayaking, and diving. In addition to this wealth of resources, park plan-

Enter Sandman: Dr. Beach and the Ratings Game

Panama City Beach has made extensive and prominent use of a number-one ranking that one of its beaches received from Dr. Stephen Leatherman, world-renowned architect of an annual beach-ratings list. The beach he rated so highly, for *Condé Nast Traveler,* was St. Andrews State Park. As anyone who's been there knows, Panama City Beach is very different from St. Andrews in that there are no Wal-Marts, pancake houses, or Matterhorn-sized condominium projects at the latter. Moreover, St. Andrews has a back-beach area with sculpted dune formations that give some inkling of what the whole of Panama City Beach must have looked like at one time. You cannot blame PCB for capitalizing on its proximity to St. Andrews, though there is something misleading about acting like they are one and the same.

The man who pronounced St. Andrews the best beach in the world is widely known as "Dr. Beach," a handle that plays off his Ph.D. in coastal geology. Professor and director of the International Hurricane Center at Florida International University, Leatherman annually rates the beaches for Condé Nast. Unfortunately, no sooner had he ranked St. Andrews number one than Hurricane Opal plowed through, ravaging the sparkling white sand, narrowing the beach, flattening the dunes. Attempts to repair the damage—beach renourishment, replanting sea oats, erecting sand fencing—have shored up the worst of it. Even though St. Andrews has not returned to Leatherman's subsequent lists, the number one rating still gets quoted as if it had been announced yesterday.

His lists, which change a lot from year to year, are received as gospel, and they are admittedly fun to read and to compare with years past. We do have to wonder a bit about the methodology, though. Take, for example, the assertion that Leatherman examines 650 beaches around the country, subjecting each destination to a very rigid rating scale. (We have an image of a guy in a white lab coat stalking the beaches, pausing to hold a stethoscope to the sand.) The scientific scale involves 50 criteria, he claims, such as sand softness, water and air temperature, number of sunny days, currents, smell, pests, trash, litter, access, crowds, and crime rate.

Not to impugn Dr. Leatherman's unimpeachable credentials. His *Barrier Island Guidebook*—a brief, nontechnical overview of processes that shape coastal barriers—is one of our bibles. Yet simple math shows that if this assertion is to be believed, he must "very rigidly" measure and assess 32,500 criteria (50 multiplied by 650) per year in order to calculate

ners have come up with excellent package deals for visitors. Seven-day and annual passes into the park will gain admission for an entire family of up to eight people. A seven-day sunup-to-sundown pass costs $10.70; if you want to use the boat launch and/or enter the park on bike or foot after hours, the fee jumps to $13.38. An annual pass costs $64.20 (day use) or $85.60 (day use plus boat launch and after-hours access). Considering that the per vehicle entrance fee to St. Andrews is $4, and that the park is by far the most well-preserved and publicly accessible beach in Panama City Beach, any of the passes qualifies as a good deal.

his final ratings. That works out to about 89 criteria assessed on a daily basis. Only on-site inspections will do, given such subjective measures of beach worthiness as "softness" and "smell." This necessitates constant travel to the coastal margins. Moreover, what about the wrenches that an atypical day at the beach might throw into the works? How is time of year accounted for? What if you visited Panama City Beach in December and Malibu in June? Would you be seeing each place at its best or worst, and is that a fair measure of overall merit? What about beaches that have been artificially renourished? Are they docked for not being natural or given added points for their people-pleasing width? No, we're not envious of Dr. Beach, who's got too much ground to cover and too many criteria to track.

Leatherman's annual Top Ten list has made him the Casey Kasem of coastal scientists. His name is cited by other Florida beach towns that have shown up on his lists. We recall a newspaper story out of Siesta Key, which felt that it had undeservedly been left off the good professor's Top Ten. They bade him visit, he was duly impressed, and Siesta Key turned up on his 1992 list.

We are somewhat amused by his celebrity in our list-addicted culture, since academics rarely get to cash in at the pop-media trough. At the same time, we've got to hand it to him for coming up with such a marketable idea. The one thing that makes it a bit of a gimmick (albeit an entertaining one) is that the beaches don't change as dramatically as his lists do. Only those beaches that experience major alterations due to hurricanes—and such events are relatively rare, and nature remarkably resilient—would become markedly different within the space of a year. Otherwise, natural processes and even human-generated changes occur on more incremental time scales.

In the appendix of this book, we've come up with a list of what we consider to be Florida's best beaches. Please don't think we're jumping on anyone's bandwagon. Just so you know, we've been drawing up such lists, both in our travel books and for magazine and newspaper articles, since we began working on our first beach-themed book in 1984—well before either Leatherman or Letterman got into the list-making game.

As for Panama City Beach, a $10 million beach renourishment project undertaken in recent years involved placing dredged offshore sand onto thinning sections of the beach. The renourishment has been a success in the short term, but it's worth noting that PCB had to go the renourishment route several times in the 1990s. Another hurricane could trigger the whole expensive dredging and renourishment cycle all over again. That's the part of the Panama City Beach story that doesn't get told quite as frequently as the bit about being ranked number one by Dr. Beach in 1995.

Stephen Leatherman, the ubiquitous "Dr. Beach" (see sidebar), rated St. Andrews the best beach in the United States in 1995. Thought it's since taken several hits from hurricanes, St. Andrews remains a stunning place, with mesa-like sand cliffs at the back of a wide beach. Along the water's edge is a teeming wealth of life forms, including starfish, urchins, and an endless field of unbroken shells. Nearby Shell Island is also park property, offering more of the same exquisite beach, unsurpassable seclusion, and a less crowded spot from which to snorkel off the jetties. Passenger ferries shuttle over every half hour from 9 A.M. to 5 P.M. in season. (Round-trip fare is $7.50 for adults and $5.50 for children 12 and under.) After Labor Day, the trips dwindle to weekends only, and by November the concession shuts down entirely until spring. The shuttle service also offers snorkel packages that include an "eco-snorkel tour" for $25: a three-hour narrated trip around the bay with stops for snorkeling in grass flats, along jetties and off Shell Island's beach. For information on shuttles and boat rentals within the park, call the **Pier Concession Store** at 850/235-4004. For the **Jetty Dive Store** on park property, call 850/233-0197.

The inlet separating St. Andrews from Shell Island is a deepwater shipping channel watched closely by the Coast Guard. Because of the prodigious mix of cross currents, the surf on either side of the jetties has earned this spot the nickname "Amazons" from the army of surfers who brave it. At certain times of year, we were told, it is among the best surfing spots in Florida, but don't let the Coast Guard catch you blocking the inlet.

6 St. Andrews State Park (Shell Island)

Location: due east of Panama City Beach, in St. Andrews Bay

Parking/fees: accessible by boat only; private operators in the Panama City Beach area run shuttles to and from Shell Island. The one within St. Andrews State Park costs $7.50 for adults and $5.50 for children, and it runs on a seasonal basis. Call the Pier Concession Store at 850/235-4004 for days and times of operation.

Hours: 8 A.M. to sunset

Facilities: none

Contact: St. Andrews State Park, 850/233-5140

Contact Information

St. Andrews State Park, 4607 State Park Lane, Panama City Beach, FL 32408; 850/233-5140; website: www.myflorida.com

MAP OF THE PANHANDLE—PAGE 547

Panama City Beach

While it's no secret that Panama City Beach (PCB, for short) is a wide-open party town and a fun and family-friendly beach town, what is often overlooked is that PCB is also a major outdoor recreation destination. PCB (pop. 5,000) has few rivals when it comes to diving, fishing, swimming, and beachcombing. It is also an arcade lover's paradise. After having endured the splendid isolation of the Nature Coast, we were happy to return to a built-up world of goofy seaside fun. And so we pummeled each other with bumper boats at Coconut Creek's Grand Maze and bumper cars at Emerald Falls Raceway, and gamely stepped up to the batting cages, driving range, and mini-golf at Tropical Island Fun Park. However, we pulled up lame at Bungee Mania. If God had meant us to plunge earthward at heart-stopping speed from a giant rubber band, we would have been born with ruptured spleens. We'd rather let the dolphins and sea lions at Gulf World attempt the heroic leaps and stunts.

Arcades and attractions aside, PCB's real drawing card is the beach. Not just any old beach, mind you, but 26 unbroken miles of great white wonder that extends from St. Andrews State Park to Phillips Inlet. This is among the prettiest beaches along the Panhandle's postcard-perfect shoreline, where blinding white sheets of quartz sand meet the clear emerald water of the Gulf of Mexico. The beach is of a healthy width in most places, thanks to ongoing renourishment projects (necessitated by hurricanes, which did their share of stripping away in the merciless 1990s). On a sunny day, the vision of polar-white sand and emerald-green sea is irresistible to anyone with a pulse.

In years past, parts of Panama City Beach were known by separate names and clearly discernible personalities. Only folks who have lived here for decades still use the older names. For example, much of what used to get called "Biltmore Beach," along Thomas Drive at the east end, now is referred to as East Panama City Beach. The one sectional identification that's still in regular (though declining) usage is Miracle Strip. This seven-mile stretch along Front Beach Road between Thomas Drive (at U.S. 98) and Panama Beach City Pier (near State Route 79) is more commonly known today as Middle Panama City Beach. Likewise, the designation West Panama City Beach serves to cover several small residential communities—Laguna Beach, Santa Monica, Sunnyside, Hollywood Beach, and Inlet Beach—between State Route 79 and Phillips Inlet. Since Panama City Beach's incorporation in 1969 as a massive linear municipality extending all the way west to Philips Inlet, those community names have served no real purpose, save as a force of habit or nostalgia. Technically, it is all Panama City Beach. Just for the record, Phillips Inlet is not an actual inlet but one of those bodies of water unique to Florida, a coastal lake.

Panama City Beach—which is not to be confused with Panama City, the larger and more drab military/industrial port town that lies in the shadow of Tyndall Air Force Base—exhibits multiple personalities, depending on what time of year you're visiting. From March through Easter, PCB is the Spring Break Capital of the Western World, with a half-million or so college-age revelers passing through town with beery smiles and Dionysian agendas. From Easter through Labor Day, PCB is a family-friendly vacation town that plies the summer tourist trade, using affordability and fun as hooks that are as effective as those that land tarpon. From Labor Day through February, PCB goes into a state of hibernation, becoming a veritable ghost-crab town.

It's worth remembering that Panama City Beach lies on the Panhandle at a lati-

MAP OF BAY COUNTY—PAGE 572

Panama City Beach + Spring Break = Fun

If you do not understand the above equation, then just skip this and move on to the next section, because this is all about the rites of spring, college-style.

Panama City Beach is king of the Spring Break mountain. In any given year since it became a nationally popular Spring Break destination in the mid-1990s, between 500,000 and 800,000 students have descended upon this lengthy anaconda of a beach town between late February and mid-April. It's no mystery why Panama City Beach has courted Spring Break or why Spring Breakers have responded. The town's core appeal can be explained with one simple statistic: Panama City Beach ("PCB," for short) lays claim to 26 unbroken miles of sandy frontage along the Gulf of Mexico. Beaches + Sun + Thousands of Party-Minded College Kids = Fun. This is a powerful equation that induces chilly, sun-starved collegians from the Midwest, the Northeast, and Texas to close their math books and head south for a week of pure hedonism. The vast majority will be heavily concentrated on a seven-mile stretch known as the "Miracle Strip"—or "Strip," for short—which runs along Thomas Drive and Front Beach Road, roughly between Club La Vela (the largest nightclub in the U.S.) west to the County Pier (the longest pier in the state of Florida).

In return for soliciting and welcoming the collegiate horde—an invitation that has largely been rescinded in such former Spring Break capitals as Daytona Beach and Fort Lauderdale—PCB receives a sizable revenue stream in the early spring, which is ordinarily a slow time of year. It's a win-win situation, you might say, with direct expenditures during Spring Break 2000 topping $51 million and total economic impact estimated at $135.7 million. More than $18 million in room revenue was generated, and $33.8 million was expended in goods and services. Spring Break is not without its detractors, but their arguments generally don't carry the day. In a community dependent on tourist revenue for its existence, it's pretty hard to argue with those kinds of figures.

For years, Spring Break in PCB was a regional phenomenon that drew mainly on schools in adjacent Southern states. The history of Spring Break as a national phenomenon in Panama City Beach commenced in 1993—the first year the community made a concerted effort to cast a larger net in marketing to students around the country. The groundwork was laid the preceding year, when student-union presidents were invited down to look around.

Spring break really took off in 1996, which is when MTV's cameras focused heavily on Panama City Beach. This was about the time that Daytona Beach, like Fort Lauderdale before it, decided that Spring Break was more bane than benefit and began discouraging collegians from balcony-jumping their way into the national headlines. In 1996, seven Spring Breakers died in largely alcohol-related mishaps in Daytona Beach.

Having set up camp in Panama City Beach, MTV based itself along Thomas Drive, where two massive nightclubs—Club La Vela and Spinnaker—host parties that attract thousands. From 1996 to 1998, MTV was all over PCB (and vice versa), throwing concerts and broadcasting such shows as *The Grind* and *Jams* from Club La Vela. In 1997, Aerosmith,

MAP OF THE PANHANDLE—PAGE 547

Stone Temple Pilots, the Mighty Mighty Bosstones, Foxy Brown, Snoop Doggy Dogg, the Spice Girls, and others performed under MTV's auspices. There was no more happening place in the world than PCB at that time.

The raucous tone of the Spring Break celebration has been softened somewhat over the past two years, as MTV has taken its Spring Break coverage elsewhere—primarily to Jamaica and Cancún, where international law sets no drinking age. But, mark our words, MTV will come back to PCB. Not every student can afford a Caribbean vacation in the middle of the school year. Just look at the hundreds of thousands of Spring Breakers who, like swallows flocking to Capistrano, return to PCB each spring.

PCB's appeal is best explained by a local business owner: "They came because they were welcomed. . . . They came because the more than 18,000 available rooms didn't cost them the next semester's tuition. They came for the 26 miles of sugary, have-to-wear-sunglasses sand, its clear 72° water. . . . They came because it's the place to leave all the worries of academia behind in the blowing snow and ivy-covered towers."

The town annually compiles a detailed list of colleges, enrollments, and break dates. This information is distributed to town businesses and any visitor who asks for it at the information kiosk beside the County Pier. The implied message is that if you mistakenly stumble into Panama City Beach during March and April, you have only yourself to blame.

"The numbers are here regardless of the presence of MTV," said one congenial "information specialist" in PCB. "It is pretty much a 24-hour-a-day event, and the cruising cars on Front Beach Road move only a few inches every 15 minutes. No one complains. That's part of the fun. I've seen so many little naked behinds you wouldn't believe it."

Upon checking in to their motel or hotel, each student gets a "welcome pack"—a kit that contains rules, tips, coupons, maps, and free samples. Clubs allow those between 18 and 21 to enter and partake of the on-premises fun, but they strictly enforce the 21-year-old minimum age for drinking. No glass containers or open fires are allowed on the beach. Severe penalties—i.e., eviction from motels without refunds and jail sentences—are meted out to balcony divers and those who tamper with fire alarms, defraud innkeepers, ignite open fires, and sleep or pass out on the beach.

Beginning in 1998, PCB initiated a unique system of dispensing instant justice for misdemeanors. They call it Spring Break Court, and it works like this: Court is set up daily in Frank Brown Park on Highway 98. Judges and lawyers are there. Large numbers of cases are handled on the spot. Guilty offenders have a choice of paying a fine ($200 or more per infraction) or doing eight hours of public service (picking up trash, cleaning the beach). The two most common infractions are underage drinking (officially, "Possession of Alcohol Under 21") and causing a public disturbance. About 90 percent of those charged pay the fine, because they want to get back to the beach. But the other 10 percent appreciate having some way to work off their fine, and so they don orange vests and fill sacks with trash. It is not a bad deal either way.

For a brochure listing Spring Break rules and regulations, along with motels, restaurants, stores, bars, and attractions that crave your business, contact the Panama City Beach Convention and Visitors Bureau, P.O. Box 9473, Panama City Beach, FL 32417; 800/PC-BEACH; website: www.800pcbeach.com.

tude that is considerably north of those year-round subtropical meccas down on the Florida Peninsula where all the snowbirds flee in winter. If you should for some reason find yourself in Panama City Beach during the winter months, you might well wind up with the shivers while dreaming longingly of Margaritaville. We certainly did. One of the coldest days we've ever spent was during a blustery December in PCB. A wicked wind chilled us to the marrow and the mercury dropped below freezing after nightfall. In Florida? Yes, in Florida. This reality check drove home the point that PCB must make hay when the sun shines warmly—which explains why it has adopted Spring Break after Fort Lauderdale and Daytona Beach sent it packing.

Not everyone is happy that this six-week party has landed in PCB. Some stuffed shirts simply do not like Spring Break. These pious souls are no doubt troubled by what H.L. Mencken characterized in his definition of "Puritanism" as "the haunting fear that someone, somewhere may be happy." Most local businesses, however, are fond of the collegiate hordes—or at least have learned to peacefully coexist with them for a month or two. After all, between the vernal influx and the more evenly spaced, family-oriented summer season, they make enough money to close down four months a year and take their own extended break.

For some properties, Spring Break accounts for a third of all revenue for the entire year. Even so, the city government has tried to "erase this Panhandle resort town's honky-tonk image," according to news accounts. (Read: they'd prefer to attract families and convention business.) Speaking to an Associated Press reporter, multi-term mayor Phillip Griffits sniffed, "We cannot let our success in Spring Break be our failure in our tourist industry the rest of the season." If he's blaming college kids for PCB's inability to fill its hotels to capacity the rest of the year, he's picked the wrong scapegoat.

Griffits went on to say, "If the legislature would allow me to regulate tacky, I could clean the beach up today. If they'd let me ride down this beach and say, 'This goes and this stays, and this sign goes and this one stays,' I could have it cleaned up tomorrow." There's a good reason the legislature won't give Griffits or others like him that power. It is because America is not Sudan or Singapore, and Panama City Beach is not Pebble Beach. PCB is 26 unbroken miles of beautiful sandy beaches and it is Party Central during March and April each year for half a million college kids.

Alas, other members of local government object to the sort of businesses that cater to people who put the bread on PCB's table: tattoo parlors, topless bars, and shops that merchandise sex paraphernalia, including condoms and other contraceptive needs. Ordinances regulating the names and signs of such places have been passed. The owner of Condom Knowledge, which was singled out as offensive, laughed at the ordinance, saying "family tourists," not college students, are his best customers. Indeed, why would college kids need adult videos or magazines when a 24-hour party is taking place on the beach?

All of this strikes us as predictably hypocritical and way too familiar. Such rumblings in Fort Lauderdale and Daytona Beach served as a prelude to giving Spring Break the bum's rush. As we predicted, those same cities are now having second thoughts about having run the students out of town. Fort Lauderdale has banked too heavily on the yuppie dollar, while Daytona Beach has placed too many eggs in the biker basket. During the weeklong Bike Fest 2000, the deadliest on record, there were 16 motorcycle-related fatalities in the Daytona Beach area. Spring Break seems safe as milk by comparison.

Should PCB get too high handed or prohibitionist, we predict that they, too, will eventually wind up singing the Spring Break blues. Fortunately, that isn't likely to happen. Indeed, the voters seem to agree that Spring Break is, by and large, a good thing. Mayor Griffits and some of the more brazen council members lost their reelection campaigns in 2000.

Beaches

From **St. Andrews State Park** to Phillips Inlet, Panama City Beach encompasses 26 miles of sandy gulf shoreline. You can stare at it for hours without growing bored. The water changes colors at different times of day, from emerald to azure to coral, and the white, nearly pure (99 percent) quartz sand provides a striking contrast. A few hundred yards offshore, dolphins can be spotted swimming giddily through the surf. Any randomly chosen part of this shoreline, if viewed from dune line to water—sans the motels and high-rises—is exactly what the word "beach" conjures in most people's desert-island fantasies.

All that said, for a city in desperate need of—no, entirely dependent upon—the public swarm from March through September, PCB has not done terrifically well at providing public beach access. West of St. Andrews State Park, a few street endings lead to dune walkovers, but parking is minimal (and more often nonexistent), and the public parks along the so-called Miracle Strip are scarce and generic. Granted, most people who come here are staying at oceanfront hotels and motels and, thus, aren't in the market for public beach access. But what about the visitors whose motels don't abut the ocean? And what about city and county residents? We're talking about a town with 26 unbroken miles of public beach. As former President Bill Clinton once put it, "We can do better." (He, of all people, should know about needing to do better.)

Beyond St. Andrews State Park, the best public-access points are **Bay County Pier and Park** (a.k.a. M.B. Miller Park), at the center of the Miracle Strip, and **Panama Beach City Pier** (a.k.a. Dan Russell Municipal Pier), the longest fishing pier on the Gulf of Mexico. Both provide free parking and facilities. The helpful Panama City Beach Convention and Visitors Bureau information center is located a stone's throw from County Pier, which has a half-mile of beach and free parking. In addition to its impressive length, City Pier (which lies west of County Pier) is home to B's Pier Cafe. The pier and beach are open all night, so you can fish around the clock, if you're so inclined.

Two smaller beach parks in PCB are

7 St. Andrews State Park (Panama City Beach)

Location: east end of Thomas Drive, in Panama City Beach
Parking/fees: $4 entrance fee per vehicle. Camping fees are $10–12 October 1–February 28, and $17–19 March 1–September 30.
Hours: 8 a.m. to sunset
Facilities: concessions, restrooms, picnic tables, showers, and visitor center
Contact: St. Andrews State Park, 850/233-5140

8 Thomas Drive Park

Location: 7,000 block of Thomas Drive in Panama City Beach
Parking/fees: free parking lot
Hours: sunrise to sunset
Facilities: restrooms and showers
Contact: Bay County Parks Division, 850/784-4066

MAP OF BAY COUNTY—PAGE 572

Thomas Drive Park, in East Panama City Beach, and **Bid-o-Wee Beach**, between the county and city piers. Thomas Drive Park lies just east of Club La Vela and Spinnaker (see "Night Moves"). It's got 80 or so parking spaces, basic facilities, and a boardwalk to the beach. Bid-o-Wee Beach isn't really a formalized access but just one of the few remaining undeveloped beachfront parcels in PCB. The county and city parks departments couldn't offer any information on it, and neither claimed responsibility for its ownership or upkeep. It lies between the Fiesta and Fountainebleau Hotels on Front Beach Road. Just park by the side of the road and walk the crossovers to the beach, noting the natural look of the dunes, which are absent elsewhere. It is, as one local put it to us, "the beach the way it used to be." Up in **West Panama City Beach**, any number of marked accesses (at least a dozen, by our rough count) lead onto the beach.

PCB has an interesting (read: not very effective) system for patrolling its beaches. Rather than station a lifeguard every 500 yards or so, as they do on Florida's densely populated east coast beaches, they hoist colored flags, displaying them prominently at numerous sites. A blue flag indicates a calm sea. A yellow flag is a caution for possible undertow, big waves, and rip currents. A red flag denotes danger, and it's illegal to go in the water when these are flying. Red can mean anything from severe undertow to sharks and/or stingrays. While lifeguards are stationed at the piers, the vast majority of PCB's 26 miles is watched over by the Panama City Beach Patrol, which scoots up and down the beach on big-wheeled carts, taking care of crises on an ad hoc basis.

The big problem at Panama City Beach is rip currents: narrow channels of water moving out to sea that can drag unwary swimmers along with them. The United States Lifesaving Association, a critic of Panama City Beach's surf-rescue system, spoke up when 10 swimmers drowned there in 1994. In their defense, the Beach Patrol has to squabble with local government for funding, and 26 miles really is a lot of beach to keep tabs on. Still, lifeguarding should become a higher priority in PCB.

Shore Things

- **Boat cruise:** Captain Davis Queen Fleet, 5550 North Lagoon Drive, 850/234-3435.
- **Dive shop:** Panama City Dive Center, 4823 Thomas Drive, 850/235-3390.

9 Bay County Pier and Park (a.k.a. M.B. Miller Park)

Location: between 13,623 and 14,401 Front Drive Road in Panama City Beach
Parking/fees: free parking lot
Hours: sunrise to sunset
Facilities: lifeguards (seasonal), restrooms, picnic tables, showers, and visitor center
Contact: Bay County Parks Division, 850/784-4066

10 Bid-o-Wee Beach

Location: between the 13,000 and 14,000 blocks of Front Beach Road in Panama City Beach
Parking/fees: free roadside parking
Hours: 24 hours
Facilities: none
Contact: Panama City Parks and Recreation Department, 850/233-5040

- **Ecotourism:** Shell Island Kayaks and Boat Trips, Pier Concession Store, St. Andrews State Park, 4607 State Park Lane, 850/235-4004.
- **Fishing charters:** Captain Anderson's Marina, 5550 North Lagoon Drive, 850/234-3435.
- **Marina:** Captain Anderson's Marina, 5550 North Lagoon Drive, 850/234-3435.
- **Piers:** Panama Beach City Pier (a.k.a. Dan Russell Municipal Pier), 16101 Front Beach Road, 850/233-5080; County Pier (a.k.a. M.B. Miller Park), 12213 Front Beach Road, 850/233-3039.
- **Rainy-day attraction:** Gulf World Marine Park, 15412 Front Beach Road, 850/234-5271.
- **Shopping/browsing:** Alvin's Big Island Tropical Department Store, 12010 Front Beach Road, 850/234-3048.
- **Surf shop:** Trader Rick's, 12208 Front Beach Road, 850/235-3243.
- **Vacation rentals:** St. Andrews Bay Resort Management, 726 Thomas Drive, 800/621-2462.

Bunking Down

There's a lot of beach, and there are a lot of hotels, motels, and condos along it in Panama City Beach. "Lots" is the operative word. The town runs on like the world's longest run-on sentence, with lots of places to stay of every quality level and description clustered along Front Beach Drive in a seemingly unbroken line.

Officially, we are told there are 18,000 rooms in and around PCB, but the actual number may be closer to 20,000. Lodgings are so abundant that even if you arrive without reservations, regardless of time of year, nine times out of ten you'll find something. The volume of rooms in PCB and the unfancy nature of a lot of the accommodations make this community the ideal site for both Spring Breakers and no-frills family vacationers. Mom-and-pop businesses are more the norm than the exception, not just in the hotel-motel trade but in the food and fun departments, too.

The quietest parts of PCB are at its west end, where the commercial buildup thins out, and east end, which belongs to St. Andrews State Park. The Miracle Strip occupies much of what lies in between. It's a densely developed seven-mile area where most of PCB's accommodations can be found. The **Holiday Inn Sunspree Resort** (11127 Front Beach Road, 850/234-1111, $$$) and the **Edgewater Resort** (11212

⓫ Panama Beach City Pier (a.k.a. Dan Russell Municipal Pier)

Location: 16,000 block of Front Beach Road in Panama City Beach
Parking/fees: free parking lot
Hours: 24 hours
Facilities: concessions, lifeguards (seasonal), restrooms, and showers
Contact: Panama Beach City Pier, 850/233-5080

⓬ West Panama City Beach accesses

Location: numerous marked accesses along Front Beach Road between City Pier and Phillips Inlet in West Panama City Beach
Parking/fees: free roadside parking
Hours: sunrise to sunset
Facilities: none
Contact: Bay County Parks Division, 850/784-4066

Front Beach Road, 850/235-4044, $$$$) anchor the Miracle Strip at the high end. The Holiday Inn offers clean rooms and balconies overlooking the gulf, plus upscale amenities like a fitness center, beachside tiki bar, swan boats, cabanas, and chaise lounges. One of the city's few lifeguard stands is directly behind the Holiday Inn, too.

The Edgewater is a sprawling golf and tennis resort spread out among 15 buildings on the beach and across the highway, where it snuggles around a nine-hole golf course. Units in the five high-rise buildings on the beach offer eye-popping views of the emerald water and white sand from their balconies. The villas on the inland side offer homey comforts and conveniences. The Edgewater experience, with a total of 540 units and a daily list of activities, is as hands-on or hands-off as you want it to be. Because it's a city-within-a-city that has a high number of monthly rentals, the Edgewater doesn't feel the off-season pinch as severely as most of PCB's lodgings.

The Boardwalk Beach Resort is a complex consisting of four hotels linked by a boardwalk that runs for a third of a mile. It's a formidable operation, with a varied lot of restaurants, bars, and beach activities—a one-stop city-within-a-city where all of your basic vacations can be met at different price points. From most to least expensive, they are **Four Points by Sheraton** (9600 South Thomas Drive, $$$), **Howard Johnson** (9400 South Thomas Drive, $$), **Beachwalk** (9450 South Thomas Drive, $), and **Gulfwalk** (9500 South Thomas Drive, $). All four hotels at the **Boardwalk Beach Resort** share the same central phone number (850/234-3484).

Just to get this on the record, the ugliest condo resort we have ever seen is located beachfront at PCB. It's called the **Summit** (8743 Thomas Drive), which is an odd name for an edifice that is, in fact, the nadir of architectural imagination. This 15-story, 30-unit-wide structure looks like the sort of institution from which you would try to escape; sling some barbed wire around the property and it could pass for a prison. In a fun and friendly beach town like PCB, just give us a clean, comfortable motel room where we can lay our sun-baked heads at night.

For assistance with motel reservations, call the **Panama City Beach Convention and Visitors Bureau** (800/PCBEACH) between 8 A.M. and 5 P.M. Central Time. They'll help you pick a place, given your needs and means, and even do the booking.

Coastal Cuisine

If, as doctors often advise, breakfast is the most important meal of the day, you're in luck in Panama City Beach. With a Waffle House, Waffle Shoppe, Waffle Iron, Golden Griddle, Pancakes Plus, Omelet & Waffle Shop, Coffee Kettle, or some other variation on this theme stationed on nearly every corner, we deduced that breakfast may be the only meal served with any regularity to most visitors (especially Spring Breakers), who nurse their hangovers with stacks of pancakes and bottomless mugs of coffee. We stumbled onto an eye-opening deal at the **All-American Diner** (10590 Front Beach Road, 850/235-2443, and 15406 Front Beach Road, 850/233-6007, $), where an all you-can-eat-breakfast goes for $5.69.

Lunch and dinner are different propositions. The choices are as staggering as the appetites brought to them by an army of people who have been playing on the beach all day. Nearly every beachfront eatery proclaims itself a "grille" or "pub." The advantage of hitting such places—**Hammerhead Fred's Grill & Bar** (8752 Thomas Drive, 850/233-3907) or the **Beach Club Grill** (10637 Front Beach Road, 850/234-6003), to name two of the more popular ones—is that you can eat, drink, and party on the same premises.

Tips for Spring Breakers

Here are some must-do's (and a few must don'ts) for those collegians coming to Panama City Beach in observance of the rites of spring:

- Get a Panama Gold Card ($30), which will gain you free admittance to a different club every night of the week. These cards can be purchased from tour operators and on-site at hotels, motels, and resort properties.
- During the day, mix and mingle on the beach behind Spinnaker and Club La Vela. This is the most happening spot on the beach.
- Try not to use the car more than you have to, or you'll wind up in endless traffic jams along Front Beach Road that move feet instead of miles per hour. On the other hand, cruising can have its up side, so make the best of it.
- At night, the party tent at Hammerhead Fred's is a hot place to reconnoiter with the opposite sex.
- You MUST go to Club La Vela at least once.
- Eat a decent meal every few days. Our suggestions: Capt. Anderson's, Hamilton's, the Treasure Ship. If you're famished, hit the all-you-can-eat buffets at places like the **Mariner Restaurant** (9104 Front Beach Road, 850/234-8450).
- Remember to apply sunscreen liberally, especially if you'll be exposing flesh that has turned polar white over the winter.
- Take advantage of corporate-sponsored events and freebies. At Spring Break 2000, for instance, Kellogg's set up a giant "cool-out cabana" that had phones where one could call home, plus lounges, saunas, Jacuzzis, etc. You'll wind up with T-shirts and ballcaps for filling out surveys and such. They're giving it all away right and left in PCB over Spring Break because (1) They want you to become a loyal consumer; and (2) They might want to hire you someday. IBM sponsored a major job fair in PCB over Spring Break 2000, though job-hunting was surely the last thing on people's minds that week.
- Obtain and use discount coupon and ticket booklets, which are freely handed out by such corporate sponsors as Coke.
- Do not taunt the police. Do not drink and drive. Do not disobey stated hotel/motel rules. Do not try to use a fake ID. Do not behave stupidly in full public view. Do not even think about balcony climbing or diving.
- Go—and go early—to the Beach Bash Beach Party on Tuesday afternoon during Spring Break at **Sharky's Beach Club** (15201 Front Beach Road, 850/235-2420). These jam-packed "all you can eat, all you can drink" bacchanals get pretty wild. Their motto: "No Shirt—No Shoes—Free Beer!"

Shuckums Oyster Pub & Seafood Grill (15614 Front Beach Road, 850/234-3214, $$), another friendly indoor/outdoor saloon, is located at the west end of the Strip. Local oysters are their forte and each order is shucked in front of you.

Also, the word "steak" is almost as prevalent as "waffle" on the PCB culinary scene, and evidently it's as popular as seafood, too. The best slabs of beef are found at **Boar's Head** (17290 Front Beach Road, 850/234-6628, $$$), which has

Wreck Dive Capital of the South

For underwater sightseers, Panama City Beach is the Hudson Valley, the Grand Canyon, and the Rocky Mountains all rolled into one. Self-described as the "Wreck Dive Capital of the South," PCB has also been chosen by Rodale's *Scuba Diving* magazine as the No. 2 wreck-diving destination in the United States. Some of these "wrecks"—lying at depths of 40 to 100 feet—are truly that, including the *Empire Mica*, a 465-foot British tanker that was sunk by a German submarine in World War II. Others have been dumped underwater for the express purpose of creating an artificial reef to attract marine animals. The 107-foot *Chickasaw*, a tugboat, is now inundated with beaugregory, snapper, and blennies.

Other popular sunken treasures include the *B.J. Putnam*, a 180-foot fish processing boat, and the U.S.S. *Strength*, a 185-foot World War II mine sweeper. In addition to these sunken treasures, the Panama City Institute has coordinated a community-wide effort to construct 50 artificial reefs in the waters offshore to create more sites for scuba divers. These man-made reefs include bridge spans and barges up to 160 feet long, and they have been deposited in water from 80 to 100 feet deep. Many are now covered with coral and rainbow-hued sponges.

Snorkelers are not out of luck, either. The jetties at St. Andrews State Park are resplendent with underwater life and are only a jump away from land. The best time for diving around Panama City Beach is between April and September. Several dive shops in the area offer customized packages and provide diving and snorkeling equipment and instruction.

Panama City Beach takes diving seriously enough to have built a museum to the history of the sport—the only such museum, interestingly enough, in the world. **The Museum of Man in the Sea** (17314 Panama City Beach Parkway, 850/235-4101) exhibits diving data that goes back to the 16th century, as well as the earliest-known relics from that time. Also on display are numerous pieces of booty and artifacts that have been recovered from wrecks by divers over the years. A 500-gallon saltwater viewing pool lets you view St. Andrews Bay from a diver's perspective. Admission is $5 for adults, $2.50 for children ages six to 16, and free for kids under six; the museum is open from 9 A.M. to 5 P.M., seven days a week.

pleased carnivores for more than 20 years with such items as "M'Lady's Cut" and "M'Lord's Cut."

The best-known seafood restaurant in town is unquestionably **Capt. Anderson's** (5551 North Lagoon Drive, 850/234-2225, $$$), which was voted the best seafood restaurant in Florida by readers of *Southern Living* magazine three years in a row. The fishing fleet unloads its daily catch outside the picture windows, and you can watch the show from the patio bar, a popular watering hole for locals and a great place to start a memorable dining experience. The decor showcases nautical artifacts around mahogany walls, slate floors, coral-tree chandeliers, and even a fireplace (in Florida?!). Crab traps filled with whelk shells hang from the ceilings. There are several large dining rooms, and you'd better carry a map if you hope to find your way back from the restroom.

Though it's a huge place, the fresh seafood is prepared consistently and well. Capt. Anderson's most popular menu items are shrimp (cooked five different ways) and grouper. If they have it, you should by all means order scamp. No, that is not a typo for "scampi." It's one of the grouper family and tastes so good that fishermen tend to keep what little they catch of it for themselves. Any grouper preparation here is a standout, and they crown their seafood platters with a meaty portion of grouper, as well. The World's Finest Seafood Platter (drum roll, please) comprises crab, shrimp, scallops, and fish, served fried ($20.95) or broiled ($22.95). A stuffed, broiled Florida lobster can be added to the platter for an additional $9.

Capt. Anderson's is open for dinner six nights a week; they also have an oyster bar and cocktail lounge on the sizable (capacity 660) premises. They do an out-the-door-popular business from Spring Break through summer's end, and then shut down from mid-November to early February. "Once school opens up, it's like turning off a spigot," owner Jimmy Patronis says.

Nearby, on Grand Lagoon, is **Hamilton's** (5711 North Lagoon Drive, 850/234-1255, $$$), another popular seafood house that specializes in cooking fresh catches over mesquite hardwood and charcoal. An interesting assortment of Greek and Cajun-tinged salads and entrées are on the menu, including snapper étouffée, snapper Lafont (stuffed with shrimp, crab, and cheese), snapper St. Charles (sautéed in olive oil), and shrimp Christo (baked in olive oil with Greek seasonings).

While we seldom mention any restaurant that is not on or near the water, **Canopies** (4423 U.S. 98, 850/872-8444, $$$) is a rare treat, offering casual fine dining on par with what any big city has to offer. The grilled grouper with crispy crawfish tails and Cajun hollandaise sauce is irresistibly fine. Ditto the trio of grouper, salmon, and tuna with a citrus beurre blanc. Best of all, you'll pay no more for your dinner than you would at fried seafood emporiums of far less luster. Canopies is located two miles east of the Hathaway Bridge in Panama City.

Night Moves

Two clubs in Panama City Beach dominate the nightlife: **Club La Vela** (8813 Thomas Drive, 850/234-3866) and **Spinnaker** (8795 Thomas Drive, 850/234-7882). Both are the size of airplane hangers, and they are adjacent to each other, along Thomas Drive at the east end of PCB. Club La Vela (see sidebar) is the more lascivious of the two, especially since Spinnaker has been repositioning itself as a family-friendly kind of place in the last few years. But even Spinnaker's reverts to form and kicks out the jams over Spring Break.

Club La Vela was home base for MTV's vaunted Spring Break coverage in the 1990s. It's the "largest nightclub in the USA," with 48 bar stations, 13 dance floors, five bandstands, and a capacity of 7,000. Regular features include wet T-shirt and bikini contests and male and female revues. The statistics at Spinnaker are only slightly less staggering: 34 bar stations and three stages for live music. During Spring Break, you might witness a "Hump the Babe" competition: guys bench-pressing willing, bikini-clad gals. At the height of Spring Break, admission to Club La Vela runs $25–30 (ouch!) and $10–15 at Spinnaker. Both are open from 10 A.M. to 4 A.M.

Sharky's Beach Club (15201 Front Beach Road, 850/235-2420) made headlines back in 1998 when it was the site of a series of Tuesday contests entitled "Sex on the Beach." Participants "gathered in a circle and simulated sex acts," according to a newspaper account. Some of the simulations went too far for the local constables, who arrested three women. Spring Break fun at Sharky's these days is less libidinous than that, but it's still a fun place to party then or any time of year. Other popular hangouts are the **Crazy Marlin** (12705 Front Beach Road, 850/235-3100), **Har-**

poon Harry's (at Breakers Restaurant, 12627 Front Beach Road, 850/234-6060), and **Hammerhead Fred's Island Grill and Bar** (8752 Thomas Drive, 850/233-3907). Incidentally, the party tent at Hammerhead Fred's is the best place to rub elbows and other body parts with members of the opposite sex during Spring Break.

Beyond these titans of the nightlife, after-dinner activities in PCB range from the virtuous to the venial. That is to say, there's praying and sinning. Praying, believe it or not, can be done at **Noah's Ark** (12902 Front Beach Road, 850/234-6062), which is housed inside a large wooden boat. It offers family entertainment to keep the young'uns from ending up at the sorts of places whose doors we happily darkened, where the only praying done is for the speedy delivery of one's next beer and all eyes are glued to scantily clad angels with dirty wings.

The best known and least shocking of these establishments is **Hooters** (12709 Front Beach Road, 850/230-9464). The Hooters concept normally seems desperately lame—waitresses with tight orange gym shorts and T-shirts proudly displaying

"Party With Thousands" at Club La Vela

Boasting of being the "largest nightclub in the USA" is a bit like Spinal Tap's claim of being "the loudest band in England." Having a large nightclub is an idle boast if there's nothing much going on inside. But **Club La Vela** (8813 Thomas Drive, 850/235-1061) has got what it takes to draw crowds and keep them coming back. Indeed, Club La Vela's motto—"Party with Thousands"—is a nightly reality, at least during the Spring Break high season. The club is open daily from February 15 through September 15 from 10 A.M. to 4 A.M. It can hold 7,000, and the staff numbers 140.

From the vantage point of the street, the club sprawls toward the beach, looming like a multi-tiered sandcastle. Its formula for success is not only to stay on top of trends but to carry them to extremes. Thus, Club La Vela constantly reinvents itself according to whatever direction the winds of popular culture are blowing. You just show up in whatever costume suits you in the role-playing cabaret of the new millennium, and they'll handle the rest.

Here are some of the "theme rooms":

- **Thunderdome**, for "hip-hop, bootie, and high-energy dance fans"
- **Underground and Night Gallery**, for "raver kids and trendy people," the music ranging from "break beats" and "progressive house" to "Chicago hard house" and "jungle." (Read: rhythmic sound and fury, signifying nothing.)
- **Rock Arena**, for live rock at high decibels, tending toward self-caricature. As we were putting this edition of *Florida Beaches* to bed, the bands that were booked at Club La Vela included Splendid Chaos, Clowndog Riot, Poptart Monkeys, and Velcro Pygmies. (Were they all named by the same antisocial miscreant?)

hoisted breasts to a construction-worker clientele—but in PCB it seems to work somehow, because they're really dressed no differently than the beach bunnies strolling the sand. The Hooters in PCB is the only outlet of this chain located directly on the beach. The food is stunningly average (cheesy, sodium-doused, cholesterol-laden wings are a specialty), but the grouper sandwich is passable and the scenery is great.

Along these same lines, but much more open about their motives, is a harem's worth of exotic dance clubs that ply their trade in Panama City (the military town across the bay) and Panama City Beach. The lovely lasses who fill the rosters at these places do some remarkable contortions. We were particularly impressed with the talent at **Show N Tail** (5518 Thomas Drive, 850/233-1717). Also noteworthy in the dangerous curves department is **The Curve** (4103 Thomas Drive, 850/234-1055). If you think we're overdoing it, keep in mind that this is the Florida Panhandle, where you're never far from a military base or rowdy beach (or both), and topless clubs are part of the landscape.

- **Galaxy Club**, the newest room, for "deep-space themes" and "stunning special effects"
- **Skybar**, overlooking the beach and Thunderdome
- **Space!**, a "super hi-tek [*sic*] club playing the latest European trance" powered by "50,000 watts of Turbosound." They add, as if this were an enticement, "It's sure to give you a chest concussion!"
- **PussyKat Lounge**, a "premium space for people-watching" (read: voyeurism), where you can attend special events like "Sex & Sushi," an "exclusive party" with free sushi and more: "The sex, well, it too is complimentary. . . . Isn't it always at Club La Vela?" For the "Erotic Pajama Party," attendees were informed that "you have to bare much of your natural good looks by attending in pajamas or lingerie." With its erotic art, candles, and animal-print furniture, the PussyKat Lounge would appear to be some sort of fetishist's den.

Other titillating enticements include features like Thong Thursday, a Ms. La Vela Bikini Contest (feminists, please note the tasteful use of "Ms."), wet T-shirt nights, male hardbody competitions, and "Lokal Weekendz [*sic*]." Club La Vela's website—www.clublavela.com—offers live webcasts, polls, message boards, and provocative photographs.

Frankly, at least to us, there's something sleazy about Club La Vela, even more so than your average topless bar. It is also quite costly: $25–30 admission at the door. Yet a night at Club La Vela is a rite of passage for Spring Breaking hedonists. Club La Vela has been MTV's Spring Break headquarters in every year the cable music channel has come down to Panama City Beach to cover the action. They did not come in 2000 and 2001, however. Nonetheless, you should shake your booty at Club La Vela at least once, if only so you can later brag to all the non–Spring Breaking drones back home that you did indeed "party with thousands."

The scenes in these places seem undignified. Hell, they are undignified: walrus-sized men and randy college boys bellying up to the stage, overly solicitous waitresses in revealing gowns, smoke and mirrors and blinking lights, grinding heavy-metal music, Wolfman Jack–voiced deejays offering sleazy repartee between each high-decibel onslaught, endless pestering to buy a "table dance," and so on. But there's something refreshingly honest, too. For one thing, they turn no one away, no matter how ugly, old, or desperate. (Even 18-year-olds get in, though the clubs enforce a 21-year-old drinking age.) For those who don't drink or imbibe only sparingly, these clubs are a bargain with their $5 cover charges. We were told by someone who works in PCB that they are favorite after-hours gathering spots for locals.

Put it this way: you're going to be in loud, smoky, and chaotic places no matter where you go at night in PCB, but in these clubs you get the added bonus of libidinous entertainment courtesy of smiling gals sporting names like Aspen, Temptation, Verandah, and Mercedes. Be sure to wait around for a "roll call," so you get to see who's on deck, or a "double trouble," where you get to see some truly inspiring teamwork. At this point, we will turn the podium over to Rasputin, who advised, "Sin that ye may be forgiven." What else are you supposed to do in a town where you might find yourself stuck in traffic behind a van, as we did, with this come-on painted on its rear: "Topless Dancers—Follow Me."

One forlorn night not long after Labor Day, we angled into a place called the **Big Easy** (10500 Front Beach Road, 850/233-3098). The choice was pretty much made for us, since nothing else was open. Big and friendly, with draft beer served in plastic pitchers and plenty of classic rock on the CD jukebox (Skynyrd, Zeppelin, Doors), it's a great place to shoot pool or throw darts and watch waves of restaurant workers wander in for their post-late shift decompression rituals. Finally, we can't resist mentioning—because of our publisher's name—**Foghorn's** (3210 Thomas Drive, 850/235-1243), a locals tavern with darts, billiards, Foos-ball, and pinball machines.

Contact Information

Panama City Beach Convention and Visitors Bureau, P.O. Box 9473, Panama City Beach, FL 32417, 850/234-6575 or 800/PCBEACH; website: www.800pcbeach.com

Panama City Beaches Chamber of Commerce, 415 Beckrich Road, Suite 200, Panama City Beach, FL 32407; 850/234-3193; website: www.pcbeach.org

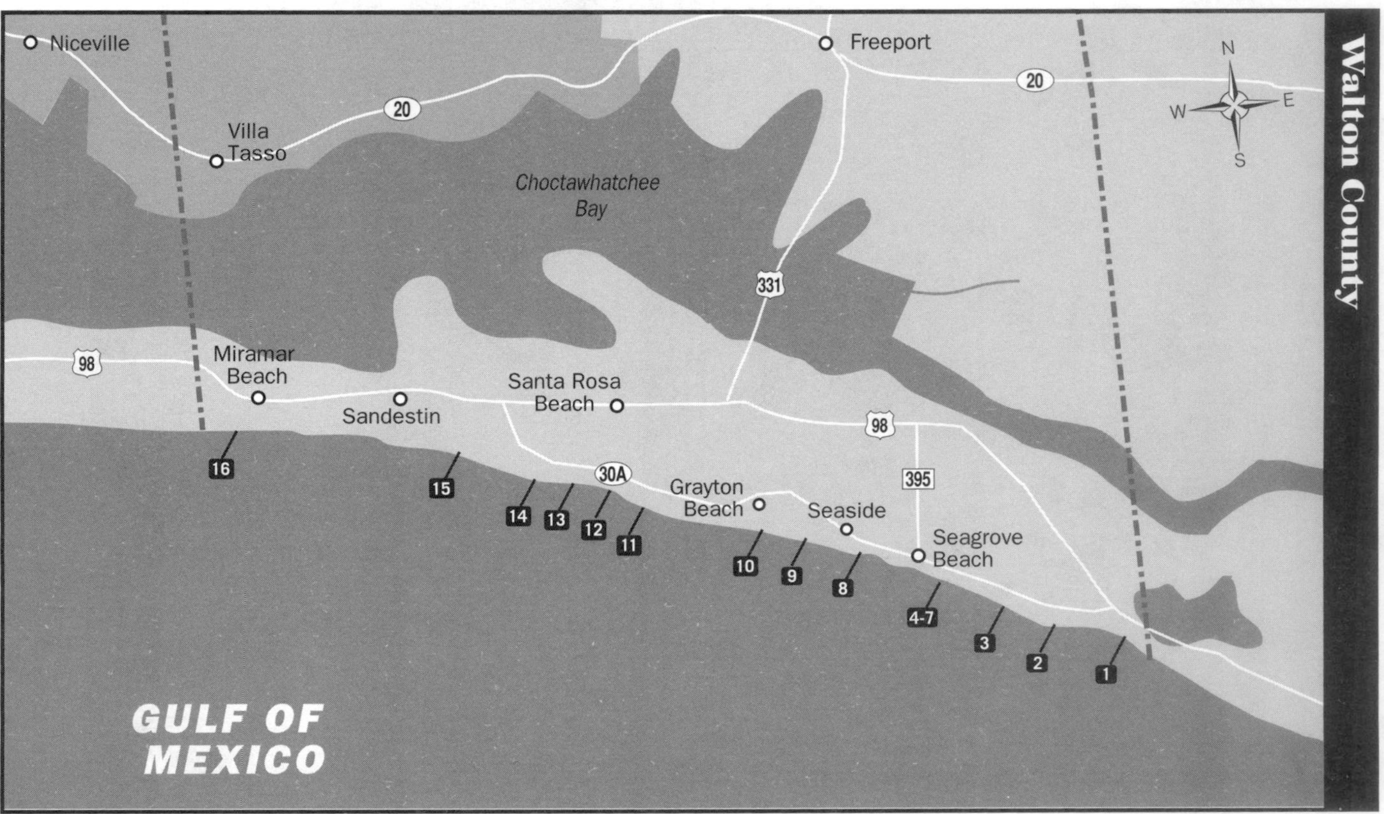
Walton County
Niceville
Freeport
20
N
E
S
W
Villa Tasso
Choctawhatchee Bay
331
98
Miramar Beach
Sandestin
Santa Rosa Beach
30A
395
Grayton Beach
Seaside
Seagrove Beach
16
15
14
13
12
11
10
9
8
4-7
3
2
1
GULF OF MEXICO

WALTON COUNTY

Walton County's 26 miles of unspoiled beaches are renowned for their blindingly white, powdery quartz sand, mountainous sand dunes (though hurricanes have pared back their height), and glistening, turquoise gulf waters. Add tasteful architecture, numerous gourmet restaurants, and miles of empty beaches, and you've got a county beloved by savvy vacationers. Walton is best known for the designer beach town of Seaside (of *The Truman Show* fame). It is also home to Grayton Beach and Topsail Hill Preserve state parks, which have breathtaking, windswept beaches. In addition, there's the older beach towns of Seagrove and Grayton Beach; the low-rise, high-end residential communities of Dune-Allen Beach and Blue Mountain Beach; and the tony stylings of Sandestin, a mammoth condo and golf resort.

Inlet Beach

Traveling from east to west, the first link in the chain of beach communities in south Walton County is Inlet Beach. As a still-embryonic community, it doesn't make much of an impression beyond the sign announcing its existence. We remember it chiefly for a roadside produce stand where oranges grown on the other side of Florida and grapes picked in California were sold. It is a kind of symbol for south Walton County, where everything is ever so slightly faux—but where faux with good taste is preferable to screwed up with bad taste.

Beaches

Camp Helen State Park, occupying 183 acres at Inlet Beach, became part of the Florida state parks system in 1997. Its centerpiece is Inlet Beach Pier, located at Phillips Inlet (which is actually an outflow for Lake Powell, a coastal dune lake). There's not much at Camp Helen—just a parking lot with an honor box, picnic tables and restrooms—and it will likely remain that way.

The state of Florida purchased the land for $13.5 million. It was spared the fate of

South Walton County

Nineteen strung-together communities make up "the beaches of south Walton County." It's a different world once you cross Phillips Inlet and leave Panama City Beach behind. Whereas Panama City Beach has turned a blind eye to the concepts of planning and zoning, Walton County's coastal communities enforce stringent local building codes. Whereas the architectural parameters that define Panama City Beach tend to be honky-tonk and high-rise, Walton County is Florida vernacular, pioneered by Seaside's experiment in New Urbanism. If Panama City Beach epitomizes the 7-Eleven mentality, Walton County's mind-set is more along the lines of Starbucks. Panama City Beach is overbuilt, while Walton County seems to be proceeding with caution, having taken heed of the mistakes made in other Florida beach communities.

At the same time, the heavily Republican south end of the county (where the beaches are) has talked of secession, chafing at the restrictions and apparently wanting to put the pedal to the metal in terms of development. It would be a shame if Walton County went the way of so many others in Florida. We do not need more Destins and Marco Islands, with shady money people subverting the public will in order to erect godawful condominium blocks for absentee owners. Please, heed a pair of beach bums who have seen it all, and leave well enough alone.

Between Inlet Beach to Dune-Allen Beach runs the 18-mile Scenic County Road 30-A Bike Path. About half its length is off-road, and the rest parallels Scenic County Road 30-A, the great gulf-hugging highway that spans the length of the county. We can imagine nothing nicer than working up a good sweat and/or appetite by spending the day cruising scenic south Walton on a two-wheeler.

Just for the record, none of south Walton's 19 "coastal communities" is incorporated. Not even Seaside.

becoming another exclusive beach community when Gulf Coast Community College drew up a management plan for the tract. The 183-acre state park is home to two dozen species of endangered or threatened plants and animals, including snowy and ploving pipers and loggerhead sea turtles. It is also the site of an old log lodge that dates back to the 1930s. Until its acquisition, the property had belonged to an Alabama textile manufacturer, which used it as a summer camp for its employees.

Long-range plans for Camp Helen State Park include the construction of an environmental education center. Eventually, it will become part of Choctaw GEOpark, a grouping of regional park units that will also include Topsail Hill, Henderson Beach, Grayton Beach, Deer Lake, and Fred Gannon Rocky Bayou State Parks. In the meantime, various groups are working to acquire more land surrounding Lake Powell—one of the largest coastal dune lakes in Florida, located on the Bay-Walton County line.

Bunking Down

Don't look for resorts or restaurants at this end of the county, but certain homes can be rented. For rentals in Inlet Beach, try **Panhandle Realty** (109 Lake Place, Panama City, FL 32413; 850/234-6823).

Contact Information

South Walton Tourist Development Council, County Road 331 and U.S. 98, P.O. Box 1248, Santa Rosa Beach, FL 32459; 850/267-1216 or 877/309-2679; website: www.beachesofsouthwalton.com

❶ Camp Helen State Park

Location: off Scenic County Road 30-A at Phillips Inlet, in Inlet Beach
Parking/fees: free parking lots
Hours: 8 A.M. to sundown
Facilities: restrooms and picnic tables
Contact: Camp Helen State Park, 850/233-5059

Rosemary Beach

Twenty-eight miles east of Destin, along Scenic County Road 30-A, Rosemary Beach is a work in progress, inspired by the example for Seaside. But where Seaside has been done up in pastels, Rosemary Beach is being executed in earth tones—rosemary green being one of them—and is described as "old Caribbean." Don't believe a word of it. The houses are so close together it looks more like New York City.

Rosemary Beach heralds and flaunts all the same features as Seaside—a town center, neighborhood pools, paths, and boardwalks—though the sense of community seems contrived because it's even more exclusive, wealth dependent, and imitative. Worse, the pace of construction has exploded like an aggravated form of cancer. In June 2001, it drove one guy off the deep end. Claiming he'd had all he could take of the runaway construction and associated noise, he anonymously threatened to blow up something, necessitating a brief evacuation.

Contact Information

Rosemary Beach, P.O. Box 4801, Santa Rosa Beach, FL 32459; 850/278-2100 or 888/855-1551; website: www.rosemarybeach.com

MAP OF WALTON COUNTY—PAGE 596

Seacrest Beach

Seacrest Beach is located 26 miles east of Destin, along County Road 30-A. It is the first in a consecutive trio of "sea"-named settlements, the others being Seagrove Beach and Seaside. Seacrest is another recently introduced development of cottages reposing between the dunes that have been modeled after the tasteful and stringently controlled example of Seaside, the mother of all "new traditionalist" coastal communities. Just west of Seacrest, a new county-owned beach access point named **Gulf Lake Beach** has appeared at Camp Creek Coastal Lake.

❷ Gulf Lake Beach

Location: at Camp Creek coastal lake on Scenic County Road 30A, just west of Seacrest
Parking/fees: free small parking lot
Hours: 24 hours
Facilities: none
Contact: Beach Services Department, South Walton Tourist Development Council, 850/267-1216

Contact Information

South Walton Tourist Development Council, County Road 331 and U.S. 98, P.O. Box 1248, Santa Rosa Beach, FL 32459; 850/267-1216 or 877/309-2679; website: www.beachesofsouthwalton.com

Seagrove Beach

Seagrove Beach predated its neighbor to the west, Seaside, by many years. Having been founded in 1949, it is the second oldest community (behind Grayton Beach) in south Walton County. People speak of "old" Seagrove and the slower, quieter life along this part of the Panhandle before it was discovered. But while Seagrove has longevity, Seaside has a master plan, which is another way of saying that the former community occupies a much longer stretch of Scenic County Road 30-A but leaves a less distinct impression. One thing that does stand out about Seagrove is an enormous high-rise condominium that shoots out of the ground to a height of 21 stories. Known as One Seagrove Place and dating back to the 1970s, it is an anomaly along Scenic County Road 30-A. While it sticks out like a sore thumb, it can claim to have been here before building regulations were put in place. We were told no more high-rises of its kind

❸ Deer Lake State Park

Location: between Seacrest Beach and Seagrove Beach on Scenic County Road 30A
Parking/fees: free parking lot
Hours: 8 A.M. to sundown
Facilities: restroom and picnic tables
Contact: Deer Lake State Park c/o Grayton Beach State Park, 850/231-4210

❹ Seagrove Beach

Location: east side of One Seagrove Place (condo tower), on Scenic County Road 30A in Seagrove Beach
Parking/fees: limited free street parking
Hours: 24 hours
Facilities: shower
Contact: Beach Services Department, South Walton Tourist Development Council, 850/267-1216

MAP OF THE PANHANDLE—PAGE 547

will be built along Scenic County Road 30-A, as four stories is the maximum permissible height for new construction.

At the same time, we've learned that a business-driven entity called the south Walton Community Council is tired of permitting delays, building restrictions, scenic corridors, and all the other things that make this stretch of coast such a delightful departure from the numbingly overbuilt Florida norm. The hue and cry that seems to be rising in south Walton County is "show us the money!" We, on the other hand, would prefer to look at the beach in its largely unmolested current state.

Seagrove Beach took its name from the groves of live oak that grow right down to the "sea" (or, more accurately, gulf). One of the most ecologically interesting aspects of the area is the mixed forest of hardwoods (oaks, magnolias, hickories, and hollies) and sand pines found among the rolling dune fields. While Seagrove is a mishmash of old Florida bungalows, new traditional cottages, and the aforementioned condo colossus, one can find nice places to rent or to take a decent meal. And, at the end of the day, there's always the beach to commend it.

Beaches

The beaches of south Walton County are broad and beautiful. Their appeal is all the more pronounced because they are so relatively unspoiled, although Seagrove Beach is more intensely built-up than some neighboring communities. Happily, public beach access is readily available in Seagrove Beach, starting east of town at Deer Lake. Surrounding one of Walton County's unique coastal dune lakes is **Deer Lake State Park.** As with Topsail Hill Preserve State Park to the west, it is more preserve than park. The lack of facilities makes the experience all the more rewarding for those who like nature in the raw. The park encompasses 172 acres around the lake and beach and 10 times that area on the inland side of Scenic County Road 30-A, for a total of 1,920 acres.

In Seagrove Beach proper, there are numerous neighborhood accesses (i.e., pedestrian easements, via dune walkovers) onto

5 Pelayo Beach

Location: beside the Pelayo development on Scenic County Road 30A in Seagrove Beach
Parking/fees: free small parking lot
Hours: 24 hours
Facilities: shower
Contact: Beach Services Department, South Walton Tourist Development Council, 850/267-1216

6 Santa Clara Park

Location: between Pelayo and San Juan accesses on Scenic County Road 30A in Seagrove Beach
Parking/fees: free parking lot
Hours: 24 hours
Facilities: restrooms, picnic tables, and showers
Contact: Beach Services Department, South Walton Tourist Development Council, 850/267-1216

7 San Juan Beach

Location: across from the south end of San Juan Street, on Scenic County Road 30A in Seagrove Beach
Parking/fees: free small parking lot
Hours: 24 hours
Facilities: shower
Contact: Beach Services Department, South Walton Tourist Development Council, 850/267-1216

Eden Gardens State Park

If you're looking for a short jaunt off the beach, take County Road 395 north from Seagrove for a few miles. You'll wind up at Point Washington, a dot on the south shore of Choctawhatchee Bay, facing Tucker Bayou. There's not much here but state forest land, a fishing dock, a ferry landing, and Eden Gardens State Park. Delightful picnic grounds look out over the bayou near Wesley Mansion, a two-story, antique-filled Greek Revival mansion dating from 1897 that serves as the centerpiece of this quiet, idyllic spot. The house and grounds belonged to William Henry Wesley, a lumber baron, and his descendents, and was deeded to the state in 1968.

The house is open for hourly guided tours from 9 A.M. to 4 P.M. Thursday through Monday. In addition to a nominal $1.50 per adult (50 cents for kids) for the tour, it costs $2 per vehicle to enter the 12-acre park. The grounds and gardens, including a gorgeous reflecting pool, are particularly attractive when in flower, with March being the peak month for color.

For more information, contact Eden Gardens State Park, 422 Harvest Road, Point Washington, FL 32454; 850/231-4214; website: www.myflorida.com.

the beach, usually beside condos or subdivisions and mainly used by their residents. More significant spots that provide public parking as well as a legal way onto the beach include the **Seagrove Beach** (adjacent to One Seagrove Place), **Pelayo Beach**, and **San Juan Beach** accesses. **Santa Clara Park**, a significant access with parking for 49 vehicle, opened in 1999. **Walton Dunes**, a three-acre parcel next to a condo of the same name, was acquired from the federal Bureau of Land Management and turned into a regional beach access.

Bunking Down

There are no motels or hotels in Seagrove Beach, but many properties—ranging from one-bedroom apartments to six-bedroom homes—can be rented through such firms as **Garrett Realty Services** (3723 East Scenic County Road 30-A, 850/231-1544).

Coastal Cuisine

Seagrove lays claim to an excellent restaurant: **Cafe Thirty-A** (Scenic County Road 30-A, 850/231-2166, $$$$). It serves a broad menu whose primary emphasis is seafood, while also whipping up beef, lamb, poultry, and vegetarian dishes with a creative, contemporary flair. Sophisticated and pricey, it's a great place to spend a long, leisurely evening. At the other extreme, **Seagrove Village Market** (3004 South County Road 395, 850/231-5736, $) has some of the best (and least expensive) grilled fish and burgers on the beach.

Contact Information

South Walton Tourist Development Council, County Road 331 and U.S. 98, P.O. Box 1248, Santa Rosa Beach, FL 32459; 850/267-1216 or 877/309-2679; website: www.beachesofsouthwalton.com

MAP OF THE PANHANDLE—PAGE 547

Seaside

Driving along Scenic County Road 30-A between Panama City and Destin, you can be forgiven for doing a double take when you pass through Seaside (pop. 1,027). It certainly brought expressions of disbelief to our faces. After we gained some familiarity with the area and its brief history, disbelief turned to admiration and, finally, the desire to return and perhaps buy homes here with the nest egg accumulated from sales of this book. (Talk about a pipedream!) Seaside is exactly what it appears to be when you first lay eyes on it: a fairy tale come to life.

The components of Seaside's fairy-tale aura would have to include such literary citations as *Gulliver's Travels* (its small-scale charm brings to mind the make-believe village of Lilliput) and Shangri-La (an idyllic place where time passes slowly and one can lead a life of contemplation and repose). After Panama City's 17-mile strip of unbroken commerce, some of it on the blue and/or tacky side, it came as a shock to stumble on a village as outwardly clean and wholesome as Seaside. It looks like *Leave It to Beaver* land, although it takes a very wealthy community of Cleaver families to afford these mortgages.

Victorian-style dwellings encircle an unpretentious town center that includes a dinky post office, upscale small shops, a village green with bandstand, a cozy bed-and-breakfast (Josephine's), one of the best restaurants in Florida (Bud & Alley's), and bicycle- and pedestrian-friendly brick streets that endeavor to discourage automobile use. Each cottage has to have a white picket fence and porch. Lawns are forbidden. Only native vegetation can be grown on a homeowner's lot. It's all laid out, chapter and verse, in the Seaside Urban Code and Construction Regulations. While it may all smack of a "father knows best" paternalism, at least father is an enlightened despot and not an irrational tyrant.

Even the dune crossovers at the street-end beach accesses break the mold. Inventive wood pavilions (designed by different craftsmen) usher one over the dunes and onto the beach. Each is architecturally distinguished and handicap accessible, providing zigzagging ramps to the sand. Of course, nothing this special happens by accident. Seaside was plotted to the nth degree by developer Robert Davis and husband-and-wife architects Andres Duany and Elizabeth Plater-Zyberk, who head the Miami firm Arquitectonica. Their idea was to interpret the "local vernacular architecture" of the Florida Panhandle in a "new traditional" community being built from the ground up. When they began hatching plans, they had a blank slate to work with. There was very little along Scenic County Road 30-A, which meant they could tailor Seaside as a community on the cutting edge of the New Urbanism, which is actually an oldfangled approach to designing neighborhoods so that people are forced to interact with one another as they did in the "old days." At least that's the theory.

Groundbreaking in Seaside dates back only to the early 1980s. Think about that: Ronald Reagan was in the White House before Seaside even began appearing on maps. Very little had to be razed before Seaside rose. Though seemingly every other square inch of Florida's coastline had long since been plundered, this prime stretch escaped notice. What has been done along Scenic County Road 30-A between Panama City and Sandestin deserves to be studied by planners looking for models of how to tastefully develop the coastline while preserving its natural assets.

In Seaside, you have a choice of places to get gourmet coffee. Italian espresso at Cafe Spiaggia? A mug of French roast at Modica Market? To put this in perspective, we had not had a good cup of coffee for so many

MAP OF WALTON COUNTY—PAGE 596

miles that we forgot what it tasted like, having adapted to the muddy rocket fuel served at gas-station convenience stores and fast-food pit stops.

Our incredulity extended to the local bookstore **Sundog Books** (Four Corners, 850/231-5481) dutifully carries best-sellers alongside fantastic collections of new and classic literature, as well as serious works of science, nature, and philosophy. Classical, jazz, and New Age music, plus the occasional reassuring purr of voices over National Public Radio, serve as background while you browse. Books are stacked with studied haphazardness in the manner of an absent-minded professor's library.

One local proudly (and accurately) referred to Seaside as the "Nantucket of the South." It does have something of the timeless look of a New England fishing village, albeit one whose age is measured in decades, not centuries. From the road, Seaside struck us as having the slightly surreal look of a Hollywood back lot or some sort of slick "Biosphere 2000" experiment whose concept of the future has a lot to do with revisiting the past. It was envisioned in much the same way by film director Peter Weir, who made Seaside the surrealistically normal centerpiece of *The Truman Show,* a film starring Jim Carrey.

Initially, Seaside's contrived normalcy had us wondering whether there was substance behind the whitewashed facade. The answer is a provisional yes. They have constructed a town that aims to reestablish connections, jump-starting the lost notion of community. There's an emerging sense that, for all our hoarded wealth and material possessions, we're a miserably estranged people. Much of the problem stems from financial inequities, notably the widening gap between rich and poor, that are beyond the ability of an urban planner to solve. Yet towns like Seaside at least represent a fresh attempt to redefine ways in which the notion of community might once again work to restore some sense of a shared existence. It is exciting to see experimental approaches undertaken and new means-ends paradigms posited by architects and developers. At least they're parting ways with the dysfunctional status quo of gray and grimly unimaginative condominium cellblocks that serve as little more than tax writeoffs for absentee owners and holding companies.

On the other hand, we're not kidding ourselves into thinking Seaside is an accessible alternative available to everyone. It is decidedly upscale, attracting moneyed aesthetes who appreciate quality. There is a world of difference between the endless cinderblock motels of Panama City Beach and the mile or so of tasteful Victoriana on display in privileged Seaside. We understand why the more bohemian residents of Grayton Beach snicker at Seaside for its stuffy airs. We know full well who owns property here: lawyers and doctors from Atlanta, Birmingham, Montgomery, and New Orleans. Granted, it's hard to elbow in on this kind of action without serious money. And yet Seaside is to be admired for erecting homes and community structures that are not typical monuments to big bucks and bad taste.

Seaside is upscale, yes, but in a casual manner that doesn't project the exclusionary paranoia of gated communities that have popped up all over Florida.

8 Seaside

Location: various street ends along Scenic County Road 30A in Seaside

Parking/fees: no public parking; accesses are for use of Seaside property owners, renters, and their guests

Hours: sunrise to sunset

Facilities: none

Contact: Seaside Visitors Center, 850/231-4224

MAP OF THE PANHANDLE—PAGE 547

What's more, it's surrounded on three sides by state parks and conservancy lands, and on the fourth by one of the prettiest beaches anywhere. In short, Seaside is unlikely to grow or change all that much. Those who come here appreciate the harmonious interplay of natural and man-made elements. In this sense, Seaside might well be the coastal community of the future and a blueprint for positive change.

Beaches

The beaches in the Seagrove, Seaside, and Grayton Beach area are perfect. We don't make this claim lightly. They rate highly on every index one can possibly apply to beaches. The sand is the texture of light brown sugar, clean and cool, singing and squeaking beneath your feet. The water is emerald inshore and azure offshore. It is a slice of Tahiti on the gulf where the water is swimmable nine months a year. Only from November through February, when water temps hover in the 60 to 65°F range, can one not slip in comfortably.

The beaches in and around **Seaside** are backed by dunes that were battered mercilessly by hurricanes in the latter half of the 1990s. They're not the mighty dunes of yesteryear, rising to heights of 30 feet or more, but they're slowly coming back. In fact, the pace of recovery has been remarkable. Many people, not only government agencies but also an army of volunteers, have worked hard on dune-restoration projects.

After Hurricane Opal in 1995, eight feet of sand were deposited on the streets of neighboring Grayton Beach, where dunes essentially vanished overnight. Sand was pumped onto area beaches and the dunes replanted with sea oats. Sand fences were erected to protect the fragile dunes from human tramping and to entrap sand particles, hastening their rebuilding. While there are still blowouts—dune-less holes in the sand ridge—and shortened, flattened dune profiles, Seaside and environs have the look of a beach well on the way to recovery. The bottom line is that if you come to Seaside, you'll find a fine beach to walk on and an emerald gulf in which to swim.

While in Seaside, check out the pavilions at the ends of Tupelo, Savannah, East Ruskin, West Ruskin, Pensacola, Odessa, and Natchez Streets. Each is unique, offering some kind of commentary on the environment that is graceful and/or playful. Our favorite is the Natchez Street Pavilion, which rises to a peak and then falls again—like a wave!—with what looks like a beach umbrella as its crowning touch.

Shore Things

- **Bike rentals:** Seaside Swim & Tennis Club, Seaside Avenue at Forest Street, Seaside, 850/231-2279.
- **Boat cruise:** Choctawhatchee River Boat Tours, Point Washington, 850/231-4420.
- **Dive shop:** Sea Cobra, U.S. 98, Sandestin, 850/837-1933.
- **Ecotourism:** Point Washington Wildlife Management Area, County Road 395, Point Washington, 850/265-3676.
- **Rainy-day attraction:** Sundog Books, Seaside, 850/231-5481.
- **Shopping/browsing:** Silver Sands Factory Stores, U.S. 98, Miramar Beach, 850/864-9780.
- **Vacation rentals:** Seaside Cottage Rental Agency, 2311 Scenic County Road 30-A, P.O. Box 4730, 850/231-4224 or 800/277-8696.

Bunking Down

There are about 260 properties for rental in Seaside and 350 cottages in all. There will be no more than that due to prohibitions on new construction. The only real-estate activity is in resales. Cottage rentals of a week or longer are an alluring option in Seaside, not only for their proximity to the superlative beach but also because the buildings themselves are so airy and architecturally distinguished. For cottage rentals in Seaside, call **Seaside Cottage Rental Agency** (2311 Scenic County Road 30-A, 850/231-4224). Two-bedroom cottages run $1,800–2,400 for a weekly rental in summer. Rates drop 12 percent in spring and fall, and 20 percent in winter.

For briefer stays, try **Josephine's Bed & Breakfast** (101 Seaside Avenue, P.O. Box 4767, 850/231-1940, $$$$), a French country inn that combines first-class elegance with the casual setting of life at the beach. The rooms are done in various color schemes and have different personalities. "Josephine" (#4) has dark green carpeting and silver fern walls, while "Napoleon" (#6) has burgundy carpeting and complementary tones throughout. These upstairs rooms share a verandah from which the gulf is visible. All seven rooms and two suites at Josephine's have a private bath, TV, VCR, microwave, coffeemaker, and fireplaces.

A full country breakfast is served to guests each morning at nine in the dining room. At night, Josephine's dining room becomes one of the premier fine-dining restaurants in the area. As a matter of fact, there's a lot of great dining to be found in the area—at least as much in the small towns of Seaside and Grayton Beach as in the larger Panhandle cities of Panama City Beach and Destin that flank them.

Coastal Cuisine

Bud & Alley's (Cinderella Circle, P.O. Box 4760, 850/231-5900, $$$$) is one of Florida's finest restaurants. The name refers not to the owners but to a pair of beloved pets. "Bud" was the name of a dachshund belonging to Robert Davis—the driving force behind Seaside, who also had an early hand in the restaurant—and "Alley" was a cat belonging to co-owner Scott Witcoski. None of this has much to do with anything, but the playful name reflects the bent of the restaurant, which occupies six areas (indoors and outdoors) and harmonizes with the beautiful beach it overlooks.

The culinary orientation is toward healthful dishes prepared with local ingredients. An herb garden out back is used extensively by the kitchen. Diving right into the menu, how about an appetizer of shrimp steamed in court bouillon and served with cocktail sauce? Or sautéed soft shell blue crab, served atop fresh tomato slices with remoulade? As for entrées, we sampled a hearty mixed grill that included homemade sausage, butter-tender filet mignon, and grilled triggerfish. A popular tuna dish consists of sushi-grade yellowfin coated with sesame seeds and quickly seared, then cut in sushi-sized portions and served with wasabi and soy sauce atop balsamic-marinated greens. You'll definitely want to press on to dessert. Everything is good, but Kahlua crème brûlée and tiramisu stand out. The latter deserves a berth in the dessert hall of fame.

In the town center is **Shades** (83 Central Square, 850/231-1950, $$), which has a studiously casual feel that, like everything in Seaside, has been meticulously cultivated. They make terrific iced tea, an essential in the South. The menu runs from peel 'n' eat shrimp, hot wings, and tasty salads to citrus crab cakes, tuna, and mahimahi. It's a good lunch stop.

Night Moves

Seaside was designed in the manner of a classic American small town, and as is the case with that model, the sidewalks roll up early. You can always hang out at the bar in Bud & Alley's or buy a bottle of wine at Modica Market to take back to wherever it is you're staying. For livelier nightlife, head to the legendary Red Bar in Grayton Beach. If you're really desperate, Panama City Beach and Destin are

Bed Taxes for Better Beaches

Walton County has beautiful beaches and a smart way of preserving them for future generations. They subsidize land acquisition, facilities, and maintenance via a bed tax. Two-thirds of the three percent bed tax levied on lodging in south Walton County goes to the beaches. It is estimated that the tax generates $2 million annually for land acquisition and beach renourishment.

"We're very serious about public beach access in Walton County," says Malcolm Patterson, executive director of the South Walton Tourist Development Council, "and we spend a lot of money on it." No public funds or ad valorem taxes have been laid out for beach projects in Walton County, where it's all been done with the bed tax. The program is relatively recent, with the first tax-subsidized beach access built in 1988.

The county classifies its accesses in two ways. "Neighborhood accesses" are public easements that give residents and renters who are not directly on the beach a means of getting there without trespassing. There's virtually no parking or facilities at a neighborhood access, though some have an outdoor shower ("freshwater washdown," in engineering parlance). "Regional accesses" are public beach accesses that offer parking and more in the way of facilities, such as restrooms and picnic tables. All accesses have crossovers to protect the dunes. In Walton County, the boardwalks, crossovers, gazebos, and so forth are built not with wood but a wood polymer that holds up against the elements by resisting weathering, splintering, and cracking.

That is just another way that Walton County is on the cutting edge of beach access. They're also bullish on land acquisition, developing regional accesses out of parcels in Seagrove Beach and west of Seaside. This is all very impressive for a sparsely populated county whose coastal residents number only about 8,500. In neighboring Okaloosa County, by contrast—especially along Destin's privatized shorefront—they look enviously at Walton County's generous bounty of public beaches. "People in Destin fuss all the time because they can't get to their beaches," notes Patterson. No such problem exists in Walton County.

There's a lesson here for planning boards, county commissioners, and enlightened developers who are willing to listen: You can't lose by making beaches accessible to the public. Besides, it's simply the right thing to do.

only a half hour east and west, respectively. But why would you want to leave a place as relaxing and quiet as Seaside? Isn't that why you paid through the nose to come here?

Contact Information

Seaside Visitors Center, 121 Central Square, P.O. Box 4730, Seaside, FL 32459; 850/231-4224 or 800/277-8696; website: www.seasidefl.com

MAP OF WALTON COUNTY—PAGE 596

Grayton Beach State Park

Grayton Beach State Park preserves a world-class beach and coastal environment. A visit to Grayton Beach makes one appreciate the vastness of Florida's dune fields in their natural state. Barrier dunes of pure quartz sand roll back from the beach for some distance, giving way to salt marsh, slash pine flatlands, and scrub-hickory hammock. It is this varied landscape, incorporating not only the beach but the environments behind it, that makes Grayton Beach an exceptional experience.

The dunes are in a cycle of recovery from hurricanes in 1995 and 1998. Hurricane Opal sheered off about half of the frontal dunes' 30-foot height in places, but sand fencing and replanting programs have accelerated their restoration. The 2,000-acre park is also dotted with lily ponds, marshes, and Western Lake, one of the brackish coastal dune lakes unique to the area that breach their boundary with the gulf several times a year. Grayton's mile-long beach runs contiguously with those of Seaside and Grayton Beach, the communities that flank it, providing opportunities for lengthy beach hikes for those up to it. The park offers 37 campsites with full hookups and a boat ramp on Western Lake. Camping at Grayton Beach is particularly pleasurable after the worst of summer's heat and bugs have died down. The clear, aquamarine water remains swimmable through October and sometimes beyond.

9 Grayton Beach State Park

Location: between Seaside and Grayton Beach on Scenic County Road 30A

Parking/fees: $3.25 per vehicle entrance fee. Camping fees are $15.40 (without hookups) and $17.54 (with hookups) per night March 1–October 31, and $8.80 (without hookups) and $10.94 (with hookups) November 1–February 28

Hours: 8 A.M. to sunset

Facilities: restrooms, picnic tables, and showers

Contact: Grayton Beach State Park, 850/231-4210

Contact Information

Grayton Beach State Park, 357 Main Park Road, Santa Rosa Beach, FL 32549; 850/231-4210; website: www.myflorida.com

Grayton Beach

If Seaside is a neoclassical sculpture, then Grayton Beach (pop. 250) is a piece of folk art: ramshackle, unpretentious, unschooled. To put it another way, Seaside takes a studied, academic approach to Florida vernacular architecture, while Grayton Beach is a mishmash of styles—including authentic tin-roofed cracker bungalows that look one hard rain shy of collapsing—and late-model vacation homes. Seaside is an instant community, while Grayton Beach has deep roots. Seaside is upscale and fussy. Grayton Beach is laid back and down to earth. Get the picture?

The town of Grayton Beach is separated from Seaside by Grayton Beach State Park. Their proximity belies the fact that the two communities are light years apart. Grayton Beach offers a truer glimpse of Old Florida, with some glancing blows from the "new traditional" imperative. Grayton Beach is by far the oldest community in coastal Walton County, having been developed in the 1920s. It was the first beach town to pop up between the Panhandle bookends of Apalachicola and Pensacola. Abutting a splendid career, Grayton Beach looks comfortably aged and unchanged, with its sandy, tree-lined streets and old homes built of weathered cypress. Its antiquarian ways have not only kept old-timers happy but attracted an artsy, offbeat element.

Most notably, from an outsider's perspective, Grayton Beach claims several excellent restaurants; a bar that exudes more personality than every club in Panama City Beach put together; Patrones, a famous hideaway, zoo, and art gallery (see "Bunking Down"); and a re-creation of impressionist Claude Monet's garden in Giverny, France, dubbed **Monet Monet** (100 East Scenic County Road 30-A, 850/231-5117).

Beaches

On the east side of Grayton Beach is Grayton Beach State Park (see separate entry). **Grayton Beach** proper has public accesses at the ends of Garfield and Pine Streets. Significant on-street parking, right before the boardwalk entrance to the beach, makes the former particularly appealing if you're just passing through town.

Bunking Down

Patrones Hideaway (307 DeFuniak Street, 850/231-1606, $$) offers an experience you'll never forget. Its seven rental units include funky bungalows, studio apartments, and a town house; daily rates begin at $90 in season. On the property is an art gallery and barnyard zoo whose highlight is a 1,000-pound pig. Patrones rents canoes for use on Western Lake.

If you're looking for longer vacation rentals, **Rivard Real Estate** (15 Pine Street, Santa Rosa Beach, 850/231-5999) has the market cornered on this hidden corner of the coast.

Coastal Cuisine

Criolla's (170 East Scenic County Road 30-A, 850/267-1267, $$$$) puts a Caribbean and Creole twist on its culinary offerings, which include pan-seared salmon served with fried, skewered soft-

⑩ Grayton Beach

Location: at the end of Garfield Street in Grayton Beach
Parking/fees: free street parking
Hours: 24 hours
Facilities: none
Contact: Beach Services Department, South Walton Tourist Development Council, 850/267-1216

shelled crawfish. (Yes, crawfish go through a molting stage just like their blue crab relations.) Prices are on the high side but worth the splurge.

Piccolo (70 Hotz Avenue, 850/231-1008, $$) is the restaurant part of an operation that also includes the vaunted Red Bar (see "Night Moves"). Entrées include half a dozen nightly preparations that go for reasonable prices. And you can always linger to hear the house jazz band, a blues band, surf group, or whatever's on the CD player at the Red Bar.

Night Moves

We fell in love with—and felt at home in—the **Red Bar** (70 Hotz Avenue, 850/231-1008) from the moment we set foot in the place. The room is indeed painted as red as Rudolph's nose, with European film posters and other bric-a-brac on the walls and red Christmas lights strung throughout. In this red-light district, you can catch live jazz or listen to CDs from an extensive collection behind the bar. We heard *The Best of Van Morrison* in its entirety one night—the perfect accompaniment to an after-dinner drink and some casual eavesdropping. Van Morrison is one of our musical heroes, and on this night at the Red Bar he never sounded better. The crowd is eclectic, making the people-watching as good as you'd find in any big-city hangout. The casual cosmopolitan ambience is not surprising, considering it's owned by Belgian brothers named Ollie and Philippe. Be aware that in summer, the Red Bar and its restaurant, Piccolo, can get out-the-door popular.

Contact Information

South Walton Tourist Development Council, County Road 331 and U.S. 98, P.O. Box 1248, Santa Rosa Beach, FL 32459; 850/267-1216 or 877/309-2679; website: www.beachesofsouthwalton.com

Blue Mountain Beach, Santa Rosa Beach, and Dune-Allen Beach

Here are three more communities in the string of pearls along the gulf in south Walton County. You'll mostly find residential cottages along this stretch of Gulf Coast. They're tasteful to a fault, being reflexively imitative of the style of Seaside without the aesthetic organizing principles that bind it all together. These houses, painted in various lollipop-inspired hues, are almost too cute (especially the orange foam ones). Since these communities are imitating Seaside, which itself is imitating an idealized past, there's a lot of faux flying around. Still, better to use Seaside as a model than to have no real models at all—or bad ones.

Blue Mountain Beach derives its name from its dunes. They rise as high as 70 feet, making this the highest point along the Gulf of Mexico in the United States. Santa Rosa Beach lies between Blue Mountain Beach and Dune-Allen Beach. Oyster

11 Blue Mountain Beach

Location: south end of County Road 83 in Blue Mountain Beach
Parking/fees: free parking lot
Hours: 24 hours
Facilities: picnic tables and showers
Contact: Beach Services Department, South Walton Tourist Development Council, 850/267-1216

Lake, one of the county's more impressive coastal dune lakes, is the primary natural feature in Dune-Allen Beach, which is otherwise distinguished by more cutesy cottages and the doubtful promise of "Caribbean-style coastal living."

Beaches

Blue Mountain Beach has a bona fide public beach, with parking for a dozen or so cars, at the south end of County Road 83. From here, you can walk onto the beach via an arty wooden gazebo reminiscent of those up in Seaside. At the south end of County Road 393 is **Ed Walline Park**, a slightly more developed beach park along this slightly less developed coastline. There are picnic tables, a decent-sized parking lot, and a boardwalk to the beach.

Santa Rosa Beach harbors a treasure known as **Gulf View Heights**. Hidden behind Goatfeathers Raw Bar and Restaurant are picnic shelters, restrooms, and parking for up to 25 cars. Finally, an access at the end of Spooky Lane provides the local condo inhabitants an easement onto the beach. A new arrival on the beach at Dune-Allen is **Fort Panic Park**, with ample off-street parking, showers, and walkways.

Bunking Down

Contact **Dune-Allen Realty** (5200 West Scenic County Road 30-A, 850/267-2121) for a listing of gulf-fronting condo and cottage rentals in the area.

Coastal Cuisine

Basmati's (Quincy Circle, 850/231-1366, $$$$), a gourmet Asian restaurant in a striking two-story wooden home, is a culinary landmark in Blue Mountain Beach. In addition to Asian dishes, they fix sushi.

Just down the road is **Donut Hole II** (6745 U.S. 98, 850/267-3239, $). Though the name suggests a Dunkin' Donuts–style hole in the wall, this is a modestly upscale bakery-diner with an excellent selection of baked goods, including key-lime glazed donuts and tarts. They serve a killer breakfast, as well as lunch and dinner from their diner-themed menu. We hit the Donut Hole on the way to Topsail

⓬ Gulf View Heights

Location: next to Goatfeathers Restaurant on Scenic County Road 30A in Santa Rosa Beach
Parking/fees: free parking lot
Hours: 24 hours
Facilities: restrooms, picnic tables, and showers
Contact: Beach Services Department, South Walton Tourist Development Council, 850/267-1216

⓭ Ed Walline Park

Location: south end of County Road 393 in Santa Rosa Beach
Parking/fees: free parking lot
Hours: 24 hours
Facilities: restrooms, picnic tables, and showers
Contact: Beach Services Department, South Walton Tourist Development Council, 850/267-1216

⓮ Fort Panic Park

Location: west of Dune-Allen Realty on Scenic County Road 30A in Dune-Allen Beach
Parking/fees: free parking lot
Hours: 24 hours
Facilities: picnic tables and showers
Contact: Beach Services Department, South Walton Tourist Development Council, 850/267-1216

Hill Preserve State Park, and it provided us with the caloric input to hike the tall dunes. The key lime–glazed items had us both smacking our lips like sated housecats. Incidentally, the original Donut Hole is in Destin.

Contact Information

South Walton Tourist Development Council, County Road 331 and U.S. 98, P.O. Box 1248, Santa Rosa Beach, FL 32459; 850/267-1216 or 877/309-2679; website: www.beachesofsouthwalton.com

Topsail Hill Preserve State Park

This recently established and therefore largely undiscovered state park has been called the most pristine coastal property in the state of Florida. Without hesitation we'd place **Topsail Hill Preserve State Park** near the top of our list of favorite Florida beaches. We must, however, attach the necessary disclaimers. As stated, Topsail is difficult to get to, though access is improving. When we first fumbled our way onto the preserve, the sandy access roads were rutted with gaping holes, and the mile-long drive to a clearing behind mountainous sand dunes was as bumpy as any hillbilly hollow.

By 2000, the main access road had been graded, and at its end was a parking lot, portable toilet, and boardwalk to the beach. Topsail increased its holdings from 350 acres in 1992 to 1,640 acres. Today, its beach extends for 3.5 miles. A network of trails is in the process of being cut; already, one runs around the south side of Morris Lake. The state recently acquired a commercial RV park on U.S. 98, which has been renamed **Gregory E. Moore RV Resort** (7525 West Scenic County Road 30-A, Santa Rosa Beach, 850/267-0299 or 877/BEACHRV) and is officially part of park operations.

Yet Topsail Hill largely remains an "undeveloped" state park, meaning that facilities are minimal. Spanish moss hangs from the trees and spongy deer moss covers the ground in this scrub forest environment. The preserve affords nesting sites for herons and egrets. Taking the road less traveled on our initial visit, we sloshed barefoot through muck and marsh that serve as a watery border between two lily ponds and a coastal dune lake. Working our way around Campbell Lake, we marveled at water as clear and calm as glass. Coastal dune lakes like this one are substantial bodies of water, occupying upward of a hundred acres. Next, we scaled a 50-foot sand cliff whose summit presented a glorious sight: a quarter-mile of dune ridges and swales between us and the Gulf of Mexico. We delicately plotted a seaward path through them, making sure not to disturb the vegetation.

Mainly, we followed other sets of footprints, using the markings to find our way back out. ("Did we turn left or right at

15 Topsail Hill Preserve State Park

Location: between Dune-Allen Beach and Sandestin, turn south on Topsail Road at U.S. 98; the beach is a 300-yard walk from the parking lot

Parking/fees: free parking lot

Hours: 8 A.M. to sunset

Facilities: restroom

Contact: Topsail Hill Preserve State Park, 850/267-1868

Map of the Panhandle—Page 547

this pile of driftwood?" was our befuddled query when we briefly lost our way.) We couldn't help but notice the number of pawprints left by animals . . . large animals. Finally, we found a break between dunes that had been sensuously sculpted by the wind. There, dead ahead, lay the aqua-blue gulf and one of the most stunningly secluded white-sand beaches we've ever seen. The only thing disabusing us of our fantasy of being shipwrecked on the perfect desert island beach was the high-rise horizon of Destin looming to the west. Even so, Topsail will always remain a special place. Let this be our little secret, okay?

Contact Information

Topsail Hill Preserve State Park, Topsail Road at U.S. 98, Santa Rosa Beach, FL 32459; 850/267-1868; website: www.myflorida.com

Sandestin

Sandestin did not exist until 1971, when an Atlanta real-estate consortium purchased a 2,400-acre parcel of land eight miles east of Destin on U.S. 98, stretching from Choctawhatchee Bay to the Gulf of Mexico. The acreage was filled with scrub pine, oak, marshes, and clear coastal dune lakes. It had previously survived Indian wars and pirate attacks, not to mention bomb detonations and rocket tests by our own armed forces. It also dodged several less appetizing attempts at development, including one by Walt Disney, who briefly considered building Disney World here. Another came from the folks who brought us the Indianapolis Speedway; they had plans to cover this exquisite area with asphalt until one of the local landowners backed out at the last minute.

After extensive planning to ensure quality development, groundbreaking took place in 1973, and the area was christened Sandestin, combining the names of neighboring towns Santa Rosa Beach and Destin. The master plan calls for 40 percent of the property to remain in a natural state at buildout. This is misleading, however, since much of that natural land will consist of golf courses, which is a wholly unnatural use of land. However, in Sandestin's favor, its Burnt Pine golf course was constructed without disturbing wetlands—and, in fact, wetland plantings were added to aid in erosion control. At least environmental issues have been factored into the developmental equation at Sandestin.

The largest self-contained resort on the Gulf Coast, Sandestin owns 7.5 miles of beach and bayshore property. In 1998, the Vancouver-based club Intrawest—which mainly owns ski resorts—acquired Sandestin. These days at Sandestin you'll find four golf courses, nine pools, tennis courts, 26 miles of biking and hiking trails, a 98-slip marina (from which fishing, sailing, and cruising charters can be arranged), a health club, four residential "villages," a gaggle of gulf-front condominiums, an excellent waterfront restaurant and lounge, and a beachside complex with a beautiful heated pool and boardwalk access ramp to the Gulf of Mexico. On the way is the village at Baytowne Wharf, a pedestrian-oriented community inspired by Charleston and New Orleans.

Beaches

The wedge-shaped Sandestin thins at the beachfront, running along the gulf for a few hundred yards. The dunes have been left relatively undisturbed, though if nothing at all were here the dune fields would roll inland for a good distance like they do at nearby Topsail Hill Preserve State Park. Regardless, the beach at Sandestin and neighboring Tops'l Beach & Racquet

Resort is exceptionally wide, white, and powdery soft, with the turquoise waters of the gulf providing eye-popping vistas. Not surprisingly, you can't access the beach at Sandestin unless you are a resort guest or property owner.

Bunking Down

Sandestin Golf and Beach Resort (9300 U.S. 98 W, 850/267-8150, $$$$) offers a full line of rentals, including rooms at a 175-unit bay-front inn and 600 units in the resort's beachfront condos and bayside golf villas. A real deal can be had in the off-season (November to mid-March), when rooms rates drop precipitously and privileges include free use of the world-class fitness center. We've stayed in both a golf villa and a beachfront condo, preferring the latter's views and easy access to the beach. (But we don't golf.)

The Southwinds condo where we bunked down had a gulf-facing balcony and was plushly appointed; there was absolutely nothing not to like. Also on the beachfront at Sandestin is the **Sandestin Hilton Resort** (4000 Sandestin Boulevard South, 850/267-9500, $$$$). Hilton leases the land from Sandestin and provides ample outdoor activities (golf, tennis) and stellar beach access.

Coastal Cuisine

For top-drawer dining, try Sandestin's sumptuously appointed **Elephant Walk** (Sandestin, 850/267-4800, $$$$), a stately beachfront restaurant and bar. The name is derived from a 1954 B-movie in is which Elizabeth Taylor plays the wife of Ceylon tea plantation owner John Whiley who, in defiance of local taboos and warnings, builds his manor in the path of the annual elephant migration.

This is indeed a fittingly symbolic though fully unintended commentary on much of the coastal development in the nearby city of Destin. The legend of the plantation owner is carried to great, imaginative leaps inside the restaurant in terms of decor, menu design, and cuisine. The signature dish, grouper Elizabeth, is named for Elizabeth Taylor. It is a sautéed grouper fillet served with crabmeat, toasted almonds, and a white butter sauce. Other tempting items include a hearty seafood gumbo (Cajun velouté with crawfish and shrimp) and snapper langoustine, served with a lobster tail.

Night Moves

Lumber into the **Elephant Walk** (Sandestin, 850/267-4800) for a drink—we'd suggest (nay, endorse) the namesake punch—as a prelude or postlude to dinner. You have your choice of patio bar or upstairs cigar room.

Contact Information

Sandestin Golf and Beach Resort, 9300 U.S. 98 W, Destin, FL 32550; 850/267-8150 or 800/622-1922; website: www.sandestin.com

Miramar Beach

Miramar Beach, the most westward of south Walton County's gulf-hugging communities, is a mixed bag that displays elements of Walton's low-key approach to beach development alongside neighboring Okaloosa County's rubber-stamping permissiveness. Because it is located along "Old Highway 98," a loop road off the modern, four-lane U.S. 98, Miramar retains vestiges of the Old Florida vacation haven it used to be. Squat homes and sunbaked apartments offer visual relief from the high-rises to the east and west. Much of the development has been smartly relegated to the north side of the road, leaving an unobstructed vista for pedestrians and motorists.

That is not to say Miramar Beach has been spared the rod of real-estate speculation. Some unsightly, aluminum-sided town houses have been built on the gulf side of Old Highway 98, and metal cranes portend upward growth with little rhyme or reason. Ultimately, we fear whatever funky character Miramar Beach still possesses is Destin-ed to be snuffed out.

Beaches

The prime public-access point onto **Miramar Beach** is located on Old U.S. 98 between Newman Drive and Avalon Estates. From the ample free parking lot, five wooden dune walkovers lead to a typical Panhandle beach, which is to say one that's nearly perfect in sand texture, coloration, size, and water temperature. The beach is backed by rounded mounds of protected dunes. Miramar Beach access is a joint venture between the South Walton Tourist Development Council, which maintains the facilities and walkovers, and a restaurant called Pompano Joe's (see "Coastal Cuisine"). There's also a pedestrian access onto the beach at Gulf Street, on the west side of the Mainsail Resort, for those in the neighborhood.

Bunking Down

East of Miramar's public beach, the beachfront assumes the names of the high-rise condominiums that have effectively usurped access to the beaches for anyone but the occasional inhabitants of these ghastly buildings. One of them, Hidden Dunes, is particularly well-named, as it blocks any view of the dunes from the highway. **Mainsail** (114 Mainsail Drive, 850/837-4853, $$$) is the most inviting of the "gulfside family resorts," offering affordable off-season rates. Next to it, however, is Edgewater, a sloping structure that looks about as inviting as a stealth bomber.

West of the public beach, the beachfront is likewise named after resort developments—in this case, Surfside and Seascape. Each of these gargantuan monoliths is claimed to be one of south Walton County's 19 beach communities, though this stretches the word *community* beyond credibility. We'd describe only five of the posited 19—Seagrove Beach, Seaside, Grayton Beach, Santa Rosa Beach, and Miramar Beach—as actual communities in the sense that we understand the term. That is to say, a place with roots, stability, a little history, a permanent population, and some meaningful interaction among them.

The final development in Walton County before crossing the Okaloosa County

16 Miramar Beach

Location: on Old U.S. 98, between Newman Drive and Avalon Estates in Miramar Beach
Parking/fees: free parking lot
Hours: 24 hours
Facilities: concessions, restrooms, and showers
Contact: Beach Services Department, South Walton Tourist Development Council, 850/267-1216

MAP OF WALTON COUNTY—PAGE 596

line is Frangista Beach, and it is the most inviting. The upscale but tastefully planned, tree-laden **Frangista Beach Inn** (1860 Old U.S. 98 East, 850/654-5501, $$$) is as relaxing a port of call as this built-up stretch of Walton County has to offer. They have single rooms and suites, and the last of the beautiful south Walton beaches is just below your balcony.

Coastal Cuisine

Pompano Joe's (2237 Old U.S. 98 East, 850/837-2224, $$) is a reasonably priced seafood house with a relaxed nautical ambience and a great location overlooking Miramar Beach. Come in at lunchtime for some inexpensive specials, which include a dynamite amberjack sandwich and salad. Fried and grilled seafood entrées include mahimahi, amberjack, and grouper, the gulf-plucked favorites you'll see on most every Panhandle menu. Our suggestion: char-grilled grouper with jalapeno pineapple salsa.

For upper-crust dining, the **Purple Rooster** (1096 Old U.S. 98, 850/650-8999, $$$$), located near the Surfside high-rise, had us crowing with delight. The restaurant displays sophistication and creativity in its menu offerings. While Steely Dan CDs played quietly in the background (a refreshing change from the usual tepid dinner music), the chefs whipped up an incomparable meal. We'd recommend cassoulet of shrimp and scallops Provençale as an appetizer and organic field greens tossed with walnut vinaigrette and Gorgonzola cheese as a salad. They do wonderful pastas and risottos (e.g., spicy duck and vegetable stir-fry with mushroom noodles and Thai curry sauce), and terrific seafood entrées, including pumpkinseed-crusted redfish, seared tuna crusted with ginger and sesame, and grilled salmon with fennel, new potatoes, leeks, and pancetta. The house specialty is a jumbo grilled veal chop, stuffed with blue crab. Items at this end of the menu run in the $24 to $28 range; pastas and risottos, $13 to $20. It's all hearty, nouveau bistro fare prepared and served with panache.

Contact Information

South Walton Tourist Development Council, County Road 331 and U.S. 98, P.O. Box 1248, Santa Rosa Beach, FL 32459; 850/267-1216 or 877/309-2679; website: www.beachesofsouthwalton.com

MAP OF THE PANHANDLE—PAGE 547

Okaloosa County

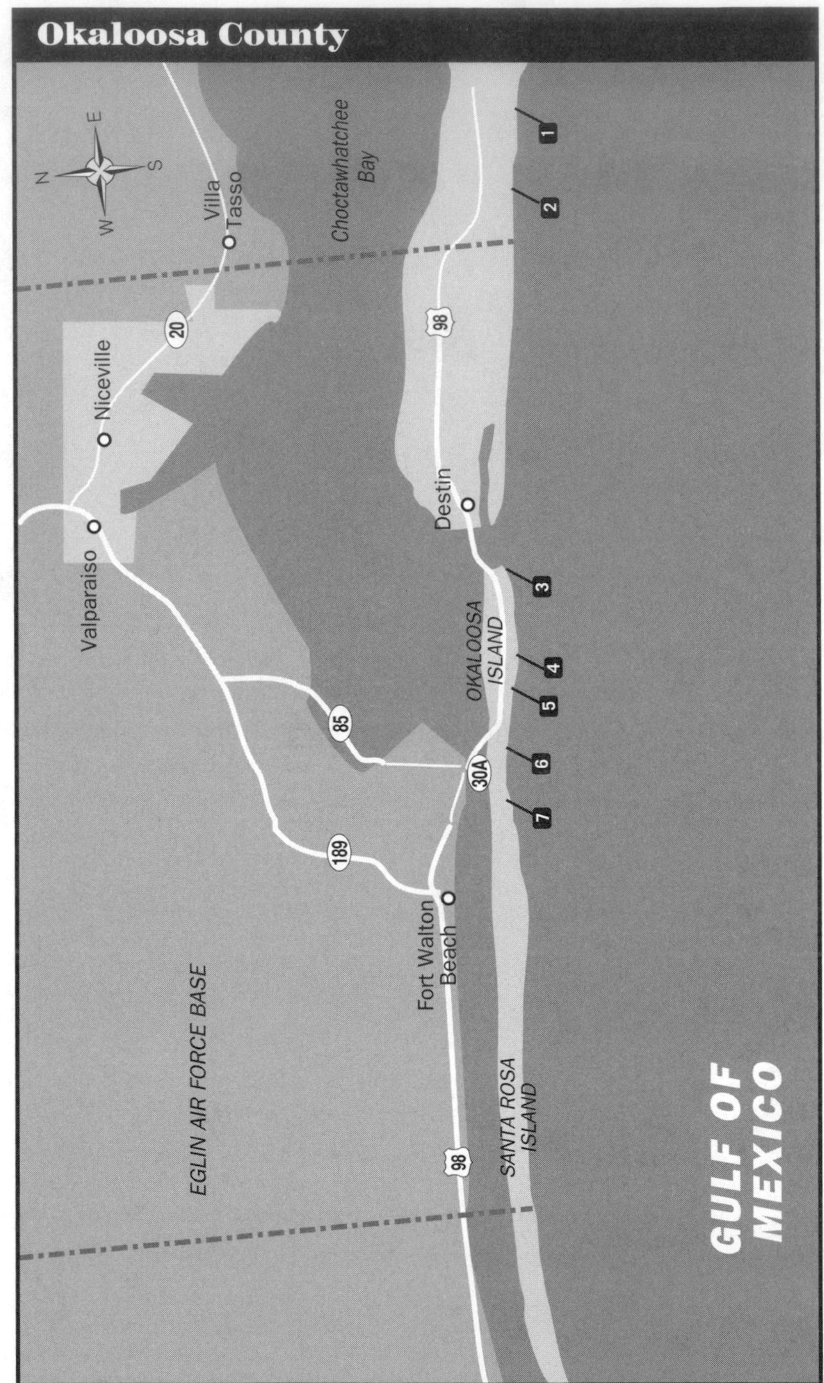

OKALOOSA COUNTY

More than half of Okaloosa County's 24-mile coastline is protected by virtue of belonging to Eglin Air Force Base, the military behemoth that occupies most of the county. In this unlikely location, you will find sand dunes whose heights rival those of the condos of Destin and Okaloosa Island, the county's main vacation meccas. Destin's principal asset is a world-class harbor with a huge charter-fishing fleet; it is the self-styled "World's Luckiest Fishing Village." Despite its name, Fort Walton Beach doesn't have gulf beaches, strictly speaking. Those fall on Okaloosa Island, a built-up area sandwiched between Eglin parcels. Okaloosa Island has beachside hotels and motels, Destin is home to fishing boats and good restaurants, and Eglin's got a lock on deserted beaches. And what beautiful, reflectively white beaches they are.

Destin

One historical note about Destin says more than 1,000 brochures. It was not an incorporated city until November 1984, about the time Ronald Reagan won his second term as president in a landslide. By then, the savings and loan frenzy was in full effect and the modus operandi was one we saw often while combing the coastline. It went something like this: Build quickly and recklessly with speculators' cash. Never ask whose money it was (Malaysians'? Germans'? Iranians'?), how they got it, why the big hurry, or what the wishes of the community might be. Block the beaches from view and access with condo towers, gates, walls, and fences erected to "protect" these investments. Put a hefty price tag on units in these horizon-obstructing monoliths. Name the developments for the very things they have destroyed or obscured (imagine an idyllic-sounding condo with Sea, Surf, Cove, Dune, Gulf, or Breeze in its name). Finally, leave the units eerily and wastefully unoccupied, as if struck by a neutron bomb, much of the year.

This is Destin, in a coconut shell. The first sight you behold upon entering the city from the east—after crossing the Okaloosa County line, near where Old U.S. 98 meets U.S. 98—is a fortress called Destiny-by-the-Sea.

Bounded by Choctawhatchee Bay and the Gulf of Mexico, Destin's real destiny is to double in size and population in the next decade. Right now, the population is said to be 13,000, though it seems much larger. One of us lives in a small town of 25,000 that seems positively rural compared to Destin. How can this be? The operative term is "full-time residents." The glut of towers is only occasionally occupied by part-timers whose Destin condo is just a second-home writeoff. Ain't America great?

Like most boomtowns, Destin has no sense of proportion or discernible identity. It's cash rich but sense poor. Every vacant plot of land on the beachfront, behind the harbor and along U.S. 98 is slated for development, though the growth here is already maxed out and overwhelming.

It did not need to turn out this way. Destin has some beautiful beaches that would otherwise receive our highest commendations. To its credit, Destin also has an intriguing harbor and a dining scene superior to the adjacent military town of Fort Walton Beach. Still, we found ourselves far preferring towns to the east (e.g., Seaside, Grayton Beach) and west (Pensacola Beach). Why? Because these other places have been through many of the

❶ James Lee County Park

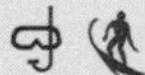  

Location: along Old U.S. 98 near the Walton County line

Parking/fees: free parking lot

Hours: 6 A.M.–8:30 P.M.

Facilities: concessions, restrooms, picnic tables, and showers

Contact: Emerald Coast Convention and Visitors Bureau, 850/651-7131

❷ Henderson Beach State Park

Location: 17000 Emerald Coast Parkway, just east of Destin

Parking/fees: $2 entrance fee per vehicle. Camping fees are $16-$18 per night

Hours: 8 A.M. to sundown

Facilities: restrooms, picnic tables, and showers

Contact: Henderson Beach State Park, 850/837-7550

MAP OF THE PANHANDLE—PAGE 547

same battles as Destin, but they've emerged with decent beach access and a better handle on development.

Destin just doesn't get it and, as a consequence, it doesn't deserve the business of beachcombers—not when so many superior options are available close by.

Beaches

After that assault, it may seem disingenuous to rave about a great public beach in Destin. That it's owned by the state came as no surprise to us. **Henderson Beach State Park** takes its name from the landowners who sold it to the state of Florida in 1983, making it the first purchase in the Save Our Coast program. At the time, Destin was still unincorporated and seemingly incapable of doing anything in the way of public beach access on its own. Thanks to the Hendersons, who wanted to see the unique natural features of the area preserved, the public has access to 6,000 feet of beachfront along the Gulf of Mexico.

The 250-acre park, located two miles west of the Walton County line and just east of Destin, is a habitat for sandpine, scrub oak, Southern magnolia, dune rosemary, and wildflowers. Henderson Beach State Park has a boardwalk, bathhouses with outdoor showers, six dune walkovers, picnic pavilions, and grills. A 30-site campground, complete with new facilities and boardwalk to the gulf, opened in February 2000.

Another fine beach park, **James Lee County Park**, lies on Old U.S. 98 near the county line. Lee has the same public-private arrangement as Miramar's county beach access. A decent and affordable restaurant called the Crab Trap is attached to the property, overlooking the Gulf of Mexico. Parking is free, and six dune walkovers, picnic pavilions, restrooms, and showers are provided. It is popular with families because the water is shallow and clear. Surfing and volleyball round out the action at this fun spot.

A small access point at 7th Street abuts the west end of Henderson Beach. Other Destin beach accesses are supposedly located south of the harbor via Gulf Shore Drive, off of U.S. 98. This jut of land is called Holiday Isle, and its condo crush rivals the upper reaches of Miami Beach. Both of the "public beach accesses" we came across were no more than niggling easements between high-rises with no parking whatsoever, so they are essentially worthless.

We did, however, stumble on an excellent parcel of state-owned land at the very end of Gulf Shore Drive. It's an unnamed but lovely dune-covered sand spit that has formed off Holiday Isle at East Pass. Park on the side of the road and have a look and a stroll. Unless you're a condo owner or resort guest, it's about all you'll see of Destin's beachfront at this end.

Shore Things

- **Bike/skate rentals:** Island Sports Shop, 1688 Old U.S. 98, 850/650-9126.
- **Boat cruise:** Southern Star Dolphin Cruises, 98 Harborwalk Marina East, 850/837-7741.
- **Dive shop:** Emerald Coast Scuba, 500 U.S. 98 East, Destin, 850/837-0955.
- **Ecotourism:** Fred Gannon Rocky Bayou State Park, 4281 State Route 20, Niceville, 850/833-9144.
- **Fishing charters:** Destin Fishing Fleet Marina Charter Service, 201 U.S. 98 East, 850/837-1995.
- **Marina:** Harborwalk Marina, 66 U.S. 98 East, 850/650-2400.
- **Rainy-day attraction:** Destin Fishing Museum, 39 U.S. 98 East, 850/654-1011.
- **Shopping/browsing:** Silver Sands Factory Stores, 10562 U.S. 98 East, Destin, 850/654-9771.

MAP OF OKALOOSA COUNTY—PAGE 618

The World's Luckiest Fishing Village

With its glut of condos and paucity of public beach accesses, Destin's crowded gulf-front real estate sounds a bum note. However, a sweeter chord is struck down by Destin Harbor, where a sizable fishing fleet gives visitors a crack at figuring out why Destin is referred to as the "World's Luckiest Fishing Village." In one sense, the deep-sea fishing bonanza doesn't have as much to do with dumb luck as submarine geology. What is referred to as the "100-fathom curve"—the point offshore where the water reaches a depth of 100 fathoms (600 feet)—draws closer to the mainland at Destin than any other spot on Florida's coastline. What this means is that when you sail out of Destin, you'll reach deep water more quickly than from any other point in the state. You can be fishing in a hundred feet of water within a few miles of shore.

The Destin Marina Fishing Fleet Charter Service represents 40 fishing boats. The scene down along the harbor bustles in summer and is considerably slower in winter. On a gray, foggy day, you can almost convince yourself that you've stumbled into a New England fishing village. Boats of all sizes take out parties of all sizes for fishing trips of varying durations, setting off as early as six in the morning. Deep-sea fishing is extremely popular in Destin, particularly on summer weekends, for which you're advised to book reservations months in advance. Weekdays in season are more flexible. Out of season, it's easier still to arrange a guided fishing trip on short notice.

Here are the bottom-line basics: Parties of up to six can expect to pay between $380 for four-hour (half-day) trips, $570 for six-hour trips, and $750 for eight-hour (full-day) trips into the Gulf of Mexico. Each additional angler beyond that will pay about 10 percent of the base cost. The most common catches are grouper, amberjack, triggerfish, king mackerel, wahoo, and dolphin. If you're after billfish—blue marlin, white marlin, and sailfish—you'll have to trek 50 to 60 miles offshore, at which point you're looking at a 12-hour trip costing around $1,075. Even if you're not dropping a grand to tussle with a marlin, it's fun to stroll the docks, watching the comings and goings, and taking stock of the catches as they're hauled off and cleaned.

Moreover, the charter-boat captains and crew genuinely seem to like what they're doing. We went out with **Capt. George Eller** (Destin Harbor, 850/650-1534) on his 42-foot sportfisher, the *Bounty Hunter.* Here's a man who obviously loves what he's doing. Of his career leading fishing charters into the Gulf of Mexico, he says, "It's not a job, it's a lifestyle. You have to want to do it. If you wake up and say, 'Damn, I have to go to work,' you won't make it. I get up and wander down to the harbor. If a trip comes along, peachy keen, but if not, 'Let's go get breakfast.'" It's a nice life. He makes the experience appealing to his passengers, too, with his enthusiasm for sportfishing. "Until you've experienced the thrill of catching a 25-pound king mackerel on a 20-pound line," he says, "you haven't lived."

For more information, contact the Destin Marina Fishing Fleet Charter Service, 201 U.S. 98 East, Destin, FL 32540; 850/837-1995; website: www.charterdestin.com.

- **Surf shop:** Sockeye's Beach and Sport, 20011 U.S. 98 East, Destin, 850/654-8954.
- **Vacation rentals:** Abbott Resorts, 35000 Emerald Coast Parkway, 850/837-4853.

Bunking Down

This may shock and amaze you (it did us), but the beach vacation mecca of Destin has few beachfront hotels and motels worth recommending. That is because it has few beachfront hotels and motels, period. Most of the motels in town, even the ones with "beach" in their names, are located on U.S. 98, away from the gulf. An exception is the **Sea Oats Motel** (3420 U.S. 98 East, 850/837-6655), an attractive, contemporary property directly on the white sand beach. Also, there's a circular, multi-story **Holiday Inn** (1020 U.S. 98 East, 850/837-6181, $$$) that sits beckoningly on the edge of the gulf and boasts of having "Destin's largest outdoor pool."

By and large, however, the most viable lodging option in Destin is a vacation rental in a beachfront high-rise. One agency that handles a plethora of these is **Abbott Resorts** (35000 Emerald Coast Parkway, 850/837-4853). The cheapest daily rate they list in summer is $166 ($95 off-season). The average weekly rental in summer is $1,500. If that's way beyond your means, you can always camp at **Henderson Beach State Park** (17000 U.S. 98, 850/837-7550, $) for $16 a night.

Coastal Cuisine

Destin's cuisine is its strongest suit, but here is yet another Pyrrhic victory. Quite simply, the prices at many seafood restaurants lining U.S. 98 are exorbitant. This is not to say the seafood isn't fresh or the preparations worthy. (After all, Destin is the self-billed "World's Luckiest Fishing Village"). But, come on—a fried seafood platter for over $20 is ludicrous! Indeed, you'll pay no more to eat at Sandestin's top-of-the-line Elephant Walk than at many less exemplary restaurants in Destin. Certain places even serve sushi, but at inflated prices that rival a raw-fish palace like Hatsuhana in Manhattan or Chicago.

Still there are so many restaurants in Destin (300, by one count) that you can't help but score a satisfying and reasonably priced meal if you know where to go. Start by following us to the **Boathouse Oyster Bar** (288 U.S. 98 East, 850/837-3645, $), a shack that sits beside a dock on the harbor. It is so refreshingly lacking in pretension that it doesn't even have a phone or restroom (you use the marina's next door). We copped a dozen cold, tasty raw oysters for $4.50, devoured while admiring the coral reef of colorful graffiti and grubstake affixed to the walls and ceiling. The Boathouse has live music seven nights a week, too.

Another perennially popular spot, right on the harbor where the charter fishing fleet does its business, is **AJ's Seafood and Oyster Bar** (168 U.S. 98 East, 850/837-1913, $$). The atmosphere is more polished, with ceiling fans, varnished picnic tables, and a chipper wait staff. But AJ's is not so upscale that it doesn't welcome—hell, it downright encourages—a biker clientele, right down to the parking area reserved "for Harleys only." They've undergone a top-to-bottom remake, but raw oysters ($5.50 per dozen) and smoked yellowfin tuna dip ($6.95) are reasonably priced, and the broiled seafood platter (shrimp, oysters, scallops, fish, crab) comes in at $18.95. If you're inclined to party, head to AJ's Club Bimini after dinner.

In the same affordable vein, we dug the **Crab Trap** at James Lee County Park (3500 Old U.S. 98 East, 850/654-2722, $$); the Back Porch (1740 Old U.S. 98 East, 850/837-2022, $$), where char-grilling fish is the name of the game; and **Joe's Crab Shack** (14055 Emerald Coast Parkway, 850/650-1882, $), where mesquite-grilled seafood items range from $10 to $15.

A great view of the water can be had at

Fish Out of Water: A Californian Cleans Up Destin Harbor

At first, we paid him little mind. He was the first mate aboard Capt. George Eller's fishing boat, the *Bounty Hunter,* out of Destin Harbor. Our group's planned deep-sea fishing excursion into the Gulf of Mexico aboard the *Bounty Hunter* got waylaid by winds and choppy seas, and the only thing we would have gotten from the gulf that day was seasick. (Just our luck: Destin's charter boats get grounded by wind and wave only once every 45 days or so.) All of the trophy fish we would have doubtlessly hauled in were given a reprieve. Instead we cruised the protected harbor and enjoyed an otherwise nice day—sunny and warm, like it usually is in Destin—shooting the breeze with the amiable Eller.

His first mate—a blond-haired, bronze-skinned sea salt who looked to be in his 30s—didn't say much at first. He paced the deck, obscured behind dark shades and a visor. Though he kept to himself, striding from stem to stern while idly tossing lines in the water to pass the time, he had an amiable smile on his face and seemed to want to join the conversation. It didn't take much prompting to draw him out. His name is Mark Walker, and he's a transplanted Californian who loves working on the water. A good guy, he headed east when his son moved to Destin so that he could be a responsible dad.

Walker brought with him a sorely needed environmental conscience that has benefited the Destin area more than the oily sorts who have overbuilt the beachfront and fouled the harbor would ever likely realize or concede. He deserves some kind of award for all the volunteer work he has done cleaning up Destin Harbor. For six months he did nothing but harbor cleanup, donating $70,000 of his own money and time. "Nobody else was going to do it," he says. With a shrug he adds, "The money's gone. The harbor lives."

He has taken a proprietary interest in Destin Harbor's health and well being. "Nobody messes with my pond," says Walker, and he's not kidding. He is the official Community Service Officer for the harbor. Among other things, he enlists smokers for his harbor-area "butt pickup patrol," forcing them to confront the litter that they and their ilk generate. "That

the **Lucky Snapper** (76 U.S. 98 East, 850/654-0900, $$$). Luckily, snapper is our favorite Florida fish, and they also do grouper all kinds of ways here. After consulting with our waiter—bronzed snapper? Caribbean-style tuna? sauteed triggerfish?—we opted for blackened grouper with fried crawfish and pineapple corn relish, served atop brown rice, and were not disappointed. Don't pass up the heads-on steamed shrimp, either.

We also lucked out by chumming U.S. 98 for early-bird offerings and posted dinner specials at the more expensive joints, hooking a nicely prepared mullet dinner at **Harbor Docks** (538 U.S. 98 East, 850/837-2506, $$$) for $8.

The finest preparations in town can be found at the very popular **Marina Cafe** (404 U.S. 98 East, 850/837-7960, $$$$), but brace yourself for sticker shock. Standout entrées include brazil-nut crusted mahimahi and grilled swordfish with lemon saffron sauce. Wood oven gourmet pizzas are a specialty, too. At least when we were in town, the Marina Cafe offered early birds an

puts them off discarding cigarette butts pretty quickly," he says, chuckling. In particular, he enjoys raising environmental awareness among children by speaking to classes at local schools. "They're good little warriors," he notes.

The more he talks, the more animated he gets and the livelier are his casts from the deck. Each toss causes the unspooling monofilament line to sing in a high-pitched tone, and then there's a small splash as the rig hits the water. "I'm trolling my favorite spots in the harbor for a trout," he explains. "I figured I might hit a 10-pounder, but I probably won't 'cause all I got's a little spoon."

Walker has mapped the harbor floor, which required countless hours diving down among toxic muck, where God knows what is buried and entrained in the sediment. Learning of this, the U.S. Environmental Protection Agency called him with one question: "Why are you not dead?' Walker claims that he's kept himself safe from the harbor's chemical horrors by coating his skin in Vaseline and treating his eyes with boric acid and ears with isopropyl alcohol. These trade secrets migrated east with him from California. He told his EPA inquisitors, "Man, I'm from Los Angeles. I grew up in a sewer.'

He's worked as a lifeguard and divemaster. He likes body surfing, but his real avocation is environmental activism. Even so, he knows what buttons not to push in Destin. "If I came out here like Greenpeace and started telling on people, I'd be dead by now," he says. "The word 'environmentalist' scares people to death." So Walker works within the system, leading by example and making friends and recruits.

On the sportfishing front, he's worked alongside Capt. Eller seven days a week for 10 months straight, but neither of them exactly looks at their days on the water as a job. "Another day in paradise," says Eller. "We believe that. Not many places can compare with this. The lifestyle here is pretty laid back. There are no smokestack industries for a hundred miles."

Even so, there is pollution. Just ask Walker if he'd eat anything he caught out of Destin Harbor, and he doesn't hesitate to answer: "No. Nevah." All the same time, between his cleanup efforts and a little boost from nature, things are looking up. The otherwise devastating Hurricane Opal, which left the harbor looking like a war zone of wrecked boats, brought a new sand floor to Destin, and 17 marine species have returned.

unbeatable deal: buy one entrée, get a second free between 5 P.M. and 6 P.M. nightly.

Another justifiably popular spot is **Cafe Grazie** (1771 Old 98 East, 850/837-7240, $$$), a bustling Italian restaurant that does everything right, from the warm bread served with an olive oil, roasted garlic, and red pepper dip prepared at your table to entrées like the house specialty grouper parmesan. You'll feel as though you've stumbled into a happening in this festive place and will enjoy the experience and the cuisine immensely, from soup to nuts, calamari to tiramisu.

Lest we forget, a good place for breakfast or a mid-day pastry is the **Donut Hole** (635 U.S. 98 East, 850/837-8824, $). We loved its kindred operation over in Walton County, and this is the original.

Night Moves

Nightown (140 Palmetto Street, 850/837-6448), with its multi-tiered dance club/disco, is the king of the nightlife. If the thought of shaking your booty to deejayed dance music in Destin is appealing, this is the place to go. As for us, we're too old and cynical to affect dance-floor moves without irony or embarrassment, and the music is egregious. Alternatives to going deaf to the turntable wizardry of DJ Doc Rock at Nightown are heading over to the harbor and hanging out at **AJ's Club Bimini** (168 U.S. 98 East, 850/837-1913) or the **Boathouse Oyster Bar** (288 U.S. 98 East, 850/837-3645), which is the most down-to-earth joint in town.

Contact Information

Destin Area Chamber of Commerce, 1021 U.S. 98 East, P.O. Box 8, Destin, FL 32540; 850/837-6241; website: www.destinchamber.com

Emerald Coast Convention and Visitors Bureau, 1540 U.S. 98 East, P.O. Box 609, Fort Walton Beach, FL 32549; 850/651-7131 or 800/322-3319; website: www.destin-fwb.com

Eglin Air Force Base

Spreading its wings to embrace 724 square miles of land plus 97,963 square miles of test and training area in the Gulf of Mexico, **Eglin Air Force Base** is the largest air force base in the free world. The 33rd Fighter Wing stationed here, heroes of the 1990 Persian Gulf incursion, are based at Eglin. The sight of parachuting pilots and the sounds of low-flying jets are not uncommon around here.

Eglin oversees 3.5 miles of beach at the east end of Santa Rosa Island and about 15 miles at the island's midsection. Sandwiched between these parcels is Okaloosa Island, the name the locals have given the unincorporated commercial area south of Fort Walton Beach. Eglin's holdings are, in the words of one lifelong local, "jewels of emptiness." Indeed, they are beautiful to behold from U.S. 98, with white sand mounded so high that it almost resembles a snowy winter landscape. The beaches of Eglin are not entirely off-limits to the public. At least the eastern parcel, near Destin Bridge, is accessible. For the military community, there's Eglin Community Beach Center, a seasonal beach club with the island's largest deck, a food concession, and a gorgeous strip of beach. The beach is open to all, with a few rules (e.g., no walking on dunes, as a beach-restoration project is in progress). Beach access is free, except for down by the jetties, which requires a $5 recreation permit obtainable at Eglin Air Force Base's Natural Resources Branch on State Route 85 in Niceville; call 850/882-4164.

North of Santa Rosa Island, much of Eglin is open to outdoor recreation. Strewn among the base's vast acreage are 15 tent camping areas, 20 fishing holes, and 52 miles of boat and canoe routes that run through eight bayous and rivers. There are no proven trails but many miles of sandy roads. To obtain a recreation permit, drop by the Natural Resources Branch or write in advance of your visit. The permitting and fee structure is somewhat complicated but basically boils down to the following: For a $5 recreational permit, you can hike, bike, or ride horses on Eglin's 264,000 acres. A permit to camp costs $5 and is good for up to five consecutive days in designated

3 Eglin Air Force Base

 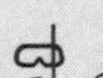  

Location: west side of Destin bridge, off U.S. 98 on Okaloosa Island
Parking/fees: free parking lot
Hours: sunrise to sunset
Facilities: none
Contact: Public Affairs office at Eglin Air Force Base, 850/882-2878, ext. 333

MAP OF THE PANHANDLE—PAGE 547

primitive campsites only. A fishing permit costs $12; a hunting permit, $40; a combined permit, $50.

Public tours of Eglin Air Force Base were canceled in the mid-1990s due to budget cutbacks. However, the **Air Force Armament Museum** (100 Museum Drive, Eglin AFB, 850/882-4062)—which sits right outside the gates at the intersection of State Route 85 and State Route 189—is open daily from 9:30 A.M. to 4:30 P.M. There is no admission charge.

Contact Information

Eglin Air Force Base, Natural Resources Branch, 107 State Route 85 North, Eglin Air Force Base, FL 32542; 850/882-4164; website: www.eglin.af.mil

Fort Walton Beach and Okaloosa Island

Fort Walton Beach is home of Eglin Air Force Base (see preceding entry). Yet even before Fort Walton Beach became home to the largest air force base in the free world, the area held strategic value.

The first settlers arrived 10,000 years ago. They were a nomadic people whose wanderings came to a halt along this coast, where they set up a sophisticated civilization with skilled artisans, intricate religious ceremonies, and a political structure. One of their temple mounds, completed around A.D. 1400, still exists right in the center of town, along with one of the largest collections of native pottery in the Southeast. They can be found at the **Indian Temple Mound Museum** (139 Miracle Strip Parkway, 850/243-6521), which offers a remarkable glimpse at pre-Columbian culture unlike any other on the Florida Panhandle. Interestingly, Temple Mound was the first municipally owned museum in Florida.

It was near this Indian temple mound that George Walton—for whom the town was named—set up camp during the Civil War to guard the coast against Union invasion. After the war, veterans of "Camp Walton" returned to the area to homestead. One of them, John Thomas Brooks, established Brooks Landing on Santa Rosa Sound, near the Indian temple mound. The town that grew from this settlement was named Fort Walton in 1932. "Beach" was added in 1953 to attract vacationers. And why not? The beaches of Fort Walton, with their blanket of nearly pure white quartz sand, are among the nicest in the state of Florida.

Today, the city of Fort Walton Beach has a population of over 22,000, and the Greater Fort Walton area a whopping 90,000. Most of the residents live on the mainland. Okaloosa Island, where the beaches are located, is technically unincorporated, although businesses out there use Fort Walton Beach as a mailing address. Thus, somewhat ludicrously, Fort Walton Beach has no gulf beaches (though it does have beaches on Choctawhatchee Bay). As military towns are wont to be, Fort Walton Beach—connected to the beaches by a bridge on U.S. 98—can get a little rough around the edges, and Okaloosa Island is the real gem of the Emerald Coast.

Beaches

Destin, Fort Walton Beach, and Okaloosa Island are marketed together as the Emerald Coast, a reference to the blue-green hue of the gulf. While Destin attracts its share of upscale vacationers, Okaloosa Island has a far more appealing and accessible beach. The fun begins just over the bridge from Destin, on land owned by

MAP OF OKALOOSA COUNTY—PAGE 618

Eglin Air Force Base. The proper name for this barrier island is Santa Rosa Island. However, the three-mile commercial corridor, between parcels owned by Eglin, is called Okaloosa Island. Santa Rosa, Okaloosa, or whatever you want to call it stretches west to Pensacola Beach and Fort Pickens, 40 miles away.

According to a local geologist, the sands that make up Santa Rosa Island "are among the whitest and most homogenous throughout the entire world." The source of this pure quartz sand is the Appalachian Mountains, and the conduit is the Apalachicola River, 130 miles east of Fort Walton Beach. As world temperatures rose at the end of the last ice age, continental ice sheets began melting and the runoff surged down rivers to the sea.

One such river was the Apalachicola, which transported chemically weathered and eroded bits of Appalachian quartz to the Gulf of Mexico. The fine-ground, polished white sand grains began arriving 5,000 years ago. Reworked by waves and currents, these deposits formed a barrier island that grew west from Destin, a process that continues today, with Santa Rosa Island extending to Pensacola Pass.

Needless to add, the beaches on Okaloosa Island are superfine in more ways than one. Starting from the east, the first public beach is **John Beasley Way-**

4 John Beasley Wayside Park

Location: along U.S. 98 on Okaloosa Island, 1.25 miles east of Fort Walton Beach
Parking/fees: free parking lot
Hours: 6 A.M.–8:30 P.M.
Facilities: lifeguards (seasonal), restrooms, picnic tables, showers, and a visitor center
Contact: Emerald Coast Convention and Visitors Bureau, 850/651-7131

5 Brackin Wayside Park and Boardwalk

Location: along U.S. 98 on Okaloosa Island, one mile east of Fort Walton Beach
Parking/fees: free parking lot
Hours: sunrise to sunset
Facilities: concessions, lifeguards (seasonal), restrooms, picnic tables, and showers
Contact: Emerald Coast Convention and Visitors Bureau, 850/651-7131

6 Okaloosa Island accesses (#1-3)

Location: marked and numbered accesses along Santa Rosa Boulevard, on Okaloosa Island
Parking/fees: free parking lots
Hours: 6 A.M.–8:30 P.M.
Facilities: lifeguards, restrooms, picnic tables, and showers
Contact: Emerald Coast Convention and Visitors Bureau, 850/651-7131

7 Okaloosa Island accesses (#4-6)

Location: marked and numbered accesses along Santa Rosa Boulevard, on Okaloosa Island
Parking/fees: free parking lots
Hours: 6 A.M.–8:30 P.M.
Facilities: restrooms (seasonal)
Contact: Emerald Coast Convention and Visitors Bureau, 850/651-7131

side Park. This free county park is located on U.S. 98, a few hundred feet east of the Visitors Welcome Center. Open 8 A.M. to 5 P.M. daily, the center is full of local literature and is staffed by helpful folks.

A quarter mile west is **Brackin Wayside Park and Boardwalk,** which has a huge pier (repaired since being heavily damaged by Hurricane Opal) as its centerpiece. There's ample free parking, a gulfside restaurant (Harpoon Hanna's), several shops, volleyball nets on the beach, and lifeguards on duty in-season.

Just around the corner, where Santa Rosa Boulevard picks up along the beachfront after U.S. 98 cuts inland, are seven numbered beach accesses. The first three have seasonal lifeguards, picnic pavilions, and facilities. **Access #1** is next to Pandora's Lounge and also bears the name Blue Dolphin Beach Walk. The smaller, unnamed **Access #2,** adjoining the Breakers, has a dirt lot. **Access #3** bears the name Seashore Beach Walk. Like #1, it has some cute gazebos, a paved lot, and a boardwalk out to the beach. **Accesses #4, #5, and #6** are unimproved, with small gravel lots and portable toilets. The fourth adjoins the Carousel Beach Resort, the fifth is next to Island Echoes Resort, and the sixth is marked with a wooden sign. A seventh access is located just before the gate to Eglin Air Force Base. The distance between accesses #1 and #7 is all of two miles, so if one lot is filled just move down to the next.

An interesting footnote: the easternmost unit of the tri-state Gulf Islands National Seashore is on Okaloosa Island. The Okaloosa Area is a bayside facility, with free parking on, and access to, Choctawhatchee Bay. The bay's calm water is ideal for sailboarding and sailing, and its shallow depths mean safe, wave-free swimming for kiddies. A concessioner rents sailboards, sailboats, paddleboats, and beach equipment, and also sells snacks and drinks.

Shore Things

- **Bike/skate rentals:** Beach Plus, 208 Perry Avenue SE, Fort Walton Beach, 850/244-6525.
- **Ecotourism:** Adventures Unlimited Canoe & Tubing, 8974 Tomahawk Landing Road, Milton, 850/623-6197.
- **Fishing charters:** Destin Fishing Fleet Marina Charter Service, 201 U.S. 98 East, Destin, 850/837-1995.
- **Marina:** Boat Marina and Boating Center, 32 U.S. 98 SW, Fort Walton Beach, 850/243-2628.
- **Pier:** Public Fishing and Observation Pier, Brackin Wayside Park and Boardwalk, 1400 block of U.S. 98 East, Okaloosa Island.
- **Rainy-day attraction:** Indian Temple Mound Museum, 139 Southeast Miracle Strip Parkway, Fort Walton Beach, 850/243-6521.
- **Shopping/browsing:** Fort Walton Beach Main Street, 180 Miracle Strip Parkway, Fort Walton Beach, 850/664-6426.
- **Surf shop:** Islander's Surf Shop, 191 Miracle Strip Parkway SE, 850/244-0451.
- **Vacation rentals:** Fort Walton Beach Resort Properties, 909 Santa Rosa Boulevard, Okaloosa Island, 850/243-0339.

Bunking Down

Plenty of spiffy new motels and hotels have opened up on Okaloosa Island in recent years. Directly in the middle of the Miracle Strip, flanking the pier and boardwalk at Brackin Wayside Park, are the recently arrived **Ramada Plaza Beach Resort** (1500 Miracle Strip Parkway, 850/243-9161, $$) and the old reliable **Holiday Inn Okaloosa Island** (1100 Santa Rosa Boulevard, 850/243-9181, $$). Both offer the predictable comforts of restaurants,

MAP OF OKALOOSA COUNTY—PAGE 618

Beaches and Buttheads: The Litter Problem

If it's true that we are what we eat, then it is also true that what we throw away reveals something about our character (or lack thereof) as people. While littering is obnoxious, it is more than just an aesthetic problem, especially at the beach, where much of it ends up in the ocean. More than two million seabirds and 100,000 sea animals die each year along U.S. shores from discarded plastic—either from ingestion or being strangled or drowned by getting caught in it. Although plastic takes up to 450 years to decompose (or so it is surmised; plastic hasn't been around that long to know for sure), 20 million tons a year of it is produced in the United States alone. Every hour Americans throw away 2.5 million plastic bottles. The problem is not just limited to plastic, either. Americans create four pounds of garbage per person every day. With only five percent of the world's population, we produce—if that's the right word—half the world's waste: plastic, paper, glass, aluminum, rubber, motor oil . . . you name it, we throw it away.

At the beach, the temptation to litter is greater than elsewhere. People are on vacation, subsisting on fast-food and convenience-store fare (with its mountains of trash). They're not focused on reducing wastage and not given many options in the way of recycling or even proper disposal. In our view, this is no excuse, because we see litter as an attitude problem. That is, when you choose to toss a cigarette butt or a wad of fast-food wrapping out the car window or on the beach sand, you're not just breaking the law, you are extending a middle finger to the world. You are, in effect, saying, "With this totally dumb and thoughtless act, I hereby make the world through which I pass an uglier place." Take a look around and you will see that Americans litter with the same pointless defiance with which they discharge their firearms, drive their greenhouse gas-emitting vehicles, fill in their wetlands, and riddle their fields and watersheds with carcinogenic chemicals. Knowing better, they choose to commit patently stupid and self-destructive acts.

The following list of "Florida's Dirty Dozen" rank-orders the flotsam deposited on Florida beaches, based on beach cleanups. The information—types of garbage, total

lounges, and poolside bars, nicely landscaped grounds, and more than adequate beach access.

All that and more is available at the **Sheraton Four Points Hotel** (1325 Miracle Strip Parkway, 850/243-8116, $$$), which is a veritable oasis of greenery and creature comforts set a comfortable distance back from the generic drabness of the Miracle Strip. A hotel tower of recent vintage faces the beach, and a landscaped courtyard with spa and heated pool feels well removed from the churning world beyond.

A number of more generic, budget-minded motels are located at the west end of Okaloosa Island, before the road ends at Eglin Air Force Base's east gate. We found an off-season rate of under $30 at a friendly beachside **Rodeway Inn** (866 Santa Rosa Boulevard, 850/243-3114, $) with spartan but adequate rooms. The super-cheap tariff was admittedly the deciding factor in our case. Arriving late in the day, and nearing the end of our itinerary with thin-

pieces reported, and percentage in terms of debris collected—was provided by Florida's Center for Marine Conservation.

Cigarette butts:	111,422 (17.6 percent)
Plastic pieces:	34,087 (5.4 percent)
Glass beverage bottles:	32,497 (5.1 percent)
Plastic food bags/wrappers:	32,211 (5.1 percent)
Plastic caps/lids:	30,669 (4.8 percent)
Plastic straws:	29,619 (4.7 percent)
Foamed plastic pieces:	29,552 (4.7 percent)
Metal beverage cans:	27,688 (4.4 percent)
Paper pieces:	22,573 (3.6 percent)
Plastic beverage bottles:	21,461 (3.4 percent)
Foamed plastic cups:	17,641 (2.8 percent)
Glass pieces:	13,328 (2.1 percent)
Total:	**402,748 (63.6 percent)**

Here's what eventually happens to litter that makes its way into the ocean. This information—the length of time it takes various items to decompose in the ocean—is provided by the Florida Sea Grant.

1. Glass bottles and jars:	maybe forever
2. Monofilament fishing lines:	600 years
3. Disposable diapers:	450 years
4. Plastic bottles:	450 years
5. Plastic six-pack rings:	400 years
6. Aluminum cans:	200 years
7. Styrofoam cups:	50 years
8. Biodegradable diapers:	one year
9. Waxed milk cartons:	three months
10. Cardboard boxes, apple cores:	two months
11. Paper towels, newspapers:	2–6 weeks

Moral of the story: don't litter the beaches, and be so kind as to pick after those pigs that do.

ning wallets and shrinking bank accounts, we decided $30 was preferable to the $75–100 rates we were being quoted down the road for a room we'd be in for all of eight hours. We wound up sharing a wing—not to mention a mess of wings, judging from the remains of a chicken dinner left on the sidewalk—with some kerchief-headed ne'er-do-wells who were partying and grilling on a hibachi outside their motel room. The Rodeway was formerly a Best Western that, as best we can figure, got pummeled by Hurricane Opal and was forced one step further down the motel franchise food chain. Some properties in the vicinity are still boarded up as a result of that devastation.

Nearby is a **Days Inn & Suites** (573 Santa Rosa Boulevard, 850/244-8686, $$). The rates are higher than they ought to be, but the place is clean, modern, and right on the beach. To put it all in perspective, the beach in back of all the aforementioned hotels and motels is polar white, with powdery soft sand that is worth whatever it costs to gain access.

Coastal Cuisine

Shoney's, Krystal Burgers, Morrison's Cafeteria, and Olive Garden are among the restaurants recommended by the Fort Walton Beach Chamber of Commerce, so you know the dining scene is nothing to write home about. But with a little rooting around, Fort Walton Beach and Okaloosa Island are capable of a surprise here and there.

Right on the beach is the **Crab Trap** (1450 Miracle Strip Parkway South, 850/243-5500, $$), the centerpiece of a complex of shops and restaurants on the rebuilt boardwalk at Brackin Wayside Park. It has a seafood-heavy menu and a great view of the water. Another "view" restaurant, **Angler's Beachside Grill** (1030 Miracle Strip Parkway South, 850/796-0260, $$) is located at the Fort Walton Pier. In addition to a seafood-heavy menu, they have a Sunday afternoon crawfish boil.

One of Florida's oldest seafood restaurant, **Staff's** (24 Miracle Strip Parkway South, 850/243-3482, $$) has been serving seafood and steaks in a family atmosphere for going on a century. Locals flock to **Seagull's** (1318 Miracle Strip Parkway SE, 850/243-3413, $$), a casual waterfront seafood restaurant serving fresh catches in ample portions. If you're in a non-seafood mood, hit **Brooks Bridge Bar-B-Que and Cafe** (240 Miracle Strip Parkway SE, 850/244-3003, $).

Night Moves

While in the Fort Walton Beach area, we opted to do as the locals do, which is to say pursue the seven deadly sins. On that note, the two most popular night spots are a raucous nightclub and a raunchy strip club. **Cash's Cabanas** (106 Santa Rosa Boulevard, 850/244-2274), including Cash's Road Kill Cafe and Cash's Faux Pas, has for 30 years offered live entertainment to servicemen, working stiffs, and party animals.

Sammy's (1212 Miracle Strip Parkway South, 850/244-0390), an exotic dance club, is home to a bevy of "Sammy's Angels" willing to take it all off for our boys in blue, as well as horny college boys, slavering construction workers, and lonely old men. As Sammy's parking lot was packed to the gills, we felt obliged to investigate. A sign inside the establishment lays out the protocol: "This is no time to be shy. . . . If you'd like an Angel at your table, just ask, 'Can I buy you a drink?'" Further pointers are offered in an essay entitled "The Naked Truth About Table Dance," which includes such irrefutable brilliance as, "Most guys offer about $20 per dance. That's about 50¢ per thrill." Finally, this disclaimer: "Sammy's is not responsible for lost or broken hearts." Or squandered paychecks.

For a local home brew, head to **Santa Rosa Bay Brewery** (54 Miracle Strip Parkway SE, 850/664-2739); try a schooner of red ale and an accompanying bowl of crawfish chowder.

Other hotspots can be found, but they get progressively seedier. One place offered male strippers and a sign that read "party with 1,000s." For further descents into Dante's Inferno, feel free to scout around town, where tattoos, palm readings, and (no doubt) knuckle sandwiches are readily available.

Contact Information

Emerald Coast Convention and Visitors Bureau, 1540 U.S. 98 East, P.O. Box 609, Fort Walton Beach, FL 32549; 850/651-7131 or 800/322-3319; website: www.destin-fwb.com

Greater Fort Walton Beach Chamber of Commerce, 34 Southeast Miracle Strip Parkway, P.O. Box 640, Fort Walton Beach, FL 32549; 850/244-8191; website: www.fortwaltonbeachfl.org

Map of the Panhandle—Page 547

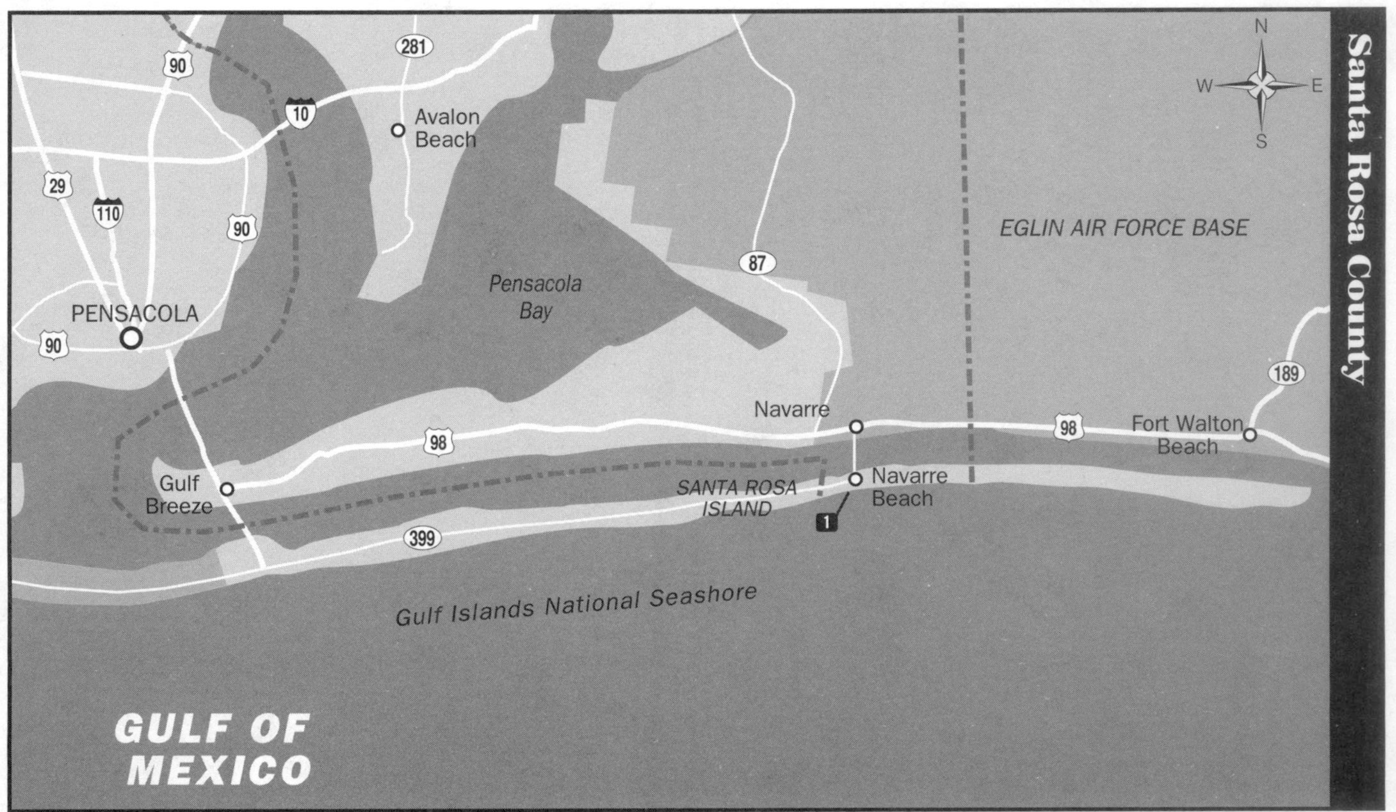
Santa Rosa County
N
W
E
S
90
281
10
Avalon Beach
29
110
90
PENSACOLA
90
Pensacola Bay
87
EGLIN AIR FORCE BASE
189
Navarre
98
98
Fort Walton Beach
Gulf Breeze
SANTA ROSA ISLAND
Navarre Beach
1
399
Gulf Islands National Seashore
GULF OF MEXICO

SANTA ROSA COUNTY

❶ Navarre Beach page 636

With the exception of Navarre Beach, Santa Rosa County gets elbowed out of the coastal picture. Even the four miles of Navarre Beach do not technically belong to Santa Rosa County but are leased from Escambia. We have never heard of such an arrangement, whereby one county "leases" a beach from another. In any case, Navarre Beach lies along a desolate stretch of Santa Rosa Island, sandwiched between Eglin Air Force Base and Gulf Islands National Seashore (whose headquarters are in nearby Gulf Breeze). Sand blows across the road, hurricanes take umbrage, and Navarre Beach has been slow to find its footing. The high-rise condos that have begun rising of late show a disappointing lack of imagination for a place surrounded by so much undefiled shoreline with which it could have harmonized. Mother Nature has sounded an alarming note, eroding away 60 feet of beach in the last few years. Mayday!

Navarre Beach

Except for a portion of Eglin Air Force Base's inaccessible coastal holdings, Santa Rosa County's only claim to gulfside real estate is staked at Navarre Beach (pop. 1,200). This town, if you can call it that, lies between Eglin Air Force Base and the Santa Rosa Area of Gulf Islands National Seashore, with the latter falling inside Escambia County. Navarre Beach is a four-mile sliver of attempted development along a forlorn, windswept stretch of Santa Rosa Island, south of the mainland town of Navarre. Every time they make some headway building condos and selling property, nature sends a hurricane Navarre Beach's way. Dunes get flattened, sheets of sand obliterate the highway, and buildings take a beating. Opal and Georges were the main offenders in the '90s.

Unlike well-established Pensacola Beach, poor Navarre Beach just can't get a leg up. There's a ghost-town aura about the place, which is seemingly too isolated from civilization to catch fire as a vacation or retirement destination. That hasn't stopped a boom in the construction of 15-story condos. Luxury high-rise condos and stilted houses are going up everywhere, but still they insist on calling Navarre Beach an "undiscovered paradise." The irony is that with the arrival of such constructions, it is no longer either undiscovered or paradisiacal.

❶ Navarre Beach

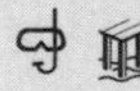   ④

Location: From U.S. 98 at Navarre, turn south on State Route 399 and cross Navarre Bridge to Santa Rosa Island. Proceed through the stop sign to the public beach.

Parking/fees: free parking lot

Hours: 24 hours

Facilities: lifeguards (seasonal), restrooms, picnic tables, and showers

Contact: Santa Rosa County Engineering Department, 850/939-2387

Beaches

About a mile's worth of Navarre Beach is undeveloped, county-owned public beach. That part of **Navarre Beach** extends from the point at which the Navarre toll bridge deposits traffic on the island to the gate at Eglin Air Force Base. We were amazed to find ourselves with virtually the whole of the beach to ourselves one fine day, sharing it only with some paratroopers on maneuvers off in the distance at Eglin. We marveled at the expanse of beach, the fineness of the sand, and the penetrating air-force blue of the water.

Navarre's free public fishing pier has been rebuilt after affronts visited upon it by hurricanes. They were catching pompano and 40-pound cobia from it last time we checked. They're open daily from 5 A.M. to 9 P.M.; it costs $5 to fish and $1 to watch. Meanwhile, they're still working on rebuilding the dunes, as each whopper of a hurricane has made it a task comparable to Sisyphus's attempt to roll a boulder up a hill.

Bunking Down

The only hotel on the island is **Holiday Inn** (8375 Gulf Boulevard, 850/939-2321, $$), a two-story beachfront hotel. For vacation rentals in Navarre Beach, try **Gulf Properties** (8460 Gulf Boulevard, 850/939-4748).

Coastal Cuisine

There are restaurants aplenty along Gulf Boulevard and Navarre Parkway. We're partial to one with good food, brew, beachside ambience, and local color: **Barracuda's Bar and Grill** (8469 Gulf Boulevard, 850/939-0093, $).

Contact Information

Navarre Beach Area Chamber of Commerce, 8543 Navarre Parkway, Navarre, FL 32566; 850/939-3267 or 800/480-7263; website: www.navarrefl.com/nbacoc

Gulf Breeze

Gulf Breeze (pop. 5,500) is six miles south of Pensacola on U.S. 98, at the western end of a spit that juts into Pensacola Bay between Santa Rosa Island and the mainland. The Santa Rosa County line extends out with the spit. Thus, even though Pensacola, Gulf Breeze, and Pensacola Beach all line up on a north-south axis, Gulf Breeze belongs to a different county. This can be problematic if you're heading out to Pensacola Beach from Pensacola (or vice versa), because Santa Rosa is a largely dry county where nothing stronger than beer can be sold. (The latest effort to change that state of affairs was voted down in November 1998.) A word to the wise: they lie in wait in Gulf Breeze for those who have been drinking and driving. The behavior is inarguably illegal and reprehensible, and you stand a good chance of getting caught in Gulf Breeze.

Gulf Breeze serves as headquarters for the Florida district of **Gulf Islands National Seashore** (1801 Gulf Breeze Parkway, 850/934-2600). You can obtain maps and literature on the six areas that make up Gulf Islands National Seashore in Florida. Three are directly on the coast: Santa Rosa (between Navarre Beach and Pensacola Beach), Fort Pickens (west end of Santa Rosa Island, near Pensacola Beach), and Perdido Key. Fort Barrancas is southwest of Pensacola, near Pensacola Naval Air Station. Okaloosa is on Choctawatchee Bay, near Fort Walton Beach.

The remaining area is Naval Live Oaks, which surrounds the headquarters and visitor center in Gulf Breeze. It is worth the short detour to drop by and orient yourself to the National Seashore's extensive holdings in the western Panhandle, and also to walk the trails and view the exhibits at Naval Live Oaks. This area is a Native American archaeological site and former federal tree farm where live oaks were grown to provide a supply of timber to build ships for the U.S. Navy from 1830 to 1860. Now it is a quiet haven for nature study where visitors can walk among salt marsh, live oak hammock, and sand-pine-scrub communities.

Contact Information

Gulf Breeze Area Chamber of Commerce, 1170 Gulf Breeze Parkway, Gulf Breeze, FL 32561; 850/932-7888; website: www.gulfbreezechamber.com

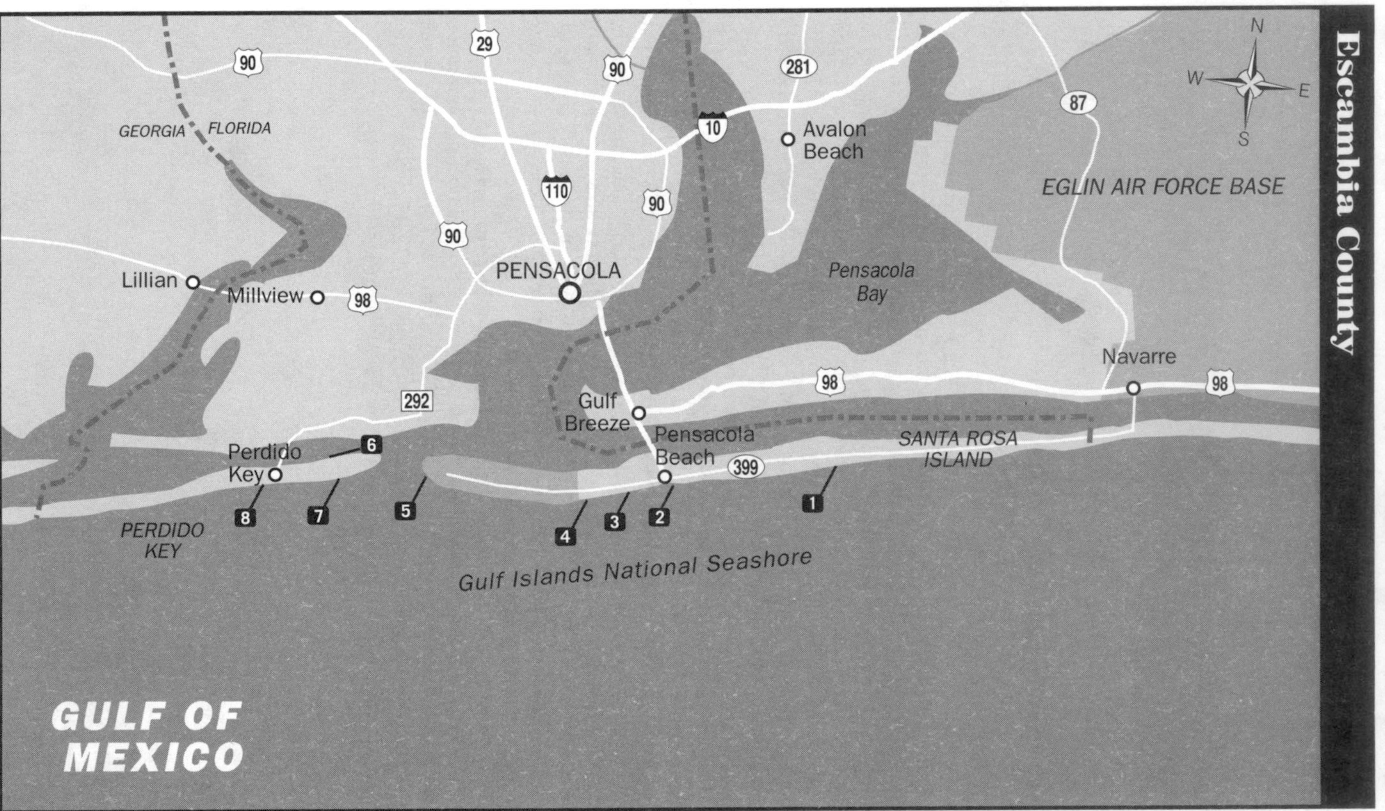
Escambia County
N
W
E
S
EGLIN AIR FORCE BASE
87
281
Avalon
Beach
90
29
90
10
110
90
90
GEORGIA
FLORIDA
Lillian
Millview
98
PENSACOLA
Pensacola
Bay
Navarre
98
98
292
Gulf
Breeze
Pensacola
Beach
399
SANTA ROSA
ISLAND
Perdido
Key
6
8
7
5
4
3
2
1
PERDIDO
KEY
Gulf Islands National Seashore
GULF OF
MEXICO

ESCAMBIA COUNTY

Escambia County is the westernmost of Florida's 67 counties, abutting Alabama on two sides. And yet Escambia is an essential part of Florida, having been one of the state's first two counties and the city of Pensacola its first territorial capital. Besides, Escambia is as blessed with beaches as any peninsular county, claiming 40 miles of fine-grained, Grade A white quartz sand. The only bad news is that severe beach erosion has been wrought by a succession of hurricanes. Two ruler-straight barrier islands—Santa Rosa Island and Perdido Key—front the Gulf of Mexico for the county's length, broken only by the narrow throat of Pensacola Pass, which leads into Pensacola Bay. The two beachside communities in Escambia County are Pensacola Beach and Perdido Key. The former is a pleasantly diverse, wisely developed beach town, while the latter is glutted with condos. Much of the county's shoreline belongs to Gulf Islands National Seashore, which also includes units in Alabama and Mississippi.

Santa Rosa Area (Gulf Islands National Seashore)

The **Santa Rosa Area** of Gulf Islands National Seashore runs for seven miles between the west end of Navarre Beach and the east end of Pensacola Beach. Three parking lots (without facilities) are strewn along its length, offering instant access to the snow-white gulf beach. A spot along this area's midsection has been named Opal Beach (after the destructive '95 hurricane), and it includes newly constructed parking lots and picnic clusters, including shelters, restrooms, showers, and dune crossovers.

Opal Beach has also become a fee-collection area, with the National Seashore's standard $6 per vehicle charge applying. Your receipt is good for seven days at Opal Beach and all other fee-applicable areas of Gulf Islands National Seashore, including Fort Pickens and Perdido Key. The road through the Santa Rosa Area and the three undeveloped roadside parking lots will remain free. Incidentally, the Florida National Scenic Trail passes through the Santa Rosa Area, with the beach itself being the trail.

1 Santa Rosa Area (Gulf Islands National Seashore)

Location: between Navarre Beach and Pensacola Beach, along State Route 399 (Gulf Boulevard) on Santa Rosa Island
Parking/fees: three free parking lots; $6 per vehicle entrance fee at Opal Beach day-use picnic area. The entrance fee is good for seven days at all units of Gulf Islands National Seashore.
Hours: 8 A.M. to sunset
Facilities: none
Contact: Gulf Islands National Seashore, 850/934-2600

Contact Information

Gulf Islands National Seashore, 1801 Gulf Breeze Parkway, Gulf Breeze, FL 32561; 850/934-2600; website: www.nps.gov/guis

Pensacola Beach

Pensacola Beach (pop. 3,000) is a gulfside community—located two bridges, 8.5 miles, and 15 minutes from downtown Pensacola, at the western end of Santa Rosa Island—which manages to maintain a relatively low-key aura reminiscent of what beach towns all over the country used to be like. In Pensacola Beach, the town overseers have kept growth in check, not prohibiting it but just slowing it down to a manageable level. The result is a community that has its fair share of condos and hotel towers (with the emphasis on "fair"), along with vast stretches of older beach homes. Pensacola Beach looks relatively unblemished compared to the reckless development that has scarred neighboring Perdido Key and big-money sellouts like Destin. All the same, some locals complain that Pensacola Beach is heading in that direction, with the governing Santa Rosa Island Authority giving realtors and developers anything they want.

In Pensacola Beach, the beach life rules. You can walk along the sand in either direction until your feet blister. You can jog, bike, or stroll an asphalt recreation trail that runs along the bay side of Via de Luna

Drive (State Route 399) for eight miles, from residential Pensacola Beach out to the gate at Fort Pickens. You can take your longboard out to the point at Fort Pickens and surf with the old-school crowd. You can eat, drink, and be merry without having to wander too far. Most of the retail/commercial buildup is located compactly in the area between the foot of Bob Sikes Toll Bridge and the public beach parking lot. Here, you'll find a water tower painted like a beach ball. Three miles west, also on State Route 399, is Pensacola Beach's other colorful water tower. These towers serve as bookends for the community, which is bordered by units of Gulf Islands National Seashore: Santa Rosa, to the east, and Fort Pickens, at the west end of the island.

Pensacola Beach is family friendly, tourist friendly, surfer friendly—just plain friendly. There's a little something for everybody out here without the interests of any one group—come-lately condo owners, longtime homeowners, transient vacationers, day-trippers from Pensacola and environs—dominating Pensacola Beach's relaxed way of life. Crowds peak in summer, when as many as a quarter million people might be out enjoying the island's beaches. Pensacola even attracts a Spring Break crowd, though it is much smaller than Panama City Beach's and tends to consist of families trying to escape college kids and college kids trying to escape other college kids.

Do bear in mind that this is not South Florida. Pensacola's climate is not subtropical, and there is no Gulf Stream warming the waters. While you'll swim comfortably from late April through September, Pensacola Beach is not a year-round playground. They do have a touch of winter here, with traces of snow from time to time. That said, the beaches of the Panhandle, especially along Santa Rosa Island, are some of the prettiest in Florida. They are also, unfortunately, disappearing. Read on.

Beaches

Santa Rosa Island is 48 miles long from stem to stern. That's a lot of beach, and Escambia County claims a fair length along its west end. The nearly pure quartz sand glistens like a bed of granulated sugar. However, there's trouble in paradise. The beaches of Santa Rosa Island have taken a beating from an onslaught of hurricanes: 1995's ferocious Hurricanes Erin and Opal, 1997's Hurricane Danny, and 1998's one-two punch of Hurricanes Earl and Georges. On the Fort Pickens side of the island, it's sad to see all the ghostly stalks of trees that have died from saltwater intrusion when the hurricane overwashed the island. Meanwhile, the beach itself has been disappearing at an alarming rate all along Santa Rosa Island. In the last two years, they've lost 74 feet of beach width. Gone with the waves. There's only one volleyball net's width of beach by the Pensacola Beach pier. They've lost 65 acres of sand, their greatest asset, along the 7.5 miles of Pensacola Beach.

This is sending area officials, resort owners and merchants into a tailspin. What do you do about an economy built on tourism when the very thing that draws people is disappearing grain by grain? You panic and go looking for 2 million cubic yards of sand and the money to pay for it. That is what is happening now in Pen-

❷ Casino Beach (Pensacola Beach)

Location: south end of Pensacola Beach Road, in Pensacola Beach
Parking/fees: free parking lot
Hours: 24 hours
Facilities: concessions, lifeguards (seasonal), restrooms, picnic tables, and showers
Contact: Santa Rosa Island Authority at 850-932-2257

sacola Beach, where they're trying to figure out how to raise the $10 to $20 million necessary for a beach renourishment project of this size. If you visit Pensacola Beach in the meantime, you will find a severely eroded and steepened beach, but a beach nonetheless. Meanwhile, an elderly Pensacola Beach activist, 75-year-old Ann Sonborn, made national headlines for her efforts to ensure that the sugar-white beaches of Pensacola remain that way. She and other watchdogs have patrolled the beaches to make sure the Santa Rosa Island Authority doesn't cheat by using red clay, rocks, dirt, and brown sand. "I like white sand," she told the *Wall Street Journal*. Don't we all?

The heart of Pensacola Beach is the enormous free public parking lot located where the bay bridge deposits traffic onto the island. At this point you can turn left toward Navarre Beach, right toward Fort Pickens, or straight into the public parking lot at Pensacola Beach. This area has long been known as **Casino Beach**, because a casino for social activities like teas and dances (not gambling) used to be out here. A concrete boardwalk runs along the beach, and the beachside Bikini Bar offers refuge from the sun. The old pier was destroyed by Hurricane Opal in 1995; a sturdy concrete replacement opened in the spring of 2001.

The beach and parking lot at Casino Beach are so oversized that they seem uncrowded even when there are significant numbers of people packing the beach. We've been to Pensacola Beach at different times of year—in early summer, at the height of Spring Break (which is but a tremor compared to Panama City Beach's annual beachquake), as well as in fall and winter (the deadest times of year)—and never failed to find a parking space. Across the way, facing Santa Rosa Sound, is Quietwater Beach Boardwalk. It's an area of shops and restaurants with a "quiet water" beach on the bayside.

In addition to all the parking by Casino Beach, smaller lots and roadside accesses are strung along the western end of **Pensacola Beach**, extending all the way to the entrance gate at Fort Pickens (see write-up later in this chapter). Only one of these free accesses, which is called **Fort Pickens Gate**, has a full complement of facilities: picnic pavilions, dune walkovers, restrooms, and showers (but no lifeguards). This is the same beach you'd pay $6 to enter via the gate at Fort Pickens. One other access, by the San de Luna condominium complex, has only a paved parking lot. Numerous "Beach Access" signs are staked in the sand at periodic inter-

3 Pensacola Beach (west accesses)

Location: 10 beach-access points (one with a parking lot) between Casino Beach and Fort Pickens, along State Route 399 in Pensacola Beach

Parking/fees: free roadside parking at dune crossovers and a free parking lot by San De Luna condominium complex

Hours: 24 hours

Facilities: none

Contact: Santa Rosa Island Authority, 850/932-2257

4 Fort Pickens Gate

Location: .1/4 mile east of the entrance gate to Fort Pickens (Gulf Islands National Seashore), on State Route 399 in Pensacola Beach

Parking/fees: free parking lot

Hours: 24 hours

Facilities: restrooms, picnic tables, and showers

Contact: Santa Rosa Island Authority, 850/932-2257

vals to allow renters and homeowners on the bay side of the road access to the beach via dune crossovers. You can also park beside the road and use the crossovers.

Shore Things

- **Ecotourism:** Naval Live Oaks, Gulf Islands National Seashore, 1801 Gulf Breeze Parkway, Gulf Breeze, 850/934-2600.
- **Fishing charters:** Moorings Charter Fleet, 635 Pensacola Beach Boulevard, 850/932-0304.
- **Marina:** The Moorings, 635 Pensacola Beach Boulevard, 850/432-9620.
- **Pier:** Pensacola Beach Pier, Casino Beach; Fort Pickens Pier, Gulf Islands National Seashore, 850/934-2600.
- **Rainy day attraction:** National Museum of Naval Aviation, Pensacola Naval Air Station, Pensacola, 850/452-3604.
- **Shopping/browsing:** Quietwater Beach Boardwalk, Quietwater Beach Road (bayside).
- **Surf shop:** Innerlight, 203 Gulf Breeze Parkway, Gulf Breeze, 850/932-5134.
- **Vacation rentals:** Sand Castles Realty, 27 Via de Luna Drive, 850/932-9723.

Bunking Down

The best spot on Pensacola Beach, in terms of location and condition, is the **Hampton Inn** (2 Via de Luna Drive, 850/932-6800, $$$). This four-story tower is a recent arrival, and unlike the Hampton Inns along interstates across America—which are geared for serviceable overnight comfort but little else—this one has been designed as a resort with vacationers in mind. Two enormous heated pools on a beach-facing deck pose an inviting detour either en route to or from the gulf. Gulfside rooms have private balconies. Rooms are spacious and airy, and the rate (averaging $135–175 per night, in season) includes a formidable continental breakfast, plus drinks and snacks at night.

Other comparably priced gulfside lodges include the **Clarion Inn and Resort** (20 Via de Luna Drive, 850/932-4300, $$$), whose low-lying architecture is more New England fishing village than corporate tower, and an eight-story **Holiday Inn** (165 Fort Pickens Road, 850/932-5361, $$$) toward the west end of Santa Rosa Island. For a drop in room rates but not room quality, the **Comfort Inn Pensacola Beach** (40 Fort Pickens Road, 850/934-5400, $$) is directly opposite the public parking lot at Casino Beach. If you don't mind being across the beach and not directly on it, you will save $20 or more a night. Besides, you're literally next door to the Sandshaker, home of the almighty Bushwacker (see "Night Moves").

Coastal Cuisine

The complex of shops at Quietwater Beach Boardwalk, on the bay side of the island near the foot of the toll bridge, houses several good restaurants. First, there's **Jubilee Topside** and **Jubilee Bushwackers** (400 Quietwater Beach Road, 850/934-3108, $$$), sister operations that face the bayside beach known as Quietwater Beach. The house-specialty barbecued oysters are brushed with a tangy barbecue butter and topped with cheese, then broiled and served with a dipping sauce. Amberjack and grouper sandwiches, a heaping fried seafood platter, and plenty of non-seafood entrées fill the menus as well. The enclosed outdoor bar in the back often jumps to the sounds of reggae bands.

Speaking of which, they serve jammin' Jamaica jerk chicken and shrimp at **Sun Ray Restaurante & Cantina** (400 Quietwater Beach Road, 850/932-0118, $$$), a Caribbean/Mexican restaurant in the same complex. Sun Ray has the bric-a-brac-strewn feel of a good old Baja surfer's bar. In fact, we heard a gaggle of old surfers, including one vintage board bum with wavy hair and ruddy complexion, waxing fondly about the surf out at "the Point" that day as they laid waste to mounds of fajitas. That seems to be the way to go here, as one sizzling pan of fajitas after another—filled with Cajun shrimp, jerk chicken, and steak—exited the kitchen. Also intriguing are the Caribbean seafood dishes: Montego Bay shrimp, red snapper, and shrimp ceviche, and a saffron-saturated paella. Wash it all down with a Corona or one of their tall, cool drinks like the Key Lime Pie—a liquid version of the popular dessert, spiked with coconut liqueur—and you'll have found a great way to beat the heat. As we were finishing dinner on a Saturday night over Spring Break, our waiter—a wiry-haired old hippie in a tie-dyed Sun Ray T-shirt—advised us to stick around for the Latin dancing. We demurred but will certainly return to Sun Ray's to further delve into their Mex-Carib menu.

A convenience store away from the Jubilee complex is the popular **Flounder's Chowder and Ale House** (800 Quietwater Beach Road, 850/932-2003, $$$). Much like Jubilee, there are indoor and outdoor dining areas, live music on occasion, and a festive beachside atmosphere that extends to the menu. "Eat, drink, and flounder" is their motto, and we happily obeyed, anteing up for Fred Flounder's Old Fashioned Florida Seafood Platter (consisting of grilled fish, shrimp scampi, fried oysters, scallops, and stuffed blue crab, all for $19.95) and a blackened sampler (chunks of grouper, tuna, and chicken). They also char-grill various fresh fish (snapper, mahimahi, grouper, yellowfin tuna), and baked stuffed flounder is a house specialty.

Flounder's shares ownership with **McGuire's** (600 East Gregory Street, 850/433-6789, $$$), a popular Irish pub in downtown Pensacola that serves steaks, burgers, ribs, and seafood in a convivial pub atmosphere, complete with an on-premises brewery and lots of dim-lit, dark-wood nooks and crannies. McGuire's ("over 20 years of feasting, imbibery, and debauchery") occupies the site of Pensacola's old firehouse. In addition to the pure, additive-free beer they turn out—we recommend a sampler of six homemade brews, lined up in a row of short glasses, with special kudos to the #2 "Irish Red"—they have a 7,500-bottle wine cellar. While touring the cellar, one of us got to handle a bottle of vino valued at $5,000. No time for slippery fingers!

Peg Leg Pete's (1010 Fort Pickens Road, 850/932-4139, $$) is a prized hangout for locals and those visitors lucky enough to stumble upon it. It's out toward Fort Pickens; turn right when you arrive on the island and head west for about a mile. There's an upstairs bar/restaurant with an outside deck, a downstairs hangout (the Underwhere Bar), and a sand volleyball court bedecked with sponsors' beer logos. Peg Leg's is a great place to come for beer and drinks, raw oysters and steamed shrimp, and ample servings of local color. And their key lime pie—which is pale yellow and not too tart, melding perfectly with its graham-cracker crust—rates high on our statewide tasting of this delicacy.

Night Moves

Begin your evening in Pensacola Beach with a Bushwacker, a local specialty that originated at a beachside bar called the **Sandshaker** (731 Pensacola Beach Boulevard, 850/932-2211). This rummy, slushy concoction migrated up from the islands with a local bartender. It's the perfect way to launch an evening in Pensacola Beach. A well-made Bushwacker tastes like a Caribbean milkshake and gives the imbiber both an alcohol buzz and a sugar rush. Several liqueurs are involved, crème de cacao prominent among them. Although it tastes like dessert, it packs a disarmingly potent punch. Locals come to the Sandshaker in late afternoon and early

MAP OF THE PANHANDLE—PAGE 547

evening for drinks, gabbing, and sunset-watching on the deck, where a troubadour can often be found strumming a tune. One we'd like to hear: "Wasting away again in Bushwackerville. . . ."

From the Sandshaker, it is a short hike across the street and toward the bay bridge to **Banana Bob's** (701 Pensacola Beach Boulevard, 850/932-1124). This multi-purpose complex, claiming to be "party headquarters on Pensacola Beach," consists of a marina, package store, deli, and bar—several of them, in fact. People dance unselfconsciously to live music in a room that resembles a gigantic screened-in porch, allowing gulf breezes to waft through. We heard a good soul-music cover band one night. A glass door separates this casual party palace from another bar area where you can talk and imbibe. Banana Bob's reminded us of nightclubs along the coast of our native Carolinas, and we felt instantly at home.

The nightlife rises to a comfortable simmer but never really boils over in Pensacola Beach. Typically, you'll see gaggles of buzz-cut military guys, baseball-capped frat boys, and dudes who pour cement and nail boards together standing around telling their latest "drunk as hell" stories while deciding where to make their next move.

Finally, a little Pensacola Beach trivia: the oldest bar on the island is the **Islander** (43 Via de Luna Drive, 850/932-9011). There's also a **Hooters** (400 Quietwater Beach Road, 850/934-9464), but don't get your hopes or anything else up, as the girls wear white T-shirts and shorts instead of the revealing get-ups into which they're squeezed like sausages at other Hooters. As we regard wholesome pulchritude more appealing than sleazy attire anyway, we actually found this Hooters to be more appealing than its sister acts.

Pensacola proper is a rocking little city, especially in the historic district around Palafox Place. You'll find all kinds of bars and hangouts on Palafox and its warehouse-lined side streets. We gravitated to an alternative club called **Sluggo's** (130 Palafox Place, 850/435-0543), where we caught the bands Sugarsmack and Squatweiler, both from back home in North Carolina. The music was loud and bracing, and we hung out till the wee hours. The good time we had in the company of Pensacola's friendly alternative community was worth the next morning's ringing in our ears.

Finally, a word to the wise: the town of Gulf Breeze, which must be crossed when going from Pensacola Beach to Pensacola (or vice versa), lies in a different county. The police force in Gulf Breeze vigilantly nabs drunk drivers en route, so don't drink and drive. We'd hate for you to party your way into a jail cell, lawyer's fees, fines, tripled insurance rates, loss of license, and other messy bringdowns that follow a DWI arrest. It's not worth the hassles, nor is it fair to put others at risk. But you already know that. Just don't forget it.

Contact Information

Pensacola Area Convention and Visitor Information Center, 1401 East Gregory Street, Pensacola, FL 32501; 805/434-1234 or 800/874-1234; website: www.visitpensacola.com

Pensacola Beach Visitor Information Center, 735 Pensacola Beach Boulevard, P.O. Box 1174, Pensacola Beach, FL 32562; 850/932-1500 or 800/635-4803; website: www.visitpensacola.com/pbeach

MAP OF ESCAMBIA COUNTY—PAGE 638

Fort Pickens (Gulf Islands National Seashore)

The west end of Santa Rosa Island is the site of an old army fort whose batteries and emplacements are open to visitors. The history is rich and the remains of the fort and its batteries, which saw active service from 1834 to 1940, are impressively large. Fort Pickens itself took 21.5 million bricks to build. It's worth taking a self-guided tour of the fort, its cannons, and emplacements. A brochure can be picked up at the visitor center. There's also a museum detailing the natural history of the area. History aside, the real marvel at Fort Pickens is seven unspoiled miles of gulf beaches. In addition, there are picnic areas, a bayside fishing pier, a bayside campground, a bike path, a camp store, and more. It's a nature lover's bonanza, and history buffs don't make out too shabbily, either.

The island thins precipitously for the first couple of miles past the entrance gate. This is due to Hurricane Opal, which nearly breached Santa Rosa Island at this spot. Actually, the island—and indeed the whole Panhandle—suffered major meteorological blows in 1995. Hurricane Erin's high winds toppled trees in August and Hurricane Opal's storm surge overwashed the island in October. Today, the park service road veers close to the lapping waves, and tendrils of sand blow across the asphalt. There was, in fact, a heated debate about relocating the road farther west, but arguments in favor of providing visitors with an ocean view won out. The trees at Fort Pickens suffered terribly from wind and waves. If the trunks didn't snap or split, the roots died from saltwater intrusion. Dunes were overtopped and flattened. The narrowed beach at Fort Pickens is still quite visibly reeling from the hurricanes of the previous decade, and it's unclear whether the future holds recovery or regression. Yet for now this end of the island remains a great place to ditch the crowd and find your own hidden sliver of beach.

5 Langdon Beach (Fort Pickens, Gulf Islands National Seashore)

Location: three miles west of Pensacola Beach, on Fort Pickens Drive at the west end of Santa Rosa Island

Parking/fees: $6 entrance fee per vehicle. The entrance fee is good for seven days at all units of Gulf Islands National Seashore. Camping fees are $15 per night (without hookups) and $20 per night (with hookups). For camping reservations, call 800/365-2267 and use the designation code GUL.

Hours: 7 A.M. to midnight (CDT) and 7 A.M.–10 P.M. (CST)

Facilities: concessions, lifeguards (seasonal), restrooms, picnic tables, showers, and a visitor center

Contact: Gulf Islands National Seashore, 850/934-2600

Beaches

Driving west from the entrance station, you hit a pair of gulfside parking lots identified only as "Public Beach." There are about 30 spaces at each and no facilities. **Langdon Beach** is the official named beach at Fort Perkins, with a large lot, picnic pavilions, dune walkovers, and seasonal lifeguards. Across the road is Langdon picnic area, a bike path, and the remains of an old battery. A short distance up the road, across from Campground Loop A, is Dune Nature Trail, a boardwalk with informative nature signage that leads a quarter mile out to the beach. A small parking lot is located near the camp store, and there is another beach boardwalk across the street. At this point, the road loops around the island's tip, where the remnants of Fort Pickens, a visitor center, and a museum are located.

You can park beside the cement wall that rims the perimeter and stroll through the fort, tour the small museum, or fish from the bayside pier. You don't need a saltwater fishing license to toss a line at Fort Pickens; it's all included in the $6 entrance fee. Continuing around the loop, you'll encounter Battery 234 and Battery Cooper. A sand trail leads to the beach from each. There's great wilderness beach strolling out at this end. As a note to surfers, the tip of the island known as "the Point" is a favorite with longboarders. People also come from all over the southeast to snorkel and dive around the jetties at Fort Pickens.

Incidentally, Fort Pickens made national headlines in July 2001 when an eight-year-old boy was attacked by a 250-pound bull shark while playing in knee-deep water. His uncle wrestled the seven-foot shark to shore, a park ranger shot it, a volunteer firefighter removed the boy's severed arm from the shark's mouth, and his aunt administered CPR to the bleeding boy on the beach. A month later, Jessie Arbogast was still recovering in the hospital, having lost most of his blood. It was a miracle he survived at all.

Just for the record: in the year 2000, there were 51 reported shark attacks in the United States, 34 of them in Florida—and only one fatal.

Bunking Down

The shaded, 200-site campground at Fort Pickens affords quick and easy walking access to gulf and bay beaches. It is, moreover, the only designated campground on Santa Rosa Island. You can camp for a week at Fort Pickens ($15–20 per night) for the cost of one night's hotel lodging in Pensacola Beach. For reservations, call 800/365-2267 and mention the designation code GUL.

Contact Information

Gulf Islands National Seashore, 1801 Gulf Breeze Parkway, Gulf Breeze, FL 32561; 850/934-2600; website: www.nps.gov/guis

Big Lagoon State Park

Big Lagoon State Park is exactly that: a big lagoon between Perdido Key and Pensacola, along a section of the Gulf Intracoastal Waterway. Its 700 acres include sandpine scrub, salt marshes, inland swamps, and sandy beaches. There's nearly a mile worth of beaches, broken into "East" and "West" designations. They're safe for children since they don't face the gulf's waves.

The park is a bonanza for nature lovers, with trails, boardwalks, an observation tower (at East Beach), abundant birdlife in the lagoons and uplands, fishing in the grass beds, and a variety of habitats in a relatively small area. A 75-site campground is shaded by tall pines. A boat ramp provides ready access to the Intracoastal Waterway. If you find yourself in the area, Big Lagoon should be an obligatory stop.

6 Big Lagoon State Park

Location: 10 miles southwest of Pensacola on County Road 292A

Parking/fees: $3.25 per vehicle entrance fee. Receipt is also good for admittance to Perdido Key State Park. Camping fees are $10 per night (without hookups) and $12 per night (with hookups) September 1–February 28, $12 per night (without hookups) and $14 per night (with hookups) March 1–August 31.

Hours: 8 A.M. to sunset

Facilities: restrooms, picnic tables, showers, and a visitor center

Contact: Big Lagoon State Park, 850/492-1595

Contact Information

Big Lagoon State Park, 12301 Gulf Beach Highway, Pensacola, FL 32507; 850/492-1595; website: www.myflorida.com

Perdido Key Area (Gulf Islands National Seashore)

The westernmost unit of Gulf Islands National Seashore in Florida occupies six glorious miles on Perdido Key. Indeed, it is by far the best thing about Perdido Key. For one thing, the road only extends three miles into the park, but the beach extends 4.5 roadless miles farther. It is possible to find solitude by walking east along the beach. You can even saddle up the backpack for a wilderness beach campout. Primitive camping is permitted and costs no more than the $6 admission to the national seashore, although they do ask that you obtain a free permit from the park ranger if you intend to park your car overnight. This formality is not required if you arrive by boat (which most campers do). The other stipulation is that campers must walk at least a half-mile east of the paved road before setting up. Call 850/934-2623 for more camping information.

Beaches

The developed beach out here is named for Rosamond Johnson, the first black serviceman from Escambia County to die in the Korean War. Before desegregation, this was the only beach in the area open to African-Americans. At **Johnson Beach**, there are covered picnic pavilions on the beach side of the road and a nature trail on the lagoon. A concession stand and lifeguards are present from Memorial Day to Labor Day. As has been noted, you can elect to ditch the crowds—not that they're ever huge, by urban-beach standards—by proceeding east to the end of the park road and then hiking along the beach to your own sandy sanctuary. At the far eastern tip of Perdido Key is the west jetty that holds open the mouth of Pensacola Bay.

Contact Information
Gulf Islands National Seashore, 1801 Gulf Breeze Parkway, Gulf Breeze, FL 32561; 850/934-2600; website: www.nps.gov/guis

7 Johnson Beach (Perdido Key Area, Gulf Islands National Seashore)

Location: 15 miles southwest of Pensacola, via State Route 292, at the east end of Perdido Key
Parking/fees: $6 entrance fee per vehicle. The entrance fee is good for seven days at all units of Gulf Islands National Seashore. There is no charge for primitive camping on the beach, but you are asked to register at the ranger station.
Hours: 8 A.M. to sunset
Facilities: concessions, lifeguards (seasonal), restrooms, picnic tables, and showers
Contact: Gulf Islands National Seashore, 50/934-2600

Perdido Key

The state of Florida's amazing shoreline and this guidebook both deserve a happier ending than the one provided by Perdido Key. The key runs for 16 miles, all but the last mile of which lie inside Florida. Between the Perdido Key unit of Gulf Islands National Seashore and Perdido Key State Park, a generous allotment of nearly ten miles of beach have been set aside for preservation and recreation. The problem here is not the key itself but the community of Perdido Key, which is actually an unincorporated part of Escambia County (read: subject to minimal building and zoning regulations). It is glutted with high-rise condos on the gulf side of the road, and more are on the way, if developers continue to have it their way (which they always seem to).

How bad is it? Bad enough that a two-year moratorium on construction had to be imposed. In 1998, however, the moratorium was lifted, and the earth movers have been at it again. The cap on living units is 4,116, but some feel that this has been ignored and that, when approved but not-yet-built developments are factored in, the construction may in fact have

8 Perdido Key State Park

Location: 17 miles southwest of Pensacola, along State Route 292 on Perdido Key
Parking/fees: $2 per vehicle entrance fee (or free with a receipt from Big Lagoon State Park)
Hours: 8 A.M. to sunset
Facilities: restrooms, picnic tables, and showers
Contact: Perdido Key State Park c/o Big Lagoon State Park, 850/492-1595

MAP OF ESCAMBIA COUNTY—PAGE 638

surpassed the cap by as many as 2,000 units. Keeping tabs on the developmental mayhem afoot on Perdido Key is bit like trying to plug a leaky dike. In June 2000, a lawyer from Destin, another ruined community, filed a $15 million lawsuit against Escambia County to force the construction of a 19-story beachfront condo called Windemere. "This project is going to get built," he fumed in a typically bullying manner. "We're going to get to develop it one way or the other. . . . They're going to get their condos."

Then, in September, a Texas developer pitched a $390 million Marriott resort and convention center that would overwhelm 213 acres of Perdido Key. It would sit next to the Lost Key. Plantation golf club and involve construction of a 300-room gulfside hotel, another 120-unit hotel on the bay side, as many as 500 time-share units and 1,455 condo units, plus a 132,000-square-foot convention center. The "project coordinator" for this abomination claimed with a straight face that it would not overload the island. He's unintentionally on the money in the sense that the island is already overloaded, so what difference would a few thousand more units make? Too much is never enough! Bring it on!

To put this in perspective, the year-round population on Perdido Key is 1,600 and the number of units is nearly triple that, which means that a lot of high-rise housing sits idle much of the time. They're mostly second residences, tax writeoffs, rental property—in short, buildings that didn't need to be built and whose dormitory-like appearance casts a ghastly, privatized pall on what should have been a more unobstructed beachfront. Why were these monstrosities not built on the north side of the road, a location no less proximate to the gulf that would have provided a buffer from hurricanes and beach erosion while allowing the public to see and use the beaches? And how could any of this have happened in a place that is a designated coastal high-hazard area—that is, an evacuation area in the event of a Category 1 hurricane?

At "buildout"—a developer's euphemism for maximum planned or permitted construction—Perdido Key will be top-heavy with 8,000 units, and the state road that runs through it will be widened to four lanes. At least some of the locals are up in arms over all this unchecked growth. The Perdido Key Association and the Escambia County Citizens Coalition are fighting the county commission and the developers as best they can with pockets that don't go nearly as deep as their adversaries'. In so doing, they run the risk of "slap suits": lawsuits filed by developers to intimidate residents who challenge their projects. It's a wonderful world (not) out here on this perfidious key.

What bothers us is that in the race for dollars, a lot of facts about beach preservation get overlooked or distorted. Consider a press release whose warm and fuzzy message misrepresented an alarming situation. One mid-August evening in 1998, a gaggle of 80 sea turtle hatchlings emerged from a nest out behind the misnamed Eden Condominium. Instinct would lead them to follow the light of the moon to the Gulf of Mexico, but they were confused by artificial lighting from the condo and headed for the pool instead. Here was the condo manager's take on what turned out to be a narrowly averted tragedy: "This was a great opportunity to see a spectacular event of nature. The [condo] visitors pitched right in and helped in the rescue effort. They just loved it!"

With four heavily developed miles of condos reaching as high as 18 stories, plus bayside developments and golf courses, it seems a little disingenuous to open a piece of visitor-information literature with the heading, "PERDIDO KEY. . . . SHHHHH-HHH!!! . . . OUR SECRET. . . ." Perdido Key is no secret—just ask the sea turtles—and this "building-frenzied key," as the

MAP OF THE PANHANDLE—PAGE 547

Pensacola News-Journal accurately described it, is home to some of the tallest and ugliest constructions anywhere on the Florida coast. What can you say about a community that sites golf courses atop wetlands, a shopping center atop an Indian burial ground, and condo towers atop a narrowing beach? Nothing more than they've got it all wrong on Perdido Key.

A final anecdote. The first edition of this book didn't go nearly so far in its criticism of development on Perdido Key, and yet one of us received a phone call at home from an outraged woman who identified herself as a member of the Perdido Key Chamber of Commerce and the manager of a condominium property. After ranting and raving for 20 minutes, she delivered her coup de grâce: "You don't know NOTHIN' about Perdido Key!"

Unfortunately for them, we know way too much about Perdido Key.

Beaches

In the middle of the developed stretch of Perdido Key is a 2.5-mile respite known as **Perdido Key State Park.** The beach here has lost a good deal of its width as the cumulative result of five hurricanes since 1995 (Erin, Opal, Danny, Earl, and Georges). There are two bathhouses at Perdido Key and a long beach to lie on. The price is right, too: $2 per vehicle or nothing at all if you can produce a receipt from Big Lagoon State Park.

Bunking Down

They call Perdido Key a family-oriented beach, but there is not a single motel or hotel room to be found on the beach. The closest you can get is **Best Western Perdido Key** (13585 Perdido Key Drive, 850/492-2775, $$), which is hundreds of yards from the beach. However, any number of high-rises like the aforementioned **Eden** (16281 Perdido Key Drive, 850/492-3336, $$$$) will rent by the week in summer and by the day the rest of the year. Rental rates at Eden run about $1,000 to $1,400 per week for a one- or two-bedroom condo in season and drop by as much as 40 percent out of season. Condo rental rates on Perdido Key vary from one concrete housing project to another, so shop around. By the way, you can't miss Eden: it's the gargantuan sloping condo that dominates the horizon like a breaching whale. It looks like anything but the biblical Eden.

Coastal Cuisine

Locals love **Triggers** (12700 Gulf Beach Highway, 850/492-1897, $$), whose specialty and namesake is triggerfish, a delicate-tasting deepwater catch that's serve fried, blackened, broiled, grilled, sautéed, char-grilled, stuffed, Cajun-style, in a salad, in a bisque, or as part of a combination plate. Give us a combination plate with triggerfish and mullet, and we're happy as clams.

Night Moves

At one end of Perdido Key is Eden, while at the other you can go about raising hell. In this case, we prefer the latter option, being big fans of a funky, down-home bar that's legendary among party animals on both sides of the Florida and Alabama state line. We're talking about the **Flora-Bama Lounge** (17401 Perdido Key Drive, 850/492-0611). This party palace literally straddles the state line. Thus, "Do it with us on the line" is their motto, and we have done it with them on several occasions. One Sunday afternoon, around the time church was letting out in most places, we wandered into the Flora-Bama Lounge to find a pair of dudes with hair down to their belt loops entertaining a packed house with a song with the refrain, "I can't wait till I get sober so I can get drunk again." The crowd, which included many women, was smiling, hoisting mugs, and singing along.

Seven different indoor/outdoor bar areas

MAP OF ESCAMBIA COUNTY—PAGE 638

are strewn around the Flora-Bama premises, and the whole ramshackle operation resembles a folk-art sculpture made out of weathered wood, canvas, and beer cans. The crowd can be as rough hewn as the architecture, looking like the sort of rowdy friends that Hank Williams, Jr. might invite over to watch Monday Night Football. Nothing dangerous, you understand, just a bunch of good ol' boys and gals blowing off steam, y'know?

The Flora-Bama Lounge hosts a number of annual events, the most notable being the Interstate Mullet Toss (yes, a fish-throwing contest, held in late April) and the Frank Brown International Songwriters Festival. Frank was a Flora-Bama employee who lived to the ripe old age of 95. The music festival named for him is an 11-day showcase in early- to mid-November that draws some of the best songwriters and performers in the Southeast. Festival venues include ten places in the vicinity of the Flora-Bama home base. The idea behind the festival is to promote the belief that "music makes the world a better place." We'd sure second that emotion! For more information, call 850/492-SONG.

Contact Information

Perdido Key Area Chamber of Commerce, 15500 Perdido Key Drive, Perdido Key, FL 32507; 850/492-4660; website: www.perdidochamber.com

BEACH BITS:
Lists, Tips, and Trivia

Florida's Top 25 Beaches

From among 400 beaches in the Sunshine State, we've selected our Top 25, presented in alphabetical order. We figured, why go through the ordeal of trying to rank them when they're all just about perfect?

- **Bahia Honda State Park**, Monroe County: You can walk way out on this shallow-bottomed beach, one of the few sandy enclaves on the Keys.
- **Bowman's Beach**, Lee County: The westernmost beach on Sanibel Island, the shelling capital of America.
- **Caladesi Island State Park**, Pinellas County: Accessible by boat only, this jewel in the Gulf of Mexico has fluffy, floury white sand.
- **Coquina Beach**, Anna Marie Island, Manatee County: The broadest beach on an island aimed at those on a blue-collar budget; blessed relief from the snob appeal of neighboring Longboat Key.
- **Daytona Beach**, Volusia County: Yes, it's big, wide, built up, noisy, a bit red in the neck, and a hell of a lot of fun. Vroom-vroom!
- **Delray Beach**, Palm Beach County: A touch of Southern California beach culture in South Florida. One of the best lifeguarding staffs in the country.
- **Fort Clinch State Park**, Nassau County: Florida begins with a bang up on the Georgia border with this sunny peach of a beach.
- **Fort Lauderdale**, Broward County: You cannot beat the sociable beach along Lauderdale's famous "Strip." Extra points for forbidding construction on the beach side of A1A.
- **Grayton Beach State Park**, Walton County: The Panhandle's elegant symphony of white sand, tall dunes, salt marshes, coastal lakes, pine flatlands, and scrub-hickory hammock reaches its crescendo here.
- **Guana River State Park**, St. Johns County: A boundless feast of wild, dune-backed beaches and a pristine estuary to explore by canoe.
- **John D. MacArthur Beach State Park**, Palm Beach County: A two-mile beach sanctuary, plus reef, mangrove, and hammock. Free trams carry visitors to the beach, or you can cross the bridged, bird-filled estuary on your own.
- **John U. Lloyd Beach State Park**, Broward County: A slice of Old Florida, with nicely preserved patches of coastal hammock and mangrove swamp bordering a wilderness beach opposite Fort Lauderdale's Port Everglades.
- **Lovers Key State Park**, Lee County: South of Fort Myers Beach, a merging of state and county parklands yields revealing glimpses of beach, mangrove swamp, inner-island habitats and—best of all—wide, driftwood- and shell-covered beaches.
- **Middle Cove Beach Access**, St. Lucie County: The best of many coast accesses on land belonging to Florida Power and Light. A short walk through the woods leads to a lovely, isolated beach.

- **Panama City Beach**, Bay County: Emerald waters, white sand, tanned bodies—the best of all possible worlds.

- **Pensacola Beach**, Escambia County: A beach town with real personality, great restaurants, acres of free parking, and water towers painted like beach balls.

- **Playalinda Beach**, Brevard County: A gorgeous sandy swatch at the south end of Canaveral's National Seashore's 33-mile beach. Warning: It's a nude beach for part of its length.

- **St. George Island State Park**, Franklin County: Miles of beaches have been preserved at the east end of St. George Island. It's great for biking, and the fishing is among the best in Florida.

- **St. Joseph Peninsula State Park**, Gulf County: Nine deserted miles of gulf beaches backed by dunes that look like snowdrifts.

- **Sebastian Inlet State Park**, Brevard and Indian Counties: Great fishing, big waves, radical surfing, and lots to do recreationally in this park, which is evenly divided between two counties.

- **Siesta Key Public Beach**, Sarasota County: Fine-grained, hard-packed white quartz sand on a wide, breezy beach at the more populous north end of Siesta Key.

- **South Beach, Miami Beach**, Dade County: The most camera-ready beach scene in the country, replete with art deco, a broad renourished beach, and slathered near-naked bodies.

- **Topsail Hill Preserve State Park**, Walton County: This isolated park has towering dunes that must be hiked over to get to the beach. It's a must-visit for those who love to escape the crowd.

- **Turtle Beach**, Sarasota County: Coarse, brown sand and lots of it on a very walkable beach at the quieter south end of Siesta Key.

- **Wabasso Beach Park**, Indian River County: Sea grape–covered dunes plunge down to a sandy beach that ranks among the finest on the East Coast—and not just the East Coast of Florida.

Fast Facts About Florida

Average hours of sunshine each year: 3,000

Capital: Tallahassee

Distance from the southern tip of Florida to the Equator: 1,700 miles

Florida sales tax: 6 percent

Greatest distance from any point in Florida to the nearest beach: 60 miles

Land area: 58,560 square miles

Land area rank: 22nd

Leading industries: tourism, citrus growing, commercial fishing

Number of acres of state parks: 500,000+

Number of annual out-of-state visitors: 73 million

Number of known springs: 320

Number of lakes of one acre or larger: 7,800

Number of miles of sandy beaches: 1,100

Number of miles of shoreline (as the crow flies): 1,800

Number of miles of tidal shoreline: 8,462

Number of rivers: 166

Number of saltwater marine species: 1,200

Number of state parks: 110+

Population rank of U.S. states: 4th

Population: 15,982,378

State animal: Florida panther

State beverage: orange juice

State bird: mockingbird

State flower: orange blossom

State freshwater fish: Florida large-mouth bass

State nickname: "The Sunshine State"

State reptile: alligator

State saltwater fish: sailfish

State saltwater mammal: manatee

State shell: horse conch

State song: "Old Folks at Home" (a.k.a. "Suwannee River"), by Stephen Foster

State stone: agatized coral

State tree: sabal palm

Time zones: Eastern (east of Apalachicola River), Central (west of Apalachicola River)

Who named Florida: Ponce de León, who called it "Pascua Florida" ("flowery Easter") on Easter 1513

Year granted statehood: 1845

Florida Beaches Scorecard

Florida's 35 coastal counties are listed below according to the number of discrete, named beaches in each that we inventoried in this book, from greatest to least.

Pinellas: 29	Martin: 15	Escambia: 8	Pasco: 3
Brevard: 28	Broward: 14	Flagler: 8	Dixie: 2
Palm Beach: 25	Indian River: 13	Duval: 7	Hillsborough: 2
Lee: 22	Bay: 12	Franklin: 7	Wakulla: 2
Monroe: 21	St. Johns: 12	Gulf: 7	Citrus: 1
Dade: 20	Volusia: 12	Okaloosa: 7	Santa Rosa: 1
St. Lucie: 20	Collier: 11	Hernando: 4	Taylor: 1
Sarasota: 17	Manatee: 9	Levy: 4	Jefferson: 0
Walton: 16	Nassau: 9	Charlotte: 3	TOTAL: 372

Toll-Free Phone Numbers

For general information on Florida, call Visit Florida (888/735-2872), the official state-funded tourist information service.

AIRLINES

Aeromexico 800/237-6639
Aeroperu 800/777-7717
Air Canada. 800/776-3000
Air Europa 800/772-4699
Air France 800/237-2747
Air Jamaica 800/523-5585
Alitalia 800/223-5730
American Airlines 800/433-7300
America West 800/235-9292
Bahamas Air. 800/222-4262
British Airways 800/247-9297
Canadian Airlines 800/426-7000
Continental Airlines 800/525-0280
Delta Airlines. 800/221-1212
Finnair 800/950-5000
Lufthansa. 800/645-3880
Mexicana 800/531-7921
National Airlines of Chile 800/238-2445
Northwest Airlines 800/225-2525
Pan American 800/359-7262
Qantas Airways 800/227-4500
Swiss Air 800/221-4750
Transbrasil 800/872-3153
TWA. 800/221-2000
United Airlines 800/241-6522
USAirways 800/428-4322
Varig 800/468-2744

Note: Miami Airport is serviced by nearly a hundred airlines and is the ninth busiest airport in the world. The above is a selective list of some of the larger airlines that fly to Florida.

CAR-RENTAL COMPANIES

Alamo Rent-A-Car 800/327-9633
Avis Rent-A-Car 800/831-2847
Budget Rent-A-Car 800/527-0700
Dollar Rent-A-Car 800/800/4000
Enterprise Rent-A-Car . . . 800/325-8007
Hertz Rent-A-Car 800/654-3131
National Car Rental 800/227-7368
Sears Car Rental 800/527-0770
Thrifty Car Rental 800/367-2277

HOTELS AND MOTELS

Best Western	800/528-1234
Clarion Hotels	800/252-7466
Club Med	800/932-2582
Comfort Inn	800/228-5150
Courtyard by Marriott	800/321-2211
Days Inn	800/325-2525
Doubletree Inn	800/222-8733
Econo Lodge	800/553-2666
Embassy Suites	800/362-2779
Fairfield Inn by Marriott	800/228-2800
Four Seasons	800/332-3442
Friendship Inn	800/453-4511
Hampton Inns	800/426-7866
Hilton Hotels	800/445-8667
Holiday Inn	800/465-4329
Howard Johnson	800/446-4656
Hyatt Hotels	800/228-9000
Inter-Continental	800/327-0200
La Quinta Inns	800/687-6667
Marriott Hotels	800/228-9290
Motel 6	800/466-8356
Omni	800/843-6664
Quality Inn	800/228-5151
Radisson Hotels	800/333-3333
Ramada Inn	800/272-6232
Red Roof Inn	800/843-7663
Renaissance Hotels	800/468-3571
Residence Inn by Marriott	800/331-3131
Ritz-Carlton	800/241-3333
Rodeway Inn	800/228-2000
Sheraton Hotels	800/325-3535
Shoney's Inn	800/222-2222
Sleep Inn	800/753-3746
Super 8 Motels	800/800/8000
Travelodge	800/578-7878
Westin Hotels	800/228-3000

Tips for Savvy Travelers

First, a rant about hotels. In general, the more you pay for a room, the less you'll receive in the way of services and amenities. Be advised that at a huge resort hotel, exorbitant room charges are only part of the story. Separate charges may be levied for parking a car, using the on-premises fitness center, getting set up with a beach cabana or lounge chair, and so on. Nothing will be given away, beyond a tiny basket in the bathroom with one-ounce plastic thimbles of shampoo and conditioner.

There is generally no free continental breakfast, either. At best, you might find a coffee urn and some Styrofoam cups in the lobby or a few bruised apples on a silver-plated tray. Moreover, there is a hidden cash economy at work on the premises. Every service provided—from the hijacking of your car by valets to the delivery of luggage to your room by bellhops to the handing of a towel by the pool—requires tipping. Why aren't these basic services covered in the inflated room charge? Why don't the big hotels remunerate their employees sufficiently so that guests are spared awkwardly digging through pockets for dollar bills?

If this is what luxury, upscale hotels are all about, we are perfectly content to stay at a Hampton, Fairfield, Comfort, or Sleep Inn, where the rooms are perfectly comfortable, parking spaces are free, and a continental breakfast is served gratis each morning. Besides, who spends that much time in a room when you're on vacation at the beach? If you are spending that many hours in a rented room, you might as well have saved your money and stayed at home, where you can watch TV for free.

Having noted all these realities of the road life, we have come up with a bunch of travel tips and advisories that have stood us good stead on our coastal wanderings:

- Snatch items off the maids' carts when they aren't looking, replenishing your stock of shampoo, pens, and writing pads. These may be the only free things you receive at higher-priced hotels.

- Stay at places that include a continental breakfast or free breakfast bar as part of the room rate. At the very least, siphon a Styrofoam cup or two of coffee from the lobby coffeemaker before checking out.

- Avoid ridiculous in-room phone charges and surcharges by using lobby pay phones for local calls and even calling-card calls. Many hotels charge a fee to call even a toll-free number from a room phone and a surcharge for using your own long-distance calling card. It's a racket.

- If you hate TV as much as we do and don't want to have its overbearing presence forced upon you in the hotel fitness center, be the earliest bird in the place, unplug the set, and then hide the remote-control device under a stack of towels.

- Carry your AAA and/or AARP card and always ask for the applicable discount.

- Avoid valets by parking on the street while registering and ask for the self-parking option, if it exists. Otherwise you will be forced to turn your car over to a youthful stranger in Bermuda shorts and will pay dearly for this larceny.

- Refuse bellhop service if you want to carry your own bags to your room. Don't even make eye contact with anyone on the premises wearing a funny uniform.

- When you pay for a breakfast buffet, or if it comes free with the room, wear a jacket and fill each pocket with fruit for the road. Then enjoy a healthy midday snack. Who says there's no such thing as a free lunch?

- Check in for at least two nights whenever possible. One-night stays are a waste of money, because you are barely on the premises for anything more than a night's sleep. With a two-day stay, you minimize the impact of late check-ins and early checkouts.

- When making reservations, make clear the type of room you want so that there will be no unpleasant surprises upon check-in. If you want two beds, nonsmoking, ground level, and an ocean view, then spell it all out to the reservation clerk.

- It's worth joining a chain motel or hotel's frequent stay club, if you are a frequent guest. At Holiday Inn, for instance, Priority Club members are automatically granted a late checkout of 2 P.M., which is worth its weight in gold.

- Don't be shy about asking for an early check-in or a late checkout. All they can say is no.

- Place the "Privacy, Please" on the door handle as you're leaving to avoid the early evening "turndown service" genies from visiting while you're out to dinner. An inviolable sense of privacy is more important to us than a five-cent chocolate on a fluffed-up pillow.

- Keeping the privacy sign on your door also spares you a rude and awkward awakening by chambermaids wanting to clean the room at an unconscionably early hour. If you hang a "Do Not Disturb" sign on your door and still get pestered before checkout time, let the manager know how you feel.

- South of Palm Beach on the East Coast and Fort Myers Beach on the Gulf Coast, Florida is a constant traffic jam. The gridlock reaches a peak in the high season, which runs from Christmas to Easter. As much as possible, plan your vacation to minimize driving once you've reached your destination.

Sun Screams: Skin Protection at the Beach

In the old days, before the ozone layer was depleted—before anyone knew what ozone was—the beach was one huge tanning salon. People who hadn't been outdoors in a year were suddenly spending two uninterrupted weeks on a towel at the beach. Slathering themselves from forehead to feet with greasy ointments, they submitted their bodies to eight hours of slow ultraviolet roasting, oblivious to anything but the fact that by vacation's end they'd have a Coppertone tan and be the envy of friends and coworkers.

We don't want to spoil your day at the beach, but we'd be irresponsible if we didn't mention the latest facts about what's really going on under the sun.

You won't get this information from the manufacturers of sunscreens and other expensive lotions designed to make you feel safe while you sunbathe under a thinning ozone layer. Many of the products on the market, in fact, misleadingly claim to offer "all-day protection," lulling sun-worshippers into a false sense of security.

However, according to research done at the Memorial Sloan-Kettering Cancer Center, no evidence can be found to show that any sunscreen on the market offers protection against malignant melanoma, which is the most severe form of skin cancer (albeit the rarest). Michael Castleman, writing in *Mother Jones,* goes so far as to call the sunscreen industry the "Sunscam" industry, claiming they willfully endanger the lives and health of beachgoers. His greatest animus is aimed at the Skin Cancer Foundation (SCF), which every year issues a warning to summer vacationers about the absolute necessity of using sunscreens if they're going to the beach. Even as follow-up studies confirm the Sloan-Kettering findings, the SCF continues to stick by its lotions, saying "sunscreen should continue to be an integral part of a comprehensive program." The SCF neglects to mention that they are heavily funded by the sunscreen industry. Castleman reports that sunscreens may even contribute to skin cancers. By prolonging people's time in the sun, they prevent "the only natural melanoma warning system human skin has—sunburn." Even in the face of statistics that show melanoma rates are rising six percent a year and that someone is 12 times as likely to contract melanoma today than in 1950, sunscreen sales are on the rise.

The real culprit is UVA radiation, a longer-wave form of sunlight than the UVB radiation that causes sunburn. While UVB radiation does its damage to the outer layer of skin, UVA penetrates the skin's elastic fibers and collagen, causing you to "leather" while you weather. More insidiously, UVA hangs around on cloudy days, too. Of course, people at the beach will continue to sit outdoors in the sun for many hours. And why shouldn't they? It's their vacation, for crying out loud. Well, to keep you from crying out loud from severe sunburn, here are some tips for safer sunbathing.

- Relax. You don't have to be a hostage to your motel room. The key to sitting in the sun is covering up. Rent a beach umbrella. Wear a hat, ideally one with a wide brim to deflect sun from the eyes. Sunlight is a contributing factor in cataract formation.

- Keep extra towels handy to lay over burning or susceptible parts of your body. Get up every hour or so and sit in the shade.
- Avoid the sun's rays between 11 A.M. and 3 P.M., when they are most intense.
- Wear protective clothing that can be easily taken off when you want to go for a swim. New lines of beachwear are on the market made from fabrics alleged to block UVA and UVB rays, but prices are high and benefits only marginally different from what normal summer clothing provides.
- Use a sunscreen that blocks UVA and UVB radiation, containing ingredients like Parsol 1789 (or avobenzone), titanium dioxide, and zinc oxide (or Z-Cote). That milky white stuff you've seen for years on lifeguards' noses is zinc oxide.
- Apply sunscreen liberally to cool, dry skin a half-hour before going outdoors, allowing it to penetrate the skin's fibers. Keep reapplying sunscreen throughout the day, because sweat and water weakens or removes it. Don't believe products claiming to be "waterproof."
- The newest sun lotions contain antioxidants (vitamins and enzymes) that are said to suppress growth of cancerous cells during sunbathing. They are indeed safer than the old sunscreens, but their claims that you can be both bronze and safe sound—and probably are—too good to be true. The most effective antioxidant is L-ascorbic acid (a form of Vitamin C). Keep in mind that the jury is out on long-term suppression of skin cancers. You are, in effect, lab rats for the antioxidant industry. You still must cover up, augment the antioxidant with sunscreens, and use common sense. As one dermatologist put it, "It's not possible to have pigment darkening without sun damage. It's too good to be true."
- Those at greatest risk for melanoma from sun exposure are fair-skinned Caucasians, people with naturally red or blond hair, and those with freckles on their upper back. Melanomas are also increasing for Chinese, Japanese, Hawaiians, and Filipinos—populations once thought immune. A family history of melanomas is also a contributing factor.
- If you feel flush later, use "after sun" lotions that contain sun-protective nutrients. Also available as topical ointments are Vitamin C and Vitamin E. Some natural substances are good, too, including aloe vera, chamomile, and marigold.
- Finally, you aren't going to die just because you didn't know all this until now. Even the lousy sunscreens and suntan lotions you used in the past gave some protection from UV radiation. Just play it smart and take added precautions from now on. That way, we'll catch you at the beach when we're all in our nineties.

Angling Florida: Fishing Regulations in the Sunshine State

No serious fisherman would ever consult us for advice on bait, tackle, boat choice, or secret fishing holes. We'd be laughed right out of the water, if not cut up for bait. However, there is one piece of advice we can unabashedly offer anglers of any level of competence who are considering a fishing trip to Florida. That is, get hold of the state government's excellent magazine, *Florida Fishing,* published each year under the auspices of the nonprofit **Florida Sports Foundation** (1319 Thomaswood Drive, Tallahassee, FL 32312, 904/488-8347). It's a detailed, lavishly illustrated journal that spells out all you need to know about Florida rules, regulations, size and bag limits, best fishing spots for every species from amberjack to tarpon, best times of year to catch each of these slithering beauties, names and numbers of reputable fishing charters, tournament information, and more.

While we are poor anglers at best, we do appreciate a good fish when it's served on our dinner plate, and Florida has some of the freshest and most readily available seafood in the United States. The state also has 7,800 lakes, and the recreational fishing industry brings in $3 billion a year in revenues. For less seasoned anglers, some general rules regarding Florida waters are worth keeping in mind.

First, everyone between the ages of 16 and 64 needs a fishing license, whether you are fishing in fresh water or salt water. The fees vary, depending on duration of license and residency status. Nonresident freshwater and saltwater licenses are $16.50 for seven days and $31.50 for one year. (Three-day saltwater fishing licenses can be obtained for $6.50.) For Florida residents, such a deal! Freshwater and saltwater licenses are each $13.50 for one year and $61.50 for five years. Additionally, a one-year snook permit costs $2 and a tarpon tag costs $51.50.

Call 888/347-4356 for more information or to obtain a license. It only takes a credit card to have a license number issued, and you can start fishing that same day, while you permanent license will be mailed out within 48 hours. There is an additional $3.95 "convenience charge" for this toll-free phone service. Lest this licensing business seem like too much government encroachment, keep in mind that the money from license fees goes to improve and restore marine habitat and to fund fisheries research and public education on these renewable but irreplaceable (if lost) resources. All revenue goes to the Florida Fish and Wildlife Conservation Commission.

Besides fish, there are established and strictly enforced saltwater limits on oysters, crawfish, queen conch, stone crab claws, blue crab, and Florida spiny lobster. There are also serious consequences for anyone harming or destroying sea turtles, manatees, porpoises, manta rays, coral, sea fans, pelicans, and other seabirds. Because some fishing regulations change from region to region, the state government advises all anglers to contact the Florida Marine Patrol District office in the area where you will be fishing. The offices for saltwater fishing are:

- **District 1**: Jacksonville Beach, 904/270-2500; Titusville, 407/383-2740.

- **District 2:** Miami, 305/325-3346; Jupiter, 407/624-6935.
- **District 3:** Marathon, 305/289-2323; Fort Myers, 941/332-6971.
- **District 4:** Tampa, 813/272-2516; Crystal River, 352/447-1633.
- **District 5:** Panama City, 850/233-5150; Pensacola, 850/444-8978; Carrabelle 850/697-3741.

Ailing Fisheries, Endangered Fish

The runaway bestseller *The Perfect Storm* is a poignant portrait of the hard lives of commercial fishermen in a world of dwindling fish. If it's hard on the fishermen, though, imagine how hard the lives of the fish have become. In early 2000, the National Academy of Sciences brought together the world's leading marine biologists to study the global fish crisis. Their unanimous conclusion: overfishing, not global warming or pollution, is the "single greatest threat to the diversity of life in the world's oceans."

It would be easy to point to the United States, third biggest exporter of fish in the world (behind Thailand and Norway), as culpable, but there's enough blame to go round the globe several times—and, in fact, the United States is one of the few nations that at least pays lip service to international ocean policies.

The bottom line, however, is that commercial fishing—the business that puts that fresh catch of the day on our beachfront platters—is a phenomenally inefficient and almost shamefully wasteful industry. Worldwide the fishing industry spends $124 billion annually to produce $70 billion worth of fish; the remaining $54 billion is covered by government subsidies. The world's fishing fleets use large nets to drag the sea floor for schools of fish, destroying coral and hauling up everything within reach. Among the haul each year are 27 million tons of fish killed in the hauling process, which are then tossed overboard. Further, of the world's major fishing grounds, 44 percent are now fished at capacity, 31 percent are exploited, 16 percent are overfished, 6 percent are depleted (no fish left), and only 3 percent are left alone to recover from overfishing.

Currently, in the waters off Florida, the U.S. National Marine Fisheries Service is considering banning fishing altogether in two 100-square-mile blocks of the Gulf of Mexico, to protect the spawning grounds of the gag grouper. Also, an extensive reserve system is being considered for the waters around the Dry Tortugas, to protect a variety of reef fish. Lest we forget, a "dead zone" approximately the size of New Jersey has also been found in the Gulf of Mexico, extending outward from the mouth of the Mississippi. Nothing lives there, and the culprit (though they deny it) is Midwestern agribusiness. Nitrogen-rich fertilizers and pesticide from factory farms run off into the Mississippi and its tributaries, running out into the Gulf of Mexico. The result is algal blooms and hypoxia (low oxygen levels) that kill virtually all life forms in the Gulf of Mexico Dead Zone three months a year. However, the agribusiness lobby has stymied any federal action on this appalling situation. Are they waiting for the entire Gulf to become as stagnant as a toilet bowl? Then what?

Aquaculture, or fish farming, is often cited as a means to compensate for loss in wild fish stocks. However, fish farming is even more devastating environmentally than old methods. In addition, horror stories are told of fish farmers (especially salmon farmers in British Columbia) slaughtering sea lions and seals to keep them from snacking on their stock. Shrimp farming is even more environmentally devastating. Thailand, in fact, has lost half its mangrove forests to shrimp farms. And so on.

We don't want to flog a dead seahorse here, but because we love seafood so much and try to encourage beach visitors to enjoy the local catch, we are disturbed by this, to say the least. We are saddened by it too, shocked by how bad the situation has grown just in the past five years. However, there are still viable ways to enjoy fresh ocean-caught seafood still, to support local fishing fleets and to take the heat off those fish species that are close to being fished into extinction. The best way is to simply refuse to order (or buy at your grocery store back home) any of the following items on any menu; you might also point out to the proprietor that these species are close to being endangered species and should be removed from the menu.

ENDANGERED SEAFOOD

Atlantic cod
Atlantic flounder
Atlantic haddock
Bluefin tuna
Chilean sea bass (a.k.a. Patagonian toothfish)
Farmed salmon
Marlin
Orange roughy
Shark
Shrimp or prawns
Red or yellowtail snapper
Sturgeon
Swordfish
Tropical grouper

SUSTAINABLE SEAFOOD

Alaskan salmon
Albacore tuna
Calamari
Catfish
Crab (all but Chesapeake blue crab)
Lobsters
Mackerel
Mahimahi
Mussels
New Zealand cod
Pacific halibut
Sardines/herring
Sole
Tilapia
Trout
Yellowfin tuna

Suggested Reading

The books listed below were helpful to us and may deserve a look from you, as well—after you've read *Florida Beaches* from cover to cover, of course!

Amory, Cleveland. *The Last Resorts*. New York: Grosset & Dunlap, 1952.

Beatley, Timothy, et al. *An Introduction to Coastal Zone Management*. Washington, D.C.: Island Press, 1994.

Carr, Archie. *A Naturalist in Florida*. New Haven: Yale University Press, 1996.

De Hart, Allen. *Adventuring in Florida: A Sierra Club Guide*. Revised edition. San Francisco: Sierra Club Books, 1995.

Exley, Frederick. *Pages from a Cold Island*. New York: Random House, 1974.

Florida Atlas & Gazeteer. Freeport, Maine: DeLorme Mapping, 1989.

Florida's Sandy Beaches: An Access Guide. Pensacola: University of West Florida Press, 1985.

Grow, Gerald. *Florida Parks: A Guide to Camping and Nature* (6th ed.). Tallahassee: Longleaf Publications, 1997.

Koster Walton, Chelle. *Florida Island Hopping: The West Coast*. Sarasota: Pineapple Press, 1995.

LaFray, Joyce. *The Guide to Florida's Best Restaurants*. Berkeley: Ten Speed Press, 1995.

Myers, Ronald L. and John J. Ewel. *Ecosystems of Florida*. Orlando: University of Central Florida Press, 1990.

Nelson, Gil. *Exploring Wild Northwest Florida*. Sarasota: Pineapple Press, 1995.

Pilkey, Orrin, et al. *Living with the East Florida Shore*. Durham, NC: Duke University Press, 1984.

Vansant, Amy. *The Surfer's Guide to Florida*. Sarasota: Pineapple Press, 1995.

Williams, Joy. *The Florida Keys: A History & Guide* (8th ed.). New York: Random House, 1997.

Index

CANOEING AND KAYAKING

ENVIRONMENTAL CRISES

FISHING

HISTORIC SITES

I

NATIONAL PARKS, PRESERVES, AND SEASHORES

STATE PARKS

SURFING

About the Authors

Parke Puterbaugh is a travel and environmental writer with a special affinity for beaches. *Florida Beaches* is the fourth book on the subject that he's coauthored with Alan Bisbort. In addition, Puterbaugh is the sole author of *Southeastern Wetlands,* published in 1996 by the U.S. Environmental Protection Agency. He is also a veteran music journalist, having written for *Rolling Stone* (where he was a senior editor) for more than 20 years. His writing has appeared in dozens of other magazines and newspapers, including *USA Today, Outside, Attaché, Stereo Review,* and *Men's Journal,* as well as such books as *The Rolling Stone Illustrated History of Rock & Roll* and *The Rolling Stone Book of the Beats.* Puterbaugh has done writing, editing, and curatorial work for the Rock and Roll Hall of Fame and Museum in Cleveland, Ohio. He coedited *I Want to Take You Higher: The Psychedelic Era, 1965–1969* (Chronicle Books, 1997) with James Henke and cowrote *Rhino's Psychedelic Trip* (Miller-Freeman Books, 2000) with Alan Bisbort. He holds bachelor's degrees in English and Sociology and a masters in environmental science from the University of North Carolina at Chapel Hill. He is a lifelong beach lover, beachcomber, surf-music aficionado, and surfer wannabe.

Alan Bisbort is a writer, editor, and researcher who has worked for the Library of Congress, both on staff and as a freelance writer/editor, for 25 years. He is coauthor of *The Nation's Library: The Library of Congress* (Scala, 2000), the authorized guide for the Library's bicentennial celebration. He's a contributor to the *Library of Congress Desk Reference to World War II* (Doubleday, 2002) and the *Library of Congress Desk Reference to the Civil War* (Simon and Schuster, 2002. His most recent works are *Famous Last Words* (Pomegranate, 2001), *Charles Bragg: The Works!* (Pomegranate, 1999), and *White Rabbit and Other Delights: East Totem West, A Hippie Company* (Pomegranate, 1996). His writings have appeared in the *New York Times, Washington Post, Washingtonian, City Paper, Rolling Stone, Creem, Biblio, Connecticut, E, Hit List,* and the *New Internationalist.* He has a degree in English from the University of North Carolina at Chapel Hill. He is a contributing columnist for the Advocate Newspapers, for which he has won two journalism awards, and is a prolific writer of letters to the editor.

Parke and Alan met at the University of North Carolina at Chapel Hill in the mid-1970s. Both work as full-time freelance writers, periodically joining forces to research and write encyclopedic beach books. *Florida Beaches* is their fourth, having been preceded by *California Beaches* (Foghorn Press, 1999) and comprehensive East Coast and West Coast travel guides, published under the series title *Life Is a Beach* by McGraw-Hill in 1986 and 1988.

Maps

Florida's Coastal Counties

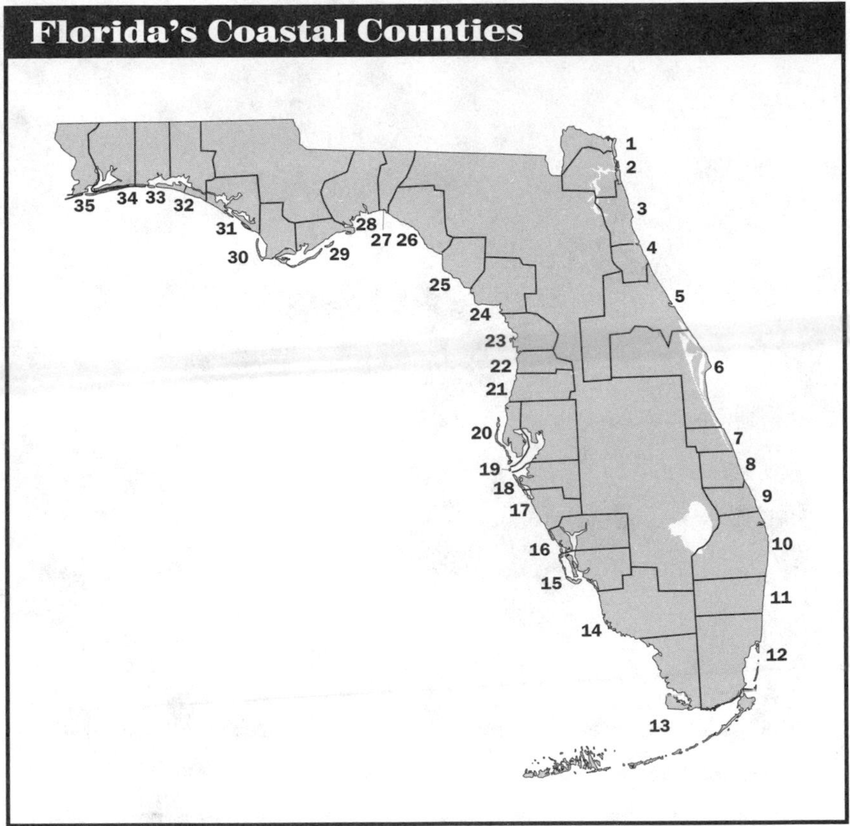

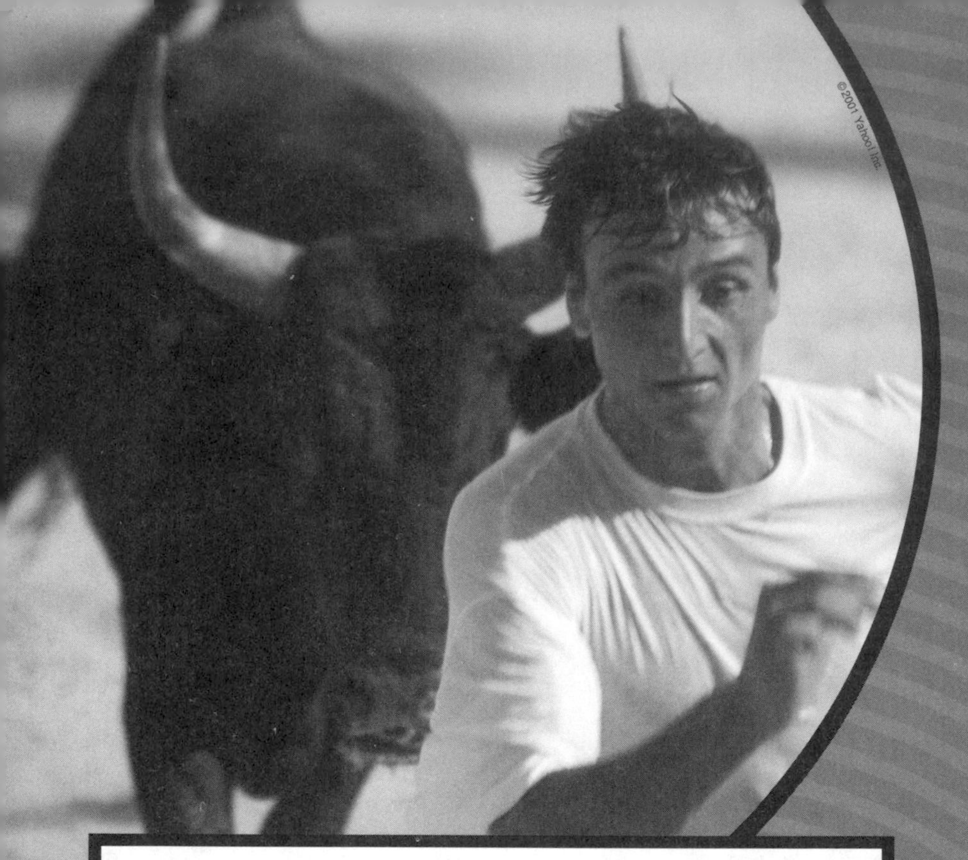
Will you have enough stories to tell your grandchildren?
©2001 Yahoo! Inc.